CONTENTS

Jon

Ste

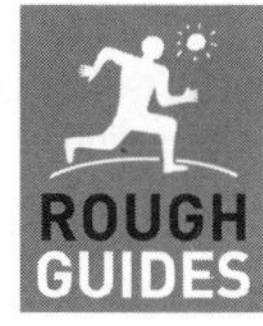

Credits

The Rough Guide to Classical Music

Editor: Joe Staines
Layout: Nikhil Agarwal
Picture research: Joe Staines
Proofreading: Jason Freeman
Production: Rebecca Short

Rough Guides Reference

Reference Director: Andrew Lockett
Editors: Kate Berens, Peter Buckley, Tom Cabot, Tracy Hopkins, Matthew Milton, Joe Staines and Ruth Tidball

Thanks to all those who ha[illegible] record and distribution companies without wh[illegible]o Elbie Lebrecht and everyone at Lebrecht Mus[illegible], the helpful staff at the Barbica[illegible]cords.

Finally, a big thank[illegible]ions of this book: Ruth Blackmore, Matth[illegible] Duncan Clark, David Doughty, Sophie Fuller, A[illegible]ameson, Francis Morris, David Nice, Francesca P[illegible], Barry Witherden and [illegible]

Publishing Information

This fifth edition published May 2010 by
Rough Guides Ltd, 80 Strand, London WC2R 0RL
375 Hudson St, 4th Floor, New York 10014, USA
Email: mail@roughguides.com

Distributed by the Penguin Group:
Penguin Books Ltd, 80 Strand, London WC2R 0RL
Penguin Putnam, Inc., 375 Hudson Street, NY 10014, USA
Penguin Group (Australia), 250 Camberwell Road, Camberwell, Victoria 3124, Australia
Penguin Books Canada Ltd, 90 Eglinton Avenue East, Toronto, Ontario, Canada M4P 2YE
Penguin Group (New Zealand), Cnr Rosedale and Airborne Roads, Albany, Auckland, New Zealand

Printed by Toppan Security Printing Pte. Ltd. , Singapore

Typeset in Minion, Myriad and DIN to an original design by Duncan Clark

The publishers and authors have done their best to ensure the accuracy and currency of all information in *The Rough Guide to Classical Music*; however, they can accept no responsibility for any loss or inconvenience sustained by any reader as a result of its information or advice.

688 pages; includes index

A catalogue record for this book is available from the British Library

ISBN 978-1-84836-476-9

1 3 5 7 9 8 6 4 2

Feature Boxes

INTRODUCTION

There are many books on composers and their works, and there are numerous guides to the countless recordings of classical music available on CD. *The Rough Guide to Classical Music* aims to be both of these things – and to do so with a degree of selectivity that will help readers get straight to the most important and enjoyable works and recordings. In short, it's an A to Z survey of over 200 of the most significant composers in the history of western music – ranging from Hildegard of Bingen, one of the great figures of eleventh-century Europe, to Thomas Adès, born in London in 1971. Each composer gets a fact-filled biography, followed by discussion of each of their most important works, along with reviews of recommended recordings.

Producing a book such as this inevitably means leaving out many composers and even more compositions and recordings. But that's partly the point. Joseph Haydn, for example, wrote 104 symphonies and while all are worth hearing, some are definitely more exciting than others – especially for someone new to his music. We've gone for what we think are the best works by the most interesting composers, mixing some underrated figures with the big names. We've also included 42 feature boxes covering such diverse topics as troubadours, the birth of opera, the rise of the virtuoso and electronic music (see opposite).

CD recommendations

Choosing which CDs to recommend requires even greater ruthlessness than selecting which composers and works to include. Beethoven only wrote nine symphonies, but there have been hundreds of recordings made of the fifth symphony alone. While it's arguable that several of these should never have been issued, a piece of music as complex as a Beethoven symphony can bear many different interpretations and a sizeable proportion of them are worth listening to.

Although some cases recordings stand head and shoulders above the competition, no performance can be described as definitive. That's one reason why we often recommend more than one version of a piece. Whereas all our first-choice CDs make persuasive cases for the music, some of the additional recommendations make valid, and sometimes provocative, alternatives.

In several instances, we've recommended a "historical", pre-stereo recording as well as a modern digital recording. While there are undoubtedly many extraordinary performers around today, and modern recordings usually benefit from technically immaculate sound quality, new is not always best. Few recent releases can match the excitement of Vladimir Horowitz's 1943 account of Tchaikovsky's *Piano Concerto No. 1* or Reginald Kell's moving performance of Brahms's *Clarinet Quintet* from the 1930s. Furthermore, it doesn't follow that a recording made more than sixty years ago will have terrible sound quality – many sound surprisingly good, and there are several companies who specialize in reissuing and remastering old recordings.

How the book works

Immediately after this introduction you'll find a list of all the composers covered in the guide, arranged chronologically, so you can see at a glance who fits where. If you find you like the music of Vivaldi, you could check the list and decide to listen to Telemann, his contemporary. Things are more complicated with the stylistically varied twentieth century: Xenakis and Arnold were born just a year apart but their music seems to come from different worlds. When a musical connection does exist (as in the case of Mozart and Haydn or Schoenberg and Berg), a cross-reference in the main text will point you in the right direction. This is followed by a list of 100 essential works that would serve as a good place to start for anyone new to classical music. At the end of the book there's a detailed glossary that defines all the technical terms we've used.

Between lies the bulk of the guide, an A to Z of composers from John Adams to Alexander Zemlinsky. Each entry starts with an introduction to the composer's life and music, followed by a run-through of the main compositions, moving from the largest-scale works to the smallest. With the most important figures – such as Bach, Mozart and Beethoven – we've generally grouped the music under generic headings (eg "Chamber Music"), giving an introduction to the composer's work in that genre before going on to individual pieces.

Each discussion of a work or works is followed by reviews of recommended recordings, with the performer details conforming to a regular format: soloist first, then orchestra/choir/ensemble, then conductor – with the name of the record company and the number of CDs in parenthesis, along with a summary of the other works featured on the disc. Take this recording of Glazunov's *Violin Concerto*:

Znaider; Bavarian Radio Symphony Orchestra; Jansons (RCA; with Prokofiev *Violin Concerto No. 2*)

Here, Nikolaj Znaider is the soloist, he's playing with the Baltimore Symphony Orchestra conducted by Mariss Jansons (we've left off first names to save space).

Purchasing CDs

If you purchase your CDs through a record store, many of those we've recommended will need to be ordered, since most stores stock just the bestsellers and new releases. Should you find that a listed CD is not in your store's catalogue, it may have been deleted or be about to be repackaged: the major companies are pretty quick to delete slow-moving items, but often reissue them, either at a lower price or combined with different music. Newly deleted and second-hand CDs can usually be located via the Internet, which is also a good place to purchase new CDs – from retailers and record companies, and, in several instances, directly from the performers or the composer.

There's been a continuous downturn in the production of classical CDs from the major companies over the last ten years. In several cases this has led to projects being curtailed and major performers and orchestras losing lucrative contracts. Not everyone has taken this lying down and a wealth of small independent companies has emerged to plug gaps in the market. Many orchestras (including the Hallé, the London Symphony Orchestra and the Chicago Symphony Orchestra) now have their own labels, and even venues, such as London's Wigmore Hall, produce their own recordings. In the case of individual composers and performers, several have bought the rights to formerly deleted recordings, repackaged them and made them available via their own websites.

Full-price recent releases can still be expensive, but the last two decades have seen an explosion of budget labels – pioneered by Naxos – and this has spurred both the big multinationals and the larger independent companies to put more effort into their own mid- and budget-price series. These reissues often feature some of the finest performances of a work ever made, so don't think for a minute that quality of a CD is always reflected in its price.

Classical downloads

Another development in the recording industry is the growth of music download services, which allow you to purchase music online and download it to your computer to then either play using a dedicated jukebox application (such as iTunes), "burn" to a CD (to use just as you would a regular CD) or transfer to an MP3 player. Apple's iTunes Store has blazed the trail for such services since 2003, its success due in part to the popularity of the same company's iPod. At first classical music was pretty poorly served by downloads but by the end of 2009 a huge amount of quality material was available. Many record labels offer their own sites where you can download new recordings, back catalogue and, in some cases, deletions. There are also several download providers with a strong classical catalogue, such as eMusic, classicsonline.com and passionato.com.

The advantages of downloading are the cost (between half and a third of the price of a CD), the fact that you can choose to purchase either an entire album or individual tracks and, of course, the fact that it delivers to your home more or less instantaneously. The drawbacks are the marginally inferior sound (not a problem for most people and, anyway, likely to improve), the lack of sleeve notes and, in the case of song and opera, the absence of the words – although such information is easily found on the Internet and is often provided on record company download sites.

CHRONOLOGY OF COMPOSERS

Born before 1400

Hildegard of Bingen	1098–1179
Perotin	c. 1170–c.1236
Guillaume de Machaut	c. 1300–1377
Francesco Landini	c. 1325–1397
John Dunstable	c. 1390–1453

Born 1400–1499

Guillaume Dufay	c. 1400–1474
Johannes Ockeghem	c. 1420–1497
Josquin Desprez	c. 1455–1521
Antoine Brumel	c. 1460–c. 1520
John Taverner	1490–1545

Born 1500–1599

Thomas Tallis	c. 1505–1585
Giovanni Palestrina	1526–1594
Roland de Lassus	1532–1594
William Byrd	c. 1537–1623
Tomás Luis de Victoria	1548–1611
Giovanni Gabrieli	1557–1612
Carlo Gesualdo	c. 1561–1613
John Dowland	1563–1626
Claudio Monteverdi	1567–1643
Michael Praetorius	1571–1621
Gregorio Allegri	1582–1652
Orlando Gibbons	1583–1625
Heinrich Schütz	1585–1672

Born 1600–1699

William Lawes	1602–1645
Francesco Cavalli	1602–1676
Giacomo Carissimi	1605–1674
Barbara Strozzi	1619–c. 1677
Jean-Baptiste Lully	1632–1687
Dietrich Buxtehude	1637–1707
Heinrich Biber	1644–1704
Alessandro Stradella	1644–1682
Marc-Antoine Charpentier	1645–1704
Arcangelo Corelli	1653–1713
Johann Pachelbel	1653–1706
Henry Purcell	1659–1695
Alessandro Scarlatti	1660–1725
François Couperin	1668–1733
Tomaso Albinoni	1671–1750
Antonio Vivaldi	1678–1741
Georg Philipp Telemann	1681–1767
Jean-Philippe Rameau	1683–1764
J.S. Bach	1685–1750
George Frideric Handel	1685–1759
Domenico Scarlatti	1685–1757
Silvius Leopold Weiss	1686–1750
Giuseppe Tartini	1692–1770

Born 1700–1799

Giovanni Battista Pergolesi	1710–1736
C.P.E. Bach	1714–1788
Christoph Willibald Gluck	1714–1787
Joseph Haydn	1732–1809
Luigi Boccherini	1743–1805
Muzio Clementi	1752–1832
Wolfgang Amadeus Mozart	1756–1791
Ludwig van Beethoven	1770–1827
Johann Nepomuck Hummel	1778–1837
Nicolò Paganini	1782–1840
Carl Maria von Weber	1786–1826
Gioacchino Rossini	1792–1868
Gaetano Donizetti	1797–1848
Franz Schubert	1797–1828

Born 1800–1824

Vincenzo Bellini	1801–1835
Hector Berlioz	1803–1869
Johann Strauss the Elder	1804–1849
Mikhail Glinka	1804–1857
Felix Mendelssohn	1809–1847
Frédéric Chopin	1810–1849

Robert Schumann	1810–1856
Franz Liszt	1811–1886
Giuseppe Verdi	1813–1901
Richard Wagner	1813–1883
Charles François Gounod	1818–1893
Jacques Offenbach	1819–1880
César Franck	1822–1890
Anton Bruckner	1824–1896
Bedřich Smetana	1824–1884

Born 1825–1849

Johann Strauss the Younger	1825–1899
Alexander Borodin	1833–1887
Johannes Brahms	1833–1897
Camille Saint-Saëns	1835–1921
Léo Delibes	1836–1891
Georges Bizet	1838–1875
Max Bruch	1838–1920
Modest Mussorgsky	1839–1881
Pyotr Il'yich Tchaikovsky	1840–1893
Emmanuel Chabrier	1841–1894
Antonín Dvořák	1841–1904
Jules Massenet	1842–1912
Arthur Sullivan	1842–1900
Edvard Grieg	1843–1907
Nikolai Rimsky-Korsakov	1844–1908
Charles Marie-Widor	1844–1937
Gabriel Fauré	1845–1924
Henri Duparc	1848–1933
Hubert Parry	1848–1918

Born 1850–1874

Engelbert Humperdinck	1854–1921
Leoš Janáček	1854–1928
Edward Elgar	1857–1934
Ruggero Leoncavallo	1858–1924
Ethel Smyth	1858–1944
Isaac Albéniz	1860–1909
Gustav Mahler	1860–1911
Hugo Wolf	1860–1903
Claude Debussy	1862–1918
Frederick Delius	1862–1934
Pietro Mascagni	1863–1945
Richard Strauss	1864–1949
Paul Dukas	1865–1935
Alexander Glazunov	1865–1936
Carl Nielsen	1865–1931
Jean Sibelius	1865–1957
Ferruccio Busoni	1866–1924
Erik Satie	1866–1925
Umberto Giordano	1867–1948
Enrique Granados	1867–1916
Franz Lehár	1870–1948
Alexander Zemlinsky	1871–1942
Alexander Scriabin	1872–1915
Ralph Vaughan Williams	1872–1958
Sergei Rachmaninov	1873–1943
Max Reger	1873–1916
Gustav Holst	1874–1934
Charles Ives	1874–1954
Arnold Schoenberg	1874–1951
Josef Suk	1874–1935

Born 1875–1899

Maurice Ravel	1875–1937
Manuel de Falla	1876–1946
Franz Schreker	1878–1934
Marie-Joseph Canteloube	1879–1957
Ottorino Respighi	1879–1936
Béla Bartók	1881–1945
Percy Grainger	1882–1961
Zoltán Kodály	1882–1967
Igor Stravinsky	1882–1971
Karol Szymanowski	1882–1937
Edgard Varèse	1883–1965
Anton Webern	1883–1945
Arnold Bax	1883–1953
Agustín Pio Barrios	1885–1944
Alban Berg	1885–1935
Heitor Villa-Lobos	1887–1959
Frank Martin	1890–1974
Bohuslav Martinů	1890–1959
Sergey Prokofiev	1891–1953
Arthur Honegger	1892–1955
Darius Milhaud	1892–1974
Lili Boulanger	1893–1918
Paul Hindemith	1895–1963
Carl Orff	1895–1982
Roberto Gerhard	1896–1970
Erich Wolfgang Korngold	1897–1957
Hanns Eisler	1898–1962
George Gershwin	1898–1937
Viktor Ullmann	1898–1944
Francis Poulenc	1899–1963

Born 1900–1924

Aaron Copland	1900–1990
Kurt Weill	1900–1950
Joaquín Rodrigo	1901–1999
William Walton	1902–1983
Maurice Duruflé	1902–1983
Aram Khachaturian	1903–1978
Luigi Dallapiccola	1904–1975
Karl Amadeus Hartmann	1905–1963
Giacinto Scelsi	1905–1988
Michael Tippett	1905–1998
Elisabeth Lutyens	1906–1983
Dmitri Shostakovich	1906–1975
Elizabeth Maconchy	1907–1990
Elliott Carter	1908–
Olivier Messiaen	1908–1992
Grażyna Bacewicz	1909–1967
Samuel Barber	1910–1981
John Cage	1912–1992
Conlon Nancarrow	1912–1997
Benjamin Britten	1913–1976
Witold Lutosławski	1913–1994
Henri Dutilleux	1916–
Leonard Bernstein	1918–1990
Malcolm Arnold	1921–2006
Iannis Xenakis	1922–2001
György Ligeti	1923–2006
Luigi Nono	1924–1990

Born 1925–present

Luciano Berio	1925–2003
Pierre Boulez	1925–
Morton Feldman	1926–1987
Hans Werner Henze	1926–
György Kurtág	1926–
Einojuhani Rautavaara	1928–
Karlheinz Stockhausen	1928–2007
Toru Takemitsu	1930–1996
Sofia Gubaidulina	1931–
Mauricio Kagel	1931–
Henryk Górecki	1933–
Krzysztof Penderecki	1933–
Harrison Birtwistle	1934–
Peter Maxwell Davies	1934–
Alfred Schnittke	1934–1998
Nicholas Maw	1935–2009
Arvo Pärt	1935–
Helmut Lachenmann	1935–
Steve Reich	1936–
Philip Glass	1937–
Louis Andriessen	1939–
Jonathan Harvey	1939–
Michael Nyman	1944–
John Tavener	1944–
John Adams	1947–
Tristan Murail	1947–
Poul Ruders	1949–
Wolfgang Rihm	1952–
Kaija Saariaho	1952–
Oliver Knussen	1952–
Judith Weir	1954–
Magnus Lindberg	1958–
James MacMillan	1959–
George Benjamin	1960–
Mark-Anthony Turnage	1960–
Michael Torke	1961–
Thomas Adès	1971–

100 ESSENTIAL WORKS

a

John Adams (1947–)

Like Philip Glass and the other minimalists with whom he is often bracketed, John Adams set out to reverse the influence of modernist cerebralism, to make it okay for composers to write unashamedly tonal music again. For Adams, "tonality is not just a cultural invention, but a natural force, like gravity". But unlike any thoroughgoing minimalist, Adams writes fairly eventful music which in a way is reminiscent of Charles Ives: never coy about using vernacular and "banal" elements, he is a crusading synthesist who is quite happy to borrow openly from sources as wide-ranging as jazz, Arab music, church music and folk tunes.

Taught clarinet by his father (a successful dance-band saxophonist) Adams was encouraged by both parents to listen to a huge variety of music, ranging from Mozart to Duke Ellington. (A cherished childhood memory is of being taken to an Ellington concert and sitting on the piano stool next to the jazz maestro.) When Adams arrived at Harvard in the late 1960s he was swept up by the radicalism of the times, and was particularly fascinated by William Burroughs' use of "vernacular, junkie language", which directly inspired him to write music that "didn't make a distinction between high art and low art, highbrow and middlebrow and lowbrow". An even greater influence was the composer John Cage (see p.125), whose *Silence*, a delightfully eccentric Zen-like collection of essays, gave Adams the courage to find his own voice as a composer.

After graduation, he headed west to San Francisco, where he encountered the minimalist works of Steve Reich, Terry Riley and Philip Glass for the first time (see p.451). Adams was immediately drawn to minimalism's resolute reliance on tonality, its insistent, hypnotic rhythms, and its absorption of Balinese, African, Indian and other non-Western musics. Yet, while Adams still stands by the view that minimalism is "the most important stylistic development in Western art music since the fifties", he soon saw the limitations of a technique that placed so much emphasis upon repetition. With *Shaker Loops* (1978) he heralded what he termed "post-minimalism", a style characterized by a more fluid and layered sound, and greater dynamic contrasts.

With his three-act opera *Nixon in China*, premiered at Houston in 1985, Adams really hit his stride. The choice of subject – President Nixon's visit to Peking in 1972 – was a daring departure for a genre that tends to fall back on ancient history or mythology for its plots, and Adams's music showed the potential of a style that amalgamated minimalist procedures with more dramatic forms

John Adams rehearsing the BBC Symphony Orchestra, January 2002.

of writing. As well as a wealth of highly kinetic repetitive rhythms, *Nixon* also has stretches of witty pastiche and parody. Audience response was positive but critics were divided, with European critics notably less enthusiastic than their US counterparts. However, by the time of his second opera, *The Death of Klinghoffer* (1991), Adams was widely recognized as a major figure on both sides of the Atlantic.

The 1990s saw Adams continuing to work on a large scale, with a series of concertos for violin, for clarinet (*Gnarly Buttons*) and for piano (*Century Rolls*). The decade culminated with *El Niño*, an ambitious meditation on Christ's nativity in the form of an oratorio – a kind of modern-day *Messiah*. Since the turn of the new century, Adams has seen his position as America's unofficial composer laureate consolidated by his thoughtful response to 9/11, *On the Transmigration of Souls* (2002) and another opera on a US historical theme, *Doctor Atomic* (2005). With a libretto by his regular theatre collaborator, Peter Sellars, the opera focused on the 1945 atom-bomb test at Los Alamos, in particular the paradox of how the sensitive J. Robert Oppenheimer came to be involved in the creation of a mass-killing machine. Generally considered dramaturgically abstruse but musically powerful, Adams reworked some of the material into the compelling *Doctor Atomic Symphony* (2007).

The Death of Klinghoffer

The Death of Klinghoffer is similar to *Nixon in China* in that it tackles an event from recent political history – the hijacking of the ocean liner *Achille Lauro* by Palestinian terrorists, and their murder of one of the passengers, Leon Klinghoffer. Adams created it in partnership with the librettist Alice Goodman and the director Peter Sellars, but there the similarities between the two operas end. While *Nixon in China* was essentially a comedy, *Klinghoffer* is preoccupied with the deep religious and economic conflicts that drove the terrible events of October 1985. Whereas *Nixon in China* is for the most part naturalistic in pace and setting, the dramaturgy of *Klinghoffer* is based, according to Adams, on largely static models, encompassing Bach's Passion settings, Greek tragedy, and Persian and Japanese drama. *Klinghoffer* is too raw to make for a comfortable night at the theatre, but it is an emotionally riveting experience, and one of Adams's most impressive achievements to date.

Maddalena, Felty, Hammons, Young, Perry, Sylvan, Friedman, Nadler; Lyon Opera Chorus & Orchestra; Nagano (Elektra Nonesuch; 2 CDs)

From the opening orchestral F minor chords Kent Nagano exerts a tight grip on this piece, and the entire performance turns out to be deep and searching. The Lyon Opera Orchestra is always impressive, while James Maddalena, as the ship's philosophical captain, and Sanford Sylvan, as Klinghoffer, are outstanding.

El Niño

In *El Niño* (The Child), a "nativity oratorio" composed 1999–2000, John Adams reworked the Christmas story as an exploration of his own faith and a wider celebration of the marvel of birth. The libretto – assembled from texts ranging from the writings of Hildegard of Bingen to extracts from the Bible and the Wakefield Mystery Plays – draws heavily on the work of Hispanic American poets such as Rosario Castellanos, whose presence gives a clue to Adams's desire to liberate the story from the West and to provide a female perspective.

Nearly two hours long and very much defined by its variety, *El Niño* is as impressive a display of Adams's compositional faculties as anything in his output. It exploits many different textural and timbral possibilities with various configurations of soloists, chorus and orchestra (guitars and deftly handled percussion add to the kaleidoscopic orchestral palette) yet there's a consistent sense of the Baroque in the mixture of directness, poignancy and rhetoric in the vocal writing.

Lieberson, Upshaw, White; Theatre of Voices; London Voices; Deutsches Symphonie-Orchester Berlin; Nagano (Nonesuch; 2 CDs)

This live recording, from the first run of performances in Paris, is a highly impressive achievement. Mezzo Lorraine Hunt Lieberson and soprano Dawn Upshaw are expressive yet controlled, the Deutsches Symphonie-Orchester Berlin sound vivid and precise, and Nagano binds the whole thing together with consummate skill.

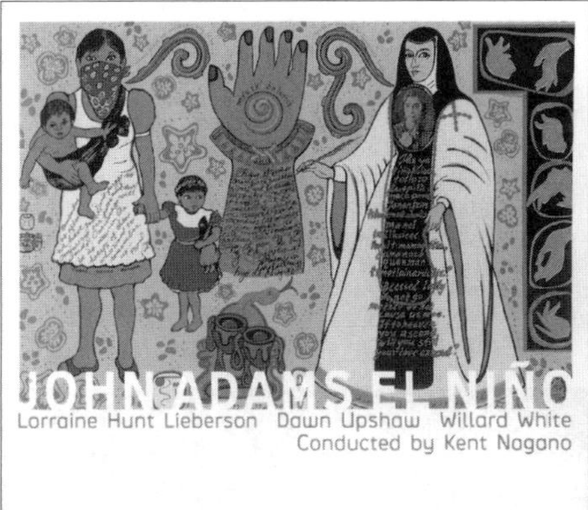

Harmonium

Harmonium came about as a result of Adams's relationship with the San Francisco Symphony Orchestra for whom he was composer in residence during the 1980s. It marks a turning point in his attempt to transform minimalism into something richer and less rigid – from, in his own words, "Great Prairies of non-event" into "forms that grow". Written for chorus and orchestra, *Harmonium* is a setting of three poems, the first of which, John Donne's "Negative Love", is a complex meditation on different types of love. It begins on a single note, around which other notes gradually accumulate, building up in size and momentum into a euphoric blaze of throbbing sound. The second and third poems are both by Emily Dickinson: "Because I Could Not Stop for Death", a poignant review of the writer's life seen from the window of a carriage, has a chant-like simplicity which is soothing and reassuring whereas "Wild Nights" is an astonishing cry of visionary ecstasy which returns to the pulsating vigour of the work's opening but this time with an electrifying, volcanic power.

San Francisco Symphony Orchestra & Chorus; de Waart (ECM)

There's little to choose between this recording and the one listed below. Edo de Waart conducted the premiere, and his commitment to the work is palpable in this 1984 live recording. The sheer excitement is electrifying with the chorus really letting themselves go in "Wild Nights".

San Francisco Symphony Orchestra & Chorus; Adams (Elektra Nonesuch; with *Klinghoffer Choruses*)

Thirteen years on and there's more restraint under the composer's direction. The sound is brilliantly clear, and the emotional core of the work, "Because I Could Not Stop for Death", comes across with heart-stopping poignancy. But the chorus, in the louder moments, sounds a little "set back", making for a more natural but less exciting atmosphere.

Shaker Loops

Shaker Loops grew out of *Wavemaker*, a string quartet in which Adams tried to merge the repetitive processes of minimalism and his own interest in waveforms. Its premiere was a failure, and Adams used his classes at San Francisco Conservatory as a means of salvaging something from it. Renamed, amended and expanded to a septet, *Shaker Loops* appeared in 1978. Its new title was inspired by the minimalist tape-loop works of the 1960s (for example *It's Gonna Rain* by Steve Reich); a pun on the musical term for a rapid tremolo; and the state of religious ecstasy attained by members of the Shaker sect.

Shaker Loops is characterized by ceaseless motion even in the slower sections, where the lines drift like mist in a forest breeze. The restless first and fourth parts ("Shaking and Trembling" and "A Final Shaking") frame the slow and languid glissandos of the second ("Hymning Slews") and the lyrical character of the third ("Loops and Verses"), which moves towards a "wild push-pull section" – what Adams calls "the emotional high point" of the work.

Orchestra of St Luke's; Adams (Nonesuch; with *Violin Concerto*)

In 1983 Adams expanded the instrumentation of *Shaker Loops* further, producing a version for string orchestra. This has become one of Adams's most popular scores, and was used in the film *Barfly*. This 1988 recording by Adams himself must be regarded as authoritative (though Edo de Waart's vibrant recording with the San Francisco Symphony Orchestra is equally impressive).

Ensemble Modern; Edwards (RCA; with *Chamber Symphony & Phrygian Gates*)

For those who think they might prefer the purity of the septet version (for three violins, two cellos, viola and bass) this Ensemble Modern recording conducted by Sian Edwards is excellent. Crisply and energetically performed, the music achieves a greater clarity with little loss of power.

Violin Concerto

Co-commissioned by the New York City Ballet, the LSO and the Minnesota Orchestra, the *Violin Concerto* was created with the knowledge that it would be choreographed, and this influenced its form as well as its content and character. It may seem odd that, writing music for dancing, Adams should tone down the strong rhythmic character of his style, but the violin part moves through the three movements in an endless line that weaves its way in and out of the orchestral texture. Though he follows the outline of the traditional concerto – a rhapsodic beginning, a slow central movement ("Chaconne"; "Body Through Which the Dream Flows") and an energetic climax ("Toccare") – the violin is always an active presence, flowing through the body of the orchestra rather than engaging with it in the usual dialogue.

Kremer; London Symphony Orchestra; Nagano (Nonesuch; with *Shaker Loops*)

The world premiere of the concerto was performed by Jorja Fleezanis in 1994, but Gidon Kremer was the soloist in the European premiere six months later, so it's hardly surprising he sounds thoroughly steeped in the music. Kremer's playing is sleek, sinuous and supple, and his tone glows richly against the varied orchestral background.

Harmonielehre

Adams was never really a pure minimalist: his music had too much harmonic momentum, too much timbral lushness – factors which gave classic early pieces like *Harmonielehre* their exhilarating feel. The opening movement, inspired by a dream in which Adams saw a gigantic tanker rise from San Francisco Bay and hurtle into the sky, begins with shattering chords dominated by brass and percussion. The second movement, "The Anfortas Wound" (a reference to the stricken guardian of the Holy Grail in Wagner's *Parsifal*), is completely different: richly expressive, its harmonic and melodic idiom recalls the late Romanticism that Schoenberg believed signalled the end of tonal music. Indeed, *Harmonielehre* is the title of Schoenberg's 1911 treatise on harmony in which he spelled out his new radical departure, and by purloining the title, Adams states his faith in tonality as a still living tradition. The last movement, "Meister Eckhardt and the Quackie", interweaves the minimalism and the neo-Romanticism of the previous movements into a marvellous fusion – a celebration of the key of E flat.

City of Birmingham Symphony Orchestra; Rattle (EMI; with *The Chairman Dances, Tromba Lontana & Short Ride in a Fast Machine*)

Simon Rattle regards Adams as one of the most significant composers of modern times, and in this vigorous performance he certainly seems to be putting his energy where his enthusiasm is. The CBSO plays with wonderful punch and precision in the minimalist episodes, and a languid grace in the neo-Romantic passages.

Thomas Adès (1971–)

Composer, performer, conductor: in these days of strict demarcation, few musicians are capable of taking on all three roles, but Thomas Adès manages it, and with prodigious success. It was as a pianist that he first attracted attention when he won Second Prize (Piano Class) in the 1989 BBC Young Musician of the Year. It proved a turning point: "It gave me quite a fright", he later recalled; "Did I want to go through all this again, play the same things again? I went home and said, 'I'm going to become a composer today, and do it properly.' I started at the top note of the piano, and went on from there."

By this time he had already studied piano and composition at London's Guildhall School, and had gone on to King's College, Cambridge, where he graduated with a double-starred first. The piece he began immediately after winning the BBC competition was *Five Eliot Landscapes* for soprano and piano, completed in 1990 as his Opus 1, and first performed in 1993. Throughout the 1990s Adès's *oeuvre* grew steadily, as did his portfolio of prestigious appointments: composer-in-association with the Hallé Orchestra (1993–95), music director of the Birmingham Contemporary Music Group (1996–2000), artistic director of the Aldeburgh Festival (1999–2008). In addition, EMI developed a close interest in his work, releasing several CDs before signing him to an exclusive seven-year contract in 1999.

Works for solo piano (usually premiered by the composer) form a significant part of his catalogue, but he has also written for chamber ensembles of various sizes, from the string quartet *Arcadiana* (1994) to the 14-piece ensemble required for *Living Toys* (1993), while major works for large orchestra include *Asyla* (1997) and *America: A Prophecy* (1999). Combining head and heart in unexpected ways, Adès has consistently shown the knack of turning tonality and rhythm on their head, and of wrily reshaping "extraneous" idioms (Ecstasy-driven dance rhythms, a slinky tango, sundry baroqueries, tough blues voicings) to his own ends.

His most celebrated work is the opera *Powder Her Face* (1995), a caustic satire on British hypocrisy that gained notoriety for its treatment of the life, divorce and death of the Duchess of Argyll: at one point the soprano impersonating the duchess has to perform what has been claimed as the world's first onstage fellatio aria. The opera's irreverent high spirits are matched by its cinematic skill in delineating location and character.

The success (or notoriety) of *Powder Her Face* led to an operatic commission from the Royal Opera House. Adès aimed high, taking as his text Shakespeare's *The Tempest* in an adaptation by playwright Meredith Oakes. Premiered in 2004, with an outstanding cast conducted by the composer, it contained some magical moments but was less musically daring and coherent than his earlier opera. It was followed, the next year, by *Violin Concerto (Concentric Paths)*, written for Anthony Marwood, and another large-scale orchestral work, *Tevot* (2007), for the Berlin Philharmonic.

A further dimension has been added to Adès's work by his relationship – both professional and personal – with the artist and filmmaker Tal Rosner. *In Seven Days* (2008), a multi-media piece inspired by the opening chapters of Genesis, created a hypnotic correspondence between swirling onscreen abstractions and Adès's dazzling, kaleidoscopic music for piano and orchestra.

Asyla

Commissioned by the City of Birmingham Symphony Orchestra and its conductor Simon Rattle, *Asyla* (the plural of the word "asylum") is one of Adès's most impressive big pieces. The opening percussion fanfare (including a quasi-Mahlerian pealing of cowbells) ushers in a keening horn melody that wakes the wind section to sympathetic muttering. Throughout, the large percussion section seems to set the agenda. In the third movement, subtitled "Ecstasio", a savage frenzy courses through the whole orchestra as Adès pays homage to rave culture and its stimulant of choice. Yet the predominant mood, established in the opening moments and elaborated in the solo for bass oboe that sets the second movement in motion, is of mournful longing, and there are passages of the most refined delicacy. Adès, evidently not overawed by the large canvas, provides a thorough workout for the modern virtuoso orchestra.

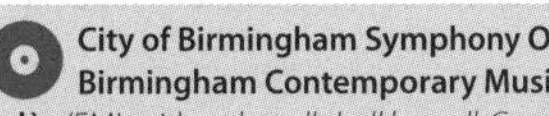
City of Birmingham Symphony Orchestra; Birmingham Contemporary Music Group; Rattle, Adès (EMI; with *. . . but all shall be well, Concerto Conciso & Chamber Symphony*)

Eight months after giving the premiere, Simon Rattle and his orchestra recorded *Asyla* over two live performances on successive days. Their reading has the stamp of experience and authority – here and throughout the CD, every detail is cleanly etched, from the very loud to the almost inaudible.

America: A Prophecy

Adès's music has usually been commissioned by British organizations or individuals, but his talent has not gone unnoticed elsewhere. In 1999 the New York Philharmonic Orchestra celebrated the new millennium by commissioning works from six composers. Adès's response was *America: A Prophecy*, a work full of menace rather than millennial optimism. It dramatizes a genuine clash of civilizations, between Spanish conquistadors and the Maya whom they annihilated. The Maya are represented by a mezzo-soprano, intoning in a voice almost drained of emotional inflection; a chorus takes the side of the Spanish, while the orchestra bridges the two, slithering and stomping for the Mayan passages, clamorous and chaotic for the Spanish. Ades's texts include such lines as "They will come from the east ... they will burn all the land, they will burn all the sky". On 11 September 2001, the whole piece suddenly seemed truly prophetic, but even without that unlooked-for relevance, *America: A Prophecy* has an unsettling power.

City of Birmingham Symphony Orchestra; Adès
(EMI; currently download only)

The City of Birmingham Symphony Orchestra and Chorus know Adès's music intimately, and it shows. No less importantly, Susan Bickley conjures up a tranced intensity for the Mayan prophecies. Adès's dark humour and restless imagination find their fullest expression in this, his most compelling work for orchestra.

Chamber Music

Adès has been fascinated by the sound-worlds opened up by period instruments, and his *Sonata da Caccia* (1993) pays tribute to the music of François Couperin (see p.148). Written for baroque oboe, horn and harpsichord, it occasionally sounds almost like a genuinely eighteenth-century work (notably at the highly melodic beginning of the third movement) but one renewed by Adès's distinctly contemporary sonic imagination and rhythmic stamp.

For his only string quartet, *Arcadiana* (1994), Adès provides the second movement with a heading that quotes from Mozart, while the third ("Auf dem Wasser zu singen") takes its epigraph from the Schubert song of that title. The musical allusions – imaginative links rather than quotations – form a network of "images associated with ideas of the idyll, vanishing, vanished, or imaginary". Tuneful fragments rise to the surface and quickly subside, as in the deliberately corny gondolier's melody that bubbles through the opening movement, "Venezia notturna", or the fourth movement's lopsided tango. The whole work is suffused with an air of wistful elegy, as befits a work evoking Arcadia.

Niesemann, Clark, Adès; Endellion Quartet
(EMI; with *Sonata da Caccia* & other pieces)

Arcadiana was premiered by the Endellion Quartet as part of the 1994 Elgar Festival, a fact reflected in the stylish finesse of the group's performance. It's matched by the graceful performance of *Sonata da Caccia*, on which the composer plays harpsichord.

Isaac Albéniz (1860–1909)

Isaac Albéniz, a crucial figure in the creation of a distinctively Spanish classical musical idiom, is associated primarily with works for the piano, and above all with *Iberia*, a suite of twelve piano pieces composed between 1906 and 1909. It's hardly surprising that the majority of his pieces were written for that instrument, given Albéniz's extraordinary gifts as a performer.

Born into a musical family, Isaac made his public debut at Barcelona's Teatro Romea at the age of 4, where some members of the incredulous audience suspected that some kind of fraud was being perpetrated. At 7 he auditioned at the Paris Conservatoire, where he was praised by Professor Marmontel – the teacher of both Bizet and Debussy – but was considered too young to become a student. In 1869 he enrolled at the Madrid conservatory but at the age of 10 he suddenly ran away from home and supported himself by giving concerts in various cities in Castile. A couple of years later he topped that escapade by stowing away on a ship to South America, travelling to the USA via Argentina, Uruguay, Brazil, Cuba and Puerto Rico, earning his bread by playing piano in so-called "places of entertainment".

Although he returned to Spain and became a diligent student, Albéniz never fully exorcized his wanderlust and spent much of the rest of his life moving between Barcelona, Madrid, Paris and London. On one trip in 1880 he followed his idol Liszt through Weimar, Prague, Vienna and Budapest, gaining invaluable instruction along the way. The fulcrum of his nomadic existence for much of the 1890s was Paris, where he taught piano and struck up friendships with, among others, Debussy, Fauré and Dukas. His encounters with the new wave of French composers, headed by Debussy and Ravel, were immensely productive – and the relationship was not the one-way process it's sometimes depicted as having been, as Albéniz contributed much to the emergence of impressionist music.

But the most significant influence on Albéniz came from the musicologist and folk-song collector Felipe Pedrell. Albéniz's earliest compositions were overindebted to Liszt, but after meeting Pedrell he began to explore and experiment with Spanish folk idioms. As the nineteenth century came to a close, it was Albéniz's music above all that defined everything that was exciting about modern Spanish piano writing. Pieces like *La Vega*, the *Cantos de España* and *Suite española* are bursting with national colour, evoking the sound of guitars, flamenco rhythms and dances like the sevillana and corranda.

As well as writing for the piano, Albéniz had a rather less successful, and slightly bizarre, career as an opera composer. On a trip to London he made an agreement with the banker Francis Money-Coutts to set his English librettos to music in exchange for a regular allowance. The results were four operas, of which the last, *Merlin* (1886), was the first of a projected but never completed Arthurian trilogy on Wagnerian lines. None has entered the repertoire, although *Merlin* has recently been revived and recorded in Spanish.

Piano Music

Written when he was 26, the *Suite española* is the finest of Albéniz's early piano works, in which he reveals a total understanding of regional Spanish dance forms, at the same time transforming them into something uniquely pianistic. The exception to this rule is *Asturias* (the fifth of the eight-part suite) in which insistently repeated notes so strongly suggest a guitar that the work has been transcribed for and is often performed on that instrument. This assimilation of folkloric elements reaches a greater level of sophistication with Albéniz's masterpiece *Iberia*, a work on which he laboured obsessively for the last three years of his life. Subtitled "12 nouvelles impressions", *Iberia* conjures up the presence of a whole array of different regions (including the then Spanish colony of Cuba), capturing the musical essence of each local culture not by merely aping and embellishing its tunes – in fact, all the tunes are original – but through a subtle snatch of rhythm here and the faintest outline of a melodic refrain there. *Iberia* was immediately recognized as the most important Spanish work for solo piano, a status it still retains, and its bold sonorities and harmonies proved an inspiration for that country's young composers.

Isaac Albéniz – pianist and composer.

Iberia; Navarra; España; La Vega; Yvonne en visite!: Hamelin (Hyperion; 2 CDs)

In this recent recording Marc-André Hamelin, a Canadian pianist of dazzling virtuosity, brings all his brilliant technique to bear on *Iberia* while also managing to convey all the subtleties and colours of Albeniz's glittering Spanish travelogue. The additional pieces are no less impressive.

Iberia; Suite española; Navarra: de Larrocha (Decca; 2 CDs)

Alicia de Larrocha studied with Frank Marshall, a pupil of Albéniz's friend Granados who in turn studied with Pedrell. This Decca set (recorded in 1973) is a glorious celebration of a great pianist. She particularly relishes the more poetic, melancholy pieces – the multi-layered subtleties of the opening *Evocación* is especially beautifully handled.

Sevilla; Mallorca; Asturias; Canción y Danza No, 1: Russell (Telarc; with additional pieces by Granados, Tarrega, Malats and Pipo)

Several of Albéniz's piano works are just as effective played on the guitar, especially when the guitarist is as gifted as David Russell. This collection of Spanish favourites, *Reflections of Spain*, contains only four of the most well-known Albéniz pieces but they are delivered with an infectious verve and great expressive warmth.

Tomaso Albinoni (1671–1750)

Albinoni is almost entirely known for a piece of music he didn't actually write. The famous *Adagio in G Minor* was not merely reconstructed by the Italian musicologist Remo Giazotto, as is usually acknowledged after Albinoni's name – it was pretty well written by him in its entirety. Giazotto came across a manuscript in the ruins of the Dresden State Library just after World War II. The music (which may not even have been by Albinoni) consisted of a bass line, a few bars of the violin part, and nothing more. Deciding that what he'd found was a church sonata, Giazotto scored the piece for organ and strings. The result is a work of solemnity and affecting simplicity, which has proved an astonishingly durable favourite, almost on a par with Vivaldi's *Four Seasons* (which was rediscovered around the same time, but is entirely genuine). If, as is rumoured, Giazotto owns the copyright to the *Adagio*, he must by now be very rich indeed.

Approaching Albinoni's genuine compositions after the lushness of the *Adagio* can come as a shock. On the whole it is bright, lively and melodious music, with an obvious debt to Corelli and more than a passing resemblance to that of Vivaldi, his contemporary and fellow Venetian – but without the same degree of energy or inventiveness.

Unlike Vivaldi, Albinoni didn't have to compose to earn his living. As the eldest son of a highly prosperous paper merchant and stationer, he approached music as a committed amateur, but soon made his mark as an opera composer, writing over fifty works (of which few have survived intact). In 1721 the family business, part of which he had inherited in 1709, was successfully claimed by one of his father's many creditors, but this loss of income coincided with the most successful period of Albinoni's career. His operas were being performed outside Italy, and he was invited to supervise one of them, *I veri amici* (The True Friends), at the Bavarian court of Maximilian II Emanuel in Munich. He even received the accolade of having three themes (from his trio sonatas, Opus 1) used as the subjects for fugues by J.S. Bach – perhaps the pinnacle of his reputation until the resurrection of the *Adagio*.

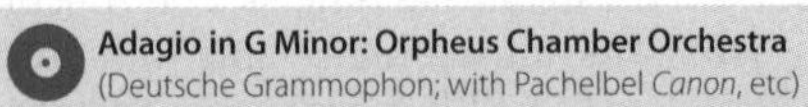
Adagio in G Minor: Orpheus Chamber Orchestra
(Deutsche Grammophon; with Pachelbel *Canon*, etc)

Performances of the *Adagio* range from the overblown to the briskly efficient. The Orpheus Chamber Orchestra take the middle line; their refined string sound makes the best possible case for the music and keeps the schmalz quotient low. The *Adagio* is coupled with a selection of Baroque favourites, including Pachelbel's *Canon*.

Concertos

Albinoni was an important figure in the development of the concerto, helping to establish the three-movement (fast-slow-fast) pattern and introducing the idea of fugal finales. The solo melodies, especially when written for the oboe, are closely modelled on the vocal ideal of smooth arching phrases with no great leaps. A feeling of balance and order prevails in most of Albinoni's instrumental writing, but this is particularly true of his twelve Opus 9 concertos (four for violin), which are outstanding for their elegance and melodic ease. The slow movements, in particular, are lyrical creations, and are often – as in the D minor oboe concerto – outstandingly beautiful.

12 Concertos, Op.9: Academy of Ancient Music; Hogwood (Decca; 2 CDs)

The whole of Opus 9 in hugely assured and elegant performances. Oboists Frank de Bruine and Alfredo Bernardini combine immaculate intonation with refined phrasing, while violinist Andrew Manze gets the pulse beating faster with his spirited accounts of the four violin concertos.

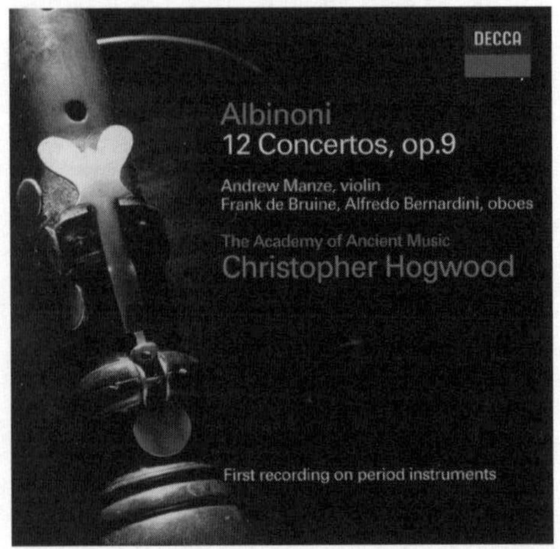

Gregorio Allegri (1582–1652)

The Sistine Chapel was built by Pope Sixtus IV to aggrandize not just himself and his family but the very office of the papacy itself. Subsequent popes contributed to its visual splendour, most notably through the frescoes of Michelangelo, but much of the chapel's fame derived from its music. The choir became a yardstick for choral excellence, and contributed to the refinement of polyphonic singing which culminated in the spiritualized serenity of Palestrina (see p.396). Its most celebrated work, however, came from an obscure composer of the next generation, Gregorio Allegri, whose setting of the *Miserere Mei* (Psalm 51 in the English Bible) was performed three times during Holy Week from the year of its creation until 1870. So renowned did this work become that its music was a closely guarded secret and illicit copyists were threatened with excommunication – though this did not stop the 14-year-old Mozart transcribing it from memory after hearing it once.

In fact the reputation of Allegri's *Miserere* derived not so much from the music itself – a simple harmonized chant – as from the astonishingly ornate embellishments improvised by members of the choir. This skill was gradually lost over the centuries so that the version that we usually hear today is one using ornamentation fixed around the end of the eighteenth century. It may be less dramatic than original performances, but its embellishment – above all the climactic top C – makes it one of the most rarefied and ethereal pieces in the whole of Catholic church music.

Allegri's musical career began in 1591 as a chorister at Rome's San Luigi dei Francesi, where he took lessons with the *maestro di cappella* Giovanni Bernardino Nanino, a follower of Palestrina. When his voice broke, Gregorio was replaced by his younger brother Domenico, but he returned as an alto in 1601. About four year later, he took holy orders and left Rome, taking up positions as composer and singer at the cathedrals of Fermo and Tivoli. After a brief spell as *maestro di cappella* of Santo Spirito in Sassia, Rome, Allegri joined the papal choir at the end of 1629. He retained the position until his death some 22 years later, and was elected *maestro di cappella* by his colleagues for the Holy Year of 1650.

In his previous appointments Allegri had adopted the new more expressive style of composition (the *seconda prattica*), but in the papal chapel, where no instruments were permitted, he returned to the *stile antico* (or *prima prattica*) as exemplified by Palestrina. Very little of this music has been recorded. At its best, as in the six-part *Missa Vidi Turbam Magnam*, Allegri breathes new life into the old forms with a wide range of contrasted voice groupings and a masterful control of sonority.

Miserere

The *Miserere*, a penitential psalm much concerned with sin, was performed at Lauds on the three days before Easter. These were Tenebrae services – as they progressed, the candles which illuminated the chapel were extinguished one by one until, in almost complete darkness, the *Miserere* was performed. In Allegri's setting the verses of the psalm alternate between plainsong (the even verses) and *falsobordone* or harmonized chant (odd verses). A further subdivision occurs: the *falsobordone* is performed in a five-part version and a four-part version by different choirs. Originally the *falsobordone* sections were a vehicle for improvised embellishments of a highly virtuosic nature in which the castrati in particular excelled. In the eighteenth century these were described by Charles Burney as "certain customs and expressions such as swelling and diminishing the notes altogether; accelerating or retarding the measure, singing some stanzas quicker than others". But already the tradition of improvisation was lost and what Burney is describing is really an interpretation of Allegri's simple harmonies onto which the embellishments had been fixed. Burney introduced the work to England but its resurgence in modern times is due to the recording made by King's College Choir in the early 1960s.

Goodman; King's College Choir; Willcocks
(Decca; with Palestrina *Stabat Mater*, etc)

Thirty or so years on and this performance still packs a punch. The treble soloist Roy Goodman (now a well-known conductor) had been cavorting around the football pitch minutes before this recording was made, but he still produced an effortless purity of tone and incisiveness which has never been bettered. The sound is warm and natural for such a notoriously difficult acoustic.

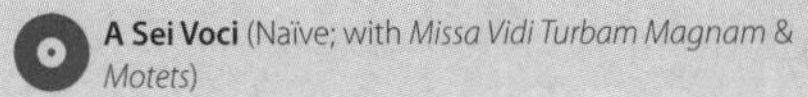

A Sei Voci (Naïve; with *Missa Vidi Turbam Magnam & Motets*)

An entire disc of music by Allegri is something of a rarity. A Sei Voci (in fact a choir of ten voices) present a cross-section of Allegri's work, including a sparkling reading of the *Missa Vidi Turbam Magnam*. There are two versions of the *Miserere* – the familiar modern edition, and one which attempts to reconstruct seventeenth-century ornamentation. The two versions are strikingly different: the ornamented version is as quirkily animated (with some odd harmonies which recall Bulgarian women's choirs) as the other is serenely predictable.

Louis Andriessen (1939–)

Louis Andriessen, Holland's foremost living composer, has a reputation as a musical iconoclast. He was one of the first European composers to break with modernism, developing a musical language which combines the hypnotic textures of minimalism, the rhythmic dynamism of Stravinsky, and the mathematical structures of J.S. Bach. Jazz is another important influence, especially bebop and boogie-woogie – music which he admires for both its coolness and its classicism. During the past twenty years Andriessen has combined his work as a composer and pianist with a teaching post in The Hague, and has become a guru to a whole generation of radical young composers.

Born in 1939 in Utrecht, Andriessen studied at The Hague Royal Conservatory with his father Hendrik and with Holland's first serial composer, Kees van Baaren, before further studies with Luciano Berio (see p.71). During the 1970s his left-wing politics led him to write for ensembles other than the conventional symphony orchestra and he created some of his most radical utterances. Two pieces, *De Volharding* (Perseverance, 1972) and *Hoketus* (1975–77), led to the formation of ensembles named after those pieces, which blurred the distinctions between "high" and "low" culture. De Volharding consisted of jazz musicians equally at home at political rallies and in the concert hall, while Hoketus were a

Louis Andriessen at work in his study.

heavily amplified group of classically trained rock musicians whose aim was to play loud, fast and dirty. Hoketus has since disbanded, but the piece of that name remains widely performed: its searing rhythmic drive and unique sound-world (saxophones, electric pianos, congas, bass guitars, panpipes) defined a new branch of urban minimalism – a far cry from the cool, laid-back quality of much American minimal music of the time.

With *De Staat* (1973–76) Andriessen began a series of pieces for large ensemble which culminated in his monumental music theatre work, *De Materie* (Matter, 1985–88) – an exploration of the relationship between spirit and matter in four interdependent non-narrative works. Andriessen continues to work on a big scale, producing pieces such as *Trilogie van de Laatste Dag* (Trilogy of the Last Day), a sardonic multi-textual disquisition on death that was first performed complete in 1998. His largest works to date, however, are the operas he has written to librettos by the filmmaker Peter Greenaway. The pair first worked together on the BBC TV film *M is for Man, Music, Mozart* (1991), a mild debunking of the more idolatrous aspects of the Mozart bicentenary. This led to further collaboration on two major theatre works: the "horse opera" *Rosa* (1994), about a fictional Mexican composer, and *Writing to Vermeer* (1999), which focused on the artist's relationship with three women (his mother, his mother-in-law and his model), and the imaginary letters they might have written to him. Besides writing the librettos, Greenaway directed the spectacular premiere productions of both works.

Andriessen has also collaborated with another filmmaker, Hal Hartley, on *The New Math(s)*, broadcast on TV in 2000, and on *La Commedia*, an opera based on Dante, which was directed by Hartley for Netherlands Opera in 2008.

De Staat

Andriessen wrote *De Staat* as a contribution to the discussion about the place of music in politics: "The moment the musical material is ordered ... it becomes culture and, as such, a given social fact." Using extracts from Plato's *Republic* which warn of the socially disruptive influence of certain types of music, *De Staat* is scored for four women's voices and twenty-five instrumentalists. The austere opening of the work – a series of canons for four oboes – has the remote and precise beauty of a mosaic. Flatulent low brass break up this restrained beginning and, throughout the work, stark contrasts of instrumental timbre are cleverly employed as if to illustrate Plato's dictum "beware of changing to a new kind of music, for the change always involves far-reaching danger". This piece frequently sounds dangerous, with its proliferation of frenzied ostinatos between cool incantatory choruses. The influence of Stravinsky and Bach is evident in the clear textures and motorized rhythms, yet the complex harmonic language and raw intensity of the work are very much Andriessen's own.

Schoenberg Ensemble; de Leeuw (Nonesuch)

The Schoenberg Ensemble and Reinbert de Leeuw have premiered many of Andriessen's works for large ensemble over the past ten years. Their playing on this 35-minute CD, in a work which makes huge demands on the performers, is both exciting and technically superb.

De Stijl

Written for the group Kaalslaag, and completed in 1985, *De Stijl* forms the third part of *De Materie*. Andriessen conceived the overall structure of the work as a translation into musical terms of the geometrical proportions of Mondrian's painting, *Composition with Red, Yellow and Blue* (1927), creating the text by juxtaposing writings on mathematical theory with reminiscences about Mondrian and his penchant for dancing. Much of the work's bristling energy is derived from the heavily amplified big band, which includes electric guitars, synthesizers, "heavy metal" percussion (i.e. four car bumpers) and boogie-woogie piano. Over a battery of strident and compulsive dance rhythms, a choir of female voices intones impassively. The perpetually restless energy of the instrumentalists conjures up more of a living and unpredictable presence than the vocalists, and despite the long, drawn-out chords that end *De Stijl* this is a work which is both exhilarating and unnerving.

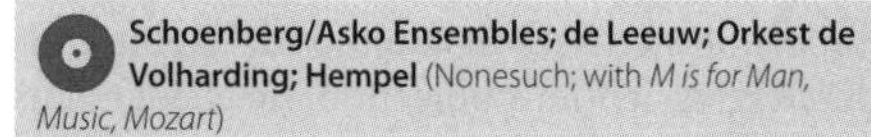

Schoenberg/Asko Ensembles; de Leeuw; Orkest de Volharding; Hempel (Nonesuch; with *M is for Man, Music, Mozart*)

This performance of *De Stijl* (also available as part of *De Materie*) is even more hard-driven than *De Staat* and it conveys much of the power of what Andriessen calls "the terrifying twenty-first century orchestra". It is coupled with the music for Peter Greenaway's film *M is for Man, Music, Mozart*.

Trilogy of the Last Day

Andriessen has what he calls a "polemical attitude" towards symphony orchestras: "They don't like my music, so why should I bother them with it? We're better off without each other." Instead he prefers to conjure up his own "terrible orchestra of the twenty-first century", as exemplified in the *Trilogy of the Last Day*, in which plaintive strings struggle to hold their own against clattering percussion, eruptive brass and woodwinds, electric guitars and synthesizers. The noisy energy generated provides a stark backcloth for the disparate texts: a choir chants a twentieth-century poem about the Last Supper, a deliberately unangelic boy sings folk poetry about a speaking skull, a *koto* player sings passages from the *Tao te Ching*, and with jaunty insouciance the aptly named De Kickers children's choir delivers grown-up truths: "Death is when … you don't shit, you don't piss any more, you don't think any more." Andriessen's "terrible orchestra" provides characteristic accompaniment, fiercely but irregularly rhythmic, usually but not invariably loud. As in his more operatic *De Materie*, the composer's choice of texts displays the elliptical wit of a philosopher-poet.

Asko Ensemble; Schönberg Ensemble; Mukaiyama; Kol; De Kickers Children's Choir; de Leeuw (Donemus Composers Voice)

The Asko and Schönberg Ensembles, like conductor Reinbert de Leeuw, are seasoned veterans when it comes to Andriessen's music, and they gave the premiere of the complete *Trilogy* in Amsterdam's Concertgebouw in 1998. This recording preserves that performance, and it is as authoritative as one could wish.

Malcolm Arnold (1921–2006)

Malcolm Arnold was one of the most traditional and at the same time individual English composers working in the post-war period, with an output based almost exclusively on strong engaging melodies supported by diatonic harmony. To an extent the apparent ease and facility with which he moved between so-called light music and more "serious" genres meant that his critical standing wavered throughout his career.

Born in Northampton, where his father owned a shoe factory, Arnold was the youngest of five children and enjoyed a comfortable upbringing. Musically precocious, he was inspired to take up the trumpet by his love for Louis Armstrong and won a scholarship to the Royal College of Music when he was 16. The decimation of the professional orchestral ranks by World War II meant that he found employment as a player even before graduation, quickly becoming principal trumpet of the London Philharmonic.

As a child Arnold had a rebellious side, and this soon manifested itself in adulthood. Having considered conscientious objection, he changed his mind and joined the army. Posted to a military band after his initial training, he shot a hole in his foot in anger and despair. It would be years before his mental condition was diagnosed as bipolar disorder, and his entire career was blighted by severe mood-swings, excessive drinking and suicide attempts.

When, in 1948, a scholarship enabled Arnold to travel to Italy and reassess his life, he gave up performing and devoted himself fully to composition. His immense fertility, and the ease with which he could get down on paper what he heard in his head, led to a highly successful career as a film composer. Beginning with short documentaries, he went on to score such classic feature films as *The Bridge on the River Kwai* (for which he won an Oscar in 1957), *The Inn of the Sixth Happiness* (1958) and *Whistle Down the Wind* (1961). Some see film as the true heart of this composer.

Arnold himself felt that his nine symphonies contained the best of him. Spanning his entire composing career, they embrace both the brilliant and the dark, and are essential listening. What lends them a deep seriousness, and sets them apart from most of the rest of his output, is the savage anger that regularly emerges: manic outbursts, related both to his troubled personal life, and to the state of the world around him.

Orchestral Music

As a professional trumpeter, Arnold developed an orchestral ear that was second to none. Berlioz,

Mahler and Sibelius were all acknowledged influences on his symphonic writing, which abounds in memorable tunes, stirring rhythms and bright primary colours, often combined with startling shifts of mood within a single movement. The elegaic *Symphony No. 5* (1961), the best known of his nine symphonies, abounds in paradoxes right from the first movement, in which the prevailing mood of unease has glints of lyricism shining through it. Even more startling is the Andante, seemingly a parody of a Mahler slow movement but becoming increasingly unstable as it progresses. His other orchestral music includes concertos written for his many musical friends, incidental pieces, and four delightful sets of dances from around the British Isles and a joyous fifth set from Cornwall – his home when he was at his most productive.

English, Scottish, Cornish and Irish Dances: Philharmonia Orchestra; Thomson (Chandos)

Bryden Thomson's recording of the *English, Scottish, Cornish and Irish Dances* is spontaneous and brimming with life. The recording is clear and well-focused and the playing of the Philharmonia is very light and responsive. It's part of a series of Arnold's music made by Chandos, which includes recordings of all nine symphonies and much of his film music.

Symphonies Nos. 2 & 5: Bournemouth Symphony Orchestra; Groves; City of Birmingham Symphony Orchestra; Arnold (EMI; with *Peterloo Overture*)

Although these two recordings date from 1970 the sound is impressively bright. Arnold's own reading of *Symphony No. 5* is especially vivid but without recourse to melodrama. The dark-hued slow movement has rarely been delivered with such burnished intensity.

Wind Chamber Music

Arnold was not exclusively a composer with a broad brush. He relaxed in smaller forms and his miniatures – many of them written for his orchestral colleagues to play – are colourful and ingenious in their often odd instrumental combinations. One of the earliest pieces to bring him to the attention of a wider public was the *Three Shanties for Wind Quintet* (1943), short pieces which develop their familiar tunes ("What Shall We Do with the Drunken Sailor?, "Boney was a Warrior" and "Johnny Come Down to Hilo") with infinite charm and with quiet, almost Haydnesque wit. Arnold's awareness of an instrument's character and capabilities, coupled with his quicksilver imagination, is also very much to the fore in the *Divertimento for Flute, Oboe and Clarinet* (1952) whose six short movements run the gamut of moods from playful good humour to quiet introspection.

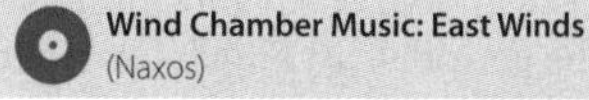
Wind Chamber Music: East Winds (Naxos)

This survey of all Arnold's wind chamber music, including the recently found *Wind Quintet* and some specially arranged works for wind octet, is performed with great flair and obvious enjoyment by the quintet East Winds and various guest artists. It makes the perfect introduction to an important aspect of Arnold's musical personality.

b

Grażyna Bacewicz (1909–1969)

Poland's most important composer between Szymanowski (see p.558) and Lutosławski (see p.311), Grażyna Bacewicz was born in Łódź into a musical family – her brother Kiejstut was a fine pianist with whom she frequently performed – and began studying at the Warsaw conservatory in 1928. She continued her musical education in Paris with two of the most influential teachers of the period, Carl Flesch for violin and Nadia Boulanger for composition. She was unfortunate to be entered for the Wieniawski violin competition in 1935, the same year as David Oistrakh and Ginette Neveu, two of the greatest violinists of the century. She did well enough, however, to gain a first-class distinction and went on to have an outstanding career as a soloist, being especially noted as an interpreter of the first violin concerto of her fellow countryman and mentor Karol Szymanowski.

Unsurprisingly much of her best writing is for the violin. She wrote no fewer than seven violin concertos and five sonatas for violin and piano, but even her orchestral writing tends to locate the dynamic drive in the string section. The music composed before the late 1950s is often described as neo-classical and, though she disliked the term, it adequately summarizes her emphasis on clear contrapuntal lines, the general brightness of her sound-world, and her avoidance of sentimentality. That is not to say her work lacks emotion – for example, the slow movement of the *Concerto for String Orchestra* (1948), one of her best works, contains a sensuous and haunting cello part set against soft but rhythmically insistent high strings.

Bacewicz's career as a violinist ended in 1955 because of injuries sustained after a serious car accident, and thereafter she dedicated herself to composing full time. The next year saw the inaugural meeting of the annual Warsaw Autumn Festival, which – following a brief political thaw – welcomed contemporary composers from around the world. The result for Bacewicz was that her work became marked by an attempt to assimilate some of the sonorities of the avant-garde, particularly those techniques, such as glissandi and clusters, often associated with her younger compatriot Penderecki (see p.401).

Orchestral Music

Bacewicz's music is still too little known, but if one work has managed to make a mark outside of her native Poland it is the *Concerto for String Orchestra* (1948), an energetic, neo-classical masterpiece that alternates a pulsating, thrusting dynamic with moments of exquisite delicacy. As a string player herself, Bacewicz seems especially sensitive to the wide range of sonorities available to her, and she exploits it to magical effect in the middle movement Andante. The *Sinfonietta* (1935) and *Symphony* (1946), also for strings only, don't have quite the same impact but are still highly impressive. Rhythmic dynamism is again to the fore, suggesting a restless inventiveness that owes much to Baroque examples but is offset by passages of intense lyricism. After these works the *Music for Strings, Trumpets and Percussion* comes as something of a shock. Written in the late 1950s, when Polish composers began to have direct contact with the Western avant-garde, it reveals a more severe harmonic language, with a particularly bleak slow movement in which menacing trumpets, vibrato strings and spooky celesta combine to mesmerizing effect.

Music for String Orchestra: New London Orchestra; Corp (Hyperion)

Released to celebrate Bacewicz's centenary, this recording plugs an important gap in the composer's discography and does so very effectively. Ronald Corp and his orchestra are enthusiastic advocates for this music and deliver performances of great clarity and vigour.

String Quartets

Bacewicz wrote a wide variety of chamber music throughout her life, much of which reveals, in the words of Adrian Thomas, "a tougher more challenging musical idiom" than her more public orchestral work. Of her seven string quartets, written throughout her career, *No. 1* (1938) already reveals a mastery of the form but the best of them date from the middle of her career. *No. 3*, written in Paris in 1947, has a restless, probing energy in its outer movements that is offset by the glorious second movement Andante – a richly harmonized lament in which a song-like melody floats over a pizzicato accompaniment. In 1951 Bacewicz's *String Quartet No. 4*, written the previous year, won first prize at the International Composers Competition in Liège. It's an arresting three-movement work with a strong individual voice: the powerful opening movement contrasts darkly sonorous music with a more abandoned rhapsodic style; the slow movement is another deeply-felt Andante which at times teeters on the brink of stasis, while the lively Rondo finale shows the composer at her lightest and wittiest.

String Quartet No. 4: The Maggini Quartet (ASV; with Szymanowski *String Quartets Nos. 1 & 2*)

The Maggini Quartet give a bold and passionate performance of the fourth quartet and really do justice to its striking sonorities. This well-planned disc allows the listener to hear one of the best of Bacewicz's quartets alongside those of her compatriot Szymanowski.

String Quartets Nos. 1 & 5: Amar Corde String Quartet (Acte Préalable; with *Piano Quintet No. 2*)

If you want to investigate the chamber music further, then these fine accounts of two Bacewicz quartets are a good place to start, from a label specializing in Polish music. As well as the quartets, there's a strong performance of the darkly brooding *Piano Quintet No. 2*.

Violin Pieces

Bacewicz composed five sonatas for violin and piano, two for solo violin, and many other pieces for the instrument, all revealing a complete understanding of its expressive range. Most were first performed by her and her brother Kiejstut, and are very much dialogues between equals. As in all her works, there's an emphasis on clarity of texture combined with a powerful sense of forward momentum. While the influence of Bartók is apparent in the fourth and fifth sonatas – in their use of folk-style material and occasionally abrasive edge – this is offset by Bacewicz's innate lyricism and love of virtuosic display for its own sake. Even in the more experimental *Sonata No. 2 for Solo Violin* (1955), in which Bachian patterning combines with avant-garde techniques, it's the passion and energy of the writing that is most striking.

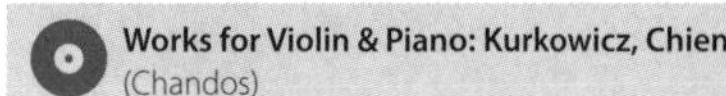
Works for Violin & Piano: Kurkowicz, Chien (Chandos)

Joanna Kurkowicz is the brilliant violinist on this selection of violin pieces written between 1946 and 1958. Her enthusiam is absolutely palpable and she has the technique to deal with Bacewicz's often demanding writing. The rather upfront sound sometimes makes the excellent piano playing of Gloria Chien seem a little clamorous.

Carl Philipp Emanuel Bach (1714–1788)

Of Johann Sebastian Bach's twenty children, three were outstanding musicians in their own right. Of these three – Wilhelm Friedmann, Johann Christian and Carl Philipp Emanuel – the last was the most influential as a composer, creating a bridge between the exuberant Baroque style of his father and the Classical style of Haydn and Mozart. While always acknowledging a great debt to his father (his only teacher), he eventually came to reject the complexity of polyphonic music, preferring a much more subjective and dramatic approach, full of unexpected and odd shifts in harmony, and with an emphasis on melody – a style known as *empfindsamer Stil* (expressive style).

Although C.P.E. Bach's educational background was broader than his father's – he trained as a lawyer and preferred the company of writers and intellectuals to that of musicians – he suffered a similar hard grind as a musician: in his case nearly thirty badly paid years as a keyboard player at the court of Frederick the Great at Potsdam. Frederick's taste was conservative, and the experimental nature of much of C.P.E. Bach's music meant that he never won preferment – indeed his principal duty seems to have been to accompany Frederick, a keen amateur flautist, on the harpsichord. Perhaps it was to widen his fame outside the narrow confines of Potsdam that he published his *Essay on the True Art of Playing Keyboard Instruments*, a highly influential treatise which was used as a teaching aid by both Mozart and Beethoven. In 1767, upon the death of his godfather, Georg-Philipp Telemann, the restless C.P.E. Bach succeeded him as music director of the five principal churches in Hamburg. His workload was enormous but, away from his church duties, the freer atmosphere of the commercial city-state made the last twenty years of his life much more stimulating.

J.S. Bach's most successful child.

Choral Music

The sheer volume of music that C.P.E. Bach had to provide for the Hamburg churches inevitably had a deleterious effect on its quality – as well as composing in a hurry, he also was obliged to knock together composite works using music by his relations and by Telemann. Of his later works the oratorio *Die Israeliten in der Wuste* (1769) is worth hearing, but his choral masterpiece is an earlier work, the *Magnificat* of 1749. The opening words of praise of the Virgin Mary are set with a thrilling energy that looks back to the Baroque, especially to the setting of the same words by his father. However, apart from a fugal final chorus, this is not a contrapuntal work but one whose impact derives from its operatic arias and its vigorous choruses.

Magnificat: Gachinger Kantorei Stuttgart; Bach-Collegium Stuttgart; Rilling (Hanssler; with J.N. Bach *Missa Brevis*)

Rilling is a veteran conductor of Baroque choral music and this recording from the mid-1970s still sounds fresh and lively, with clear and incisive singing from the chorus. The soloists are extremely fine, with soprano Arleen Auger excelling in her long and tender aria "Quia respexit humilitatem".

Symphonies

With their emphasis on the emotional manipulation of the listener, the symphonies of C.P.E.

Bach exemplify the *empfindsamer Stil* just as much as his keyboard pieces. They are intense, compact works whose three movements tend to follow a pattern: fast and agitated, followed by slow and sorrowful, and concluding fast and cheerful. The best and most adventurous of them, the six *Hamburg Symphonies*, were commissioned by Baron van Swieten (later a patron of Mozart), who allowed the composer a completely free hand. The result is startlingly original: audacious changes of key, sudden contrasts in dynamics and complete breaks in the musical flow all contribute to the music's restless excitement.

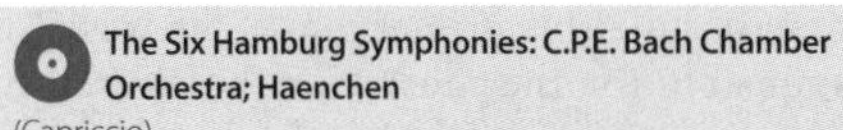

The Six Hamburg Symphonies: C.P.E. Bach Chamber Orchestra; Haenchen
(Capriccio)

These volatile symphonies can sound incoherent in performance, but Haenchen avoids the pitfall by taking the mood-swings completely seriously. The fast movements really rattle along, while the slow movements have a languidness that seems entirely authentic. Occasionally the ensemble becomes a little ragged, but this is a small price to pay for such energy and commitment.

Cello Concertos

The three delightful cello concertos of C.P.E. Bach are thought to date from around 1750. They are unlikely to have been composed for Potsdam and may have been first performed by Berlin amateurs with Christian Schale (the court orchestra cellist) as soloist. Their outer movements, which display the kind of restless, stop-start energy of the *Hamburg Symphonies*, follow the pattern of Baroque concertos by having alternate solo and tutti sections. The striking slow movements are notable for their poetic solo lines, which seem to aspire to the intensity of vocal expression. In particular, the melody of the doleful slow movement of the A minor concerto is made up of short-breathed phrases that seem to suggest sighing or even sobbing.

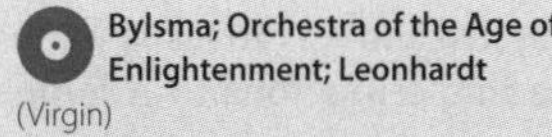

Bylsma; Orchestra of the Age of Enlightenment; Leonhardt
(Virgin)

Anner Bylsma is the doyen of Baroque cellists, and this disc shows him at his best, with performances of great sensitivity especially in the slow movements, which he draws out with great tenderness. The orchestral support is a little brash in the fast movements, but this disc is worth buying for Bylsma's playing alone.

Keyboard Music

C.P.E. Bach was one of the greatest keyboard composers of the eighteenth century, a fact that has been undermined by his historical status as a "transitional" composer – neither purely Baroque nor fully Classical. He was hugely prolific, writing some 150 sonatas and a slightly lesser number of shorter pieces. His favourite keyboard instrument was the clavichord, a soft and delicate-sounding instrument whose strings were struck like those of the piano, rather than plucked like the harpsichord, and whose dynamics could therefore be controlled by touch. An immensely sensitive performer, he was famed above all for the emotional intensity of his improvisations, a quality most evident in his fantasias and the slow movements of his sonatas, which are more harmonically quirky and unconventional than those of his great successors Haydn and Mozart.

Sonatas & Rondos: Pletnev
(Deutsche Grammophon)

Though most commonly played on period instruments, C.P.E. Bach's keyboard music can sound equally convincing on a modern piano. From the explosive opening rush of the *Sonata in G Minor*, Mikhail Pletnev utilizes the piano's dynamic and tonal range to emphasize the music's modernity and idiosyncrasy. The playing is often angular and stylized, but always to great effect.

Sonatas: Cerasi
(Metronome)

On this outstanding recording of six little-known sonatas, each from a different decade of the composer's life, the earliest three pieces are performed on a double-manual harpsichord while the more mature works are performed on the fortepiano. Carole Cerasi's performances are fresh and effervescent, combining a solid technique and musical vigour with a lightness of touch and free-wheeling spirit.

Johann Sebastian Bach (1685–1750)

Johann Sebastian Bach is unquestionably the greatest composer before Mozart, and arguably the greatest ever. On one level, his music is an example of supreme craftsmanship – he mastered with mathematical precision the formal problems of counterpoint, and produced keyboard music in which as many as five separate lines of argument are simultaneously sustained. Yet this is also music of the deepest humanity, and not just in the most overtly dramatic of Bach's works, such as his depiction of Christ's suffering in the *St Matthew Passion*. To listen to a complete performance of the *Goldberg Variations* – as purely abstract as anything he wrote – is to participate in a journey of extraordinary transformations, in which the final return of the original theme is a deeply moving and satisfying experience.

Bach came not so much from a musical family as from a musical dynasty: the line of musical Bachs begins all the way back in the sixteenth century and extends to the middle of the nineteenth. And to a large extent, despite his superior talent, Johann Sebastian's career was no more distinguished than those of several of his forebears. For Bach there was none of the international experience and renown of his contemporary Handel.

After spells as church organist at Arnstadt and Mulhausen, Bach's first important position was at Weimar, where in 1708 he became the court organist and a chamber musician to the duke, Wilhelm Ernst. When eight years later a disgruntled Bach overinsistently applied for permission to leave, having been passed over for the senior post of *Kapellmeister*, the duke's response was to jail him for one month for his impertinence. (Disagreements with employers were to dog his career.) The position he was attempting to leave for, and which he took up in 1718, was *Kapellmeister* at the small court of Prince Leopold of Anhalt-Cöthen. Here he composed most of his instrumental and orchestral music, since the prince belonged to the Calvinist Church, whose austere services employed little music beside psalm singing. When the prince married, his enthusiasm for music waned and in 1722 Bach applied to be cantor at the Thomasschule (the school of St Thomas) in Leipzig – rather reluctantly, since it seemed like a demotion. He got the position, but only after his friend Telemann (see p.581), among others, had turned the job down.

Bach was to spend the last 27 years of his life dealing with the gruelling workload at Leipzig, where his duties were almost impossibly demanding. As well as teaching at the Thomasschule (his primary task), he was also responsible for the music for the church of St Thomas and three of the town's other churches, and on top of that was expected to provide music for important civic occasions. In his first six years there he composed a staggering amount of music, including five cycles of cantatas for the main services in the Lutheran Church calendar, and his two magnificent settings of the Passion. He also found time, during the Leipzig years, to father thirteen children by his second wife Anna Magdalena (of whom only six grew to adulthood) to add to the four surviving children of his first marriage.

Such were the stresses of work that by 1729 there was sufficient friction between Bach and his employers for him to consider moving on once again. Among the problems, according to Bach, was the fact that "the place is very expensive and the authorities are hard to please and care little for music". In the end he stayed put, but he diversified his compositional activities, most significantly by writing for the Collegium Musicum of Leipzig, a musical society of students and professionals, originally founded by Telemann, which met and performed in Zimmermann's popular coffee house.

He died in July 1750, leaving unfinished his last extended project, a complex and theoretical exploration of counterpoint called the *Art of Fugue*. Even before his death he was regarded as hopelessly old-fashioned and was attacked for his "turgidity" by a leading critic, Johann Adolphe Scheibe. Bach's work remained under-performed – though not completely neglected – until well into the nineteenth century, and the most talented of his sons, Carl Philipp Emanuel (see p.16), was to develop a style markedly different from that of his father.

CANTATAS

The Lutheran Church has always regarded music as an integral component of its liturgy, with a strong emphasis on congregational participation in the form of chorales – hymns – often with words and music by Luther himself (see p.413). Along with the setting of biblical texts, chorales were the Church's dominant musical form until about 1700, when the theologian-poet Neumeister published a collection of religious verses in German that were intended to be sung. These so-called cantatas were not narrative pieces, but rather commentaries on the biblical texts used in the service – most importantly on the Gospel reading. Texts were extremely pious, often emphasizing God's mercy in the face of the abject nature of man. All the major German composers wrote them, but no one as ambitiously or lavishly as Bach, whose cantatas often combine recitatives and arias, choruses and chorales into one dramatic whole. Bach also wrote several secular cantatas, either to celebrate civic or royal occasions or – as in the so-called "Coffee" and "Peasant" cantatas – purely as quasi-operatic entertainments. About three-fifths of Bach's cantata output – over two hundred works – has survived, but most of them remain little-known, partly because of their number but also because their often morbid texts do not appeal to modern tastes. Not all of them are great works – some contain unidiomatic and occasionally meandering vocal lines – but the best are masterpieces and should not be ignored.

Complete Cantatas: Amsterdam Baroque Choir and Orchestra; Koopman (Challenge Classics; 17 three- or four-disc volumes)

The pioneering complete cantata series on Teldec, directed by Nikolaus Harnoncourt and Gustav Leonhardt, now sounds rather bald and prosaic. Helmuth Rilling's cycle, on Hänssler, has more warmth and emotion but the sound is often dry and ungiving. Better than either of these is Ton Koopman's series, which was begun on Erato but is now available on Challenge Classics, the cycle on BIS by Masaaki Suzuki, with a mostly Japanese cast of singers and instrumentalists, and the ongoing live series from John Eliot Gardiner and his Monteverdi Choir on his own SDG label. Koopman's set is the most consistently good, but all are worth investigating, perhaps after checking out some of the better-known cantatas listed below.

Cantata No. 80

One of the most famous of all Bach's cantatas is No. 80, *Ein' feste Burg* (A Mighty Fortress), originally written in 1715 but revised for use at Leipzig in 1723 (numbering does not signify the order in which the cantatas were written). It is a typical

The school (left) and church of St Thomas, Leipzig.

example of a cantata in which Bach takes a simple chorale tune – in this case one by Luther – and builds a large and magnificent musical edifice around it. On one level the cantata is a set of variations on a theme with which the congregation were completely familiar: from the opening chorus, in which the voices create an elaborate fantasia around the chorale, through various permutations of soloist and thematic material until the final singing of the chorale, in which the congregation may well have joined.

Cantata No. 80: Schlick, Lesne, Crook, Kooy; Ghent Collegium Vocale; Herreweghe (Harmonia Mundi; with *Magnificat*)

Herreweghe's approach emphasizes the way the strands of polyphony move in and out of each other like living organisms. There's very little aggression in his performances – some may find them underdramatized – but he achieves an engaging musical coherence without recourse to stylistic idiosyncrasies.

Cantata No. 82

As well as large-scale works involving combinations of soloists and chorus, Bach also wrote a number of solo cantatas of which the best is No. 82, *Ich habe genug* (It is enough). The text is a response to the biblical story of Simeon who, having seen the Christ child, felt he could die in peace. It is one of Bach's most intensely personal and consolatory works, with the opening words reiterated throughout its length. A solo oboe magically interweaves itself around the vocal line in the yearning opening aria (a very characteristic device in the more lyrical cantata arias); the second aria is a gentle, reassuring lullaby, and the third is a joyous welcoming of death.

Hunt Lieberson; Orchestra of Emmanuel Music; Smith (Nonesuch; with *Cantata No.199*)

This is one of the great recordings of recent years. Mezzo-soprano Lorraine Hunt Lieberson invested everything she sang with a heartfelt intensity that never seemed strained or contrived. The result in this recording of two of Bach's solo cantatas is almost unbearably moving, as if the listener were eavesdropping on some private agony.

Hotter; Philharmonia; Bernard (EMI; with Brahms songs)

This cantata is frequently a showcase for singers who don't usually sing Bach. Few have brought such a degree of sensitivity to it as the great bass-baritone Hans Hotter, renowned as a Wagnerian and as a lieder singer. In this 1950 recording, his awareness of textual meaning is effortlessly conveyed through an unforced shaping of Bach's long lines.

Cantata No. 106

Cantata No. 106 (known as "Actus Tragicus") is not part of the cycle of cantatas written for the liturgical year but a funeral cantata composed for a specific memorial service, possibly that of Bach's uncle Tobias Lämmerhirt, who died in 1707. If this early date is correct, it would signal a turning point in Bach's choral music, for this is a mature and profound work, which, like *Cantata No. 82*, creates a remarkable mood of calm serenity and consolation from its very beginning. Bach's talents as a subtle dramatizer of words (which here come mainly from the Bible) is everywhere apparent. At the heart of the work a beautiful tenor arioso gives way to an admonitory bass aria, which leads to a sombre choral fugue that diminishes into a lone soprano voice exclaiming the word "Jesu!" – a moment of touching vulnerability and an expressive masterstroke.

Argenta, Chance, Rolfe Johnson, Varcoe; Monteverdi Choir and English Baroque Soloists; Gardiner (Archiv; with *Motet BWV 118b & Mourning Ode BWV 198*)

This gentle and reassuring work gets a suitably sensitive performance on this CD. Gardiner usually prefers to point up the drama of Bach's choral works, but although there is much spirited singing – notably in the final God-glorying chorus – what most impresses here is the eloquent restraint, which establishes exactly the right mixture of seriousness and joy.

Cantatas Nos. 140 & 147

No. 140, *Wachet auf* (Sleepers Wake), and No. 147, *Herz und Mund* (Heart and Mouth), are two of the most popular of the cantatas. The theme of the former is that of the soul eagerly anticipating the arrival of Christ like a bride awaiting the bridegroom. The joyous, expectant mood is established in the opening chorus by the underlying restless rhythm, over which Philipp Nicolai's soaring chorale tune is spun out by Bach in ever richer configurations. *Herz und Mund*, more monumental and varied in mood, is a meditation on receiving Jesus – into the womb of the Virgin Mary and into the hearts of man. It is famous for the chorale that closes each of its two sections, a melody popularly known as "Jesu, Joy of Man's Desiring".

Monteverdi Choir; Gardiner (Archiv)

A wonderful recording of two of Bach's most popular cantatas, this disc would make a perfect introduction to the cantatas as a whole. The choral singing in particular has an energy and bounce that is positively uplifting.

OTHER CHORAL WORKS

While the cantatas constitute most of the volume of Bach's choral music, they don't include his very greatest pieces for choir, such as the magnificent *B Minor Mass* and his settings of the Passion, written for performance at Easter time. In his Passions, as with his cantatas, Bach took an already existing genre – in this case the musical setting of the Gospel accounts of Christ's suffering and death – and turned it into a monumental epic which emphasized, above all, the human dimension of the story. Passion settings had existed since medieval times but from the mid-seventeenth century additional texts were added to the basic narratives as meditations and commentaries on the proceedings. Again, like the cantatas, the Passions aroused mixed feelings in their listeners. Many disapproved of what they perceived as an opera performance in a sacred setting, and indeed the swift changes of mood, from the consoling tone of the chorales to the sheer viciousness of some of the crowd choruses, are shockingly direct in the way they involve and implicate the listener in the story. According to Bach's obituarist, he wrote a total of five Passions but only two, the Passions of St Matthew and St John, have survived.

St Matthew Passion

Written in the late 1720s, the *St Matthew Passion* is Bach's grandest and arguably his greatest work. The narrative, taken from chapters 26 and 27 of St Matthew's Gospel, is sung in a highly expressive recitative by a tenor Evangelist. Direct speech is allocated to soloists – a bass singing the role of Christ and the remaining "characters" distributed among a range of voices – with the most animated and contrapuntal music given to the chorus in their capacity as crowd. Throughout the narrative Picander's additional words (for both soloists and chorus) balance the urgency of the story and provide an element of inward meditation that is highly personal. The prevailing mood of the work is more contemplative than dramatic and, though a terrible feeling of tragedy pervades the music, there is also an overwhelming sense of community that binds all the participants together, in particular through the vehicle of the Passion chorale which punctuates the drama at five points.

Rolfe Johnson, Schmidt, Bonney, Monoyios, Von Otter, Chance, Crook, Bär, Hauptmann; London Oratory Junior Choir & Monteverdi Choir; Gardiner (Archiv; 3 CDs)

The *St Matthew Passion* has been staged several times and Gardiner's ardently dramatic interpretation immediately makes you realize why. His speeds are fast and his dynamics extreme, but always in the service of narrative momentum. The excellent soloists, all with a clear and open delivery, match the bright and incisive style of the chorus, but they're tender and sensitive in the more contemplative moments.

Gooding, York, Kozená, Bickley, Gilchrist, Padmore, Harvey, Loges; Gabrieli Consort; Gabrieli Players; McCreesh (Deutsche Grammophon; 2 CDs)

Bach's choral works may originally have been performed without a choir, the soloists providing the choral sections one voice per part. The approach brings extra clarity and dramatic directness to Bach's complex writing, and it pays dividends in this superb recording from Paul McCreesh. Mark Padmore is perhaps the best Evangelist on record, and Magdalena Kozená is wonderful wherever she appears.

Pears, Fischer-Dieskau, Schwarzkopf, Ludwig, Gedda, Berry; Philharmonia Choir and Orchestra; Klemperer (EMI; 3 CDs)

Klemperer's *St Matthew Passion now* sounds very old-fashioned: forces are big and speeds slow to the point of stateliness. Yet this account has an unrivalled grandeur and solemnity, thanks to Klemperer's ability to control a large chorus, and his unfailing sense of the shape and direction of a phrase. A devotional intensity is sustained through the whole work, making the final chorus almost unbearably powerful.

St John Passion

The *St John Passion*, first performed on Good Friday 1724, has until recently been judged the lesser of the two extant Passions. It is certainly on a smaller scale – lasting less than two hours – and the additional texts, selected from a number of authors, add up to a less coherent whole than Picander's *St Matthew* additions. However, it is a remarkably powerful work, which conveys the story of Jesus' last hours with startling immediacy. Some wonderful arias provide individual responses to the events – such as the dilemma faced by Pilate – but arguably the greatest music is found in the writing for choir. A powerful opening chorus sets the foreboding tone, with a pair of oboes cutting through the vocal textures and adding an incisive edge to the sound. Later on, Bach's contrapuntal choral writing in the crowd scenes creates an astonishing sense of confusion and cruelty – so much so that some people have described the work's representation of the Jews' treatment of Christ as being anti-Semitic.

Argenta, Holton, Rolfe Johnson, Varcoe, Hauptmann, Chance; Monteverdi Choir; Gardiner (Archiv; 2 CDs)

Gardiner's bright, forceful style is admirably suited to the *St John Passion*. As usual the Monteverdi Choir are superbly versatile: sinister and aggressive in the choruses at the Crucifixion, powerful but tender in the chorales. They are matched by the fine soloists, with Anthony Rolfe Johnson immensely authoritative as the Evangelist and a pure-toned Nancy Argenta outstanding in the soprano arias.

Schmidthusen, Mera, Türk, Sakurada, Hida, Urano, Kooij; Bach Collegium Japan; Suzuki (BIS; 2 CDs)

Masaaki Suzuki's period-instrument Bach recordings have made a big impact in recent years. This *St John Passion* shows why: the solo singing is first-rate, the orchestral playing sparkling, and the conducting demonstrates a genuine closeness to the music. There are moments of great drama, but the choir sounds broader than Gardiner's, making for a more devotional atmosphere, especially in the chorales.

B Minor Mass

Like the *Christmas Oratorio*, the *B Minor Mass* is a composite work largely put together over two decades from cantata movements, and it was possibly intended as a compendium to show off Bach's skill as a choral composer, rather than as a piece for a specific occasion. Bach sent the Kyrie and the Gloria to the Catholic Elector of Saxony in 1733, along with a letter complaining about his Leipzig employers and asking for a job, which he did not get. From such unpromising beginnings emerged one of his greatest works. Its first chorus, a stately fugue, establishes the sense of solid and unshakable faith with which the work is imbued. Not all the music is so solemn, however. The glorious Sanctus is an animated rush of energy for six-part choir and high trumpets, with rhythms that suggest dancing rather than worship.

Argenta, Dawson, Chance, Varcoe; English Baroque Soloists and Monteverdi Choir; Gardiner
(Archiv; 2 CDs)

Gardiner's urgent and tightly sprung account is distinguished by some fine solo performances (Michael Chance's Agnus Dei and Nancy Argenta's Laudamus Te are outstanding), but above all it's the characteristically precise and highly charged singing of the Monteverdi Choir that gives this recording its sense of majesty.

Les Musiciens du Louvre; Minkowski
(Naive; 2 CDs)

This is not the only stripped-down version of the Mass, but it's by far the most persuasive. Using an orchestra of 25 musicians and with choruses divided between the ten first-class soloists, Minkowski achieves textures that are transparent but ever-changing, and though his tempi are generally quick, there's rarely any sense of undue haste: indeed, Nathalie Stutzmann's ravishing Agnus Dei is an episode of wonderful serenity.

Christmas Oratorio

Though there is a narrative to the *Weichnachts-Oratorium*, or Christmas Oratorio, this is not really an oratorio at all, but a series of cantatas to be performed at the six services that begin with Christmas Day and end with Epiphany (6 January). Plundered from already composed secular cantatas, it would never have been performed as a single work in Bach's time, but it does form a musically unified whole. The author of the text is unknown (it was probably Picander, who wrote parts of the *St Matthew Passion* and many of the cantatas) and, although not as theatrical as the Passion settings, the joyfulness of the text is perfectly evoked by some thrillingly exuberant music. Nowhere is this more evident than in the work's brilliant opening, which combines kettledrums, a fanfare and a rousing chorus to the words "Jauchzet, frohlocket!" (Rejoice, Exult!).

Larsson, von Magnus, Prégardien, Mertens; Amsterdam Baroque Choir and Orchestra; Koopman
(Erato; 2 CDs)

Koopman's approach is to treat this work as one of varying moods and colours without resorting to theatricality. The forces are quite small-scale but there is an intensity to the choral singing which is never overstrained. The recording also boasts, in Christophe Prégardien, a sweet-toned and convincing Evangelist – direct, unfussy and sincere.

Schlick, Chance, Crook, Kooy; Collegium Vocale; Herreweghe (Virgin; 2 CDs)

Herreweghe captures the prevailing festive mood of the work with a sparkling opening, in which the instrumentalists acquit themselves brilliantly. Howard Crook makes a strong and sympathetic Evangelist, and there are no weak links among the other soloists. As with Koopman, the dramatic elements are never overplayed.

Motets

Despite his hectic schedule in Leipzig, Bach was also required to compose for occasional church events. He responded with at least seven choral works, which he called motets: settings of sacred texts written, like the cantatas, in German. But instead of being miniatures in the manner of the Renaissance, Bach's motets are near-orchestral in scope, small-scale symphonies that balance music of luminous simplicity with some of his most dazzling contrapuntal writing. Several stand out. *Singet dem Herrn* (Sing unto the Lord) opens as a buoyant waltz that transforms into a chorale; it closes with a fugue shared between eight voices. Written for a funeral, *Jesu, Meine Freude* (Jesus, My Joy) is the most monumental of the lot: an eleven-movement setting (based on St Paul's Epistle to the Romans) woven around a Lutheran hymn. From texts struggling with the essence of belief, Bach wrests music of high drama and turbulent emotion: as heart-rending as anything he would write in the Passions.

Rubens, Kiehr, Fink, Türk, Kooy; RIAS-Kammerchor; Akademie für Alte Musik Berlin; Jacobs
(Harmonia Mundi)

Some recordings of the motets emphasize their emotional impact at the cost of technical precision; others are too arithmetical. These young singers get it just right, producing beautifully nuanced performances that have plenty of bite but still sound spontaneous and clear. René Jacobs uses light instrumental accompaniment and intelligently offsets the choir with soloists for greater dramatic colour.

Magnificat

A Magnificat is a musical setting of the Virgin Mary's words of joy ("My soul doth magnify the Lord"), that she spoke to her cousin Elizabeth after she had conceived. Bach's first setting, his only surviving one, was written for the Christmas celebrations of 1723, and is one of the most Italianate of all his choral works, with a splendid Vivaldi-like blast of rippling semiquavers in the opening chorus. It's broken up into sections like a cantata, and involves soloists as well as a chorus, providing them with some melodies that are disarmingly simple and direct by Bach's normally complex standards. Though comparatively short (lasting less than half an hour), the work ranges in tone, from the elegiac "Quia respexit humilitatem", in which a solo soprano interweaves with a plangent *oboe d'amore*, to the jubilant closing chorus, "Gloria patri".

Ghent Collegium Vocale; Herreweghe (Harmonia Mundi; with *Cantata No. 80*)

There's a fluidity in evidence here, a sense of the polyphonic lines all flowing together in one direction, that is completely captivating. Herreweghe's balance of voices and instruments is exemplary: he treats them as part of one integrated texture. Especially telling is "Quia respexit humilitatem", effectively a duet between the soprano and a highly vocalized oboe line.

ORCHESTRAL MUSIC

It was at Weimar that Bach first came into contact with the Italian style of concerto writing in which a large instrumental ensemble is contrasted with one or more soloists (see p.610). This style was exemplified by the works of Vivaldi, several of which Bach arranged for solo keyboard or as concertos. Bach composed his first original concertos in Cöthen, and they were still largely based on the Vivaldian model, with three movements arranged fast-slow-fast. The outer movements are characterized by vigorous forward-driven rhythms and the regular reappearance of the opening material (the "ritornello"), while the slow movement has an aria-like lyricism. As well as the concertos mentioned below, he also wrote several that survive only in part – mostly for oboe – some of which have been reconstructed for performance. If the dynamism of the concertos was inspired by Italian models, then the elegance of the four *Orchestral Suites* shows the influence of French forms, which by the end of the seventeenth century were highly popular in German aristocratic circles. Bach almost certainly composed all four while at Cöthen, though it is also likely that they were later adapted, along with various concertos, for the Collegium Musicum at Leipzig.

Brandenburg Concertos

First printed in 1721, the six *Brandenburg Concertos* were dedicated to the Margrave of Brandenburg, who had commissioned them after hearing Bach play two years earlier. All but the first, and possibly the third, were written at Cöthen, and they were undoubtedly conceived primarily for the court orchestra, since the unusual orchestration of several of them is known to have matched the players at Bach's disposal there. Largely assembled from other compositions – some of them written around the same time, others earlier – the *Brandenburgs* were probably intended to demonstrate the potential of the concerto form. From the jubilant first to the intimate sixth, Bach develops his thematic material in a much more complex and extended fashion than Vivaldi ever did, and the relationship between the soloists and the orchestra similarly breaks new ground – the extended role of the harpsichord in the fifth sounds in places like an anticipation of Mozart's piano concertos.

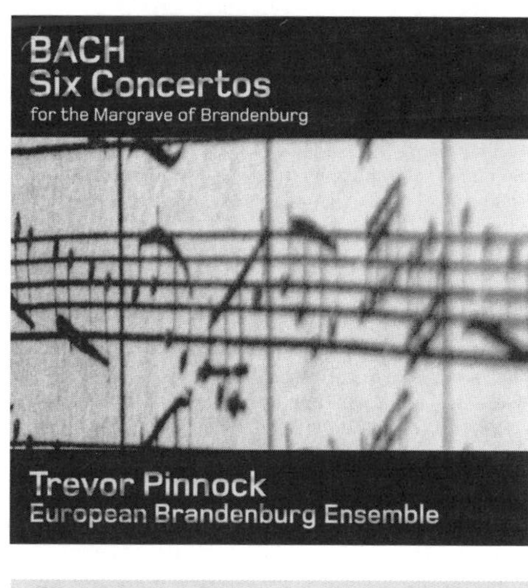

European Brandenburg Ensemble; Pinnock (Avie; 2 CDs)

Directed from the harpsichord by Trevor Pinnock, this scratch ensemble (made up of some of the finest Baroque instrumentalists in Europe) achieves wonders in their very first recording. Though essentially a conventional approach in terms of speeds and dynamics, the sense of joyous, spontaneous music-making is completely infectious.

Il Giardino Armonico; Antonini
(Teldec; 2 CDs)

This is an extremely dynamic performance by a young Italian group. The ensemble is tight, tempos are fast and there is some vivid tone colour, especially in the brass section. There are occasional moments of eccentricity but what is lost in subtlety is gained in the sheer panache and evident enjoyment of the playing.

Violin Concertos

The two *Violin Concertos*, in A minor and E major, and the marvellous *Double Violin Concerto in D Minor* also probably date from Bach's Cöthen period, although this is by no means certain. The E major concerto, which opens with three bold chords – a classic Vivaldian device – comes close to the buoyant mood of the *Brandenburgs*, and also contains one of Bach's most inspired and poignant slow movements, in which the delicate solo melody is framed by slow and sombre music in the lower strings. The A minor concerto is another first-rate composition, but best of all is the *Double Concerto*, a marvel of contrapuntal inventiveness which stands as one of Bach's very greatest works. The piece's imitative solo lines weave in and out of each other with a playful brilliance in the outer movements, and with a tender lyricism in the slow movement.

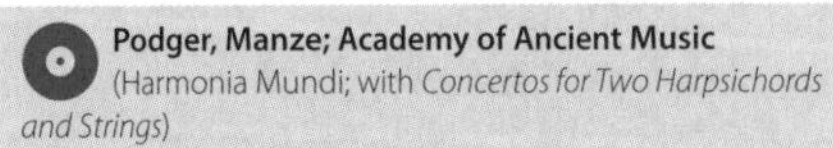

Podger, Manze; Academy of Ancient Music
(Harmonia Mundi; with *Concertos for Two Harpsichords and Strings*)

This is an original-instrument performance, but in Andrew Manze the Academy of Ancient Music has a director of such chutzpah that such designations seem irrelevant. At the same time that the music is revealed in a fresh light, the sheer enjoyment of the players is vividly communicated.

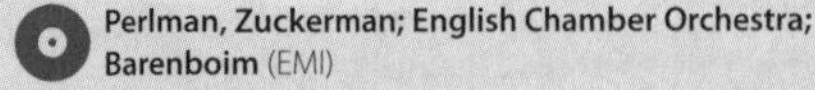

Perlman, Zuckerman; English Chamber Orchestra; Barenboim (EMI)

This recording dates from the1960s when Perlman, Zuckerman and Barenboim frequently played together, and there is a rapport between them which is genuinely thrilling. Perlman plays the solo concertos with his characteristic sweetness of tone, and there is a competitive edge to the swagger that both soloists bring to the *Double Concerto*.

Harpsichord Concertos

Most of Bach's concertos for one, two, three or four harpsichords started life in another form, usually as concertos for different instruments and in one case, the *Concerto for Four Harpsichords*, as a concerto by Vivaldi. In the process of taking music for a single-line instrument or instruments and transcribing it for the harpsichord – which can play polyphonically – Bach often completely changed the character of the pieces, making the textures denser and the elaboration of thematic ideas more complicated. Several of these harpsichord concertos were written for the Collegium Musicum of Leipzig, and would have been performed with Bach himself at the keyboard.

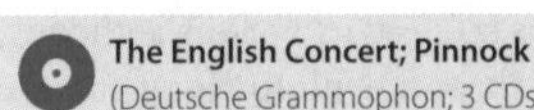

The English Concert; Pinnock
(Deutsche Grammophon; 3 CDs)

In Trevor Pinnock's complete recording of the harpsichord concertos, dating from the early 1980s, the playing is very focused and forward-moving, with tempi sometimes extremely fast. With excellent co-soloists in the concertos for multiple harpsichord, and bright, vivid sound, this budget reissue represents excellent value.

Orchestral Suites

In Baroque music a suite consisted of a set of contrasting movements based on dance forms. All four of Bach's *Orchestral Suites* (which were probably not written as a set) begin with the kind of grandiose and stately overture that suggests a debt to French music, in particular to Lully. But even here Bach makes the form his own, by writing the fast middle section of each overture in the more complex style of the Italian concerto. Generally the overall mood of the suites evokes the easy-going elegance of court music: the German dance form – the allemande – is discarded, and the optional forms of bourrée, gavotte and minuet dominate. Bach's melodic invention, especially in the second and third suites, is at its most easy and inspired – notably in the serene air from *No. 3* (the famous "Air on a G String") and the electrifying flute solo (the *Badinerie*) from *No. 2*.

Boston Baroque; Pearlman
(Telarc; 2 CDs)

This recent recording is remarkable not just for the stylish playing of Boston Baroque but the bright yet natural sound achieved by Telarc's engineers. This is a period instrument band but with absolutely no interpretative point scoring, instead there's a freshness and buoyancy to the playing which reflects the dance origins of much of the music.

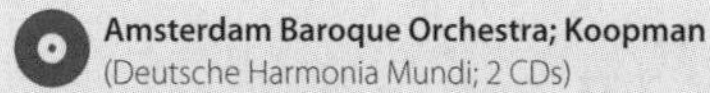
Amsterdam Baroque Orchestra; Koopman
(Deutsche Harmonia Mundi; 2 CDs)

This is one of Koopman's best recordings. The mixture of formal elegance and excitement that these works require is perfectly achieved with wonderful nobility of phrasing and finely judged speeds. The ensemble playing is unruffled and flawless, and the more brilliant moments are dazzlingly realized.

KEYBOARD MUSIC

Bach's renown in his own lifetime was less as a composer than as a keyboard player, both at the harpsichord and at the organ. His great ability was summarized in his obituary: "How strange, how new, how beautiful were his ideas in improvising. How perfectly he realized them! All his fingers were equally skilful; all were capable of the most perfect accuracy in performance." Such skill and knowledge could be put to a variety of uses. Not only did Bach write keyboard music in every known form of his time (both for performance and for education), but he was also known for his ability to maintain and repair harpsichords, organs and other instruments.

Bach would have played on a range of keyboard instruments: the soft-toned clavichord, the strings of which sounded by being hit, as well as the fuller-toned harpsichord, the strings of which were plucked. Nowadays argument rages as to whether Bach's keyboard music sounds better played on the harpsichord or the modern piano. It undoubtedly sounds good on both, but the tone and volume of a piano (unlike the harpsichord) is modified by the pressure of the fingers, thus allowing a performer a wider range of sounds with which to explore the intricacies of Bach's contrapuntal style.

The Well-Tempered Clavier

The Well-Tempered Clavier consists of two books (though only the first was given the name) of twenty-four preludes and fugues, each book working through the twelve major and twelve minor keys. Unequalled in the profligacy of their inventiveness, the books were intended partly as a manual of keyboard playing and composition, partly as a systematic exploration of harmony, and partly as a celebration of new developments in tuning technique – the "tempering" of the title (see box on p.26) – that allowed a keyboard instrument to be played in any key without being retuned. The fugues, in as many as five voices, are brilliantly constructed and full of sprightly dance-like passages and strong, concise melodies, and the preludes that introduce them can be seen as prototypes for the poetic distillations of Chopin's *Préludes* and *Études* – indeed, Chopin revered the "48", as *The Well-Tempered Clavier* is often known. Of the two books, the slightly earlier first is marginally more playful and the second a little more complex and dense.

Leonhardt
(Deutsche Harmonia Mundi; 2 CDs x 2)

The most authoritative and satisfying of the several harpsichord versions available is this one from Gustav Leonhardt, a veteran Bach specialist whose playing is always flexible but carefully argued.

Nikolayeva
(Mezhdunarodnaya Kniga; 2 CDs x 2)

Tatiana Nikolayeva exploits the full range of the piano's sonorities: a crisp, hard touch is used for the more rhythmically motorized preludes yet there are no qualms about using the sustain pedal to add colour and warmth. Her speeds can be slow, especially in some of the fugues, but the shape and direction of a piece is never in any doubt.

Gould
(Sony; 2 CDs x 2)

As with all his Bach performances, Glenn Gould doesn't touch the pedal, preferring to emphasize line above tone. Often hailed as one of the greatest piano recordings ever, this is an extraordinary set, with some fugues played so slowly they almost fall apart and others taken at a speed your ears can only just keep up with.

Goldberg Variations

This set of thirty variations on a theme were supposedly commissioned by Baron von Keyserling – the Russian ambassador to the Dresden court – in order to relieve the wearisome hours of his insomnia, and were named after the baron's harpsichordist, who was to play them. The work begins with a highly ornamented but rather demure theme, around whose bass line Bach proceeds to fashion an astonishing series of transformations, from the ebullient to the introspective. The variations are grouped in threes, each group ending with a canon, except for the very last variation which is a quodlibet – a rousing piece which combines two popular songs. The epic scope of the work is due not simply to its length, but to its enormous variety – both stylistically and in terms of mood – and the way the whole piece is held together by the constant underlying presence of the original

Tuning & Temperament

A central tenet of music-making is the desirability of singing or playing "in tune", accurately producing sound waves that vibrate at the correct frequency. In practical terms, this means different things to different types of musician. Singers, violinists, trombonists and others who can slide smoothly between an infinite number of pitches rely on their ears and fingers to "tune" each as they go along; keyboard players simply call in a professional tuner every few months; while harpists, according to Stravinsky, "spend 90 percent of their lives tuning ... and 10 percent playing out of tune." For all this, tuning is today a highly standardized affair. An F sharp in Madrid is the same as an F sharp in Melbourne, and pianos in New York are tuned using the same system as those in Paris or Tokyo. But it wasn't always so simple, as modern tuning relies on two basic principles, both of which took centuries to establish their global hegemony.

The first of these two principles is *concert pitch*, which ensures uniform tuning around the world by defining the exact frequency of one benchmark note: the A below middle C. Today's concert-pitch A vibrates 440 times per second, but old tuning forks suggest that the figure varied from around 350 to 550 in pre-Baroque Europe, with standardization slowed down by the fact that retuning the most important and expensive instrument in each town – the church organ – meant completely rebuilding it. In the Renaissance era, it wasn't uncommon for neighbouring towns to have totally incompatible ideas of pitch (creating serious problems for travelling musicians) and even during the late Baroque period, pitch was usually around a whole tone lower than what we use today – something clearly audible in many recordings made by period-instrument performers.

The second basic tuning principle – *equal temperament* – is a bit more complicated, and requires some background explanation. At the heart of Western music is the twelve-note chromatic scale that makes up each octave: the scale that creates the repeating pattern of black and white notes on a piano keyboard. This chromatic scale isn't entirely man-made: it can be reached by rearranging a few basic musical "intervals" that are grounded in both nature and mathematics. A "do", for example, in the do-re-mi scale, vibrates two-thirds as fast as the "so". And if you strike a bell tuned to the pitch of "do", you will hear subtle extra notes – overtones – in the sound, including "so". This neat relationship between music, mathematics and nature has fascinated thinkers since the time of Pythagoras.

But there's a problem. When you try to tune an instrument according to these neat mathematical ratios, it becomes apparent that they are not quite compatible with Western music's twelve-note scale. As you get one interval right, another will start sounding sour. You might be able to tune the instrument so that it sounds good in one key – for example, build up just intervals from G and the instrument might sound okay in G major – but move to another key and everything will sound terrible.

All this became an increasingly pressing concern from the Renaissance era onwards, as composers began combining ever more keys in single pieces of music. The growing dominance of keyboard instruments – which, unlike voices and violins, couldn't circumvent the problem by tweaking each note's tuning depending on its context – also raised the stakes. The result was a race to find an ideal compromise: a tweaked, or "tempered", scale that allowed more flexibility, but without losing the pure sound of the "just" intervals. From the many contenders, the system that finally emerged victorious was equal temperament, in which the octave is divided into twelve identical semitones – the rungs of the chromatic ladder are evenly spaced out. This neat solution, which involves tempering every interval in the scale, allows an instrument to sound equally in tune in all 24 major and minor keys.

Looking back, equal temperament seems like a glaringly obvious idea, but it was only widely accepted after centuries of debate among Europe's musical and intellectual elite. It met resistance both from religious figures – who called it unholy for doing away with all of God's "natural" intervals – and from many musicians, who pointed out that, while everything sounded acceptable in equal temperament, nothing sounded perfect. Another complaint was that, since each key sounded the same, the new system didn't provide subtle shifts of colour as music moved from one key to another, a by-product of earlier temperaments that became an intrinsic part of Baroque musical thought. Today, our ears are so used to the equally tempered world that we don't notice these downsides. But during Bach's day, musicians were much more aware that every fixed tuning system represented a compromise. As Johann Georg Neidhardt commented in 1732, "equal temperament brings with it its comfort and discomfort, like blessed matrimony".

Legendary Bach pianist Glenn Gould.

thematic material, including a descending stepwise bass line. The *Goldbergs* stand deservedly as one of Bach's best-loved compositions.

Rousset
(L'Oiseau-Lyre)

This is a refreshingly forthright and decidedly wide-awake performance on a suitably bright-sounding instrument. Christophe Rousset's speeds tend to be brisk and he limits his changes of registration, letting the instrument do the work in crisp and buoyant style.

Gould
(Sony)

Glenn Gould's 1955 recording of the *Goldberg Variations* revolutionized people's perception of how Bach should be played. This 1981 recording, released shortly before his death, is even more remarkable for the vivid precision of his touch, and the way that each line of the music is so clearly articulated. Speeds are sometimes idiosyncratic, but you'll be swept along by Gould's verve and enthusiasm.

English & French Suites

The titles of the *English Suites* and *French Suites* were not chosen by Bach, and their significance is unclear, as they do not define any substantial differences between these two sets of dance movements. Written purely for enjoyment rather than for instruction, they follow approximately the same format, with a steady allemande followed by a more rapid courante, a stately sarabande and an extremely lively gigue, sometimes with additional short movements – such as a bourrée – inserted between the sarabande and gigue. The *English Suites*, however, begin with a prelude which is often, as in the third suite, a large-scale concerto-like movement. The *French Suites* are less grandiose: the sarabandes and briefer additional movements are less contrapuntal than the equivalents in the *English Suites*, and bear a slight resemblance to the easy-going and flowery style of Couperin (see p.148), with whom Bach is known to have corresponded.

English Suites: Gould
(Sony; 2 CDs)

French Suites: Gould (Sony; 2 CDs; with *Overture in the French Style*)

Though there is no shortage of objectors to Glenn Gould's cavalier treatment of the printed page, nobody can match the clarity that he brings to Bach's multi-stranded keyboard music. These two sets show Gould at his most enjoyable – astonishingly fleet-fingered and full of argumentative intelligence.

Partitas

The six keyboard *Partitas* were the first works of Bach to be published. Intended to form the first part of a *Clavierübung* (Keyboard Exercise), the *Partitas* are an obvious development from the *English Suites* and *French Suites* and progress in difficulty and grandeur as the series unfolds. A partita is essentially the same as a suite, a collection of movements based on dance forms. Bach's six are among the last great examples of a genre which was already beginning to be superseded by the sonata. They are all highly individual works: from the sprightly delicacy of *No. 1* to the monumental *No. 6*, each contains its own assortment of *galantarien*, optional movements, like the minuet, which were added to the core movements of allemande, courante, sarabande and gigue, and each begins with a different form of opening movement.

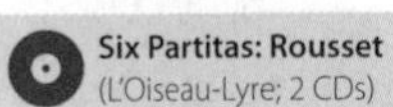

Six Partitas: Rousset
(L'Oiseau-Lyre; 2 CDs)

These are sparkling accounts of the *Partitas* from Rousset, full of spring and excitement. Again his instrument has a bright, forward sound but he uses a greater variety of registration than in his *Goldberg Variations*, finding just the right tone and touch for the great range of moods that are present.

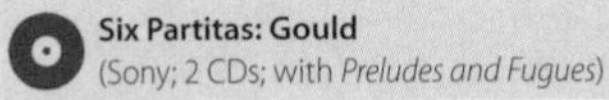

Six Partitas: Gould
(Sony; 2 CDs; with *Preludes and Fugues*)

Recorded in the late 1950s and early 1960s, this sequence is a typically thrilling, strong-willed and occasionally strange Gould production. Critics (and later Gould himself) expressed reservations about its tendency to overassertiveness, but no other pianist has conveyed so powerful an impression of passionate analytical intelligence.

The Italian Concerto

In 1735 the second part of Bach's *Clavierubüng* appeared, which contained two works: a partita, published as *An Overture in the French Manner*, and the *Italian Concerto*. Here the emphasis is on contrast, both works mimicking orchestral music of two different national styles: the concerto in a major key, and the partita in a minor one. The *Italian Concerto*, one of the most popular of Bach's keyboard works, is a clever translation of a typical three-movement Vivaldian concerto into keyboard form. Bach specifically indicates that it should be played on a two-manual harpsichord, the main manual representing the orchestra, the other, softer, manual representing the soloist (not that this has stopped many pianists from recording the work). The middle slow movement has a long solo part, rich in ornament, that is highly suggestive of a lyrical oboe line.

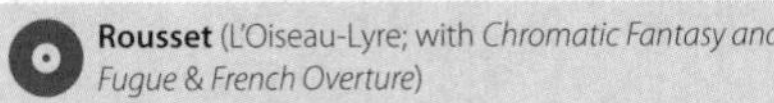

Rousset (L'Oiseau-Lyre; with *Chromatic Fantasy and Fugue & French Overture*)

As well as a brilliant account of the *Italian Concerto*, Rousset gives a fleet-fingered performance of one of Bach's most mercurial keyboard pieces, the *Chromatic Fantasy and Fugue*, making this a near ideal introduction to Bach on the harpsichord.

ORGAN MUSIC

It's difficult to overstate the significance of the organ in Bach's life. He came from a family of organists, and the instrument formed the basis of his early musical training. During his extended stay with his elder brother Johann Christoph in Ohrdruf, he not only worked his way voraciously through Christoph's collection of organ music (to the extent, according to legend, of copying a forbidden manuscript by moonlight), but learned how to repair and maintain the local church instrument – a skill that remained valuable later in life. Every one of Bach's professional posts involved playing the organ, and he performed some of his most majestic displays of virtuosity at its keyboard. One story tells of a French soloist who was due to challenge Bach's supremacy at improvisation, but ran off, terrified, after hearing him practising the night before; another contemporary gasped that Bach could "by the use of his feet alone … achieve such an admirable, agitated and rapid concord of sounds … that others would seem unable to imitate it even with their fingers".

Bach wrote for the organ throughout his career, encompassing a variety of musical genres: chorale preludes for use in Lutheran church services, technically demanding trio sonatas, in which the two hands and feet operate as if three different instruments, and numerous individual pieces and orchestral transcriptions – not to mention the monumental preludes and fugues he completed while working at Weimar. Given the importance of the instrument in his career, it's perhaps appropriate that Bach's first surviving works, the "Neumeister" chorales, were written for organ, just as tradition has it that his final piece, an organ prelude on "Wenn wir in höchsten Nöten sein" (When in the hour of greatest need), was dictated from his deathbed.

Preludes & Fugues

Bach is thought to have once walked some 200 miles to hear the greatest organist of the era, Dietrich Buxtehude, play in Lübeck. The extended leave of absence landed him in trouble with his employers back at Arnstadt, but the trip was worth it, as Bach was deeply affected by what he heard. Congregations soon began complaining that his playing was too florid, and he began to compose virtuosic preludes and toccatas – the most familiar example being the early *Toccata and Fugue in D Minor* (originally written, many scholars suspect, for violin or some other instrument). This improvisatory style was ideally suited to the massive Baroque organs then being built in north Germany, and Bach was later to gripe that, after his Lübeck trip, he never again had access to an instrument on this scale. Ironically, it may have been this very limitation that encouraged him to refine his organ writing into something more rigorous. Soon after moving to the small chapel at Weimar, he set to work on a group of two-part organ preludes and fugues, ambitious pieces in which the influence of Vivaldi's orchestral writing often makes itself heard. These tightly unified compositions foreshadow *The Well-Tempered Clavier* in their determination to test the musical and intellectual possibilities of counterpoint.

Organ Masterpieces: Koopman
(Regis; 2 CDs)

This excellent set includes practically all the Weimar preludes and fugues, plus a smattering of other masterpieces, recorded on four fine Dutch Baroque organs. Ton Koopman plays with such invention and flair that even old warhorses like the *Toccata and Fugue in D Minor* sound fresh. Terrific value, and probably the best way in to Bach's organ music.

Organ Works Vol. 1: Oortmerssen
(Challenge Classics)

On this disc, alongside the monumental *Prelude and Fugue in B Minor* and its C major counterpart, you get the third trio sonata and a Bach transcription of a Vivaldi concerto. All receive committed and thoughtful readings on historic instruments: Jacques van Oortmerssen is a more austere player than Koopman, but his insights into the music's architecture are unsurpassed.

Chorale Preludes

Chorale preludes were originally short pieces – often improvised – that served simply to remind a Lutheran congregation of the tune they were about to sing (see p.413). Some of Bach's 150 compositions in the genre could fulfil this liturgical role: notably the joyful Christmas prelude *In dulci jubilo*, which alternates a block-chord version of the chorale with sparkling improvisatory interludes, and the 45 miniatures of the teaching manual *Orgelbüchlein* (Little Organ Book). But it seems unlikely that Bach's two major collections of chorale preludes – the third part of the *Clavierübung* (Keyboard Excercise) and the eighteen so-called "great" Leipzig preludes – were ever intended for religious use. Both collections set chorale melodies in an encyclopedic variety of ways: buried in dense contrapuntal textures or appearing as a richly decorated solo voice; used as rigorously worked-out fugal subjects or grounds for complex sets of variations. Perhaps the boldest example – and typical of Bach's blurring of the distinctions between genres – is the "St Anne" *Prelude and Fugue in E Flat Major*, which crowns Part III of the *Clavierübung*. After a swaggering French-style prelude in Vivaldian concerto form, Bach closes with a resplendent three-part fugue – a structure that has been interpreted as Bach's celebration of the Holy Trinity.

Organ Works Vol. 4: Kee
(Chandos)

The "St Anne" prelude and fugue gets a glittering performance here on the vibrant (and vibrantly recorded) eighteenth-century Schnitger organ in Groningen. Piet Kee also offers winning versions of the "Schübler" chorales – among them the well-known "Wachet auf", adapted by Bach from his cantata – and an energetic version of the ankle-twisting fourth trio sonata.

Organ Works Vol. 2: Amsterdam Baroque Choir; Koopman (Teldec)

As well as the complete Schübler and Leipzig chorale preludes, this ingenious disc includes sprucely sung versions of the chorales themselves, mostly harmonized by Bach himself. Koopman's organ performances are sometimes a little too exuberant – his love for ornamentation might grate – but there's no doubting the sincerity of his playing.

OTHER INSTRUMENTAL MUSIC

The main forum for Bach's orchestral and instrumental music was Cöthen and the Collegium Musicum at Leipzig. Cöthen possessed a wealth of talented instrumental players: Prince Leopold himself was a gifted amateur who played the harpsichord, the violin and the viola da gamba. Oddly enough, apart from the keyboard music already discussed, there is not a great deal of instrumental music from this, or any other, period of Bach's career, and much of what has survived is of dubious authorship. Undoubtedly the greatest of the non-keyboard instrumental pieces are the three partitas and three sonatas for unaccompanied violin and the six suites for unaccompanied

What is a Fugue?

Music in which two or more independent melodies are woven together (known as contrapuntal music or counterpoint) can be written in many different ways. The melodic lines, which are referred to as "voices" whether they are sung or played, may be freely composed or written according to some kind of organizing principle, such as having a recurring theme that each of the voices plays in turn. The simplest example of this style (called "imitative" counterpoint because the voices sound like they're imitating each other) is the round, in which all the voices perform a single theme over and over again, each starting at a different time. The most complex imitative style is the fugue, in which a short recurring theme (the "subject") is mixed with freely composed lines in a complex conversational texture.

Though there is no fixed structure that defines the fugue, most examples have a very similar form, which starts with an easy-to-recognize opening section – the exposition. One voice starts off by playing the subject, then another voice enters presenting the subject at a different pitch, while the first voice continues with a complementary melody. The piece then builds up line-by-line until all the voices (there are usually between three and five) have entered.

A fugue would become a bit tiresome if the composer simply continued passing the subject around the voices, so before another "entry" of the subject occurs, a new section is usually inserted. Called an episode, this section consists of a short piece of music, generally derived from the subject, being treated sequentially – repeated at gradually higher or lower pitches – leading the piece into a new key. The rest of the fugue consists of the alternation of entries, in various keys, and more episodes, but to add to the excitement the composer can show off by treating the subject in increasingly complex ways, such as overlapping it with itself (stretto), turning it upside down (inversion), playing it back to front (retrograde), extending the length of the notes (augmentation), or shortening the notes (diminution).

Fugue writing developed in the Renaissance, but at that time there was no concept of "a fugue" as such. The term simply described the texture of voices entering in a fugue-like way. It wasn't until the early Baroque that composers such as Frescobaldi and Sweelink started forging whole pieces in a fugal style. Often making use of more than one subject, these works had various names, including the canzona, ricercar and fantasie. The fugue developed throughout the seventeenth century and reached its zenith in the eighteenth, in the output of the greatest ever contrapuntalist, J.S. Bach.

In the Baroque, the fugue was considered the most "learned" of musical styles, appreciated only by the educated. When used in church music, its multi-layered richness was intended to fill the congregation with a sense of confused wonder. For lesser composers, writing fugues could be a somewhat slow and mathematical process, but not for a master like Bach, who could improvise eloquent fugal textures at the keyboard and see at a glance the unique possibilities of a given subject.

Fugues became less fashionable after the Baroque period but remained, and still remain, a curriculum staple for students of composition. Many composers – from Mozart in the finale of his "Jupiter" Symphony to Schoenberg in *Pierrot Lunaire* – have reinvented the genre for their own time. One of the most striking examples is by Beethoven, who described his massive and powerful *Grosse Fuge* (the original final movement of the Op. 130 string quartet, see p.57) as the high point of his chamber output.

Fugue: Bach and His Forerunners: Tilney
(Music & Arts)

Veteran harpsichordist Colin Tilney has had the bright idea of selecting eight of the fugues from the *Art of Fugue* and interspersing them with fugues by three predecessors, Frescobaldi, Gabrieli and Froberger, and one near-contemporary, Louis Couperin. He also plays on an instrument without equal temperament (see p.26), which makes for some pleasingly odd-sounding harmonies. It all adds up to an intriguing recital and a great demonstration of how brilliantly Bach developed an already well-tested musical idea.

cello, works which push the expressive and technical possibilities of their respective instruments to unprecedented extremes. However, the flute sonatas form a highpoint of that instrument's repertoire, and the *Art of Fugue*, which could be categorized as a work for either keyboard or chamber ensemble, reveals the remarkable depth of Bach's genius with counterpoint.

The Art of Fugue

Bach's very last work is one of his most baffling. The *Art of Fugue* is a collection of fugues and canons that display the full gamut of fugal transformational techniques, such as augmentation and diminution (see box opposite). The theory that the work was intended as an intellectual exercise rather than for performance is borne out by the fact that no instruments are specified in the score, yet it is written in such a way that it can be played at the keyboard. It may have been created for the members of the Corresponding Society of the Musical Sciences, a society formed by Bach's former pupil Lorenz Mizler, which explored music's theoretical basis in mathematics. But although the *Art of Fugue* (the title was not Bach's own) reveals Bach in his most academic and puzzle-solving guise, it is no mere pedantry and there is much here of great energy and inspiration. Since Bach did not specify any instrumentation, the big question is: what instrument or instruments should the *Art of Fugue* be played on? There are many keyboard recordings, but versions are available for everything from saxophone quartet to orchestra.

Keller Quartet
(ECM)

The *Art of Fugue* lends itself remarkably well to string quartet, and such performances bring out a lyricism in Bach's counterpoint that can't be articulated at the keyboard. This recording from the Keller Quartet is one of the best available. The Hungarian players, alternately bold and dance-like, eschew excess vibrato to create a wonderful translucent sound reminiscent of a consort of viols.

Violin Sonatas & Partitas

Although a stringed instrument is capable of playing two notes at the same time, one expects a work for a solo stringed instrument to produce a single line of music, without much harmony and without counterpoint. The extraordinary achievement of Bach's violin sonatas and partitas is the way in which harmony and counterpoint are implied through the frequent spreading of the component notes of a chord. Listening to these works for the first time it is difficult to believe that you are hearing just one instrument – especially in the second movement of each sonata, where Bach provides a fully realized fugue. At the same time this is not simply intellectual wizardry: these works abound with vivid melodies and some of the movements, such as the famous chaconne from the *D Minor Partita*, rank among the most deeply emotional moments in all of Bach's music.

Grumiaux
(Philips; 2 CDs)

These pieces are the Everest of the violin repertoire, extremely difficult to play and utterly exposed, with no orchestra or piano to cover imperfections. Grumiaux makes it all sound terribly easy: his playing is clean and incisive, with a stylish sense of line, and double-stopping that is boldly and clearly articulated.

Podger
(Channel Classics; 2 CDs)

Rachael Podger, on a Baroque violin, produces every note with great shape and colour, especially in the pathos-imbued movements like the "Chaconne" and the "C Major Prelude". Yet her overall approach is characterized by a joyous spirit and exquisite articulation that makes these works seem incredibly light and airy in places.

Cello Suites

There is no fugal writing in the *Cello Suites* but they share with the unaccompanied violin works the same capacity to create a multi-textured sound from a single-voiced instrument. A spectacular example of this is the prelude of the first suite, in which succeeding chords are separated out into their individual notes – what you hear is both the gently rocking, forward momentum of the separated notes, and the underlying harmonic structure. The last two suites are the most technically demanding: *Suite No. 5* involves unconventional tuning, or *scordatura*, while *No. 6* is written for a five-stringed instrument, rather than the usual four-stringed one. Like the violin works, these are virtuosic pieces – the first ever written for cello – and may have been composed for one of the most talented of the Cöthen players, the cellist and viola da gamba player Christian Ferdinand Abel.

Bylsma
(Sony; 2 CDs)

Anner Bylsma has recorded the suites twice, both times on Baroque instruments with gut rather than metal strings, thus making for a warmer and more diffuse sound. This suits his style of playing, which tends to stress the delicacy and intimacy of these pieces. He is a master of phrasing and of touch, with subtle shifts of emphasis that refashion phrases in an unexpected but utterly convincing manner.

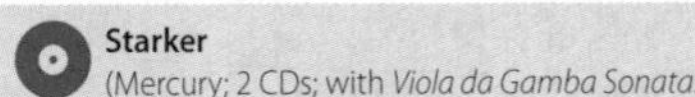

Starker
(Mercury; 2 CDs; with *Viola da Gamba Sonatas*)

Janos Starker has recorded these works at many times, the best of which – made in the late 1950s for EMI – is only available as part of a six-CD set. This slightly later performance is still remarkable, however, possessing a sinewy vigour and a dynamism which revolutionized the playing of these works. Poor CD remastering is the only drawback.

Casals
(Naxos; 2 CDs)

Until Casals came along, the *Cello Suites* were virtually unplayed, and the fact that they are now core repertoire is almost entirely due to his trail-blazing performances. His personal identification with the music comes across strongly in this recording from the 1930s. With his warm tone and idiosyncratic phrasing, these classic accounts convince by virtue of Casals' deep musicality.

Musical Offering

In 1747 Bach, still with a reputation as a brilliant keyboard improviser, travelled to Potsdam at the request of King Frederick the Great of Prussia. He arrived in the evening just as the king (a talented flautist) was beginning his regular concert with his court musicians, among whom was Bach's second son Carl Philipp Emanuel. The older Bach requested a theme from the king on which he improvised a three-part fugue, later improvising a six-part fugue on a theme of his own devising. Back in Leipzig the king's theme was written up and extended into a work containing a three- and a six-part ricecar for keyboard, and a trio sonata in four movements for flute, violin and continuo, together with ten scholarly canons. The whole thing, lavishly printed, bound and presented to the king as a *Musical Offering*, can be seen as a sophisticated calling card – Bach flexing his musical and intellectual muscles with, perhaps, half an eye on a possible royal appointment.

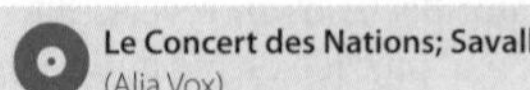

Le Concert des Nations; Savall
(Alia Vox)

Jordi Savall's highly expressive recording commences with the brief "royal theme" on solo flute – an effective innovation, which has the effect of tuning your ear to the dazzling ingenuity with which Bach develops his material. Arranged so that the four-movement sonata forms the hub of the recital, the recording features two different versions of the mighty six-voice fugue (for solo harpsichord and, right at the end, for chamber ensemble).

Flute Sonatas

By the early eighteenth century the transverse flute (as opposed to the recorder) had become hugely popular, and there was a continuous demand for new music for it. Of the six flute sonatas traditionally ascribed to Bach, two are now thought to be not by him, though both are delightful works. The genuine ones are marked by the intricacy of the writing, in which the equal importance of each line (the flute part, and the bass and right-hand harpsichord lines) makes them more like trio sonatas than sonatas for a soloist and accompanist. They are generally characterized by cool restraint, rarely matching the energy or dynamism of the unaccompanied violin or cello pieces, yet there is much of great beauty in this tightly reined music.

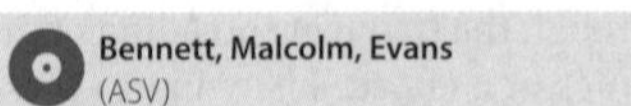

Bennett, Malcolm, Evans
(ASV)

William Bennett possesses a full and controlled tone, and makes an eloquent soloist, especially impressive in the long elegant phrases of the *E Minor Sonata*. The dynamic control of these performances (recorded in 1978) makes them livelier than most, and the emphasis shifts naturally from instrument to instrument where necessary.

Samuel Barber (1910–1981)

Right back in the 1930s, when Samuel Barber was being lauded in some quarters as one of the most talented American composers of his generation, his music was being labelled as utterly anachronistic by modernists. Totally unperturbed, Barber went on writing in his neo-Romantic vein, turning out essentially dramatic and lyrical works in a tonal language rooted in the late nineteenth century. In the 1970s, with a large and varied body of work behind him, Barber was able to state with a certain satisfaction, "it is said that I have no style at all but that doesn't matter. I just go on doing, as they say, my thing. I believe this takes a certain courage."

It's hardly surprising that many of Barber's compositions are vocal settings – he was an excellent baritone, and as a young student at the Curtis Institute he entertained notions of becoming a professional singer. By the time Barber graduated in 1932 he was already a confident composer with several highly accomplished works under his belt, including *Dover Beach* (a song singled out for praise by Vaughan Williams) and the *Serenade for String Quartet*. From the start his music exhibited many of the Barber hallmarks, notably extended lyrical lines and a remarkable facility for instrumental colour and text-setting. Barber was never coy about wearing his heart on his sleeve – his music was always first and foremost to do with the expression of profound personal emotion, a quality which soon got him noticed, not least by Toscanini. Once Toscanini had performed the *Adagio for Strings* in 1938, Barber never looked back. Numerous awards came his way, including Pulitzer prizes for the opera *Vanessa* (1958) and for his *Piano Concerto* (1962), and it must have seemed as though his star would never stop rising.

The bubble was to burst, however, with the failure of Barber's biggest work of the 1960s, the full-scale Shakespearean opera *Antony and Cleopatra*. Franco Zeffirelli's libretto was decidedly over the top, as was his production for the 1966 premiere, which with all its live animals and hundreds of extras looked like a second-rate Cecil B. de Mille movie. The opera was revised by his lifelong companion Gian Carlo Menotti, and restaged in 1975 at the Juilliard School in New York, but never found many admirers. Although Barber had a spate of commissions in the early 1970s, his writing tailed off at the close of the decade, due in no small part to the cancer that was to kill him.

Adagio for Strings

Barber's name is synonymous with one composition, the undeniably beautiful *Adagio for Strings* which began life as the slow movement of his 1936 *String Quartet*. Two years later Barber arranged it for string orchestra and, with the help of Toscanini, it lodged itself indelibly in the American psyche. With its slow-building melodic lines, breath-like pauses and general mood of subdued sadness, it is not difficult to see why it has taken on the status of a twentieth-century classic. It was broadcast at the death of President Roosevelt and more recently provided catharsis in Oliver Stone's Vietnam film *Platoon*. Unfortunately the *Adagio* has tended to overshadow all Barber's other work, but there is now an increasingly wide cross-section of his music appearing on CD.

Atlanta Symphony Orchestra; Levi (Telarc; with *Knoxville, Essays Nos. 1 & 2, School for Scandal Overture & Medea's Dance of Vengeance*)

This is a broodingly atmospheric account of the *Adagio*, with Levi perfectly judging the work's dark ebb and flow and resisting the temptation to underline the pathos. The disc also includes a selection of Barber's orchestral works, including the two concentrated *Orchestral Essays*, and a delightfully fresh performance of *Knoxville*.

Violin Concerto

Barber's *Violin Concerto* was commissioned in 1939 by the businessman Samuel Fels for his young protégé the violinist Iso Briselli, who rejected it as too easy when Barber submitted the first two movements. It is true that, though unabashedly Romantic in tone, the Allegro and Andante contain no technical fireworks. What they do possess is a rhapsodic exuberance in the Allegro and a defiantly vocal melancholy in the Andante. There's a Mendelssohnian fervour to both movements, but it's saved from being a nineteenth-century pastiche by Barber's characteristic spare and loose-limbed orchestration. For the finale (marked "Presto in moto perpetuo") Barber tapped into a more modern, though hardly avant-garde, vein in which woodwind and brass scuttle alongside the frenetic soloist as if in pursuit. Briselli rejected this movement as unplayable and the work was eventually premiered by Albert Spalding and the Philadelphia Orchestra in 1941.

Shaham; London Symphony Orchestra; Previn
(Deutsche Grammophon; with Korngold *Violin Concerto & Much Ado About Nothing)*

It's interesting to hear the Barber concerto alongside that of Korngold. Both are Romantic works but Barber has more of a modern take – more neo-Romantic than Korngold's blatant heart-tugging. Gil Shaham and André Previn make an excellent team, bringing out the brilliance and vivacity of the Barber rather than milking its more emotional side.

Knoxville: Summer of 1915

When, in 1947, the soprano Eleanor Steber asked Barber for a new work for her to perform with the Boston Symphony Orchestra, the composer turned to the prose and poetry of James Agee, which he had recently been reading. The result was *Knoxville: Summer of 1915*, an unashamedly nostalgic evocation of a child's view of small-town family life, as American as Thornton Wilder's *Our Town* or Frank Capra's *It's a Wonderful Life*. Barber sets Agee's prose poem (a mix of the simple and the overly poetic) in a largely syllabic and straightforward manner which stays close to the rhythms and inflections of the original. Musically it is dominated by a gentle rocking melody – suggesting a lullaby – that frames the work. A more animated middle section (representing the clatter of the streetcar) leads into a brief rhapsodic passage as night falls. Barber's restraint and real identification with the material means that sentimentality is avoided and a genuinely moving picture emerges.

McNair; Atlanta Symphony Orchestra; Levi
(Telarc; with *Adagio, Essays Nos. 1 & 2, School for Scandal Overture & Medea's Dance of Vengeance*)

Knoxville is a marvellous vehicle for a lyric soprano, but it's not that easy to bring off. Sylvia McNair has a beautiful, full and rounded voice and does as well as any at expressing the easy-going, everyday innocence of the work, especially in the opening. Just occasionally, in the more rapturous passages, the words get lost, but overall her enunciation is good and this is the best of recent recordings.

Songs

Perhaps the most attractive of all Barber's works are his songs, in even the earliest of which – such as *Slumber Song of the Madonna* (1925) – he shows an impressive facility with vocal colour and word-setting. By the time of *Dover Beach*, for string quartet and baritone, he was completely in control of the medium, exploring rich harmonic textures and complicated polyphony. His range of expression is unrivalled among modern songwriters, encompassing every mood from Schubertian tenderness and simplicity (as in *A Nun Takes the Veil*, 1937) to the artfully decadent (as in the café-style *Solitary Hotel*, 1968–69).

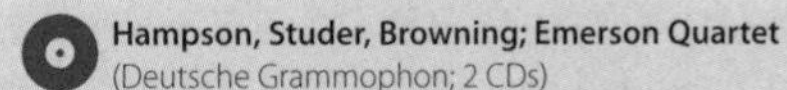

Hampson, Studer, Browning; Emerson Quartet
(Deutsche Grammophon; 2 CDs)

The DG set of Barber's songs is a splendid chronological survey, excellently performed by all involved. Thomas Hampson is especially fine, effortless in Barber's protracted lyrical melodies yet also intensely dramatic wherever necessary.

Agustín Pio Barrios (1885–1944)

Paraguayan composer-performer Agustín Pio Barrios is sometimes described as the "Chopin of the guitar", and there is some justice in this designation. Like much of Chopin's work for piano, Barrios's guitar pieces stand out in the repertory for their elegant beauty, poetic ease, and for being perfectly conceived for their instrument in a way that only a virtuoso could achieve.

Born in a small town in southern Paraguay in 1885, Barrios started learning the guitar at a very young age. Recognizing his talent, his parents sent him for a formal education in Asunción, where he excelled as a performer and spent time developing transcription skills, reworking keyboard masterpieces by the likes of Bach and Beethoven for the guitar. He also developed keen interests in mathematics, literature, poetry and philosophy, which he maintained throughout his life, later claiming that "one cannot become a guitarist if he has not bathed in the fountain of culture".

In 1910 Barrios headed to Argentina to give a short series of recitals. They proved so successful that he ended up spending most of the next two decades on the road, performing in most of the countries of South and Central America. In the late 1920s he became increasingly fascinated by his Guarani Indian ancestry, and in the early 1930s, under some pressure from his concert agent, he started giving recitals not in standard concert dress but in traditional Indian attire, complete with feather headdress. He billed himself as "Chief Nitsuga Mangoré" (the first name Agustín spelled backwards and the second borrowed from a legendary anti-colonialist Guarani chieftain), adding the curious shout-line "the Paganini of the guitar from the jungles of Paraguay". Often he would appear for one half of a recital as Mangoré, performing pieces in a folk style, and then reappear after the interval in a dinner jacket and offer Bach and other transcriptions. In the mid 1930s, he spent a year in Europe, performing in Germany, Spain and Belgium. A few years after his return he took a position as professor at the conservatory of San Salvador, where he died in 1944.

Barrios composed throughout his life and his works are highly innovative, both in terms of their unique use of Romantic harmony and in the way they maximize the guitar's resources without ever sounding like mere studies. Barrios was also probably the first classical guitarist ever to make recordings, the earliest dating from 1913. His own recordings, which are the only sources for many of his pieces, are available on the Chanterelle label.

Works for Guitar

Barrios's output consisted entirely of works for solo guitar, and of the 300 or so he probably wrote, more than 100 have survived. He admired the musical traditions of his native continent, and many of his pieces are rhythmically and melodically modelled on local forms such as *choros*, *tangos* and *cuecos*. Good examples can be found in the first and second *Danza Paraguaya*, in which tunes and rhythms from Barrios's homeland are presented in the style evocative of the Paraguayan harp. Yet little that he wrote sounds completely South American, as his musical language was marked by the influence of the Spanish guitar greats like Tárrega and Sor, while pieces such as the *Preludio in G Minor* and *Mazurka appasionata* bear the imprint of the European classical tradition from Bach to Chopin.

One of Barrios's best-known pieces is the three-movement *La catedral*, inspired by an experience at the Cathedral of San José in Montevideo, Uruguay. After a lyrical prelude comes a reverent Andante religioso, the broad chords of which pay tribute to the Bach organ music that was being played in the cathedral. Finally, a lively Allegro solemne brings us back to the reality of the jostling outside world. Equally popular is Barrios's last piece, the serene *Una limosna por el amor do Dio* (Alms for the Love of God). Its initially melancholic but eventually resolved melody is wonderfully articulated with tremolo technique, in which long notes are created by the rapid repetition of short notes.

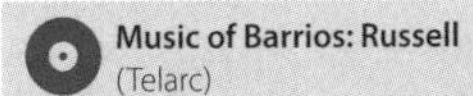

Music of Barrios: Russell
(Telarc)

David Russell's subtly expressive and technically assured playing makes this collection the best Barrios disc available. It includes many of the famous pieces, including *La catedral*, *Una limosna* and the *Danza Paraguayas*, which flow effortlessly and unpretentiously.

The Great Paraguayan: Williams
(Sony Classical)

John Williams has long been a keen advocate of Barrios and his fans will doubtless enjoy this CD. His playing is technically excellent as ever, though in places he lacks the expressive ease of Russell. Including *La catedral*, *Una limosna*, the *Preludio in G Minor* and the *Mazurka appasionata*, the collection overlaps with about half of Russell's disc.

Béla Bartók (1881–1945)

During the first two decades of the twentieth century, the tonal basis of classical music – the tyranny of major and minor keys, as Stravinsky termed it – finally collapsed. For Schoenberg and his Viennese followers, the logical progression from the lush ambiguities of Wagner was the development of serialism, replacing the exhausted principles of tonality with the rigours of the twelve-tone system. Béla Bartók, however, found another way out of the impasse, producing music in which the Germanic tradition was given new life by incorporating it into a strongly nationalist style. In this he was, of course, not unique. Nationalism had been an increasingly powerful force since the European wave of revolutions in 1848, and received crucial impetus with the outbreak of worldwide conflict in the 1910s, as can be heard in the work of such diverse figures as Dvořák, Prokofiev, Janáček, Grieg, Sibelius and Vaughan Williams. But no other composer managed to produce work in which folk and art music were assimilated with such power and modernity.

Bartók's early music was the product of years of studying the German tradition at the Budapest Academy. Bearing the imprint of Wagner, Brahms, Liszt and Strauss, it was traditional, slightly old-fashioned and full of unfettered melodic expression. In 1902 Bartók was inspired by a performance of Strauss's *Also Sprach Zarathustra* to write his own tone poem *Kossuth*, but for all his composing ambitions he spent the next five years pursuing the career of a travelling piano virtuoso, specializing in the music of Liszt. The partial exorcism of these Romantic influences began in 1905, when he interrupted his touring to begin an exploration of Hungarian peasant music; the following year, he and his friend Kodály (see p.282) published a collection of twenty Magyar songs. However, his own music was persistently rejected and in 1907, recognizing the futility of life as a composer, he took a position as head of piano studies at the Budapest Academy, where he continued his ethnological studies. Bartók's immersion in Hungarian folk traditions – and his discovery of Debussy's impressionism – encouraged him to look beyond the confines of purely tonal expression and he developed a fascination with dissonance, a feature of nearly all his music written after his extraordinary opera *Duke Bluebeard's Castle* (1911).

Bartók was not the first composer to write "Hungarian" classical music, but, whereas Brahms and Liszt had written pieces in a style that was Hungarian in atmosphere rather than substance, Bartók marked a clear break with tradition by treating his folk melodies and rhythms as truly raw material, emphasizing their "primitive" elements. On the other hand, though his music was often aggressive and harsh, its essential language didn't diverge completely from tonality, and the structural principles of his greatest compositions – such as the astringent string quartets – justify the description of Bartók as one of the last and most original Romantic composers. His ardent nationalism and his refusal to adopt the methods of the Second Viennese School placed him outside the mainstream of the European avant-garde, and Bartók's name did not feature prominently on concert programmes during his lifetime. His successes in the USA, where he spent the last five unhappy yet productive years of his life, were engineered by extremely prominent performers whose advocacy did more to persuade the promoters and press than did the music itself. He remains a slightly eccentric figure in the history of modern music – though his music is now featured widely in concert halls and record catalogues, he's arguably the least influential of the twentieth century's indisputably great composers. There is no school of Bartók.

Duke Bluebeard's Castle

Bartók composed only three stage works: the two ballets, *The Wooden Prince* and *The Miraculous Mandarin*, and the one-act opera *Duke Bluebeard's Castle*. *Bluebeard's Castle*, the finest of the three, is a disturbing, static drama with just two characters – Bluebeard himself (bass/baritone) and his new wife, Judith (soprano). The opera, written in 1911, represents Bartók's departure from his intoxication with German music in general and Richard Strauss in particular, though his debt to Strauss's chromatic indulgence is revealed in the Romantic grandeur of the music he assigns

Béla Bartók recording folk songs in Transylvania, c.1908.

to Judith. Her sinister husband sings in contrastingly dour and stark tones, setting up a tension that is quintessentially Bartók.

The action of this deeply disturbing tale is simple. Against his wishes, Bluebeard allows his new wife the keys to the seven doors that open onto the hall of his castle. Behind each door she discovers something terrible – from a torture chamber to a magic garden where the roses are spotted with blood – until finally she realizes that she is to be imprisoned forever, along with his three other wives, behind the seventh door. The opening of the fifth door is an awesome moment: as it opens, Judith is confronted by a blinding ray of sunshine, an event for which Bartók found one of his greatest inspirations – a simple but amazingly effective C major chord, from which develops some of the opera's most stunning music. This scene is a staggering visual coup, but *Bluebeard*'s general lack of narrative incident makes it one of the few operas that's as effective on disc as it is on stage.

Ramey, Marton; Hungarian State Orchestra; Fischer (Sony)

This is arguably the best of the dozen or so available recordings. Eva Marton delivers a rainbow of vocal colours, and Samuel Ramey similarly makes the most of his role's potential. Adam Fischer directs the whole thing with a sometimes overwhelming passion, and creates a translucent sound that highlights the mastery of Bartók's orchestrations.

Berry, Ludwig; London Symphony Orchestra; Kertész (Decca)

Kertész's vision of *Bluebeard* is febrile, restless and edgy. He pays a great deal of attention to detail which, with his manic and fluctuating tempi, makes the score sound less flowing than it really is – but it is an approach that works well. Walter Berry and Christa Ludwig sing with their usual strength and commitment, though the former's tone occasionally seems too smooth and generous.

The Miraculous Mandarin

Bartók, whose introspection bordered on the pathological, was clearly attracted to stories of loneliness and alienation in which the power of love could both redeem and destroy. In 1917 he read the scenario for a ballet, *The Miraculous Mandarin*, in the Hungarian literary magazine *Nyugat*. Bartók immediately decided to set it to music, enthusiastically describing the grisly tale to a journalist as "beautiful". The plot tells of three thugs who force a young girl to lure passers-by into a room where they will rob them. After two unsuccessful attempts, a strange Chinese man appears. The girl arouses his desire by dancing. The men try to kill him but he will not die. Only when the girl satisfies his desire do his wounds begin to bleed and he dies.

Like *Duke Bluebeard's Castle*, *The Miraculous Mandarin* exudes a tangible claustrophobia and an almost suffocating sexual tension. The work's swirling, restless energy and profusion of jagged cross-rhythms clearly owe much to *Petrushka* and the *Rite of Spring* but, whereas Stravinsky's rawness conjures up the exotic, Bartók evokes a much more modern vision – an alienating cityscape of glaring lights and blaring klaxons. This is certainly his most aggressive score, with only the beguiling and virtuosic clarinet solos of the three enticement scenes offering much in the way of lyricism. The nightmarish and percussive violence of the score is made bearable by the brilliant richness of the orchestral colouring which, though consistently sinister, has several highly sensuous moments.

Hungarian Radio Chorus; Budapest Festival Orchestra; Fischer (Philips; with *Hungarian Sketches*, *Romanian Folk Dances*, etc)

Fischer gets a finely detailed and energetic performance from his Budapest players. There is an engaging clarity and bite to the orchestral playing (qualities that also serve the accompanying *Romanian Folk Dances* well) and the solo passages are excellent. The seduction scenes, in particular, are beautifully played by an uncredited clarinettist.

Piano Concertos

Bartók was an excellent pianist and his first two piano concertos, dating from 1926 and 1931, were clearly written to suit his own particular style of playing. In both concertos, Bartók treats the piano as primarily a percussive instrument, and their raw ferocity can still shock listeners as much as they did at their first performances. Unlike his violin concertos, there is no lyricism or Romantic lilt here – you might be seduced by the music of these other works, but the first two piano concertos batter you into submission.

The third piano concerto was one of Bartók's final pieces and was left incomplete at his death – after the final seventeen bars had been completed by a former student Tibor Serly, the work got its first performance on 8 February, 1946. Written for Bartók's wife Ditta, the third concerto is considerably less aggressive and more classical in form – indeed it is one of the most conventionally constructed works he wrote. The music reflects the composer's contentment at the very end of his life: America may not have turned out to be the land of milk and honey, but the Nazis had been defeated and he had been restored to all his official musical posts in his absence, encouraging him to consider a return to his native Hungary.

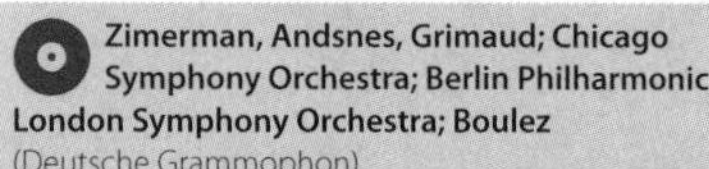

Zimerman, Andsnes, Grimaud; Chicago Symphony Orchestra; Berlin Philharmonic; London Symphony Orchestra; Boulez (Deutsche Grammophon)

A different soloist and orchestra for each concerto but with the same conductor. Sounds like a gimmick but, surprisingly, it works incredibly well, not least because Boulez gives each of his soloists their head. Krystian Zimerman's is the most scintillating performance but the others are not far behind.

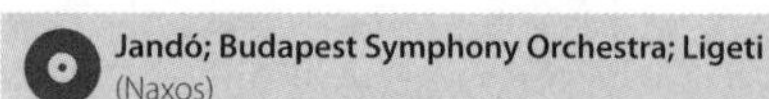

Jandó; Budapest Symphony Orchestra; Ligeti (Naxos)

Jandó, who has recorded a wide range of repertoire for Naxos, is clearly very much at home with Bartók. These are vigorous, idiomatic accounts which hold their own with the best – especially in view of the budget price.

Violin Concertos

Bartók wrote his two-movement first violin concerto in 1908, soon after returning from his first folk-song-collecting expedition. This headily Romantic piece was written for the young violinist Stefie Geyer, but sadly she did not reciprocate the emotion so clearly expressed in the lovely first movement, and she left the composer shortly after the work's completion. Bartók duly shelved the concerto, which remained unperformed until two years after Geyer's death and fifty years after it was written.

In 1938, the Hungarian violinist Zoltán Székely asked Bartók to have another go. The composer preferred to write an extended set of variations but Székely maintained that, as he was paying for the work, he should get what he asked for. Not wishing to be defeated, Bartók then cheated by writing a three-movement concerto which is, in fact, an extended set of variations – though it requires close analysis to find the relation between the opening pizzicati and the finale. It has its moments of dissonance, but predominantly it is as melodic as the earlier one, and repeated listening reveals a flood of ideas that seem to tumble over each other.

Midori; Berlin Philharmonic Orchestra; Mehta (Sony)

Midori's recording of the Bartók concertos was the one that showed that the Japanese-American whizz kid amounted to a lot more than just an amazing technique: this disc is a marvel, her interpretations are well measured, understated and deeply thought out.

Pauk; National Polish Radio Symphony Orchestra; Wit (Naxos)

The Hungarian violinist György Pauk may not achieve the total effortlessness that some virtuosos have achieved, but he more than makes up for it with sensitive lyrical playing in the first concerto and vivacious energy and idiomatic treatment of the Gypsy material in the second.

Concerto for Orchestra

The genre of the "concerto for orchestra" was a twentieth-century invention inspired by the rapidly increasing technical abilities of American orchestras in the period after World War I. Kodály and Lutosławski both wrote pieces in this format, but neither quite matches Bartók's intricately constructed showpiece, which gloriously displays the virtuoso talents of each of the orchestral sections.

One of the composer's last works, the *Concerto for Orchestra* was commissioned in 1943 by the conductor Serge Koussevitzky, whose Boston Symphony Orchestra gave the first performance at the end of the following year, an event received with great acclaim. The five movements present a gradual transition from the severity of the first to a life-affirming finale, with interruptions along the way – thus the satirical and light-hearted second movement is followed by a "Song of Death", which in turn gives way to an Intermezzo that has a dig at Shostakovich by quoting his seventh symphony.

Oslo Philharmonic Orchestra; Jansons (EMI; with *Music for Strings, Percussion and Celesta*)

This 1990 recording combines outstanding performances with the kind of bright modern sound that really benefits the clean textures of Bartók's orchestral music. Jansons' account is invigoratingly dynamic, and the Oslo Philharmonic meets the challenge head on, nowhere more excitingly than in the sparking finale.

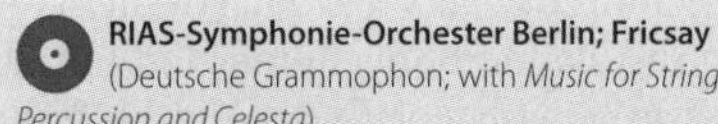

RIAS-Symphonie-Orchester Berlin; Fricsay (Deutsche Grammophon; with *Music for Strings, Percussion and Celesta*)

Ferenc Fricsay was a close associate of the composer (he conducted a Bartók premiere aged 22), and this 1957 performance reveals a profound knowledge of every detail of the work. The sound quality is remarkably vivid, and at mid-price this coupling is a real bargain.

Music for Strings, Percussion and Celesta

Commissioned by one of the twentieth century's most important patrons, Paul Sacher, and first performed by him and his Basle Chamber Orchestra in 1937, *Music for Strings, Percussion and Celesta* is one of Bartók's most unorthodox, complicated and demanding works. It's written in four continuous movements, lasts around thirty minutes, and is scored for a unique ensemble: two groups of strings, a phalanx of percussion instruments including cymbals, drums, tam-tam, timpani and xylophone, plus piano, harp and celesta, a piano-like instrument with metal bars instead of strings. It's an extremely eerie piece of music (Kubrick used it on the soundtrack of *The Shining*), and a seminal one, too – its monothematicism (the way the whole thing is generated from a single theme), and its emphasis on rhythmic power rather than on melody, established a mature style from which Bartók did not stray until his last five years.

Oslo Philharmonic Orchestra; Jansons (EMI; with *Concerto for Orchestra*)

Mariss Jansons' strong rapport with the Oslo orchestra has produced several fine recordings, and this is one of the best. Jansons brilliantly conjures the translucent texture demanded by Bartók – the Adagio sounds particularly spooky —and he doesn't labour the work's thematic reinventions.

RIAS-Symphonie-Orchester Berlin; Fricsay (Deutsche Grammophon; with *Concerto for Orchestra*)

Throughout his career Fricsay was famed both as an interpreter of Bartók's music and as a fastidiously precise director of his orchestras. His reading of the *Music for Strings, Percussion and Celesta* (dating from 1953) won awards when it was first released, and still has few serious rivals.

String Quartets

Bartók's six string quartets are his greatest achievement and span his entire creative life: the first was completed in 1908, the second in 1917, the third in 1927, the fourth in 1928, the fifth in 1934 and the last in 1938. As with Beethoven and Shostakovich, Bartók translated his deepest and most personal thoughts into his quartets, and each of the six is the purest distillation of his immersion in folk song. The two central quartets, the third and the fourth, have the most astringent and difficult music, but they are also the two most challenging and exciting to listen to. The third is a short, highly concentrated exercise in expressionism that teeters on the brink of atonality. Though Bartók was not a string player, he manages to create an astonishing variety of deeply anguished and mysterious sounds, culminating in the hard-driven and cathartic finale. The sections of the third's single-movement structure form a palindrome; a pattern repeated in the fourth quartet, a more expansive and less introspective work. At its heart is an extraordinary slow movement, full of the wild "night sounds" of nature – rustling trees, birdsong, the movement of insects. It's followed by a short Scherzo entirely made up of manic pizzicato strumming. The finale is one of the most disturbingly driven and dissonant works in the whole of quartet literature.

Takács Quartet
(Decca; 2 CDs)

There are plenty of recordings that have more polish than these performances, but few that bring such a high level of commitment, flair and excitement. The Takács Quartet sound completely at home in Bartók's extraordinary soundworld. The rhythmic contortions, unexpected changes of mood and lurking folk elements are all perfectly judged and handled with a complete assurance of the idiom.

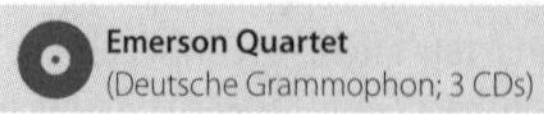

Emerson Quartet
(Deutsche Grammophon; 3 CDs)

On a technical level the Emerson Quartet's award-winning recording of the complete cycle is unrivalled. However, these works need a lot more than concentration on precision, and you can't help feeling – especially in the last two quartets – that the Emersons are sometimes preoccupied with accuracy at the expense of expression.

Violin Sonata

After the string quartets, Bartók's most important chamber music is his *Violin Sonata, Op. 117*, one of the greatest works ever written for unaccompanied violin. It was commissioned by Yehudi Menuhin in 1944, the year after Bartók had praised Menuhin's performance of the composer's first sonata for violin and piano. Although it was written in America, a period of almost unrelieved unhappiness for Bartók, the sonata is an incredibly positive piece of music, showing an understanding of the violin's capabilities that's extraordinary for a composer who didn't play this difficult instrument. With the exception of Ysaye's six sonatas, Bartók's was the first sonata for solo violin to be written since Bach's, and the example of Bach's compositions is never far away in this neo-classically structured piece. Bartók's imagination was inspired by these self-imposed restraints – with its strange cross-rhythms and harmonics, the sonata gives the violin a wholly original voice.

Faust (Harmonia Mundi; with *Sonata No. 1 for Violin and Piano*)

Isabelle Faust combines sustained intensity, a shining sound, a wide dynamic range and perfect intonation in a gripping and powerful performance that makes Bartók's dissonant writing sound haunting and immediate. The *Sonata* is coupled with an excellent recording of the first sonata for violin and piano.

Pauk
(Naxos; with *44 Duos for Two Violins*)

György Pauk's performance – as in his other Bartók recordings – is characterized by a raw, gutsy tone and a sense of complete identification with the material. It comes with a superbly idiomatic and sensitive account of Bartók's extraordinary folk-inspired *44 Duos for Two Violins*.

Solo Piano Music

Like Prokofiev and Rachmaninov, Bartók was a brilliant pianist, destined to lead the life of a virtuoso until he met Kodály and turned his attention to ethnomusicology. His piano music reflects a complete understanding of the instrument's possibilities – in particular its percussive aspect – and is frequently shot through with the quirky rhythms and modality of the folk music he collected. Several of his piano works, like the *Six Romanian Folkdances* (1915), are, in fact, relatively simple arrangements of folk music, but in other instances, having imbibed the spirit of a musical region, he produced complex works of an extreme originality. The short, popular *Allegro barbaro* (1911) is a case in point: its swirling rhythms are like an encapsulation of every wild, Eastern European dance one has ever heard. But even in more tightly structured works, like the *Suite* (1916) or the *Sonata* (1926), propulsive rhythms and modal melodies never disappear for long. *Out of Doors* is another work that dates from 1926 (sometimes called his piano year). Though not strictly programmatic, it's clearly meant to evoke rustic sounds and sights from croaking frogs to droning bagpipes. Bartók also wrote a number of lively pedagogical works, of which *Mikrokosmos*, in six progressively difficult volumes, is the most famous.

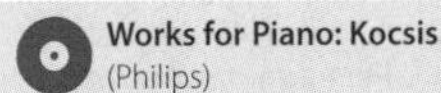

Works for Piano: Kocsis
(Philips)

Zoltán Kocsis is a Hungarian pianist absolutely steeped in Bartók's music (he edited the Hungaraton CD set "Bartók at the Piano", a historically valuable collection of recordings of the composer and associates in performance). He was therefore a good choice for Philips' enterprising seven-volume series of Bartók's complete solo piano output. This sampler disc is a great place to start, containing superb accounts of the *Sonata* and *Out of Doors*, among other works.

Sonata for Two Pianos and Percussion

About a year after writing the *Music for Strings, Percussion and Celesta*, Bartók received a commission from another Basle group to write the *Sonata for Two Pianos and Percussion*. Like the earlier work, this is very much an exercise in exploring the specifically percussive timbres of the piano and the expressive capacity of percussion – a fascination that can be traced back to the slow movement of the *Piano Concerto No. 1* (1926). Once again the relationship of the two pianos – placed on either side of the platform – to the percussion section is that of first among equals. There is also a similar mood of mystery to the work, not least in the brooding build-up of its opening section, and the weirdly funereal march that constitutes the slow movement. There is something almost anthropomorphic about the disconcertingly varied range of voices in this movement – Bartók may have stopped writing for the theatre but he hadn't lost his sense of drama. The final movement is a madcap romp with a witty xylophone part that recalls Shostakovich at his most exuberant.

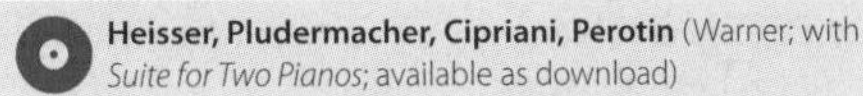

Heisser, Pludermacher, Cipriani, Perotin (Warner; with *Suite for Two Pianos*; available as download)

With neither of Martha Argerich's brilliant accounts of the *Sonata* available as a single CD, this excellent performance from the French duo of Jean-François Heisser and Georges Pludermacher is the one to go for. Supported by the lively percussion team of Gérard Pérotin and Guy-Joel Cipriani, there's a real feeling of excitement and enjoyment in evidence.

Arnold Bax (1883–1953)

Vaughan Williams may have produced the finest of all British symphonic cycles (see p.594), but for many discerning critics Arnold Bax ran him a close second. Bax's seven symphonies – written between 1922 and 1939 – are late-Romantic in style but never soft-centred; the best of them effectively evoke the power and grandeur of the natural world through brilliantly coloured orchestration and tautly energetic melodies. Along with his orchestral tone poems, these constitute Bax's finest achievement, but he also wrote a wealth of chamber music and vocal works, and several pieces for piano solo.

Born into an affluent middle-class English family and brought up in London, Bax was already a gifted pianist by the time he entered the Royal Academy in 1900. He was taught composition by Frederick Corder and piano by Tobias Matthay, but by far the greatest impact on his artistic development was the poetry of W.B. Yeats – in particular *The Wanderings of Oisin*. Bax's passion for Yeats propelled him to Ireland, a country which became his spiritual and, for a time, his real home. So great was his youthful identification with all things Irish – including the country's Republican struggle – that he wrote stories and poems under the pseudonym Dermot O'Byrne, and several of his early compositions have self-consciously "Celtic" themes.

Russian music also made a tremendous impact on the young composer: an outstanding sight-reader, he often played through scores with his friend Arthur Alexander, including all of Rimsky-Korsakov's orchestral works, the symphonies of Borodin, Balakirev and Glazunov, and even Stravinsky's *Rite of Spring*. This passion was cemented by a trip to Russia and the Ukraine in 1910, and was further reinforced by the London seasons of Diaghilev's Ballets Russes (see p.547), all of which Bax attended. His early tone poems and the first three of his symphonies are all infused with Russian colouring – Rimsky-Korsakov and early Stravinsky being particularly strong influences.

Though he escaped military service, World War I was a difficult period in Bax's life. He began a love affair with a young pianist, Harriet Cohen, eventually leaving his wife and family; then in 1916 he was deeply affected by the failure of the Dublin Easter Rising. Despite, or perhaps because of, these emotional upheavals, he was extremely productive, composing several big orchestral works including the best of his tone poems. After the war's end Bax became established as one of Britain's leading composers: both Myra Hess and Harriet Cohen championed his piano music, and several conductors – including Thomas Beecham, Henry Wood and Eugene Goossens – were enthusiastic advocates of his orchestral works.

After two decades at the top of his profession Bax was knighted in 1937 and five years later made Master of the King's Music – ironic since by this time he had virtually given up composing, and was living alone in a room in a Sussex inn. An engaging autobiography, *Farewell My Youth*, appeared in 1943 but the only music of any real significance in his later years was the powerful score that he wrote for David Lean's film adaptation of Dickens's *Oliver Twist*.

Despite a largely successful career, Bax's music virtually dropped off the radar of British concert life following his death. This neglect has been partially reversed in the last twenty years and nearly all his works are now available in good recordings. This revival of interest is still to be reflected in the concert hall, however: only the popular *Tintagel* is performed with any real regularity.

SYMPHONIES

As a composer of large orchestral works, Bax started off by writing a series of highly evocative tone poems, and when it came to symphonies there is a strong sense of him simply extending the language of these earlier works into something more epic and wide-ranging. All seven of his symphonies, beginning with *No. 1* in 1922, are frequently rhapsodic and have a spontaneous – almost impulsive – character, as if the material is controlling him rather than the other way round. Just occasionally this makes the music seem directionless, but the best of these symphonies are works of great power and originality. All are worth hearing, but *Nos. 3, 5* and *6* – written while wintering in Scotland – are arguably the finest.

Complete Symphonies: BBC Philharmonic; Handley (Chandos; 5 CDs; with *Rogue's Comedy Overture & Tintagel*)

Of the three complete cycles of the symphonies available on CD, the most recent, conducted by Vernon Handley, is the most consistently brilliant. Handley's awareness of detail means that all the orchestral colouring is evident, but never at the expense of the music's shape. He also inspires some great playing from the BBC Philharmonic. The only slight cavil is that the CDs are not available individually.

Symphony No. 3

Written during the winter of 1928–29, the *Symphony No. 3* has proved the most performed and recorded of all Bax's symphonies. Scored for a large orchestra, including xylophone, celesta and anvil, it's an expansive work that is both highly dramatic and astonishingly rich in thematic material. This is especially true of the long first movement, in which – following a mysterious opening bassoon solo – changes of mood, from the languid to the urgently angry, come thick and fast. The slow movement is more serene, with some exquisite brass writing (the horn and trumpet solos in particular) creating a feeling of almost religious rapture. In the enigmatic finale a dark introductory passage soon gives way to a jaunty minor-key melody that is part folk song and part nursery rhyme. It's followed by an epilogue (a favoured Baxian conclusion) in which a haunting melody rising above a steady three-note ostinato establishes an atmosphere of overwhelming tranquillity.

Royal Scottish National Orchestra; Lloyd-Jones (Naxos; with *The Happy Forest*)

If the Chandos complete set seems too extravagant an outlay, you can buy the symphonies individually conducted by David Lloyd-Jones in a superb series for Naxos. Lloyd-Jones is especially persuasive in *No. 3*, where he's very much alive to the elemental nature of the music (though he doesn't quite achieve the Handley/Chandos luminosity of sound).

Halle Orchestra; Barbirolli (Dutton; with *Violin Concerto*)

This recording from the 1940s, now meticulously remastered, is something of a classic and well worth hearing. Barbirolli was a notable Bax interpreter and his performance positively throbs with passion. It's coupled with Eda Kersey's account of the relatively uninspired *Violin Concerto* with the BBCSO under Sir Adrian Boult.

Symphony No. 5

Bax's fifth symphony was dedicated to Sibelius, whom he greatly admired, and written in 1932 during yet another stay at Morar on the west coast of Scotland – and it's difficult to keep these two facts at bay when listening to this work. There's a distinct whiff of northern forests, sweeping hills and stormy seas throughout, while the vivid opening, by turns threatening and mysterious, is very close to Sibelius (though the way the predominantly funereal material builds towards a climax only to subside before it reaches it is very Baxian). The slow movement, introduced by shimmering strings and a bright trumpet fanfare, is an exhilarating seascape that shows off Bax's total mastery as an orchestrator. The finale starts with some darkly heavy chordal writing which leads straight into a kind of restless *moto perpetuo* with an almost militaristic feel. The edginess gives way to a slow section, before a euphoric climax heralds the arrival of the epilogue, in which the movement's solemn opening theme rises majestically above a stately ostinato – a glorious ending to one of Bax's most endearing works.

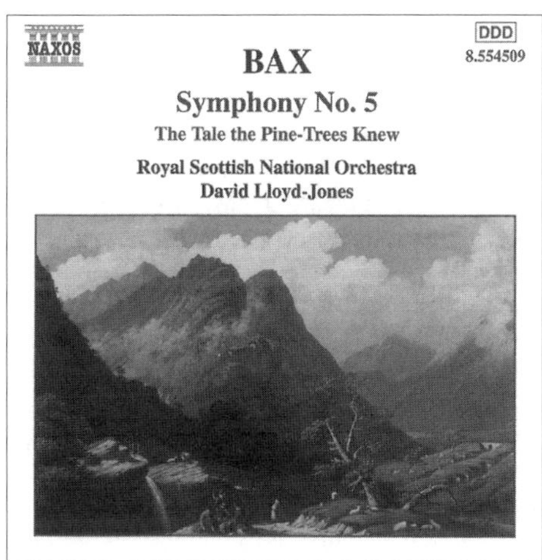

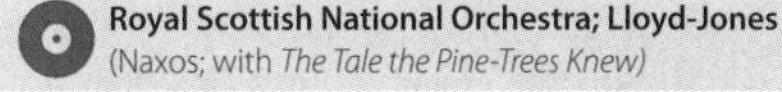
Royal Scottish National Orchestra; Lloyd-Jones
(Naxos; with *The Tale the Pine-Trees Knew*)

Another fine performance from Lloyd-Jones and the RSNO, who seem to get better as the cycle progresses. The last movement is especially well-handled, with the build-up of the epilogue creating a real sense of excitement. The contemporary *The Tale the Pine-Trees Knew* is another work with a touch of northern chill to it.

Symphony No. 6

A darker and more intense work than its predecessors, the *Symphony No. 6* is regarded by many as Bax's masterpiece. Completed in 1934, it is another nature-inspired work but this time the vision is much harsher. Bax's development of his material has such a relentless quality that, at times, it resembles Shostakovich at his most biting. There are also – especially in the first and last movements – those sudden, disturbingly rapid, changes of mood that are so quintessentially Baxian. The heavy-footed ostinato that underpins the work's opening is interrupted by an Allegro with a hint of an Irish dance to it; this leads to a central section in which a lilting melody alternates with storm music of great ferocity. The slow movement is thoughtful and subdued, with a more animated second theme whose dotted rhythm suggests a "Scotch snap". The finale's fantastical journey takes in a haunting clarinet solo at the beginning, through another manic jig-like dance to an overwhelming ecstatic climax before subsiding into the most visionary of all Bax's epilogues.

Royal Scottish National Orchestra; Lloyd-Jones
(Naxos; with *Into the Twilight*)

This is arguably the jewel in the crown of Lloyd-Jones's Bax cycle. There's a real sense of how the musical ideas grow out of each other, and the RSNO play as if their lives depended on it. A highly convincing account of one of the finest of British symphonies.

TONE POEMS

Many of Bax's early orchestral works were inspired by Ireland, including a cycle of three tone poems entitled *Eire*. The second of these, *In the Faery Hills* (1909), was his first real success and sees his signature sound taking shape. As with the symphonies, the tone poems are, in his own words, "…based upon aspects and moods of extreme nature and their relation to human emotion." They are usually in ternary form, with the most lyrical and expansive music reserved for the central section. The most celebrated, *The Garden of Fand*, *Tintagel* and *November Woods*, were all written during World War I, and from the 1920s Bax concentrated more on symphonies. Even so, some of the later orchestral pieces are worth investigating, in particular the three *Northern Ballads* and *The Tale the Pine-Trees Knew*.

The Garden of Fand

Bax reached full maturity as an orchestrator with *The Garden of Fand*, which he wrote in 1913 but didn't fully orchestrate until 1916. The inspiration was the Irish legend of the warrior Cuchulain's seduction by the sea goddess Fand, although Bax was at pains to point out that the piece didn't represent the events of the story. Instead, as in so many of his works, it evokes the sea – specifically, in Bax's words, "the atmosphere of an enchanted Atlantic completely calm beneath the spell of the Other World". The opening is particularly magical, with a falling figure in the woodwind suggesting a scene-setting, once-upon-a-time quality. Indeed, the rich but transparent orchestral colouring and the languid pace are just as suggestive of an awakening forest as of the sea, and there are times when Bax's debt to the Debussy of *L'après-midi* is very apparent. It's an extremely effective piece, nevertheless, climaxing in Fand's "song of immortal longing", a powerfully emotional "big tune" that suggests that the work had strong personal connections to Bax's own life.

London Philharmonic Orchestra; Boult
(Lyrita; with *Tintagel, November Woods, Northern Ballad No. 1 & Mediterranean*)

Adrian Boult was a regular champion of Bax's music, his association with it going all the way back to 1919. This recording of *Fand* was made towards the end of his conducting career in 1967 and his complete understanding of the music is apparent, not least in the transparency of the sound he gets from the orchestra.

Tintagel

Like *The Garden of Fand*, *Tintagel* is part seascape and part love song, the two being inextricably bound together in true Romantic fashion. Bax wrote it following an illicit six-week holiday in Cornwall with his new lover, the nineteen-year-old Harriet Cohen, and the music makes explicit his overwhelming and elemental passion for her. Perhaps it's the directness and relative succinctness of *Tintagel* that have made it the most popular and enduring of all Bax's work. It is certainly a gloriously exhilarating experience, both in the concert hall and on disc. Bax begins the piece gently enough, before introducing a stirring brass motif that represents the ruined castle of Tintagel rising up above the ocean. To reinforce the site's association with King Mark – and for personal reasons – Bax introduces a motif from the last act of Wagner's opera *Tristan und Isolde,* which he develops throughout the second half of the work, before a rousing climax suggests the tumultuous crashing of the waves against the cliffs.

London Philharmonic Orchestra; Boult
(Lyrita; with *Garden of Fand, November Woods, Northern Ballad No. 1 & Mediterranean*)

With *Tintagel* Boult adopts quite a brisk pace (compared to many), but it pays off in an account that is always exciting and never indulgent. His sense of where the music is going and how to build to a climax is especially finely judged.

London Symphony Orchestra; Barbirolli
(EMI; with Vaughan Williams *Symphony No. 5*)

Barbirolli and *Tintagel* were made for each other, and this EMI recording from the 1960s does not disappoint. Like Boult, he doesn't hang around, but the sheer power and grandeur that he manages to achieve in this performance is awe-inspiring.

November Woods

November Woods, written in 1917, is Bax at his most vividly pictorial, and makes you wonder why the composer wasn't snapped up by Hollywood in the 1930s. It also illustrates how deft an orchestrator he was: the large forces – including a contrabassoon, two harps and a celesta – are employed with the greatest precision, while the individual layers of orchestral texture are always wonderfully clear. The opening bars immediately conjure up an image of the wind in the trees, via shimmering harps and fluttering flutes – a chromatic rising and falling that harks back to Tchaikovsky's *Francesca da Rimini.* The piece is dominated by a three-note motif that suggests a feeling of unease, an effect reinforced by sudden shifts from major to minor. The prevailing mood is dark, despite a sensuous middle section for strings and celesta (for Bax, "a dream of happier days"), and although the work ends on a quiet note, the storm never feels as if it's very far away.

London Philharmonic Orchestra; Boult
(Lyrita; with *Tintagel, Garden of Fand, Northern Ballad No. 1 & Mediterranean*)

Boult's 1972 recording of *November Woods* is still the best available. Bax's quicksilver score, with its rapid changes of mood and pace, of delicacy and power, has never sounded so magical.

Ludwig van Beethoven (1770–1827)

Beethoven the demigod, the tragic yet otherworldly genius, scornful of society and oblivious of life's trivialities, is the product of almost two centuries of mythologizing. Dubious biographies with titles such as *Beethoven, the Man Who Freed Music* and *Beethoven, Life of a Conqueror* are typical of the awestruck image-creation that has been going on since the composer's day, extrapolating an astounding character from the astounding music. Yet the facts of Beethoven's life – such as are known for certain – create a rather more complicated and disturbing picture.

Born in the elegant but provincial city of Bonn, Beethoven's earliest musical training was at the hands of his singer father, a hard and unbending man whose decline into alcoholism made Ludwig the virtual head of the family during his teenage years. In 1787 a brief spell of study with Mozart in Vienna was interrupted by the death of his mother, but he returned there on a permanent basis three years later and began studying again – first with Haydn (from whom he "never learned anything"), then with Albrechtsberger and finally with Salieri, who taught him Italian vocal style. In Vienna, the musical capital of Europe, Beethoven rapidly established himself as a virtuoso pianist of the highest calibre: his initially rough style was refined after hearing the pianist Johann Sterkel and thereafter his pianistic supremacy was rarely challenged. He was admired, above all, for his amazing powers of improvisation, whether it be on a given theme or in developing an idea within a sonata movement.

Beethoven's success, however, was clouded by hearing difficulties, which had begun troubling him as early as 1797. In 1802, when medical treatment brought no improvement, he took himself off to the nearby village of Heiligenstadt for a rest cure. When this too proved fruitless, Beethoven, in near-suicidal depression, wrote a desperate and poignant letter to his two brothers explaining why he hadn't told them of his affliction earlier and outlining what he saw as his future as "an outcast; I can enter society practically only as true necessity demands". Only his art prevented him from taking his life: "it seemed to me impossible to leave the world until I had brought forth all that I felt was within me".

Beethoven out walking. Caricature by J.P. Lyser.

All the stories of Beethoven's misanthropy, his eccentricity and wildness, date from the decline in his hearing, which frequently caused him acute physical pain. Never the easiest of men, his frustration and anger at his condition made him intensely prickly, and the patience of his friends and family was frequently tested. Karl, his nephew and ward, was so oppressed by his uncle's heavy hand (Beethoven forbade him from seeing his mother) that he attempted suicide in order to be free of him. Even so, the power and charm of the composer's personality was such that he had a number of close relationships with women, though most of them were married nobility and therefore unattainable. The identity of Beethoven's greatest love, his "Immortal Beloved", remains a mystery to this day. The most likely candidate seems to be Antonie Brentano, whose youngest child Beethoven might just conceivably have fathered.

Despite moving within an aristocratic milieu, Beethoven's attitude to the upper classes was ambivalent. He was at heart a republican, and though nearly all of his patrons were titled – beginning with Count Waldstein in Bonn – he would not be condescended to. He ended his close friendship with the generous Prince Lichnowsky in 1806 by declaring: "There have been, and will be, thousands of princes. There is only one Beethoven." Whereas Mozart and his predecessors were craftsmen who supplied a commodity to a paying master, Beethoven insisted on asserting his independence and the absolute importance of self-expression: "What is in my heart must come out and so I write it down."

If Beethoven's confidence as a performer was gradually diminished by his deafness (he finally stopped playing publicly in 1815), then his imaginative powers as a composer grew greater and greater. Cushioned by an annuity provided in 1808 by his friend and pupil the Archduke Rudolph and two other nobles, his maturity as a composer was signalled two years earlier by the *Eroica* symphony, arguably the most significant single work of his entire life. As a broad generalization, Beethoven prior to the *Eroica* had been a composer of the eighteenth century; with this symphony music entered the age of Romanticism.

The post-*Eroica* decade produced a succession of masterpieces, including the opera *Fidelio*, the *Rasumovsky* string quartets, the *Violin Concerto*, the fourth and fifth piano concertos, symphonies four to eight, and some magnificent works for solo piano – notably the *Waldstein* and *Appassionata* sonatas. These "middle period" works, containing most of Beethoven's great melodic writing, have remained the most popular, but in terms of intensity and originality the finest was yet to come. Around the middle of the 1810s, his retreat from the outside world almost complete, Beethoven commenced perhaps the greatest continuous cycle of composition in history: the last five piano sonatas, the last five string quartets, the *Diabelli Variations*, the *Missa Solemnis* and, most famous of all, the gargantuan *Symphony No. 9*, all come from this, his so-called "late period". Never doubting the validity of his ground-breaking departures from convention, his last music is without precedent, characterized by ever greater abstraction and contrast; by the proximity of episodes of stridency and violence with lyrical passages that seem to melt into silence; and by a sense of agonizing self-revelation.

As Beethoven plumbed the depths of introspection, his fame grew so far that, by 1824, when his final symphony was given its first performance, his name and music were international in a way that not even Mozart's had been. When he died, aged 57, obituarists recorded that a terrible storm had raged in Vienna, and that the dying man had shaken his fist at the heavens as thunder and lightning struck the town.

OPERA

Beethoven was not a natural operatic composer, only managing to write the one opera – albeit in three separate versions and with four different overtures. He was approached in 1803 by Schikaneder, the librettist of Mozart's *Die Zauberflöte*, to write a work for the Theater an der Wien, but he soon abandoned this scheme and turned his attention to a newly translated French play, *Léonore*. The resulting opera (of the same name) was premiered in 1805 and poorly received, so Beethoven revised it, reducing the three acts to two and giving it a new overture. This too failed and it wasn't until 1814 that a further revised version (with a new name and yet another overture) finally won the recognition it deserved. A later plan for an operatic treatment of Goethe's *Faust* came to nothing.

Fidelio

Said to be based upon an event during the French Revolution, the plot of *Fidelio* concerns the unjust imprisonment of Florestan, husband of Leonore, who attempts to free him by disguising herself as a man and entering the service of Pizarro, the prison governor. Pizarro, a veritable emblem of *ancien régime* repression, tries to have Florestan executed before the arrival of Don Fernando, the minister of state, but his plot is thwarted by Leonore. Don Fernando arrives at the prison, sets Florestan free and duly punishes Pizarro. This simple narrative gives rise to some astonishing moments, perhaps the most powerful being the prisoners' chorus, a slow and deeply moving song of solidarity that opens with a simple set of shifting chords quite unlike anything ever written before. With its themes of unselfish love, loyalty, courage, sacrifice and heroic endurance, *Fidelio* is the nearest thing Beethoven ever produced to an explicit political-philosophical creed.

Ludwig, Vickers, Frick, Berry, Crass, Hallstein; Philharmonia Orchestra and Chorus; Klemperer (EMI; 2 CDs)

Klemperer's intense, slow-moving performance of *Fidelio* (made for EMI in 1961) is a very fine achievement, with Jon Vickers a splendid Florestan and Christa Ludwig unrivalled in the role of Leonore. Throughout his long career Klemperer had a profound affinity with this opera and, although at the time of this recording he was old and ill, his resolve and integrity produced an awe-inspiring performance.

Nielsen, Winbergh, Titus, Moll, Lienbacher; Hungarian Radio Chorus; Nicholas Esterházy Sinfonia; Halász (Naxos; 2 CDs)

Michael Halász's *Fidelio* on Naxos offers a superb version at a budget price. With unbridled enthusiasm, and a natural, unfussy approach, the soloists and chorus give a performance that flares into life as if for the first time. Halász conducts the opera with a muscular fervour that proclaims the youthfulness of Beethoven's masterpiece, to make – despite some cuts in the dialogue – a first-rate recording.

SACRED MUSIC

Beethoven's distinctly personal Christian faith, a faith that denied conventional observances and public display, was sorely tested throughout the years of his deafness. But three large religious works came out of this period. The first of them, *Christus am Olberge* (Christ on the Mount of Olives) is an oratorio written in 1803 – perhaps as an attempt to emulate Haydn's *Creation*, which was first performed just five years earlier. Despite Beethoven's close identification with the subject, *Christus* has not been popular in modern times and is rarely performed. *The Mass in C* – though not as neglected as the oratorio – is likewise underrated; despite some uneven moments it is well worth digging out. Only Beethoven's second mass, the *Mass in D* (commonly known as the *Missa Solemnis*) has got close to receiving unqualified praise, and is widely seen as the greatest mass setting of the nineteenth century.

Missa Solemnis

Intended for the installation in 1820 of Beethoven's friend and pupil Archduke Rudolph as Archbishop of Olmütz, this mighty, uncompromising work was not finally completed until 1823, and had its first performance a year later in St Petersburg. There's no piece of religious music to compare with the *Missa Solemnis*, for this is a composition that externalizes its creator's struggle to achieve inner peace, with extraordinary dynamic contrasts and passages that make enormous demands of the soloists. Perhaps the most remarkable section is the Benedictus, a huge, Gothic conception culminating in a ten-minute violin solo of extreme beauty that leads, like some massive papal procession, into the Agnus Dei, a section that incorporates an episode of brash, almost militaristic declamation. The polar opposite of most masses, it's a disconcertingly exposed work, sometimes tranquil, sometimes strenuous, but always profoundly and directly spiritual.

Janowitz, Ludwig, Wunderlich, Berry; Berlin Philharmonic Orchestra; Karajan (Deutsche Grammophon; 2 CDs; with Mozart *Mass in C*)

This recording, featuring one of the finest vocal quartets of the century, is one of Karajan's best, and has few serious rivals. It's not perfect – the tempi are sometimes too slow, the balance is odd in places, and the solo violin wanders out of tune – but the pathos and weight of the performance are profoundly moving.

Margiono, Robbin, Kendal, Miles; Monteverdi Choir; English Baroque Soloists; Gardiner (Archiv; 2 CDs)

Far from imposing an orderly, monumental approach, Gardiner and his team let us hear just how titanically eccentric Beethoven's "Solemn Mass" is. Instead of trying to smooth over the paradoxes, riddles and dislocations, Gardiner reveals how they all add up to a complex but thrillingly vital statement, hopeful yet also hauntingly ambiguous – surprisingly modern, in fact.

Mass in C

An altogether more searching, intimate work than the titanic *Missa Solemnis*, the *Mass in C* was commissioned by Nikolaus Esterházy II in 1807. To some extent Beethoven was working in homage to Haydn, who wrote six masses for the family, but he attempted to reimagine the text and underscore its human drama – something that didn't impress the prince, who branded Beethoven's efforts "unbearably ridiculous". The *Mass in C* has not always been much rated by critics either, but it has a freshness and lack of bombast not often found in Beethoven's choral music. The opening Kyrie, in which warm chords sung by the choir open into long-spun solo lines, is as lyrical as anything written by Mozart; and although stormier forces make themselves felt in the Gloria and Credo, the opening of the Sanctus, in which sighing woodwind calls and unadorned choral responses are suspended over ominous drum rolls, is perhaps the most dramatic moment of all. The Agnus Dei moves anxiously between major and minor keys before returning to the serene confidence of the opening movement.

Evans, Stephen, Padmore, Varcoe; Collegium Musicum 90; Hickox (Chandos; with *Meeresstille und glückliche Fahrt* and *Elegischer Gesang*)

Hickox's straightforward, unaffected approach is perfectly suited to this music, which benefits from his lively tempi and sensitive ear for balance. The orchestral playing – on period instruments – is nicely shaped, the choir sounds full-bodied without being overripe, and an excellent team of soloists is led by Mark Padmore's forceful tenor and Rebecca Evans's honeyed soprano.

SYMPHONIES

With a mere nine symphonies, Beethoven revolutionized the orchestra and overturned all previous attitudes to symphonic form. The first two, completed in 1800 and 1802 respectively, are openly based upon the examples of Mozart and Haydn, but the third – the *Eroica* – heralded an entirely new concept of scale. Numbers five through to nine increasingly free the structure from classical restraints and move swiftly towards the more Romantic, subjective approach that was to prevail in mid-nineteenth-century Europe. Beethoven completed his *Symphony No. 9* in 1824; just six years later, Berlioz completed his first symphonic work, the *Symphonie Fantastique*. The first complete recorded cycle of the symphonies was made in the 1930s by Felix Weingartner. Since then over fifty conductors have recorded these immense works, though frankly some of them shouldn't have bothered. There are, however, a few whose overview justifies the cost of buying the full set.

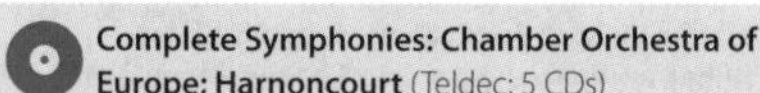

Complete Symphonies: Chamber Orchestra of Europe; Harnoncourt (Teldec; 5 CDs)

For a superb modern interpretation, Harnoncourt's 1990 set is outstanding for the way it assimilates many of the discoveries of the period-instrument brigade without making a fetish out of it – these are powerful and highly expressive performances.

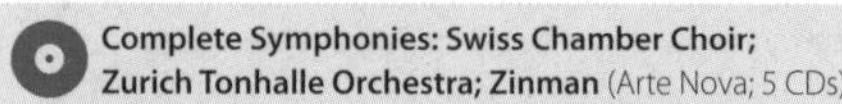

Complete Symphonies: Swiss Chamber Choir; Zurich Tonhalle Orchestra; Zinman (Arte Nova; 5 CDs)

This is an amazing bargain: recent recordings of first-rate performances based on a new edition of the symphonies. Zinman follows Beethoven's often surprisingly fast metronome markings and the results are exhilaratingly fresh and exciting. Each CD in the set is available individually and all make good alternatives to those listed below.

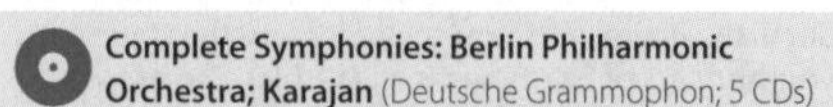

Complete Symphonies: Berlin Philharmonic Orchestra; Karajan (Deutsche Grammophon; 5 CDs)

Karajan recorded no fewer than four complete Beethoven symphony cycles. Some prefer his first, more traditional (mono) recording with the Philharmonia from the 1950s, but this second set, recorded in 1961, has a new-found energy and excitement in the works that is truly infectious.

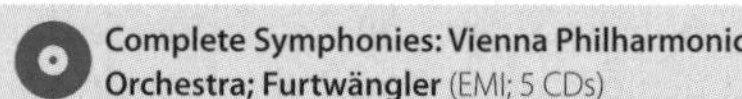

Complete Symphonies: Vienna Philharmonic Orchestra; Furtwängler (EMI; 5 CDs)

If interpretative vision matters to you more than sound quality, then Furtwängler's post-war cycle will offer genuine insights, though the playing is variable since the "cycle" was put together from performances given over quite a long spread of time.

Symphony No. 1

Though neither of Beethoven's first two symphonies is comparable to the majesty and innovation of the *Eroica*, it is a mistake to look upon them as mere preludes to that amazing piece – by the time Beethoven came to write the first symphony he was already 30 and had a considerable body of music to his name. *Symphony No. 1* clearly reflects Haydn's towering presence in late eighteenth-century Vienna, but Beethoven brought his own, rough-edged manner to the old master's style – Beethoven's fingerprints are especially in evidence in his reworking of Haydn's trick of slow introductions to the outer movements.

Chamber Orchestra of Europe; Harnoncourt (Teldec; with *Symphony No. 2*)

Harnoncourt's reading of *No. 1* (coupled with an excellent account of *No. 2*) brings out the wit and sprightliness of the piece in an utterly winning manner. Tight ensemble and an overriding sense of energy are employed with a control and a lightness of touch that is in marked contrast to the more grandiloquent later symphonies.

Symphony No. 2

The *Symphony No. 2* grew out of a period of intense despair as Beethoven struggled to come to terms with his increasing deafness. Amazingly, it's a work that bears little sign of this torment – rather, it bubbles with life and optimism. This is more obviously a piece by Beethoven than is the first symphony – the leg-pulling Scherzo, for example, is unmistakably his, with its innovative scoring and its unexpected exchanges, stops and starts. On the other hand, the finale – while maintaining the mood of the preceding movement – plainly looks to the eighteenth century as it slips into a polyphonic style that owes considerably more to Bach than to Mozart or Haydn.

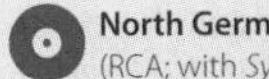

North German Radio Symphony Orchestra; Wand
(RCA; with *Symphony No. 7*)

The live cycle by the veteran German conductor sparkles with life and the sheer joy of music-making, nowhere more so than in the performance of *Symphony No. 2*. Speeds are lively without sounding rushed, and the bright sound quality heightens the effect of spontaneity and celebration.

Symphony No. 3

Beethoven's *Symphony No. 3* is better known as the *Eroica*, a title thoroughly befitting what many people consider the greatest symphony ever written. Completed in the spring of 1804, this amazing score contains the very foundations of Romanticism in its grandiose gestures and burgeoning themes, and in its unprecedented scale – the outer movements are enormous structures that virtually ignore the accepted conventions of sonata form.

The thunderous opening chords – like those launching the fifth symphony – are some of the most recognizable in all music, and the last movement is the most exciting and thrilling of all his symphonies. On the way to this finale one crosses extremes of exultation and misery that belong to a world unknown to the music of the eighteenth century. Another crucial characteristic of the *Eroica* is its anticipation of programme music – i.e. music with a narrative. That said, the extra-musical references are more elusive than those to be found in Berlioz or Strauss, for example. Some have suggested that the second movement's funeral march was inspired by a real-life cortege or by a poem describing one, while others – on slightly surer ground – have inferred that the references to English and Hungarian music in the last movement were intended as tributes to the nations uniting to defeat Napoleon (the symphony's dedicatee until he went and crowned himself emperor, whereupon Beethoven tore the title page in half and rededicated it to Prince Lobkowitz).

Chamber Orchestra of Europe; Harnoncourt
(Teldec; with *Leonore III* & *The Creatures of Prometheus*)

From the very beginning this performance announces itself as an electrifying one. The opening movement is highly dynamic, with the great clattering chords being given an extra impact by the use of natural trumpets. The funeral march achieves an astonishing aura of dignified despair, while the triumphant finale has a fluidity and flow which few other conductors have matched.

Symphony No. 4

Beethoven's fourth symphony, completed in 1806 and performed the following year, is often dismissed – along with the other even-numbered symphonies – as one of his "lighter", unclouded pieces. The categorization is hard to fathom, as this rather neglected symphony, though certainly witty, is an often disturbing creation, with an opening movement that recalls the titanic strength of the first movement of the *Eroica* and an Adagio not far removed from the *Eroica*'s funeral march. Tellingly, the symphony is written in the mysterious key of B flat, which it shares with some of Beethoven's most profound music – including the "Archduke" *Piano Trio*, the *Piano Sonata No. 29* and the *String Quartet No. 13*.

Bavarian State Orchestra; Kleiber
(Orfeo)

This is a truly remarkable performance. Kleiber's rhythmic flexibility verges on the extreme, but he maintains a flowing, uninterrupted sense of line that holds the music together no matter what his chosen pulse. Though it contains little over half an hour's music, this live recording is special enough to justify the full price.

Symphony No. 5

The first five bars of the fifth symphony – perhaps the most famous musical motif ever written – are so terrifyingly direct that commentators have been unable to resist attributing some autobiographical "meaning" to them. "Fate knocking at the door" is a more noble interpretation than the one that links the orchestral hammering to the arrival of Beethoven's bad-tempered cleaner, but this exceptional work really doesn't benefit from any narrative additions. Those opening beats provide the impetus for a first movement that is as concentrated as anything in symphonic

The late Carlos Kleiber, a great Beethoven conductor.

literature, and the unrelenting forward motion is maintained right through the whole symphony. The impact of the finale – again announced by united chords – is heightened by the addition of trombones, piccolo and contrabassoon, instruments that heralded enormous advances in orchestration. The headlong rush into C major at the close is almost as euphoric as in the *Eroica*, concluding with emphatic chordal repetitions that still sound shocking.

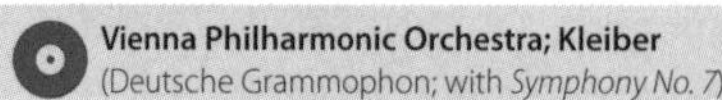

Vienna Philharmonic Orchestra; Kleiber
(Deutsche Grammophon; with *Symphony No. 7*)

There are numerous fine recordings of the fifth, but Kleiber's is the most celebrated of the last forty years. The finale may be slightly undercharged, but the drive that Kleiber imparts to the first movement and the Scherzo is unequalled by any other conductor in the studio – this is one of the very few performances that doesn't make this symphony sound hackneyed.

Symphony No. 6 – The Pastoral

It is remarkable that the fifth and sixth symphonies were both written in 1808 and were performed on the same evening shortly before Christmas the same year. Subtitled the "Pastoral" in response to its obvious representation of the countryside, the *Symphony No. 6* is replete with characteristic Beethoven touches, with a profusion of contrasting ideas following hard on each other's heels, but is completely unlike its Promethean predecessor in atmosphere. Its five highly melodic movements are predominantly sunny, and Beethoven attached unambiguously bucolic titles to each of them – "Awakening of joyful feelings on arrival in the country", "Merry-making of the country folk" and so on. He was anxious, though, that the symphony should not be taken as a sequence of naively descriptive episodes – as he wrote in his notebook, "the meaning of the work is obvious without verbal description". Of all Beethoven's symphonies, the sixth is the one that most clearly looks forward to the tone-poems of the late nineteenth century.

NDR Sinfonieorchester; Wand
(RCA; with *Symphony No. 1*)

This CD came as a surprise when it was released late in 1993. Günther Wand was 80 when he made this live recording but his performance is bursting with energy. Some of Wand's earlier work was excessively concerned with fidelity to the score, but here he delivers a fresh and personal view of a piece that can too often sound hackneyed.

Symphony No. 7

The seventh symphony, composed during 1812, plainly reflects the terrible circumstances in which it was written. The Napoleonic wars were wreaking havoc across Europe, Beethoven's deafness was far advanced and, to make things worse, he was in love with a woman who was already married – recognizing the futility of his affections, he wrote letters to her which he never sent. Amongst this anguish he created the gigantic *Symphony No. 7*, a work that was one of Beethoven's notable financial successes.

It opens – as does the first – with a slow introduction, but this one leads into a thrilling Vivace, in which Beethoven juxtaposes rhythms derived from Sicilian dance music with a cleverly syncopated theme. The following Allegretto is an almost unrelievedly doom-laden episode, with its relentlessly repeated statements of grief and mourning. An austere Presto then precedes an Allegro of manic fury, which is dominated by monumentally grand themes, the orchestral texture being dominated by the timpani and horns.

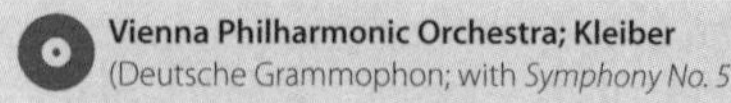

Vienna Philharmonic Orchestra; Kleiber
(Deutsche Grammophon; with *Symphony No. 5*)

Carlos Kleiber's astounding vision of the seventh, now coupled with the fifth (see above), is still the most thrilling performance of this symphony on disc. As with most of his work, there is a tautness to his conducting that keeps the tension running high, but never out of control. His is one of the few performances that takes the Allegretto at the snappy tempo Beethoven intended.

Symphony No. 8

The eighth symphony – often disparagingly known as the "Little" Symphony – was written at the same time as the heroic seventh, though you'd never guess it. This is a much lighter piece, with a vein of humour that's apparent from the start. The polite-toned first movement, which at first hearing might seem something of a regression into nostalgia, is a self-consciously slight piece of music in which Beethoven makes fun of the recently invented metronome, a mechanism recently devised by his friend Johann Maelzel. The sense of fun continues throughout the Scherzo (for once a genuinely jokey movement), the Trio and, finally, into a bizarrely constructed Finale, in which Beethoven plays one last trick by beginning the coda extremely early, and using it to create entirely new themes rather than bring the music to a swift conclusion. Formally, this is Beethoven's oddest symphonic creation; it's also his most entertaining.

 **Royal Liverpool Philharmonic Orchestra; Mackerras** (Classics for Pleasure; with *Symphony No. 2*)

In the absence of Thomas Beecham's delightfully witty account, this equally effervescent performance is a fine alternative. Mackerras is a superb Beethoven conductor who communicates his enthusiasm for the piece and gets some wonderfully lively playing from the Liverpool Philharmonic.

Symphony No. 9

The idea of setting Schiller's "Ode to Joy" came to Beethoven as early as 1793, but it was not until the winter of 1823–24 that he completed the work for which that poem provided the climax – the *Symphony No. 9*, or *Choral Symphony*. It's a work so stupendous that later composers felt a superstitious dread of completing their ninth symphony, as if it were tempting fate to attempt to venture beyond the number marked by Beethoven's final work in the genre. For others, however, the ninth symphony was a catalyst. Beethoven's fusion of poetry and orchestral music inspired Berlioz's epic vision and was the starting point for Wagner's obsession with developing an art form that would make possible the expression of unbounded feeling.

Lasting over an hour, the four movements of the ninth symphony are extraordinarily diverse and can be a draining experience. The long opening movement – combining innovative orchestration with formal restraint – leads to a fiery Scherzo, an amazing piece of music that seems to be on the brink of being forced apart under its own head of steam. Nothing in these two movements prepares one for the deep solemnity of the long Adagio, a creation that's almost unbearably moving in its troubled tranquillity. The finale's clamorous introduction leads to a review of all the symphony's previous themes before rejecting them in favour of the "Ode to Joy" theme, an amazingly simple melody that employs a mere five notes. Beethoven introduces it gently at first, then allows it to grow in boldness. A repetition of the opening is halted by the poem's opening lines, delivered like a clarion by the bass soloist: "O friends, not these tones, but let us rather sing more pleasant and joyful ones". The chorus and other soloists respond to the call. The melody then transforms into a jaunty march led by the tenor and is followed by a long orchestral interlude which leads to the core of the movement – a religiose invocation to universal fraternity that suddenly explodes into a rapturous statement of joy. After a short meditative section by the soloists, the symphony ends with a final euphoric rush of energy.

 **Tomowa-Sintow, Baltsa, Schreier, Van Dam; Berlin Philharmonic Orchestra; Karajan** (Deutsche Grammophon; 2 CDs; with *Symphonies Nos. 5 & 6*)

Karajan's legendary 1976 recording has been remastered, making an already vivid performance even more exhilarating. With a striking team of soloists, each in their prime, there is a real sense of individual talent making common cause to exhilarating effect.

 **Rodgers, Jones, Bronder, Terfel; Royal Liverpool Choir and Orchestra; Mackerras** (EMI)

This performance by Mackerras is remarkable for the extent to which the conductor refuses to impose a "reading" on the work: here, respect for the score is absolutely paramount. The result is neither bland nor anonymous, but sounds fresh and consistently exciting – high on joy and low on solemnity.

 **Briem, Höngen, Anders, Watzke; Bruno Kittel Choir; Berlin Philharmonic Orchestra; Furtwängler** (Music and Arts)

If you're not fussy about sound quality, try Wilhelm Furtwängler's March 1942 performance, recorded live in Berlin. This is the finest of his ten recordings of the symphony, and arguably one of the greatest recordings ever made. It's a reading unlike any other, imbued with religious devotion and yet full of anguish and torment.

CONCERTOS

Beethoven's first concerto was composed for the piano in 1795 and his last, again for piano, in 1809. In between he composed a further three concertos for piano, one for violin and one for piano trio – one of the very few ever written for violin, cello and piano, and the only Beethoven concerto to fall short of greatness. The concerto for solo violin, on the other hand, is a highly melodic masterpiece with a sense of cohesion and an understanding of the instrument that has remained unequalled.

The piano concertos were the first to challenge the formula of the eighteenth century. Until Beethoven's emergence, the piano repeated or developed an opening theme played by the orchestra, and sometimes took over the material on its own. Beethoven recognized the form's dramatic potential and gave the protagonists material to be played independently of each other while working towards a common goal. The result was that the concerto ceased to be a series of delicate exchanges between soloist and orchestra and became, by the fifth concerto, the embodiment of Romantic conflict – one individual voice set against the many.

Piano Concertos Nos. 1–5: Perahia; Concertgebouw Orchestra; Haitink (Sony Classical; 3 CDs)

Finding a version that succeeds equally in all these richly contrasted works is just about impossible. But with Perahia and Haitink there's an exceptional range of colour and character, and so often they seem to get it just right. Both are also super-refined technicians with a strong sense of each concerto as a living dramatic whole. Superb recordings too.

Piano Concertos Nos. 1–5: Kempff; Berlin Philharmonic Orchestra; Van Kempen (Deutsche Grammophon; 3 CDs)

If there's one characteristic above all that emerges here, it's delight – in the range of Beethoven's imagination, the power and delicacy of his invention, the intensity of feeling and the sheer compass of his musical intellect. Some of the most riveting moments are the quietest, but Kempff can certainly do drama and dance energy. The 1953 mono recordings have worn very well.

Piano Concertos Nos. 1 & 2

Beethoven's first two piano concertos were written in the reverse order that they are numbered: *No. 2* in B flat dates from the late 1780s, *No. 1* in C major from 1795. They are distinctly eighteenth century works but already sound more "advanced" than Mozart's, especially in the radical and inventive way Beethoven develops and transforms his thematic material. *Concerto No. 1* is one of the most infectiously lively of all his works. In the first movement the soloist acts as a rather mischievous presence in the face of the grand, martial-sounding orchestral passages. The classic Rondo finale shows Beethoven at his most skittish, having something of the nature of a chase between soloist and orchestra. *Concerto No. 2* follows a similar pattern: brilliant outer movements containing some startling changes of key and spectacular passage work but with considerably lighter textures (there are no clarinets, trumpets or drums). Both concertos have at their centre wonderfully serene slow movements in which the emotion is both expansive and intensely concentrated.

Piano Concerto No. 1: Michelangeli; Vienna Symphony Orchestra; Giulini (Deutsche Grammophon; with *Piano Sonata No. 4*)

No. 1 is the most quixotic and lively of the early concertos. Michelangeli might not be an obvious choice for this work (several critics loathed this recording) but, in tandem with Giulini, he really lets his hair down, bringing out the work's wit and energy – above all in the brilliant and carefree finale.

Piano Concerto No. 2: Argerich; London Sinfonietta (EMI; with Haydn *Piano Concerto No. 11*)

Argerich's earlier recording of the second concerto, which she conducts from the keyboard, is to be preferred to her recent recording with Sinopoli: there's a lightness and crispness of articulation to her playing which makes the concerto come alive in a way that only rarely happens.

Piano Concertos Nos. 3 & 4

The shadow of Mozart's late piano concertos hovers around Beethoven's *Piano Concerto No. 3*, although the sense of Romantic anguish is more pronounced, particularly in the outer movements which combine symphonic grandeur with eloquent pathos. The Largo begins with a sombre and intensely ruminative solo that is answered by more serene orchestral passages – as if to offer comfort and relief.

Piano Concerto No. 4, the last of Beethoven's piano concertos to be performed by him, was completed in 1807. It begins unusually, with the piano alone stating a gently rocking opening theme which the orchestra then takes up, leaving the piano silent. A sense of mystery has been established and when the soloist reappears it's with an almost improvisatory flourish. It's a long and expansive movement, essentially sunny in mood but with a definite undertow of melancholy, in which the soloist ranges from the rapturous to the introspective. The short Andante takes the form of a dialogue between fierce, pithy statements from the orchestra and reticent responses from the piano which suddenly blossom into a cadenza-like passage of great poignancy. The Rondo finale is extremely dramatic: a predominantly feverish abandon is interrupted by a wistful second subject which is exquisitely echoed by the woodwind.

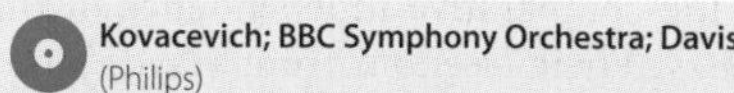

Kovacevich; BBC Symphony Orchestra; Davis (Philips)

Stephen Kovacevich is one of the great Beethoven pianists of the last thirty years. His recordings of the concertos with Colin Davis, available individually, are all good but this is the best of the set. Where Pollini is all precision, Kovacevich is expansive and poetic. His treatment of the slow movement has an intensity that is awe-inspiring.

Piano Concerto No. 5 – The Emperor

With his last and greatest piano concerto, written in1809, Beethoven forces the genre into the most heroic of forms (though its nickname, the *Emperor*, was not of his choosing). The piano now really stands up to the orchestra which, at the outset, does little more than announce the soloist's entry with a few chords. The piano then lets loose a flood of sound that washes over the orchestra before attacking a cadenza of great difficulty which, eventually, allows the orchestra back in to pursue a long exposition of all the movement's main themes. The piano is first among equals here, though in Beethoven's day it would have had a real struggle asserting itself. No such problem occurs in the spiritually charged delicacy of the Adagio, where after a sombre but deeply felt orchestral introduction (whose ending is tantalizingly delayed) the piano enters high up with the simplest of descending melodies against a minimal accompaniment. It's the most extraordinarily touching moment, the crystalline purity of the piano's tone conveying both confidence and frailty. A bridge passage of lightly touched chords leads into the last movement, as spirited a Rondo as Beethoven wrote but with an extra symphonic dimension to it.

Kempff; Berlin Philharmonic Orchestra; Leitner (Deutsche Grammophon; with *Piano Concerto No. 4*)

Perhaps the best single CD of the *Emperor* is the one from Wilhelm Kempff, no show-stopping virtuoso but a musician with a deep affinity with Beethoven's music. Eschewing the overblown gestures that some pianists resort to in this work, he is strong without being overassertive, and in the slow movement he achieves an almost liquid sonority.

Levin; Orchestre Révolutionnaire et Romantique; Gardiner (Deutsche Grammophon; with *Choral Fantasy*)

This period-instrument recording uses an 1812 piano which is both harder-sounding and more limited in volume than a modern piano. In the slow movement this means a less singing line than usual, but the piano's reticence and frailty in the face of the orchestra is oddly touching.

Violin Concerto

Beethoven's *Violin Concerto* was first performed on 23 December, 1806 by Franz Clement, who hadn't seen the piece before its premiere, let alone rehearsed it. The press found little to praise in the work – except for Clement's "entertainment" between the first and second movements, when he played a sonata of his own composition on one string, with the violin held upside down. The concerto remained lost in obscurity until it was rescued by the young Joseph Joachim who gave a series of memorable performances conducted by Mendelssohn.

The concerto's opening is beautifully simple: four crotchets, tapped out on the kettledrum, followed by a simple hymn-like melody in the woodwind that establishes a mood of supreme tranquillity, which is maintained throughout the long first movement. The orchestral introduction lasts about three minutes, at which point the violin appears, as if from nowhere, in a serene rising phrase like a bird taking flight. All the thematic material stated by the orchestra is repeated and embellished by the violin. The slow movement Larghetto is even more ethereal: again the principal theme is simple and dignified, featuring brief silences which, in the theme's second statement, are filled with exquisite decorative sallies from the soloist. The exquisite tenderness of this movement is rudely shattered by the earthy boisterousness of the finale, a Rondo in which the soloist finally gets to show off a bit.

Zehetmair; Orchestra of the 18th Century; Brüggen (Philips; with *Two Romances*)

Few of Beethoven's major works have become so barnacle-encrusted with performance traditions as the *Violin Concerto*. Zehetmair and Brüggen gleefully strip away distorting late Romantic preconceptions, in the process revealing a work that can be urgently dramatic for all its many beautiful moments, and whose originality can still startle.

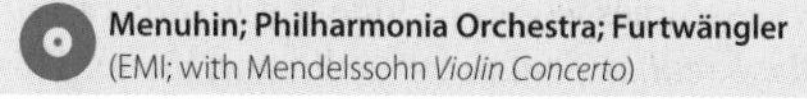

Menuhin; Philharmonia Orchestra; Furtwängler (EMI; with Mendelssohn *Violin Concerto*)

Made in 1954, this is one of Furtwängler's very last recordings and it makes an eloquent swan song. Menuhin – perhaps the work's greatest modern interpreter – is on his very best form: the tone is sweet but never simpering, and the sense of line assured and firm.

Triple Concerto

The so-called *Triple Concerto* for violin, cello and piano is something of an oddity and until quite recently was regarded as one of Beethoven's weaker (or lighter) works. It certainly lacks the dramatic impact of the violin concerto, and seems to look back to the slightly earlier genre of the *sinfonia concertante*, in which the soloists were more closely integrated with the orchestra. The relative easiness of the piano part reflects the fact that an "amateur" pianist, the Archduke Rudolph, gave the first performance with two professionals, Seidler and Kraft, on violin and cello.

There's a strange and elegiac quality to the concerto's opening, and the cello's statement of the sombre main theme makes you regret that Beethoven didn't write a concerto for that instrument alone. If the first movement slightly outstays its welcome, then the second – again in subdued mood – simply serves as a dark introduction to the bravura finale, an energetic polonaise which really wears its dance origins on its sleeve.

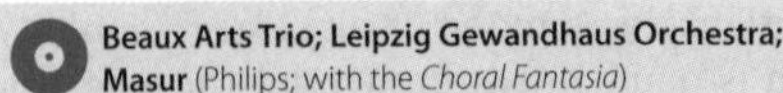

Beaux Arts Trio; Leipzig Gewandhaus Orchestra; Masur (Philips; with the *Choral Fantasia*)

Using a chamber group as soloists for this work has the obvious advantages of tight ensemble and a built-in rapport between the players. That's certainly the case in this performance, which under Masur's dynamic direction packs considerably more of a punch than usual. The cello part, which really dominates the solo writing, is played with great warmth and feeling by Peter Wiley.

CHAMBER MUSIC

Chamber music is, by definition, an intimate and personal means of expressing musical ideas, and much of Beethoven's most beguiling music can be found in small forms like the piano trios (for piano, cello and violin) and the violin sonatas (for piano and violin). But Beethoven's restless and probing mind meant that nearly every chamber genre that he attempted more than once had its formal limits challenged and extended. Thus many works have a complexity and a depth of feeling that have led some critics to describe them as symphonic in scope. Examples would include the *Archduke Trio* and the *Kreutzer Sonata* for violin and piano. This sense of development, of pushing a genre to its formal and emotional limits, is most dramatically exemplified in the string quartets, which range from the utterly conventional to works so subjective and experimental that Beethoven's contemporaries could scarcely acknowledge them as music at all.

Piano Trios

Beethoven's first published works – his Opus 1 – were three trios for piano, cello and violin, and already they show a marked advance on Haydn's trios in the comparative independence of the three parts. Their freedom from Haydn's frequently oppressive formality looks forward to the first mature trios, the pair that comprises Op. 70: displaying all sorts of harmonic twists, thematic innovations and structural idiosyncrasies, these trios make much of the piano part and contain plenty of those dramatic outbursts that are typical of Beethoven's middle period. Even more arresting is the first of the two Op. 70 trios (1808), nicknamed the *Ghost* because of its mysterious and haunting Largo; its sibling boasts a cheerful, bombastic finale that's the most entertaining music Beethoven composed for this combination of instruments.

The so-called *Archduke Trio*, Op. 97 (1811), was Beethoven's last full-scale work for piano trio, and is typically conclusive. The third movement is its centre of gravity: a highly moving set of variations, with the cello dominating the thematic content, it opens with a hymn-like theme and progresses to a coda which magnificently sums up the movement's ideas. The finale might be less powerful than that of Op. 70 No. 2, but it nevertheless has a sweeping rhythmic power.

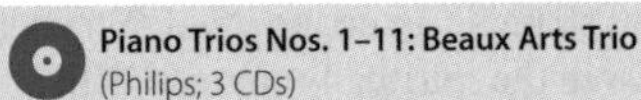

Piano Trios Nos. 1–11: Beaux Arts Trio (Philips; 3 CDs)

The best currently available overview of the trios, though at times a little hectic, are these 1965 recordings by the great Beaux Arts Trio. Their trademark is a rich and full tone and the kind of rapt and attentive ensemble that only comes from years of playing together.

Piano Trios Nos. 4, 5 & 7: Beaux Arts Trio (Philips)

A coupling of the *Ghost* and the *Archduke* makes the best introduction to Beethoven's trios. With the excellent recording by Szeryng, Fournier and Kempff on Deutsche Grammophon now available only as part of a 5-CD set, the Beaux Arts recording is the one to go for. Their deeply communicative and musical playing is well suited to these majestic works.

Violin Sonatas

Beethoven was the first composer to write sonatas for "Piano and..." as opposed to the classical norm of sonatas for "... and Piano", an arrangement that had subjugated the keyboard to the role of accompanying instrument. In Beethoven's violin sonatas the piano carries as much responsibility for the musical argument as the violin, and many of his violin sonatas are fearsomely difficult for the pianist.

Of the ten violin sonatas, *Sonata No. 5*, subtitled the *Spring*, and *Sonata No. 9*, known as the *Kreutzer*, are recorded and performed almost to the exclusion of the remaining eight. They do indeed warrant the attention, yet they are very different pieces indeed. As its nickname suggests, the *Spring* sonata is a light-hearted and airy work: opening with one of the most charmingly lyrical of all Beethoven's melodies, it's a piece that demands beauty of tone rather than trailblazing virtuosity. The *Kreutzer*, on the other hand, might initially seem to require nothing but virtuosity. Named after a leading French violinist who never played it, it was premiered by the Afro-English violinist George Bridgetower, who Beethoven greatly admired but later fell out with. Both parts are fiendishly difficult, although the piano is very much the dominant party and carries much of the weight – especially in the first movement. The passionate exchanges and heavy counterpoint of this movement are particularly dramatic and inspired Tolstoy to write his novella, *The Kreutzer Sonata*, about a wife-murderer in which music is condemned as being a powerful and morally subversive force. (Tolstoy's story in turn inspired Janáček to write his brilliantly disturbing *String Quartet No. 1* – see p.274.)

Complete Sonatas for Piano and Violin: Szeryng, Haebler (Philips; 2 CDs x 2)

If you're seeking a complete set of the sonatas, then Henryk Szeryng and Ingrid Haebler take the honours, with the budget price an added bonus. They are at their best in the more lyrical moments, with Szeryng's incisive violin tone and unerring sense of line especially effective in the *Spring* sonata. The *Kreutzer* is just a little undercharged – but it's a notoriously difficult piece to really bring off.

Sonatas Nos. 5 & 9: Perlman, Ashkenazy (Decca)

Several performers couple the *Spring* and *Kreutzer* sonatas on one disc. Itzhak Perlman and pianist Vladimir Ashkenazy achieve the best results because both performers have a wide enough emotional range in their playing to encompass the very different moods within these pieces.

"Kreutzer" Sonata: Szigeti, Bartók (Hungaroton; with Bartók *Sonata for Violin and Piano No. 2* & Debussy *Violin Sonata*)

Recorded during a recital at the Library of Congress in 1940, this is probably the most nerve-tingling *Kreutzer* on disc. In the first movement, particularly, the emotional temperature is high, with both artists willing each other on to ever more expressive heights. The rapport between the players is almost uncanny, and if there are occasional ragged edges it all adds to the sense of immediacy.

Cello Sonatas

Beethoven's first two sonatas for cello and piano were written in 1796, apparently on the hoof, for the French cellist Jean-Louis Duport – the first major chamber works for the instrument since Bach's *Cello Suites*. Both sonatas follow the same two-section pattern, with a weighty first movement offset by a spirited Rondo. Anxious that the cello would dominate proceedings, Beethoven avoided writing melody-led slow movements and described the cello's role as mere "obbligato".

The third sonata (1807) is a more ambitious three-movement work, one in which the piano and cello speak as genuinely equal partners. One of Beethoven's greatest chamber compositions, it shows the influence of the exploratory "Razumovsky" quartets and the experimentalism of the *Symphony No. 5*, written at the same time. The last two cello sonatas foreshadow Beethoven's late-period radicalism: he called *No. 4* a "free sonata" because of its daringly unconventional format, while its successor was described by one baffled reviewer as "among the most unusual and peculiar" works the 45-year-old composer had yet come up with.

Rostropovich, Richter (Philips; 2 CDs)

Mstislav Rostropovich has a reputation for forthright and big-boned playing, but on these discs Sviatoslav Richter gives as good as he gets. There's a real buzz between the pair, gloriously evident in the argumentative third sonata, and even if the sound is rather constricted the breadth and energy of their dialogue more than makes up for it.

Perényi, Schiff (ECM; 2CDs)

If Rostropovich and Richter go for the heart of these works, Miklos Pérenyi and Andras Schiff aim for the head. But these performances are never cold: Schiff's pianism is alert and rhythmically incisive, while Pérenyi's willingness to sacrifice tonal beauty for musical insight comes into its own in the late sonatas especially. Another bonus is that the rest of Beethoven's music for piano and cello is included.

STRING QUARTETS

The string quartet genre had come to prominence during the latter half of the eighteenth century, when Mozart and Haydn started to produce quartets of exceptional quality. Beethoven's first set of six quartets (Op. 18) bear his individual stamp but are clearly written in the shadows of his great predecessors. His seventh quartet, Op. 59 No. 1 (1806) – first of three quartets named after Count Rasumovsky, their dedicatee – is the turning point and initiates a departure from accepted rules quite as radical as that brought about by the *Eroica* symphony.

The Takács Quartet in full flight.

The subsequent middle-period quartets are characterized by slow introductions, lengthy four-movement structures, complicated dramatic counterpoint and the development of an elaborate sonority far removed from the decorous formality of Haydn. Even more startling are the last five quartets. As spare and intense as the last five piano sonatas, these astonishing compositions are marked by an increasing predilection for a polyphonic style, evident not only in movements that are overtly fugal but also in episodes where the four separate parts finally become thematically indivisible, creating a sense of four minds combining for the perfect expression of a single idea.

Complete String Quartets: Takács String Quartet
(Decca; 7 CDs)

These recent recordings by the Hungarian Takács Quartet find a near-ideal balance between unbridled emotional commitment and technical control. The performances are spontaneous, inventive and daring, yet the players refrain from unnecessarily milking every dramatic moment. Excellent recorded sound completes an outstanding set.

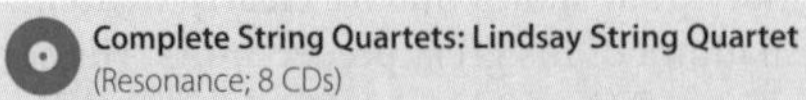
Complete String Quartets: Lindsay String Quartet
(Resonance; 8 CDs)

The Lindsays recorded the complete Beethoven quartets twice. Both cycles have an electric sense of occasion normally found only in the concert hall, but this first set also offers exceptional value for money. Despite the occasionally imperfect intonation, these readings have an urgency and a vital sense of discovery that touches every movement.

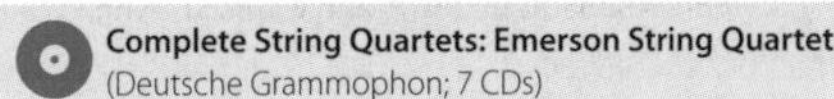
Complete String Quartets: Emerson String Quartet
(Deutsche Grammophon; 7 CDs)

If you want gleamingly accurate modern recording, look no further than this award-winning set from the Emerson Quartet, an American group whose technical expertise and panache are truly breathtaking. Deutsche Grammophon provide suitably detailed and vivid sound.

Early & Middle Quartets

There is a lot of fine music in Beethoven's first six quartets, but the debt to his great predecessors is everywhere apparent, and only in the melancholy last movement of *Quartet No. 6* does a unique voice really emerge. Perhaps the best place for the newcomer to start is the *Quartet No. 7*, the first of the quartets dedicated to Count Rasumovsky, written when Mozart and Haydn's influences were completely assimilated. The *Quartet No. 7* still respects the classical forms, but employs such idiosyncratic harmonic and melodic devices that, at the first performance, the instrumentalists laughed at what they were expected to play and the audience launched an angry protest. The middle two movements epitomize Beethoven's innovative writing: the Scherzo juggles numerous ideas, each passing within sight of the others but never uniting, while in the impassioned and poignant third movement, Beethoven reverses the accepted hierarchy of the opening motifs – the first being lithe and elegant, with the second taking on the punchy, dominant role normally given to the opening statement. Apart from the second and third "Rasumovsky" quartets, the other middle-period pieces are the tenth, known as the *Harp* (1809) because of the pizzicato exchanges in the first movement, and the eleventh, the *Serioso* (1810) – unlike most, a title ascribed by Beethoven – which is the last and most powerful quartet before the final five.

String Quartets 1–9: Takács String Quartet
(Decca; 4 CDs)

With their richly textured sound and probing musicality, the Takács players bring out a distinctive Beethovenian voice even in most Mozart-esque sections of the early quartets. Their middle quartets are equally good, employing wide-ranging dynamics and never lacking a great sense of purpose.

Late Quartets

Beethoven began the late quartets in 1822, after a gap of twelve years, prompted by an amateur cellist, Prince Galitzin, who commissioned the first three. Each of the five is a titanic piece but two of them, the *Quartets Nos. 13* and *14*, reach levels of profundity astonishing even for Beethoven. *Quartet No. 13* contains some of the most troubling of all Beethoven's music – the achingly beautiful "Cavatina" and the torrential last movement, "Grosse Fuge" (Great Fugue). The Schuppanzigh Quartet, who gave the first performances, were quite unable to understand this music, and refused to play the "Grosse Fuge" – their protests over its impossible technical demands allegedly prompted Beethoven to remark "what do I care about you and your fucking fiddles".

In the Schuppanzigh's defence, the fugue is a terrifying piece. Running to 745 bars and lasting over twenty minutes, it reaches new extremities of anguish and violence, making terrible demands of the four performers. Beethoven agreed to write an alternative ending for the quartet and, in a moment of exasperation, gave the musicians a feeble replacement finale that bore no relation to the remainder of his late music. Beethoven claimed that the "Grosse Fuge", published separately as Op. 133, was "the high point to my entire chamber music" but arguably *Quartet No. 14* is an even greater work. It begins with a slow and gentle fugue which builds to an almost unbearable intensity and has at its core a set of variations of increasing complexity. All of these last quartets communicate a sense of the composer thinking out loud, with the listener as a kind of privileged eavesdropper. They are frequently difficult, though not as relentlessly serious as some have suggested, but what makes them so satisfying is precisely the demands that they make: this is music which, unlike some, calls for an active and concentrated listening response before it will yield up its magic. It is certainly worth the effort.

Takács Quartet
(Decca; 3 CDs)

The Takács Quartet's focused but restless energy is ideally suited to these profoundly emotional late works. They plumb the depths of this music without ever sounding histrionic, and their probing intelligence is matched by excellent recorded sound.

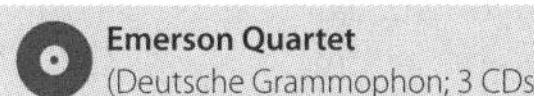

Emerson Quartet
(Deutsche Grammophon; 3 CDs)

The Emersons' complete Beethoven set is at full price, but their *Late Quartets* are available separately in this excellent-value set. Some may find that the technical perfection of the playing seems to occasionally contradict the raw and vulnerable spirit of the music, but these are stunning performances that only improve with repeated listening.

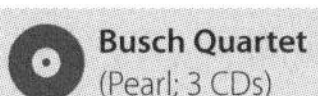

Busch Quartet
(Pearl; 3 CDs)

The Busch Quartet were one of the last quartets to play in a style that had its foundations in the nineteenth century. In this set, recorded in the 1930s, they swoop between notes and only use much vibrato when the music demands a sweetening of the texture. The recorded sound is not brilliant, but the sheer sense of immediacy and of struggle within the group makes for many electrifying moments.

PIANO MUSIC

Just as Beethoven's string quartets are the finest body of quartets created by one person, so his piano sonatas are the peak of that instrument's repertoire. All 32 sonatas are masterpieces, while his final major work for solo piano, the *Diabelli Variations*, represents a profound summation of his lifetime's work. The crucial thing to remember when listening to these works is that every note that Beethoven wrote for the piano was written solely with himself in mind. Beethoven's independence and self-reliance colour each of the 32 sonatas, from the three pieces that comprise Opus 2, begun when Beethoven was only 23, to the final Opus 111, a composition so extraordinary that Thomas Mann devoted part of his novel *Doctor Faustus* to an exposition of its form. His attitude towards the piano was typical of his attitude towards all instruments, in that everything he wrote posed a challenge to the piano's resources. In fact piano technology was

Sonatas and Sonata Form

Between the thirteenth and seventeenth centuries the term *sonata*, from the Italian "to sound", had no precise meaning when applied to music. Depending on where and when it was used, it could imply a collection of dance pieces; a lute work; a work for one or more solo instruments with or without accompaniment; and in some cases even a vocal work. During the Baroque period it most commonly referred to the trio sonata: a chamber piece, usually with multiple movements, in which two melody instruments are supported by one keyboard and one bass instrument. They could be religious, the *Sonata da chiesa*, or secular, the *Sonata da camera*. But the term is also found at the top of Baroque solo pieces – such as Bach's for violin – which could just as easily be referred to as suites or partitas.

In the mid-1700s, the transition to the Classical era, the term was increasingly associated with works for solo keyboard. Domenico Scarlatti, who wrote over 500 sonatas for harpsichord, was a major figure in this development, as was C.P.E. Bach, whose sonatas for the clavichord (a forerunner of the piano, see p.472) were especially significant because he usually adopted a pattern of three movements, arranged fast-slow-fast. It was this model that was taken up by Haydn and Mozart, and later by Beethoven. The latter is particularly important for the way he developed what was a sophisticated and essentially elegant genre into something symphonic in its proportions and emotional weight.

Most sonatas from the Classical period onward are written almost exclusively for solo piano or for a piano and one other instrument (such as violin or cello) and usually conform to the three-movement fast-slow-fast plan (one critic declared that in the first movement composers showed what they could do, in the second what they could feel, and in the third how glad they were to have finished). Mozart rarely deviated from this pattern, but Haydn and Beethoven regularly inserted an extra movement before the finale (either a minuet or a scherzo) and both wrote a few two-movement sonatas.

It's not just the pattern of movements that defines a Classical sonata, though; it's the way the individual movements are written. The first movement (and sometimes other movements) generally follows a structure known as *sonata form*. Confusingly, though, this term doesn't only refer to sonatas: most symphonies and chamber music of the Classical era (and much later music) make use of sonata form, especially in the first movement, hence the alternative phrase, *first movement form*. In the most basic terms, sonata form is a three-part scheme, consisting of an *exposition*, in which the thematic material is introduced, a *development*, the dramatic heart of the piece where the themes are further explored by the composer, and the *recapitulation*, an altered restatement of the exposition. As well as a way of approaching themes, though, sonata form is a way of approaching tonality and the relationship between keys. The exposition usually contains two groups of themes, separated by a *transition*; the first is sounded in the home key (the key the piece is "in"), and the second is in another key. In the development section, various keys are visited, adding to a sense of drama and instability, and the recapitulation usually repeats the material of the exposition, but plays both theme groups in the home key, providing a sense of finality and closure. This form is true of most Classical sonatas, but it is not a strict set of rules – it was the works that defined the genre, not the genre that defined the works.

Though its heyday was the Classical era, the sonata was carried forward by Romantic composers such as Schubert, Chopin, Schumann, Liszt and Brahms, though only the latter firmly maintained the principles of sonata form. The twentieth century, too, yielded its fair share of sonatas – Debussy, Bartók, Shostakovich, Cage and Carter are just a few of the composers who reworked the genre in a modern style.

progressing at an astonishing rate during this period: the range of notes was extended by two and a half octaves, the sustaining pedal was developed and there was a marked difference between the light-toned Austrian instruments (which Beethoven seems to have preferred) and the heavier actions of French and English pianos. Even so, with the last five sonatas Beethoven went as far as the instrument could possibly take him, and then looked towards the string quartet as the ultimate means of expression.

As with the symphonies and the quartets, you should really listen to all of the piano sonatas, and the easiest way to do this is to buy one of the complete recordings listed below. However, if you want to get to know the sonatas slowly, begin with the ones we've singled out; they are not necessarily the greatest, but each one vividly characterizes certain crucial aspects of Beethoven's approach to the form.

Complete Piano Sonatas: Goode
(Elektra Nonesuch; 10 CDs)

Richard Goode's cycle is at its best with the late sonatas, which are available in a separate box. The middle-period works sometimes suffer from a percussive, over-weighted strength, while the early sonatas suggest that Goode is happier with introspection than with humour. Still, this superbly recorded and annotated set is a personal and revealing cycle that can stand up to any of the competition.

Complete Piano Sonatas: Perl
(Arte Nova; 10 CDs)

Alfredo Perl is a young Chilean pianist with an amazing technique and plenty of passion. He never shies away from the weird and quirky aspects of Beethoven and is especially strong in the most turbulent sonatas, like the *Appassionata*. Occasionally the more lyrical and introspective moments evade his grasp, but in the end the sheer energy of his playing sweeps you away. A real bargain.

Complete Piano Sonatas: Kempff
(Deutsche Grammophon; 8 CDs)

Mono sound, but Kempff's 1950s set of the complete sonatas is still one of the finest ever recorded. The lucidity and intensity of his concerto recordings are both present, but now there's an added edge of directness – as though you're listening to something acutely relevant and confidential. It's most telling in the great slow movement of the *Hammerklavier*, or the variation-finales of Opp. 109 and 111, yet Kempff can also sparkle and soar, as in the finale of Op. 2, No. 3.

Sonata No. 8 – The Pathétique

The *Pathétique*, the most important of Beethoven's early sonatas, was written in 1798–99 during his "C minor period", when this was almost the only minor key he used for important works – other examples being the *Piano Concerto No. 3*, *String Quartet No. 4* and the third of the Op. 1 piano trios. It's a key well-suited to the expression of pathos – hence one element of the title that Beethoven gave to this work: *Grand sonata pathétique*. The other component of the title – the sonata's scale – has less to do with mere length than with the size of the sound, for the orchestral sonority of the *Pathétique* must have placed a great deal of strain on the instruments of the day. Showing obvious signs of Beethoven's dissatisfaction with the rigidities of Classical form, this is a mighty, sometimes desperate work, reflecting Beethoven's awareness of the deterioration in his hearing. There's a terrible sense of loneliness in the weightily solemn central movement, a section which – as in the *Appassionata* – is framed by contrastingly dramatic outer movements.

Gilels (Deutsche Grammophon; with *Sonatas Nos. 23 & 31*)

The Russian pianist Emil Gilels was revered for his granite-like performances of Beethoven's music. In the *Pathétique*, he adopts slower than average tempi but the playing never drags, such is his grasp of the music's structure. His tone is expressive and resonant, notably in the Adagio, where his massive, weighted sound produces such an atmosphere of oppression that the finale comes as a welcome relief.

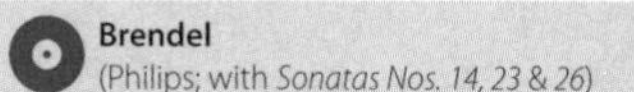

Brendel
(Philips; with *Sonatas Nos. 14, 23 & 26*)

This recording of *Pathétique* is superb. Captured with a gorgeously round yet clear tone, Brendel takes the opening movement more slowly than many players – especially the introduction, which sounds tragic and ominous here – but is absolutely captivating throughout.

Sonatas Nos. 13 & 14 (The Moonlight)

By the end of 1801 Beethoven had completed a further seven sonatas, including the two sonatas of Op. 27. The second of these, the so-called *Moonlight Sonata*, opens with Beethoven's most famous piano passage, a dreamy, melancholic movement that's now too well-known to be heard as the revolutionary idea it was. By labelling this sonata and its twin as "Quasi una fantasia" (Like a fantasy), Beethoven was explicitly differentiating his work from the weighted, formal structures of his predecessors, and by opening the *Moonlight* with a slow movement he was instantly establishing a sound-world in which the certainties of Classical form no longer applied. The second movement, an Allegretto, was described by Liszt as a "flower between two abysses" and it really is little more than an interlude before the stormy finale – a movement built upon a rhythmic idea rather than a melody.

The other Op. 27 sonata is also a marvellous work, but has never achieved the same popularity, perhaps through the lack of so memorable an opening. Comprising four movements that are unbroken in performance, it's a strangely prophetic work – with its inward-looking freedom of construction, and its alternating moments of unannounced restfulness and sudden near-dementia, it looks forward to the late sonatas.

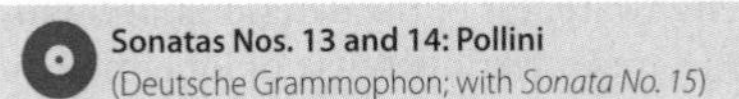

Sonatas Nos. 13 and 14: Pollini
(Deutsche Grammophon; with *Sonata No. 15*)

There are over one hundred recordings of the *Moonlight* in the current catalogue, and many of them treat the music as if it were little more than a Romantic scribble. With Pollini you certainly don't get anything wishy-washy: this performance is well thought out and fanatically secure in its technique. The other two sonatas on the CD are similarly serious and thoughtful.

Sonata No. 14: Kempff (Deutsche Grammophon; with *Sonatas Nos. 8, 15 & 24*)

Kempff's third Beethoven sonata cycle, a stereo set from the 1960s, provided a refined antidote to the kind of Beethoven-playing which is all sound and fury. His restrained, elegant and lyrical approach works especially well in the *Moonlight*, in which sensitivity and spontaneity create a sense of wondrous discovery. The coupled versions of the *Pathétique* and *Waldstein* sonatas are also wonderful, though the *Appassionata* isn't a first choice.

Sonata No. 21 – The Waldstein

In 1804, Beethoven generously repaid the support he'd received from Count Ferdinand von Waldstein by dedicating a piano sonata to him. Written a year after the *Eroica*, the *Waldstein* is a similar landmark in the evolution of its genre, accelerating the dissolution of conventional cyclic forms and pushing towards a great expansion in scale. The *Waldstein* had begun as a relatively normal three-movement sonata, albeit one with a monumental opening movement constructed from an audaciously simple rhythmic conceit – the whole movement is generated by just two bars of chopping quavers. The masterstroke of Beethoven's rewriting was to remove the central movement and replace it with a slow and haunting section which is little more than an introduction to the Rondo finale. Where an eighteenth-century sonata would pause for contented reflection, the *Waldstein* merely halts long enough to catch its breath before hurrying onward.

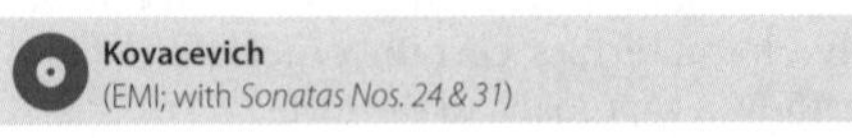

Kovacevich
(EMI; with *Sonatas Nos. 24 & 31*)

The weight and tension of Kovacevich's playing is the product of many years' experience, and there is nothing flashily impressive about this performance – though his uninhibited prestissimo ending to the finale is as thrilling as any crowd-pleasing virtuoso could muster. The accompanying performance of the Op. 110 sonata is stupendous, and the recorded sound is faultless.

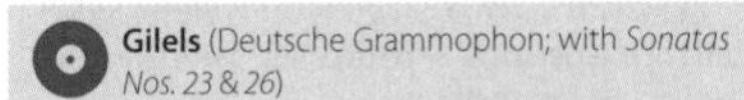

Gilels (Deutsche Grammophon; with *Sonatas Nos. 23 & 26*)

The recordings on this disc were made in the first half of the 1970s, and instantly acquired the status of classics. Both fastidious and fiery, Gilels' *Waldstein* is one of the peaks of an extraordinary career.

Sonata No. 23 – The Appassionata

In the opinion of Beethoven his greatest sonata was the *Sonata No. 23* (1804), a titanic four-movement work of unprecedently extreme emotional and technical challenges. The initial Allegro and the succeeding Andante (a huge set of variations) are magnificent creations, but it is the last movement that justifies the name *Appassionata*, which was bestowed on it a few years after Beethoven's death. This tempestuous finale is introduced by crashing, repeated chords which are followed by a simple series of semi-quavers, in turn punctuated by shockingly violent outbursts. After a number of unexpected pauses, introduced by aggressive high-speed octave passages, comes the coda – one minute of uninterrupted, surging mayhem. This final section is extraordinarily difficult to play and is always disturbing, no matter how often you listen to it. Its first audience must have been utterly perplexed.

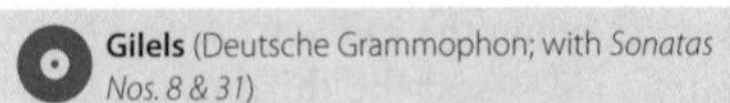

Gilels (Deutsche Grammophon; with *Sonatas Nos. 8 & 31*)

Emil Gilels' 1974 version is weighty yet always controlled and incisive, with sharply distinguished rhythmic punctuation and, when necessary, a biting, metallic piano sound. This performance is so celebrated that it's also been released on another coupling, with the *Waldstein* and *Les Adieux*.

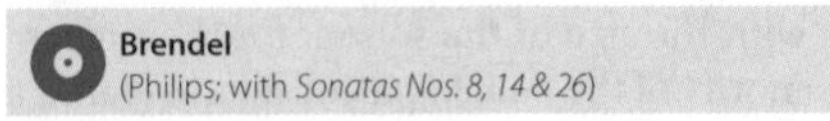

Brendel
(Philips; with *Sonatas Nos. 8, 14 & 26*)

Recorded in 1994, Brendel's account of the *Appassionata* is refined yet intense. He is a little more cerebral than some players in this mighty work, but his interpretation is never dry and his authoritative playing pulls you in completely. This excellent disc would make a good introduction to Beethoven's sonatas – and to Brendel's pianism.

Sonata No. 26 – Les Adieux

No. 26 is unique among Beethoven's piano sonatas in being the only one which contains a specific programme, or exterior reference, woven into its structure. The "farewell" of its title is to Beethoven's friend and pupil Archduke Rudolph who, between 1809 and 1810, was forced to leave Vienna because of the advance of Napoleon's army. (The cannon fire during this dark time caused Beethoven to take refuge in a cellar in order to protect his ears.) In fact there is nothing overtly pictorial in the music; rather the three movements establish the appropriate moods indicated by their titles ("Farewell", "Absence" and "Return"). In the case of the first, the central motif is based on three notes, G-F-E flat, which in German spells Le-be-wohl – "Farewell". The second, Andante espressivo, has a wonderfully understated poignancy with gleams of light shining through, which finally breaks into a fast movement of undisguised elation.

Kempff (Deutsche Grammophon; with *Sonatas Nos. 21 & 23*)

Kempff's approach to Beethoven is particularly well suited to *Les Adieux*, with its subtle changes of mood and inflection. This gentle but penetrating reading is especially good in the slow movement, where it brings out the music's bitter-sweet quality.

Gilels (Deutsche Grammophon; with *Sonatas Nos. 21 & 23*)

Gilels adopts a more heroic stance, but there's no bluster to this technically peerless playing – coupled with stupendous accounts of the *Waldstein* and *Appassionata* sonatas, this performance on its own confirms Emil Gilels as one of the most remarkable of all pianists.

Late Sonatas

With his last five sonatas, Beethoven took keyboard writing into a new realm, and at their completion he almost decided to finish with the piano for good, declaring that it was an "unsatisfactory instrument" – though he went on to compose the *Diabelli Variations*. A brief glance at some of the movement headings gives a good idea of what the composer was looking for in his music – the words *appassionato*, *molto sentimento*, *espressivo* and *dolente* litter the scores. Striving for absolute expression, Beethoven ventured into a complex revaluation of tradition, in which the standard forms of classical music were invested with extraordinary emotional potency. The impetus of each sonata's musical argument propels one towards the final movement, and the finales of Op. 109 and Op. 111 are in variation form, while the finales of Op. 106 and Op. 110 are fugal. Beethoven had, in effect, come full circle: tormented by the most unclassical of impulses, he followed the old paths in search of new freedoms.

Beethoven's longest and most difficult sonata is the twenty-ninth, Op. 106, subtitled the *Hammerklavier* – technically a pointless title, since *Hammerklavier* is German for "pianoforte", but one that has appropriately aggressive connotations. No other sonata covers as vast a terrain as this one. Once you've recovered from the percussive opening movement, you find yourself in a strange lopsided march that is then hammered by petulant chords before expiring mid-phrase. After that comes a slow movement of heart-wrenching intensity, in which the music persistently ebbs away to the verge of silence; the desperate conclusion is a colossal fugue, an almost unmanageably complex construction which is attacked by Beethoven almost as if he wants to beat it into submission.

The last sonata, Op. 111, is the most mysterious. It contains only two movements, a disconcertingly unclassical structure that has prompted much speculation. In Thomas Mann's *Doctor Faustus*, one of the characters gives a lecture entitled "Why Did Beethoven Write No Third Movement to Op. 111?" – and the answer, in a nutshell, was that the second movement had effectively nailed the sonata form into its coffin. This second movement is a monumental set of variations based upon a beguilingly simple "Arietta" theme that becomes the basis for some of Beethoven's most agonized, most serene and most eccentric writing – including one heavily syncopated section which sounds like a jazz break. As the piece comes to a close, the exhausted pianist is required to play a huge series of trills, turning a device that in the eighteenth century was merely a decorative convention into a devastatingly moving episode, a suggestion of refuge after the preceding storms.

The Late Sonatas: Pollini
(Deutsche Grammophon; 2 CDs)

Pollini's technically astonishing recording of the last five sonatas is rightly famous, admired even by those who generally find his perfectionism too clinical. The performance of Op. 101 is unsurpassable in its delicacy, while the *Hammerklavier* gets the full powerhouse treatment – it might seem overdone, but this is surely how the composer imagined the music would sound on a piano more muscular than the ones at his disposal.

Sonata No. 31: Kovacevich
(EMI; with *Sonatas Nos. 21 & 24*)

Op. 110 gets an incredible performance from Kovacevich: there's a profound and intense concentration about his playing which culminates in an almost spiritualized reading of the fugal last movement.

Bagatelles

Of the shorter pieces that Beethoven wrote for the piano, the three sets of *Bagatelles* (24 in total) are the best known. A bagatelle literally means "a trifle" and, though such pieces are predominantly light, in Beethoven's hands they become finely wrought and highly characterful works which look forward to the concentrated piano miniatures of such Romantic composers as Chopin and Schumann. All three sets exhibit strong contrasts and a range of moods between the individual pieces, but only the last set, *Six Bagatelles* (Op. 126), was actually conceived as a cycle. Composed in 1824 they are close in style to the late sonatas in their complexity, quixotic mood changes, and in the way rhythmic predictability is constantly undermined. The *Bagatelles* have long proved highly popular with amateur pianists, although the best-loved *Bagatelle* of all, a piece known as "Für Elise", was written as a single work.

Bagatelles 1–25: Brendel
(Philips)

Brendel approaches the *Bagatelles* in a refreshingly matter-of-fact manner, bringing out the vigour and the fluidity of the pieces but not at the expense of their poetry. His "Für Elise" is pointedly unsentimental but exquisitely shaped.

Diabelli Variations

Beethoven's *Thirty-Three Variations on a Theme by Diabelli* were completed in 1823 in response to a commission from publisher and composer Anton Diabelli. Thinking he'd hit upon a way to make a fast buck, Diabelli asked fifty composers to submit a variation on a theme that Diabelli had written, with a view to publishing the results as a composite creation. He received one from Schubert, one from the eleven-year-old Liszt, and thirty-three from the insulted Beethoven. Diabelli had never seen the like of them before, but, immediately recognizing their greatness, he published them as a separate album. In this incredible work, Beethoven realized a new mode of variation in which each variation radically reinterpreted the original theme, instead of merely parodying it or playing upon its basic framework. At the end of the *Diabelli*'s colossal trajectory, in which a host of musical forms has been quoted and transformed, Beethoven comes up with an astonishing gesture of reconciliation – a Haydnesque theme ending in a simple C major chord.

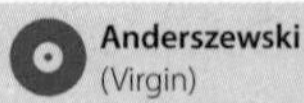

Anderszewski
(Virgin)

This recording is a dazzling display of Piotr Anderszewski's tight rhythmic articulation, his perfectly chiselled phrasing, the clarity of his counterpoint, and his attention to detail. But what makes it so special is the sense that the performer is simultaneously in control of this huge work and lost in its limitless possibilities. It's not always a comfortable listen, but it's very human and deeply affecting.

Kovacevich
(Philips)

Stephen Kovacevich's 1968 recording of the *Diabelli* is a classic, as free-flowing as Beethoven's approach to the variation form. His playing is muscular yet supple, accentuating the integrity of each variation without sacrificing the sense of overall structure. That all-important final chord is like a goal reached at the end of a long, long journey.

SONGS

Beethoven's songs are the most neglected part of his output, even though his subtle word-setting and complex piano parts paved the way for the better-known achievements of Schubert and Schumann. His range was wide – from simple strophic songs (where the musical material is repeated from verse to verse) to ambitious through-composed pieces like the quasi-operatic *An die Hoffnung*. He also made over 100 arrangements of mostly British folk songs for the Edinburgh publisher George Thomson. Even his finest songs are never as obviously accessible as Schubert's, largely because he avoids vivid, descriptive texts in favour of rather lofty subject matter (he set Goethe more than any other poet). Just occasionally an intensely personal tone impinges, as in his greatest achievement as a songwriter, *An die ferne Geliebte* (1816).

An die ferne Geliebte

Regarded as the first important song cycle, Beethoven's *An die ferne Geliebte* (To the Distant Beloved) took art song to a new level of profundity, through both the variety of the accompaniments and the extra psychological dimension added by the subtle shifts of harmony. Though the six songs are mostly strophic with relatively simple melodies, Beethoven unifies them by such devices as having the last song in the same key as the first and re-employing some of the same material. The poems, by Alois Jeitteles, merge the thoughts of a lover separated from his beloved into his reflections on the landscape. It is possible that Beethoven chose what was for him fairly untypical texts, because the theme had some extra personal significance. Despite the profusion of nature imagery, he avoids the kind of pictorial effects that Schubert so delighted in. Instead, his touches of colour are more sparing, as in the second song where the relatively conventional harmonies suddenly give way to chromaticism on the words "Innere Pein" (inner pain).

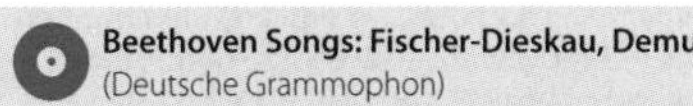
Beethoven Songs: Fischer-Dieskau, Demus
(Deutsche Grammophon)

A good selection of Beethoven songs with the baritone Dietrich Fischer-Dieskau at his interpretative peak in the mid-1960s makes for a highly winning combination. *An die ferne Geliebte* is especially well handled, made all the more moving by subtle understatement, and the sensitively restrained piano playing of Jorg Demus – arguably the finest of Fischer-Dieskau's accompanists.

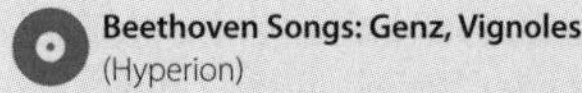
Beethoven Songs: Genz, Vignoles
(Hyperion)

Stephan Genz is an ideal Beethoven singer: his well-focused voice draws you into the music with a restrained, but highly effective, expressiveness that seems exactly right. As well as *An die ferne Geliebte*, he gives particularly powerful accounts of the slightly chilly *Sechs Lieder von Gellert*. The accompaniment of Roger Vignoles is always beautifully judged.

Vincenzo Bellini (1801–1835)

It can be difficult to appreciate what it was that made Vincenzo Bellini so remarkable, as modern audiences tend to have a problem with his abundance of oom-pah-pah orchestral passages, bombastic choruses and solo histrionics. But it's worth persevering, for there's more to Bellini than first meets the ear. Italian opera composers immediately prior to Bellini saw themselves primarily as creators of melodies, and those melodies had little or no connection with the words that the singers were singing. Effectively, the libretto and the orchestra were operating independently of each other. Bellini set about writing intense yet melodic music which related closely to the attitudes and sentiments of his characters, thus laying the foundations for the dramatic masterpieces of Donizetti, Verdi and Puccini. Whereas Rossini and his predecessors had relied on formula, enabling them to dash off an opera in seven days, Bellini took time and effort over his work, struggling towards a poised and well-proportioned form that appealed to the emotions as well as to the ear. He was, as Wagner wrote after Bellini's death, "all heart".

Born three years before Beethoven completed the *Eroica*, Bellini lived for only 34 years, leaving his eleventh opera incomplete. His first great success was *Il pirata*, commissioned by La Scala in 1827 and written (as were *I puritani* and *La sonnambula*) for the expressively lyrical voice of Giovanni Rubini, a man famous all over Europe as "the King of Tenors". Bellini's music is the summit of the bel canto style, requiring voices of massive flexibility and range – and, as far as the lead roles are concerned, enormous stamina. Even though the tenor parts are now transposed downwards, as they were written for falsetto voices rather than the full chest voice of the present day, Bellini's male leads are among the most demanding in the repertoire.

In 1831 he wrote his masterpiece, *Norma*, which ever since has been the vehicle for some of the world's greatest sopranos – Maria Callas, Montserrat Caballé and Joan Sutherland have all excelled in the title role. This fabulously emotive score, in which the words carry as much of the meaning as does the music, and the pace of the action is dictated by dramatic necessity, clearly represented a turning point in the development of Italian opera. The passionate ecstasy and elegiac melancholy of Bellini's music, allied with his fragile good looks, led to his idolization as the very personification of Romanticism, though not everyone was susceptible to his charm. The German poet Heinrich Heine wrote of him acidly: "He was coquettish, ever looking as though just removed from a bandbox ... his features had something vague in them, a want of character, something milk-like; and in this milk-like face flittered sometimes a painful-pleasing expression of sorrow. The whole man looked like a sigh in pumps and silk stockings."

Bellini's early death compounded the Romantic myth. Exhausted by the effort of composing *I puritani*, he fell ill and died, alone, in a dreary house in a suburb of Paris, where his last opera had just had its premiere. Rossini was among the bearers of the funeral shroud at the Requiem mass; Bellini was later buried in the cathedral of his native Catania.

La sonnambula

As its title suggests, the plot of *La sonnambula* (The Sleepwalker) is not exactly a model of plausibility. Amina is to marry Elvino. Lisa also loves Elvino but agrees to entertain Count Rodolfo, a handsome lord recently returned from abroad. Unknown to everyone, Amina is a sleepwalker, and she winds up, all unwitting, in the bed of Rodolfo. Elvino then agrees to marry Lisa, but Rodolfo attempts to explain the mistake. Everyone scoffs at his story but, as they do, Amina is seen walking along the roof of a mill, which collapses as soon as she is safely across. Elvino and Amina duly marry. Bellini's essentially simple music transforms this tale into a touching rustic idyll. *La sonnambula* contains a substantial amount of beautifully expressive writing for soprano and tenor, especially in the second act, and the role of Amina features some real show-stopping coloratura singing.

Sutherland, Pavarotti, Ghiaurov, Buchanan, Jones, Tomlinson, de Palma; London Opera Chorus; National Philharmonic Orchestra; Bonynge (Decca; 2 CDs)

Richard Bonynge's recording is blessed with the incredible voice of the young Luciano Pavarotti as Elvino. His voice has the texture and confidence of a singer at the height of his powers, and his phrasing is pure and enthrallingly musical. Pavarotti's pairing with Joan Sutherland works wonderfully – her singing might occasionally be over-stylized but she revels in Bellini's expressive artistry.

I puritani

The excessively complicated plot of *I puritani* is set in England at the time of the Civil War, the action revolving around two rival families – one Roundhead, the other Cavalier. Yet, for all its complexity, the libretto provided Bellini with considerably more substantial characters than *La sonnambula*, and it inspired him to create some of his most perfect and demanding music for the tenor voice. The first act's "A te, o cara" is one of his most beautiful solo arias, while the final act's "Vienni, fra queste braccia" demands two high D naturals – two full notes higher than the penultimate note of "Nessun Dorma". Elvira, the soprano lead, is less involving than Amina or Norma but suffers no dearth of lyrical music, and the concluding "Credeasi, misera!" is one of the saddest, most affecting tenor/soprano duets ever written.

Sutherland, Pavarotti, Ghiaurov, Cappucilli, Luccardi; Royal Opera House Chorus; London Symphony Orchestra; Bonynge (Decca; 3 CDs)

This recording boasts four of the protagonists featured in Decca's *La sonnambula* and they are similarly effective here. Pavarotti steals the show with an awesome performance of seemingly effortless flair. Sutherland is slightly self-conscious at times, as if in awe of her partner's abilities, but she produces some wonderful moments, not least when singing of her supposed betrayal.

Norma

Norma is Bellini's greatest opera, its glorious music triumphing in the face of a plot that degenerates into near farce. The action takes place in Gaul during the Roman occupation. Pollione, a Roman, has abandoned the Gaul high priestess Norma and their two children in favour of another priestess, Adalgisa. Discovering Pollione's infidelity, Norma moves to kill her children but is unable to go ahead with the terrible deed. Adalgisa implores Pollione to return to Norma but fails. Norma then incites war between the Gauls and Romans, a conflict which leads to Pollione's capture and death sentence. Norma, still in love with her husband, offers her life in exchange for his, and mounts the funeral pyre, where Pollione joins her.

From this raw material Bellini creates a lyric drama which, in the last act, takes on a truly tragic grandeur. Bellini's mastery of long and deeply expressive melodies is at its most sublime in "Casta Diva", the ultimate bel canto soprano aria, and in two soberly moving duets for soprano and tenor, "In mia man" and "Qual cor tradisti". It's no overstatement to say that the final act is the single greatest example of dramatic bel canto ever composed.

Callas, Corelli, Ludwig, Zaccaria, de Palma, Vincenzi; La Scala Orchestra and Chorus; Serafin (EMI; 3 CDs)

The title role of *Norma* demands a soprano who can act as well as she can sing. Maria Callas possessed this combination of qualities and is stunning in this 1960 version, the later of her two studio recordings. It also boasts the amazing Pollione of Franco Corelli, who delivers some of the most impressive Bellini tenor singing on record.

George Benjamin (1960–)

It is disappointing when prodigies turn out to be less prolific than they are prodigious, but in George Benjamin's case disappointment fades in the face of painstakingly consummate craftsmanship. In seeking different techniques for every piece, Benjamin eschews reach-me-down grids and systems, and though composing seems not to have become easier as he gets older, there is no sense of grinding labour in listening to his music, only of a sensuous delight in organizing sound.

Benjamin began composing at the age of 9, showing such early signs of musical precocity that by the age of just 14 he was studying composition at the Paris Conservatoire with Olivier Messiaen (and also piano with Messiaen's wife, Yvonne Loriod). For one whole year, his studies consisted solely of writing thousands of chords, exploring the nuances and possibilities of harmony, a discipline which bore fruit in his *Piano Sonata* of 1978, a work which already announces Benjamin's natural affinity with French music and his characteristic love of rich and unusually coloured sonorities. In 1980 he became the youngest composer to have a work – *Ringed by the Flat Horizon* – performed at the BBC Proms. The appearance soon afterwards of *A Mind of Winter* (1981) and *At First Light* (1982), two of the most magical works of the 1980s, announced, it seemed, the arrival of a major new talent.

Instead, a long period of creative near-silence ensued – almost as if Benjamin had realized, as he himself has said, that "sound is lovely, but unless it is somehow more than itself, it's of no interest". Returning to Paris to work at Pierre Boulez's music research centre IRCAM, the resulting work, *Antara* (1987), marked a new departure, with its adroit electronic manipulation of the sound of Peruvian panpipes, accompanied by an unlikely instrumental ensemble of flutes, trombones, strings and two anvils.

The encounter with computers and electronics was not to be pursued, however. Instead, Benjamin's next work, *Upon Silence* (1990), looked backwards for its instrumental line-up, using a viol consort to accompany a setting for soprano

George Benjamin (centre) discusses a point with pianist Paul Crossley.

of W.B. Yeats's poem "The Long-Legged Fly". The sudden switch from computers to period instruments was typical of Benjamin's constant search for fresh sonorities; more disquieting was the fact that, by 1993, he had written barely half an hour of music in an entire decade. The first signs of Benjamin's escape from what appeared to be an interminable creative impasse was signalled, in 1993, with the orchestral work *Sudden Time*, which takes up and extends a preoccupation of *Upon Silence* – namely, the contrast between the elasticity of "dream time" and the more regular and mechanical motion of "real time".

Since then, a relative spate of new works has followed, including two major orchestral pieces, *Three Inventions* (1995) and *Palimpsests* (2002); a chamber opera, *Into the Little Hill* (2006); and, most recently, a miniature piano concerto, *Duets* (2008). All these works show the fruits of Benjamin's long creative introspection: the musical detail is as original and as beautiful as ever, but the gossamer textures and ear-teasing sonorities are now married to a sense of large-scale form and dramatic purpose – all offering further evidence of an increasing assurance, one which promises great, if not numerous, things for the future.

At First Light

Benjamin's early works all show his acute feeling for harmonic and instrumental colours, a sensual delight in sounds for their own sakes, and a wonderful ability to translate visual or poetic images into music of haunting vividness. Nowhere is this clearer than in *At First Light* (1982), inspired by the hazy radiance of Turner's painting *Northiam Castle: Sunrise*, which is mirrored in an impressionistic musical haze in which sounds emerge from musical textures just as objects emerge from the mist in Turner's canvas. So detailed is Benjamin's deployment of his forces (the score calls for "large newspaper" and "ping-pong ball with flat-bottomed glass") that it's hard to believe there are only fourteen players producing the work's kaleidoscopic range of sounds.

At First Light; A Mind of Winter; Ringed by the Flat Horizon; Antara; Panorama: Walmsley-Clark; London Sinfonietta; BBC Symphony Orchestra; Benjamin, Elder (Nimbus)

Benjamin conducts the London Sinfonietta in lucid performances of *At First Light* and *Antara*, while Mark Elder directs a dramatic account of *Ringed by the Flat Horizon*. Penelope Walmsley-Clark is the fearless vocal soloist in *A Mind of Winter*, an exquisitely frosty setting of Wallace Stevens' poem "The Snow Man".

Sudden Time & Three Inventions

Sudden Time, an orchestral work conceived in 1983 but not completed for another decade, was the first result of Benjamin's decade-long process of musical self-examination. The title refers to a poem by Wallace Stevens: "It was like sudden time in a world without time", and Benjamin recalls how the work was inspired "by a dream in which the sound of a thunderclap seemed to stretch ... as if in a spiral through my head. I then awoke, and realized that I was experiencing the first second of a real thunderclap." This sense of time simultaneously condensed and extended is magically realized in the fugitive and contradictory pulses which flow through an orchestral landscape of characteristic luxuriance and originality.

Benjamin's next work, *Three Inventions*, is a marvellously fluent and original work for chamber orchestra. There's an acute sense of musical drama here, in the diaphanous plucked textures and mournful flugelhorn solo of the first invention, for example; or in the evanescent gong-strokes and mighty bass-drum blows which punctuate, and eventually terminate, the third.

Bickley; Fretwork; London Sinfonietta; London Philharmonic Orchestra; Benjamin (Nimbus; with *Upon Silence & Octet*)

Benjamin and the London Sinfonietta again, with John Wallace taking the flugelhorn solo in *Three Inventions*. The disc also includes performances of both versions of *Upon Silence* – one for viol consort, one for modern strings (Susan Bickley the excellent soloist in both) and the *Octet* from 1979.

Palimpsests

A palimpsest is a kind of old manuscript in which the original text has been erased or overwritten so that different layers of writing remain visible, in various stages of legibility and completeness. Benjamin's two-movement, twenty-minute orchestral work *Palimpsests* exploits the obvious musical possibilities of this concept, with different strata of music appearing and disappearing as the work progresses, starting with a faintly medieval-sounding canzone for clarinets which is rapidly buried beneath layers of often strikingly energetic and full-blooded music – with a minatory brass section frequently to the fore. This work's hard-edged sonorities show just how far Benjamin has travelled since the delicate impressionism of *At First Light*.

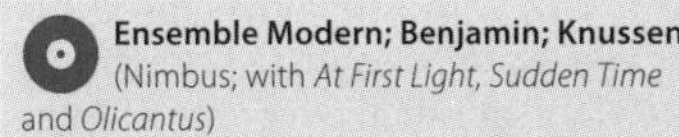

Ensemble Modern; Benjamin; Knussen (Nimbus; with *At First Light, Sudden Time* and *Olicantus*)

Benjamin directs the excellent Ensemble Modern in a gloves-off account of *Palimpsests*, coupled with live recordings of *At First Light* and *Sudden Time* which make for interesting comparisons with the studio versions listed above. The brief, eloquently understated little ensemble piece *Olicantus* (written for – and conducted here by – Oliver Knussen) completes the disc.

Sometime Voices & Into the Little Hill

The increasing dramatic range of Benjamin's later music is perfectly encapsulated by the magical *Sometime Voices* (1996), for baritone, chorus and orchestra. The work sets part of the famous speech of Caliban's in *The Tempest* ("Sometimes a thousand twangling instruments / Will hum about mine ears; and sometime voices"), with Caliban's words declaimed in roaring declamatory lines by the baritone soloist while orchestra and chorus provide a teasingly muted, tantalizingly suggestive musical background – as if (says Benjamin) the "music was happening, as in a dream, within Caliban's mind".

The chamber opera, *Into the Little Hill*, is something of a landmark in Benjamin's *oeuvre*, clocking in at around forty minutes, twice as long as anything else he had previously written. The unusual line-up comprises two female soloists playing multiple roles and a fifteen-piece ensemble featuring a characteristically eclectic instrumental selection (including bass flute, two basset horns, contrabass clarinet, cimbalon, banjo and mandolin). The opera shares *Sometime Voices*' mysterious nocturnal atmosphere, featuring some of Benjamin's most spare and haunting music, although the piece is hamstrung by Martin Crimp's tub-thumpingly tedious libretto (a mangled reworking of *The Pied Piper of Hamelin*), meaning that it perhaps works better as a concert piece (or on CD) than in the theatre.

Ensemble Modern; Ollu, Nagano, Knussen, Komsi, Summers, Henschel (Nimbus; with *Dance Figures*)

Excellent performances of *Sometime Voices* (with Dietrich Henschel as Caliban) and *Into the Little Hill*, with Anu Komsi and Hilary Summers the two accomplished singers – the latter's distinctively androgynous voice is particularly well matched to her twin roles of minister and mother. The entertaining ballet score, *Dance Figures* (2004) for orchestra is an additional bonus.

Alban Berg (1885–1935)

Despite their reputation, the composers known as the Second Viennese School (Schoenberg, Berg, Webern) did not turn their back on the past. Following Schoenberg's lead, they saw the twelve-tone system of composition (see p.478) not as a negation of tonality, but as its logical development. This is nowhere more apparent than in the music of Alban Berg, which marries an expressive richness – the equal of any late Romantic music – to a complexity that even now retains some of its coded secrets.

Berg already had a substantial body of songs to his credit when, in 1904, he enrolled in Schoenberg's classes. Anton Webern had already signed up, and the two were to remain close friends. Over the next seven years, Berg's music achieved astonishing maturity under Schoenberg's watchful eye: there can be few more masterly works labelled "Opus 1" than his *Piano Sonata* (1908), and the last piece he wrote while a Schoenberg student, the *String Quartet* (1910), remains a cornerstone of twentieth-century quartet literature. The last of his *Four Songs* (1910) was his first atonal work.

Shortly before Schoenberg's move to Berlin in 1911 put an end to Berg's studies, Berg attended Mahler's funeral, and later the Munich premiere of Mahler's *Das Lied von der Erde*. Within weeks he had begun composing his first orchestral work, the *Five Orchestral Songs on Picture-Postcard Texts* by Peter Altenberg (Altenberg was known in Viennese intellectual circles as "the Socrates of the coffee house"). When Schoenberg premiered two of these songs in Vienna in 1913, a riot ensued. Schoenberg himself soon added his voice to the detractors, suggesting that Berg would do better to write longer, more discursive pieces than these songs, and the epigrammatic *Four Pieces for Clarinet and Piano* which followed.

Chastened, Berg duly embarked on his *Three Orchestral Pieces*, which were much more what Schoenberg had in mind. Meanwhile, shortly before war broke out in 1914, he was in the audience for the Viennese premiere of *Woyzeck*, a play written eighty years earlier by Georg Büchner. Immensely moved, Berg vowed to make an opera from the play. War and military service interrupted his work, and it was not until 1922 that he completed *Wozzeck* (as the play was then, and the opera still is, known). Excerpts were successfully performed in 1924, by which time Berg was working on his *Chamber Concerto*.

Erich Kleiber conducted the premiere of *Wozzeck* in Berlin in 1925: it required 34 full orchestral rehearsals, so revolutionary was Berg's language, both musical and dramatic. Performances followed throughout Europe and the United States. It was the first international success for an atonal work from the Schoenberg school, and Berg confirmed his growing status with the *Lyric Suite* (1927). Then in 1929 he signed a contract for the rights to the "Lulu" plays (*Earth Spirit* and *Pandora's Box*) of Franz Wedekind, which had enjoyed a *succès de scandale* ever since *Pandora's Box* was banned in 1904 (Berg saw a private performance in 1905). Work on the opera *Lulu* had begun before Berg signed the contract; now it proceeded apace.

With the Nazis a growing threat, the whole country, as Berg wrote, was "dancing on a volcano". Hitler became chancellor in January 1933, Schoenberg left Berlin in May, finally emigrating to the United States in October. In May 1934, Berg wrote to Webern that he had finished *Lulu*, bar some finishing touches. Nearly a year later, he set the opera aside to compose the *Violin Concerto* in memory of Manon Gropius. Soon after completing what is now his most popular work, Berg was stung by an insect. An abscess developed, the infection worsened, and on Christmas Eve 1935 Alban Berg died of general septicaemia. He was just 50 years old.

Wozzeck

Fragmentary, hallucinatory and profoundly pessimistic, Georg Büchner's play *Woyzeck* (left incomplete when the playwright died in 1837, aged 23) is an astonishingly prescient piece, "the first real tragedy of low life" according to George Steiner. When Berg saw the Vienna premiere in 1914, he knew that he had a subject for his first opera and, although he did not serve at the front, his experiences of World War I only confirmed his realization. *Wozzeck* tells, with cinematic immediacy, the story of a simple soldier's brutalization and humiliation by a sadistic and repressive system; pushed to the brink, Wozzeck kills his wife, then himself.

Wozzeck is Berg's most expressionist work, with a dissonant score that creates an atmosphere of mounting paranoia and oppressiveness. The opera's musical structure is formidably complex, but as Berg himself wrote, "there must not be anyone in the audience who, from the moment the curtain rises until it finally descends, notices anything of these various fugues, inventions, suites and sonata movements, variations and passacaglias. Nobody must be filled with anything except the idea of the opera." In a performance which does justice to the music, Berg's wish is fulfilled: the form of *Sprechgesang* (speech-song) he evolves suits the characters' halting attempts to communicate, while the orchestra tells us everything they can't express.

Waechter, Silja, Winkler; Vienna Philharmonic Orchestra; Dohnányi (Decca; 2 CDs; with Schoenberg *Erwartung*)

Eberhard Waechter's characterization of Wozzeck is a terrifying portrayal of fear and desperation. Through varying the quality of his voice he gives a chilling impression of Wozzeck's instability without resorting to the sort of barking and wailing found on some other recordings. Anja Silja's Marie, a powerfully lyrical reading, perfectly matches Dohnányi's visceral view of the score.

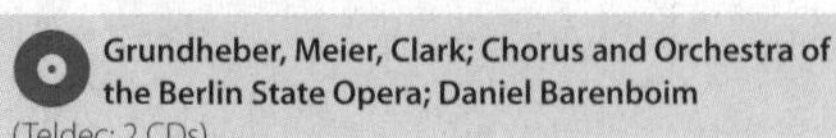

Grundheber, Meier, Clark; Chorus and Orchestra of the Berlin State Opera; Daniel Barenboim (Teldec; 2 CDs)

Barenboim's live recording from 1994 is superb, the conductor demonstrating a genuine affinity with Berg's complex orchestral writing, especially in terms of detail and architecture. The main roles are brilliantly performed by Franz Grundheber, who conveys Wozzeck's self-pity as well as his rage, and Waltraud Meier, who is an electrifying Marie.

Lulu

Berg's second opera was incomplete at his death, his substantial sketches hidden, almost as a sacred relic, by his wife Hélène. Only the first two acts were performed at its 1937 Zürich premiere, with a mainly pantomimed episode from Act 3 concluding the work. For forty years, the work survived as a two-act torso, but when Hélène died in 1976 Friedrich Cerha undertook the completion, which required less intervention than Berg's widow had suggested. The third act was crucial to Berg's plan of the opera as a kind of palindrome, the turning point occurring in Act 2 Scene 1, where a silent film depicts Lulu's arrest, trial and imprisonment. Pierre Boulez conducted the Paris premiere of the completed *Lulu* in 1979.

While Strauss's *Salome* epitomizes the fantasy of the destructive allure of female sexuality, Berg's *Lulu* is a rather more complex and human representation of that *fin de siècle* archetype, the *femme fatale*. Lulu is both a self-determining, modern woman who uses her sexuality as a weapon, and at the same time the victim of the men, and women, who objectify her (the libretto even hints at childhood abuse). The last act finds her reduced to walking the streets of London, where she finally falls victim to Jack the Ripper. Berg's flexible twelve-note technique produces music that is tough and lyrical, expressionist and dramatic. The harmonies are richer than in *Wozzeck*, the musical and dramatic shape more immediately appreciable, thanks in large part to the theme associated with Lulu, a point of reference throughout.

Stratas, Mazura, Riegel, Minton, Tear; Paris Opera Orchestra; Boulez (Deutsche Grammophon; 3 CDs)

This studio recording, which largely re-creates the 1979 premiere performance, is a highlight of Boulez's conducting career. There is a freedom and spontaneity to the performance, an ease and inevitability to the changes of pacing and subtleties of rubato that is simply breathtaking. Teresa Stratas, famous for playing neurotic heroines, has long been associated with Lulu, and her interpretation is exceptional.

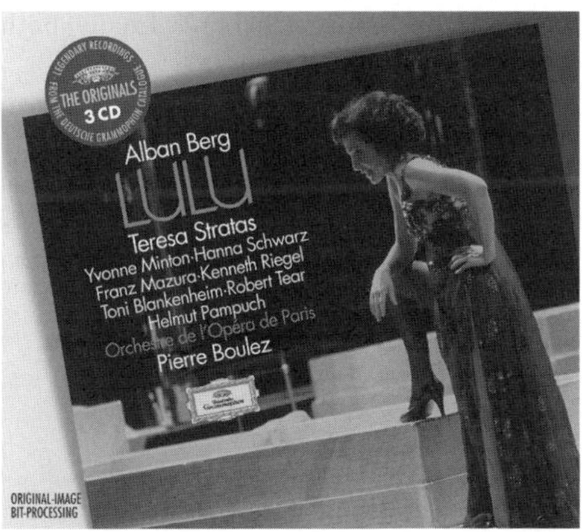

Songs

As you might expect of one of the greatest opera composers, Berg also wrote some extremely fine songs. Many of the earliest pieces (those without opus numbers) are, as Schoenberg suggested, "in a style between Wolf and Brahms", but with the set known as *Seven Early Songs*, written under Schoenberg's tutelage between 1905 and 1908, a more distinctive voice emerges. Originally written for piano accompaniment, they achieve greater impact in Berg's 1928 orchestration.

More remarkable still are the *Altenberg Lieder*, settings of texts which the poet Peter Altenberg sent to the Bergs on postcards from the Alps. A riot greeted the premiere of two of the songs under Schoenberg's baton in 1913: the audience didn't like the epigrammatic texts, or the use of a large orchestra to produce such quiet, chamber-like textures. Now, those very qualities are what make the songs so appealing. Also worth mentioning is Berg's concert aria "Der Wein", which the composer saw as no more than an occasional piece, but which today seems to breathe the same air as *Lulu* (for a recommended recording, see below, under "Three Pieces for Orchestra").

Norman, Schein; London Symphony Orchestra; Boulez (Sony Classical)

It's regrettable that Jessye Norman so rarely records such repertoire. Her sumptuous voice revels in Berg's music, her attention to detail, and to the sense of the words, making her an ideal interpreter. In addition to the *Altenberg Lieder* and the *Seven Early Songs*, the disc also includes a handful of mostly early songs with piano accompaniment: Norman again excels.

Violin Concerto

Few twentieth-century works are as wrenchingly moving as Berg's *Violin Concerto*, written in response to the death in 1935 of Manon Gropius, the 18-year-old daughter of Alma Mahler and the architect Walter Gropius. The violinist Louis Krasner had already commissioned a concerto from Berg, who broke off from *Lulu* to write the piece, dedicated "to the memory of an angel". Berg scholars, who enjoy nothing more than the composer's cryptological and numerological obsessions, have uncovered "a secret programme" of references to Berg's mistress, Hanna Fuchs-Robettin, and to Berg's illegitimate daughter, progeny of a youthful affair with a servant girl in the Berg household.

Be that as it may, the *Violin Concerto* needs no secret programme to work its magic. Reconciling the twelve-note system with traditional tonality, Berg quotes from a Carinthian folk tune in the opening movement, and from the Bach chorale *Es ist genug* (It is enough) in the second movement. The concerto begins as if the soloist were tuning the violin against the orchestra, but tension quickly mounts as the music becomes more agitated. As in *Lulu*, Berg then reverses the process, the music slowing, growing ever quieter until the Bach chorale steals in, and violin and orchestra sink into a mood of loss and resignation.

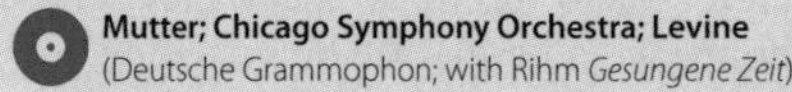

Mutter; Chicago Symphony Orchestra; Levine
(Deutsche Grammophon; with Rihm *Gesungene Zeit*)

Anne-Sophie Mutter's panache pays rich dividends in a work demanding a match between free fantasy and cast-iron discipline. Under James Levine, the Chicago Symphony Orchestra provides sumptuous but delicate support throughout.

Krasner; BBC Symphony Orchestra; Webern
(Testament; with *Lyric Suite*)

Made in 1935, Krasner's version, accompanied by Webern, is the first recording ever made of this work and, despite the inevitable crackle on the transfer from 78s, this is a deeply moving performance with a wonderfully idiomatic authority. An added bonus is the *Lyric Suite* in a 1936 recording by the Galimir quartet.

Three Pieces for Orchestra

The *Three Pieces for Orchestra* were completed in 1915, shortly before Berg was conscripted into the Austrian Army's war effort, but they did not receive their first complete performance until 1930. It is difficult to understand why, since the music so clearly honours the example of Mahler – the composer whose work first pointed Berg towards orchestral composition. Yet the piece is mature Berg, a complex structure yielding a richness of musical incident that is both exhilarating and unsettling, as at first thin, then eventually massive, sounds emerge from the opening silence. The world of *Wozzeck* is just around the corner.

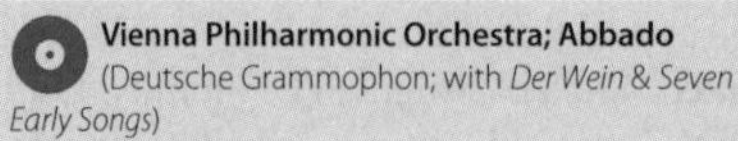

Vienna Philharmonic Orchestra; Abbado
(Deutsche Grammophon; with *Der Wein* & *Seven Early Songs*)

Abbado brings bite to the Vienna Phil's sheer lustrousness, working wonders in this dense score; the climactic march is hair-raising. In the accompanying orchestral songs, Anne Sofie von Otter is beautiful but a touch cool for the *Seven Early Songs*, but her aristocratic tones marry perfectly with the jazzy pungency of *Der Wein*, written while the composer was already at work on *Lulu*.

Lyric Suite

Berg's six-movement *Lyric Suite* for string quartet, written in 1925–26, contains, like the *Violin Concerto*, coded references to his affection for Hanna Fuchs-Robettin, as well as quotations from Wagner's *Tristan und Isolde* and from Zemlinsky's *Lyric Symphony* (see p.642). When, at his publisher's request, Berg prepared an arrangement for string orchestra, he orchestrated only movements two to four – the expressive core of the work. If in the process he smoothed away some of the quartet version's toughness, he also added an emotional richness, and the closing moments of the third movement (marked Adagio appassionato) are as touching as anything he ever wrote. It was premiered by Jascha Horenstein in Berlin in 1929.

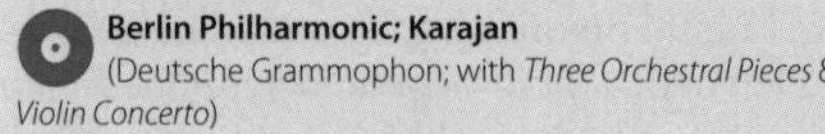

Berlin Philharmonic; Karajan
(Deutsche Grammophon; with *Three Orchestral Pieces* & *Violin Concerto*)

These recordings, made by Karajan and the BPO in the 1970s, are established classics. The lushness and intensity of Berg's writing is fully realized, largely thanks to the BPO's extraordinarily opulent and varied string sound, but Karajan also articulates the fastidious orchestral fabric and the overall structure. The coupled accounts of the *Three Orchestral Pieces* and the *Violin Concerto* are equally impressive.

Chamber Concerto

Its short score completed on Berg's fortieth birthday (9 February, 1925), and dedicated as a belated fiftieth birthday present to Schoenberg, the *Chamber Concerto* also marks the twentieth anniversary of the friendship between Berg, Schoenberg and Webern. No wonder, then, that to honour these associations Berg derived the work's opening motifs from the composers' names (the German system of notation favours such musical tributes). By restricting the concerto's accompaniment to thirteen wind instruments, Berg produced some marvellously unusual colourings, while the solo parts for piano (first movement), violin (second movement) and, finally, both together, are virtuoso showpieces.

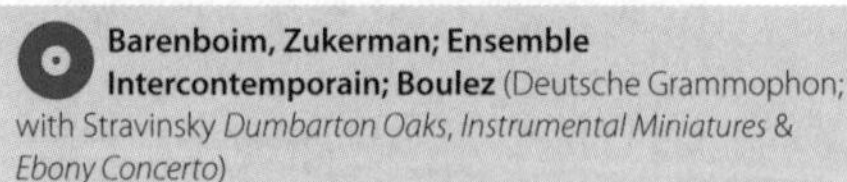

Barenboim, Zukerman; Ensemble Intercontemporain; Boulez (Deutsche Grammophon; with Stravinsky *Dumbarton Oaks*, *Instrumental Miniatures* & *Ebony Concerto*)

There's a fruitful tension here between the soloists' expansive Romanticism and the no-nonsense rigour of Boulez, a tension that matches the conductor's statement, "what I find most striking [in Berg's music] is the combination of immediate expressiveness with outstanding structural powers".

String Quartet

Effectively marking Berg's graduation from Schoenberg's class, the *String Quartet* is the composer's first conclusive foray beyond tonality. Like the *Piano Sonata*, it displays great rhythmic flexibility and a broad expressive range, immediately apparent in the way the blunt opening statement quickly softens into a kind of question. There are moments of aching lyricism, but also bursts of fiery declamation, both stretching the players' techniques: it at times feels as if the young Berg is trying to fit everything he knows into one piece, but the quartet deserves its status as a twentieth-century classic.

Schoenberg Quartett (Brilliant Classics; with the *Lyric Suite* and other chamber works)

In the absence of both Alban Berg Quartett recordings, this makes a more than adequate alternative. In both the *String Quartet* and the original version of the *Lyric Suite* the group finds just the right balance between Berg's heady mix of agony and ecstasy. Great value for money, since it contains all of the chamber music at budget price.

Piano Sonata

The hegemony enjoyed by tonality was already decaying when, in 1908, Berg completed his Opus 1. As Pierre Boulez wrote of the piece, Berg "feels the attraction of the distant future, but is still tied to the recent past". There are traces of Liszt and, unsurprisingly, of Schoenberg, but there is already originality in the way Berg manipulates tiny fragments of melody and rhythm into a statement dense with dramatic gesture and packing a powerful emotional punch, not least in the closing moments, which seem to imply not so much rest as exhaustion.

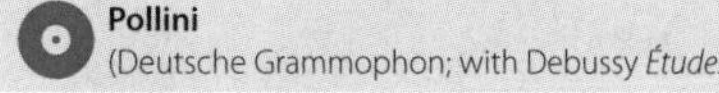

Pollini
(Deutsche Grammophon; with Debussy *Études*)

Not everyone enjoys Maurizio Pollini's crisp attack: he plays the sonata much faster than, for example, Glenn Gould, who recorded this "music from the twilight of tonality" several times. But Pollini's cerebral clarity pays dividends in a work that, though short, makes great demands on the player if the lines are to emerge uncongested.

Luciano Berio (1925–2003)

Luciano Berio's work is characterized above all by his love of the theatrical, his fascination with the voice, and his constant willingness to engage with music of the past as well as of the present. Drawing on a range of influences that reaches from the poetry of Dante to the politics of Martin Luther King, and from the operas of Monteverdi to the sounds of modern jazz, his output embraced all the major musical developments of its time, including electronic music, music theatre, and works using quotation and collage – hence one critic's description of him as an "omnivore".

Berio's leaning towards vocal music was fostered by his relationship with the remarkable American singer Cathy Berberian, for whom he wrote many of his earlier works, and whose vocal versatility and charismatic stage presence was richly exploited in works such as *Recital 1* and *Sequenza III*, both of which interestingly blur the boundaries between traditional song and music theatre. At the same time as he was composing his Berberian-inspired vocal pieces, Berio was also exploring more complex interactions of music and text in three major works of the 1960s: *Épiphanie* (1962), *Laborintus 2* (1965) and *Sinfonia* (1969), which between them set an enormous variety of texts (ranging from Dante to Levi-Strauss) in a baffling range of musical styles, most famously in the third movement of the *Sinfonia*, which creates a complex musical labyrinth around the third movement of Mahler's *Symphony No. 2*.

Given the sense of the theatrical which was implicit in all these works, it was no surprise that Berio soon began to turn to opera – albeit a form of opera which owed little to traditional models. His experiments in the genre are best represented by his third opera, *Un re in ascolto* (*A King Listens*, with a libretto by Calvino), an opera about the rehearsals and auditions for an opera – not so much a musico-dramatic story as an extended meditation on the meaning of listening, singing and memory.

The interleaved musical and verbal texts which characterize so many of Berio's vocal and theatrical works find their counterpart in much of his purely instrumental works. In 1958 he embarked on a sequence of pieces for solo instruments, the *Sequenzas*, whose sometimes zany virtuosity offers an instrumental parallel to the Berberian vocal works. These were followed by a further series of linked works, the *Chemins*, in which the existing *Sequenzas* are recycled within new layers of musical accompaniment and commentary, rather as the third movement of *Sinfonia* had supplied fresh layers of musical and verbal commentary around the kernel of Mahler's symphonic movement.

A similar preoccupation with recomposition and "commentary techniques" can be found in

Luciano Berio at work on his "restoration" of Schubert's tenth symphony.

Berio's rich sequence of (mainly instrumental) works based on popular and folk music. Though this interest dates back to his *Folk Songs* of 1964, it was in instrumental works of the 1970s and 1980s that this aspect of his music become especially important, most memorably in *Voci* (1984), a haunting reworking of Sicilian folk melodies for viola and orchestra, and *Ritorno degli snovidenia* (1977), based on fragments of Russian revolutionary songs, for cello and orchestra. Berio's constant dialogue with musical tradition can also be seen in his various orchestrations of works by de Falla, Mahler and Brahms, among others, and, most notably, in *Rendering* (1989), his typically creative completion of unfinished symphonic sketches by Schubert.

Vocal Works

As Berio expert David Osmond-Smith puts it, "the seminal works of the early sixties were written not for 'the voice', but for a voice: that of Cathy Berberian". The Berberian work *par excellence*, *Recital I* (1971), encapsulates her vivid theatrical gifts, offering a "deconstructed recital" in which the soloist tries to work through her repertoire with a chamber orchestra while supplying a Beckett-like stream-of-consciousness commentary. A similar sense of drama underpins *Sequenza III*, for solo voice, with its surreally dramatic (if largely unintelligible) stream of sung, muttered and garbled phonetic fragments. The theatrical element is more muted in the earlier *Circles* (1960), where the singer's circular movement around the stage is mirrored by a musical circle in which three poems by e. e. cummings are progressively deconstructed into their constituent phonetic parts, then put back together again. A very different type of vocal writing is explored in *Folk Songs* (1964), a knowing but engaging compendium of folk tunes from around the world which has proved Berio's most popular work.

Recital I for Cathy; Folk Songs: Berberian; London Sinfonietta; Juilliard Ensemble; Berio
(RCA; with songs by Weill)

A classic recording from Berberian: it's hard to imagine anyone surpassing her marvellously deranged performance of *Recital I*, while the full reach of her expressive abilities is beautifully captured in the more mainstream *Folk Songs*.

Circles; Sequenza I, III, V: Berberian, Nicolet, Globokar (Wergo)

Berberian's unique variety of vocal theatre is superbly captured in this historic recording from 1967, featuring *Circles* along with three of the early *Sequenzas* in outstanding performances by Berberian, trombonist Vinko Globokar in *Sequenza V* and flautist Aurèle Nicolet in *Sequenza I*.

Sinfonia

Sinfonia (1968–69), for eight amplified voices and orchestra, was part of a wider pattern of response to the musical crisis of the 1960s, during which avant-garde composers began once again to look to music of the past for material and inspiration – a turn towards so-called "meta music", or music about music. The third movement of *Sinfonia* is one of the most famous and remarkable examples of this approach: a dense fabric of verbal quotations contained within a musical quotation, the Scherzo from Mahler's *Symphony No. 2*, which is borrowed virtually wholesale and then used as a kind of musical armature around which Berio concocts a dazzling semantic and musical labyrinth, including further quotations (from Mahler, Ravel and Debussy, among others) and chattering texts drawn from Samuel Beckett's *The Unnameable*. The four outer movements frame this central *tour de force* with further, though more understated, explorations of the relationship between text and note – most tellingly in the second movement, "O King", a moving homage to Martin Luther King which gradually constructs a quietly intoned vocal setting of his name out of its constituent vowel sounds – a procedure analagous to that used in *Circles*.

Concertgebouw Orchestra; Electric Phoenix; Chailly (Decca; with *Folk Songs & Formazioni*)

The expressive breadth and richness of Berio's music is beautifully captured in these sumptuous performances, with Electric Phoenix the accomplished protagonists in the verbal and vocal pyrotechnics of *Sinfonia*, and Jard van Nes the excellent soloist in *Folk Songs*. *Formazioni* (1987), one of Berio's most striking orchestral works, completes the disc.

Concertos

The musical possibilities inherent in the concerto form – or at least a rather unusual version of it – have been particularly important in Berio's music. His earliest experiments in the genre can be found in the *Chemins* cycle, a group of pieces based on the *Sequenza* cycle, in which each original *Sequenza* becomes the solo part in a kind of miniature "concerto" – as in *Chemins II* and *Chemins IV* and *Corale* (based on the *Sequenzas* for oboe, viola and violin respectively), in which the original solo piece is embedded within a fresh layer of musical commentary.

A sequence of concerto-like pieces has further extended the idea of creating entire works out of the kernel of a virtuoso solo line, as in the ruminative *Ritorno degli snovidenia* (1977), in which the solo cellist's contemplative endless melody is sustained, extended and embroidered by the surrounding orchestral instruments, or the dazzling *"Points on the curve to find..."* (1974), for piano and chamber orchestra, a breathtaking study in musical perpetual motion. In typical Berio fashion, this latter work has itself since become the basis for a further concerto for piano and orchestra, *Concerto II (Echoing Curves)* (1989).

Chemins II & IV; Corale; "Points on the curve to find..."; Ritorno degli snovidenia: Ensemble Intercontemporain; Boulez (Sony; available as a download)

A miraculously lucid performance by Pierre-Laurent Aimard of the stunningly virtuosic *"Points on the curve to find..."* is the highlight of this fascinating disc, whilst violinist Maryvonne Le Dizès and violist Jean Sulem offer incandescent accounts of the feisty *Corale* and *Chemins II*.

Rendering

Rendering (1990) is one of Berio's most impressive feats of musical legerdemain, offering a musical "restoration" of sketches for Schubert's tenth symphony (which the Austrian composer left unfinished at his death) and somehow managing to combine the musical worlds of the early nineteenth and late twentieth centuries into a convincing whole. As Berio put it: "I set myself the target of following those modern restoration criteria that aim at reviving the old colours without, however, trying to disguise the damage that time has caused, often leaving inevitable empty patches in the composition." Thus the Schubert sketches have been beautifully orchestrated and pieced together in period style, while the "empty patches" have been filled in with music composed by Berio himself – what he describes as "musical cement", a rather unflattering description for his magically hushed interconnecting material, itself incorporating reminiscences of other works by late Schubert, with the tinkling of a celeste marking the joins between Schubert's music and Berio's.

London Symphony Orchestra; Berio; Lucchesini (RCA; with *Concerto II "Echoing Curves" & Quattro versioni originali della "Ritirata notturna di Madrid"*)

Conducted by the composer, the LSO manage to be idiomatic in both Schubert and Berio and accomplish the slightly surreal transitions between the two sound-worlds with impressive fluency. The striking, large-scale *Concerto II* for piano and orchestra makes an interesting comparison, while Berio's witty arrangement of Boccherini's *Ritirata notturna di Madrid* provides a brief but engaging encore.

Hector Berlioz (1803–1869)

The life of Hector Berlioz – as related in his dazzling, if overimaginative, memoirs – is classical music's Byronic epic. Yet this quintessential Romantic began rather inauspiciously, in the backwater of Grenoble. Whereas most musical giants displayed prodigious gifts in childhood, Berlioz learned neither the piano nor the violin, though he did develop an enthusiasm for the flute and, later, the guitar. Notwithstanding his lack of practical musical ability, he wanted to pursue a career in music, but his father insisted that he enter the medical profession. Berlioz did as he was told, but in 1822, while studying medicine in Paris, he began to take serious music lessons for the first time.

Owing to the fact that his father's allowance was forthcoming only for as long as he remained at medical school, Berlioz hesitated over making a serious break until 1826, when he mustered the courage to leave the medical school and enter the music conservatory. His subsequent development was bewilderingly fast, and was actually aided by his inability to play the piano well – other composers tended to work out their ideas at the piano, but Berlioz found himself free of such creative limitations and soon realized that the orchestra and large ensembles were his true métier.

In 1827 he experienced one of many life-changing events when he went to see a performance of *Hamlet*. Even though his English was far from fluent, the play hit him "like a thunderbolt", as did the beauty of the leading lady, Harriet Smithson. It was to be the start of a lifelong addiction to Shakespeare and an equally intense, if less durable, passion for Miss Smithson (they married in 1833 and separated nine years later). During the first five months of 1830 – having in the interim immersed himself in Goethe's poetry and attended a revelatory series of Beethoven concerts in Paris – he composed his *Symphonie Fantastique*, a huge orchestral piece in which he attempted to sublimate his passion for the actress; its subtitle, "Episodes in the life of an artist", betrays an autobiographical element that was never far below the surface of Berlioz's music.

Not long after, Berlioz finally succeeded in winning the Prix de Rome, a scholarship given to artists to enable them to study at the Villa Medici in Rome – and Italy was duly to become another of his great inspirations. Berlioz proceeded to produce a string of similarly colossal and innovative works that secured the admiration of composers such as Liszt, Paganini and Chopin, but had difficulty obtaining a wider audience, not least because his music usually demanded very large and expensive forces.

A sombre Berlioz photographed by Pierre Petit.

The work that posed the greatest problems in this respect was his penultimate opera, *Les Troyens*, a five-act, four-hour monster which the Paris Opéra refused to produce in its entirety. Berlioz then divided the work into two parts and, eventually, he saw the second of these, *Les Troyens à Carthage*, staged at the Théâtre-Lyrique in 1863. As with so many of his works, the performance was a grand failure, but this failure hit him harder than any.

He found occasional solace through conducting, but his last seven years were overshadowed by illness, despair and resentment at his country's inability or unwillingness to recognize his talent – a situation that has not really changed, for Berlioz is far more widely respected abroad than he is at home. His music was doubtless very strange for its time, with its irregular rhythms and almost boastfully complicated orchestration, and certainly it can be pompous and overblown. However, Berlioz is one of music's great originals, spurning traditional formulas to blend literary, pictorial and musical elements into highly energetic and highly personal creations.

STAGE WORKS

Of Berlioz's five stage works, two are masterpieces – the classically inspired *Les Troyens*, and his homage to Goethe, *La damnation de Faust*. The early *Les francs juges* is lost, apart from a lengthy overture which is sometimes programmed in orchestral concerts. *Benvenuto Cellini*, the story of the intrigues surrounding the Renaissance sculptor and his rivals, gets an occasional performance and recording, but is too lengthy for its content, although Berlioz created one of his best overtures – *Le carnaval Romain* – out of its carnival scene. His late Shakespearean comedy, *Béatrice et Bénédict*, a hotchpotch of styles with heavy reliance on spoken scenes, has never been a success, despite containing one or two musical highlights and an attractive overture.

La Damnation de Faust

Berlioz read a translation of the first part of Goethe's *Faust* in 1828 and fell under its spell at once. He immediately set to work on eight *Scenes from Faust*, which he sent to the poet for approval – a bad move, as it turned out. Goethe showed the score to a composer friend who was appalled by Berlioz's outrageous music, and the result was that he withdrew the work. Many years later, he reworked the scenes into *La damnation de Faust*, a hybrid work, more closely resembling an oratorio for concert performance than an opera – Berlioz himself called it a "dramatic legend".

Berlioz sticks much closer to his source than many other composers who have set the Faust legend, such as Gounod and Busoni, and his kaleidoscopic work crams an extraordinary range of music into its two-hour span. Between the crashing "Hungarian March" of the opening scene and the climactic ride to hell, there's a rowdy tavern scene, a supernatural ballet as Faust dreams of Marguerite (Gretchen in the original), a love scene, a mad aria and a great pantheistic invocation of nature, one of the most advanced parts of this amazingly vivid score. No previous work for the stage had risked such violent contrasts, and few subsequent composers could bring them off so successfully.

Lewis, Terfel, von Otter; Philharmonia Chorus and Orchestra; Chung (Deutsche Grammophon; 2 CDs)

The most recent recording of *Faust* is in many ways the best and the most theatrical. The stellar cast is led by veteran tenor Keith Lewis who brings genuine anguish and horror to the necromancer's fall. Bryn Terfel as his adversary projects sufficient malice to offset the innate generosity of his voice while Anne Sofie von Otter is simply the most effortless Marguerite on record.

Les Troyens

Berlioz's epic tale of the Trojan War, written in the late 1850s, brought together the obsessions of several decades – primarily the poetry of Shakespeare and Virgil, and the operas of Gluck, whose finely structured libretti provided a model for the text of this most un-Gluck-like extravaganza. Berlioz never lived to see *Les Troyens* performed complete: after years of waiting for the Paris Opéra to agree to a production, he split the opera in two and let the second section, *Les Troyens à Carthage*, be performed separately. It wasn't until 1957 that a nearly uncut version was played one evening at Covent Garden.

The opera begins in war-ravaged Troy, quickly introducing the prophetess Cassandra, the pivotal figure of the first two acts (together entitled *La prise de Troie*), and the role with perhaps the noblest music in the entire score. The whole of this first part of *Les Troyens* is full of grandiose and doomstruck music. Berlioz creates a wholly different sound-world for the sensuality of the court of Queen Dido at Carthage. After this comes the best-known music of the opera, the symphonic interlude known as "The Royal Hunt and Storm", commencing a succession of beautiful set pieces that culminates in a great love duet for Aeneas and Dido, incorporating words from Shakespeare's *Merchant of Venice*.

Heppner, DeYoung, Lang, Mingardo; London Symphony Orchestra and Chorus; Davis (LSO; 4 CDs)

For his second recording of *Les Troyens*, Colin Davis found himself another top line-up, including Canadian heldentenor Ben Heppner. The clarity of Heppner's diction is exceptional, as is the luxuriant nature of his voice. Davis moves the score on more than he did on his pioneering 1969 Philips set, and the chorus provide strong, if utterly un-French, support. At budget price this is a great way to discover Berlioz's masterpiece.

CHORAL & VOCAL WORKS

Berlioz wrote a considerable amount of vocal music apart from the operas, including a number of cantatas (several of which are lost), some lovely orchestral songs and two large-scale religious works – the *Grande Messe des morts* and *L'enfance du Christ* (The Childhood of Christ). Written in 1837 and 1850–54 respectively, they are total opposites in style – the *Grande Messe* is a hyperbolically massive affair, *L'enfance* a gentle series of musical tableaux.

Grande Messe des morts

In 1837 the minister of the interior commissioned Berlioz to write a Requiem mass for a great public ceremony. Like the *Requiem* of Verdi, the *Grande Messe des morts* (as it is usually called) was created by a man with apparently no real religious convictions. Written almost entirely for chorus and orchestra, it features just one soloist, a tenor, and he appears in one movement only. Comparable to Beethoven's *Missa Solemnis* in its dynamic extremes, the *Grande Messe* is famed for its vast scale, notably the use of four brass bands in the "Tuba Mirum" movement – placed at the four compass points (in effect the four corners of the orchestra) – to conjure the Day of Judgement in an ear-splitting display. Certainly nothing else in the work matches the sheer theatricality of this moment, but there is much to admire in this austerely grand and sometimes lurid composition, not least an unexpected moment of contemplative calm in the "Quaerens me" section which is sung completely unaccompanied.

Dowd; Wandsworth School Boys Choir; London Symphony Chorus and Orchestra; Davis (Philips; 2 CDs; with *Te Deum*)

Though Bernstein's outstanding recording is not currently available, this makes a more than worthy substitute (though tenor Ronald Dowd is not as dramatic as Stuart Burrows is for Bernstein). Davis brings out the power and the anguish of the work and the Philips engineers capture the full impact of the brass bands.

Ainsley; Choeur et Orchestre de Montréal; Dutoit (Decca; 2 CDs; with other Berlioz choral works)

Although this lacks the raw power of Colin Davis's version, it makes up for it with brilliant engineering: the balance between choir and orchestra is ideal and the massed brass of the Dies Irae has never sounded so unclouded. Dutoit's interpretation is less dark than Davis's, focusing more on the work's optimism than on its morose undertones.

L'enfance du Christ

L'enfance du Christ is so distinctly archaic in style that it hardly seems possible that it's written by the composer of the *Grande Messe*. A self-confessed agnostic, Berlioz presents the story of the young Christ as a legendary narrative rather than as an uplifting religious experience. The work is in three sections: the first centres on the birth of Christ and the predicament of King Herod; the second is a pastoral interlude in which the Holy Family flee into Egypt, a scene containing some of the composer's most placid music; and the final part depicts the hospitality given to them in Egypt, an episode featuring some fairly crass scene-painting but a serene choral ending.

Gens, Agnew, Naouri, Lallouette, Caton; La Chapelle Royale; Collegium Vocale; Orchestre des Champs Élysées; Herreweghe (Harmonia Mundi; 2 CDs)

This live performance on period instruments is an absolute revelation. The soloists are all French (with the exception of Paul Agnew's narrator) and the combination of native singers and the more pungent sonorities of the instruments (especially the woodwind) creates some wonderfully rich, individual sounds, which Herreweghe shapes with great subtlety.

Les nuits d'été

Les nuits d'été (Summer Nights), a cycle of six songs to words by Berlioz's friend and fellow journalist Théophile Gautier, was first written in 1841 as a composition for voice and piano. A couple of years later Berlioz orchestrated the third song, "Absence", and in 1856 he decided to make orchestral versions of the other five. It is impossible to overstate the importance of this piece to French music: whereas Beethoven, Schubert and Schumann had already established the concept of the song cycle in Germany, it was Berlioz who single-handedly introduced the form to France. Yet its novelty is but a small part of the appeal of *Les nuits d'été*, for these are among the loveliest songs of the nineteenth century, thanks to music that's completely attuned to the melancholic languor of Gautier's poems which are mostly concerned with love – though usually within the context of death or separation.

Crespin; Orchestre de la Suisse Romande; Ansermet (Decca; with Ravel *Shéhérazade*)

In 1963, when this recording was made, soprano Régine Crespin was at the height of her powers, with a depth of understanding and an ability to communicate that remain unsurpassed in this repertoire. Hers is a quintessentially French voice – incisive, sensuous, characterful and with a real relish for the nasal quality of the vowels.

ORCHESTRAL WORKS

Berlioz's early overtures – especially *Le Corsaire* and *Le Carnaval Romain* – generate a certain fidgety excitement, but there's no disputing which two compositions stand out as the best of his small output of orchestral work: the *Symphonie Fantastique*, the first and greatest Romantic symphony, and *Harold en Italie*, a sort of travelogue for viola and orchestra.

Symphonie fantastique

Both as a first symphony and as a work by a 27-year-old, the *Symphonie fantastique* is a staggering achievement. Written just three years after Beethoven's death, at a time when he was still regarded as a radical, this hour-long and five-movement work took several steps beyond Beethoven's symphonic structures. For one thing, this is the first symphony to make thorough use of the *idée fixe*, a single melody that reappears in different guises throughout the work – a concept that is the forerunner of the leitmotifs in Wagner and Richard Strauss. Furthermore, although composers had written scenic music before the *Symphonie fantastique* and simple musical onomatopoeia had been common for centuries (for example Vivaldi's *Four Seasons*), no composer had used instrumental music to present so specific a narrative drama. In short, this symphony is an opera without words.

Mythologizing Berlioz's neurotic obsession with Harriet Smithson, the "plot" of the *Symphonie fantastique* is an opium-induced phantasmagoria, in which the hero imagines the torrid progress of a love affair that ends ultimately in his execution for the murder of his lover. Berlioz supplies sub-titles to explain events: "Reveries – Passions"; "A Ball"; "Scene in the Country"; "March to the Scaffold" and "Dream of a Witches' Sabbath". The *idée fixe* runs chillingly through each movement and reaches its gruesome climax when it is coupled with the terrifying Dies Irae plainchant – Romanticism's ultimate musical theme.

Vienna Philharmonic Orchestra; Davis (Philips)

The symphony, with its vast forces, wild rhythms and extremes of loudness and softness, is a *tour de force* of orchestral writing and no one knows it better than Sir Colin Davis. His third recording of it, with the Vienna Philharmonic, has the advantage of superb sound and excellent playing.

Detroit Symphony Orchestra; Paray (Mercury; with *Hungarian March, Roman March, Corsair Overture & Roman Carnival Overture*)

This is an absolutely spine-tingling account by an orchestra and conductor completely of one mind. They present Berlioz as the high priest of Romanticism: brooding, darkly imaginative and with a ferocious energy which borders on the demented.

Harold en Italie

Although it was composed in 1834, the gestation of *Harold en Italie* began three years earlier. While crossing from Marseille to Leghorn, Berlioz met a sea captain who claimed to have ferried Byron – author of *Childe Harold's Pilgrimage* – around the Greek islands. But the real catalyst was Paganini (see p.393), who approached him for a viola concerto. Berlioz immediately abandoned the idea of a strict concerto in favour of what amounted to a symphony with obbligato viola, with the solo part conceived as a portrayal of "a kind of melancholy dreamer in the style of Byron's *Childe Harolde*". When Paganini realized that there was nothing in the score to display his notorious abilities he refused to play it and the two fell out. But when, later, he heard *Harold* performed, he threw himself at Berlioz's feet to beg forgiveness and later sent the composer a note comparing him to Beethoven – along with a gift of 20,000 francs.

The work is dominated by a central thematic idea, but Berlioz now takes the *idée fixe* a stage further – whereas in the *Symphonie fantastique* the *idée fixe* recurs unchanged, here the "Harold" idea appears in every movement but serves as the basis for thematic development. The rhythmic pungency is even more engaging than the symphony, and the melodies – especially in the adrenaline-pumping finale – are much more immediate. In effect Berlioz's second symphony, it has proved less popular than the first, but is arguably the superior work.

Imai; London Symphony Orchestra; Davis (Philips; with *Tristia*)

Davis correctly sees the piece as more a symphony than a concerto, and Nobuko Imai is an ideal partner, embedding the viola in the integral musical soundscape, and never clamouring for the limelight. Excellently recorded, the disc also includes the fascinating but little-known *Tristia* pieces.

Golani; San Diego Symphony Orchestra; Talmi (Naxos; with *Les francs juges* & *Rêverie et caprice*)

A very good and dramatic performance at budget price, with Rivka Golani a warm-toned soloist, is slightly marred by the rather "boxy" acoustic which rather lessens the immediacy of the playing.

Leonard Bernstein (1918–1990)

Leonard Bernstein's big break is the stuff of legend – substituting for the sick maestro Bruno Walter for a New York Philharmonic concert on 14 November, 1943, he became famous overnight, launching a meteoric and controversial career as a conductor. For some, Bernstein got right to the heart of Beethoven, Mahler and other great symphonists, giving himself unreservedly to the music's emotional pulse; for others, he was a self-indulgent showman, besotted with himself and with the audience's applause. Yet conducting was but one strand of a career that was remarkably varied and at the same time consistent.

From the mid-1950s Bernstein presented dozens of TV programmes – the most famous being the *Young People's Concerts* (1958–73) – in which he played and brilliantly explicated the works that he so manifestly loved. The basis for Bernstein's lectures was his belief that all music is rooted in a universal language that is basically tonal. This belief was fundamental to his own compositions, in which Bernstein strove to forge a connection between art music and the music of the American people. More specifically, he felt that jazz was the essential sound of the USA – though the jazz you hear in Bernstein's music is not so much a direct legacy of Duke Ellington or Jelly Roll Morton, but jazz as reworked by Gershwin and Aaron Copland.

As a composer his greatest successes were in music for the stage, and he created a string of hit shows that culminated in *West Side Story* (1957), a classic of American musical theatre. His theatrical instincts frequently spilled over into his concert works, Bernstein himself admitting to "a deep suspicion that every work I write, for whatever medium, is really theatre music in some way". Such compositions as his three symphonies, *Jeremiah*, *The Age of Anxiety* and *Kaddish*, are indeed profoundly dramatic, but they also draw sustenance from Bernstein's Jewish heritage, with its basis in synagogue chant.

As the 1960s progressed, Bernstein came under increasing fire from radical young musicians, for whom the serialist principles of Schoenberg, Berg and Webern, and their hardline successors Boulez and Stockhausen, were the new orthodoxy. Although Bernstein fought a vigorous rearguard action against the dogmatic rejection of the general public's taste, he began to lose his confidence as a composer, preferring instead to develop his role as the guardian of what he felt was best in music.

Yet even in the face of vilification Bernstein never relinquished his musical values, and his principles have come to be more relevant now than they were at the time. There may be some truth in the accusation that Bernstein's concert music is often nothing more than skilled pastiche, but it's equally true that he could be seen as the precursor of a generation of American composers – Adams, Glass, Reich and so on – who are as effusively theatrical, eclectic and tonal in their leanings as Bernstein was.

West Side Story

Of all Bernstein's music, it's the stage works that sum up best what he was all about, and

George Chakiris (Bernardo) leads three dancers in a scene from the film version of *West Side Story.*

of these *West Side Story* is the most mould-breaking as well as the most consistently tuneful. Transposing *Romeo and Juliet* to the gangland of New York's West Side in the 1950s, the score successfully modernizes the Broadway musical idiom, infusing it with a restless energy by way of complex rhythms and occasionally acerbic harmonies. It was not a huge success at its premiere – its reputation soared after the release of the film version in 1961. Though *West Side Story* is full of great songs, including "America", "Maria" and "Tonight", it's equally remarkable for the quality of its extensive dance music (which Bernstein later rearranged as a concert suite) and for its decidedly downbeat ending, breaking one of the cardinal rules of music theatre.

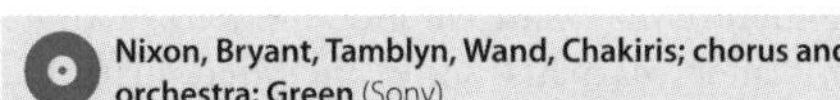
Nixon, Bryant, Tamblyn, Wand, Chakiris; chorus and orchestra; Green (Sony)

There are now a handful of recordings of *West Side Story*, but for those wanting the authentic buzz of the original the best place to go is to the film soundtrack. It's not the complete score but it's more than just highlights and it packs more of a punch than any subsequent version.

Te Kanawa, Carreras, Troyanos, Horne, Ollman; chorus and orchestra; Bernstein
(Deutsche Grammophon; 2 CDs; with *On the Waterfront* & *Symphonic Suite*)

Bernstein's own recording of the complete score remains controversial because of the way it gives the piece the full-blown operatic treatment. While exploiting his soloists' ability to elicit the kind of subtle vocal effects that would not be possible from Broadway singers, it's a moot point whether such vocal finesse is appropriate.

Heinrich Biber (1644–1704)

In the seventeenth century the violin consolidated its position as expressively the most wide-ranging of non-keyboard instruments. This was an age of great violin makers, like Amati and Stradivari, as well as outstanding performers like Corelli (see p.147). Italy was the centre of instrumental prowess, but the finest of all seventeenth-century virtuosos was Heinrich Biber, who spent most of his working life in Salzburg. A composer as well as a performer,

Biber was fascinated by the doctrine of the affections: the belief that emotional states such as tenderness, fear and anger could be given direct musical expression. Many Baroque composers pursued this idea but none did so with such a degree of quirkiness, flair and sheer experimental verve as Biber. Above all else in his violin sonatas, he reveals an astonishing combination of profound feeling and technical wizardry that suggests a brilliant improviser at work.

Biber was born in Warttenberg in Bohemia but probably received his early training in Vienna under Johann Schmelzer, the leading Austrian violinist of the day. Some time around 1668 he entered the service of Archbishop Karl von Liechtenstein-Kastelkorn, a music lover whose castle in Moravia boasted a fine musical establishment. In 1670, while on official business, Biber mysteriously abandoned his position while in Salzburg and entered the employ of another powerful churchman, the Prince-Archbishop of Salzburg, Maximilian Gandolph. He was to remain there for the rest of his life: beginning as a court violinist and rising to the rank of court *Kapellmeister* and cathedral choirmaster in 1684 before his eventual ennoblement in 1690. In his later years his duties included writing a substantial amount of large-scale choral music for the cathedral, among which the *Requiem in F* is outstanding. Despite his renown as a performer, there is no evidence to suggest that he travelled anywhere much farther than Munich. Nor was there any known contact with other major composers, apart from his colleague at Salzburg, George Muffat (a student of both Lully and Corelli), who shared Biber's enthusiasm for writing sonatas.

Violin Sonatas

The normal tuning of instruments of the violin family is in intervals five notes apart (fifths). However, much of Biber's music employs a device called *scordatura* whereby an instrument is tuned differently from piece to piece. This was done for a variety of reasons: to extend the possible range of notes, to make certain chords playable, and to change the character of the instrument by creating new sonorities. In *The Mystery Sonatas*, composed for a religious ceremony celebrating the Rosary, Biber takes the use of *scordatura* to imaginative extremes. Each sonata corresponds to an event in the life of Jesus or the Virgin Mary and, though they employ stylized dance forms and sets of variations, each attempts to evoke a particular devotional mood and sometimes to create a particular scene – such as the fluttering of angelic wings in No. 1 (*The Annunciation*) or the rising of the sun in No. 11 (*The Resurrection*). The set ends with a passacaglia for unaccompanied violin, the earliest known extended work for solo violin and an obvious forerunner of J.S. Bach's great *Chaconne*. In the other outstanding set of violin sonatas of 1681, *scordatura* is rarely used: they are, nevertheless, highly inventive and technically demanding works. Once again, sets of variations abound, as does brilliant passage work, often over a sustained note in the bass part. Certainly, these works are occasionally flashy for the sheer hell of it, but more often their sudden changes of mood reveal a brilliant, restless and essentially improvisatory musical temperament.

The Mystery Sonatas: Holloway (Virgin; 2 CDs; available as download)

John Holloway's sinewy and rather bare violin tone is well-suited to the generally austere nature of this music. Though it is possible to ignore the religious aspect of these sonatas, and to listen to them individually, Holloway communicates a real sense of progression (despite varying the continuo instruments) so that the cumulative effect of the full set, culminating in the solo passacaglia, is extremely powerful.

Eight Violin Sonatas; Sonata Representativa; Two Passacaglias: Romanesca (Harmonia Mundi; 2 CDs)

Andrew Manze, the violinist of Romanesca, is a Baroque specialist whose panache and lack of inhibition are ideal for these works. He is particularly adept at an almost throwaway manner with Biber's more filigree passage work and displays an appropriately wide range of tone colour. The slight fluctuations of mood are judged with all the nonchalant ease of a good jazz musician.

Harmonia Artificiosa-Ariosa

As well as vehicles for his own prodigious virtuosity, Biber also wrote music for larger ensembles. Most of these chamber works employ conventional string tuning; the exception is one of his most striking works, the *Harmonia artificiosa-ariosa*, a collection of seven partitas for two instruments and bass, six of which employ *scordatura* tuning. These are magical works: more tightly formed and less capricious than the violin sonatas but with a similar depth of feeling and abounding in contrapuntal vigour and strange harmonies.

Biber was an exact contemporary of Pachelbel (see p.392) and there are moments in these works which resemble the latter's famous *Canon and*

Gigue. Biber, however, was a more sophisticated composer and the partitas' many variations display an endless capacity for unpredictable invention. Particularly spectacular are the air and thirteen variations of *Partita VI* (the non-*scordatura* partita), which include a canon in which the voices are only separated by half a beat's difference.

Musica Antiqua Köln; Goebel
(Archiv; 2 CDs)

Reinhard Goebel and Musica Antiqua Köln sound as though they have this music in their veins, so assured and full of flair are these performances. They don't play up the eccentricity, as some other recordings do, instead there's a prevailing sense of *joie de vivre* tempered by an acute awareness of Biber's amazing sonorities.

Missa Salisburgensis

Although Biber's work as a violinist is what made his reputation, recent scholarship has begun to uncover the full range of his talents – notably in the field of choral music, much of which has been rediscovered in the last 30 years. His appointment to Salzburg's new Baroque cathedral in the 1680s made Biber responsible for major church events there, resulting in a number of extravagant compositions that use the epic space to the full. His most ambitious choral work is the *Missa Salisburgensis*, the 1682 "Salzburg Mass", composed to mark 1100 years since the archdiocese was founded. Lost until the nineteenth century, when one of Biber's successors as choirmaster reputedly discovered pages of the manuscript being used to wrap vegetables, it was only attributed to Biber in the 1970s. Scored for no fewer than 53 vocal parts and a battalion of instrumentalists, it is an extraordinary piece, contrasting great sheets of sound with delicately traced duets and energetic instrumental interludes. Like Biber's nine or so other settings of the mass, it points in very different directions at once: undeniably influenced by the complex multi-choir writing of Venetian composers such as Gabrieli, but also reflecting the intimate expressiveness of Buxtehude.

Gabrieli Consort & Players; Musica Antiqua Köln; McCreesh (Archiv)

From the awe-inspiring opening chords you know that you're in for something spectacular, and this disc doesn't disappoint. Paul McCreesh has forged a reputation for restaging long-lost liturgical spectaculars, and this spaciously recorded, high-octane performance is one of his finest. Other accounts register more of the *Missa Salisburgensis*'s detail, but none has this one's fierce drama.

Harrison Birtwistle (1934–)

The raw and visceral music of Harrison Birtwistle often sounds as if it has sprung into being from a point before or beyond the modern world, evoking elemental human or natural forces, whether the stylized violence of Greek tragedy, the elemental cycles of the natural world or the destructive march of time itself. Many of Birtwistle's earlier compositions possess the massive, rough-hewn quality of a prehistoric monument, though as his career has progressed he has also shown an increasing ability to produce music of spare lyrical beauty and, on occasion, haunting delicacy.

During the 1950s, English music was dominated by the homespun pastoral aesthetic of Vaughan Williams and his followers, while European experimentalism was largely viewed with suspicion and disdain. It was in this claustrophobic environment that the so-called "Manchester School" – a group of students at the Royal Manchester College of Music consisting of composers Birtwistle, Peter Maxwell Davies and Alexander Goehr, plus conductor Elgar Howarth and pianist John Ogdon – began their careers, looking to the latest developments on the continent for inspiration. Birtwistle bided his time, studying clarinet and keeping his ambitions as a composer to himself. It wasn't until 1965 that he scored his first major critical success with the ensemble piece *Tragœdia*. The violent musical imagery of the work – choruses of shrieking woodwind and madly plucked harp alternating with hushed interludes of intense but muted lyricism – owes something to the example of Greek tragedy, an influence which also gave the work its title (meaning "goat dance") and which was to have a lasting impact on Birtwistle.

Harrison Birtwistle in discussion with conductor Martin Brabbins.

The ritualized violence of *Tragœdia* reappears in even more extreme form in Birtwistle's notorious chamber opera, *Punch and Judy* (1967), a work which somehow manages to combine burlesque seaside entertainment, the stylized forms of Greek tragedy and an acerbic, ultra-modernist score into a convincing – if extremely disquieting – whole. The work that really signalled the arrival of Birtwistle as one of the major composers of his generation, however, was *The Triumph of Time* (1972), a monumental orchestral procession inspired by Bruegel's depiction of the remorseless progress of Time and Death. The snatches of doleful cor anglais melody which memorably punctuate the work exemplify the vein of plangent lyricism which was increasingly to temper and enrich Birtwistle's style. From the 1970s, his often more muted and sombre soundscapes seemed to owe something to the bleak and depopulated landscapes of Birtwistle's native northern England – an unexpected reinvention of the pastoral idiom against which the members of the Manchester School had so determinedly fought.

In 1986 came the long-awaited premiere of Birtwistle's second opera, *The Mask of Orpheus*, which represents the summation of his love of ritualized, quasi-mythological narratives. Another six operas have followed since (along with other music-theatre works), including the "mechanical pastoral" *Yan Tan Tethera* (1988), a supernatural tale of two shepherds, their sheep and the devil, the monumental *Gawain* (1991), whose bleak narrative counterpoints the Arthurian hero's trials against the remorseless cycle of the seasons, and the innovative recent music-theatre work *Semper Dowland, semper dolens* (2009), using material (freely arranged and adapted) by John Dowland. Alongside his operas, Birtwistle's prolific output has also begun to include an increasing number of vocal works (most notably the hour-long *Pulse Shadows* of 1996, setting poems by Paul Celan), as well as many purely instrumental pieces, such as the masterful *Secret Theatre* (1985), the massive *Earth Dances* (1986) for orchestra and, most recently, the innovative *Theseus Games* (2002) for large ensemble and two conductors – works in which the savagery of earlier pieces seethes, volcanically, beneath an often richly poignant lyricism.

The Mask of Orpheus

Birtwistle laboured from 1973 to 1984 on his "lyric tragedy" *The Mask of Orpheus* (1986), arguably his greatest work. Vast and unwieldy, the opera presents the story of Orpheus and Eurydice, not cleansed as it was in Baroque operas, but as a tale of fundamental violence and tragedy; and it tells that tale over and over again, viewing it and reviewing it from every possible angle in 42 "trinities of action". It is a work like no other, yet it also seeks to encompass the whole history of opera, music, dance, theatre, and language itself. The principal characters appear in three guises: the mythical, the heroic and the human; and each is played by three performers: a singer (with a puppet double), a dancer and a mime. There is also an elaborate electronic score. On paper this sounds impenetrable; if performance does not make everything crystal clear, it nevertheless carries a powerful physical weight that transcends narrative clarity.

Garrison, Bronder, Rigby, Owens, Angel; BBC Singers and Symphony Orchestra; Davis (NMC; 3 CDs)

It was brave of Andrew Davis to revive the opera in 1996, albeit in semi-staged form; and braver still of NMC to issue this live recording of a piece that cries out for theatrical presentation to make sense of its convolutions. Excellent documentation casts light where it can, but in the end it's the sheer commitment of all involved that carries the listener to a point where the score's fathomless riches overcome all doubts.

The Triumph of Time

Birtwistle often describes his works as "imaginary landscapes", and this is one of his finest, a monumental, thirty-minute orchestral procession-cum-funeral march (inspired by and named after the macabre etching by Pieter Bruegel the Elder) in which the listener is led slowly through ever-changing musical scenery, viewing the same landmarks from constantly evolving perspectives. This geographical, rather than chronological, approach to time is typical of Birtwistle's music, as is the work's hauntingly sombre lyricism – powerfully muted for most of its length, but rising at its centre to a vast and shattering climax. Two musical signposts stand out from the constant flux: a three-note melodic fragment for soprano saxophone and a more elaborate cor anglais solo, reminding us of Birtwistle's lyrical gifts, all the more moving for never being overindulged.

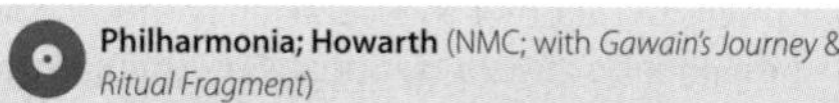

Philharmonia; Howarth (NMC; with *Gawain's Journey & Ritual Fragment*)

Elgar Howarth has been a champion of Birtwistle's music from the beginning of the composer's career, and here delivers a performance of tremendous power – suitably monolithic but never excessively static. Also included are *Gawain's Journey*, a surprisingly successful precis of Birtwistle's opera *Gawain*, with vocal parts reassigned to solo instruments, and the eloquent, elegaic *Ritual Fragment*.

Silbury Air & Secret Theatre

The burgeoning lyricism of Birtwistle's music during the later 1970s and early 1980s was accompanied by an increasingly sophisticated attitude to rhythm and musical time – a marriage of the pastoral with the mechanical which has become a leading feature of many of his pieces. Perhaps the classic instrumental example of this is *Silbury Air* (1977), in which a "pulse labyrinth" – a kind of road map of different musical speeds – determines the routes along which the composition travels as it wends its way through one of Birtwistle's most memorable and dynamic landscapes.

The lyrical and the mechanical are again leading themes in *Secret Theatre* (1985), a work which magnificently sums up all Birtwistle's musical achievements to that date. The work is scored for chamber ensemble divided into two parts: a "Cantus" (of mainly wind instruments), whose stream of endless melody runs virtually unbroken throughout, and a "Continuum", whose mechanical accompaniment, like a kind of ceaselessly ticking musical clock, counterpoints and contradicts the Cantus's lyrical effusions.

London Sinfonietta; Howarth
(Etcetera; with *Carmen arcadiae mechanicae perpetuum*)

The definitive Birtwistle recording, performed by the excellent London Sinfonietta, who commissioned all three works on the CD – the third is *Carmen arcadiae*, a brilliant jigsaw puzzle of brightly coloured musical fragments which are dismantled and reassembled in constantly shifting patterns as the work progresses.

Earth Dances

Birtwistle's exuberant, forty-minute orchestral showpiece, *Earth Dances*, takes its title and structure from a geological metaphor, dividing the orchestra into six different layers – or "strata", as the composer describes them – whose shifting relationships evoke the massive natural forces that shape the planet. Sometimes the strata stack up immensely; at other moments, they thin to the most diaphanous textures; but always there is the sense of returning to the same point, only to discover that the view has changed in the interim. On top of these seismic musical processes, Birtwistle creates a virtuoso orchestral superstructure whose riotous details suggest the teeming surface life of the Earth in all its protean variety.

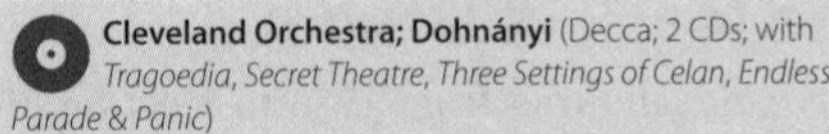

Cleveland Orchestra; Dohnányi (Decca; 2 CDs; with *Tragoedia, Secret Theatre, Three Settings of Celan, Endless Parade & Panic*)

Christoph von Dohnányi's aristocratic orchestra tussles mightily with the Lancastrian grit of one of Birtwistle's grandest structures. With fine accounts of the jazzy "concertos" for trumpet (*Endless Parade*) and saxophone (*Panic*), plus Boulez's accounts of *Secret Theatre* and *Tragoedia*, this set offers an excellent cross-section of Birtwistle's career.

Georges Bizet (1838–1875)

Like so many nineteenth-century opera composers, Bizet attained immortality through a single score – *Carmen*. He completed its fourth and final act in 1874; a year later he was dead. Bizet packed a lot into his short life. By the age of nine he had entered the Paris Conservatoire and within months was winning every major prize for piano, organ and composition. In 1857, aged nineteen, he won the coveted Prix de Rome, which set him on a steady course to security and fame. An example of his abilities at this time can be found in his *Symphony in C Major*, an astonishing work which reflects the influence of Gounod, whom Bizet had befriended in 1856.

His first major opera, *Les pêcheurs des perles* (The Pearl Fishers), was produced at the Opéra Comique in 1863. It was written to an appalling libretto whose authors later admitted that, had they been aware of Bizet's talents, they would not have saddled him with such a "white elephant". However, the public warmed to Bizet's sensual and melodic music, and *Les pêcheurs des perles* became one of Bizet's very few immediate successes – though its continued survival is primarily due to one lovely duet for tenor and baritone. He went on to compose a number of comic and dramatic operas, many of which were left incomplete, and none of which suggested anything more remarkable than proficiency. Then in 1872 Bizet began to take an interest in Prosper Merimée's short novel *Carmen*; the Opéra Comique, however, was far from enthusiastic – they didn't want death on their stage, and neither were they keen on a project dominated by thieves, Gypsies and cigar-makers. Despite these misgivings, the manager finally committed himself to a production and on 3 March, 1875, *Carmen* was given its premiere.

Bizet described the result as "a definite and hopeless flop" (an exaggeration) and, ever prone to psychosomatic illness, took to his bed. Four hours after the curtain had fallen on the 33rd performance, he died from the second of two major heart attacks.

Carmen

Carmen is the first "realistic" French opera, merging spoken dialogue, intense local colour and well-crafted tragic drama into a compelling masterpiece. It soon attracted praise from influential quarters: Wagner wrote of it, "Here thank God ... is somebody with ideas in his head"; both Brahms and Tchaikovsky adored it; and Nietzsche used the opera as a stick with which to beat Wagner. However, the hot-blooded characterization of Carmen, and of her rival lovers Don José and the bullfighter Escamillo, scandalized the first audiences, as did the tragic ending, in which Don José murders the heroine.

Bizet's evocation of the opera's Spanish locales displays amazing abilities as an orchestrator, while Carmen is arguably the most successful mezzo-soprano role in all opera. Her manipulative and magnetic personality is articulated through music of graphic sensuality – her opening habanera and seguidilla are especially sexy. It is hard to imagine how critics could have attacked *Carmen* for being tuneless. It boasts more memorable tunes than any other French opera except Gounod's *Faust* – the only French opera as popular as *Carmen*.

Berganza, Domingo, Cotrubas, Milnes; Ambrosian Singers; London Symphony Orchestra; Abbado (Deutsche Grammophon; 3 CDs)

This is a superbly professional *Carmen* and the most Spanish ever recorded. Placido Domingo makes a smooth

but powerful Don José, while Teresa Berganza is a very sexy Carmen, suggesting a youthful capriciousness that's absent from most interpretations. Sherill Milnes delivers the "Toreador Song" with real oomph, and Ileana Cotrubas is a vibrant, if unusually weighty, Micaëla.

Price, Corelli, Freni, Merrill; Vienna Boys Choir; Vienna State Opera Chorus; Vienna Philharmonic Orchestra; Karajan (RCA; 3 CDs)

Franco Corelli is an outstanding Don José: his massive voice is incomparably thrilling, and he produces a genuinely tragic portrayal. Leontyne Price is not the most characterful Carmen, but brings an effective sense of malice to the part. Karajan's approach is exciting if unsubtle, but with Mirella Freni and Robert Merrill in marvellous form this set is the most entertaining introduction to Bizet.

Symphony in C Major

Bizet's finest orchestral score, the *Symphony in C Major*, was composed in 1855, when he had only recently turned seventeen – though it was not performed until 1935, having been discovered two years earlier in the archives of the Paris Conservatoire by Bizet biographer D.C. Parker. Like its model, Gounod's *Symphony No. 1*, Bizet's work makes no claims to originality, but it's a fresh, ingenious and uninhibited piece, something like a French version of Schubert in its beautiful melodic writing (though Bizet could not have known Schubert's large-scale works) and scored with a wonderful transparency. Like Mendelssohn's early music, this is more than mere juvenilia.

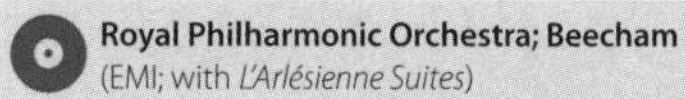

Royal Philharmonic Orchestra; Beecham (EMI; with *L'Arlésienne Suites*)

Sir Thomas Beecham's charming and light-footed account of the symphony is full of wit and colour. His moulding of Bizet's intricate architecture is unfailingly secure and the Royal Philharmonic Orchestra responds to his demands with engaging immediacy.

L'Arlésienne Suites Nos. 1 & 2

In 1872 Bizet wrote the incidental music for Alphonse Daudet's play *L'Arlésienne*, a tragedy set in the author's native Provence about a man who kills himself because of his unrequited love for a girl from Arles. Bizet's discreet and sensitive music did not guarantee the play's success and it closed after a few weeks. Rather than waste the music, Bizet took four of the pieces and turned them into a concert suite which proved extremely popular, and soon after his death, his friend Ernest Guiraud made a second suite, again of four pieces, which included a minuet based around a duet from Bizet's opera *La jolie fille de Perth*. Both are frequently performed and contain a wealth of sparkling and inventive music: particularly delightful is the Prélude from *Suite No. 1* in which a set of variations around a strident melody is followed by a plaintive solo for the (then new) saxophone.

Royal Philharmonic Orchestra; Beecham (EMI; with *Symphony in C Major*)

Beecham gives an equally lively performance of the two *L'Arlésienne* suites. Once again, the approach is nimble and stylish, but these performances also communicate a strong sense of dramatic spontaneity.

Luigi Boccherini (1743–1805)

Though Boccherini was a highly successful cellist and a prolific composer – especially of chamber music – he is largely known today for just one work, the minuet from his *String Quintet in E*, a piece that gained a new lease of life when it was used on the soundtrack of the classic British comedy film *The Ladykillers*. He was almost an exact contemporary of Haydn, and his music possesses a similar classical elegance and charm – indeed, the minuet bears a marked

resemblance to Haydn's equally popular *Serenade* (now thought not to be by Haydn). It is true that he rarely matches the depth or passion of the older composer, but to dismiss him, as the violinist Giuseppe Pupo did, as "Haydn's wife" is grossly unfair. His music might occasionally be insipid, but it's full of good tunes, always pleasant, and sometimes startlingly original.

Boccherini was born in Lucca, the son of a double-bass player and cellist, who gave him his first lessons. His early career was spent as a cello virtuoso, and he took part in the first ever public string quartet concerts in Milan in 1765, at the same time forming a friendship with one of the violinists, Filippo Manfredi. The two decided to tour together, travelling to Paris in 1767 and then on to Madrid a year later, where Boccherini gained the patronage of the Infante Don Luis, the king's younger brother. He was to remain in Madrid for the rest of his life, serving Don Luis until 1785 and then the Benavente-Osuna family until 1798, while at the same time providing music for Prince Frederick-William of Prussia.

His final years were full of misfortune. The Parisian music publisher Pleyel took advantage of Boccherini's good humour and generosity, refusing to return manuscripts and demanding changes in his style to match public taste. Two daughters died in 1802, and his wife and another daughter in 1805 – events that almost certainly contributed to his mental decline. He died in poverty, although ironically his music was to enjoy a real vogue almost immediately after his death.

String Quintets

"There is perhaps no instrumental music more ingenious, elegant and pleasing, than his quintets", wrote Charles Burney in 1770. Boccherini went on to write over a hundred of them plus nearly as many string quartets, so it is unsurprising that some of his chamber music is bland and repetitious. That said, several of the quintets involve the interesting imitation of non-musical sounds, like birdsong, in his quintet *L'Ucelliera*, or – even more strikingly – street sounds in the quintet entitled *Night Music in the Streets of Madrid*. Boccherini's quintets mostly employ two violins, two cellos and a viola, a combination partly dictated by the musicians available in Don Luis's retinue. The fact that this is court music doesn't prevent a dark and sometimes edgy mood appearing – most frequently in the form of sombre and introspective slow movements.

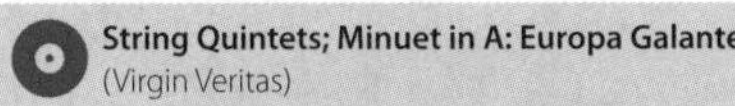

String Quintets; Minuet in A: Europa Galante (Virgin Veritas)

These are performances of real flair from Europa Galante, led by their first violinist Fabio Bondi, which reveal Boccherini's depth as well as his sophistication. The chosen quintets, all from Opus 25, are exceptionally lively and inventive – No. 6 in A minor is particularly distinctive for its quirky and restless outer movements. The group also give a highly spirited rendition of the famous minuet.

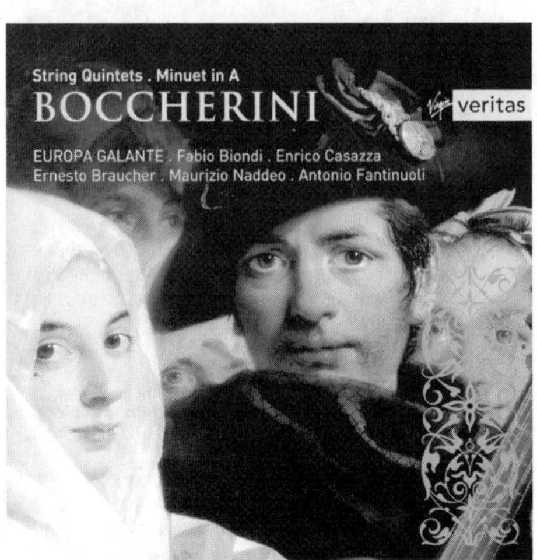

Guitar Quintets

The Marquis of Benavente-Osuna was a talented amateur guitarist, for whom Boccherini wrote six guitar quintets which evoke the sunny, easy-going atmosphere of the early paintings of Goya (another of the marquis's employees). One remarkable aspect of these quintets is the variety of effects that Boccherini spins out of this combination of instruments. In some pieces the guitar is clearly the dominant voice; in others, like the boldly dramatic first movement of the first quintet, it is the violin that prevails. The most extraordinary single piece, though, is the last movement from the fourth quintet where, after a slow introduction, a full-blooded fandango lets rip, complete with strumming guitar, insistent rhythmic repetitions and even castanets.

Romero; Academy of St Martin-in-the-Fields Chamber Ensemble (Philips; 2 CDs)

This is a fine introduction to Boccherini's music. Delicacy and wit predominate, but Pepe Romero and the Academy chamber players are not afraid to let go where necessary – the performance of the *Fandango Quintet* is particularly thrilling.

Cello Concertos

Boccherini wrote at least eleven cello concertos, and all of them were written for himself to perform, thus they often make difficult technical demands on the soloist, with much of the solo writing not just richly ornamented – as in the wonderfully decorative passage work of the third concerto's slow movement – but also placed consistently high in the register. As with most of his music, the prevailing mood of these works is of an easy gracefulness and poise. In the nineteenth century a cellist named Grützmacher took movements from two of the best concertos and arranged them into a single work, a romanticized hybrid that is still, after the minuet, Boccherini's best-known work.

 **Cello Concertos Vol.1, Nos. 1–4: Hugh; Scottish Chamber Orchestra; Halstead** (Naxos)

These works really benefit from period instrument performances but, sadly, the two best versions (Coin on Astrée and Bylsma on Sony) aren't currently in the catalogue. Track them down if you can. In their absence, this disc (part of a three-disc survey of all the concertos) is extremely enjoyable and includes the glorious G major concerto. Tim Hugh is the eloquent and persuasive soloist, well supported by the Scottish Chamber Orchestra.

Alexander Borodin (1833–1887)

Like many of his Russian contemporaries, Borodin was essentially an amateur composer, in the sense that he had a flourishing career in a completely different field and composed in his spare time – which accounts for both his relatively small output and the high proportion of works that he never found time to finish. Yet Borodin made a distinctive contribution to the Russian musical nationalist cause in the 1870s and 1880s. In addition to his fertile melodic talent, he had a good ear for exotic orchestral sounds, and created some pungent harmonic writing that gives his music a real strength and originality.

He was the illegitimate son of a Georgian prince and by the tradition of such things was given the name of one of the prince's serfs. Despite displaying a childhood passion for music, he trained as a chemist and physician and it was as an academic chemist that he first made his name, engaging in important research as a professor at the Academy of Medico-Surgery in St Petersburg.

Although he had been attempting to compose since his teens, he began to exploit his compositional skills only when, as a young man, he came under the influence of Mily Balakirev (1837–1910), the figurehead of a group of radical musicians based in St Petersburg (the others were César Cui, Modest Mussorgsky and Nikolai Rimsky-Korsakov). He refused to contemplate cutting down on his scientific responsibilities, and the five years it took for him to complete his first work, his *Symphony No. 1*, set the pattern for his rate of composition. Characteristically, he worked on the opera *Prince Igor* for some eighteen years, from penning the first ideas in 1869 to his death in 1887, when it was still not complete. In the meantime, he did manage to finish one of his most popular works, his *Symphony No. 2* (after nearly seven years' work), though its successor, begun in 1885, also remained incomplete on his death and, like much of the opera, was made performable by Alexander Glazunov (see p.212).

Prince Igor

Borodin's first and only complete opera, *The Bogatyrs* (1867), was an unsuccessful comic parody of grand opera and was followed by an equally futile bid to write a serious opera, *The Tsar's Bride*. But in *Prince Igor*, rambling though some of it may be, he created a worthy counterpart to Russian opera's greatest historical tragedy, Mussorgsky's *Boris Godunov*. Set in twelfth-century Russia, the story tells of Igor and his son Vladimir, who leave home to fight the Polovtsi tribe. They are captured and treated well – the Polovtsi chief Khan Konchak entertains them with dancing (the "Polovtsian Dances") and Vladimir falls in love with the Kahn's daughter, Konchakovna. Igor escapes, to continue fighting and return to his wife Yaroslavna; Vladimir stays with his captors, and marries Konchakovna. It is more an opera of tableaux than of forward-moving action, and gave Borodin the chance to reveal his flair for oriental imagery and orchestral colour, best demonstrated in the orchestral highlights that, despite the opera's rarity on stage, have always been popular in the concert hall and on record. The overture, reputedly written by Glazunov from memories of Borodin's piano improvisations, is a vivid foretaste of what's to come; the other famous excerpts – a "Polovtsian March", the "Dance of the Polovtsian Maidens" and the choral "Polovtsian Dances" – all come from the scene set in the encampment of Igor's enemies.

Prince Igor: Kit, Gorchakova, Grigorian, Ognovenko, Minjelkiev; Kirov Theatre Chorus and Orchestra; Gergiev (Philips; 3 CDs)

Recorded in conjunction with a 1993 Kirov production, this is by far the best *Prince Igor* ever recorded. Gergiev gives a dynamic, sometimes ferocious, reading of the score, animating even the weakest scenes. Mikhail Kit's ringing bass lacks definition, but he is a formidable presence as Igor. Galina Gorchakova's soprano has a glorious bloom and she brings both dignity and sweetness to Yaroslavna.

Overture & Polovtsian Dances: National Philharmonic Orchestra & Chorus; Tjeknavorian (RCA; with *Symphony No. 2* & *In the Steppes of Central Asia*)

The *Price Igor* orchestral excerpts can be found on any number of Russian music compilations. This is one of the best simply because conductor Loris Tjeknavorian so clearly relishes the fevered energy of the music and his performers respond in kind. The inclusion of two of Borodin's best orchestral works makes this the perfect single disc introduction to the composer.

Symphonies & Orchestral Works

Although Borodin in effect wrote only two and a half symphonies, they represent a significant contribution to the history of the form in Russia. Like Tchaikovsky's earlier symphonies, Borodin's employ typically Russian harmonies, melodies and rhythms against a fairly conventional Germanic formal background. *Symphony No. 1*, in particular, looks back to Schumann, one of Borodin's prime influences at the time, yet is a distinctly Russian work, particularly in the use of a folk song in the Scherzo and the oriental lyricism of the slow movement. *Symphony No. 2* – the best of them – represents his first fully mature work and demonstrates all his most characterful features: rhythmic drive, grandeur, nostalgia and exuberance. Much of it was derived from sketches for *Prince Igor*, and it inhabits the same world of epic romance. From reminiscences by his colleagues Borodin clearly had the whole of his *Symphony No. 3* in his head, but only completed the spellbinding second movement and sketched the first.

Of Borodin's other orchestral works only one is a self-contained original work for orchestra. *In the Steppes of Central Asia* is a marvellously rich tone poem depicting an oriental caravan (evocatively suggested by a cor anglais melody) crossing the central Asian plains with an escort of Russian soldiers.

Symphonies Nos. 1–3: CSR Symphony Orchestra Bratislava; Gunzenhauser (Naxos)

The budget-price CD from Stephen Gunzenhauser and the authentically Slav-sounding Czechoslovak Radio Symphony Orchestra of Bratislava is among the most successful in the Naxos catalogue, with brilliant performances and a vivid recording quality that's better than several bigger-name companies.

Symphony No. 2 & In the Steppes of Central Asia: National Philharmonic Orchestra; Tjeknavorian (RCA; with *Overture & Polovtsian Dances*)

The second is arguably the best of Borodin's, symphonies and Tjeknavorian and his forces do it proud bringing out all the rich orchestral colouring and communicating the work's epic sweep. *In the Steppes of Central Asia* gets a no less powerful account, making this the perfect one-stop Borodin disc.

String Quartets

Borodin's mature chamber music comprises two delightful string quartets, the composition of which was prompted by the formation of the first professional Russian string quartet in 1871. The second is by far the more popular, largely because of its famous slow movement, a ravishing, orientally flavoured nocturne that has gained a separate life of its own in versions for string orchestra as well as in its original scoring. This is framed by two elegant movements that are essentially dialogues between the cello (Borodin's own instrument) and first violin, and the work finishes with a rigorous finale, which opens with question-and-answer exchanges and continues with some energetic contrapuntal writing. Written during a summer holiday in 1881 and dedicated to Borodin's wife, it's a highly personal work, but it exudes an overriding sense of contentment.

Lindsay Quartet
(ASV; with *String Sextet in D*)

These finely judged and sensitively nuanced performances are an absolute joy, with the Lindsays emphasizing the warm lyricism of the quartets without ever slipping into sentimentality. The rare but charming *String Sextet* is an added bonus.

Borodin Quartet
(Chandos)

Named after the composer, the legendary Russian quartet recorded these works for the state label, Melodiya, in 1983. They are delightful, engaging performances which, now remastered by Chandos, still stand the test of time despite the slightly enclosed sound.

Lili Boulanger (1893–1918)

Lili Boulanger was an astonishing talent whose reputation has been largely eclipsed by that of her older sister Nadia, one of the most influential teachers and musicologists of the twentieth century. Yet in her tragically short life she produced music – in particular for the voice – that can stand comparison with virtually anything written at that time in France, and had she lived longer it's almost certain that she would have become one of the century's great composers. Despite the advocacy of her sister and a phalanx of other musicians, she remains shamefully neglected.

The sisters came from a long line of musicians and were educated by their aristocratic Russian mother, establishing a cultural connection that was strengthened by the Parisian vogue for all things Russian following the first season of Diaghilev's Ballets Russes in 1909. In fact her music shows a greater debt to Debussy and her teacher and mentor Fauré than it does to Rimsky-Korsakov or Stravinsky. In 1913 Boulanger became the first woman ever to win the coveted Prix de Rome, which was awarded for her dramatic cantata *Faust et Hélène* (her father had also won the prize in 1835). This was one of her most substantial works, along with the unfinished opera *La Princesse Maleine* which, like Debussy's *Pelleas et Mélisande*, was based on a play by Maeterlinck.

Boulanger was an invalid for most of her life, seriously weakened by bronchial pneumonia at the age of 2 and eventually dying of cancer at the age of 24. Yet by all accounts she was also remarkably self-assured and determined, attributes that are mirrored in her music. In view of her illness, and the social context of a country mired in the hell of World War I, it's scarcely surprising that much of her small, largely vocal, output is often tinged with desolation.

Faust et Hélène & Choral Music

Candidates for the Prix de Rome had to set a prescribed text, which in 1913 was Eugène Adenis's *Faust et Hélène*, loosely based on Part II of Goethe's *Faust* – Mephisto's conjuring up, at Faust's command, of Helen of Troy. Boulanger's achievement was to elevate her material into a completely convincing world of dark and claustrophobic passions. There's a debt to Wagner in its expansive chromaticism and to Debussy in the directness of its utterance, and yet, at the same time, the voice is entirely her own. While there's a prevailing sensuousness to the vocal writing, the dramatic momentum of this half-hour scene never subsides.

Boulanger was a Catholic who poured a deeply religious intensity into much of her choral music. Of her three settings of the psalms, *Psalm 24* is a declamatory cry of jubilation for four-part chorus and tenor soloist in which powerful brass writing and modal harmonies provide a raw, primitive edge. Even finer is her setting of *Psalm 130*, the "De Profundis", for alto and tenor soloists, chorus and orchestra, composed between 1910 and 1917. This is a highly personal creation of great solemnity, resembling Fauré in its harmonies if not in its sentiment. An overwhelming sense of mystery pervades the music – there are hints of plainsong – suggesting a deeply felt awe at the power of God's presence.

Faust et Hélène; Psalms 24 & 130: BBC Philharmonic; City of Birmingham Symphony Chorus; Tortelier (Chandos; with *D'un matin de printemps* & *D'un soir triste*)

Justifiably hailed on its release in 2000, this outstanding disc should help to redress the neglect that Boulanger's music still suffers. *Faust et Hélène* is especially well served: a trio of fine soloists – Jason Howard, Bonaventura Bottone and Lynne Dawson – create a powerfully dramatic atmosphere, while conductor Yan Pascal Tortelier brings out the richly varied sonorities of each piece with subtlety and restraint.

Songs

Boulanger always loved the music of Fauré and many of her songs reveal his influence, particularly in the way the soloist and pianist are equal partners. Her outstanding work in this genre, *Clairières dans le ciel* (Clearings in the Heavens), is a cycle for male singer of thirteen songs written during her residency in Rome in 1914. The poems are by the symbolist Francis Jammes who was a close friend of Henri Duparc (see p.169) and there is something of Duparc in the music's subtle chromaticism and, more significantly, in the way Boulanger identifies so completely with the texts she sets. The music perfectly captures the bittersweet mood of the poems in which memories of a lost love are prompted by chance association with nature or everyday impressions, and which like Schubert's *Winterreise* ends in profound despair. Word-painting and some exquisitely delicate piano writing make this an exceptionally effective and poignant cycle.

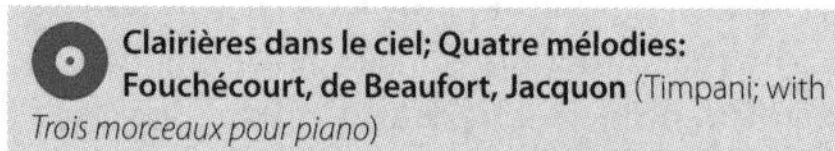

Clairières dans le ciel; Quatre mélodies: Fouchécourt, de Beaufort, Jacquon (Timpani; with *Trois morceaux pour piano*)

Tenor Jean-Paul Fouchécourt, with his light but rounded tone, makes a near-ideal soloist for *Clairières dans le ciel*, finding just the right balance between the sensuous and the melancholy, and conveying the protagonist's gradual loss of hope. Mezzo-soprano Sonia de Beaufort is the effective soloist on the early *Quatre mélodies*.

Pierre Boulez (1925–)

Composer, conductor, theorist, visionary: Pierre Boulez has been many things to many people. To some he is quite simply the single most significant classical musician of the past fifty years; to others he's a superannuated modernist whose natural gifts have been stifled by his constant need to intellectualize and pontificate. Whatever one's attitude, Boulez's pervasive influence on today's musical culture – from avant-garde compositional theory to the concert repertoire of the world's major symphony orchestras – is impossible to ignore.

Born in 1925, in Montbrison in southeastern France, Boulez studied composition with Messiaen in Paris before bursting spectacularly into view in the late 1940s with a sequence of remarkably accomplished pieces such as the first two piano sonatas and the cantatas *Le visage nuptial* and *Le soleil des eaux* – works which at once summarize and surpass all that was then most modern in music. Repudiating all the compromises with tradition which, he claimed, marred the work even of composers as progressive as Schoenberg and Stravinsky, Boulez set about creating a brave new musical world, untouched by sentiment or retrospection – as in the fearlessly complex and nerve-janglingly dissonant *Piano Sonata No. 2*, which expresses an exuberance bordering almost on rage, making clear Boulez's determination, not so much to wipe the slate clean as to smash it to bits.

Thus established as the *enfant terrible* of French music, Boulez embarked on a period of research into ways of writing music that was completely new, an enterprise he shared with other young iconoclasts such as Stockhausen and Nono – the so-called "Darmstadt School" (see p.384), named after the German town which hosted a summer school devoted to their ideals. It was Messiaen's uncharacteristically austere *Mode de valeurs et d'intensités* which showed how, by systematically ordering pitch, rhythm and dynamics in strict numerical sequences, one could write "automatic" music. And it was Boulez who produced, in *Structures I* for two pianos, the classic work of what has come to be known as "total serialism": music (in its first movement at least) of absolute abstraction and pure process.

Boulez, the figurehead of the hyper-modernist cause, continued to promulgate the doctrine loudly in his many writings and pronouncements. Nevertheless, his next major work, *Le marteau sans maître*, was remarkable more for its pure love of musical colour and its incantatory melodic lines than for any theoretical advances, as was the still grander work for voice and ensemble which followed, *Pli selon pli*. As the 1950s and 1960s progressed, Boulez's effortless creative confidence seemed to evaporate, though there was no slackening in his protean intellectual speculations. He flirted with electronics in *Poésie pour pouvoir*, with open-ended form in *Figures, doubles, prismes*, and with indeterminacy in the *Piano Sonata No. 3* – all accompanied by self-justificatory essays, and all subsequently withdrawn, revised or left unfinished.

It was at this time that Boulez emerged as a conductor of international standing – perhaps finding in conducting a surrogate outlet for his increasingly stifled compositional urges. By 1970 he was holding prestigious but onerous positions as chief conductor of both the BBC Symphony Orchestra and the New York Philharmonic, and the compositions had virtually dried up. The uncharacteristically sombre orchestral work *Rituel* was the only finished work to emerge during the entire 1970s, and the remainder of his diminishing compositional output consisted not of fresh projects, but of revisions and recompositions of earlier pieces.

Then, in 1977, came the greatest public challenge of Boulez's career, when he secured a colossal grant from the French government for the establishment of the Institut de Recherche et Coordination Acoustique/Musique (IRCAM), a futuristic musical laboratory buried under the Pompidou Centre in the heart of Paris. Overseen by Boulez, IRCAM was to provide a hi-tech venue in which leading composers and scientists would work together to investigate the possibilities of technology in music, educating musicians and public in a set-up complete with its own resident ensemble, the Ensemble Intercontemporain. In the history of music only Wagner previously had been able to command patronage on this scale, and expectations were high, the greatest one being that Boulez himself would use the resources of IRCAM to produce the masterpiece which seemed to be demanded by investment on such a massive scale. Boulez's response, *Répons*, premiered in 1981, rose magnificently to the challenge of producing a huge public statement using the latest computerized gadgetry and represented a high-water mark in his career as a composer.

Pierre Boulez studying a score.

Répons was to be Boulez's (as yet) last major original undertaking using the IRCAM set-up, although he has continued to work intermittently with computer music in a series of smaller works, most notably *...explosante-fixe...* for flute and chamber ensemble (this being the latest reworking of a piece that now exists in no fewer than four different versions). Other works of the past two decades have included exquisite miniatures such as *Dérive 1* & *2* and further revisions and recompositions of earlier works – notably a refulgent new version of *Le visage nuptial* – which have made clear just how far Boulez's earlier theoretical postures were at variance with his natural leanings towards the sumptuous, the sensuous and the quintessentially French.

Pli selon pli & Other Vocal Works

Boulez's two "cantatas", *Le visage nuptial* and *Le soleil des eaux*, are amongst his finest and most accessible works. Both originally date from the late 1940s, both are written for solo female vocalist(s), choir and orchestra, both set poetry by René Char, and both underwent interminable revisions before achieving their definitive form – *Le visage*, in particular, took four decades to complete, growing in the process from a modest and somewhat dry chamber work to the gloriously technicolour final version. Both show Boulez at his most musically self-indulgent, capturing the essence of Char's erotic-surreal texts in music of languorous sensuality which casts more than a passing glance in the direction of earlier French masters Debussy and Messiaen.

Boulez's most ambitious vocal work, *Pli selon pli* (Fold by Fold), setting poems by Mallarmé, was written in 1957–62, with inevitable later revisions. The three central movements comprise a set of "improvisations" in which Mallarmé's elusive poems are gradually dismantled into their constituent images, and are flanked by two outer movements for much larger ensemble in which the voice is only fleetingly present. The fantastically sculpted vocal lines, ringing percussion sonorities and outbursts of propulsive energy exude a quality of hypnotic stasis, and capture Boulez's style at its most typical.

Pli selon pli; Le visage nuptial; Le Soleil des Eaux; Figures, doubles, prismes: BBC Symphony Orchestra; Ensemble Intercontemporain; Bryn-Julson, Laurence; Boulez (Warner; 2 CDs)

This 2-CD set offers the perfect introduction to Boulez's music, beautifully conducted by the composer himself and with the excellent Phyllis Bryn-Julson – perhaps the finest of his vocal interpreters – the soloist in all three works (joined by mezzo Elizabeth Laurence in *Le visage*). The 1958 orchestral piece *Figures, doubles, prismes* makes an interesting accompaniment – listen out for the wonderful, Berg-inspired string writing of its conclusion.

Le marteau sans maître

Le marteau sans maître (The Unmastered Hammer; 1953–55) again uses poetry by René Char, whose texts are set in four of the nine interlocked movements. What's most obviously novel about the music is its scoring, featuring contralto, alto flute, viola, guitar, vibraphone, xylorimba (a large xylophone), and unpitched percussion – creating a percussive, strangely hypnotic sound-world which sometimes suggests the influence of African music. Scarcely less original is *Le marteau*'s complex rhythmic structure, with capricious bursts of instrumental crossfire making such enormous demands of the performers that some fifty rehearsals were required before the premiere.

Ensemble Intercontemporain; Summers; Boulez (Deutsche Grammophon; with *Dérive 1 & 2*)

This is the most recent of Boulez's three recordings of *Le marteau*, with the Ensemble Intercontemporain in fine form, while the rich contralto tones of soloist Hilary Summers bring a distinctive quality of seductive languor to the vocal movements. The two chamber pieces, *Dérive 1 & 2*, make an attractive coupling, showing Boulez's later style at its most direct and enjoyable.

Eclat/Multiples & Rituel

The seven-minute chamber work *Eclat* (1965) sounds like a direct continuation of the musical world of *Pli selon pli*, with its shiny percussion sonorities and mesmeric fixity. In 1970, Boulez added a continuation, *Multiples*, to the original *Eclat*, with the intention, he said, of eventually writing a forty-minute piece using ever greater numbers of instruments – though thirty years later he has yet to fulfil this promise and the work remains unfinished. Despite this, the existing torso contains some of his most thrilling music, as the stasis of *Eclat* is gradually transformed into the propulsive energy of *Multiples*.

Boulez's next major work is very different. Composed in an uncharacteristic fit of decisiveness in 1974, *Rituel* is Boulez's least typical work, but also one of his most effective. Designed as a tribute to the late Italian composer-conductor Bruno Maderna, the work's austere sound-world and ritualistic effect are quite unlike anything else in Boulez's music, achieving an overwhelming effect as an ever-expanding sequence of wind refrains slowly piles up – accompanied by an exotic array of percussion instruments, which supply a constant accompaniment of assorted chimings, bangings and scratchings.

BBC Symphony Orchestra; Ensemble Intercontemporain; Boulez (Sony)

Boulez's recording of *Rituel* was made with the BBC Symphony Orchestra in 1976, shortly after his stint as their chief conductor had finished, and this fine performance offers eloquent proof of their long and fruitful association. The Ensemble Intercontemporain, which Boulez helped found in 1975, give a characteristically virtuosic account of *Eclat/Multiples*.

Répons

Répons is perhaps Boulez's single greatest achievement, and the work that most happily marries his natural gifts with his constant desire to blaze new musical trails. Using IRCAM technology plus a unique instrumental line-up and layout – nine solo percussionists, surrounded by a small chamber orchestra, surrounded by the audience, who are themselves surrounded by a ring of loudspeakers – *Répons* unveils rich and strange new musical territory, achieving a scale and an energy virtually unmatched in Boulez's music. Its trajectory is elegantly simple, as the thrillingly energetic music of the opening section (for live performers only) is gradually transformed into a surreal and marvellously textured landscape of ringing electronic sounds. Sadly, the work's formidable demands – not only the virtuoso requirements of the score itself, but also the practical problem of transporting and assembling the relevant digital hardware, plus the difficulty of finding a concert hall big enough to stage it in – have meant that *Répons* has rarely been heard in performance.

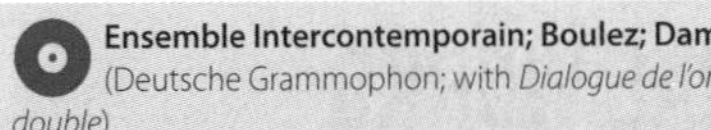

Ensemble Intercontemporain; Boulez; Damiens (Deutsche Grammophon; with *Dialogue de l'ombre double*)

Unsurprisingly, this is the work's only recording, though that's hardly a problem, given the outstanding quality of this performance by Boulez and the Ensemble Intercontemporain. The altogether more modest *Dialogue de l'ombre double*, for solo clarinet and electronics, completes the disc.

Piano Music

The piano sonatas stand either side of the brief foray into "total serialism" represented by *Structures I* for two pianos: the two-movement *Sonata No. 1* was written by the 21-year-old composer in 1946, and the more ambitious *Sonata No. 2* followed two years later – a furious keyboard assault whose jagged lines and unremitting rhythmic pile-ups gave something absolutely new to the world of classical music. The notion of "mobile form" was pioneered by Boulez and Stockhausen at the same time, the latter in *Piano Piece XI* (1956), the former in his *Piano Sonata No. 3* (1955–57), one of the many Boulez works that remains "unfinished", though the sonata's use of indeterminacy (the pianist selects the order of movements, as well as tempo and dynamics) means that this is less of a problem than you might expect.

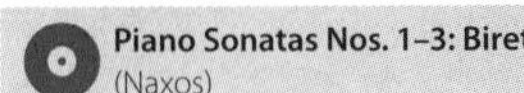

Piano Sonatas Nos. 1–3: Biret (Naxos)

Of the four recordings of the three piano sonatas currently available, this is perhaps the best (and certainly the cheapest), with Idil Biret's volatile and highly strung performances bringing out the expressionistic convulsions of Boulez's keyboard writing with terrific force, as well as sensitively capturing its brief instants of faltering lyricism.

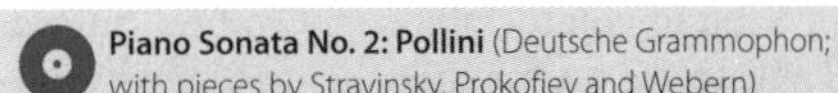

Piano Sonata No. 2: Pollini (Deutsche Grammophon; with pieces by Stravinsky, Prokofiev and Webern)

Maurizio Pollini's taut recording of the formidable second sonata is the best performance of a Boulez keyboard composition yet recorded, and a wonderful example of how a great pianist can bring clarity and musical logic into the heart of even Boulez's densest contrapuntal textures.

Johannes Brahms (1833–1897)

In the face of Liszt, Wagner and the "New German School" of music, it was Brahms who upheld the long-established ideals of the German tradition. He was not, however, the reactionary figure he's sometimes portrayed as being. No less a revolutionary than Arnold Schoenberg praised Brahms's combination of "economy and riches", and his best music (of which there's a great deal) generates a remarkable power from the tension between its seething emotions and the propriety of its Classical structures.

As with so many composers, Brahms's life lacked much in the way of incident. His childhood in Hamburg was devoted to study and it was not until he was 15 that he began to play in public. Although some biographers doubt the veracity of the story, it's still widely believed that he often played in brothels in order to gain some limited financial independence, and various writers have linked this to Brahms's precarious and fruitless relationships with women in his mature years. Whatever the cause of his notorious reticence and boorishness, Brahms

Brahms relaxes with a cigar.

always felt uncomfortable with women, but was still able to see the positive side to his awkwardness – it saved him, he observed (with a candour that was very much the mark of the man), from "both opera and marriage".

One of the defining influences upon his creative life was the great violinist Joseph Joachim, whom Brahms met for the first time in Hanover in 1853 while touring with another Hungarian violinist, the self-styled "Gypsy" virtuoso Eduard Reményi. Upon hearing the young Brahms perform some of his own work, Joachim provided him with letters of introduction to Liszt and to Schumann, who hailed the young man as a genius – not the first time he'd become overexcited by a new young artist, but on this occasion he was right. The ensuing friendship with Schumann and with Schumann's wife, the pianist Clara Wieck, did much to nurture Brahms's talent, but it was not until after Schumann's death, in 1856, that Brahms began to devote serious energies to composing.

In 1860 he put his name to a declaration – also signed by Joachim – that dissociated the signatories from the new trends championed by Liszt and his circle. This professed conservatism meant that success remained elusive for years, and it was not until 1869, when his *Deutsches Requiem* was first performed, that Brahms was finally recognized as a major creative force. In 1872, having moved to Vienna, he succeeded Rubinstein as artistic director of the Gesellschaft der Musikfreunde, a post he held for only three years. From 1875 until his death, his time was dominated by composition, and by occasional engagements as a conductor or pianist.

The symphonies, all but one of the concertos and most of the chamber works for which Brahms is now chiefly revered date from his last extraordinarily fertile quarter-century, years which also saw him drift ever further away from public life. Brahms was happiest on his own. In 1885 Clara Schumann, his friend and rumoured lover, said of him: "To me he is as much a riddle – I might almost say as much a stranger – as he was twenty-five years ago." There is, however, little sense of distance in his work, which includes some of the most profound, elegiac and unsentimental music of the nineteenth century.

CHORAL WORKS

Brahms wrote many unaccompanied choral pieces for women's choral societies as well as a huge output of songs for solo voice, duet and other combinations. Much of this output was for amateur musicians and is of mixed quality, so comparatively little of it is now regularly recorded or performed in public. That said, however, two works stand out from the rest: *Ein deutsches Requiem* – Brahms's greatest vocal work and his first orchestral score to receive widespread praise – and the *Alto Rhapsody*, one of his most moving creations.

Ein Deutsches Requiem

The idea of writing a Requiem mass first came to Brahms after the death of Schumann in 1856, but for various reasons – not least of them his lack of true faith – the intention lapsed until 1865, when the death of his mother plunged him into inconsolable grief. Four years later he completed his tribute to her, *Ein deutsches Requiem* (A German Requiem), a mass quite unlike any previous Requiem. Spurning the conventional Latin texts, Brahms set sections of Luther's translation of the Bible in a composition that was primarily intended to reconcile the living to their loss, and dwelt more on the hope of the Resurrection than on the fear of Judgement Day. It first appeared without its central and most beautiful section, the soprano solo which makes up the fifth movement.

Schwarzkopf, Fischer-Dieskau; Philharmonia; Klemperer (EMI)

Klemperer's famous 1961 recording is a highly reverential affair, distinguished by excellent solo contributions from Fischer-Dieskau and Schwarzkopf, supported by fine choral work from the Philharmonia Chorus. For some tastes it's too slow and clotted, but for many it's an awe-inspiring experience. EMI's new transfer is bright and cleanly balanced.

Margiono, Gilfry; Orchestre Révolutionnaire et Romantique; Gardiner (Philips)

John Eliot Gardiner's recording is at the other end of the stylistic spectrum. He uses period instruments and produces amazingly clear sonorities and sparser, lighter textures – not perhaps what you'd expect in Brahms, but highly convincing nonetheless. The thoroughly competent soloists hardly match up to Klemperer's legendary pair, but this is a thrilling and revealing performance.

Alto Rhapsody

The *Rhapsody for Alto, Chorus and Orchestra* – to give the *Alto Rhapsody* its full name – was written in a fit of despair. Brahms's feelings for Clara Schumann had subsided after her husband's death and he had transferred his affection to her daughter Julie – one of many such futile infatuations. Julie, oblivious to Brahms's true motives, saw him merely as a benevolent "uncle" figure, and in 1869 she married her partner of choice, unaware of the depth of Brahms's feelings for her. As a wedding gift Brahms presented her with the *Rhapsody*, a setting of Goethe's poem "A Winter Journey in the Harz Mountains". It was indeed a thunderous example of Brahms's gift for self-pity, a fact which Clara noticed even if her daughter did not. The mood of the piece is decidedly unmatrimonial, but the despairing bleakness of its opening is soon left behind – the point at which the chorus finally joins the soloist is one of the most heart-warming moments in all Brahms's output.

Ludwig; Philharmonia; Klemperer (EMI; with *Symphony No. 1 & Tragic Overture*)

The Klemperer–Ludwig performance of the *Alto Rhapsody* is essential to any Brahms collection. Christa Ludwig, one of the last century's greatest German altos, gets marvellously restrained orchestral accompaniment from the Philharmonia at its peak.

SYMPHONIES

Brahms's four symphonies are unique in that they are all products of the composer's maturity. During his early years, constant fear of comparison with Beethoven affected him ("You have no idea how hard it is to compose when always you can hear the footsteps of that giant behind you", he wrote) so deeply that he struggled for decades with the idea of writing his first symphony, which finally saw the light only in 1876. Within a decade, Brahms had completed his second, third and fourth symphonies, a sequence of distinctive compositions that encompass a vast range of styles, forms and emotional states. In the opinion of many, it's the most important body of symphonic music after Beethoven's. For example, Hans von Bülow, conductor of the premiere of *Symphony No. 4*, famously declared that his favourite key was E flat, for its three flat notes (signified by the letter b in German) symbolized for him the "Holy Trinity" of Bach, Beethoven and now Brahms.

Complete Symphonies: Berlin Philharmonic Orchestra; Harnoncourt (Teldec; 3 CDs ;with overtures & *"St Anthony" Chorale Variations*)

Harnoncourt reveals the inner logic and structural grandeur of the Brahms symphonies with the kind of exemplary clarity and inner detailing you'd usually expect from a period performance specialist. These magnificently engineered recordings have thrilling sonic impact, while offering a more cerebral approach to this composer than Karajan or Furtwängler.

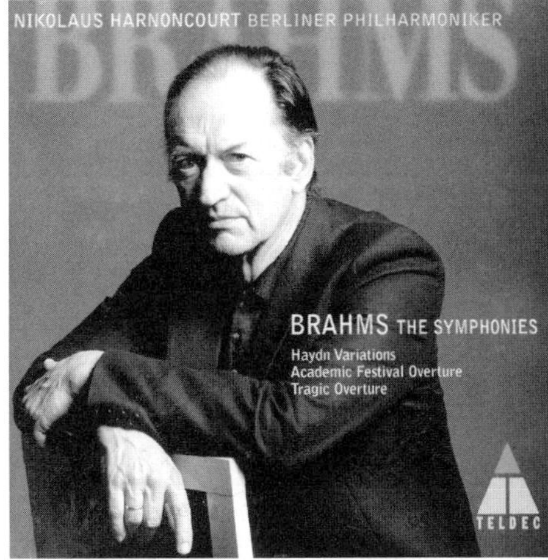

Complete Symphonies: Berlin Philharmonic; Karajan (Deutsche Grammophon; 2 CDs)

Karajan's 1978 DG cycle offers lovingly cultivated and highly distinguished performances and fine recorded sound at mid-price. This is very much a traditionalist's view of

Brahms, however. Karajan's readings can be over-inflated and grandiloquent at times perhaps, but the richness of the string tone and the conductor's unerring sense of line and structure make for a very satisfying listening experience.

Complete Symphonies: Vienna Philharmonic Orchestra; Berlin Philharmonic Orchestra; Furtwängler (EMI; 3 CDs)

If it's drama and power that you're looking for, then Furtwängler provides it in large quantities. Recorded live in the late 1940s and early 1950s, these performances (all but the first with the Berlin Philharmonic) seethe with a brooding energy and an overriding sense of tragedy.

Symphony No. 1

Although the first symphony was only received politely at its premiere in Karlsruhe, by the time it reached Vienna it was already being nicknamed "Beethoven's Tenth", affirming Brahms's elevation to the ranks of the great Austro-German symphonic masters. The epic strivings of its first movement certainly owe much to Beethoven, but it is when the finale's principal theme (announced in unison by the violins after the dark and ominous introduction) is first heard that the influence of the "Ode to Joy" from the final movement of Beethoven's ninth becomes unmistakable. The exultant, striding triumphalism of this movement is unmatched in the other symphonies; above all else, this music conveys a palpable sense of Brahms's own understandable relief at having finally managed to complete his first symphony at the age of 44.

Berlin Philharmonic Orchestra; Karajan
(Deutsche Grammophon; with Schumann *Symphony No. 1*)

Karajan recorded this symphony several times, but it's in this 1963 version that his grip on the music is at its strongest. The many great moments are lithe, muscular and unswerving in their sweep and authority, but there's also a greater degree of poetry than you find in most accounts, and the orchestral playing is superb throughout.

Philharmonia Orchestra; Klemperer
(EMI; with *Alto Rhapsody* & *Tragic Overture*)

Some critics find Klemperer a ponderous rather than inspired Brahms interpreter. It's true that his reading of the first symphony is extraordinarily stately, but it's also majestic, with grandeur and warmth going hand in hand.

Symphony No. 2

With the monumental creative struggle of the first symphony behind him at last, Brahms had the confidence to relax as he began work on his second symphony, which from the outset is a much more genial and less craggy piece than its predecessor. It repeated the success of the first in Vienna, and duly attracted more comparisons to Beethoven, acquiring the nickname "The Pastoral" in reference to Beethoven's sixth. The *Symphony No. 2* marked a crucial point in Brahms's career – on the back of its favourable reception both his first and second symphonies were published, and he embarked on a series of triumphant European concert tours.

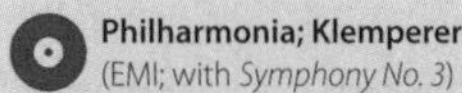

Philharmonia; Klemperer
(EMI; with *Symphony No. 3*)

Refined and lustrous playing, and from Klemperer a beguiling yet epic vision. An overwhelming sense of pastoral ease is summoned here, and Klemperer maintains a flow and a charged, noble grandeur which keeps its sense of yearning where lesser performances falter.

New York Philharmonic; Masur
(Teldec; with *Academic Festival Overture*)

This recording was one of the highlights of Masur's New York years. It's a lithe and powerful reading, and tremendously well played throughout. Particularly impressive are the massed cellos in their great melody in the slow movement, and the finale develops bounding energy as it progresses.

Symphony No. 3

The Viennese public had to wait another six years for Brahms's third symphony, but when it finally arrived it was received with even more enthusiasm than the first two. Eduard Hanslick, vociferous anti-Wagnerite and ultra-conservative doyen of Vienna's music critics, declared that the third symphony united the titanism of the first symphony with the untroubled pastoral charm of the second. It's certainly a magnificent achievement (some would say Brahms's greatest symphony), but it's not the most ingratiating composition. The third symphony is a tightly wrought and subtly argued piece and its drama is generally low-key: there are no fireworks here, but rather an atmosphere of subdued and resigned confession. With this symphony it's essential to give the music time to work on you.

Columbia Symphony Orchestra; Walter
(Sony; with *Symphony No. 2*)

Walter's use of pivotal phrases to change the pace and emotional temperature allows him to suggest immense breadth of emotion coloured by an autumnal resignation. With its sense of spaciousness and powerful urgency when necessary, Walter's classic interpretation makes this music seem to dance.

Philharmonia; Klemperer
(EMI; with *Symphony No. 2*)

Klemperer does not quite evoke Walter's depth of introspection or his sheer range. This is nonetheless a performance of wise humanity and great strength, which on Klemperer's own terms is superlatively judged..

Symphony No. 4

With his *Symphony No. 4* Brahms reached the culmination of his symphonic style – the outer movements are virtually symphonies in themselves, containing ideas that are almost too grand to be fully worked out, even in the context of the vast, gauntly imposing canvas of this overwhelming creation. The defiant opening movement is packed with truly epic and gripping melodic ideas, while the equally momentous finale, a passacaglia with thirty individual variations on its ground-bass theme, has the same air of finality as the conclusion of Beethoven's ninth. Yet this is no paean of universal brotherhood, but rather the spiritual struggle of the solitary thinker striving to confront finality and extinction.

Vienna Philharmonic Orchestra; Kleiber
(Deutsche Grammophon)

Brahms's gravest symphony elicits from Kleiber one of the most memorable recordings of the digital era. It's a fair bet that Kleiber heard Furtwängler conduct this symphony many times, for this is a performance characterized by the same command of orchestral colour and possesses comparably electrifying dynamism.

Cleveland Orchestra; Szell
(Sony; with *Academic Festival & Tragic Overtures*)

Recorded in the mid-1960s, this provides a markedly different approach to Kleiber's emotional rollercoaster but is highly convincing in its own right. George Szell's Cleveland band are tightly drilled and, while at times a bit more give seems desirable, this has the advantage of highlighting the inner logic of the work with greater clarity than usual.

CONCERTOS

Brahms wrote four concertos – two for piano, one for violin and one for violin and cello (the so-called *Double Concerto*) – and all except the last have become regular fixtures on concert programmes. Though each is quite distinct in character, these works are united by Brahms's conception of the concerto as a symphonic form, in which the soloist becomes at times subservient to the independent-minded orchestra. Thus in the *Violin Concerto* the second movement is introduced by a theme that the soloist never gets to play, and in the *Piano Concerto No. 2* the third movement is dominated not by the pianist but by the principal cellist, whose long and beautiful theme is taken up by the rest of the orchestra. As in Beethoven's concertos (on which Brahms's were often based), there are moments of cut-and-thrust drama as the soloist and orchestra contend supremacy, but generally, as with Brahms's works in other genres, it is a compelling sense of organic unity which prevails.

Piano Concertos

Brahms began work on his first piano concerto at the age of 21, shortly after Robert Schumann's attempted suicide. It was intended as a joint tribute, to Robert and to Clara, who had given the first performance of Schumann's own piano concerto. The work was premiered by Brahms himself in 1859, three years after Schumann's death, and proved a critical disaster. Subsequently, however, with Clara's help, its quality was recognized and even now it remains the more popular of the piano concertos. Though it begins with a powerful orchestral introduction that keeps the soloist out of the picture for some four minutes, it's a more flamboyant and virtuosic piece than the second concerto, building to an unforgettable Hungarian finale, whose momentous and percussive principal theme dominates from beginning to end.

The second concerto – one of the longest ever written – was composed some twenty years later, while Brahms was basking in the acclaim accorded to his third symphony. And like that work, it reflects the mellower aspects of the composer, particularly in the slow movement, with its innovative use of a second solo instrument (the cello) to carry the main theme. It's by no means an entirely placid work however – the tussle between piano and orchestra in the second movement is one of the most exhilarating episodes in the entire concerto repertoire.

Piano Concertos Nos. 1 & 2: Freire; London Gewandhaus Orchestra Leipzig; Chailly (Decca; 2 CDs)

Nelson Freire is one of the most instinctive of contemporary pianists, but also blessed with a staggering technique; he brings an enormous depth of feeling to these works and, when necessary, a volcanic energy. It's a live performance and the sense of occasion is well captured, with Riccardo Chailly and the Gewandhaus Orchestra in complete accord with Freire's reading of the work.

Piano Concertos Nos. 1 & 2: Gilels; Berlin Philharmonic Orchestra; Jochum (Deutsche Grammophon; 2 CDs; with *Op. 116*)

Gilels' deeply humane performances are now presented in marvellously refreshed sound, and the combination will be hard to beat irrespective of price. This is playing which penetrates the music and possesses it from within: tender, fervent, striking for its refined judgement, and glowing with a majestic poise. The concertos are also available singly, at mid-price, in DG's Galleria series.

Violin Concerto

For years Brahms promised to write a concerto for Joseph Joachim, but as with so many of his major projects he kept putting it off. Finally, spurred by the success of the second symphony, he set to work on the piece, taking guidance from Joachim as to what was possible for the instrument. Although it was originally conceived in four movements, Brahms was persuaded to drop one of the central movements to keep the concerto down to a more conventional length – the excised portion later reappeared as part of the second piano concerto. Essentially lyrical in character, the final version shares much of the second symphony's mood: the key of D major is common to both works, as it is to the Beethoven violin concerto which Brahms greatly admired. By the time of its premiere, on New Year's Day 1879, Brahms had become somewhat eccentric in his mode of dress, and the staid Leipzig audience watched in horror as the composer-conductor's trousers, tied up with an old necktie, began to slip. Fortunately, Brahms's corpulent form ensured the trousers remained in place, but the initial verdict on his new concerto was lukewarm. Its breakthrough came shortly afterwards, when Joachim introduced the work to England, and since then it has been one of the most popular concertos in the violin repertory.

Vengerov; Chicago Symphony Orchestra; Barenboim (Teldec; with *Violin Sonata No. 3*)

Maxim Vengerov may well become the Heifetz of this century. Certainly, his magnificent performance of the Brahms concerto is no less masterful nor less brilliant in any way, and this disc also includes a definitive live performance of the third sonata with Barenboim at the piano. Both works are warmly and atmospherically recorded.

Heifetz; Chicago Symphony Orchestra; Reiner (RCA; with Beethoven *Violin Concerto*)

From the "King of Violinists" comes this supremely effortless and indeed (before its exhilarating finale) almost undemonstrative performance. Heifetz's attack is crisp and vigorous, and yet he knew better than almost anybody how to make this music sing. There is the artlessness that conceals art in the darting invention and luscious cantabile of his fastidiously spun lines, and a touching candour about every bar.

Neveu; Philharmonia; Dobrowen (EMI; with Sibelius *Violin Concerto*)

Ginette Neveu, who died in a plane crash in 1949 at the age of only 30, left what is widely considered to be the finest recorded version of this concerto. This is a marvellously poetic and dramatic performance, and it has been well transferred from original 78s – though inevitably the sound lacks the subtleties of modern engineering.

Double Concerto

The *Double Concerto*, like the *Violin Concerto*, owes its creation to Joachim, whom Brahms had alienated by supporting Joachim's wife during their unpleasant divorce. Brahms intended this concerto as a gesture of reconciliation, though some commentators have suggested that another violin concerto might have been a more appropriate gift – indeed, it's almost as if Brahms were baiting the violinist, because nothing of great importance is given to the solo violin. Written after the symphonies and piano concertos, it's a particularly angular and unsettled piece, and as a result of its great seriousness of purpose, some passages can seem too thickly orchestrated. Yet, while this might not be Brahms's greatest work, it does feature some wonderful fiery interplay between cello and violin.

Oistrakh, Rostropovich; Cleveland Orchestra; Szell (EMI; with Beethoven *Triple Concerto*)

Rostropovich and Oistrakh knew each other's style so intuitively that they move through the music with a singleness of mind that's uncanny. While their pugnacity might well take some getting used to, their bluster often mingles with lyricism of great beauty. It's coupled with a classic 1969 Berlin recording of the Beethoven *Triple Concerto*.

CHAMBER MUSIC

Brahms was happiest at the piano, the instrument at which he excelled as a virtuoso, and, to an extent, he appeared somewhat reluctant to explore the unknown territory of chamber music involving instruments with which he was less familiar. Indeed, his first ventures into the genre were undertaken in part as technical exercises, as preparation for orchestral composition; they have not survived, as Brahms had a habit of destroying music of which he did not approve. It's the more remarkable, then, that his mature chamber music is among the greatest of the nineteenth century. Only Beethoven wrote so successfully for so many different ensembles: Brahms's output includes sonatas for violin, viola, cello and clarinet; trios for clarinet, horn and piano; sextets; string quartets; quartets for piano; string quintets; a piano quintet and – perhaps his masterpiece in this field – a quintet for clarinet and strings. There are no duds among this group: the pieces we've singled out will take you to the heart of things.

Clarinet Quintet

The autumnal *Quintet for Clarinet and Strings* is the finest of four clarinet pieces written for Richard Mühlfeld, a dazzling instrumentalist who also inspired Mendelssohn. Composed in the calming atmosphere of the alpine resort of Bad Ischl in 1891, the quintet seems to show that its morose and difficult creator had found peace in his final years – only Mozart's clarinet quintet can strike quite as deeply as this resonant masterpiece. The unprecedented range of expression and unrivalled understanding of the solo instrument's capabilities give this work a sense of completeness that few of Brahms's other chamber works can boast.

Stoltzman; Tokyo Quartet
(RCA; with Weber *Clarinet Quintet*)

This account remains one of the finest around. Richard Stoltzman has an ideally fluid and mellifluous tone, and he is supported by sensitive and alert playing from the Tokyo Quartet. The slow movement is especially beautiful here, but the sense of valediction that's fundamental in late Brahms is allowed to work its spell throughout.

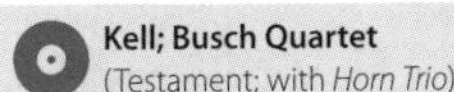

Kell; Busch Quartet
(Testament; with *Horn Trio*)

The playing of the Busch Quartet and Reginald Kell is the closest thing you'll hear to the sort of playing that Brahms would have heard, and it's been relatively well preserved on this vintage mono recording. Giving the music's weighted counterpoint a rare freedom and sense of direction, this is one of the most moving Brahms recordings ever made.

Piano Quintet

In his 1853 article "New Paths", Schumann described Brahms's chamber music as "symphonies in disguise". That description was never truer than with the Op. 34 *Quintet*, in which Brahms's own beloved instrument takes centre stage. The *Quintet* was originally planned with two cellos – only for Brahms's friend, the violinist Joachim, to dismiss it as opaque. The introduction of a piano came to the rescue, by turns incisive, quizzical, introspective – driving the music on, interrogating and lightening the mellow confidences of the strings, whipping the finale from diffidence into defiant exultation. The work in its finished form has been seen as an attempt to combine the resonances of orchestral music with the differentiated textures of chamber music. It is certainly one of the masterpieces of Brahms's maturity.

Quartetto Italiano; Pollini
(Deutsche Grammophon)

Maurizio Pollini offers a legendary interpretation which stands above the rest for its high drama: its impulsive accelerations, ominous pauses which shrink from a whisper, and moments of deliberation which suddenly explode into life. The piano line is meticulously articulated and there is an electrifying rapport between the strings, who bring exceptional fire and brilliance to the proceedings.

String Quartets

In the nineteenth century, the rise of the symphony as a melting pot for innovation meant that chamber music had become displaced, except as a vehicle for more intimate ideas. But Brahms kept his allegiance to a classical past, and for him the quartet remained a proving ground for experiments of striking originality. From his youth he made sketches for chamber pieces, all of which he destroyed, and only in 1873 did he complete something he felt ready to publish. The first of this Opus 51 set has the striving spirit characteristic of his middle period; and with customary high craftsmanship Brahms toys with our expectations, as if discovering the medium of the quartet afresh. The *Quartet No. 3* (1876) harks back to the world of Mozart and Haydn. Yet, throughout the cycle, nostalgia is muted, and it serves only to allow Brahms's interplays and musical tensions to be resolved with greater impact.

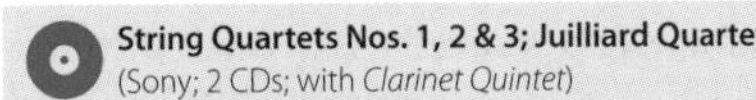

String Quartets Nos. 1, 2 & 3; Juilliard Quartet
(Sony; 2 CDs; with *Clarinet Quintet*)

There's such a high level of empathy from these American players that you can almost imagine that this music was written for them. A combative aspect is the key to the greatness of their account of the third quartet, which comes close to realizing in sound the tremendous mental effort it cost the composer. Now comes with a marvellous perfomance of the *Clarinet Quintet* with Charles Neidich.

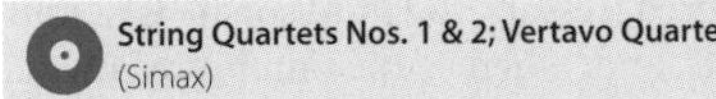

String Quartets Nos. 1 & 2; Vertavo Quartet
(Simax)

The playing of the Vertavo Quartet is magnificently controlled, but they obviously enjoy living dangerously, particularly in the epic outer movements, where the torrential force of their playing will have you on the edge of your seat. It's not often that you're left feeling that Brahms is actually a modernist – but here everything sounds novel, questing and dramatic.

Piano Trios

The piano trios form an important if less well-known aspect of Brahms's creativity within the world of chamber music. To an extent, Brahms took up the torch at the point at which Beethoven had laid it down, but although he used Beethoven's quartets, along with those of Schubert, as a point of departure, these trios are also highly individual creations, with a sound-world that's altogether novel. Each of the three instruments is stretched to its limits at times, as if Brahms wanted to create orchestral depth and colour using just three players. Another fascinating aspect of the trios (particularly the last one, the C minor work of 1886) is Brahms's treatment of the string players as soloists, giving both the violin and cello some sonorous passages that are ideally suited to their respective characteristics. Just occasionally, Brahms's handling of his material is so scholarly (particularly in the final trio) that the music becomes almost indigestibly complex, but his wealth of powerfully sculpted ideas amply rewards attentive listening.

Beaux Arts Trio
(Philips; 2 CDs)

These are without question the most authoritative and distinguished accounts of these works in the catalogue. The Beaux Arts Trio play with unique breadth of insight and a feeling of spontaneous inspiration, a quality that comes all too infrequently to studio recordings like these. The 1960 Philips sound is at once brilliant and truthful, but it also has exceptional spaciousness.

Violin Sonatas

The three violin sonatas, written between 1878 and 1886, epitomize Brahms's remarkable ability to reconcile heartfelt expression with classical discipline. The first – in fact his fourth, as three earlier ones were destroyed – is perhaps the most lyrical and is an outstanding example of his use of cyclic form: the whole work is unified by a single idea, three repeated notes that are first heard at the work's beginning. The second sonata exudes an optimistic and confident atmosphere, but the third – also written in the summer of 1886 – is a bleak, melancholic and introspective piece. Unlike its predecessors, the third sonata is in four movements, and, whereas the outer movements dominate the earlier sonatas, here it is the central movements that form the crux.

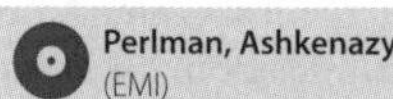

Perlman, Ashkenazy
(EMI)

Perlman and Ashkenazy give outstanding, mellow performances, complemented by the recording's rich and warm sound. There are plenty of rivals in this field, but no other violin and piano partnership quite matches the way this pair evince the subtle undertow of repressed emotion that underlies these fine works.

String Sextets

Brahms's two sextets, both scored for two violins, two violas and two cellos, are among his finest works. The first, composed in 1858, is fairly straightforward in its construction, with an almost complacent feel that contrasts starkly with the deliberate contrapuntal introspection of the second, written six years later in absolute privacy – almost certainly in response to the breakdown of a friendship with one of his lady friends, Agathe von Siebold. Both works have a similarly constructed opening movement but it is in the finales that Brahms's expression most obviously differs. The first ends with cheerful exuberance while the second concludes with a turbulent and complex reworking of a single idea that, in well-disguised form, reappears throughout the other movements. In short, the second sextet is Brahms at his most engagingly melancholic.

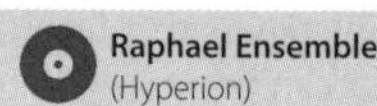

Raphael Ensemble
(Hyperion)

This CD has been around for some years now, in which time several other fine rival versions have appeared, but none has eclipsed it. The Raphael Ensemble really warm to Brahms's typically independent part-writing – each of the players shines in these rich and enthusiastic performances, assisted throughout by clear and spacious recorded sound.

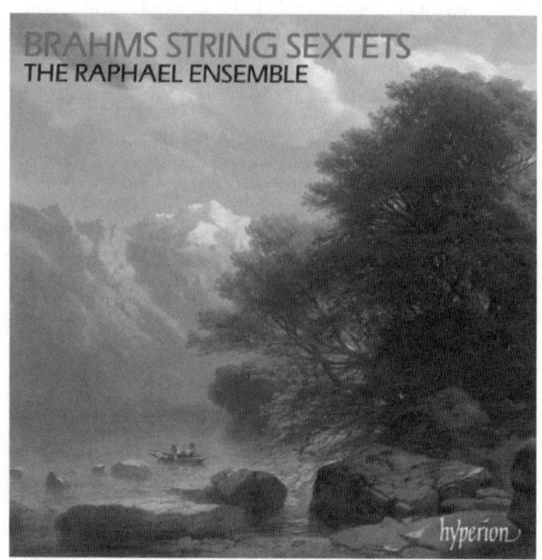

PIANO WORKS

Brahms was a formidable pianist, who produced a large amount of music for the instrument throughout his creative life, for only on the piano, as he once told Clara Schumann, did he feel fully at ease and at home. Though there is more virtuoso display in his early piano works and more of an emphasis on chordal writing in the later ones, Brahms's piano style evolved only slightly once he had achieved maturity. In consequence, there is not, as with Beethoven, the palpable sense that the piano music traces the course of a long creative journey. You'll certainly find some lovely melodies here, but an equally important aspect of most of the works listed below is their quasi-orchestral texture, a quality that again allies Brahms with Schumann. Brahms thought with all ten fingers, and the resulting music can sometimes seem distinctly heavyweight; but when played by a pianist with the requisite sensitivity to timbre, Brahms's piano works are revealed as masterpieces of condensed, almost refractory writing.

As is the case with Schumann, Brahms's sonatas are relatively neglected, and his reputation as a composer for the piano rests almost exclusively upon a group of short, condensed pieces – the *Ballades* Op. 10, the two *Rhapsodies* Op. 79, and the piano pieces of Op. 117, Op. 118 and Op. 119.

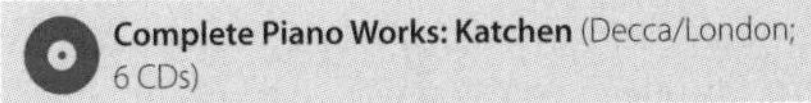

Complete Piano Works: Katchen (Decca/London; 6 CDs)

If you want to tackle all of Brahms's piano music, pick Julius Katchen's set from the mid-1960s. Playing on a beautifully warm-toned piano, Katchen is a master of effective understatement: avoiding any tendency to heaviness, his playing has invigorating refinement and spirit. A selection from these performances is also available as a 2 CD budget set.

Ballades and Rhapsodies

Listening to the four *Ballades*, composed in 1854 when Brahms was only 21, you can hear why Schumann so readily proclaimed him a genius. Inspired by the brooding fatalism of folk ballads (the first by the Scottish poem "Edward", which described an act of matricide), all of them share a basic ternary structure. The first three are almost demonic in character, as Schumann remarked at the time, but the last and longest of the four is something quite different. A sighing Adagio of immense beauty, it seems to reveal an act of reticent soul-searching, almost an ingenuousness, that was never again to be heard in Brahms's music. The two thrilling *Rhapsodies* in B minor and G minor (1879) are kindred spirits to the first three *Ballades* – marked "agitato" and "molto passionato", they are music of primal urgency, offset by lambent interludes of introspection.

Four Ballades: Gilels (Deutsche Grammophon; with *Piano Quartet No. 1*)

This is playing of profound composure and inner wisdom, whose measured sensibility permits a unique command and variegation of phrase and texture – whether in the shifting clouds of *No. 2*, the clipped pedal work of *No. 3*, or the sullen fog of *No. 4*. This performance is also available, un-remastered, at budget price.

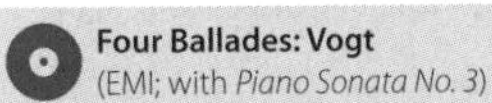

Four Ballades: Vogt (EMI; with *Piano Sonata No. 3*)

These are not only among the most lithe and impulsive accounts you're likely to hear of the *Ballades*, they're also among the most determined and intellectually purposeful. But that's not to suggest that Lars Vogt is any less convincing in more introspective passages, where he plays with the taste and sensitivity that are usually the province of lifelong experience.

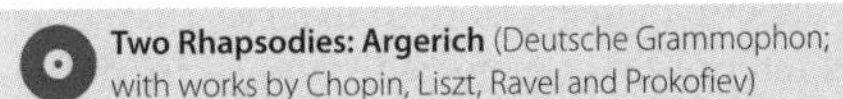

Two Rhapsodies: Argerich (Deutsche Grammophon; with works by Chopin, Liszt, Ravel and Prokofiev)

There are many performances of these thrilling pieces, but none better than these. Martha Argerich, in her debut recital recording, brings passion tempered by eloquence: each shift of nuance is given its proper intensity, and no other pianist has allowed this music to breathe so freely and grow with a wider range of colour.

Piano Sonatas

The three piano sonatas were what a 20-year-old Brahms carried under his arm for his first historic meeting with Robert Schumann. The third and best of them he had just penned; the other two he'd dashed off the previous year, with a young man's proud disdain for any humbling comparisons with Beethoven, or for that matter any other antecedent. For this is music which seizes the sonata form and remakes it into a gargantuan receptacle for teeming ideas: "that young eagle" observed Schumann in his subsequent magazine editorial, seemingly staggered by this poetic onslaught, and eager to think that a successor to Beethoven might have arrived. Perhaps it was Schumann's exuberant reception that induced Brahms's subsequent caution towards his own art, and interestingly enough, he never wrote another sonata. Be that as it may, these works align a mastery of thematic organization with the boundless fertility of one who revels in his own mastery of the mightiest of instruments.

Piano Sonatas Nos. 1 and 2: Richter (Decca; 2 CDs; with *Paganini Variations, Schumann, Fantasie etc*)

Richter's grand manner may drain a little of the essential youthful impetuosity from this music, but it gets to the heart in so many other ways: seeking out Brahms's premature nostalgia as well as his fulminating grandeur. This is a live recital of the highest order but for those preferring the safety of the studio, Richter has recorded both sonatas on a single disc for Decca.

Piano Sonata No. 3: Kissin (RCA; with selections from the *10 Hungarian Dances*)

With Radu Lupu's account of this sonata now deleted, Evgeny Kissin is the next best thing. It's a very different performance, however, one that treats the work as a showpiece of high-octane, no-holds-barred virtuosity. Some may find it lacks soul, but it's an undeniably exhilarating display that in the end dispels all reservations.

Late Piano Works

The most intensely personal of all Brahms's piano compositions are the pieces gathered under the titles Op. 116, Op. 117, Op. 118 and Op. 119. Composed around 1892 for an ailing Clara Schumann, these ballades, romances, rhapsodies and intermezzos (terms with no precise definition) offer a kaleidoscopic image of the composer, compacting an extraordinary range of emotion into a brief span. Each of these miniatures is a marvel of immediacy, making them perhaps the best place to start an exploration of Brahms's piano music.

Piano Pieces Op. 116: Gilels (Deutsche Grammophon; 2 CDs; with the piano concertos)

Profoundly contemplative, this is outstanding playing, with an extraordinary refinement and quality of judgement. The clarity with which Brahms's overlapping melodic strands and patterns of narrative tension are weighted, articulated and brought together is something to marvel at.

Piano Pieces Opp. 117–119: Lupu (Decca; with Op. 79 *Rhapsodies*)

Radu Lupu is a master of Brahms's late style, allowing each detail room to breathe, and defining all the varied inner voices that are so important to the Opp. 117–119 pieces. He may not be the most exciting pianist to have recorded these works, but his unshowy approach makes him one of the most revealing.

LIEDER

Brahms wrote over 190 songs for voice and piano throughout his career, as well as many vocal duets and quartets. While he set poems by leading writers including Goethe and Heine, he has been criticized for also using texts by many minor fashionable poets and translations of folk poetry. In fact, Brahms was an avid and discerning reader of literature who felt that a poem should only be used as the basis of a song when music could add something to it. Once drawn to a text, he would recite it aloud, studying it until he felt that he could achieve an effortless, natural musical setting. A highly skilled pianist, Brahms gave his songs richly textured, very expressive and often virtuosic piano accompaniments.

Die schöne Magelone and other songs

Brahms's only song cycle, *Die schöne Magelone*, is loosely based on a novella by Ludwig Tieck, about a brave knight from Provence who falls in love with a king's daughter, is captured by bandits and separated from his beloved before their eventual reunion. The best of the songs (the exquisite lullaby "Ruhe, Süssliebchen" and the despairing "Verzweilung") give a vivid portrayal of a young man in love. Brahms's many other lieder depict an enormous range of moods and states of being, including rollicking good humour ("Unüberwindlich"), ecstatic mutual love ("Von ewiger Liebe"), youthful flirtatiousness ("Vergebliches Ständchen") and joy in nature ("Feldeinsamkeit").

Two popular late sets of lieder are the *Zigeunerlieder* Op. 103 (with texts from Hungarian folk poetry, and a musical style influenced by Eastern European Gypsy music) and Brahms's last songs, *Vier ernste Gesänge* (1896), with texts taken from Martin Luther's translation of the Bible. These moving meditations on death were inspired in part by the final illness of Brahms's beloved friend Clara Schumann; he outlived her by under a year.

Brahms Lieder: Fischer-Dieskau, Moore, Barenboim, Sawallisch, Richter (Brilliant Classics; 6 CDs)

This budget set gathers together all the songs except those explicitly for female voice. Fischer-Dieskau, accompanied by four equally fine pianists, was in top form when these recordings were first released in the 1970s. As well as a wonderful version of *Die schöne Magelone*, there are many other treasures, including a dramatic rendition of the *Vier ernste Gesänge*, moving beautifully from the dark thoughts of the first song to the exultant end of the fourth.

Lieder: Von Otter, Forsberg (Deutsche Grammophon)

This album remains a great introduction to Brahms songs. Highlights include an exciting rendition of the *Zigeunerlieder*, and stunning performances of the virtuosic paean to love '"Meine Liebe ist grün" and the tender *Zwei*

Gesänge for voice, viola and piano. Anne Sofie von Otter sings with great beauty of tone and emotional commitment, superbly accompanied by Bengt Forsberg.

Deutsche Volkslieder

As a north German from Hamburg who moved to Vienna, Brahms had ample opportunity to experience a wide range of German folk music. The folk song was important to him throughout his career, as a basis for many of his original songs and as inspiration for some of his instrumental music. He often expressed his intention of producing a major collection of folk song arrangements and eventually did so, publishing the forty-nine *Deutsche Volkslieder* in 1894. Brahms took words and tunes from a number of sources (not always totally authentic), adding his own piano accompaniments and sometimes making small alterations to text and melody. Although Brahms felt the songs were written more for private enjoyment than the concert hall, he was very pleased with them, stating that: "It is the first time I look back with tenderness on what I have produced."

Schwarzkopf, Fischer-Dieskau, Moore
(EMI; 2 CDs)

Recorded before either singer had become at all mannered, this set provides 42 of the *Deutsche Volkslieder*. From sombre tales of women in distress to humorous or romantic courtship duets and songs of chivalry, the songs are performed with great feeling and energy accompanied by Gerald Moore in sparkling form.

Benjamin Britten (1913–1976)

Benjamin Britten was arguably the most significant British composer since Purcell, with almost one hundred major compositions to his credit, ranging from full-scale operas to accessible but unpatronizing music for schoolchildren. Although he was an emphatically tonal composer and a committed melodist, Britten's style was unmistakably modern in its economy, clarity and energy. He was especially brilliant at descriptive writing – the "Four Sea Interludes" from his opera *Peter Grimes* are astonishingly evocative – but he rarely indulged in the uninhibited lushness of his contemporary Michael Tippett. As Yehudi Menuhin once memorably put it, "If wind and water could write music, it would sound like Ben's."

Britten was born in Lowestoft on Saint Cecilia's day (22 November) – appropriately, as she is the patron saint of music. His mother, a keen amateur musician and singer, was the formative influence in his early years, and by the age of five he was already writing. Britten went on to take lessons from the composer Frank Bridge, who introduced him to the music of progressive European composers such as Bartók, Berg and Schoenberg. After studying at the Royal College of Music, Britten got a job with the Post Office film unit and wrote music for a number of innovative documentary films (including *Night Mail*), a crucial experience in refining his technique as a dramatic composer. He also met and collaborated with the poet W. H. Auden, who was to be one of the most important influences of his life, reinforcing Britten's pacifism and providing the text for his first important song cycle, *Our Hunting Fathers* (1936).

Discontented with life in England, Auden emigrated to America in 1939, followed a few months later by Britten and Peter Pears, the tenor who was to be Britten's partner for almost forty years – it's hard to find a partnership that so dominated the creative output of a composer as did this one. Britten and Pears spent nearly three years in America, where Britten wrote his first big orchestral work, the *Sinfonia da Requiem* (1940), and his first dramatic work, the operetta *Paul Bunyan* (1941) to a libretto by Auden. This period in the States was crucial in bringing out Britten's profound attachment to his English heritage, and his feelings for his native East Anglia were heightened by an article he read on the Suffolk poet George Crabbe. He determined to go back to England and to set Crabbe's work as an opera.

Britten returned home in 1942 and had soon written some of his very best music – *A Ceremony of Carols* and a song cycle for Pears titled *Serenade for Tenor, Horn and Strings*. But it was the opera

Peter Grimes (1945), based on a story by Crabbe, that put him firmly on the map, establishing him not just as a brilliant composer but also as a sincere commentator on social and political events, something that runs through most of his output. At the time of *Peter Grimes* there were only two established opera companies in Britain, so Britten turned to the medium of chamber opera and created his own company, the English Opera Group (with the producer and librettist Eric Crozier and his regular designer John Piper) to perform these small-scale pieces. They became the centrepiece of the annual Aldeburgh Festival, which Britten started in 1948 in the Suffolk seaside town that he and Pears had made their home.

Throughout the rest of his life, in addition to writing works for Aldeburgh and for amateur groups and schoolchildren (*Noye's Fludde*, 1957, is the best of these), Britten received several major commissions, the greatest of which was the *War Requiem* (1961), composed for the consecration of Coventry Cathedral after its post-war reconstruction. Britten had been a conscientious objector during the war and several of his works carry a pacifist message, the *War Requiem* foremost among them. A few years later the opening of the Snape Maltings just outside Aldeburgh allowed for larger-scale opera productions, and *Death in Venice*, the last of Britten's fifteen operas, was produced there in 1973. Giving Pears his most demanding stage role, *Death in Venice* was Britten's most public statement about his long-standing relationship with the singer. In 1976 Britten accepted a life peerage – the first musician to be so honoured. He died in December of that year, of the heart disease that had weakened him in his last few years.

Benjamin Britten (left) with Peter Pears.

OPERA

In Britten's operas there is a sense of austerity that suggests an essentially pessimistic view of humanity, and his music, which is often powerfully elemental, reflects this. His greatest opera, *Peter Grimes*, encapsulates many of the themes that preoccupied him throughout his life – the vulnerability of innocence, the abuse of power, and the susceptibility of the outsider to the pressurizing norms of society. These ideas even surface in his lighter operas – the bittersweet comedy *Albert Herring* (1947) and the exotically scored *A Midsummer Night's Dream*. Of his other major operas, *Billy Budd* has an all-male cast and another maritime setting, while *The Turn of the Screw*, from the ghost story by Henry James, was a commission from the 1954 Venice Biennale.

Peter Grimes

Peter Grimes, which reopened Sadler's Wells theatre after the war in June 1945, marked a watershed for Britten and a rebirth for British opera. It was so widely publicized and well received that a bus conductor on the route to the theatre is reported to have announced "Sadler's Wells! Any more for *Peter Grimes*, the sadistic fisherman?"

The story is a grim one: Grimes is a fisherman whose temperament and conduct have put him at odds with the Aldeburgh community in which the opera is set. At the outset he is acquitted of the murder of his young apprentice, who has died at sea. Here Grimes has music of great beauty and vulnerability that is sharply contrasted with the gossips and busybodies of the Borough. But we see his darker side as he bullies his new apprentice, who then accidentally falls to his death. Grimes sets sail in his ship and sinks it out at sea.

Though the action of *Peter Grimes* is focused on the ambiguous fisherman and his finely drawn social background, its magnificent orchestral score evokes another principal character, the sea itself. The opera's four vivid *Sea Interludes*, which allow for scene changes, have become concert pieces in their own right, and the music conjures up tempests throughout the piece.

Vickers, Harper, Bailey; Royal Opera House Chorus & Orchestra; Davis (Philips; 2 CDs)

Vickers' terrifying portrayal of Grimes' frustration displays a mixture of violence, anguish and fragility that has a Lear-like quality. Heather Harper makes an earthy Ellen Orford, and the supporting cast are uniformly excellent. Colin Davis lacks the confident drive of Britten (see below) but he brings out the colours of the score beautifully.

Pears, Watson, Pease; Royal Opera House Chorus & Orchestra; Britten (Decca; 2 CDs)

Most of Britten's recordings of his own operas stand as classics, and nowhere is that truer than with *Peter Grimes*, recorded complete for the first time in 1958, with Peter Pears superb in the title role and Britten bringing a pacy energy to the score. Pears' singing of "Now the Great Bear and Pleiades" in Act I poignantly evokes the loneliness of the fisherman at the mercy of fate and the elements.

Billy Budd

In *Billy Budd*, based on the story by Herman Melville, Britten recapitulates the maritime setting and several of the themes of *Peter Grimes*. Billy Budd, a sailor unjustly accused of murder, is driven to his execution by the vindictive Claggart and by Captain Vere, a decent man forced by circumstance to sacrifice him. Much has been made of the homoeroticism that runs through *Billy Budd* (the cast is exclusively male), and indeed the heaviness of Britten's orchestration does suggest a sense of sexual tension. The drama is remarkably direct and the presentation of good and evil in the forms of Billy and Claggart is among the most intense in all opera, with Britten employing easily recognizable tonalities for each. Though *Billy Budd* was highly acclaimed at its first performances – some proclaiming it greater than *Grimes* – it hasn't enjoyed the same popularity since.

Keenlyside, Langridge, Tomlinson; London Symphony Chorus and Orchestra; Hickox (Chandos; 3 CDs)

Where this performance scores over Britten's own Decca recording is in the superb casting, with Simon Keenlyside as Billy and Philip Langridge as Vere achieving a remarkable degree of subtlety in their characterizations. The conducting of Richard Hickox while always exciting is occasionally a little too belligerent.

The Turn of the Screw

Britten's next major opera, *The Turn of the Screw* (1954), inhabits a totally different world. It's the finest of his chamber operas, tailor-made for six singers and thirteen instrumentalists whose musical abilities Britten knew intimately. The libretto was written by Myfanwy Piper (wife of the painter John Piper, who designed the sets for many of Britten's operas), based closely on the story by Henry James. It tells of Miles and Flora, two children in a remote country house haunted by the ghost of Peter Quint, the man who may have sexually corrupted them. The exact nature of what went on between Quint and the children is unclear, as is the contribution made by the imagination of the children's governess.

Britten composed the opera at lightning speed, yet it is one of his most brilliant scores. It is very tightly constructed as a sequence of variations on a theme using all twelve notes of the chromatic scale, yet because it requires two child performers the music also has a wonderful simplicity and transparency – indeed, some nursery rhymes are cunningly woven into the score. The sheer range and delicacy of the sounds Britten gets from the chamber orchestra is quite remarkable.

Lott, Langridge; Aldeburgh Festival Ensemble: Bedford (Naxos; 2 CDs)

This 1994 recording is so wonderful it even supersedes the version recorded by Britten himself. Felicity Lott is both heroic and vulnerable as the governess and Philip Langridge makes a highly menacing Quint. Much of the special atmosphere of this piece is created by the orchestral textures, which have never sounded as luminous as here.

CHORAL MUSIC

Britten's choral writing, another crucial part of his output, ranges from small-scale pieces for boys' choir to massive works like the *Spring Symphony* and the *War Requiem*. Although he is regarded as standing firmly in opposition to the pastoralism which prevailed in English music in the first half of the twentieth century, there is a recurring fascination with the cycles of nature and the traditions of the countryside in both his choral music and his songs. Where he differs from composers like Vaughan Williams or Finzi is in his almost total avoidance of a nostalgic or reassuring version of pastoral – a dark element is rarely far from the surface of his work.

Hymn to St Cecilia & Spring Symphony

Hymn to St Cecilia (1942) for unaccompanied five-part chorus and soloists is quintessential Britten, with text (by Auden) and setting that emphasize not just the emotional and aesthetic power of music, but its eroticism as well. Britten's music, like Auden's poem, combines a classical tightness of form with a complexity of ideas about the role of the artist in the face of a disintegrating civilization. Each section ends with a unison exaltation to "Blessed Cecilia", a simple device but one which serves to create a sense of structural unity.

The *Spring Symphony* (1949), commissioned by Serge Koussevitsky for the Boston Symphony Orchestra, was inspired directly by the experience of the Suffolk countryside. Organized in four movements, it sets a series of fourteen poems for soloists and chorus, evoking the progress of winter to spring and the onset of summer. The orchestra is large, but Britten scores the music for small and contrasted instrumental groups. Given the nature of the poems, it is a testament to his ingenuity that the music steers well away from the hackneyed English pastoral tradition while containing some wonderfully atmospheric music – not least in the languorous but edgy setting of another Auden poem ("Out on the lawn I lie in bed") which forms the emotional heart of the work.

Spring Symphony; Hymn to St Cecilia: Hagley, Robbin, Ainsley; Choristers of Salisbury Cathedral; The Monteverdi Choir; Philharmonia Orchestra; Gardiner (Deutsche Grammophon; with *Five Flower Songs*)

John Eliot Gardiner and his Monteverdi Choir are renowned for their lucid and dynamic performances of Baroque music. Their approach works spectacularly well with Britten – revealing the contours and the structure of the *Spring Symphony* as never before. The performance of the *Hymn to St Cecilia* is no less fresh and invigorating.

War Requiem

The *War Requiem* (1961) was commissioned for the consecration of a new cathedral at Coventry – the previous building having been destroyed by the Luftwaffe in World War II. Britten's text is an interweaving of the Latin mass (for soprano, chorus and orchestra) with nine poems by Wilfred Owen (for tenor and baritone soloists with chamber orchestra), while a third element is provided by a distant choir of boys' voices accompanied by an organ. Britten had a clear message and he wanted to communicate it as strongly as possible: "My subject is War, and the Pity of War. The Poetry is in the pity ... All a poet can do today is warn" is the Owen inscription on the title page.

The *War Requiem* is fundamentally a work of reconciliation, and Britten wanted this fact to be represented by the three soloists in the first performance: Peter Pears, Dietrich Fischer-Dieskau and Galina Vishnevskaya, from Britain, Germany and Russia respectively. In the event the Soviets wouldn't give Vishnevskaya a visa and the part was taken at short notice by Heather Harper. Some critics have argued that in taking on the grandiose form of a large-scale "official" choral work, Britten was compromising the individuality of his voice, but while there are moments when the inspiration flags this is a hugely powerful and affecting work.

Harper, Langridge, Shirley-Quirk; London Symphony Orchestra & Chorus; Hickox (Chandos; 2 CDs; with *Sinfonia da Requiem & Ballad of Heroes*)

The original Britten version, featuring the trio of Pears, Fischer-Dieskau and Vishnevskaya, is a classic, but equally impressive is this 1991 recording conducted by Richard Hickox. It provides the kind of clean modern sound that really benefits a work of this size and complexity, and the soloists are deeply rooted in the music.

A Ceremony of Carols & Missa Brevis

A Ceremony of Carols (1942) was composed at the same time as the *Hymn to St Cecilia* and has a similarly cool economy of means. Written for the unusual combination of boys' voices and harp, what especially impresses is the sheer variety of moods Britten achieves in his setting of the nine medieval texts, from the serene lullaby "Bululalow" to the almost aggressive urgency of "This Little Babe". This capacity to surprise is even more in evidence in the short setting of the mass which he wrote in 1959 for the boy choristers of Westminster Cathedral at the request of their choirmaster, George Malcolm. The choir were famed for the clarity and hard-edged quality of their sound, qualities which Britten was keen to exploit. The result is decidedly austere and angular, with the setting of the Agnus Dei – usually a consoling moment – particularly striking for its spooky dissonances.

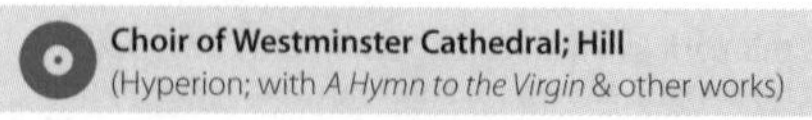
Choir of Westminster Cathedral; Hill (Hyperion; with *A Hymn to the Virgin* & other works)

The best all-round recording of Britten's smaller-scale choral music is this disc from David Hill and the Westminster Cathedral Choir. The voices are clear and pure, and the acoustic gives the music just the right amount of bloom.

SONGS

Britten composed his *Quatre Chansons Français* for soprano and orchestra at the age of fifteen, and song cycles were to form a prominent part of his output from then onwards. This was something of a rarity in English music, and demonstrates Britten's admiration for the music of Mahler, who influenced the rich and original instrumental colouring of many of his songs. Nearly all Britten's songs were written with the uniquely plangent tones of Peter Pears in mind. His first major cycle, *Our Hunting Fathers* (1936), revealed him as something of an *enfant terrible*, with its wild orchestral writing, strenuous vocal line and political message. W. H. Auden's text ostensibly deals with cruelty to animals, but the real subject is anxiety at the current situation in Europe.

Les Illuminations

Les Illuminations (1939) is a setting of eight obliquely erotic and elusive verses by Arthur Rimbaud for soprano and string orchestra. Britten almost certainly turned to the French language in order to liberate himself from the rather constricting (and often precious) world of English song. The cycle evokes a hallucinatory world in which images of the modern city and a luxurious depiction of the god Pan exist side by side. There is also a tightness and economy to the music that reflects Britten's awareness of contemporaries like Stravinsky. He creates some glorious effects, and there is often a harmonic disjunction within songs which increases the poetry's sense of ambiguity. The line that frames the cycle, "J'ai seul la clef de cette parade sauvage" (I alone hold the key to this savage parade), suggests that this piece had a special significance to Britten: it is certainly one of his most vivid and inspired shorter works.

Pears, Tuckwell; London Symphony Orchestra; Britten (Decca/London; with *Serenade & Nocturne*)

Pears' recordings of these major song cycles, made in the early 1960s, represent the essential disc of Britten's vocal music and not just for historical reasons. Of course Pears brings a special quality to this repertoire, but the technical and artistic quality of the whole disc is unbeatable.

Serenade for Tenor, Horn and Strings

Britten's finest song cycle, the *Serenade for Tenor, Horn and Strings*, was written for Pears in 1943 and takes the night as its subject. The unusual instrumentation was the result of Britten's admiration for the brilliant horn playing of Dennis Brain, who demonstrated the possibilities of using the instrument's natural harmonics rather than the valves for creating an eerie, slightly "out of tune" sound. Britten employed this in the mysterious scene-setting prologue, with its suggestion both of a hunting call and of reveille. The technique gives the music a sound which is highly effective. The *Serenade* reveals Britten's astonishing capacity to get right to the heart of his chosen texts. Setting six English poems, chosen with the help of the critic Edward Sackville-West, Britten's vision of night is of a time beset with shadows and spiritual angst – despite the serenity of the opening poem, Charles Cotton's "Pastoral". Guilt, pain, love and death all flit across the landscape of the unconscious: most terrifyingly in the pared-down and harmonically troubling setting of Blake's "O Rose thou art sick" and the medieval "Dirge" in which the tenor's melody seems half chant and half wail.

Bostridge, Neunecker; Bamberger Symphoniker; Metzmacher; Britten Sinfonia; Harding (EMI; with *Our Hunting Fathers*)

There's been a recent spate of fine recordings of Britten's masterpiece, none better than this one by the outstanding English tenor Ian Bostridge. The voice is light but, like Pears, Bostridge's diction is crystal clear and his ability to convey the nuances of the text is outstanding.

Pears, Tuckwell; London Symphony Orchestra; Britten (Decca/London; with *Les Illuminations & Nocturne*)

Though recorded when Pears was in his fifties, this is a tremendously powerful and authoritative performance, rather freer in interpretation than his earlier recording with Dennis Brain. The "Dirge", in particular, has never sounded so extreme.

ORCHESTRAL MUSIC

Britten wrote relatively little purely orchestral music, but some of it ranks amongst his best work. Perhaps his best known orchestral work is the *Young Person's Guide to the Orchestra* (1946), a set of variations on a theme of Henry Purcell. Originally the soundtrack for an educational film, each variation is presented by a different section of the orchestra culminating in an exuberant fugue for the full orchestra. More serious are the *Variations on a Theme of Frank Bridge* (1937), which marks his coming of age as a composer and has proved one of his most durable works, and the *Sinfonia da Requiem* (1940), the closest Britten came to writing a purely orchestral symphony.

Variations on a Theme of Frank Bridge

The *Variations on a Theme of Frank Bridge* is a tribute to his teacher – Britten said that each of the movements portrayed a different aspect of Bridge's character. Written for the Boyd Neel Orchestra, it is a tremendously confident and extrovert work which reveals Britten's interest in the neo-classicism of Stravinsky. The variations take the form of a series of parodies of different musical genres – a Viennese waltz, a bourrée, a funeral march etc – and there's some brilliant fugal writing. Inevitably, it also has its darker moments and the return to the original theme adopts a more serious language reminiscent of Mahler.

Tomter; Norwegian Chamber Orchestra; Brown
(Virgin; with *Simple Symphony & Lachrymae*)

Both the *Frank Bridge Variations* and the *Simple Symphony* are given wonderfully spritely and generous performances. There's an added bonus in the passionate performance of *Lachrymae*, a work for viola and string orchestra inspired by Dowland.

Sinfonia da Requiem

There are no light moments in the *Sinfonia da Requiem* (1940). A profoundly mournful memorial for his parents and for the war dead of Europe, each of its three movements has a title derived from the Requiem mass. The first movement ("Lacrymosa") reveals Britten at his most Mahlerian: an ominous drumbeat heralds a naggingly persistent motif which builds slowly in the strings with chilly interjections from the wind. The prevailing dark despair is suddenly shattered by the next movement ("Dies irae"), a demented *danse macabre* in which a Scottish jig is thrown back and forth across the orchestra with mounting hysteria and a growling saxophone solo adds to the sense of unease. Only in the finale ("Requiem aeternam") is there any sense of reassurance with another slowly building theme – oddly similar to the end of Stravinsky's *Firebird* – that offers some kind of fragile hope.

London Symphony Orchestra; Bedford
(Naxos; with *Four Sea Interludes* and *Passacaglia* from *Peter Grimes & Gloriana Suite*)

Originally recorded for Collins, this excellent recording is now on Naxos at budget price. Stuart Bedford, who worked with Britten, is especially strong in the *Sinfonia da Requiem*, bringing an extra layer of emotion to this austere work. He is no less impressive in sparklingly atmospheric accounts of the *Sea Interludes* and the *Passacaglia*.

Max Bruch (1838–1920)

That Max Bruch is widely known for just one work, his *Violin Concerto No. 1*, is both unfair and misleading. One of the most prominent German composers of the nineteenth century, he produced a large amount of lush, tuneful music but his innate conservativism meant that by the end of the century he was completely out of step with the innovations of Mahler, Reger and Richard Strauss – all of whose music he loathed – let alone the more radical experiments of Schoenberg.

Bruch's career was something of a procession along the establishment path, winning competitions, studying with well-respected figures (notably Ferdinand Hiller), composing for the theatre, concert hall and church, and accepting various prestigious positions. He was in his early twenties when he achieved his first major success as a composer with *Frithjof*, a choral work based on an old Norse saga. Several more choral blockbusters cemented his reputation and established him as the natural successor to Mendelssohn in the field of grandiose oratorios. In 1867 he was appointed director of the court orchestra at Schwartzburg-Sonderhausen but decided to become a freelance musician after three years (Brahms then applied for the vacated post). He was in Liverpool from 1880–83 as music director of the Liverpool Philharmonic Society, and it was there that he wrote the *Scottish Fantasy* and *Kol Nidrei* – his best known works after the first violin concerto. Finally, in 1891 he was made a professor at the Berlin Academy where he taught composition until 1910.

Like Pfitzner, who in 1916 organized a revival of Bruch's opera *Die Loreley*, he lived out of academia's palm, producing music that was designed first and foremost to appease the institutions that supported him, and, secondarily, to entertain the public in the least demanding fashion. He lacked the genius of his great contemporary Brahms (with whom he had a rather spiky relationship) but was sometimes associated with him in opposition to the "New German School" of Wagner and Liszt. He had the modesty to recognize himself as a lesser talent, predicting that: "Fifty years from now he (Brahms) will loom up as one of the supremely great composers of all time, while I will be remembered for having written my G minor violin concerto."

Symphony No. 3

Bruch's symphonic style owes much to Mendelssohn and Schumann. And even more to Brahms, whose influence is clear in Bruch's *Symphony No. 3* – the last and best of his symphonies – which was written in 1883, during his Liverpool sojourn but later revised. Bruch is actually a more colourful orchestrator than Brahms, but his sense of structure is far less assured, and the symphony has a rather episodic character to it. That said, it's a touching work pervaded by a powerful mood of nostalgia (Bruch called it "a work of life, of joy") especially in the grand sweep of the slow movement. The most engaging movement is the finale, whose glorious opening theme has more than a hint of English folk song to it.

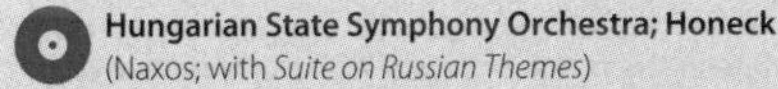

Hungarian State Symphony Orchestra; Honeck (Naxos; with *Suite on Russian Themes*)

There have been quite a few recordings of Bruch's *Symphony No. 3* in the last couple of decades, but this budget recording is probably the most convincing. This is not least because conductor Manfred Honeck clearly believes in the work, relishing but not wallowing in its gloriously old-fashioned melodies.

Violin Concerto No. 1

Although its success was practically instant, the *Violin Concerto No. 1* (1866) took Bruch four years and a great deal of effort to write. Technical advice came from the violinist Joseph Joachim, who was extremely encouraging, and the conductor Hermann Levi, who was not – he disparaged the work for its structural shortcomings. Bruch's most original idea was to write the first movement as a Prelude to an ensuing Adagio rather than as a completely autonomous movement. It begins with a series of quiet exchanges between orchestra and soloist, the violin tentative at first and then more confident in its main theme, which is stated over a tense orchestral background of timpani and tremolando strings. It's an exhilarating opening movement, alternating between the sweeter more relaxed quality of the violin's second theme and a recurrent tension generated by the interval of a minor third and a restless short-long rhythmic motif. A moment of calm leads into the Adagio, in which the influence of Mendelssohn is clearly apparent in the subdued but powerful emotion of the main theme. Like Brahms, ten years later, Bruch closes the concerto with an energetic Hungarian-style Allegro, perhaps a gesture to the Hungarian-born Joachim, the work's dedicatee and first performer.

Heifetz; New Symphony Orchestra; Sargent (RCA; with *Scottish Fantasy* & Vieuxtemps *Concerto No. 5*)

The finest version of Bruch's *Violin Concerto No. 1* is the historic account from Jascha Heifetz – the quality of his sound and his response to the music's inflections are stunning, and his phrasing encourages Sargent and the orchestra to wallow in the score's sensual beauty.

Lin; Chicago Symphony Orchestra; Slatkin (Sony; with Mendelssohn *Violin Concerto* & Vieuxtemps *Concerto No. 5*)

For the classic coupling of the Bruch and Mendelssohn concertos, there is no finer modern recording than the one from Cho-Liang Lin and Leonard Slatkin, a performance that's particularly beautiful and intense in the slow movement of the Bruch.

Scottish Fantasy

Bruch's only other work to approach the first concerto in popularity is the *Scottish Fantasy*, written in Liverpool in 1880 for the brilliant Spanish virtuoso Pablo de Sarasate. Inspired (inevitably) by the writings of Sir Walter Scott, the four-movement piece quotes a number of Scottish folk songs and is scored for violin and orchestra, with a prominent harp part to give it a suitably "bardic" feel. Its Scottishness is about as authentic as *Brigadoon* but it's highly enjoyable if you surrender to its kitsch charm. A gloomy processional opening, from which the wavering violin line emerges, conjures up a kind of misty "days of yore" atmosphere before the soloist lets rip with a heart-tugging version of the song "Auld Robbie Morris". It's followed by a lively dance over a bagpipe-style orchestral drone, a relatively restrained slow movement, and a rousing finale with some spectacularly acrobatic writing for the soloist.

Heifetz; New Symphony Orchestra; Sargent (RCA; with *Violin Concerto No. 1* & Vieuxtemps *Concerto No. 5*)

Heifetz's playing of the *Scottish Fantasy* is no less brilliant than his account of the *Violin Concerto*. It's a performance that throbs with energy and a marvellous ebullient spontaneity. Sargent and the New Symphony Orchestra provide the perfect platform for Heifetz's magic.

Lin; Chicago Symphony Orchestra; Slatkin (Sony; with *Violin Concerto No. 1*)

Like Heifetz, Lin is technically pretty well flawless but what impresses most is the way he takes the music at face value: by not playing to the gallery he manages to make the work's sentimentality seem touching rather than sugary.

Kol Nidrei

Bruch could spot a good tune as well as write one, and when in 1881 he finally succumbed to one of several requests to write a cello work, he took as his starting point the haunting Jewish melody "Kol Nidrei", traditionally chanted on the eve of Yom Kippur (the Day of Atonement). Bruch's masterstroke was to break up the tune, when it first appears in the solo part, into groups of three notes with a rest between each group. The result, in the hands of a fine performer, suggests the idea of a voice so full of emotion that it is forced to take a breath between each short phrase. Like the *Scottish Fantasy*, the work is episodic (there's another borrowed tune, "O Weep for Those"), but in *Kol Nidrei* each section seems to grow out of the previous one, making it a much more unified work. Bruch was not, as is commonly thought, Jewish but he was perfectly aware of the appeal that *Kol Nidrei* would have for Jews. It was premiered in Liverpool in 1882 by its dedicatee Robert Hausmann.

Wispelwey; Die Deutsche Kammerphilharmonie Bremen (Channel Classics; with Tchaikovsky *Rococo Variations* & Saint-Saëns *Cello Concerto No. 1*)

This recent account from Peter Wispelwey adopts a comparatively cool approach: rubato is kept to a minimum and there's little sense of the cello "vocalizing" the melody. The restraint pays off, however, in a performance that allows the music to speak for itself rather more than is usual.

Casals; London Symphony Orchestra; Ronald (Pearl; with *Violin Concerto No. 1* & *Scottish Fantasy*)

Despite the crackles, this 1936 recording is a classic – highly expressive but without ever lapsing into sentimentality. Casals' tendency to mimic vocal phrasing seems particularly appropriate in the music of Bruch. The disc comes with an understated but effective first concerto by Nathan Milstein and another scintillating *Scottish Fantasy* from Heifetz.

Anton Bruckner (1824–1896)

Throughout much of the century following his death, Anton Bruckner's name was routinely paired with that of Gustav Mahler. After all, the external similarities seemed obvious: both were Austrian, both wrote vast symphonies and both needed many years of proselytizing from dedicated interpreters before their music was truly appreciated. Beyond these resemblances, however, they were very different characters: Mahler was an intellectually sophisticated, neurotically egotistical composer-conductor, laden with psychological paradoxes; Bruckner was a pious and naive church organist with a lumbering manner, ill-fitting suits and rustic accent, whose massively simple music attests to the redemptive force of the divine.

Bruckner's grandfather and father were both village schoolteachers. As the position traditionally went hand in hand with that of church organist, young Anton was surrounded by the worlds of the schoolroom and the church from an early age, and by the time he was ten years old he could often be found deputizing for his father at the organ. His formal musical education began in the following year, and in 1836 he was accepted as a choirboy at the famous monastery of St Florian near Linz in Upper Austria.

He spent 1840–41 in Linz itself, completing his teacher training, after which he secured his first paid position as schoolmaster in a small village on the Bohemian border. But his true ambition was realized when he gained a teaching post at St Florian itself, where he remained for ten years. During this period he continued his musical education and composed his first works, mainly liturgical pieces. In 1855 he moved back to Linz to take up the position of cathedral organist, and rapidly established himself as one of Europe's greatest exponents of the instrument. But all the while his private studies of theory and composition continued, initially under the celebrated Viennese theoretician Simon Sechter, and later with a teacher some ten years his junior, Otto Kitzler.

It was with Kitzler's help and encouragement that the diffident Bruckner found his true musical vocation, when the former conducted a performance of Wagner's *Tannhäuser* in Linz. It proved a revelation. Bruckner had spent almost forty years assimilating every theoretical rule of composition, but his discovery of Wagner showed him that his way forward was to break these rules, as Wagner had done, in order to create symphonic music that mirrored Wagner's achievements as a master of music drama.

Until this point, Bruckner's music hardly stood out from the run-of-the-mill material being written for day-to-day use in the Catholic Church's liturgy. Now, as if to make up for lost time, he immediately began a series of truly original scores, including the *Symphony in D Minor* (1863–64), which he later numbered No. 0, the three mature masses (1864, 1865–66 and 1867–68), and his acknowledged *Symphony No. 1* (1865–66), all of them recognizably Brucknerian in scale and content. During this period of frenetic and unrelenting activity, he suffered a mental breakdown which manifested itself in a number of perplexing symptoms, including numeromania (an obsession with counting), and spent the spring and summer of 1867 in a sanatorium until he was fully recovered. The following year Bruckner moved to Vienna to succeed his old teacher Sechter at the city's music conservatory, where he taught theory and the organ, and later became a lecturer at the university.

Here, between 1871 and 1876, Bruckner composed his next four symphonies, beginning each one as soon as he had finished its predecessor. He then spent the next three years making revisions to these, before embarking on his next great surge of creative effort, which saw the completion of his *String Quintet* (1879), symphonies *No. 6* (1879–81),

Anton Bruckner in his work room, c.1885.

No. 7 (1881–83) and *No. 8* (1884–87) and the *Te Deum* (1881–84). A further period of revisions followed, largely spurred on by friends who urged Bruckner to find new ways to make his music more approachable. Ever eager to comply with well-meaning suggestions, Bruckner often found himself unable to finish his works to his satisfaction, and indeed, he never managed to complete his last symphony, *No. 9* (1891–96). He died in Vienna in October 1896 and in accordance with his wishes was buried beneath the organ at St Florian.

Throughout all his years in Vienna, Bruckner had to put up with continual barracking from the anti-Wagnerites and in particular the venomous critic Eduard Hanslick, who wielded far-reaching powers in Viennese musical life. Only *Symphony No. 7* brought him unchallenged success and led to international recognition during his last decade. Some still carp at the crudities and naiveties that many of Bruckner's works apparently display, yet there was arguably no other composer who spent so many years studying his art before establishing his unique voice. He remained a devout Catholic for the whole of his life and his faith pervades all his music, though it was with the traditionally secular symphony – Gothic cathedrals in sound, as they have often been described – that his originality was established.

Famous First Words

Throughout musical history certain powerful critics have informed the general opinion to such an extent that even celebrated composers and performers found it difficult to withstand their influence. This is all the more alarming when one considers just how often the opinion-formers got it so completely and spectacularly wrong.

Of the first performance of Beethoven's ninth symphony, for example, Louis Spohr wrote: "The fourth movement is, in my opinion, so monstrous and tasteless and, in its grasp of Schiller's *Ode*, so trivial that I cannot understand how a genius like Beethoven could have written it." One would think that as a composer himself Spohr might have resisted the temptation to raise his pen against a colleague, but even Weber, himself battleweary from critical abuse, wrote a review of Beethoven's seventh symphony in which he suggested that its composer was "ripe for the madhouse" and that the later works were "a confused chaos, an unintelligible struggle after novelty." When the last four of Beethoven's quartets were performed in concert in 1826 one critic suggested that their composer had "finally lost all grasp of reason, and stands before us like a madman rocking on his haunches."

While some attempted to ride out the abuse – such as Max Reger, who famously wrote to one hostile critic: "I am sitting in the smallest room of my house. I have your review before me. In a moment it will be behind me" – others were less resilient. Bruckner would suffer terrible depressions before each of his premieres, primarily on account of his overwhelming fear of Eduard Hanslick, the doyen of Austrian critics and the major opponent of Richard Wagner and the New German School. According to Bruckner: "With him one cannot fight. One can only approach him with petitions." Hanslick was Bruckner's nemesis. The composer was once asked by the Emperor Franz Josef what he might do for him, to which Bruckner replied: "Do something about Hanslick".

Of Hans Richter's first performance in Vienna of Bruckner's eighth symphony (1892) – a work now regarded generally as one of the summits of the entire symphonic canon – Hanslick wrote: "I found this newest one, as I found the other Bruckner symphonies ... strange as a whole and even repugnant ... characteristic of Bruckner's newest symphony is the immediate juxtaposition of dry schoolroom counterpoint with unbounded exaltation. Thus, tossed between intoxication and desolation, we arrive at no definite impression and enjoy no artistic pleasure. Everything flows, without clarity and without order, willy-nilly into dismal long-windedness..." Hanslick's words were decisive. Not until the rise to primacy of conductor Wilhelm Furtwängler during the early 1930s would Bruckner's star finally begin its rise to ascendancy.

CHORAL MUSIC

Before Bruckner had any idea about how to write for an orchestra, he had excelled in his writing for choir with basic instrumental accompaniment. Indeed, his liturgical output exceeds his symphonic, though many of these early works are best left to the dedicated. Much more worthwhile are the mature masses, which bring to the mass tradition of Mozart and Haydn both the lyricism of Schubert and the austerity of Bach. On a grander scale is the *Te Deum*, a work Bruckner felt to be one of his best. "When God finally calls me", he once said, "and asks 'What have you done with the talent I gave you, my boy?', I will present him with the score of my *Te Deum* and hope he will judge me mercifully."

Masses Nos. 1–3 & Te Deum

Bruckner wrote as many as seven masses, but only the last three, dating from the 1860s and known confusingly as nos. 1, 2 and 3, are performed with any regularity. These works were no more immune from Bruckner's revisionary practices than were his symphonies, and the third, in F minor, was reworked at least four times before he arrived at a definitive version. The first (D minor) and last have orchestral accompaniment, but the middle work (E minor) has only an accompaniment of wind instruments in response to the more austere sect for whom he wrote the work.

Bruckner's setting of the great hymn of praise to God, the *Te Deum*, was written between the seventh and eighth (1881–84) symphonies and is thus his most mature vocal composition. It is on the same scale as his symphonies, requiring four soloists, a choir, organ and orchestra, and, despite its key of C major, it has even been used, following Bruckner's own misguided suggestion, as a choral finale to the ninth symphony, which is in D minor.

Corydon Singers & Orchestra; Best (Hyperion; 3 CDs; with other choral pieces)

Matthew Best and his Corydon Singers have made their names in this music and these Hyperion discs provide some of the most intensely moving Bruckner available, sensitively performed and recorded. The discs are all available individually, but there is a discount if you buy the full set.

Motets

The motets span almost the whole of Bruckner's adult life. They are among the finest liturgical music of the last 150 years, in which Bruckner's love of Renaissance polyphony is fused with his own ripe chromaticism. Many are written to be performed without accompaniment and, as expressions of devotion, they possess a touching simplicity in their directness of expression. High points include the deeply moving but unsentimental settings of *Ave Maria* of 1861 (which marked the beginning of his stylistic maturity), *Tota pulchra es Maria* (for tenor, four-part choir and organ), *Os justi*, *Christus factus est* and the more intense *Locus iste*.

Ave Maria; Locus iste; Christus factus est; Vexilla regis; Os justi; Virga Jesse floruit; Pange lingua: Polyphony; Britten Sinfonia; Layton (Hyperion; with *Mass No. 2*)

Seven of Bruckner's most beautiful motets are included here, and in performances that have never been bettered. Polyphony are firm and assured in even the most difficult writing, and always completely absorbing. With these comes a stunning account of Bruckner's most original mass setting – all stunningly recorded.

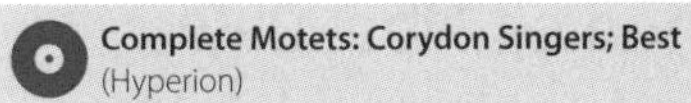

Complete Motets: Corydon Singers; Best (Hyperion)

Luxurious but pure singing from the Corydon Singers of all eleven motets. Their radiant performances bring out the quiet sincerity of Bruckner's religious convictions without a hint of heaviness or sentimentality.

SYMPHONIES

Bruckner was 40 before he found his symphonic vocation. He went on to write ten symphonies on a scale not heard before. While his contemporary Brahms was happy to follow the example of Beethoven's classicism, Bruckner sought a much more modern and novel development of the form, an enterprise in which he was immensely influenced by the operas of Wagner. Bruckner's orchestral forces are on a truly Wagnerian scale – the late symphonies, for example, call for a quartet of Wagner tubas in addition to the already substantial brass section, and their textures demand vast numbers of string and woodwind instruments.

Yet the music itself often betrays Bruckner's background as an organist. Huge sections of the symphonies concentrate exclusively on a particular combination of instruments, as if a particular selection of organ stops had been chosen; these blocks of sound often change abruptly, sometimes with a naive pause to divide them; themes are presented and developed in long strands that are often achieved by simply repeating phrases before moving on; climactic sections often find the full orchestra reiterating a single chord; and, at his most basic, Bruckner has the whole orchestra playing in unison – a dramatic stroke, but one which often sounds coarse and unsophisticated. So Bruckner is not the most subtle or natural of symphonists, but there is so much in the way of harmonic ingenuity, melodic sweep and sheer orchestral magnificence in his music that, despite its scale, diffuseness and clumsiness, it invariably repays your patience. The best works for a first try are symphonies *No. 4* and *No. 7*.

Symphonies Nos. 0–9: Concertgebouw Orchestra; Haitink (Philips; 9 CDs)

Haitink's cycle, recorded throughout the 1960s, did much to establish his reputation as a conductor of enormous integrity and power. Haitink's conducting is classically clear and direct. His sense of structure is as good as anyone's, but he can also pull the stops out, as in his scintillating reading of the *Symphony No. 4*, and intellectually forceful accounts of the last three Bruckner symphonies.

Symphonies Nos. 0–2

Though less distinguished than the later symphonies, the first three nevertheless established many of Bruckner's most distinctive characteristics, from the sense of scale to the organ-like washes of orchestral sound and the construction of long expanses from short, repeated phrases. Bruckner's stylistic development was very much a gradual process, however, so there is often little to distinguish one symphony from the next.

Much of the music of *No. 0* postdates *No. 1*: Bruckner at first abandoned it then revised it before embarking on *No. 2*, but felt that the work now known as *Symphony No. 1* was worthier of the title, so relegated *No. 0* to its zero status. *No. 1* was the first to be performed, at a concert in Linz in 1868 conducted by the composer. Shortly afterwards, he moved to Vienna and from time to time over the next twenty or more years tinkered with the score of the work, finally producing a complete revision in 1891 (the so-called Vienna version) that left hardly a bar untouched. The second symphony was the first to be completed after his move to Vienna and before the anti-Wagner claque began directing its venom towards him. It had a successful first performance in 1873, but his friend Johann Herbeck encouraged him to make changes and cuts, resulting in the 1877 version, though Robert Haas restored the cuts in his edition and it is this version that is invariably played today.

Symphony No. 0: Ireland National Symphony Orchestra; Tintner (Naxos; with *Symphony No. 8*)

With Riccardo Chailly's radiant account of this symphony no longer available, Georg Tintner's performance is the

The "Bruckner Versions" Problem

Bruckner was a compulsive reviser. Various explanations have been put forward as to why: that he was too ready to take advice from well-meaning but uncomprehending friends; that his quest for perfection developed into a kind of "revision mania"; or that his success as an improviser at the organ gave him an unconscious prejudice against setting his work in stone for all time. Whatever you choose to believe, it is an enduring headache for conductors, concert-planners and record-buyers. And modern research has only complicated the issue still further. Some would argue that if you take into account all the changes apparently sanctioned by Bruckner to his *Symphony No. 3*, for instance, then the music could be said to exist in as many as nine different versions.

To make matters worse, there are two scholarly editions of the symphonies and major choral works. When the "original" versions of Austrian musicologist Robert Haas began to appear in the 1930s, they were hailed as revelatory, purging the music of the cuts and "improvements" inflicted on the music by others. But Haas's sometimes "creative" approach (his edition of the *Symphony No. 8* appears to conflate two separate Bruckner versions), plus the awkward fact that he was sponsored by the Nazis, resulted in demands for a new edition in the years after World War II. As a result another Austrian musicologist, Leopold Nowak, created a second, more extensive edition, based on a more literal reading of the handwritten scores Bruckner submitted for performance or publication. But anyone who has ever seen a Bruckner manuscript – with its multitudinous deletions, additions and pastings-over – would surely concede that deciding what actually represents the "definitive" Bruckner is a nightmare in itself. Haas's idiosyncratic solution to the problems of the *Symphony No. 8* has continued to find support from some of the finest Bruckner conductors: for example Herbert von Karajan, Bernard Haitink, Jascha Horenstein, Günter Wand and Daniel Barenboim, with Pierre Boulez recently joining the ranks of those arguing that the Haas score of *No. 8* makes more "musical" sense, whatever the historical pros and cons.

Recent performances and recordings of Bruckner's earlier versions have convinced many that subsequent revisions by no means always improved things. The final version of *Symphony No. 3* (1889) may be the most sophisticated from a harmonic and orchestral point of view, as well as being the most concise, but the original score (1873) is arguably the most structurally successful – Bruckner's best shot at creating a "cathedral in sound". And even when later versions are generally preferred – as in the case of *Symphony No. 4* – the originals remain fascinating: more like different improvisations on the same material than first faltering footsteps. The best advice for the newcomer is probably to go for the most highly recommended recordings and then explore. Comparing and contrasting can only enhance one's understanding, and enjoyment, of this extraordinarily original composer.

one to turn to. His Irish orchestra may not be the best in the world, but there's a freshness and a lightfooted easiness on display here that makes this early work seem utterly convincing.

 **Symphony No. 1 (1866 version): Vienna Philharmonic Orchestra; Abbado** (Deutsche Grammophon)

This electrifying live performance, with the leonine power of the Vienna Phil in full throttle, is shaped with fantastic conviction by Claudio Abbado. His speeds are sometimes quite leisurely, but this only increases the symphony's sense of scale and magnitude. A terrific achievement.

 **Symphony No. 2 (1877 version, ed. Haas): Houston Symphony Orchestra; Eschenbach** (Koch International)

Christoph Eschenbach turns in a lucid and thoroughly convincing account, proving himself very adept at handling Bruckner's often perplexing structures. In this performance, the majesty of this still underplayed Bruckner symphony is never in doubt.

Symphony No. 3

In September 1873, Bruckner took an incomplete symphonic score to Richard Wagner at Bayreuth, along with the score of *Symphony No. 2*, to ask Wagner which one he would like to have dedicated to him. He chose the unfinished piece, and from then on Bruckner always referred to his *Symphony No. 3* as the "Wagner Symphony". Its first version contained a string of quotations from Wagner's operas, but these were eradicated before the premiere in 1877, and Bruckner made a further revision in 1889. It is one of his most enjoyable early symphonies, full of original harmonic and melodic touches, and with a concluding section that, more than any of his other works, looks forward to the grandeur of Mahler.

 **Symphony No. 3 (1873 version): Royal Scottish National Orchestra; Tintner** (Naxos)

In his complete cycle for Naxos, Georg Tintner strove to present Bruckner's symphonies in their earliest versions. Not all the performances are of equal quality, but this one is a must. There are more visceral and dynamic versions available, but Tintner conducts with outstanding naturalness and brings an ease and spontaneity to the music that few have matched.

 **Symphony No. 3 (1889 version, ed. Nowak): Vienna Philharmonic Orchestra; Böhm** (Decca; 2 CDs; with *Symphony No. 4*)

When it comes to the truncated and urgent 1889 version, which has superseded that of 1877, the choice must fall on Böhm, who makes the most of the work's rich sonorities in a subtle performance. This is a fine and beautifully played version, with a special charisma and dignity that only great Bruckner conductors could attain.

Symphony No. 4 – The Romantic

Bruckner himself referred to his fourth symphony as the "Romantic", but when Bruckner uses the term he's not thinking of any Byronic human drama, but rather of nature and all its wonders. This symphony is in essence an allegorical representation of the Austrian countryside. Following the example of Weber's *Der Freischütz* (see p.609), in which the sound of the horn first acquired Romantic connotations, Bruckner makes the instrument dominate this symphony: the opening movement features avalanches of brass tones, but the horn really comes into its own in the Scherzo, an evocation of a hunting scene that alludes to the rustic Austrian dance known as the Ländler. This movement first introduces a characteristic triplet rhythm which became known as the "Bruckner rhythm", so often did he use it subsequently.

There were as many as four versions of this symphony, though only three survive: the first from 1874, a revised one from 1878–80, when he added the "hunting-horn" Scherzo, and an unauthorized, bastardized version by his pupil Ferdinand Löwe, made in 1888 but long since superseded by the Haas edition of the 1878–80 (though there are still recordings available of this version).

 **Symphony No. 4 (1880 version, ed. Nowak): Vienna Philharmonic Orchestra; Böhm** (Deutsche Grammophon)

Karl Böhm's performance just about has it all: Schubertian lyrical grace and rock-like structural integrity; visionary grandeur and very worldly warmth. Hearing this helps explain why Bruckner called *Symphony No. 4* the "Romantic", yet at the same time one can sense how "unique" and "untimely" Bruckner was – in particular that his sense of God in Nature goes way beyond nineteenth-century German Romanticism.

 **Symphony No. 4 (1878–80 version): Berlin Philharmonic Orchestra; Wand** (RCA)

Günter Wand lived long with this music, and nurtured an interpretation that's rarely been equalled. From the horn calls at the start to the overwhelmingly magnificent conclusion, this is a reading that never puts a foot wrong throughout its 69-minute duration. Recorded live, it has a unique electricity and sense of occasion – and the orchestral playing is pretty well unique, too.

Symphony No. 5

This was the first of Bruckner's mature symphonies to survive in a single version and was his most monumental to date, being both longer and more finely worked-out than its predecessors. It has a sense of solemnity not found in the earlier symphonies, with a dramatic sense of conflict generated by the suggestion that passion is always being kept in check. Bruckner's characteristic use of rich brass chorales is here becoming an increasingly prominent feature, while the finale is a marvellously constructed amalgam of fugue and chorale. Bruckner's *Symphony No. 5* is perhaps his most powerful expression of his religious faith: where others would have used voices to articulate belief, Bruckner obviously felt that "The Loving God" (as he liked to call him) was best praised by a score whose epic dimensions seem to elevate humanity to the heavens.

Berlin Philharmonic Orchestra; Wand
(RCA)

What's especially impressive about Günter Wand's live performance is the way momentum is always maintained, even in the tricky last movement, where he sails through with the same unmannered eloquence and power that have been the hallmarks of this great performance from the beginning. The devotional, awestruck intensity of the moment is effectively captured by the recording.

BBC Symphony Orchestra; Jascha Horenstein
(BBC Legends)

Bruckner's fifth symphony is a song of affirmation written at a time of personal desolation. Jascha Horenstein's 1971 Proms performance ends in the pure splendour of praise, yet – especially in the sombre Adagio and the weirdly mercurial Scherzo – it lets us know what Bruckner had to contend with before regaining solid ground. For a pre-digital radio broadcast the sound is more than satisfactory.

Symphony No. 6

Bruckner's next symphony proved to be a lighter, more congenial work than its predecessor – the equivalent, say, of Beethoven's eighth or Brahms's second. Still, it would be wrong to dismiss the work as being somehow less serious than its siblings: the majestic and deeply profound slow movement, for example, has a depth and eloquence that almost demands an attitude of reverence. This is not one of his most frequently performed symphonies, perhaps because of its relative coolness and detachment, but it is typical Bruckner to the core, and again it required no revision on Bruckner's part.

Symphony No. 6 (ed. Haas): New Philharmonia; Klemperer (EMI; with Wagner *Wesendoncklieder*)

Made in 1964, this has long been regarded as a classic Bruckner recording and it wears its age well. Klemperer handles the New Philharmonia with serene confidence, and both orchestra and conductor revel in the symphony's joyous climaxes. Although some find Klemperer's Bruckner a little too stiff, there are plenty of moments in the slow movement that afford real poetry.

Symphony No. 7

The *Symphony No. 7* is the work that brought Bruckner most success in his lifetime, and has always been his best-loved symphony. It has the most enraptured opening of all Bruckner's works: a long radiant phrase played by the cellos and first horn, which is unfolded over tremolando strings. A second, more purposeful, rising theme emerges from the first, a process that exemplifies the amazing clarity with which Bruckner arranges his raw material. The Adagio, written in anticipation of Wagner's death, is the most heart-wrenching episode, with the sombre, glowing tone of four Wagner tubas used to state the melancholy opening phrase of the first theme. A meandering linking passage leads to a lyrical second subject – consolation after the initial gloom – but a mood of extreme tension is generated by the violins' restless, scurrying accompaniment. A near-demonic energy dominates the strident Scherzo, a typically lively Austrian Ländler, which is in marked contrast to the warmth of the trio that accompanies it. The finale takes up the airy pastoral character of the trio and is essentially jubilant. Only a leaping brass phrase hardens the mood, but even this builds to a euphoric climax which culminates in the glorious apotheosis of the closing bars.

Vienna Philharmonic Orchestra; Karajan
(Deutsche Grammophon)

Karajan recorded the seventh symphony more than once, but this 1989 performance with the Vienna Philharmonic is the most incandescent. It is also the most sculpted, with Karajan shaping Bruckner's arching phrases with extraordinary precision. The exactness of his control and the sumptuousness of the orchestral tone tend to reinforce the idea of Bruckner the master builder.

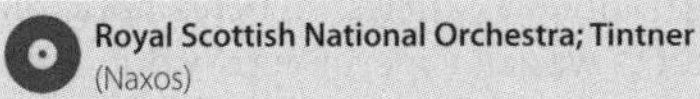

Royal Scottish National Orchestra; Tintner
(Naxos)

The orchestral playing on this Naxos account isn't quite in the big league, but Tintner knows that the key to Bruckner's music is simply to allow the material to evolve naturally and at its own pace. The first movement is taken very broadly without getting bogged down, the Adagio is deeply felt, and the climax is as visionary as any on disc.

Symphony No. 8

The *Symphony No. 8* is Bruckner at his grandest, most uplifting and most religious. At around eighty minutes long, with a slow movement lasting up to half an hour, it can seem daunting and diffuse on first hearing, but it repays repeated acquaintance for the sumptuousness of its orchestral sound and grandeur of its themes. Like nearly all his symphonies, Bruckner opens with pianissimo tremolo strings, an allusion to the opening of Beethoven's ninth, where similarly the music seems to emerge from nothingness – and the theme the strings accompany even matches the rhythm of Beethoven's at the same point. There is a sense of Bruckner wrestling with demons throughout the course of this symphony, yet by the end all is resolved as the main themes come together into the serene, uplifting key of C major. Bruckner completed his symphony in 1887 but then bowed to the inevitable pressure to make cuts, and a new version was completed in 1890.

Symphony No. 8 (ed. Haas): Berlin Philharmonic Orchestra; Wand (RCA; 2 CDs)

A fitting memorial to a great Brucknerian. At a time when conductors have tended to concentrate on Bruckner's architecture at the expense of his soul, Günter Wand balanced structure and humanity to something like perfection. The eighth may on one level be a great monument, but it is also a moving record of a personal journey from darkness to light, as this remarkable live performance shows.

Symphony No. 8 (ed. Nowak): Vienna Philharmonic Orchestra; Giulini (Deutsche Grammophon; 2 CDs)

Giulini opts for the Nowak edition in this rapt and highly charged reading. Though the pace is stately to a degree, which many find wearing, he never loses sight of the overall scheme of things, nor does the slightest detail elude him. He's more theatrical than most, moulding orchestral effects in a way that's usually calculated to thrill, whereas Karajan's more sublime approach seems often to resonate from another world.

Symphony No. 8 (1887 version, ed. Nowak): Ireland National Symphony Orchestra; Tintner
(Naxos; 2 CDs; with *Symphony No. 0*)

Bruckner certainly improved the *Symphony No. 8* technically when he revised it, but Tintner's powerful reading of the original 1887 score shows how radically his conception changed in the process. The original fortissimo ending to the first movement clearly represents both death and transfiguration; in the revision we hear only death. A fascinating insight into the workings of a great symphonic mind.

Symphony No. 9

So preoccupied was Bruckner with making needless revisions of his earlier symphonies that he never managed to complete his last work in the form. Attempts have been made to furnish it with a finale from Bruckner's sketches, but it has long been accepted in the form of a three-movement torso. More approachable than *No. 8* (and, if completed, it would probably have been even longer), it is a musical summation of his life: the great Adagio subtly alludes to earlier works, while the symphony's drama expresses the resolution of his self-doubts in the solace of overpowering religious faith.

Berlin Philharmonic Orchestra; Wand
(RCA)

Günter Wand's depth of insight makes for a deeply moving and humbling experience in this incomparable live recording of the *Symphony No. 9*. It's a gaunt, craggy, unforgiving affair, doubtless much as Bruckner intended it should be, and you're left in no doubt about the agonizing effort its composition required. A magnificent, chastening and ultimately uplifting musical event.

Vienna Philharmonic Orchestra; Giulini
(Deutsche Grammophon)

In this astonishing live recording of 1988, Giulini adopts the broadest of tempi (particularly in the outer movements) but manages to keep everything perfectly balanced. Nothing ever sounds exaggerated or forced and the orchestra clearly revel in being allowed to produce the most sumptuous of sounds, which is beautifully captured by the DG engineers.

CHAMBER MUSIC

Until recently, few would have acknowledged Bruckner as a significant composer of chamber music, and his finest work in the genre, his *String Quintet* of 1879, remains relatively obscure. It was composed at the request of the Viennese violinist Hellmesberger, who was far from happy with it, deeming the Scherzo to be unplayable, thus prompting the accommodating Bruckner to compose a replacement *Intermezzo*, now performed as a separate work. Hellmesberger was only convinced of its viability after a successful performance by a rival ensemble, the Winkler Quartet, with Franz Schalk (who later butchered the *Symphony No. 5*) taking the second viola part. Bruckner's only *String Quartet* and the charming *Rondo* for strings were written as technical studies, and it was never intended that they should be performed in public.

String Quintet

Bruckner's *String Quintet* is a work which in microcosm manages to capture the structural grandeur of his symphonies. Though seldom performed, it ranks as one of the most significant examples of the form since Schubert's C major quintet of 1828. Bruckner's work actually sounds very different to Schubert's since he follows the precedent of Mozart in using two violas (rather than a second cello), thus giving the work a "thick" sonority that seems characteristically Brucknerian. There's never any sense that this was an experimental work. Every theme is perfectly crafted and its overall structure is so cogent and lucid that the quintet immediately registers as a masterpiece. At its heart is a long Adagio – the most symphonic of the movements – in which an underlying sadness finally resolves into a mood of peaceful resignation.

String Quintet; String Quartet; Rondo: L'Archibudelli
(Sony Classical)

This fascinating recording includes each of Bruckner's string chamber works. The performances by L'Archibudelli – who play on gut strings – are outstanding, above all for the way the organic development of Bruckner's style is allowed to unfold. The warmth and naturalness of the recording ideally suits such radiant and affectionate performances.

Antoine Brumel (c.1460–c.1520)

Antoine Brumel, born near Chartres around the middle of the fifteenth century, was one of the most respected musicians and composers of his time. Josquin's *Deploration sur la morte d'Ockeghem* mentions Brumel as one of four followers of Ockeghem who should "weep great tears of grief" at the loss of their "good father" (the others are Josquin himself, Pierre de la Rue and Loyset Compère), and although the theorist Glareanus sourly notes that Brumel excelled through his industry rather than his natural gifts, most writers of his period showered him with praise.

Like many of his contemporaries he travelled widely: probably beginning his career in the choir of Chartres Cathedral, he was last heard of in Italy, where he settled in Rome for some time. Brumel had a reputation as a difficult man to deal with, and this may be borne out by the rapidity with which he moved from job to job – for example, he held a post at Notre Dame in Paris for no more than a year before leaving in some haste. Nonetheless, he was sufficiently valued for Alphonso I of Ferrara, an important patron, to make more than one attempt to hire him. The duke finally succeeded in enticing him to his court in 1505 with the offer of a large salary augmented by a travel allowance. He remained there for five years before his move to Rome. Neither the date nor the place of his death is known.

Sacred Music

Although we know of over fifty *chansons*, Brumel's greatest works are religious. Of his sixteen surviving settings of the mass, the late *Missa de Beata Virgine* is probably his masterpiece. Possibly written in competition with Josquin's setting, it suffers little in comparison, showing an easy control of counterpoint, a sometimes insouciant approach to dissonance, and a daring degree of melodic and rhythmic invention. There's an especial delight in raising the tension towards the end of a movement as the voices chase each other in a flurry of cross-rhythms and ever-decreasing note-values before coming to satisfying rest. No less impressive is the astonishingly assured and flamboyant *Missa "Et Ecce Terrae Motus"* for twelve voices, one of the earliest large choral works, which mixes strict canonic techniques with free invention, contrasts of timbre and impressively full textures when all twelve voices are singing at once.

Missa "Et Ecce Terrae Motus": Tallis Scholars; Phillips
(Gimell; with *Lamentations* and *Magnificat*)

The two other recordings of this mass beef up its massive sonorities by adding instruments to the voices. In contrast, Peter Phillips's Tallis Scholars rely on their pure, and distinctly English, vocal sound to convey the complexities of Brumel's counterpoint. With its mysterious rhythmic ebb and flow, this is one of the great glories of Renaissance music – a work to rival Tallis's better-known *Spem in alium*.

Ferruccio Busoni (1866–1924)

Ferruccio Busoni is one of the forgotten men of twentieth-century music, a situation largely due to the diversity of his talents and his resistance to easy classification. The child of professional musicians, Busoni was born in Tuscany but spent most of his professional life in Germany where, although he always regarded himself as primarily a composer, his early fame was achieved as one of the greatest pianists of his generation.

Like Schoenberg – with whom he enjoyed a mutually respectful relationship – Busoni was a formidable theoretician, and his *Outline of a New Aesthetic of Music* (1907) established him as one of the leading figures of the avant-garde and the first musician to espouse microtonality (music with 36 notes to an octave) and electronic music.

Busoni was one of the finest pianists of his day.

His theories on new music made him the target of musical conservatives, notably Hans Pfitzner, who attacked him for his "sterile intellectualism". Yet Busoni was never able to escape the pull of tradition and his more daring notions were never incorporated into his own compositions. Instead he preferred to write music that looked back to the eighteenth century for inspiration, an approach he termed "Young Classicism" and defined as "the mastering, sifting and exploitation of all the achievements of preceding experiments".

Ultimately Busoni was hamstrung by his own analytical intelligence and by his reverence for the past, and is probably most likely to be remembered as a formidable pianist. The only works you are likely to come across regularly in the concert hall are his fine transcriptions of Bach for the piano. However, there are a few works of his own in which Busoni manages to struggle free of the weight of history: his gargantuan piano concerto, his operas and some of his original piano works. The stage works are not ingratiating pieces – Busoni hated the sensationalized realism of verismo opera, aspiring instead to create a hieratic music drama in which a perfect fusion of music and text would facilitate the spiritual elevation of the audience. The results can be turgid in places, but *Doktor Faust* in particular has moments of great power, and each of the operas is clearly the product of a questing intelligence.

Doktor Faust

Busoni began the libretto of *Doktor Faust* in 1914, basing it not on Goethe's poem but on an old German puppet-play and on Marlowe's *Doctor Faustus*. The finished article, however, is a metaphysical drama that bears little resemblance – beyond its sixteenth-century setting – to Marlowe's semi-farcical creation. Having invoked Mephistopheles to help him gain "riches, power, fame" etc, Busoni's Faust runs away with the recently married Duchess of Parma, whom he abandons when she becomes pregnant. Later he meets the duchess, now destitute, carrying the body of their child. Stricken by the scene, Faust offers his own life that the child might live; as Faust dies, defiant of God and the Devil alike, a young man rises from his child's corpse.

Completed after Busoni's death by Philip Jarnach, *Doktor Faust* is a work of immense power that confronts the complexities of the Faust legend more completely than any other operatic treatment of it. Though written in strict Classical form, its orchestration is lush and inventive, and the heavily chromatic vocal parts infuse the rigid structure with a sweeping sensuousness not found in Busoni's other work for the stage. The text is difficult and the opera does demand repeated listening for its ideas and leitmotifs to have any effect, but, as with so many twentieth-century progressive operas, the effort does reap rewards.

Henschel, Begley, Hollop, Jenis, Fischer-Dieskau; Orchestre et Choeur de l'Opéra National de Lyon; Nagano (Erato)

Released in 1999, this is the only complete recording of *Doktor Faust*, reinstating the 700 bars missing from Ferdinand Leitner's brilliantly performed, but heavily cut, version on DG. It also offers Antony Beaumont's remarkable new realization of the final scene, which Busoni left unfinished at the time of his death in 1924. The work finds worthy exponents in Kent Nagano and a magnificent cast.

Concerto for Piano and Orchestra

Busoni's *Concerto for Piano and Orchestra* is a massive creation, requiring the pianist to play almost continually for over an hour and – come the last movement – to do battle with a male chorus as well as a hundred-strong orchestra. It shows Busoni as a consummate synthesist: there is a great deal of Brahms's influence here (especially the opening theme) and a constant recourse to traditional Italian rhythms and melodies – each of the first three movements is built around folk songs, while the fourth is a highly developed quasi-Neapolitan song. The work contains perhaps Busoni's most accessible and memorable writing, with grand melodies that surge through the piano part and some fine passages of orchestration. The last ten minutes of the fifth and final movement are particularly beautiful, and the music's transformation into its conclusive glowing resolution is a remarkable achievement.

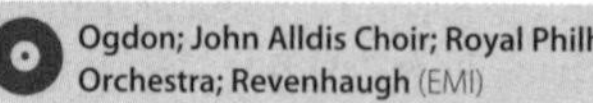

Ogdon; John Alldis Choir; Royal Philharmonic Orchestra; Revenhaugh (EMI)

There are now several fine performances of this epic work, but the legendary 1968 recording of John Ogdon (who studied with Busoni pupil Egon Petri) is still the best, not least because of Ogdon's unmatched grasp of its colossal structure.

Piano Music

The seventh of Busoni's rules for practising the piano reads: "Bach is the foundation of piano playing, and Liszt the summit. The two make Beethoven possible." His considerable output of original compositions and transcriptions for solo piano reflect this slightly confusing view of the relationship between past, present and future, and also point to Bach and Liszt – the greatest keyboard transcribers of the past – as pivotal influences. By far the best known (and the most often performed) of his pieces are his transcriptions of Bach, such as his thrillingly tumultuous reworking of the "Chaconne" from Bach's *Partita No. 2* for solo violin (also transcribed by Brahms for piano left hand). Listening to this epic piano piece it's difficult to believe the material was ever conceived for violin, such is the refulgence of Busoni's textures. Many of his original pieces also incorporate transcriptions or quotations from other composers. In his *Fantasia Contrappuntistica*, for example, the unfinished movement from Bach's *Art of Fugue* is transformed into a massive, frighteningly virtuosic meld of Baroque and modern contrapuntal writing. Not all his pieces are immediately appealing, but in certain works, including some of the *Sonatinas* and *Elegies* (partly based on folk material), Busoni effectively reconciles his various stylistic approaches and finds a unique, cogent voice, characterized by a beautiful, unaffected sense of harmony.

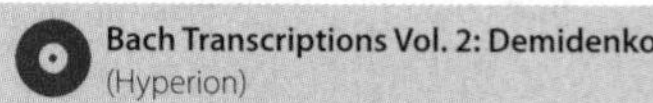

Bach Transcriptions Vol. 2: Demidenko (Hyperion)

With his flawless technique, Romantic sensibility and assured sense of line, Nikolai Demidenko makes the ideal interpreter of Busoni's Bach transcriptions. This volume contains the famous "Chaconne" along with two preludes and fugues and a series of chorale preludes. All are given electrifying performances on a rich-toned Fazioli piano.

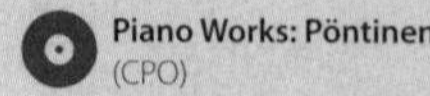

Piano Works: Pöntinen (CPO)

The visionary and sometimes eccentric nature of Busoni's piano writing means that there are few pianists either willing or able to get to grips with him. Roland Pöntinen is one who has penetrated the mercurial nature of these works better than most. In his hands the *Six Sonatinas*, *Indianische Tagebuch* (four pieces based on American Indian themes) and the *Carmen Fantasy* come across with a rare profundity.

Dietrich Buxtehude (c.1637–1707)

By the last years of his life, Dietrich Buxtehude's fame as an organist was so great that in 1706 the young J.S. Bach took four weeks leave from his employment at Arnstadt and travelled (allegedly on foot) over 200 miles to Lübeck in order to hear the great man play. Ironically, Bach's far greater importance as a composer has meant that, until very recently, Buxtehude was primarily known simply as a forerunner of Bach. In fact, he was a major composer in his own right, who exploited recent technical developments in organ building to produce a large body of organ music that was both highly virtuosic and expressive. Both this and his vocal music (which covers a wide variety of styles and genres) were first performed at the innovative public concerts in Lübeck which made him so famous in his lifetime.

Not much is known about Buxtehude's early life. He may have been born in Helsingborg, in Sweden, where his father Johannes was organist at the church of St Mary. In the early 1640s the family moved to Elsinore in Denmark where Johannes took up the position of organist at the St Olai Kirke. The young Dietrich almost certainly received his musical training from his father and probably studied at the Latin school in Elsinore. Appointed organist at his father's old church in Helsingborg in his early twenties, he was back in Elsinore within a few years as organist at the German Marienkirche. Then in 1668, following the death of Franz Tunder, he was appointed to the highly prestigious post of organist at the Marienkirche in Lübeck – one of the prosperous Hanseatic League mercantile towns – and soon after married one of Tunder's daughters.

Buxtehude's principal musical duties at the Marienkirche were playing the organ at the main morning and afternoon services on Sundays and on feast days. As well as this, he held the separate office of *Werkmeister*, an important administrative role with responsibility for the church's finances for which he received an additional salary. Outside of his church duties Buxtehude developed a tradition, started by Tunder, of performing and directing concerts held within the church. These took place on five Sundays of the year, and were known as *Abendmusiken* (Evening Music). The scope of these concerts, performed for the edification of Lübeck's merchant families, was greatly increased by the construction of two new balconies, in addition to four already existing, which together were able to hold around forty musicians.

As well as Bach, other musicians made the journey to Lübeck: Johann Mattheson and Georg Friedrich Händel (both youthful employees of the Hamburg opera) arrived in April 1703 as potential successors. However, neither candidate seemed willing to accept the condition of marrying Buxtehude's youngest daughter, and the post was eventually filled by his assistant, J.C. Schieferdecker (who was), four months after Buxtehude's death in 1707.

Membra Jesu Nostri

Buxtehude's sacred vocal works have survived because they were sent to and copied by his friend Gustav Düben, *Kapellmeister* to the king of Sweden. His most celebrated vocal work, *Membra Jesu Nostri*, may have been commissioned by Düben who was known to have liked Latin settings (Buxtehude mostly set texts from the Lutheran Bible). *Membra Jesu Nostri* combines Biblical quotations with a medieval text which, like the more frequently set *Stabat Mater*, concentrates on the pain and suffering of the Crucifixion, each of its seven cantatas being a meditation on a different part of Christ's body. The mood is quiet and contemplative: there is nothing of the thrust of the Passion narrative but rather the clear, emotional intensity that you find in the best Lutheran chorales. At the same time, Buxtehude's vocal style shows a clear debt to the expressive power of Venetian music with its striking dissonances and sensitive word setting. The most magical moment occurs at the beginning of the third cantata *Ad manus* (to his hands) when, after a sombre instrumental introduction, two sopranos weave an exquisitely delicate phrase around each other that is answered homophonically by the other voices before the same phrase is repeated by two lower-voiced soloists.

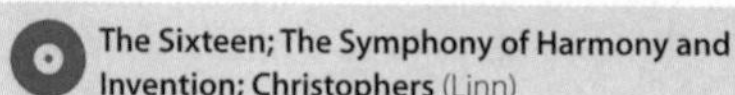
The Sixteen; The Symphony of Harmony and Invention; Christophers (Linn)

This fine account of Buxtehude's masterpiece combines a surprising amount of drama with the intimacy achieved by having only one voice to a part and a delicate continuo of cello, organ and theorbo. The voices are closely recorded so that individual timbre is apparent, and speeds are often on the slow side, but the performance is saved from self-indulgence by the rhythmic suppleness of Christophers' direction.

Keyboard Music

The organists of north Germany were renowned for their ability to improvise, and much of Buxtehude's output for the instrument, notably his praeludia, alternates relatively free sections with more tightly structured, often fugal, ones: a contrast which enabled the performer to display flights of fancy and intellectual rigour within the same piece. Even more common in north Germany are those works which are based on a melody from one of the Lutheran chorales (or hymns). Buxtehude concentrated on the chorale prelude, a meditative response to the words of the chorale in which melody and accompaniment were played on separate manuals – and the more complex chorale fantasy in which each line of the chorale was treated separately and often very elaborately. Among his most impressive works are three ostinato pieces (works built over a continuously repeated bass theme), which reveal a less typical, more Italianate, vein.

Buxtehude also wrote secular music for other keyboard instruments, mostly suites and variations. The latter includes the celebrated *"La Capricciosa"* in which a simple, fifteenth-century Italian dance is brilliantly transformed into a dazzling, virtuosic *tour de force*. The theme was also used by Bach in *Goldberg Variations*, a work that may have been partly inspired by *"La Capricciosa"*.

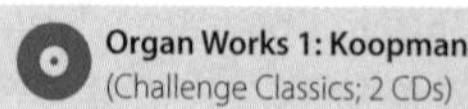
Organ Works 1: Koopman
(Challenge Classics; 2 CDs)

The mastermind behind a project to record all of Buxtehude's music, Baroque specialist Ton Koopman takes the honours on all the keyboard discs. With plenty of rival recordings of the organ works, his consistent brilliance makes him the top recommendation. In Volume 1 he takes on the works of Buxtehude's maturity, performing them on the historic organ of St Nikolai at Altenbruch.

Harpsichord Works 1: Koopman
(Challenge Classics; 2 CDs)

Ton Koopman's survey of all the surviving harpsichord music takes up three CDs in two volumes. Playing on modern copies of instruments by Giusti and Ruckers, he focuses on the suites and variations, with a particularly scintillating account of *"La Capricciosa"*. Always flexible as a player, Koopman's spirited and immediate playing is vividly captured in clear, bright sound.

William Byrd (c.1537–1623)

William Byrd was called by his contemporaries "Britanniae Musicae Parens", the father of British music. It was a title he fully deserved: though writing in the Golden Age of English music, he stands out for his combination of sensuousness and formal precision. It was an achievement all the more remarkable since Byrd was a lifelong Catholic during one of the most violent periods of England's religious history. What saw him through was probably a combination of shrewdness, friends in high places (the Earl of Worcester and Lord Lumley, leading Catholics, were patrons), and his outstanding musical ability.

Little is known about his family background. He may have been the son of Thomas Byrd, a gentleman of the Chapel Royal and a colleague of Thomas Tallis (see p.564), with whom the younger

Byrd is thought to have studied. In 1563 he was appointed organist and choirmaster of Lincoln Cathedral, a post he held until 1572 when he moved to London to become joint organist at the Chapel Royal with Tallis. The two men also held the exclusive right to print and publish music and in 1575 they published *Cantiones Sacrae*, a collection dedicated to Queen Elizabeth and containing seventeen motets by each composer. After the enterprise's financial failure the pair petitioned the queen and were granted the lease of the manor of Longney in Gloucestershire. In his later years Byrd became more and more uncompromising about his religious beliefs and on several occasions he and his wife were fined for recusancy (failure to attend Church of England services). In 1593 he moved to a large property at Stondon Massey in Essex, possibly to be near the Catholic Petre family, in whose chapel one of the three Latin masses, his greatest music, was almost certainly first performed.

Byrd was a prolific composer of church music, and of all the great masters of the sixteenth century only Lassus (see p.287) has a similar range. As well as the *Cantiones Sacrae* of 1575 he published two more collections of motets with the same title in 1589 and 1591, and two sets of *Gradualia* (cycles of music for the Catholic liturgical year) in 1605 and 1607. These last two publications had Byrd's name printed on every page, even though, as Catholic works, they were illegal. In the first volume he wrote of the effect the scriptural texts had upon him: "I have found that there is such a power hidden away and stored up in those words that ... all the most fitting melodies come as it were of themselves, and freely present themselves when the mind is alert and eager."

Byrd is equally important as a composer of secular music – with the exception of lute music, he left examples of virtually every musical form current during his lifetime. He excelled especially in the composition of solo keyboard music and made an important contribution to the development of consort music (see p.296).

The Great Service

The *Great Service*, consisting of settings of six lengthy liturgical texts, is Byrd's finest music for the Anglican Church. Scored for a ten-part choir divided into two semi-choirs, it is conceived on a truly grand scale. Byrd uses the size of the choir not so much for volume or declamatory effects, but for a marvellously rich variety of vocal textures and sonorities. As well as constantly changing the combination of voices, Byrd is endlessly inventive in other ways: he varies the phrase lengths and rhythms, throws in unexpected harmonies and repeats lines in ever more elaborate ways. The effect on the listener is one of being caught up in an absorbing narrative.

The Great Service and Anthems: Tallis Scholars; Phillips (Gimell)

This measured and unruffled music particularly suits the Tallis Scholars, with their well-balanced voices and emotionally controlled sound. They are alive to every nuance and subtle shift in mood, and shape each phrase with care, never allowing the long lines to sag for a moment.

Masses and Motets

Byrd produced some of his most intense and expressive music for the Latin rite, including three Latin masses and numerous motets. There were very few opportunities for the public performance of this music and it must have been designed primarily for use in private chapels in Catholic houses.

The texts that Byrd chose for his motets were often pleas for deliverance or laments for Jerusalem in captivity – texts which would have been interpreted by the Catholic community as references to their plight. In these works Byrd makes much use of imitative polyphony, a style that he absorbed from contemporary Italian composers such as Palestrina. With its expressive and rich harmonies, Byrd must have found it perfectly suited to the highly personal nature of his subject matter. The three masses are also polyphonic works, but more concise and all the more powerful as a result. Each is written for a different voice combination – for three parts, four parts and five parts – but they share a similar clarity and directness, with the vigorous counterpoint never obscuring the audibility of the words.

The Masses: The Cardinall's Musick; Carwood (ASV)

Andrew Carwood's group produces a rich, warm tone which nicely counterbalances the sometimes austere nature of the music. The four-part mass is sung, unusually, by male voices only and their dark, sonorous tone well suits its solemnity. It also contrasts wonderfully with the light, ethereal quality of the high voices used for the three-part mass.

Cantiones Sacrae 1575: The Cardinall's Musick; Carwood (ASV)

Most of the pieces in this collection of Byrd's early motets are sung one to a part, thus heightening the intensity of this highly expressive music. The singers are masters at building phrases to create drama, as in the motet *Libera me, Domine* where tone and volume are steadily increased before the explosion on the words "in die illa tremenda".

Keyboard Music

Byrd revolutionized the writing of keyboard music, creating complex and inventive pieces which sound surprisingly modern. Mostly contained in two collections, *My Ladye Nevells Virginal Booke* and the *Fitzwilliam Virginal Book*, they include several sets of variations based on popular English airs, like "The Carman's Whistle" – a relatively banal tune which Byrd brilliantly transforms into ever more elaborate figurations. The forms that Byrd returned to again and again, however, were the pavan and galliard. These dance movements gave Byrd endless scope for experimenting with different phrase lengths and rhythms. One of the best-known pairs of pavan and galliard that Byrd wrote was the *Quadran*, in which he brings into play all his skills of counterpoint and harmony to create extended paragraphs of music obeying nothing but their own internal logic.

English Virginals Music: Yates (Chandos; with works by Gibbons, Tomkins, Bull, etc)

This is a well-chosen collection from the high point of English keyboard music, firmly centred on William Byrd, who is represented by nine pieces including *The Bells* and *The Woods So Wild*. Sophie Yates's playing, on a bright-sounding virginal (a copy of an old Italian instrument), is a model of elegance and refinement.

The Complete Keyboard Music: Moroney (Hyperion)

Davitt Moroney's seven-disc survey – in which he plays some 127 pieces on harpsichord, virginal, clavichord and organ – is superb. At the heart of the set are the 56 stately pavans and sprightly galliards, played with great precision and eloquence. Hyperion have also issued a single CD selection from this set by way of a taster.

Consort Music and Songs

Consort music (see p.296) was a genre that Byrd adopted and made his own in a way that attracted few serious imitators. His compositions for viols alone mostly took the form of elaborate contrapuntal fantasias and dances, notable for their expressiveness and dynamic rhythms. His works for voice and viols consisted of settings of English poems, in which the viols are no mere accompaniment but very much an integral part of the action, pursuing their own independent lines. It is interesting that Byrd should have favoured this song form over the madrigal (see p.203), which was very much in vogue at the time – evidently he was less interested in the madrigalists' rather obvious pictorial devices, and more concerned with exploring form, structure and mood. Byrd chose to set mostly elegies and laments – such as the doleful "Oh That Most Rare Breast", composed on the death of Sir Philip Sydney – which are perfectly served by this more sober song form.

Consort Songs: Kirkby; Fretwork (Harmonia Mundi)

This delightful disc, recorded in 2004, intersperses a good selection of Byrd's consort songs with five instrumental consorts (including two fantasias). Emma Kirkby makes an ideal soloist in this repertoire, combining near-perfect diction with a sensitivity to textual meaning. Fretwork, a leading viol consort, provide warmly beguiling accompaniment.

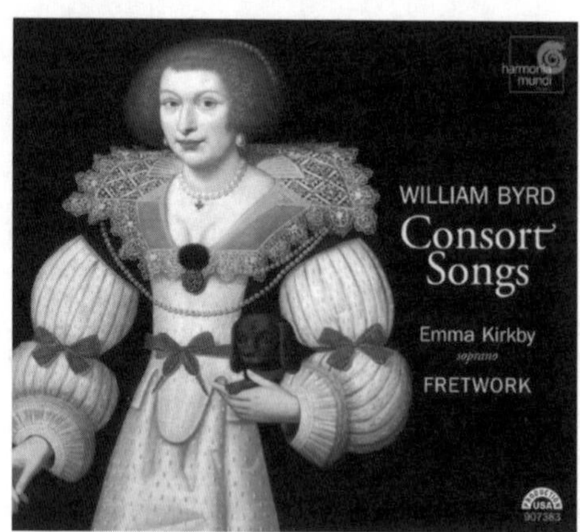

C

John Cage (1912–1992)

Guru to some, charlatan to others, John Cage constantly challenged the very idea of music, using randomness as a basis for composition, doctoring instruments to produce new sonorities, and including the widest array of sounds in his works. He wanted to break down the barrier between art and life, "not to bring order out of chaos ... but simply to wake up to the very life we're living". His most famous work, *4'33"* (1952), requires a pianist to lift the lid of a piano and then not play it for four minutes and thirty-three seconds – the point was to reveal to the audience the impossibility of total silence and to focus their attention on the wealth of sounds that surround them. This blurring of the conventional separation of real life and the concert hall reached its extreme in certain notorious performances in which Cage would sit on stage frying mushrooms – he was a notable expert on fungi, and in 1958 he won $6000 on an Italian TV quiz show answering questions on the subject.

In his twenties Cage studied with the composer Henry Cowell, who had already written pieces for piano in which the performer plucked and beat the strings directly. He also studied with Schoenberg, and their arguments about harmony (Cage thought it unimportant) led Schoenberg to say of him: "He's not a composer, he's an inventor – of genius." Cage's works of the 1930s, mainly for percussion, are based around numerically ordered rhythmic patterns, and are more akin to Eastern than Western music – another aspect of Cowell's influence. In 1938, developing Cowell's ideas, he started inserting objects like screws, wood or paper onto the strings of a piano in order to produce a wide range of percussive sounds. Much of his most expressive music was written for what Cage called the "prepared piano".

In the late 1940s Cage's attitude to music underwent a profound change as a result of his study of Zen Buddhism. In an attempt to rid his music of all vestiges of self-expression and intentionality he started to introduce chance as a guiding principle first in the compositional process and then into performance. *Music of Changes* (1951) is the pivotal work: it was Cage's last fully determinate piece, but was composed using chance processes. Most of his chance works were written out, not in conventional notation, but as visually startling and often ambiguous graphic designs. As these became increasingly irrational and anarchic, Cage developed a cult following during the 1960s, though many fellow musicians, such as Pierre Boulez, believed that his emphasis on randomness was a conceptual blind alley. In the last twenty years of his life, Cage returned to more organizational methods of composing.

Guru to the avant-garde – John Cage in 1966.

Keyboard Music

One of Cage's major contributions to the music of the twentieth century is his "prepared piano", an instrument he invented out of necessity: unable to fit a percussion ensemble onstage to accompany a dance performance, he modified a piano to produce "a percussion ensemble controllable by one player". The potential of this construction is best shown in his *Sonatas and Interludes*, a cycle of pieces written between 1946 and 1948, in which he exploits a wide range of sonorities, some bright and bell-like, others more delicate and subdued. Rhythmic motifs and patterns recur, producing an incantatory and hypnotic quality close to that produced by the gamelan, the percussion orchestras of Java and Bali.

In *Music of Changes* (1951) – written for conventional piano – Cage employed chance compositional processes but the results were completely fixed. The result is fragmented and pointillistic music very much like the total serialist works that Boulez and Stockhausen were writing at the same time, but the spirit is worlds away from their violence and hyper-complexity. *Music for Piano 1–85*, a series of pieces written from 1952 to 1962, allows the performer complete freedom in choice of dynamics, rhythm and tempo. In the hands of a sensitive performer this music breathes the unique Cagean spirit of Zen in which sounds are liberated to be themselves.

Sonatas and Interludes for Prepared Piano: Tilbury
(Explore)

This 1974 recording, unavailable for years, made a welcome appearance on CD in 2006. John Tilbury's experience as an improviser (he is a member of legendary free improv outfit AMM) makes its presence felt in his tactile articulation of Cage's driving rhythms and percussive ungrooves.

Complete Piano Music Vol. 2: Music for Piano 1–85; Electronic Music for Piano: Schleiermacher
(Dabringhaus and Grimm)

Schleiermacher's deeply committed and meticulously prepared performance produces magical results. If you think Cage's introduction of radical indeterminacy in performance is the negation of music listen to these CDs.

Vocal Music

Less well-known than the prepared-piano works are Cage's works for the voice, but they are equally inventive in their treatment of the singer as an instrument of endless possibilities.

"The Wonderful Widow of Eighteen Springs" (1942), his most recorded song, matches the poetic words of James Joyce to a simple folk-like melody, mostly using just three notes over the restless scurrying of the pianist drumming on the outside of the piano. Rather more bizarre is the *Solo for Voice 52,* which employs a fragmentary text of vowels, consonants and words from five languages, all rendered at odd and unpredictable pitches.

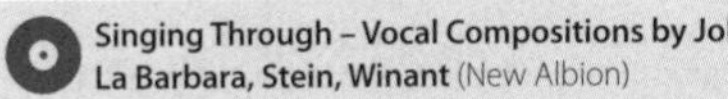

Singing Through – Vocal Compositions by John Cage: La Barbara, Stein, Winant (New Albion)

Joan La Barbara's selection features vocal music from right across Cage's career, ranging from the lyrical to the difficult and disturbing. There's a fine performance of *The Wonderful Widow of Eighteen Springs*.

Atlas Eclipticalis

When Leonard Bernstein led a performance of Cage's *Atlas Eclipticalis* – a 1961 work generated from maps of stars, with constellations transformed into patterns of notes – with his New York Philharmonic, mutiny broke out within his normally adoring orchestra. At issue: each musician was required to play off their own independent instrumental part. The positioning of Cage's angular, scattering notes was technically challenging, and Bernstein had stressed the importance of practising each part to perfection. But then the players realized they were to be wired into a network of contact microphones that were to be switched on and off at random. The result? Their diligent practice could well be rendered inaudible. From a listeners' perspective, however, the gorgeously untidy counterpoint of so many instrumentalists colliding and dovetailing at random can be thrilling, provoking a liberated sound plasma that subjective compositional choice would have been unlikely to stumble across. Good thing, too, some might say. Therein lies Cage's enigma.

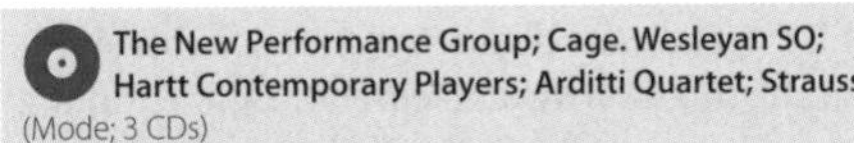

The New Performance Group; Cage. Wesleyan SO; Hartt Contemporary Players; Arditti Quartet; Strauss (Mode; 3 CDs)

This 3-CD set anthologizes two *Atlas Eclipticalis* performances, recorded in 1983 and 1988. What a fascinating comparison: the first (conducted by Cage) lasts for nearly three hours, and is stacked with dense vistas of randomly flowing and overlapping material. It's a trip. The second performance, a mere half-hour long, is sparse and disciplined.

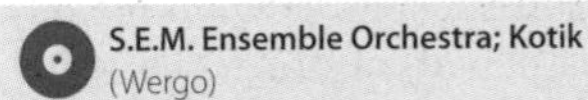

S.E.M. Ensemble Orchestra; Kotik (Wergo)

Wergo's budget alternative is no less impressive. Petr Kotik's view of the piece is tighter than Cage's own, and shifting perspectives of foreground and background emerge through his uncluttered textures.

Joseph Canteloube (1879–1957)

Around the beginning of the twentieth century, many European musicians began assiduously to explore and study their own indigenous musical traditions. Earlier composers, for instance Dvořák, had already tapped into folk music in order to stimulate their own work and to give it a nationalistic element, but this was something different. The new ethnomusicology aimed to make an accurate record of a vanishing world, either through annotation or through sound recordings. The best known of these researchers were Béla Bartók in Eastern Europe, Ralph Vaughan Williams in England and Joseph Canteloube in France.

Canteloube was born at Annonay in the eastern part of the Auvergne, the ancient heart of France's Massif Central – a vast, isolated and proudly independent region. As a young man he studied music at the Schola Cantorum, a Paris music school (more progressive than the Conservatoire) that had been founded by Vincent D'Indy. It was D'Indy's teaching that encouraged Canteloube to continue his investigations into French folk music, an interest that had been kindled by childhood walks in the mountains and which was to become his life's work. Initially, he concentrated on the music of his own native region but he later produced collections of songs from all over France – in particular, the Languedoc and the Basque country.

As with Bartók and Vaughan Williams, Canteloube's fascination with folk song and rural life permeated his own music, including his operas – *Le Mas*, set in a Provençal farm, and *Vercingétorix*, about the Averni chieftain who resisted Julius Caesar's invasion of Gaul. Though both were performed at the Paris Opéra, they have long since disappeared from the repertoire, as has the rest of Canteloube's music with the sole exception of the ever popular *Chants d'Auvergne* (Songs of the Auvergne).

Chants d'Auvergne

The main body of Canteloube's folk-song collections was published in four volumes between 1923 and 1930. They include a wide range of songs, from poignant romances to boisterous dances. As a composer, Canteloube was decidedly unsympathetic towards the fashions of modernism and, controversially, he decided to arrange this simple peasant music with extremely luscious, and at times overwrought, orchestral accompaniment, full of glittering instrumental detailing that owes something to Debussy. The best-known song, "Baïlèro", is a case in point. Canteloube purportedly heard it sung across the mountains between a shepherd and a shepherdess, but what you hear in the concert hall is a slow, languid melody, cushioned by a warm body of strings and embellished with an oboe line imitating a shepherd's pipe. Canteloube's aim was to evoke the missing element, the Auvergne landscape, through deft touches of orchestral colour, but the result bears no more relation to folk music than do Mahler's *Knaben Wunderhorn* settings. Dismissed as nostalgic kitsch by some critics, the great strength of these song settings is the way that the vocal line is always paramount and rarely swamped by the orchestral wash. Above all, like the contemporary *Bachianas brasileiras No. 5* of Villa-Lobos (see p.593), these songs have proved a wonderful vehicle for pure and incisive soprano singing.

Upshaw; Orchestre de l'Opéra de Lyon; Nagano (Erato; 2 CDs; with Emmanuel *Chansons Bourguignonnes*)

Some singers, including Kiri Te Kanawa on Decca, wallow in the heavy sensuousness of these songs. Dawn Upshaw has a lighter and more idiomatic approach: her tone is full but never overwhelming and there is a pleasant reediness to her voice that sounds particularly appropriate. The orchestral playing is stunning, successfully creating the unobtrusive rustic ambience that Canteloube strove for.

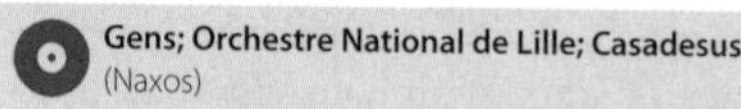

Gens; Orchestre National de Lille; Casadesus (Naxos)

This is that rare phenomenon, a recording of *Chants d'Auvergne* (in fact a selection) by a French singer. Véronique Gens is best known as a Baroque performer, but her relatively light voice works well in this repertoire, combining with the orchestra as if it were another instrument. Needless to say her pronunciation is exemplary.

Giacomo Carissimi (1605–1674)

The oratorio – the musical setting of a religious text in the form of a dramatic narrative – emerged as a distinct form at the same time as opera, at the end of the sixteenth century. Like opera, it employed solo singers, recitative, a chorus and instrumentalists, but unlike opera it usually had a narrator and was rarely intended for staging. It developed in Rome, out of an initiative by Filippo Neri to provide a more accessible and emotionally direct form of worship for Catholics in the wake of the Reformation, and was performed at informal gatherings in which readings and a sermon were combined with the musical performance. The venue for these gatherings was not the church itself but a nearby hall called an oratory – hence the name of the new genre.

Giacomo Carissimi, a name now almost forgotten, was the leading oratorio composer of the mid-seventeenth century. Despite several prestigious job offers, including that of successor to Monteverdi at St Mark's in Venice, Carissimi spent almost his entire professional life as *maestro di cappella* at the powerful Jesuit centre, the Collegio Germanico. His numerous oratorios were not composed for the Collegio, however, but for the upper-crust confraternity of the Most Holy Crucifix, who every Lent celebrated the miraculous survival of a crucifix from the fire that destroyed the church of San Marcello in Rome.

Carissimi's most celebrated work, *Jepthe*, so impressed Handel that he borrowed its final chorus for his own oratorio *Samson*, and it has continued to be performed since it was written. The overt emotionalism of the music, largely conveyed through an aria-like style of recitative that gives a melodic tenderness to the rhythms of speech, makes it the most appealing of his compositions.

Jepthe

The text of *Jepthe*, taken from the Book of Judges, tells of the dilemma of Jepthah (Jepthe in Italian): having promised to sacrifice the first person to greet him when he returns home, if God will grant him victory over the Ammonites, he is met by his beloved daughter. The story is short and intense, and contains striking contrasts of feeling, as when the daughter's joyous praises to God at her father's homecoming are followed by a touching and intimate dialogue between them as he explains her fate. Most famous of all is her final lament, an extended recitative which achieves its emotional impact largely through dissonances in the accompaniment. Even more beautiful is the ensuing grieving chorus, in which, according to a contemporary, "you would swear that you hear the sobs and moans of the weeping girls".

Gabrieli Consort and Players; McCreesh (Brilliant Classics; with *Judicium Salomonis* & *Jonas*)

This heartfelt and dramatic performance is still the best *Jepthe* available. Contrasts of mood are pointed up by extreme changes of speed – the slowness of the final chorus, for instance, draws out the emotion ever more painfully. Of the other two oratorios, *Jonas* (Jonah) is the more varied and contains a marvellously energetic evocation of a storm at sea. The English text is included but not the original Latin.

Elliott Carter (1908–)

Elliott Carter belongs to that great line of American musical pioneers, stretching from Charles Ives to Conlon Nancarrow, whose works have done so much to turn the old world of European classical music on its head. Like Ives in particular, Carter creates a very American sense of place, evoking both the wide-open horizons of its deserts and plains, and the dense urban landscapes of its great cities, whose relentless energy and colliding narratives have done so much to shape his rich and dynamic style. Tough and challenging it certainly is, but at its finest Carter's music has a cyclonic sweep and complexity which few other composers of the past century have been able to match.

Carter came late to composition, despite early encouragement from Charles Ives, who sold insurance to his parents until they discovered the subversive influence he was exercising on their son. Instead Carter studied English and mathematics at Harvard before, in the face of parental opposition, going to Paris to study with the celebrated teacher and Stravinsky ally Nadia Boulanger. Returning to America, Carter began to compose works combining elements of Boulanger's neo-classicism (a style he later characterized as "a masquerade in a bomb shelter") with a more populist American voice, as in his *Symphony No. 1* (1942) and *Holiday Overture* (1944) – though the gung-ho, Coplandesque idiom of these pieces soon gave way to works of increasing originality. The complex rhythmic structures of the 1946 *Piano Sonata* – "like jazz improvisation, with the beat left out", as Wilfrid Mellers has described it – pushed the populist neo-classical style to its limits. The *Cello Sonata* of 1948 went still further, exploring the contrasting personalities of the cello and piano, the first effusively emotional (representing psychological time), the second percussive and admonitory (representing chronometric time) – a model of the type of character drama that was to form one of the bases of Carter's mature work.

Still dissatisfied, however, Carter retired to the solitude of the Arizona desert to work on his *String Quartet No. 1* (1951), the work which signalled his final coming of age. Reflecting something of the grand wilderness amidst which it was composed, the quartet's heroic scale and exhilarating sweep create a sense of a musical world in constant and majestic evolution, as the intersecting narratives move in and out of focus. Shortly after its composition, the quartet won a major European prize, propelling Carter to international prominence.

Encouraged by this success, over the next two decades Carter launched into a series of increasingly innovative works. The theatrical *String Quartet No. 2* (1959) further explored the *Cello Sonata*'s technique of dramatically opposed and interacting instrumental characters, while a sequence of three concertos – the *Double Concerto* (1961), the *Piano Concerto* (1965) and the *Concerto for Orchestra* (1969) – raised the first quartet's principle of multi-layered musical narrative to heights of even greater complexity. His quartet cycle continued in 1971 with his formidable *String Quartet No. 3* which, with the *Symphony for Three Orchestras* (1976), marks the outer limits of his strenuous technical experiments.

In 1975, the appearance of *A Mirror on which to Dwell*, Carter's first vocal work for thirty years, ushered in a new period of creative ease. The three decades since then have seen an astonishing outpouring of music, with landmarks including a fine *Violin Concerto* (1990) and the monumental *Symphonia* (1996) for orchestra, while in 1998, at the age of 89, Carter embarked on his first opera, the aptly titled *What Next?* An apparently inexhaustible stream of orchestral pieces, concertos, chamber compositions and vocal works continue to appear, most recently *Interventions*, for piano and ensemble, premiered at the composer's 100th birthday concert in Carnegie Hall in 2008 – further evidence of musical history's most astonishing example of creative longevity.

Elliott Carter at work.

Concerto for Orchestra

One of only three compositions Carter completed in the 1960s, the *Concerto for Orchestra* represents his music at its most titanic and impetuous, unleashing elemental forces to devastating effect. After he'd started writing the piece, Carter came across St John Perse's poem "Vents", with its evocation of mighty winds destroying and then renewing America. This provided a metaphorical focus for the drama of a piece in which everything is in a process of constant transformation until the material of the entire concerto is swept up into the last movement, before finally disintegrating into the silence from which it emerged.

London Sinfonietta; Knussen (Virgin; with *Three Occasions for Orchestra & Violin Concerto*)

Oliver Knussen has a special authority in Carter's music, and with an ensemble as proficient and committed as the London Sinfonietta, the *Concerto* gains a transparency that makes its progress inexorable, yet still mysterious. The *Violin Concerto*, here performed by Ole Bohn, who gave its premiere, is one of the most strikingly lyrical of Carter's recent works.

Double Concerto

The *Double Concerto* for harpischord, piano and two chamber orchestras is one of Carter's strangest but most original and entertaining works. Like the second quartet, the concerto is built around the conflicting musical personalities of the two soloists and their accompanying ensembles, sounding in places like a Baroque concerto gone mad, or a museum full of clockwork instruments all running at different speeds ("I feel more like a traffic cop than a conductor", as Gustave Meier, the work's first conductor, put it). An elegant symmetry underlies the arch-shaped work, inspired by passages from Lucretius's *De Rerum Natura* ("All things keep on, in everlasting motion … Speeding above, below, in endless dance") – like a musical version of the creation, evolution and destruction of the universe, emerging from and returning into silence, with a pair of hyperactive cadenzas for piano and harpsichord framing a hushed central Adagio.

Jacobs, Kalish; Contemporary Chamber Ensemble; Weisberg (Nonesuch; 4 CDs; with other Carter works)

The only one of the three recordings of the concerto currently available, dating from 1973, with Paul Jacobs (harpsichord) and Gilbert Kalish (piano) – two performers long associated with Carter's music – the accomplished soloists, and virtuoso support from the Contemporary Chamber Ensemble.

Symphonia

Composed in Carter's mid-eighties, *Symphonia* is the most recent and perhaps the finest of all his pieces for orchestra – a work which, as the title suggests, both is and is not a symphony. Its first two movements were actually premiered separately, but it's impossible to argue with the strange but compelling logic of the final three-movement work. The generous scale (three quarters of an hour) and dynamic energy are astonishing, but *Symphonia* also, in common with other recent creations, possesses a new-found clarity – at least in Carter's terms. After the muscular opening Partita, the central slow movement, Adagio tenebroso, shows Carter at his simplest but most eloquent, touching rare expressive depths. The finale, Allegro scorrevole, is a magical, will o' the wisp creation which flies past before ending on the single, high voice of a solo piccolo – one of twentieth-century music's most daring conclusions.

BBC Symphony Orchestra; Knussen
(Deutsche Grammophon; with *Clarinet Concerto*)

Carter's supreme interpreter, Oliver Knussen, leads the magnificent BBC Symphony Orchestra through a breathtakingly confident performance of *Symphonia* which is unlikely to be surpassed. The puckish *Clarinet Concerto* completes the disc, with Michael Collins the excellent soloist.

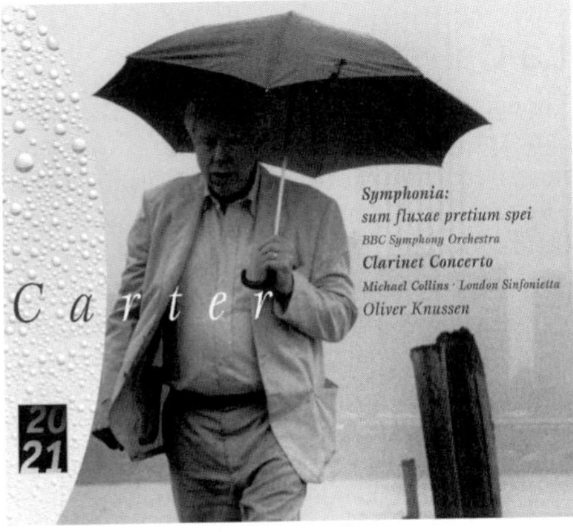

String Quartets

Complexes of simultaneous musical events constitute the most arresting and challenging feature of Carter's music. While one instrument may accelerate to vanishing point, another slows to immobility; effusive lyricism may be set against complex metronomic pulses; as many as four independent musical streams can run in parallel. This multi-dimensional approach was first expounded in the seminal *String Quartet No. 1* and is vividly exemplified in the *String Quartet No. 2*, in which the music is composed out of the confrontations between the different instruments, each one of which has its own way of behaving, rather like (as Carter has suggested) the different characters in a Mozart operatic ensemble, though with a very different musical effect. A dozen years later, Carter's next quartet went one step further, dividing the instruments into two contrasting duos, each playing in different tempi – so that, in effect, there are actually two separate pieces running simultaneously from beginning to end. The fourth and fifth quartets continue the theme, though with less memorable results.

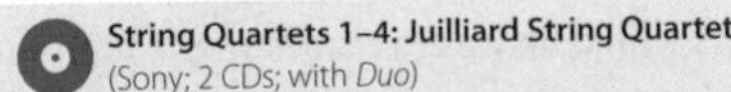

String Quartets 1–4: Juilliard String Quartet
(Sony; 2 CDs; with *Duo*)

The Juilliard premiered the second and third quartets, and the composer supervised these recordings, which have a unique and palpable authority. Of the available versions, these also strike the best balance between muscularity and lyricism, which is such a feature of Carter's quartet writing.

String Quartets 1 & 2: Composers Quartet
(Nonesuch; 4 CDs; with other Carter works)

The world-premiere recordings of the first two quartets, made in 1970 under the supervision of the composer, and still reckoned to be the best available, making marvellous musical and expressive sense of Carter's complex, multilayered constructions.

Sonatas

The revolutionary evolution that Carter's musical style underwent in the years between 1945 and 1952 can be traced in the three superb sonatas written during that period. The *Piano Sonata* (1945–46) marks the high-water mark of Carter's neo-classical style – a considerable work in its own right, although inevitably overshadowed by later pieces. The *Cello Sonata* (1948) is an exhilarating transitional work, largely neo-classical but showing the first signs of Carter's increasing fascination with unusual rhythmic structures and contrasting instrumental "personalities" (here the pedantic, metronomic piano versus the lyrical and improvisatory cello). Separated from the earlier sonatas by the seminal first quartet, the *Sonata for Flute, Oboe, Cello and Harpsichord* (1952) seems to have sprung out of a different musical universe entirely, an exhilarating musical *jeu d'esprit* in which the modernist techniques pioneered in the quartet are given a second outing – with oblique neo-classical nods.

Piano Sonata; Cello Sonata; Sonata for Flute, Oboe, Cello and Harpsichord: Jacobs; Krosnick; Sollberg; Kushkin; Sherry (Nonesuch; 4 CDs; with other Carter works)

One of Carter's most important interpreters, Paul Jacobs gives a fine rendition of the *Piano Sonata* before joining Joel Krosnick for an edge-of-your-seat reading of the *Cello Sonata* and then switching instruments to lead the *Sonata for Flute, Oboe, Cello and Harpsichord*. Definitive recordings.

Pier Francesco Cavalli (1602–1676)

By the middle of the seventeenth century the Venetian mania for opera was at its height, with sixteen opera houses in operation to satisfy public demand. Cavalli, a pupil of Monteverdi (from whom he learned a lyrical tenderness which he was to maintain throughout his career), was one of the first to exploit the situation: in 1639 he signed a contract with the Teatro San Cassiano which involved him in running the company as well as composing for it, a position that made him acutely sensitive to the needs of his audience. Cavalli was the first composer to set out to produce an accessible, repeatable operatic formula, and though he's not of the same stature as Monteverdi, his best works have a vitality and a dramatic atmosphere that makes them immediately engaging.

Cavalli's first teacher was his father, Giovanni Battista Caletti, the *maestro di cappella* of Crema cathedral. In 1616 Cavalli was taken to Venice by the governor of Crema, Federico Cavalli, whose name he adopted. Before his involvement in the theatre, Cavalli gradually rose through the ranks at St Mark's, beginning as a fifteen-year-old singer, becoming second organist in 1639, and first organist six years later. As in the case of Monteverdi, working at St Mark's was not regarded as being incompatible with writing for the theatre, although by the time Cavalli finally attained the ultimate position of *maestro di cappella* in 1668, his career as an opera composer was largely over.

Cavalli's early operas are still dominated by recitative (a kind of sung speech) but this was supplemented by a more lyrical form known as arioso, which stood halfway between recitative and aria. Songs, or arias, were initially employed sparingly in Venetian opera, as moments of contemplation or emotional outpouring outside of the narrative, but by the 1660s opera had become crammed with arias as vehicles for star performers. Of the several librettists who worked with Cavalli, the most important was the poet Giovanni Faustini, who was also the impresario of San Cassiano. The typical Cavalli–Faustini opera abandoned mythology for invention (*La Calisto* is the exception to this rule), combined comic and tragic elements, and usually involved two pairs of noble lovers having to overcome a range of obstacles before attaining perfect happiness.

By 1660 Cavalli's fame was so great that he was invited to Paris by Cardinal Mazarin to write an opera, *L'Ercole amante*, for the wedding of Louis XIV to Maria Teresa of Austria. He reluctantly accepted. It was an enormously lavish production, with ballet interludes written by Lully (see p.310), but the premiere was delayed by a series of disasters (Cavalli's *Xerse* was performed as a stopgap), and it was received with little enthusiasm. Dejected by this failure, Cavalli entered semi-retirement until 1668, when he was persuaded to return to the theatre. By now his style was outdated and the fickle Venetian public largely ignored him; he retained his position at St Mark's until his death, however, by which time he had amassed a considerable fortune.

La Calisto

Though not a success on its premiere at the Teatro San Apollinare in 1651, *La Calisto* is today the most frequently performed of all Cavalli's operas. The excellent libretto combines two stories from Ovid's *Metamorphoses,* both about the amorous adventures of the gods. Jove lusts after the nymph Callisto, finally seducing her by disguising himself as her mistress Diana; meanwhile Diana herself is infatuated with Endymion, a beautiful shepherd boy. By turning the stories into something that at times resembles a *Carry On* film – there's a great deal of sexual innuendo, cross-dressing and furtive coupling – Faustini was simply forcing classical legend, which was no longer very popular on the stage, into the shape of the comedy of sexual intrigue, which was. Cavalli matches his librettist for inventiveness, employing different types of music for different characters: sensual sweetness for Callisto; opulent lyricism for Diana and her lover Endymion, heard at its most beautiful in his song to the moon, "Lucidissima face"; and punchy arioso recitatives for Pan and his satyrs, which effectively suggest a completely alien culture. The popularity of love duets with Venetian audiences was such that Jove and Callisto are given two, the first an extraordinarily rhapsodic exchange of short phrases that is very close in feeling to the end of Monteverdi's *L'incoronazione di Poppea*.

Baker, Bowman, Cotrubas, Trama; Glyndebourne Festival Chorus; London Philharmonic Orchestra; Leppard (Decca; 2 CDs)

This 1972 recording features James Bowman (Endymion) and Janet Baker (Diana), both in their vocal prime. Their scene together at the start of Act 2 contains some wonderful singing that is absolutely in keeping with the suppressed eroticism of Cavalli's music. The lushness of Leppard's edition of the score perfectly matches the full-blooded approach of the singers.

Bayo, Lippi, Pushee, Mantovani; Concerto Vocale; Jacobs (Harmonia Mundi; 3 CDs)

Jacobs' generous and energetic direction brings this period-instrument performance to life. Marcello Lippi's Jove is a *tour de force*, Maria Bayo's Callisto is appropriately languorous, while Graham Pushee's Endymion is close in timbre to James Bowman (see above) but rather sparer in tone. The one small disappointment is the hard tone and slight wobble of Alessandra Mantovani's Diana.

Sacred Music

Considering his sixty-year connection with St Mark's, Cavalli's surviving sacred compositions are surprisingly few. Of his two published collections the most significant is the *Musiche sacre* of 1656 which contains twenty-eight works, including a setting of the mass, psalms and hymns for Vespers, and six instrumental canzonas suitable for church use. Like Monteverdi's *Vespers* of 1610, this collection is a virtual compendium of music for the liturgical year and is also as stylistically varied. Several pieces, including the Mass, are in the grandiose style associated with St Mark's, with two separated choirs, strings, continuo and optional trombones. The Mass is described as a *Messa Concertata*, which means that the full force of the twin choirs and accompaniment is contrasted throughout with various solo combinations. There are also passages for instruments alone (ritornelli) which act as a kind of musical punctuation between sections of the longer movements – the Kyrie, Gloria and Credo. The overall effect is dramatic, with moments of great solemnity juxtaposed with passages of the most delicate intimacy, as in the central section of the Credo when the serene setting of the words "et incarnatus est" suddenly gives way to a rapt series of duets on the word "Crucifixus" (he was crucified).

Messa Concertata: Seicento; The Parley of Instruments; Holman (Hyperion)

This spacious, airy performance of the *Messa Concertata* is given the suggestion of a liturgical context by being interspersed with four instrumental canzonas and two motets, one of which, "O bone Jesu" (a duet for high voices), is remarkably close in style to *La Calisto*. Despite the small vocal forces, the work's ceremonial nature and serene moments come across powerfully and atmospherically.

Emmanuel Chabrier (1841–1894)

Emmanuel Chabrier was an early collector of Manet and the impressionists, and like them he made a break with the methods of his immediate predecessors, albeit in a more limited way. In his first significant instrumental work, *Dix pièces pittoresques* (1881), he rejected virtuosity and academicism to produce ten atmospheric piano miniatures of great expressive freedom in which frequently blurred tonality and richly hued harmonies seem to point the way to Debussy. His celebrated rhapsody *España*, written two years later, is an equally vivid orchestral evocation of Spain (a country he adored), full of flashing colours, whirling skirts and stamping feet.

For the first 39 years of his life, Chabrier's music-making was that of the gifted amateur. As

Emmanuel Chabrier.

a child his prodigious talent had always been nurtured but his bourgeois father insisted on a broad education, hoping that Emmanuel would follow his own profession – the law. In 1856 the family moved from their home town of Ambert in the Auvergne to Paris, and five years later Emmanuel began work at the Ministry of the Interior. The move to Paris at least brought him into the orbit of successful artists – writers and painters as much as musicians. He was particularly close to the poet Verlaine, whose words he set, and to the painter Manet, who painted his portrait at least twice and who died in Chabrier's arms in 1883. Chabrier's friends admired him for his skill at the piano and loved him for his sense of humour: the composer D'Indy used to call him "the angel of drollery". This potential for comedy led to two operettas: in *L'étoile* (1877) an overcomplicated and pedestrian plot is set to sparkling and witty music, while the risqué *Une éducation manquée* (1879) is similarly marred by a vapid spoken text which limited it to just one performance.

The turning point for Chabrier's musical career – and, in one sense, a false step – came in 1879 when he absented himself from the ministry in order to attend a performance of Wagner's *Tristan und Isolde* in Munich. Overwhelmed by the experience, Chabrier quit his job the following year in order to pursue composition full time. The very un-Wagnerian *España* made him an overnight success but it was as an opera composer that he wished to succeed. In *Gwendoline* (1886) he wears his enthusiasm for *Tristan* on his sleeve but it failed to endear him to French audiences. More successful was the comic opera *Le roi malgré lui* (1887), a complex plot redeemed by inventive melodies and unconventional harmony.

Chabrier's final years were painful ones. Racked by depression and terrible headaches (probably brought on by syphilis), composition became more and more difficult for him, and his last work, a Wagnerian lyric drama called *Briséïs*, remained uncompleted at his death.

Orchestral Music

When Chabrier visited Spain in 1882, he seems to have been equally impressed by the shapeliness of Spanish women as he was by the dance rhythms which he jotted down in his notebook. The result was *España*, an exuberant musical homage which Poulenc, in his short book on Chabrier, saw as "a portrait of Spanish music by a brilliant apprentice" – though several Spanish musicians have dismissed it as a lurid tourist's view of their country. For most listeners it's the sheer energy of the work which sweeps them away, a quality equally in evidence in the driving urgency of the *Gwendoline Overture*, the only part of the opera regularly performed today. In fact, Chabrier's orchestral output is disappointingly small. The most popular work after *España* is the *Suite pastorale*, an orchestration of four of the *Pièces pittoresques*, which conjures up the sultry and sensuous warmth of a Monet landscape.

Bourrée fantasque; España; Gwendoline Overture; Suite pastorale: Detroit Symphony Orchestra; Paray
(Mercury; with Roussel *Suite*)

This is one of the best of the Mercury label's legendary recordings from the 1960s. Paul Paray was a scintillating interpreter of French repertoire, extremely sensitive to nuance but quite able to pull out all the stops when needed, as in his hard-driven rendition of the *Gwendoline Overture*. The sound has weathered extremely well and, despite strong competition, this is a clear first choice for *España*.

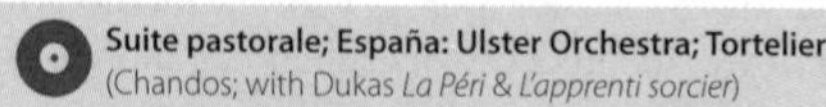

Suite pastorale; España: Ulster Orchestra; Tortelier
(Chandos; with Dukas *La Péri* & *L'apprenti sorcier*)

Tortelier is marginally less successful with Chabrier than with Dukas on this disc: tone colour and instrumental detail is emphasized, sometimes at the expense of shape and momentum (especially in the *Suite pastorale*) but these are still first-rate accounts.

Dix pièces pittoresques

Chabrier was a brilliant and fiery pianist, who frequently broke the piano strings in his enthusiasm. His piano music rarely reflects this aggressive side but, like his orchestral music, it does express an underlying concern with colour and sonority. *Dix pièces pittoresques* was the breakthrough work – Poulenc thought these pieces "as important for French music as Debussy's *Préludes*". In their ability to pin down a mood or an image, they recall Schumann's more poetic miniatures, like *Kinderszenen*, but with an added humour. The most famous of the set is the exquisite "Idylle", a lyrical, bittersweet melody given an added urgency by a regular staccato pulse in the left hand. Almost as beautiful is "Sous-bois" (much loved by Ravel), another piece which contrasts a rather dark left-hand presence with a sweet, almost throwaway, nursery tune in the right-hand. The piano-breaking side of Chabrier can be heard in "Tourbillon", "a typical salon gallop" in Poulenc's words, which lets rip some rapid passage work with a characteristically Chabrieresque mixture of delicacy and bravado.

Dix pièces pittoresques and other piano works: Planès
(Harmonia Mundi; with Ravel *À la manière de Chabrier*)

Alain Planès is an exceptional pianist who brings to everything he plays a probing intelligence and sensitive touch. In Chabrier this means taking the music seriously without being austere. There is a wealth of poetic detail in his playing which brings out the melancholy undertow in a piece like "Idylle". Angela Hewitt's recent recording offers stiff opposition on Hyperion but this is a more subtle interpretation.

Marc-Antoine Charpentier (1643–1704)

Neglected for centuries, Charpentier has recently emerged as one of the greatest French composers of sacred music in the seventeenth century, arguably superior to his more successful contemporary, Lully (see p.303). His music shows more diversity than Lully's, ranging – often within the same work – from the stately to the intimate. The key to this achievement was his adoption of a style, based on the new Italian concerto, which employed dramatically telling contrasts between different groupings of voices throughout a work. Moreover, Charpentier softened the predominantly formal and grandiose style of French music, introducing a more Italianate sensuousness and a greater sensitivity to word-setting.

Little is certain about Charpentier's early life. He was born in Paris, and is known to have been in Rome in the mid-1660s, where he studied with the leading oratorio composer Carissimi (see p.128). Back in Paris he served a series of aristocratic patrons, beginning with the Duchess of Guise, noted for her piety and for the excellence of her musical establishment, which Charpentier directed and sang in as a countertenor. He succeeded Lully as the playwright Molière's collaborator, writing the music for his last play, *Le malade imaginaire*, in 1673. In the 1680s he was on the fringes of the court, serving the dauphin as music director and acting as teacher to the Duke of Chartres, but illness intervened when he seemed close to an appointment at the Royal Chapel. It was also in the 1680s that Charpentier gained the position of composer and *maître de musique* of the principal Jesuit church of St Paul, a position he held until 1698, when he moved to the even more prestigious post of *maître de musique* at Sainte-Chapelle du Palais. He wrote just one full-length opera, *Medée* (1693), but the taste for Lully was strong enough to eclipse all rivals, even after his death, and Charpentier's work ran for only ten performances.

La Descente d'Orphée aux Enfers

La descente d'Orphée aux enfers is a short chamber opera composed for the household of the Duchess of Guise in 1686. It received just one performance, but the occasion for which it was composed is unknown. The opera takes the Orpheus myth (already a rather hackneyed subject for an opera) and provides it with a happy ending – Orpheus leads Eurydice out of the Underworld and back to Earth.

In its economy and concentration, *La descente d'Orphée* is comparable to Purcell's almost exactly contemporary *Dido and Aeneas*, though it lacks that work's overwhelming sense of tragedy. Indeed Charpentier's music – although extremely beautiful – is relatively undramatic: the easy-going pastoralism of its opening scene is followed by a generalized and rather subdued melancholy (at the moment when Eurydice is bitten by the snake) which is largely sustained throughout the work. Orpheus is the most substantial role and, in his journey through the Underworld, his vocal line becomes appropriately more elaborate and seductive. As in *Dido and Aeneas*, there is a final chorus of heart-breaking beauty in which the various inmates of Hades bewail the departure of the voice that has eased their suffering.

Agnew, Petibon, Zanetti, Bernadi; Les Arts Florissants; Christie (Erato)

The revival of interest in Charpentier's music is largely due to the advocacy of the American conductor William Christie, whose long familiarity with the music makes him a highly persuasive interpreter. This is not a work where Christie can exercise his usual dramatic flair; instead, what comes across is the way his careful control of the small orchestra enhances Charpentier's subtle shifts of mood and colour.

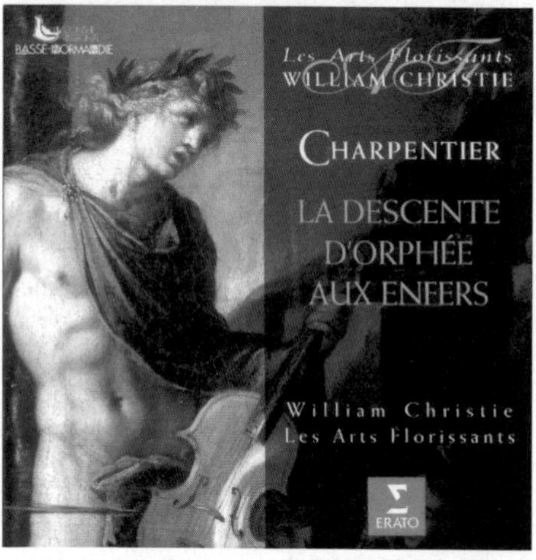

Sacred Music

The most striking aspects of Charpentier's choral music are the refined elegance of the melodies, and its rich and expressive harmonies. Though religious sobriety characterizes the overall tone, this is lush music, with subtle underlining of key moments in the text, and marked contrasts between succeeding episodes. Even a large-scale, celebratory work like the D major *Te Deum*, written for the church of St Paul, is broken up into distinct sections with clearly distinguished moods – thus it begins with kettledrums and trumpets, but contains moments of quiet devotional intensity, like the soprano solo to the words "Te ergo quaesumus" (Therefore we beseech thee). Similarly in the greatest of his masses, the *Missa Assumpta est Maria*, the prevailing mood is sombre but there are subtle shifts of emphasis achieved by various combinations of the eight soloists.

Te Deum; Missa Assumpta est Maria; Litanie de la Vierge: Les Arts Florissants; Christie (Harmonia Mundi)

It would be hard to find a better introduction to Charpentier than this CD. The balance and control are exemplary, with the switches from full chorus to small vocal groupings never sounding abrupt. There are many outstanding moments, from the *Te Deum*'s triumphant orchestral prelude to the Mass's meltingly tender Agnus Dei.

Frédéric Chopin (1810–1849)

Frédéric (or Fryderyk) Chopin, the only son of a French father and a Polish mother, was born near Warsaw, and his Polishness always remained immensely important to him, even though most of the latter half of his life was spent in Paris. The music of Poland permeates his compositions, which were written almost exclusively for the piano, an instrument that by then had become the supreme means of Romantic self-expression. But, whereas his great contemporary Liszt used the piano to create heroic self-portraits and vast panoramas, Chopin was an introvert and a miniaturist, infusing conventional forms such as the sonata and the prelude with an intimacy and an emotional intensity which the poet Heine described as the "poetry of feeling".

The young Chopin's early tuition was at the hands of provincial piano teacher Adalbert

Zwyny, whom he always held in the highest regard – not least for the fact that his teaching focused on the keyboard music of J.S. Bach and Mozart at a time when it was far from fashionable. At twelve he began attending the Warsaw Conservatoire, studying composition with the principal, Josef Elsner, who more or less allowed him to follow his own direction. He left in 1829 and in that year wrote a piano concerto (published as *No. 2 in F Minor*) which he performed in Warsaw the following year. In 1830 he left Poland, travelling to Vienna where his playing made a profound impression on Schumann, although he became deeply depressed by the news of Russia's invasion of his native land. At the end of 1831, he headed for Paris, the scene of his greatest artistic successes and where he was to make his home for the remaining eighteen years of his life.

The dominant influence of Chopin's adult life was the free-thinking novelist Aurore Dudevant, better known as George Sand. Their affair began in the summer of 1838 and they spent the following winter together in Majorca, where, because of Chopin's tuberculosis, they were made to occupy a deserted monastery – a situation that considerably worsened his condition. Back in Paris they lived in nearby apartments and spent each summer at Sand's country house at Nohant, where many of Chopin's greatest works were composed. Their relationship was turbulent, and Sand became increasingly irritated by what she saw as his excessive demands on her affections. In 1847 they finally separated, and Chopin composed very little after that date. After undergoing a purgatorial concert tour of Britain in 1848, he finally succumbed in October of the following year to the tuberculosis which had dogged him for most of his life.

Chopin was essentially an experimental composer, exploiting the potential of the recent developments in piano construction, like the increase of their range to a full seven octaves and the use of heavily felted hammers which could produce a more refined tone. But although his works are often extremely difficult to play they are rarely – unlike much of Liszt – virtuosic for virtuosity's sake. Another feature that crucially distinguishes Chopin from Liszt, Schumann and most Romantic composers is that he did not write music that carried literary, pictorial or biographical significance – his works are to be understood in purely musical terms. Not that this has stopped people from finding non-musical meanings in his music. And in fact the concentrated and volatile nature of his imagination does invite such

The young Frédéric Chopin – heart-throb of the salons.

speculation. Though Chopin found the process of composition extremely arduous, his solo pieces in particular often sound like spontaneous improvisations that have been forced from the unconscious by overwhelming emotion.

Piano Concertos

Of the several works for piano and orchestra that Chopin wrote, the two concertos are the most significant. Both were composed shortly before Chopin finally left Poland (in the reverse order to which they are numbered), and both show the influence of Hummel and the Irish composer John Field in their emphasis on long unbroken lines in the right hand – especially in the two highly poetic slow movements. What marks them out as uniquely his own is the way he decorates a simple phrase not as ornament for ornament's sake but as the expression of deeply felt emotion. The orchestra's role is strictly subordinate (something for which Chopin has been criticized), either simply accompanying the piano, or providing long introductions that create a sense of expectation before the piano's entrance. Both end with Polish-tinged finales: *No. 1* with the distinctive 2/4 rhythm of the Krakoviak dance, while *No. 2* is close in feel to a mazurka.

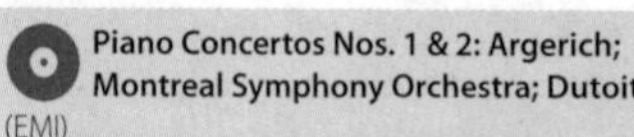

Piano Concertos Nos. 1 & 2: Argerich; Montreal Symphony Orchestra; Dutoit (EMI)

Martha Argerich has recorded the concertos before, but the passing of a couple of decades seems to have ignited an even greater enthusiasm for these works. Her performances are high on spontaneity and abound in small imaginative touches – she is particularly good at bringing out the playfulness of the fast movements.

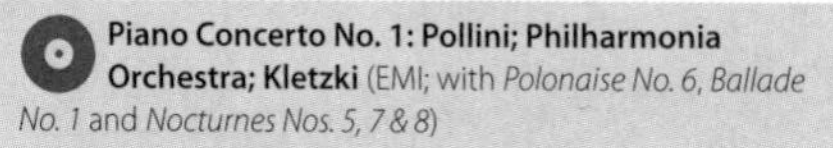

Piano Concerto No. 1: Pollini; Philharmonia Orchestra; Kletzki (EMI; with *Polonaise No. 6, Ballade No. 1* and *Nocturnes Nos. 5, 7 & 8*)

This recording of the first concerto was made shortly after Mauricio Pollini won the 1960 Chopin Competition. Pollini's approach is unsentimental and combines a strong touch with quicksilver imagination. There's no lack of drama but he never loses sight of the essentially vocal conception of many of the melodic lines.

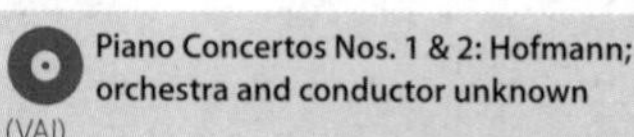

Piano Concertos Nos. 1 & 2: Hofmann; orchestra and conductor unknown (VAI)

Josef Hofmann was one of the supreme interpreters of these works. He possessed an extraordinary touch – delicate and strong at the same time – and used a rubato so spontaneous and unsentimental that it sounds as if he is making the music up as he goes along. These radio performances date from the 1930s (the orchestra is probably the New York Phil under Barbirolli), and the sound is a little rough.

Piano Sonatas

Structure and thematic development have long been held up as the weak areas of Chopin's work, particularly in longer pieces such as the three piano sonatas. But these are Romantic works that should not be straitjacketed by the rigours of sonata form. The best of them, the second in B flat minor (1839) and the third in B minor (1844), are tumultuous displays of sustained energy. The former is justly famous for its slow movement, the "Marche funèbre" (written as a single piece two years earlier), to which Chopin added a highly dramatic first movement, a demented Scherzo and a no less agitated finale – "four of his most reckless, unruly children under one roof" is how Schumann peevishly described it. The third sonata is even more epic in scope and more lyrical, with a huge sweep of shifting moods. It begins with the most declamatory of openings before an intensely lyrical figure impinges itself – like sunlight breaking through clouds. The slow movement sounds close in spirit to the resigned introspection of late Schubert, its sombre main theme followed by a slow rippling figuration in the right hand.

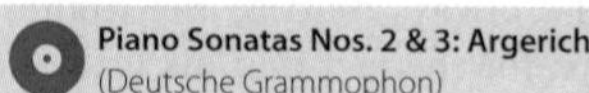

Piano Sonatas Nos. 2 & 3: Argerich (Deutsche Grammophon)

Martha Argerich's playing stresses the restlessness of Chopin's imagination, nowhere more dramatically than in these two sonatas. The second is taken at a breakneck pace (even the funeral march is faster than usual), but with a sense of urgency rather than rush; the third has a grandeur which is largely generated by her brilliant range and control of dynamics.

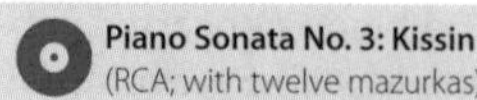

Piano Sonata No. 3: Kissin (RCA; with twelve mazurkas)

This live performance from a 23-year-old Evgeny Kissin is outstanding for its authority and depth of imagination. It's a less volcanic reading than Argerich's, but no less passionate and with, arguably, a greater breadth of conception. His selection of twelve mazurkas is played with a seemingly effortless ease of expression.

Préludes

The 24 *Préludes* (Op. 2) were completed in Majorca during the winter of 1838. They have been compared to the similarly concise preludes of Bach's *Well-Tempered Clavier*, which work through every major and minor key in the same way. The comparison is reasonable enough, as Chopin took a copy of that score with him to Majorca, but whereas each of the Bach preludes prepares the way for a fugue, there is nothing remotely introductory about Chopin's. These are highly concentrated poetic miniatures, and the most atmospheric works he ever wrote. George Sand's account of their stay at the old monastery tells of Chopin's "morbid anxiety created by his own imagination"; her version of events might be slightly romanticized, but the *Préludes* certainly fluctuate wildly between euphoria and despair, ranging from the restrained melancholy of *No. 6* to the delicate capriciousness of *No. 11* to the passionate drive of *No. 24.*

26 Préludes: Argerich (Deutsche Grammophon; with *Piano Sonata No. 2*)

This is the most celebrated of all Argerich's recordings, and deservedly so: every note sounds fresh and alive, and her varied touch perfectly matches the mood of each piece – all are conjured up with a marvellous sense of elation. The CD also includes two posthumous *Préludes*, a wonderfully warm performance of the *Barcarolle* and scintillating accounts of the sixth *Polonaise* and the second *Scherzo*.

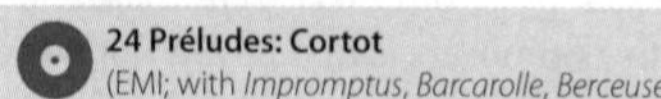

24 Préludes: Cortot (EMI; with *Impromptus, Barcarolle, Berceuse*)

Alfred Cortot's 1930s account of the *Préludes* is justly hailed as one of the truly great piano recordings of the period. Though the sound quality is predictably uneven, Cortot's almost religious vision of these extraordinary miniatures is always clear, articulated with extreme but completely natural sounding rubato and dynamics.

Études

Piano studies were something of a growth industry in the early nineteenth century – practically every virtuoso, from Clementi to Kalkbrenner, was prepared to impart the method behind his prowess via a book of études or studies. Chopin's two collections of twelve études, Op. 10 (dedicated to Liszt) and Op. 25, are something rather different, however. Although individual pieces are concerned with conventional technical problems, Chopin transforms them into music of real depth and feeling – travelling through a wide range of moods – while at the same time exploring the boundaries of the technically possible and the harmonically acceptable.

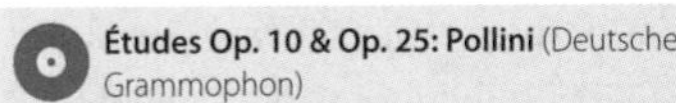

Études Op. 10 & Op. 25: Pollini (Deutsche Grammophon)

Pollini's approach to Chopin is calm and precise, though not as glacial as some critics have suggested. In the *Études* his measured style and near-flawless technique produce brilliant results. The abundant rapid cascades of notes, as in the eleventh étude from Op. 25, are managed with an almost imperious ease, but in the quieter and warmer moments, he is no less convincing.

Polonaises

The polonaise is a Polish national dance of a rather stiff and stately nature, written in triple time – it had much the same status in Polish culture as the waltz did in the Austro-Hungarian Empire. Chopin's polonaises, as one might expect, greatly transcend the formal restraints of the genre, which in his hands becomes a vehicle for his impassioned feelings about his native land – a land that in his lifetime was partitioned between the great powers of Europe, then invaded by Russia. Of the sixteen polonaises that Chopin wrote, only the seven later ones are regularly performed. There is a bold and defiant character to these pieces, not just in the overtly vigorous examples such as the "Heroic" Polonaise, which shows Chopin at his most fiery, but also in those, such as the *C Minor Polonaise*, which are shot through with a melancholy anxiety. Chopin also composed a *Polonaise-fantaisie*, a remarkable piece that commences with one of his most arresting ideas then continues into what sounds like an extended improvisation.

Polonaises Nos. 1–7; Polonaise-fantaisie: Pollini (Deutsche Grammophon)

Pollini's unshowy strength makes these accounts utterly compelling. His articulation of the polonaise's martial rhythms is superbly crisp and arrogant, an effect assisted by his technique of slowly building to the climax of each big tune without ever quite reaching it, enabling the tune to retain all its vigour each time it returns. Pollini's *Polonaises* are also available in a mid-price box of three CDs, with his recordings of the *Études* (see above) and the *Preludes*.

Mazurkas

The mazurka is another Polish dance form in triple time, but with a dotted rhythm that makes it resemble a kind of lurching waltz; it was usually danced slightly faster than the polonaise but not as fast as the waltz. Chopin clearly did not intend his mazurkas to be danced to, but rather to evoke a more elusive, bittersweet image of Poland than was projected by the more forthright *Polonaises*. The *Mazurkas* are also more varied in mood than the *Polonaises*, ranging from the sparklingly energetic opening piece from Op. 7 to the quiet despair of the fourth from Op. 17. They must have been dear to Chopin's heart, since he wrote more of them than of any other genre.

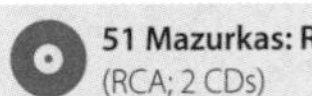

51 Mazurkas: Rubinstein (RCA; 2 CDs)

Artur Rubinstein is another great Chopin interpreter, who by his direct and unfussy performances did much to dispel the image of the composer as a sentimental lightweight. The *Mazurkas* reveal him at his best, with a light and subtle touch, completely attuned to the music's quiet charm and the quirky ebb and flow of its rhythms.

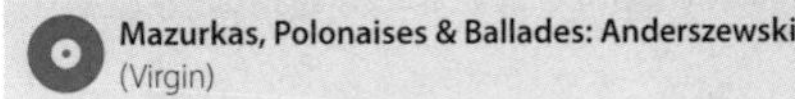

Mazurkas, Polonaises & Ballades: Anderszewski (Virgin)

Piotr Anderszewski begins this Chopin recital disc with the six late Mazurkas of Opp. 59 & 63 and ends – after a pair of Ballades and a pair of Polonaises – with a Mazurka from Op. 68. It's an intelligently conceived programme, and the playing is magnificent throughout, from the swaggering introduction to Op. 59 No. 3 to the delicate melancholy of Op. 63 No. 2.

Waltzes

The craze for waltzes began in the late eighteenth century and by Chopin's time was in full stride. Though he began writing them himself when he was just 16, a trip to Vienna in 1830 left him markedly unimpressed by the popular waltzes of Lanner and the older Johann Strauss. A greater influence was Weber's *Invitation to the Dance*: a brilliant and sophisticated piano showpiece that had enjoyed huge popularity since its appearance in 1819. Chopin's *Waltzes* are a similarly personal response to the dance form, an imaginative evocation of the gaiety and abandon, and sometimes the sadness, of the ballroom.

Waltzes: Ohlsson
(Hyperion)

Garrick Ohlsson won the Chopin Prize in 1970 and, like Argerich and Pollini, has become something of a Chopin specialist. This disc, part of a Chopin series, doesn't have the vibrancy of Lipatti (no one on disc does) but it's brilliant playing that sparkles with life.

14 Waltzes: Lipatti (EMI; with *Barcarolle, Nocturne Op. 27 No. 2 & Mazurka Op. 50 No. 3*)

Dinu Lipatti recorded fourteen of the *Waltzes* in 1950, the year he died aged only 33, and the recording has remained a benchmark for this music ever since. His delicacy of touch and elegance of conception were matchless: the shimmering passage work and his unforced rubato effortlessly convey the music's evanescent brilliance. The mono sound is a little restricted, but more than acceptable.

Nocturnes

John Field invented the piano nocturne as a lyrical and dreamy short piece (not necessarily indicative of night-time) in which an expressive melody in the right hand was gently supported by broken chords in the left hand. Their singing quality was partly derived from the bel canto arias of Bellini's operas. Field's charming but essentially languorous creation was transformed and extended by Chopin into something with a greater emotional range, though a sense of wistfulness generally prevails. These are the pieces that established Chopin's reputation in the aristocratic salons of Paris, and their absolute simplicity and directness of expression have made them the most popular of all his works.

Rubinstein
(RCA; 2 CDs)

The gentle lyricism of the *Nocturnes* is perfectly suited to Rubinstein's unassertive style and limpid tone. But his readings stand out, above all, for the way the long, meandering right-hand phrases, with their finely spun ornamentation, are delicately shaped through subtle shifts of emphasis that bring out every nuance.

Pires
(Deutsche Grammophon; 2 CDs)

These are amazingly delicate readings from Maria João Pires, who builds up each nocturne slowly, shaping them with minutely modified inflections. Among the many recent recordings currently in the catalogue, this is definitely the one to go for.

Scherzi

A scherzo was originally a light-hearted piece which had taken over from the minuet and trio as a short animated movement within a symphony or sonata. Beethoven developed it into an even livelier component of a large-scale composition, but in Chopin's hands the form achieved complete independence and, while Chopin retained the mercurial nature of the scherzo, he almost emptied it of any humour. Like the *Ballades* (see below), the *Scherzi* are extended pianistic tone poems, into which Chopin pours some of his most tempestuous writing. In the *Ballades* there is, perhaps, a suggestion of narrative, which is wholly absent from the *Scherzi*.

Richter
(Regis; with *13 Preludes from Op. 28*)

Sviatoslav Richter plays these pieces like a man inspired, with such presence and seriousness that every moment sounds carefully weighed up. Yet there's no sense of calculation or strain, and it would be hard to find playing of greater immediacy. High points include his handling, in *Scherzo No. 1*, of the transition from its frantic opening to the rapt tenderness of the middle section.

Pollini (Deutsche Grammophon; with *Barcarolle & Berceuse*)

Pollini, in the four *Scherzi*, is no less convincing than Richter. He's so much in command technically that he can bring an added dimension and a drama to these pieces without needing to posture.

Ballades

The four *Ballades* are among Chopin's most extraordinary and powerful works, abounding in quite startlingly dramatic contrasts, with moments of lyric tenderness being followed by passages of tumultuous energy. The narrative implications of the name "ballade" (here applied to music for the first time) have led many commentators to link these pieces with the longer poems of Chopin's Polish contemporary Adam Mickiewicz, several of whose works Chopin set to music as songs. However, though the poems and the music share a certain volatile and episodic quality, there is no evidence that the composer had any specific programme in mind when writing the *Ballades*.

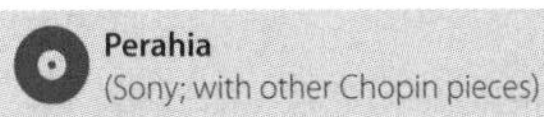

Perahia
(Sony; with other Chopin pieces)

Murray Perahia is a superbly poised and elegant pianist whose tone always sounds perfectly measured and weighted. Yet there is a magical flow to his playing here – each *Ballade* unfolds with the most eloquent and unruffled grace.

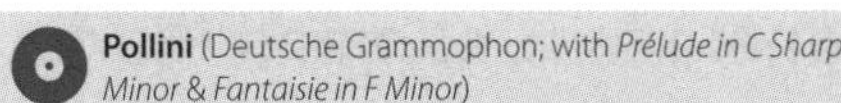

Pollini (Deutsche Grammophon; with *Prélude in C Sharp Minor & Fantaisie in F Minor*)

In the hands of some pianists the four *Ballades* can come across as somewhat self-indulgent rather than revolutionary creations, but Pollini's accounts – tender, intelligent, impassioned yet perfectly controlled – are the very antithesis of effusive salon music.

Rivals at the Piano

When Chopin arrived in Paris in 1831 he was simply one piano virtuoso among many, and his concert debut, early the next year, was on a bill which included the most celebrated performer of the day, Frederic Kalkbrenner (1785–1849) – then at the height of his career. Kalkbrenner had just published his *Méthode* for playing the piano and had set up a training course which he proposed to Chopin that he join – for three years! Although Chopin was a great admirer ("I long to play like Kalkbrenner. If Paganini is perfection itself, Kalkbrenner is his equal but in quite a different field. It is difficult to describe his calm, his enchanting touch, his incomparable evenness…"), he wisely resisted the invitation.

Despite the presence of Kalkbrenner, Chopin – who played his F minor piano concerto and *Mozart Variations* – proved a huge success. Liszt and Mendelssohn were present, and both were greatly impressed by him, despite their own utterly different styles. Chopin's playing was particularly admired for the variety of his touch, and for the singing quality (or cantabile) of his right hand. He was also adept at using a highly distinctive interpretative device called rubato (literally "robbed"), whereby rhythm, instead of being applied in strict time, was expressively distorted by shortening some notes and lengthening others, an effect likened by Liszt to the movement of a tree's leaves in the breeze.

But, neither physically nor temperamentally, was Chopin cut out for a career as a virtuoso, and he performed infrequently in public, preferring private recitals in the salons of the aristocracy – a milieu which better suited the poetic intimacy of his style. Kalkbrenner's true successor was Chopin's younger contemporary Franz Liszt who, having been mesmerized by the technical brilliance of the violinist Paganini, determined to extend the piano's range so that it was simultaneously capable of virtuosic display and expressive depth. Liszt's ascent was temporarily halted when – to avoid scandal – he fled to Switzerland in 1835 with his mistress Countess Marie d'Agoult, and Sigismund Thalberg (1812–71) arrived in Paris. A Kalkbrenner pupil, who had also studied with Hummel and Ignaz Moscheles, Thalberg was a crowd-pleaser and a brilliant technician who was portrayed by the cartoonist Dantan as having ten arms. Renowned for his extraordinary singing tone and his aristocratic *froideur*, his immediate and overwhelming success prompted Liszt to return to Paris the following spring.

There then followed a protracted critical debate, both in print and among the *beau monde*, on the relative merits of each pianist: the critic and composer Fétis championed Thalberg, while Liszt was supported by both Berlioz and Chopin. Liszt himself was not above stirring things up by attacking the superficiality of Thalberg's compositions in an article in the *Revue musicale* – a slightly hypocritical charge when one considers the flashy brilliance of so many of Liszt's own piano pieces. Things came to a head when the salon hostess, the Princess di Belgiojoso, organized a concert for Italian refugees at which both men performed – Liszt a fantasy on Pacini's *Niobe*, Thalberg a fantasy on Rossini's *Moses*. When no consensus emerged as to the victor, the princess organized an even more ambitious concert, this time inviting no fewer than six of the capital's top pianists – including Herz, the veterans Pixis and Czerny, and Chopin – to write and perform a variation on the march from Bellini's opera *I Puritani*, collectively entitled *Hexameron*. After each pianist had performed his variation at a separate piano, Liszt delivered the unexpected *coup de grâce* in the form of a further three variations parodying the styles of Pixis, Herz and Thalberg (but sparing his former teacher Czerny and his ally Chopin). While the immediate humiliation of Thalberg may have re-established Liszt's position as the supreme piano virtuoso of the age, it seems to have done little damage to Thalberg's own reputation or career.

Sonata for Cello and Piano

Of the little chamber music that Chopin wrote, the outstanding item is the grave and autumnal *Sonata for Cello and Piano in G Minor*, his last composition of any importance. He had written for the cello before, but the inspiration behind the sonata was his friendship and admiration for the cellist Auguste Franchomme, who helped him with the technical aspects of the work and to whom it is dedicated. The piece stresses the differences between the two instruments – the piano part is full of agitated passage work, whilst the cello is calmer, with longer and more subdued phrases.

Argerich, Rostropovich (Deutsche Grammophon; with *Polonaise brillante* & Schumann *Adagio and Allegro for Cello and Piano*)

This is a near-perfect pairing of musicians for the work, with Argerich's passion tempered by the insinuating warmth of Rostropovich's tone. Even the rather rambling first movement sounds compelling, but most moving is the third movement, which contains one of Chopin's most poignantly elegiac melodies.

Muzio Clementi (1752–1832)

If it were not for the affection with which Vladimir Horowitz regarded his music, Muzio Clementi's prolific contribution to piano literature would by now have faded to the edge of oblivion. As it is, he's known more as a pianist, scholar, theorist, teacher, piano manufacturer, and as Beethoven's friend and publisher, than as a composer. However, as a child Clementi was paraded as a prodigy of Mozartian abilities, and for most of his eighty years he was one of the most famous and highly respected musicans in Europe.

Italian born, Clementi was entrusted by his father to the care of Peter Beckford MP, and in 1767 the 15-year-old was moved to England, where he made his home, with Beckford, in Dorset. In 1774 he was freed of his obligations to his mentor and went to London where, from 1777, he conducted Italian opera. Four years later he began to tour Europe, engaging with rival pianists in public battles of improvisation and sight-reading. Mozart, who was one of his opponents, was not impressed: "He has great facility with his right hand, his star passages are thirds. Apart from this, he has not a farthing's worth of taste or feeling; he is a mere *mechanicus*." In 1810 he made a semi-permanent return to London, where he settled down to composing symphonies, concertos, piano sonatas and the famous *Gradus ad Parnassum*, a series of one hundred keyboard studies which remains a foundation of piano technique. Among his pupils were Hummel (briefly) and the Irishman John Field (the inventor of the nocturne) who toured Europe demonstrating his master's pianos.

After 1810 Clementi made sporadic trips into Europe – two of them extended – with the intention of impressing his symphonic music upon audiences in Paris and Leipzig. These efforts were mostly wasted, for by 1824 his music had all but disappeared from concert programmes, due principally to the increasing fame and popularity of Beethoven's work. Some time after 1830 Clementi retired from professional life and moved to Lichfield and, soon after, to Evesham. Such was his reputation that his funeral was held at Westminster Abbey, and so many people turned up that mourners were obliged to stand; Clementi was then buried in the abbey cloisters, where his tombstone describes him as "The Father of the Pianoforte".

Piano Sonatas

Clementi composed over one hundred piano sonatas, and their influence is hard to overestimate (see p58) – many of them were highly regarded by Beethoven, for example, and by John Field. The early sonatas are little more than homages to Domenico Scarlatti, but between the Op. 10 and Op. 14 sonatas a distinctive Clementi style comes to the fore. Rejecting the conventional Italianate two-movement form, these sonatas inaugurated the three-movement structure, and in their use of thematic development and generally more abrasive melodic style they anticipated Beethoven's keyboard writing. However, Clementi's music has none of Beethoven's heroics or purposeful self-scrutiny – it's predominantly

light in nature, and most of the sonatas up to the end of the century have the feel of harpsichord pieces. Come the advent of the full-grown piano, his style had advanced harmonically to such an extent that some of his late music foreshadows the early work of Field and Chopin. If Clementi never fulfilled the promise of his youth, he nonetheless developed a solid personal style that is instantly recognizable and immediately charming.

Piano Sonatas Op. 24 No. 2; Op. 25 No. 5; Op. 4 Nos. 2 & 3: Demidenko (Hyperion)

Nikolai Demidenko is a more circumspect performer than Horowitz (see below). Though he uses a modern piano, his approach is restrained and sensitive. Instead of drama he employs a very refined variety of touch and, when required, some wonderfully clear and quiet playing. It doesn't disguise the fact that Clementi is a derivative composer but it does persuade you that he's a good one.

Piano Sonatas Op. 33 No. 3; Op. 34 No. 2; Op. 14 No. 3; Op. 26 No. 2; Op. 47 No. 2: Horowitz (RCA)

Horowitz was an important advocate for Clementi. His interpretations sometimes take expressive liberties, but even if these performances have as much to do with Horowitz as with the composer, that is all part of their appeal – these are delightful displays of two prodigious musical imaginations at work.

Aaron Copland (1900–1990)

Aaron Copland is best known for his morale-boosting ballets and patriotic pieces of the 1930s and 1940s, and these are certainly among the most remarkable compositions of their time, particularly when you bear in mind that their cowboy hoedowns and jigs were written by a sassy New Yorker of Russian-Jewish background. It would be wrong, however, to view scores like *Billy the Kid*, *Rodeo* and *Appalachian Spring* in isolation. Masterpieces though they undoubtedly are, they are only one side of the work of a highly inquisitive and analytical artist who was always on the lookout for a new challenge.

The seeds of Copland's independence were sown way back in his student years, a period when American music was squarely provincial. To show just how entrenched things then were, Copland was fond of telling how Rubin Goldmark, his highly conservative composition teacher, once caught him looking at the score of Ives' *Concord Sonata* and warned him not to contaminate himself with such things. It is lucky for posterity that he followed the advice of a friend, gathered together his hard-earned savings, and headed for Paris, the haven of every artistic revolutionary from Joyce to Hemingway and Picasso to Stravinsky.

When Copland arrived he set about enrolling at the New School for Americans at Fontainebleau, where he was taught by Nadia Boulanger, the remarkable woman who coached an entire generation of budding American composers between the wars. The four years with Boulanger (1921–25) were the most important musical experience of his life: she opened him up to a huge variety of musical influences and taught him all about the virtues of clarity and restraint, as well as giving him a solid technical grounding and a thorough knowledge of orchestration. Stravinsky's neo-classicism made a particularly strong impact on him, as did the music of Les Six and the exciting new sound of jazz then sweeping Europe. Copland never looked back. On returning to New York in 1925 he resolved to forge a distinctively American-sounding music, a project not without controversy in the narrow and back-biting world of American contemporary music. The fact that much of his music has subsequently been

Aaron Copland in rehearsal.

identified in the popular imagination as quintessentially American is a measure of his success. But Copland was also a generous proselytizer on behalf of American music in general, tireless in his efforts to win it an international reputation.

In a long and fruitful career Copland went through four highly distinct phases: an exuberant jazzy first phase from 1925 to 1929 (as typified by *Music for the Theatre* and the *Piano Concerto*); a severe avant-garde period from 1930 to 1936 (for example the *Piano Variations*); the hugely popular "Americana" phase of 1936–49; and a final return to difficult serial territory (in such works as the *Piano Fantasy*). Yet despite these abrupt stylistic shifts there is a distinctive Copland sound, a sound largely determined by his brilliant abilities as an orchestrator. The American composer Virgil Thomson described Copland's orchestration as "plain, clean-coloured, deeply imaginative ... theatrically functional", and its transparency is the key factor – even in the midst of the busiest textures everything is lucid and opaque. Boulanger had taught him the knack of "keeping instruments out of each other's way", a skill to which he allied a knack of making each part of the orchestra carry its own "expressive idea", bringing a specific emotional connotation to the unfolding drama of a piece.

Copland was also a master of rhythm. The nervous energy of his orchestral music relies heavily on dance and march rhythms, spiced with the displaced accents of jazz, but at the other end of the spectrum he could achieve very complex trance-like effects, as in the slow finale of the *Piano Sonata*. His harmonies were no less expressive and elegant. Time and again Copland found new contexts for conventional intervals and familiar chords, dropping them unexpectedly into very dissonant passages, making them sound fresh and new.

Symphonic Ode & Ballets

The *Symphonic Ode*, written in 1927 for the 50th anniversary of the Boston Symphony Orchestra, marks the beginning of a new austerity in Copland's music, with markedly transparent textures and extremely complex rhythms. Copland rated the *Ode* among his finest works but he was aware of what he called its "bony" outline, and "softened" it up in a later revision. By the mid-1930s he had changed direction once again. Politicized by the Depression, he had become aware that a "new public for music had grown up around radio and the phonograph. It made no sense to ignore them ... I felt it was worth the effort to ... say what I had to say in the simplest possible terms." Among the numerous creations of this new listener-friendly Copland are *El salón México* (1936), which with its sinewy orchestration, jaunty dance rhythms and use of folk tune is a pointer to the ballets to come. *Billy the Kid* (1938) continued the pattern with a vivid depiction of the Wild West, right down to the obligatory shoot-outs. Even more celebrated is the much-loved dance score *Appalachian Spring*, written for the dancer Martha Graham and completed in 1944. It's a work that deals, in quasi-mythic terms, with hope and aspiration – it tells of a newly wedded couple setting up home in Pennsylvania in the early nineteenth century – and it struck an immediate chord with American audiences. Copland's skill in creating lucid, open textures is combined with strong affirmative melodies, culminating in his extended treatment of the Shaker hymn "Simple Gifts" at the end of the work.

Appalachian Spring; Billy the Kid; Rodeo; Fanfare for the Common Man; Quiet City: Cincinnati Pops Orchestra; Kunzel (Telarc)

This disc has the three major Copland ballets (*Appalachian Spring* and *Billy the Kid* in concert suite versions), plus the famous *Fanfare for the Common Man* and the delightful *Quiet City* for cor anglais, trumpet and strings. It thus presents a good cross-section of the orchestral music, and the performances are sparkling and idiomatic.

Symphonic Ode; Appalachian Spring: Seattle Symphony Orchestra; Schwarz (Delos; with the *Piano Concerto*)

Gerard Schwarz and the Seattle Symphony Orchestra are exemplary interpreters of his music, giving performances that are clean and precise without being ungiving. In the wrong hands *Appalachian Spring* can slide into cutesiness, but there's no hint of that in the original 13-instrument version performed here.

Symphony No. 3

Commisioned by Sergei Koussevitsky and written between 1944 and 1946, the *Symphony No. 3* marks the culmination of the new lean, clean style that Copland had developed in the ballets *Rodeo* and *Appalachian Spring*. The scale is very much larger, however, with the symphony orchestra supplemented by a range of percussion instruments (including piano), which are given brief but effective cameo roles. Copland insisted that there was no specific programme attached to the symphony, but it is possible to see it as a public statement of affirmation after the dark days of the war, and Copland himself said that he "... was reaching for the grand gesture." Certainly there's an epic sweep to it, established by an arching phrase from the woodwind that builds in richness and complexity as other sections join in. There are moments of tension – the second movement Scherzo is like a more strident version of *Rodeo* – but the prevailing sense is of a kind of grandiose serenity, climaxing in the finale which opens with, and then develops, Copland's famous *Fanfare for the Common Man*, written four years earlier.

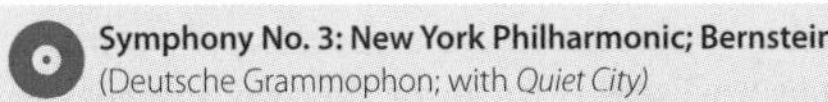

Symphony No. 3: New York Philharmonic; Bernstein (Deutsche Grammophon; with *Quiet City*)

With Leonard Bernstein at the helm of the New York Phil, the *Symphony No. 3* comes across as a major achievement – arguably the greatest of all American symphonies. From the rapturous calm of the opening through the manic leaps of the Scherzo and the grandeur of the finale, Bernstein never stints on the drama, and the work emerges radiant and brightly coloured.

Piano Concerto

The last of Copland's jazz-influenced works was the *Piano Concerto* of 1926, written one year after Gershwin's *Piano Concerto in F* (see p.204) but without that work's button-holing charm. Copland's two-movement concerto is more angular and abrasive, concerned with rhythm rather than melody. A restrained, almost alienated, mood prevails throughout the first movement, beginning with the opening bluesy fanfare and continuing with the introspective piano writing. In contrast, the second movement is all dash: the piano's syncopations lurching unsteadily before getting into their stride. Copland conceived of his concerto as a dramatic work, and the piano does indeed seem like a character moving through a modern city, negotiating the brash sounds, the bright lights and the jostling crowds.

Hollander; Seattle Symphony Orchestra; Schwarz (Delos; with *Symphonic Ode & Appalachian Spring*)

The performance of the *Piano Concerto* is no less impressive than the other works on this disc: Lorin Hollander is the ideal Copland pianist, being discreet and sympathetic in the first movement, and witty rather than aggressive in the lively finale.

Clarinet Concerto

Copland's 1948 *Clarinet Concerto* was commissioned by Benny Goodman – an accomplished player both in swing and classical music – who gave its first performance two years later. It's a work, like *Appalachian Spring*, which makes a simple contrast between quiet, serene music and something more lively and abandoned. The slow, lilting opening movement, in which the clarinet is very much part of the spare orchestral fabric, has been described by one critic as "a perfect fusion of Satie and Mahler". It leads, via a short cadenza, into the second and last of its movements, marked simply "rather fast". This has been compared to jazz, but though it employs spiky, syncopated rhythms and an abundance of ostinati it's unmistakably Copland in its airiness and feeling of space, and seems to point the way towards the lyrical minimalism of John Adams.

Goodman; Columbia Symphony Orchestra; Bernstein (Sony; with Stravinsky *Ebony Concerto*, Bartók *Contrasts*, Bernstein *Preludes, Fugues and Riffs*)

This classic recording collects together the various classical works that Benny Goodman either commissioned or premiered. Copland's concerto was written with Goodman's manner of playing very much in mind, and there's a relaxed air to the performance which seems entirely appropriate.

Songs

Copland's songs are not numerous, but they have established themselves as permanent fixtures in the recitals of American singers. The outstanding set is the *Twelve Poems of Emily Dickinson*, which Copland completed in 1950 after working on them for six years. Dickinson was a unique voice in nineteenth-century American literature, and it is Copland's achievement to convey her powerful mix of the personal, the quietly resolute and the visionary so convincingly and so sympathetically. This is one of the greatest song cycles written since World War II.

As a relief from the concentrated effort that he'd exerted on the Dickinson settings, Copland decided to make arrangements of some of his favourite American songs. The result was two sets of five songs entitled *Old American Songs* Sets 1 and 2. Originally written for voice and piano, the songs' easy-going charm proved so popular that Copland orchestrated them. The first set is the most lively and contains the Shaker song "Simple Gifts" that was employed in *Appalachian Spring*, and the delightful children's song "I Bought Me a Cat".

Old American Songs Sets 1 & 2; Twelve Poems of Emily Dickinson: Hampson, Upshaw; St Paul Chamber Orchestra; Wolff (Teldec)

Exemplary performances of the orchestrated versions of these songs. Thomas Hampson sings the *Old American Songs* with immense panache and good humour – no other singer on record sounds so at home with them. Dawn Upshaw brings a purity and intensity to the Dickinson settings which emphasize their visionary aspect.

Twelve Poems of Emily Dickinson: Bonney, Previn (Decca; with songs by Barber, Previn & Argento)

Arguably the Dickinson songs have a more concentrated impact when performed just with a piano – there's more intimacy and greater immediacy. Barbara Bonney, like Dawn Upshaw, has a light clear voice but she manages to convey a greater wealth of detail, and brings out the songs' quirky humour in her performance. She's brilliantly supported by André Previn.

Piano Music

As well as being a fine pianist, Copland the composer used the piano to work out his ideas: it's not surprising, therefore, that throughout his career he wrote several pieces for the instrument which though not as well-known as his orchestral pieces are among his most challenging and original compositions. Both the *Piano Variations* (1931) and the *Piano Sonata* (1941) are uncompromisingly modernist works which owe something to both Prokofiev and Bartók in their percussiveness and angularity but which are also shot through with Copland's characteristic "Americanisms" – sparse textures, widely spaced intervals, jazz-inspired rhythms. The *Sonata* is more epic in scope. Copland referred to it as grandiose, albeit "... a very dry and bare grandiosity, instead of the fat grandiosity of a big orchestral work ..." There is also a definite sense of wartime anxiety in its restlessness, ominous hints of tolling bells and generally elegaic undertow.

The *Piano Fantasy* (1957) is one of the least Coplandesque of his works. While adopting the twelve-tone system, Copland adapted it by using just ten notes for the tone row with the remaining two notes of the chromatic scale being reserved for cadences. The resulting exploratory and improvisatory work runs the gamut of pianistic effects from delicate intimacy to pounding declamatory statements that occasionally border on the bombastic.

Piano Variations; Piano Sonata; Piano Fantasy: Lively (Etcetera)

These are brilliant and persuasive performances of Copland's three most important piano pieces from David Lively. There's a real sense that the performer knows the works inside out and he's especially good at conveying the dynamic and fluid inner pulse of the music.

Arcangelo Corelli (1653–1713)

Though instrumental music was becoming increasingly important by the middle of the seventeenth century, Corelli is still unusual in that he wrote absolutely no music for the voice. Instead he worked exclusively in the three genres which he helped to establish and refine: the concerto grosso, the trio sonata, and the solo sonata. His published output was small but his influence was enormous. All subsequent composers who worked in these genres, up until the last quarter of the eighteenth century, used Corelli's work as a model and some – like Couperin in his *L'Apothéose de Corelli* – paid open homage to him.

Corelli was born in Fusignano, between Bologna and Ravenna, into a family of well-to-do landowners with no history of musical talent. He reputedly studied with a local priest but his main musical education took place at the Accademia Filarmonica at Bologna, then an important centre for instrumentalists. From 1675 he was based in Rome, where he gradually established himself as one of the city's leading violinists, playing in church ensembles but also in theatre orchestras.

Engraving after a portrait of Corelli by Hugh Howard.

Corelli was employed by three of the most important patrons of the day beginning with Queen Christina of Sweden (who had been living in Rome since 1655) whose service he entered in 1679 and to whom he dedicated his first twelve trio sonatas two years later. He also arranged musical events, including musical academies, for the enormously wealthy Cardinal Pamphili who in 1687 employed him as his music master. Soon after, Corelli moved in to the cardinal's palace, taking with him his pupil Matteo Fornari with whom he lived until his death. When Pamphili moved to Bologna in 1690, Corelli was snapped up by the third of his patrons, the young Cardinal Ottoboni, and went to live at his palace the Cancelleria. For all three patrons Corelli organized and composed for ensembles of different sizes, often working with other composers. He also directed operas at Ottoboni's private theatre and at the public Teatro Tordinona.

As a performer Corelli was renowned for the elegance and pathos of his playing: "I never met with any man", wrote a contemporary, "that suffered his passions to hurry him away so much whilst he was playing on the violin." He was no virtuoso, however, and occasionally his technique let him down – indeed, during a visit to Naples in 1701 he had the embarrassing experience, while leading the orchestra in an opera by Alessandro Scarlatti, of being unable to play a high note which the Neapolitans could manage with ease.

Such was Corelli's renown, that even in his lifetime composers were slavishly imitating his style, the widespread influence of which was due, to a large extent, to the massive increase in music publishing at the beginning of the eighteenth century. He died a rich man, leaving not just the predictable collection of instruments and manuscripts (which he bequeathed to Matteo Fornari) but also a fine collection of paintings, one of which went to Cardinal Ottoboni. He is buried in the Pantheon, in a tomb adjacent to that of the painter Raphael.

Concerti Grossi

The concerto grosso, a form of orchestral music that appeared towards the end of the seventeenth century, was like most other instrumental music of the time, in that it consisted of a series of contrasting quick/slow movements based on dance forms. What was new about it was the way that the orchestra was organized into two different groups: a small group called the concertino and a larger group called the concerto grosso (later known as the ripieno or tutti). These two groups played in alternation, with the concerto grosso for the most part simply echoing the material of the concertino, creating a contrast between loud and soft passages. Corelli's concerti grossi have a prevailing mood of balance and control: even in their exuberant fast movements these concertos are quite different from Vivaldi's, which are full of unbridled energy and unpredictability. These are easy-going and graceful pieces, and they contain much of great beauty, particularly in *Concerto No. 8* (Christmas Concerto) with its dramatic opening, its varied and inventive melodies and its grave and sonorous slow movements.

Twelve Concerti Grossi: The English Concert; Pinnock (Archiv; 2 CDs)

This double CD contains all the concerti grossi that Corelli published (though he evidently wrote many more). The performances, typical of director Trevor Pinnock, are clearly argued and always forward-moving, though rarely at the expense of the music's poise and elegance.

Trio & Solo Sonatas

A key genre in the Baroque period, the trio sonata consisted of three parts played by four instruments: two upper parts, usually violins, plus a bass part, called a continuo, played by a keyboard and a low stringed instrument. Generally a distinction was made between the chamber sonata, which employed dance forms, and the more serious church sonata, which usually did not, but in Corelli's hands the difference between the two forms became increasingly blurred. All his trio sonatas are refined and elegant works in which the violin parts, especially in the slower movements, have a lyrical quality akin to the human voice. This is enjoyable but undemanding music, which avoids extremes of register and of emotion.

The twelve "solo" sonatas that make up Corelli's Op. 5 resemble the trio sonatas but they feature only one violin part and include an additional fast movement. Corelli was as influential a performer and teacher of the violin as he was a composer, and these works can be seen as summarizing his understanding of the best qualities of the instrument. Even in the most technically difficult moments the brilliance of the passage-work serves the music rather than the performer. The most famous – and energetic – sonata is the last in the collection, a set of sparkling variations on the famous popular dance tune "La Folia".

"La Folia" and other sonatas: The Purcell Quartet (Hyperion)

For this excellent CD, the Purcell Quartet have picked some of the high points of the different sets, mixing solo and trio sonatas. Their generally light but lively approach provides the most persuasive account of Corelli on disc. The "La Folia" sonata gets a highly spirited rendition from violinist Elizabeth Wallfisch, who combines a delicate touch with a gutsy attack and enormous flair.

François Couperin (1668–1733)

François Couperin, known as Couperin le Grand to distinguish him from his various musical relations, was the outstanding French composer of the period between Lully and Rameau. In his music he strove to reconcile the graceful lyric qualities of the prevailing French style, as represented by Lully, with the energy of the Italian style, as exemplified by Corelli. Indeed, one set of his instrumental pieces is entitled *Les goûts réunis* (The Styles Reunited), and he wrote musical tributes to both composers which imagined their harmonious afterlife in the Elysian Fields. Couperin is probably best known for his four books of harpsichord pieces (*Pièces de clavecin*): some 220 brilliantly crafted miniatures, whose mysterious titles and delicate wit have frequently been compared to the elegant and enigmatic paintings of his contemporary Antoine Watteau.

The Couperins were a musical dynasty to rival the Bachs. Indeed, François Couperin's first job, as organist at the Paris church of St Gervais, had been held by his father and uncle before him, and was to remain in the family until 1826. At the age of 25 he succeeded his teacher, Jacques Thomelin, as organist to the king, and a few years later consolidated his position at court when he became harpsichord teacher to several of the royal children. Few other details are known about his life. He acquired a coat of arms shortly after arriving at court, and in 1702 was made a Chevalier of the Order of Latran. None of his correspondence with J.S. Bach has survived (it is thought to have finished up as jam-pot covers), but from the tone of his surviving letters and of his famous keyboard treatise *L'art de toucher le clavecin* (The Art of Playing the Harpsichord) he seems to have possessed a sardonic sense of humour. Perhaps it was this that kept him from any further appointments at court until 1717, when he took over from d'Anglebert as the king's harpsichordist, a position he retained until his death.

Vocal Music

The wit and inventiveness which is a characteristic of much of Couperin's music gives way in his sacred vocal pieces to something much more simple and direct, though still with an emphasis on melody. These works tend to be small-scale and intimate, following the model of Carissimi and his French pupil Charpentier, and none of them is more beautiful than the *Leçons de ténèbres*, settings of the Lamentations of Jeremiah to be performed on the three days before Easter and one of the greatest glories of French Baroque music. The title, which means "lessons of shadows", refers to the fact that during the services held on those three days all the church candles are gradually extinguished to symbolize the sufferings of Christ. Couperin wrote the full quota of nine lessons (three for each day) but only the first three (for Maundy Thursday) have survived. Each lesson opens with a Hebrew letter sung to an exquisitely sensuous and fluid vocal line; thereafter the vocal style is a fusion between the declamatory and the lyrical, providing restrained but eloquent anguish to Jeremiah's lament at the fall of Jerusalem.

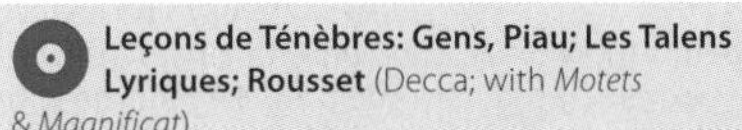

Leçons de Ténèbres: Gens, Piau; Les Talens Lyriques; Rousset (Decca; with *Motets & Magnificat*)

Sandrine Piau's incisive dark-toned voice brings real gravitas to the *Première leçon*, while the lighter and more fluid tone of Véronique Gens emphasizes the tenderness of the *Deuxième*. When the two come together for the *Troisième*, it's their sensitivity to each other, as much as the rich blend of their voices, which makes this account so compelling. They're equally effective in the *Motets* and *Magnificat*.

Keyboard Music

Couperin's four books of harpsichord pieces are organized into 27 suites which he called *Ordres*. Though based on dance forms, most of the individual pieces within these suites have fanciful titles, such as *Les barricades mystérieuses* (his most famous individual piece), *L'arlequine* or *Les Idées heureuses*, some of which are evidently descriptive while others may have had some private significance. The music's expressiveness is enhanced by rich ornamentation, which – unusually for the time – is never left to the discretion of the performer, but always precisely specified. In some pieces he adopts what was known as the *style brisé* (broken style) in which the notes of a chord are not all played together but one after the other (originally in imitation of lutenists). Though lacking the formal fascination and rich counterpoint of Bach's keyboard works, Couperin's are more personal and idiosyncratic, with an emphasis on melody and a wide variety of moods, from the light and elegant to the sombre and subdued.

Barricades Mystérieuses: Verlet (Naive)

Blandine Verlet has recorded nearly all of Couperin's keyboard music over the years, and this disc is a rich selection from those various recordings. She plays on three different harpsichords, all of which have a generous but unclattery sound, and she uses the registration with subtlety and discretion to mirror the music's quixotic changes of mood.

Harpsichord Works: Beaumont (Warner Classics)

Another fine selection of Couperin keyboard works, personally chosen by harpsichordist Olivier Beaumont from the complete recordings he made in the early 1990s. Only two works overlap with the Verlet disc, *Les barricades mystérieuses* and *Le réveil-matin*, but Beaumont also includes three homages to Couperin by his contemporaries.

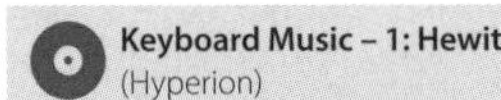

Keyboard Music – 1: Hewitt (Hyperion)

Couperin on a modern concert piano is an unusual proposition, but Angela Hewitt (a skilful Bach pianist) is a convincing advocate, selecting pieces carefully, and negotiating Couperin's tricky ornamentation with great sensitivity. The result is extremely seductive: delicate, elegant and with elements of both mystery and playfulness.

Pièces de violes

The outstanding item from Couperin's other solo instrumental music is a late work, the *Pièces de violes* (1728). Viol music had been particularly appreciated in France but was now in decline. Couperin's *Pièces* were written the year after the death of Marin Marais, the great viol master of the period (and the subject of the film *Tous les matins du monde*), and perhaps were intended as a tribute to him. Made up of two suites, this is music of rare inventiveness and charm – from the opening wistful prelude of the first suite to the scurrying activity of the second's concluding movement (mysteriously entitled "La chemise blanche"). Although the bass viol – also known as the viola da gamba – does not have the same incisiveness as the modern cello, the husky quality of its string tone gives it a mellowness and a vulnerability that perfectly complements the essentially melancholic nature of this music.

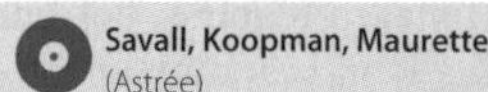

Savall, Koopman, Maurette
(Astrée)

Despite the fact that nowadays there's an abundance of fine viol players, these pieces have only been recorded a handful of times. This version from Jordi Savall, made in 1975, is outstanding. Savall is a musician who always places an emphasis on both expressive depth and beauty of tone, and on this disc the results have a beguiling intimacy and tenderness.

Jordi Savall with his bass viol.

d

Luigi Dallapiccola (1904–1975)

The theme of human liberty and subjection is a recurrent feature of both Luigi Dallapiccola's life and his music. Born in 1904 in Pisino, Istria, an ethnically Italian region of the Austro-Hungarian Empire, Dallapiccola was just ten years old when he and his family were interned in Graz after the Austrian authorities began to suspect his father of Italian nationalist leanings – an early and formative experience of the fate of political and racial minorities living under an authoritarian regime. Nevertheless, although the forced removal disrupted the young Dallapiccola's musical education, it was in Graz that he heard the performance of Wagner's *Flying Dutchman* which made him decide to become a composer, and in 1923 he entered the Florence Conservatory, an institute with which he would maintain a lifelong connection.

Dallapiccola's early works show him grappling with a range of influences: Debussy especially, along with earlier Italian composers such as Monteverdi and Gesualdo, and – after hearing a performance of Schoenberg's *Pierrot Lunaire* in Florence in 1924 – the music of the Second Viennese School. A decade of study and consolidation followed. In 1934 Dallapiccola was appointed professor of piano at the Florence Conservatory (a post he held until his retirement in 1967), while his own compositions continued to absorb lessons learned from Busoni, Schoenberg and, especially, Berg, as he began to incorporate the twelve-note system into his own music. Meanwhile, the growing shadow of Fascism reawakened his concern with the plight of ordinary human beings living under despotism. In 1938 Mussolini's adoption of Hitler's racial policies (with the consequent threat to Dallapiccola's own wife, who was Jewish) provided the impetus for the *Canti di prigionia* (Songs of Imprisonment), the first of his triptych of works concerned with imprisonment and freedom. As Dallapiccola noted in his diary: "In a totalitarian regime the individual is powerless. Only by means of music would I be able to express my anger."

Dallapiccola's public opposition to Mussolini made his position increasingly untenable until, in 1942, he was forced first out of Florence and then into hiding in the countryside. For all his personal difficulties, however, the years immediately before and during World War II were musically fecund ones, as Dallapiccola established the lyrical version of twelve-note music – with a distinctly Italian turn of phrase – that was to serve him for the remainder of his career, and which he first expounded in a sequence of vocal works, most notably the *Liriche greche* (Greek Lyrics), written during the 1940s. As a well-known opponent of Fascism, Dallapiccola emerged from the war with his personal reputation enhanced, while the premiere in 1950 of his most famous work, the opera *Il prigioniero* (The Prisoner), established his international reputation as the leading Italian composer of his generation. Yet as his public fame increased, so his musical style became increasingly abstract and personal, eschewing big public statements in favour of a lyrical understatement, as exemplified by the third of his "prisoner" pieces, the *Canti di liberazione* (Songs of Freedom) of 1955.

Il prigioniero

Written in the aftermath of World War II, Dallapiccola's one-act opera *Il prigioniero* offers a twentieth-century reworking of the old operatic theme of imprisonment and attempted escape – a kind of anti-*Fidelio* in which evil rather than good wins out, or a latter-day *Tosca*, but without even the brief amorous consolations of that earlier Italian masterpiece. The dramaturgy could hardly be simpler: the (nameless) Prisoner is allowed to escape from his cell and given the illusory promise of freedom, only to be recaptured and put to death, having learnt that "the ultimate torture was hope". Musically under the spell of Berg's *Wozzeck*, the Prisoner's wildly fluctuating emotions are mirrored in an expressionistic orchestral score which packs into its single nightmarish act a kaleidoscopic range of incident, creating a sense of knife-edge intensity matched by few other operatic works of the past hundred years – and whose sustained dramatic power Dallapiccola himself was never subsequently able to repeat.

Bryn-Julson, Hynninen, Haskin; Swedish Radio SO & Choir; Salonen (Sony; with *Canti di prigionia*)

This fine performance was recorded live in Sweden in 1995. Jorma Hynninen is a capable Prisoner, ably supported by Phyllis Bryn-Julson as the Mother and Howard Haskin as the Grand Inquisitor. Esa-Pekka Salonen makes the best possible sense of a score that can sometimes sound wayward and fragmentary. A vivid performance of the *Canti di prigionia* completes the disc.

Liriche greche

The fame of *Il prigioniero* has tended to obscure the fact that Dallapiccola was pre-eminently a composer of small-scale vocal and instrumental pieces. Nowhere is his talent for the miniature more apparent than in the rich sequence of works for female voice and ensemble dating from the late 1930s and 1940s – including the three miniature song-cycles collectively known as the *Liriche greche* (1942–46), with which he established his own unique brand of Italianized twelve-note music.

Like Berg, Dallapiccola employed the twelve-note method in a sometimes unsystematic manner, using it in combination with traditional harmonies and a decidedly Mediterranean lyricism, as in the first set of *Liriche greche*, the radiant *Cinque frammenti di Saffo*. The second and third sets – the *Due liriche di Anacreonte* and *Sex carmina Alcaei* – are more abstract and reticent, showing Dallapiccola's increasingly rigorous twelve-note technique and structure, and a concentrated brevity that is more reminiscent of the music of Anton Webern, another enduring influence on his music.

Ensemble Intercontemporain; New London Chamber Choir; Zender; Wood; Moffat; Jansen; Gwynne (Warner; with *Canti di prigionia, Tempus destruendi – Tempus aedificandi* and *Due cori di Michelangelo Buonarroti il giovane*)

A fine performance of the *Liriche greche* (Julie Moffat the excellent soloist) along with the *Canti di prigionia* and a pair of choral works: the early *Due cori di Michelangelo Buonarroti il giovane* (1933), an engaging exercise in neo-Madrigalian style, and the altogether more severe *Tempus destruendi – Tempus aedificandi* (1971), one of Dallapiccola's last pieces.

Claude Debussy (1862–1918)

Claude Debussy was a radical from the outset. As a student, he continually failed his harmony exams because, like Beethoven over a century before him, he refused to accept the absolute authority of the textbook. A brilliant pianist, he would irritate and shock his contemporaries by inventing harmonies and chords that effectively were reinterpreting tonality – already he was moving towards the creation of musical impressionism. In 1882 he failed to win the Prix de Rome, just as the previous great French musical revolutionary, Hector Berlioz, had done, but two years later he took the coveted prize and moved to Rome. He spent the next two years there, meeting Liszt and Verdi, among others, and hearing dozens of contemporary works, including Wagner's *Lohengrin*.

His attendance at the 1888 and 1889 Bayreuth festivals deepened his understanding of Wagner's operas, but although he recognized the importance of *Tristan und Isolde* and *Parsifal* he also saw that these gargantuan, mythic works were something of a dead end. While other French composers such as Chabrier and Chausson responded to Wagnerism by composing their own grand Norse dramas, Debussy looked beyond the mainstream Western traditions as a way of expanding the vocabulary of music. A Javanese gamelan performance at the Paris Exposition of 1889 had a profound effect, overwhelming him with the elemental beauty of its indeterminate harmonies. However, it was within Russian music that Debussy found the clearest guidance as to how he might create a musical aesthetic as distinctly French as the art of the impressionist painters and Symbolist poets with whom he was so close. For Debussy, Russian music was primarily suggestive and evocative, a corrective to Wagner's sternly philosophical and self-consciously profound dramas.

Debussy began to explore a compositional process that avoided conventional thematic development, instead moving its material through constantly shifting harmonic and orchestral backgrounds – impression mattered more than direction. The first great example of this carefully crafted vagueness was his only opera, *Pelléas et Mélisande* (begun in 1893), followed a year later by his orchestral *Prélude à l'après-midi d'un faune*, an apparently free-floating composition that was attacked for formlessness but turned out to be one of the most influential pieces of music ever written.

His three *Nocturnes*, performed in 1900 and 1901, marked an increasing sophistication of technique, and four years later Debussy produced what many regard as his masterpiece, the symphonic sketches titled *La Mer*. At the same time he wrote one of the finest of his many piano works, the *Images*; evocative music in which he came close to realizing his ideal of the "hammerless piano". His remaining orchestral works, among them the ballet *Jeux*, were received with great enthusiasm in more adventurous circles, but his final years, during which he produced mainly chamber and piano pieces, were clouded by illness and World War I.

Claude Debussy à la plage, 1911.

By reason of his influence, Debussy could be classed as perhaps the most important composer of the twentieth century – figures as diverse as Stravinsky, Bartók, Ravel, Webern, Messiaen and Boulez all admitted a debt to him. He is also one of the most approachable. However abstract and ambiguous his work may seem, Debussy believed fervently that music should be communicative. As he once wrote: "Love of art does not depend on explanations, or on experience as in the case of those who say 'I need to hear that several times'. Utter rubbish! When we really listen to music, we hear immediately what we need to hear".

Pelléas et Mélisande

Debussy had a clear idea of what he required from opera: "I wanted from music a freedom which it possesses perhaps to a greater degree than any other art, not being tied to a more or less exact reproduction of Nature but to the mysterious correspondences between Nature and Imagination." With Maurice Maeterlinck's play, *Pelléas et Mélisande*, he found his perfect libretto, a misty tale of doomed love that proceeded by hint and implication rather than by dramatic incident. He began setting the play, virtually uncut, in 1893 and revised it obsessively until the first performance at the Opéra Comique on 30 April, 1902. It was immediately recognized as a watershed in the history of opera and classical music.

The influence of Wagner's *Parsifal* is clear in Debussy's orchestration, yet this dramatically static work is the very antithesis of Wagnerian heroics. It's an opera in which music doesn't so much emphasize the meaning of the text as complement or revise it. In a letter to Chausson he wrote of *Pelléas*: "I have found ... a technique which strikes me as fairly new, that is silence as a means of expression and perhaps the only way to give the emotion of a phrase its full power." Debussy's conception of silence as a dramatic device is certainly one of his most lasting innovations. There are no big tunes in *Pelléas*, and it contains few moments of traditional lyricism – on the whole, Debussy writes vocal parts that correspond to the patterns of French speech. Some people find it boring, others regard it as the greatest of all French operas, but there's no disputing its status as a ground-breaker.

Shirley, Söderström, McIntyre, Ward, Minton, Britten, Wick; Royal Opera House Chorus & Orchestra; Boulez (Sony; 3 CDs)

Pierre Boulez's recording of Debussy's opera is a brilliant and rare example of one composer expressing his total sympathy for the work of another. He clarifies the complex orchestral colours and shapes each of the brief scenes as part of the overall structure. Elisabeth Söderström is glowing as Mélisande, while George Shirley conveys Pelléas's confusion without resorting to overemphasis.

Prélude à l'après-midi d'un faune

Pierre Boulez once remarked that "just as modern poetry surely took root in certain of Baudelaire's poems, so one is justified in saying that modern music was awakened by *L'après-midi d'un faune*". Saint-Saëns's took a rather less positive approach – "It's as much a piece of music as the palette a painter has worked from is a painting" – but his dismissal comes close to capturing the essence of this amazing tone poem. Debussy based his composition upon the poem of the same name by Mallarmé and, like the poem, the music works by suggestion rather than statement. A trance-like flute theme opens the work, establishing a uniquely hedonistic and languid atmosphere that is then extended by some marvellously deft and harmonically innovative writing for woodwind.

Concertgebouw Orchestra; Haitink (Philips; 2 CDs; with *Images, Jeux, Nocturnes, La Mer*, etc)

Haitink's outstanding Debussy survey from the late 1970s, now at mid-price, is an irresistible bargain. In *L'après-midi d'un faune* he marshals his brilliant orchestral forces with the most delicate touch, producing an extraordinary sense of heaviness and otherworldliness.

Philharmonia; Cantelli (EMI; with *La Mer, Nocturnes* and excerpts from *Le martyre de Saint Sébastien*)

Cantelli's 1954 reading makes the *L'après-midi* into a less evanescent piece of music, and highlights its structural cohesion. This may not be as close to the composer's spirit as some performances, but it's a memorable and legitimate approach.

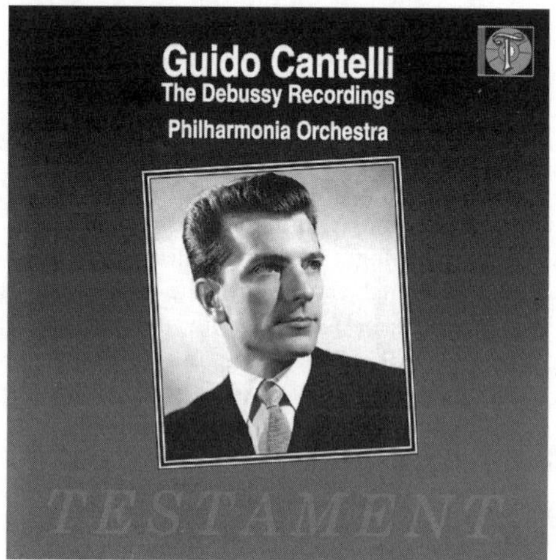

Nocturnes

The three *Nocturnes* feature some of Debussy's most imaginative orchestral writing. Untypically, he provided an explanatory note to the set, providing as fine an introduction as could be wished for: "The title *Nocturnes* is ... not meant to designate the usual form of a nocturne, but rather all the various impressions and the special effects of light that the word suggests. "Nuages" renders the immutable aspect to the sky and the slow, solemn motion of the clouds, fading away in grey tones lightly tinged with white. "Fêtes" gives us the vibrating atmosphere with sudden flashes of light. The background remains persistently the same: a festival, with its blending of music and luminous dust, participating in the cosmic rhythm. "Sirènes" depicts the sea and its countless rhythms and presently, among the waves silvered by the moonlight, is heard the mysterious song of the sirens as they laugh and pass on."

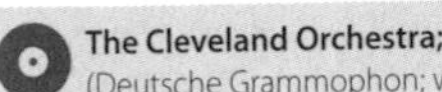

The Cleveland Orchestra; Boulez (Deutsche Grammophon; with *La Mer, Jeux & Rhapsodie pour clarinette*)

This recent recording by Pierre Boulez is one of the best he has ever made. It's got all the insight and discipline you expect from this conductor, and with the Cleveland Orchestra in top form, the result is a breathtaking, layer by layer revelation of the extraordinary delicacy of Debussy's score.

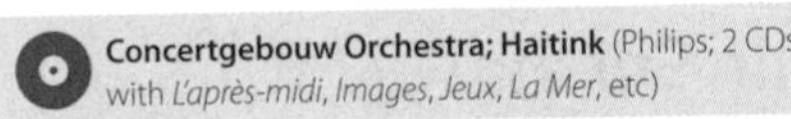

Concertgebouw Orchestra; Haitink (Philips; 2 CDs; with *L'après-midi, Images, Jeux, La Mer*, etc)

Bernard Haitink really excels in this recording of the *Nocturnes*. Only a conductor with a really close bond to an orchestra could produce such utterly specific refinements of mood and colour.

La Mer

In the summer of 1904 Debussy left his wife for another woman, provoking his wife into a suicide attempt. Debussy fled, mistress in hand, to the English resort of Eastbourne in Sussex, and there he composed his finest orchestral work, *La Mer*. The first performance in 1905 excited hostility in some quarters that seems scarcely credible today, with the critic from *The Times* remarking: "As long as actual sleep can be avoided, the hearer can derive great pleasure from the strange sounds that enter his ears if he will only put away all ideas of definite construction or logical development."

The piece is in three movements titled "From dawn to mid-day on the sea", "Play of the Waves" and "Dialogue of the Wind and the Sea". At the first rehearsal, Erik Satie facetiously commented that he "particularly liked the bit around half-past ten". While the music is not as programmatic as anything by Strauss, it still conveys clear images of the sea through flickering, fragmentary themes and some of Debussy's finest orchestration, such as a remarkable section in the first movement when the sixteen cellos are divided into four groups of four.

The Cleveland Orchestra; Boulez (Deutsche Grammophon; with *Jeux, Nocturnes & Rhapsodie pour clarinette*)

Boulez's commendable achievement in this performance is to create the perfect balance between *La Mer* as a great symphonic tone poem, evoking the primal force of the ocean, and as a ground-breaking work of almost chamber-like delicacy with the subtlest of instrumental coloration.

Concertgebouw Orchestra; Haitink (Philips; 2 CDs; with *L'après-midi, Images, Jeux, Nocturnes*, etc)

Haitink's delicate command of nuance and texture, and his refinement and fluidity of gesture, have been justifiably praised. But, above all, it is his combination of grace and his majestic sense of architecture that illuminates one of the twentieth century's most fastidiously conceived scores.

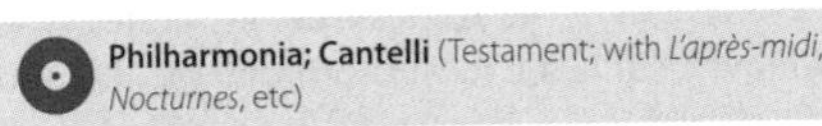

Philharmonia; Cantelli (Testament; with *L'après-midi, Nocturnes*, etc)

This performance is the highlight of Guido Cantelli's famed "Debussy sessions", recorded in London with one of the world's finest orchestras. Cantelli's worship of his mentor Toscanini is clear from the opening bars – every nuance and colour is achieved with startling immediacy.

Jeux

Debussy's last three orchestral works were all ballets. The first and finest of them, *Jeux* (Games), was composed in 1912 and premiered in 1913 by Diaghilev's Ballets Russes (see p.547). Debussy based the work's construction upon a basic, undulating phrase which is then developed into a wild variety of musical gestures, vaguely corresponding to the strokes of a tennis game. Stravinsky hailed the work as a masterpiece, with the reservation that he found some of the ideas over-kind on the ear – though Stravinsky was probably alone in this reaction to a score which, in its emphasis on percussive orchestration, prefigures much of the twentieth century's avant-garde music.

The Cleveland Orchestra; Boulez (Deutsche Grammophon; with *La Mer, Nocturnes & Rhapsodie pour clarinette*)

A brilliant account of *Jeux* brings out the work's quirky modernisms and angularity. The Cleveland players clearly relish this music and the finely judged account of the clarinet rhapsody by Franklin Cohen is the icing on the cake.

Concertgebouw Orchestra; Haitink (Philips; 2 CDs; with *L'après-midi, La Mer, Images, Nocturnes*, etc)

Jeux is Debussy's most difficult score to bring off, but, once again, Haitink – through a mixture of precision and flexibility – produces a beguiling account, in which individual timbres shine through with amazing clarity.

String Quartet

Debussy's early forays into chamber music are not particularly successful, but by the time he got round to writing his *String Quartet* in 1893 he had achieved complete mastery of the medium. Following the example of César Franck, Debussy employs cyclical form, which means that the heavy declamatory opening theme occurs in different manifestations throughout the entire work. But there are also many other themes that come and go with a profligate generosity, including two wistfully lyrical melodies in the first and third movements. The Scherzo is the most dramatic movement, dominated as it is by a plucked accompaniment over which a light but restless melody glides. The slow movement is the most profound: mellow and subdued, with at its heart a folk melody of great tenderness.

Quator Ebène
(Virgin; with Ravel & Fauré string quartets)

Utterly exquisite playing from a young French quartet. The fact that they are also jazz musicians may explain why these performances have such a spontaneous and flexible feel to them, but there is also great warmth and tenderness in their playing.

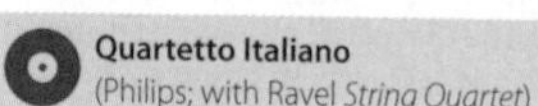

Quartetto Italiano
(Philips; with Ravel *String Quartet*)

This account from the mid-1960s does not have the finesse that some quartets have achieved, but it is, nevertheless, a very beautiful performance, full of warmth and of brilliantly controlled dynamics that give the works an extra dramatic dimension.

Cello Sonata

Completed in 1915, the *Cello Sonata* was intended as the first of six instrumental sonatas. In the end, the cancer from which Debussy was dying meant that he completed just three (the others being the *Violin Sonata* and the *Sonata for Flute, Viola and Harp)*. Remarkable for the range of ideas it packs into its small time span, the *Cello Sonata* begins with a declamatory piano introduction before the cello almost sidles in, sombre and unflamboyant, with a decidedly resigned air to its main theme. A bittersweet tone prevails throughout the work: moments of introspection are suddenly interrupted by bursts of energy. This is most apparent in the extraordinary middle movement which has a stream-of-consciousness quality somewhat akin to a jazz improvisation.

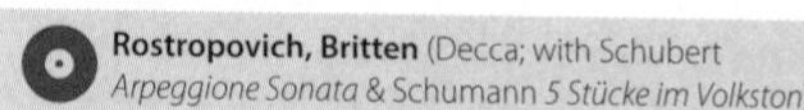

Rostropovich, Britten (Decca; with Schubert *Arpeggione Sonata* & Schumann *5 Stücke im Volkston*)

Cellist and pianist need an almost uncanny understanding to make the restless ebb and flow of this work achieve true magic. Fortunately the combination of cellist Mstislav Rostropovich and Benjamin Britten is about as good as it gets, with both artists completely alive to all the sonata's complex colours and moods.

Violin Sonata

Written a year after the *Cello Sonata*, by which time Debussy was extremely ill, the *Violin Sonata* is a little longer than its predecessor but no less enigmatic. If anything it is even more acerbic and inward looking in feel; a mood immediately apparent in the mercurial first movement in which the violin's spontaneous outpourings have something of Gypsy music to them. The second movement is rather more light and playful, but even here dark shadows obtrude. The last movement has been criticized as insubstantial – Debussy struggled with it – but it's just as valid to see its tension between frantic striving and resignation, its rapid switches between fantasy and desperation, as poignant. The sonata was the last work Debussy performed in public.

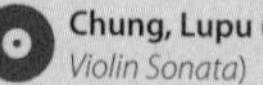

Chung, Lupu (Decca; with Chausson *Poème* & Franck *Violin Sonata*)

In this classic recording from the 1970s, violinist Kyung-Wha Chung and pianist Radu Lupu are acutely sensitive to the subdued, elegaic nature of this sonata. Their close rapport is always apparent – an essential requisite in music where the mood fluctuates so readily.

Suite Bergamasque

Composed between 1890 and 1905, the *Suite bergamasque* shows Debussy hankering after the elegance of an earlier period of French music – as the Baroque dance titles of two of the four pieces indicate. Hovering between major and minor keys, fusing mock-archaisms with Debussy's own freshly minted style, this music is at the same time deeply considered and slightly fey. Debussy always had a fondness for moonlight music, and the third piece, "Clair de lune", has achieved the status of a classic with its melodic charm and easy grace.

Rogé (Decca; 2 CDs; with *Children's Corner, Images & Préludes*)

Pascal Rogé is one of the outstanding interpreters of *fin de siècle* French piano music. On this two-CD set his wonderfully lucid and fluent pianism seems perfectly suited to Debussy's quicksilver imagination. With excellent accounts of most of Debussy's major piano works, this is an excellent budget alternative to the Michelangeli set (see below).

Children's Corner

Of all Debussy's piano compositions, the most transparent is the *Children's Corner* suite, written for his daughter in 1906. These are sprightly and good-humoured pieces, some of them satirical – such as "Doctor Gradus ad Parnassum", a joke at the expense of Clementi's finger exercises (see p.142) – others brilliantly pictorial, like the delicious "The Snow is Dancing". Inspired by his daughter's governess, Debussy gave English titles to each of these six miniatures, but his English wasn't quite as perfect as his piano writing, which is how one piece came to be called "Jimbo's Lullaby" – Debussy meant it as a lullaby for a baby elephant.

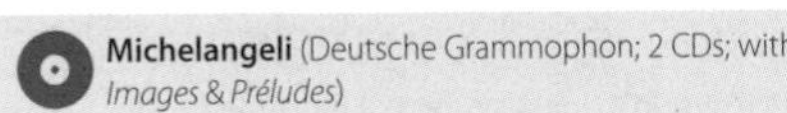

Michelangeli (Deutsche Grammophon; 2 CDs; with *Images & Préludes*)

Michelangeli's studio recording of *Children's Corner* is a showcase for his astonishing control of tone and weight, drawing out nuances and establishing layers of sound that few other pianists are equipped even to investigate. This performance is also available as part of a double-CD set, with *Images* and *Préludes I & II*.

Images

Debussy's two sets of *Images* (1905 and 1907) are musical homages to pure sensation, conjuring the sound of bells through leaves, sunlight reflected from the scales of goldfish, and a multitude of other transient moments. The opening piece, "Reflets dans l'eau", straight away establishes Debussy's unique understanding of the keyboard's potential, translating the rhythms of water into hypnotic, refreshing music that's as vividly pictorial as anything Liszt could have created. However, the *Images* require a degree of patience if you're coming to them from the incident-packed music of the nineteenth century, for their dynamic levels are generally very low, and the sense of silence, so mastered in *Pelléas*, is again a central feature of these aural landscapes. Whatever you do, don't reject them on first hearing – these miniatures are among the richest of all piano works.

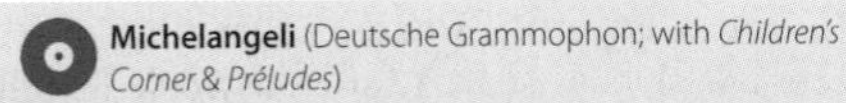

Michelangeli (Deutsche Grammophon; with *Children's Corner & Préludes*)

Michelangeli's performances of these works are astonishing, creating an ever-shifting and constantly fascinating world of sound. This account, one of the finest Debussy recordings ever made, is also available as part of a double-CD set.

Préludes

Debussy's two books of *Préludes* (1910 and 1913) are the last of his descriptive piano works. Titles such as "La cathédrale engloutie" (The Drowned Cathedral) indicate an affinity with the allusive world of the *Images*, but others, such as "Feux d'artifice" (Fireworks) and "La danse de Puck", are indicative of a more outgoing element to the *Préludes* – indeed several of these pieces make use of popular musical influences, including Neapolitan songs and music-hall numbers. They might be slightly more accessible than the *Images* (though bear in mind that Debussy did not intend all 24 to be heard in one session), but if anything they are technically even more demanding – only the *Études* require more of the pianist.

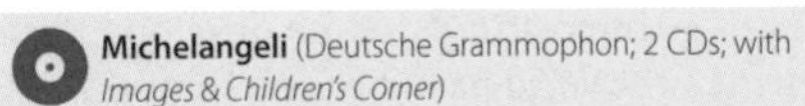

Michelangeli (Deutsche Grammophon; 2 CDs; with *Images & Children's Corner*)

For some critics Michelangeli is too preoccupied with seductive sonorities at the expense of musical depth, and the playing here is sometimes idiosyncratic. But his Epicurean style, with its marvellous gradations of dynamics and timbre, is perfectly suited to Debussy's most macroscopic piano music.

Gieseking (EMI; 2 CDs)

Walter Gieseking's recording of the *Préludes*, made in 1953–54, late in the pianist's life, is a legendary set. The sound is not digital-pure, but this playing transcends any such considerations. No one has evoked the diaphanous quality of Debussy's apparitions quite so well, or summoned the orchestral quality of his piano music with such effortless power.

Études

The *Études*, Debussy's last major works for piano, were written in 1915 yet they reflect nothing of his depression during the war years. Early in that year, Debussy had edited the complete piano works of Chopin and he duly dedicated his own two books of six studies to the memory of his great precursor. Like Chopin's *Études*, these pieces explore different aspects of piano technique, but are far more than mere technical exercises – though extremely difficult, they are among the most entertaining of all his piano works. The first book is the more traditional, experimenting with problems of overall dexterity, whereas the second is concerned with the very vocabulary of music and displays some typically advanced harmonic and melodic ideas.

Aimard (Teldec; with *Images*)

Pierre-Laurent Aimard regularly plays contemporary music, so it's no surprise that this performance emphasizes the modernity of Debussy. It's uningratiating, even aggressive at times, but Aimard never sacrifices tonal subtlety, and the precision of his fingerwork is astounding.

Uchida
(Philips)

Mitsuko Uchida is on top of even the most demanding studies, playing with a crispness, style and sophistication that mark her out as a brilliant Debussy pianist. On top of this, the recorded sound is exceptional.

Mélodies

Throughout his career Debussy wrote songs (the term *mélodie* is the French equivalent of the German lieder) which, though never as central to his output as those of Fauré, were more formally daring. Interestingly, as he developed as a songwriter, the vocal parts became simpler – less concerned with display and more with the integrity of the poem – to the extent that his vocal lines sometimes seem like melodic realizations of the spoken text. At the same time, the piano parts became richer and more atmospheric, almost able to function as pieces in their own right: as in "Le tombeau des Naides", the third song of the *Trois chansons de Bilitis* (1897–98), in which the delicate piano part suggests falling snow while the singer's part is close to recitative.

Debussy set the words of several poets but he shared with Fauré a particular enthusiasm for Paul Verlaine, whose dream-like, ambiguous early poems represented a break with the strict metrical forms of the past in a way that is comparable to Debussy's destabilizing of tonality. Among the most popular of his Verlaine settings is his second version of "Clair de lune", from *Fêtes galantes* (1882–91), in which a sense of a flickering twilight world is created by a gently rippling piano part over which the long vocal lines seem to float.

Nuit d'étoiles: Gens, Vignoles
(Virgin; with songs by Poulenc and Fauré)

One of the world's finest singers of Baroque music, Véronique Gens proves her versatility here in a superb recital that includes the *Trois chansons de Bilitis*, *Fêtes galantes* and five other Debussy songs. Her voice is elegant and balanced, her phrasing beautiful throughout, and though she's never over-dramatic, the texts in her native French are carefully articulated, in the manner of an intimate storytelling.

Léo Delibes (1836–1891)

Friedrich Nietzsche said he liked Léo Delibes because he made "no pretensions to depth". Like his teacher Adolph Adam, who wrote "my only ambition is to compose music that is transparent, easy to understand and amusing to the public", Delibes was a committed populist, and his music is full of personality – albeit the personality of Meyerbeer, Gounod, Bizet and countless other French composers, rather than his own. He may have possessed no strong musical identity, yet Delibes achieved considerable fame during his lifetime, and is the founder of modern, symphonic ballet music. As a composer of opera he had just one enduring claim to fame, *Lakmé*.

After a youthful career as a chorister and as organist of Saint-Pierre de Chaillot, Delibes was employed as an accompanist at the Théâtre Lyrique where he came into contact with Gounod, Bizet and Berlioz. While there Delibes composed several enormously successful comic operas and operettas, written very much in the style of Offenbach. In 1863 he moved to the Opéra where he eventually reached the exalted rank of second chorus master. However, he was driven by a desire to compose for the ballet, and in 1866 the success of *La source* (co-written with Louis Minkus) convinced him that his talents were indeed best suited to dance. In 1869 he composed his last operetta and the following year he completed his ballet *Coppélia*, another huge hit. Delibes pursued his métier with renewed enthusiasm, achieving more success with *Sylvia* in 1880 – a work which was a significant influence on the ballets of Tchaikovsky. Although he had abandoned operetta, he did not neglect the opera, and in 1883 (a year after the first performance of Wagner's *Parsifal*), *Lakmé* was staged at the Opéra Comique. It too was an immense success, and his reputation has rested securely upon it – and *Coppélia* – ever since.

Lakmé

Lakmé is a particularly egregious example of European exoticism, set in mid-nineteenth-century India. An English lieutenant named Gerald is smitten by Lakmé, the daughter of a Brahmin priest, who eventually stabs Gerald upon discovering his identity. Lakmé tends Gerald's wounds in her forest hut, but he is unable to decide between his love for her and his responsibility to his regiment. Lakmé decides for him by eating a poisonous leaf.

Delibes's deliciously light melodic writing saves the day – the first act's beautiful "Flower Duet" for two sopranos is one of the best-known moments in opera, though that's largely due to the fact that British Airways used it as their theme tune for a while. Lakmé's show-stopping "Bell Song" is the opera's other high spot, but this is not just a virtuoso showpiece for soprano. The male lead role is well drawn and theatrically compulsive, and the music's oriental inflections are consistently entertaining, for all *Lakmé*'s conservatism.

Dessay, Kunde, van Dam, Haidan; Toulouse Capitole Chorus and Orchestra; Plasson (EMI; 2 CDs)

The latest recording of this opera to be released is also one of the best. It stars the French coloratura soprano Natalie Dessay whose voice has an almost Baroque purity to it, a quality well suited to this music. Though recorded in the studio, the cast work well together under Michel Plasson's tight direction with an ease suggestive of a live production.

Sutherland, Vanzo, Bacquier, Sinclair; Orchestre National de l'Opéra de Monte Carlo; Bonynge (Decca; 2 CDs)

Bonynge's recording stars his wife, Joan Sutherland, as a technically superb heroine – the "Bell Song" poses no problems for her. She is admirably partnered by Alain Vanzo, and the supporting cast is good too, with a delightful plummy English lady from Monica Sinclair. For those mainly interested in the "Flower Duet", Decca have issued a mid-price single CD of highlights from this performance.

Coppélia

Coppélia prompted Tchaikovsky to remark that he preferred Delibes to Brahms. Admittedly, Tchaikovsky had a special love of ballet and a special hatred of Brahms ("that talentless bastard", as he once called him), but there can be little doubt that, together with Tchaikovsky's dance music, *Coppélia* is one of the seminal nineteenth-century works in this genre. Based upon E.T.A. Hoffmann's short story "The Sandman", which concerns the toymaker Doctor Coppelius and his dancing doll (a story Offenbach used in his *Tales of Hoffmann*), the music is full of fine melodies, vivid characterization and brilliantly conceived dances. It is not a sophisticated score, but this is one of the few classical ballets that will bear close attention away from the stage.

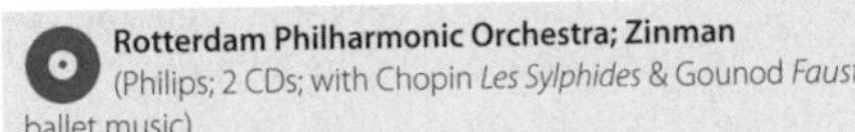

Rotterdam Philharmonic Orchestra; Zinman (Philips; 2 CDs; with Chopin *Les Sylphides* & Gounod *Faust* ballet music)

David Zinman conducts an excellent version of the complete ballet here, with an alert and theatrical sounding Rotterdam Philharmonic Orchestra. The fine sound, the generous fill-ups and the mid-price tag add up to make this the number-one choice.

Frederick Delius (1862–1934)

Born in England to a German father, Frederick Delius turned to composing while in Florida, then spent most of his working life in rural France. His music is similarly cosmopolitan and difficult to classify, but it was largely inspired by the composer's deep love of nature, whose beauty and impermanence he tried to evoke in rich, diaphanous orchestral textures, full of shifting chromatic harmonies. A late Romantic composer, he regarded his music as a means of expressing his spiritual values, which were largely an amalgam of the philosophy of Nietzsche and the pantheistic writings of Walt Whitman.

Delius was brought up in Bradford, the son of a prosperous wool merchant who at first insisted that the boy join the family business. But it had no appeal for him, and in 1884 he left for Florida in order to run an orange plantation. It was here, on hearing the workers' songs wafting across the

St John River, that he decided to become a composer. He took some lessons with a local organist named Thomas Ward, a course of instruction he later claimed taught him more than his eighteen months at the Leipzig Conservatorium between 1886 and 1888.

One thing he did gain from Leipzig was the friendship and support of Edvard Grieg, who persuaded Delius's father that Frederick's future was as a composer. Delius came to regard Norway as his spiritual home, and his bohemian spell in Paris, in the early 1890s, was largely spent in the company of Scandinavian artists, including the painter Edvard Munch and the playwright August Strindberg. Paris was also where he met Jelka Rosen, a painter whom he later married. In 1897 the couple moved to the village of Grez-sur-Loing near the forest of Fontainebleau; it was to be their home for the rest of his life, with the exception of the war years, which were spent in England and Norway.

In contrast to the roistering years in Paris, Delius's life at Grez was deliberately reclusive, and it was here that he gradually developed his individual impressionistic style. His music gained its initial success in Germany, but its biggest following was in England (a country he claimed to loathe), principally through the advocacy of his greatest interpreter, Sir Thomas Beecham, who organized major Delius festivals in 1929 and 1946. The latter stage of his life, however, was marked by increasing ill-health, which eventually left him blind and paralysed – the result of syphilis contracted in his youth.

Choral Music

The orchestral miniatures may be the most popular of Delius's compositions, but it is the orchestral songs for soloists and chorus that are his greatest achievement, and all of them combine, to varying degrees, a sense of the thrilling vitality of life with an underlying sadness at its transience. *Sea Drift* (1903–04), a setting of a Whitman poem, tells of a sea bird that has lost its mate and waits faithfully, but in vain, for her return. The *Songs of Sunset* (1906–07) are even more melancholic, setting poems that are permeated by the evanescence of happiness and love. In both works there are no breaks in the music, and Delius employs an idiosyncratic and informal style of vocal writing – part recitative, part arioso – that gives each work a sense of an unfolding awareness.

By contrast, the *Mass of Life* (1904–05) is a rapturous celebration of the life force (though even here there are moments of despair), taken from Nietzsche's *Also Sprach Zarathustra* – also the inspiration for one of Richard Strauss's most popular works. Zarathustra is Nietzsche's idea of the Superman, a man disdainful of weakness and conventional morality, and the *Mass of Life* is a fittingly huge and powerful work, full of sinewy and vigorous choral writing, and – especially in the night-time music – some remarkable orchestration. In scope and ambition it stands alongside Mahler's *Symphony No. 2* and Schoenberg's *Gurrelieder*.

Sea Drift; Songs of Sunset; Songs of Farewell: Terfel; Bournemouth Symphony Chorus & Orchestra; Hickox (Chandos)

Hickox's second recording of *Sea Drift* is gloriously impassioned and utterly convincing. In Bryn Terfel he has a soloist who knows how to pace a role dramatically – characterization is far more vivid than on rival recordings. And the chorus are superb, utterly responsive to Hickox's sensitive shaping and colouring and, in turn, beautifully served by the wonderfully open and expansive Chandos sound.

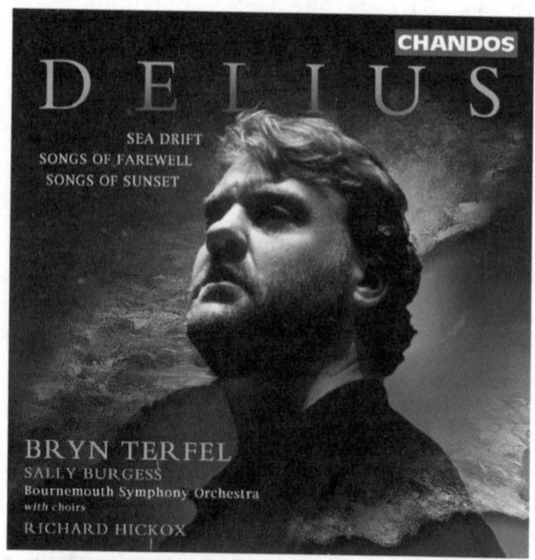

A Mass of Life; Requiem: Evans, Rodgers, Rigby, Robson, Coleman-Wright; Waynflete Singers; Bournemouth Symphony Orchestra and Chorus; Hickox (Chandos; 2 CDs)

The *Mass of Life* has been called a pagan oratorio, and in this 1997 recording Hickox manages to whip up an even greater mood of frenzy and abandonment than Groves did in his EMI recording. This is a marvellous performance which deserves to establish this work, once and for all, as one of the choral masterpieces of the early twentieth century.

Orchestral Music

Delius's most immediately accessible music is found in short orchestral pieces such as *Brigg Fair* (1907), *Summer Night on the River* (1911), *On Hearing the First Cuckoo in Spring* (1912) and

A Song Before Sunrise (1918) – works whose very titles evoke a benign, pastoralist image of nature. He is not a composer whose strength comes from melodic inventiveness (though he does have some good tunes) or from tightly structured forms; rather it is the orchestration and harmony that make his sound-world unique. Subtle combinations of instruments (including beautifully evocative woodwind writing), gently lilting rhythms, chromaticism that is hazy yet coherent – these are the things that create the overwhelming sense of tranquillity and spaciousness that colours so much of his orchestral work.

On Hearing the First Cuckoo; Brigg Fair; Summer Night on the River; A Song Before Sunrise: Royal Philharmonic Orchestra; Beecham (EMI; with other orchestral works)

Beecham was the supreme interpreter of Delius, his attention to phrasing and the detailing of dynamics always producing remarkable results – nowhere more hauntingly than in *Brigg Fair*, a work which in terms of sumptuousness and delicacy of colouring matches the best of Debussy or Ravel. Though recorded in the late 1950s to early 1960s, the sound is remarkably fresh and bright.

Brigg Fair; In a Summer Garden; On Hearing the First Cuckoo; Paris; Summer Night on the River; A Village Romeo and Juliet: Walk to the Paradise Garden: BBC Symphony Orchestra; Davis (Warner)

If you are looking for bright, clean modern sound, this disc fits the bill and at a highly competitive price. Andrew Davis makes a skilful advocate for these pieces, and shows a real sensitivity to the Delian ebb and flow – knowing when to push the music along and when to hold back.

Violin Concerto

Of the four concertos Delius wrote – for piano, violin, cello, and for violin and cello together – it is the *Violin Concerto* (1916) that is the most satisfying work. Though Delius was himself a talented violinist and the work was written for the brilliant English violinist Albert Sammons, it is markedly not a virtuosic showpiece. The solo part might often soar and glide rhapsodically over the orchestral texture, but it is always connected harmonically with the orchestral writing and seems to grow out of it. The work is in one long movement divided into three clear sections, and abounds in moments of passionate spontaneity, sometimes dream-like, sometimes fervent.

Little; Welsh National Opera Orchestra; Mackerras (Decca; 2 CDs; with *Piano Concerto* & *Orchestral Works*)

Mackerras is an ideal Delius conductor, unerringly judging the music's shape and direction, while Tasmin Little is an inspired soloist, bringing to the work an ardour which is utterly compelling. Balance between soloist and orchestra is perfect, with the musical momentum seeming to pass effortlessly from one to the other.

Gaetano Donizetti (1797–1848)

It is hard to understand how two adjacent European countries could produce such disparate musical styles as did nineteenth-century Italy and Austria. Gaetano Donizetti and Franz Schubert were born in 1797, the former in Bergamo, the latter in Vienna, and yet there have surely never been two less similar neighbours. Whereas Schubert's music trawled the deepest recesses of the mind, Donizetti's exhibitionistic operas required no one to think too deeply. "Music for the Italians", noted Berlioz, "is a sensual pleasure and nothing more. For this noble expression of the mind they have hardly more respect than for the art of cooking. They want a score that, like a plate of macaroni, can be assimilated immediately without having to think about it." And yet, though it's true that Donizetti's crowd-pleasers won't bear examination by the rigorous standards of contemporaries such as Beethoven, Schubert, Schumann or Chopin, he nonetheless had a genuine artistic vision. Like Bellini – the other master of bel canto opera – he wanted to bring music and drama into a "closer, more direct conjunction", to quote the composer himself.

In all, he wrote some 73 operas, and the majority of them are populated either with historical personalities (for example *Lucrezia Borgia*, *Anna Bolena* and *Maria Stuarda*) or with characters lifted from writers such as Schiller, Hugo and Walter Scott. It was the last of this

Gaetano Donizetti by Joseph Kriehuber.

trio who provided him with the material for his finest opera, *Lucia di Lammermoor* (1835), a daring attempt to reconcile his post-Rossinian devotion to exquisite vocal line with the need for real character development. Like Bellini and Rossini before him, Donizetti was more than happy to accommodate the bravura talents of his star singers (many of whom had worked closely with Bellini), but his career showed an increasing willingness to subordinate display to the needs of the drama. His move away from the strict framework of "aria–recitative–chorus" was gradual, but by the end of his life he was writing through-form operas, in which the action remained constant without interruptions for set-piece singing.

Donizetti undoubtedly wrote too much too quickly, but it should be remembered that the conditions in which he worked were hardly conducive to the creation of profound or sophisticated art. To get further work, the opera composer had to complete his current commission quickly, and when confronted by an impatient, fee-paying impresario, Germanic concepts of self-expression mattered for nothing. For all his "commercialism", Donizetti is, with Bellini, nineteenth-century Italy's most important composer of opera before Verdi, a composer who wrote pastiche Donizetti for his first twenty years – then paid his precursor the compliment of stealing one of his tunes for the Grand Chorus of *Aïda*.

L'elisir d'amore

In 1832, Donizetti completed his first great comic opera, *L'elisir d'amore* (The Elixir of Love), a tongue-in-cheek reinterpretation of the Tristan and Isolde myth. A "love potion" is bought from a quack doctor by Nemorino, in the hope of winning the love of Adina. She chooses to marry another man but, before doing so, is forced to realize that she loves Nemorino after all, and they finally marry. The quack then does a roaring trade. *L'elisir d'amore* is a great sentimental-pastoral comedy, and it features some of the composer's finest music, with Nemorino's second-act "Una furtiva lagrima" standing out as one of the most affecting bel canto tenor arias ever written. Adina, the soprano lead, has plenty of beautiful writing, including a first-act duet with Nemorino and a solo in the second act, "Prendi, prendi per me sei libero".

Sutherland, Pavarotti, Cossa, Malas, Casula; Ambrosian Singers; English Chamber Orchestra; Bonynge (Decca; 2 CDs)

Luciano Pavarotti's early recording with Joan Sutherland and Dominic Cossa is the most rewarding of the many versions in the current catalogue. Pavarotti's voice might not quite catch Nemorino's naive innocence, but he and Sutherland establish a genuine relationship, and Cossa is endearingly convincing as the roguish charlatan Dulcamara.

Gheorghiu, Alagna, Scaltriti, Alaimo, Dan; Chorus and Orchestra of the Opéra de Lyon; Pidò (Decca; 2 CDs)

The husband and wife team of Angela Gheorghiu and Roberto Alagna make an impressive double act in this 1997 recording. It's a very theatrical performance, with Gheorghiu bringing a toughness of characterization to Adina and dealing with the most difficult passage work with an almost contemptuous ease.

Lucia di Lammermoor

Sir Walter Scott's *The Bride of Lammermoor* afforded Donizetti with a perfect vehicle for intensely emotional writing. Basically, the tale recounts the long-standing feud between the families of Lammermoor and Ravenswood and the love between Lucia and Edgardo – Lucia being the sister of the head of Lammermoor, and Edgardo the head of Ravenswood. Lucia dies after killing her enforced husband-to-be and, upon seeing her coffin carried towards burial, Edgardo kills himself in desperation.

The superb characterizations of *Lucia di Lammermoor* and its string of glorious melodies – at once fresh and sentimental – make this his most successful opera, and it received frequent productions when bel canto enjoyed a vogue back in the 1950s. The archetypal Romantic Italian opera, *Lucia* is renowned for the extraordinary soprano pyrotechnics of the "Mad Scene" in Act 3, but it contains some magnificent tenor passages as well – in fact, the male role attracted more attention from Donizetti's first audiences.

Sutherland, Pavarotti, Milnes, Ghiaurov; Royal Opera House Chorus and Orchestra; Bonynge (Decca; 2 CDs)

This 1971 recording, Sutherland's second Lucia, is one of her lasting achievements. The voice is magnificent, more vibrant and varied than in 1961, and richer in character. The young Pavarotti is in resonant voice, while Sherrill Milnes and Nicolai Ghiaurov are in roaring good form as Enrico and Raimondo.

La fille du régiment

One of Donizetti's most light-hearted operas, *La fille du régiment* (1840) was also one of his most successful, receiving 44 performances in its first year in Paris. A tale of love triumphant against the odds, it is famous for two episodes, one for the soprano lead, the other for the tenor. The former, Marie's "Song of the Regiment", is full of flowing ideas that will stick in your mind for days after you first hear it. However, it is her suitor Tonio's "Ah mes amis" that is the show-stopping *tour de force*, requiring the tenor to sing for upwards of five minutes before a terrifically demanding sequence of nine consecutive high Cs. Few singers have been able to manage such acrobatics, which is why this greatly enjoyable opera rarely reaches the stage.

Sutherland, Pavarotti, Sinclair, Bruyere, Malas, Garrett, Coates, Jones; Royal Opera House Orchestra and Chorus; Bonynge (Decca; 2 CDs)

In the 1960s, when this record was made, Luciano Pavarotti was unrivalled in bel canto roles, and it was his New York Met appearance as Tonio that made him a superstar. This is a really remarkable performance, powerful, accurate and bursting with character. Joan Sutherland is extremely fine if a bit precious, and Richard Bonynge binds the whole together with his brisk and enthusiastic accompaniment.

Don Pasquale

In *Don Pasquale* (1843), his late comic masterpiece, Donizetti plundered the classical heritage of Mozart to create a sort of operatic *commedia dell'arte*. Centring on an old man's attempt to find himself a young wife, the opera is remarkable for its free-flowing conversational recitative and the lightness of its orchestration and vocal writing. The small cast, headed by nineteenth-century opera's most perfect soubrette role, makes *Don Pasquale* ideally suited to small opera houses, yet it's infrequently performed, perhaps because it doesn't deliver the heart-stopping vocal tricks that people have come to expect from Italian opera. Fortunately, it works extremely well on record, where the quality of its tightly written libretto comes to the fore.

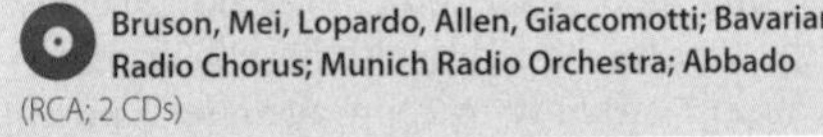

Bruson, Mei, Lopardo, Allen, Giaccomotti; Bavarian Radio Chorus; Munich Radio Orchestra; Abbado (RCA; 2 CDs)

This 1993 recording, made under Roberto Abbado's nimble direction, shoots along with infectious brio and real panache. Renato Bruson is an impressive-sounding Don, whose comedic instincts never desert him, and Eva Mei manages the difficult coloratura moments with wit as well as technical distinction.

John Dowland (1563–1626)

The lute was the most popular solo instrument in Europe at the end of the sixteenth century and John Dowland was one of its most skilful practitioners. But, despite his prowess, he repeatedly failed to gain the position he so coveted at the English court, a failure he felt strongly in spite of a highly successful career abroad. Perhaps his Catholicism, to which he had converted while resident in France in the 1580s, had hindered him at the English court (though it did not affect his older contemporary William Byrd; see p.122). At any rate Dowland abandoned his new faith in 1597 prior to returning briefly to England from Italy where, as an itinerant performer, he had fallen in with a group of disaffected English Catholics whose treasonable plans had considerably alarmed him. The following year he obtained an extremely lucrative position

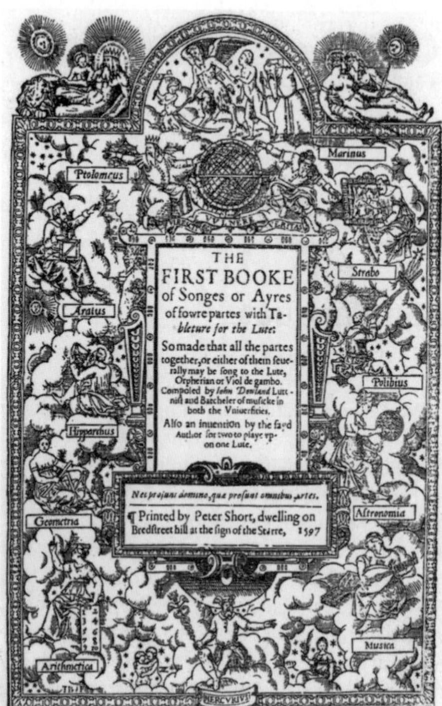

THE
FIRST BOOKE
of Songes or Ayres
of fowre partes with Ta-
bleture for the Lute:
So made that all the partes
together, or either of them seue-
rally may be song to the Lute,
Orpherian or Viol de gambo.
Composed by *Iohn Dowland* Lutenist and Batcheler of musicke in
both the Vniuersities.
Also an inuention by the sayd
Author for two to playe vp-
on one Lute.

Nec prosunt domino, quae prosunt omnibus, artes.

¶ Printed by Peter Short, dwelling on
Bredstreet hill at the sign of the Starre, 1597

The title page of *The First Booke of Songs*.

as lutenist to King Christian IV of Denmark, remaining there until 1606 but making several lengthy trips to London to visit his wife and son – and, almost certainly, to apply again for a post at the English court. Ironically, when he was finally appointed as one of the king's lutenists in 1612, his inspiration – at least as a composer – seems to have deserted him.

Dowland was greatly admired in his lifetime by fellow musicians as well as by writers: the poet Richard Barnfield, in his sonnet "In Praise of Music and Poetry", wrote that his "heavenly touch upon the lute doth ravish human sense". Yet despite this esteem he appears to have been a profoundly discontented and melancholic man, a fact reflected in his music, which dwells almost obsessively on sadness and death.

Lachrimae

Perhaps Dowland's most famous work is the collection of pieces for viol consort and lute entitled *Lachrimae, or Seaven Teares Figured in Seaven Passionate Pavans*. This is a series of subtle divisions (variations) on a slow and sombre melody in which the opening motif of a falling fourth recurs throughout the sequence. The melody, which also existed as both a lute solo and as the song "Flow My Tears", became the most famous in Europe, parodied and imitated by numerous composers. The collection also contained other consort music, including one of Dowland's saddest and most complex pieces entitled, appropriately, "Semper Dowland, semper dolens" (Always Dowland, Always Doleful).

Seven Teares: The King's Noyse; O'Dette; Douglass
(Harmonia Mundi)

A very fine set indeed, as good as the previously recommended Hesperion XX recording which is now hard to find. Like that group, The King's Noyse favour a rich, burnished tone but they create it with Renaissance violins rather than viols so the sound is less heavy. In addition to the pavanes and galliards there are a handful of Dowland songs, performed with flair by soprano Ellen Hargis.

Songs

"Flow My Tears" had originally appeared in 1600 in the second of the four books of songs that Dowland published, most of which consistently reflect the cult of melancholy that was so prevalent in Elizabethan court circles. In fact, though Dowland set the words of several leading poets, many of the most lugubrious texts ("In Darkness Let Me Dwell", "Go Crystal Tears") were anonymous. Dowland's greatness as a songwriter lay in his ability to match exactly the music to the feeling of the words, a preoccupation that places him closer to Italian madrigalists, like Monteverdi and Marenzio (whom he knew), than to his English colleagues. *The First Booke of Songs* is the least morose of Dowland's song compilations.

The First Booke of Songs: Muller; Wilson
(ASV)

The First Booke of Songs is well served by Rufus Muller's clear and firm-toned voice. The meaning of the sometimes complex texts is well conveyed, although Muller ocassionally over-enunciates consonants at the beginning of words. He is at his best in the slower more introspective songs, such as *Go Crystal Tears*, where he allows himself a greater degree of expressiveness and a more intimate tone quality.

Lute Songs: Padmore, Kenny
(Hyperion; with Britten *Nocturnal*)

Tenor Mark Padmore is renowned for his attentiveness to the words he sings, conveying meaning in a completely unforced way – perfect for the intimate quality of Dowland's songs. Lutenist Elizabeth Kenny (who also wrote the excellent sleeve notes) is an ideal partner; both singer and instrumentalist seem to draw inspiration from each other.

Solo Lute Music

Dowland wrote more than a hundred lute solos in a wide variety of musical forms, including dance forms like the slow pavane or the sprightly galliard (frequently played as a pair). He was particularly adept at divisions (as variations were then called), and much of his lute music displays a contrapuntal sophistication far in excess of most of his contemporaries. The expressive range of his music is wide, although the self-consciously melancholic nature of much of it is what he is best known for. In fact many lute pieces display a sly wit, not least in their titles: thus we have *The Frogg Galliard*, *Mrs Winter's Jumpp*, and the mysterious pair *Mrs White's Thing* and *Mrs White's Nothing*.

Complete Lute Works Volume 1: O'Dette
(Harmonia Mundi)

Paul O'Dette's five-disc set of the complete lute music, available as separate CDs, is unlikely to be bettered for fluency and spontaneity. An added bonus is that he plays on three different instruments, including a steel-stringed orpharion. The pieces collected on this first volume provide an ideal introduction to this beguiling music.

Guillaume Dufay (c.1400–1474)

Dufay is one of an outstanding group of Franco-Flemish composers that emerged from the Dukedom of Burgundy, the most opulent and artistically fertile of the courts of fifteenth-century northern Europe. Dufay was connected to the Burgundian court but never formally attached to it, instead spending much of his working life in Italy, where his reputation grew so high that he was described by Piero de' Medici as "the greatest ornament of our age". Like Machaut, Dufay was a priest and he received a substantial part of his income from largely honorary church appointments, but unlike Machaut much of his music was written for the Church. He is a seminal figure in the field of sacred music, helping to establish the mass as a coherent and unified whole, a development that made it the principal vehicle of elaborate polyphony for the next century and a half.

Dufay was born in or near Cambrai, an important centre of religious music, and he began his career there in 1409 as a chorister at the cathedral. While still a young man he went to Italy to work for the Malatesta family at Pesaro before joining the papal chapel in 1428. Apart from two years as *maestro di cappella* to the Duke of Savoy, he remained a member of the papal choir until 1437, based firstly at Rome, then at Bologna and Florence. He returned to Cambrai in 1440 and, apart from another brief spell with the Duke of Savoy from 1452 to 1458, he never left. In preparation for his death in 1474 Dufay paid for no fewer than three sung masses (including his own setting in honour of St Anthony), thirteen low masses and an annual ceremony to be held in his memory. Such expenditure was far from excessive and is one of the reasons why the fifteenth-century Church grew so phenomenally rich.

Sacred Music

Polyphonic music – which in Dufay's time was reserved for occasions of great importance – was transformed by him into a clearer, richer and more sonorous musical language, with harmonies and carefully placed dissonances that give the music a feeling of forward progress. In his later masses, his finest works, he employs the cantus firmus method, in which the musical material is built around an already existing melody, usually a section of plainchant. One of the best of these late masses is the *Missa Ecce Ancilla Domini* (Behold the Handmaid of the Lord), its name taken from the plainsong chant that forms its cantus firmus. It is written for four voices, but at least half the Mass, as a means of contrast, uses just two voices in different combinations. It's a remarkably powerful and attractive piece, in which slow, reverent passages are balanced by more rhythmically lively sections in the two-part writing. Dufay also helped to develop the isorhythmic motet (see p.316) in which rhythm and pitch patterns are repeated while the melody evolves separately. One of his finest motets, *Nuper Rosarum Flores*, is based on the mathematical proportions of Florence Cathedral and was composed for the consecration of the cathedral shortly after the completion of Brunelleschi's stupendous dome.

Missa Ecce Ancilla Domini: Ensemble Gilles Binchois; Vellard (Virgin)

In keeping with increasingly common practice, the mass is here placed within a liturgical context which includes the various chants and hymns appropriate to the service for which it was written, thus helping to create a vivid sense of occasion. The all-male voices have a warmth and a suppleness which bring out the zest of the music without recourse to overt expressiveness.

Motets: Huelgas-Ensemble; Van Nevel (Harmonia Mundi)

This CD presents all of Dufay's isorhythmic motets in chronological order, including *Nuper Rosarum Flores*. Most of these works were commissioned for church and municipal occasions, yet there is nothing rigid or pompous about them. The Huelgas-Ensemble's outstanding performances vividly bring Dufay's waves of sumptuous, colourful sound to life.

Secular Music

Dufay wrote many secular songs (or *chansons*) and, although he rarely set words as refined as Machaut's, they mostly deal with the same theme of unrequited courtly love. Most of the songs are *rondeaux*, with sections of words and music recurring throughout, and many of them are polyphonic, employing three and sometimes four voices. Although he composed *chansons* throughout his career there is no obviously discernible change of style between the early and the late songs: all are characterized by a refined and lyrical quality, with memorable melodies that are often tinged with a hint of melancholy.

Dufay and Binchois: Ballades, Rondeaux, Lamentation: Ensemble Gilles Binchois; Vellard (Harmonic Records)

Though difficult to track down, this is by some way the outstanding recording of Dufay's songs, eleven of which are included here, along with seven by Binchois. Vellard adopts a flexible approach; some songs are performed by voices, some by instruments and some by both. There is a delightful lightness and purity to the singing, with the plaintive tones of Brigitte Lesne making an outstanding contribution.

Paul Dukas (1865–1935)

Outside of France Paul Dukas is known for a single work, *L'Apprenti sorcier* (The Sorcerer's Apprentice), which reached its widest audience in the shape of a cartoon. One of the most successful episodes in Walt Disney's *Fantasia* (1940) has a hapless Mickey Mouse confidently conjuring up a broom to carry water for him, only to find, as the house begins to flood, that he's unable to make it stop. Dukas's own problem was almost the reverse: an extremely self-critical and fastidious man, he composed very little and at the end of his life destroyed much of what he had written. What survives reveals a consummate craftsman, but one who found it hard to establish a strong, individual voice.

Dukas's career parallels that of his slightly older contemporary, Debussy. Both men studied composition with Guiraud at the Paris Conservatoire (in 1888 Dukas narrowly missed winning the prestigious Prix de Rome which Debussy had won in 1884); both of them wrote music criticism; and both wrote an opera based on a play by Maurice Maeterlinck. But, whereas Debussy was a naturally experimental composer, Dukas was a conservative who took a strong lead from others and tended to use established forms.

Before *L'Apprenti sorcier* brought him overnight fame in 1897, Dukas had written two substantial orchestral works. *Polyeucte* (1891), an overture to Corneille's play, reveals a debt to both Franck and Wagner in its rich chromaticism. More impressive is the *Symphony in C Major*, in which a tightening of structure and greater rhythmic incisiveness is combined with skilful atmospheric writing in the slow movement. For some, Dukas's greatest achievement is his opera *Ariane et Barbe-Bleue*, based on Maeterlinck's retelling of the Bluebeard legend. First performed in 1907, five years after the premiere of Debussy's *Pelléas et Mélisande*, it creates a similarly twilit world (with occasional quotes from *Pelléas*), but lacks the depth and intensity of Debussy's masterpiece.

From the time of his last major orchestral work, *La Péri* (1911), until his death in 1935, Dukas composed no more major works that have survived. Instead he spent much of his time as an editor of earlier French composers (including Rameau and Couperin) and as a Conservatoire teacher of future ones – most notably Olivier Messiaen (see p.346).

Orchestral Music

L'Apprenti sorcier, inspired by a Goethe ballad, is one of the few works by Dukas which is uniquely his own. It's a brilliantly concentrated piece in which a central, jaunty theme is magically transformed from a mood of engaging confidence to one of sinister power through a deft employment of orchestral colour. Brass and wind seem to dominate the changing character of the theme, while shimmering strings are mainly used to establish a "once upon a time" feel at the beginning and end of the work. Tension is maintained, despite a series of false climaxes, through an unnerving dotted rhythm in the lower instruments which never seems to go away.

La Péri displays a similar gift for theatrical suspense. It was commissioned by Diaghilev's Russian Ballet in 1911, but the company never performed the piece (despite Bakst's beautiful costume designs) because Dukas insisted that the lead should be performed by an outside dancer, Nathalie Trouhanova. The story tells of Prince Iskender's theft of the lotus-flower of immortality which is guarded by a beautiful *péri* or fairy. She dances for him, he falls in love with her and returns the flower, only for her to disappear. Dukas's ballet shares the same exotic sound-world as Rimsky-Korsakov's *Scheherazade* and Stravinsky's *Firebird* (two earlier Russian Ballet successes). As with both those works, there is an emphasis on diaphanous textures, rhapsodic climaxes and striking atmospheric effects, which is both magical and seductive.

La Péri; L'Apprenti sorcier: Ulster Orchestra; Tortelier (Chandos; with Chabrier *Suite pastorale & España*)

Yan Pascal Tortelier is one of the finest interpreters of early twentieth-century French repertoire. On this disc he elicits beautiful and dynamically varied sounds from the Ulster Orchestra, and employs a keen sense of dramatic pacing, so that the sections grow out of each other naturally. There are some moments of real incandescent beauty, especially in *La Péri*.

Piano Sonata

The great French pianist Alfred Cortot called Dukas's *Piano Sonata* "one of the most important efforts ever made to adapt Beethovenian characteristics to the French pianistic style." It's a four-movement work on the grandest possible scale, which daringly juggles many disparate and seemingly contradictory elements into a largely coherent whole. The first movement resembles late Beethoven filtered through the sensibility of Scriabin: there seems to be a permanent and breathless build-up to a climax that never quite happens. The middle two movements evoke the organ loft, first through a radiant and serene religiosity that sounds like an improvisation, then through a fierce and fiery toccata. The final movement, the longest, is a strenuously passionate rhapsody paying obvious homage to the last act of *Tristan und Isolde*. This is a work that makes strong demands on both performer and listener alike and should be approached with caution.

Ogdon (EMI; with Dutilleux *Piano Sonata* & Schmitt *Deux mirages*)

Though not easy to find, this recording repays the effort. This is music that requires a pianist of skill, daring and vision. John Ogdon had all these qualities and more, and here he gives a torrential performance that has never been bettered – passionate but never bombastic.

Hamelin (Hyperion; with Decaux *Clairs de Lune*)

If you can't find the Ogdon recording, this performance makes an excellent substitute. Marc-André Hamelin certainly has the technical ability to match Ogdon and he brings a wide range of tone colour to Dukas's shifting kaleidoscopic vision without quite reaching the delirious heights attained by Ogdon.

John Dunstable (c.1390–1453)

Very little is known about the English composer John Dunstable (or Dunstaple), but there is no doubt that his music exerted a profound and far-ranging influence throughout fifteenth-century Europe. Even during Dunstable's lifetime, the commentator Martin le Franc was remarking on the debt composers such as Dufay and Binchois owed to their older contemporary. Copied manuscripts of his music are found in libraries in Italy and Germany and even as far afield as Estonia. Dunstable's special impact on European composers can partly be explained by his probable service in the entourage of the powerful Duke of Bedford, regent of France between 1422 and 1437, who had Joan of Arc burnt as a witch. While in France Dunstable may have written music for the coronation of Henry VI in Paris, a possible French connection further strengthened by the fact that he was granted lands in France on the Duke of Bedford's death.

His major patrons in England were the dowager Queen Joan and the Duke of Gloucester (Bedford's brother). Both had links with St Albans Abbey, for which Dunstable wrote at least one motet (*Albanus roseo rutilat*), although he does not seem to have held a position there, nor ever to have taken holy orders – unusually for a composer of this time. It was the abbot of St Albans, John Whethamsteade, who wrote one, if not both, of the two Latin epitaphs commemorating the composer. Each of these refers almost as much to Dunstable's fame as an astronomer as they do to his musicianship, and it seems likely that his later years were devoted to study of the Quadrivium (arithmetic, astronomy, geometry and music). His talents may even have extended to the visual arts: a Dunstable manuscript in Cambridge, concerned with astronomical and astrological speculations, contains a number of fine and imaginative drawings which some scholars have attributed to the composer.

Sacred Music

Dunstable was working at the start of a musical Golden Age in England – indeed some of the music ascribed to him may have been written by his equally talented English contemporary Leonel Power. Both men seem to have written exclusively sacred music and both had fully assimilated the technical innovations of the Ars Nova (see p.293), in particular a more rigorous and numerically ordered approach to rhythm. Dunstable composed several motets for three or four voices, in which the two higher parts were supported by a lower voice moving at a slower speed. Often these motets were isorhythmic, which means that the under part is made up of a repeated rhythmic unit. Most isorhythmic motets were divided into three progressively faster sections and most employed different words in each part. This made for some rich and complex textures, and it was this richness of sonority which made such an impression on Dunstable's continental colleagues. An even greater impact was achieved by the English invention of the cantus firmus mass, in which a borrowed melody – usually sung in the tenor part – was employed as the structural basis for each movement of the mass. In an age when the expression of the meaning of the sacred words was of marginal importance, this went a long way towards imposing a stylistic unity on the mass. Dunstable (or perhaps Power) wrote one such mass, the *Missa Rex seculorum*, which is based on a plainsong antiphon for St Benedict.

John Dunstable: The Hilliard Ensemble
(Virgin)

This disc first appeared in 1984 and still sounds fresh and exciting, with the usual Hilliard strengths of perfect intonation, meticulous ensemble and rhythmic suppleness well to the fore. The group concentrate on the motets and include two sections of an incomplete mass.

John Dunstaple: Orlando Consort
(Metronome)

The advantages of this disc are twenty minutes more music and first ever recordings of the *Missa Rex seculorum* and the extraordinary *Gloria in canon*, discovered just as the Orlando Consort went into the studio. The group's approach is more robust than that of the Hilliards, and the sound is much more forward and not so homogeneous – what you lose in solemnity and purity of voice you gain in liveliness.

Henri Duparc (1848–1933)

In the aftermath of the Franco-Prussian War, the guardians of France's musical culture reaffirmed their rejection of all things German, in particular the dangerously progressive ideas of Richard Wagner. The exception to this rule was César Franck (see p.196) – always something of an outsider – who as a teacher attracted to himself the more adventurously minded composition students. Among the most gifted of the "bande à Franck" (as his early pupils were known) was Henri Duparc, who studied privately with Franck while training to be a lawyer. Duparc rapidly developed into an exquisite talent, producing a small body of highly atmospheric songs which stand as the finest written in the period between Berlioz and Fauré. Tragically, he suffered from a debilitating, neurotic sensitivity (neurasthenia was the contemporary diagnosis) which led him to stop composing at the age of thirty-seven.

Duparc was born in Paris into a well-to-do family and educated at the Jesuit College of Vaugirard, where César Franck taught music. Duparc was a regular visitor to Germany, and first heard Wagner's music performed at Munich in 1869, and was introduced to the composer by Liszt in the same year. Ten year later, a trip to Bayreuth with Chabrier (see p.133) consolidated his assimilation of Wagner's harmonic ideas, an influence clearly discernible in several of his best songs. His first published work, *Feuilles volantes* for piano, appeared in 1869, but like several of his compositions it was later rejected by him. A symphonic poem *Lénore* (1875), based on a poem by Bürger, was regularly performed (and was later arranged as a piano duet by Franck), but his attempt at an opera, *Roussalka*, was abandoned.

Many of the first performances of his works were given by the Société Nationale de Musique, an important forum for new music which Duparc helped to set up (along with Franck, Saint-Saëns, Fauré and others). His taste in all the arts was for the progressive: he admired Ibsen, Verlaine and other "advanced" writers long before it was fashionable to do so. He even criticized Wagner to his face for the over-literalness of his Bayreuth productions. The emphasis of Duparc's own aesthetic was always on feeling: "Je veux être ému" (I want to be moved), he stated, a principle elaborated in a letter to his friend the poet Francis Jammes, in which he wrote that "music inspired by poetry can only be justified if it adds something to the poetry, if it makes it more touching for souls who are moved by musical expression."

Gérard Souzay, the doyen of Duparc singers.

After leaving Paris in 1885, Duparc moved to south-west France and then to Switzerland. In relative isolation, his life became extremely quiet and uneventful: his main creative outlet was drawing in sepia and watercolour, until this too was curtailed by failing sight. In 1906 a visit to Lourdes with the writer Paul Claudel and Francis Jammes led to an intensifying of his religious faith and an increasingly resigned attitude to his physical suffering. Apart from a few brief sketches for *Roussalka* (which he later burned) he never composed another note.

Songs

Duparc wrote the seventeen songs for which he is remembered – though he later thought only thirteen were worthwhile – between 1868 and 1884. The carefully chosen texts mostly generate a mood of wistful nostalgia, a yearning for the unattainable or for pleasures now lost. The sensuous, dream-like quality of Duparc's music is offset by an emotional intensity which raises them above the salon fare of most French song of the period, and suggests a kinship with both Schubert and Schumann. Indeed, one of the rejected songs, "Le Galop", is a very obvious homage to Schubert's "Erlkönig". Several of Duparc's songs are masterpieces: in particular, his setting of "L'invitation au voyage" is striking for the way the anxiously rocking accompaniment and contrastingly calm refrain captures the voluptuous but suffocating mood of Baudelaire's original. Undulating chordal accompaniment also characterizes "Chanson triste", a subtle, bittersweet setting of a poem by Jean Lahor, whose *Extase* wrung from Duparc a highly chromatic *liebestod* inspired by Wagner's *Tristan*. No less Wagnerian is the glorious "Phidylé", a sensuous paean to nature in which a simple modal melody rises to a glorious and radiant climax in the last stanza.

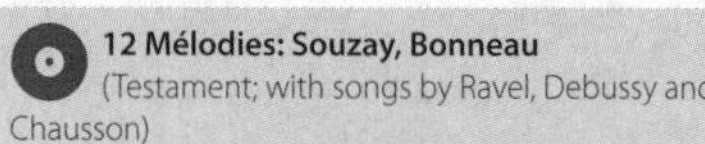

12 Mélodies: Souzay, Bonneau (Testament; with songs by Ravel, Debussy and Chausson)

Gérard Souzay was one of the supreme interpreters of Duparc's songs and in these recordings, taped by Decca in 1953, he can be heard at his finest. His meticulous control of both tone and dynamics means that every nuance – from the morbid to the passionate – comes across as if personally directed at the listener.

Complete Songs: Delunsch, Le Texier, Kerdoncuff (Timpani)

This recent recording divides all seventeen songs between an outstanding soprano, Mireille Delunsch (who sings eleven of them), and a merely adequate baritone, Vincent Le Texier. Fortunately the best songs fall to Delunsch, and while her interpretations are understated (almost to the point of coolness), her radiant, full tone brings an incisive clarity to each song.

Hendricks; Orchestre de l'Opéra de Lyon; Gardiner (EMI; with Ravel *Shéhérazade* & *Cinq Mélodies Populaires Grecques*)

Duparc orchestrated eight of his songs (six of which appear here), bringing their latent operatic qualities to the fore and losing something of their intimacy. In this recording by the American soprano Barbara Hendricks, the voice sits very much within the texture of the orchestra, each piece resembling a kind of miniature tone poem, but the overall effect arguably oversweetens the songs' original fervour.

Maurice Duruflé (1902–1986)

Though his name is often coupled with (and overshadowed by) that of Gabriel Fauré, Maurice Duruflé possessed one of the most distinctive voices in French twentieth-century music. His poignant and monumental *Requiem* (1947) closely echoes Fauré's own, and in other ways, too, Duruflé seemed isolated from the revolutions within post-war music. Although Messiaen was a contemporary at the Paris Conservatoire, Duruflé resisted experimentalism and moved quietly within the Parisian musical establishment – organist for 45 years at the tranquil church of St Étienne-du-Mont, tutor at the Conservatoire and responsible for just a handful of works, many of them inspired by the connection between Gregorian chant and French Catholicism. Tellingly, Duruflé once confessed himself "bewildered" by the direction music had taken during the course of his lifetime.

Despite the talent he displayed at the Conservatoire (he won five prizes there in the 1920s), it was Duruflé's training as a chorister at Rouen Cathedral that would dominate his imagination. Like many French religious institutions, Rouen boasted a strong plainsong tradition, formalized during the nineteenth century and sung daily. This environment had a profound influence on Duruflé, and the fluid contours and modal colours of chant make themselves felt in much of his music. Sometimes the plainsong is placed over a simple accompaniment, as if in a liturgical context, but more often it acts as an imaginative cue, Duruflé weaving deft and rhythmically intricate textures from its sparse lines.

Like his teacher Paul Dukas, Duruflé was obsessively self-critical and published just ten compositions, predominantly writing for organ and voices. Among the organ works, the *Prelude,*

Adagio and Choral Variations on the "Veni Creator" theme (1930) is an early masterpiece, but in every sense his greatest work is the *Requiem*, which faithfully transcribes the Latin chants from the Office for the Dead, transforming them into an ambitious composition for choir, large orchestra and organ. Although Duruflé, characteristically, was unsatisfied with his efforts – later writing that "by enclosing [Gregorian chant] within the bar-lines of present-day notation, we risk the destruction of its poetry, of its immaterial nature, its elusiveness" – the *Requiem*, with its refined balance of introspection and emotion, made his name internationally.

From the 1950s, however, as his teaching duties took precedence, Duruflé found it increasingly difficult to compose, and after a near-fatal car crash in 1975 retired from musical life altogether. His final work, *Notre Père* (1977), a tender piece for unaccompanied choir, was written with the aid of his wife (herself a talented organist). As a conclusion to his career it was bittersweet: the motet's text is a vernacular translation of the Lord's Prayer, commissioned because, following new Vatican guidance, the Catholic authorities had decided to retire Duruflé's beloved Latin service and use French instead.

Requiem

Though the composer's wife once dismissed Fauré's *Requiem* as "salon music", it's undeniable that Duruflé took it as his starting point. This is evident not only in the biblical texts he selected (the blazing Dies irae is omitted, the otherworldly In Paradisum inserted), and use of mezzo-soprano and baritone soloists, but also in the *Requiem*'s restrained and sombre tone. Duruflé is arguably more adventurous, however, reproducing Gregorian plainsong yet clothing it in vibrant harmony, and delivering some genuinely spine-tingling moments – the Pie Jesu, a duet between mezzo and solo cello, is astonishingly delicate, while the arching Sanctus makes Fauré's seem saccharine by comparison. Like much of Duruflé's music, the *Requiem* was much revised, and no less than three separate versions survive: one for chorus, full orchestra and organ; another for cut-down chamber forces; and a last version for organ and choir alone. Also worth hearing among the choral works are the *Four Motets on Gregorian Themes* (1960), miniatures as beautifully crafted and spiritually involving as anything in the *Requiem*.

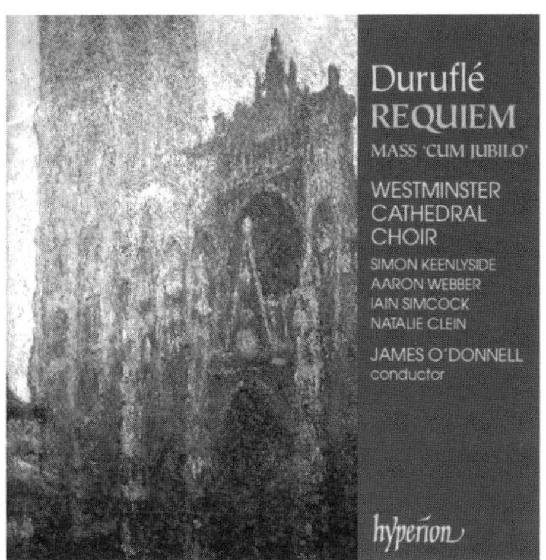

Requiem (organ version): Keenlyside, Webber, Simcock, Clein; Westminster Cathedral Choir; O'Donnell (Hyperion; with *Mass "Cum Jubilo"* and other choral works)

This scintillating performance by the Westminster Cathedral Choir conveys the airy clarity of Duruflé's writing while never losing sight of the work's profound drama. The cathedral's acoustic offers plenty of incense-laden atmosphere, and the rest of the choral works, including the lovely *Four Motets*, receive committed readings.

Requiem (orchestral version): Te Kanawa, Nimsgern; Ambrosian Singers; Desborough School Choir; New Philharmonia Orchestra; Davis (Sony; with Fauré *Requiem*)

The organ version of the *Requiem* is the more frequently performed, but the large-scale orchestral alternative provides a grander vision of eternity. Andrew Davis's recording is currently the best on offer. Although occasionally lugubrious, the chorus sings with conviction and Kiri Te Kanawa's full-blooded Pie Jesu is terrific.

Organ Works

Duruflé was a virtuoso organist – he premiered Poulenc's *Organ Concerto* – and the instrument remained a driving force behind his music. While his writing builds on the symphonic tradition of the great French organ luminaries Franck, Widor and Vierne, it also draws upon the freer style of Charles Tournemire, another plainchant aficionado. Though only amounting to around an hour of music, the organ pieces form an impressive body of work in which the composer's meticulous use of the instrument combines with a taut sense of drama. It's ferociously challenging to play yet never needlessly flamboyant. Indeed, Duruflé attempted to withdraw his one nod to the bravura French tradition, the blistering final Toccata from the *Suite* (1933), because he felt it had become too much of a showpiece. More typical are the *Veni Creator* variations, a symphonic composition that buries the plainsong melody deep within the musical texture, only for it to erupt joyously in the final movement, and the defiant *Prelude and Fugue on the Name of Alain* (1942), which uses a motif spelling out the surname of a young composer killed in action two years earlier.

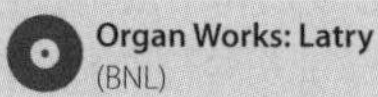

Organ Works: Latry
(BNL)

Several respectable recordings of Duruflé's organ works have appeared in the last few years, but Olivier Latry outclasses them with gripping performances recorded on Duruflé's own instrument, the grand Cavaillé-Coll at St Ètienne-du-Mont. If at times the organ sounds a little rough around the edges, Latry's sure technique and brilliant dramatic awareness more than win through.

Henri Dutilleux (1916–)

Dutilleux is one of the major figures of recent French music, but his severe self-criticism has meant that his reputation rests on a fairly small body of work. Like his older contemporary Messiaen, he has no qualms about writing music that is richly sonorous, abounding in luminous and sensuous timbres. Unlike Messiaen, however, Dutilleux's work reveals an interest in traditional forms, which he has sought to renew in the light of his fascination with the workings of time and memory.

Dutilleux was born into a highly artistic family in Angers, France. While he was still a boy, the family settled in Douai and shortly after Henri's grandfather – a composer taught by Saint-Saëns and a lifelong friend of Fauré – advised that he should study at the local music school. His musical training continued at the Paris Conservatoire where he won the Prix de Rome in 1938 with the cantata *L'anneau du roi*. In normal circumstances the award would have entailed a four-year period of residency in Rome but Dutilleux was only there for four months due to the pressure of events leading up to World War II. Enlisted as a stretcher-bearer, after demobilization he worked for a brief period as *chef de chant* (chorus master) at the Paris Opéra, before joining the staff of Radio France in 1943. From 1945 he was director of music productions there, resigning in 1963 in order to concentrate on composing.

Dutilleux now regards his juvenilia as too derivative of Fauré, Debussy and Ravel to be worth preserving and has rejected nearly all the music that he wrote prior to his sinewy *Piano Sonata* of 1947. He also considers that his work prior to that time conformed too closely to a stereotype of an entertaining French music that is all charm, elegance and wit. With the *Piano Sonata*, composed for his wife, the pianist Geneviève Joy, he found a voice of his own.

The majority of Dutilleux's mature works are marked by a technique of developing variation that he likes to term "progressive growth". To some extent derived from his reading of the novels of Marcel Proust, this involves the gradual development of small melodic or rhythmic cells into themes that reappear throughout a work – as opposed to the statement of a fully formed theme at the opening of each movement. This has been an important feature of his music since the thematically linked third and fourth movements of his *Symphony No. 1* (1950–51).

Symphonies Nos. 1 & 2

Dutilleux's preoccupation with memory, combined with his obvious passion for creating glittering and lush musical textures, means that his large orchestral works often seem to evoke a landscape redolent of dreams. The *Symphony No. 1* is a case in point: there is a distinct feeling of circularity to it, as if the startling instrumental gestures and musical arguments always take you back to the same place.

The *Symphony No. 2 – La double –* is Dutilleux's orchestral masterpiece. Begun in 1955 but not finished until 1959, it is scored for large orchestra with a separate group of twelve soloists (including harpsichord and celesta) positioned around the conductor. This suggests the Baroque concerto grosso form, but what Dutilleux had in mind was the idea of the orchestra having a "double", with all the disorienting qualities that this suggests. In the final version of the piece, Dutilleux replaced the stable tonal harmony with which it originally ended with a more ambiguous chord, thereby emphasizing the questioning quality of the music.

BBC Philharmonic; Tortelier (Chandos)

Yan Pascal Tortelier, who conducts both of Dutilleux's symphonies here, is very highly regarded by the composer as an interpreter of his music. The pacing of both works is exemplary, but the outstanding feature of the performances is the perfectly realized orchestral sonorities.

Tout un monde lointain...

In the early 1960s Dutilleux was asked to compose the score to a ballet based on Baudelaire's collection of darkly erotic poems *Les fleurs du mal.* He eventually withdrew from the project, considering the poems to be unsuitable for a ballet scenario. But his response to the poetry eventually found musical expression in *Tout un monde lointain...* (A Whole Distant World...), a concerto for cello and orchestra commissioned by the great Russian cellist Mstislav Rostropovich and written between 1967 and 1970. Dutilleux added epigraphs taken from *Les fleurs du mal* to each of the work's five movements, though these were added as an afterthought – the music inhabits the same imaginative world as the poetry rather than illustrates it. It's an immensely sensuous and mysterious world in which the soloist journeys, and – as in the first symphony – the music emerges from a silence to which it eventually returns. Progressive growth is again in evidence with the germ of the concerto's two poignantly lyrical slow movements already present in the first.

Mørk; Orchestre Philharmonique de Radio France; Chung (EMI; with *L'arbre des Songes & Trois strophes*)

In this performance, soloist and orchestra coexist as equals with the one emerging from the other. If anything this intensifies the hypnotic dream-world quality of this work. Truls Mørk also gives powerful accounts of the three short pieces for unaccompanied cello.

Rostropovich; Orchestre de Paris; Baudo (EMI; with Lutosławski *Cello Concerto*)

This performance from Mstislav Rostropovich and the conductor and orchestra who premiered the work has tremendous authority and power, with the soloist rather more prominent than on the Mørk/Chung account. It's coupled with a no less compelling version of Lutosławski's concerto.

Ainsi la nuit

Of all Dutilleux's works, his string quartet *Ainsi la nuit* (Thus the Night), seems the most concerned with time and memory and, in this respect, the most indebted to his reading of Proust. Composed between 1973 and 1976, the quartet contains four "parentheses" interpolated between the first five of its seven movements. These either anticipate or recall material found elsewhere in the work, contributing to the quartet's manifold interrelationships. The music is at times expressionistic in tone and demonstrates a familiarity with the quartets of Bartók, Berg and Webern, though Dutilleux makes of these influences something entirely his own. *Ainsi la nuit* contains a panoply of beautifully evocative gestures and tone colours – often suggestive of a mysterious, nocturnal world – as well as a striking and highly imaginative textural variety.

Orpheus String Quartet (Channel Classics; with Debussy and Ravel string quartets)

Although Dutilleux chose to distance himself from the music of certain more mediocre French talents he never removed himself from the fundamental traditions of French music. Here his string quartet is presented alongside those of Debussy and Ravel in remarkably warm recordings by a very impressive ensemble.

Antonín Dvořák (1841–1904)

With the tide of revolutions that swept across the continent during the 1840s, nationalism became a dominating factor in European art. Nowhere was this process more important than in Czechoslovakia, and no composer was more prominently nationalistic than Antonín Dvořák. Of the three great Czech composers – Smetana (see p.527) and Janáček (see p.271) are the others – Dvořák was the one whose influence upon the development of a national voice was the most original and lasting, and it was Dvořák who was most successful in reconciling folk traditions with symphonic music. Few composers of his time could match his flair for infectious melody or his ability to orchestrate with kaleidoscopic colour and nuance.

Antonín Dvořák by Hugo Boettinger.

Born in Bohemia, Dvořák spent his uneventful early life in study and practice, then in 1863 played in a concert of Wagner excerpts, conducted by the composer himself – an experience that had a significant impact on his approach to opera. From 1864 he played viola in the Prague National Theatre Orchestra, where from 1866 the chief conductor was Smetana, the fountainhead of Czech musical nationalism. In 1873 Dvořák left the orchestra to devote himself to composition, and within a year his *Symphony No. 3* had won him an Austrian national prize as well as the respect of Brahms, who was on the jury. Two years later, Dvořák's *Moravian Duets* brought him the same prize, and again Brahms was delighted by the young man's progress, going so far as to recommend his music to a publisher.

With the appearance of such distinctively Czech works as the *Slavonic Dances* (1878) Dvořák was soon gaining ever widening recognition: the great violinist Joseph Joachim commissioned a concerto from him (but had to wait years for it); conductor Hans Richter commissioned a symphony; while another leading conductor, Hans von Bülow, promoted Dvořák's work through concerts and tours. Numerous trips to England, where he was championed for his conducting as much as his composition, extended Dvořák's fame, brought him money and produced several of his greatest works, including the *Symphony No. 7*.

Dvořák's success reached one of its peaks in 1891, when he was appointed professor of composition at the Prague Conservatory, awarded an honorary doctorate by Cambridge University and invited to take up the directorship of the National Conservatory of Music in New York, with an annual salary of $15,000. In October 1892, after a five-month farewell tour of Bohemia and Moravia, Dvořák finally moved to the US, where he remained for three years. This period was not especially happy but it was very fruitful, as Dvořák's discovery of America's folk heritage combined with his aching homesickness to produce a string of masterpieces, including the violin concerto and the *New World Symphony*.

In 1895 he returned to teach at the Prague Conservatory, becoming its director in 1901 – the year of his sixtieth birthday, which was celebrated in Prague by performances of his work. His final years were extremely contented, and most of his time was spent working on tone poems and operas. Unfortunately, though Dvořák produced a total of ten operas, only one of them, *Rusalka*, has achieved any popularity, and that's largely down to one extremely famous soprano aria ("O Silver Moon"). His reputation continues to rest primarily on his orchestral music.

SYMPHONIES

Admiration for the music of Beethoven and Schubert was what first led Dvořák to consider writing symphonic music, and his early symphonies (the first, the *Bells of Zlonice*, was completed in 1865) reveal these Viennese influences quite strongly, as well as the impact Brahms had on him. It was not until his wholehearted commitment to Czech nationalism in the mid-1870s that Dvořák's voice began to be heard properly, and though there's a strong Czech element to his fourth symphony (1874) the sequence improves markedly with *Symphony No. 6*. The best-known of his symphonies is the last, the *New World*, which contains one of the most famous of all symphonic movements.

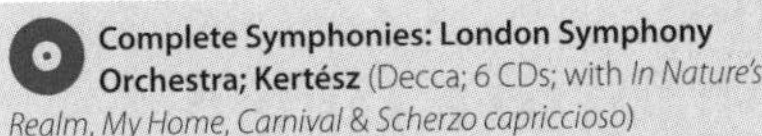

Complete Symphonies: London Symphony Orchestra; Kertész (Decca; 6 CDs; with *In Nature's Realm, My Home, Carnival & Scherzo capriccioso)*

Istvan Kertész did much to help re-establish Dvořák's earlier symphonies as works to be taken seriously in the complete cycle, which he recorded in the 1960s. These are classic accounts: there's a palpable rapport between orchestra and conductor, and the result is playing of an amazing warmth and enthusiasm, even in the weaker symphonies.

Symphony No. 5

Like its Wagner-inspired predecessor, *Symphony No. 4*, the fifth symphony has been eclipsed by the later four. However, Dvořák's contemporaries rated his *Symphony No. 5* very highly, and it's not difficult to see why. It's among the composer's most tightly knit and demonstrably classical formulations, yet it contains a wealth of Bohemian-inspired melodies that simply couldn't have been written by anyone else. All four movements – but especially the first and last – contain unforgettably strong ideas, expressed with a conciseness that's often suggestive of the symphonies of Brahms and Schumann.

Oslo Philharmonic Orchestra; Jansons (EMI; with *Scherzo capriccioso & Othello)*

Mariss Jansons and the Oslo Phil taped this symphony in 1989. It's a stunning account: the playing is often electrifying, though there's also an affecting poignancy in the slow movement. The sound is equally impressive and there are effective fillers in the shape of the *Scherzo capriccioso* and *Othello*.

Symphony No. 6

The marvellous *Symphony No. 6* (1880) owes much to Brahms's second symphony – which is also in D major – and in places displays somewhat over-weighted orchestration, but at the same time it's unmistakably the work of Dvořák. Typical of the composer's mature style are the frequent, quasi-Romantic key modulations within the determinedly classical structure, and the use of the Scherzo movement to express fervently nationalist sentiments. Based on the *furiant* – a Czech dance – the Scherzo of this symphony was the first movement to establish Dvořák as a truly Slavonic composer, clearly distancing him from the plethora of German symphonists (most now forgotten) who were then jostling for attention.

Czech Philharmonic Orchestra; Bělohlávek (Chandos; with *The Wild Dove*)

In the absence of the fine Decca recording of Dohnányi and the Cleveland Orchestra, this is the performance to go for. The Czech Philharmonic could probably give a good performance of this work without a conductor, but under Jiří Bělohlávek they really skip along with amazing verve and passion.

Symphony No. 7

In stark contrast to the sixth symphony's atmosphere of well-being, the *Symphony No. 7* is overshadowed by intimations of tragedy. In this respect, and in its sense of retrospection, it is not unlike Brahms's third symphony, of which Dvořák was almost certainly aware. Both symphonies were written in the same year – 1885 – and it is probably no accident that Dvořák chose to use D minor, the bleak relative minor key to the F major of Brahms's third. The emotional gravity of this mighty work gives the symphony a strong claim to being Dvořák's greatest. The Scherzo and finale, in particular, contain some of the composer's most remarkable writing, and their combination of rhythmic vitality and free-form melody make these movements two of the finest of the late nineteenth century.

Oslo Philharmonic Orchestra; Jansons (EMI; with *Symphony No. 8)*

Jansons' interpretation has a driving, almost impulsive, zeal and his control over the music's surging momentum is absolute. There is a polish and all-pervading warmth in evidence and the many fine strands of Dvořák's most disparate orchestral work are successfully drawn together.

Royal Concertgebouw Orchestra; Davis (Philips; 2 CDs; with *Symphonies Nos. 8 & 9* and *Symphonic Variations)*

This account of the seventh is among the most urgent and punchy in the catalogue. Sir Colin Davis gets just about everything right and the highly atmospheric and cultivated orchestral playing is well served by an outstanding digital transfer. With superb renditions of Dvořák's last two symphonies, this two-disc set is a bargain.

Symphony No. 8

Dvořák's *Symphony No. 8* (1889) again stands in complete contrast to its immediate predecessor. In many ways it harks back to the exuberant cheerfulness and Czech feeling of the sixth, and only in the first movement's introduction is there any sign of the seventh's sobriety. Although the main theme from this opening is repeated later in the movement, the bulk of it is dominated by one of Dvořák's most inspired melodies. The Adagio, almost a tone poem of birdsong and country life, is similarly melodic, while the third movement is a rustic dance of infectious good humour. The finale is a set of variations (rare for

Dvořák) that builds towards a rousing and suitably conclusive climax.

Berlin Philharmonic Orchestra; Kubelík (Deutsche Grammophon; with *Symphony No. 9*)

Kubelík's is an intense and exciting account – Dvořák seized by the collar and propelled, like one long glowing fanfare. There's some particularly fine sectional playing in this warm and expansive reading, with the BPO in sparkling, virtuosic form. The accompanying ninth is also superb.

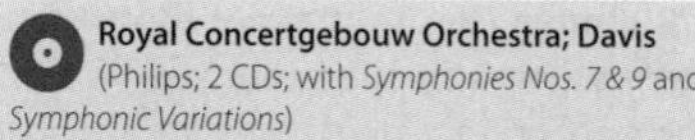
Royal Concertgebouw Orchestra; Davis (Philips; 2 CDs; with *Symphonies Nos. 7 & 9* and *Symphonic Variations*)

Better engineered than DG's Kubelík recording, Sir Colin Davis moulds and propels this work with rare dedication and insight. Magnificently played by the Concertgebouw, there's never been a finer-paced or more accomplished Dvořák eighth.

Symphony No. 9

The best-known tune in all Dvořák is the main theme from the third movement of the *Symphony No. 9* (1893), a mournfully nostalgic piece of music that has been appropriated by countless TV producers and advertising types. The symphony was intended to celebrate the fourth centennial of Columbus's "discovery" of America, and its title, *From the New World*, might lead you to expect a more upbeat tone. Dvořák wrote of it that "the influence of America can be felt by anyone who has a nose", but the symphony's American-influenced rhythmic patterns and tunes are turned into an expression of acute homesickness and thus of Czech identity – similar to his "American" quartet (see p.178). The music is tirelessly melodic and brilliantly scored for a large orchestra, but it is very long and in the wrong hands can become tedious.

Berlin Philharmonic Orchestra; Kubelík (Deutsche Grammophon; with *Symphony No. 8*)

Kubelík's recording of the ninth is very different in spirit – if not in technique – from his eighth. Indeed, his *New World* is soul-searching and intensely dramatic. Never has Dvořák's finale hung together so convincingly as it does here; but, throughout, the playing is shatteringly powerful.

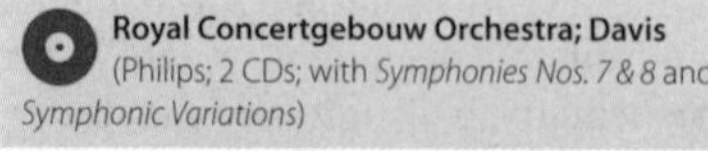
Royal Concertgebouw Orchestra; Davis (Philips; 2 CDs; with *Symphonies Nos. 7 & 8* and *Symphonic Variations*)

This thrilling account brings Sir Colin Davis' survey of Dvořák's last three symphonies to an arresting climax. Davis is fully alive to every nuance and subtlety of Dvořák's scoring, and the full-on tension attained in the first movement is sustained even in the slow movement. Again, the orchestral playing and sound are first-rate.

OTHER ORCHESTRAL MUSIC

Dvořák composed a considerable amount of orchestral music on top of his nine symphonies, including four concertos: two for cello and one each for violin and piano. The piano concerto is a Beethoven-ish hybrid that never really gets off the ground, and the first of the two cello concertos is a fairly insubstantial work which was only discovered seventy years ago in sketch form and needed to be orchestrated by a third party. But the other two are very fine works and have established themselves as staples of the Romantic repertory, especially the majestic concerto for cello. Dvořák's other orchestral works include the ever-popular *Slavonic Dances* and some remarkable symphonic poems, which display even stronger expressions of nationalist feeling than his symphonies, the genre allowing him to transform the material of Czech folklore without the constrictions of classical form.

Cello Concerto

The second cello concerto, the last major composition that Dvořák composed during his stay in America, has become one of the most popular of all his works and perhaps the most popular concerto ever written for the instrument. Dvořák was asked to write the piece by a friend of Wagner, the cellist Hanus Wihan, who gave the first performance of Strauss's cello sonata as well as this concerto. The music that Dvořák composed is richly inventive, full of deep feeling (the final movement was revised after the death of his wife), and perfectly fitted to the cello – Dvořák's experience as an orchestral player enabled him to appreciate the problems of balance and blending that arise when orchestrating for a solo instrument with a low register. Dvořák's understanding of orchestral sonority and of the cello's distinct textural qualities makes this grand and emotionally intense piece one of his finest achievements.

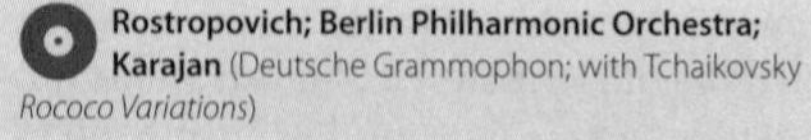
Rostropovich; Berlin Philharmonic Orchestra; Karajan (Deutsche Grammophon; with Tchaikovsky *Rococo Variations*)

Modern orchestras tend to distort the concerto's intricately studied proportions, but Karajan was aware of this potential for imbalance and controlled the Berlin Philharmonic with uncommon clarity. Of Rostropovich's many recordings of this work, this 1969 version is the best, bursting with energy and fresh ideas.

Violin Concerto

As with Brahms's violin concerto, Dvořák's was dedicated to and written with the help of the great Hungarian violinist Joseph Joachim. It may not be a great work – it's much less frequently played than the Brahms, and Joachim himself never performed it – but it is certainly rich in strong and beguiling melodies. The first movement begins with a bold, even angry, orchestral phrase, while the soloist's response is by turns wistful and rhapsodic – a contrast that characterizes the movement as a whole. The slow movement is the concerto's high point: a tender song that is poignantly nostalgic in mood. With the finale we enter the world of the *Slavonic Dances*, with a boldly syncopated main theme that allows the soloist a good deal of brilliant and often skittish passage-work.

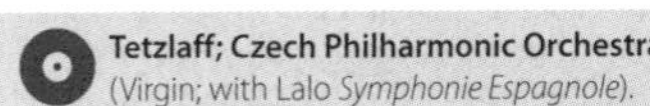

Tetzlaff; Czech Philharmonic Orchestra; Pesek (Virgin; with Lalo *Symphonie Espagnole*).

Christian Tetzlaff takes a thoughtful yet heroically intense stance to this work. He's more measured and acerbic than some, but he leaves you in no doubt that this is a masterpiece. The solo playing is unfailingly vital and full of character, and there's sympathetic and idiomatic support from Pesek and the Czech Phil.

Symphonic Poems

Dvořák's four best-known symphonic poems – *The Water Goblin*, *The Noonday Witch*, *The Golden Spinning Wheel* and *The Wild Dove* – were written in 1896, and were based upon gruesome folk ballads by the nationalist writer Erben. Following the examples of Liszt, Smetana and Richard Strauss, Dvořák uses a single theme for each central character and transforms it as the situation demands, thereby creating musical continuity while projecting a sense of narrative development. If he is less successful than Strauss, it is because he follows the very specific source material too closely but, despite this, Dvořák's masterly orchestration brings considerable life and colour to these Grimm-like creations.

Complete Symphonic Poems: Bavarian Radio Symphony Orchestra; Kubelík (Deutsche Grammophon; 2 CDs; with *Overtures & Slavonic Dances*)

Again, Kubelík is highly sympathetic to Dvořák's rich orchestral style and he allows the music to follow its natural course without straining to score interpretive points. He brings entertaining flair to these pieces, and the Bavarian Radio Symphony Orchestra respond with an enthusiasm that sounds spontaneous.

Slavonic Dances

The *Slavonic Dances* began life as folk-dance rhythms, became piano duets, and ended up not only as Dvořák's introduction to the world beyond Bohemia, but as staples of the orchestral encore repertory. In 1874 the struggling composer had applied for an Austrian state stipendium, for which one of the judges was Brahms's colleague Eduard Hanslick. In November 1877, Hanslick wrote to Dvořák, "Brahms has taken a lively interest in your splendid talent and was particularly pleased by your two-part Bohemian songs". The upshot was an introduction to Brahms's publisher, Simrock, who immediately commissioned "two volumes of Bohemian and Moravian Dances". The reward for the gaiety and buoyant movement of these eight pieces was, for Dvořák, overnight celebrity. A second set of *Slavonic Dances* followed eight years later.

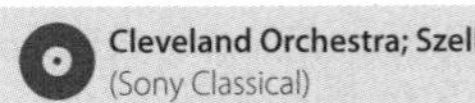

Cleveland Orchestra; Szell (Sony Classical)

These are masterful accounts from George Szell, whose rhythmic pointing adds much to the drive and passion of the dances. The Clevelanders are on top form, and the 1963 and 1965 recordings never show their age thanks to sensitive digital remastering.

CHAMBER MUSIC

Dvořák composed a large amount of chamber music, which is hardly surprising for a viola player who greatly admired the chamber work of the classical masters. His Op. 1 and Op. 2 were both for string quartet, an ensemble for which he wrote some fourteen of his forty chamber pieces, one of which – the *String Quartet No. 12* (known as the "American") – is one of the most popular quartets ever written. Much of the chamber music has an obvious kinship to that of Brahms, particularly in its contrapuntal weight, but Dvořák's style is invariably lighter, more sweetly melodic and more freely inventive.

String Quartets

As with the early symphonies, Dvořák's later string quartets have almost completely eclipsed their predecessors. There is some sparkling and memorably melodic music in the early examples, which document the rapid development of Dvořák's compositional technique, but the late quartets are in a different league.

String Quartet No. 12 (the "American") was the first of three chamber works composed in 1893 while Dvořák was living in the US, and it was soon established as his best-loved quartet and his most popular chamber work. Although its opening was modelled on the introduction to Smetana's first quartet, there is little of that composer's raw misery here – frustrated energy and nostalgia are the prevailing moods, the latter element typified by the Lento, with its plaintive, soaring violin melody.

Dvořák's last works, written during a burst of creative activity at the end of 1895, reveal his musical imagination at its most visionary – subtle, complex and harmonically advanced. The last two quartets – *No. 13* in G major and *No. 14* in A flat major – are both characterized by a deeply ambivalent emotionalism. The soulful Adagio variations of *No. 13* are shot through with more joyful moments but ultimately its mood is one of resignation. Similarly, *No. 14* has a slow movement of almost unbearable pathos which is only relieved by the exuberant and folk-inspired finale.

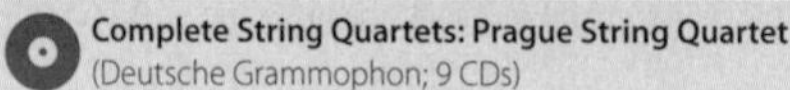

Complete String Quartets: Prague String Quartet (Deutsche Grammophon; 9 CDs)

This justly famed cycle was recorded during the late 1970s by the Prague Quartet, whose fresh and spontaneous interpretations bring out both the nationalistic colour of much of the melodic material and the more forward-looking structural innovations of the later works. The digital transfers are excellent, making this the ideal way to investigate Dvořák's complete quartets.

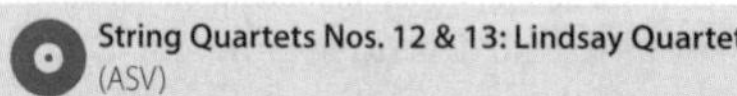

String Quartets Nos. 12 & 13: Lindsay Quartet (ASV)

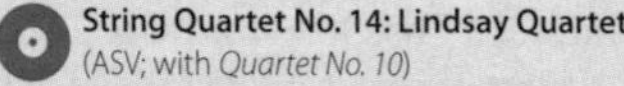

String Quartet No. 14: Lindsay Quartet (ASV; with *Quartet No. 10*)

The Lindsay Quartet's Dvořák readings are particularly fresh and revealing. All their hallmarks are in evidence here – the widest range of expressive gestures and, above all, an emphatically spontaneous way of performing. The performance of the last quartet, with biting incision and spring-like eagerness, is a revelation: a superlative rendering of a rarely acknowledged masterpiece.

String Quintets

Like Schubert, and Mozart before him, Dvořák recognized the potential of the string quintet, a genre in which he composed freely and over quite a long period. Usually he favoured Mozart's chosen instrumentation, in which a second viola is added to the customary quartet line-up. This gives a particularly rich sonority, especially in the middle register, which Dvořák managed to fully exploit. However, the second quintet is scored for unconventional forces – string quartet plus double bass. The music is even more disarmingly original than the instrumentation, merging Czech and classical idioms with North American Indian melodies. In the Larghetto, Dvořák follows Haydn's example of composing a set of variations with a double theme.

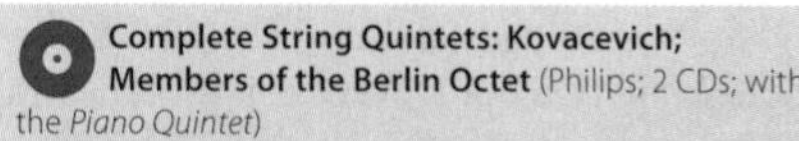

Complete String Quintets: Kovacevich; Members of the Berlin Octet (Philips; 2 CDs; with the *Piano Quintet*)

These are sonorous and deeply considered accounts of the string quintets from the highly adroit and disciplined Berlin Octet, who show rare facility and depth of understanding in this music. They are coupled with a thrilling and emotionally concentrated account of the piano quintet with Stephen Kovacevich.

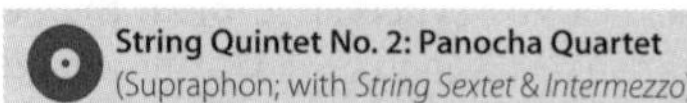

String Quintet No. 2: Panocha Quartet (Supraphon; with *String Sextet & Intermezzo*)

The augmented Panocha Quartet is always alive to the Bohemian eagerness of the *Quintet No. 2*. The players negotiate every twist and turn in a performance which never loses its spring and metrical wit. Their crisp, deft articulation is a constant pleasure.

Piano Trios

Of the four piano trios that Dvořák wrote, the later two are the most enticing. The third, from 1883, is the most orchestral and dramatically charged of Dvořák's chamber compositions, its four movements containing almost every distinctive feature of his music. Characterized by an unprecedented seriousness of purpose, it marked a decisive step forward in his career and foreshadowed the epic expression of the seventh symphony, which came two years later. The Allegretto grazioso contains music of haunting pathos but this tendency towards sadness is restrained by some entrancing, disruptive cross-rhythms. The fourth and final trio, known as the *Dumky*, was completed in 1891 and is one of Dvořák's most bittersweet creations. The *dumka* was a Slavonic folk ballad, predominantly elegiac in mood, and Dvořák transformed it into a musical form in which a melancholic slow idea was contrasted with sections of a faster dance-like character. The richly eloquent cello part was composed for the virtuoso Hanus Wihan, who premiered the work with the composer and the violinist Ferdinand Lachner.

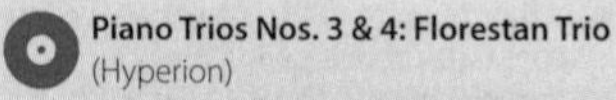

Piano Trios Nos. 3 & 4: Florestan Trio (Hyperion)

The British Florestan Trio recorded these works in 1996. They're technically superb, and in places there's an admirable fire and brilliance, but most important is the sensitivity and allure of the playing – especially in slow movements, where the Florestan are completely beguiling.

Complete Piano Trios: Beaux Arts Trio
(Philips; 2 CDs)

Brightly energetic performances from the Beaux Arts Trio, who play with all their customary flair and imagination. The recording dates from the late 1960s, and the sound is good, if occasionally a little harsh.

Piano Quintet

The *Piano Quintet* of 1887 is arguably Dvořák's greatest chamber piece, and it's certainly one of the most popular, thanks to both its memorable melodies and sheer panache. Demonstrating clear debts to Brahms, it's a work of passionate extremes in which a typically Dvořákian lyricism is alternated with music of greater drive and urgency. It has a virtuoso keyboard part and equally demanding and brilliant parts for the string players, though there are also some very reflective moments, such as the opening of the slow movement, where the piano weaves a delicate accompaniment around the cello's sombre melody.

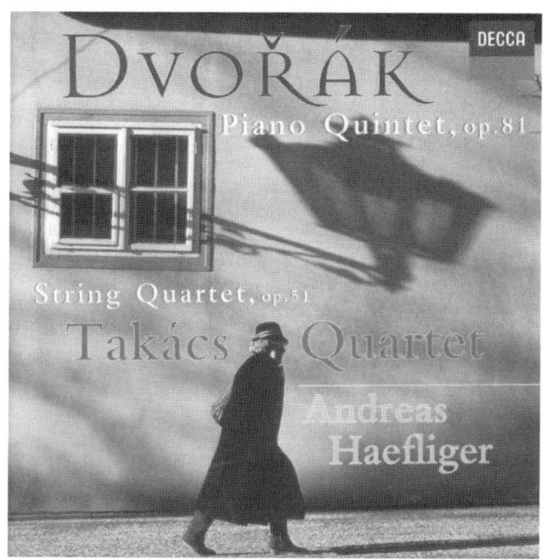

Takács Quartet; Haefliger
(Decca; with *String Quartet No. 10*)

In this superbly played and brightly recorded version, the Takács Quartet and pianist Andreas Haefliger make near-perfect collaborators, with the former's warm, velvety tone held in check by the latter's more classical approach. The Takács' full-blooded, slightly old-fashioned approach gets full rein in the delightful folk-tinged *Quartet No. 10*.

e

Hanns Eisler (1898–1962)

For a long time Hanns Eisler remained confined to the ranks of cult musicians, largely on account of his politics – he was a committed Communist for most of his life and one of the few decent composers to function effectively in the former East Germany (whose national anthem he wrote). However, Eisler was no socialist-realist hack: a pupil of Arnold Schoenberg in the early 1920s, he later felt the need to break with a teacher whose ideals were irreconcilable with Eisler's desire to make serious music a part of the daily lives of ordinary people – an attitude he had in common with Hindemith (see p.258).

This mission to create radically politicized art led him from Vienna to Berlin where he met the actor and singer Ernst Busch, for whom he wrote many hard-hitting ballads. These were often in the form of bitingly satirical verses (many written by Kurt Tucholsky) set to music that always strove to highlight the meaning of the text. Accompaniment was either a piano or the kind of light, jazz-style ensemble that was becoming increasingly popular. In 1930 Eisler began his long-standing collaboration and friendship with the Marxist poet and playwright Bertolt Brecht, writing music for his play *Die Mutter* and for the film *Kuhle Wampe*. When the Nazis came to power in 1933, Eisler's music was banned and he was forced into exile, spending time in Denmark, Spain and Mexico before eventually settling in Hollywood. Here he renewed his partnership with Brecht, writing the music for the play *Galileo* and the film *Hangmen Also Die* (about the assassination of Heydrich), for which Brecht wrote the screenplay. In 1947 both men fell victim to Senator McCarthy's witch-hunt of Communists and appeared before the infamous Un-American Activities committee. Despite the intercession of a group of intellectuals, including Einstein and Thomas Mann, Eisler was deported to East Germany in 1950 and remained there for the rest of his life, continuing to work with Brecht on theatre productions at the famous Berliner Ensemble.

Deutsche Sinfonie

Eisler had the idea of writing a large-scale anti-fascist work, provisionally entitled *Concentration Camp Symphony*, in 1935 and had completed the first two movements a few years later. However the Nazis and exile intervened and the work became a work-in-progress, only receiving its first performance in 1959. Brecht supplied nearly all of the text, which ranges from the crudely hectoring ("the class struggle alone can liberate the masses in cities and countryside…") to the bitterly ironic

("If God doesn't bother about the rain what does he bother about?"). Eisler puts it all together as a series of cantatas for different soloists and chorus with orchestral interludes, in a style that occasionally recalls others (Hindemith, Schoenberg and, at times, even Mahler) but which is notable, above all, for its lucidity and lack of bombast. The cumulative effect is surprisingly powerful and by the end very moving.

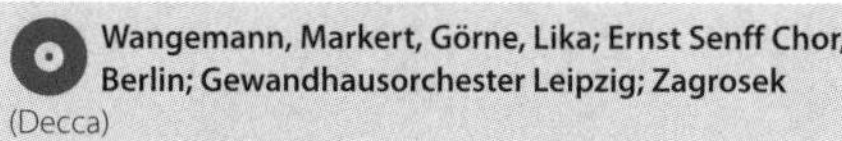

Wangemann, Markert, Görne, Lika; Ernst Senff Chor, Berlin; Gewandhausorchester Leipzig; Zagrosek
(Decca)

This is one of two Eisler works to be included in Decca's Entartete Musik series, dedicated to composers suppressed by the Nazis. It's a marvellous performance that should persuade many people to take Eisler's work more seriously.

Film Music

Eisler was a highly distinguished film composer, winning Oscars for the Hollywood films *Hangmen Also Die* (1942) and *None but the Lonely Heart* (1944), and collaborating with Alain Resnais on his film *Nuit et brouillard* (1955). In the 1930s he worked with a number of left-wing documentary makers and subsequently adapted his own music as orchestral suites. These included *Niemandsland*, an anti-war film by Victor Trivas, which became *Suite No. 2*; *Kuhle Wampe*, a feature film made by Brecht about a workers' holiday camp (*Suite No. 3*); and *Die Jugend hat das Wort*, a documentary by Joris Ivens (*Suite No. 4*) set in the Urals. This is the kind of objective "utility" music that radical German composers like Hindemith and Weill had proposed as an alternative to the subjective emotional wallowing of expressionism and Romanticism. It's bright, lightly scored music (with wind instruments, as opposed to strings, very much to the fore) with an acerbic and unsentimental edge to it.

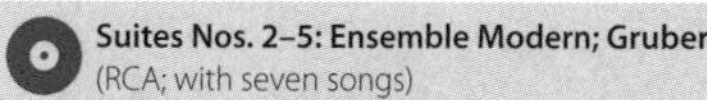

Suites Nos. 2–5: Ensemble Modern; Gruber
(RCA; with seven songs)

These are wonderfully fresh and invigorating accounts from the virtuosic Ensemble Modern, directed by composer and Eisler enthusiast, H.K. Gruber, who ensures that the performances have the requisite abrasiveness. Gruber also performs seven of Eisler's political songs, in a highly effective rough-toned but clearly enunciated fashion.

Songs

Brecht, who wrote the bulk of Eisler's song texts, frequently used the most scathing irony, not just to point up the exploitation and depredations of the working class but also to denounce political passivity (for instance in the *Ballad on Approving the World*). Eisler perfectly matches the Brechtian tone with music that is clear and direct. Like Weill, he consciously tries to bridge the divide between popular styles and classical music, and many songs are good enough to survive separation from their theatre or cabaret context. In the *Hollywood Liederbuch* (Hollywood Songbook), both Brecht and Eisler temper the sarcasm and bitterness with moments of tenderness and lyricism worthy of Schubert. Written during the years in exile, the songbook mixes texts by Brecht with classic poems by, among others, Goethe and Eichendorff in a cycle of personal suffering, but one in which the anguish is not morbidly interiorized (as in Schubert's *Winterreise*) but placed within a broader picture of war-torn Europe.

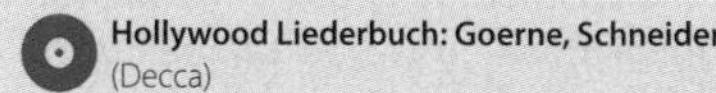

Hollywood Liederbuch: Goerne, Schneider
(Decca)

Matthias Goerne is one of today's great lieder singers, and he treats the *Hollywood Liederbuch* as a collection of art songs, with none of H.K. Gruber's rough edges. It works very well, with Goerne exploiting great tonal and dynamic variety to communicate the songs' poignant subtleties.

Edward Elgar (1857–1934)

The so-called English musical renaissance got underway in the years immediately following World War I, as Vaughan Williams and his contemporaries began to write pieces that reflected their research into English folk music. Edward Elgar, on the other hand, though he was the progenitor of this renaissance in the sense that he gave international stature to British music, was an essentially European composer, whose musical language derived more from Wagner and Brahms than from anything native. In his own day his older contemporaries Stanford and Parry were equally well respected, but history has established him as the greater

Sir Edward Elgar in his study annotating a score.

original – and arguably the first great English composer since Purcell.

Despite his aristocratic appearance and later recognition by the Edwardian establishment, Elgar was always a provincial countryman at heart – although he lived in London during the early years of the twentieth century, he found refuge from city life in the Sussex hills. He was born in a village outside Worcester, where his father served as organist at the Catholic church and ran a music shop and piano-tuning business. Edward never received much in the way of formal musical education. Initially he picked up his skills from the environment in which he lived, helping his father by playing the organ in church and teaching himself the violin in order to play in the local orchestra. His compositional technique was acquired by similar means, trying out his early works with the help of his siblings.

His ambitions grew when in 1889 he married one of his piano pupils, Caroline Alice Roberts, the daughter of a retired army general. The combination of the warmth of this relationship and his acceptance into upper-middle-class circles seems to have inspired him, and the 1890s saw a great increase in his prowess. The *Serenade for Strings* (1892) was his first work to be published, though international fame eluded him until the first performances of the *Enigma Variations* in 1899. His greatest choral work, *The Dream of Gerontius*, was premiered the following year, but to little acclaim at the time, though the succeeding years were to be his most successful.

Elgar became a household name following the appearance of his *Pomp and Circumstance March No. 1* – the first of a series of five military marches that, though they don't constitute the composer's greatest music, are written with an undeniable panache. *No. 1* was finished in 1901, but patriotic words by A.C. Benson were added the following year when Elgar had to provide music for King Edward VII's coronation. Elgar did not approve of the text's triumphalist sentiments, but the resulting work – "Land of Hope and Glory" – soon became an unofficial national anthem. Elgar was knighted in 1904, and in 1911 was awarded the Order of Merit. In the intervening years he composed some of his largest works, among them *The Apostles* (1903), the *Introduction and Allegro for Strings* (1905), *The Kingdom* (1906), *Symphony No. 1* (1908), the *Violin Concerto* (1910) and *Symphony No. 2* (1911). The symphonic study *Falstaff* followed in 1913.

Just a few patriotic works emerged during the war years, but the end of the conflict brought forth perhaps his greatest work: the *Cello Concerto* (1919). Three major chamber works composed at the same time – a violin sonata, a string quartet and a piano quintet – share its valedictory, autumnal mood, as if Elgar were pouring out his disillusionment with the changes the war had brought. The death of his wife in 1920 put a virtual stop to his creativity, and for the fourteen years that remained to him he composed little, concentrating instead on conducting and making recordings of his music.

Elgar was one of the consummate masters of orchestral writing of his day – his scores are almost mosaic-like in their selective, ever-changing use of instrumental sounds. Moreover, he was one of the least parochial English composers: Wagner's *Parsifal* pervades the music of *Gerontius*, while the melodic lines and harmonic idiom of Brahms are particularly noticeable in the late chamber works. Yet the grandeur and nostalgia of Elgar, his pastoralism and occasional pomposity, make him the epitome of a particularly Edwardian English style.

CHORAL & VOCAL MUSIC

Though choral music was a preoccupation of Elgar's early years, nothing of lasting value emerged until *The Light of Life* (1896) and the historical oratorios of the late 1890s, *King Olaf* and *Caractacus*. Most rewarding of his choral compositions is the series of works from the turn of the century, beginning with *The Dream of Gerontius* (1900). From the success of *The Dream of Gerontius* emerged a plan to compose a trilogy of oratorios detailing the founding of the Christian Church, a project abandoned when the first two – *The Apostles* and *The Kingdom* – failed to achieve a positive response from their audiences.

The Dream of Gerontius

Elgar had been brought up a Roman Catholic, but his faith had never been particularly strong. *The Dream of Gerontius*, a setting of Cardinal Newman's long poem dealing with the soul's passage from life into death, can be seen as Elgar's attempt to establish his faith more fully – and indeed he followed it up with two biblical oratorios. This is one of his most deeply felt works, a sensitive yet stirring setting of a text that tackles the most fundamental concepts, as Gerontius (tenor) moves through his final illness and is led on his journey to heaven by the figure of an angel (contralto). Elgar's dramatic imagination and the absence of any sentimentality lifts *Gerontius* clear of the morass of forgettable Victorian oratorios. When he had completed it, Elgar wrote on the score "This is the best of me", and arguably *The Dream of Gerontius* is his greatest achievement.

Palmer, Davies, Howell; London Symphony Chorus and Orchestra; Hickox (Chandos; 2 CDs; with *The Music Makers*)

Richard Hickox creates a particularly bright and vivid impression of *Gerontius* without losing sight of the mystical core of the work. Arthur Davies is an unusually dynamic Gerontius, Felicity Palmer is movingly intense as the angel and Gwynne Howell particularly strong in the double role of Priest and Angel of the Agony.

Baker, Lewis, Borg; Hallé Choir; Sheffield Philharmonic Chorus; Ambrosian Singers; Halle Orchestra; Barbirolli (EMI; 2 CDs; with *The Music Makers*)

There have been at least fourteen complete recordings of *Gerontius*; all have their strengths but none is definitive. This 1964 version is one of the best: highly dramatic and with the plangent voice of Janet Baker providing the most moving angel on record.

Sea Pictures

Elgar was not a particularly distinguished songwriter, but he excelled himself in the cycle of five songs that he wrote for contralto and orchestra (premiered by Clara Butt in 1899). The sea evidently inspired him, for his orchestral writing successfully represents its powerful presence through several deft touches – from the heavy chords conveying the swell of the sea in the first song, to the storm-tossed fervour of the last. The choice of verses is typically Edwardian: a mixture of over wrought religiosity ("Sabbath Morning at Sea"), bombast ("The Swimmer") and a touch of fairy-land ("Sea Slumber Song"). But Elgar manages to raise his material into something genuinely moving, nowhere more so than in the simple directness with which he sets his wife's poem "In Haven".

Baker; London Symphony Orchestra; Barbirolli
(EMI; with *Cello Concerto & Cockaigne*)

It's unfortunate for other contraltos that Janet Baker has made this work so utterly her own. Her reading abounds in fervour and commitment, every word sounds meant, and the whole thing simply sweeps you along. Barbirolli and the LSO are always alive to the score's more subtle detailing.

ORCHESTRAL MUSIC

"Gentlemen, let us now rehearse the greatest symphony of modern times, written by the greatest modern composer, and not only in this country." Thus the conductor Hans Richter greeted the London Symphony Orchestra when preparing Elgar's first symphony for its London premiere. Not unlike his mentor Brahms, Elgar struggled long and hard for many years before embarking on this most exacting of instrumental forms, and he managed to complete only two, both extremely fine works. Compared with the contemporary symphonies of Mahler they are traditional works, but these are arguably the first great British symphonies, revealing often highly original solutions to form and structure. A third symphony, which existed only in sketch form when Elgar died, was "completed" by the composer and musicologist Anthony Payne in 1997. More of a joint work than the completed *Symphony No. 10* of Mahler, it achieved great acclaim at its premiere and has already had several recordings.

Some of Elgar's finest music is to be found in his other pieces for full orchestra – the outstanding works being the famous *Enigma Variations* and the rich orchestral tapestry of *Falstaff*. Just as Elgar completed only two symphonies, so he turned to the concerto form only twice in his life, with a violin concerto and a cello concerto. And in the same way that the two symphonies have quite distinct characters, so these works also show widely different approaches to the form and its traditions.

Symphony No. 1

As early as 1898 Elgar had contemplated a symphony in memory of General Gordon, the British governor of Sudan killed at Khartoum in 1885. Elgar wrote to a friend that "the thing possesses me, but I can't write it down yet", but when he did come to compose his *Symphony No. 1*, in 1907–08, it seemed to have lost its specific historical reference: as Elgar again wrote, "There is no programme beyond a wide experience of human life with a great charity [love] and a massive hope in the future." It was first performed to great acclaim in Manchester in December 1908, conducted by its dedicatee, Hans Richter. The symphony is dominated by a melody that's given Elgar's characteristic expressive marking of *nobilmente* (nobly); returning at salient points throughout the four movements, this melody encapsulates the mood of this grand, optimistic and distinctly Germanic work.

London Philharmonic Orchestra; Boult
(EMI; with *Serenade for Strings, Chanson de matin & Chanson de nuit*)

For a performance of real majesty and sweep, without interpretative quirks but with plenty of bite and character, Adrian Boult's last recording of the work for EMI is unbeatable, with the London Philharmonic Orchestra, which has probably recorded the work more times than any other orchestra, in superb form.

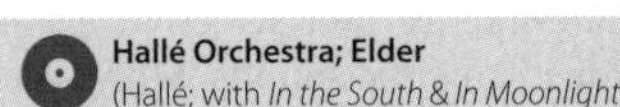

Hallé Orchestra; Elder
(Hallé; with *In the South & In Moonlight*)

Since his appointment as principal conductor of the Hallé, Mark Elder has emerged as one of the most exciting Elgarians around. This is a hugely passionate interpretation. Elder is completely attuned to the structure of the symphony, with a wonderful sense of momentum but never at the expense of feeling.

Symphony No. 2

His confidence boosted by the warm reception of his *Symphony No. 1*, Elgar soon began a second. Completed in 1911, the work was dedicated to the memory of the late King Edward VII, but despite the slow movement's funereal tread Elgar intended no programmatic link to be made. Indeed, according to the composer "…the spirit of the whole work is intended to be high and pure joy." Even so there are moments when this spirit subsides into passages of hesitancy and introspection, not just in the slow movement, but also in the fleet-footed Rondo and the consoling finale. Overall, the work's discursive structure, with its wealth of thematic cross-references, make the second symphony more complex and subtle than the first – which may well account for the less than overwhelming reception it received at its early performances.

London Philharmonic Orchestra; Boult
(EMI; with *Cockaigne Overture*)

There's a grandly expansive quality to this interpretation from Boult (who recorded the symphony a number of times). The London Philharmonic Orchestra's wonderfully burnished string sound brings out the symphony's poignancy as well as its generosity of spirit.

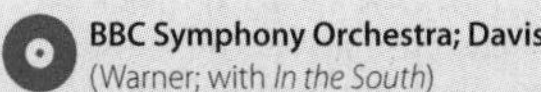
BBC Symphony Orchestra; Davis
(Warner; with *In the South*)

This is an absolutely outstanding recording from Andrew Davis and the BBC Symphony Orchestra – and a bargain at budget price. Davis, more than most, gets to the heart of the emotional complexities of this enigmatic work. The recorded sound is excellent.

Enigma Variations

The true title of this work is *Variations on an Original Theme*, as the "Enigma" is strictly speaking only the title of the section that introduces the theme. Ever since the work first appeared, musicologists have tried to unravel what this enigma might be: the consensus has long been that the theme was composed as harmony and counterpoint to another theme that is never itself heard, so the crux of the argument is over the identity of that implied theme. The conundrum is irrelevant to the glorious music of the variations themselves, which were all given cryptic titles referring to Elgar's "friends pictured within", as his dedication has it. These friends have long been identified, as Elgar often tagged their initials and nicknames onto the music. Thus the first variation *CAE* is a portrait of his wife Caroline Alice Elgar, while the serene *Nimrod* is a tribute to his publisher friend A.E. Jaeger whose surname is German for "huntsman" – hence the allusion to the Old Testament figure of Nimrod the hunter.

Philharmonia; Barbirolli
(EMI; with *Falstaff*)

Few conductors have equalled John Barbirolli in the *Enigma Variations*, and his 1962 performance with the Philharmonia is a classic. The recorded sound is admittedly somewhat dated, but the nobility and finesse of the interpretation easily outweigh such a drawback.

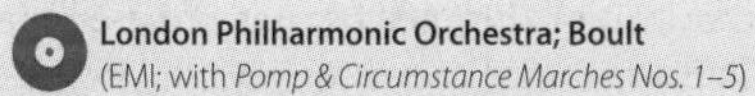
London Philharmonic Orchestra; Boult
(EMI; with *Pomp & Circumstance Marches Nos. 1–5*)

Adrian Boult and the London Philharmonic Orchestra provide a more aristocratic but equally enjoyable reading of the *Enigma Variations*, distinctive for its structural rigour. It comes coupled with lively but earnest accounts of the celebrated *Pomp and Circumstance* marches.

Serenade for Strings & Introduction and Allegro

Composed in 1892, the *Serenade for Strings* is the first recognizably Elgarian work – "I like 'em", he later wrote of the *Serenade*'s three movements, "the first thing I ever did." The *Serenade* is undoubtedly a beautiful work, but the second of his two major works for strings, the *Introduction and Allegro*, is a great one. Composed in 1905 for the newly formed London Symphony Orchestra, Elgar described working on it in a postcard to his friend Jaeger: "I'm doing that string thing ... no working out part but a devil of a fugue instead ...with all sorts of japes & counterpoint." With its juxtaposition of a string quartet against a full string orchestra, the work sparked off a succession of English string works that have their roots in the Baroque concerto grosso idea of "competing" string ensembles.

Allegri Quartet; Sinfonia of London; Barbirolli
(EMI; with Elgar *Sospiri* & *Elegy* and Vaughan Williams *Greensleeves Fantasia* & *Tallis Fantasia*)

This is an absolutely classic recording of the finest early twentieth-century English string works in performances of great fervour. John Barbirolli was always a passionate exponent of Elgar's music, but he is never self-indulgent, concentrating on producing a beautiful and refulgent sound without lapsing into self-indulgence.

In the South

In the South, called an overture but more of a tone poem, is Elgar at his most Straussian. Written while he and his wife were holidaying in Italy, it's a kaleidoscopic evocation of the landscape and historical associations of that country and it possesses a sustained exuberance which is almost unique in his output. It opens with a great swirling rush of energy which leads straight into a typically passionate and pulsating Elgarian big tune before subsiding into a quietly poetic passage. There's a homage to Berlioz's *Harold in Italy* by way of a melancholic viola solo, but the work ends with a triumphal blaze of orchestral sound with the brass very much to the fore.

Bournemouth Symphony Orchestra; Silvestri
(EMI; 2 CDs; with *Symphonies Nos. 1 & 2* and *Serenade*)

It may seem perverse to recommend a recording by a provincial orchestra and a largely forgotten conductor, but few versions of *In the South* get close to this one in terms of sheer *joie de vivre*. In Constantin Silvestri's hands the piece crackles with an infectious energy from beginning to end. It comes with spirited accounts of both symphonies from Barbirolli and the Hallé.

Hallé Orchestra; Elder
(Hallé; with *Symphony No. 1* & In Moonlight)

As a single disc alternative to Silvestri, Mark Elder and the Hallé Orchestra's recent performance is the one to go for. Clearly relishing every bar, they treat the work as the bravura showpiece it is, wringing every inch of drama from it with thrilling exuberance.

Falstaff

Elgar's penultimate orchestral work (the *Cello Concerto* came later) is arguably his finest. Unlike Verdi's opera, which concentrates on the womanizing side of Falstaff's character as portrayed in Shakespeare's *Merry Wives of Windsor*, Elgar's "symphonic study" dwells on his relationship with Prince Hal in *Henry IV* and *Henry V*, culminating in the newly crowned king's rejection of his old friend, and Falstaff's death – perhaps symbolic of the passing of the age in which Elgar had grown up and felt secure. The score is marvellously detailed and reveals a sense of humour not heard so openly in any of Elgar's music, though the grandiose and melancholy elements play equally important roles.

Hallé Orchestra; Barbirolli
(EMI; with the *Enigma Variations*)

This performance has enormous panache and brio. There's a wonderfully theatrical feel about Barbirolli's approach, but without ever lapsing into exaggeration or histrionics. A classic performance from the most passionate of Elgarians.

Violin Concerto

"It's good! Awfully emotional, too emotional, but I love it." Elgar's *Violin Concerto* displays all his characteristic trademarks of wistfulness, grandeur and rapturous lyricism, but it is immensely virtuosic as well – indeed, some rate it as the most difficult violin concerto in the repertory. Composed in tandem with the second symphony, the finished manuscript bears the inscription "Here is enshrined the soul of …?", almost certainly a reference to Alice Stuart-Wortley who encouraged him to complete the work, and for whom he had a very deep affection. Though melodically rich, there is an interconnectedness between all the concerto's main themes and a prevailing sense of ardour tinged with sadness, most pointedly in the central slow movement where the soloist enters quietly in its middle, most "vocal" register. The concerto marks a real development of the form, notably in the last movement's extended accompanied cadenza in which the soloist mulls over themes from the whole work.

Kennedy; City of Birmingham Symphony Orchestra; Rattle (EMI; with Vaughan Williams, *The Lark Ascending*)

Kennedy's second recording of the *Violin Concerto* is even more thoughtful and intense than his first. It really sounds like the performance of someone who knows the concerto inside out: no nuance is missed, no detail left untouched. Some may find the emphasis on the introspective a little self-indulgent, but overall it's a highly convincing account.

Menuhin; London Symphony Orchestra; Elgar
(EMI; with *Cello Concerto*)

Fritz Kreisler premiered the concerto but wouldn't record it, so in 1932 the seventeen-year-old Yehudi Menuhin was hired for the job. The composer was immediately impressed and it's easy to understand why: there's a naturalness and a fluency to Menuhin's playing which is utterly beguiling. The performance comes with a recording of the Cello Concerto by Beatrice Harrison made in 1928.

Cello Concerto

World War I took its toll on Elgar. Although he was not directly involved in any participatory way, he saw in it the destruction of the world he had known since childhood, and there is a tangible sense of regret and dejection in his last major works. Along with three important chamber works (see below), the most famous of these is the *Cello Concerto*, a work that conveys the impression, in the words of the Elgar scholar Michael Kennedy, of "a man wearied with the world … finding solace in the beauty of music". The texture has something of the transparency of chamber music, and the form of the concerto reflects a state of emotional flux – it's divided into four movements which further divide into sections with quite contrasting moods, though mournfulness is the dominant tone. Resonant cello chords frame the whole piece, opening the concerto with buttonholing immediacy, and making a poignant comeback towards the end.

Du Pré; London Symphony Orchestra; Barbirolli (EMI; with *Sea Pictures*)

Jacqueline du Pré's magnificent recording with John Barbirolli has dominated the catalogue since it was issued in the mid-1960s. Few cellists have penetrated the concerto's inner recesses so deeply, or produced a performance of such burning intensity. This is the place to begin any Elgar collection.

CHAMBER MUSIC

Elgar composed a lot of chamber music in his youth, notably the series of so-called "shed music" he wrote for himself and his young wind-playing friends to play in his garden. But his only works of significance, apart from the various salon pieces for violin, date from the end of World War I, when he rented a quiet cottage in the wooded uplands of Sussex and composed his *Violin Sonata*, *String Quartet* and *Piano Quintet*, works expressing with deep seriousness his disillusionment with post-war life, yet also conveying some of the "wood magic", as Elgar's wife called it, of their surroundings.

Piano Quintet & String Quartet

The *Piano Quintet* (1919) is Elgar's most overtly Brahmsian work though it is equally dominated by Elgar's highly personal way of creating a pervasive atmosphere of ghostliness – a mood supposedly inspired by a group of dead trees near to his Sussex home. At its core is a slow movement of almost unbearable poignancy which begins like a procession before moving into a richly chromatic second subject. The *String Quartet* (1918) is more intimate in style but no less wistful and melancholic. There's plenty of power in it too and its outer movements have an edginess and an anxiety lurking beneath the mellow sonorities. The sombre, plaintive slow movement was a particular favourite of Lady Elgar and was played at her funeral.

Piano Quintet; String Quartet: Donohoe; Maggini Quartet (Naxos)

This would be a remarkable recording at any price. Both the Maggini Quartet and pianist Peter Donohoe clearly feel a real affinity with this music and they capture its melancholy charm more profoundly than most.

Violin Sonata

The three-movement *Violin Sonata* is Elgar at his most openly Romantic, the very antithesis of strait-laced Englishness; the theme of the opening movement is the most arresting idea in all Elgar's chamber music, with a restless energy – one moment passionately expansive, the next painfully withdrawn – that borders on the neurotic. The second movement maintains this bittersweet quality with a tentative soliloquizing opening which seems uncertain whether it belongs to the salon or the confessional. The long finale is no less impressive with similarly mercurial mood changes to the first movement but with an underlying warmth to it which Elgar likened to the last movement of the second symphony.

Kennedy, Pettinger (Chandos; with other violin pieces)

Nigel Kennedy has a real rapport with Elgar's works, which he plays with a raw emotion that is utterly genuine and completely at the service of the music. This is among the best recordings of the *Sonata*, and the disc also includes Elgar's lighter violin pieces, including the charmingly insinuating *Salut d'Amour* for violin, cello and piano.

f

Manuel de Falla (1876–1946)

Glimpses of Manuel de Falla's personality, as seen by his contemporaries, are tantalizingly rare, but two images of him are well-known: one is Picasso's melancholy drawing of 1920; the other is Stravinsky's remark that he was "the most unpityingly religious person I have ever known – and the least sensible to manifestations of humour". Yet this austere man, a lifelong bachelor, wrote some of the most sensuous and alluring music to have come out of Spain.

Born into a prosperous family in the seaport of Cadiz, Falla had every encouragement to immerse himself in music, receiving piano lessons first from his mother and then from an array of eminent teachers. Yet for several years he could not decide between a musical or a literary career. He was about 17 when he finally committed himself to becoming a composer, around the time that he encountered the music of Grieg. Immediately impressed by Grieg's strong national character and his rejection of Teutonic notions of musical structure, Falla conceived "an intense desire to create one day something similar with Spanish music".

After a distinguished spell at the Madrid Conservatory (1898–99), when he took top marks and prizes in all his classes, Falla persuaded Felipe Pedrell, the seminal figure of Spanish musical nationalism, to take him on as a pupil. Pedrell's influence on budding Spanish composers of the day was profound, as important as that which the Russian teacher-composer Rimsky-Korsakov had over the young Stravinsky. Pedrell exhorted Falla, as he had Albéniz and Granados before him, to develop a style based on folk music, and showed him how to achieve this within a wider European framework. Although Falla took many of his teacher's ideas to heart, his own style differed from Pedrell's in two fundamental ways. Firstly, his inclination throughout his life was to write sparely, and he had an abhorrence of music with too many notes – Pedrell's own compositions and those of his other students are decidedly expansive. Secondly, Falla chose not to quote folk tunes directly as Pedrell would do, but to extract the essence of the music, to build something new from this raw material. As he put it in an essay of 1917, "I think that in popular song the spirit is more important than the letter."

In 1907, two years after winning a prestigious competition for his opera *La vida breve*, Falla bought a one-week return train ticket to Paris, and ended up staying seven years. Soon after arriving he was befriended by Debussy, Ravel and Dukas, and got caught up in the anti-Wagnerianism sweeping French musical circles. Even though he was never particularly successful financially, Paris was the making of him as a composer, enabling him to reassess the musical heritage of his homeland in the context of the impressionist masterpieces of the French innovators. The first fruit of this process was *Noches en los jardines de España* (1911–15), a lush composition for piano and orchestra.

At the outbreak of World War I Falla returned to Spain. Many of the compositions of this period, including the two ballet scores *El amor brujo* (1915) and *El sombrero de tres picos* (1917–19), derive their character from the *cante jondo*, the highly evocative song style of Andalucía, of which Falla had been making a thorough study. These ballets were highly popular, and suites of dances from *El sombrero* soon became international concert favourites. Falla could have gone on profitably mining the rich orchestral style of his ballets but, inspired by the neo-classicism of his friend Stravinsky, he set off on a new phase, working to condense and distil his style.

In 1919 he moved to Granada, where he gathered around him a circle of intellectuals, the most notable of whom was the writer and poet Lorca. Though each new work took ever longer to write, with Falla poring over every note and phrase, the music of Falla's neo-classical phase attained a lapidary perfection, for example in the small-scale theatre piece *El retablo de maese Pedro* and the *Concerto for Harpsichord* (1923–26).

Never a man to repeat himself, Falla then embarked on *Atlantida*, a huge oratorio for soloists, chorus and orchestra. This was the most ambitious work he had ever undertaken and he was to devote the rest of his life to it, but it remained unfinished and was not performed until 1962. Falla's last years were lived out in self-imposed exile in Argentina, where the composer had moved to escape the regime of General Franco.

Nights in the Gardens of Spain

It was the great Spanish pianist Ricardo Viñes who persuaded Falla to transform *Noches en los jardines de España* (Nights in the Gardens of Spain) from a solo work into one for piano and orchestra. The result is one of Falla's most impressionistic and poetic works, full of shimmering and diaphanous textures that recall Debussy but which also possess a hard-edged precision through the presence of the piano. Its three sections are descriptive: the first evokes the Generalife gardens of the Alhambra in Granada; the second – the most animated – is described as a distant dance; and the third was inspired by the gardens of the Sierra de Córdoba. The whole work is shot though with Spanish colour, not through the precise quotation of specific folk songs, but by the subtle utilization of effects – strumming chords, insistently repeated phrases, declamatory unison passages in the piano – which suggest the rhythms and cadences of flamenco song, as filtered through the memory of a dream.

Manuel de Falla enjoying himself in a Paris restaurant.

de Larrocha; London Philharmonic Orchestra; Frühbeck de Burgos (Decca; 2 CDs; with *The Three-Cornered Hat, El amor brujo, Harpsichord Concerto*, etc)

There's a wholely natural feeling to the way the climaxes and sudden changes of direction are so perfectly judged in this performance – a measure of how well the conductor and soloist (both Spanish) know this work. From the perfumed heaviness of the opening to the rapturous piano arabesques of the last movement, a richly mysterious mood is beautifully sustained.

El amor brujo

The one-act ballet *El amor brujo* (Love the Magician) was finished in the same year as the *Nights in the Gardens of Spain*, and like that work is imbued with the spirit of Gypsy music. The story tells how the affair between the beautiful Gypsy girl Candelas and her lover Carmelo is thwarted by the interruptions of the jealous ghost of her former lover (indicated by a strident fanfare motif). Only by luring the ghost away – through the charms of another Gypsy girl – can Candelas and Carmelo be free of him. Falla conveys all this in ten highly concentrated sections, four of which include song (the work was commissioned by the Gypsy dancer and singer Pastora Imperio). The music is vividly atmospheric and creates a genuine sense of supernatural danger, a mood which culminates in the serene but spooky "Magic Circle" and the more famous (and often anthologized) "Ritual Fire Dance". On a more seductive note comes the delightful "Pantomime", a luxurious slow tango in 7/8 with which Candelas's friend Lucía successfully captivates the offending ghost. Originally scored for eight instruments, Falla revised it for full orchestra in 1916 and that is how it is commonly heard today.

Mistral; New Philharmonia Orchestra; Frühbeck de Burgos (Decca; 2 CDs; with *The Three-Cornered Hat, Nights in the Gardens of Spain, Harpsichord Concerto*, etc)

Once again Rafael Frühbeck de Burgos proves himself to be a masterly conductor of Falla. There's an intensely theatrical feel to the proceedings and in Nati Mistral he has an authentic flamenco singer able to do justice to the passionate vocal outpourings that punctuate the score.

The Three-Cornered Hat

Commissioned in 1916 by the impresario Diaghilev for his Russian Ballet company, *El sombrero de tres picos* (The Three-Cornered Hat) was first performed in London in 1919. It boasted an incredible wealth of talent (choreography by Massine, designs by Picasso, Karsavina dancing the role of the miller's wife), and was one of the company's greatest successes, putting Falla on the international map as a composer. Based on the novel by Alarcón, it tells of the failed attempt by an elderly local magistrate (whose three-cornered hat is a symbol of authority) to seduce the miller's lovely wife. His failure ends in complete humiliation and his effigy is tossed in a blanket amid general rejoicing. Falla's score offers a strong rebuttal to the charge that he lacked a sense of humour. It abounds in the most sparklingly exuberant array of melodies and the principal characters are all wittily characterized, often through association with a specific Spanish dance rhythm. But there is also greater bite in this score, as if, in writing for the Russian Ballet, Falla felt obliged to acknowledge the rhythmic adventurousness of the company's previous successes, in particular Stravinsky's *Petrushka*.

Montreal Symphony Orchestra; Dutoit (Decca; 2 CDs; with *Nights in the Gardens of Spain, El amor brujo, Harpsichord Concerto*, etc)

Charles Dutoit's 1984 recording of *The Three-Cornered Hat* is absolutely electrifying, with brightly vivid sound and energetic playing from an obviously enthused Montreal Symphony Orchestra. A major achievement which communicates the sheer theatrical excitement of the piece.

de los Angeles; Philharmonia Orchestra; Frühbeck de Burgos (EMI; 2 CDs; with *La vida breve & El amor brujo*)

EMI repackage this 1963 recording of the complete ballet at regular intervals. The current set showcases the thrilling voice of Victoria de los Angeles, with Frühbeck de Burgos delivering a sparklingly theatrical account of *The Three-Cornered Hat*, brilliantly played by the Philharmonia.

Gabriel Fauré (1845–1924)

Like Delius, Fauré is a composer whose music does not seem to travel well: revered in his native France – above all as a composer of songs – he is known elsewhere almost solely for his hugely popular *Requiem*. Unfortunately this excludes a wealth of highly refined and beautiful music. Fauré's style reveals a Romantic sensibility held in check by a classical sense of form and decorum – it is music of feeling, sometimes of passion, but it never aspires to the epic or the transcendent, preferring a more discreet and intimate means of expression. Some have dismissed him as never aspiring much higher than the salon and, although there are insipid moments in his music, at its best it possesses elegance, harmonic adventurousness, and an understated but intense degree of feeling.

Fauré, the youngest of six children (possibly an unplanned addition to the family), proved to be an extremely precocious talent. When he was nine he was sent to the École Niedermeyer, a Paris music school with a bias towards ecclesiastical music. In much of Fauré's music, throughout his life, there are hints of the church

Gabriel Fauré playing the piano for his friend Albéniz (far right).

modes that he would have learned there. In 1861 the 25-year-old Saint-Saëns (see p.465) arrived at the school to teach piano, and proceeded to broaden his students' outlook, introducing them to the music of Liszt and Wagner. The friendship that he formed with Fauré lasted until Saint-Saëns's death in 1921.

Fauré's career began as an organist, firstly at Rennes and then, after serving in the Franco-Prussian war of 1870, at the Paris church of St Honoré d'Eylau. In 1879 he heard the whole of Wagner's *Ring* cycle in Munich, and although he later acknowledged its effect on him ("Such things seep into you just like water seeps through sand") he was not swept up in the Wagner mania that hit Paris a few years later – unlike many other French composers. In 1896 he won two major appointments, as organist at the church of La Madeleine and professor of composition at the Paris Conservatoire where he exerted a strong influence on a succession of pupils, including Maurice Ravel and Nadia Boulanger, the twentieth century's most important composition teacher. Even though he gave up the Madeleine job in 1905 when he was appointed director of the Conservatoire, the time he could set aside for writing music decreased substantially, a problem exacerbated by his growing deafness which left him feeling increasingly alone. This sense of isolation almost certainly contributed to the development of a more introspective style. Fauré's later work is characterized by a paring down of his musical language, an unfashionable restraint that probably accounts for the relative failure of his second opera, *Pénélope* (1913).

Choral Music

Of the great Requiems of the nineteenth century, Verdi's sounds as if it was written for the opera house and Brahms's for the concert hall – Fauré's alone has the odour of incense, doubtless thanks to his career as an organist and his familiarity with church music. This is a work to comfort and to reassure the faithful in the face of death, rather than to overwhelm them with the finality of judgement; significantly it omits the full, fearsome text of the Dies Irae (Day of Wrath), allowing only a passing reference to it in the Libera Me (Deliver Me) section. The overwhelming impression is one of peace and serenity, which, in the Agnus Dei, is transformed into an almost joyous resignation. One of the most innovative features of the work was its orchestration, which omitted violins and woodwind to create a warmly mellow sound. At the request of Fauré's publisher, however, the *Requiem* was re-scored for full orchestra in 1900, and that is the version most commonly used today.

Fauré wrote several other liturgical works, of which the short *Messe basse* (Low Mass) for high voices is the best known. Originally written in collaboration with Messager, when it was known as the *Messe des pêcheurs de Villerville*, it was revised by Fauré in 1906 to make it entirely his own, creating a work that's striking for the clarity and simplicity of its religious sentiment.

Requiem (1893 version); Messe des pêcheurs de Villerville: Mellon, Kooy, Van Doeselaar; Petits Chanteurs de Saint-Louis, Paris Chapelle Royale; Musique Oblique Ensemble; Herreweghe (Harmonia Mundi)

Herreweghe's recording is unusual for giving us the original version of the *Messe basse* and an earlier and simpler version of the *Requiem*. His decision is fully justified by performances in which the closer balance between orchestra and choir creates a wonderful sense of intimacy.

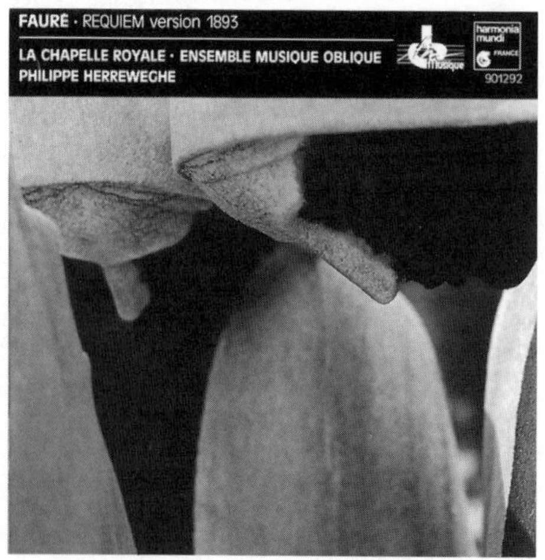

Requiem (1900 version): Auger, Luxon; Choir of King's College Cambridge; English Chamber Orchestra; Ledger (EMI; with *Messe basse*, Poulenc *Mass in G* & Duruflé *Requiem*)

For an account of the *Requiem*'s more full-blooded 1900 version, this performance by the Choir of King's College under Philip Ledger is particularly good value. Soprano Arléen Auger is an outstanding soloist in the haunting Pie Jesu.

Orchestral Music

Much of Fauré's orchestral music was written either as commissions for the theatre or transcriptions of existing instrumental pieces. There are no symphonies or concertos, and, perhaps because of this, his orchestral works are rather neglected – a shame, since most of it is of the highest quality and displays his characteristic freshness and clarity. The suite *Masques et bergamasques* started life as a choreographic divertissement inspired by the paintings of Watteau. It's essentially light music, airy and undemanding and, in truth, a little insipid. The incidental music that Fauré wrote for Maeterlinck's play *Pelléas et Mélisande*, also turned into a suite, has considerably more bite, and contains in the third-movement Sicilienne one of the best of those hauntingly melancholic tunes that he seemed to turn out at will. In the one movement *Elégie for cello orchestra*, this melancholy comes as close as anything Fauré wrote to a genuinely tragic expression of grief. A more wistful tone is found in the *Pavane* for orchestra, a gentle unassuming work that has proved the most popular of his orchestral works.

Orchestral Works: BBC Philharmonic; Tortelier (Chandos)

This disc contains a good selection of most of the better-known orchestral works (but not *Pelléas et Mélisande*), which the BBC Philharmonic plays with great sympathy. The emotional range of this music is not wide, and Tortelier finds just the right degree of warmth and elegant charm.

Chamber Music

If Fauré was unduly self-critical and nervous about writing orchestral works, then in his chamber music he had no such inhibitions, producing an array of works of a consistently high standard that is unrivalled in French music at that period. Much of it, particularly the two piano quartets, has the breadth and energy that you associate with orchestral music, and nearly all of it includes a piano part. Of his early chamber music, the two most celebrated works are the *Violin Sonata No. 1* and the *Piano Quartet No. 1*, both written in the mid-1870s and both characterized by an underlying melancholy that is offset by sparkling Scherzo-like movements. Both the *Piano Quartet No. 2* (1886) and the *Violin Sonata No. 2* (1917) are darker, less effusive works, in which thematic material from their first movements is skilfully developed in subsequent sections.

Piano Quartets Nos. 1 & 2: Domus
(Hyperion)

Domus have all the qualities required for a perfect chamber group: distinctive instrumental voices that can shine individually when necessary, but above all a strong sense of a common cause. Both piano quartets are held together by some brilliantly nimble piano playing, and there is an emotional depth to the slow movements which is utterly compelling.

Violin Sonatas Nos. 1 & 2: Grumiaux, Crossley
(Philips; with Franck *Violin Sonata*)

Grumiaux and Crossley respond warmly and imaginatively to the violin sonatas, treating their rhythmic ebb and flow with a flexibility that brings out their quicksilver charm. Grumiaux's variety of tone is particularly apparent in the slow movements, where his highlighting of details heightens the sense of personal utterance.

Piano Music

Like his chamber music, Fauré's piano works are extremely personal pieces which are largely introspective in mood. The choice of forms – nocturnes, barcarolles, preludes, impromptus – reveals a debt to an earlier generation: to Chopin for a poetic concentration and clarity of utterance; and to Liszt (whom Fauré knew well) for the more mercurial and capricious colouring of his work. Fauré's own unique contribution was a harmonic adventurousness, and a tendency for unexpected modulations which create a restless and elusive quality as if the music is not always quite sure where it is going. In his later piano works, in particular the last three nocturnes, this uneasy dreaminess intensifies, creating music that is curiously enigmatic but strangely moving.

Paik
(Decca)

All of Fauré's piano music has been well recorded by Paul Crossley on CRD and Kathryn Stott on Hyperion. However, the best place to start is an introductory compilation, and, with Pascal Rogé's excellent disc currently unavailable, this one from Kun Woo Paik is a good choice. It contains an ideal selection of works (including five nocturnes) in performances of admirable clarity and tonal beauty.

Songs

Fauré wrote nearly one hundred songs throughout his career, and they show off his lyric gift at its subtle and eloquent best. They include settings of poems by Baudelaire, Gautier and Victor Hugo, but the poet with whom he seems to have the strongest sympathy was Paul Verlaine, who inspired some of his most sensuous and concentrated writing. Both poet and composer are concerned with atmosphere more than description, and the instrumental part in these songs never acts just as accompaniment but rather shapes and directs the vocal line in ways that delicately alter the mood. *La bonne chanson* (1892–94), the finest of his song cycles, possesses a fresh and heartfelt ardour that reflects Fauré's feeling towards the work's first performer, his mistress Emma Bardac.

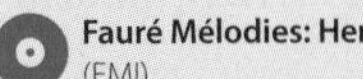

Fauré Mélodies: Hendricks, Dalberto
(EMI)

American soprano Barbara Hendricks is a seasoned exponent of French song, and this selection of Fauré's *melodies* – including *La bonne chanson* and favourites such as *Nell* and *Les roses d'Ispahan* – doesn't disappoint. Michel Dalberto makes a profoundly sympathetic and idiomatic accompanist.

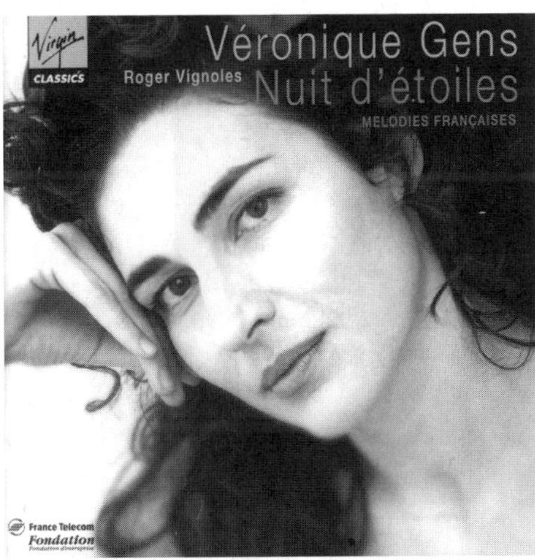

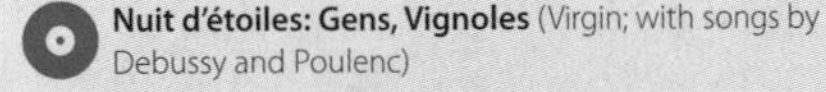

Nuit d'étoiles: Gens, Vignoles (Virgin; with songs by Debussy and Poulenc)

This disc contains just eight, mostly early, songs by Fauré (plus a selection of songs by Debussy and Poulenc) sung by one of the most eloquent and persuasive of recent French singers, Véronique Gens. The intimacy and restraint of her interpretations is absolutely compelling and this disc makes the perfect introduction to the seductive world of twentieth-century French song.

Morton Feldman (1926–1987)

As a broad generalization, the music of the American avant-garde differs from its European counterpart in being primarily concerned with the sensual qualities of sounds themselves rather than the shaping and ordering of those sounds. Morton Feldman is typical of this tendency: his sound-world, especially in his later works, consists of small, soft and unhurried musical gestures which emphasize the physical detail of instrumental timbre. With this comes a fondness for repetition and an absence of rhythmic momentum which is, in Feldman's own words, "a conscious attempt at formalizing a disorientation of memory". The cumulative effect is of a hallucinatory stasis, not dissimilar to the large canvases of Mark Rothko, a painter Feldman knew and admired. It is a music where little happens – very beautifully.

Feldman was born in New York and studied composition, unsatisfactorily, with Stefan Wolpe and then Wallingford Riegger. The catalyst for his attempts to liberate sound from structure came when he met John Cage in 1949. *Projections* (1950–51) was a Cage-influenced work, written on squared paper with fairly general instructions, allowing the performer almost limitless freedom of choice over pitch and note duration. This was fairly rapidly replaced as a working method by

A laughing Morton Feldman at CalArts in 1987. A seated John Adams shares the joke.

more precise notation, but with note duration still left relatively free. The effect, in works like *Piece for Four Pianos* (1957) or *The Swallows of Salangan* (1960), is of a kind of anarchic counterpoint in which material disconcertingly overlaps and shifts. In Feldman's later work the emphasis changes again, from a preoccupation with the exploration of timbre to a fascination with time – a fascination exemplified by the *Piano and String Quartet* of 1985.

Rothko Chapel

In 1971 Feldman attended the opening ceremony of the Rothko Chapel in Houston, Texas. Feldman was asked to write a piece of music specifically for the building and as tribute to Mark Rothko, fourteen of whose large canvases were hung in the chapel, a non-denominational meditative space. The paintings were Feldman's starting point: "Rothko's imagery goes right to the edge of his canvas, and I wanted the same effect with the music – that it should permeate the whole octagonal-shaped room and not be heard from a certain distance." Using very spare forces – viola, celeste, percussion, chorus and soprano solo – in a way that treats them as discrete abstract elements, Feldman creates a musical-spiritual ambience not dissimilar to the later music of Arvo Pärt. The difference is that Feldman's sound-world is cooler, with a greater emphasis on details of timbre as a means of communication. Each of its five sections unfolds with an unruffled glow that seems to heighten the listener's sensitivity as it progresses.

Abel, Rosenak, Winant; UC Berkeley Chamber Chorus; Brett (New Albion; with *Why Patterns?*)

It is sometimes suggested that interpretation is irrelevant in music of such an undemonstrative nature. Suffice it to say that the forces assembled here respond to the music in an appropriately sensitive and self-effacing manner, and the result is extremely powerful.

Piano and String Quartet

In the *Piano and String Quartet* the piano, with the sustaining pedal held down, plays an arpeggiated chord as the string quartet plays a sustained chord. Notes change, harmonies shift, individual notes are sounded, but the essential pattern of broken chord plus sustained chord continues, to increasingly mesmerizing effect, for the eighty-minute duration of the work. The piece seems to have no beginning or end, no intention or direction, and yet listening to it heightens aural awareness to such a degree that the smallest modification of the chords possesses a resonance and an intensity that is startling.

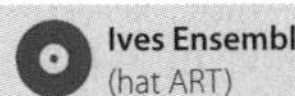

Ives Ensemble
(hat ART)

The premiere recording by the Kronos Quartet and pianist Aki Takahashi is still worth checking out, but this new one from the Amsterdam-based Ives Ensemble reaches for greater extremes of softs and muted-louds, orientating a clearer pathway through the distorting repetitions of Feldman's structural labyrinth.

For Samuel Beckett

In the work of Irish playwright and novelist Samuel Beckett, Morton Feldman found a remarkably seamless counterpart in words for his own ideas about sound. They collaborated on two works, *Neither* (1977) and *Words and Music* (1987), and Feldman's last completed work (also from 1987) was a dedication to his friend. Scored for a standard orchestra, with added tuba and an important part for vibraphone, this eerie and otherworldly music seems to step into a haunted twilight world. Feldman's ear for blending orchestral timbres reaches a logical endpoint here, as the opening wind, brass and string sonorities resonate as a single voice. This sonic puree is helped along by the all-encompassing dark modality of Feldman's harmonies, which neuters any possibility of overly empathic expressive hooks, mirroring Beckett's trademark existentialist woe.

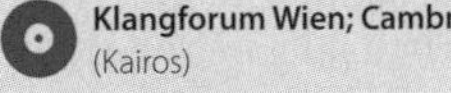

Klangforum Wien; Cambreling
(Kairos)

More deliberately paced than rival versions, this brilliantly detailed and soulful performance captures the marrow of *For Samuel Beckett*'s deathly chill. The Kairos recording engineers place you directly inside the orchestra – the perfect vantage point to eavesdrop on the curious unfolding of an orchestral riddle.

César Franck (1822–1890)

Although Belgian, César Franck became the figurehead for a generation of French composers who had little interest in the predominantly operatic fare on offer in France, being instead attracted to Germanic ideas of symphonic form and musical abstraction. Acclaim for his work was meagre in his lifetime, but Franck brought a new seriousness to French music that ultimately would resonate in the compositions of later figures like Debussy and Delibes.

He was born in the Walloon city of Liège to a Flemish family; hence the mixture of French and Flemish in his name. At the age of 11 he made his first tour as a virtuoso pianist and two years later the whole family moved to Paris so he could study there. Mercilessly exploited by his avaricious father, he left home in 1848 in order to marry his pupil Félicité Desmousseaux and shortly after took up the post of organist at Notre Dame de Lorette – the church where he had been married. Franck's earliest compositions were chiefly vehicles for his piano tours, followed by a series of religious works, then by pieces for the organ – at which he showed stunning prowess after the move to Paris – and for full orchestra. For many of his middle years his energies were given over to teaching and disseminating a musical philosophy that wanted to take French music away from its perceived frivolity and mediocrity.

Nearly all Franck's finest and best-known works seem to have been inspired by his unrequited infatuation with one of his former composition students, Augusta Holmès. Before his friendship with the beautiful Holmès, Franck specialized in rather earnest religious music, but in the last decade of his life his music took on a more sensuous quality and a greater adventurousness. These later works include the *Piano Quintet* (1879), the symphonic poem *Le chasseur maudit* (1882), the *Prelude, Chorale and Fugue* for solo piano (1884), the *Symphonic Variations* for piano and orchestra (1885), the *Violin Sonata* (1886), the *Symphony in D Minor* (1888), the *String Quartet* (1889) and the three *Chorales* for organ (1890). He also wrote two long-forgotten operas, *Hulda* (1885) and *Ghisèle* (1890) – the last left unfinished when Franck died after being knocked down by a bus.

Franck's first-rate orchestral works amount to just a single symphony, one concertante work for piano and orchestra and a handful of symphonic poems. His reputation rests primarily on his instrumental pieces, the best of which are his *Piano Quintet*, *Violin Sonata* and organ music, most of which comes from the years of his maturity, whereas the piano pieces are mainly the product of his years as a touring virtuoso, when his compositional technique lagged some way behind his dexterity.

Symphony in D Minor

When Franck began his *Symphony in D Minor* in 1886, he had few French examples except Berlioz to follow – his most obvious influences were Liszt's symphonic poems, in which a rigid structure is combined with the inventive transformation of themes that metamorphose as their harmonies and contexts change. Franck's symphony marks a development of the concept of cyclic form, in which music from one movement reappears later on, providing unity and coherence – thus ideas from the symphony's first two movements are recalled in the third. The slow movement is famous for its cor anglais solo, an instrument French critics of the time thought unsuitable for a major role in a serious symphony.

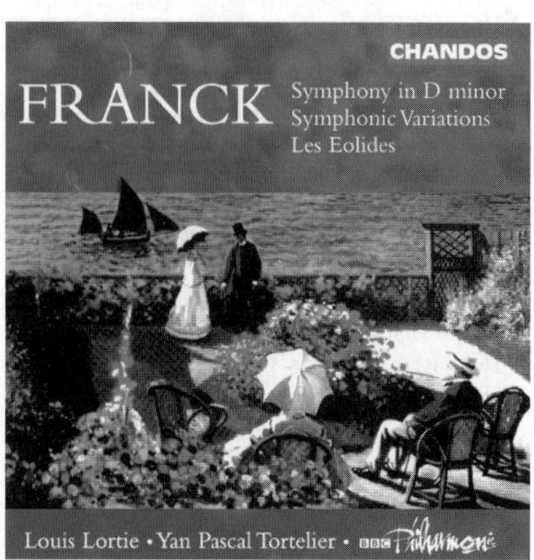

BBC Philharmonic; Tortelier (Chandos; with *Symphonic Variations & Les Eolides*)

One of the great modern interpreters of French music, Yan Pascal Tortelier invests this performance with an immediate sense of mystery and profundity. He's equally convincing at the lighter, more quicksilver moments which he puts over with an insouciant freshness.

Chicago Symphony Orchestra; Monteux (RCA; with Stravinsky *Petrushka*)

Similarly light-footed is Monteux's 1961 account for RCA, re-released as part of a splendid fifteen-disc Monteux Edition, but available as a single CD. This clear-sighted and unfussy account does justice to a work that has suffered at the hands of conductors straining for interpretative novelty.

Symphonic Variations

Often regarded as Franck's masterpiece, the *Symphonic Variations* for piano and orchestra is an engaging showpiece in which Liszt's principle of thematic metamorphosis is once more employed, this time to develop a rather introspective double theme in a miraculous series of transformations, culminating in a breezy final section that is more a full symphonic movement than a mere coda. Unlike Liszt's works for piano and orchestra, there are very few moments of attention-seeking virtuosity, the piano part is often closely integrated with the orchestral writing, and there is an emphasis on sonority of which the best example is the strikingly atmospheric reverie of variation six.

Lortie; BBC Philharmonic; Tortelier (Chandos; with *Symphony in D Minor & Les Eolides*)

The *Symphonic Variations* can sound rather rambling and is a difficult work to pull off convincingly. This performance gets it just right, establishing the perfect balance between the expansive orchestral writing and the more delicate solo part, played with exquisite poise by Louis Lortie.

Curzon; London Philharmonic Orchestra; Boult (Decca; with Brahms *Piano Concerto No. 1*)

Clifford Curzon's 1955 account of the *Symphonic Variations* is highly Romantic but at the same time wonderfully deft and delicate. It comes coupled with his blazing performance of the Brahms *Piano Concerto No. 1*, conducted by Georg Szell.

Piano Quintet

The *Piano Quintet* (1879), written at the beginning of Franck's productive final decade, is his most passionate and personal work and was almost certainly inspired by Augusta Holmès. Franck is sometimes accused of having too much of the solemnity of the organ loft to his music, but in the *Piano Quintet* the rawness of the emotion and the vigour with which it is expressed is overwhelming – harmonies are richly chromatic and it is said to contain more fortissimos and pianissimos than any other chamber work. Saint-Saëns was the pianist at the first performance, but he stomped off immediately afterwards – allegedly annoyed by the work's unpredictable key changes but more likely because he too was an ardent (but rebuffed) admirer of Augusta Holmès.

Levinas; Ludwig Quartet (Naxos; with Chausson *String Quartet*)

With Clifford Curzon's wonderfully passionate version with the Vienna Philharmonic Quartet only available on a four-CD set, this budget recording makes a valuable alternative. The players are more restrained than in the Curzon performance but it's an account that is both fresh-sounding and exciting.

Violin Sonata

Franck's other main chamber piece, the melodious *Violin Sonata* (1886), was written as a wedding present for his fellow Liégeois, the great violinist Eugène Ysaÿe. A triumphant example of cyclic form, it has four movements: a languid Allegretto, which was changed from an Adagio after Ysaÿe convinced Franck it worked better at a faster tempo; a fiery Allegro; a recitative-fantasia recalling earlier themes; and a gentle finale which is one of the finest examples of a canon written after Bach. (The first movement, a serenely resplendent dialogue between violin and piano, may have been the inspiration for Marcel Proust's brilliant description of the sonata by the fictitious composer Vinteuil in his novel *Swann's Way*.)

Chung, Lupu (Decca; with Debussy *Violin Sonata* & Chausson *Poème*)

Kyung Wha Chung's classic account of the *Violin Sonata*, coupled with some fine Debussy and Chausson, is an essential mid-price CD. Chung has the poise for this music, not swooning over the main theme like some of her competitors, and she has a highly sympathetic partner in the pianist Radu Lupu.

Perlman, Ashkenazy (Decca; with Brahms *Horn Trio*)

More than most, Perlman treats Franck's gloriously long-breathed phrases like song. His sense of line, subtle shifts in pace and dynamics have all the naturalness and control of a great opera singer. Ashkenazy is the most sensitive of partners, bold and eloquent but never overwhelming the violin sound.

Organ Works

Franck's reputation as a composer for the organ rests on the masterful series of about a dozen works written in the early 1860s and during the last ten years of his life, most notably the *Prelude, Fugue and Variation* (1862) and the three magisterial *Chorales* (1890). Franck was a prodigiously talented organist, and at the church of Sainte Clotilde (where he played from 1858) he had the advantage of a new organ constructed by the most innovative organ builder in France, Cavaillé-Coll. This allowed for more orchestral scope, and it was in this medium that Franck felt most at home. The organ pieces do not necessarily represent him at his most adventurous and forward-looking, but they nonetheless contain some magnificent music.

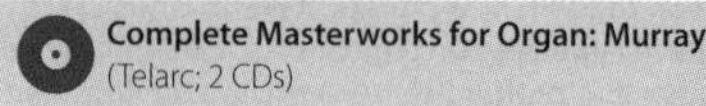

Complete Masterworks for Organ: Murray
(Telarc; 2 CDs)

This two-disc set contains all the major organ works, including the *Prelude, Fugue and Variation* and the *Chorales*. Michael Murray's faithful performances were recorded on a Cavaillé-Coll organ that has changed little since Franck's day.

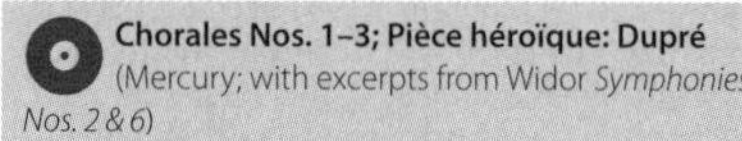

Chorales Nos. 1–3; Pièce héroïque: Dupré
(Mercury; with excerpts from Widor *Symphonies Nos. 2 & 6*)

Marcel Dupré's accounts of the *Chorales* and one of the *Trois Pièces* is more imaginatively played and more sonically impressive – giving little sign that it was recorded as long ago as 1959.

g

Giovanni Gabrieli (c.1553–1612)

Towards the end of the sixteenth century many composers were looking for alternatives to the polyphony that had dominated church music for the last 150 years. Among the new styles to appear was one that was peculiar to the state of Venice, a style that had developed out of the lavish ceremonial music performed at the city's magnificent church of St Mark. This Venetian style was called polychoralism because it employed no fewer than two, and sometimes as many as five, separated choirs (*chori spezzati*), which were placed in different locations around the high altar, including the galleries on each side of it.

Much of the most sumptuous music written for St Mark's in the polychoral style was by Andrea Gabrieli and his nephew Giovanni, both of whom served as organists there. The music itself was homophonic; that is, made up of chords rather than the independent lines of polyphony. Great blocks of sound, with an emphasis on sonorous textures and dramatically varied dynamics, acted as the aural equivalent of the sumptuous but hieratic splendour of St Mark's itself, the most Byzantine of all great European churches. In Giovanni's music the textures were further enriched by the use of instrumental music, especially violins, cornetts (an early wooden version of the trumpet) and sackbuts (close to the modern trombone).

Not much is known about Giovanni Gabrieli's life: he studied with his uncle Andrea and, like him, spent some time at the Munich court of Albrecht V, where he would have worked with Lassus (see p.294). He succeeded Merulo as organist at St Mark's in 1585, and when his uncle died the following year he became the church's principal composer of ceremonial music. He was also an organist at the Scuola di San Rocco, a confraternity given to lavish celebration on its patron saint's day. Much of Gabrieli's music was published in 1597 in a collection titled *Sacrae Symphoniae*, and his subsequent fame led to him being sought out as a teacher, especially by pupils from Germany. The greatest of these was Schütz (see p.508), who assimilated Gabrieli's style and perpetuated it in Germany long after it had been forgotten in Venice. He was obviously a favourite pupil of Gabrieli, since he received a ring from him on his deathbed.

Polychoralism was replaced in Venice by the more eclectic and expressive style of Monteverdi (see p.351), who became *maestro di cappella* at St Mark's a year after Gabrieli's death.

Ceremonial Music

Gabrieli's career coincides with one of the most opulent periods of Venetian history, presided over by one of its most lavish doges, Marino Grimani, who spent colossal amounts on state occasions. Obviously such occasions involved the church, but it was Venice rather than God that was being celebrated, and at St Mark's priests could actually be fined if they interrupted the music. Gabrieli clearly revelled in the musical extravagance that was expected of him, and he was one of the first composers to make highly specific instructions about dynamics: one piece is actually entitled *Sonata pian e forte* (loud and soft sonata). Instrumental music was as important as choral for creating the right atmosphere of solemnity, and St Mark's could muster players of the highest ability. Gabrieli responded by producing music of great virtuosity. Writing mostly canzonas and sonatas – which would have been performed with the organ and from the organ loft – he raised the quality of such music to the same levels of sophistication that already existed in vocal and choral music.

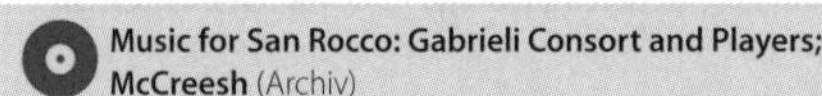

Music for San Rocco: Gabrieli Consort and Players; McCreesh (Archiv)

Paul McCreesh has recorded several of his "reconstructions" of Venetian ceremonial events. This one features music to celebrate the feast day of San Rocco, and is made up almost entirely of music by Gabrieli – including several canzonas, which take on a greater immediacy when performed in context. Recorded at San Rocco, it's an outstanding achievement that communicates a genuine sense of occasion.

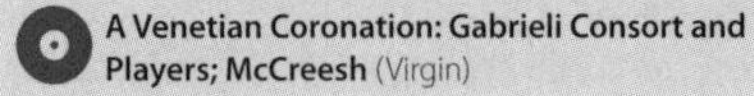

A Venetian Coronation: Gabrieli Consort and Players; McCreesh (Virgin)

Another "reconstruction", this time concentrating on music that might have been performed in St Mark's at the coronation of Marino Grimani in 1595. Slightly less than half the music is by Giovanni Gabrieli, while the rest is a setting of the mass by his uncle Andrea, plus some fanfares and a small amount of plainsong. Beautifully performed, this is a powerfully evocative disc.

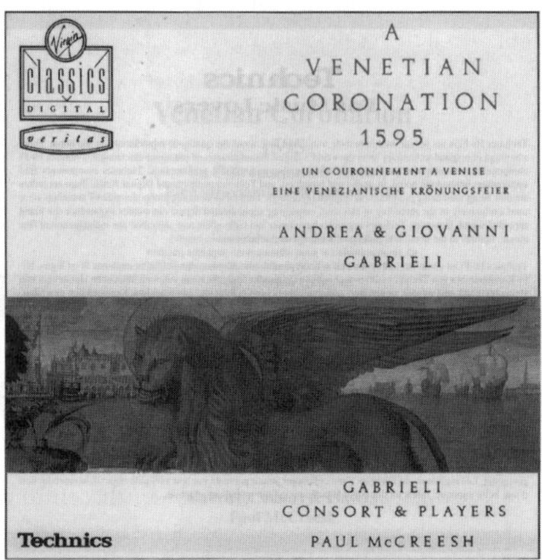

Roberto Gerhard (1896–1970)

One of the most important and distinctive Spanish composers of the twentieth century, Roberto Gerhard absorbed the lessons of atonality while forging a distinct style that always remained in touch with his Catalan musical roots. His music has a luminous clarity of texture, and reveals a vivid awareness of the intense physical impact of instrumental sounds and colours, yet even in his most abstract and experimental works recognizably Catalan fragments of melody and rhythm suddenly emerge when one least expects them.

He was born in Valls into a cosmopolitan family. After studying with the distinguished Spanish composer Felipe Pedrell – a pioneering expert in Spanish folk music – he travelled to Berlin and then Vienna, where he was briefly a student of Schoenberg. A supporter of the Republicans in the Spanish Civil War, he was forced into exile after the victory of the Fascists in 1939, finishing up in Britain, where he spent the rest of his life.

Gerhard's early work shows a deep engagement with Catalan folk music: *Sis cançons populars Catalanes* (1928–29) and *Cancionero del Pedrell* (1941) are both captivating arrangements of Spanish folk songs, and his cantata *L'alta naixença del rei en jaume* (1932) is an ardent affirmation of Catalan nationalism. But Schoenberg's influence was strong, and Gerhard soon adopted his teacher's twelve-tone method. This gradually became tempered, though, with a more flexible approach to atonality, which concentrated not on theme but on texture and colour.

In the 1950s he pioneered electronic music on tape, largely as a result of working in theatre and radio, working closely with the BBC Radiophonic Workshop. The culmination of this work was the *Symphony No. 3* (*"Collages"*) (1960) in which he combined taped sounds with a live orchestra. His experimentation with electronics also had a clear impact on his instrumental music, inspiring an ever wider range of sonorities and textures. His large output includes works in all genres: songs, arrangements, chamber music, cantatas, an opera called *The Duenna* (based on a play by Sheridan), concertos, and, in his last decade, a series of large scale orchestral works which are his finest achievements.

Initially Gerhard's music was little appreciated in the conservative musical environment of post-war Britain but by the mid-1950s, with the support of the BBC (especially its music controller William Glock), he at last began to receive the recognition he deserved, not only in Britain but also in Europe and the US. Regular major commissions began to come his way allowing him to compose the series of large-scale masterpieces of his last decade. Since his centenary in 1996 nearly all of Gerhard's major works have become available on CD.

Orchestral Music

The four symphonies, together with the *Concerto for Orchestra* (1965) and *Epithalamion* (1965–66), are among Gerhard's finest achievements. In these works his orchestration reaches a new level of brilliance in a dazzling kaleidoscope of sounds and textures, and he succeeds completely in creating coherent large-scale orchestral forms unified not thematically but by a balance of texture, colour and rhythm. Gerhard described how the *Symphony No. 3* (1960) was inspired by seeing the sunrise at 30,000 feet on a flight back to Britain, an experience which he described as like hearing "the blast of ten thousand trumpets". In this work Gerhard combines a large orchestra with taped electronic sounds, and the result is a visionary soundscape with a feeling of infinite spaces and distances.

Epithalamion, written at the same time, is a similarly superb showpiece for large orchestra, with a prominent role for the large percussion section. However, its prevailing mood is sombre, despite the fact that its title derives from a wedding ode by Edmund Spenser. Gerhard uses his large forces with great restraint, only on rare occasions unleashing the full weight of the orchestra. In particular, the long slow dialogue between solo flute and strings over slow hypnotic drum beats is one of the most hauntingly beautiful passages he ever wrote.

Symphony No. 3 ("Collages"); Epithalamion: BBC Symphony Orchestra; Bamert, Tozer (Chandos; with *Concerto for Piano and Strings*)

Matthias Bamert and the BBC Symphony Orchestra, who have recorded all Gerhard's symphonies, are ideal interpreters of the finest of the four, revelling in his exuberant sound-world. The balance between tape and orchestra is perfectly judged, and the spacious recording allows Gerhard's massive orchestral gestures to make their full impact. The performance of *Epithalamion* is magnificent, with some ravishing playing from the solo flute.

Chamber Music

The first of Gerhard's two string quartets (1950–55) employed his own personal version of the twelve-tone method, while the second (1960–62) introduced an extraordinary range of odd, percussive sounds, anticipating later experiments with varying combinations of instruments, often including pitched and non-pitched percussion, to create scintillating new sound-worlds. Without question, his best chamber pieces are the works with astrological titles which he wrote in his last decade, the beginning of a projected cycle he did not live to complete. *Gemini* is a dazzling compendium of unorthodox sound effects obtained from the conventional combination of violin and piano. *Libra* (1968), for six players, is very much a self-portrait (it was his own astrological sign), in which a Spanish flavour is clearly discernible in the prominent guitar part, with its rapid, loud flamenco-style strumming and plangent fragments of melody. *Libra* ends with a haunting quasi-modal melody on the clarinet accompanied by mysterious glissandi on timpani, guitar and violin, a passage which reappears in a slightly different scoring at the end of *Leo* (his wife's star sign), Gerhard's last completed work.

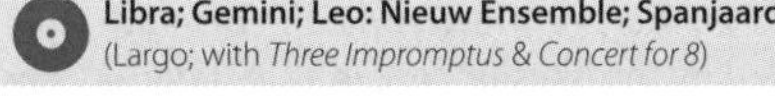

Libra; Gemini; Leo: Nieuw Ensemble; Spanjaard (Largo; with *Three Impromptus* & *Concert for 8*)

These superb performances brim with rhythmic energy and life, especially in Gerhard's valedictory masterpieces *Leo* and *Libra*. All the performances do full justice to Gerhard's unerring ear for novel and utterly effective instrumental effects. The close recording gives a presence to the instrumental sound that suits this music very well. This CD is the best introduction to Gerhard's fascinating sound-world.

George Gershwin (1898–1937)

Like many other songwriters who held sway over American popular music in the 1920s and 1930s, George Gershwin was a New Yorker of European-Jewish extraction. During his boyhood his family was constantly on the move from one Manhattan tenement to another, and his parents were far too busy trying to support their children to have much time for any cultural pursuits. The young George, however, had a home-grown artistic collaborator in the shape of his older brother Ira, who in later years was to write the lyrics to most of his classic songs. The purchase by the Gershwins of their first piano in 1910 was to change George's life. Originally intended for Ira, the instrument was soon monopolized by George, who quickly went through a variety of neighbourhood piano teachers, rapidly outgrowing what each one had to offer.

By the age of 16 Gershwin had dropped out of business school and was working on Tin Pan Alley as a plugger of other people's songs. In 1919 he had his first hit with "Swanee", taken from his comedy *La La Lucille*. It was the start of an unending stream of hit shows, peppered with songs that are a roll-call of twentieth-century popular music's high points, including "Fascinatin' Rhythm", "Someone to Watch Over Me" and "Lady be Good".

But despite the money and fame Gershwin was not satisfied. Fascinated since childhood by classical music, he started to entertain the idea of writing extended instrumental works that would use American musical forms, like ragtime, blues and jazz, to convey the vibrant everyday life of the American people. The catalyst for this new departure was provided by the band leader Paul Whiteman, who invited Gershwin to contribute a piece to a concert advertised as "An Experiment in Modern Music". In under a month Gershwin wrote his *Rhapsody in Blue*, and he played the piano part himself at the premiere on 12 February, 1924. Attended by the likes of Toscanini, Stravinsky and Rachmaninov, the concert was a sensation, and it made Gershwin famous overnight.

From that time on his reputation was sealed, although he occasionally had periods of insecurity that drove him to snatch lessons wherever he could. On a trip to Paris he even approached Ravel for tuition. Ravel's answer was: "Why do you want to become a second-rate Ravel when you're already a first-class Gershwin?" Legend has it that he also asked Stravinsky for compositional guidance, but that the latter, upon hearing what the young man earned in one year ("about 250,000 dollars"), asked him for lessons instead.

Apart from Stravinsky, the classical composers who most fascinated Gershwin in the mid-1920s were Schoenberg and Berg, yet it was the music produced by the group of French composers known as Les Six which directly inspired the half-jazzy, half-classical *An American in Paris* (1928). His final "serious" work, the opera *Porgy and Bess* (premiered in Boston on 30 September, 1935), was not universally popular at first – some eminent black

Gershwin playing the piano on the roof of a Miami hotel.

composers, including Duke Ellington, were less than complimentary – but its array of wonderful songs has ensured its place on the stage ever since.

With *Porgy* he had gone further than ever in fusing popular and classical styles, and at no cost to his mass audience appeal. But at this peak in his career Gershwin was cut down with a brain tumour while working on his third Hollywood film score, *The Goldwyn Follies*. Among those who most keenly felt the loss was his friend Arnold Schoenberg, who said of Gershwin: "Music was what made him feel, and music was the feeling he expressed. Directness of this kind is given only to great men, and there is no doubt that he was a great composer."

Porgy and Bess

It would have been easy for Gershwin to go on repeating the formula that had made his musical comedies such successes, but in 1926 he came across a novel called *Porgy and Bess* by Dubose Heyward, and the book immediately fired his imagination. He soon determined to turn this story of a South Carolina black community into an opera – "If I am successful", he wrote, "it will resemble a combination of the drama and romance of *Carmen* and the beauty of *Meistersinger*." He succeeded beyond all expectations: just as in *Carmen* there are plenty of beautiful songs, effortlessly woven into the score, and like *Meistersinger* it displays a highly skilful use of leitmotifs and large choral numbers, creating a sense of tight community in Catfish Row similar to that in Wagner's Nuremberg. It didn't please everybody, though: jazz fans were dismissive of his use of African-American music, while opera critics complained that it was just a string of hit tunes. Gershwin responded to this last charge by pointing out that "nearly all of Verdi's operas contain what are known as 'song hits'". He might have added that few twentieth-century composers of any type had written songs as tuneful and powerful as "Summertime", "I Got Plenty o' Nuttin", "Bess You is My Woman" and "It Ain't Necessarily So".

Carey, Haymon, Blackwell, Evans, White; Glyndebourne Chorus; London Philharmonic Orchestra; Rattle (EMI; 3 CDs)

Based closely on the Glyndebourne production, this recording has a highly spontaneous feel to it with an exhilarating atmosphere. Under Rattle's exuberant direction the LPO inject just the right rhythmic fluidity into their playing, while all the main roles are brilliantly characterized. There is also a highlights disc available.

Rhapsody in Blue

Paul Whiteman had achieved enormous success by diluting jazz in order to make it acceptable to white middle-class Americans. In commissioning *Rhapsody in Blue* he wanted to go further and make it acceptable to a classical audience (probably unaware that Milhaud had got there a few months earlier with *La création du monde*). His 1924 concert "An Experiment in Modern Music" was a success largely because Gershwin's work (programmed near the end) came as a blast of exuberant and original energy amid the anodyne orchestral arrangements of popular songs that made up the rest of the programme. Consisting of one long movement (loosely divided into three sections – fast/slow/fast), the *Rhapsody in Blue* is essentially a collection of inspired show tunes connected by the kind of virtuosic effects that wouldn't be out of place in a Liszt piano concerto. Orchestration was by Whiteman's arranger Ferde Grofé, and the famous wailing glissando on the clarinet which opens the work emerged in rehearsal. None of which alters the fact that it still makes an incredible and immediate impact, especially in Grofé's original orchestration.

Previn; London Symphony Orchestra (EMI; with *Piano Concerto in F & An American in Paris*)

This is not an easy work to pull off: both orchestra and soloist need to shake off their inhibitions without being brash and noisy – in the right hands *Rhapsody in Blue* is extremely sexy music. André Previn makes an ideal interpreter: his own experience as a jazz pianist means that the Gershwin style offers no surprises. This is a fresh, exhilarating and utterly idiomatic performance.

Piano Concerto in F

The conductor Walter Damrosch was at the Whiteman concert and as a result Gershwin was commissioned to compose a "proper" piano concerto for the New York Symphony Orchestra. In fact, though there is greater thematic development and the work is divided into clear-cut movements, the mixture is very much as before – a combination of a Romantic-style concerto, Dixieland rhythms, and the melancholy of both the blues and Yiddisher popular music. Gershwin described it thus: "The first movement employs the Charleston rhythm. It is quick and pulsating, representing the young and enthusiastic spirit of American life ... The second movement has a poetic nocturnal atmosphere ... The final movement reverts to the style of the first. It is an orgy of rhythms, starting violently and keeping to the same pace throughout."

Previn; London Symphony Orchestra (EMI; with *Rhapsody in Blue & An American in Paris*)

Previn is equally impressive in the concerto: light-touched and spring-heeled, never wallowing in the more sentimental passages, and above all tapping into the humour that seems to elude so many performers.

An American in Paris

Gershwin's third orchestral work (again premiered by Damrosch) was clearly inspired by two trips that he made to Paris: "My purpose here is to portray the impressions of an American visitor in Paris as he strolls about the city, listens to the various street noises, and absorbs the French atmosphere." It is thus a kind of easy-going tone poem, unspecific in programme, though Gershwin did purchase some genuinely French car horns to add to its authentically urban feel. There's also a much more assured sense of structure than in his previous orchestral works, with less of a stop-start feel to it. Gershwin thought of it as a "rhapsodic ballet" and its combination of wide-eyed innocence and brash boulevardier spirit were perfectly captured by Gene Kelly's choreography in the 1951 film inspired by the piece.

Previn; London Symphony Orchestra (EMI; with *Piano Concerto in F & Rhapsody in Blue*)

Again this is a work that demands complete sympathy and understanding of the idiom for it not to sound heavy-footed and pedestrian. It certainly gets it in this kaleidoscopic performance, which brings out all the jauntiness and sleaze that you could possibly want.

Carlo Gesualdo (c.1561–1613)

The music of Carlo Gesualdo is among the strangest ever written. Even in the context of a period when composers were constantly experimenting with ways of enlivening the words they set, his music startles through its bizarre and almost neurotic sensitivity to meaning. His later madrigals – in which chromaticism and dissonance are the norm – make for especially fascinating but at times uncomfortable listening. The eccentricity of the music is mirrored by the details of Gesualdo's extraordinary life.

Gesualdo was a member of one of the principal families of the Neapolitan aristocracy, inheriting the title of Prince of Venosa on the death of his elder brother in 1586. Shortly after, having obtained special papal permission, he married his cousin, the twice-widowed Maria d'Avalos. Four years later Gesualdo discovered that his wife was conducting an affair with the Duke of Andria. One night, having left his palace on the pretext of a hunting trip, he returned home suddenly and found the lovers in bed together, whereupon he had them both murdered – allegedly skewered on a single sword. Gesualdo escaped punishment but this event seems to have overshadowed the rest of his life. Although he married again, he seems to have become increasingly melancholic, largely cut off from society in the isolation of his castle in southern Italy. In his later years he became excessively devout and had himself regularly scourged.

It was not unusual for members of the aristocracy to be musically adept, but it was rare for them to pursue their interest as single-mindedly as Gesualdo did. In 1593 his second marriage, to Leonora d'Este (who later tried to divorce him for his violent behaviour towards her), brought him into close contact with the Duke of Ferrara (Leonora's brother). Ferrara was a lively artistic centre with a particularly strong

The Madrigal History Tour

Vocal compositions described as madrigals were written and performed throughout the Renaissance: as early as the 1320s, when a homespun style of secular music first emerged in northern Italy, and as late as the early 1600s, when madrigals reached a pinnacle of expressiveness and sophistication. However, not much connects the late sixteenth-century madrigal and its older, simpler counterpart. The earliest surviving fourteenth-century madrigals are two- or three-voice pieces, settings of pastoral texts with little ambition to seriousness, and by the end of the century they had largely passed out of fashion. The origins of the word itself are obscure: despite efforts to find a pastoral root (from the Latin mandra, meaning "flock"), it's more likely to derive from matrix, "mother" – indicating that the songs were sung in Italian dialect (the "mother" tongue), rather than Latin, the language of Church, power and politics.

Yet even if early and late examples have little in common, it was enthusiasm for poetry written in the fourteenth century that encouraged the development of a new kind of madrigal two hundred years later. One spur came when Pietro Bembo (1470–1547) promoted the writing of Dante Alighieri, Francesco Petrarca (Petrarch in English) and others as the model for modern poets to follow. It was Bembo's 1501 edition of the poems (revealingly entitled the *Canzoniere*, or "songbook") that introduced many composers to Petrarch's work, and which later became the basis for countless madrigal settings. Of later writers, only Giovanni Battista Guarini (1538–1612), the author of the pastoral drama *Il pastor fido*, would rival Petrarch in popularity with composers.

Among the earliest musicians to respond to Petrarch's combination of literary refinement and torrid psychological realism were Philippe Verdelot, Constanzo Festa and Jacques Arcadelt, all of whom worked for the powerful Medici dynasty in Florence in the 1530s and whose work – much of it in four parts, and designed for unaccompanied private performance – circulated together in manuscript. Arcadelt in particular honed the madrigal into a poetically expressive form: his most celebrated madrigal, "Il bianco e dolce cigno" (The Sweet White Swan) is an early example of expressive musical "word-painting".

A determination to spotlight the text persisted with the next generation of Italian madrigalists, but they also stretched musical boundaries much further, writing for five or six voices and experimenting with imaginative polyphonic structures. Cipriano de Rore (1516–75), a Flemish composer who spent most of his working life in Italy at the courts of Ferrara (see p.553) and Parma, crafted highly polished madrigals, often using pungent chromaticism to illuminate the texts he set. By contrast, the Venetian Andrea Gabrieli (c.1533–86), uncle of Giovanni (see p.199), developed a "hybrid" style of madrigal, lighter and more musically immediate, in which pastoral verses again began to dominate. Gabrieli's style was followed by Luca Marenzio (c.1553–99), who produced no fewer than nine books of madrigals, many of which showcase the brilliant virtuosity of his singers and suggest that the madrigal was gradually becoming a species of enjoyable concert music.

Marenzio's late compositions announce a move back towards more serious matter – a direction that was decisively followed by the last great Italian madrigalists of the period, Claudio Monteverdi (1567–1643), Carlo Gesualdo (c.1561–1613) and Sigismondo D'India (c.1582–1629). When one commentator saw fit to criticize Monteverdi's style for being off-kilter, Monteverdi responded by announcing what he called the *seconda prattica* (second manner), a compositional style that strove to squeeze out every nuance of emotional meaning from the words (see p.355). But even Monteverdi rarely went as far as Gesualdo, some of whose madrigals are so harmonically audacious that they seem to foreshadow the atonality of Schoenberg and other modernists.

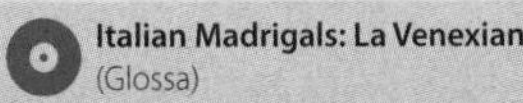

Italian Madrigals: La Venexiana
(Glossa)

This sampler disc by the outstanding vocal group La Venexiana is the perfect introduction to the beauties of the Italian madrigal, with pieces by Monteverdi, Luzzaschi, Marenzio and Sigismondo D'India extracted from the group's single discs of these composers. Currently out of the catalogue, snap it up if a copy comes your way.

Il Pastor Fido: Cantus Cölln; Junghänel
(Deutsche Harmonia Mundi)

This CD comprises settings of Guarini's influential verse drama *Il pastor fido* (The Faithful Shepherd) by madrigalists ranging from the well-known (Marenzio and Monteverdi) to the more obscure (Casentini and Saracini). Cantus Cölln employ one voice per part but their approach is slightly more expressive. The one drawback is that no texts are supplied.

musical tradition (see p.5553). Here he met Luzzasco Luzzaschi, a skilled madrigalist and one of a succession of Ferrara-based composers who were concerned with finding ever more expressive settings for words. A favoured means of achieving this greater intensity was through chromaticism – in other words, composers began exploiting the interval of the semitone, with the result that the progress of the music became less predictable and regularly threw up peculiar harmonies. This was the catalyst that Gesualdo needed: before Ferrara his work is interesting but relatively conventional; after Ferrara it becomes increasingly original and, at moments, extreme.

Back at his castle, Gesualdo intensified his musical activities, surrounding himself with musicians, including his equerry, Count Alfonso Fontanelli, and Pomponio Nenna, a madrigalist (previously employed by the Duke of Andria) whose work is often very similar to Gesualdo's. Recent Gesualdo scholarship has attempted to downplay his oddity by linking him to a tradition, fostered in the academies of Naples, for musical experimentation.

Madrigals

Gesualdo wrote six books of madrigals, the best of which – books three to six – were written after his return from Ferrara. His favoured texts were usually short and dealt, almost exclusively, with death and the sufferings of love. They tend to be set so that the most highly charged words are always dramatically emphasized, either by dissonance or a change of speed or an unexpected modulation. Unlike Dowland's similarly morbid songs, where consistency of mood invites the listener's identification, Gesualdo's madrigals are distinguished by disruptive and restless changes of mood, so that the end result is rather like eavesdropping on some unresolvable, private agony.

One of his best-known madrigals, "Moro, lasso", is typical of his approach to word-painting. The opening theme of death is conveyed by a series of startling chromatic progressions, followed by a sudden lightening of mood that is underlined by a rapid ornamental flourish on the word "vita" (life). A dramatic shift from major to minor signals the appearance of a new idea – the denial of help to the suffering lover. The last section is a lament over the lover's fate and consists of short outbursts, which gradually build up to a final resolution on the word "morte". It is possible that "death" has a sexual connotation here; the anguished cries of "ahi" and the mounting tension would certainly bear this out.

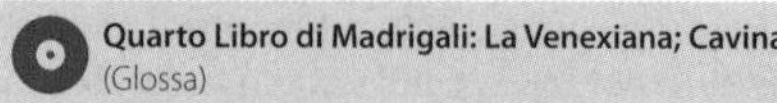

Quarto Libro di Madrigali: La Venexiana; Cavina
(Glossa)

This disc provides the whole of book four of the madrigals in performances that are beautifully controlled and with marginally less emotional underlining than Concerto Italiano employ (see below). Both ensembles adopt one voice to a part which adds to the almost claustrophobic intensity of this music.

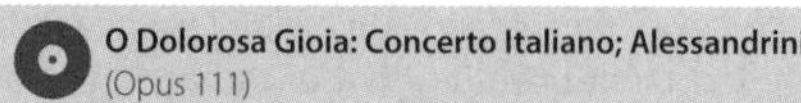

O Dolorosa Gioia: Concerto Italiano; Alessandrini
(Opus 111)

This recording features madrigals from books five and six alongside works by contemporary composers Nenna, Monte and Luzzaschi, setting Gesualdo's work in context. The five solo voices of the Concerto Italiano are perfectly balanced and their sonorous tone is well suited to the intensity of Gesualdo's music which they invest with just the right amount of drama and emotion.

Sacred Music

Gesualdo appears to have been a devoutly religious man – he greatly admired his uncle Carlo Borromeo (later St Carlo Borromeo), a leading figure behind the Council of Trent and a patron of Palestrina (see p.396). Church music accounts for about a quarter of Gesualdo's output, and although it is sombre and restrained in comparison with his madrigals, it still carries a far greater sense of the personal and extravagant than that of his contemporaries. Motet settings of gloomy and penitential texts – chosen presumably to reflect his own predicament – comprise the bulk of these works, and stylistically they tend to follow the pattern of Palestrina, but with occasional startling changes of speed that break up the meditative stillness. His greatest religious work, and the closest to his madrigal writing, is the set of responses for Holy Week, published in 1611.

Tenebrae: Hilliard Ensemble
(ECM New Series; 2 CDs)

The Hilliard Ensemble's celebrated disc presents all the music that Gesualdo wrote for the Tenebrae services of Holy Week (including the Holy Week music reviewed above). This is the most anguished moment in the Christian calendar and the music perfectly matches the intensity of the mood. The performance is immaculate: heartfelt but not over-demonstrative, and perfectly judged in terms of both phrasing and intonation.

Orlando Gibbons (1583–1625)

Gibbons was the outstanding composer of English church music in the generation that succeeded William Byrd. He excelled as a writer of anthems (the English equivalent of Latin motets), building on Byrd's richest and most demonstrative Anglican settings to produce his own vigorous and expressive musical language. He was also a renowned composer of keyboard music, notable for its contrapuntal rigour and inventiveness, and as a keyboard player he was described by the French ambassador as "the best hand in England".

He was born in Oxford into a musical family: his father William was a player in the city band and his brother Edward was master of the choristers at King's College Cambridge, where Orlando served as a chorister and later studied as an undergraduate. In 1603 he joined the Chapel Royal in London and became organist there some two years later – a position he held until his death. His success continued with preferment at court: a gift of £150 in 1615, and four years later an appointment as "one of his Majesty's musicians … to attend in his highnes privie chamber". In April 1625, as organist of Westminster Abbey, he played at the funeral of King James I, and two months later was summoned to Canterbury as part of the royal household to await the arrival from France of King Charles I's new bride, Queen Henrietta Maria. On Whit Sunday, a few days before the queen's arrival, Gibbons died suddenly from an apoplectic fit and was buried in Canterbury Cathedral.

Sacred Music

By Gibbons' time English was the language of the liturgy in Britain, and the anthem had become the main choral display piece. There were two forms: the full anthem, which was closest to the motet, was a polyphonic piece for full choir – *Hosanna to the Son of David* is probably the best known example – while the more dramatic verse anthem contrasted solo sections with choral sections, both accompanied by either organ or strings. Gibbons' most dramatically appealing music is found in his verse anthems, of which the finest, *This is the Record of John*, is a gentle yet compelling narrative, sung for the most part by an alto soloist with the chorus echoing the closing chords of each section. It is a peculiarly English mixture of solo and choral interplay, pointing the way towards Purcell's more dramatic style.

Gibbons also wrote two settings of the Evening Service (Magnificat and Nunc Dimittis): the first is a homophonic but highly tuneful setting for full choir, the second is a more elaborate version with several verses.

Anthems: Winchester Cathedral Choir; Blaze, Varcoe; Hill (Hyperion)

At last a recording that really does justice to this marvellous music. David Hill is one of the most talented of British choir directors and the Winchester choristers have a wonderful rounded tone that is perfectly suited to this subtle music, and which is perfectly captured by Hyperion's engineers. Robin Blaze is the understated but highly effective soloist in *This is the Record of John*.

Instrumental Music

Gibbons was a versatile and wide-ranging composer. Along with Byrd and John Bull he contributed to *Parthenia* (1613), the first collection of keyboard music to be published in England. He also wrote thirty or so pieces for viols using three, four and sometimes five instruments supported by a keyboard – either a small organ or more commonly a harpsichord. These included a handful of *In Nomines*, which took as their starting point a melodic fragment from a mass by John Taverner (see p.571).

In both keyboard and consort music, Gibbons' preferred form was the fantasia, a freely composed work in several sections, described by Thomas Morley in 1597 as "…when a musician taketh a point at his pleasure and wresteth and turneth it as he list…" Fantasias were the most common form of instrumental music in seventeenth-century England and in the hands of a master like Gibbons were developed using imitative counterpoint in a highly imaginative fashion. Less melancholic than Dowland's instrumental music and less cerebral than Byrd's, some have seen Gibbons' fantasias as anticipating J.S. Bach in the way formal adventurousness is combined with deep feeling.

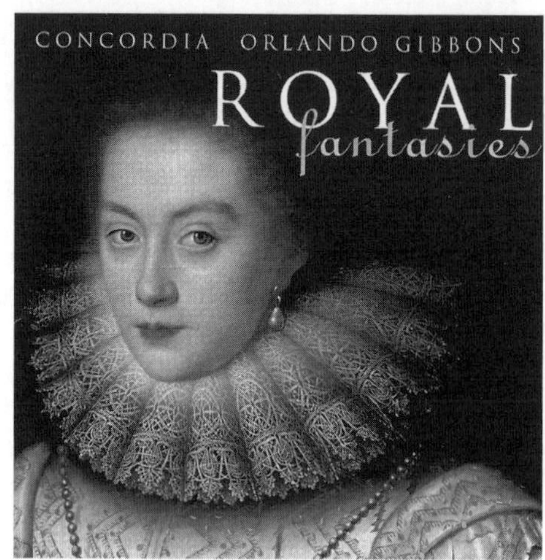

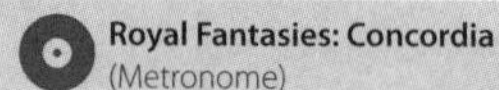

Royal Fantasies: Concordia
(Metronome)

This is the first volume of a complete survey of Gibbons' consort music by the outstanding group Concordia who really communicate the richness and variety of this music. Their sound is light and sinewy, and they favour an expressive approach (with discreet harpsichord support) which is never overbearing.

The Woods So Wild: Toll
(Linn)

The inventive genius of Gibbons the keyboard composer is vividly conveyed in John Toll's exquisite and imaginative playing. Of the 24 works included here, just over half are played on a bright and unclattery harpsichord, the rest (mainly fantasias and preludes) on a recently restored early English organ of great charm.

Umberto Giordano (1867–1948)

As is the case with several *verismo* composers (such as Leoncavallo and Mascagni), Umberto Giordano's name has survived on the strength of a single opera. Typically for an Italian composer of his time, Giordano was drawn to opera almost from the start, and his early life was spent battling with parents who strongly objected to his pursuing a life in music. It was not until 1890 that he graduated from the Naples Conservatory, but by then he had already completed his first opera, the one-act *Marina*, which he had submitted as an entry in the 1889 Sonzogno opera competition. *Marina* fared no better than sixth place, but it secured him a commission for a full-length work, the result of which, *Mala vita*, was one of the most sensational of all *verismo* operas, with a plot that contrived to bring together a prostitute and the Virgin Mary. It was violent, crude and, for a short time, extremely popular.

His next opera, *Regina Diaz*, was ditched after only two performances, but in 1896, having moved to the warmer audiences in Milan, Giordano composed his masterpiece, *Andrea Chénier*. Unfortunately its premiere came less than two months after the first staging, also in Milan, of Puccini's *La Bohème*, and *Chénier* was inevitably overshadowed to a large extent. Nonetheless, *Chénier* brought its composer considerable acclaim, and two years later he produced another extremely popular opera, *Fedora* – a work which gave rise to the witticism "Fedora fè d'oro" (Fedora made money). Its success was guaranteed when Caruso, who sang on the first night, gave a thrilling performance of the opera's only tenor aria "Amor ti vieta", which was so well received that he was obliged to sing it twice.

Of his other operas, only *Madame Sans-Gêne* achieved anything like the success of *Andrea Chénier* or *Fedora*, and he composed his last, *Il re*, in 1929. For the remaining nineteen years of his life he composed nothing but songs and a few light salon pieces.

Andrea Chénier

Like Puccini, Giordano was heavily influenced by the lyricism of Massenet but he is on the whole less subtle than both – he was generally at his best when writing fervent music for fervent situations. Yet with *Andrea Chénier* he created a group of three-dimensional personalities, a string of memorable tunes, and some of the most dramatic scenes in all opera.

The eponymous hero is based upon the real-life Andrea Chénier, an eminent poet in Revolutionary France, but the events are a romanticized tale of love across the social classes, political intrigue, injustice and tragic death. There are some remarkable moments in the course of the four acts – notably Chénier's improvised poem "Un di all'azzuro spazio" in Act 1, his beloved's Act Three aria "La mamma morta" (used to great effect in the film *Philadelphia*), and Chénier's reflection on his imminent death, "Come un bel di di Maggio" – but the overall orchestration and pacing are just right as well. The eighteenth-century pastiche shows a masterly understanding of the orchestra and Giordano's word-setting must have been the envy of all his contemporaries, excepting Puccini. *Andrea Chénier*'s absence from the opera-house stage has more to do with a dearth of genuine heroic tenors than with any intrinsic weaknesses in the music.

Corelli, Stella, Sereni, De Palma; Rome Opera Chorus and Orchestra; Santini (EMI; 2 CDs)

Andrea Chénier is the part Franco Corelli was born to perform and he sings it here at the peak of his form. Full and baritonal, his voice is nonetheless capable of glass-breaking heights. His two big solos are sung with all the self-indulgent but thrilling mannerisms for which his performances were so memorable, while the final "Vicino a te" is uniquely moving.

Philip Glass (1937–)

Philip Glass is the most famous and financially successful serious composer alive, thanks mainly to the instant accessibility of his brand of minimalism. Whether he's writing for ballet, opera, theatre, film or even for a TV jingle, Glass's style is unmistakable, with its repetitions of cell-like phrases, often built from brightly coloured keyboard sounds enhanced by soothing vocals and bright horns. Though often criticized as shallow and uneventful, Glass's music is insidiously effective – and hugely catchy.

Of immigrant Jewish parentage, Glass grew up in Baltimore and got a taste for commercial music when he sold Elvis Presley records in his father's music store. He was an accomplished flautist and violinist by the age of 15, when he attended Chicago University to major in maths and philosophy. By the late 1950s he was in New York studying with Steve Reich (see p.448) at the Juilliard School, and went on to study with Darius Milhaud (see p350) at Aspen and Nadia Boulanger in Paris.

While in Paris, Glass assisted sitarist Ravi Shankar with the soundtrack for Conrad Rooks' film *Chappaqua*. Received wisdom says that minimalism was a reaction against the dry, elitist modernist schools, but Glass explains it somewhat differently: "There was a generation about ten years older than me, like Xenakis, Stockhausen and Boulez, who were so damn good at what they did that there was no need to write any more of that kind of music. Working with Ravi, I saw there was another way music could be organized, around rhythmic ideas instead of around structure. Rhythm could be the structural basis of the music instead of just an ornament."

Returning to New York in 1967, Glass threw himself into the bohemian art scene, giving loft concerts with Terry Riley and Steve Reich, and forming the Philip Glass Ensemble. From this period came *Music in Similar Motion* (1969) and *Music in Changing Parts* (1970), both written for organs, flute, trumpet and saxes, and combining rock-type grooves with perpetual drones, all played at incredible volume.

Glass's breakthrough as a theatrical composer came when he met theatre conceptualist Robert Wilson, with whom he produced the hallucinogenic four-hour opera *Einstein on the Beach* (1976). A sellout at the Met, this was the work that pushed minimalism into the mainstream. Assisted by engineer Kurt Munkacsi, Glass built up a reputation for technical brilliance in the studio, and his first digital album, *Glassworks* (1982), was a hit across a wide spectrum of musical taste. On a larger scale, the operas *Satyagraha* (1980) and *Akhnaten* (1984), drawing on the lives of Gandhi, Tolstoy, Martin Luther King and a sun-worshipping Egyptian pharaoh, completed the trilogy begun with *Einstein*, and thrillingly combined his trademark repetitions and overlappings with the ceremonial grandeur of the stage.

Amongst the most stimulating projects of the 1990s were his reunion with Ravi Shankar, *Passages* (1991), in which each gave the other basic material to expand into full compositions, and the 1998 collaboration with Robert Wilson, *Monsters of Grace*, an audiovisual extravaganza based on

Philip Glass at the Kiev Restaurant, New York, 1993.

the writings of the thirteenth-century Sufi poet Rumi. The decade also saw him embark on works in conventional classical forms, including the symphony (he has written seven so far, including two based on the albums *Low* and *Heroes* by David Bowie and Brian Eno) and the concerto (two for piano and one for cello).

Glass currently lives in the East Village, where he spends each morning composing before taking the short stroll to his hi-tech Living Room Studios where he oversees record production and the rehearsal of opera and ensemble pieces. As the first composer to develop a production-line system, which uses sampling techniques so that every musical sketch can be speedily turned into finished product, he continues to maintain a brisk rate of output.

Akhnaten

Glass is fascinated by visionaries, by people who have changed the world by the sheer force of their ideas. Einstein and Gandhi formed the basis of the first two operas in his epic trilogy; for the third he turned to Velikovsky's book *Oedipus and Akhnaten*. The original idea was to have two operas on stage simultaneously, one telling the story of Oedipus and the other that of Akhnaten, but in the end Glass decided to focus on the latter, and his attempt to introduce monotheistic religion to Egypt. Glass's omission of violins from the score creates a dark, warm sound which – along with some stunning music for brass – perfectly evokes the mysterious and the exotic. This orchestral sound also contrasts with the solo voices and emphasizes the otherworldly quality of the music for Akhnaten himself – sung by a countertenor. *Akhnaten* is one of Glass's most majestic, lyrical works, with several long-limbed, graceful arias leavening the familiar restless, staccato instrumental music, and even without the visual spectacle it's a compelling experience.

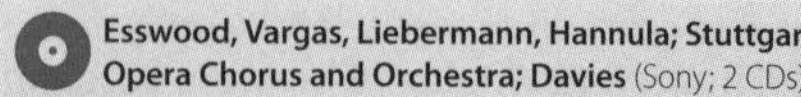

Esswood, Vargas, Liebermann, Hannula; Stuttgart Opera Chorus and Orchestra; Davies (Sony; 2 CDs)

Russell Davies here conducts many of the original cast from the Stuttgart premiere of *Akhnaten*. Paul Esswood makes the pharaoh a convincing and touching figure, and the remaining players are all well cast. However, *Akhnaten* is an opera in which the orchestra is the leading voice and the Stuttgart players really rise to the occasion.

Koyaanisqatsi

In his work for film Glass insists on working on a project from the beginning, so that "the music has a totally functional relation to the image. It's not something that's carved out and stuck on a film, they're made together." Glass has worked with Schrader (*Mishima*) and Scorsese (*Kundun*), but the best known of his soundtracks were written for Godfrey Reggio's non-narrative documentaries *Koyaanisqatsi* and *Powaaqatsi*. *Koyaanisqatsi*, filmed entirely in North America, was a portrait of the US seen in terms of an imbalance of technology (the title is a Hopi word meaning "life out of balance"). It used filmic devices like freeze-frame and slow motion to create a mesmeric visual impression, which is perfectly matched by Glass's hypnotic score. Much of the music is filled with Glass's typically restless and rippling surfaces but it is the slower, more reflective moments that stay in the memory, in particular the title track – a slow portentous organ and deep chanting voices – which is reprised at the end of the film over a haunting image of rocket remains slowly tumbling to Earth.

Glass, Western Wind Vocal Ensemble; The Philip Glass Ensemble
(Elektra Nonesuch)

This 1998 re-recording contains considerably more of the film's soundtrack than the earlier Island recording, although the personnel is very similar – Glass's band augmented by brass, strings and the Western Wind Vocal Ensemble. What has improved almost beyond recognition is the sound quality which is startlingly fresh and brilliant.

Music in Twelve Parts

Written between 1971 and 1974, *Music in Twelve Parts* summed up Glass's work so far, while signalling a change of direction. The music still has all the characteristics of stereotypical minimalism: short, repetitive motifs rather than legato melodies, little harmonic variety, relentless rhythms and hard, glittering textures. But it was also "a breakthrough", Glass commented, containing "many of the structural and harmonic ideas that would be fleshed out in later works." Part One, written in 1971, was originally intended to stand alone. The most meditative of the twelve pieces, the strands of its twelve-voice counterpoint create an acoustical phenomenon that especially fascinated Glass: overlapping figures suggesting a drone of a fifth that is not actually written into the music. He continued with the series and with Part Eight had completed what he had set out to do; the final four parts pursue a slightly different direction. The twelve parts are modular – designed to be played in any sequence or combination. Overall it lasts more than three hours, but it's a crucial part of the Glass canon and should be heard.

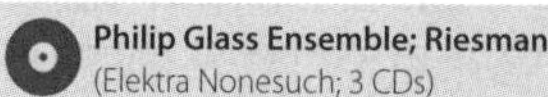

Philip Glass Ensemble; Riesman
(Elektra Nonesuch; 3 CDs)

This set, recorded in 1993, is markedly more human than the original Virgin recordings in which the performances had the precision and, in many passages, the coldness of machines. The sound is softer and the effect is more hypnotic and less forbidding than the earlier version.

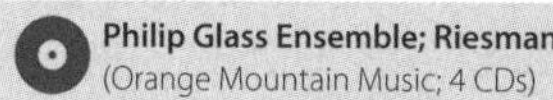

Philip Glass Ensemble; Riesman
(Orange Mountain Music; 4 CDs)

This 2006 recording, cut live in Italy, retains the honed pizzazz of earlier versions, but adds "lived in" seasoning to the ensemble sound. Listen to the near-Lisztian virtuosity of Part Six and those "wrong note" key changes in the final part – Glass, purveyor of soporific arpeggios? Not in this soulful performance.

Book of Longing

Premiered at Toronto's Luminato Festival in 2007, *Book of Longing* is a collaboration between Glass and songwriter Leonard Cohen. It functions as a song cycle crossed with an oratorio as the sentiments of Cohen's poetry, recited by the man himself, are amplified by a quartet of singers and Glass's own ensemble. As earlier projects with Allen Ginsberg and Patti Smith had already demonstrated, Glass moves beyond the margins of "classical" performance with ease. Cohen, however, wryly commented: "This work is like a bumble bee. Aerodynamically it really shouldn't fly but, somehow, it does." And it flies because Glass and Cohen – two phenomenally successful Jewish men in their early seventies, both interested in other faiths, and with an apparently undiminished appetite for the fairer sex – are in complete empathy, as they ponder their Jewish heritage and the challenges of growing (relatively) old.

Cohen, Plaisant, Hugo, Erat, Keeling; Philip Glass Ensemble; Riesman
(Orange Mountain Music)

Recorded shortly after that first performance in Toronto, this recording of *Book of Longing* sounds bedded-in and assured. The rich, peachy tones of Leonard Cohen's speaking voice have unique majesty, while an extraordinary group of vocalists pitch in somewhere between pukka classical diction and Broadway theatrics.

Alexander Glazunov (1865–1936)

Glazunov is best known for things other than his own compositions: for helping complete some of Borodin's music, for example, or for teaching Shostakovich, or for conducting the premiere of Rachmaninov's first symphony while allegedly drunk and thereby triggering the young composer's nervous breakdown. With its undisguised assimilations of Tchaikovsky, Rimsky-Korsakov and Scriabin, Glazunov's music might not have the individuality of the music of some of his compatriots, yet it is often attractive and colourful, and it brought him worldwide acclaim in his day.

Glazunov's main problem was his conservatism. This was the charge laid against him long ago by both Prokofiev and Shostakovich, and there is no denying that by the standards of his friend Scriabin, for example, his music showed little advance on that of the nationalist circle surrounding Mily Balakirev, though he did manage to fuse their general techniques with the European-oriented style of Tchaikovsky.

His musical talents were nonetheless prodigious and he soon outgrew Rimsky-Korsakov's tutelage. His first mature works date from the 1880s, when he produced the first two of his eight symphonies (a ninth got no further than a single movement). Three more date from the 1890s, as do the two ballets which brought him more acclaim than anything else he wrote, *Raymunda* (1897) and *The Seasons* (1899). In the year of the latter work he was appointed professor at the St Petersburg conservatory, where he remained until 1930, having become its director in 1905. In the early years of the century he produced the *Violin Concerto* (1904) and the *Symphony No. 8* (1906), and from then on he composed little of any consequence, concentrating instead on his academic responsibilities, thereby managing to stay in favour with the regimes both before and after the Revolution. He settled in Paris in 1932, where he died four years later.

Ballet Music

When Tchaikovsky died in 1893, the director of the Imperial Theatres, Vsevolozhsky, needed a composer in a similar vein to maintain the standards set by Tchaikovsky's three great ballet scores. Glazunov's reputation was already fairly high when, in 1897, he was invited to compose a full-length ballet, *Raymunda*, to be choreographed by the legendary Marius Petipa. The result was such a success that Glazunov wrote two more ballets for St Petersburg, *Les Ruses d'amour* and *The Seasons*, before turning his back on the theatre. Of these three, *The Seasons* is the finest: its debt to Tchaikovsky is always apparent, but it is not the pale imitation that some have suggested, and its fifteen short sections (none longer than four minutes) sparkle with brilliantly conceived, and highly danceable, ideas. Each of the seasons is vividly but lightly characterized: best of all is winter, which consists of a shimmeringly delicate theme followed by four witty variations representing frost, ice, hail and snow.

Scottish National Orchestra; Järvi
(Chandos; with *Violin Concerto*)

Neeme Järvi is something of a Glazunov specialist (he has recorded all the symphonies) and his enthusiasm for this music is apparent in every bar. *The Seasons* is more lightly textured than Tchaikovsky's great ballets, and Glazunov's delicate instrumental colouring is exquisitely presented by the Scottish National Orchestra.

Violin Concerto

Glazunov's *Violin Concerto* was written in 1904 for the virtuoso Leopold Auer (a future colleague at the St Petersburg Conservatoire). It's very much a Romantic showpiece in the manner of Mendelssohn or Tchaikovsky, but with the violin's melodic material more closely related to its orchestral background than in their concertos. There are two sections (bridged by a cadenza): the first is dominated by a gently lyrical melody with a hint of Slavic melancholy; the second is heralded by a jaunty fanfare-like motif in the trumpets which is then developed by the soloist into an ever more spectacular display of technical bravura. This is the one work by Glazunov to have established itself as a repertoire standard outside of Russia, not least because of the advocacy of Auer's most brilliant pupil, Jascha Heifetz.

Znaider; Bavarian Radio Symphony Orchestra; Jansons (RCA; with Prokofiev *Violin Concerto No. 2*)

Nikolaj Znaider's debut disc in 2002 is a fine example of matching a relatively new artist with works at which he truly excels. In the face of some top-class competition, Znaider more than holds his own in a guileless, perfectly judged performance of the Glazunov concerto: while alive to all its sweetness, he never over-strives for dramatic effect.

Symphonies

Master of the well-made symphony, Glazunov received increasingly little credit for his essentially late-Romantic inspiration as the twentieth century advanced and new masters weaned on this music, among them Prokofiev and his older friend Miaskovsky, turned their backs on the old guard. An increasingly tolerant view now means that Glazunov's impeccable constructions and his often piquant orchestration may be enjoyed without too much soul-searching. None of the eight provides the chronicle of self-discovery in Tchaikovsky's last three symphonies, but Glazunov's essentially robust creativity does offer a healthy alternative – especially in the music of the 1890s. The two most immediately likeable of his symphonies are the warmly Romantic fourth and the sharply focused and bucolic seventh.

Symphonies Nos. 4 & 7: Bamberg Symphony Orchestra; Järvi (Orfeo)

Järvi's Glazunov cycle offers fresh-faced pleasures throughout, especially in the Bamberg woodwind's cultivated handling of the many delightful solos. Like most Russian composers, Glazunov never wrote a dull Scherzo, and Järvi makes a special case for the fourth's scintillating example – a worthy encore-piece if ever there was one.

Mikhail Glinka (1804–1857)

Glinka was the father of Russian musical nationalism, the first Russian master of operatic writing, and the first Russian composer to find acceptance in the rest of Europe. He was born into a wealthy landowning family, and as a 13-year-old took piano lessons with the Irish pianist-composer John Field, the creator of the nocturne (see p.140). But in 1824 he abandoned his musical studies in favour of a post at the Ministry of Communication, and even though he gave recitals as an amateur singer he did not fully devote himself to music until 1828, when he began full-time composition lessons.

Two years later he moved to Milan, where his exposure to Italian music forced him to acknowledge the weakness of his native national tradition – every aspect of Russian music at this time, even its folk songs, was contaminated by the overbearing influence of Western European culture. In 1833 he moved on to Vienna, but homesickness and the death of his father forced him to return to St Petersburg where, in 1835, he set about writing his first opera – *A Life for the Tsar*, the first serious attempt at creating classical music with a genuinely Russian character, though Italian lyricism is an important element of its style. *A Life for the Tsar* is always being brought out for the openings of operatic seasons in Russia, but it's not the subtlest opera ever written, and its interest remains chiefly historical.

The opera's successful production in 1836 proved that Glinka had struck a chord, and his subsequent appointment in 1837 as Imperial *Kapellmeister* cemented his position as Russia's most important composer. Midway through that year, Glinka began to plan an opera based upon Pushkin's poem "Ruslan and Lyudmila" and, even though the poet's death prevented their collaboration, a libretto was patched together. Glinka's second opera was produced in 1842 and its massive success finally secured his fame outside Russia. Numerous aspects of *Ruslan and Lyudmila* marked it out as essentially Russian: its use of Russian folk polyphony and melodic themes; the recitatives based upon the rhythms of the Russian language; the texture of its sounds, in which instruments such as the balalaika played a significant part. It was a declaration of musical independence, and at Glinka's death in 1857 a generation of composers was ready to continue writing music that was Russian in style, flavour and inspiration – the first such generation in Russia's history.

Ilya Repin's portrait of Glinka (1887).

Ruslan and Lyudmila

From the famous, toe-tapping overture to the tuneful, boisterous finale, Glinka's second opera is a thoroughly entertaining piece. Based upon Pushkin's poem, Glinka's magical tale can be seen as anticipating the fantastic and grotesque elements of the operas of Rimsky-Korsakov and Stravinsky. Basically, Lyudmila vanishes from a feast organized for her three suitors. Her father promises her hand to the one who finds her first. Ruslan, the heroic knight, learns that she has been stolen by an evil dwarf, and then battles with a giant decapitated head to win a magic sword with which to defeat the dwarf and rescue Lyudmila. The tale may have its dramatic weaknesses, but the music's overall stylistic cohesion, melodic invention and idiomatic Russian harmonies more than compensate.

Ognovienko, Netrebko, Diadkova, Bezzubenkov, Gorchakova; Kirov Opera; Gergiev (Philips; 2 CDs)

This 1996 live recording is one of only two versions of *Ruslan* in the catalogue, and it's so good that it's unlikely anyone will try to challenge it. The intensity of the orchestral playing is white-hot and all the soloists are outstanding. There's a fair amount of audience noise but it's a minor price to pay in the context of such a fine performance.

Orchestral Works: BBC Philharmonic Orchestra; Sinaisky (Chandos)

The overture to *Ruslan and Lyudmila* is one of the great Russian orchestral showpieces, and it gets a suitably dynamic performance here. The disc also contains two dances from Act 3 of the opera plus a selection of Glinka's less well-known orchestral music, including the two sparkling *Spanish Overtures* and the brilliant orchestral variations *Kamarinskaya*.

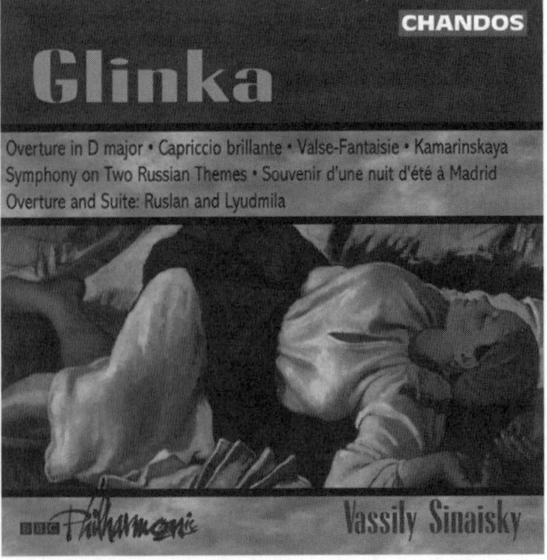

Christoph Willibald Gluck (1714–1787)

It was Gluck who put into practice the principle defined by his near-contemporary Pietro Metastasio – "when the music in union with drama takes precedence, then the drama and music itself suffers in consequence". Gluck was the first composer to deny his singers any opportunity to indulge mere display, for in Gluck's operas the role of the music is to transmit the meaning of the libretto. Technically he may not have been the most accomplished of eighteenth-century composers, but he was the first to write operas in which music and drama achieved a state of complete balance.

German-born, Gluck was educated in Prague then moved to Vienna in 1736, where he played cello in a nobleman's private orchestra. In 1737 the orchestra travelled to Milan where Gluck took lessons with Sammartini (a pioneer of sonata form), under whose guidance he composed his first opera *Artaserse*. Its success led to the completion of a further seven operas before he left for London in 1745 and, although his two London operas failed, his friendship with Handel was to prove of inestimable musical benefit.

Upon leaving London in 1746, Gluck spent the next four years in travel, during which his operas *Semiramide riconosciuta* and *La clemenza di Tito* were well received, and then settled in Vienna. At the end of 1752 he was appointed *Kapellmeister* to the Prince of Saxe-Hildburghausen, a position that cemented his dominance of Vienna's musical life. Giacomo Durazzo, the manager of Vienna's state theatres, saw in Gluck's talent an opportunity to capitalize on the popularity of the lively and flexible French *opéra-comique*, and he engaged Gluck to adapt various existing works in the genre. Gluck responded by producing his own series of "French" comic masterpieces, following the successful premiere of *La fausse esclave* in 1758.

Inundated with requests for operas, it was not long before Gluck was working directly with his librettists, rather than accepting completed texts as part of a commission. His collaboration with the poet Raniero de' Calzabigi brought about radical reforms in the composition and production of opera, as typified by *Orfeo ed Euridice* (1762), a work whose dramatic use of orchestration and overall sense of direction were enthrallingly original. *Alceste*, composed in 1767 to a libretto by Calzabigi, furthered the development of Gluck's mission to "restrict music to its true office by serving poetry by means of expression and by following the situation of the story" and "to strive for a beautiful simplicity".

Alceste was not immediately the success it would later become, and in 1770 Gluck left his Vienna position, settling three years later in Paris, in order to fulfil the Opéra's commission for *Iphigenie en Aulide*. Its production was a sensation, as were his revisions of *Orfeo* and *Alceste*. However, his fame resulted in jealousy and, in an episode worthy of a Feydeau farce, a quarrel was engineered between Gluck and his bitter rival Piccini by asking the latter to set *Iphigénie en Tauride*, a libretto on which Gluck was working at the time. Piccini's version was moderately successful, Gluck's was his masterpiece: boasting an astonishingly integrated fusion of dance, drama, chorus and song, it rapidly eclipsed the competition. In 1779, Gluck retired to Vienna where, living in regal splendour, he died after refusing his doctor's orders that he drink no alcohol after dinner.

Orfeo ed Euridice

Gluck composed *Orfeo* twice: in 1762 for Vienna (in Italian), and in 1774 for Paris (in French, as *Orphée et Euridice*). In the Viennese version the title role was scored for castrato, and dramatic fluency was its main aim. In the longer Paris version, this role was given to a soprano and two new ballets, the "Dance of Furies" and the "Dance of the Blessed Spirit", were added – rather at the expense of the emotional gravity and dramatic cohesion. The opera is based on the legend of the musician Orfeo (Orpheus), who is mourning the death of his wife Euridice. Allowed by Zeus to try and reclaim her from Hades, Orfeo must first persuade Pluto to release her, and then guide her back to Earth without looking at her until they have crossed the River Styx. Orfeo succeeds until Euridice, who can't understand his behaviour, claims she would rather be dead than be rejected by him.

He turns to look at her, and she is lost. Then, in an artificially happy ending typical of the eighteenth-century stage, she is restored to life.

Stripped of all ornament, Gluck's vocal writing possesses a simple beauty that reaches its highest pitch in Orfeo's "Che faro senza Euridice?" (What shall I do without Euridice?). Gluck's recitative is a far more fluid use of a convention that had too often dragged the action to a standstill. Choruses are sumptuous and are allocated sparingly throughout the whole.

Ragin, McNair, Sieden; Monteverdi Choir; English Baroque Soloists; Gardiner
(Philips; 2 CDs)

This digital set of the Viennese version of Orfeo features Derek Lee Ragin's countertenor and Silvia McNair's soprano, an ideal partnership. McNair, one of the outstanding lyric talents of our time, is especially impressive, giving an effortless portrayal of Euridice. Under Gardiner's flexible direction this performance is wonderfully fresh, and benefits from well-spaced recording and full documentation.

von Otter, Hendricks, Fournier; Monteverdi Choir; Lyon Opera Orchestra; Gardiner
(EMI; 2 CDs)

For the French *Orfeo* Gardiner turned to Berlioz's edition of the score, which is a sort of hybrid of the two versions, with a chorus from *Echo et Narcisse* tacked onto the finale. (Berlioz also cut the *Dance of the Furies*, which Gardiner reinstates.) The recording's prime attraction is the beguiling mezzo-soprano of Anne Sofie von Otter, who brings a disciplined suffering to her portrayal of Orphée.

Iphigénie en Tauride

First performed in Paris on 18 May, 1779, *Iphigénie en Tauride* was Gluck's last important work. Its libretto, by Nicholas-François Guillard, is the finest poem set by Gluck, and the opera as a whole comes as close as possible to the composer's ideal of a modern revival of the spirit of Greek tragedy. Ultimately derived from the plays of Euripides (the twists and turns of the plot are too complicated to detail here), *Iphigénie en Tauride* contains some extraordinary moments of great drama, not least the introductory storm (there is no overture) and the chorus of the Furies in Act 2, when Orestes' terrible, haunting conscience (he has murdered his mother) is portrayed as if in a dream. The arias throughout are innovatively plain and eloquent, while the finely realized orchestration lifts the ensemble high above the status of mere accompaniment. *Iphigénie en Tauride* is an extraordinarily colourful but plaintive work, which, for all its heroic subject matter, set opera squarely on the path to realism.

Montague, Aler, Allen, Argenta, Boulton, Alliot-Lugaz, Massis; Monteverdi Choir; Lyon Opera Orchestra; Gardiner (Philips; 2 CDs)

This is a masterly account that buzzes with a sense of purpose and engagement. In the title role, Diana Montague produces an extraordinary, glowing performance. Gardiner rushes some of the ensembles, but his control of the choruses and his attention to clarity are superb.

Henryk Górecki (1933–)

Henryk Górecki's third symphony, the "Symphony of Sorrowful Songs", is one of the most remarkable musical success stories of the recent past. Written in 1976, this cathartic vision of post-Holocaust, post-industrial humanity was recorded several times in Górecki's native Poland, and was beginning to develop a cult following in the rest of Europe (a small section features at the end of Maurice Pialat's 1990 film *Police*). Then in 1992 a version was recorded featuring soprano Dawn Upshaw with the London Sinfonietta, which within a few weeks of its release hit the top of the classical charts in both Britain and the United States. To date it has sold over a million copies, transforming its previously obscure creator into a major international figure.

Born near the bleak industrial town of Katowice, Górecki studied at its academy of music in the late 1950s, quickly establishing a reputation for his fierce individualism. He utilized a frenzied form of serialism in his *Symphony No. 1* (1959), which duly outraged the Communist officials, as did the subsequent *Scontri* (Collisions) for orchestra, an even more scorching work. After the short-lived post-Stalinist thaw in Poland, the disillusioned composer sought solace in his country's folk songs and in religion, as exemplified by his *Symphony No. 2* (1972), with its setting of texts

Górecki (right) and Warner's Bill Holland celebrate the huge sales of the Nonesuch recording of his *Symphony No. 3*.

from the Psalms. Spending much of his time walking in the Tatra mountains, an agricultural area rich in ancient cultural traditions but close to the site of Auschwitz, he then began to conceive of unifying the emotional history of Poland in one great work. The result was the awesome *Symphony No. 3*, for which he took words from the Holy Cross lament and an inscription left by a girl imprisoned by the Nazis at Zakopane, in the Tatras.

Three years later Górecki's frail health forced him to withdraw from teaching, but since then he has written a harpsichord concerto, *O Domina Nostra* for soprano and organ, and *Lerchenmusik* for cello, piano and clarinet, while the Kronos Quartet have recorded his difficult string quartet *Already it is Dusk*. Sales of the *Symphony No. 3* CD have now allowed him to buy a house in his beloved Tatra mountains and enjoy his worldwide celebrity for a work which he views as an "intensely felt revelation of the human condition".

Symphony No. 3

For his "Symphony of Sorrowful Songs", written in 1976, Górecki evidently took inspiration from Ives and Szymanowski, particularly in the use of overlapping melodies drawn from folk song and church music. The opening wells up from deep bass melodies, developing the first half of a canon for strings until, eventually, a bell-like figure from a muffled piano ushers in the soprano singing a fifteenth-century hymn. In the second movement – the emotional heart of the work – yearning, radiant orchestral writing frames an exceptionally lovely song for the soprano. The contrast between the beauty of the sounds and the horror of their origins (they were scratched onto the wall of a Gestapo cell by an 18-year-old girl) intensifies the effect of the song – the listener clings for comfort to the tenderness of the music as a way of softening the nightmare vision of the circumstances in which they were written (a markedly different approach to that of Nono in his response to Nazi brutality,

Il canto sospeso – see p.383). The final movement sets a folk song mourning a lost son who may have been killed in combat, ending in a soft, extended and rather inconclusive cadence.

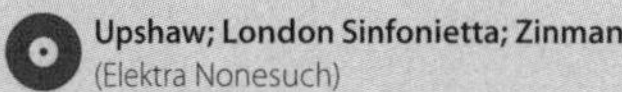

Upshaw; London Sinfonietta; Zinman (Elektra Nonesuch)

Dawn Upshaw's pure and incisive tones are certainly breathtaking, but what sets this recording apart from others is the incredibly wide panoramic sound (mastered by rock engineer Bob Ludwig) which gives an extraordinarily embracing resonance to the performance.

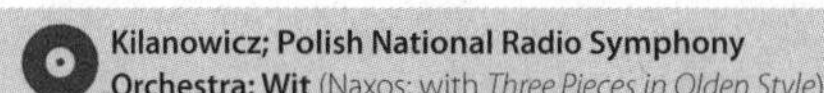

Kilanowicz; Polish National Radio Symphony Orchestra; Wit (Naxos; with *Three Pieces in Olden Style*)

A performance of Górecki's most popular work which not only holds its own against the Nonesuch version but arguably surpasses it. While the sound quality is not as rich nor as transparent, Antoni Wit seems to get closer to the heart of the work in a reading which is more austere but also more spiritual. Zofia Kilanowicz is the outstanding soloist.

Choral Music

The 1981 *Miserere* is, unusually for Górecki, overtly political. In March of that year a sit-in by members of Rural Solidarity was violently ended by the militia. The unaccompanied *Miserere* was Górecki's immediate response, though censorship prevented its public performance until 1987. Employing an outwardly calm manner, couching his anger in rich solemn sonorities, Górecki contrasts secure religious faith with the perilous unpredictability of political repression. After about twenty minutes, a sudden outburst of volume seems more like an outburst of pent-up grief than a threat of retribution. Less than five minutes later, at the insistent repetition of the word "Domine", it is as if the choir is hyperventilating and the music finally allowing itself to sob.

Like Henze's *Requiem*, *Good Night* (1990) was written in memory of Michael Vyner of the London Sinfonietta, who did much to promote Górecki's music in the West. Scored for soprano, alto flute, three tam-tams and piano, *Good Night* is an austere, heartfelt work constructed in three movements from the simplest of materials. Tiny melodic fragments evoke the difficulty of resolving grief, symbolizing things left unfinished and the forlorn attempts of mourners to find meaning in the sudden absence of someone close.

Miserere: Chicago Symphony Chorus; Chicago Lyric Opera Chorus; Nelson (Elektra Nonesuch; with *Three Pieces in Old Style & Kleines Requiem für eine Polka*)

An outstanding performance of this emotionally compelling and powerful work. John Nelson controls his combined choirs with a sure grasp, building the work gradually to its shattering climax. One small, but unimportant, drawback is the occasional presence of background noise.

Good Night: Szmytka, Edmund-Davies, Gleizes, Righarts: I Fiamminghini; Werthen (Telarc; with *Three Pieces in Old Style & Kleines Requiem für eine Polka*)

A reverential and moving account of *Good Night*, in which the performers communicate a powerful atmosphere of quietly shared pain.

Chamber Music

After annoying Polish officialdom with his serial style in the early 1960s, Górecki spent some time in Paris before returning to Katowice and writing *Three Pieces in Old Style* in 1963. These miniatures for string orchestra (the longest is three and a half minutes) are significant examples of Górecki's developing individual voice. The first sets a wistfully lyrical modal melody against a diatonic background, the second suggests a folk dance, while the last moves the grave chorale-like tune from serene harmonies through dissonance to a final tussle out of which a consonant sound (like a final "amen") emerges triumphant.

The flavour of Górecki's chamber music is typified by *Kleines Requiem für eine Polka* for piano and thirteen instruments (1993). Fast and slow tempi interact during four movements, where episodes of boisterousness contrast with funereal bells and horn solo. Although the opening Tranquillo is soft, simple and pensive, the succeeding Allegro reminds the listener that Górecki's music often contains echoes of Bartókian dances, Stravinskian fanfares or implacable Messiaen-like chords, illustrating that he is quite capable of running amok in outbursts of parody, anguish or defiance. The work is usually translated as "Requiem for a Polka" but it can also mean "Requiem for a Polish Woman". Górecki refuses to elucidate, and the music continues to tantalize, suggesting an underlying story whose plot we cannot deduce.

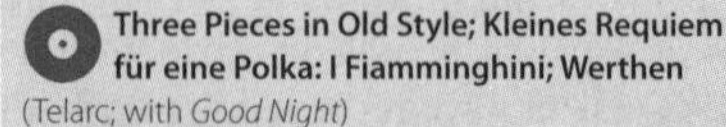

Three Pieces in Old Style; Kleines Requiem für eine Polka: I Fiamminghini; Werthen (Telarc; with *Good Night*)

The excellent Flemish orchestra I Fiamminghini gives moving performances of these intensely personal yet accessible works. Under their founder and director, Rudolf Werthen, they give full value to Górecki's characteristically high, shimmering, patiently sustained chords as well as to the hollow, bell-like ones which mirror the intervals of his confined, tentative melodic cells.

Charles François Gounod (1818–1893)

For most of the first seventy years of the nineteenth century, Paris was the great centre of musical Romanticism, but this situation arose more from the city's ability to attract foreign talent – Chopin, Liszt, Meyerbeer, etc – than from the recognition of its native talent (such as Berlioz). Between 1852 and 1870 only five new French works were added to the Paris Opéra's repertory, and it was thanks only to the Théâtre-Lyrique that any new French music was heard in the capital at all. Charles François Gounod was the first home-grown composer to break the trend. Although his debt to German music is undeniable (he had a fondness for Beethoven's late quartets), Gounod is the most thoroughly representative French composer of the mid-nineteenth century, and is the man chiefly responsible for leading French opera away from the elephantine spectaculars of Meyerbeer, France's most popular operatic composer at the time.

Gounod's first operatic attempts were far from successful, being pastiche Gluck with thin plots and weak texts, and it was not until 1859 that he hit upon an operatic subject that really stimulated him – Goethe's *Faust*. Deeply religious but with a great weakness for women, Gounod concentrated on that aspect of the poem that spoke to him most directly – he and his librettists duly pulled *Faust* to pieces in order to emphasize the love story of Faust and Marguerite rather than Goethe's wider metaphysical considerations (which is why German writers call the work *Margarethe* rather than honouring it with the same title as their national poet's masterpiece). Reductive though it may be, Gounod's *Faust* is an inspired mixture of melodic invention, religious solemnity and vivid characterization, and gave the country's composers a new sense of direction and identity. It also became the most successful French opera in history. As early as 1863, an English critic was complaining – "Faust, Faust, Faust, nothing but Faust. Faust on Saturday, Wednesday and Thursday; to be repeated tonight, and on every night until further notice." To date, *Faust* has been performed in over fifty countries and translated into 25 different languages.

Keen to build upon *Faust*'s success, Gounod produced *Philémon et Baucis*, *La colombe* and the five-act *La reine de Saba*; but the last of these attracted accusations of "Wagnerism", a cardinal offence in Paris. The opera was an overnight failure, and its successor, *Mireille*, was similarly rejected after its first performance in 1864. It began to look as if Gounod would never repeat the glory of *Faust*, but in 1867 his reputation was saved by Shakespeare – *Roméo et Juliette* was vigorously promoted by the Théâtre-Lyrique, who were desperately in need of critical prestige, and both theatre and composer got the hit they needed.

Faust

Gounod's *Faust* is but a distant relative of Goethe's, but the libretto has a directness and lack of pretension that's perfect for the operatic stage, and the score is so stuffed with memorable tunes that it has served as the basis for more instrumental transcriptions, fantasies and variations than almost any other opera. The tenor lead is especially memorable, with the third act's "Salut! demeure chaste et pure" standing out as a sublime example of Gounod's lyric style. Similarly, the duets in Act 1 for Faust and Mephistopheles, and in Acts 3 and 5 for Faust and Marguerite, are irresistibly appealing. In short, *Faust*'s seemingly endless stream of hummable melodies make this one of the most completely enjoyable operas ever written.

Gedda, de los Angeles, Christoff, Blanc; Paris Opera Chorus and Orchestra; Cluytens (EMI; 3 CDs)

This 1958 recording has an authentically theatrical atmosphere. Nikolai Gedda's Faust is beautifully stylish and Gallic, Victoria de los Angeles's Marguerite projects an appropriate purity, and the demonic Boris Christoff gives the most over-the-top performance of his life, roaring and bawling his way through the score. Excerpts from this performance are available on a single mid-price disc.

Hadley, Gadia, Ramey, Agache; Welsh National Opera Chorus and Orchestra; Rizzi (Teldec; 3 CDs)

Recorded in 1993, this is by some considerable margin the outstanding *Faust* of recent times. Having assembled a well-balanced cast (with bass-baritone Samuel Ramey at his insinuating best as Mephistopheles), conductor Carlo Rizzi brings a convincing French style and considerable dramatic flair to the proceedings.

Percy Grainger (1882–1961)

Percy Grainger is one of twentieth-century music's strangest figures, a man whose eccentricity, both in his music and in his life, teetered on the brink of insanity. Possessing enormous energy and a restless, inquisitive mind, he produced compositions that frequently employ weird instrumental combinations in unconventional musical forms. Yet he is best known for a handful of unremittingly jolly folk-song arrangements like "English Country Gardens" or "Molly on the Shore". To explore his output a little more deeply is to discover much that is dark and disturbing, though rarely in a way comparable to any of his *fin de siècle* contemporaries. Only the music of Charles Ives (see p.263) emits a similar uneasy tension between the desire to be both experimental and easily expressive.

Grainger's early years were deeply distressing. Born in Melbourne, the only child of a drunken architect father, he was regularly beaten by his dominating mother, who also instilled in him some bizarre ideas about racial purity. In 1895 mother and son went to Frankfurt in order to improve Percy's youthful piano skills, and it was here that he first began composing under the tutelage of an inspired amateur musician, Karl Klimsch, who introduced him to the central inspiration of his career, folk song. Forced by his mother's ill-health to pursue a career as a concert pianist, Grainger moved to London in 1901. When not performing, he was a diligent and pioneering collector of folk song and established some vital musical friendships, notably with Grieg, to whom he dedicated his British folk-song arrangements, and with Delius, who encouraged him to have his works performed.

With the onset of World War I, Grainger and his mother moved to the United States, where they took up citizenship at the war's end. His mother's suicide four years later was both deeply traumatic and a liberation. In 1926 he married the Swedish-born Ella Ström. The wedding took place in front of 20,000 people at the end of one of Grainger's concerts at the Hollywood Bowl, and a choral work, *To a Nordic Princess*, composed especially for the occasion, was performed.

In later years Grainger's interests continued to range widely: he particularly admired Duke Ellington and invited him and his band to illustrate one of his lectures at New York University. He also began to design and build his own "free music machines", strange contraptions with which he aimed to develop a beatless music capable of a vast range of different pitches. By this time, however, few people took him seriously and at his death Grainger was regarded as a completely marginal figure, despite the enthusiasm of such figures as Benjamin Britten. Today, with the Chandos record company committed to recording everything he ever wrote, a more reasoned assessment of Grainger's value is becoming possible.

Percy Grainger supervising a piano roll recording of one of his performances.

Choral Music

Grainger's passion for folk song is reflected in the highly imaginative arrangements that he made of them. It's as if, through quirky harmonies or by vivid orchestral colouring, he was trying to distil not just the essential mood of a song but also to re-create the emotion of its original singer. The haunting "Brigg Fair" pits a lone tenor soloist against a hushed but fervent choral backgound; "The Lost Lady Found" contrasts, with increasing urgency, a vigorous unison line of women's voices against a crisply accented orchestral part. Best of all is the sea shanty "Shallow Brown", in which a desperate woman bemoans the loss of her lover, her words echoed by an indifferent chorus against the furious tremolando rise and fall of guitars, mandolins and ukuleles.

Works for Chorus and Orchestra: Varcoe, Padmore, Gritton; Joyful Company of Singers; City of London Sinfonia; Hickox (Chandos)

Volume 3 of Chandos's Grainger edition is a complete delight, with Richard Hickox and his forces clearly enjoying themselves in a nicely varied programme. Baritone Stephen Varcoe has the lion's share of the solos (including excellent renditions of "Shallow Brown" and "Shenandoah") but Mark Padmore's "Brigg Fair" is no less affecting.

Orchestral Music

Grainger avoided conventional forms, preferring to write orchestral miniatures, which he sometimes gathered together in the form of a suite. Refusing to acknowledge any distinction between light and serious music, he had no qualms about bringing widely disparate types of music together. The first two movements of *In a Nutshell* (1916) are typically high-spirited: an energetic romp of a tune – the sort, Grainger stated, that you might hum on a railway platform while waiting for your lover – is followed by a pastiche music-hall song which is all sauntering, easy-going charm. After this comes the extraordinary "Pastoral", which begins as a lilting Delius-like nature picture then gradually disintegrates into something dark and disturbing.

In the same year Grainger wrote one of his longest and strangest pieces, *The Warriors*. Originally planned for the Russian Ballet (though never performed by the company), it's a wild and passionate work in which seemingly incongruous styles seem to fight it out. Scored for orchestra, three pianos and an endless array of percussion, it has been described by Simon Rattle as being like Holst's *The Planets* with Stravinsky's *Les Noces* laid on top of it. For Grainger, rich and striking sonorities were half the battle.

In a Nutshell; The Warriors; Country Gardens; A Lincolnshire Posy: City of Birmingham Symphony Orchestra; Rattle (EMI)

There's some really sparkling and energized playing here, with Rattle (a former percussionist) clearly relishing the spectrum of percussive sonorities at his disposal. *The Warriors* is particularly exciting, while in Grainger's transcriptions of Ravel's *La vallée des cloches* and Debussy's *Pagodes*, each work's oriental inspiration is made startlingly manifest. If this disc doesn't convert you to Grainger, nothing will.

Piano Music

Despite his international reputation as a concert pianist, Grainger claimed to loathe the instrument: "I consider it an affront to destroy a melodiously conceived idea by trying to fit it into the limitations of two hands and a box full of hammers and strings." He managed, however, to "dish up", as he called it, a substantial body of pieces for the piano, although most were arrangements of his own and other composers' works. All are marked with detailed instructions in pointedly Anglo-Saxon English (Grainger wished to "free" the language of its Latin and Greek "impurities"), for example "louden hugely", "heavily but clingingly", "harped all the way", etc. Many of these piano pieces are extremely difficult, despite their insouciant air, frequently combining traditional dance forms with elaborate counterpoint. *Handel in the Strand* mixes Handelian vigour with musical-comedy swagger; *In Dahomey* is Grainger's stupendously virtuosic tribute to black American music, while a more contemplative mood is found in *Harvest Hymn* and his marvellously sentimental homage to Australia, *Colonial Song*.

Piano Music: Hamelin (Hyperion)

Marc-André Hamelin is that rare thing: an internationally acclaimed pianist prepared to expend his energies on non-mainstream repertoire. Hamelin brings out all Grainger's technical wizardry – like his capacity to juggle more than one melody simultaneously – without it sounding merely flash. His own technical ability allows the more emotional pieces, such as *Colonial Song*, room to speak for themselves.

Enrique Granados (1867–1916)

It is with good reason that Enrique Granados is banded together with his compatriots Isaac Albéniz and Manuel de Falla in most histories of music. Like them he was taught by the eminent musicologist Felipe Pedrell, who inspired all three to forge an individual style based on indigenous folk music; and, just as Albéniz and Falla had, Granados made the *de rigueur* student trip to Paris, hotbed of the European avant-garde. All three became masters at taking native folk melodies and overlaying them with a highly spiced chromatic idiom, more often than not French in derivation. When it came to character, however, it was a different matter. The spontaneously warm Granados was closer in temperament to his friend Albéniz than to the drier Falla, and the similarities did not end there. Both Granados and Albéniz were concert pianists of international repute who chose to write primarily for the piano, and their reputations rest primarily on just one concert suite – though the quality of Granados's *Goyescas* and Albéniz's *Iberia* is of the highest order.

Granados started off by composing pretty, salon-type pieces in a post-Lisztian manner. However, with the 1892 premiere of an orchestral version of three of his *Danzas españolas* for piano, it was clear that a new direction in Spanish music was opening up. The *Danzas españolas* were much admired by Massenet, Saint-Saëns and above all Grieg, an endorsement which must have given Granados much satisfaction, as the nationalism of Grieg's music was much appreciated by Spanish audiences and young composers alike. Granados, well aware of prevailing fashions, knew that the best way to get noticed in Spain was to write a *zarzuela* (a distinctly Spanish type of operetta), and a few years later he composed the highly successful *Maria del Carmen* (1898), which gained him a commendation from the king. Although he cashed in on his success with a string of other *zarzuelas*, over the next decade or so he devoted himself as much to teaching and performing as to composition. From time to time Granados's talents took him away from music altogether – he once said of himself, "I am not a musician but an artist", and by all accounts he was a fine writer and excellent painter. But despite these creative diversions Granados remained first and foremost a musician, and was in great demand as an accompanist by such virtuosos as the cellist Pablo Casals and the violinist Jacques Thibaud.

During the early 1900s Granados composed a variety of works, most of which are now unknown, but all the while he was contemplating the music of what was to be his most ambitious work to date, *Goyescas*. It was *Goyescas* that made Granados a name to be reckoned with. After its French premiere in 1914, at the Salle Pleyel in Paris, all sorts of honours came his way, including election to the Légion d'honneur and a commission from the Opéra to compose a piece of music theatre derived from *Goyescas*. The outbreak of World War I soon scotched the idea of a production, but interest then unexpectedly came from New York's Metropolitan Opera.

The composer travelled over with his wife to be present at the resoundingly successful premiere on 26 January, 1916, then prolonged his stay to play at the White House at the invitation of President Wilson. Consequently they missed a direct boat back to Spain, so decided to travel back to Europe via England. The SS *Sussex*, the boat they took from Liverpool to Dieppe, was torpedoed by a German submarine with the loss of many lives, including that of Granados and his wife. Just two months before his death, Granados had written to a friend: "I have a whole world of ideas ... I am only now starting my work."

Piano Music

Among Granados's earliest piano works are the delightful *Danzas españolas* (Spanish Dances), written between 1892 and 1900. In these twelve pieces arranged in four sets, Granados was attempting to create piano pieces that were completely infused with the character of Spanish dance. It was a similar project to that of his fellow countryman Albéniz (see p.6), but Granados's approach is less wild than that of his contemporary; although some pieces employ the rhythms of specific dance forms, the overall flavour is rather more urbane than Albéniz's *Suite española*.

Granados's masterpiece *Goyescas* conjures up a fantasy world of gentility and style. All eight pieces in the suite were inspired by the paintings of Goya, and rarely has a composer captured the underlying mood of the work of another artist with such clarity and insight. Eighteenth-century Spanish music plays an important part in the sound-world of *Goyescas*, but, as the critic Harold Schonberg wrote, it's the general "scent of Spanish rhythms, Spanish melodies, and Spanish life" which makes the suite so memorable. The Andalusian flamenco elements sometimes have a tendency to be a touch over-repetitive, but in the most famous piece, "Quejas, o la maja y el ruiseñor" (known in English as "The Maiden and the Nightingale"), every statement of the plaintive melody and its concluding arabesque is beautifully constructed, with nothing overstated.

Danzas Españolas: de Larrocha
(Decca)

Alicia de Larrocha is the doyenne of Spanish pianists and one of the great interpreters of Granados. She has recorded these pieces several times but this performance is the brightest sounding and the most subtle.

Goyescas: de Larrocha
(Decca; with Albeniz *Iberia*; 2 CDs)

The music of *Goyescas* can sound flat if the pianist can't muster a supercharged rhythmic vitality, but de Larrocha rises to the occasion – this account of the complete *Goyescas* is beautifully fashioned and marvellously flexible in its response to the music's fluidity and evocative magic.

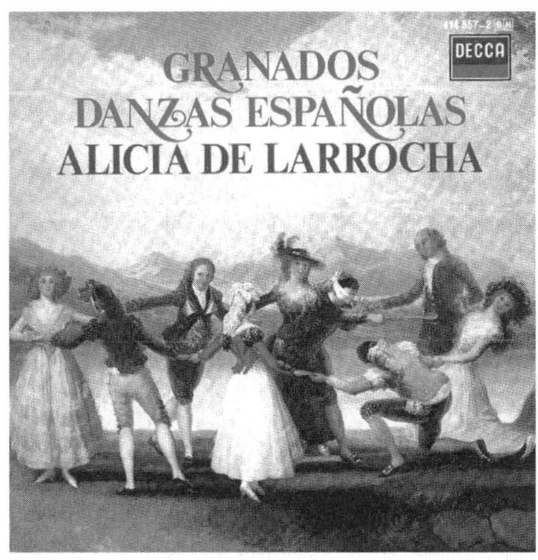

Guitar Transcriptions: Kerstens
(British Guitar Society)

As with Albéniz, many guitarists have made versions of Granados piano pieces, but it is rare to hear a whole CD of such transcriptions. Dutch guitarist Tom Kerstens makes the idea seem an inspired one. Playing on a reproduction of an 1888 Torres guitar, and using his own versions, he generates all the requisite passion and excitement of this music.

Edvard Grieg (1843–1907)

Grieg may have been the only internationally successful composer to have come out of Norway, but it would be a mistake to regard him as a peripheral figure. He ranks with names such as Sibelius and Dvořák in the late nineteenth century's upsurge of musical nationalism, inspiring musicians across Europe to follow his example in looking to his country's folk heritage for source material. In Spain, for example, the impact of Grieg's music on the likes of Manuel de Falla (see p.187) was instrumental in the formation of an essentially national school of music. The depth of Grieg's influence is all the more remarkable when you compare his output to that of Sibelius and Dvořák, for, whereas they were devoted to mighty large-scale compositions, Grieg was a committed miniaturist. His *Piano Concerto* might be his best-known creation, but it's not at all typical.

His first lessons came from his mother. Then in 1858 the Norwegian violinist and folk enthusiast Ole Bull heard Grieg play the piano and persuaded his reluctant parents to send the boy to the Leipzig Conservatory. Bull was delighted, Grieg was not. He hated his time there, but had the good fortune to attend concerts at which the likes of Clara Schumann and Richard Wagner were regular artists.

In the spring of 1862 his Opus 1 was published, and in May of the following year he settled in Copenhagen, where he was taken under the wing of Niels Gade, Denmark's leading Romantic composer and a close friend of Schumann and Mendelssohn. Gade was enthusiastic about the young composer's potential but his optimism was tempered by misgivings about his lack of large-scale work, and so he set Grieg the task of writing his first

The elderly Grieg at the piano.

and only symphony, something for which he was neither technically equipped nor temperamentally suited.

Soon afterwards he met his cousin, the singer Nina Hagerup; a year later, the two were engaged to be married and Grieg was back in Norway, living in the house of Ole Bull. From this point, his artistic personality began to change as he started taking a studious interest in his country's musical heritage, having previously spent a long time away from home or immersed in a middle-class milieu that had been dominated by Danish culture. His commitment to Norwegian nationalism was confirmed by his encounters with Rikard Nordraak, Norway's great hope for the formation of a national school (Rikard died in 1866 aged just 24, having written what is now Norway's national anthem), and by a meeting with Henrik Ibsen in Rome in 1865.

He returned to Norway confident of his mission, and after promoting concerts of his own music he was quickly recognized as one of his country's foremost composers. In 1867 he married Nina and settled in Oslo, where he became a teacher and conductor of international renown. A year later he and his family moved back to Denmark where he composed his *Piano Concerto*; in Italy the following year he presented Liszt with his very badly handwritten draft of the piece and, to his amazement, Liszt played the whole concerto right through. "Go on, you have the stuff", Liszt is said to have encouraged him.

By 1874 Grieg was so famous and so highly valued that the Norwegian government voted to grant him an annuity, and Ibsen similarly paid his respects by asking him to provide incidental music for his play *Peer Gynt*. His popularity took him to England, where he and his wife gave numerous recitals and, in an extraordinary display of affection, both Oxford and Cambridge granted him honorary degrees. The last twenty years of his life followed a rarely changing pattern of holidays, composition and concert tours and he became one of the elder statesmen of European music.

One year after Grieg's death, Schoenberg composed his first atonal works and within five years Grieg's name had become synonymous with everything outdated in music. There is indeed nothing too challenging in Grieg. His music is on the whole a sweetly harmonic synthesis of folk song and German-based Romanticism – the Romanticism of Schumann, not of Wagner, for whose lofty ambitions Grieg felt no affection. Within these limits, however, he is one of the most distinctive and enjoyable composers of his time, a master of small-scale form whose greatest music is, in a sense, his slightest.

Piano Concerto

Grieg was an excellent pianist and hardly a year passed when he did not give concerts either as a soloist or with his wife. He wrote his *Piano Concerto* as a vehicle for his own talents, and its youthful exuberance – reminiscent of Schumann's only concerto, also in A minor – has ensured its place in the repertoire of most of today's concert pianists. Composed in 1868 while Grieg was holidaying with his wife and young child in Denmark (although revised to the version played today in 1907), it is replete with a sense of tenderness and wellbeing, expressed in a proliferation of enchanting thematic ideas. The opening motif – an idea as well-known as the opening of that other virtuoso warhorse, Tchaikovsky's first concerto – is built upon a descending second followed by a descending third, intervals typical in Norwegian folk music. The Adagio boasts a touchingly beautiful melody – sombre in its orchestral form, gloriously refulgent in its piano version. The work closes with a spirited rondo containing at its centre an extremely tender new theme that is triumphantly restated at the work's conclusion.

Andsnes; Berlin Philharmonic Orchestra; Jansons (EMI; with Schumann *Piano Concerto*)

Performances of the Grieg concerto helped establish Norwegian pianist Leif Ove Andsnes as one of the most exciting musicians around. His second recording of the work, from 2002, is revelatory, thanks to Andsnes' ability to make even the most familiar music sound newly minted. His tender yet strongly pulsed playing is partnered perfectly by the sonorous Berlin Philharmonic under Mariss Jansons.

Kovacevich; BBC Symphony Orchestra; Davis (Philips; with Schumann *Piano Concerto*)

Stephen Kovacevich's mid-1970s recording (as Stephen Bishop) still holds up extremely well. His playing is clear, unaffected and lyrical, showing a great overall awareness of shape and colour.

Peer Gynt

In 1874 Henrik Ibsen decided to adapt his verse play *Peer Gynt* for a performance at the theatre in Christiania (now Oslo). Norway's theatrical tradition at the time was based upon operettas and musical plays, and Ibsen recognized that his sprawling play needed a soothing soundtrack in order to succeed – and accordingly asked Grieg to supply incidental music. The new production was first staged in February 1876 and was hugely successful, playing for several nights until a fire destroyed the sets and costumes.

To give his music an existence apart from Ibsen's drama, Grieg extracted two suites for concert performance, and these two spin-offs – Op. 46 and Op. 54 – contain his most striking orchestral music, showing a directness and freshness that generally eluded him when he came to write for large forces. Its best-known section is the flute's principal theme from "Morning", but this is one of many examples of a piece of music being identified with a sound bite from one of its less remarkable moments. Most of the other self-contained episodes make "Morning" sound banal, none more so than "Solvejg's Song", a piece of wonderfully fragile lyricism.

Peer Gynt (complete): Bonney, Eklöf, Sandve, Malmberg; Gothenburg Symphony Orchestra; Järvi (Deutsche Grammophon; 2 CDs; with *Sigurd Jorsalfar*)

Neeme Järvi conducts the whole of the musical score of *Peer Gynt* but includes just the bare bones of Ibsen's text to keep the action clear (the full play can go on for four hours). The Gothenburg Symphony Orchestra respond with delightful enthusiasm to the sensitive but direct conducting. There is also a highlights disc of this performance.

Peer Gynt (excerpts): Hollweg; Royal Philharmonic Orchestra; Beecham (EMI; with orchestral pieces)

This classic recording from 1956–57 presents Beecham's own selection of purely musical highlights from *Peer Gynt* – which includes all the music from the suites. His performances with the Royal Philharmonic are excellent, by turns radiant and waspish.

Songs

"I loved a young girl who had a wonderful voice and an equally wonderful gift for interpretation. That girl became my wife and my lifelong companion to this very day. For me, she has been – I dare admit it – the only genuine interpreter of my songs." Grieg's adoration of his wife was the wellspring of his songs, his greatest body of music and, though she could not be regarded as the sole inspiration for all 140, there is little doubt that she had a defining influence on their evolution.

As with Schubert, Grieg's emotional range is vast, and the melodic directness and limpidity of his music allows anyone to grasp immediately the nature of each song – but you'll need a translation to hand in order to appreciate the delicacy with which Grieg augments the content of each text. In contrast to Schubert, most of Grieg's songs are strophic (whereby the same music is repeated with each successive stanza), in honour of their folk inspiration.

von Otter, Forsberg
(Deutsche Grammophon)

Anne Sofie von Otter gives marvellously characterful interpretations, beguilingly frank in the folksy pieces, deeply moving in the more intimate songs such as "I Love You" and "Last Spring" – the latter song possessing a melody so perfect that Grieg couldn't resist recycling it for a couple of other compositions. Her regular pianist, Bengt Forsberg, provides exemplary accompaniment throughout.

Violin Sonatas

Grieg's three violin sonatas were particularly close to his heart. All have a freshness and the composer's characteristic lyrical facility, but the third – his chamber masterpiece – possesses a deeper emotional level and a complete mastery of form. The first two are early works, written in the 1860s, when the composer was looking to his native folk song as a means of forging a distinctly Norwegian national style. With the *Sonata No. 3 in C Minor* (1886), the folk elements are completely assimilated into the music and the whole work is infused with a very much darker tone. This is immediately apparent in the turbulent opening which exudes an air of anxiety despite a more serene second subject. The second movement begins with one of Grieg's most touchingly poignant melodies which starkly offsets the insistent energy of the second theme. Following a wonderfully mysterious and atmospheric opening (conjuring the world of *Peer Gynt*), the finale returns to the raw power of the opening with a dance-like melody set over pounding fifths in the piano part.

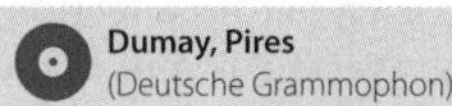

Dumay, Pires
(Deutsche Grammophon)

Highly expressive accounts by violinist Augustin Dumay and pianist Maria-João Pires. Theirs is a regular partnership, and there is a real sense of digging deep into the music's emotional depths – the slow movement of the third sonata, in particular, has rarely sounded so heartfelt.

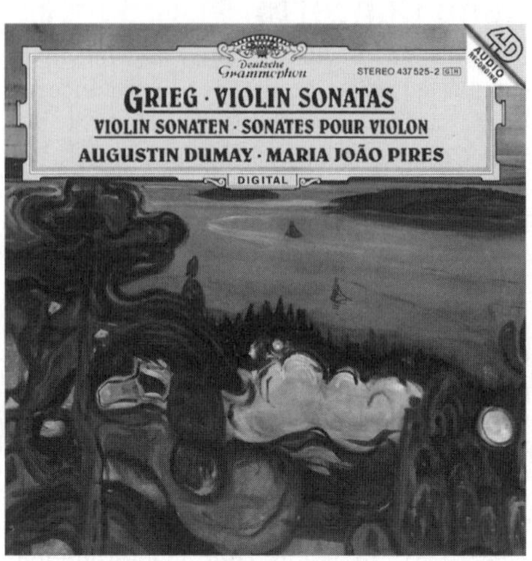

Lyric Pieces

Grieg's talent for uncomplicated, sincere and brief musical ideas is well displayed in his *Lyric Pieces*, ten sets of piano pieces spanning his career from 1867 to 1901. Ranging from forty seconds to four minutes in length, they are extraordinarily crafted compositions, defining a mood in the space of a bar or two, giving it enough time to completely infiltrate the listener's mind, then letting it go. At their best the *Lyric Pieces* are as touching as some of Chopin's miniatures, and even when they amount to little more than whimsical musings they are never less than tunefully pleasant.

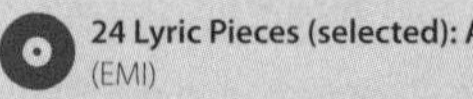

24 Lyric Pieces (selected): Andsnes
(EMI)

Leif Ove Andsnes, a great advocate of the music of his fellow countryman, has made one of the more substantial selections of the *Lyric Pieces*, which he plays on Grieg's own piano. The result is a complete triumph, with all the quiet intimacy of these delightful pieces communicated in utterly focused and poetic readings.

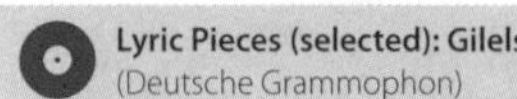

Lyric Pieces (selected): Gilels
(Deutsche Grammophon)

Emil Gilels' selection of nineteen pieces from all ten books of *Lyric Pieces* is justifiably regarded as a classic. It's a performance of sublime, fluid romanticism, with Gilels perfectly attuned to the mood of each piece.

Sofia Gubaidulina (1931–)

Sofia Gubaidulina has said of herself, "I am the place where East meets West", which is as good a categorization as any. One of the leading innovative composers in the former Soviet Union, she comes from a mixed Tartar and Slavic background, and the influence of Eastern philosophies is clear in many of her attitudes towards spirituality and its expression – whether writing for huge orchestral forces or a few solo instruments, she tends to explore a wide range of sonorities in order to create music that is extraordinarily still and serene, leaving the listener with a sense of timelessness rare in Western music.

She started writing music at an early age and then studied in Kazan (the capital of the present-day Tatar Republic) before moving to Moscow, where she attended the conservatory until 1963. Until around that time the Soviet regime had been diligent in keeping Russian composers isolated from the corrupting influence of modern Western music, but as the 1960s wore on there was a gradual thawing of official attitudes, marked by visits from avant-garde composers such as Luigi Nono and Pierre Boulez. Having started her career writing in straightforward tonal idioms, Gubaidulina took every possible chance to explore the new languages and techniques, such as serialism, electronics and the use of numerical patterns in composition. As one of the country's most interesting avant-garde composers – alongside the more turbulent Alfred Schnittke (see p.476) – she experienced the inevitable criticism from the Communist Party's cultural controllers.

For much of her life in the Soviet Union Gubaidulina supported herself by writing music for films and the theatre, disciplines that enabled her to experiment with a wide variety of sounds and procedures. Another crucial contribution to her work has come from the traditional music of the Soviet Union – in 1975 she founded an improvisation group called Astreya, which made

Sofia Gubaidulina regards composing as a religious act.

wide use of folk instruments and forms, and had a great influence on her concert-hall pieces. Her breakthrough work, in terms of wider recognition, was *Offertorium* (1980) which was written for (and championed by) the violinist Gidon Kremer. Since then her artistic stock has risen and she is now regarded as one of the most significant of living composers. Since 1992 she has lived in Hamburg.

If there is one common denominator to Gubaidulina's output, it is her belief in the transforming power of art. Much of her music is rooted in religious imagery, and she believes passionately in the ability of music to establish a sense of connection with the transcendent.

Offertorium

Gubaidulina's violin concerto, *Offertorium* (1980, revised 1982 & 1986), was her first work to become known outside the Soviet Union. It's a moving and virtuosic piece, built entirely around the theme from J.S. Bach's *Musical Offering*, which is stated at the beginning, spread between different instruments in the style of Webern's orchestral transcription of the work. For Gubaidulina, *Offertorium* represents an attempt "... to unite the two personalities in the history of music who have produced the greatest impression on me." In the first part of the work's single movement the theme is heard several times, but with each variation it gradually disintegrates; by the end of *Offertorium* the theme has been transfigured and is played in retrograde by the soloist – a moment of calm beauty and resolution.

Kremer; Boston Symphony Orchestra; Dutoit (Deutsche Grammophon; with *Hommage à T.S. Eliot*)

The best performance comes from Gidon Kremer, for whom the work was written; his passionate account is coupled with *Hommage à T.S. Eliot* (1987) for soprano and octet, a setting of lines from *The Four Quartets* in which Gubaidulina explores Eliot's concept of the transformation of time.

Stimmen ... Verstummen ...

The twelve-movement *Stimmen ... Verstummen ...* (Voices ... Fall Dumb ...), written in 1986, opens with one of Gubaidulina's most original flourishes – an ecstatic D major triad in the wind instruments, over strange scurrying sounds from the strings. The triad is disrupted at the end of the first movement by a menacing D flat from the brass instruments, and throughout this massive and entrancing work movements of static tonal calm are broken by uneasily chromatic episodes. The work reaches an extraordinary climax in the minute-long ninth movement, which is almost completely silent – rhythmic gestures for the conductor are notated in the score at this point, but even without this visual contribution it's a powerful and strange moment.

Royal Stockholm Philharmonic Orchestra; Rozhdestvensky (Chandos; with *Stufen*)

These excellent performances are conducted by Gennady Rozhdestvensky, a champion of so much new Russian music. The intensity of *Stimmen ... Verstummen ...* carries the listener through the almost silent ninth movement, when the pulse of the rhythmic patterns that Gubaidulina has established can still be felt.

Choral and Vocal Works

Gubaidulina has set a wide range of texts demonstrating the breadth of her philosophical, spiritual and artistic concerns – from ancient Egyptian and Persian texts through the writings of St Francis of Assisi to the works of poets such as Marina Tsvetayeva and Rainer Marina Rilke. *Perception* (1983), for soprano, baritone and seven strings, sets writings by Francisco Tanzer and uses a variety of different vocal techniques including sprechstimme. Rather more striking is the recent *Jetzt immer Schnee* (Now Always Snow, 1993), a hauntingly beautiful setting of Gennady Aigi's mystical and impressionistic verses. A vast landscape, both serene and threatening, is evoked through spare orchestral writing over which the voices sound intimate and vulnerable. The opening is especially memorable: an incantatory phrase is repeated between the voices with a whispered intensity, while scuttering strings animate the background.

Jetzt immer Schnee; Perception: Kleindienst, Lorenz; Netherlands Chamber Choir; Schönberg Ensemble; De Leeuw (Philips)

Striking performances from all concerned on this CD, particularly in *Jezt immer Schnee* (sung in Russian). The devotional qualities of the music are conveyed with a hallucinatory vividness by the Netherlands Chamber Choir. This is currently out of the catalogue but well worth looking out for.

Chamber Works

One of Gubaidulina's most frequently performed chamber works is the radiantly contemplative *Garten von Freuden und Traurigkeiten* (Garden of Joys and Sorrows). Written in 1980, this piece creates an enthrallingly beautiful sound-world using all the resources of just three instruments – flute, viola and harp. In *Seven Last Words*, written in 1982, Gubaidulina creates an equally unusual but quite different texture. Here two solo instruments – a cello and a traditional Russian *bayan* or button accordion – play beautiful lamenting melodies and strange, agitated scratching sounds over chant-like passages from the string orchestra. *In croce*, for cello and organ, is another work in which the exploration of unusual sonorities produces an extraordinary atmosphere of spiritual struggle and resolution. The *String Trio* (1988) is a demanding work for the more conventional line-up of violin, viola and cello – "three characters who reveal their individual wills", to quote the composer's description. The first movement travels from a violently sparse opening through to full rich harmonies, and is followed by a second movement of floating pizzicato and ethereal harmonics. The often disturbingly agitated final movement ends with a feeling of uneasy peace.

Seven Last Words; In croce; Five Pieces "Silenzio": Rabus, Kliegel, Moser; Camerata Transylvanica; Selmeczi (Naxos)

With Gidon Kremer's live recording of *Garten von Freuden und Traurigkeiten* and the *String Trio* currently out of the catalogue, this CD becomes the first choice as an introduction to Gubaidulina's chamber music – outstanding performances of three of her most mysterious works.

Garten von Freuden und Traurigkeiten: Debussy Trio München (Cavalli; with music by Jan Bach, Arnold Bax & Fredrik Schwenk)

In a programme of relatively obscure twentieth-century chamber works, *Garten von Freuden und Traurigkeiten* stands out for its radiant beauty. This is a rapturous account from the Debussy Trio of Munich who are consistently sensitive to the work's intricate subtleties.

h

George Frideric Handel (1685–1759)

The death of Henry Purcell in 1695 (see p.426) ended two remarkable centuries of achievement in English music. But Purcell had no obvious successor, and by 1700 English music was in the doldrums – though London continued to be a major centre of musical excellence. Salvation came in the form of George Frideric Handel, whose arrival in 1710 injected a new vitality into English musical life. Handel's melodic flair and his cosmopolitanism – he had successfully assimilated the Italian and French styles – made an immediate impact. If his attempt to establish opera in England was ultimately a failure, then his transformation of oratorio into a quasi-operatic form had a deep-rooted effect on English taste that was to last until Elgar. Of his contemporaries, only J. S. Bach produced work in which the qualities of robustness, lucidity and passion were so finely balanced.

Handel was born in the north German town of Halle in 1685, son of a surgeon who was convinced that the law was the proper calling for his son. Yet the musicians at the Court of Saxe Weissenfels, where his father worked, soon introduced Georg Frideric Händel (as he was then) to their profession, and recognized his remarkable potential. His teacher, F.W. Zachow, gave him a grounding in counterpoint and instrumentation as well as a bravura keyboard technique, and by 1702 Georg was a major figure in the region – cathedral organist, composer and friend of Telemann (see p.581).

In 1705 he presented several operas in Hamburg. Their mixed fortunes convinced him he should learn his operatic trade in Italy: he duly went to Florence, where he came to know both Alessandro and Domenico Scarlatti; and to Venice, where his opera *Agrippina* was a huge success and where he met Prince Ernst of Hanover. At the prince's recommendation, Handel was appointed court conductor to the Elector of Hanover, Georg Ludwig. But, aware of the limitations of his new position, Handel took official leave of absence and set out for England in search of a more lucrative marketplace for his operatic skills. Shortly after his arrival, Handel persuaded the management of the Haymarket Theatre to stage an opera by him. The result was *Rinaldo*, written in fifteen days flat. The furore it produced – not least when Handel released a flock of sparrows for one aria – made him an overnight success.

Despite his poor English, Handel seems to have been adept at making good contacts: the influential Earl of Burlington was an important early patron, while the composition of a magnificent

George Frideric Handel at work, after a portrait by Philippe Mercier.

Te Deum in celebration of the Peace of Utrecht secured him a state pension from Queen Anne. There was a brief moment of embarrassment in 1714 when his Hanoverian employer succeeded to the English throne as George I, but the success of another opera, *Amadigi* (1715), quickly restored his fortunes. In 1716 Handel accompanied George I on a return visit to Hanover, where he persuaded an old friend, Johann Christoph Schmidt, to return to England with him as his amanuensis. Shortly after his return, Handel was employed by the rich Duke of Chandos in the unusual position of composer-in-residence.

In 1719 a society of wealthy amateurs founded the Royal Academy of Music. Handel was appointed music director and composed operas alongside his chief rival Giovanni Bononcini. Its nine seasons drew from him a stream of masterpieces (including *Giulio Cesare*) but the squabbles and enormous fees of competing prima donnas crippled the Academy, as did the long-running popular success of John Gay's satirical *Beggar's Opera* (1728), a work which lampooned the contrivances and downright idiocies of opera seria. Handel himself remained solvent, however, and a patriotic potboiler, *Riccardo I, Re d'Inghilterra*

(1727), ensured that he stayed in grace with the newly crowned George II. In 1729 he formed another company, but his new works were not so well received as before. Four years later a rival group, the Opera of the Nobility, was set up with many of the stars of Handel's old company and with the backing of the Prince of Wales. Handel retaliated with a new style of opera in which singing was interspersed with ballet, but a revival of one of his early oratorios, *Esther*, suggested a new direction, a notion confirmed by the reception of another oratorio, *Deborah*, in 1733.

Yet by 1741, again a victim of fickle public taste, his finances were ailing once more, and Handel was thrown into despair when his *Messiah* failed to enthrall its first audiences. He was reported "disordered in mind", but the late 1740s saw his reputation revive through oratorios of operatic power and splendour – *Samson*, *Judas Maccabaeus* and then *Solomon*, written in the same year that the *Music for the Royal Fireworks* was produced to celebrate the peace treaty of Aix-la-Chapelle.

In April 1759 Handel fainted during a performance of *Messiah*, and died soon after. He was buried in Westminster Abbey, the only possible resting place for the figure who had become in effect the composer to the nation.

OPERAS

Handel was the greatest of all composers of opera seria, the dominant operatic genre of the eighteenth century. Opera seria had been formulated by the Italian poet Pietro Metastasio in an attempt to get rid of opera's more absurd aspects. A typical Metastasian libretto revolved around a conflict between love and duty: there were three acts in which recitative and aria were alternated – recitative usually expressing dialogue, arias being reserved for soliloquy. Handel's achievement was not so much to transform the conventions of the genre as invest them – especially the da capo arias – with a new emotional conviction and psychological insight. His operas possess both tenderness and vigour, which perhaps explains why they alone, out of all the thousands of Baroque operas, have been regularly and effectively staged over the last fifty years – despite their often static quality and implausible plots. Though all of them contain music of rare beauty, their length often puts potential listeners off. With this in mind, we have selected a recital disc of some of the most celebrated arias and recommended two of the most famous, and frequently performed, of all Handel's operas – *Giulio Cesare in Egitto* and *Ariodante*.

Handel Arias: Daniels; Orchestra of the Age of Enlightenment; Norrington (Virgin)

Handel routinely employed castrati in his operas (*Rodelinda* has three). In modern times, these roles are taken either by a female mezzo-soprano or a male counter-tenor. David Daniels is one of the most outstanding of recent counter-tenors, and this disc shows off the full range of his skills with arias from *Tamerlano, Rinaldo, Rodelinda, Ariodante, Giulio Cesare* and *Serse*.

Giulio Cesare in Egitto

Giulio Cesare in Egitto, written for the Royal Academy of Music in 1724, is perhaps Handel's most fully wrought example of the heroic ideal. Voluptuous and exotic, introducing a new orchestral brilliance and magnificence of spectacle, it was a success from its first appearance – "the house was just as full at the seventh performance as at the first", noted a courtier, Monsieur de Fabrice. The story tells of Julius Caesar's Egyptian campaign, the machinations of the Egyptian ruler Ptolemy, and the love of his sister Cleopatra for the Roman emperor.

Handel's music matches the drama's scale, but principal amongst this opera's qualities is its concentration on solo arias – Cleopatra and Caesar have eight each. The role of Cleopatra is one of Handel's greatest creations for the female voice, and her Act 2 recitative and aria "Se pietà di me non sento" (If you feel no pity for me), in which she laments her fate, yearns for revenge and longs for the love of Caesar, is especially wonderful – with a melody of effortless conviction, this is the opera's most emotive episode. The accompanied recitatives are significant for their startling number of modulations, while the vocal lines themselves are both longer and more complex than in any of Handel's previous operas. The title role (originally played by the castrato, Senesino) is weakly defined by Haym's text, however, and it is left entirely to the music to bring Caesar's idealized nobility and courage to life.

Larmore, Schlick, Fink, Rorholm, Ragin, Zanasi, Visse; Concerto Köln; Jacobs (Harmonia Mundi; 3 CDs)

Where this recording triumphs is in the richness of characterization. Jennifer Larmore has real brio as Caesar (originally a castrato role) but the crucial role is Cleopatra. Handel matches Shakespeare in the infinite variety he reveals in Cleopatra's eight arias, and Barbara Schlick rises marvellously to the occasion, moving from frothy innocence through pathos to seductive insinuation.

Castrati

The castrato came into being at around the same time as opera. Throughout the Middle Ages the Church had upheld Saint Paul's injunction to "Let your women keep silence in the churches" by using children and falsettists (counter-tenors) for choral music. It's not known exactly when their ranks were joined by castrated adult males, but they seem to have become commonplace by the middle of the sixteenth century, though the earliest castrati whose names have survived were Pietro Folignato and Girolamo Rossini, who were drafted into the Sistine Chapel choir in 1599.

If medical assistance could not be afforded, the child's mother usually conducted the operation, which was recorded by the French lawyer Charles d'Ancillon, who wrote one of the first books about castration. The testicles were removed by "putting the patient into a bath of warm water, to soften and supple the parts, and make them more tractable. Then the jugular veins were pressed, making the party so stupid and insensible that he fell into a kind of apoplexy." Castration of one's offspring was technically punishable by death or excommunication, but the Church was prepared to believe the stories of childhood mishap – a kick from a horse or a bite from a wild pig – that virtually every castrated soprano offered to explain his mutilation. Powerless to reverse the dreadful deed, choirmasters took the view that the unfortunate child might as well be put to good use. These uses were initially exclusively church-bound, and a top-class castrato could earn good money if he agreed to remain faithful to one diocese. Such was the allure of the potential income that by the end of the sixteenth century, according to one estimate, some four thousand children were being castrated annually in Italy alone. The Church was soon full to overflowing with male sopranos, and supply would have far outstripped demand had Peri's *Euridice* not revealed the opportunities for stardom in the new genre of opera. From 1600 until the time of Mozart, the castrato was an essential component of opera, and in their eighteenth-century heyday star singers, such as Senesino, Caffarelli, Carestini and – most famously of all – Farinelli, commanded astronomical fees. Indeed such was their allure that Handel, in his opera *Giulio Cesare* (see opposite), wrote important roles for no less than three castrati.

Although only a tiny number of castrated children ever found fame or fortune, other consequences of amputation were more predictable: the castrato could expect to develop uncommonly thick hair on his head but remain bald everywhere else; he was certain to suffer from obesity and grow rapidly upwards, often reaching far greater than average height (the ludicrously mannered poses of many castrati were adopted to counter their ill-formed gait); his face would be inclined to a crimson corpulence; and his chest would become abnormally developed – hence the freakish breath control demonstrated by the successful castrati, who were able to hold a single line of music for up to two minutes.

Another aspect of the adult castrato's life remains controversial. Marriage for castrati was banned by both Catholics and Protestants, but many of them seem to have been singularly popular as consorts for both sexes. Modern endocrinology suggests that the sexual activities of the castrati could not have involved the use of their undeveloped genitals, so there remains some doubt as to what exactly they got up to. But there is no doubt that some retained their sexual drive while presenting no risk of conception, and enjoyed a thriving parallel career as high-class prostitutes.

Carestini – The Story of a Castrato: Jaroussky; Le Concert d'Astrée; Haim (Virgin)

The great castrati roles are nowadays sung either by a female soprano or male countertenor. Philippe Jaroussky is one of the best of the latter, with a beautifully consistent tone across the range of his voice – a characteristic of the great Carestini. His material, by Handel, Gluck and more obscure figures, includes both the virtuosic and the heart-rending.

Farinelli, Il Castrato: Ragin, Mallas-Godlewska; Les Talens Lyriques; Rousset (Naive)

For the sumptuous (if factually inaccurate) biopic of Farinelli, the filmmakers decided to create their idea of a castrato's sound by electronically fusing the voices of countertenor Derek Le Ragin and soprano Ewa Mallas-Godlewska. Several critics sniffed at the result but it is certainly striking and remarkably convincing. The selection includes arias by Handel, Hasse and Ricardo Broschi – Farinelli's brother.

The Last Castrato. Complete Vatican Recordings: Moreschi (Opal)

If you want to know what an actual castrato sounded like, this is the only place to go. Alessandro Moreschi, first soprano of the Sistine Chapel for thirty years, was in his forties when he made these recordings in Rome in 1902 and 1904. The ethereal voice that emerges over the crackle is like nothing you'll have heard before. But be prepared: it as disturbing to listen to as it is poignant.

Ariodante

For the libretto for *Ariodante* Handel turned to an existing text, by Antonio Salvi, based on Ariosto's *Orlando furioso*. A complex tale of skulduggery, the drama unfolds in Scotland, where Ariodante and Ginevra are celebrating their engagement. Ariodante's rival, Polinesso, uses the maid Dalinda to help him falsify evidence of Ginevra's infidelity and when this is presented to the court, together with news that Ariodante has thrown himself to his death, Ginevra goes mad. Ginevra is saved when Polinesso confesses his plot and Ariodante returns, having faked his suicide.

Ariodante's most striking quality is that both Ariodante and Polinesso are travesti roles – i.e. male roles played by women. This means that nearly all of the opera's leads are sopranos. Consequently, most of the duets and ensembles involve the heady union of female voices, a combination that is particularly exquisite in the duets between Ariodante and Ginevra, such as Act 1's soaring "Prendi da questa mano" (Take from this hand), in which the lovers pledge their devotion. Ariodante's "masculine" qualities are expressed through some of the composer's most intricate coloratura. But it is Ginevra who provides the opera's emotional core by undergoing a transformation – from happy innocence to resignation – movingly expressed in the haunting "Il mio crudel martoro" (My cruel torment), in which she prays for death.

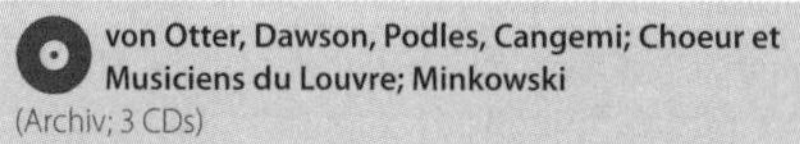

von Otter, Dawson, Podles, Cangemi; Choeur et Musiciens du Louvre; Minkowski
(Archiv; 3 CDs)

Marc Minkowski's recording of *Ariodante* is exceptional, first and foremost, for its casting. The partnership of Anne Sofie von Otter in the title role and Lynne Dawson as Ginevra is intoxicating, with both singers articulating their feelings, as well as their words, with wonderful commitment. The supporting cast and chorus are excellent, and Minkowski's small but resonant orchestra creates a generous background for the vocal score.

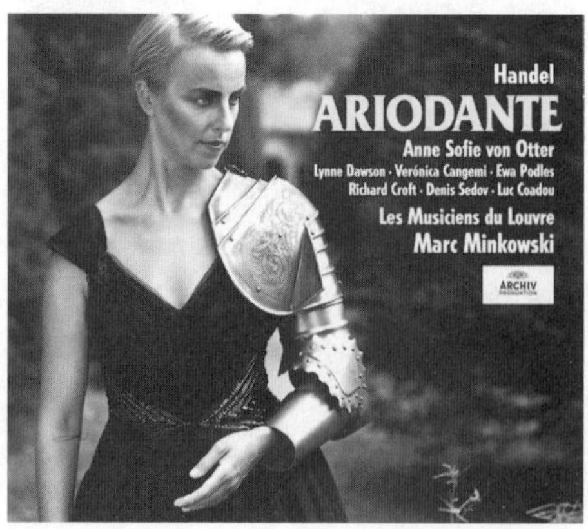

ORATORIOS

Oratorio had emerged in Italy at the end of the sixteenth century (see p.128), at about the same time as opera, to which it provided a religious counterpart. Composers who wrote for one almost inevitably wrote for the other. Handel was no exception: during his stay in Italy he wrote an oratorio, *La Resurrezione*, for Rome, and an opera, *Agrippina*, for Venice. In England, where oratorio was largely unknown, Handel fashioned his own version of the genre in a manner calculated to appeal to middle-class Protestant taste. Most of the stories were taken from the Bible; they were sung in English; and they had substantial choruses, which drew on the varied tradition of the English anthem. They were not church music – most were performed in the concert hall or in the theatre – but neither were they opera, although the narrative of many makes effective staging perfectly feasible. *Messiah*, by far and away the most celebrated oratorio, is actually the least typical because it doesn't tell a story.

Messiah

By 1740 Handel realized that his operatic career was finished and, facing an indifferent audience, he contemplated retirement. But in the summer of 1741 came an invitation from Dublin to write a sacred oratorio to be performed in the city. Handel collaborated with his friend Charles Jennens, who fashioned a skilful libretto combining both Old and New Testament texts – the subject being a non-dramatic presentation of Christ as the world's saviour. The essential mood that Jennens established is one of contemplation: characters are not named, though there is a slight suggestion of narrative in the Nativity sections. All of this is communicated by music which bears intense meaning in every bar, and has a visionary quality in its evolution from darkness to light.

In his deployment of soloists and choruses, Handel's sense of timing and proportion is matchless, and the sheer physical pleasure of the sound is remarkable too. There's a plethora of beautiful arias (recitative is minimal), which vary greatly in both type and mood: from the grandiose da capo aria of "He Was Despised" to the more simple lyricism of "How Beautiful are the Feet". Equally memorable are the magnificent choruses in which grand ceremonial music is frequently combined with elaborate, often fugal, counterpoint, thus emphasizing how the religious experience is as joyful as it is reverential.

Rodgers, Jones, Robson, Langridge, Terfel; Collegium Musicum 90; Hickox (Chandos; 2 CDs)

This recording has a fine group of soloists – all seasoned opera singers – who really sound as though they mean what they are singing. Particularly outstanding are Bryn Terfel and Philip Langridge, whose first recitative, "Comfort Ye", immediately establishes the right mood of fervent expectation. Richard Hickox's conducting conjures up the sense of occasion that is so vital for this work.

Marshall, Robbin, Rolfe-Johnson, Hale, Brett, Quirke; Monteverdi Choir; English Baroque Soloists; Gardiner (Philips; 2 CDs)

Gardiner's version is remarkable for the transparency of its sound and the way the music's development, from gravitas to celebration, is so sensitively captured. Dramatic impact and a sense of joy are strong – the Monteverdi Choir bring a lightness of touch and rhythmic spring to the choruses – and there is a real sense of the work being approached as if for the first time.

Judas Maccabaeus

Ever the consummate opportunist, Handel dashed out *Judas Maccabaeus* by way of a compliment to the Duke of Cumberland, who in April 1746 had defeated the Jacobite rebels at the Battle of Culloden. In his haste Handel lifted sections from his existing oratorios *Joshua* and *Belshazzar*, the rest of the libretto being patched together by the congenial Reverend Thomas Morell, who could match something of the composer's breakneck speed. In the event the premiere had to wait until April 1747. Perhaps out of fear that his dedicatee might find something offensive in the portrayal of the oratorio's military hero, Handel here avoided the intense personal drama that had characterized *Belshazzar* – which in any case seemed to have baffled a public used to milder fare. *Judas* deals with the anticipation of events and of reactions to them, rather than with events themselves, yet its contrasts of mood and tempo sustain it well over three acts, and it has endured as one of the finest of all celebratory compositions.

De Mey, Saffer, Spence, Thomas, Asawa, Kromm; Berkeley Chorus; Philharmonia Baroque Orchestra; McGegan (Harmonia Mundi; 2 CDs)

Nicholas McGegan's small forces add crisp refinement to music which, on the whole, is more contemplative than theatrical; resiliently phrased, this performance rarely sounds undernourished, as it so easily could.

Solomon

Opening on 17 March, 1749, Handel's most sumptuous and musically thrilling oratorio was unveiled to a nation in the midst of exuberant mass celebration – the War of the Austrian Succession was over, and in Green Park stood a wooden structure over a hundred feet high, depicting the king amid the Greek gods. "Record him, ye bards, as the pride of our days ... Ev'ry object swells with state, All is pious, all is great" – this is the heart of *Solomon*, a piece that idealizes Georgian England through implicit historical comparison. Pantheistic rather than narrowly Christian, *Solomon* is more a pastoral idyll and pageant than a dramatic narrative (the dispute of the two harlots being the only moment of excitement), combining episodes of ceremonial with an enraptured lyricism. This is especially true of the glorious Act 1 in which, after a grand opening, Solomon and his queen seem to do very little but exchange increasingly sensuous blandishments.

Watkinson, Argenta, Hendricks, Rodgers, Rolfe Johnson, Varcoe; Monteverdi Choir & English Baroque Soloists; Gardiner (Philips; 2 CDs)

John Eliot Gardiner's performance has won many awards for its ebullient pace and lyrical sensitivity. With Joan Rodgers and Barbara Hendricks in especially luscious voice, and with the Monteverdi Choir superlatively clear and precise, this is an outstanding Handel recording.

SACRED MUSIC

Handel's operas and oratorios have tended to eclipse his achievements in the less ambitious areas of choral music. In fact he wrote a great deal of excellent music for the church, though this does tend to lean towards the grandiose and the ceremonial. His travels had given him a highly detailed knowledge of different styles and, by the time he settled in England, Handel had appraised what was needed and then enhanced it with a fusion of Italian harmonic intensity, German polyphony, elements of French music and Purcellian grandeur.

Dixit Dominus

Handel reached maturity as a composer while in Italy, and of all his Italianate works the best known and most exuberant is the setting of Psalm 110, *Dixit Dominus*, from 1707. The influence of Vivaldi is evident in the animated opening (underlined by

Baroque: A Period or a Style?

Of all musical-historical terms, Baroque has the most surprising pedigree – descended from the Portuguese word "barroco", referring to a rough or imperfectly shaped pearl. For hundreds of years it was an insult, implying something bizarre or grotesque. Yet it has ended up describing one of the most colourful and magnificent periods in the arts. Baroque has been called the first truly international style, shaping everything from epic buildings to tiny decorative artefacts, epic canvases to intimate chamber music.

Modern commentators agree that the Baroque era began around 1600, immediately after the Renaissance, and stretched until around 1750. The movement is often connected to the Counter-Reformation – an attempt by the Vatican to provide theological answers to Protestant criticisms that spilled over into a vast programme of artistic patronage affirming the Church's power. Magnificent Baroque churches filled with dazzling new art sprang up in Catholic Germany, Spain, Sicily, France and Poland, and the style was sufficiently expansive that its effects were felt as far north as Protestant countries such as England and the Netherlands. In Italy, Bernini and Borromini forged the motifs of Baroque in architecture and sculpture, adopting the serene forms of the Renaissance but pushing them in radical new directions: twisting columns and tearing apart facades, introducing extravagant decoration and bold contrasts between light and shade. Caravaggio, Rubens and Rembrandt attempted similarly expressive techniques in painting, experimenting with intense lighting effects and pungent colours to bring new drama to familiar subjects and take spectators to the heart of the action.

In music, the term carries similar connotations, but contemporaries were not always impressed. In the 1730s the French critic Jean-Baptiste Annet noisily complained about composers who "wrest laboriously from the bottom of the sea some baroque pearls, when diamonds can be found on the surface of the earth", while by 1768 the philosopher and music-lover Jean-Jacques Rousseau had written off baroque music as "that in which the harmony is confused, charged with dissonances, in which the melody is harsh and little natural, intonation difficult and the movement constrained".

Despite these harsh words, it's possible to detect more than a hint of what we understand by the term today: Baroque was a newly energetic style, inventive in its harmony, restless in its melodic effects. As with Baroque painting and architecture, Baroque music often contains thrilling contrasts and elaborate decoration. And in addition to making the most of new discoveries about temperament (see p.26), Baroque composers were able to capitalize on rapid technical developments in keyboard instruments such as the harpsichord and organ, and had access to string and wind instruments of greater power and flexibility. They forged new musical forms such as the concerto (see p.610), which experimented with the sonic effects of different groups of instruments; the cantata, which infused religious texts with humane drama; and opera, which placed secular stories in the most elaborate of theatrical contexts.

It can be hard to say precisely what connects, say, the restrained religious cantatas of someone like Buxtehude with the exuberant operas of Handel – still less what makes them both Baroque, a style that extended across many artistic and geographical boundaries. The answer might lie in the determination of Baroque artists to extract the maximum emotional effect from their work, to make art feel as intense and varied as life. In the words of Heinrich Wölfflin, the nineteenth-century art historian who brought the term into currency, "the baroque never offers us perfection ... only the unrest of change and the tension of transcience".

some lively string writing) and vivid harmonies – in particular the spine-tingling soprano duet of the last verse ("De torrente in via"). Corelli is another influence, notably in the way solo and tutti passages are frequently contrasted. But the sheer energetic vigour of the contrapuntal writing, in particular the toe-tapping and exuberant Gloria, is unmistakably Handelian.

Massis, Kozená; Les Musiciens du Louvre; Minkowski (Archiv; with *Saeviat tellus*, *Laudate pueri* & *Salve Regina*)

To a large extent the disc is a vehicle for the two brilliant sopranos who perform on it. The two come together (with other soloists) on *Dixit Dominus*, and rarely has the duet sounded so thrillingly ethereal. Throughout the work the chorus finds just the right balance between robust involvement and delicate restraint.

Anthems

In England the anthem was a more sober and ceremonious affair than the continental motet. The eleven so-called *Chandos Anthems*, written in between 1717 and 1720 for the first Duke of Chandos, are typical examples of Handel's prowess in the genre. By turns stately, penitential and joyful, these early works were significant in laying the foundations of Handel's career as a composer of oratorios. The sixth of the group, *As Pants the Hart*, is an absolute *tour de force* of choral writing. But in terms of dramatic impact nothing can quite match *Zadok the Priest* – one of the anthems written for the coronation of George II in 1727. Its opening is a masterpiece of mounting tension, with a long orchestral introduction of arpeggiated strings gradually building to an explosive choral entry. It's an ecstatic moment and, perhaps unsurprisingly, has been played at every subsequent coronation.

Chandos Anthems Nos. 4–6: Dawson, Partridge; The Sixteen Choir and Orchestra; Christophers (Chandos)

The Sixteen's recordings of the *Chandos Anthems* are available as a four-CD set or as individual discs. This volume, including the outstanding *As Pants the Hart*, would make a good introduction. The sound quality is full-bodied but the clarity of the singing is never compromised. The soloists are at the heart of these performances, lustrous in tone yet capturing the essential directness of the music.

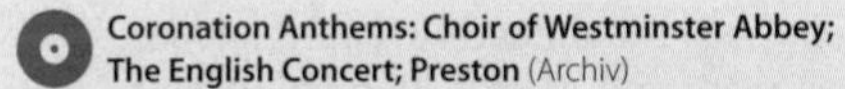

Coronation Anthems: Choir of Westminster Abbey; The English Concert; Preston (Archiv)

This outstanding disc presents radiant interpretations of this often jubilant music. *Zadok* is the best-known item here, but the highlight is *My Heart is Inditing*, with the Westminster Choir as smoothly assured in the lyrical inner sections as in the cumulative grandeur of the conclusion.

ODES

The duty of writing a celebratory ode in honour of the monarch's birthday was one of the tasks of the Master of the Queen's Musick. It's a measure of both Handel's impact in England and his opportunism that he managed to appropriate this task soon after his second stay. Another annual celebration was the festival in honour of St Cecilia (the patron saint of music). Since 1683, this was an occasion when London musicians gathered together to honour both the saint and their profession in the form of a church service and a banquet at which an ode was performed.

Ode for the Birthday of Queen Anne

The *Ode for the Birthday of Queen Anne* was written around the same time as the *Utrecht Te Deum* during Handel's second visit to London. It celebrates the Queen as a peace-maker (the Peace of Utrecht had ended the eleven-year War of the Spanish Succession) but its imagery is predominantly pastoral. It opens with a stunning masterstroke: a slow, sinewy phrase sung by the alto soloist is repeated by a solo trumpet before the two voices interweave themselves in elegant combination. It's a brilliant fusion of the stately and the sonorous, a pattern that recurs throughout the work.

Fisher, Bowman, Ainsley, George; New College Oxford Choir and the King's Consort; King (Hyperion; with *Te Deum in D & Sing Unto God*)

This is the second recording of the *Ode* by countertenor James Bowman who gives a beautifully poised account of the *Ode*'s opening lines in which his rounded tone blends seamlessly with the trumpet solo. Robert King's direction is always lively and there is some first-rate choral singing from the New College Choir.

Ode for St Cecilia's Day

The *Ode for St Cecilia's Day*, written in 1739, sets words by John Dryden (who also wrote a longer work honouring the saint, "Alexander's Feast", that Handel set three years earlier). Dryden's poem is a work rich in classical allusion: in its outer sections it ascribes to music a role in both the creation and the end of the world, while its central verses – divided between tenor and soprano arias – celebrate the qualities of individual instruments. Handel's music matches the verve of Dryden's text with some highly colourful word-setting. The *Ode* culminates in a marvellously stirring climax evoking the final trump: a chorale-like melody is sung accompanied by the soprano and echoed by the chorus before a trumpet heralds a final joyous chorus – "The dead shall live, the living die, And Music shall uptune the sky".

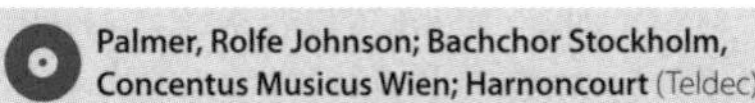

Palmer, Rolfe Johnson; Bachchor Stockholm, Concentus Musicus Wien; Harnoncourt (Teldec)

Recorded in 1977, this performance still holds its own. It's very much a work that relies heavily on its two soloists, especially the soprano. Felicity Palmer's incisive and slightly hard tone may not appeal to everyone, but the very instrumental quality of her voice comes into its own in the final section. That she is also capable of the most delicate singing can be heard in her tender account of the long-phrased opening solo.

ORCHESTRAL SUITES

The orchestral suite was developed in Germany, where the formal elegance of French court music had been introduced by German followers of Lully. The suite consisted of a set of contrasting dances modelled on the type found in Lully's operas and ballets. They were also known as overtures because of the two-movement overture which always preceded the dances. The form became highly popular in German aristocratic circles (Bach and Telemann both wrote them for princely patrons). Handel had no qualms about plundering previously written works for his two famous sets, the *Water Music* and *Music for the Royal Fireworks*. With bright clear sonorities of woodwind and brass (i.e. sounds that were meant to carry), these are both very clearly music for the outdoors.

Water Music

On 17 July, 1717, King George I and his entourage enjoyed a lavish trip down the Thames from Lambeth to Chelsea. As reported in the *Daily Courant*: "... a City Company's Barge was employ'd for the Musick, wherein were 50 Instruments of all sorts, who play'd ... the finest Symphonies, compos'd express for this Occasion, by Mr Hendel." These "Symphonies" were actually a group of orchestral suites which collectively became known as the *Water Music*. No autograph score exists of the *Water Music*, so the order of the dances is a matter of guesswork. What is generally agreed is that there are three distinct suites for various combinations of instruments. Each suite has its own particular character. The F major is the most radiant and the most grandiloquent: scored for two oboes, bassoon, two horns and strings, it's the first use of Baroque horns in English music and they dominate the set even though they're not used in every movement. The five-movement D major suite adds two trumpets and kettle drums to the band and the result is much more martial in tone. The most intimate of the suites, the one in G, was probably played as the royal party dined at Lord Ranelagh's villa at Chelsea. Its mixture of recorder, flute and strings has a much more "indoor" feel to it, as does the delicate sprightliness of its French-style dances.

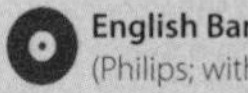

English Baroque Soloists; Gardiner
(Philips; with *Fireworks Music*)

This recording is an object lesson in the articulation of textures and accenting. John Eliot Gardiner's sense of the natural growth and fluctuating tension of the music is the key to this performance's spontaneity – the slow movements have a dying fall to them, and rarely have Allegros or Prestos been so effervescent.

Fireworks Music

Within a few weeks of *Solomon*'s first performance, another spectacular Handel premiere took place. As part of the celebrations for the ending of the war, a pavilion over four hundred feet long was erected in Green Park, and Handel was asked by George II to create a suite for an immense pyrotechnic display to be held there on 27 April, 1749. Handel wanted to use strings but the king insisted on "martial instruments". The final forces used for the *Music for the Royal Fireworks* are unclear, but included nine trumpets, nine horns, twenty-four oboes, twelve bassoons and three pairs of kettledrums. A rehearsal on 21 April went well, with a hundred musicians playing to a crowd of over twelve thousand, and bringing the centre of London to a standstill. The same could not be said of the big night: "The rockets succeeded mighty well; but the wheels, and all that to compose the principal part, were pitiful ... and then, what contributed to the awkwardness of the whole, was the right pavilion catching fire, and being burnt down in the middle of the show."

The overture is one of Handel's most exhilarating, brilliant creations, and if the remaining numbers are slighter, there is no finer demonstration of Beethoven's comment that Handel knew best how to achieve grand effects with simple means.

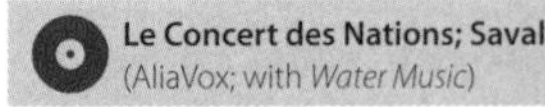

Le Concert des Nations; Savall
(AliaVox; with *Water Music*)

Handel's ceremonial music really benefits from a vigorous and energetic approach – which it certainly gets from Jordi Savall and Le Concert des Nations. There is none of the

politeness and emphasis on a clean sound at all costs that you get with some period orchestras. This is an outfit that does not shy away from the more gutsy and lurid colours that their instruments are capable of producing.

CONCERTOS

The concerto grosso, in which the main body of an orchestra (called the ripieno or concerto grosso) is in dialogue with a small group of instruments (the concertino), achieved its definitive form in the concertos of Corelli, written at the end of the seventeenth century. Handel was prompted to turn to the genre after the great success of two sets by a rival in London, Francesco Geminiani. Handel's Opus 3, published in 1734, and his Opus 6, of six years later, constitute the concerto grosso's final grand flourish. Thereafter concertos were largely a dialogue between the orchestra and an individual soloist. Handel's own main contribution to the solo concerto were the two sets of organ concertos, Opus 4 and Opus 7. Organ concertos were, more or less, a form invented by Handel, who wrote them to be performed as interludes between the acts of his oratorios.

Concerti Grossi

Handel's first great contributions to the genre, the Opus 3 of 1734, are six concerti grossi with woodwind, featuring a mix of new writing and pieces reworked from existing compositions by Handel and others. These are robust and clearly articulated pieces which make the most of the form's dramatic contrasts of solemn grandeur and vitality. Outstanding among them is the second, in B flat, which displays Handel's fascination with combining sweet melodies with unusual sonorities.

Handel's orchestral masterpiece appeared five years later – the Opus 6 concerti grossi, published as *Twelve Grand Concertos*. Amongst the most powerful works of the Baroque era, these concertos form part of a family tree that begins with Corelli, but Handel brings a new vibrancy and motion – his dances are fresh and flexible, his instrumentation lyrically ripe, his polyphony adventurous and tantalizing. The very last concerto, *No. 12 in B Minor*, forms a suitable climax: bristling with restless energy and yet full of mystery, it has in its central movement a quintessentially serene Handelian melody (hard not to imagine it being sung) that is twice repeated in variation form.

Concerti Grossi Opus 3: The English Concert; Pinnock (Deutsche Grammophon Archiv)

Trevor Pinnock's performance of the Opus 3 concerti is one of great charm. The English Concert play with a delicate fragility where necessary, and achieve a moving dignity in the slow movements.

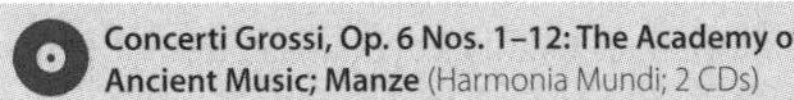
Concerti Grossi, Op. 6 Nos. 1–12: The Academy of Ancient Music; Manze (Harmonia Mundi; 2 CDs)

Andrew Manze directs the Academy from his position of leader of the orchestra with a good deal of verve and energy. His generally fleet-footed and light approach brings out the mercurial brilliance of these concerti, but the sound is always rich and refined.

Organ Concertos

Sir John Hawkins, Handel's contemporary, leaves a description of him at the organ: "His amazing command of the instrument, the grandeur and dignity of his style, the copiousness of his imagination, and the fertility of his invention were qualities that … no one ever pretended to equal." Handel's delight in improvisation is crucial to his finest works for this instrument, his organ concertos – the form of keyboard music to which he devoted himself after 1730. These works were written to be played on the organ or harpsichord, since English organs normally lacked the pedalboards and multiple manuals fitted to their hefty continental counterparts, and the consequence is that the texture of these pieces is extremely transparent. Many passages were left as skeletons to be fleshed out with improvisation, which is why they demand a performer with both knowledge and flair to bring them to life.

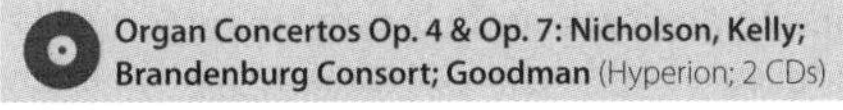
Organ Concertos Op. 4 & Op. 7: Nicholson, Kelly; Brandenburg Consort; Goodman (Hyperion; 2 CDs)

Admirably fresh and lively performances from Paul Nicholson played on the organ of St Lawrence Whitchurch – an instrument that Handel himself played on. The sixth concerto of Op.4 is played by Frances Kelly in the version arranged for harp.

KEYBOARD MUSIC

Handel was a brilliant keyboard player and during his stay in Italy he took part in one of those keyboard duels between competing virtuosos that aristocratic patrons so loved to set up. This one was at the palace of Cardinal Ottoboni in Rome, and pitted Handel against his Neapolitan contemporary Domenico Scarlatti (see p.471). According to Handel's first biographer, "there was a total difference in their manner. The characteristic excellence of Scarlatti seems to have consisted in a certain elegance and delicacy of expression. Handel had an uncommon brilliancy and command of finger: but what distinguishes him from all other players ... was that amazing fullness, force, and energy, which he joined with them." Handel wrote more than twenty keyboard suites, of which the most distinguished are the first published set, sometimes known as the eight *Great Suites.*

Eight Suites for Keyboard

As had happened before with his music, Handel was prompted into revising and publishing his keyboard suites in an attempt to undermine the sale of pirated versions that had appeared. The first set of eight were published in 1720 but were probably written quite a bit earlier. They incorporate a wide range of styles – French, Italian, German – sometimes within the same suite. Thus the glorious second suite has as its first movement an aria-like Adagio but culminates in a fugue of enormous wit and invention. The fifth suite is the most frequently recorded, popular above all for its last movement air and variations in which can be heard, according to legend, the clear sound of the blacksmith's hammer against an anvil – hence its nickname *The Harmonious Blacksmith.*

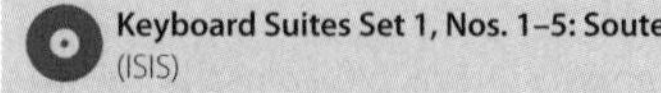

Keyboard Suites Set 1, Nos. 1–5: Souter (ISIS)

If you feel that this music is best served by being played on the kind of instrument for which it was written, then you won't find anything more authentic than this. Martin Souter plays an instrument from the Bate collection at Oxford University that almost certainly belonged to Handel himself. It's a one-manual instrument, surprisingly warm in tone and well recorded, which Souter plays with real flair and energy.

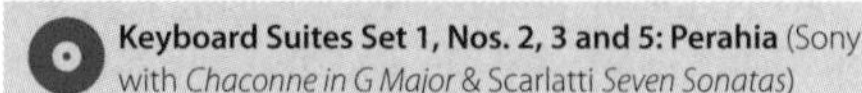

Keyboard Suites Set 1, Nos. 2, 3 and 5: Perahia (Sony; with *Chaconne in G Major* & Scarlatti *Seven Sonatas*)

Handel's suites lend themselves to being played on the piano as well as any Baroque keyboard music. When the playing is this good it is hard to imagine them on any other instrument. Murray Perahia brings a quality to this music which is both mellow and incisive, and above all his playing emphasizes the brilliance of the music rather than the brilliance of his own playing.

Karl Amadeus Hartmann (1905–1963)

By turn savage and mournful, lyrical and despairing, the music of Karl Amadeus Hartmann gives voice to the convulsions that gripped Europe from the 1930s to the 1960s. Working predominantly in large-scale forms, he produced a body of work – until recently largely neglected – that maintains a respect for nineteenth-century ideals of expression while at the same time forging a distinctly personal twentieth-century language.

Hartmann's early compositions, such as the *Jazz Toccata and Fugue* for solo piano (1928), reveal the influence not only of jazz but of Hindemith and Bartók. For several years before Hitler became chancellor, he organized new music concerts in Munich, and throughout his life he kept abreast of the latest musical developments while aligning himself to no particular school. A vehement anti-fascist, Hartmann dedicated his *Miserae*, begun in 1933, to victims of the internment camps that Hitler had already established: "My friends, who had to die a hundred times over, who sleep for all eternity: we shall not forget you (Dachau 1933–34)". The following year he began work on *Des Simplicius Simplicissimus Jugend* (The Simplest Simpleton), an opera based on a seventeenth-century account of the Thirty Years War, in which he drew parallels between the Germany of that era and the Germany of the present; it was not performed until after World War II.

Throughout the Nazi era Hartmann remained in self-imposed "internal exile" in Munich, withdrawing himself and his music from concert life from 1933 to 1945. He may have participated in underground resistance, and at one point buried his manuscripts in a remote location, fearing that they would be destroyed. In 1942 he began a period of study with Anton Webern (see p.625). While Webern's serialism exerted little direct influence, Hartmann learnt much from the older composer, not least a formal discipline to balance what he acknowledged were his own more anarchic tendencies. As the war neared its conclusion, Hartmann witnessed the death-march of prisoners out of Dachau. His response was the Piano Sonata "*27 April 1945*", which bears the inscription "endless was the stream, endless the misery, endless the sorrow". By the time he completed the sonata, the war had ended.

Appointed to oversee the reconstruction of musical life in Bavaria, he established a long-running series of highly influential concerts under the title *Musica viva*. From 1947 onwards, Hartmann undertook the parallel task of reconstructing his own oeuvre, partly to provide it with a context free of the taint of the Nazi era. Some works he revised or withdrew, others he plundered for ostensibly new pieces. With the 1953 publication of his *Symphony No. 6* (derived from music written in 1938), the reordering seemed complete, although further revisions followed, as did two wholly new symphonies. Besides the eight numbered symphonies, Hartmann's symphonic works include the *Sinfonia tragica* (1943) and *Klagesang* (1945). Taken together, these are the backbone of his work, synthesizing elements of the Austro-German tradition from Bruckner through Mahler to Berg, yet always with a strong personal inflection born of profound humanism and a broad musical knowledge.

Portrait of Karl Amadeus Hartmann by his brother Adolf.

Symphony No. 1

The subtitle of the *Symphony No. 1 – Versuch eines Requiem* (Attempt at a Requiem) – might serve for all of Hartmann's symphonies. Derived from his pre-war *Symphonic Fragment* (premiered in 1948, then revised in 1955), it opens with a fanfare of thundering intensity before the mezzo-soprano soloist enters to intone Hartmann's German-language adaptation of Walt Whitman's poem "Misery": "I sit looking out at all the sorrows of the world … all the meanness and agony without end". The fanfare returns, bringing with it intimations of apocalyptic despair, to which the soloist seems already to have succumbed. Four of the five movements are Whitman settings, giving the work a Mahlerian form that freely mixes symphony, orchestral song and dramatic cantata. The whole is suffused with aching desolation, reflected in the pained *parlando* to which the soloist frequently resorts so as not to beautify the sentiments expressed. Only the purely instrumental third movement seems to offer hope, or at least relief, but that is soon extinguished by the last two movements, "Tears" and "Supplication". After the singer's final words ("O my dead! Exhale them perennial sweet death, years, centuries hence"), the latter builds to the briefest of orchestral climaxes over funereally tolling bells.

Kallisch; Bamberg Symphony Orchestra; Metzmacher (EMI; with works by Martin, Nono and Schoenberg)

Ingo Metzmacher's three-CD set of the symphonies makes a persuasive case for hearing all eight as a cycle. But many of the individual performances are also available in powerful and imaginative anthologies. This one collects works united in their response to war and tyranny. Metzmacher's refined performances capture the music's anger, restlessness and only occasional serenity.

Symphony No. 3

The *Symphony No. 3*, which was premiered in Munich in 1950, consists of music written during the war, plus a movement each from *Klagesang* (composed in response to the arrest of a friend) and the *Sinfonia tragica* (1943). Yet far from being a patchwork, the result is an organically integrated piece. The first movement, labelled "Virtuoso fugue" by the composer, begins with barely audible percussion which clears the way for a doleful melody played first on double bass, then picked up by string quintet before the whole string section adds its voice. Never quite amounting to a crescendo, the build-up is superbly handled. An abrupt explosion of percussion and winds briefly shatters the mood, ushering in a passage of almost martial brightness that never quite disperses the melancholy. The concluding movement was originally the first movement of the *Sinfonia tragica*, a work that went missing in Hartmann's lifetime but which was rediscovered in the 1970s. The opening march establishes a funereal atmosphere from which the rest of the work offers no escape, although yearning woodwind melodies struggle briefly but vainly to break free. It closes so quietly that it is as if the music, rather than reaching a climax, has simply ceased to be.

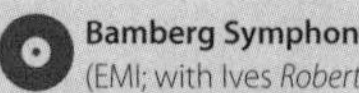

Bamberg Symphony Orchestra; Metzmacher
(EMI; with Ives *Robert Browning Overture*)

Metzmacher's recording is as persuasive as any in his Hartmann cycle; the Bamberg musicians deliver playing that is heartfelt but without exaggeration. Charles Ives' *Robert Browning Overture* makes a by no means obvious but appropriate companion piece.

Concerto funèbre

When in 1959 Hartmann revised his *Musik der Trauer* (Mourning Music) of 1939, he re-titled it *Concerto funèbre* (Funeral Concerto), in which form it has become his most performed work. The violin's heart-rending solo rhapsody, as virtuosic as in any of the great Romantic concertos, never obscures the profound conviction that lies behind the work. The tension between soloist and string orchestra, between moments of stillness and, at times, a headlong forward momentum, is superbly maintained throughout. The concerto opens with an instrumental quotation from a medieval Czech hymn, giving voice to Hartmann's dismay at the German invasion of Czechoslovakia in 1938. This leads quickly into the second movement Adagio in which the solo violin's long, singing lines are a cry of despair for the future, beneath which the orchestra (strings only) throbs in sympathy. A febrile anger permeates the third movement, finally subsiding as it succumbs to the numbed march of the fourth-movement Chorale.

Faust; Munich Chamber Orchestra; Poppen
(ECM; with *Symphony No. 4* & *Chamber Concerto*)

An outstanding interpreter of Bartók, Isabelle Faust is an ideal soloist in Hartmann's most-recorded work. The purity of her tone is matched by a willingness to cut up rough, particularly in the Adagio, while Christoph Poppen and the MCO deliver committed performances in both the concerto and the *Symphony No. 4* (also scored for strings alone). This is the obvious single-CD introduction to the composer.

Jonathan Harvey (1939–)

Almost uniquely among contemporary composers, Jonathan Harvey strives to make music of a consciously spiritual nature without rejecting the methods and strategies of modernism. While his contemporaries Arvo Pärt and John Tavener – inspired by the simple harmonies of pre-Renaissance polyphony – have sought the numinous by paring down their musical language, Harvey embraces complexity, revelling in the infinite sonic possibilities afforded by modern electronics. One of his most celebrated works, *Mortuos Plango, vivos voco* (1980), mixes the sounds of his young son's treble voice with the tolling of the great bell of Winchester Cathedral. The result is both poignant and reassuring in the way recognizable sounds are atomized via electronics into something timeless and ethereal.

Born at Sutton Coldfield in England, Harvey began his musical career as a chorister at St Michael's, Tenbury. While at Cambridge University he had private lessons in composition with Erwin Stein and in analysis with Hans Keller. His early works reveal the influence of Britten as well as interest in Schoenbergian serialism and the modalism of Messiaen. In 1969 a scholarship to Princeton brought him briefly within the orbit of Milton Babbitt, whose total serialism taught him the value of disciplined structural procedures. A more liberating influence was Stockhausen (the subject of a book by Harvey), whose experiments in rhythmic duration, the use of silence and the division of the orchestra into separate groups helped Harvey to develop a more personal and individual musical voice. Stockhausen's interest in Eastern ideas – both musical and mystical – has clear parallels with Harvey's own spiritual preoccupations.

Harvey's Christianity, which is informed by Indian spiritual traditions as well as the ideas of Rudolf Steiner and Carl Jung, is at the heart of his music. Much of what he writes for the voice (be it liturgical music or opera) is deeply contemplative and informed by a strong sense of ritual. But in all his music there is an extraordinarily ecstatic quality, a sensual enjoyment of the purely physical qualities of the – sometimes violent – sounds that he conjures up. This quality, or the way that, as Harvey puts it, "music perpetually plays between the physical sound and our subjectivisation of it", is graphically realized in *Bhakti* (1982) – the most thrilling and visionary of all his works to date.

Much of Harvey's working life has been taken up with teaching. He was professor of music at Sussex University from 1977 to 1993, and at Stanford University between 1995 and 2000. Since then he has received many commissions, and was composer-in-association with the BBC Scottish Symphony Orchestra from 2005 to 2008.

Bhakti

In the early 1980s, at the invitation of Pierre Boulez, Harvey worked at IRCAM, where he created *Bhakti*, a work for chamber orchestra with quadrophonic tape. Bhakti, a Sanskrit word meaning "to revere", is a Hindu movement emphasizing deep devotion to an individual god. Each of the work's twelve movements has a quotation from one of the ancient *Rig Veda* hymns, which encompass a range of moods, feelings and images and act as a stimulus to the musical ideas. *Bhakti* begins with a powerful representation of nothingness and the first stirrings of thought: it focuses on a single note, played by different instruments, which quietly builds and expands before a sudden flurry of more complex musical material. The tape (which is mostly composed of the electronically transformed sounds of the ensemble) acts as a contrasting voice in a dialogue with the acoustic material, and as a means of conveying a tangible sensation of space, both outer and inner.

Bhakti: Nouvel Ensemble Moderne; Vaillancourt (Naïve)

This second recording of *Bhakti* illustrates how a "difficult" contemporary can become clearer and more coherent the more often it is performed. There is a stronger sense of the development of ideas in this performance, as if the performers were thinking in terms of a journey – spiritual or otherwise. It's a quality enhanced by the stunning sound, wonderfully atmospheric in both depth and detail.

Cello Concerto

Harvey was a professional cellist for a brief time and the cello is the instrument with which he has made some of his most personal utterances. He regards it as the most human of instruments: "... it speaks with every aspect of the human voice, masculine, feminine, powerful, tender, poetic, exclamatory, dreamy". The 1990 *Cello Concerto* was inspired, like *Bhakti*, by a Hindu text (a quotation from *The Mahabharata*) and it too unfolds as a journey – in this case the individual's journey towards a state of bliss. The soloist is, for the most part, surrounded by a web of bright percussive sounds (vibraphone, celeste, glockenspiel) which suggests an aura of protective light carrying it across the more earthbound sounds of the rest of the orchestra.

Cello Concerto: Uitti; Arturo Toscanini Orchestra; Encinar (Etectera)

This disc generates a remarkable sensation of spaciousness and grandeur with the soloist, at times, an extremely vulnerable presence. Frances-Marie Uitti seems able to respond with ease to all the technical difficulties Harvey throws at her and the result is an aural experience quite unlike any other.

Orchestral Works

Not all of Harvey's music uses electronics, as a series of orchestral commissions written over the last ten years reveals. In their place he often employs an extended percussion section to create a glittering panoply of other-wordly sounds. Inspired by a purification ritual in a Tibetan Buddhist monastery, *Body Mandala* (2007) includes woodblocks, Tibetan bells and bamboo clusters; the resulting sense of ceremony is enhanced by the addition of two bass trombones that evoke the sound of the low Tibetan *tungchen*. A dramatic tension between agitated striving and stillness is evident in much of Harvey's music, nowhere more so than in ... *towards a Pure Land* (2005) where the overall sensation is one of travelling between different states of consciousness. The contempative wins out in the profoundly meditative *Tranquil Abiding* (1999), a contemporary classic in which the regularly pulsed rise and fall between two notes suggests a slow and steady inhalation and exhalation of breath.

Body Mandala, Tranquil Abiding, ... towards a Pure Land: BBC Scottish Symphony Orchestra; Volkov (NMC; with *Timepieces* & White as Jasmine)

Body Mandala and ... *towards a Pure Land* were both written for the BBC Scottish SO during Harvey's residency in Glasgow, and the orchestra's familiarity with his music is reflected in performances of great power and conviction. NMC's production has brilliantly captured every detail of this kaleidoscopic music.

Joseph Haydn (1732–1809)

Until relatively recently, Joseph Haydn was commonly regarded as John the Baptist to Mozart's Jesus Christ; a great man, certainly, but a secondary figure nonetheless. Haydn did the spadework, entrenching the symphony and the string quartet in the cultural landscape, and then dazzling Mozart came along, refining and perfecting what Haydn had doggedly constructed. This misjudgement of Haydn's music was supported by the image of "Papa Joe", a nickname bestowed on him many years before his death. Apart from his occasionally brutish treatment of Frau Haydn, he does seem to have been an agreeable person, well-respected by all, concerned about the wellbeing of others, and – when compared to someone like Beethoven – generous to a fault. But this genial portrait obscures the truth, for Joseph Haydn was one of the great revolutionaries of classical music, making huge advances in structure, harmony and melody, investing every form with inexhaustible potential for expression. He was born into the Baroque age, and went on to write music which prefigures the stormy creations of Beethoven.

Joseph Haydn at the time of his London successes.

Haydn was born in the Austrian town of Rohrau, and in 1761, after a conspicuously ordinary early life, was engaged as vice-*Kapellmeister* by Prince Paul Esterházy, a Hungarian nobleman. He remained exclusively in that family's employment for the next thirty years, working for Prince Paul and then for his son Nikolaus, at their palaces of Eisenstadt and Esterháza. Unlike Mozart, whose relationships with his patrons were neither easy nor consistent, Haydn lived happily within the confines of his master's world and benefited enormously from the seclusion and from having a permanent orchestra with which to work. As he later remarked, "there was no one there to confuse me, so I was forced to become original". His duties demanded that he compose almost constantly, but as he travelled rarely and was overawed at the prospect of having to perform as a pianist, violinist or conductor outside the palaces, his fame as a composer was spread almost solely through publishing.

In 1790 Nikolaus Esterházy died and the court musicians were dismissed by his successor. Haydn was also deemed surplus to requirements but, as a sign of the family's respect for his loyalty, they continued paying his salary and allowed him to keep his *Kapellmeister* title. He moved to Vienna, but shortly afterwards he received an invitation from the impresario J.P. Salomon to visit England. Feted by the music world and entertained by royalty, his first stay in England (1791–92) was a remarkable success and his time in London remains the most fascinating episode in what was a fairly uneventful life. He remained in England for some eighteen months, and took enormous satisfaction in receiving an honorary degree from Oxford University.

Having returned from London, he bought a house in Vienna where he taught Beethoven, among others, but in 1794 he was commissioned by Salomon to write six new symphonies and so made the journey back to England. This second visit lasted from February 1794 to August 1795 and brought him even greater fame and success. After his return, he moved back into employment with the Esterházys, but he worked for their household only on special occasions, devoting most of his time to composing. Between 1796 and 1802 Haydn produced some of his greatest music (in particular, the oratorio *Die Schöpfung*), but from 1802 his health began to fail, leading towards an illness from which he died in 1809.

Haydn's life may have been unenthralling, but his music is not. In some ways he was more radical than Mozart: whereas Mozart was obsessed with symmetrical perfection, in which the four- and eight-bar phrase reigned unchallenged, Haydn experimented with phrases lasting three, five, seven, and even nine bars; and while Mozart almost never veered from the sonata convention of first and second subjects, Haydn sometimes built movements on single themes, a procedure that didn't become a convention until the nineteenth century. As with any prolific composer, his output has its pedestrian moments, but his best music is outstandingly fresh and sprightly. Above all, Haydn is the most humane and comforting of composers. In his own words, he wrote music so that "the weary and worn, or the man burdened with affairs, may enjoy a few moments of solace and refreshment".

CHORAL MUSIC

Haydn was a deeply religious man and much of his most heartfelt and passionate music can be found in his sacred choral works. In his early masses and in works like the *Stabat Mater* (1767) there is a freshness and vigour to the writing which suggests that his faith was an essentially joyful aspect of his life. Unfortunately his activities as a composer for the church were curtailed by an imperial edict of 1783 restricting the use of orchestral music in the Catholic liturgy. The advantage of this was that when he returned to writing sacred music in 1796 he had a new-found confidence as a composer which enabled him to produce choral works of a hitherto unknown power and profundity. Supreme among these were the six final masses that he wrote, commissioned on a yearly basis by Prince Nikolaus Esterházy for his wife's name day, and his greatest oratorio *Die Schöpfung* (The Creation), a work largely inspired by hearing several of Handel's oratorios while in London.

Masses Nos. 11 & 12 The Nelson and the Theresa

Haydn wrote the third of his last set of masses in the summer of 1798, naming it *Missa in angustiis* – "Mass in anxious times". The anxiety was caused by Napoleon Bonaparte who had shelled Vienna the year before and was now in Egypt. It is more commonly known as the *Nelson Mass* in honour of the British admiral who destroyed the French fleet in August 1798 and for whom it was performed two years later. Scored for three trumpets, timpani, strings and organ, it begins in the most thrilling fashion with a restless Kyrie in which the soprano soloist has some brilliant soaring runs. This and the unusually sombre Benedictus are in D minor; the rest of the Mass is more celebratory but with the nervous energy of its opening never far from the surface.

The so-called *Theresa Mass* (named after the empress Maria Theresia but not, in fact, dedicated to her) is a less hard-driven work, more ample and confident and full of the most glorious melodies, in particular a beautiful alto solo in the Gloria. Both masses divide the Gloria and Credo into sections which are distributed between solo voices and the chorus, thus increasing the impact of the words and creating some telling contrasts in mood. There is also a new prominence given to the orchestra, which adds an even greater element of grand drama to these works.

Brown, Bruce-Payne, Butterfield, Finley; Monteverdi Choir; English Baroque Soloists; Gardiner (Archiv; 2 CDs)

You would be hard pressed to find a recording of these works more thrilling than this one. John Eliot Gardiner's usual trademarks of incisive attack and beautifully clear choral singing pay real dividends, especially in a work so abounding in dramatic flair as the *Nelson Mass*. The *Theresa Mass* gets a no less impressive performance.

Leipzig Radio Choir and Staatskapelle Dresden; Marriner (EMI; 2 CDs; with *Masses Nos. 7 & 10*)

Neville Marriner never loses sight of the sheer drama of the late masses, and there's plenty of atmosphere in both these performances. He's helped by some excellent soloists – in particular some powerful and incisive singing from soprano Margaret Marshall in the *Nelson Mass* and the warm tone of mezzo Doris Soffel in the *Theresa Mass*.

Die Schöpfung

The original English text for *The Creation* – a fusion of the early chapters of Genesis with sections of *Paradise Lost* – was put together with Handel in mind. When Haydn saw the text, he realized its potential and asked his friend Baron van Swieten to translate it into German. Like a Handel oratorio, *Die Schöpfung* is full of fresh and vivid imagery, depicting all the manifold glories of the Creation with a startling pictorialism.

The overture, depicting Chaos before the first day, is a bleak, formless and dissonant introduction to the arrival of the Archangel Raphael, who shares with the other archangels the narration of subsequent events – the first being the creation of light. With a lapidary simplicity typical of Haydn, the dawning of light is achieved by modulating from the darkness of C minor into a stupendous C major fortissimo chord. The subsequent arias achieve a transcendent simplicity that, perhaps, only Haydn could have brought to such a demanding subject. The choruses are similarly clear in their expression and, notably in "The Heavens are Telling the Glory of God", Haydn shows his genius for multiple voice part-writing.

McNair, Brown, Schade, Gilfry, Finley; Monteverdi Choir; English Baroque Soloists; Gardiner (Archiv; 2 CDs)

John Eliot Gardiner marshals his forces with superb discipline, producing a wonderfully fresh sound which still manages to possess the requisite amount of mystery – essential for this work. His excellent soloists are nicely contrasted: baritone Gerald Finley in particular brings a wonderful combination of the noble and the sympathetic to the role of Raphael.

Janowitz, Ludwig, Wunderlich, Krenn, Fischer-Dieskau, Berry; Vienna Singers; Berlin Philharmonic Orchestra; Karajan (Archiv; 2 CDs)

This *Die Schöpfung* boasts a great cast, though tragically tenor Fritz Wunderlich died before completing the sessions. Karajan employed two singers for the roles of Raphael and Adam and brought in Christa Ludwig for the final movement's "Let Every Voice Sing unto the Lord". This might suggest a fragmentary performance, but in fact this is a brilliantly realized and cohesive interpretation.

Massey, Harvey, Padmore, Persson, Davies, Piau; Vienna Singers; Gabrieli Consort & Players with Chetham's Chamber Choir; McCreesh (Archiv; 2 CDs)

If you want an outstanding version sung in English, this recent recording of *The Creation* is the one to go for. Paul McCreesh is particularly alive to the sheer theatre of the work, and his excellent soloists and outstanding chorus have a level of commitment that is often electrifying.

Die Jahreszeiten

Encouraged by the success of *Die Schöpfung* (1798), Haydn promptly set to work on another libretto prepared by Baron van Swieten – a German-language adaptation of episodes from *The Seasons*, by the English poet James Thomson. Premiered in May 1801, *Die Jahreszeiten* (The Seasons) was received with such enthusiasm that publication of the score earned Haydn four times the salary he'd been paid by Prince Esterházy.

The oratorio represents spring, summer, autumn and winter through a sequence of bucolic scenes, in which the rustic protagonists make observations on the cycle of nature as a metaphor for the trajectory of human existence on Earth. The climax of the piece is a vision of the eternal spring that awaits the righteous in heaven. The arias and choruses have all the vitality you'd expect of Haydn, and are spiced with some vivid scene-painting, in which the orchestra imitates crowing, a summer storm, a hunt, croaking frogs, and so on. Haydn had his doubts about these dashes of colour ("I was forced to write this Frenchified rubbish", he wrote), but they play a vital role in the delightful sound-world of his final masterpiece.

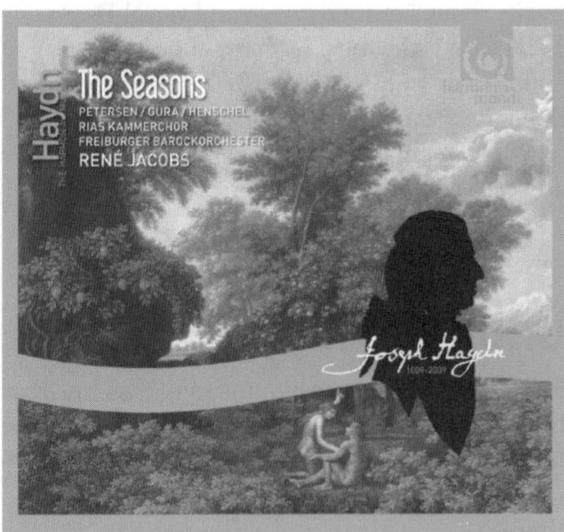

Petersen, Güra, Henschel; Monteverdi Choir; RIAS Chamber Choir; Freiburg Baroque Orchestra; Jacobs (Harmonia Mundi; 2 CDs)

An irresistible performance: the soloists are strong, the choir is tight, the period-instrument orchestra puts a real zing into the music, and René Jacobs keeps the whole thing moving with great ebullience and grace. When you've listened to this set, you'll find it hard to understand why *Die Jahreszeiten* isn't more often performed.

SYMPHONIES

Between 1757 and 1795 Haydn composed some 104 symphonies, refining the form from the relatively simple early works – based on the Italian sinfonia of three movements (fast–slow–fast) – to the highly sophisticated symphonies of his maturity which served as a model for practically every composer of the nineteenth century. All the symphonies after *No. 31* are in four movements (usually arranged fast–slow–fast–fast), each with a second- or third-movement minuet and a finale that functioned as a fast-moving and dramatic climax to the whole work. All but one of the last fourteen symphonies open with a slow introduction. However, these similarities are largely superficial, for each of these symphonies is a markedly original blend of deep feeling and elegance, with the final twelve manifesting a perfect, Mozartian synthesis of form and substance.

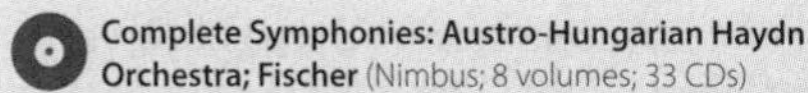

Complete Symphonies: Austro-Hungarian Haydn Orchestra; Fischer (Nimbus; 8 volumes; 33 CDs)

Many record companies have attempted a complete set of Haydn symphonies but few have reached the finishing line. With Antal Dorati's pioneering edition for Decca (recorded in the early 1970s) no longer available, the best place to turn (if you want the whole lot interpreted by the same conductor) is to the Nimbus recordings directed by Adam Fischer. These are excellent performances, played by an orchestra especially assembled for the task and recorded in the Haydnsaal of the Esterházy Palace in Austria.

Symphony No. 44 The Trauer

Almost a third of Haydn's symphonies have acquired nicknames, most of which fit the music well. *Symphony No. 44*, known as the *Trauer* or "Mourning" symphony, dates from the early 1770s when Haydn's symphonic writing took on a more emotional and dramatic character. Critics have dubbed such works *Sturm und Drang* (Storm and stress) after an eighteenth-century German literary movement. The musical precedent for this darker more restless style can be found in the work of C.P.E. Bach (see p.16). Haydn applied it to certain of his minor key symphonies and to various choral works. From the very beginning the *Trauer* symphony is full of startling contrasts: in the first movement a strong unison statement is immediately followed by a restless scurrying figure, and there are frequent dynamic extremes and the repetition of major key phrases in the minor. It is one of Haydn's most brilliantly inventive works, which apparently gained its nickname from Haydn's desire that the stately Handelian slow movement be played at his funeral.

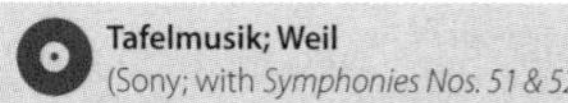

Tafelmusik; Weil (Sony; with *Symphonies Nos. 51 & 52*)

Tafelmusik are a medium-sized period instrument outfit but their relative leanness of sound really benefits these works. There's something effortlessly idiomatic about their playing, which is crisp and energetic but without any sense of strain.

Symphony No. 45 The Farewell

Symphony No. 45 – The Farewell – culminates in a piece of musical industrial action organized by Haydn on behalf of his disgruntled musicians. Near the end of the last movement an Adagio coda commences, during which the musicians stop playing one by one and leave the stage until only two violins are left. This was a hint to Prince Nikolaus Esterházy that the stay at his summer residence had gone on too long and that the musicians missed their wives. This is not Haydn's most tuneful symphony but it is one of his most highly charged and one of the finest of the *Sturm und Drang* symphonies.

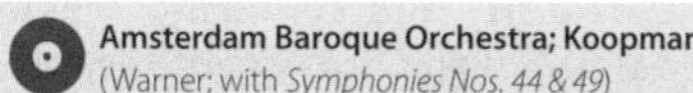

Amsterdam Baroque Orchestra; Koopman (Warner; with *Symphonies Nos. 44 & 49*)

Ton Koopman and the Amsterdam Baroque Orchestra are better known for their performances of Baroque music, J.S. Bach in particular. But the band's sinewy and energized playing is remarkably effective in Haydn's *Sturm und Drang* symphonies.

Symphonies Nos. 48 & 49

The empress Maria Theresia visited Esterháza in the autumn of 1773 and for a long time the *Symphony No. 48* was thought to have been written to celebrate the event – hence its nickname *Maria Theresia*. Despite the fact that it is now known to have been written several years earlier, the symphony certainly has a festive quality and opens with a grand flourish – a lively fanfare in which two high horns are strikingly prominent. It's a C major work (traditionally a key of celebration) but the general sense of bustle in the outer movements is offset by the long, tranquil slow movement in which there are some marvellous moments for the horns and oboes. The *Symphony No. 49*, nicknamed *La passione*, could not be more different. It begins slowly in a mood of almost funereal solemnity, a feeling that never entirely deserts it even during the frenetic second-movement Allegro. A decidedly sombre minuet and a Presto that fizzles with nervous energy make this one of the most darkly coloured of all Haydn's symphonies.

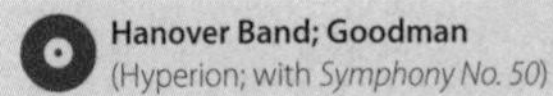

Hanover Band; Goodman
(Hyperion; with *Symphony No. 50*)

Roy Goodman's excellent cycle with the period instrument Hanover Band looked all set to finish but was axed halfway through. They are similar in style to Tafelmusik, powerful and direct (with a prominent harpsichord continuo), more concerned with momentum and inner drama than with refinement.

Symphonies Nos. 82–87 The Paris Symphonies

In 1779 Haydn signed a new contract with Nikolaus Esterházy whereby his music was no longer the exclusive property of the prince. The result was a wealth of commissions from publishers and, eventually, from impresarios throughout Europe. One such – for six symphonies – arrived from the Comte d'Ogny, one of the financial backers of a Parisian concert society called "Concerts de la Loge Olympique".

Written during 1785 and 1786, symphonies nos. 82–87 display an extremely wide-ranging imagination both formally and in terms of orchestral virtuosity and colouring. Haydn was clearly aware of the prowess of the Paris orchestra, which was one of the biggest and best in Europe, and there are extensive wind parts in all six works. The Paris symphonies are among Haydn's most scintillating; all are worth hearing but three have proved especially popular.

Symphony No. 82 – The Bear – is a C major work, predominantly jovial but with a melancholy tinge running through it. It gets its name from the last-movement Vivace in which a rollicking "Bear dance" over a drone of fifths recurs throughout the movement. The animal association of *Symphony No. 83 – The Hen* – derives from the "clucking" second subject of its first movement. It's the only minor-key symphony in the Paris set and its opening subject and cantabile slow movement seem like a return to the angst-laden feel of the *Sturm und Drang* symphonies.

Symphony No. 85 was a favourite of the French queen Marie Antoinette and was therefore nicknamed *La Reine* (The Queen). It has something of the elegant fake rusticity which the queen so much enjoyed, especially in its second movement – a set of variations on the French folk song *La gentille et jeune Lisette*.

Concentus Musicus Wien; Harnoncourt
(Deutsche Harmonia Mundi; 3 CDs)

More ambitious in terms of orchestration, the Paris symphonies really allow an ensemble to show off, and with Harnoncourt and the Concentus Musicus you get performances of real character and bite, with Haydn's innovative orchestral timbres emphasized to occasionally startling extremes.

Symphonies Nos. 88 & 92

Symphony No. 88 continues the rich orchestration of the later Paris symphonies and has a large wind and brass section. Throughout the first movement (Adagio-Allegro) Haydn contrasts different sections of the orchestra, a tactic he employs to even more telling effect in the Largo – a movement greatly admired by Brahms. This is essentially a set of variations on a simple chorale-like theme first heard in the wind section, then by the strings, before being repeated in various permutations (with periodic sinister interruptions from the whole orchestra playing fortissimo). There is also a very striking rustic Trio complete with simulated hurdy-gurdy sounds.

In 1791 Oxford University conferred an honorary doctorate on Haydn who conducted his *Symphony No. 92 – The Oxford* – at the celebrations (though it was actually composed two years earlier and dedicated to Comte d'Ogny). It's one of the most warm and serene of all Haydn's later symphonies, full of cantabile melodies reminiscent of Mozart. Its broad and sunny slow movement is occasionally startled by dark minor-key outbursts, and the fizzing finale injects an element of almost neurotic fussiness into the otherwise untroubled proceedings.

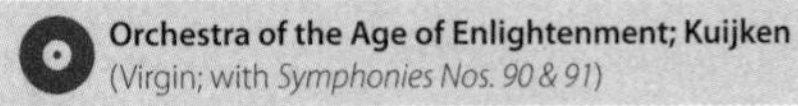

Orchestra of the Age of Enlightenment; Kuijken
(Virgin; with *Symphonies Nos. 90 & 91*)

Sigiswald Kuijken and the OAE follow up their huge success with the Paris symphonies with no less exciting accounts of two of Haydn's greatest. They particularly excel themselves in the glorious slow movement of *No. 88* – the string playing has a warmth and an expansiveness that is truly inspiring.

Symphonies Nos. 93–104 The London Symphonies

London was a demanding and sophisticated musical centre, and to satisfy demand the impresario J.P. Salomon tried to secure the services of both Haydn and Mozart for his concerts in the Hanover Square Rooms. Only Haydn arrived, composing the first six symphonies for seasons in 1791 and 1792, and the second six for the season of 1794. These last twelve symphonies are arguably

Haydn's greatest achievement in the genre. The orchestra is even larger than for the Paris symphonies, and the harmonies more daring, with frequent unexpected moves to different keys. The slow introductions are as grand as before but with an added tension which sets you up for the splendours which follow. All twelve are inventive and infinitely rewarding works, but we have singled out three of the most celebrated.

Symphony No. 94 – The Surprise – was written in Hertfordshire, in the course of Haydn's first visit to England in 1791. The "surprise" of the nickname comes in the second movement when, halfway through a light and seemingly insignificant Andante, there comes a fortissimo bang from the timpani. It was suggested that Haydn had placed the explosion there in order to wake up any dozing members of the audience, but he insisted that he had merely wanted to surprise the listener with something new.

Symphony No. 100 – The Military – was performed at the eighth concert on 31 March, when it was introduced as a "Grand Military Overture", a reference to the use of a military battery of kettledrums, triangle, cymbals and bass drum in its second movement. The work became especially famous for the final movement, a rondo whose main theme managed to find its way into England's ballrooms. The military flavour returns near the end of the symphony with great grandeur, but the parade-ground pomp is ultimately absorbed into the atmosphere of the salon.

The very first bar of *Symphony No. 103* – an unannounced drum roll – is a marvellous, unprecedented coup, which inevitably led to the symphony becoming known as the *Drum Roll*. This dramatic flourish announces one of Haydn's most original works, leading into a quiet, sustained phrase for bassoons, cellos and basses which has a mystery comparable to the opening of Schubert's *Unfinished Symphony*. Later in the symphony you get a masterful set of double variations on two themes derived from folk tunes, a Trio that makes intriguing use of the clarinets, and a finale that is ingeniously based upon a single theme.

Royal Concertgebouw Orchestra; Harnoncourt (Warner Classics; 5 CDs; with *Symphony No. 68*)

Nikolaus Harnoncourt has proved himself to be an absolute master of the symphonic repertoire of the Classical era, and these sparkling accounts of the London symphonies form the high point of his Haydn recordings for Teldec. The rhythmic buoyancy and the contrapuntal vigour of these great works are always to the fore.

CONCERTOS

Haydn composed numerous concertos for violin, cello, flute, oboe, trumpet, horn, bassoon, piano and organ. The problem is that not all of them were published during his lifetime and many known works are lost (some presumably in the fires that destroyed Haydn's home in 1768 and again in 1776). The good news is that several works in manuscript have reappeared relatively recently: the *Cello Concerto in C*, for instance, was accidentally discovered in 1961 in the Prague National Library and, for all anyone knows, there may be more such gems scattered across Europe. None of Haydn's concertos reach the same level of profundity as the best of Mozart's, but there is much to enjoy here, in particular the brilliant *Trumpet Concerto* – the most important ever written for the instrument.

Trumpet Concerto

In the late eighteenth century the trumpet attained great prominence as a solo instrument, its natural limitations gradually being overcome by developments which culminated in a fully chromatic instrument – but with keys, like a keyboard instrument. It was for this keyed trumpet – later superseded by the valved instrument – that Haydn wrote his *Trumpet Concerto* in 1796, for the Viennese trumpet player Anton Weidlinger. It was Haydn's last fully orchestral work, and strangely it found little popularity at first, probably due to the unusual sound of the keyed trumpet. Nowadays it's a favourite vehicle for trumpet virtuosos, who get plenty of opportunity to show off in the first movement's thrilling cadenza. The slow movement is extremely lyrical (making it as demanding for a trumpet player as the fireworks of the cadenza), while the last movement is typical of the restrained exuberance of all Haydn's concerto finales.

Hardenberger; Academy of St Martin-in-the-Fields; Marriner (Philips; with concertos by Hummel and Stamitz)

Beautiful playing from Håkon Hardenberger, one of today's great trumpet virtuosos. His playing has everything, a pure burnished tone when necessary and the most breathtaking articulation, all of which help to breathe new life into what is something of an old chestnut.

Cello Concertos

The two cello concertos widely attributed to Haydn (the first is still regarded as spurious in some quarters) were almost certainly written for Joseph Weigl, a cellist in the Esterházy court orchestra – which suggests that their standard of ensemble playing must have been high, as the technical demands of both works are extreme. The first concerto, in C major, was probably written between 1761 and 1765, and opens with a movement that is really nothing more than a virtuoso display; a cheery mood generally prevails throughout the concerto, and the Adagio boasts an extremely affecting and well-extended melody. The second concerto, in D major, is notable for the exquisite beauty of its Adagio, but the first movement is far too long for the material upon which it is based. Though written in 1784, when Haydn was at the height of his powers, the second concerto is less involving than its predecessor.

Rostropovich; Academy of St Martin-in-the-Fields; Brown (EMI)

Rostropovich is well suited to the vivacity of these concertos. He favours quick tempi and a big gruff sound, forgoing the twee delicacy of some other cellists, and the enthusiasm with which he attacks the works' outer movements is highly engaging. His playing of the central Adagios is exquisite – in the C major concerto he produces an ethereal sense of stillness that is breathtaking.

Keyboard Concertos

Haydn wrote several relatively simple organ concertos, plus some for the harpsichord or fortepiano (an early version of the piano). Of these, one in particular stands out. The *Keyboard Concerto No. 11* in D major, written around 1780, is full of the strikingly dramatic contrasts that Haydn so much enjoyed. In the opening Vivace the rather skittish main theme – delicate filigree right hand over thumpingly insistent left – is systematically transformed and undermined by quixotic major–minor contrasts. The highlight is the slow movement, which is dominated by the soloist's marvellously long-breathed and expressive cantabile melody. The concerto ends with a spirited Rondo all'Ungherese in which the piano quotes a frenetic Balkan dance, the "Siri Kolo", with the orchestra in very much a supporting role.

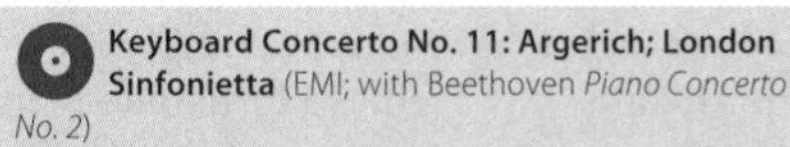

Keyboard Concerto No. 11: Argerich; London Sinfonietta (EMI; with Beethoven *Piano Concerto No. 2*)

Martha Argerich is a great champion of this concerto and has recorded it twice. The earlier version, in which she directs from the keyboard, is the better of the two, despite some overly romantic playing in the slow-movement cadenza. Apart from that, this is an exemplary account, notable, above all, for the way she combines a vigorously incisive touch with expressive delicacy.

STRING QUARTETS

Like Mozart, Haydn wrote a large amount of chamber music, including more than 120 trios and more than thirty duos for the baryton, a stringed instrument resembling the cello that was played by Prince Nikolaus Esterházy. The core of Haydn's legacy as a chamber composer, though, is his work for string quartet. Whereas Mozart composed a mere 23 string quartets, Haydn completed around ninety – the exact number remains unknown.

Not a single quartet written before Haydn's has survived to modern times, but Haydn wrote within the context of a suffocating Viennese tradition whereby every work ended with a fugal finale. By the time he came to write his *Opus 20* quartets, around the age of forty, Haydn had taken the quartet so far from the formulaic sterility of his predecessors that he could allow himself to end his works with fugues once again – but fugues of such inventiveness as to further widen the gap between himself and the past. Musicologist Hans Keller wrote of Haydn's quartets: "On a conservative count, he composed 45 profound and profoundly different, absolutely flawless, consistently original master quartets, each a violent, multi-dimensional contrast to any of the others." Indeed Haydn seems to have given his quartets more intense attention than his symphonies, for they display a greater thematic, structural and textural richness than any of his orchestral music. No other composer has so completely understood the expressive capabilities of the quartet's four parts, and this body of work represents the apogee of Haydn's genius for outward simplicity and inward complexity.

Complete String Quartets: Kodály Quartet
(Naxos; 26 volumes)

The Kodály Quartet's cycle of Haydn's quartets features some excellent quartet playing which, at budget price, is superb value. As is essential with Haydn's music, the leader directs the performances with absolute clarity of intention, and the result is at once extremely lyrical, dramatic and spontaneous.

String Quartets Op. 1

It's emblematic of the importance of the string quartet to Haydn that his Opus 1 should be a group of six string quartets. Published in 1764 (it's not known exactly when they were completed), they follow a standard pattern of five short movements – Presto/Allegro, Minuet, Adagio, Minuet, Presto/Allegro – with the central Adagio nearly always the longest. It is the Adagio of the E flat quartet, the first of the set, that singles it out as the finest of them – the Italianate beauty of the very long principal melodic line is unparalleled in his writing for quartet. Accompanied by simple harmony, this seamless music melts off the page. Of the other Opus 1 quartets, *No. 6* is also outstanding for its Adagio, less liquid in form than that of *No. 1*, but almost as moving.

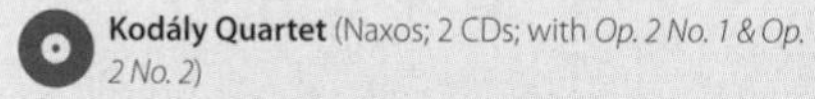

Kodály Quartet (Naxos; 2 CDs; with *Op. 2 No. 1 & Op. 2 No. 2*)

The Kodály Quartet's playing of these very simple works is nothing short of spiritual, especially in the Adagios, where their sonority becomes a single voice. Tempi are always quick and the players avoid anything akin to sentimentality. In short, as an introduction to Haydn's quartets, this cannot be beaten.

String Quartets Op. 20

With the six quartets of Op. 20, written in 1772, Haydn brought the form to a state of maturity: all four instruments are employed as equal voices (with the cello used as a solo instrument on occasions) and the musical material is much more complex – both rhythmically and harmonically, and in the way ideas are developed. These are probably the darkest and most intellectual of all Haydn's quartets, there is strong emphasis on counterpoint, and several of the final movements are written as fugues. But they are also extremely varied in mood: *Quartet No. 2* has a fulsome ripeness, especially in its slow movement; *No. 4* abounds in a kind of radiant joyfulness; while *No. 5* is the most subdued and melancholy of the whole set.

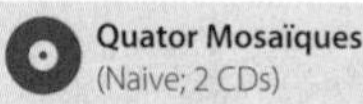

Quator Mosaïques
(Naive; 2 CDs)

The Quator Mosaïques are the most consistently fine period-instrument quartet around, and they possess immense flair and style. The individuality of the four voices comes across very strongly here, and the gut strings of the instruments produce a sound which is thicker and more sinewy than those of the Kodály Quartet.

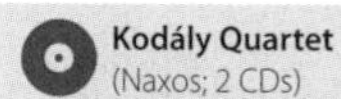

Kodály Quartet
(Naxos; 2 CDs)

The more introspective the work, the more the Kodály Quartet seem to invest themselves into the music. There's some marvellously rapt and concentrated playing and the closeness of the ensemble is exemplary.

String Quartets Op. 33

The six quartets of Op. 33, composed in 1781, are no less complex than those of Op. 20 but they are cast in a very much lighter vein. Dedicated to the future Tsar Paul II (which is why they're sometimes known as the "Russian" Quartets), these works reveal Haydn at his most playful and light-hearted – a fact that some have attributed to Haydn's love affair with the Italian singer Luigia Polzelli. The arioso-like slow movements of several of them may also be a kind of homage to Luigia. Nicknames reflecting their whimsicality have accrued to the three most popular quartets in the set. *No. 2 – The Joke* has an easy-going last movement with a coda whose sudden unexpected silences give you no idea when the work has finished. *No. 3* in C major, the most enchanting of the set, is called *The Bird* because of the grace notes that adorn the principal theme of the first movement and the trills in the second-movement Trio. *No. 5* goes by the unlikely name of *How Do You Do?* on account of its opening phrase. It's rather more notable for the yearning nature of its cantabile slow movement.

Quator Mosaïques
(Naive; 2 CDs)

In these works, the Quator Mosaïques are more on top of the listener than the Kodály Quartet, and their dynamic shading

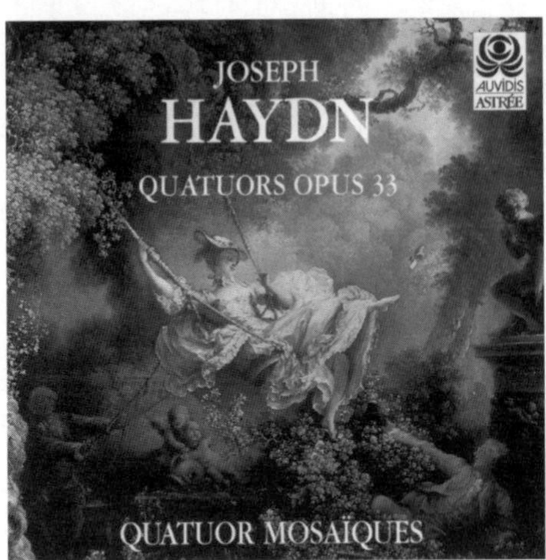

is much more pointed. Like Tafelmusik in the symphonies, there's a sense that it's the character and colour of these quartets which they find attractive.

Kodály Quartet
(Naxos; 2 CDs)

The Kodály Quartet's slow movements are considerably slower than the Mosaïques' but there is never any sense of indulgence; rather there's a feeling that they want to present the music in as pristinely classical a manner as possible. The slightly recessed sound contributes to this sense of distance.

String Quartets Op. 76

The six Op. 76 quartets are, understandably, Haydn's most famous, for they mark the culmination of his quest for expressive perfection. Commissioned by a Viennese nobleman named Count Joseph Erdödy, who retained their exclusive use for two years, they were completed in 1797, when Haydn had turned 65. He must have felt some satisfaction with the outcome, for they are the strongest and most finely wrought of all his chamber compositions and clearly inspired Beethoven's first attempts at quartet writing – even if he was reluctant to admit the influence.

In the Op. 76 set you can find everything with which Haydn's style is synonymous – ingenious variation, complex fugal writing, folk-influenced melodies, perfect ensemble writing and general transparency. The range of expression is astonishingly wide: the slow movement of *No. 3*, *The Emperor*, is a deeply moving, hymn-like theme composed in response to England's national anthem (it was adopted as the Austrian national anthem and is now the German); the slow movement of *No. 5*, marked *mesto* (sadly), is proto-Romantic in its supple beauty; the forcefulness of Beethoven is prefigured by the first movement of *No. 1*, with its sudden fortissimo outbursts; and the so-called "Witches' Minuet" of *No. 2* is a fine example of Haydn letting his hair down.

Quator Mosaïques
(Naive; 2 CDs)

The Quator Mosaïques really come into their own with these performances of the greatest of Haydn's quartets. They are never scared of bringing out some of the stranger sonorities in these pieces, which coupled with their sparing use of vibrato, makes for powerful and intense listening.

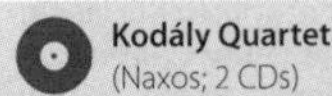
Kodály Quartet
(Naxos; 2 CDs)

The Kodály Quartet's performances of Op. 76 possess a steady, reliable elegance that's typical of their entire Haydn cycle. They are expressive without sentimentalizing the often lush writing, and their sense of experimentation makes this sound like music freshly minted.

Seven Last Words

The *Seven Last Words* occupies a unique place within Haydn's output. It was commissioned in 1785 by the administrators of Cadiz Cathedral, who asked him to provide instrumental music for a special Good Friday service, to be performed between meditations on Christ's seven last words on the Cross. As Haydn wrote: "Each time, at the end of the sermon, the orchestra would begin again and my composition had to be in keeping with the presentation." To compose seven consecutive Adagios, each lasting ten minutes, was a taxing proposition, and Haydn missed his deadline – the first Cadiz performances took place in Holy Week of 1787, though there were performances in Vienna and Bonn the month before.

Haydn's achievement was extraordinary. Not only did he avoid monotony, he produced some of his most innovative and expressive work in the *Seven Last Words*, building music of almost symphonic density around the weighty, declamatory melodic lines that represent the words of Christ. The fact that he reworked the orchestral score into a string quartet (among other formats) shows he was justly proud of this remarkable work.

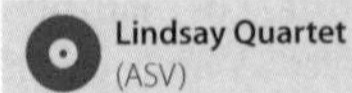
Lindsay Quartet
(ASV)

This splendid recording demonstrates that this piece sounds best played by string quartet, as the four voices define the harmonic and thematic material more clearly than an orchestra. The Lindsays give full scope to the music's pathos and reverence, while losing nothing of its momentum. The ensemble playing isn't faultless, but for spontaneity and depth, the Lindsays are without equal.

KEYBOARD MUSIC

Haydn's keyboard music owes most to the instrumental traditions of north Germany, in particular C.P.E. Bach (see p.16), which means that it possesses an expressiveness and an occasional whimsicality that contrasts with the more lyrical spirit of Mozart's work in the same medium. But even among those concert pianists who specialize in the core classical repertoire (Mozart, Beethoven and Schubert) there is disagreement over the merits of most of Haydn's keyboard sonatas – Glenn Gould played the late ones and was rumoured to have planned to record them all, and Sviatoslav Richter played just a few of them – but the *Sonata in C Minor* is an unqualified masterpiece, as is the astonishingly inventive *Variations in F Minor*.

Sonata in C Minor & Variations in F Minor

The *Sonata in C Minor* (No. 33) dates from 1771 and is something of a watershed, marking a decisive move away from dance-music style and towards the storm and stress of early Romanticism. It is also Haydn's first sonata to carry specific dynamic markings, suggesting that the work was intended for a fortepiano and not a harpsichord, as were all works previous to this. The work's emotional contrasts and overall pacing make it a stylistic companion to the *Farewell Symphony* and the Op. 20 string quartets, and the combination of outright drama and reflective melody – especially in the outer movements – marks the inauguration of the Viennese Classical style, the style which Beethoven was eventually to bring to the point of dissolution.

Described by Haydn as "Un piccolo divertimento" the *Variations in F Minor* stand as one of the pinnacles of the keyboard repertoire. The theme is brilliantly conceived for variation form and the variations themselves are notably innovative, but it is the finale, with its sixty bars of Beethoven-like fury, that is the most striking aspect of this piece. The intensely personal nature of this music has prompted various theories as to the identity of the person to whom Haydn was so openly baring his soul. In all probability there was no such person – in 1773 Haydn had simply written a piece of music so expressive as to have generations of Romantics looking for an answer to a question that had never been posed.

Brendel (Philips; 4 CDs; with other Haydn keyboard works)

Brendel plays Haydn with just the right blend of wit and meticulousness. He's a gentle advocate, never pushing too hard: his reading of the *Sonata*'s Andante brings out all its quirky charm, while in the *Variations* he lets the music do its own persuading without any forced bravura. His performances of these two masterworks are currently only available in a 4-CD set, but it's well worth investigating what is some of the greatest and most neglected of piano literature.

Pletnev (Virgin; 2 CDs; with *Sonatas Nos. 60, 62* and piano concertos)

Mikhail Pletnev makes an interesting contrast to Brendel. Where Brendel is fairly restrained in his approach, Pletnev takes a more extreme interpretative line, shaping the phrases more overtly and often varying his touch between hands. It works extremely well, though it may be a little mannered for some tastes. Discs also include two later sonatas and three piano concertos.

Hans Werner Henze (1926–)

Henze is one of the most significant, most approachable and most political of post-war European composers. His social commitment, which grew out of disgust with the Nazi Germany of his youth and his disappointment with the failure of post-war Germany to fully confront its past, eventually led him into the espousal of Communism, an infatuation with the idea of world revolution, and a lengthy sojourn in Cuba. In a whole series of works, concentrated between 1968 and 1980, Henze gave vent to his disaffection with Western capitalism, but he is far from being a straightforward propagandist – on the contrary, Henze is a highly subtle and complex composer.

His early works show the influence of Stravinsky, Hindemith, Bartók and Schoenberg, yet Henze has always retained a loyalty to Classical forms – he has, after all, written ten symphonies. He has always been a profoundly theatrical composer as well: he has stated that all his work ultimately derives from the theatre, and has referred to his hearing *The Marriage of Figaro* as a formative childhood experience. His eclecticism meant that he was intolerant of the hard-line experimentalism of Stockhausen, Boulez and Nono (see p.384), who in turn disapproved of his music to the extent that they organized a walkout of a performance of *Nachtstücke und Arien* in 1957. Henze summarized his aesthetic credo as follows: "With my music I would very much like to be in touch with the people, but not with those whose criteria permit no divergence from certain fundamentalist norms. My certainty lies in my wavering. My wavering is ambivalence about a world that has populated itself with people whose papers are all in order." This position first found a direct and lucid voice in the hard-hitting style he developed for the small-ensemble political works he composed in the 1960s and 1970s, such as *The Raft of the Medusa*, *La Cubana* and *El Cimarrón*.

One essential component in Henze's work is its sensuousness, a quality that came to the fore after he left his native country at the age of 27 to live in Italy, which is still his home. Italy has stimulated his work in innumerable ways: through its light and colour; through its freer attitude towards his homosexuality; and, perhaps above all through its emphasis on community. Of the various popular projects with which Henze has been involved, none has been more important than the festival he created at the Tuscan town of Montepulciano. Here, working with professional musicians and local people, Henze established a forum for the performance of a range of projects, from new works to little-known Italian operas, most of them staged in the town square. Innovative and highly popular, the festival in Montepulciano epitomizes the best qualities of this prolific composer.

The Bassarids

The Bassarids (1965) is Henze's greatest opera. Taking a reworked version of Euripides' *The Bacchae* by W.H. Auden and Chester Kallmann, Henze creates a highly complicated structure which is in effect a single-spanned two-hour symphony with voices. The formal aspects of the opera are demonstrations of a remarkable technical proficiency, but what matters most is Henze's ability to portray the conflicts of sense and sensuality in music that is immediately effective. Praising the libretto he had been given, Henze wrote that Auden "… understood the ability of music to forget itself … the crude shamelessness of musical expression", and *The Bassarids* abounds with correspondingly rich and expressive music. Agave's haunting description of her first exposure to the cult, the wild hunt of the Bassarids, and the appearance of Agave carrying her son's head are all extremely intense episodes, and throughout the opera the conflict between rationality and sensuality is mirrored in clashes between harmony and cacophony. The cumulative impact is extraordinary. The most original moment comes right at the end when, with disorder triumphant, Pentheus dead, Cadmus and his court banished, and Dionysus in total command, the music becomes subdued – a moment more dreadful in its calm acceptance of the new order than any Dionysian orgy.

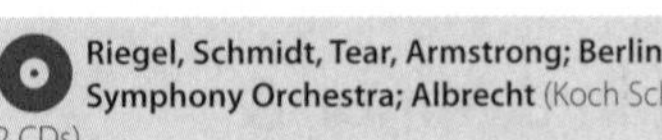
Riegel, Schmidt, Tear, Armstrong; Berlin Radio Symphony Orchestra; Albrecht (Koch Schwann; 2 CDs)

Gerd Albrecht is a noted champion of Henze's music, and this 1986 performance of the German-language version of *The Bassarids* is full of conviction and confidence. The casting is exceptional, with the baritone Kenneth Riegel and Andreas Schmidt outstanding as Dionysus and Pentheus. The sound is full, capturing the sumptuous Berlin forces with clarity and warmth.

Symphonies

The ten symphonies that Henze has composed since 1947 cover an even wider ground than the operas, from the Classical forms of the first and the sumptuous late-Romantic textures of the second to the agitprop of the sixth and the grief-stricken bombast of the ninth (choral) symphony. They form the best introduction to a prolific output that is stylistically very diverse – often bewilderingly so. *Symphony No. 7* (1984), the finest of them all, has been explained by Henze in the following terms: "Again and again I have felt drawn towards the Beethovenian tradition … My seventh symphony is a German symphony and it deals with matters German." If this is the case, then his view of his native land is a profoundly ambiguous one. Only the first of the four movements, an energetic, almost bullish Allemande, exudes optimism; the other three are predominantly melancholy, with the Scherzo and the finale both inspired by the tragic figure of the Romantic poet Friedrich Hölderlin. Most elegiac of all is the grandiose second movement, which exudes an almost funereal sense of darkness and resignation.

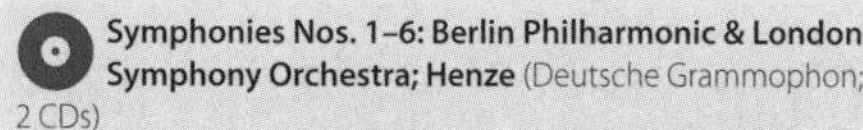

Symphonies Nos. 1–6: Berlin Philharmonic & London Symphony Orchestra; Henze (Deutsche Grammophon; 2 CDs)

This mid-price symphony set, conducted by the composer, gives you a fair slice of his best music. The sixth symphony is the problem piece, tending towards a rather stale political attitudinizing, but the set is well worth having for a concise history of Henze's musical development up until the Cuban years.

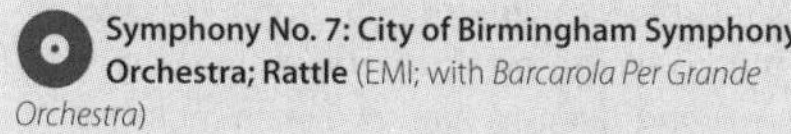

Symphony No. 7: City of Birmingham Symphony Orchestra; Rattle (EMI; with *Barcarola Per Grande Orchestra*)

The finest single Henze recording is Simon Rattle's amazing performance of the *Symphony No. 7* and the *Barcarola*, recorded live in Birmingham. These are near-perfect interpretations of frequently complex and always rich music – Rattle brings total conviction to the four contrasting dance movements that make up the symphony, and manages the sweep of the *Barcarola* with real panache.

String Quartets

Henze once remarked that the string quartet "should at least lean towards a reflection of the demands of classical music", and his own quartets are some of Henze's most obviously coherent works. The first two, from 1947 and 1952, are rather hard-boiled – neo-classical and serial works respectively. The series picks up considerably with the sudden rush of three quartets in 1975–77 commissioned by the Schwetzingen festival. Much of their musical material derives from Henze's opera *We Come to the River*, and all three were written in memoriam: the third, a single-movement work of a burnished intensity, was dedicated to Henze's mother; the fourth, a more densely argued work with a heart-rending slow movement, to the left-wing Chilean musician Victor Jara; while the fifth, the most episodic and pithy of the three, commemorates Benjamin Britten.

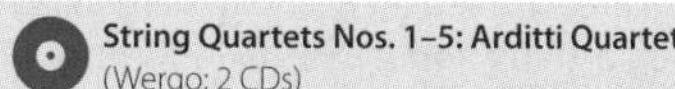

String Quartets Nos. 1–5: Arditti Quartet (Wergo; 2 CDs)

It's a mark of fashion, or maybe of the composer's prolific output, that there's only one available recording of these rewarding works. The Ardittis are on predictably good form: in particular, they eloquently express the intensely elegiac mood of the fourth quartet, with its long and beautiful slow movement. The recording is, as is usual with Wergo, rather dry but well projected.

Hildegard of Bingen (1098–1179)

The tenth child of a noble family, Hildegard of Bingen was sent, at the age of eight, to live in an enclosed cell with the anchoress Jutta at the Benedictine monastery of Disibodenberg in southern Germany. Jutta died in 1136 and Hildegard became the leader of the small group of nuns attached to the monastery. Between 1147 and 1150, against the wishes of her abbot, she left with her eighteen nuns and her secretary – the monk Volmar – to found an independent convent on the Rupertsberg near Bingen and remained there for the rest of her life.

Hildegard was an ecstatic mystic and from 1141 she had a series of 26 visions which were dictated to Volmar and recorded in a book, *Scivias* (Know the Ways). The language of these visions, and of the religious poetry that she set to music, is highly personal and full of startling images, both apocalyptic and sensual – "When I was forty-two years and seven months old, the heavens were opened and a blinding light of exceptional brilliance flowed through my entire brain. And so it kindled my whole heart and breast like a flame, not burning but warming." The widespread fame Hildegard achieved during her lifetime – she was known as the "Sybil of the Rhine" – was due not so much to her music as to her intellect and influence. She led four preaching missions throughout Germany and her many correspondents included two popes, the Holy Roman Emperor Frederick Barbarossa (whom she berated for failing to reply promptly) and the powerful head of the Cistercian order, Saint Bernard of Clairvaux. As well as two more books of mystical writings she produced important works on natural history (*Physica*) and medicine (*Causae et Curae*) and a secret language (probably used by her nuns). Much of her work centres on a notably feminine theology, celebrating the female figures of the Virgin Mary, Ecclesia (the community of the Church) and Sapientia (holy wisdom). After her death she was considered for, but never achieved, canonization.

Gregorian Chant

Christianity has a long history of chant: religious texts set to single-line melodies for one or more voices. Of the various types of Christian chant – collectively known as plainchant or plainsong – the most important is Gregorian chant, which is the official chant repertory of the Roman Catholic Church and the oldest surviving music of the Western tradition.

From its foundation until the eighth century, Christianity grew without an overall regulatory body, and this meant that as the liturgy expanded, so regional variants developed around Europe. This was especially the case when it came to chant, as there was no means of writing down the melodies and rhythms. As the first monarchs of the Carolingian dynasty – ruling over an empire which included France and parts of Italy and Germany – King Pepin III and his son Charlemagne took steps to unify the different strands of the Christian liturgy, aiming to supplant the various local traditions with the rite of the Roman Church. Pepin liaised with the papacy in Rome, and in 752 Pope Stephen II came to inform the Carolingians on the details of the Roman liturgy and its music. However, Roman chant was not assimilated immediately and it merged with the Gallic traditions for a period of 150 years before it achieved a stable form with the advent of notation in the tenth century. The earliest manuscripts of this hybrid chant are the basis of Gregorian chant – a name probably adopted because the Franks believed that the celebrated St Gregory the Great, who was pope from 590 to 604, composed the music brought from Rome, though this is almost certainly untrue.

With texts mostly drawn from the biblical *Book of Psalms*, the chants are monophonic melodies based on a mode (a set of notes, similar to a scale), but they vary greatly in length and complexity. The simplest, syllabic chants, in which each syllable is set to one note, were probably intended to be sung by the choir or congregation, whilst the more florid melismatic examples, which have many notes to each syllable, were probably performed by soloists.

In the earliest sources, which date from around 900, the chants are notated with neumes, little marks written above the text that indicate melodic shapes but not specific pitches or intervals. Only in the eleventh century were various methods employed to write down specific notes, including the drawing of coloured lines on the page (the earliest form of today's musical stave), and even then there was no indication of rhythm. During the Counter-Reformation, the chants were extensively re-edited, and only in the middle of the nineteenth century was there a renewed interest in returning to the original sources, as the monks at the monastery of Solesmes in France, and then others, attempted to re-create original performance practice.

Various schools of interpretation began to emerge: one Solesmes monk suggested that all the notes should have the same value; another thought the rhythm should be much freer, with notes grouped into twos and threes; later, W.A. Vollaerts propounded the "mensuralist" theory that two different note lengths were usually used. These theories are still the subject of much debate, and they're all represented in the ever-growing Gregorian chant discography.

Canto Gregoriano: The Monks of the Abbey of Santo Domingo de Silos (EMI)

This is the recording that took Gregorian chant from obscurity and placed it on the bestseller lists. The Silos monks, who have links with the Solesmes monastery, sing with a very round sound and broad tempi. This, combined with the reverberant acoustic, makes for a highly devotional, meditative atmosphere.

Adorate Deum – Gregorian Chant from the Proper of the Mass: Nova Schola Gregoriana; Turco (Naxos)

Adorate Deum contains chant for the proper of the mass, the parts that change from day from day. Nova Schola Gregoriana's performance is very balanced: the rhythm and dynamics are neither too dramatic nor rigid and the quality of singing is high. Their sound is highly translucent, partly due to the comparatively unreverberant recording.

Chant Cistercien: Ensemble Organum; Péres (Harmonia Mundi)

This disc focuses on Cistercian chant – Gregorian chant that was "purified" in the twelfth century by Cistercian monks, who removed what they saw as unnecessarily elaborate passages to clarify the modes (scales). Ensemble Organum sing with a more penetrative tone than either of the above groups; they're very musically responsive, with relatively free rhythms yielding to the text.

Symphonia harmoniae

In the 1150s Hildegard gathered together her 77 liturgical songs (antiphons, responsories, sequences and hymns) into a collection which she called *Symphonia harmoniae caelestium revelationum* (Symphony of the harmony of heavenly revelations) and which were used for worship at the convent. The word "Symphonia" signified for her not just the harmonious combination of different musical sounds but also the divine harmony of the cosmos, and she saw the act of making music as a union between the physical and the spiritual that brought the participant closer to the divine: "Words symbolize the humanity of the son of God but music symbolizes his divinity." Hildegard's musical language has the same inspired quality as her poetry. It is not based on the traditional formulas of plainchant but consists of freely composed single melodic lines using frequent embellishments and a wide melodic range to convey a lyrical and sensual quality.

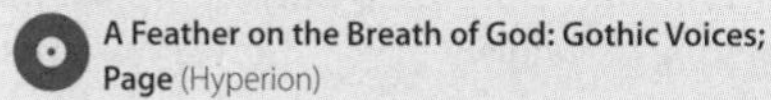

A Feather on the Breath of God: Gothic Voices; Page (Hyperion)

This pioneering recording first appeared in 1984 and remains one of the best introductions to Hildegard's music, with all the singers conveying a powerful sense of joy and spontaneity. Page varies male and female voices, solo and ensemble singing to produce an absorbing collection of hymns and sequences from the *Symphonia*.

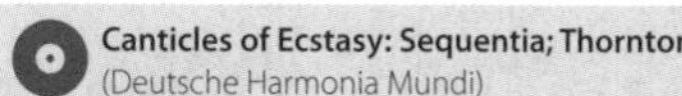

Canticles of Ecstasy: Sequentia; Thornton (Deutsche Harmonia Mundi)

The all-female group Sequentia are in the process of recording all Hildegard's music. On this disc the singers, accompanied in places by fiddles and harps, bring a passionate, soaring intensity to a collection of antiphons, responsories and sequences dedicated to the Virgin Mary and the Holy Spirit.

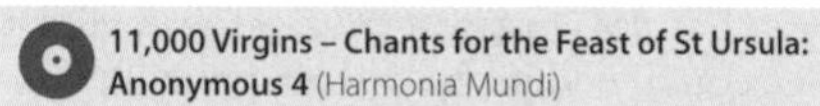

11,000 Virgins – Chants for the Feast of St Ursula: Anonymous 4 (Harmonia Mundi)

St Ursula, who was said to have been martyred with eleven thousand companions in Cologne, seems to have had a special significance for Hildegard, who wrote several works for her feast day. Anonymous 4's recording is based on those works, which they have interspersed with chants from other sources to re-create something of their liturgical context. The singing is resonant yet retains an exquisite purity.

Ordo Virtutum

One of Hildegard's most remarkable achievements is a musical morality play – a drama in which the characters are personifications of moral or abstract qualities. Dating from about 1150, *Ordo Virtutum* (Play of Virtues) is the oldest surviving Christian music drama and the earliest of Hildegard's dated works. Probably written for the opening of the convent in Rupertsberg in 1152, *Ordo* contains around twenty female parts that were almost certainly performed by the twenty nuns in Hildegard's community. The play tells the story of the human soul – represented by a character called Anima – caught between the forces of good (sixteen Virtues, with such allegorical names as "knowledge of god", "humility" and "discipline") and evil (the devil Diabolus, who shouts his part instead of singing it, and was possibly played by Hildegard's male secretary). After a long struggle, the Virtues win and Alma rises to immortality. There are 82 melodies within the work, which are syllabic and more direct in style than most of Hildegard's other music. Unusually for spiritual works of the period, *Ordo*'s text is not drawn from the Bible.

Thornton; Sequentia; Bagby (Deutsche Harmonia Mundi; 2 CDs)

Sequentia originally recorded *Ordo* in 1984 and re-recorded it for the 900th anniversary of Hildegard's birth in 1998, by which time they were firmly established Hildegard experts. Their wealth of experience is evident on this well-recorded and comprehensively annotated double-CD: the singing is subtle yet confident and the use of instruments is unusually sensitive and effective.

Paul Hindemith (1895–1963)

Paul Hindemith was one of the twentieth century's greatest musical polymaths, equally adept as a string player, conductor, theorist and composer. His style was similarly varied, ranging from the dense expressionism of his early one-act operas to the sinewy contrapuntalism of his neo-Baroque maturity. Like several German composers during the interwar period, Hindemith saw himself as an opponent of bourgeois culture, with a political commitment to the idea of making "useful" music (*Gebrauchsmusik*) that was direct and accessible ("for people with ears my stuff is really easy to grasp"), and throughout his life he wrote regularly and extensively for amateurs. His standing as one of the seminal figures of modern music was partly undermined by his extraordinary facility (it took him less than six hours to write *Trauermusik* to commemorate George V's death) and by his stylistic diversity, but if his reputation sharply declined at his death it has undergone a steady reappraisal since the late 1980s.

Hindemith came from a poor, working-class background but his father, recognizing his children's talent, had them coached in music. Between 1909 and 1914 Paul studied at the Hoch Conservatory in Frankfurt and then, at the start of the war, got a job at the Frankfurt Opera orchestra and the position of second violinist in the string quartet of his teacher, Adolf Rebner. It was while at the Frankfurt Opera that Hindemith came to the attention of the conductor Fritz Busch, who was looking for new operas by up-and-coming composers. Busch gave the premieres of Hindemith's first two operas, *Mörder, Hoffnung der Frauen* (Murder, Hope of Women) and *Das Nusch-Nuschi* at Stuttgart in 1921. Both were extreme works: the first a setting of a violent play by the expressionist

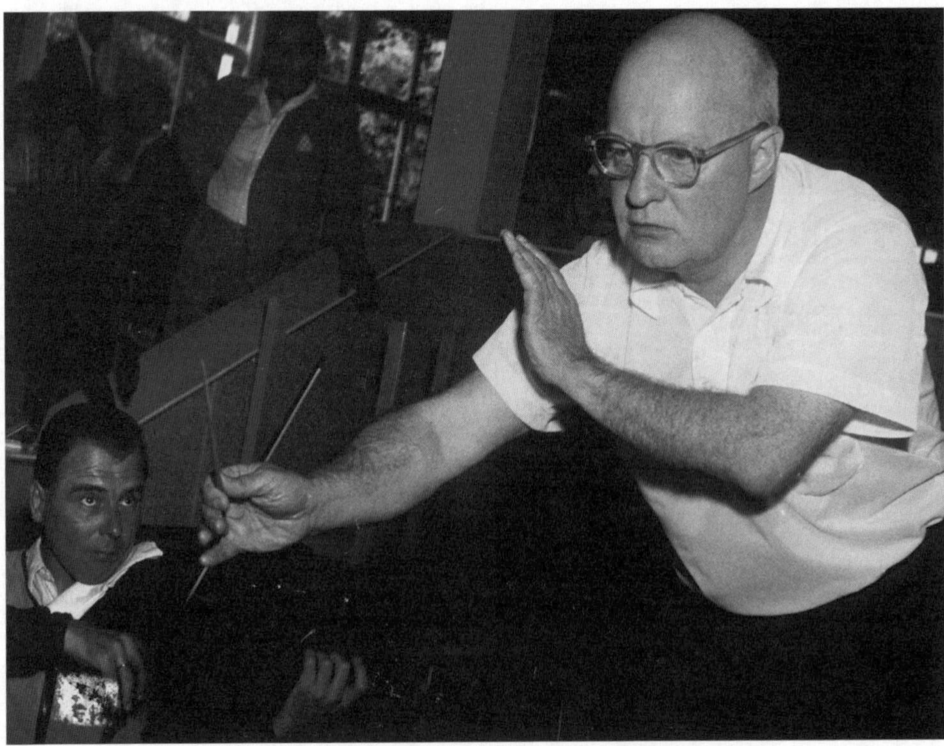

Paul Hindemith conducting a rehearsal in 1953.

Expressionism and After

The devastation – both physical and spiritual – that afflicted Europe as a result of World War I not only shattered political certainties but aesthetic ones as well. It is true that some major artists, Richard Strauss for instance, carried on as if nothing had happened, but for more radical figures it was time to change direction, to formulate a new musical language for new, leaner times. The first thing to be rejected was Romanticism and its final, most extreme, manifestation, expressionism. The latter was an artistic movement which attempted to exteriorize the (usually troubled) inner life of the artist, which in musical terms meant using fractured forms and atonality to create a nightmare world of instability and anxiety. Expressionism was primarily associated with the avant-gardes of Germany and Austria – with works like Schoenberg's *Erwartung* (1909) and Hindemith's *Mörder, Hoffnung der Frauen* (1919) – but it is arguable that an expressionistic impulse also lay behind the raw energy of Stravinsky's *Le sacre du printemps* of 1913 (see p.548).

In place of the formal freedoms of the pre-war years, composers now sought the discipline of a structured framework, and they found the models for this in the work of certain pre-Romantics. The music of J.S. Bach and Mozart was especially admired for its clean lines, rhythmic tightness and textural lucidity – and for the fact that it referred to nothing outside of itself or, as Stravinsky put it, was "powerless to express anything at all, whether a feeling, an attitude of mind … a phenomenon of nature, etc…" Stravinsky's *Pulcinella* (1917) was the turning point: written for Diaghilev's Russian Ballet (see p.547), it consisted of a number of pieces ascribed to the eighteenth-century Italian Pergolesi, wittily but affectionately arranged for a chamber orchestra using odd instrumental combinations and decidedly spare and modern harmonies. For Stravinsky, this dynamic relationship with the past offered a new way forward, and neo-classicism (as the style was called) would remain a significant stimulus until after his "Mozartian" opera *The Rake's Progress* (1951).

In Austria and Germany, the abandonment of expressionism by the avant-garde led to two separate developments both pulling in different directions but both involving a dialogue with tradition. For Schoenberg, the old diatonic system of major and minor keys was over (see "The Crisis of Tonality", p.480). In its place he invented an alternative system, serialism, whereby the twelve notes of the chromatic scale were fixed in a specific order (or series) for each composition, which would act as the fundamental basis from which all subsequent ideas derived. This radical departure was held in check by the fact that Schoenberg wished to employ serialism within the framework of traditional forms.

For other Austro-German composers – like Hindemith, Weill and Eisler – there was a political dimension to their rejection of expressionism which, with its preoccupation with the unconscious, they saw as a manifestation of bourgeois neuroticism. They wished to create music that was clear, objective and incisive – that turned an unflinching (rather than a sentimental) eye on the post-war reality. In common with Stravinsky, such composers favoured woodwind instruments over strings and drew their inspiration partly from jazz-style combos (Weill and Eisler) and – in the case of Hindemith – from the pulsating motor rhythms of Baroque music.

To a significant extent, neo-classicism became the dominant influence on young experimental composers working in the interwar years. It had an impact on the French group known as Les Six (in particular Poulenc) and was transmitted further afield through the Paris-based pedagogue Nadia Boulanger whose pupils in the 1920s and 30s included the Americans Aaron Copland and Elliott Carter, and the Pole Grazyna Bacewicz. What all these different composers had in common was an interest in the ordered forms of the past, which resulted in clearly developed thematic processes and translucent textures. Where they differed from the doctrinaire Schoenberg, and his most faithful pupil Webern, was in their adherence to diatonic harmony and what one critic has called a "contemporary multiplicity of awareness", an attitude not dissimilar to the postmodern composers of today.

painter Oscar Kokoschka, the second containing a castration scene. Busch drew the line at conducting Hindemith's third one-act opera, *Sancta Susanna*, which centred on the sexual fantasies of a young nun.

Such shock tactics made Hindemith's name but in the 1920s he began to review his musical language, gradually developing a more disciplined style based on Baroque composers like J.S. Bach; this first appeared in *Kammermusik*

No. 1 of 1921 and can be heard in his fourth opera, *Cardillac*. His ability to startle, however, had not deserted him: *Neues vom Tage* (News of the Day, 1929) had a scene featuring a woman in the bath (which upset Hitler) as well as a fashionable jazz element to the score. Hindemith then undertook another change of direction, writing a series of staged cantatas (including *Lehrstück*, with a polemical text by Brecht) in which thinly disguised political messages were set to archly neo-Baroque music. In 1929 he visited London for the first time, where his friend William Walton (see p.620) engaged him as soloist at the first performance of Walton's *Viola Concerto*; in 1930 he returned to give the premiere of his own *Viola Concerto*.

In 1933, with Hitler's rise to power, Hindemith began work on *Mathis der Maler* (Mathis the Painter), an opera based upon the life of the painter Mathias Grünewald (c.1460–1528) during a time of bitter and violent struggles between Catholics and Lutherans. It had to wait a long time to reach the stage, but in March 1934 Wilhelm Furtwängler – a champion of Hindemith's music – conducted the first performance of the *Mathis der Maler Symphony*, which consists of three interludes extracted from the full score. Its success was immediate but the authorities – in particular Hitler – expressed their anger at the subject matter. In November, Furtwängler defended the music and its composer in an open letter, but the controversy resulted in the banning of the symphony and the opera, and, ultimately, to Hindemith's departure for Turkey, where he helped establish a music school. Upon his return, the Nazis were better disposed towards him, but worryingly "demonstrative" applause at the first performance of his new *Violin Sonata* in 1936 led to a ban on all Hindemith's work.

After another brief spell in Turkey, Hindemith returned to Germany to resign from his post, and left for America. In 1938 *Mathis* was staged in Zurich, but its production was never reported in the German press. In 1940 he was appointed visiting professor at Yale and head of advanced composition at Tanglewood, where he taught Leonard Bernstein (see p.78). After the war his music again began to circulate in Germany, and his fiftieth birthday was marked by numerous performances. The majority of his remaining years were spent teaching in America and Switzerland, devoting ever less time to composition.

Mathis der Maler Symphony

Mathias Grünewald was a German painter whose work – most famously the *Isenheim Altarpiece* – is characterized by intensely heightened colour and graphic depictions of physical suffering. In the early years of the twentieth century he had become something of a talismanic figure for, in particular, expressionist artists. In his opera about the painter, Hindemith clearly intended his audience to draw parallels with their own time, describing Mathis as a man "plagued by the devilish torments of a doubting, seeking soul, who experiences ... the breakdown of a new era". *Mathis der Maler* is a powerful, if somewhat prolix, work and, though two complete recordings exist, you're best advised to listen first to the *Mathis der Maler Symphony* – arguably the composer's masterpiece. Completed before the opera, in order to give something for Furtwängler to take on a planned tour with the Berlin Philharmonic, the symphony was banned by the Nazis as degenerate. This might seem odd, in view of the fact that the music represents a distinct move back towards traditional melody rather than away from it, but the symphony was incriminated by the anti-war message of the opera, and its depiction of the corruption of power. Each of the symphony's three movements – "The Angelic Concert", "The Entombment" and "The Temptation of St Anthony" – represents a panel from the Isenheim Altarpiece. The final movement, and in particular its brass chorale, is one of Hindemith's greatest achievements.

San Francisco Symphony Orchestra; Blomstedt (Decca; with *Symphonic Metamorphosis* & *Trauermusik*)

This recording is something of a benchmark. Herbert Blomstedt has an unmatched empathy for Hindemith's inner torment, and the San Francisco Orchestra respond with amazing sensitivity, revealing layers of inner voices that are commonly ignored. The performances of the accompanying pieces are equally fine.

Requiem for Those We Love

Hindemith's *Requiem* was composed in 1946 as a lament for President Roosevelt and the victims of World War II. In tribute to his adoptive country during the war years, Hindemith took the text not from the Latin mass but from Walt Whitman's great elegy for the dead of the American Civil War, "When Lilacs Last in the Door-yard Bloom'd". The *Requiem* displays Hindemith's great technical expertise as a composer (there are fugues, marches and even a passacaglia), but is far from being a didactic display of classical orthodoxy (there's enough of that in the chamber music) – everything here is subjugated to deeply felt personal expression. The sonorous opening prelude, in which heavy brass chords suggest the tolling of bells, is occasionally performed separately, but you should hear the work complete – it's one of those rare twentieth-century scores that can invoke the unqualified spiritual devotion of earlier centuries without seeming phoney.

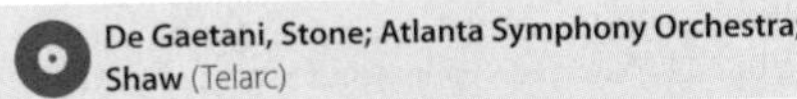

De Gaetani, Stone; Atlanta Symphony Orchestra; Shaw (Telarc)

Robert Shaw, the conductor of this performance, commissioned the *Requiem* for the Collegiate Chorale of New York and his detailed knowledge and deep sympathy for the work are apparent in every bar.

Kammermusik

Kammermusik literally means "chamber music", which the seven works of that name written by Hindemith in the 1920s clearly are not. The first is a suite for twelve solo instruments, the other six are concertos – all with different solo instruments. They were written for a festival of contemporary chamber music, and mark the start of a new phase in Hindemith's development in which he strove to translate some of the dynamism, clarity and contrapuntal vigour of Baroque orchestral music into a modern form. Hindemith's youthful delight in shocking bourgeois taste is still to the fore in *Kammermusik No. 1*, the scoring of which includes parts for siren, accordion and a canister of sand. The first two movements, dominated by edgy motor rhythms, are followed by a haunting slow movement whose spare scoring recalls Stravinsky's *Soldier's Tale*. The last movement, the longest, is a swirling rush of energy, culminating in the quotation of a contemporary foxtrot by the trumpet and an ensuing wail from the siren.

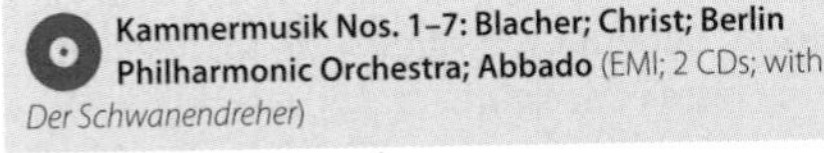

Kammermusik Nos. 1–7: Blacher; Christ; Berlin Philharmonic Orchestra; Abbado (EMI; 2 CDs; with *Der Schwanendreher*)

Claudio Abbado points up the quicksilver wit of *Kammermusik No. 1* rather than making it sound strident as do many conductors. The remaining *Kammermusik* works get just as lively performances, with Abbado brilliantly illuminating Hindemith's clean textures. The viola concerto, Der Schwanendreher, gets an equally convincing performance from Tabea Zimmermann and the Bayerischen Rundfunks Orchestra under David Shallon.

Viola Sonatas

Hindemith trained as a violinist but by 1919 the viola was his instrument of choice. Two years later he was the viola player of the Amar-Hindemith Quartet (later the Amar Quartet) which had been founded to give the first performance of his *String Quartet No. 2*. Hindemith raised the profile of an instrument with a lowly reputation, and was much in demand as a soloist for other composers' works as well as his own. His eight viola sonatas (four for viola alone and four accompanied by the piano) contain his most personal voice, and two, in particular, are among his finest works. The *Sonata for Viola and Piano Op. 11/4*, written in 1919 (ostensibly during Hindemith's expressionist phase), has a quiet intensity and an elegiac warmth reminiscent of Vaughan Williams, above all in its opening rhapsodic Phantasie. Three years later came the Second Sonata for solo viola (Op. 25/1) and a striking change of tone. Where before the instrument's mellow sonority had been emphasized, now there is a concentration on line and contrapuntal energy, which reaches extremes in the infamous fourth movement, marked by Hindemith: "Raging tempo. Wild. Beauty of tone of secondary importance".

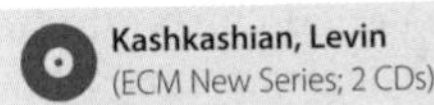

Kashkashian, Levin (ECM New Series; 2 CDs)

Kim Kashkashian, one of the finest viola virtuosos around, really has the measure of these works. There is an electricity to her playing (coupled with a ripe tone) which eclipses all other recordings. In particular, the solo sonatas have a rigour and an intensity that is truly compelling.

Ludus tonalis

Ludus tonalis (Tone Games, 1942) is Hindemith's finest work for the piano. Written when he was visiting professor of music theory at Yale University, and subtitled "Studies in Counterpoint, Tonal Organisation and Piano Playing", it consists of a sequence of alternating fugues and interludes with an opening prelude mirrored by a closing postlude. The inspiration is clearly the didactic keyboard works of J.S. Bach – the *Well-tempered Clavier* and the *Art of Fugue* – and several of the twelve fugues employ traditional contrapuntal devices like inversion or stretto. But these pieces are no more dry academic exercises than are Bach's, and throughout there is a palpable sense of excitement in the imaginative treatment of the fugue subjects. No other twentieth-century

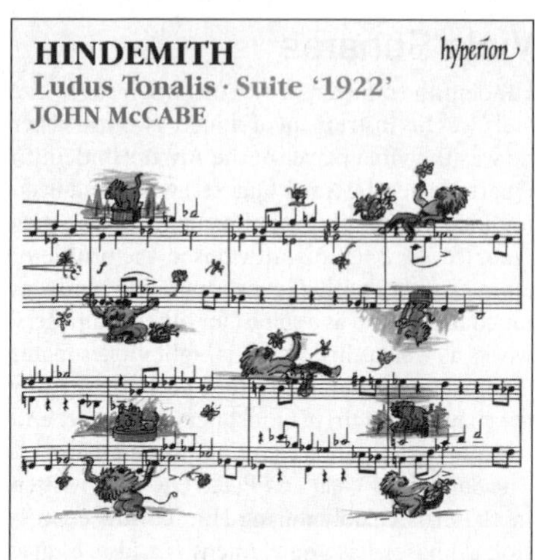

keyboard work, with the possible exception of Shostakovich's *Preludes and Fugues*, reinvents an archaic form with such a spirit of adventure.

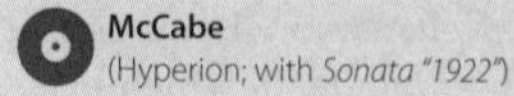

McCabe
(Hyperion; with *Sonata "1922"*)

John McCabe presents these pieces with a clarity and incisiveness that emphasizes their contrapuntal rigour. These are compelling and unsentimental accounts, but there are times when you feel that the pianist could afford to be a little more giving.

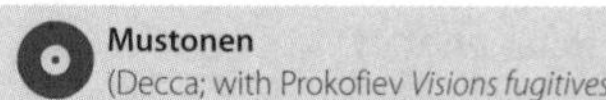

Mustonen
(Decca; with Prokofiev *Visions fugitives*)

This disc is currently out of the catalogue but well worth seeking out. Olli Mustonen approaches every piece on its own terms. His touch is remarkably varied but never heavy or percussive, and the prevailing mood is sunny with many instances of a sly puckish humour at work.

Gustav Holst (1874–1934)

Gustav Holst – an Englishman with a Swedish name – was to a large extent hampered by the period into which he was born, a period in which there was no English musical tradition from which to draw and little chance of a favourable reception for new English music. He composed only as and when he felt the urge, was rarely performed in his lifetime, and relied on classroom teaching for his income. Holst is one of the many composers for whom popularity was posthumous.

Holst was born in Cheltenham, the son of a piano teacher (his father) and one of his pupils. A somewhat sickly child, his piano playing was slowed up by his neuritis, and his early attempts at composition failed to win him a scholarship at the Royal College in London. He stuck at it, however, and, heavily influenced by the work of Gilbert and Sullivan, he composed his first operetta – *Lansdown Castle* – which was performed in 1893. This impressed his father enough to convince him to borrow money and send Gustav to the Royal College, where he studied composition with Charles Stanford and also took up the trombone, his neuritis having finally killed his ambitions as a keyboard player.

It was while at the College that Holst met and became friends with Ralph Vaughan Williams, who introduced him to English folk music, a passion they shared until Holst's death in 1934 (the same year as Elgar's and Delius's). Yet Holst did not respond to these folk influences as readily as his mentor, partly because the presence of Wagner loomed too powerfully. A London performance of *Götterdämmerung*, conducted by Gustav Mahler, made a big impression and a large proportion of Holst's early music veered towards the grandeur of Wagner's operas.

His passion for Wagner soon became less all-pervasive, partly due to other influences such as Stravinsky and Strauss – whose orchestra music Holst was familiar with through his trombone playing – and Sanskrit literature, which lay behind works such as the *Choral Hymns from the Rig Veda*, the chamber opera *Savitri* and the symphonic poem *Indra*. Now a composer with a unique voice, Holst wrote a steady stream of original music, most notably *The Planets*, a seven-movement orchestral suite that gave him his only taste of acclaim.

The Planets, and the late, grim *Egdon Heath*, show what Holst was capable of when he allowed himself to think on a large scale. However, much of his music was written in the certainty that professional performances would never come his way, which is one reason why so much of his output was composed for amateur and children's groups, such as the two London schools for girls where he spent most of his career teaching. This lack of recognition was one reason for the depression that, along with physical ill-health, bothered Holst for much of his life.

The Planets

The Planets, Holst's most brilliantly inventive and famous score, was one of many pieces inspired by the composer's extra-musical interests. In 1913 a friend introduced him to astrology, thus sparking the idea of creating a seven-part tone poem in which the characters of each of the planets would be evoked. This often turbulent and melancholic music was first performed on 29 September, 1918, and it was inevitable that *The Planets* would be perceived as an expression of the nation's collective emotions during the war years. Listening to "Mars" they heard the fury of the Somme and Passchendaele, yet Holst declared that there was no programme to his orchestral suite, and in the case of this particular episode such a programme was impossible – Holst had finished the movement before August 1914.

"Jupiter" – source of the patriotic hymn "I Vow to Thee my Country" – is perhaps the best-known episode, but listening to *The Planets* for the first time is bound to produce several moments of strange familiarity, as this is one of the most often quoted and plagiarized scores of the twentieth century.

Mitchell Choir; London Philharmonic Orchestra; Boult (EMI; with Elgar *Enigma Variations*)

Sir Adrian Boult gave the first performance of *The Planets* in 1918 and, sixty years later, shortly before his ninetieth year, he entered the studio to record it for the third and final time. His interpretation is coloured by intense passion but also suggests the deep reflectiveness of advancing years. Well recorded, this is a fine and moving introduction to Holst.

BBC Symphony Orchestra; Davis (Warner; with *Egdon Heath*)

If you want a single disc of Holst's two finest orchestral works, look no further than this recording. Andrew Davis just falls short of Boult's incisive interpretation, but with exemplary sound and at budget price this is, nonetheless, highly recommendable.

Egdon Heath & St Paul's Suite

The tone poem *Egdon Heath*, composed in 1927 in homage to Thomas Hardy, was Holst's first full-scale orchestral work after *The Planets*. The music is based upon a passage from *The Return of the Native* in which the heath is described as "a place perfectly accordant with man's nature – neither ghastly, hateful, nor ugly; neither commonplace, unmeaning, nor tame; but like man, slighted and enduring; and withal singularly colossal and mysterious in its swarthy monotony". Witheringly bleak at times, this music is the polar opposite of sunny English bucolicism and Holst believed it to be his finest orchestral work.

St Paul's Suite, Holst's most famous score for amateurs, was written for the orchestra of St Paul's girls' school in 1912–13. Famous for a final movement that quotes and builds upon the perennial English folk tune "Greensleeves", it's a good-natured piece of music, with none of the depths of *The Planets* or *Egdon Heath*, but essential listening if you want an idea of Holst's range.

Gustav Holst in thoughtful mood.

Egdon Heath & St Paul's Suite: London Philharmonic Orchestra; Boult (Decca; 2 CDs; with *The Planets, The Perfect Fool Ballet Music & Hymn of Jesus*)

Boult excels himself in *Egdon Heath*, getting as close to the soul of the composer as one is likely to hear on record. This two-for-the-price-of-one CD set (called *The Essential Holst*) includes fine performances by Boult of *The Perfect Fool* and *The Hymn of Jesus*, a hard-driven *Planets* from Solti, and a lively account of the *St Paul's Suite* from Christopher Hogwood.

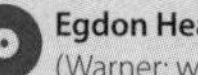

Egdon Heath: BBC Symphony Orchestra; Davis (Warner; with *The Planets*)

In recent years Andrew Davis has become an outstanding exponent of English twentieth-century music, and in this performance he does full justice to the score's dark and mysterious fatalism.

Arthur Honegger (1892–1955)

Though Honegger spent much of his life in Paris, he retained close links with the German-speaking heritage of his native Switzerland, hence the hybrid Franco-Teutonic character of much of his music. Honegger's earliest significant compositions, such as his violin sonata of 1918, were written around the time that he became one of the chic group of French composers known as Les Six (which included Milhaud and Poulenc), but his relationship with the other five was always ambiguous, chiefly because of the distinct lack of humour in his outlook – manifested particularly by Honegger's antipathy to the quirky Erik Satie, spiritual guru of Les Six. Honegger wrote at the time: "I have no taste for the fairground, nor for the music-hall, but, on the contrary, a taste for chamber music and symphonic music in its most austere form." When it came to modern French music, Honegger's preference was for Debussy, whom most of Les Six considered decidedly passé, but he was just as likely to draw upon German, central European and Russian music for inspiration.

Honegger's opera *Antigone*, a collaborative venture with Jean Cocteau, was a disaster on stage, but early success came with the semi-dramatic biblical oratorio *Le Roi David* (1921) and a series of orchestral works including *Pacific 231*, the piece with which he's associated as strongly and unfairly as Ravel is associated with *Bolero*. From the mid-1920s he entered a very productive period, composing several dramatic works, a cello sonata and his first symphony, as well as pursuing the parallel careers of lecturer, writer, music critic and accompanist – he often appeared with his wife, the pianist Andrée Vauraborg, on international and transatlantic tours. Even though Honegger was based in Paris, he maintained firm ties with Switzerland through his close connection with Paul Sacher, the founder and conductor of the Basel Chamber Orchestra. Sacher premiered a significant number of his works and even commissioned two symphonies, the best known being the *Symphony No. 2* (1941).

Honegger held that music required not a change in the rules but "a new player in the same game". This he duly became, producing works that were essentially a natural outgrowth from the tradition of Bach, Beethoven and Richard Strauss. Stravinsky's neo-classicism was also an important influence, and in general Honegger was a surprisingly cosmopolitan composer – his extensive output shows that he was happy to experiment with all sorts of forms, including populist ones such as jazz, which he used to great effect in the 1925 *Piano Concertino*. Characterizing himself as "an honest workman", he even tried his hand composing for the film and radio industries, most notably for two Abel Gance films, *Napoléon* (1927) and *Les Misérables* (1934).

World War II profoundly affected Honegger, whose troubled state found expression in works such as *Cris du Monde*, *Jeanne d'Arc* and the *Symphony No. 3*. After the war he could never quite shake off the depression that that conflict had brought him, and although he continued to create he frequently made it plain that he had become disillusioned with his life – "the profession of a composer is peculiar", he once wrote, "in that it is the principal activity and occupation of a man who exerts himself to produce wares for which no one has any use". As if continuous depression were not bad enough, Honegger contracted angina on a tour of the USA in 1947, a debilitating condition from which he was never to recover.

Symphonies Nos. 2 & 3

Symphony No. 2 was commissioned in 1936, but by the time Honegger had completed it World War II had begun and his mental state had completely altered. This is the work of a deeply unhappy man, full of a troubled energy that suggests the frustration of someone unable to stop (or to come to terms with) the madness that surrounds him. It is scored for strings and a trumpet, which only enters in the last movement to reinforce the chorale tune played by the first violins – a supremely moving moment.

Five years later, with the war ended, Honegger's mood was still one of despair. *Symphony No. 3* (1946) was subtitled "Liturgique", as each of its three movements is headed by a quotation from the Requiem mass. It's the most programmatic of all his works: "I wanted to portray man's terror in the face of Divine anger – to depict the brutal, eternal feelings of persecuted tribes which are subjected to the whims of fate..." A clamorous and angry first movement of endless chugging strings and strident brass is followed by an Adagio (De profundis) in which a lyrical melody seems always on the point of disintegration. The finale begins even more darkly: an ominous march ("the rise of collective stupidity") builds inexorably before subsiding into a warm Mahlerian Adagio, which ends in a solo piccolo rising, birdlike, above the rest of the orchestra – a symbol of peace after the preceding gloom.

Berlin Philharmonic Orchestra; Karajan
(Deutsche Grammophon; with Stravinsky *Concerto in D for String Orchestra*)

Stunning accounts of both symphonies from Karajan and the BPO, who resist the temptation to soften the rugged contours of the *Symphony No. 3* by being overly expressive. Instead, both symphonies are beautifully served by the orchestra's immaculate technical finesse – the end of the third is like emerging out of a terrible storm.

Three Symphonic Movements

Honegger's *Three Symphonic Movements* was actually written as three separate works and that is the way it is usually performed. The first and best known, *Pacific 231* (1923), was seen at the time as the height of modernity (largely because of its subject matter). In fact it's a kind of miniature tone poem that aimed to conjure up a visual impression of "... the quiet turning-over of the machine at rest, the sense of exertion as it starts up, the increase in speed and then finally the emotion, the sense of passion inspired by a 300-ton train racing through the night". *Rugby* (1928) also attempted to translate extreme physical exertion ("the attacks and counters of the game"), this time through a delightful freewheeling rondo of sinewy, contrapuntal energy. The last of the three, finished in 1933, is purely abstract: a restless Allegro marcato in which strings and brass awkwardly co-exist as two distinct battling elements, and an Adagio whose lugubrious saxophone opening and spare orchestration is reminiscent of Hindemith and Weill.

New Zealand Symphony Orchestra; Yuasa
(Naxos; with *Symphony No. 3* & *Pastorale d'été*)

An excellent budget disc that contains all three symphonic movements in vigorously committed performances. The orchestra is not in the same league as the Berlin Phil, but the playing has an attention to detail that suggests both familiarity with the music and enthusiasm for it. This is equally true of the orchestra's fine reading of the langourous early tone poem *Pastorale d'été* and the *Symphony No. 3*.

Johann Nepomuck Hummel (1778–1837)

Hummel's career has many parallels with his older contemporary Beethoven. Both studied with several of the same teachers (including Salieri and Haydn), and both developed careers as virtuoso pianists. But, whereas Beethoven was a daring innovator, both as a composer and as a pianist, Hummel was essentially a conservative – which is why his relationship with Beethoven was rather uneasy, and why his music has been largely ignored since his death. This is unfortunate since at his best, particularly when writing for the piano, he is a composer of elegance and charm, with a special facility for producing ornate and lyrical melodies spun out over light and delicate accompaniments.

Lithograph of Hummel, after a portrait by Grünler.

Hummel began his career as an infant prodigy, impressive enough to be given free lessons by Mozart. Like Mozart he was touted around Europe by an ambitious father, and it was during a trip to England in 1790 that he got to know Haydn, through whom he later obtained the position of *Konzertmeister* at the court of Prince Nikolaus Esterházy (Haydn was still the prince's *Kapellmeister*, in title if not in practice). Hummel's time there was not especially successful, but he remained at the court, on and off, until 1811 when he returned to Vienna. Thereafter his career alternates between that of a jobbing composer (*Kapellmeister* to the Grand-Duchy of Weimar from 1819 until his death) and a concert pianist. His piano playing epitomized the classic Viennese style, and was described by Czerny, Beethoven's most successful piano pupil, as "a modern cleanness, clarity and of the most graceful elegance and tenderness". It was a style that made Hummel, during the 1820s, one of the most celebrated performers in Europe, but the following decade he had been superseded by the more expressive and passionate playing of Romantic pianists such as Chopin and Liszt.

Concertos

The *Trumpet Concerto* is Hummel's most-recorded work, in part because trumpet players have so limited a repertoire that they gratefully accept any halfway decent piece that comes their way. That said, it is one of the liveliest concertos for the instrument, with a lyrically wistful slow movement and a virtuosic last movement. Even better are the concertos Hummel wrote for his own instrument, the piano. These are bravura works, written to show off Hummel's pianistic skills, especially his ability to play long highly ornamented melodies. They may not be as poetic as Chopin's two concertos (on which they exerted a very powerful influence) but they are better orchestrated and far more extrovert works, whose neglect over the years is hard to understand.

Trumpet Concerto: Hardenberger; Academy of St Martin-in-the-Fields; Marriner (Philips; with concertos by Haydn, Hertel and Stamitz)

Håkan Hardenberger plays all four concertos on this CD with astonishing technical expertise and an enormous amount of flair – it's rare to hear a trumpet sounding so light. His articulation is always clear and bright, and there is wit and warmth in his playing of the Hummel, particularly in the way he rattles through the ebullient last movement.

Piano Concertos in A Minor & B Minor: Hough; English Chamber Orchestra; Thomson (Chandos)

The success of Stephen Hough's recording of the two piano concertos did much to re-establish Hummel's reputation. He tackles the amazingly difficult solo parts not just with ease but with a great deal of artistry, shaping the music's sometimes abrupt transitions from boldness to lyricism with delicacy and style.

Piano Music

As the most celebrated pianist of the first two decades of the nineteenth century, Hummel composed a large body of piano works for his own use, ranging from flamboyant display pieces to the more substantial Piano Sonatas. The latter contain the best of him, and while they reveal Hummel's awareness of what other composers were up to, a strong individual voice is evident. The opening theme of the *Sonata in F minor* of 1807, for instance, is obviously Mozartian but the rest of the movement has a most un-Classical freedom of expression. This is even more marked in the later sonatas, which are distinguished by their virtuosity and dramatic flourishes. The grandiose *Sonata in F sharp minor* (1819) has a power worthy of Beethoven, though lacking his inventiveness, while the elaborate ornamentation of the slow movement's lyrical melody set a stylistic precedent that Chopin was quick to develop.

Piano Sonatas: Hough (Hyperion)

There's a new found interest in Hummel's music, to which Stephen Hough has made a major contribution, most recently with this selection of three of Hummel's best sonatas. To the two discussed above, Hough adds the D major sonata of 1824, playing all three with such flair and conviction as to make their neglect all the more mystifying.

Engelbert Humperdinck (1854–1921)

Humperdinck's masterpiece, *Hänsel und Gretel*, is a fairy-tale opera that's emphatically not for children. Operas with supernatural themes had dominated German opera since the days of Weber (see p.622), but Humperdinck gave these subjects a new gravity by turning the harmony, orchestration and mythic power of Wagner's operas to the service of the fairy tale. Lightening the ponderousness of his master's music with the use of folk-style music, he perpetuated the Wagner line while taking it to a more populist level.

Humperdinck was a highly gifted child and began composing operas before formal studies at Cologne University, where he won dozens of prizes. It was there that he fell under the spell of Wagner's music, joining a Wagnerite student society in Munich called The Order of the Grail. He met the man himself in Naples in 1880 and was invited to Bayreuth to help with preparations for the first performance of *Parsifal* in 1881–82. After Wagner's death the following year, Humperdinck returned to Cologne, worked for the music publishers Schott, then tried his hand at teaching and music criticism. In 1890 he returned to composition and three years later Humperdinck's friend and champion Richard Strauss – then the *enfant terrible* of German music – conducted the first performance of *Hänsel und Gretel* in Weimar. The opera's popularity was enormous, and it made the composer a household name in Germany almost overnight. (The reception abroad was initially less rapturous; the English impresario Augustus Harris hardly helped when he introduced the opera to an American audience as "the wonderful work of this great composer Pumpernickel".) The royalties from *Hänsel und Gretel* allowed Humperdinck to devote the remaining years of his life to composition, his major later achievement being *Königskinder* (Royal Children), first performed at the New York Met in 1910. At his death he was acknowledged as one of the last great Romantic composers, through whom the line of Beethoven could be traced through Wagner and on to Richard Strauss.

Music from Hänsel und Gretel; Königskinder; Dornröschen and The Blue Bird: Bamberg Symphony Orchestra; Rickenbacher (Virgin)

Though now difficult to track down, this CD is the best introduction to Humperdinck if you don't feel ready to jump into one of the full-length operas. It contains the best-known orchestral passages from *Hänsel*, as well as excerpts from *Dornröschen* (Sleeping Beauty), his ballet *The Blue Bird*, and *Königskinder*.

Hänsel und Gretel

Humperdinck's first opera began as a commission from his sister – she asked him to write music for a children's play that she'd adapted from the famous story by the Brothers Grimm. The resulting three-act opera has been a mainstay of the Christmas operatic season since its first performance. Described by Richard Strauss as "a masterpiece of the highest quality", it was translated into some twenty languages within a couple of decades of its premiere, and in 1923 became the first opera ever to be broadcast live on radio. Combining the artless charm of German folk songs with a Wagnerian orchestral magnificence, it brings the natural and supernatural worlds vividly to life, particularly in the interludes of the "Witch's Ride" (shades of the *Ride of the Valkyries*) and "Dream Pantomime".

Moffo, Donath, Fischer-Dieskau, Augér, Ludwig; Tolz Boys Choir; Munich Radio Orchestra; Eichhorn (RCA; 2 CDs)

With such an array of vocal riches as the radiant Helen Donath as Gretel, the ham-theatrical Christa Ludwig as the Witch and the noble but lovable Dietrich Fischer-Dieskau as the Father, conductor Kurt Eichhorn might have been tempted to let them get on with it; instead he produces a reading that brings out the detail and colour of the score more than any other.

Grümmer, Schwarzkopf, Metternich, Schürhoff; Bancroft's School Choir; Philharmonia; Karajan (EMI; 2 CDs)

It would be perverse not to recommend Karajan's 1953 *Hänsel und Gretel*, a performance famed for his insight into the symphonic texture of the orchestral score. Elizabeth Grümmer's Hänsel is an equally remarkable achievement, and remains one of the most beautiful vocal performances ever recorded, rather overshadowing the wispily self-conscious Gretel of Elisabeth Schwarzkopf.

I

Charles Ives (1874–1954)

Charles Ives was one of the most extraordinary innovators Western music has produced, and an equally fascinating man – for years he led a double life, working as a highly successful insurance agent by day, and as a composer by night. His music uses collage, atonality, polytonality, dissonance, quarter tones, asymmetrical rhythms and elements of jazz and ragtime – a panoply of devices that anticipated many of the experiments of Stravinsky, Debussy, Schoenberg, Berg and Webern, before some of them had written their first note. Apart from his wife and a handful of friends and contemporaries, no one understood what he was up to for years, but Ives could not care less. Composing in virtual seclusion, he went on following his instincts until he stopped writing in his fifties.

Almost every work he wrote contains quotes from the tunes, patriotic songs, hymns and marches he heard while growing up in Danbury, Connecticut, where he received a highly unorthodox musical education from his army bandleader father. He became an intensely patriotic man, whose adoration of his country was often expressed by referring back to his happy childhood. Ives had a virtually photographic memory and everything he heard and saw as a child made a lasting impression on him – nothing more so than a baseball rally he once attended, where two marching bands met head on, each playing totally different music. Ives was so entranced by the sound that in adulthood the juxtaposition of different musics became a favourite compositional ploy.

Despite moments of wistfulness and tenderness in works like the *Symphony No. 3*, *The Unanswered Question* and *Three Places in New England*, Ives did not write pretty music, the sort admired by the conventional public. His hardy background gave him an aversion to "cissy sounds", and his opinions on many revered figures were not flattering – Chopin he considered to be "soft … with a skirt on", while Mozart was "effeminate". He was a musical Ernest Hemingway – where he came from people "got up and said what they thought regardless of the consequences". Allied to this forthrightness was an earthy idealism, central to which was the belief that art should become part of the fabric of humanity; he looked forward to the day when "every man, while digging his potatoes, will breathe his own Epics, his own Symphonies (Operas if he likes)".

It's no wonder that Ives became a hero to America's twentieth-century musicians. Every marginalized composer has at some time or another taken courage from his bold and stoically independent stance, epitomized in his declaration that "the impossibilities of today are the possibilities of tomorrow".

Symphony No. 3

If Gustav Mahler had lived a little longer he might well have put Ives on the musical map decades before the old man received his long overdue recognition. Evidently Mahler had come across a score of Ives's *Symphony No. 3* (1901–04) towards the end of his tenure as conductor of the Metropolitan Opera and the New York Philharmonic, and had copied it out ready to perform when he returned to Vienna. It was not to be. The third was indeed to be the first of Ives's symphonies to receive a complete performance, but that was not until 5 April, 1946 in New York. To Ives's immense surprise and satisfaction it took the Pulitzer prize. One of his most popular symphonic works, it is based on music he had played as a young organist at the Central Presbyterian Church in New York, using favourite hymns like "What a Friend We Have in Jesus" to build the outer movements' melodic and harmonic structures. The end result is a highly ingratiating piece, which is by turns gentle, jaunty and devotional in mood.

Saint Louis Symphony Orchestra; Slatkin
(RCA; with *The Unanswered Question & Three Places in New England*)

When it comes to the interpretation of robust American music there are few American conductors to match Leonard Slatkin. His performance of the *Symphony No. 3* is muscular where necessary, but never at the expense of the work's nuanced folksy imagery.

Symphony No. 4

Massive, transcendent, wholly impractical and like nothing else in music – although every note could be traced back to a source from American folklore or Classical tradition – Ives's *Symphony No. 4* (1910–16) symbolizes everything that made him unique and important. Although lasting little over thirty minutes, Ives wrote for orchestral forces that imply an epic of Cecil B. DeMille proportions: three saxophones, eight percussionists, two harps, organ, theremin (an early electronic instrument) and a piano tuned in quartertones join an augmented body of strings, wind, brass and a choir. Why such excesses? Ives wanted to create music that felt bigger than earthly life, posing "the searching questions of What? And Why? which the spirit of man asks of life", he said. After a stentorian Prelude, the piece lurches towards a vastly complex fugue, with parts jump-cutting around displaced tempos and asymmetrical rhythmic ratios, throwing fragments of quoted hymns around like ticker-tape. The piece ends with a grand battle between atonal and tonal material, before finding its affirmative choral conclusion.

Charles Ives relaxing at home.

Dallas Symphony Orchestra; Litton
(Hyperion; with *Symphony No.1 & The Unanswered Question*)

American conductor Andrew Litton's performance is triumphantly ballsy and noisy, taking Ives's challenges head on. The Dallas orchestra are not fazed by such unheralded rhythmic demands and the choral finale is deeply affecting, especially after the powerful tug-of-war between peaceful tonality and disruptive atonal intrusions.

The Unanswered Question

In 1906 Ives wrote *The Unanswered Question*, which definitely has a claim to being his watershed piece. This was the first composition in which he juxtaposed contrasting groups of instruments, each having its own distinctive style. Described as a "Cosmic Landscape", *The Unanswered Question* is a symbolic drama in which the "Perennial Question of Existence" is asked seven times by a solo trumpet against a background of muted offstage strings that represent "the Silences of the Druids – Who Know, See and Hear Nothing". Four woodwinds are unleashed to seek "the Invisible Answer", but to no avail, and they leave the scene before the trumpet reiterates the question for the last time.

Saint Louis Symphony Orchestra; Slatkin (RCA; with *Symphony No. 3 & Three Places in New England*)

Slatkin is as impressive in *The Unanswered Question* as he is in the *Symphony No. 3*. He seems completely in control of the work, and the Saint Louis Symphony Orchestra respond admirably, bringing out the poetry of the music with remarkable warmth and finesse.

Three Places in New England

The ten years following *The Unanswered Question* were marked by feverish activity. One of the classic works produced in this decade was *Three Places in New England* (1903–14), the second part of which – "Putnam's Camp" – is one of the most celebrated instances of Ives's love of clashing sounds, with a wild march full of duff notes and players missing the beat. This section is preceded by a piece subtitled "Col. Shaw and His Coloured Regiment", a memorial to America's first black army company, taking the form of a highly effective dreamlike blues, spiced with dissonant harmonies. The final part, "The Housatonic at Stockbridge", was inspired by Ives's memory of an autumn walk he and his wife took soon after they were married; it's a stunning piece, memorable for the way it sets a simple folk tune against a turbulent orchestral texture and then, at the end, fades into silence.

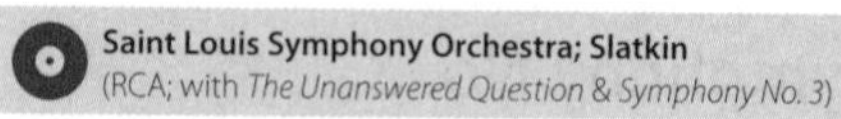

Saint Louis Symphony Orchestra; Slatkin
(RCA; with *The Unanswered Question & Symphony No. 3*)

Slatkin and the SLSO take hold of Ives's more wildly extravagant moments in the *Three Places* and, rather than taming them, actually stoke up the drama – the result is a performance with a genuine electric charge. All in all, this disc is definitely the best way into Ives's orchestral music.

The "Concord" Sonata

Ives was a talented pianist, known for his skills of improvisation, and he wrote a number of works for the piano. The greatest of these was his second sonata, nicknamed the "Concord" after the town in Massachusetts associated with the transcedentalism school of literature and philosophy. Each of the four movements is an "impressionistic picture" of a leading transcendentalist figure, including Emerson, Hawthorne, the Alcotts and Thoreau. Ranging in style from angular modernism to Debussy-esque impressionism – and quoting Beethoven's fifth symphony in various places – it's a huge work that makes enormous demands of the performer. "Is it the composer's fault that man has only 10 fingers?", Ives once asked. In places it feels as though he is taking pleasure in overstepping the piano's limits, and, as if acknowledging this, he wrote small optional parts for viola and, in the last movement, flute. The second movement, meanwhile, requires the pianist to strike huge clusters of notes with a piece of wood exactly 14¾ inches in length.

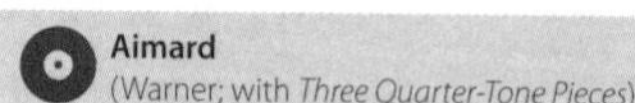

Aimard
(Warner; with *Three Quarter-Tone Pieces*)

Pierre-Laurent Aimard delivers a typically supercharged account of the "Concord" (complete with viola and flute parts). He's a highly disciplined performer and his intense, dynamic approach ensures that this sometimes rhapsodic work never sounds unstructured.

J

Leoš Janáček (1854–1928)

Although he was born halfway through the nineteenth century, Janáček's best music belongs decisively to the twentieth. His finest works – the last four operas, the *Sinfonietta*, *Glagolitic Mass*, *The Diary of One Who Disappeared* and the two string quartets – were composed in an astonishing burst of creativity in his last decade, and they are among the most impressive and accessible pieces of the last hundred years, distinguished by terse dramatic power, emotional lyricism, eccentric orchestration and rhythmic bite.

Janáček was the fifth of nine children born into a poor teacher's family in Hukvaldy, northern Moravia. He was educated in Brno, the Moravian capital, and spent most of his life there – the National Theatre in Brno premiered the operas that are the basis of his reputation, and the Czechs' reluctance to place him alongside their beloved Smetana and Dvořák is perhaps due to his being perceived as too Moravian.

As with so many central European composers, folk music was the liberating ingredient in his career. In 1888 he set off on a tour of northern Moravia with the ethnographer František Bartoš, and this intense encounter with the indigenous culture led to a decisive change in his compositional style. Certain folk tunes made their way into his orchestral and choral compositions, but more generally the short, irregular melodic phrases of Moravian music became integral to Janáček's idiosyncratic constructions, while echoes of folk ensembles influenced his distinctive orchestral sound.

Janáček's work can be seen as a fight against the German domination of his country, and the foundation of the Czechoslovak republic in 1918 was a factor behind the amazing creativity of his last years. But as well as being a Czech patriot, he was also an ardent believer in a pan-Slavic culture – he learned Russian, visited that country twice, sent his daughter to study in St Petersburg and founded a Russian club in Brno. In 1900 he conducted a concert featuring dances from the various Slav nations, for which he wrote a *Serbian Kolo* and *Russian Cossack Dance*. The Russian writers Gogol, Ostrovsky, Tolstoy and Dostoevsky inspired some of his greatest works (the libretto of *From the House of the Dead* was translated by Janáček from Dostoevsky), and the monumental *Glagolitic Mass*, with its text in Old Church Slavonic, can be heard as a sort of manifesto for a pan-Slavism.

The other dominating feature of much of Janáček's work is its erotic charge. His marriage, to a pupil ten years his junior, was never very successful

Leoš Janáček in a studio photograph of 1904.

– they were formally separated in 1917, when Janáček had an affair with Gabriela Horvátová, singer in the Prague production of *Jenůfa*. Soon afterwards he began the crucial relationship of his last decade when at the Moravian spa town of Luhačovice he met Kamila Stösslová, a married woman half his age. Janáček conceived an all-consuming but unreciprocated passion for Kamila, to whom he wrote over 700 letters, the most passionate ones being written almost daily in the last sixteen months of his life. (They have recently been published in English, edited and translated by John Tyrrell.) *The Diary of One Who Disappeared* was the first work to be inspired by Kamila, who was then transformed into the heroines of three of his finest operas, *Káťa Kabanová*, *The Cunning Little Vixen* and *The Makropulos Case*. However, the most direct expression of their relationship is his *String Quartet No. 2 "Intimate Letters"*, one of the most intimate pieces of music ever written. Less than six months after it was composed, Janáček died of pneumonia from a chill he caught while the aloof Kamila was staying with him in Hukvaldy.

Jenůfa

The creation of *Jenůfa* lasted nine years (1894–1903), a period in which Janáček's whole musical style was undergoing changes. In addition to finding a way to fully integrate folk music into large-scale pieces, he was abandoning the idea of opera as a series of set pieces in favour of a through-composed dramatic form. He also became interested in the melodies of everyday speech, deciding that his vocal music should define "a melodic curve which will, as if by magic, reveal immediately a human being in one definite phase of his existence".

The opera is based on Gabriela Preissová's play *Její pastorkyna* (Her Foster-Daughter) – a slice-of-life drama set in a Moravian village. Two men, Steva and Laca, are rivals for Jenůfa's affection; she gets pregnant by the former, the unreliable one, but is truly loved by the latter; Steva moves on to another girl, whereupon Jenůfa's stepmother drowns the baby; finally Jenůfa and Laca are reconciled, in one of the great moments of opera. Janáček's absorption of Moravian folk music underpins the entire score, which has a rough-edged veracity that's typical of his mature work. Janáček very often writes for only the high and low strings, leaving out the middle registers for a more unsettling effect. Where a shade more emotional warmth is required, he fills out the string texture to cover the full spectrum.

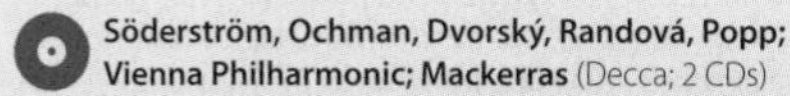
Söderström, Ochman, Dvorský, Randová, Popp; Vienna Philharmonic; Mackerras (Decca; 2 CDs)

Mackerras's Decca series of Janáček's operas is unsurpassed, and this premiere recording of the opera's original version is magnificent in every way. As the stepmother, Eva Randová brings out every nuance of this tyrannical yet well-meaning character. Elisabeth Söderström and the two male leads are also finely cast, while the orchestral playing is superb.

Kát'a Kabanová

Kát'a Kabanová, a story of adultery in a tyrannical family setting, was written in 1919–21 and is based on *The Storm* by the Russian playwright Ostrovsky – one of several works Janáček based on Russian literature. His love for Kamila Stösslová is crucial to the psychological portrait of Kát'a, whose love for another man can be read as Janáček's wish-fulfilment. The action is concise and dramatic: Kát'a is reluctantly attracted to Boris, with whom she has an affair while her husband is away, then confesses to her mother-in-law (another strong female character) and is driven to commit suicide in the river. This is probably Janáček's best-constructed work, and it contains some quite extraordinary love music. The opening is especially fine – a brooding orchestral prelude in which the melodic line keeps turning in on itself before reaching the glorious melody that is associated with Kát'a throughout the opera. The timpani then burst in ominously, to return at decisive moments later in the opera.

Beňačková, Straka, Randová, Pecková, Knopp; Czech Philharmonic Orchestra; Mackerras (Supraphon; 2 CDs)

This is Mackerras's second recording of *Kát'a*, made in 1987, more than twenty years after his first. This time it's an exclusively Czech affair, with a rawer more urgent sound from the orchestra and, in Gabriela Beňačková's Kát'a, a more febrile performance than Söderström's.

The Cunning Little Vixen

Kamila Stösslová was again an inspiration for *The Cunning Little Vixen*, this time as self-sacrificing wife and mother – but an equally crucial inspiration was the countryside around his native village of Hukvaldy, where Janáček bought a house in 1921, shortly before starting work on this opera. Derived from a regular cartoon strip that appeared in a Brno newspaper, *The Cunning Little Vixen* is the beguiling anthropomorphic tale of a young vixen called Bystrouska (Sharp Ears), who is caught and raised by a gamekeeper. She kills his chickens, escapes, finds a mate, and is finally shot by a poultry dealer; at the end of the opera the gamekeeper is found back in the forest, surrounded by a troop of animals including a young vixen, Bystrouska's cub. Conjuring a broad vision of life's richness and transience, and nature's capacity for renewal, *The Cunning Little Vixen* shows Janáček at his most sumptuous and lyrical.

Popp, Jedlička, Randová; Vienna Philharmonic Orchestra; Mackerras (Decca; 2 CDs)

Full of luscious orchestral interludes, this is probably the most entrancing Janáček opera, and this recording of it is another triumph from Mackerras. Lucia Popp is immensely lively and characterful in the title role, and the Czech supporting cast is very fine indeed.

Glagolitic Mass

For several years Janáček conducted a male choir in Brno, and choral music actually comprises the largest element of his output. His masterpiece of the genre is the *Glagolitic Mass*, a piece bursting with brassy fanfares and rhythmic energy, though it has some quieter moments of rapt contemplation. It was written at white heat in a single month in 1926, after an inspirational walk in the woods at Luhačovice, the spa where he had met Kamila. "I felt a cathedral grow out of the giant expanse of the woods", he wrote. "A flock of sheep were ringing their bells. Now I hear the voice of an arch priest in the tenor solo, a maiden angel in the soprano and in the choir – the people. The tall firs, their tips lit up by the stars, are the candles and during the ceremony I see the vision of St Wenceslas and I hear the language of the missionaries Cyril and Methodius."

The text of the *Glagolitic Mass* is written in Old Church Slavonic, and the piece is a patriotic hymn to the greatness of the Czech nation and Slavic culture. Judging by his letters to Kamila, he also imagined the piece as a celebratory wedding mass for the two of them.

Palmer, Gunson, Mitchinson, King, Parker-Smith; City of Birmingham Symphony Chorus and Orchestra; Rattle (EMI; 2 CDs; with *Sinfonietta, Concertino, The Diary of One Who Disappeared* and other works)

This may be an almost exclusively English performance of the Mass but it certainly lacks nothing in raw energy and gusto. Felicity Palmer is an incisive soloist with something of a Slavic edge to her tone, and the Birmingham chorus give all they've got.

Sinfonietta & Taras Bulba

Janáček's orchestral *tour de force*, and his most popular work, is the *Sinfonietta*, which was written at the same time as the *Glagolitic Mass* and is comparable in its exuberance and overall tone. Encapsulating Janáček's patriotic pride in the newly formed Czechoslovakia, it also – inevitably – has its connection with Kamila. A military band that she and Janáček heard playing in her hometown of Písek gave him the idea of the massive brass fanfares that open and close the piece. The five movements are dramatically scored and highly contrasted, but it's a remarkably coherent piece, thanks mainly to a melodic motif that underpins each part.

Taras Bulba is an exceptionally vivid and rather gory "Rhapsody for Orchestra" which tells of the death of the Ukrainian Cossack leader Taras Bulba and his two sons in the 1628 war against the Poles. Based on the story as told by Gogol, it's in three sections: the first two evoke the battle at Dubno and the death of the two sons; the third tells of the capture of Taras and his subsequent execution.

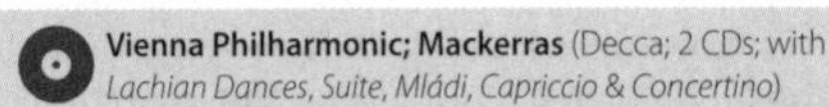

Vienna Philharmonic; Mackerras (Decca; 2 CDs; with *Lachian Dances, Suite, Mládi, Capriccio & Concertino*)

Under Mackerras's baton the VPO produce recordings of the *Sinfonietta* and *Taras Bulba* which are rugged and highly charged. Recently repackaged as a double CD along with Janáček's other orchestral works, this set is remarkably good value for money.

The Diary of One Who Disappeared

The first composition to emerge from Janáček's infatuation with Kamila Stösslová was the song cycle *The Diary of One Who Disappeared*, a piece which, like *The Cunning Little Vixen*, was spurred by something printed in the Brno paper *Lidové noviny* – in this instance some poems about a young man becoming infatuated with a Gypsy girl and forsaking his family. The form of the work is unprecedented: it's a cycle of 22 numbers for tenor and piano, a combination joined in the middle three songs by a female chorus plus a mezzo-soprano to personify the Gypsy girl, Zefka. "While writing the *Diary*", Janáček wrote to Kamila, "I thought only of you. You were Zefka!"; unsurprisingly, in view of its heavily autobiographical burden, the story is told principally through the thoughts of the young man, while the Gypsy's true feelings remain ambiguous – despite an episode of lovemaking, discreetly masked by a piano solo.

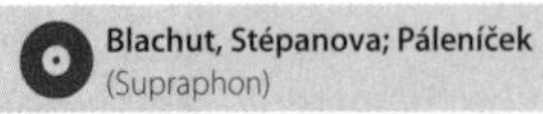

Blachut, Stépanova; Páleníček (Supraphon)

This *Diary* performance, recorded in the 1950s, is something of a classic not because it's the most beautifully sung but because it's the most heartfelt and intense. Tenor Beno Blachut really inhabits the role in a way few other singers manage and he's well supported by pianist Josef Páleníček. The same disc also contains a later performance (with the same pianist) sung by tenor Nicolai Gedda with more refinement but less dramatic impact.

String Quartets

Janáček's two string quartets are amongst the greatest ever written, containing extraordinary textures and sudden juxtapositions of contrasting ideas. The first, written in a week in 1921, is based on Tolstoy's novella *The Kreutzer Sonata*, a portrait of jealousy in a loveless marriage. It's possible to find musical correspondences to the incidents in the story, but it's better to ignore these programmatic elements and simply enjoy the outstanding lyrical and dramatic invention of the score. The same goes for the second quartet, which was written in about three weeks in 1928 and to which Janáček gave the unambiguous subtitle *Intimate Letters*. Judging by Janáček's letters to Kamila, the quartet contains depictions of specific characters and events – the stormy opening theme must represent the composer and the chilling viola reply introduces us to Kamila – but it's futile to speculate on the extra-musical meanings. The passion is what matters, and that's evident in each phrase – in Janáček's own words, "This piece was written in fire." After hearing it played he wrote: "It's a work as if carved out of living flesh. I think that I won't write a more profound and a truer one." Little more than a month later he was dead.

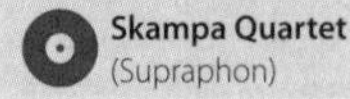

Skampa Quartet (Supraphon)

Many couplings of Janáček's two quartets are available, but these electric performances stand out. The Skampa Quartet play with real bite, bringing out the detail of this music (especially the dynamic variations) without ever sacrificing its rough-edged beauty. These are intense, encapsulating accounts, with the players demonstrating a complete naturalness with Janáček's sound-world.

Piano Music

The solo piano works of Janáček contain his most intimate and spontaneous music and, in the *Sonata 1. X. 1905 "From the Street"*, some of his greatest. The sonata's unusual title refers to the death of a Czech worker during a demonstration demanding a Czech university in the predominantly German town of Brno. The response to this tragedy is heartfelt and unmistakably Janáčekian; simple thematic material is developed improvisatorily; unexpected harmonies and changes of mood abound; scurrying sub-textural figurations suggest inner turmoil and unease. There are just two movements (a third was destroyed just before the first performance): the first entitled "Presentiment", the second "Death". Both are extremely atmospheric: in the second a repeated dotted motif evokes a funeral procession where anger slowly mounts and then recedes.

The collection of ten short pieces, *On an Overgrown Path*, was written between 1901 and 1908. As a group they resemble Schumann's *Kinderszenen* and were partly written as a response to the death of Janáček's daughter Olga. The individual titles were added just before publication but they reinforce the themes of sadness and reminiscence. These are incredibly intense poetic miniatures, which pinpoint a mood or an image with a laconic ease. The most striking of them all is the dramatic "The Barn Owl Has Not Flown Away", where clamorous arpeggios represent the cry of the owl – a portent of death in Czech folklore.

Sonata 1.X.1905; On an Overgrown Path; In the Mists: Firkušný (Deutsche Grammophon; 2 CDs; with *Concertino for Piano and Chamber Orchestra*)

Czech pianist Rudolf Firkušný plays with the authority of somebody with a deep knowledge of this music and he gets right to its heart. There is no straining after poetic effects in his playing, which is straightforward and restrained and gives a clear sense of the shape of each of the sonata's movements. Again in the miniatures a compelling urgency is achieved through the clarity of his phrasing.

In the Mists; Sonata 1.X.1905; On an Overgrown Path; Reminiscence: Schiff (ECM)

A completely different approach is provided by András Schiff on this recent recording. In place of Firkušný's incisiveness, he offers a gentler sound and more detailed interpretations that bring out the music's poetry and in no way lessen its impact.

Josquin Desprez (c.1455–1521)

Josquin Desprez (usually referred to simply as Josquin) dominated western Europe's musical landscape at the end of the fifteenth century in much the same way as Dufay (see p.165) had dominated it in the middle. Like Dufay he came from northern Europe, possibly from St Quentin in the Hainaut region of France, and established, if anything, an even greater reputation. Contemporaries compared him to Michelangelo, and Luther memorably announced: "Josquin is master of the notes, which do what he wants, while other composers must do what the notes want." Polyphony came of age with Josquin: he consolidated the achievements of his great predecessors, Dufay and Ockeghem, turning their essentially linear style into something more harmonically complex and expressive. For the first time, real attention was paid to conveying the meaning of words, but it is the sheer beauty of the sound which is most striking. It was Josquin who established the pattern for Renaissance sacred music, creating rich vocal textures made up of long arching phrases in which consistent imitation between the voices creates a sense both of unity and of progression.

What little was thought to be known about Josquin's early years is now in doubt, as recent research indicates that he was born c.1455 rather than 1440 as was previously believed, and was the son of one Gosard Lebloitte. Confusion arose because of the existence of another Josquin, a singer based principally in Milan. Any connection between Milan and Josquin the composer is now regarded as suspect, and the earliest information we have about him relates to his presence at the court of King René of Anjou in 1475.

More adequately substantiated is Josquin's presence early in 1483 in the Burgundian town of Condé-sur-l'Escaut, and from 1498 (when the other Josquin died) we can be fairly sure that he was in France, attached to the court of Louis XII. By 1502 he was certainly at the court of Duke Ercole of Ferrara, recommended by one of the duke's talent scouts – although another had suggested a different composer, Isaac, on the grounds that Josquin was irascible, composed only when he wanted to and charged too much. The duke chose Josquin and was rewarded with a mass setting based on his name. When the plague hit Ferrara a year later, Josquin sensibly left and returned north (his successor, Obrecht, died of the plague in 1505), returning to Condé-sur-l'Escaut, where he became provost of the collegiate church of Notre Dame, a position he held until his death.

Sacred Music

Though Josquin wrote a substantial number of courtly songs, it is as a composer of motets and masses that he exerted the widest influence. In much of Josquin's sacred music the technique of imitation, whereby one voice repeats part or more of what another voice has just sung, becomes increasingly apparent. Another device which he exploits is that of suspension, in which a note in one voice is held while the other voices move onto a new chord – the resulting discord sets up a tension which is only resolved when the held note moves onto the correct note. Josquin also makes plentiful use of the old technique of basing music on an existing tune, called the cantus firmus: he based one of his last and best-known masses, the *Missa Pange Lingua*, on a plainsong Corpus Christi hymn. However, rather than emphasize the borrowed material (which is what his contemporaries tended to do), Josquin treats the plainsong melody very freely and largely disguises it within the overall musical fabric by distributing it between the different voices, which he combines with great variety and with an acute sensitivity to the text. He also wrote masses that employ a secular cantus firmus, two of them using the popular song "L'homme armé" (The Armed Man).

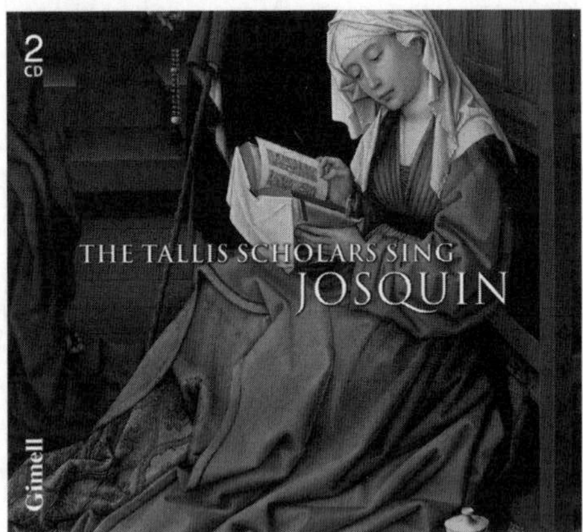

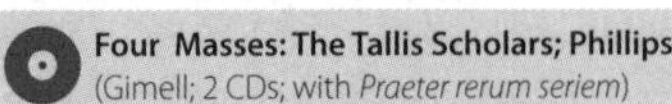

Four Masses: The Tallis Scholars; Phillips
(Gimell; 2 CDs; with *Praeter rerum seriem*)

This Tallis Scholars two-CD set makes a great introduction to Josquin's music. It includes the *Missa Pange Lingua*, both *L'homme armé* masses, the *Missa Mi-mi* and the glorious motet *Praeter rerum seriem*. The range of his stylistic development is conveyed by the two *L'homme armé* masses: the first has a medieval feel, with the four voices overlapping in pitch, while the later work spreads them wider, creating a striking sense of space.

Missa Pange Lingua: Ensemble Clément Janequin; Ensemble Organum; Pérès
(Harmonia Mundi)

In contrast to the Tallis Scholars, the two combined all-male choirs on this disc give a much more robust performance. The mass is placed within a larger liturgical context by the inclusion of plainchant and this succeeds in highlighting the rich splendour of the polyphony. Matters of speed, volume and, above all, attack are very much attuned to the meaning of the words, and the result is expressive and passionate.

Mauricio Kagel (1931–2008)

Though his output was hugely diverse, and many of his works were intensely serious, Argentinian-born composer Maurizio Kagel remains best-known for his subversive and surreal side – as an artist unafraid to raise a smile. Filmmaker and playwright as well as musician, he brought a more daring sense of bizarre theatricality and biting irony to post-war music than any other member of the avant-garde. *Finale*, a work for chamber orchestra, provided a typical example of his desire to turn the concert-going experience on its head: the Stravinskian texture is interrupted when the conductor feigns death on the podium. In *Abduction from the Concert Hall*, meanwhile, the orchestra are kidnapped, and the conductor has to negotiate their release by telephone.

Born and raised in Buenos Aires, Kagel failed the entrance examination to his local music conservatory. Instead, he studied literature and philosophy at the University of Buenos Aires – with Jorge Luis Borges among others – and took private lessons in music theory, conducting, singing, piano, cello and organ. He also started composing (without a teacher) and in 1957, on the recommendation of Boulez, who was impressed by one of his scores, he moved to Europe, settling in Cologne. There he combined his unique brand of instrumental theatre – in which the physical actions of the performers were as important as the actual notes – with a desire to criticize accepted musical conventions.

The results included works such as *Match* (1964), which alludes to the competitiveness of Western musical culture: two cellists, seated on opposite sides of the concert platform, try to outdo each other, with a percussionist positioned between them acting as referee. Similarly, *Anagrama* (1957–58) is a subtle critique of the claims of formal control: it claims to be as strictly constructed as the total serialism of Boulez's *Structures Ia*, yet is composed with rules that are decidedly illogical. And in *Ludwig van* (1969–70), he repeats Beethoven quotations until they seem banal.

However, Kagel was more than just a satirist. Even his more surreal works – whether influenced by his constant desire to question conventions, by recurring dreams or (as some have suggested) by his clinically supervised mescaline and LSD experiments – are never simply flippant. In the last two decades of his life, Kagel's music, in such works as the *Sankt-Bach-Passion* (1981–85), the *String Quartet No. 3* (1986–87) and the Stravinskian *Doppelsextett* (2000-2001), espoused neo-tonality and seemed more concerned with relating to history than subverting it. Although he never forgot

Kagel's sense of humour was central to his work.

how to lampoon – his radio piece *Playback Play* (1997) was inspired by a visit to a music instrument fair, the resulting collage of instrumental clichés and febrile sales-talk satirizing the hard-nosed commercial wing of the music business: its tendency to know the cost of everything, but the value of nothing.

Sankt-Bach-Passion

More than an hour and a half long and scored for speaker, mezzo, tenor, baritone, three choirs, organ and orchestra, the *Sankt-Bach-Passion* is a decidedly large-scale work that reveals Kagel's unqualified veneration of the great German composer. Kagel compiled his own text to tell the story of Bach's life, based on historical documents and adapted from cantata texts – references to God and to Jesus Christ are replaced with the name of J.S. Bach – while following the structure of the Lutheran service. Premiered in Bach's tercentennial year, 1985, the piece largely eschews the irony central to much of Kagel's music, and avoids any direct quotations from Bach's work or overt parodies of his style. Due to the work's focus on narration there is a marked absence of extended arias, and the choruses are less substantial than in Bach's own *Passions*. Still, this is a solemn and impressive work, remarkable for the audacity of its conception.

von Otter; Blochwitz; Hermann; Roggisch; Zacher; Limburger Domsingknaben; NDR-Chor Hamburg; Südfunk-Chor Stuttgart; Radio-Sinfonie-Orchester Stuttgart; Kagel (Naive; 2 CDs).

Part of an ongoing Kagel edition, this disc was recorded soon after the *Sankt-Bach-Passion* premiere, with Kagel at the podium and an impressive group of soloists. The performance, sound quality and accompanying documentation are all of the highest order.

..., den 24. xii. 1931

Written in the period 1988–91, the bizarrely named *..., den 24. xii. 1931* – subtitled "Garbled News" and scored for baritone voice, violin, viola, cello, double bass, two pianists and two percussionists – had its beginnings in Kagel's wish to discover interesting news items from the time of his birth. As such, the text is collated and edited from newspaper reports, an advert and a reader's letter, all published during the days surrounding his birthday. Over the course of the work's seven movements the mood ranges from the threatening machismo of the Japanese general occupying Manchuria (complete with crashing cymbals and pentatonicism) to the pathos of a man who finds himself unemployed and homesick at Christmas. It's an oddly compelling work that is cuttingly satirical, mysterious and joyful by turns.

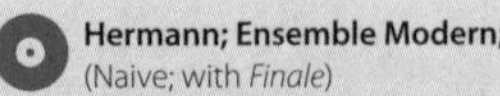

Hermann; Ensemble Modern; Kagel (Naive; with *Finale*)

These are splendid performances from Ensemble Modern under the direction of the composer. Baritone Roland Hermann provides a vivid and assured performance in *..., den 24. xii. 1931*, which is coupled with a compelling recording of *Finale*.

String Quartets

Kagel composed four string quartets. *Nos. 1* and *2* (1965–67), which were published together and essentially form two movements of the same work, demonstrate their composer's unique brand of instrumental theatre. They begin with the cellist walking onto the stage while glancing reproachfully behind him at the other three players who, for the time being, remain behind the scenes. He stands hesitantly at his own chair before walking over to that of the first violinist, where he sits before returning to his own chair. There follow plentiful examples of the dramatization of the psychological tensions that exist between the players, who are required to use a variety of materials – including knitting needles, matches and paperclips – to take the music into the realm of noise. While these have an undeniable comic effect, they are also capable of a strange beauty. By contrast, the *String Quartet No. 3*, dating from 1986–87, forgoes the antics of its predecessors (though it does feature a wide array of advanced bowing techniques). In this work, wistful, almost Romantic themes are starkly juxtaposed with more dissonant, Bartokian sections.

String Quartets Nos. 1-3; Arditti String Quartet; Wiesner (Naive; with *Pan*)

The *String Quartets Nos. 1 & 2* should ideally be seen as well as heard, but the Arditti players do an excellent job of bringing a sense of theatre to this recording. Kagel insisted that, in performance, these two early quartets should be separated by a work composed by a living composer. On this disc, Kagel's own *Pan* (1985), a miniature for piccolo and string quartet, fulfils this curious obligation.

Aram Khachaturian (1903–1978)

In 1948, at the infamous conference of the Composers' Union in Moscow, Khachaturian (along with his colleagues Shostakovich and Prokofiev) was denounced for the "formalist" tendencies in his music. That is, for deviating from the melodious, flag-waving jollity as prescribed by Stalin's cultural ideologue, Andrei Zhadanov. In retrospect it's difficult to see why this happened, for, with the exception of the more experimental *Symphony No. 3* (1947), Khachaturian's unashamedly Romantic and folk-inflected works, in which he gave international voice to the distinctive melodies and harmonies of Armenia (from where his family came), seem the ideal Soviet mixture of conservatism and nationalism. It is precisely these qualities that have seen him looked down on by Western critics (despite the popularity of several of his works), and it is true that his music, while always strong on melody, is frequently rather weak in structure and the development of ideas.

Khachaturian showed little musical talent until his brother persuaded him to go to Moscow in 1921, where he somehow managed to gain a place at the Gnesin Music Academy to study the cello, an instrument he had never played before. By 1925 he was studying composition with Myaskovsky and making rapid progress; his first work – a dance for violin and piano – was published only a year later. His international reputation was established by his *Piano Concerto*, which was written in 1936 and followed up four years later by the *Violin Concerto*. By the close of the 1940s he had completed three symphonies, but it was two full-length ballet scores – *Gayaneh* and *Spartacus* – that brought him the most widespread attention.

Khachaturian's symphonies lack the immediate impact of his concertos and ballets, but they all have an individual stamp. The three-movement *No. 1*, first performed in 1934, introduced a new personal way of combining his native folk music with symphonic processes. Although having no specific programme, *No. 2* (1943) undoubtedly reflects the wartime circumstances of its composition, with its ominous bells and musical calls-to-arms suggesting the darkness, sacrifice and heroism of the USSR's "Great Patriotic War".

Violin Concerto

Khachaturian's *Violin Concerto*, written in 1940 for the great Russian violinist David Oistrakh, is a brash and exuberant work completely lacking in any subtlety. The overblown orchestral writing frequently teeters on the banal and ideas often outstay their welcome. The work's saving grace is the violin part, whose insinuating and pushy charm can overcome nearly all critical resistance when in the hands of an outstanding performer. It's an exceptionally vocalized solo line, coloured by the Eastern inflections and ornamentation of Armenian folk music, and dominated by a yearning, rhapsodic quality. This is given a nocturnal sultriness in the second movement and an almost rowdy air of abandon in the third. For those who are won over by its naive energy, there will be as many who dismiss it as shameless kitsch. It won a coveted Stalin Prize in 1941.

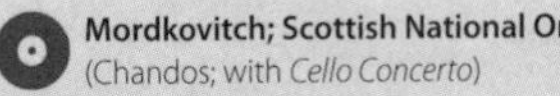

Mordkovitch; Scottish National Orchestra; Järvi (Chandos; with *Cello Concerto*)

Chandos have gone for broke with this disc: an extremely rich and detailed sound with the soloist placed well forward. Lydia Mordkovitch, a David Oistrakh pupil, is just the kind of violinist to revel in all its sensual overloads and she plays it as if it were a true masterpiece. It's coupled with a strong perfomance of the *Cello Concerto* by Raphael Wallfisch.

Ballet Music

Khachaturian's particular gift for brightly memorable melodies and boisterous orchestral writing is far better suited to the frequently episodic nature of ballet music, and his ballets *Gayaneh* and *Spartacus* are the works that have maintained his international reputation. *Gayaneh* is a classic example of Socialist Realism in which the eponymous heroine is a worker on a collective farm who wins the love of a Red Army commander. Filled with a sparkling array of folk-inspired tunes, its most famous episode, the manic "Sabre Dance", has had a life of its own, even materializing as a pop single. *Spartacus*, which tells of the famous slave revolt against the Romans, though equally propagandist, has survived the collapse of Communism and is still performed as a ballet. The music is very much geared to the energetic leaps of the Bolshoi's male dancers, but like *Gayaneh* it's famous for one hit tune – the surging Adagio, danced by Spartacus and his wife Phrygia, which was used as the theme music for the BBC TV series *The Onedin Line*.

Suites from Gayaneh & Spartacus: Armenian Philharmonic Orchestra; Tjeknavorian (ASV; with *Masquerade* & Ippolitov-Ivanov *Caucasian Sketches*)

Armenians are extremely proud of Khachaturian and this recording by Loris Tjeknavorian and an Armenian orchestra is both lively and passionately committed. Rather than play either of Khachaturian's own suites from *Spartacus*, Tjeknavorian has made his own selection in both ballets, with more of the same in the shape of five pieces from the incidental music to *Masquerade*.

Oliver Knussen (1952–)

Oliver Knussen is one of British music's great originals, and a rare example of a contemporary composer who has succeeded in writing music that is at once thoroughly modern but also shamelessly enjoyable. Knussen's combination of artfulness and accessibility informs every aspect of his music. It is technically complex and often fiendishly challenging for performers, but also vivid and direct in its appeal. It is painstakingly crafted (Knussen is a notoriously slow composer) but in performance sounds captivatingly effortless and spontaneous. His pieces are typically short (few movements exceed five minutes), and yet Knussen generally packs so much musical incident into even the briefest timespans that one hardly thinks of him as a miniaturist. And although some of his works have a childlike quality and a certain undersized, toy-box charm, they conceal, like the children's books of his operatic collaborator Maurice Sendak, complex and very adult depths.

Born in 1952 into a musical family (his father, Stuart, was principal double bassist of the London Symphony Orchestra for many years), Knussen was something of a prodigy as both composer and performer, conducting the London Symphony Orchestra in the premiere of his first symphony at the age of just fifteen. Two further symphonies followed during the 1970s, along with a sequence of beautifully crafted pieces for smaller ensembles such as *Ophelia Dances* (1975), *Cantata* (1975) and *Coursing* (1979). Most of the 1980s were occupied by work on a pair of chamber operas, *Where the Wild Things Are* and *Higglety Pigglety Pop!*, which confirmed Knussen's stature as one of the brightest talents of his generation. The operas also saw a new playfulness creeping into his musical style, along with an increasing opening up to past influences (such as when, in *Wild Things*, Max is crowned King of the Wild Things to a famous phrase borrowed from the coronation music in *Boris Godunov* – a small but wonderfully apt comic touch). Meanwhile, Knussen was taking on an increasingly busy conducting schedule, appearing with many leading ensembles and accepting the post of artistic director at the Aldeburgh Festival.

Following the completion of the two operas, Knussen returned to mainly instrumental formats in the 1990s, often writing for relatively modest forces and crafting works that were small in scale, but not in effect. The results included the *Horn Concerto*, *Two Organa*, *Songs Without Voices* (1992), and, most recently, the *Violin Concerto* (2002). Although entirely of their time, these works often cast loving backward glances towards past masters such as Perotin, Mussorgsky, Mahler, Debussy and Britten – reflecting Knussen's desire to establish "an active relationship with music that attracts me from afar", and his instinct "that a whiff of something recognizable can help the first-time listener find some bearings in what is sometimes a profusion of activity – a sense that while the settings of some of these fairy tales may be forests, and quite dense ones at that, they are neither necessarily forbidding nor unwelcoming ones."

Chamber Operas

Maurice Sendak's classic children's book, *Where the Wild Things Are*, provided the perfect subject for Knussen's first opera, telling the story of a mischievous boy, Max, who, having been sent to bed without any supper, sails off to a land inhabited by the strange and frightening Wild Things – and comes back home again to find his dinner still warm on the table. Sendak's marvellous book has many of the qualities of Knussen's music. Simultaneously knowing yet naive, it combines a sense of childlike wonder with a trace of the emotional murkiness which gives both book and opera their psychological power. The story also provides plenty of gilt-edged musical opportunities – from the moonstruck magic of Max's sea-crossing to the bacchanalian frenzy of the Wild Rumpus – all of which Knussen seizes gleefully.

Wild Things forms part of an operatic double bill with Knussen's second chamber opera, *Higglety Pigglety Pop!*, also to a libretto by Sendak. Although the latter work doesn't quite match *Wild Things* for dramatic cogency and expressive power, its surreal fairy-tale plot and unusual cast of characters (the lead role is taken by a dog, accompanied by various other animals, plus a baby, a tree and a potted plant) offer Knussen scope for plenty of off-beat musical fun and games, culminating in the mock-Mozartian finale – a miniature opera within an opera.

Where the Wild Things Are; Higglety Pigglety Pop!: Buchan, Saffer, Hardy, Gillett, Wilson-Johnson, Richardson, King; London Sinfonietta; Knussen
(Deutsche Grammophon)

Knussen remains unchallenged as a performer of his own works, making light of complex textures and attacking the more energetic passages with exhilarating bravado. Lisa Saffer pulls off the challenging part of Max in *Wild Things* with wonderful vocal agility and a bright, boyish tone, while Cynthia Buchan makes an unforgettably tragi-comic Sealyham terrier in the lead role of *Higglety Pigglety Pop!*

Symphonies

Knussen's *Symphony No. 1*, completed when he was fifteen, was subsequently withdrawn, so his first extant orchestral work is the *Symphony No. 2* (1971), completed at the advanced age of nineteen. Displaying an astonishing assurance and originality for one so young, this symphony-cum-song cycle (setting poems by Trakl and Plath) shows his rare ability to evoke mood and scene through vivid vocal and instrumental writing which was later to bear fruit in his operas. By contrast, the *Symphony No. 3* (1979) is purely instrumental, although again an implicit drama (a musical depiction of Shakespeare's Ophelia) underpins the character of the instrumental writing. The dramatically deranged first movement depicts Ophelia's madness, while the magical second – one of Knussen's most majestic creations – evokes her drowning and death in seven luminous variations on twelve huge chords, which develop into a gigantic, solemn processional before dissolving back into the music of the symphony's opening.

Symphonies Nos. 2 & 3: Philharmonia Orchestra; London Sinfonietta; The Nash Ensemble: Barry; Hirst; Tilson Thomas; Knussen (Unicorn-Kanchana; with *Trumpets, Ophelia Dances, Coursing & Cantata*)

An excellent introduction to Knussen's music of the 1970s, with dramatic accounts of *Symphonies Nos. 2 & 3* (the latter in a sumptuous account by the Philharmonia conducted by Michael Tilson Thomas) alongside several of his finest early works for smaller ensembles, such as *Ophelia Dances* and *Coursing*, performed with magnificent elan by the London Sinfonietta.

Horn Concerto

Perhaps the finest of Knussen's orchestral works, however, is the *Horn Concerto* (1994). Comprising a single movement lasting some twelve minutes, it carries an expressive punch far greater than its modest length would suggest. The ghost of Mahler (with a hint of Britten) hovers over much of the piece – the concerto's working title was *Night Air*, and Knussen himself has compared it to one of the *Nachtmusik* movements from Mahler's symphonies. The work's tantalizingly oblique nods to tradition, its nocturnal harmonies and haunting post-Romantic melodic writing are irresistible, and its closely argued structure (an ingeniously twisted sonata-form movement) and harmonic logic ensure that, like all Knussen's music, it rewards careful and repeated listening.

Horn Concerto: Tuckwell; Shelton; London Sinfonietta; Knussen (Deutsche Grammophon; with *Whitman Settings, Flourish with Fireworks, The Way to Castle Yonder, Two Organa & Music for a Puppet Court*)

A wonderful performance of the *Horn Concerto* by dedicatee Barry Tuckwell is just one of the highlights of this immensely rewarding CD, conducted by the composer and collecting together some of his most memorable orchestral and chamber works of the 1980s, as well as the virtuoso *Whitman Settings* for soprano. A joy from start to finish.

Zoltán Kodály (1882–1967)

Zoltán Kodály's career was unremarkable until after his graduation from Budapest University in 1905. It was then that he encountered Béla Bartók, with whom he was to change the direction of Hungarian music. Shortly after meeting, they embarked upon a pilgrimage to collect folk songs, the first of several expeditions which helped formulate their musical identities and cement their lifelong friendship. Kodály later recalled the inspiration behind their studies: "This vision of an educated Hungary, reborn from the people, rose before us. We decided to devote our lives to its realization." This devotion resulted in a book of Hungarian folk songs with a preface by Kodály, published in 1906, and, later that year, the premiere of his symphonic poem *Summer Evening*.

In 1908 Kodály took over the composition classes at Budapest's Liszt Academy from his own teacher, Franz Koessler, and from then on became closely involved with the formation of the musical curriculum in Hungary's schools. With Bartók, he formed a society for the promotion and performance of contemporary music, a scheme that met with official hostility and public indifference, and their attempts to promote folk song were no more successful, although the pair continued compiling information until the outbreak of war.

In 1923, however, Kodály's fortunes changed with the widespread success of his *Psalmus Hungaricus*, written for the fiftieth anniversary of the unification of Buda and Pest. Soon afterwards a contract with Universal Edition resulted in the publication of a large amount of his music. In 1926 he composed his folk-opera *Háry János*, which was followed by *The Spinning Room* (1932), a work steeped in the folklore of Transylvania. In 1933 Kodály and Bartók were requested by the Hungarian Academy of Sciences to compile a compendium of the country's folk music; with Bartók's departure for America, Kodály assumed editorial control of a project that finally reached the presses in 1951.

Kodály remained in Hungary during World War II, and after Bartók's death in 1945 was hailed as Hungary's greatest living composer, being inundated with invitations to head colleges, universities and artistic institutions, and receiving dozens of governmental decorations. Most of his remaining years were devoted to the composition of choral music and to tours as a conductor, musician and lecturer. He died happy in the knowledge that his two greatest ambitions – the

Kodály was as important a teacher and pedagogue as he was a composer.

publication of his books of Hungarian folk music and the introduction of daily music lessons into Hungarian schools – had been fulfilled.

Kodály remained a conservative composer throughout his life, in that he had no interest in subverting the established classical forms, and was devoted primarily to melody. Yet his music has a distinctive voice, thanks in large part to the rich mix that went into it – in addition to the folk songs of his native land, he was fascinated with Debussy, and Bach, Palestrina and Gregorian chant all became components of Kodály's sound. Kodály might lack cosmopolitan flair, but his music is an instantly enjoyable and consistently rewarding alternative to the more demanding idiom of his friend and colleague Bartók.

Psalmus Hungaricus

The *Psalmus Hungaricus* represents the climactic fusion of two fundamental elements in Kodály's musical philosophy – his belief in the supremacy of the human voice, and his belief that any musical culture was dependent upon the nurture of amateur performance. He wrote a large amount of choral music for amateur societies, and *Psalmus Hungaricus* is by far the finest. It's a piece that's redolent of the spirit of Hungarian music, yet surprisingly it contains no direct folk quotations: stylistically, the chief influences are Gregorian melody, Bachian polyphony and Renaissance harmony. For all these decorous influences, *Psalmus Hungaricus* is an urgent and often barbaric composition, showing Kodály at his most thrilling.

London Symphony Orchestra; Kozma; Brighton Festival Chorus; Kertész (Decca; with Dvořáks's *Requiem*)

Kertész's pulsating performance is a marvellous tribute to Kodály, his friend and teacher. This is a controlled but beautifully coloured and passionate account, and the tenor Lajos Kozma gives a finely considered performance, singing with ample weight.

Concerto for Orchestra

Kodály's *Concerto for Orchestra* was composed for the Chicago Symphony Orchestra, who first performed it in 1941 – two years before they gave the premiere of Bartók's *Concerto for Orchestra*.

Unlike Bartók's five-movement virtuosic score, Kodály's concerto is a one-movement, twenty-minute piece that rejects what he characterized as "false brilliance" in favour of "melancholy and uncertainty". Again, unlike Bartók's massive score, Kodály's heavily contrapuntal piece is scored for an ordinary orchestra, the only addition to standard forces being the appearance of a triangle. A tension between modernity and more folkloric rhythms and harmonies runs through the concerto, producing music of wonderful emotional intensity.

Philharmonia Hungarica; Dorati (Decca; 2 CDs; with *Háry János Suite, Dances of Galánta, Dances of Marosszék, Peacock Variations, Summer Evening & Symphony in C*)

Antal Dorati was a great advocate of Kodály's music, recording it on several occasions. This recording of the *Concerto for Orchestra* dates from the early 1970s and is currently the only one in the catalogue. Fortunately, the performance is a very eloquent one and these two discs make a splendid introduction to Kodály's range as an orchestral composer.

Háry János Suite

Háry János is a Baron Münchhausen-type tale of a soldier whose fantastic adventures are, to quote the composer, "the personification of the Hungarian story-telling imagination". First produced in October 1926, it's a delightful comic opera (or, rather, a play with music), but because of the language barrier and its uneven construction it is rarely staged outside Hungary. The Kertész recording of the complete work is currently available, but it is far better to approach it through the orchestral suite that Kodály created from the opera's main ideas, a translation that secured the opera's fame. You know what you're in for right from the start, when the full orchestra explodes in a huge musical "sneeze", signifying that what follows is not to be taken too seriously. Among the ensuing episodes are a battle scene in which János single-handedly defeats Napoleon, and the representation of a Viennese musical clock. Beautifully orchestrated and superbly constructed, the *Háry János Suite* is Kodály's most entertaining score, the perfect follow-up for the child who has enjoyed Prokofiev's *Peter and the Wolf* or *Lieutenant Kijé*.

Philharmonia Hungarica; Dorati (Decca; 2 CDs; with *Concerto for Orchestra*, etc)

Dorati's is the kind of performance that makes it almost impossible to keep still when listening to it. The *Dances of Galánta* is no less vivid a work in its rich profusion of orchestral colour and sweeping melodies, even if there is just a hint of the tourist board in its folksiness. Similarly the *Peacock Variations* occasionally conjure up Hollywood in the way it so blatantly wears its heart on its sleeve.

Sonata for Unaccompanied Cello

The prodigious *Sonata for Unaccompanied Cello*, written in 1915, is one of the peaks of twentieth-century music for that instrument. Anyone thinking Kodály too safe a composer should listen to this. It's a *tour de force* that takes the folk tradition, in which Kodály had immersed himself so thoroughly, and gives it the kind of acerbic modern spin that you normally associate with Bartók. Every technical skill is employed here – from double-stopping and harmonics to playing with the bow and plucking the strings at the same time – to create a wild, improvisatory fantasy (albeit constructed as a sonata) which one moment suggests a mournful Transylvanian dance and the next moment, Bach.

Starker (Delos; with *Duo for Violin and Cello*, Bottermund *Variations on a Theme by Paganini for cello solo*)

There are nearly twenty performances currently listed in the catalogue, making this one of the most recorded of all Kodály's works. This has claims to be as near-definitive as you can get, challenged by Janos Starker's own 1950s recording on the Period label. Starker has this music in his bloodstream (he played it for the composer when he was a teenager) and his combination of technical precision and sinewy intensity is unbeatable.

Janos Starker in action.

Erich Wolfgang Korngold (1897–1957)

Erich Wolfgang Korngold, the son of the leading Viennese music critic, Julius Korngold, was one of the most astonishing musical prodigies of the century. At the age of 9 he wrote a cantata, *Gold*, which so impressed Gustav Mahler that he proclaimed the boy a genius and arranged for him to study with Zemlinsky (see p.641). His ballet-pantomime *Der Schneemann*, written in his thirteenth year, was premiered under Zemlinsky's baton and subsequently performed all over Austria and Germany. Both Puccini and Strauss – the dominant influences on his style – were admirers, the latter remarking that "this firmness of style, this sovereignty of form, this individual expression, this harmonic structure – one shudders with awe to realize these compositions were written by a boy."

Korngold's first two operas, *Der Ring des Polykrates* and *Violanta*, were produced in 1916 as a double bill at the Munich Staatsoper, conducted by Bruno Walter. Both were emotionally charged works employing a rich post-Wagnerian chromaticism that became even more intense for his next opera, *Die tote Stadt* (The Dead City), which is generally considered his masterpiece in the genre. *Die tote Stadt* was staged simultaneously at Cologne and at Hamburg (where Korngold was musical director) to huge acclaim.

Throughout the 1920s Korngold was involved with the renowned producer Max Reinhardt, making arrangements of operettas for him. He also wrote another opera, *Das Wunder der Heliane* (1924–26), which he considered his finest work but which was overshadowed by the extraordinary success of Ernst Krenek's jazz opera *Jonny spielt auf*. But his success in Germany was not to last. By the early 1930s the growing intensity of anti-Semitism in Germany led his publishers, Schott, to warn him that future performances of his music would be extremely difficult. In 1934 Max Reinhardt invited him to accompany him to Hollywood to work on a film version of *A Midsummer Night's Dream,* for which Korngold rescored Mendelssohn's incidental music. He returned briefly to Vienna to work on his final opera, *Die Kathrin,* before returning to Hollywood, where over the next twelve years he was to write eighteen outstandingly imaginative and atmospheric film scores, mainly for Warner Bros., two of which –*Robin Hood* and *Anthony Adverse* – were to win him Oscars.

Korngold and family arrive in Los Angeles.

Arguably his American years ruined his career. Leaving Hollywood for Vienna in 1949, he was now disparaged as much for having worked in the cinema as for the old-fashioned style of his music. After the critics panned the belated Viennese performance of *Die Kathrin* (the Nazis had cancelled the 1937 production), he gave up the idea of a sixth opera and he devoted the remaining years of his life to orchestral music, including a violin concerto which was performed and recorded by Jascha Heifetz. Many of these later works employed material previously used in his film scores.

Korngold is one of several candidates for the title of "last of the great Romantics", for as a boy he brilliantly assimilated a late Romantic style from which he never later deviated. His work is full of warm and expansive melodies and the lushest of harmonies while lacking the contrapuntal adventurousness of Strauss or Pfitzner. But in the last twenty years there has been a major revival of interest in his work: *Die tote Stadt* is now staged fairly regularly and several young virtuosos have added the *Violin Concerto* to their repertoire. The hothouse emotionalism of his work will not appeal to everyone, but those unafraid to wallow will not be disappointed.

Die tote Stadt

Puccini declared *Die tote Stadt* to be "among the most beautiful and the strongest hope of new German music", but Korngold's masterpiece never achieved the worldwide popularity of Strauss's operas, even though the musical line dividing them is extremely thin. Perhaps it was the rather morbid subject matter, closer in spirit to Schreker, that has put people off. The story tells how the recently widowed Paul meets a dancer who resembles his wife, but when she mocks him he eventually strangles her. Julius and Erich Korngold's adaptation of George Rodenbuch's symbolist novel *Bruges-la-Morte* retains the dreamy atmosphere of the original but relegates the brooding presence of the city to the background, making the psychological vulnerability and anguish of the protagonist its main concern. The trauma of World War I lies just beneath the surface.

The score veers between a quasi-religious profundity and a honeyed sweetness which to many ears comes dangerously close to kitsch, but Korngold marshals his huge orchestral forces with great precision, and the opera also contains some powerful melodic writing – as in the Act 1 aria "Glück, das mir verblieb" (Joy sent from above), sung first by Marietta and then by Paul. This inspired episode, made famous by Lotte Lehmann and Richard Tauber, illuminates Paul's despair with wonderful clarity and is the opera's finest vocal moment.

Kollo, Neblett, Luxon, Wageman, Prey; Bavarian Radio Chorus; Munich Radio Orchestra; Leinsdorf (RCA; 2 CDs)

This recording is perhaps the finest achievement of both René Kollo and Erich Leinsdorf. The tenor's voice is never under any strain, and sounds smooth and dark throughout. Carole Neblett taps into the work's sentimentality with shameless abandon, and Leinsdorf is clearly in love with Korngold's orchestrations, holding suspensions beyond their natural length and revelling in the chromatic wash.

Violin Concerto

Written in 1945 for Bronislav Hubermann, the *Violin Concerto* was actually premiered in 1947 by Jascha Heifetz, who became its greatest champion. It's a good example of how Korngold plundered parts of his film scores in order to create a concert work, and the insinuating, heart-tugging opening theme is indeed pure Hollywood (taken from the film *Another Dawn*). The second movement is, if anything, even more lachrymose, with a lyrical melody (from *Anthony Adverse*) and a shimmering vibraphone creating a suitably febrile atmosphere. The Rondo finale is the most distinctly American-sounding (as opposed to Hollywood) movement: a rhythmically lively opening suggests a hoedown though in fact the movement's main melody was taken from the costume drama *The Prince and the Pauper*. The critic of the *New York Sun* famously called the work "more corn than gold": it's an unfair dismissal though it is true that Korngold plays around with each of the big tunes rather than seriously developing them. It does not stop it from being a hugely enjoyable, if essentially superficial, piece.

Shaham; London Symphony Orchestra; Previn (Deutsche Grammophon; with Barber *Violin Concerto*)

This is a performance that takes this concerto completely seriously as an orchestral work, rather than merely treating it as a collection of radiant moments. Balance between orchestra and soloist sounds more realistic than is usually the case, and Shaham's warm tone is held in check – he only pulls out all the stops for the really syrupy moments.

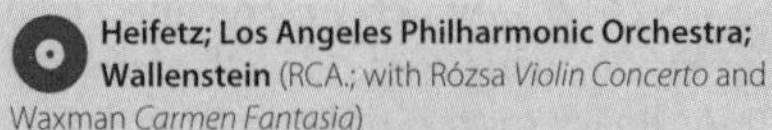
Heifetz; Los Angeles Philharmonic Orchestra; Wallenstein (RCA.; with Rózsa *Violin Concerto* and Waxman *Carmen Fantasia*)

Heifetz's classic recording of the *Violin Concerto* from 1953 is still one of the best available. The violin sound is recorded well forward of the orchestra, and Heifetz treats the concerto entirely as a showpiece for his talents. It's an extremely old-fashioned, vocalized reading – all throaty tone colour and delicate swoops, which tends to point up its Hollywood origins.

Symphony

Korngold's *Symphony* (1952) is the most uncompromisingly modern of all his works, more angular than his earlier compositions, yet no less enjoyable. Written five years before his death, it

Composers at the Movies

Saint-Saëns was the first major figure to compose for the cinema when he agreed to write the music for the costume melodrama *L'assassinat du Duc de Guise* in 1908. Although music had been employed since film's beginnings, primarily as a means of covering up the noise of the projector, a commissioned score was the exception rather than the rule: the norm was to employ a pianist (or a small ensemble) who would play, or improvise, a live accompaniment to the film using cue sheets in which the classical repertoire and popular hits of the day were shamelessly plundered.

A leap forward for so-called "silent" films came in 1915, when director D.W. Griffiths created a score with composer J.C. Breil for his Civil War epic *The Birth of a Nation*. This consisted of both original and traditional material arranged so that it could be precisely cued with the onscreen action. The score was then published, allowing it to be performed, in one form or another, at subsequent screenings around the country. On the whole, however, original scores for early Hollywood movies tended to be rather crude affairs and it was in Europe that a more sophisticated and experimental approach prevailed with the cinema attracting several leading figures of the avant-garde. These included Erik Satie, whose witty, modern score forms the perfect complement to René Clair's Surrealist short film *Entr'acte* (1924); and Shostakovich, whose powerful music for *New Babylon* (1929), a film about the Paris Commune, convincingly encompasses biting satire and deep-felt emotion.

With the coming of sound to the movies in 1929, Hollywood producers realized the advantages of commissioning new music for a film, and as studio music departments became ever larger, so they were boosted by an influx of talent from Europe – some of whom were escaping from the Nazis. Among the many European composers who were to have a profound impact on the "sound" of Hollywood in the 1930s and 40s were Erich Korngold, Max Steiner, Franz Waxman, Miklós Rósza and Dimitri Tiomkin. All of these composers worked within a fairly narrow, essentially Romantic, style – dubbed by Rósza "Broadway-cum-Rachmaninoff". Significantly, the major figures of European modernism, Schoenberg and Stravinsky (both of whom lived in Hollywood), resisted the Hollywood dollar, while the acerbic Hanns Eisler (see p.180) only survived there until it was discovered that he was a communist.

In America, the composer was the servant of the studio and few Hollywood composers had the kind of close working relationship that Prokofiev enjoyed with Sergei Eisenstein and which produced the masterpieces *Alexander Nevsky* and *Ivan the Terrible* (see p.419). One who did was Bernard Herrmann, a composer whose sense of dramatic pacing was such that the director Alfred Hitchcock used to consult him before he started shooting. Herrmann's scores for Hitchcock – in particular the hypnotically somnambulant *Vertigo* and the edgy nervousness of *Psycho* – are major elements of the success of his films. Herrmann had a strong musical identity and was not afraid to break out of the Romantic straitjacket, often employing simple, pared-down motifs which were repeated in such a way as to get, unnervingly, under the skin.

In the 1950s there was a gradual loosening up of the whole notion of what sort of music was appropriate to accompany a film. Elmer Bernstein's jazzy score for *The Man with the Golden Arm* (1956) was followed by actual jazz scores like Duke Ellington's *Anatomy of a Murder* (1959), while the schoolroom drama *The Blackboard Jungle* (1955) came with a tailor-made rock'n'roll soundtrack. Meanwhile in France, director Jean-Pierre Melville used Bach piano music as the background to his version of *Les enfants terribles*, a decision which was to influence forthcoming directors like Truffaut and Rivette, as well as the American Stanley Kubrick, who came to specialize in the telling juxtaposition of disparate pieces of classical music, as in *2001 – A Space Odyssey* in which Richard Strauss, Johann Strauss and Ligeti are combined to brilliant effect.

Despite the diversity of music now employed in the cinema, the composer is still the dominant figure when it comes to film music, and his or her task is much the same as it was sixty years ago – to unify the action and underline the emotional high points. Currently, no figure looms as large as John Williams, the composer of *Jaws*, the *Star Wars* series and *Schindler's List*, who sees himself as part of a grand tradition. Williams acknowledges a debt, not only to Hollywood legends Korngold and Steiner, but also to the major Romantic composers of the past like Tchaikovsky and Elgar.

sounds like a final bid for respectability, with all the thick luscious orchestration that one associates with him cut away to a leaner and more eloquent mix. It's an epic work in four long movements, with an underlying tension between major and minor, tragedy and resolution. Its startling opening, in which a battery of percussion creates a mood of foreboding, gives way to a long mysterious clarinet tune. A bold and brassy Scherzo precedes a rich, deeply felt Mahlerian Adagio of unrelieved sombreness, while the seemingly playful finale is interspersed with moments of an almost bitter edginess.

London Symphony Orchestra; Previn (Deutsche Grammophon; with *Much Ado About Nothing Suite*)

Since Rudolf Kempe's trailblazing account in 1972, this symphony has been recorded no fewer than four times. André Previn's is the latest and the best, with the conductor judging the work's ambiguity and subtle changes of mood with great precision.

György Kurtág (1926–)

Shortly after World War II, György Kurtág and György Ligeti (see p.300) were fellow composition students at the Franz Liszt Academy in Budapest. Artistic freedoms were severely limited in Hungary at that time, and it was not until the 1950s that the two men had any direct contact with the European avant-garde. Both were completely transformed by the experience, but whereas Ligeti stayed away from his homeland and completely embraced new ways of organizing sound, Kurtág returned to Hungary where his newly acquired experimental techniques became another element of an extremely idiosyncratic musical personality. Kurtág's mature musical language, in which a sense of alienation and human frailty is never far from the surface, shows an awareness of the concentrated and concise forms of Webern in combination with a highly charged expressiveness that has much in common with Bartók.

In Paris, where he studied with both Darius Milhaud and Olivier Messiaen, Kurtág also came into contact with the Hungarian psychologist Marianne Stein, who encouraged him to go back to first principles as a composer. Performances of Stockhausen's *Gruppen* for three divided orchestras and Ligeti's electronic *Artikulation* were further formative influences, as were the Domaine Musical concerts organized by Pierre Boulez. In 1959, shortly after returning to Budapest, Kurtág composed a string quartet (*Quartetto per archi*) in six short and densely argued sections – designated his Opus 1 (and dedicated to Marianne Stein), it marked a new beginning.

Kurtág's strong tendency to self-criticism meant new works came slowly throughout the 1960s and 1970s – between 1959 and 1973 his total output amounted to less than ninety minutes of music. A set of whimsical semi-pedagogical piano pieces, *Játékok* (Games, 1973–76), grew from his work as professor of piano at the Franz Liszt Academy, and a song cycle, *Messages of the Late Miss R.V. Troussova* (1976–80), helped to establish his wider reputation when it was performed at IRCAM in Paris. *Messages* was the first of several settings of the work of a Russian poet, Rimma Dalos, resident in Budapest, and it marked the start of Kurtág's fascination with Russian language and literature, in particular the novels of Dostoevsky.

More recently Kurtág has begun to write for larger forces, although his utterances are no less pithy and gesture-packed than before. If anything, in pieces such as *Grabstein für Stephan* and *Stele*, his preoccupation with mortality has generated an even more personal musical language, one in which the characteristically vulnerable voices of small instrumental groups are made all the more acute through a background setting of grand statements and rich sonorities.

Messages of the Late Miss R.V. Troussova

The success of the Paris performance of *Troussova* has helped to make it the best known of all Kurtág's works. Written from the viewpoint of a woman looking back on a life of love, frustration and despair, it comprises 21 songs divided into three sections entitled *Loneliness*, *A Little Erotic* and *Bitter Experience – Delight and Grief*. Dalos's stark imagery and the cycle's fragmentary nature allows Kurtág to give full rein to his brilliance in depicting sudden shifts of mood and tone through unpredictable instrumental combinations and virtuosic vocal effects. *Troussova* is suffused with a restless energy and is the most obviously expressionist of all Kurtág's works, but there are also moments of great lyricism, like the haunting seventh song, "You Took My Heart". There's also an obvious kinship with Bartók's opera *Bluebeard's Castle* – in the overriding sense of loneliness, and in the way the non-vocal music seems like a projection of the central character's troubled psyche.

Hardy; Ensemble Modern; Eötvös
(Sony; *Quasi una fantasia & Scenes from a Novel*)

This performance of *Troussova* wins out over the rival with Erato recording on account of its clear sound quality, which allows the precise, painterly qualities of Kurtág's sound-world to emerge with great vividness. Soprano Rosemary Hardy manages her fearfully difficult part not just with ease but also with great expressiveness and musicality. The two other works are equally well performed. Currently out of the catalogue but worth tracking down.

Grabstein für Stephan & Stele

Grabstein für Stephan (Gravestone for Stephan) was written in 1989 as a memorial to the husband of Marianne Stein. At its centre a solo guitar seems to represent a static, human presence around which groups of instruments are placed like mourners. It opens with the soloist's gentle plucking of open strings – the work's central motif – over which a shifting array of grief-suggesting sounds (low strings, assorted percussion, wailing alarm signals) are layered. *Stele* (1994), essentially a three-movement symphony, employs the orchestra in a more conventional manner, though with a large tuned percussion section which includes pianos, celesta and cimbalom. At times the sensuousness of its richly clotted textures sounds almost Mahlerian. This is intensely sad music: a tentative, ghostly opening movement moves, without a break, into a clamorous, angry lament before culminating in a finale of immense and terrible gravity in which, once again, the shadow of Bartók's *Bluebeard* is never far away.

Berlin Philharmonic Orchestra; Abbado
(Deutsche Grammophon; with Stockhausen *Gruppen*)

The Berlin Philharmonic respond brilliantly to this music. There's a strong sense, in both works, of the different sections of the orchestra functioning like actors in some powerful tragedy. Abbado controls his forces with an unfailing sense of the right emphasis at the right moment to deliver performances of affecting power and simplicity.

Music for Strings

Small-scale string ensembles have been central to Kurtág's work, ever since he chose to mark his first string quartet as his Opus 1. His music for strings exemplifies the creative processes of a composer who combines an uncompromisingly questing intelligence with a real consciousness of his place within a tradition. His output in this medium includes homages to forerunners as diverse as Mussorgsky, J.S. Bach, Schubert, Verdi and Schumann. However, Bartók – "my mother tongue" – and Webern occupy the foreground of Kurtág's mental landscape, as is clear from the first quartet, a fifteen-minute assemblage of splintered, scurrying episodes and charged silences. It's clearly the creation of a major composer, but a greater cohesion (and lyricism) is evident in the "12 microludes for string quartet" that make up *Hommage à András Mihály* (1977).

Compression and expressivity are equally manifest in the third quartet, *Officium breve in memoriam Andreae Szervánsky* (1989), a typically allusive work (referring notably to Webern, Beethoven, Bach and Szervánsky) that condenses fifteen movements into a span of just thirteen minutes. These delicate melodic fragments were composed in the same year as *Ligatura – Message to Frances-Marie*, Kurtág's response to the musical interrogation of Charles Ives's *Unanswered Question*. Written for Frances-Marie Uitti, a cellist who has developed a technique of using two bows simultaneously, *Ligatura* is an aphoristic yet texturally rich piece, as is *Aus der Ferne III* (1991), an elegiac quartet which is constructed around a slowly pulsing low C on the cello and finally fades "into the distance", as its title suggests.

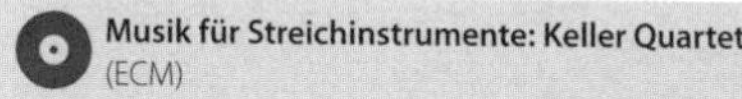

Musik für Streichinstrumente: Keller Quartett
(ECM)

This disc offers a panoramic survey of Kurtág's career, containing all the works discussed above plus a second version of *Ligatura*, scored for two cellos in addition to two violins and celesta (played by Kurtág himself). The performances by the Keller quartet are technically precise and deeply committed, as you might expect from a group that studied with the composer.

Játékok

The word *játékok* translates as "games", and the dozens of brief piano pieces that Kurtág has gathered under this title began in the 1960s with a few playful exercises written for his young son. In the 1970s he wrote dozens more, and since then the open-ended series has continued to grow: Book Nine is now in progress. Like a more skittish version of Bartók's *Mikrokosmos*, many of the pieces in the first books of *Játékok* are instructional, being intended to introduce the young pianist to the potential of the instrument, while making the learning process as much fun as possible – some are to be played with the palms of the hand, for example, and others with elbows or fists. In the later books, *Játékok* has evolved into something less pedagogical and more akin to a pianistic sketchbook or workshop, featuring numerous homages to other composers, tributes to friends and a miscellany of fleeting ideas. Deeply personal and consistently brilliant, *Játékok* is one of the most fascinating creations in contemporary music.

Csalog
(Budapest Music Center)

Gábor Csalog – a pupil of Kurtág's – has here gathered 58 pieces from books one to eight of *Játékok*, many of them under a minute in length (and one a mere fourteen seconds). Released to mark the composer's eightieth birthday, it's an unflaggingly engaging set, on which Csalog is assisted by András Kemenes, Kurtág himself, and Kurtág's wife Marta. He's recorded a second and equally fine selection for the same label, and more are in the pipeline.

L

Helmut Lachenmann (1935–)

According to Helmut Lachenmann "Tradition is a wonderful reality", but "...not understanding that the inner dynamic of tradition is always to innovate, is a prison." Since his first acknowledged works surfaced during the late 1950s, Stuttgart-born Lachenmann has chiselled his uniquely beautiful, but defiantly provocative, body of work from out of the bedrock of Austro-German tradition. But while that might imply pastiche of archetypal Classical and Romantic models, such as symphonies and sonatas, instead Lachenmann forces his listeners to reconsider what tradition is. In his *Gran Torso* for string quartet (1972) and *Ausklang* (Sounding-Out) for piano and orchestra (1985), he positions himself in creative conflict with age-old protocols about how string quartets and piano concertos "ought" to work. By actively throwing overboard melodic, structural and harmonic hooks that have become expressively blunted through overuse, he builds from what might – or might not – be left.

This instinctive radicalism has made Lachenmann the source of endless controversy. In 1976 he was charged with cultural vandalism when his *Accanto* for clarinet and orchestra brutally disjointed, then shredded, familiar strains from Mozart's *Clarinet Concerto*, puréeing Mozart's sublime gestures into agitatedly ticking motor rhythms, volatile white noise and the absurdist theatrics of the solo clarinettist (Eduard Brunner) wrenching his instrument apart and blowing through the debris. To whom was this musical assault aimed? Not Mozart himself, a composer who Lachenmann reveres, but, more pointedly, at the consumerist mentality hell-bent on cheapening Mozart's true achievements by cherrypicking the most "beautiful" passages of an iconic work like the *Clarinet Concerto* on compilation albums.

Definitions of "beauty" are, in fact, central to Lachenmann's aesthetic credo. He argues that artists must make a distinction between the overly perfumed, audience-ingratiating beauty typical of commercial music – which he regards as disturbingly manipulative – and "authentic' beauty. In interviews he often evokes the German word *Geräusch* – meaning noise, but in the sense of natural noise like wind blowing or trees rustling – to explain himself. His 1990s opera *Das Mädchen mit den Schwefelhölzern* (The Little Match-Girl) requires wind players to blow through their instruments without producing defined notes and, in one scene, the violin section play with guitar plectrums to represent in sound the icy, dulled chill of his scenario – the little girl who

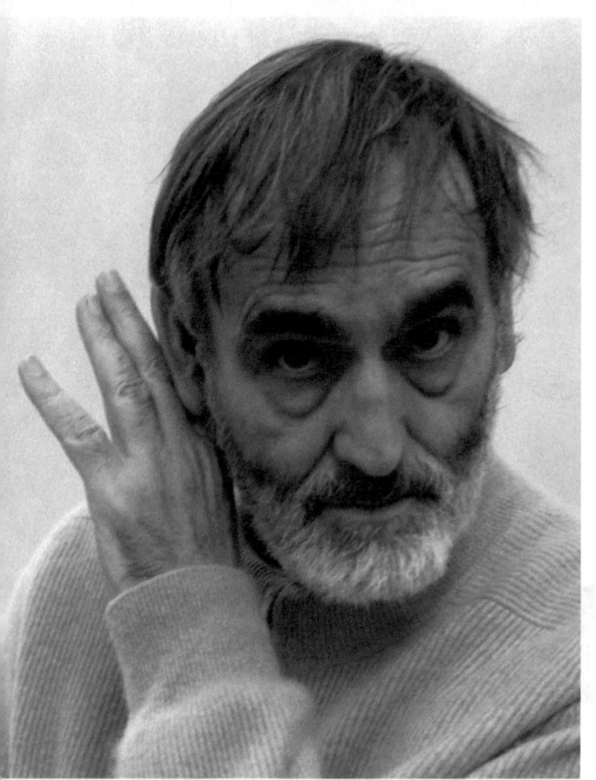

Helmut Lachenmann in 2006.

in Hans Christian Andersen's fairy tale freezes to death in the snow.

Such non-traditional techniques have required Lachenmann to fundamentally rethink how he notates his sounds on manuscript paper. A typical Lachenmann sound – like, for instance, combining a pizzicato note with a simultaneous flick of the finger against the wooden body of a violin – needs a specifically invented symbol, one beyond the reach of conventional notation. Because Lachenmann is looking beyond music towards noise, his notation is often even more dense and detailed than composers like Kagel, Cage or Carter. Lachenmann's polemic engagement with the classical music establishment makes him a hero or villain, depending on your point of view. In 1958 he had relocated to Venice to study composition with Marxist composer Luigi Nono, but Lachenmann has often spoken about how his presence in the more conservative Italy, rather than Germany, meant he missed epoch-moulding occasions like the first performance of Stockhausen's *Gruppen*. This made him more dependent on his own resources, giving him an outsider perspective from the start.

Schwankungen am Rand

Lachenmann's supple philosophical distinction between music and noise can take some acclimatization, but his 1975 orchestral piece *Schwankungen am Rand* (Fluctuations at the Boundaries) articulates the arguments with clarity, and is the perfect primer. String and brass players must bend their technique to Lachenmann's characteristically exacting specifications – blowing, hitting and scraping their instruments to harvest mint-fresh timbres. In the unfolding musical argument another layer is provided by thunder sheets – large sheets of metal, modified by Lachenmann himself for this piece – which percussionists play with conventional percussion mallets and with nails, hammers and their fingers. As the jagged sounds overlap and blend, Lachenmann explains that his thunder sheets "turn into radically deformed monster violins with super-pizzicato-fluido sounds" – while the actual orchestral violins, by extension, are transformed into resonating sound objects resolutely turned away from their usual orchestral function. Inside this viciously expressive music is another kind of beauty.

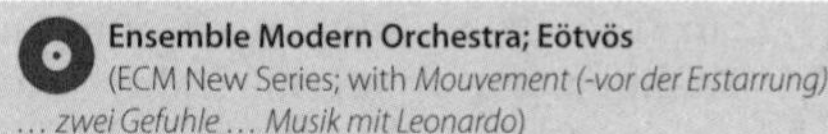

Ensemble Modern Orchestra; Eötvös
(ECM New Series; with *Mouvement (-vor der Erstarrung)* & *... zwei Gefuhle ... Musik mit Leonardo*)

This landmark 2002 release put *Schwankungen am Rand* on the map as a forgotten masterpiece of modernist music. Hungarian conductor Peter Eötvös – himself a composer – shepherds those crack musicians of the Frankfurt-based Ensemble Modern through Lachenmann's thirty-minute structure without compromising his elemental sound-world.

Gran Torso

It's no coincidence that the title of Lachenmann's first string quartet, *Gran Torso*, completed in 1972 and revised six years later, has echoes of Beethoven's *Grosse Fuge*. Beethoven's work is considered the most technically demanding quartet writing of the nineteenth century and Lachenmann, similarly, aims to re-radicalize the language of the string quartet. Beginning with hushed sonorities perched at the edge of audibility, he generates structural arcs that his extended instrumental techniques simultaneously shatter – long sustained passages are ripped apart by abrupt scrapings, while manic pizzicatos send melodic cells scattering to the outer limits of our ability to hear them. Beethoven's *Grosse Fuge* trashed the formality of the fugue by twisting its conventions against itself. Lachenmann applies a comparable mindset to every parameter of the string quartet. And like Beethoven, *Gran Torso* defined a wholly fresh approach to the string quartet that generations of younger composers have been keen to follow up on.

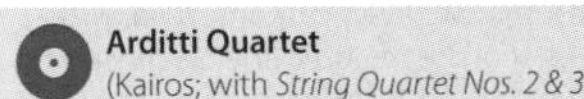

Arditti Quartet
(Kairos; with *String Quartet Nos. 2 & 3*)

Not easy music to nail, but no group performs this repertoire better than the Arditti Quartet. If the sounds Lachenmann hears in his inner ear move off the radar of conventional instrumental timbre, the Ardittis unerringly zone into his intentions, realizing his ideas faithfully.

Das Mädchen mit den Schwefelhölzern

When it was announced Lachenmann was writing a work for that most bourgeois of musical institutions – the opera house – there were raised eyebrows. Nor did its composition proceed smoothly. His briefcase was stolen and the score went missing for months, but the opera finally premiered in 2001. Lachenmann's approach to opera is typically revisionist. Overriding the usual relationship between music and libretto, he instead fuses music and text at a deep structural level. Lachenmann's characters – taken from Hans Christian Andersen's Christmas fairy tale – shiver as they sing, their vocal lines coloured by sharply inhaled breaths and chattering teeth; sounds that are amplified by the orchestra, who don't so much accompany in the traditional sense as extend and amplify the vocal timbres. The music comes full circle as Andersen's little girl meets her sad end, and hints of tonality follow her ascension into heaven.

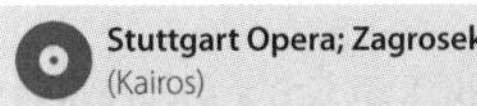

Stuttgart Opera; Zagrosek
(Kairos)

This recording was culled from the premiere run of performances in 2001 and is more vivid and dramatic than the alternative studio-bound performance offered by ECM. Lothar Zagrosek shapes a pacey whole from Lachenmann's fragments, while a stellar cast of singers (including Sarah Leonard) relish his extended vocal techniques.

Francesco Landini (c.1325–1397)

Francesco Landini was Italy's first great composer, the most prolific and gifted musician of the trecento (the fourteenth century). Like Machaut, his better-known contemporary from France, he was a prodigiously talented man and not just as a composer: he had strong literary, philosophical and scientific credentials, and, despite being blinded by smallpox at an early age, was a revered organist and organ builder.

The son of a painter in the school of Giotto, Landini was raised in Florence at one of the most exciting times in the city's history. The Church had started to lose its total domination over all aspects of life, and humanist, secular activities were burgeoning in the arts, with the *tre corone* – Dante, Boccaccio and Petrarch – championing the use of the vernacular in poetry. With this new way of writing – *dolce stil nuovo*, the "sweet new style" – came a new lyrical approach to music, in which the beauty of the melody line was the all-important consideration (initiating a melodic focus that has been a defining feature of Italian music ever since). The carefully shaped, highly ornamented and virtuosic melody lines were supported by simple harmonic activity, usually with a bass moving "in parallel", and the resulting texture was, essentially, decorated monophony. The pieces served as sensual, secular entertainment for social occasions.

Although Landini spent most of his life working for the Church – his powers of improvisation at the organ were greatly revered – he devoted all his compositional energies to the development of the secular vocal tradition, expanding the pre-existing musical language into a cohesive, organic style. He put less emphasis on embellishment and virtuosity, enriched rhythm and harmony, and developed a more goal-orientated style of writing. The increased homogeneity of his music is partly the result of the influence of French music, which marks the beginning of a fusion of the Italian and French styles that culminated in the more intricate *Ars sublitor* style of the fifteenth century.

Songs

Landini's surviving output – quite possibly everything he ever wrote – consists of 154 songs for one, two or three voices. The madrigal had dominated Italian secular music until the 1360s with its rustic style, pastoral texts and a two-line closing section that was markedly different from the rest of the piece. Landini wrote some madrigals but focused mainly on the *ballata*, which has dance form origins and generally sets texts of a more self-revealing, personal nature. In structural terms, the ballata makes use of two repeated sections – similar to the *virelai*, which was used extensively by Machaut.

The earliest manuscripts of works by Landini and his contemporaries date from some time after they were written. The most important source is the beautifully illuminated *Squarcialupi codex*, probably created in 1415, but copies of many of Landini's pieces have been found in various manuscripts throughout Italy. The lack of original sources makes it nearly impossible to know exactly how the works were originally performed. The most contentious point is which lines, if any, were intended to be played on instruments, and consequently a work may be sung unaccompanied on one recording and supported by harps, bagpipes and drums on another.

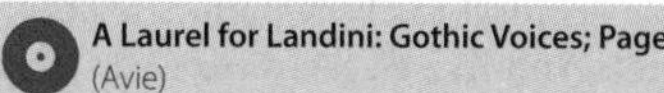

A Laurel for Landini: Gothic Voices; Page
(Avie)

An appropriately celebratory title for a disc that does full justice to this quirky, elegant and compelling music. Gothic Voices' familiarity with the music shines through in performances of seventeen of his songs (and a handful by his contemporaries) that are lively but unforced, with an emphasis on expressing the melodic line cleanly and clearly. Accompaniment on some of the songs is provided by Andrew Lawrence-King on medieval harp.

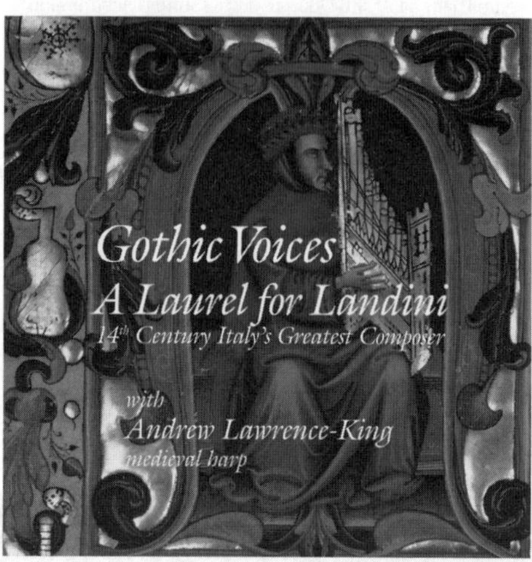

Roland de Lassus (1532–1594)

Roland de Lassus (or Orlando di Lasso as he was known in Italy) was a contemporary of Palestrina and, like him, was one of the truly outstanding composers of the sixteenth century. They almost certainly knew each other, since in 1555 Palestrina succeeded Lassus as *maestro di cappella* at the church of St John Lateran in Rome, and their respective careers make an interesting comparison. Lassus travelled throughout Europe, while Palestrina was firmly based in the region of Rome. Both men wrote polyphonic music but, whereas Palestrina evolved a style that was notable for its calmness and serenity, Lassus wrote pieces that were altogether more individual and quirky. He was also far more versatile than Palestrina, and his works encompass every major musical genre of the time.

Lassus was born at Mons, in the Franco-Flemish province of Hainaut. He may have been a chorister at the church of St Nicholas, but there is nothing to substantiate the legend that he was kidnapped by talent scouts, on account of the beauty of his voice. However, he was in Italy by the age of twelve, in the service of Ferdinand Gonzaga, the viceroy of Sicily. His prestigious appointment at St John Lateran at the age of 21 is a tribute to his remarkable talent, but he was there for only eighteen months before returning north to Antwerp. Shortly after his return, Lassus was summoned to Munich to join the ducal court of Bavaria, firstly as a singer and then, in 1562, as *Kapellmeister*. He was to remain there for the rest of his life, enjoying a unique familiarity with the duke, Albrecht V, and with his son and successor Wilhelm. Lassus's correspondence with Wilhelm has been preserved: written in a mishmash of languages and full of puns and bad jokes, it shows him as a remarkably spirited and affectionate person. He also had a dark side, however, and in his last years suffered from such extreme depression that his music almost dried up.

Sacred Music

From the middle of the sixteenth century the term *musica reservata* (reserved music) was applied to those composers who were concerned with trying to convey the meaning of the words they set. Of Lassus a contemporary wrote that he could make "… the things of the text so vivid that they seem to stand actually before our eyes". Devices such as chromaticism, whereby the melody was made more expressive by employing notes apart from those from the key it was written in, became increasingly common at this time, and in his early work – especially in his songs and madrigals – Lassus employs quite extreme chromaticism, as well as frequent declamatory passages. But as his career progressed his writing became more subtle and economic in its expressiveness. The eight-part *Missa Bell' Amfitrit'altera* has an ineffably radiant but simple opening and its shifts of mood are achieved mostly by varying the musical texture and the rhythm. His final work, *Lagrime di San Pietro* (Tears of St Peter), is an extraordinarily powerful cycle of sacred madrigals in which the music's austerity and intensity of feeling perfectly match the clarity of the poetic imagery.

Missa Bell' Amfitrit'altera: Westminster Cathedral Choir; His Majesty's Sagbutts and Cornetts; O'Donnell (Hyperion; with music by Hassler & Erbach)

Through the addition of instrumental and choral music by Hassler and Erbach, this recording represents how a festal celebration in Bavaria might have sounded around 1600. Including the more grandiose ceremonial music of his contemporaries succeeds in emphasizing the serene beauty of Lassus's mass setting. The beautifully measured performances enhance the sense of occasion.

Lagrime di San Pietro: Ensemble Vocal Européen; Herreweghe (Harmonia Mundi)

The Ensemble Vocal Européen adopt a strikingly vivid approach in this music. Their seven voices combine perfectly but are strong and individual, with some wonderfully judged contrasts in dynamics. They are helped by a sympathetic recording, which brings out the immediacy of the voices yet also suggests the space that surrounds them.

William Lawes (1602–1645)

Though still relatively little-known, William Lawes composed some of the most compelling and strikingly original instrumental music of the early seventeenth century. Decades ahead of his time, he took the sound-world of English consort music (see p.296) and invested it with an unprecedented richness through the use of daring, emotionally laden harmonies and adventurous instrumental combinations. His "setts", or suites, for viols and other instruments contain beautiful, introspective music that is elegant yet wonderfully unpredictable, with polyphonic lines interweaving like the gnarled branches of a majestic old oak tree – an image reinforced by the luxuriant woody timbre of the ensembles he wrote for.

The son of a lay preacher, Lawes was born in Salisbury in 1602 and, as a child, probably sang in the local cathedral choir. He was reportedly talent-spotted by the Earl of Hertford, who "obtained him from his father", and tutored him "of his own cost … under Master Giovanni Coprario, an Italian, and most Exquisite Musician". Coprario was not actually an Italian: he was an Englishman called John Cooper who thought an Italian pseudonym would help his career. But he *was* one of the great musicians of his day, and his influence on Lawes was all-important. Not only did he give him a solid compositional grounding based on his treatise *Rules of Composition* (rules that Lawes would soon master and then start breaking with abandon). He also introduced his pupil to all of England's most esteemed musicians – and to Lawes's future employer, Charles I, who as a prince was a fellow pupil of Coprario.

Lawes's breakthrough came in 1633, when he was commissioned to write the music for *The Triumph of Peace,* a hugely elaborate and expensive masque put on by London's Inns of Court (law schools) to prove their allegiance to the king. Soon after, he was given an official post in Charles's court as "musician in ordinary for the lutes and voices", an honour achieved some years

Consort Musick

In the sixteenth and early seventeenth centuries, European composers focused primarily on writing for the human voice. But the period did see the creation of some superb instrumental works, especially in England, where so-called *consorts* – small instrumental ensembles – were prevalent both in theatres and in the homes of aristocratic connoisseurs. Consort was a very loose term, "a company of Musitions together", according to one contemporary definition, but roughly speaking consort groups fell into two categories. The first, anachronistically referred to as "broken" consorts, featured instruments of various different types, a typical line-up being bass and treble viol, recorder or flute, and two or three plucked instruments, such as lute, theorbo, cittern and bandora. This kind of mixed ensemble was especially popular at masques, banquets and other such festivities, and English mastery of the genre was recognized across Europe from the Elizabethan era onwards, thanks to composers such as Thomas Morley and Philip Rosseter.

However, it was the second format – the "whole" consort, which featured instruments of just one family, perhaps with keyboard or lute accompaniment – that produced the greatest music. Whole consorts were written for recorders, violins, sackbuts and many other instruments, but by far the most popular choice were the various members of the viol family: the bowed, fretted, flat-backed string instruments that were eventually eclipsed by violins, violas and cellos. The popularity of viol consorts was helped by the fact that many of the royal and aristocratic figures who employed composers at the time were themselves keen amateur violists (in the early seventeenth century, especially, a "chest" of viols was an essential accessory for any well-to-do household). But this wasn't the only reason for the success of the genre: composers must have revelled in an instrumental combination that – much like the string quartet, which would become popular more than a century later – offered great flexibility and unrivalled expressive power.

All the most significant English musical figures of the sixteenth and seventeenth century wrote works for viol consort. Thomas Tallis and William Byrd found the medium an ideal alternative vehicle for many of the techniques of vocal polyphony. A few decades later John Dowland, who always had a penchant for musical melancholia, used the sound of the viol consort to explore the darkest depths of pathos in his *Lachrimae*. Dowland's successors, Orlando Gibbons and William Lawes, excelled in the wonderfully free-flowing fantasias that had long been associated with these instruments. The last jewels in consort repertoire were provided by Matthew Locke and Henry Purcell, who added a late-Baroque finesse to the viol sound.

The richness of consort music isn't only down to these major figures, however, but also to lesser-known but hugely talented musicians such as John Jenkins and Anthony Holborne (an Elizabethan composer who, despite his obscurity, impressed NASA employees sufficiently to ensure that a sample of his work was included on the Voyager spaceshot as an example of human achievement). After the age of Purcell, consort music quickly declined. It was probably inevitable that viols would soon become unfashionable, and give way to the brighter, louder alternatives: violins, violas and cellos. But it can't have helped that, after the death of Purcell, the next great musical genius to compose in England was one whose background was far removed from this uniquely British tradition: George Frideric Handel, a German trained in Italy.

Crye: Concordia (Metronome)

Concordia are a leading consort ensemble and this disc – which comes with a Glyn Maxwell narrative poem inspired by this melancholy music – shows them at their best. The selection combines well-known and obscure consorts by Tobias Hume, Anthony Holborne, Henry Stonings, Thomas Tallis and others.

Anthony Holborne – The Teares of the Muses: Hespèrion XXI; Savall (Alia Vox)

Anthony Holborne (c. 1545–1602) published an important consort collection entitled *Pavans, Galliards & Almains* in 1599. Though his music lacks Lawes's daring or Byrd's polyphonic genius, it's still highly compelling, and sounds superbly rich and warm in this performance from Jordi Savall's group. The viols are complemented by keyboard instruments and occasional percussion.

Matthew Locke – The Broken Consort: The Parley of Instruments; Holman (Hyperion)

Matthew Locke (c. 1620–1677) influenced Purcell, but has now been largely eclipsed by him. This delightful disc shows this to be an injustice: Locke's Suites, here played by a mixed group of violins and viols, reveal a rich and inventive imagination. They are presented here interspersed with four duos for bass viols.

previously by his brother Henry (himself a celebrated composer of songs, and good friend of the poet John Milton). Charles held the Lawes brothers in the highest esteem, and William spent a highly productive decade in his employment. He wrote many songs as well as numerous sacred anthems, but his angular contrapuntal style was best suited to instrumental music, which he composed both for the theatre and for courtly consort groups. It was the latter genre in which he really excelled, most notably in the extraordinary setts for viols, and various works for unusual combinations of instruments, such as the *Royall Consorts* and the *Harp Consorts* (for harp, viol, violin and theorbo).

On the outbreak of civil war, Lawes entered the Cavalier army. Presumably at the king's request, he was given a specifically low-risk position as commissary in a general's regiment. But in a cruel twist of fate, this very regiment happened to be present at the bloody siege of Chester in September 1645, when Lawes, along with hundreds of others, was killed by Roundhead muskets.

Setts for Viols

Lawes's greatest works are his "setts" – suites – for four, five or six viols. This is music that's remarkable for the tunefulness of every line of the contrapuntal texture, and for its sheer harmonic audacity. Lawes revels in dissonances and unexpected changes of key, sometimes to the point that the results sound positively strange – as in the end of the first movement of the *Sett in F Major*. Each sett consists of a few movements, the dominating forms being fantasies – richly polyphonic pieces that look back to the Renaissance era – and more stately aires and pavans that look forward to the late Baroque period. The setts were written with organ accompaniment, though some modern-day performers prefer to leave this out, as a viol-only format helps present this "dazzling and dangerous music" (as one performer described it) with the maximum clarity and incisiveness.

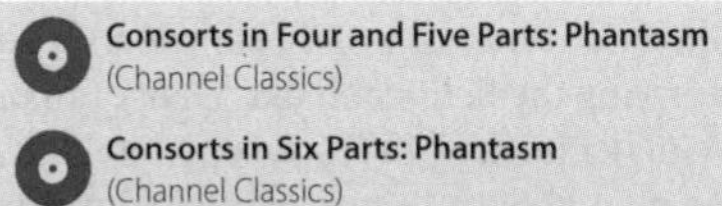

Consorts in Four and Five Parts: Phantasm
(Channel Classics)

Consorts in Six Parts: Phantasm
(Channel Classics)

Phantasm are an extraordinary ensemble: technically superb and always able to invest their chosen repertoire with a living, breathing energy. Performed without the organ accompaniment, these recordings provide the best possible introduction to Lawes's music.

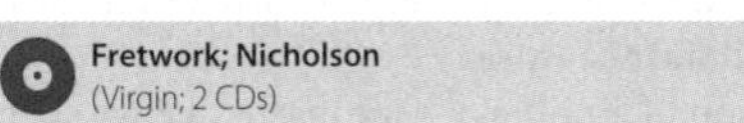

Fretwork; Nicholson
(Virgin; 2 CDs)

At budget price, this complete recording of the five- and six-part viol setts is truly excellent value. Fretwork don't quite have the steely panache and dynamism of Phantasm, but their more reticent performances – this time with keyboard accompaniment – are impressive nonetheless.

Royall Consort suites

There is surprisingly little chamber music that combines viols and violins. But Lawes, always the rule-breaker, used this combination of instruments in many of his greatest works, most notably the ten suites that make up the *Royall Consort* collection. Here, two bright-sounding violins take the upper voices, while the lower register is provided by the more velvety sonority of a pair of bass viols. To fill out the texture, continuo support is provided by not one but two theorbos (large double-necked lutes), their plucking and strumming adding a strong theatrical edge to the proceedings. Indeed, if the viol consorts are defined by their passionate introspection, the *Royall Consort* has an air of public display and celebration. Each suite comprises several stylized dance movements – Alman, Corrants, Sarabands and the curious "Ecco" – plus the occasional fantasy and many wonderful aires, which show Lawes at his most effortlessly lyrical.

The Purcell Quartet; North, O'Dette
(Chandos; 2 CDs)

For this premiere recording of the complete *Royall Consort* suites, released in 1995, the Purcell Quartet are joined by two of the world's leading lutenists, Nigel North and Paul O'Dette. The performances succeed in conveying both the scuttling vivacity of the dance movements and the more elegiac sound-world of the aires and fantasies.

Franz Lehár (1870–1948)

Franz Lehár was the Andrew Lloyd Webber of his day: within two years of the premiere of *Die lustige Witwe* (The Merry Widow) in 1905 he was a dollar millionaire, and the show ran for a record 778 performances in London – King Edward VII saw it four times. *The Merry Widow* pioneered the concept of merchandizing, with "Merry Widow" hats, corsets, cigarettes and cocktails going on sale in New York. Several other operettas virtually repeated the success of his best-known work, and were exported to theatres right around the world.

The son of a military bandmaster, Lehár spent his childhood stationed with his father's regiment in various towns across the Austro-Hungarian Empire, and for a short while he studied with Dvořák at the Prague Conservatory – "Hang up your fiddle and start composing", he is reputed to have been advised. He had already composed a couple of fairly successful operettas by the time he was given the libretto of *Die lustige Witwe* by Oscar Léon and Leo Stein, the authors of Strauss's hugely popular *Wiener Blut*. In fact Lehár was the second choice as composer – he got the job after being set a trial song, which he composed in a single day and played down the telephone to Léon.

By the time the show was in rehearsal, the Theater an der Wien (Vienna's main operetta theatre) had little faith in the piece, and at one point offered Lehár five thousand crowns to withdraw it. The premiere on 30 December, 1905 went well enough, but business was slow and free tickets were handed out to fill the house. Eventually word got round, and *Die lustige Witwe* is still a regular fixture at the Theater an der Wien, even displacing *Cats* from the summer season's programme. After a couple of flops, Lehár hit a winning streak with *Der Graf von Luxemburg* (1909) and *Zigeunerliebe* (1910), both of which had highly successful worldwide runs and are still regularly performed in central Europe.

Lehár's career then took another downturn until it was revitalized by the tenor Richard Tauber, who became the most celebrated performer of Lehár's music and gave his name to *Tauberlied* – songs that have become far more popular than the operettas that spawned them. The most famous of these, "Dein ist mein ganzes Herz" (You are my Heart's Delight), comes from Lehár's last international triumph, *Das Land des Lächelns* (The Land of Smiles), premiered in Berlin in 1929. At Christmas 1930, Lehár's sixtieth birthday year, some two hundred productions of *Das Land des Lächelns* were in progress in Europe, and five hundred different Lehár productions in total. His last major work, *Giuditta*, was premiered at the Vienna State Opera in 1934, the only operetta to have been given that honour, and the show was relayed internationally by 120 radio stations.

Many musicians of Jewish extraction decided to emigrate when the Nazis came to power, but – although his wife was Jewish – Lehár stayed in Vienna. He is said to have been the favourite composer of Hitler, who as a young man was a regular visitor to the Theater an der Wien's production of *Die lustige Witwe*. After the Anschluss Lehár composed a new overture to *Die lustige Witwe*, which he dedicated to Hitler to protect himself and his wife. This didn't help Lehár's Jewish colleagues, however, and Fritz Löhner-Beda, one of the librettists of *Das Land des Lächelns* and *Giuditta*, was murdered in a concentration camp while his work was playing in Vienna. After moving to Switzerland for a few years Lehár returned to his villa in Bad Ischl, where he died in 1948.

Marilyn Hill Smith Sings Lehár and Kálmán: Smith; Chandos Concert Orchestra; Barry (Chandos)

This CD is by far the best compilation of Lehár (and Kálmán) arias, partly because Marilyn Hill Smith steers away from the popular favourites and comes up with some little-known but high-quality numbers from *Giuditta*, *Zigeunerliebe* and others. Hill Smith's tone is usually just right, while Stuart Barry brings out the fine orchestration and transparency of the scores.

Die lustige Witwe

The story of *Die lustige Witwe* is one of absurd aristocratic intrigue to prevent a wealthy widow, Hanna Glawari, marrying a Frenchman and thereby depriving the fictional Balkan kingdom of Pontevedro of her fortune. In typical operetta style, Danilo, the man chosen to lure Hanna from the Frenchman, turns out to be her former heart-throb, although there are plenty of diversions on the way. Lehár throws Balkan spice into the score with some folk dances and Hanna's famous "Vilja-Lied" – the *vilja* is a wood spirit from Montenegrin folklore. (Furthermore, Danilo's costume for the premiere was closely modelled on that of the Crown Prince of Montenegro). The celebrated "Merry Widow Waltz" and some splashes of French nightclub music further enrich the mix.

Studer, Skovhus, Bonney, Trost, Terfel; Vienna Philharmonic; Gardiner (Deutsche Grammophon)

In this vivid and seductive set, all the singers bring a quality of unforced clarity and ease to the vocal lines, although only Bo Skovhus (Danilo) is a regular performer of operetta. The other great pluses of this recording are that it is contained on one CD, includes all the music, and cuts the spoken dialogue down to a minimum.

Schwarzkopf, Waechter, Gedda, Steffek; Philharmonia Chorus and Orchestra; Matačic
(EMI; 2 CDs)

This classic recording, made in 1962 and recently remastered, has never been bettered. Elisabeth Schwarzkopf has all the alluring mystery that Hanna Glawari requires, and her seductive performance of the "Vilja-Lied" has just the right delicacy and poise. Eberhard Waechter and Nikolai Gedda are suitable foils, and the more rumbustious parts of the score are dashed off with splendid abandon.

Ruggero Leoncavallo (1857–1919)

Just as Italians in the eighteenth century would have nothing to do with Gluck, so in the nineteenth century they were extremely uncomfortable with Wagner, an attitude typified by the career of Ruggero Leoncavallo. Enamoured of Wagner's music as a young man, he came to write one of the two great examples of operatic verismo, the low-life counterblast to Wagnerian epic music drama.

Leoncavallo first experienced Wagner's music in 1878 and was deeply affected by it – or rather, by its literary and dramatic scope. He set about writing *Crespuculum*, a quasi-Wagnerian Renaissance trilogy, but was soon sidetracked into completing a project that had occupied him since his student days, an opera called *Chatterton*, about the young English poet who killed himself by taking strychnine. When the promoter of the premiere disappeared with all the money before the first night, Leoncavallo approached a publisher with a view to issuing *Chatterton* in print. However, the publisher felt Leoncavallo to be a better librettist than composer, and commissioned him to write the text for Puccini's *Manon Lescaut*. Puccini had him removed from the project.

After two years' further dissatisfaction, the ever-ambitious Leoncavallo found his inspiration in the success of Mascagni's *Cavalleria rusticana*, the work that launched verismo opera in 1890, and promptly dominated the limelight in Italy. As he later wrote: "I shut myself in my house … and in five months I wrote the poem and music of *pagliacci*." Toscanini gave the first performance of *I pagliacci* (The Clowns) on 21 May, 1892, and overnight Leoncavallo found his fame and made his fortune.

On the back of this success he arranged for the first part of his *Crespuculum* to be performed and, after a blaze of pre-publicity, *I Medici* was duly premiered on 9 November, 1893. The evening was a disaster, and from then on he was embroiled in a losing battle with Puccini for the affections of the Italian people. Leoncavallo's *La Bohème* was performed almost a year after Puccini's and, even though it met with some success, he never came to terms with its inevitable disappearance from the stage.

Leoncavallo was one of the first composers to take a serious interest in the gramophone, composing the song *Mattinata* expressly for the G&T record company (Caruso recorded it in April 1904), but life went steadily downhill after *pagliacci*. The man who had once proposed writing a music drama to rival Wagner's spent his dying months composing an operetta entitled *A chi la giarettiera?* – or *Whose Garter is This?*

I Pagliacci

The central idea of *I pagliacci* – a travelling actor discovers that his younger wife has been having an affair with a friend and colleague, and wreaks a dreadful revenge – was taken from a case that Leoncavallo's magistrate father had judged, and it typified the verismo ideal. From this sordid tale he made one of the finest dramatic operas ever written, showing a command of proportion, timing and characterization that is absent from the rest of his output. The cheated husband (Canio) is one of the greatest dramatic tenor roles in all opera; Nedda, the cheating wife, is a less involved part than that of the adulterer Tonio, but their set pieces and exchanges are riveting in their energy and conviction. The last ten minutes, during which Leoncavallo's play within a play reaches its shocking conclusion, are the ultimate in verismo.

Corelli, Amara, Gobbi, Zanasi, Spina; La Scala Orchestra & Chorus; Matačic (EMI; 2 CDs; with Mascagni *Cavalleria rusticana*)

Matačic's 1960 recording is a masterpiece of base emotion and divine inspiration. Franco Corelli's awesome Canio is unmatched before or since, and Tito Gobbi brings all Tonio's contradictory qualities to the surface. Lucine Amara's Nedda lacks malice, but Matačic's driving direction makes up for it. Unfortunately, the accompanying *Cavalleria rusticana* is not in the same league.

Bergonzi, Carlyle, Taddei, Panerai; La Scala Orchestra & Chorus; Karajan (Deutsche Grammophon)

Karajan's lush 1965 recording is a fabulous testament to his transformation of the Scala forces from a second-rate band into the most expressive orchestra ever to record this work. Carlo Bergonzi's voice lacked steel, but the fluency of his phrasing is intoxicating. Joan Carlyle's light soprano is beautifully produced, and Giuseppe Taddei is a feverish Tonio.

György Ligeti (1923–2006)

Ligeti's creative outlook was formed by his experiences under two dictatorships – those of Hitler and Stalin. A Jew born in Transylvania just as Hungary was losing that region to Romania, he survived World War II in a labour camp (his brother and father both died in Auschwitz). Following the war, he studied and taught at the Budapest Academy, but fled after the crushing of the anti-Soviet uprising in 1956. Arriving in Cologne, he became an associate of Stockhausen at the WDR electronic music studio, where he rapidly caught up on the musical developments from which he had been cut off in Hungary. In the 1960s he emerged as a leading member of the international avant-garde. By now living mostly in Hamburg and Vienna, he became an Austrian citizen in 1967.

Of the traumatic experiences that shaped his life and artistic outlook, Ligeti remarked: "I am permanently scarred; I will be overcome by revenge fantasies to the end of my days." And yet, despite his work's penchant for the surreal and the grotesque, he emerged as the most approachable, as well as one of the most fascinating and compelling, of post-war composers. A feeling of loss and nostalgia characterizes much of his output, often evoked by the haunting modalities of East European folk music – most obviously in the early Hungarian period directly influenced by Bartók, from which come the *Concert Românesc* (1951) and the delightful *Six Bagatelles for Wind Quintet* of 1953. But pathos is balanced by absurdist humour, as in the notorious twenty-minute *Poème symphonique for 100 Metronomes* (1962), a piece of "mechanical music" which lasts until the last device finally stops beating.

The mechanical is one aspect of the "clocks and clouds" ethos that made Ligeti's name in the early 1960s (a piece with that title appeared in 1973). In *Atmosphères* (1961) and other "cloud" pieces such as *Apparitions* and *Lontano*, Ligeti rejected the serial complexities favoured by contemporaries such as Stockhausen and Boulez in favour of music in which pulse and harmony are suspended. Clusters of adjacent sounds were used to achieve slow, seamless change, most famously in *Lux Aeterna* for unaccompanied voices, in which fine gradations of pitch create a kind of warped polyphony. (It was used, without permission, in Stanley Kubrick's film *2001*.) At the same time, Ligeti's maverick sense of humour expressed itself in the quasi-theatrical *Aventures* and *Nouvelles aventures*, a pair of exuberant vocal works setting nonsense phonetic texts, and the imposing *Requiem*, Ligeti's summatory early work, which combines the sound-mass textures of the orchestral pieces and the zany theatricals of *Aventures* to disturbing effect.

The cloudy sound-masses of these early works are typically created out of microscopic tangles of intertwined instrumental lines – a kind of musical spider's web, described by the composer as "micropolyphony". In Ligeti's works of the

Ligeti at his home in Hamburg.

later 1960s and early 1970s the lines gradually become clearer, reintroducing a sense – albeit a rather peculiar one – of melody, counterpoint and harmony, while rhythm also resurfaces, often in the form of crazily superimposed pulses or psychotically fast instrumental outbursts, like the deranged functioning of some vast mechanical instrument. In works such as the *Chamber Concerto*, *Melodien* and the *Double Concerto* for flute and oboe Ligeti pushes this style to its limits, creating a compellingly strange musical world, at once eerie and beautiful.

Ligeti's major project of the 1970s, the opera *Le Grand Macabre*, summed up all his previous creative preoccupations and sowed many of the seeds which were to germinate in subsequent works.

Set in "Breughelland", a world derived from the visionary paintings of Breughel and Bosch, the opera depicts the end of the world, as experienced by a gang of grotesques. Musically, the opera shows Ligeti at his most diverse, featuring such strikingly offbeat inspirations as a parodic overture for twelve car horns and the portentous orchestral march – composed out of snatches of ragtime and cha-cha superimposed on a mutilated theme from Beethoven's "Eroica" Symphony.

Following the opera's premiere in 1978 and a period of serious illness, Ligeti's style underwent a profound evolution, as first demonstrated by the moving *Trio for Violin, Horn and Piano* of 1982, a work in which a kind of tonality and traditional metre reappear in his work for the first time in over two decades, but lopsided or dislocated to comic or disturbing effect. It was in subsequent works – most notably two prodigious concertos, for piano and violin, and a sequence of eighteen *Études* for piano – that Ligeti's creative trajectory reached its destination. In all these works there are overt references to traditional classical (and other) music, often with a decidedly Eastern European flavour, but recontextualized in Ligeti's inimitably personal manner and often expressed in a complex rhythmic style in which conflicting layers of tempi are used to drive the music forward.

Ligeti's music is beyond tonality and atonality, and beyond postmodernism – "the ironic theatricalizing of the past is quite foreign to me". His sound-world is utterly unique, but until recently he has been sparsely served on disc; Sony began to rectify this with a superb Complete Ligeti Edition, a commendably adventurous series that was completed by Teldec.

Requiem

While in Hungary Ligeti had twice considered setting the Requiem, the Latin mass of the Dead, attracted in particular by the doom-laden words of the Dies irae. He finally did so following a commission from Swedish Radio in 1961, the same year that he first directly encountered the apocalyptic images of Bosch and Breughel in Madrid's Prado museum. In the end Ligeti only set three sections of the Requiem: the Introitus, Kyrie and Dies irae, isolating the last part of the Dies irae (Lacrimosa) into a coda-like conclusion. The work opens with a low orchestral growl from which the basses emerge with a tonally indeterminate drone. While there's some sense of development from darkness into light, as higher voices are added, the overall feeling (continued in the Kyrie) is disconcerting – like listening to the desperate, swirling voices of the damned. In the Dies irae these voices become increasingly clamorous, with shrill, demented outpourings from the soprano soloist and increasingly violent instrumental interventions. Whether the hushed and tentative Lacrimosa, for the two female soloists, offers any real sense of hope or redemption is a question left open.

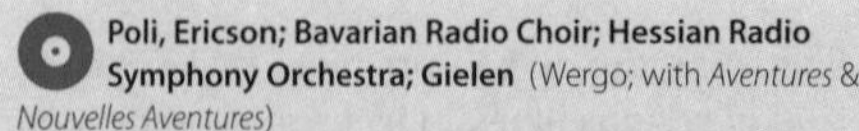

Poli, Ericson; Bavarian Radio Choir; Hessian Radio Symphony Orchestra; Gielen (Wergo; with *Aventures & Nouvelles Aventures*)

The enormous difficulty of the *Requiem*'s vocal writing (Ligeti permitted the chorus some leeway over pitches) is weathered with apparent ease by the choir and the two soloists, Liliana Poli and Barbra Ericson. Michael Gielen's direction brings out both the structural logic and the terrible pathos of a work that many see as Ligeti's personal monument to the Holocaust.

Atmosphères & Lontano

In the early 1960s Ligeti was exploring the possiblity of creating a monumental, pulseless music made up of great blocks of seemingly static, but subtly changing, textures whose component parts flowed seamlessly in and out of each other. One spectacular example is *Atmosphères* (1961) which begins with a vast chord covering over five octaves played by strings and wind, the sound changing as the wind players gradually withdraw. The impact of *Atmosphères* is overwhelming: one moment it seems to evoke a vast wheezing organ, another a swarm of demented bees. Texture is everything: there are no silences, instead the music is punctuated by a series of enormous crescendos. *Lontano*, written six years later, is more of the same but the overall effect feels very different. This time the clusters – chords made up of closely adjacent notes – are built up gradually in overlapping layers. There is still a sense of sculpted sound but the combination of instrumental timbres is often radiantly beautiful, suggesting something bejewelled and glowing.

Berlin Philharmonic Orchestra; Nott (Teldec; with *Concert Românesc, Apparitions & San Francisco Polyphony*)

A disc that provides an ideal survey of Ligeti's orchestral work from the earlier part of his career in the West (along with the first recording of the Kodaly-influenced *Concert Românesc*). Using such an outstanding orchestra as the Berlin Phil makes these works seem especially visionary, and highlights Ligeti's extraordinary talent for creating hauntingly memorable sounds.

Chamber Concerto

The *Chamber Concerto* (1969–70) is perhaps the finest of the rich sequence of concerto-like works which Ligeti composed during the late 1960s and early 1970s (others are the *Cello Concerto* of 1966, *Melodien* for chamber orchestra of 1971, and the *Double Concerto* for flute and oboe of 1972). The work is scored for a small ensemble of thirteen virtuoso performers, featuring winds, strings and two keyboard players – a relatively traditional instrumental line-up, though one from which Ligeti managed to conjure the most outlandish sonorities, while a Hammond organ adds a distinctively sepulchral touch to some of the concerto's spookier moments. The *Chamber Concerto* explores in characteristically Ligetian fashion the contrast between dream-like stasis and frantic activity, as the drifting, underwater sonorities of the first two movements are gradually transformed into the headlong finale, with its helter-skelter instrumental crossfire. Standing somewhat apart is the third movement, a kind of crazy Scherzo composed out of a deranged mêlée of conflicting pulses, like a room full of machines gone haywire – one of Ligeti's most memorable creations.

Schönberg Ensemble; de Leeuw (Teldec; with *Melodien, Piano Concerto & Mysteries of the Macabre*)

In the wrong hands, works like the *Chamber Concerto* can sound merely grotesque, but Reinbert de Leeuw and his excellent performers deliver the work's outlandish textures with consummate musicality, allowing its obscure logic and strange beauty to emerge with compelling force. With top recordings of *Melodien* and the *Piano Concerto*, this is the best single-CD introduction to Ligeti's work.

Ensemble Intercontemporain; Boulez (Deutsche Grammophon; with *String Quartet No. 2, Ramifications, Aventures & Lux Aeterna*)

Though less ingratiating than de Leeuw's, Boulez's classic reading of the *Chamber Concerto* has its own palpable authority and it comes with a good selection of Ligeti's chamber, vocal and choral works from the 1960s (the La Salle Quartet offer a still unsurpassed reading of the *String Quartet No. 2*, composed the year before the *Concerto*).

Piano & Violin Concertos

Written back-to-back between 1985 and 1992, the *Piano Concerto* and *Violin Concerto* together demonstrate the full expressive range of Ligeti's later output. The driving force behind the mercurial *Piano Concerto* (as behind the contemporaneous *Piano études*) is essentially rhythmic, particularly in the work's first, third and fifth movements, which generate an irresistible verve out of their endlessly colliding cross-rhythms and jauntily swung melodies. These enclose two further movements: the second, a strange lament (joined at one point, to memorable effect, by a slide whistle); the fourth, a kind of musical jigsaw puzzle, whose initially fragmentary and stuttering utterances gradually freewheel into chaos, with irresistibly comic effect.

Compared to the precise, mechanical fantasies of the *Piano Concerto*, the *Violin Concerto* is an altogether more rhapsodic work, employing a wider range of musical material and reference – most strikingly in the second movement, based on a chorale-like melody of disarming directness which teeters on the brink of outright nostalgia until, with characteristic humour, being rudely reprised on mistuned pipes. As in the *Piano Concerto*, the vigorous outer movements delve deeply into Ligeti's box of rhythmic tricks, though here the effect is wilder and more impassioned, evoking the fiddle traditions of Eastern Europe.

Piano Concerto; Violin Concerto: Gawriloff, Aimard; Ensemble Intercontemporain; Boulez (Deutsche Grammophon; with *Cello Concerto*)

In this superb recording of the *Violin Concerto* Saschko Gawriloff (who premiered the work and helped compose the fifth-movement cadenza) is ably supported by Boulez and the EI. The *Piano Concerto's* supple rhythms fare less well under Boulez's direction, and the recorded sound does no favours to soloist Pierre-Laurent Aimard, who labours mightily but often inaudibly amongst the orchestral mayhem.

Piano Concerto: Aimard; Schönberg Ensemble; de Leeuw (Teldec; with *Chamber Concerto, Melodien & Mysteries of the Macabre*)

Pierre-Laurent Aimard's second recording of the *Piano Concerto* is an altogether happier affair, with Reinbert de Leeuw's more sympathetic accompaniment allowing the work's rhythmic snap and comic verve to emerge with irresistible effect.

Piano Études

Ligeti completed his first book of piano études in 1985, the second in 1993, and the third set in 2001. As ambitious and profound as the studies of Chopin and Debussy, Ligeti's études virtually reinvent an instrument which had been largely sidelined by the musical avant-garde, creating effects of a complexity which is all the more compelling for being produced by just a single performer. Like much of his later music, the études are founded on the complex interplay of different rhythms and tempi. Many of the pieces are fast and furious, with conflicting rhythmic layers emerging out of a flurry of notes, as in the anarchic first étude, "Désordre", or the Mephistophelean thirteenth, "L'escalier du diable"; others are more reflective, as in the radiant "Arc-en-ciel" or the haunting "Cordes vides". Finest of all, however, is the sixth étude, "Automne à Varsovie", in which as many as four overlapping tempi are used to conjure up a mistily impressionist veil of sound – a marvellous union of poetry and technique, at once beautifully evocative and utterly original.

Aimard (Sony; with *Musica Ricercata*)

This is by far the best of the various recordings of the first two books of études. Aimard manages the technical and polyrhythmic challenges with complete assurance, and brings out a kaleidoscopic array of nuances and colour. Also included are a single étude from the third book and the wonderful *Musica Ricercata* sequence (which was sampled by Stanley Kubrick for the soundtrack of *Eyes Wide Shut*).

Magnus Lindberg (1958–)

Magnus Lindberg began his compositional career committed to the idea of pushing the language of music into uncharted territory: "Only the extreme is interesting. Striving for a balanced totality is nowadays an impossibility." The music he wrote in the 1980s reflects this dictum – it is dense, monolithic and gritty, often evoking images of a harsh and unyielding landscape. More recently, however, there has been a pronounced mellowing in his style, in works that are far more linear, with an emphasis on brighter and more sonorous textures. As the composer describes it himself: "Earlier I used to hack away at stone; these days my approach has been softer, gentler, as if I were moulding in clay."

Born in Helsinki, Lindberg studied composition at that city's Sibelius Academy with Rautavaara (see p.440) and Paavo Heininen, who introduced him to a wide range of contemporary music. With fellow-student Essa-Pekka Salonen (then a horn player, now a conductor) he founded the instrumental ensemble Toimii as a means of working out and performing his compositions. After graduating, he travelled widely in Europe, studying in Paris with Vinko Globokar and Gérard Grisey, and taking courses with Franco Donatoni in Italy and Brian Ferneyhough in Germany.

Lindberg's early works were strongly influenced by serialism but he was also interested in computers, which he used to calculate the highly complicated rhythmic transformations of *Kraft* (1985). The percussive impact of this work – which uses objects from a scrap-metal yard – and its punk-inspired sounds summarize Lindberg's rather brutal musical preoccupations at this period. The post-*Kraft* works, such as *Marea* (1989–90) and *Joy* (1989-90) show a gradual change of direction to a sound-world in which there is greater sense of momentum and details of instrumental timbre are far more apparent.

By the 1990s Lindberg was reinventing himself with bewildering regularity, first employing the chaconne as an organizational method, then abandoning it in favour of pulsating ostinati that seem to derive from Stravinsky, with a sideways glance towards minimalism. Significant works from this period, including *Aura* (1994) and *Arena* (1995), helped establish Lindberg as one of the most successful composers of his day, a reputation he has continued to build on since, with a number of large-scale orchestral works including four concertos.

Lindberg has almost entirely avoided writing for the human voice, a seemingly deliberate decision which ended in 2009 with *Graffiti*, a half-hour work for chamber choir and orchestra which set inscriptions found on the walls of Pompeii.

Works for Chamber Orchestra

Lindberg's compositions of the 1990s are much more listener-friendly than his earlier works and are a good place to start for someone new to his music. *Corrente* (1992) takes a look at a Baroque dance form and transforms its rapid, flowing character into a kaleidoscopic melee of scurrying voices which are built up layer by layer. There's an ominous undertow to the piece running through to the three darkly dramatic chords with which it ends. *Coyote Blues* (1993) started life as a commission for a vocal work, but Lindberg's interest in rhythmic complexity meant that it soon developed into another orchestral piece, albeit one with a more pronounced lyrical strain than usual. Its brilliant opening fanfare and obsessively repeated ostinati suggest a clear debt to Stravinsky's *Les noces* and *Octet* but there's also a distinctly American feel to it, not least in the bright open sonorities of its closing moments. His move to a more vividly hued instrumental palette climaxes in *Arena* (1995), a commission for a conducting competition which is his richest score to date, even in its pared-down version *Arena II*. Its use of repeated motifs, vivid colours and the edgy anxiety of its first half suggest a *hommage* to the more experimental Hollywood film scores – in particular, the work of Bernard Herrmann.

Arena II; Coyote Blues; Tendenza; Corrente: Avanti! Chamber Orchestra; Oramo (Ondine)

This is a remarkably well recorded and performed disc, with Lindberg's vivid orchestral colours coming across in all their brilliance thanks to the individual virtuosity of many of the players. The dramatic, and at times restless, element that underlies Lindberg's more recent work is pushed to the fore by Sakari Oramo, and it even comes across in such a solid and ungainly work as the early *Tendenza*.

Aura

Dedicated to the memory of Lutosławski (see p.311), *Aura*, composed in 1994, is Lindberg's largest and most symphonic work to date. It's made up of four movements (which are played without a break), the first two of which combine a monumentality of scale with a tangible sense of purpose. Opening with a low orchestral growl and thumping timpani, which seem to be leading to something primal and monolithic, the music constantly confounds expectation through sudden detours, usually to explore strange instrumental combinations from which exquisite flashes of colour often emerge – like the fusion of glockenspiels and piano which produces a restless, shimmering energy-burst at the end of the second movement. Throughout *Aura*, this tension between a sense of the orchestra as a single, massive voice and as a collection of myriad, individual protagonists – each with its own particular character – is what generates the work's momentum. The final movement climaxes in a frantic chorus of unrestrained excitement which is resolved by a serene coda, behind which the ghost of Sibelius seems to hover.

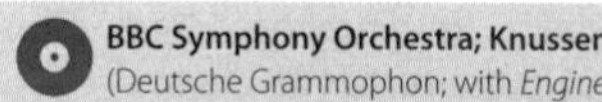

BBC Symphony Orchestra; Knussen (Deutsche Grammophon; with *Engine*)

What comes across here so strongly is Knussen's complete engagement with the music and his ability to communicate his enthusiasm to the orchestra. An immaculately produced recording, it reveals the BBC Symphony Orchestra as an outfit of entrancing virtuosity and confidence – it sounds as if they have been playing this music for decades.

Concertos

Lindberg's conception of the orchestra as a complex mechanism of interlocking parts does not readily accommodate a virtuoso soloist. What finally persuaded him to tackle the concerto format were longstanding relationships with specific musicians. The first of these was Lindberg himself; he wrote his *Piano Concerto* in 1991, but then took three years bringing it to a state he was happy with. Other concertos followed: the *Clarinet Concerto* in 2002 for Kari Kriikku and the *Cello Concerto* (2001) for Anssi Kartunen (both players had been members of Toimii). Then in 2006 came the *Violin Concerto*, written not for a Finnish colleague but for the young Georgian violinist Lisa Batiashvili. All the concertos delight in testing the soloist's virtuosity to the limit, but while displaying all Lindberg's skill in manipulating rhythmic intricacy and dense harmonies, they also mine a vein of lyricism which opens up unexpected possibilities for something akin to melody.

Clarinet Concerto: Kriikku; Finnish Radio Symphony Orchestra; Oramo (Ondine; with *Gran Duo & Chorale*)

Kari Kriikku nonchalantly handles every challenge, not least the improvised cadenza, a canny suggestion of Classical style. In a piece teeming with ideas, hyper-modern squeaks and squawks jostle with reminiscences of Gershwin, revealing Lindberg's born-again lyricism.

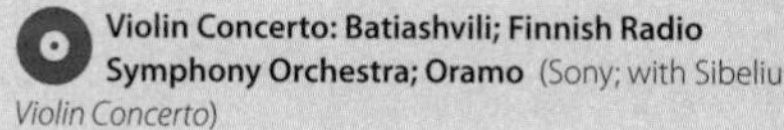

Violin Concerto: Batiashvili; Finnish Radio Symphony Orchestra; Oramo (Sony; with Sibelius *Violin Concerto*)

This is the most openly expressive of Lindberg's concertos, and Batiashvili has the requisite gamut of colours, to say nothing of the technical panache, to do it justice. She twins Lindberg with the Sibelius Concerto, a choice that would once have seemed provocative; now the two pieces make good companions.

Franz Liszt (1811–1886)

In certain circles Franz Liszt is still not taken seriously, and the reason for this lies in his brilliance as a performer – Liszt, the argument goes, was all self-promotion and no substance. The accusation is nothing new. In 1874 the critic Eduard Hanslick wrote: "The main objection against Liszt is that he imposes a much bigger – an abusive – mission on the subject of his work: namely either to fill the gap left by the absence of musical content or to justify the atrociousness of such content as there is."

Certainly Liszt was a large-scale character. Born Ferenc Liszt, the son of a minor Hungarian court functionary, he became the greatest pianist of his age – indeed, possibly of any age. Like Paganini (see p.386), he developed his technique to the

Franz Liszt at the piano.

point at which he had to create his own style of music to do justice to his capabilities, and much of that music did little more than show off his technique. Instead of working from his own ideas, he quarried all available musical sources and reworked the material into show stoppers that would demonstrate that he could play octaves faster than anyone else, and hit the keys harder (he used to break his wooden-framed pianos). His offstage character hardly suggested serious devotion to music. Liszt was the ultimate Romantic blend of immorality and piety, an infamous womanizer who had the face of St Francis carved on his walking stick – alongside Mephistopheles and Gretchen, heroine of Goethe's *Faust*.

There was indubitably more than a dash of the showman in Liszt, but his contribution to the development of nineteenth-century music was immense. On a practical level, he was an uncommonly generous man who gave freely of his time and money to champion the music of other composers. As for his own compositions, the fireworks represent just the surface, for in his symphonic music he anticipated the tone poems of Strauss and the vast fluid structures of Wagner (his son-in-law), while in his austere late piano music he created perhaps the most prophetic work of his time. As Schoenberg once wrote – "one must not overlook how much there is in his music that is new, musically, and discovered by genuine intuition. Was he not after all one of those that started the battle against tonality?"

Liszt invented the piano recital and the career of travelling virtuoso, but his first major works were created after making a break with his self-established tradition. In 1847, after nearly thirty years as Europe's most revered pianist, Liszt met and fell in love with the Princess Carolyne von Sayn-Wittgenstein, who convinced him that, having sown more oats than most could imagine, he should settle down. Somewhat in awe of the princess, Liszt renounced his career as a roaming virtuoso and in 1848 accepted an invitation to become *Kapellmeister* to the Grand Duke of Weimar. During his ten years at Weimar he wrote or revised most of the pieces for which he is now best known, and made the city a pre-eminent musical centre by conducting a vast number of new works, including music by Schumann, Berlioz, Verdi, Donizetti and Wagner. Weimar became the centre of the progressive faction of which Wagner was the figurehead, a group opposed by Brahms, Hanslick and the traditionalists of Vienna.

In 1860 he moved to Rome, where five years later he took minor orders. His music from this time was soaked in religious sentiment, but his heart was never really in it and in 1869 he began to divide his time between Rome, Weimar and Budapest. The more he travelled, the more he reverted to his old ways, and his amorous adventures once again became the talk of Europe. As his increasing years began to take effect, however, he devoted ever larger amounts of time to teaching and, together with Clara Schumann, he helped produce some of the early twentieth century's greatest pianists. In the 1870s his music entered its final and most radical phase, and he remained active as a composer and performer right to the end of his life – his jubilee tour, marking his 75th birthday, was reported across the world. He died soon after. His career had bridged a whole era in the cultural development of Europe: had he been born two years earlier, his life span would have overlapped with both Haydn and Stravinsky.

Faust Symphony

In 1846 Berlioz dedicated his dramatic cantata *La damnation de Faust* to Liszt. It was to be nearly ten years before Liszt repaid the compliment by dedicating his own interpretation of Goethe's two-part poem to Berlioz. The *Faust Symphony* was one of the major works to emerge from the years in Weimar (along with Liszt's only other symphony, the weaker *Dante Symphony*), but was constantly revised – nineteen years after the first performance in 1861, he was still revising the slow movement.

There are three movements – "Faust", "Gretchen" and "Mephistopheles" – and each is, essentially, a character study. The grand and sweeping first movement is an extraordinary example of Liszt's technique of transforming his basic themes: lasting nearly half an hour, it is built on just five short phrases. After a second movement of almost chamber-music delicacy, which looks towards the anti-Wagnerian simplicity of his final decade, the finale represents Goethe's "spirit of negation" by grotesque parody of the themes heard in the opening movement. The latter half of "Mephistopheles" depicts "the great struggle" and concludes with his defeat, in which the "Chorus mysticus" (end of Part Two of Goethe's *Faust*) is strikingly set for tenor, male chorus and full orchestra.

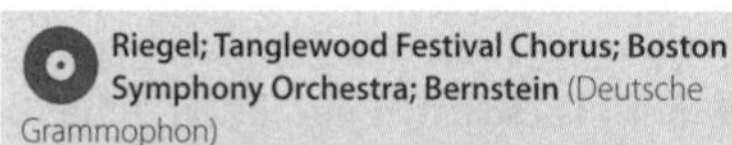

Riegel; Tanglewood Festival Chorus; Boston Symphony Orchestra; Bernstein (Deutsche Grammophon)

One consummate showman meets another: this was one of Bernstein's calling cards, and he gives it his all in this 1976 recording. It's an electrifying and highly passionate account – the "Gretchen" movement in particular has a real glow. Kenneth Riegel is the fine tenor soloist.

Les Préludes

Liszt can be credited with inventing the genre of the symphonic poem, an extended orchestral piece presented as the interpretation of a non-musical subject. He completed thirteen of them, illustrating subjects taken from classical mythology, Romantic literature, recent history or imaginative fantasy and, while not all of them are successful, *Les Préludes* (another product of the Weimar years) is a masterpiece. Liszt actually composed the twenty-minute piece before deciding that the music was a paraphrase of a poem by Lamartine, in which life is presented as a series of preludes to the afterlife. As with the *Faust Symphony*, the opening theme appears in many guises throughout the work and, more than almost any other of his orchestral compositions, *Les Préludes* is a brilliantly organic, well-structured creation.

Berlin Philharmonic Orchestra; Karajan (Deutsche Grammophon; with *Mazeppa & Hungarian Rhapsodies* and Smetana *Ma vlast)*

Liszt's grand and spectacular music brings out the best in Karajan and his orchestra – this is one of his most exciting recordings, and in the closing measures the music simply tears off the page. This two-disc set is an excellent introduction to Liszt's large-scale work.

Piano Concerto No. 1

The more famous and certainly more enjoyable of Liszt's two piano concertos is the first, in E flat. It was begun in 1830 then revised for years until, in what must have been one of the concerts of the century, Berlioz conducted the first performance, with Liszt himself at the piano, in 1855. With its unison opening theme, leading into a series of startling octave leaps, the concerto's opening is one of the most dramatic of any Romantic piano concerto. This introduction is followed by a fiery cadenza which, in turn, leads to a series of calmer, more reflective passages, and the concerto carries on in this exchange of moods, keeping you on the edge of your seat in anticipation of the next burst of pyrotechnics. Moments of incredible banality are dotted through the score, but there are enough Romantic gestures to distract your attention.

Richter; London Symphony Orchestra; Kondrashin (Philips; with *Piano Concerto No. 2* and Beethoven *Piano Sonatas Nos. 10, 19 & 20*)

Richter gives overwhelmingly powerful and authoritative readings of the concertos. He was at his technical peak when he recorded them in the 1960s, and his fingerwork has a steely energy to it which is remarkable. He is well supported by Kondrashin, one of the most sympathetic of concerto conductors, and the LSO.

Zimerman; Boston Symphony Orchestra; Ozawa
(Deutsche Grammophon; with *Totentanz*)

For a more recent recording of both concertos, Krystian Zimerman is unsurpassed. He takes this music completely seriously, investing it with enormous weight and profundity without stinting on the pyrotechnics – particularly in the first concerto. The disc also includes a death-defying performance of *Totentanz*.

Études d'exécution transcendante

Liszt's eight *Études d'exécution transcendante* (or *Transcendental Studies*) comprise one of the great documents of musical Romanticism and a landmark in the history of the piano, amounting to nothing less than the creation of modern piano technique. These studies teem with such outrageous difficulties that, in their day (1831), they were the most difficult works ever written for the piano; even now, there's but a handful of pianists able to play them authoritatively. The versions most commonly performed today are Liszt's revisions of 1851, which cut back on the pyrotechnics but, even so, are as fiendish as anything written since. If played well, this music rises above mere display to reach a plateau of intense emotional conviction – especially the first four.

Berezovsky
(Warner)

To play these works at all requires a formidable technique; to play them so that the poetry (rather than the effort) shines through requires a gift afforded to very few. Boris Berezovsky has the technical prowess to deal with the pyrotechnics but also knows how to enter the introspective core of such pieces as the beautiful "Harmonies du soir" and "Ricordanza".

Berman
(Melodiya)

As an alternative to the Berezovsky version, the late Lazar Berman's old Melodiya recording is worth snapping up – if you find it. Though recorded in mono, it's an absolutely mesmerizing account, powerfully played and with an unsurpassed visionary sweep.

Hungarian Rhapsodies

A lot of Liszt's music bears the stamp of his Hungarian heritage, and of all his quasi-Gypsy compositions the most inventive and popular are the nineteen *Hungarian Rhapsodies*. Growing out of the composer's renewed interest in the folk music of his native country, the first fifteen were written between 1840 and 1847; the last three were not added until the 1870s. These are not Liszt's greatest works – they often sound rather contrived and superficial – but the rhythms and melodies are immediately infectious, and the transcriptions of the sounds of a Gypsy orchestra (solo violin, clarinet, cimbalom and strings) are breathtaking. Best-known is the second rhapsody – Tom and Jerry, and Daffy and Donald, have all skittered around to it.

Hungarian Rhapsodies Nos. 2, 6, 8–15: Cziffra
(EMI)

Unpredictable and risk-taking, György Cziffra produces just about the most hair-raising playing on record. Marvellous entertainment, this disc is a worthy tribute and a superb introduction to the very best and the very worst of Liszt's piano music by one of the greatest Lisztians in history.

Sonata in B Minor

Composed between 1851 and 1853, and dedicated to Schumann, the *Sonata in B Minor* is cast (like Schumann's *Fantasie in C*) in three movements that are played without a pause. It's a vast work, underlaid by a series of themes and motifs that grow, fuse and eventually expire. Three of the main motifs are stated in the opening bars: a softly ominous descending phrase, a wildly animated one, and a low growl of repeated notes in the bass. Liszt weaves these together and drives them along in a whirl of furious semi-quavers, exploring a kaleidoscope range of thematic transformations. The first motif is escalated into a "big tune" of grandiose dimensions; another becomes a lyric melody of Chopinesque tenderness.

The second movement ushers in a mood of subdued, even religous, solemnity. Some of Liszt's pupils associated this movement with the character of Gretchen in Goethe's *Faust*, with the finale representing Mephistopheles. There's no evidence that Liszt intended this Faustian subtext, but it's certainly not difficult to project a demonic fury onto the last movement. Marked "energico", it begins with a brilliant and extremely manic fugue, and builds into a phantasmagorical review of the work's themes. It's a *tour de force* of bravura virtuosity that in its most exhibitionist passages seems to anticipate Tchaikovsky.

Zimerman (Deutsche Grammophon; with other Liszt piano works)

Many pianists treat the *Sonata in B Minor* either as a barnstorming melodrama or as a rather unwieldy successor to Beethoven's late sonatas. In Krystian Zimerman's hands the music's visionary dimension stands out, but it feels as if every phrase has been carefully thought out in terms of weight and colour; the work's undoubted histrionic quality is tempered by moments of iridescent delicacy and inner calm.

 **Argerich** (Deutsche Grammophon; with Schumann *Piano Sonata No. 2* and Brahms *Rhapsodies*)

Martha Argerich's recording of the sonata is a magnificent high-voltage account, pulsating with the most astonishing energy but always remaining utterly coherent. In the opinion of many commentators, it is the finest thing she has ever recorded.

Années de pèlerinage

The first two volumes of Liszt's *Années de pèlerinage* (composed and revised from the 1830s to the 1870s) are perhaps the most complete overview of his talents as a composer. (The third volume, compiled against Liszt's will and published posthumously, is inferior to the other two.) Standing in complete contrast to the glitter and dazzle of the études, these pieces are principally lyrical miniatures, and are more concerned with the creation of atmosphere than the construction of a literal narrative. The first book, dealing with his travels through Switzerland, includes the exquisite "Au bord d'une source" and "Vallée d'Obermann", both of which are as fresh as the landscapes they portray. In the second volume, the so-called "Italian book", art and literature are the subjects, and here the music is, if anything, even more beautiful. "Sposalizio" and "Petrarch Sonnet 104" are two of the most translucent, unaffected piano pieces he ever wrote, and if "Après une lecture du Dante – Fantasia quasi Sonata" looks back to the virtuosic indulgence of his youth, it does so in the spirit of re-evaluation.

 **Années de pèlerinage vols. 1–3: Berman** (Deutsche Grammophon; 3 CDs; with *Venezia e Napoli*)

These are radiant, incandescent performances of all three *Années* from one of the greatest Liszt pianists of the post-war period. Lazar Berman is the complete Lisztian, able to make what in other hands sounds merely exhibitionistic into a discursive stream of consciousness of the highest poetic quality.

 **Années de pèlerinage vols. 1–3: Jandó** (Naxos; 3 CDs)

The highlight of the Naxos survey of Liszt's piano music is the three volumes of *Années de pèlerinage* recorded by their principal house pianist, the Hungarian Jeno Jandó. These are still wonderful performances – lacking the grandiosity of Berman, certainly, but with plenty of charm and brilliance.

Operatic Transcriptions

Liszt's operatic transcriptions served a double function: on the one hand they enabled Liszt to create a fund of bravura piano music without the sweat of arduous creative thought; and on the other they assisted his colleagues by publicizing contemporary operas – before the age of the gramophone, piano transcriptions were the way most people got to hear the operas of Wagner, Berlioz, Verdi, Tchaikovsky, Bellini, Donizetti, Gounod and Meyerbeer. Sometimes Liszt made a straightforward bar-for-bar transcription, as in the works of Rossini and Wagner (whose music he felt was perfect to begin with), but of his sixty works in this genre a number are a good deal better than the originals upon which they were based. He composed an opera as a child of thirteen, and you can only regret that his interest in opera was stifled by his enthusiasm for the work of others.

 **Piano Works Volume 30: Howard** (Hyperion; 2 CDs)

As an introduction to Liszt's operatic transcriptions, there is nothing finer than Leslie Howard's two-disc survey, which includes *Faust*, *Norma*, *Don Giovanni*, *Aida*, *Eugene Onegin* and *Tristan*, to name just a few. Howard's playing is at times splashy and thumping, but he's an excellent, dramatic pianist and his complete recording of Liszt's solo piano music is one of the great recording feats of the last century.

Mephisto Waltz No. 1

The first of Liszt's three *Mephisto* waltzes – an orchestral piece transcribed for piano in 1881 – is a virtuoso's delight and one of his most popular works for piano. Lasting only ten minutes, it is full to bursting with Romantic imagery, including evocations of violins, nightingales, the play of starlight and village dances. When it first emerged, *Mephisto No. 1* caused a sensation, provoking the *Boston Gazette* into suggesting that "it has about as much propriety on a programme after Schumann and Handel as a wild boar in a drawing room".

 **Ashkenazy** (Testament; with *Feux follets* and music by Chopin, Rachmaninov & Prokofiev)

Although Vladimir Ashkenazy has never been particularly associated with Liszt's music, this blistering performance (from the 1950s) sees him adopting dangerously fast tempi which no other recorded pianist has been able to pull off. The disc also includes *Feux follets* (the fifth of the *Transcendental Studies*).

Late Piano Pieces

While his contemporaries were piling more and more notes into their scores and trying desperately to out-Wagner Wagner, Liszt pushed music to the opposite edge in his late piano works. With their raw dissonances and attentuated textures, their use of silence as a dramatic means, their denial of absolute tonality and their lack of any audible themes, these terse utterances are prophetic of the world of Schoenberg and Webern. Many of them speak of an obsession with death and repentance, as typified by the two pieces entitled *La lugubre gondola*, which were inspired by Liszt's premonition of Wagner's death two months before it occurred, in Venice in 1883. Clashing chords and ideas that offer no centre or direction suggest an emptiness and despondency that is nothing short of desolate.

Howard
(Hyperion)

Leslie Howard gives superb accounts here of thirty of Liszt's final works for piano, five of which have never been recorded before. His playing is always deeply infused with emotion, and in the four pieces associated with Wagner's death the sense of loss and desperation is movingly portrayed without any recourse to sentimentality. Brilliantly programmed, and memorable performances.

Jean-Baptiste Lully (1632–1687)

Rarely has a composer so dominated a cultural environment as Lully dominated the French court in the reign of Louis XIV. Through his friendship with the king, and some unscrupulous wheeler-dealing, he managed to achieve almost complete control of the musical life of Paris and Versailles. He was also extremely talented: he wrote sprightly and energetic dance music which, collected together as suites, exerted a strong influence on European orchestral music until the middle of the eighteenth century; and much of his more serious music, including his operas, possesses a powerful stateliness – though it can, on occasion, subside into pomposity.

Lully was born an Italian but went to France at the age of fourteen as a servant to a cousin of Louis XIV. Though an outstanding violinist, he first attracted attention as a dancer and a mime, performing alongside the young king in a court ballet in 1653. In the same year he joined the royal household as Composer of the King's Instrumental Music, and composed a number of ballets that were performed by his own orchestra, La Petite Bande – an ensemble that he moulded into one of the finest of the age. During the 1660s he produced a series of *comédies-ballets* in collaboration with the playwright Molière, the most famous of which was *Le bourgeois gentilhomme* (1670).

Lully's increasing control of French theatre music was consolidated in 1672 by his purchase of the exclusive right to produce opera, or *tragédie lyrique* as it was known in France. Lully virtually created the genre, by fusing the courtly ballet with the conventions of classical French tragedy into one enormous and lavish spectacle in which the setting, scenic effects and choreography were all as important as the music. The elaborate, often fantastical, plots – usually taken from Greek myths or from the epics of chivalry – were combined with the examination of moral issues in such a way as to pay flattering tribute to the sagacity of the king for whom they were written.

Lully's first theatre was a converted tennis court, but with Molière's death he moved, rent-free, into the theatre of the Palais Royal. For the next fifteen years he produced an opera per year, mostly to librettos by the tragedian Philippe Quinault. His unrivalled power – he even forbade music in the marionette theatre – made him many enemies. One resentful entrepreneur, Henri Guichard, allegedly tried to have him poisoned by putting arsenic into his snuff. More damaging were reports of Lully's homosexuality, which reached the ears of the king, who threatened to make an example of him.

His death was a strange mixture of grandeur and farce: while conducting his *Te Deum*, in celebration of the king's recovery from illness, he jabbed one of his toes with the stick he was using to beat time. A gangrenous abscess developed but he refused amputation, and died – an immensely wealthy man – some two months later.

L'Orchestre du Roi Soleil: Le Concert des Nations; Savall (Alia Vox)

This disc reflects the full range of Lully's non-vocal music in three suites: the *comédie-ballet Le bourgeois gentilhomme*, a collaboration with Molière; *Le divertissement royal*, written for court celebrations; and the instrumental music from the opera *Alceste*. Le Concert des Nations play every dance, march and

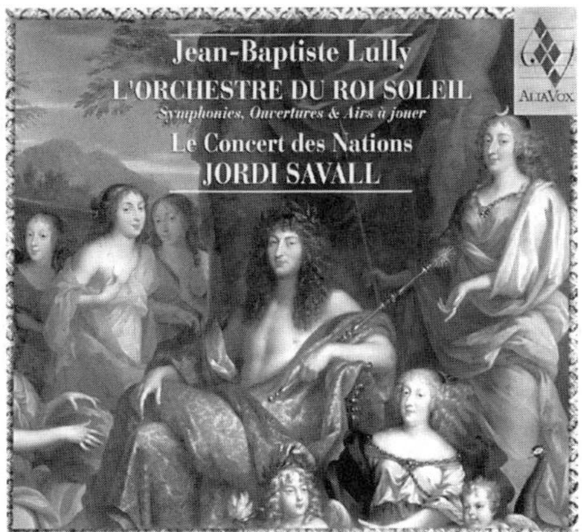

air with total conviction, perfectly judged tempi and delicate ornaments, capturing the gaiety and tragedy, as well as all the stateliness and pomp, of Lully's music.

Armide

Lully's operas are rarely staged outside France. To a modern audience, the elaborate proceedings, and much of the music, can seem cumbersome and laboured. However, they do contain some majestic moments, and none more so than *Armide*, a late work which stands as Lully's masterpiece. The libretto, by Quinault, is based on a story from *Gerusalemme Liberata*, the great chivalric poem of Renaissance Italy. Armide (Armida) is a sorceress obsessed by the Christian knight Renaud (Rinaldo), who seems impervious to her beauty. She captures and plans to kill him, but instead falls in love with him. Renaud is bewitched into loving Armide but he is rescued by two of his fellow knights and she flies away as her palace is destroyed by demons. It is a plot with a similar outline to Purcell's *Dido and Aeneas*: a noble warrior is unmanned by love until duty prevails and the joys of the flesh are abandoned. That Lully turns this into such a compelling drama is a tribute to his flexible vocal writing, which generates a powerful dramatic momentum. His recitatives are never far away from the rhythms of normal speech and even the more elaborate airs do not stop the action in the manner of an Italian operatic aria.

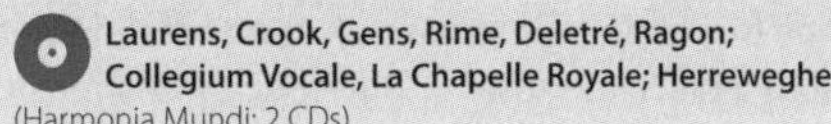

Laurens, Crook, Gens, Rime, Deletré, Ragon; Collegium Vocale, La Chapelle Royale; Herreweghe
(Harmonia Mundi; 2 CDs)

No recording of a Lully opera can reflect the totality of the proceedings, but this persuasive performance goes a long way to making the music seem dramatically feasible on its own. Guillemette Laurens is brilliant at conveying the ambivalent emotions of Armide; Howard Crook's Renaud is necessarily a rather bloodless characterization, but he has an unerringly elegant sense of the music's line.

Witold Lutosławski (1913–1994)

Lutosławski was Poland's greatest composer between Szymanowski and Penderecki, and his output exhibits a few key influences from across twentieth-century music: the angular, folk-inspired style of Bartók in his early pieces, Cage's chance techniques in his post-1960 compositions, and a French fastidiousness and delight in colour throughout.

Lutosławski matured late as a composer, and then suffered from the restrictions imposed by the post-war Communist government in Poland. He was a non-political figure, as far as that was possible for a Polish composer of the time, and forty years later he claimed – probably disingenuously – that he "never felt any pressure to write a certain way". However, his *Symphony No. 1* (1947) was banned for being "formalist", and soon after he turned to Polish folk material, producing his remarkable *Concerto for Orchestra* (1954), in which he used folk themes as "raw material to build a large musical form". One of his most popular works, the *Concerto* clearly betrays the influence of Bartók, to whose memory Lutosławski dedicated another early milestone: the often searingly intense *Funeral Music*. The latter, however, sees the emergence of a more dissonant, quasi-serialist style.

After the post-Stalin thaw, Poland became the most liberal artistic environment in the Soviet bloc, and in 1958 Lutosławski heard on radio the chance-based *Concert for Piano and Orchestra* by John Cage. The impact was great – "I suddenly realised I could compose music differently from that of my past" – and soon after Lutosławski composed *Venetian Games* for chamber orchestra, which marked the beginning of his modernist period. In this and other works, he developed a technique that has been described as "aleatory counterpoint": the melodic material is defined, but the precise coincidence of the various strands is left open. Unlike Cage, Lutosławski insisted on "a clear delineation of duties between composer and performers ... I have no wish to surrender even the smallest part of my claim to authorship of even the shortest passage".

Chance under tight compositional constraints and "experimenting within tradition" governed Lutosławski's way of working for the rest of his career. Among his key later works were his second, third and fourth symphonies, and the three orchestral pieces entitled *Chain*. In these pieces, Lutosławski's love of finely shaded orchestra colour comes to the fore, and sound in itself is often the primary element. Some listeners find this approach difficult (as the composer himself acknowledged in writing that some people "feel alien in the world of sound; their thoughts escape to a realm of images or feelings that do not exist in a piece of music"). But none of this music could be described as being impressionistic – it always shows a deep concern with form – and in *Chain*, especially, the aleatoric approach is diluted by more straightforwardly melodic elements.

Concerto for Orchestra

"I do not like this work of mine very much, but apparently it has preserved some freshness", said Lutosławski in 1973. Maybe its effects became too obvious for his refined sensibilities, but audiences and critics beg to differ – the *Concerto for Orchestra* (1950–54) is one of the few great post-war works with immediate audience appeal. The *Concerto* was, he said, "the only serious piece among the folk-inspired works" which he wrote in response to official criticism. The presence of Bartók looms large: the stamping chords of the "Intrada" immediately grab the attention, and the writing uses some bold and vivid colours. The second movement ("Capriccio notturno e Arioso") is distinctive for its atmospheric timbres while the finale is a set of variations on a passacaglia theme, followed by a chorale reminiscent of the one in Bartók's own *Concerto for Orchestra*.

BBC Philharmonic Orchestra; Tortelier
(Chandos; with *Mi-parti* & *Musique funèbre*)

This is a gripping interpretation, charged and committed from the opening chords, and aided by sound quality that has superb presence and clarity. The masterly *Mi-parti* is one of the later aleatoric works, and its shimmering, subtly shifting sonorities are ideally captured here.

Witold Lutosławski.

Chicago Symphony Orchestra; Barenboim
(Warner; with *Symphony No. 3*)

Daniel Barenboim and the Chicago Symphony provide another fine, and resonantly recorded, performance of the *Concerto*, alive to all of Lutosławski's textural nuances. This time, the coupling is an impassioned account of the third symphony.

Symphonies

Indebted to both Hindemith and Bartók, the first symphony is a fairly conventional piece full of easily recognizable tunes, but with the *Symphony No. 2* Lutosławski employed aleatory techniques to a large-scale work for the first time. It's a two-movement structure, the first preparatory to the second: the shimmering, tremulous textures and motifs of the episodic opening movement "Hésitant" are put forward tentatively then taken up in the second movement, "Direct", with firmer purpose. Within each section there is a "rhythmically elastic counterpoint", a kind of "collective ad lib" in which each musician plays, in effect, as a soloist. When the sign for the end of the section is given, the performers stop immediately. If before this time a player has played their part to the end, they repeat it from the beginning. The *Symphony No. 3* is also in two connected movements, integrated by an insistent four-note motto which dramatically opens the work – as in the "fate" motif of Beethoven's *Symphony No. 5* – and also closes it. The fourth symphony, completed in 1992, two years before his death, reintroduces a melodic aspect that Lutosławski had previously downplayed.

Symphony No. 2: Los Angeles Philharmonic; Salonen (Sony; with *Piano Concerto & Chantefleurs et chantfables*)

Symphony No. 2 receives a performance of great drive and intensity from Esa-Pekka Salonen, and the recording has excellent clarity. The *Piano Concerto*, a late work, is given persuasive advocacy by Paul Crossley, while Dawn Upshaw offers magical interpretations of Lutosławski's settings of the surrealist poetry of Robert Desnos.

Symphony No. 3: Chicago Symphony Orchestra; Barenboim (Warner; with *Concerto for Orchestra*)

Barenboim is as impressive in the third symphony as he is in the *Concerto for Orchestra*, eliciting first-rate playing from the Chicago Symphony and bringing out all of the work's drama and passion in what feels like a huge single sweep.

Chain

The three orchestral pieces known as *Chain* were composed in the mid-1980s in the wake of the third symphony and share that work's intense musical language. Constructed so that each forms a self-contained unit that nonetheless connects with the other two, like links in a chain, they incorporate fully written sections as well as episodes in which the instrumentalists are given some leeway to improvise. Of the three, the best is the second, subtitled "dialogue for violin and orchestra". The work was written for the violinist Pinchas Zuckerman but was premiered, and has been enthusiastically championed, by Anne-Sophie Mutter, who describes it as "a very expressive work, rather like a Monet painting in its colours."

Chains II & III: Mutter; BBC Symphony Orchestra; Lutosławski (Deutsche Grammophon; with *Partita & Piano Concerto*)

With her confident but subtle approach, Mutter is an ideal soloist in this performance conducted by the composer. With equally fine accounts of *Partita* (which was written for Mutter), and the *Piano Concerto* (with Krystian Zimerman), this nicely packaged DG disc would make a great place to begin exploring the composer's work.

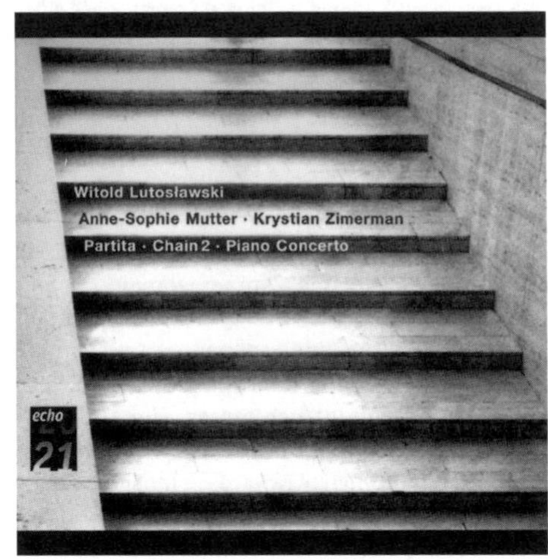

Chain II: Bakowski; Polish National Radio Symphony Orchestra; Wit (Naxos; with *Symphony No. 4, Partita for Violin and Orchestra, Funeral Music & Interlude*)

Krzysztof Bakowski's interpretation is slightly less precise than Mutter's, but his performance has plenty of emotional charge. With a selection of other key works, this budget-price CD represents excellent value for money.

String Quartet

As with the second and third symphonies, Lutosławski's only string quartet (1965) is in two movements, the first being introductory, and it is aleatory in the same way as those orchestral works. The members of the quartet play distinctly characterized short segments together, but then diverge, thus subverting the traditional conversational dynamic of the quartet medium – as with some of Elliott Carter's quartets. As the composer described it, "Each of the interpreters is to play his part as if he alone existed... When playing as a soloist ... his playing [can be] flexible, free and individual." Paradoxically, however, in different performances the overall effect is quite similar, and is characterized by the way that texture becomes more important than individual lines.

Arditti Quartet (Montaigne; with string quartets by Kurtág and Gubaidulina)

The Ardittis are the leading exponents of contemporary music for string quartet, and this recording is typically compelling. This is a taut and dramatic performance with a violent impact that is enhanced by a dry acoustic. Currently out of the catalogue but likely to return before too long.

Elisabeth Lutyens (1906–1983)

Nicknamed "twelve-tone Lizzie", Elisabeth Lutyens was one of the most radical British composers of her generation. Although music by the Viennese serialists Schoenberg and Webern was being played in London while she was a young woman, Lutyens always claimed that she had developed her twelve-note technique independently of them, and certainly she was to display a staunch self-reliance throughout her career. Her style was constantly changing and developing, and her complex but ultimately rewarding music has gone in and out of fashion, although the best of it has never received the attention it deserves.

She was born into a well-to-do artistic family: her father was the architect Edwin Lutyens and her mother, Lady Emily Lytton, became a devoted follower of Krishnamurti and theosophy. Determined from an early age to become a composer, Lutyens studied briefly at the École Normale in Paris in her late teens and then at the Royal College of Music. It took her some years to find a musical language with which she was satisfied, and she later withdrew most of her works before the ground-breaking *Chamber Concerto No. 1* (1939–40).

The early 1940s were a period of experimentation, culminating in her glorious cantata *O Saisons, O Châteaux!* (1946), to words by Rimbaud. By this time she had left her husband, the singer Ian Glennie, for Edward Clark, a former pupil of Schoenberg and a leading figure in contemporary music circles. Unfortunately Clark was also frequently unemployed, leaving Lutyens with the responsibility of providing for him and her four children, which she did by writing scores for film and radio. She became a well-known figure amongst the writers and artists who frequented the pubs of London's Fitzrovia, hanging out with such luminaries as Dylan Thomas, Louis MacNeice and Francis Bacon.

After overcoming a nervous breakdown and alcoholism at the beginning of the 1950s, Lutyens started to produce some of her most striking works. Yet compositions such as the *String Quartet No. 6* (1952), and her Wittgenstein-inspired *Excerpta tractatus-logico philosophici* (1952), were simply too advanced for the British musical establishment, and she was rarely performed. The successful first performance in 1962 of the powerful *Quincunx* for baritone, soprano and orchestra saw the beginning of a change in the reception of her music. The more adventurous musical climate of the 1960s and 1970s was more open to her uncompromising ways, and she produced a stream of important works, such as *And Suddenly It's Evening* (1966), a setting of four poems by Salvatore Quasimodo for tenor and instrumental ensemble, and *Essence of Our Happiness* (1968), which used Islamic texts and words by John Donne.

During this period, film score commissions provided Lutyens with a much-needed financial lifeline. These were almost exclusively written for low-budget horror movies made by Hammer Films and their main rivals in the 1960s, Amicus Films. There's a certain irony in the fact that a musical language regarded as difficult in the concert hall was seen as perfectly accepable in such films as *The Skull* (1965) and *Theatre of Death* (1967).

In her later years Lutyens' music became less dry and more immediately lyrical, but by the time of her death she had become almost as well-known for her caustic wit and outspoken opinions on the British musical establishment as for her music.

Quincunx

Lutyens' critical fortune, if not her financial one, improved markedly following the reception given to *Quincunx* (1960) after its premiere at the Cheltenham Festival in 1962. A quincunx is an arrangement of five objects: four forming the corners of a square, and the fifth at its centre. Though essentially a large orchestral work, at the heart of *Quincunx* is a short setting of a particularly enigmatic passage by the seventeenth-century writer Sir Thomas Browne ("... the Quincunx of Heaven runs low, and 'tis time to close the five ports of Knowledge"). A sense of mystery permeates the whole work, which is formed of five short movements for full orchestra alternating with four for different groups of instruments (woodwind, strings, percussion, brass) and one for solo baritone. The dense and slow moving tutti sections are in marked contrast to the exquisite writing of the solistic passages which have a chamber-like transparency. One of her most structurally coherent works, much of the impact of *Quincunx* derives from its beautiful – sometimes unnerving – sonoroties.

Shirley-Quirk, Nedlick; BBC Symphony Orchestra; Del Mar (Lyrita; with *And Suddenly it's Evening* and Bedford, *Music for Albion*)

Sensitively conducted by Norman Del Mar, and with outstanding engineered sound, this 1960s recording does full justice to all the poetic subtleties of what is arguably Lutyens' finest work. The song cycle for tenor and chamber orchestra, *And Suddenly It's Evening*, gets an equally powerful performance.

Chamber Music

Luytens' large-scale works are mostly absent from the CD catalogue, but there is a wealth of dramatic and expressive music to be found among the chamber works that have been recorded. One of the earliest pieces she was later prepared to acknowledge was her *Chamber Concerto No. 1*, the first of six chamber concertos composed during the 1940s. Its bare textures and serial language must have seemed unrelentingly austere to its first audience in 1943. By 1957, when she wrote *6 Tempi for 10 Instruments*, Lutyens was experimenting with different ways of using rhythm: this work, admired by Stravinsky, comprises six short movements which are all of the same duration but use that time in very different ways.

Chamber Concerto No. 1; 6 Tempi for 10 Instruments; Triolet I and Triolet II: Jane's Minstrels; Manning (NMC; with *The Valley of Hatsu-Se*, etc)

All credit to NMC for issuing the only currently available CD to consist entirely of music by Lutyens. It presents a wide-ranging selection of her chamber music in excellent and incisive performances.

Other Vocal Music

O Saisons, O Châteaux!, a setting of Rimbaud's short poem for soprano and string orchestra, guitar, mandolin and harp, is one of Lutyens' better-known works. First performed in 1947, it is an immediately appealing piece with the soprano soaring over an accompanying ensemble that Lutyens described as being like "an enlarged amplified guitar".

Much of Lutyens' work in the 1960s was vocal, and her music from this decade includes *The Valley of Hatsu-Se* (1965), settings of eight ancient Japanese poems for soprano, flute, clarinet, cello and piano, and *Lament of Isis on the Death of Osiris* (1969), which was extracted from Lutyens' unsuccessful opera *Isis and Osiris*. Using writings by Plutarch and from the Egyptian Book of the Dead, the *Lament* makes strenuous use of the soprano soloist's full emotional and technical range. Her later, more lyrical writing can be heard in two works dating from 1971: *Requiescat* for soprano and string trio, and *Driving out the Death* for oboe, violin, viola and cello. Brief yet deeply moving, *Requiescat* was commissioned by the music magazine *Tempo* in memory of Stravinsky and uses as its text a passage from *The Couch of Death* by William Blake. *Driving out the Death*, probably the most frequently performed of all Lutyens' work, was inspired by ancient rituals marking the changing seasons; in six sections, it opens with an oboe call, and the expressive voice of this instrument dominates the whole work.

O Saisons, O Châteaux!: Cahill; Brunel Ensemble; Austin (Signum; with *Six Bagatelles* and works by McCabe, Saxton and Williamson)

Soprano Teresa Cahill is utterly convincing on this recording of *O Saisons, O Châteaux!*, her strong tones ringing out over the rich string colour. On the same disc the Brunel Ensemble give a well-judged account of the complex *Six Bagatelles*, a work of which they gave the first performance in 1996, twenty years after it was written.

The Valley of Hatsu-Se; Lament of Isis on the Death of Osiris; Requiescat: Jane's Minstrels; Manning (NMC; with *Chamber Concerto No. 1*, *6 Tempi for 10 Instruments*, *Triolet I & Triolet II*)

Jane Manning, for whom both *The Valley of Hatsu-Se* and *Lament of Isis on the Death of Osiris* were written, gives finely characterized and expressive readings of the vocal works on this disc, which would be the obvious starting point for anyone wanting to explore Lutyens' music.

Guillaume de Machaut (c.1300–1377)

Round about the year 1320 the French composer and theoretician Philippe de Vitry wrote a treatise entitled *Ars Nova* (New Art) in which he claimed that the recent technical innovations in music amounted to a major break with the music of the immediate past. Musicologists later employed the term Ars Nova for the developments that took place in French and Italian music in the fourteenth century, designating the previous period – the period of early polyphony (c. 900–1250) – Ars Antiqua.

Guillaume de Machaut was the outstanding Ars Nova composer, exploiting new musical techniques that make much of his work sound startlingly modern. One of the most significant innovations was that of isorhythm, whereby a fixed rhythm was applied to the cantus firmus, the borrowed melody that often underpinned a new composition. This fixed rhythm might have a different number of notes from the main melody, so that each time it was repeated it would begin at a different point along that melody – a numerical system of composing that has led to Machaut being bracketed with Schoenberg as an essentially intellectual composer. In addition, Machaut also employed musical forms that were in decline, and many of his most moving songs are monophonic.

Machaut was almost certainly born in Rheims, a city where he spent most of his later years. Around 1323 he joined the household of John of Luxembourg, the king of Bohemia, serving as his secretary on many military and diplomatic expeditions. When King John died at the Battle of Crécy in 1346, Machaut went on to serve a succession of aristocratic patrons including the king's daughter Bonne, King Charles the Bad of Navarre, the king of Cyprus and the dukes John of Berry and Amadeus of Savoy. As a priest much of his income came from a number of largely honorary positions awarded him by various churches throughout France.

Machaut's fame during his lifetime was gained as much by his skills as a poet as by his musicianship, and he was admired as such by his great English contemporary Geoffrey Chaucer. In his later years, he fell in love with a woman much younger than himself and he tells their story – the source of much biographical detail – in a long poem, *Le Voir Dit* (The Tale of Truth). "All my works", wrote Machaut to his beloved, "were made from your feelings, and are for you especially."

Songs

Machaut exemplifies the poetic and courtly conventions of his day. Despite his income from the

Church, nearly all of his compositions are secular songs about love, the courtly, spiritual love of the Middle Ages which requires the love object to be an unattainable woman of unrivalled beauty. Her devoted admirer pays extravagant tribute to her, and swears undying devotion, even though she is the cause of as much pain as pleasure. Machaut's language is in the tradition of the troubadours of southern France, poet-musicians who performed their work at the chateaux of the nobility (see below). One of his favoured song forms is the *virelais*, in which a refrain alternates with three stanzas, and these compositions have all the simple directness of folk song. His polyphonic songs, on the other hand, are more adventurous and possess greater rhythmic variety, often using a form of syncopation called the hocket (from the Latin for "hiccup"), which breaks up the line of

Troubadours and Trouvères

The troubadour, the poet-musician of thirteenth and early fourteenth-century southern France, is often thought of as a lovesick, lute-carrying minstrel wandering from one chateau to the next – a stereotype that tells only part of the story. In fact, the troubadours were a diverse collection of men, and some women, from all social levels (the first troubadour was the Duke of Aquitaine) who developed a sophisticated, pleasure-loving court culture, in which poetry and music were the primary source of entertainment.

The emergence of the troubadours marks the initial rise of non-religious artistic activity in Europe. Instead of Latin, they wrote in *langue d'oc*, the colloquial dialect of southern France, and their poems focus on secular subjects. Occasionally they wrote political satire or on moral issues, but mostly they stuck to their overriding cultural preoccupation – the idea of courtly love, *fin'amors*. In troubadour society, ladies were treated as examples of divine perfection, and the complete surrender to love's power was thought of as life's most important goal. Troubadour music consisted of expressive single-line song settings of their poems which may have been sung unaccompanied, though there is evidence that instruments sometimes accompanied the tunes.

We know of 450 troubadours – 42 of whom were also composers – who over 200 years wrote roughly 2600 poems and 175 melodies. Their influence was immense, and though their culture was forced into decline by the Albigensian Crusades in around 1220, their achievements were carried forward across Europe. The use of the vernacular spread widely as did the fascination with courtly love (as displayed in Machaut's songs).

The culture that most directly grew out of the troubadours was that of the trouvères of northern France, who composed more than 2000 songs. Though they wrote in a different dialect (*langue d'oil*), trouvère music and poetry often involved imitation, parody or reinvention of troubadour material. One of the most famous trouvères is Blondel de Nesle, who according to legend was responsible for saving his master, Richard the Lionheart, who was imprisoned in a secret location in Austria in 1191. The story goes that Blondel wandered from castle to castle singing a song that only he and the king knew. Eventually, Richard answered by singing the second verse from inside his prison, and Blondel was then able to tell the English where Richard was held captive.

As with most medieval music, it is very difficult to know exactly how the songs of the troubadours and trouvères were actually performed, and reconstructions of the music vary wildly. Very little troubadour music was written down at all until the trouvères undertook the task: few sources indicate rhythmic notation and none specify how or when instruments were used.

Troubadours and Minnesänger "En chantan m'aven a membrar": Ensemble Lucidarium; Gosfield & Biggi (L'empreinte digitale)

This collection from Ensemble Lucidarium includes songs by the troubadours, the trouvères and the minnesänger (who developed the lyric tradition in Germany). The performances are vivacious and improvisatory, and feature diverse and rich instrumental work.

The Spirits of England and France – 2: Gothic Voices; Page (Hyperion)

Focusing specifically on the works of the trouvères, this outstanding disc ranges from contemplative *grands chants* (the most popular trouvère form) to more rhythmic genres such as the *pastourelle*. The solo singing is exquisite and the instrumental work, where present, is subtle and sensitive. It's currently out of the catalogue but Hyperion are likely to reissue it soon.

a melody in one voice by inserting sudden gaps which are then filled by the other voices, thus creating a gentle undulating quality.

The Mirror of Narcissus – Songs of Guillaume de Machaut: Kirkby, Philpot, Covey-Crump; Gothic Voices; Page (Hyperion)

Gothic Voices perform these three- and four-part songs unaccompanied, which shows off their complexity and energy in a more immediate way. This is especially true of the one sacred work on the disc, the motet *Inviolata genitrix*, where it really does sound, at moments, as if three people are singing completely different songs simultaneously.

Messe de Notre Dame

Machaut's most important work for the Church was the four-part *Messe de Notre Dame*, the first polyphonic setting of the Ordinary of the Mass which shows some kind of stylistic unity between the sections. The Ordinary of the Mass is those parts of it which are constant – i.e. the Kyrie, Gloria, Credo, Sanctus and Agnus Dei – as opposed to those sections whose texts vary according to the occasion, and which are called the Proper of the Mass. Austerity is the chief characteristic of the *Messe de Notre Dame*, in which the general simplicity of the word-setting places the few dramatic moments in particularly sharp relief.

The Hilliard Ensemble; Hillier (Hyperion; with *Le Lai de la fonteinne & Ma fin est mon commencement*)

The Hilliard Ensemble's approach to this music is to avoid the obviously expressive and to concentrate on making the music's constant rhythmic ebb and flow sound coherent. The result is an air of extraordinary devotional intensity.

Oxford Camerata; Summerly (Naxos; with songs from *Le Voir Dit*)

With one singer per part and slower tempi, the Oxford Camerata lack some of the rhythmic dynamism of the Hilliards but make up for it with melodic clarity and meditative atmosphere, aided by the spacious acoustic of Rheims cathedral (for which the *Messe* was probably originally composed).

James MacMillan (1959–)

James MacMillan is one of that rare breed of contemporary composers whose works readily find an audience. In 1993 the Edinburgh Festival featured no fewer than eighteen of his compositions, and in 1997 the South Bank Centre in London put on a retrospective tribute called *Raising Sparks*, after a work written by MacMillan that year. Although it is impossible to separate his music from his socialism, his Catholicism and, not least, his Scottish patriotism, his work is far from didactic, its appeal far from parochial. In the five years after its 1992 BBC Proms premiere, his percussion concerto *Veni, Veni, Emmanuel* received more than 100 performances around the world, and his 1996 *Cello Concerto* was first performed by no less illustrious an advocate than Mstislav Rostropovich. His work is often linked with that of other deeply religious modern composers, notably Arvo Pärt and John Tavener, but his music is more raw and turbulent than that implies. As MacMillan himself has remarked of his kinship with Tavener: "Tavener has always said that for him the most important image is that of the Risen Christ. For me, it's Christ Crucified. It shows in our music: in Tavener's, it's as if Heaven is already attained. In mine, it's still to be fought for."

For polemical as well as practical purposes, MacMillan has often stood against "the old guard of the avant-garde" who "are deeply suspicious of any significant move towards tonality, any hint of pulse that is actually discernible, and any music which communicates successfully with a non-specialist audience". Nevertheless his early music grew from an engagement with Polish modernism, and with the then avant-garde Peter Maxwell Davies, and more recently he might be said to have reached a rapprochement with some of the ideas of Harrison Birtwistle, as well as the distinctly Russian styles of Sofia Gubaidulina and Galina Ustvolskaya.

Yet everything that MacMillan does aims at direct emotional and dramatic communication, an enterprise in which Scottish traditional music is an important source of inspiration. His largest work to date is the opera *Inés de Castro* (1996), a work which divided the critics more deeply than most. One described it as "pornography" because it "tempts us with the thrill of transgression without the slightest challenge to our values or experience". Others applauded its vision of a woman who pays the highest price for allowing love to intrude on realpolitik. Significantly, the opera was well received by audiences, no doubt grateful for a work that, in the tradition of Verdi and Mussorgsky, engaged heart and mind in its musical drama. In that sense it could be said to be a companion piece to the purely orchestral *The Confession of Isobel Gowdie* (1990), the Proms debut of which marked a turning point in MacMillan's professional life.

Recent new works include *Symphony No. 3 "Silence"* (2003) inspired by Shusaku Endo's novel *Silence* about a massacre of Christians in seventeenth-century Japan, and *A Scotch Bestiary* which inaugurated the organ at Frank Gehry's Disney Hall in Los Angeles. MacMillan's latest opera, *The Sacrifice*, based on a story from the medieval Welsh epic the *Mabinogion*, was premiered by Welsh National Opera in 2007.

The Confession of Isobel Gowdie

It's not difficult to see why this large orchestral work became such a firm favourite in the wake of its ecstatic reception at its premiere. With its references to the Scottish ballad tradition and to Gregorian chant, not to mention its occasional echoes of Stravinsky, Messiaen, Berg, Vaughan Williams and Purcell, this is a composition in which resonant textures and violent dynamics achieve a transformative immediacy, the effect of which more than one critic has likened to listening to a Mahler symphony. The title refers to a Scottish woman who, in 1662, was tortured into confessing herself a witch, an incident that serves as a metaphor for MacMillan's "fears about the new rise of fascism" in Europe.

BBC Philharmonic Orchestra; MacMillan
(Chandos; with *Symphony No. 3*)

Isobel Gowdie has become something of a contemporary classic, with three recordings in ten years. This one, conducted by the composer, is certainly the most gut-wrenchingly powerful, with the BBC Phil really piling into its most violent passages. It's coupled with the Japanese-inflected *Symphony No. 3*.

BBC Scottish Symphony Orchestra; Maksymiuk
(Universal Koch Schwann; with *Tryst*)

Jerzy Maksymiuk premiered *Isobel Gowdie*, and his recording sensitively moulds every phrase of MacMillan's slow-moving lament, handling the abrupt and shocking change of gear in the work's *Rite of Spring*-like middle section with easy virtuosity. *Tryst* is another single-movement work of great power, its melody deriving from a MacMillan setting of the poem "The Tryst".

Veni, Veni, Emmanuel

In a series of works written in the 1990s, MacMillan harnessed the implicit drama of concerto form in a way that considerably enriches his musical vocabulary. This is nowhere more apparent than in the one-movement percussion concerto *Veni, Veni, Emmanuel*, which fully exploits the vast battery of instruments available to the modern percussionist. The musical material, drawn from fifteenth-century French Advent plainchant, represents, the composer says, "a musical exploration of the theology behind the Advent message", and what is most striking about the work is its balance of exuberance and contemplative calm. MacMillan makes the utmost demands of his soloist, who is rewarded with not only a showpiece but a work of immense communicative force. Evelyn Glennie premiered *Veni, Veni, Emmanuel* at the 1992 BBC Proms, a performance that repeated the earlier Proms impact of *Isobel Gowdie*.

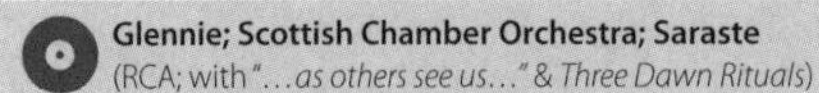

Glennie; Scottish Chamber Orchestra; Saraste
(RCA; with *"…as others see us…"* & *Three Dawn Rituals*)

Evelyn Glennie (a compatriot of MacMillan) is a tireless champion of new music for percussion, but few of the pieces she has ushered into the world have the integrity and power of *Veni, Veni, Emmanuel*, which she performs here with a commanding authority.

Currie; Ulster Orchestra; Yuasa
(Naxos; with *Tryst*)

Percussionist Colin Currie, another Scot, has built up a strong relationship with this concerto and here gives a tremendous and wonderfully supported performance full of élan. This warm and lively recording at budget price is highly recommendable.

Triduum

MacMillan's orchestral triptych *Triduum* incorporates *The World's Ransoming* (1995–96), the *Concerto for Cello and Orchestra* (1996) and the *Symphony "Vigil"* (1997) – three interconnected pieces that relate to the events and liturgies of Maundy Thursday, Good Friday and the Easter Vigil. The first panel of the triptych, *The World's Ransoming*, concentrates on Maundy Thursday and features a plangent cor anglais whose lament is ornamented in a manner that recalls Scottish traditional bagpipe music. During the course of this single-movement work a Bach chorale (*Ach wie nichtig*) is quoted on two occasions, each time forming one layer of a multi-layered texture. The *Concerto for Cello and Orchestra* includes music originally from *Inés de Castro*, the most substantial borrowing being the music of the "Executioner's Song", which appears in the first of the concerto's three movements, where its sardonic tone and vulgar rhythms evoke Christ's mockers. The *Symphony "Vigil"*, a potent musical journey from darkness to light, from divided lower strings at its opening to high violin harmonics at the work's close, was MacMillan's first symphony.

The World's Ransoming; Concerto for Cello and Orchestra: Pendrill, Wallfisch; BBC Scottish Symphony Orchestra; Vänskä (BIS)

The splendid performances of the first two panels of MacMillan's orchestral triptych feature as soloists Christine Pendrill, who performed the concertante part in *The World's Ransoming* at the work's premiere, and Raphael Wallfisch, for whom MacMillan wrote his first cello sonata in 1999.

Symphony "Vigil": Fine Arts Brass Ensemble; BBC Scottish Symphony Orchestra; Vänskä (BIS)

Osmo Vänskä's reading of the *Symphony "Vigil"* is no less powerful, with the recorded sound exceptionally clear and alive and the music consistently well paced.

Elizabeth Maconchy (1907–1994)

Elizabeth Maconchy described her work as "an impassioned argument", and indeed her compositions are characterized by the combination of heartfelt lyricism and clear logical structures. Her vigorous music, which remained rooted in tonality except for an experiment with twelve-note techniques during the 1940s, is among the most dynamic to have been produced in twentieth-century Britain, and deserves to be far more widely heard than it is at present.

Maconchy spent most of her childhood in the countryside of England and Ireland, with little exposure to any music other than what she played on the piano or made up for herself. At sixteen she went to the Royal College of Music in London, where she studied with Ralph Vaughan Williams and explored new music by composers like Bartók, while developing her own highly personal musical language. She first sprang to public attention at the age of 23 when her powerful orchestral work *The Land*, based on a poem by Vita Sackville-West, was premiered at the Proms in August 1930, to enthusiastic reviews.

In 1932 Maconchy developed tuberculosis, the disease which had killed her father ten years previously. She cured herself by moving out of London and living in a shed at the bottom of the garden of her house in Kent. In spite of this enforced isolation, her music continued to be performed all over Europe throughout the 1930s, although some British critics found the modernity and intellectual power of her music hard to accept in a woman. Having married in 1930, Maconchy had two daughters in 1939 and 1947 (the younger of whom is the composer Nicola LeFanu), and had to spend much of her time looking after her family. Nonetheless, in the face of resistance from the male-dominated establishment, she continued to develop her musical voice, composing a powerful collection of works in many different genres, from chamber music to opera. An increasing volume of commissions from performers, institutions and festivals came her way in the 1970s and 1980s, but her innovative edge was not blunted by her increasing success. In 1987 her contribution to British music was fully recognized when she was made a Dame of the British Empire.

Orchestral Music

The success of *The Land* was followed by various smaller works for orchestra, including the prizewinning overture *Proud Thames* and the highly contrapuntal *Symphony for Double String Orchestra* – both from 1953. The string orchestra was to remain a favoured medium, as is shown by later works such as the expansive *Music for Strings*, first performed at the Proms in 1983. Maconchy's two works for clarinet and orchestra show clearly the changes in her style over the years. The *Concertino No. 1* (1945) is a richly ominous work in three movements with exciting, driving rhythms and dramatic brooding passages. *Concertino No. 2* (1984) is a shorter, more exposed work, in which the clarinet is accompanied by an orchestra which includes wind, brass and timpani creating an enthralling sound-world where stark harmonies and textures are reconciled with lyrical warmth.

Proud Thames; Symphony for Double String Orchestra; Music for Strings: London Philharmonic Orchestra; London Symphony Orchestra; Handley; Wordsworth (Lyrita; with *Serenata Concertante for Violin and Orchestra*)

A welcome release of Maconchy's main orchestral works, all lovingly conducted by Vernon Handley, except the *Music for Strings* which has Barry Wordsworth at the helm. These works, more than others, reveal the pull between the composer's flair for counterpoint and her innate Romanticism.

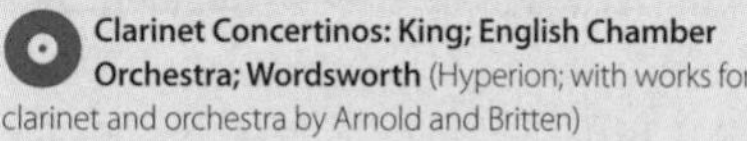
Clarinet Concertinos: King; English Chamber Orchestra; Wordsworth (Hyperion; with works for clarinet and orchestra by Arnold and Britten)

This recording of the *Clarinet Concertinos* is one of the few to contain any of Maconchy's orchestral writing. Clarinettist Thea King, who has recorded many little-known works by British composers, gives gloriously persuasive performances with sensitive accompaniment from the English Chamber Orchestra.

String Quartets

Maconchy wrote string quartets throughout her life, and her thirteen works in the genre make up a sequence as rewarding as those by Bartók or Shostakovich. The string quartet was the perfect medium for her closely argued musical language, clearly demonstrating her fascination with melodic and rhythmic counterpoint.

Maconchy described her *Quartet No. 1*, written when she was 25, as "extrovert, direct and rhythmical"; its high-spirited energy is apparent from the characteristic driving rhythms of the opening bars. The dramatic and darkly brooding *Quartet No. 4*, written during World War II, demonstrates her technique of building the material of a work from one cell, in this instance an idea first heard in the opening cello pizzicato. The prizewinning *Quartet No. 5* – her own favourite – contains an achingly beautiful slow movement, while *Quartet No. 8* (1966) is the most dissonant. *Quartet No. 9*, with its deeply moving, elegiac slow movement, was written in August 1968 at the time of the Soviet occupation of Prague.

The viola was Maconchy's favourite instrument and this can be clearly seen by its central role in the two single-movement quartets of the 1970s, *Quartet No. 10* and *Quartet No. 11*, both characteristic of Maconchy's later, more condensed style. The latter she described as like "a piece of woven material, with contrasting colours and patterns running through it".

Complete String Quartets: Hanson, Bingham & Mistry Quartets (Regis; 3 CDs)

Recorded by three different quartets and released by Unicorn Kanchana in the 1980s, this outstanding set of Maconchy's complete quartets has recently been licensed to Regis and is now available at budget price. The discs also contain interesting sleeve notes written by Maconchy herself.

Gustav Mahler (1860–1911)

Until little more than forty years ago, Mahler's heady, epic compositions were regarded with a degree of suspicion similar to that which still dogs many of his contemporaries, such as Zemlinsky and Schreker. In his own time he was known far more for his conducting than for his music and it took many decades of proselytizing by conductors such as Bruno Walter, Wilhelm Mengelberg and, later, Leonard Bernstein before the symphonies became the audience-pullers they are today – though there were always pockets of support, notably in the Netherlands and New York, both places where Mahler frequently conducted. That the symphonies finally caught on in a big way after World War II is doubtless due to an affinity between their unstable, angst-ridden content and the complex world of the late twentieth century.

Sigmund Freud, to whom Mahler turned for analysis in later life, found the roots of the composer's neuroticism in his childhood, which was spent in a somewhat tense family atmosphere. One memorable event occurred when the young Gustav rushed out into the street to escape a particularly heated parental argument, to be confronted with the playing of a military band (they lived next to a barracks) – an incident often seen as prophetic of Mahler's later juxtaposition of widely contrasting moods in his music. In a Mahler symphony one passes from the tragic to the commonplace, from the ingenuous to the ironic, from rustic folk song to spiritual ecstasy, in the space of a moment.

Mahler was born into a Jewish-Bohemian family at a time when official attitudes to Jews in the Austro-Hungarian Empire were relaxing after years of residence restrictions. Thus he was able to benefit from a decent education in Prague and later at the Vienna Conservatory, where his fellow pupils included Hugo Wolf (see p.635) and Hans Rott. A recently rediscovered symphony by Rott (available on Hyperion) gives an intriguing insight into Mahler's early work: it predates Mahler's own symphonies yet prefigures many of their musical themes, suggesting that Rott, who died insane at the age of 26, was a significant influence. Among the many other influences on Mahler in Vienna was the music of Bruckner who, though only beginning to receive the recognition he deserved, was idolized by Mahler and his fellow students.

Gustav Mahler photographed in about 1900.

Just as he was beginning to find his voice as a composer in the dramatic cantata *Das klagende Lied* (1880) and other early songs, Mahler discovered his talents as a conductor and soon won renown for his performances of the operas of Mozart, Beethoven and Wagner. By 1888 he was chief conductor at the Budapest Opera and within a few years was in charge at the more prestigious house in Hamburg, where his thoroughly prepared performances – at a time when rehearsal was often seen as an encumbrance – gained him more plaudits. It was also during this period that

The Cult of the Conductor

Although the birth of the modern conductor can be dated from 1820, when Louis Spohr became the first musician to use a baton while directing an orchestral performance, the cult of the conductor as demigod began with (and has never really recovered from) the athletic, exaggerated eccentricities of Beethoven. His bizarre approach to the performance of his own music, while generally thought mad by most of those fortunate enough to see him on the podium, nonetheless set the tone for much of what was to follow, since the cult of the conductor has thrived for the most part off the appearance of things.

It is easy to forget that conductors between the 1820s and 1880s served a largely metrical purpose. The general standard of orchestral performance was so poor that a conductor was necessary, primarily, to ensure that everyone remained together; but when Wagner set about training his own orchestras he became the first conductor to concentrate on the expressive potential of the conductor's art, and his impact on the appearance as well as the practice of conducting was almost as great as Beethoven's. While Beethoven and Wagner were composers who achieved fame as conductors of their own music, but little else, the most celebrated of Wagner's peers (Louis Antoine Jullien, Hans von Bülow and Hans Richter) were professional conductors – re-creative, rather than creative musicians. Jullien knew what the public expected of such people, and would conduct Beethoven wearing a fresh pair of white kid gloves, with a jewel-encrusted baton that he had brought to his podium on a silver salver.

By the end of the nineteenth century, when Bülow's Meiningen Court Orchestra could play perfectly well without him, the standard in performance became so high that time beating was made redundant. The conductor could, therefore, concentrate on the expressive and theatrical qualities of performance to the exclusion of almost every other factor. Conductors who had once felt compelled to "bring in" a section of instruments were (and still are) seen to be wasting their time, since modern players have the same music as the conductor before them, and can count just as well. Consequently, Gustav Mahler was revered for his embodiment of the epic potential of symphonic and operatic performance. His status as a philosopher-conductor – as a musician capable of bringing something to a work of music not enshrined in its score – raised the art to a point just short of perfection. Orchestra members were torn between reverence and fear, but for all that Mahler achieved in performance, he nonetheless paved the way for an unstoppable wave of charlatanism.

The success of Stokowski and Koussevitsky (who was rumoured to conduct his scores from the double-bass part, having never learned to read the treble clef) emphasized the air of high camp that characterized a great many of the twentieth century's most famous conductors. Others, such as Otto Klemperer, would play up their gravitas to the point of high theatre (he would pretend to fall asleep during rehearsals), while the deeply philosophical Furtwängler employed a technique so random that he was known by the LPO as "the demented rag doll." The leader of the Berlin Philharmonic during the 1950s was asked how the orchestra knew when to come in when Furtwängler was conducting. "Oh, that's easy" replied the violinist. "We close our eyes and hope for the best."

With the notable exception of Sir Thomas Beecham, the greatest conductors of the past have always endeavoured to appear as autocratic, severe and humourless as the European dictators to whom they are best compared. Indeed, it was more than a little ironic that the most sanctimoniously anti-fascist conductor of the twentieth century, Arturo Toscanini, should himself have been hysterically dictatorial on and off the podium. It is fair to say, however, that not everyone managed to preserve this carefully nourished air of austerity. The Swiss conductor Ernst Ansermet, for example, employed an idiosyncratic pidgin English that would frequently reduce British orchestras to tears of laughter. On one now famous occasion he lost his temper with the players of the BBC Symphony Orchestra and yelled: "You think I know fuck nothing, but you are wrong, I know fuck all!"

he established the pattern of composing that would last until his death: with concert and opera seasons taking up most of the year from autumn to spring, he had to confine his writing to the summer months, usually retiring to the idyllic surroundings of the Carinthian lakes in southern Austria. To Mahler, it was a life of great continuity, for he saw little distinction between bringing masterpieces to life in the concert hall and opera house, and expressing his innermost thoughts in his own music. Refusing to separate life from art, Mahler embodied the apotheosis of Romanticism.

As Mahler became disenchanted with musical life in Hamburg he set his sights on Vienna and went to the lengths of converting to Roman Catholicism to make himself acceptable to the anti-Semitic Viennese court that ran the opera house. He was duly appointed principal conductor at the Vienna State Opera in 1897 and survived ten acrimonious years at the head of one of Europe's top musical establishments, where he raised musical and dramatic standards to unforeseen heights, but at the expense of never-ending battles with orchestral players, singers and critics. (The top job at Vienna is still one of the toughest posts in the music world.) Mahler rarely conducted his own music in Vienna, not wanting to be seen taking advantage of his position, but toured widely through northern Europe with his symphonies and song cycles.

In 1907 he resigned from his Viennese post and accepted the offer of a contract at the Metropolitan Opera in New York, but ended up becoming more involved in the regeneration of the New York Philharmonic. At the same time a serious heart disease began to manifest itself, a bacterial infestation brought on by the throat infections that had plagued him throughout his life. His last compositions, the ninth and tenth symphonies and the song cycle *Das Lied von der Erde*, are overwhelmingly imbued with premonitions of his death, which finally occurred on 18 May, 1911, after a fruitless visit to a bacteriologist in Paris on the way back from his final American trip.

SYMPHONIES

"The symphony is a world", proclaimed Mahler to Sibelius, and indeed few if any composers have crammed so much into their symphonies, from funeral marches to vast images of nature, from ironically quoted popular tunes and dances to great apostrophes to love. These are not purely abstract works in the tradition of Brahms and Bruckner: all have strong extra-musical elements, incorporating poems or religious texts, or possessing an ambitious philosophical "programme". On the other hand, these programmes are not the detailed paraphrases that you'll find in the symphonic poems of Berlioz or Strauss, and it's not necessary to know the "meaning" of the piece before listening to it – Mahler himself regarded his explanatory subtitles as mere crutches, and often deleted them from his revisions. Most of the symphonies describe a dramatic progression of some sort, and accordingly demonstrate "progressive tonality", where the symphony ends in a different key from that in which it began.

The first four were influenced by the folk-like verses of *Des Knaben Wunderhorn* and his own settings of them, and three of them incorporate solo singers and/or choirs. There followed three purely instrumental works of enormous power and range, but he returned to the vocal symphony with *Symphony No. 8* – in terms of number of performers required, his most massive work. After that came the incomparable, valedictory *No. 9* and an attempt at completing a tenth (since reworked into a performable version). Of the ten, the first and fifth are probably the best places to start.

Symphonies Nos. 1–9; Adagio of Symphony No. 10: Bavarian Radio Symphony Orchestra; Kubelík
(Deutsche Grammophon; 10 CDs)

Inevitably in a body of work with such a range of challenges it would be a miracle if a single conductor were to produce the ideal performance of each and every symphony, but the most consistently satisfying attempt is Rafael Kubelík's. Though none of the symphonies merits an outright first choice individually, this is a low-cost way of getting hold of the lot in consistently excellent performances.

Symphony No. 1

Mahler's *Symphony No. 1* (1885–88) began life as a symphonic poem, and a vestige of this early draft survives in the subtitle that is occasionally attached to it, "Titan", and in the appearance on some recordings of a subsequently discarded movement entitled "Blumine". The flower imagery of this movement provided an interlude in the rather confused narrative of the original, which was based on a novel by Jean-Paul, in which the hero figure's contemplation of nature leads to a fatal self-absorption. Suggestions of this extra-musical programme remain in the work's evocative, primordial opening, the slow movement's funeral march (based upon "Frère Jacques") and the presence of song tunes from Mahler's own *Lieder eines fahrenden Gesellen* (see p.322). It is remarkably original for a first symphony and its direct influences are hard to define, beyond a melodiousness recalling Schubert and a sense of scale derived from Bruckner.

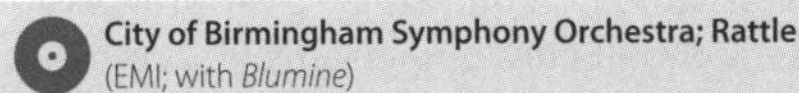

City of Birmingham Symphony Orchestra; Rattle (EMI; with *Blumine*)

Simon Rattle's live recording best captures the music's scale, with the twilight opening played at an extreme pianissimo and evolving into a most magical evocation of awakening nature. The rustic Scherzo has a real Austrian rumbustiousness, with the horns playing at full tilt, while the sense of irony in the funeral march is never far from the surface, and the climax of the finale is truly breathtaking.

Bavarian Radio Symphony Orchestra; Kubelík (Deutsche Grammophon; with *Lieder eines fahrenden Gesellen*)

Rafael Kubelík's account is somewhat undercharged when compared to that of Rattle, but it's an approach that is utterly convincing, emphasizing the work's delicacy and poetry. Speeds tend towards the brisk, but the lightness of Kubelík's touch and his complete control of the orchestra mean that an idiomatic lilt is always guaranteed.

Symphony No. 2 – The Resurrection

The first movement of the *Symphony No. 2* (1888–94) also began life as a symphonic poem, *Totenfeier*, or "Funeral Rites", in which Mahler claimed to show the "hero" of his first symphony being "borne to his grave". He later reworked this as the first movement of a symphony broadly expressing the concept of the life force's ability to rise again from the ashes of fate through faith in God – hence the symphony's subtitle.

The first three movements are purely instrumental, the self-explanatory funeral march being followed by two interludes looking back on the happy and bitter times of life; in the fourth movement, the "hero" hears the call of God in an evocative alto solo, "Urlicht" (Primeval Light); and in the finale he has to face the Day of Judgement before being granted immortality. Such a grand theme called for grand treatment and Mahler uses a vast orchestra (including ten horns and eight trumpets), together with two solo singers and a choir, in a work that lasts some ninety minutes.

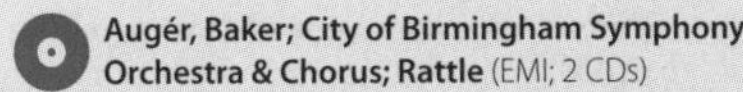

Augér, Baker; City of Birmingham Symphony Orchestra & Chorus; Rattle (EMI; 2 CDs)

Simon Rattle is again the first recommendation here. He shapes phrases with attention paid to every nuance of the score, while the grand sweep remains paramount; his performers play and sing magnificently and the recording is often overwhelming.

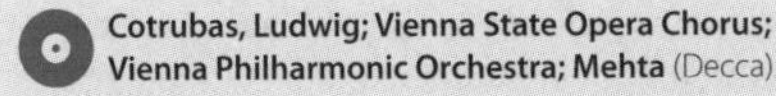

Cotrubas, Ludwig; Vienna State Opera Chorus; Vienna Philharmonic Orchestra; Mehta (Decca)

Zubin Mehta has made some marvellous recordings and this is among the best of them. The Vienna Philharmonic Orchestra plays with an incandescent fervour, but what impresses the most is Mehta's control of the overall shape of the symphony, which ensures that by the time you reach the finale there is an extraordinary sense of culmination and resolution.

Symphony No. 3

Whereas *Symphony No. 2* is a hymn to humanity's salvation through spirituality, *Symphony No. 3* (1895–96) is a hymn to the natural world. Conceived as a seven-movement paean entitled *The Joyful Knowledge* or *A Summer Morning's Dream*, it originally bore movement headings such as "Summer Marches In", "What the Meadow Flowers Tell Me" and "What Love Tells Me", and ended in a child's view of heaven. In the event, Mahler turned this last movement into the finale of *Symphony No. 4* and, as with *No. 1*, he suppressed the somewhat twee details of the programme.

Although written for a slightly smaller orchestra than *No. 2*, the third symphony uses extravagant vocal forces (soprano, boys' chorus, women's chorus) for two brief movements. This was to be Mahler's broadest work in terms of scale, with a vast first movement suggesting the awakening of primeval life from the depths of winter, four contrasting middle movements (one a setting of Nietzsche's "Midnight Song", another of a naive *Wunderhorn* poem), and an extended, slow-building Adagio finale culminating in an apotheosis in which, in Mahler's words, "Nature in its totality may ring and resound".

Procter; London Symphony Orchestra; Wandsworth School Boys' Choir; Ambrosian Singers; Horenstein (Unicorn-Kanchana; 2 CDs)

For the best recording of this symphony you have to go back to Jascha Horenstein's classic recording with the LSO in the 1960s: no one has delved deeper into this majestic work. The sound quality might leave something to be desired by modern standards, but this is one of those cases where the music has to come before technology.

Ludwig; New York Choral Artists; Brooklyn Boys' Chorus; New York Philharmonic Orchestra; Bernstein
(Deutsche Grammophon; 2 CDs)

Leonard Bernstein was a renowned interpreter of Mahler, but his epic readings will not appeal to everyone. Bernstein's Mahler is, above all, a creature of emotional extremes, and there are times when he wallows in the angst to excessive lengths. This is not the case here: rather there is a sense of grandeur without bombast, and depth of feeling without sentimentality.

Symphony No. 4

The projected finale of *Symphony No. 3*, a soprano setting of the *Wunderhorn* song "Das himmlisches Leben" (The Heavenly Life), became the climactic last movement of *Symphony No. 4* (1899–1901). This symphony is a much more restrained work than its predecessors: the orchestra is of a normal size (and features no trombones), there are only four movements (usually lasting around an hour in total), and the childlike sentiments of the finale's text affect the whole work. The mood is established in the opening bars – a kind of "trotting" introduction, complete with jingling bells, which breaks into an expansive, pastoral big tune that is joyously affirmative. The symphony is not devoid of weightier moments, however – the Scherzo requires the lead violinist to tune the violin up a tone to add a sinister touch to proceedings.

Raskin; Cleveland Orchestra; Szell
(Sony; with *Lieder eines fahrenden Gesellen*)

Mahler's sunniest symphony is handled with a perfect touch by Georg Szell in this 1964 recording. The Cleveland Orchestra was at a high point at this period and there is great subtlety and colouristic variety throughout. In Judith Raskin (as has often been pointed out) Szell had the ideal soloist for the last movement's ingenuous charm. One of the great Mahler recordings.

Price; London Philharmonic Orchestra; Horenstein
(Classics for Pleasure)

Another great performance from Jascha Horenstein, this time with the London Philharmonic Orchestra. A more indulgent conductor than Szell, what comes across more than anything is a feeling of spontaneity and sheer joy in the music. Margaret Price makes a radiant soloist in the final movement.

Symphony No. 5

The *Symphony No. 5* was written between 1901 and 1903, but Mahler continued to revise it until his death in 1911. Following a clear progression from a mood of dark despair to joyful reconciliation, its five movements are divided into three distinct parts. Part I begins with an unnerving minor-key fanfare that seems to herald some dreadful tragedy. A funeral march of quiet desperation follows, periodically interrupted by passages of extreme emotional violence, a mood which is intensified in the second movement. Part II consists entirely of one movement, a Scherzo, which in its initial guise of forceful jollity provides a shocking contrast to the preceding movements.

The Adagietto that commences Part III was conceived as a love-poem for the beautiful Alma Schindler whom he married in 1902. Made famous by its subsequent use in Visconti's film *Death in Venice*, its radiant combination of strings and harp provides a serene oasis at the heart of the work. And yet there's an underlying sadness to it, the frailty of the sound perhaps suggesting the ephemerality and fragility of life. The finale, which follows without a break, has no such vulnerability: an initially rustic feel is established via an exchange of wind instruments – horn calling to bassoon, clarinet and oboe. The movement builds in speed with a scurrying fugal passage that reveals Mahler's admiration for Bach. Textures become increasingly thick and complex but the overwhelming sensation is of an exuberant, pulsating energy which Mahler expert Deryck Cooke describes as an "artistic joy in symphonic creation, of building up a large musical structure". This sense of affirmation climaxes with a glorious chorale-like figure in the brass that is rapidly overwhelmed by an explosive flurry of a conclusion.

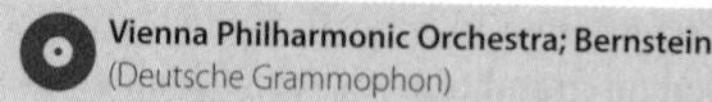
Vienna Philharmonic Orchestra; Bernstein
(Deutsche Grammophon)

The most invigorating account of the *Symphony No. 5* is Leonard Bernstein's live recording with the Vienna Philharmonic: his self-indulgent way with Mahler has always had its detractors, but here his empathy with the composer's intentions is unsurpassed. The playing conveys the excitement of a live event and the recording is unusually spacious.

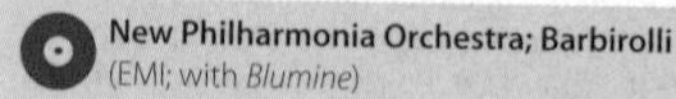
New Philharmonia Orchestra; Barbirolli
(EMI; with *Blumine*)

This is a justly famous account. In particular it is the warmth and geniality of Barbirolli's reading that sticks in the memory – this is Mahler with a very human face. It doesn't have the detail or incisiveness of Bernstein's reading, and there are a few moments when the music seems to lose its way, but nevertheless this is well worth investigating.

Symphony No. 6

The *Symphony No. 6* (1903–04) was Mahler's only symphony to follow the conventional four-movement pattern and to be centred on a single key, A minor. He at first toyed with the idea of naming it the *Tragic* and, while there may be no specific text attached to the work, it's a powerful, pessimistic composition. In its first version, the last movement contained three crashing blows, marked to be played with a sledgehammer on a resonant surface; intended to represent the hammer-blows of fate, they were to prove prophetic when a year after the first performance in 1906 he lost his position at the Vienna Opera, his daughter died and his heart condition was diagnosed. Mahler was highly superstitious and later excised the third of the blows from the score as if to ward off his death, yet the bleakness of the work's ending is matched only by Tchaikovsky's sixth symphony and Mahler's own ninth.

Vienna Philharmonic Orchestra; Boulez
(Deutsche Grammophon)

Pierre Boulez is perhaps not an obvious choice as a Mahler interpreter but in this, the bleakest of all his symphonies, he excels himself in a performance of unrivalled cumulative impact. It's a highly controlled performance but by no means unemotional and the Vienna Philharmonic's sumptuous sound really benefits from having such a firm hand at the tiller.

Israel Philharmonic Orchestra; Mehta
(Teldec; 2 CDs; with *Lieder eines fahrenden Gesellen)*

Zubin Mehta's approach is more expansive and luxuriant than that of Boulez but he never becomes self-indulgent (as some conductors do in this symphony). The Israel Philharmonic has a reputation for being an orchestra of individuals, but the response to Mehta's direction is electrifying in its level of commitment and this is a tremendously exciting performance.

Symphony No. 7

As if trying to exorcize the gloom of *No. 6*, Mahler's *Symphony No. 7* (1904–05) ends with his most uninhibited attempt at being cheerful, in a finale that combines allusions to Offenbach's *Can-Can* and Wagner's *Die Meistersinger* in a general melange of C major joyfulness that can seem merely gaudy in the wrong hands. It is probably this movement that has led to the work's relative neglect until recent years, when the glories of its other movements have at last been recognized. The funereal first movement may not be one of his most profound symphonic essays, but is made up for by the three movements that follow. The outer pair are entitled "Nachtmusik" (Night Music) and combine the moods of the nocturne with those of a serenade (the song-like second includes important parts for mandolin and guitar), while the central movement is one of Mahler's most miraculous creations – a ghostly Scherzo revealing his mastery of orchestral colour.

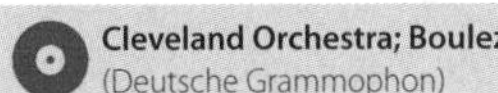

Cleveland Orchestra; Boulez
(Deutsche Grammophon)

In what is arguably Mahler's most problematic symphony, Boulez gives a vigorously assured performance that brings out the work's richly various sonorities and rhythmic energy. Boulez is one of the few conductors who manages to bring real coherence to the last movement.

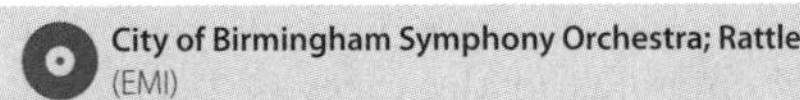

City of Birmingham Symphony Orchestra; Rattle
(EMI)

Simon Rattle brings this music vividly to life. The symphony has been in the CBSO's repertoire for many seasons and this live recording combines the advantages of familiarity with the risks inherent in live performance. The acoustic is perhaps a little dense for the large forces used, but the whole enterprise is thrillingly executed.

Symphony No. 8 – The Symphony of a Thousand

If *Symphony No. 6* descends to Hell, *Symphony No. 8* (1906) rises heavenward. It is in two parts – the first a setting of the Pentecostal Latin hymn "Veni Creator Spiritus", the second a setting of the closing scene from Goethe's *Faust*. Thus Mahler returned to the use of vocal forces, and not simply for the odd movement, as in the second, third and fourth symphonies: here he calls for eight soloists, a boys' chorus and large mixed chorus, hence the nickname of the *Symphony of a Thousand*. The result is a wide-ranging work, the rigorous counterpoint and earnestness of the opening hymn contrasting with the lush treatment of the Goethe; but the two parts are linked by certain musical themes and by their conceptual similarity – the first is a humanist interpretation of a Christian text concerning the search for enlightenment, the second a portrayal of Faust's redemption through wisdom and love.

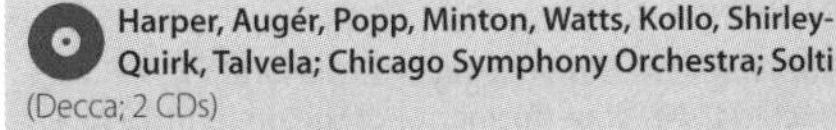

Harper, Augér, Popp, Minton, Watts, Kollo, Shirley-Quirk, Talvela; Chicago Symphony Orchestra; Solti
(Decca; 2 CDs)

The choice of recordings rests between Solti and Tennstedt, both superb but quite different in approach. Solti's is an operatic reading, stunningly recorded and with a first-class roster of singers; the engineers capture the scale of the work like no others, from the pungent organ at the opening and close to the tintinnabulating pianos and harps in the second movement.

Connell, Wiens, Lott, Schmidt, Denize, Versalle, Hynninen, Sotin; London Philharmonic Orchestra & Choir; Tiffin School Boys' Choir; Tennstedt (EMI; 2 CDs; with *Das Knaben Wunderhorn*)

Klaus Tennstedt's recording, on the other hand, while no less massive in overall concept, is a more personable account, with greater care taken over orchestral detail and more air around the notes. A difficult choice, then: Solti for greater physical impact, Tennstedt for greater musical qualities.

Symphony No. 9

Mahler was a very ill man by the time he wrote his *Symphony No. 9* (1908–11). Ever superstitious, he attempted to trick fate out of its habit of terminating composer's lives after their ninth symphonies (as in the cases of Beethoven, Bruckner and Dvořák) by pretending that this was really his tenth, with his intervening symphonic song cycle *Das Lied von der Erde* as the true *No. 9*. This sleight of hand did nothing to lighten the tone of the music, for this symphony is the most desperately death-ridden piece Mahler ever wrote. The opening movement, in which you can hear ominously tolling bells, the tread of a funeral march and a faltering heartbeat, gives way to a deliberately charmless rustic Ländler with a vulgar, distorted waltz at its centre. The Rondo-Burlesque third movement is, in the words of Mahler scholar Deryck Cooke, a "contrived chaos ... a ferocious outburst of fiendish laughter at the futility of everything". From this emerges the Adagio finale, in which death is stoically accepted and the music fades into tranquillity.

Berlin Philharmonic Orchestra; Karajan (Deutsche Grammophon; 2 CDs)

The ninth's colossal structure, drastic changes of tone and profound solemnity require the greatest conductors and orchestras to do it justice. Herbert von Karajan and the Berlin Philharmonic are such a partnership. Their live concert performance, recorded in 1982, is immaculate, displaying an intensity rarely found in other performances of the work, with the orchestra playing as if their lives depended on it.

Vienna Philharmonic Orchestra; Walter (Dutton Labs; 2 CDs)

Mahler's friend and chief acolyte, Bruno Walter, conducted the first performance of the ninth in 1912. Twenty-six years later he gave another performance in Vienna, just before the Nazis invaded Austria. Dutton Labs have now improved the previously constricted sound into something unmissable – here is a highly charged and intensely dynamic reading which makes a uniquely powerful impact.

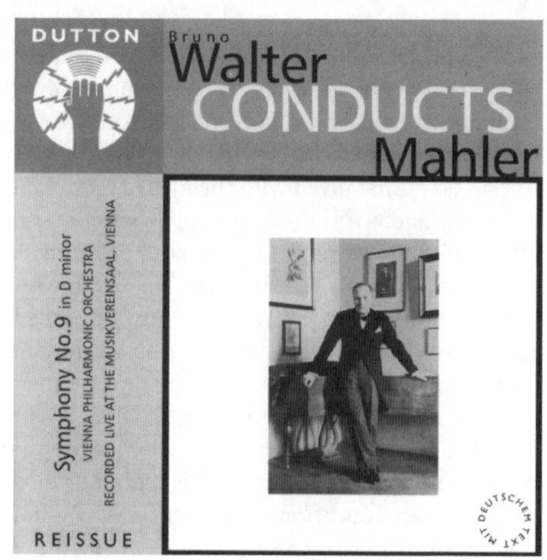

Symphony No. 10

In the summer of 1910 Mahler made a sketch of a new symphony, but left it in an unfinished state when he died the following spring. All five movements of the *Symphony No. 10* had a continuous line of music and three of them were filled out in more detail and partially scored for orchestra. Two movements were edited for performance in 1924, but it wasn't until the early 1960s that Deryck Cooke produced a performing version of the whole work, judiciously filling out passages that Mahler had not had time to expand beyond a single melodic line. This version took a while to be accepted by the musical establishment and there are still many eminent conductors who refuse to touch it on the grounds that it never can be a true representation of Mahler's intended completion. Yet those who do ignore it ignore a valuable insight into Mahler's state of mind a year after completing the doom-laden ninth. Here, death is again very much a subject of the work, but the overall impression is one of achieved peace, as if Mahler had at last exorcized his terrors.

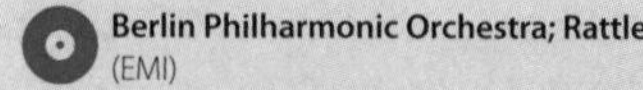

Berlin Philharmonic Orchestra; Rattle (EMI)

One conductor who has never had any doubts about the completion of the work, and indeed has included his own editorial additions in performance, is Simon Rattle. His live recording with the Berlin Philharmonic supersedes his earlier version with the Bournemouth SO, because of both the extra maturity and subtlety of Rattle's conducting and the orchestra's superbly musical playing.

VOCAL MUSIC

A smaller but no less important part of Mahler's heritage is his contribution to German song, as significant in its own way as that of Schubert, Wolf and Strauss. Like Schubert, he had a supreme melodic gift, with a vocal style that was honed by setting various folk texts in his early songs – and indeed the folkloric element remained central to all his vocal work, including the solo and choral sections of his symphonies. Virtually all his songs exist in versions accompanied by piano or orchestra (even the symphonic *Das Lied von der Erde* has an authentic piano version), but, given Mahler's skills in orchestration, the fuller alternatives are almost invariably more effective.

Das klagende Lied

Das klagende Lied, a cantata for four soloists, chorus and orchestra, setting Mahler's own poem relating a folk tale about a fratricide, sounds too accomplished to be the work of a twenty-year-old. This immensely accomplished piece is the composition in which he "found himself as Mahler", as he once said, and apart from a few songs and a movement for piano quartet he destroyed everything that had preceded it. In the 1890s he revised the cycle and discarded its first movement, which he felt to be superfluous to the storytelling, but fortunately this inspired if sprawling movement has now returned to circulation – though beware that some older recordings still omit it.

Dunn, Baur, Fassbaender, Hollweg, Schmidt; Berlin Radio Symphony Orchestra; Düsseldorf City Music Society; Chailly (Decca; 2 CDs; with other orchestral songs)

Riccardo Chailly's recording of the complete work is magnificent in every way. He has a superb orchestra and a fine quintet of soloists – a quintet, since the imaginative decision has been taken to have a boy treble sing the murdered brother's lament, rather than a mezzo-soprano, an evocative and eerie touch.

Songs

The text of Mahler's first song cycle, *Lieder eines fahrenden Gesellen* (Songs of a Wayfarer; 1883–85), is again his own, and is once more written in the style of the poetry from the immensely popular collection of folk texts titled *Des Knaben Wunderhorn* (The Boy's Magic Horn). There are four songs, all dealing with a rejected lover's attempts to find solace in nature and, ultimately, in death – the second song became the main theme in the first movement of *Symphony No. 1*, the composition of which followed immediately on from these songs.

Mahler's settings from *Des Knaben Wunderhorn* itself do not form a cycle as such, but are a collection of individual songs composed between 1892 and 1901. The range of these songs – some of which percolated into the symphonies written during this period – is impressively wide, from the mournful "Das irdische Leben" (Earthly Life) to the witty "Lob des hohen Verstandes" (Praise of Lofty Intellect), and they are usually shared between a female and a male singer.

After such folksiness, the *Kindertotenlieder* (Songs on the Deaths of Children; 1901–04) are made of sterner stuff. Although these settings of five poems by Friedrich Rückert predate the tragic death of one of Mahler's children, they seem an expression of an overwhelming fear for their wellbeing. While working on these songs, Mahler composed five more settings of poems by Rückert; these *Rückert-Lieder* are no more a cycle than is the *Wunderhorn* series, instead dwelling on a variety of Mahlerian themes, from love and life to loneliness and death.

Lieder eines fahrenden Gesellen; Kindertotenlieder; Rückert-Lieder; Des Knaben Wunderhorn (three songs): Fassbaender; German Radio Symphony Orchestra; Chailly (Decca; 2 CDs; with *Das klagende Lied*)

The mezzo-soprano Brigitte Fassbaender has no equal in the early cycles, and her disc with Chailly is nothing short of stunning, giving each song a character and personality of its own. In terms of tone quality, her voice is perhaps coarser than many of her rivals (both male and female), but its innate expressiveness is totally involving.

Des Knaben Wunderhorn: Schwarzkopf, Fischer-Dieskau; London Symphony Orchestra; Szell (EMI)

For the *Wunderhorn* songs, Elisabeth Schwarzkopf and Dietrich Fischer-Dieskau are the most effective pairing in their classic 1968 recording with Georg Szell conducting the London Symphony Orchestra. Both singers are renowned for the way they stress the meaning of the words, and the result here is particularly characterful and communicative.

Des Knaben Wunderhorn: Hampson, Parsons (Teldec)

Thomas Hampson and Geoffrey Parsons have resurrected Mahler's original piano versions of the *Wunderhorn* songs on a splendidly sung and played recording. Most other piano-accompanied recordings use an edition made from piano reductions of the orchestral score, whereas this version uses a piano score which preceded the orchestration.

Das Lied von der Erde

The valedictory song cycle *Das Lied von der Erde* is one of Mahler's most personal works and is perhaps his most beautiful, combining symphonic scale and structure with the narrative clarity of a song cycle. The six songs are settings of translated Chinese poems conveying the relationships between death and nature, with human life presented as a transient stage in the ever-renewing processes of the Earth. Mahler emphasized the message with some words of his own at the end of the last song, as the music fades away: "The dear Earth everywhere/Blossoms in spring and grows green again!/Everywhere and eternally the distance shines with a blue light!/Eternally ... eternally ...". The cycle calls for a tenor and mezzo-soprano, who alternate between songs of defiance and resignation, but the dominant performer is the mezzo, who has the final thirty-minute movement to herself.

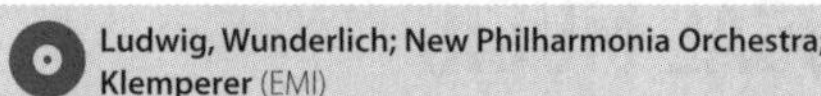

Ludwig, Wunderlich; New Philharmonia Orchestra; Klemperer (EMI)

In terms of vocal quality, this 1964 recording has not been bettered. Fritz Wunderlich's golden tenor deals effortlessly with the unrewarding tenor part, and Christa Ludwig's brings an ideal ease and warmth to her delivery. Under Klemperer the New Philharmonia rarely played better than this.

Fischer-Dieskau, King; Vienna Philharmonic Orchestra; Bernstein (Decca)

Replacing the mezzo with a baritone was sanctioned by Mahler but is rarely performed. This 1966 recording makes a persuasive case for it, with Dietrich Fischer-Dieskau is at his most intense as Bernstein and the Vienna Phil wring every inch of pathos from this great score.

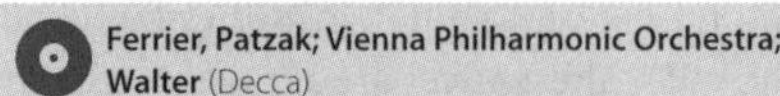

Ferrier, Patzak; Vienna Philharmonic Orchestra; Walter (Decca)

Kathleen Ferrier became a noted exponent of this work, and that is the principal reason for getting this 1952 mono recording (Julius Patzak's voice was by this time a little frayed at the edges). Ferrier's voice has a poignant vulnerability which is deeply moving, especially in the final song.

Frank Martin (1890–1974)

Swiss culture has always been a bridge between the Germanic and Latin worlds, a situation embodied in the person and music of Frank Martin, who was born into a Geneva-based family of French Protestant descent but was more inclined towards the German approach to art. Martin composed from the age of 8 (Bach's *St Matthew Passion* was an early inspiration), and was taught harmony and counterpoint but never underwent any formal conservatory-level training – he actually began, but never completed, a course in mathematics and physics. Initially he was more interested in music theory and education than in composition (he became a renowned teacher and lecturer), and the now more or less forgotten works from the 1920s were let down by their excessively theoretical basis – the exception is the remarkable *Mass for Double Choir* (1926). During the 1930s his work gained more focus with the development of a personal language, albeit one which drew on various aspects of modernism including Schoenberg's serialism and the neo-classicism of Stravinsky. Martin was essentially a craftsman, and though analogies with watch-making are a little far-fetched, there is a consistently meticulous and ordered quality to much of his work.

His best-known orchestral works date from the 1940s, in particular the ingeniously neo-classical *Petite Symphonie Concertante* (1945) and the *Concerto for Seven Wind Instruments* (1949). But it is as a setter of words that Martin comes into his own: his choice of usually mythic texts is always intensely personal and often highly original, and his settings exude a sincerity and a respect for the words that reminds one of Britten. These include the oratorios *Le Vin herbé* (1941) and *In terra pax* (1944), and the song cycles *Der Cornet* (1943) and *Sechs Monologe aus "Jedermann"* (1943). Martin later wrote a pair of operas, *Der Sturm* (1955), based on Shakespeare's *The Tempest*, and *Monsieur de Pourceaugnac* (1962), based on Molière, and there are numerous chamber and vocal works sprinkled throughout his career, as well as a series of concertos. Only a small portion of his output is performed with any regularity outside of Switzerland, but an increasing number is now available on CD.

Orchestral Works

The *Petite Symphonie Concertante*, arguably Martin's masterpiece, was written as a commission from the Basle-based conductor and impresario Paul Sacher, who asked Martin to compose something that gathered together all the common stringed instruments – harp, harpsichord, piano and string orchestra. Martin came up with a piece that used the eighteenth-century concerto grosso as its model, but reversed the priorities of that form by giving prominence to the harp and harpsichord, the parts conventionally associated with the accompanying role. Martin's deployment of this unique combination of instruments is highly resourceful, and like many of his works it is constructed from themes using all twelve tones of the chromatic scale, but clothed in a harmonic style that makes the music sound almost tonal.

The most intriguing of Martin's other orchestral works is the *Concerto for Seven Wind Instruments*, an instantly appealing and occasionally astringent piece, spiced with musical allusions – a jibe at a Ravel-like waltz in the first movement, and references to Haydn's *Clock* symphony in the steady tread of the slow movement.

Petite Symphonie Concertante; Concerto for Seven Wind Instruments: Guibentif, Ruttimann, Jaccottet; Suisse Romande Orchestra; Jordan (Warner; with *Sechs Monologe aus "Jedermann"*)

The Suisse Romande Orchestra is absolutely steeped in this music which they play with enormous flair and excitement under Armin Jordan's direction. The balance between soloists and orchestra is just right in the *Petite Symphonie* and there's a spiky humour in evidence in the *Wind Concerto*. Comes with a good rendition of the *Sechs Monologe aus "Jedermann"* by Gilles Cachemaille.

Sechs Monologe aus "Jedermann"

The *Sechs Monologe aus "Jedermann"* (Six Monologues from "Everyman") is a song cycle extracted from the play *Jedermann* by Hugo von Hoffmannstahl (Richard Strauss's librettist), which is in turn based on the English medieval morality play *Everyman*. Its theme is the destructive power of excessive wealth. No knowledge of the play is necessary, and in fact dropping the listener straight into these contextless but connected monologues only heightens the sense of the mythic and the mysterious. The prevailing mood of intense foreboding is created by some powerfully atmospheric orchestral writing which has a distinctly *fin-de-siècle* feel to it. Indeed, in its overriding sense of an unnamed horror being faced by a lone, morally lost figure, it has a strong emotional kinship with Bartók's *Bluebeard's Castle*, though it is more lightly scored. For a dramatic and characterful baritone it is among the most rewarding of modern song cycles, a fact that has not escaped Dietrich Fischer-Dieskau who has recorded it at least twice.

Wilson-Johnson; London Philharmonic Orchestra; Bamert (Chandos; with *Maria-Triptychon* and suite from *Der Sturm*)

This is the most satisfying of recordings currently available (the better of the Fischer-Dieskau recordings is not available) and boasts some beautifully controlled orchestral playing from the LPO and a searingly dramatic interpretation from David Wilson-Johnson – although Gilles Cachemaille on the previous disc runs him close.

Mass for Double Choir

The glorious a cappella *Mass for Double Choir* was completed in 1926 but not performed until 1963 – Martin apparently regarded it as a purely personal offering to God. It is one of the greatest of twentieth-century liturgical works, very much rooted in the tradition of early Christian music (chant-like passages are a major feature) but with an unmistakable modernity – above all in its imprecise tonality. There is something similar to the music of Arvo Pärt (see p.399) in the startling simplicity of its opening Kyrie, in which an undulating line in the altos is passed back and forth between the voices, building and overlapping with a supplicatory eloquence. Martin's sensitivity to words is everywhere apparent, but what is so effective is the way he applies a variety of devices – chant-like repetitions, melismatic passages, declamatory writing – and manages to weave them all together into a seamless and perfectly unified whole. The most exuberant writing occurs in the Gloria and Credo (the "Et Resurrexit" has all the eagerness of a nursery rhyme) but the work ends with a mood of stillness and peace in the Agnus Dei.

Westminster Cathedral Choir; O'Donnell (Hyperion; with Pizzetti *Messa di requiem* and *De profundis*)

There are several recordings of the *Mass for Double Choir* currently in the catalogue. This is one of the very best, with the Westminster Cathedral Choir sounding technically assured but also communicating a real sense of the work's devotional joy.

Bohuslav Martinů (1890–1959)

After Janáček, Martinů was the leading Czech composer of the last century, but his reputation has suffered because he was both prolific and inconsistent. He often wrote at high speed, almost never revised his scores and was curiously indifferent to performance or acclaim. There's always a lyrical ingredient in his work, a strong rhythmic drive and, often, a sense of ebullience and fun.

Martinů was born in the little town of Polička in the Bohemian-Moravian highlands, an area remarkable for the richness of its musical traditions (Smetana and Mahler came from this region too). His family lived in a tiny room at the top of a church tower, where his father – a cobbler by trade – earned money by keeping an eye open for fires in the town below. For the rest of his life Martinů carried a postcard of the view from the tower, and his home town was to remain an inspiration for him even after World War II had forced him permanently into exile. A sickly child, he spent most of his time closeted in the tower until the age of 6, when school brought his first real confrontation with the outside world – a disorienting experience later echoed when he uprooted himself to live in Prague, Paris and the USA.

Martinů learned the violin, started composing aged 10, and in 1907, thanks to local donations, was sent to the conservatory in Prague, where he was not a very successful student. Though his *Czech Rhapsody*, written to celebrate the founding of the new republic in 1918, was played in the presence of President Masaryk, Martinů was a late developer as a composer – it wasn't until he was regularly playing the violin in the Czech Philharmonic in the early 1920s that his musical education really began. In 1923 he took advantage of a small grant from the ministry of education and went to Paris, intending to stay just a few months. He remained there for over seventeen years.

Paris was then the artistic capital of Europe, and Martinů – despite his shyness and inability to speak French – threw himself into the maelstrom. He went to the composer Albert Roussel for lessons and, fascinated by Stravinsky, popular music and jazz, dashed off a couple of noisy orchestral pieces and some experimental ballet scores, culminating in *La revue de cuisine* (1927), in which various kitchen utensils dance the charleston, tango and foxtrot. Later Parisian works included the most interesting of his fourteen operas, *Julietta*, a number of works on Czech folk themes – notably the ballet *Špalíček* (a huge success in Prague in 1933) and the beautiful cantata *Kytice* – and several concertos and concertante pieces in a sort of neo-Baroque style. In 1940, soon after the premiere of the magnificent *Double Concerto* (his best work), Martinů was blacklisted by the Nazis and his music was banned in Czechoslovakia. He and his wife fled Paris with no more than a suitcase and went to start a new life in America.

Martinů in the garden of his lodgings in Ridgefield, Connecticut.

Like Bartók, Martinů didn't feel at home in the US, although he was highly regarded by influential conductors such as Serge Koussevitsky and Eugene Ormandy, and received plenty of commissions. After the war ill-health prevented Martinů returning to Czechoslovakia, and with the arrival of the Communist regime in 1948 he decided reluctantly to stay in America.

The most important works from this period of exile were the six symphonies composed between 1942 and 1951, but some of Martinů's best and most deeply Czech music was written after his return to France in 1953. There he composed a series of four cantatas inspired by the poems of Miroslav Bureš, a poet from his home town, and an opera, *The Greek Passion*, based on a story by Nikos Kazantzakis of *Zorba the Greek* fame. Martinů died in a Swiss hospital before the first performance; twenty years later his body was transferred to the family grave in Polička, in sight of his beloved tower.

Choral Music

All of Martinů's finest choral music was written to folk texts, and perhaps the most beguiling examples of the genre are the four chamber cantatas composed as an act of homage to his home town at the end of his life. Setting texts by local writer Miroslav Bureš, the cycle follows a seasonal sequence beginning with *Otvírání studánek* (The Opening of the Wells), celebrating a May-time custom in the Moravian countryside when processions go into the hills to cleanse the wells and springs. Written for soloists, female chorus and a chamber group of two violins, viola and piano, this piece is fresh and naive, whereas there's a greater intimacy and softness to *Romance z pampelišek* (Romance of the Dandelions), for unaccompanied mixed chorus and soprano solo. *Legenda z dymu bramborové nati* (The Legend of the Smoke from Potato Fires) recounts the harvest-time legend of how the Virgin Mary steps down from a stained-glass window to work in the fields as a peasant; the soloists and chorus are accompanied by an ensemble of piano, recorder, clarinet, horn and accordion, which creates a sound rather like a band of village folk musicians. *Mikec z hor* (Mikec of the Mountains), for the same ensemble as the first cantata, tells how a shepherd boy settles his flock on a mountain so that the frost mistakes their white coats for snow and moves elsewhere, leaving them to enjoy a mild winter.

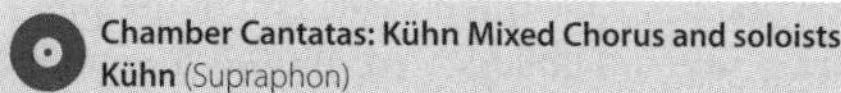

Chamber Cantatas: Kühn Mixed Chorus and soloists; Kühn (Supraphon)

The Opening of the Wells is sung with unsentimental freshness and is given a spirited instrumental accompaniment, though it's a little spoiled by an overintrusive narrator – thankfully, he's absent from *The Legend of the Smoke* and *Mikec of the Mountains*. The recording of all three is crystal clear.

Ballets

Martinů wrote a series of ballets in Paris, several of which were experiments involving film, puppets, projections and impossible sets. Typical of this period is *Vzpoura* (Revolt), a ballet-fantasy in which bedlam breaks out among the musicians and sounds: black notes fight against white notes, high notes against low ones; the gramophone mutinies against ragtime and jazz; critics commit collective suicide and Stravinsky emigrates to a desert island. From the chaos a Moravian girl in national costume emerges singing a folk song, and a lyrical order is restored. *Špalíček*, written in the early 1930s, was Martinů's first large-scale work drawing primarily on Czech folk material – he called it a ballet of "popular plays, customs and fairy-tales". It's a piece that also bears the influence of Stravinsky's *Les noces*, in that the texts sung by the soloists and chorus are integral to the score.

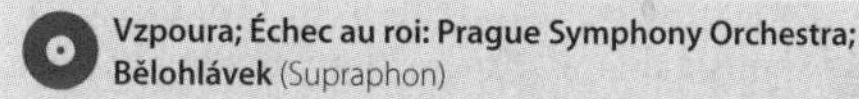

Vzpoura; Échec au roi: Prague Symphony Orchestra; Bělohlávek (Supraphon)

This CD is the premiere recording of *Vzpoura* and the chess ballet *Échec au roi*. Bělohlávek's lively direction really underlines the cartoon-like high spirits of Martinů's music in the 1920s.

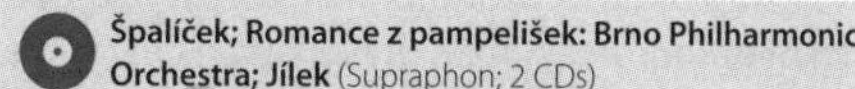

Špalíček; Romance z pampelišek: Brno Philharmonic Orchestra; Jílek (Supraphon; 2 CDs)

This colourful and fresh recording of *Špalíček* also includes *Romance z pampelišek*, one of the four cantatas to verses by Miroslav Bureš composed in the 1950s.

Symphonies

Martinů's orchestral sound is very recognizable, with its driving momentum tempered by Czech lyricism, and the texture of the orchestra almost always given extra bite by a piano part. The remarkably varied six symphonies, all of which were written in America, are the most impressive of his orchestral pieces. *Symphony No. 1*, written in only fifteen weeks, is very lyrical and epic in scale; *No. 2* is pastoral and distinctly Czech-sounding; *No. 3* has an undertow of tragedy, reflecting its creation in wartime; *No. 4* is closer in spirit to the first symphony, and is reminiscent of Dvořák; *No. 5*, written at the end of the war, is more gentle and understated; and *No. 6*, subtitled "Fantaisies symphoniques", is full of changing moods and intriguing textures, and includes a quotation from his fantasy opera *Julietta*.

Symphonies Nos. 1–6: Bamberg Symphony Orchestra; Järvi (BIS; 3 CDs)

Of the several available recordings of Martinů's symphonies, Neeme Järvi's are the best. The playing is lyrical and dynamic, with a splendid sinewy quality in the syncopated rhythmic passages, and the sound is very clear. The three discs of this box-set are also available individually (at full price); if you want to sample just one, go for the nicely contrasted pairing of *Nos. 3* and *4*.

Double Concerto

Many of Martinů's huge number of concertos and concertante works settle into a note-spinning neo-Baroque groove which can be long-winded and tedious, but his *Double Concerto* – for two string orchestras, piano and timpani – is one of the masterpieces of twentieth-century music. Written in 1938 for Paul Sacher and his Basle Chamber Orchestra, this taut and powerful work was composed as a direct response to the imminent Nazi invasion of Czechoslovakia, and marks a turning point in his life. After 1938 Martinů was never to see his family or homeland again.

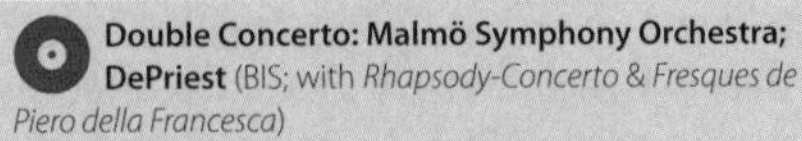

Double Concerto: Malmö Symphony Orchestra; DePriest (BIS; with *Rhapsody-Concerto & Fresques de Piero della Francesca*)

The *Double Concerto* is one of Martinů's most widely recorded works, and several fine versions are available. We have selected this rugged performance by the Malmö Symphony Orchestra, not least because – coupled with the unashamedly romantic *Rhapsody-Concerto* and the powerfully atmospheric *Fresques de Piero della Francesca* – this would be the ideal disc with which to start a Martinů collection.

Pietro Mascagni (1863–1945)

Verismo opera, which flared onto the musical landscape of Italy during the last ten years of the nineteenth century, was largely inspired by the literary realism of writers like Zola and the Sicilian Giovanni Verga, and it, in turn, foreshadowed the world of soap opera. In verismo operas emotions are extreme, characters are one-dimensional, the tension is high, the pace is fast, and the attention span is short – the two most successful verismo operas, Mascagni's *Cavalleria rusticana* and Leoncavallo's *I pagliacci* (see p.299), last only an hour.

Pietro Mascagni, the father of "realistic" opera, shot to prominence on 17 May, 1890, with the Rome premiere of *Cavalleria rusticana*, or "Rustic Chivalry". Things might have turned out very differently. Reading, by chance, of a competition for one-act operas, he prepared to send in the fourth act of his full-length opera *Ratcliff* but, unknown to him, his wife had already submitted the recently completed *Cavalleria* on his behalf. It was one of three winners, and received its first performance in front of a half-empty but wildly enthusiastic house.

The rapid international vogue for *Cavalleria* was unprecedented and its popularity remains undimmed – every opera house plays it once every few years, invariably on a double bill with *I pagliacci* (*Cav & Pag*, as it's known in the trade). However, unlike Leoncavallo, Mascagni found success beyond his name-maker, and went on to produce some extremely fine music, most notably the three-act opera *L'amico Fritz*. He was also a respected conductor and assumed some of Toscanini's duties at La Scala when the maestro resigned in protest over the Fascist regime. Mascagni had no such qualms and blithely launched each performance with the Fascist hymn – indeed he was swiftly adopted by Mussolini's government as their official composer. Though this move earned him the obloquy of the victorious allies, by the 1950s he was back in the ranks of the one-hit wonders.

Cavalleria rusticana

Set in Sicily, the plot of *Cavalleria rusticana* revolves around the relationship between Santuzza and Turiddu. Before the action starts, the latter has seduced the former, then deserted her for Lola, a previous lover, now the wife of Alfio. In revenge, Santuzza reveals all to Alfio, who takes it rather badly and ends up killing Turiddu in a duel behind the church (to heighten the pathos, this all takes place on Easter Sunday). It's a cheap and cynical tale, similar to that of *I pagliacci*, but *Cavalleria rusticana* is musically the superior – melodically, it stands up to comparison with the bulk of Puccini. The Intermezzo has been used time and time again in advertising campaigns, but the best part of the opera is the final fifteen minutes, during which Turiddu, the tenor lead, sings his marvellous testament to the wonders of wine, "Viva il vino", and his concluding lament, "Mama, quel vino e generoso" – the latter is an extraordinary, highly moving bit of music. Alfio's involvement is one part bluster and one part ballast, but Santuzza gets some excellent writing, not least "Voi lo sapete", in which she sings of her betrayal.

Carreras, Caballé, Manuguerra, Varnay; Ambrosian Opera Chorus; Philharmonia Orchestra; Muti
(EMI; 2 CDs; with *I pagliacci*)

Cavalleria rusticana requires a strong-minded conductor to keep the pace rapid. Riccardo Muti pushes the drama with great intensity, especially during his laudably unsentimental reading of the duet between Turiddu and Santuzza. Carreras is a virile anti-hero and Montserrat Caballé is in beautiful voice as Santuzza. The accompanying performance of *I pagliacci* is no less outstanding.

Arragal, Evstatieva; Bratislava Radio Symphony Orchestra; Slovak Philharmonic Chorus; Rahbari
(Naxos)

You can buy versions with flashier singing and finer sound quality, but Naxos's account with the splendid Giacomo Arragal as Turiddu and Stefka Evstatieva as Santuzza wins out on musical terms. Rahbari's conducting is solid and unselfconscious and, while the Slovak Philharmonic does not stand comparison with Muti's Philharmonia, the performance has great integrity and a sense of occasion.

Jules Massenet (1842–1912)

With the advent of Wagner, French composers such as d'Indy, Chausson and Chabrier reacted by creating their own vast Gothic operas, which usually amounted to little more than Teutonic heroics in French fancy dress. Jules Massenet, nineteenth-century France's finest prolific composer of opera, offered an alternative by redefining the lyrical French tradition – the tradition of Gounod (see p.219) – in the light of Wagner's advances in dramatic structure. Massenet was uninterested in profundity of any sort, but few composers have ever created such attractive surfaces.

After studies with Ambroise Thomas, Massenet won the Prix de Rome in 1863, then spent three years in Italy, where he visited Liszt, and got married. He had his first opera performed in 1867 and, after interruptions from the Franco-Prussian war, achieved his first major success in 1872 with *César de Bazan*. This was followed a few months later by the yet more popular *Marie-Magdeleine*, a work of "discreet and pseudo-religious eroticism", to use d'Indy's words. This eroticism, together with an affection for orientalism, coloured most of Massenet's subsequent work, and he was openly cynical about pandering to the French taste for religiose

Jules Massenet poses in his garden.

themes, declaring: "I don't believe in all that creeping Jesus stuff, but the public likes it and we must always agree with the public."

In 1881, after a string of finely constructed oratorios, he produced *Herodiade*, a work whose free and semi-declamatory melodies can be seen as anticipating Debussy's *Pelléas* (see p.153). His next success, *Manon* (1884), used leitmotifs and weightier brass, a development that led to the composer being labelled "Mademoiselle Wagner", a jibe produced partly by envy, for by now Massenet was the country's most popular opera composer. After *Manon*, Massenet produced three notable failures – *Le Cid*, *Le Mage* and *Esclarmonde* – but in 1892 he came up with his masterpiece, *Werther*. Taking his inspiration from Wagner's *Parsifal* and Goethe's *Sorrows of Young Werther*, Massenet here achieved a genuinely moving work which contrasts the Germanic sobriety of Charlotte, Werther's love, with the Gallic charm of Sophie – and in the character of Werther himself he created his finest tenor role.

For a while Massenet produced verismo operas (after all, the French opera *Carmen* was the progenitor of verismo), but he finally settled back into his natural style of light, lyrical and saccharine music. His younger contemporaries were, however, unimpressed by his crowd-pleasing rhetoric. Indeed, it was Debussy's hatred of Massenet and his easily won success that drove him to complete *Pelléas et Mélisande*, a work which set the seal on Massenet's fall from grace. After *Sapho* (1897), only *Don Quichotte*, produced in 1910, brought Massenet any reminder of past glories, and he died bitter at the direction in which, in Debussy's hands, French music was now heading.

Manon

The source for Massenet's *Manon* is the same as that to which Puccini turned for his third opera – *Manon Lescaut*, by Abbé Prevost. As with *Werther*, the tale offers plenty of opportunities for lavish emotionalism – humble Manon elopes with the young nobleman Des Grieux, abandons him, returns to him after he has joined the priesthood in despair, is accused of prostitution and finally dies in a prison cell, in the arms of her lover. Though Massenet doesn't go for the extreme passions that Puccini wrung out of his source, his most affecting music is to be found in the five acts of this melodious tragedy – not least in the seminary scene, where Manon begs Des Grieux to leave the priesthood, and in Manon's death scene. Less dramatic but more emotional than *Werther*, this is a beautifully written opera and, of all his heroines, Manon is the most alive.

Gheorghiu, Alagna, Patriarco, van Dam; Chorus and Symphony Orchestra of La Monnaie; Pappano
(EMI; 2 CDs)

Roberto Alagna is the consummate French tenor and he sounds completely at home as Des Grieux, catching all the character's psychological fluctuations. As Manon, Angela Gheorghiu finds an ideal expression for the sacred–profane tensions that define the role. Together, as in the grand Act 3 duet and Act 4's glorious "Sphinx étonnant", they are in a class of their own.

Cotrubas, Kraus, Quilico, van Dam; Chorus and Orchestra of the Capitole de Toulouse; Plasson
(EMI; 2 CDs)

In Michel Plasson's 1982 set, Ileana Cotrubas makes a lyrical, beautifully paced but nicely theatrical Manon – even if she lacks the darker qualities needed for the last two acts. Alfredo Kraus is as stylish as ever, and Gino Quilico is a huge success as Lescaut, making much of Massenet's rather one-dimensional material. The supporting cast are all excellent and the recorded sound is fresh and flexible.

Werther

With *Werther* Massenet achieved a perfect balance between drama, characterization and beauty of sound. Based upon Goethe's novel, the tragedy principally concerns the affections of Werther, Charlotte and Albert. The poet Werther loves Charlotte, who loves Werther but is engaged to marry Albert. Werther leaves, returning to find Charlotte married. She begs him to leave her alone but upon finding that her husband has loaned him his pistols she rushes through a blizzard to find him dead. As you might imagine, the opera is remarkable for the pathos of much of the music, and it boasts moments of thrilling atmosphere. It also shows Massenet's fascination with the psychology of women, and if Charlotte lacks the insight of some of Puccini's heroines, Massenet nonetheless gives her a highly convincing and sympathetic gravity. The first act contains the majority of *Werther*'s finest writing, but the Act 3 reconciliation scene is perhaps the most impressive demonstration of Massenet's understanding of the human voice, while the finely constructed development towards the tragedy of Werther's death is unforgettable.

Vargas, Kasarova, Schaldenbrand, Kotoski; German Symphony Orchestra, Berlin; Jurowski (RCA; 2 CDs)

As Werther, Ramón Vargas is the undoubted star of the show, and it's a pleasure to hear a singer turn Massenet's music to such consistent advantage. His Charlotte, Vesselina Kasarova, sings beautifully and with great confidence. Valdimir Jurowski directs a nervously energetic performance, opting for subtle shifts in texture and temperature, which the Berlin orchestra respond to with great flair and sensitivity.

Kraus, Troyanos, Manuguerra, Barbaux; London Philharmonic Orchestra; Plasson (EMI; 2 CDs)

Alfredo Kraus and Tatiana Troyanos make a perfect couple, the latter's dark tone nicely placed against Kraus's lighter voice. Manuguerra's Albert conveys just the right level of arrogance and cruelty, and Plasson allows the heavy orchestrations their due without letting them overwhelm things. A highlights disc is also available.

Nicholas Maw (1935–2009)

Like his British contemporaries, Peter Maxwell Davies and Harrison Birtwistle, Nicholas Maw absorbed the legacy of serialism, and yet his strongest affinities were with the luxuriant opulence of the late Romantic movement. The reconciliation of these influences took years to achieve, but produced at least one work of major status.

Maw studied at the Royal Academy of Music in the mid-1950s, and in 1958 produced his first significant piece, *Nocturne*. Written under the tutelage of the neo-classicist Lennox Berkeley, and owing much to Bartók, *Nocturne* won him a French government scholarship which allowed him to study in Paris with two of the most eminent teachers of his day, Max Deutsch (a pupil of Schoenberg) and Nadia Boulanger. A period of creative sterility followed, in which Maw eked out a living as a writer and teacher.

His breakthrough came with the *Scenes and Arias* of 1962, a setting of twelfth-century texts for three sopranos and orchestra, in which the lushness of Richard Strauss – and something of the attack of the Second Viennese School – found fresh chromatic richness. Developing this new idiom took the next eight years, an evolutionary process which Maw referred to as "my second apprenticeship". It was a fruitful time, however, in which Maw produced a series of operas: *One Man Show*, *The Voice of Love* and *The Rising of the Moon*. These are full of lyrical music, as deeply argued as before, yet more clear-cut in its effects and now revealing the influence of Alban Berg alongside Strauss, Britten, Wolf and Brahms. Despite their quality, however, Maw's operas enjoyed limited success, which some have attributed to the crassness of some of the librettos – they include, for example, the sexual initiation rites of British soldiers in nineteenth-century Ireland.

In the 1970s Maw further developed his finesse in orchestration, blending colours and timbres in a way that gave clarity to music in which melodic motifs were elaborated with increasing drama, and at ever greater length. The period – which saw the composition of the massive orchestral piece, *Odyssey* – also saw Maw become more overtly tonal in his musical language, a tendency that was confirmed by the highly Romantic *Violin Concerto* of 1993. A recording of this work won a Grammy in 2001, helping to raise Maw's profile; but the following year's Covent Garden premiere of *Sophie's Choice*, an operatic treatment of William Styron's novel, garnered mixed reviews, despite Simon Rattle describing it as the most significant opera of the last fifty years.

Odyssey

Written between 1973 and 1979, then revised until 1985, *Odyssey* is the summation of Maw's expressive progress up to its time of writing,

Joshua Bell – the dedicatee of Maw's violin concerto.

and is a journey in itself. It was composed in its playing order, and during its development Maw's style became less ambiguous, his debt to tonal music more blatant. Lasting ninety minutes, the whole gigantic structure is spun out of a 44-bar melody and owes something to Bruckner's sense of epic symphonic form. It begins with an introduction which the composer summarized as "a gigantic upbeat groping towards articulation", and moves through four contrasting movements before reaching an epilogue which closes the music serenely.

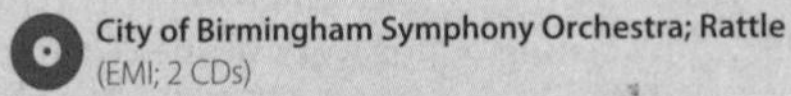

City of Birmingham Symphony Orchestra; Rattle
(EMI; 2 CDs)

Simon Rattle, the conductor in this premiere recording, rates Maw as the spiritual heir to William Walton, and has described Odyssey as "... a masterpiece, a whole world of ideas miraculously welded together: new, alert and alive." Rattle's interpretation, transparent and unforced, makes a case for *Odyssey* as a solid contribution to the English lyric tradition.

Violin Concerto

Although he had considered writing a violin concerto for many years, Maw was inspired to do so only after hearing Joshua Bell, a violinist whom he perceived to be "the real thing ... A real Romantic soloist." Romanticism is what Maw was attempting to refashion here, but the concerto is no pastiche, and nor is it particularly Brahmsian, as some have suggested. Rather, the warm-blooded lyricism and rhapsodic gestures of the soloist – which at times suggest the violin concertos of Syzmanowski – are subsumed into a grandiose and elemental symphonic vision. The risk of such an enterprise, especially one in which richly beautiful sounds are an end in themselves, is that a sense of structure and direction can be dissipated, and that is only partially avoided. There are many wonderful moments, however, not least the opening of the third (slow) movement in which the ruminative voice of the soloist emerges out of the burnished glow of the orchestral strings.

Bell; London Philharmonic Orchestra; Norrington
(Sony)

Joshua Bell is not a violinist who is particularly focused on contemporary music, and although he premiered this work – and made this recording – it has not become part of his repertoire. Still, he gives an utterly committed performance with Norrington and the London Philharmonic, and really seems to relish Maw's opulent sound-world.

Life Studies

Life Studies (1976), an eight-movement work for fifteen solo strings, clearly has strong affinities with some of the classics of twentieth-century string writing – Schoenberg's *Verklärte Nacht* and Tippett's *Concerto for Double String Orchestra*, for example – and yet has a unique and powerful energy of its own. Maw was obviously fascinated by the wide range of sonorities that can be obtained from limited forces, and the work abounds in mysterious contrasts of timbre: in the third study (*poco agitato*) a restless scurrying is countered by a slower, smeary string sound, while the next movement is dominated by jazzy pizzicato cadenzas on the double bass. Maw divides his forces into two groups and there is a constant sense of antiphonal argument in each of the studies, a tension that is finally dissipated only on the last note of the final study, where all the instruments come together.

Life Studies; Sonata Notturna: English String Orchestra; Boughton (Nimbus)

This is the second time that *Life Studies* has been recorded, but William Boughton's reading has a depth and an understanding of the music, not to say a marvellously thick sound, which makes it a clear first choice. It is coupled with the intensely lyrical *Sonata Notturna* for cello and strings, in which the soloist is Raphael Wallfisch.

Peter Maxwell Davies (1934–)

With the English pastoral tradition largely put out to grass, and with serialism a battle seemingly won, Peter Maxwell Davies emerged in the 1960s as one of the freshest and most innovative voices in British music. A questing and experimental musician, he found a fresh source of inspiration in quotation from past ages and styles – but quotation lifted beyond pastiche onto an entirely individual level. His preoccupations have never been merely stylistic, however: he describes himself as a composer "torn by the fundamental question of good and evil", who writes music in the face of a modern world which seems to look upon past atrocities and pronounce, "They couldn't happen now."

Born in Manchester, he studied at the Royal Northern College of Music with Harrison Birtwistle, John Ogdon and Alexander Goehr, and soon became identified with the "Manchester Group" and its commitment to the serialist avant-garde. At the same time he developed an affection for medieval music – not just for its rhythmic devices but also for its notions of damnation.

In 1957 Maxwell Davies won a scholarship to study composition in Rome, and two years later his orchestral piece *Prolations* won the Olivetti Prize. He returned to England and took up the post of music director at Cirencester Grammar School, at first just to make ends meet. The experience proved invigorating, however, giving him a chance to write simpler, sparer music for young people – something he has enjoyed doing ever since.

The life and music of early English composer John Taverner (who lived through troubled times, see p.571) became a particular focus, giving rise to two orchestral fantasias, the opera *Taverner* (1962–70) and other works developed from plainsong fragments. Maxwell Davies' methods here were similar to those used in "parody" masses in the fifteenth and sixteenth centuries, where the material of one composition is used to create another.

In 1968 – after periods at Princeton and at Adelaide University – Maxwell Davies returned to Britain and founded, with Harrison Birtwistle, the Pierrot Players, later renamed the Fires of London. Before long he was writing most of his music for this group, including *Eight Songs for a Mad King* (1969) and several other music-theatre spectacles exploring extremes of delusion and hysteria. He also wrote chamber pieces for the ensemble, refining his elaborations of the rhythmic involutions of medieval scores, and developing an interest in the astringent tones of out-of-tune instruments, which connected with Maxwell Davies' fascination for "music of the absurd".

In 1971 he moved to the Orkney islands, off the north coast of Scotland. The sounds, landscapes, literature and history of the place have inspired many works since, including the first and second symphonies (1976 and 1980). Increasingly mystical religious views have also proved important,

Peter Maxwell Davies perched on a bollard.

as have the works of local writer George Mackay Brown, whose texts were used in *Hymn to St Magnus* (based on a twelfth-century psalm to the Orcadian saint) and *Black Pentecost*.

Maxwell Davies' more recent works are his most immediately appealing, not least due to their approachable (though non-tonal) harmonic language. High points include a fruitful collaboration with the Scottish Chamber Orchestra on a series of ten concertos (1987–96), a cycle of string quartets commissioned by the Naxos recording company and two full-length operas – *The Doctor of Myddfai* (1996) and *Mr Emmett Takes a Walk* (2000). But even the most craggy and uncompromising music by this challenging and theatrical composer is well worth exploring. In 2004 this former *enfant terrible* was appointed Master of the Queen's Music.

Worldes Blis

Worldes Blis (1969) took three years to create, and painstaking craft is evident in every section of this granitic work. In the composer's own words, *Worldes Blis* develops "slowly in extremely articulated time-spans ... with a minimal presentation of the material in such a way as to make the structural bones as clear as possible". The title is taken from a thirteenth-century monody ("worldes blis lasts no time at all"), and the piece flows from isolated musical cells towards the theme of this source material through ever-changing melodic, rhythmic and harmonic contours, moving from serenity through tension to an explosive climax. It's as if traditional symphonic development, which sets out with the exposition of the subject, has here been thrown into reverse.

Manchester Cathedral Choir; Royal Philharmonic Orchestra; BBC Philharmonic Orchestra; Maxwell Davies (Collins; with *The Turn of the Tide*)

Maxwell Davies paces this performance immaculately, maintaining the flow through each successive part. The coupled work, *The Turn of the Tide* (1992), depicts the creation of life on Earth and the threat that humanity poses to the rest of nature; intended to be played by professionals, with interludes in which schoolchildren can improvise, it shows Maxwell Davies at his most accessible.

Black Pentecost

Written in 1979, the polemical *Black Pentecost* is a four-movement symphony with voices. Its title is taken from George Mackay Brown's poem "Dark Angels" ("Now, cold angels, keep the valley from the bedlam and cinders of a Black Pentecost") and the text is from his novel *Greenvoe*, set on the imaginary island of Hellya as it is ripped to bits by commercial exploitation. What set Maxwell Davies working was the threat of uranium mining in Orkney. "But it could be anything", he has said. "The pollution is there, and the kicking of people out of their houses is there, and the destruction of a way of life is there. The LSO commissioned it", he added, "but when they found out what it was, they didn't want to touch it."

The piece plays out a dramatic encounter between a baritone, in the role of Operation Black Star, and a mezzo-soprano who takes on the personae of both narrator and of Bella Budge, one of Black Star's innocent victims. An orchestral introduction, which hovers between menace and meditative stasis, sets the scene before the singers explore the moral consequences of "the catastrophe of nations" as "piecemeal a village died, shrivelled slowly with the radiance of Black Star." Relentlessly slow-paced, with episodes of savage parody and near-chaos, vocal interludes that vacillate between lament and hysteria, cavernous resonances and abrasive outbursts, *Black Pentecost* is an arduous masterpiece, comparable in its fatalism and ambition to Mahler's *Das Lied von der Erde*.

Jones, Wilson-Johnson; BBC Philharmonic Orchestra; Maxwell Davies (Collins; with *Stone Litany*)

The composer's insight is invaluable in teasing out the dense musical rhetoric of *Black Pentecost*, and the performance is excellently recorded. The coupling, *Stone Litany* (1973), again features a haunted orchestral landscape that is shattered by vocal interpolation, here symbolizing the birth of speech. Della Jones handles with aplomb the pyrotechnics which Maxwell Davies imposes on the sparse Old Norse text.

Symphony No. 5

Completed in 1994, the *Symphony No. 5* is one of Maxwell Davies' most impressive compositions, a single-movement symphony which in its elemental starkness recalls Sibelius's seventh (which Maxwell Davies had conducted just prior to starting work). The tone is austere but eloquent and, rather like the work of another Finnish symphonist, Rautavaara, it conjures up images of unyielding northern landscapes – there is even a suggestion of bird cries towards the end of the work. Maxwell Davies employs his customary device of using plainchant to underpin the thematic material, which gives the work its unity, but there is also a developing sense of tension within the symphony, as nervous, scherzo-like music is set against long-drawn-out music of translucent expansiveness.

Philharmonia Orchestra; BBC Philharmonic Orchestra; Maxwell Davies (Collins; with *Chat Moss, Cross Lane Fair & Five Klee Pictures*)

The Philharmonia give an enthrallingly and highly concentrated performance of the *Symphony No. 5*, one that really communicates its monumentality and its charged atmosphere. The symphony developed material from *Chat Moss*, a short work inspired by the barren marshes near Maxwell Davies' childhood home.

Felix Mendelssohn (1809–1847)

The conductor Hans von Bülow said of Mendelssohn that he began as a genius and ended as a talent, and Mendelssohn was indeed a terrifyingly gifted child. He painted with skill, wrote fine poetry, was an excellent athlete, spoke several languages, played many instruments and, in 1825, aged only sixteen, he composed one of the great chamber works of the nineteenth century – his *Octet for Strings*. With this work he set himself impossible standards, and though he went on to produce much excellent music, he never again came so close to perfection.

He was born into a wealthy Jewish-German family, and his talents were encouraged by his mother and elder sister, Fanny, who was almost as gifted a pianist as her brother. He made his concert debut in 1818 and had some of his music performed the following year. In 1821, aged 12, he was taken to meet the 72-year-old Goethe in Weimar, and the two became strong friends. In 1826, a year after the composition of the *Octet*, he wrote his overture to *A Midsummer Night's Dream*, a work that established his name internationally, yet remarkably it was not until he had completed three years' study at Berlin University that he finally decided upon a career in music. In March 1829 he gave the first performance of Bach's *St Matthew Passion* since the composer's death in 1750, and he was to be one of the principal influences behind the European revival of Bach's music. Near the end of that year he made his first visit to England where, apart from conducting concerts of his own work, he played the piano in the first English performance of Beethoven's *Emperor Concerto*. The English loved him and for many years he was the country's most popular foreigner.

After touring Scotland (where he met Sir Walter Scott) he returned to mainland Europe, to spend two years touring Germany, Austria and Italy. Further visits to England in 1832 and 1833 cemented his position within that country's musical life and he became a frequent guest artist with the Philharmonic Society Orchestra. In 1835 he became conductor of the Leipzig Gewandhaus Orchestra, and in 1837 he married. The next few years saw him produce a wide range of superb music, including his *Violin*

Concerto. In 1843 he established a new conservatory of music in Leipzig, where he was assisted by Robert Schumann, and in 1847 he made his tenth and last visit to England, when he became friends with Queen Victoria and Prince Albert, teaching the latter at the piano. In May of that year his beloved sister Fanny died and the shock of this loss, together with the pressure of severe overwork, led to his own death six months later.

It had been a brilliant career and yet also something of an anticlimax. Mendelssohn was described by von Bülow as the most complete master of musical form after Mozart, and this very mastery is perhaps the chief reason for his relapse into self-conscious politesse – the creation of pleasing, impeccably structured music came easily to him. His music is as bereft of struggle as was his life. Never did he lack money, praise or support, and not until the death of his sister did he experience genuine misery – and by then it was too late. No other great composer experienced such complete insulation from hardship, and there is little question that his cushioned existence impaired his creative development. His emotional range never really broadened, so is it surprising that his music remained consistent? One example tells the whole story – his *A Midsummer Night's Dream*. He wrote the overture in 1826 and, seventeen years later, added the incidental music. So identical in style is the additional material that it seems more like seventeen days: there's not the slightest evidence of creative evolution in its hugely enjoyable, supremely elegant and completely untroubling pages.

Elijah

Mendelssohn's extraordinary popularity in England was due mostly to his oratorios and other religious works, in which he satisfied the Victorians' craving for pious tunes and grand choruses. Of the pious tunes the finest is his beautiful hymn *Hear My Prayer*, which contains *O for the Wings of a Dove*. Of the more grandiose sacred compositions, the most rewarding is his oratorio *Elijah*, written in the summer of 1844, some eight years after Mendelssohn had first approached his librettist, Julius Schubring, about a possible collaboration on a work celebrating the prophet. Dominated by the bass role of Elijah and the chorus, the oratorio is very dramatic in a civilized sort of way, combining vivid sound-pictures of oceans, earthquakes and fires with more urbane passages of orchestral music. As you'd expect from someone who spent so much time in England, Mendelssohn pays homage to Handel in his choral writing, and he also shows his proficiency in Bach-like counterpoint. *Elijah* is an engaging piece, but it is long and potentially demanding.

Drawing of Mendelssohn by Johann Schmeller.

Terfel, Fleming, Bardon, Ainsley; Edinburgh Festival Chorus; Orchestra of the Age of Enlightenment; Daniel (Decca; 2 CDs)

Elijah comes in English and German versions (both sanctioned by the composer), and arguably packs more of a punch if you understand what's going on. This English-language performance has real narrative drive and boasts the most powerful Elijah on disc in the shape of Bryn Terfel. Just occasionally it feels that more drama is being squeezed out of the work than is in fact there, but if this performance doesn't convince you of the work's merits, nothing will.

Symphony No. 3 – the Scottish

At twilight on 30 August, 1829, during a holiday to recover from a gruelling concert series in London, Mendelssohn visited Holyrood Palace. He knew from Schiller of the tragic Mary Queen of Scots, and of the murder of her secretary Rizzio at Holyrood. Steeped in the gloom, he jotted down the first sixteen bars of a new symphony, an unbroken stream of melody later to be christened the *Scottish*. A week later, on a trip to Fingal's Cave on the island of Staffa, the opening of *The Hebrides* overture also came to him, but years passed before either work reached its final form. Mendelssohn returned to the symphony in 1841, and the following year introduced it to England, dedicating it to two new friends: Queen Victoria and her consort Albert. The third symphony opens with an impassioned recitative, and rises from a warlike Allegro to a noble closing hymn. Schumann pinpointed the relationship of these two movements when he wrote, "We consider it most poetic – like an evening corresponding to a lovely morning."

London Symphony Orchestra; Maag (Decca; with *A Midsummer Night's Dream*)

With Herbert Blomstedt's beautifully poised account now out of the catalogue, Peter Maag or Abbado (see below) are the next best bet. Maag and the LSO's 1960 performance is justly celebrated for its vivid sense of excitement and atmosphere, and it's coupled with an equally magical selection from A Midsummer Night's Dream.

Symphony No. 4 – The Italian

Of Mendelssohn's five mature symphonies (he wrote a group of string symphonies as a child), the fourth, the *Italian*, is the one that shows the composer at his most winning. Written in Berlin in the winter of 1832, a few weeks after his return from Italy, the symphony's ebullient mood reflects the wealth of pleasures he found there, in the country's landscapes, art and people. Apart from the brilliant and lively Neapolitan tune that forms the basis to the last movement, there's nothing that's specifically Italian about the music – indeed, one of Mendelssohn's contemporaries insisted that the Andante was based upon a Czech pilgrim folk song, while the boisterous Scherzo that follows it was inspired by Goethe's poem, "Lilis Park". The overall ambience, however, is one of Mediterranean spontaneity and expansiveness, and its life-affirming attitude is established right at the outset with the opening movement's skipping main theme, prelude to one of the composer's most delightful movements.

London Symphony Orchestra; Abbado (Deutsche Grammophon; with *Symphony No. 3*)

There's an adroitness, a boundless impression of urgency and power, underpinning Claudio Abbado's reading which puts him in ahead of most of his competitors. Wonderfully judged and sprung, this is one of those performances that makes the inevitable into a surprise. Coupled with a marginally convincing account of the *Symphony No. 3*.

A Midsummer Night's Dream

Mendelssohn's most popular work is now the *Violin Concerto* but it hasn't always held that place in the public's affection – previously his best-loved piece was the overture to his *A Midsummer Night's Dream*, source of the famous "Wedding March". Deeply impressed by Schlegel's translations of Shakespeare, Mendelssohn composed the overture when he was only seventeen, and it beautifully captures the elfin atmosphere of the original. The incidental music, composed in 1843, is rarely performed complete, which is a pity, for as Schumann rightly commented, it glows with "the bloom of youth". Innovatively constructed from motifs heard in the overture – thus, for example, the opening chords are used as the basis for the entry of Oberon and Titania in the finale – it's a wonderfully evocative series of musical tableaux.

Watson, Wallis; Finchley Children's Music Group; London Symphony Orchestra; Previn (EMI)

This is currently the best of the complete versions of the incidental music. Previn is not a theatre conductor, but there's a strong dramatic element to this reading and some suitably spirited singing from the Finchley Children's Music Group.

Other Orchestral Music

His overtures combine two of Mendelssohn's earliest passions: for travel and for the stage. By the age of twenty he had written seven operas, which the Berliners resolutely ignored; but nowhere else would Mendelssohn continue to fuse form and dramatic tension as effectively as he does in his overtures. His youthful discovery of *A Midsummer Night's Dream* had been made with his sister Fanny, and his response was originally scored for two pianos, so that they could play it together before family and friends. The memory of a buffeting at sea would, in Rome, be worked into *The Hebrides* overture; this was in 1830. Goethe's paired poems "A Calm Sea" and "A Prosperous Voyage" had drawn a choral-orchestral setting from Beethoven before Mendelssohn wrote his concert piece in 1829; and Mendelssohn echoes his predecessor in theatrical sense and structural rigour. Yet even the slightest of Mendelssohn's stage music keeps evergreen freshness, and its place in the staple orchestral repertoire is deserved.

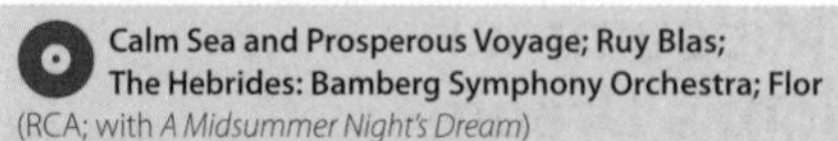

Calm Sea and Prosperous Voyage; Ruy Blas; The Hebrides: Bamberg Symphony Orchestra; Flor (RCA; with *A Midsummer Night's Dream*)

Always animated, these are actually rather dark performances which leave the big-band approach far behind. The result has no false gloss, but a lightness of touch which brings one far closer than usual to the fresh intimate nature of Mendelssohn's vision.

Violin Concerto in E Minor

As a young boy Mendelssohn wrote two concertos for violin, both of them immensely accomplished works, but scarcely anticipating the breathtaking originality of his *Violin Concerto in E Minor*. Written in 1844, it's a late work and one that firmly rebuts the idea that the precocious composer lost most of his inspiration after the age of twenty. Dispensing with any orchestral introduction, the soloist pitches straight in with a passionately surging melody that verges on the melodramatic. In contrast the movement's second subject is quiet and confiding, a moment of intimacy before the restlessness of the first theme returns. Even more moving is the song-like simplicity of the Andante, a movement that has been accused of sentimentality but which has all the lucid directness of a great Mozart aria. With the finale, Mendelssohn returns to the energetic lightness of his *A Midsummer Night's Dream Overture* with an elusive dance in which the violin's playful scamperings are frequently shadowed by a woodwind instrument as if in hot pursuit. It's a suitably high-spirited ending to what is the most straightforwardly enjoyable of all nineteenth-century concertos.

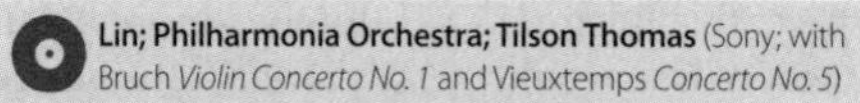

Lin; Philharmonia Orchestra; Tilson Thomas (Sony; with Bruch *Violin Concerto No. 1* and Vieuxtemps *Concerto No. 5*)

Lin's vibrant reading is an ideal mix of fire and tenderness. He regularly wrong-foots clichéd expectations – as good performances are apt to do – with delicate dynamic shading and finely tapered phrases. Both soloist and conductor play this so-familiar music with poise, delicacy and an unfailing sense of newness. A marvellous bargain.

Heifetz; Boston Symphony Orchestra; Munch (RCA; with Tchaikovsky *Violin Concerto*)

This 1959 account by Jascha Heifetz is in a class of its own. It's a recording that shows signs of its age but no other violinist could match Heifetz's effortless technique and unique "singing" tone.

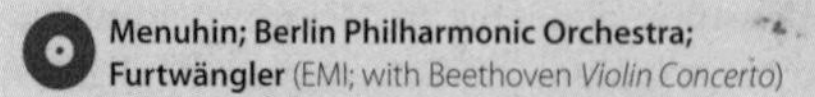

Menuhin; Berlin Philharmonic Orchestra; Furtwängler (EMI; with Beethoven *Violin Concerto*)

This is another "classic" account in a rather different vein. Menuhin was very much at his peak in the early 1950s, and the rare sweetness of his tone and his impeccable phrasing are at their most beguiling in the slow movement.

Piano Concertos

"He played the piano as a lark soars", Ferdinand Hiller recalled of Mendelssohn the performer. The corollary might be that he had little notion of conflict or any propulsive inner need; and the piano concertos, heard in a weak performance, seem to sum up Mendelssohn's idiom at its most garrulously trite. But in the right hands they reveal a genuine dramatic clout and irresistible flow of melody.

The *Concerto No. 1,* in G minor, was "thrown off", as Mendelssohn himself put it, in Rome during November 1831. The premiere came in Munich a year later: "I was received", the composer recalled, "with loud and long applause... but I was modest and would not appear." The second concerto, in D minor, was composed in 1837 for the Birmingham Festival. "The people made such a fuss over me that I was quite dumbfounded." Its second movement is as restful as any *Song Without Words* (see p.346), but there are innovations too: the way in which soloist and orchestra weave together from the outset, the unity of three seamless movements connected by fanfares.

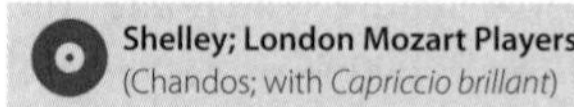

Shelley; London Mozart Players (Chandos; with *Capriccio brillant*)

Howard Shelley's bravura is combined with an acute sensitivity over matters of pacing and of light and shade. Within the overall fleetness of tempo and touch there are interludes of lush intimacy in which sentimentality is kept firmly at bay.

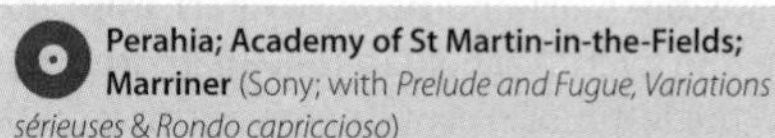

Perahia; Academy of St Martin-in-the-Fields; Marriner (Sony; with *Prelude and Fugue, Variations sérieuses & Rondo capriccioso*)

Incisive playing too from Murray Perahia, and at a more competitive price. Perhaps his conception of the music is not quite as organic or as variegated as Shelley's, but this is persuasive and beautiful playing nevertheless. The three famous solo encores are excellent.

Octet

Mendelssohn's *Octet* is scored for double string quartet, an ensemble that combined the intimacy of the quartet with the fuller sound of a small orchestra. On the score he indicated that the soft and loud markings "must be strictly observed and more strongly emphasized than is usual", and the *Octet* is a work that abounds in strong contrasts. The long first-movement Allegro opens with an exuberant opening phrase that bounds along with a youthful eagerness, while the movement's second subject, with its sweeter, more languid melody, introduces a subdued atmosphere that borders on the melancholic. In the Andante that follows, textures are lightened but the mood is darkened into something autumnal: it's the richest and least sentimental of all Mendelssohn's slow movements, with a depth of feeling that he reached on very few occasions.

In the wisp-like Scherzo (often used as an orchestral showpiece) Mendelssohn asks for playing that is fast but as light as possible. Inspired by lines from Goethe's *Faust* describing the motion of the clouds, the Scherzo's scampering, evanescent energy connects it with Mendelssohn's *Overture to A Midsummer Night's Dream* and the finale of his *Violin Concerto No. 2*: compositions that evoke the world – so dear to him – of fairies and hobgoblins. But it is the final movement that clinches the greatness of the *Octet* – its buoyant jubilation and tight fugal construction give it a power that's equalled by few other finales in chamber music, and the final three minutes are the most exciting thing Mendelssohn composed.

Cleveland Quartet & Meliora Quartet
(Telarc; with *Quartet in A Minor*)

In this recording two of America's best string quartets join forces for a splendidly characterful performance of the *Octet*. They follow Mendelssohn's instructions to the letter, and the result is a pulsating account that goes from bold declamation to hushed intimacy in a few bars. The finale is a *tour de force*, charging along at breakneck speed but with total coordination between the players.

String Quartet No. 2

Two years on from the *Octet*, Mendelssohn wrote his remarkable *String Quartet in A Minor* whose harmonic richness and subdued melancholy reveal a debt to the late quartets of Beethoven (who had died that year). After a slow opening, the first movement is developed with a contrapuntal vigour that is typical of early Mendelssohn in the way an initial yearning quality is built to a passionate height. The slow movement possesses a quiet dignity in which the main theme is treated fugally; it is followed by a classically elegant intermezzo, with a bustling central section, and a remarkably dramatic finale that reprises material from other movements before ending with the quartet's opening Adagio.

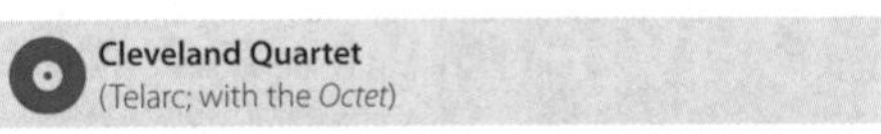

Cleveland Quartet
(Telarc; with the *Octet*)

The Cleveland Quartet give a touchingly emotional account of the *String Quartet in A Minor*, with a wide range of touch and timbre, and a greater emphasis on the inner voices than is usual. Especially magical is the whispered delicacy of the slow movement fugue and an almost throwaway lightness of touch in the intermezzo.

String Quintet No. 2

Mendelssohn completed his second quintet in 1845, more than twenty years after his first essay in the genre and nearly twenty after the *Octet*, a work with which it has some similarities. As with the *Octet*, each of the instrumental parts is given almost equal weight, and any good performance will clearly reveal Mendelssohn's genius for counterpoint. The first-movement Allegro is a perfect example of multi-thematic writing, showing his consummate ability to juggle more than four voices at once. Full of elegiac tunes, especially in the haunting Adagio, the *String Quintet No. 2* looks forward to the world of Brahms's mature chamber music, and is Mendelssohn's most rewarding chamber piece after the *Octet*.

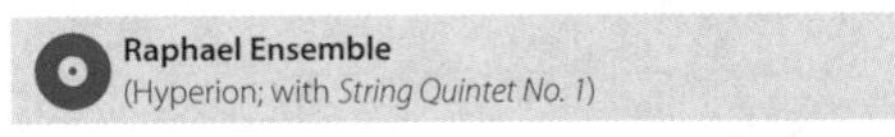

Raphael Ensemble
(Hyperion; with *String Quintet No. 1*)

Beautifully fresh and energetic music-making from the Raphael Ensemble, who really get to the heart of these pieces. There is a real sense of playing for each other while managing to retain a sense of five individual voices. An exhilarating experience.

Songs Without Words

Mendelssohn wrote three large-scale piano sonatas, a fantasia and a major set of variations, but his reputation as a composer for the piano is dominated by the *Lieder ohne Worte* or *Songs Without Words*. Composed from 1830 onwards, these forty-eight miniatures were published in six cycles of six during his lifetime, with two other sets issued posthumously. Combining surface virtuosity with a lyrical sense of line, they are exquisitely constructed and intimate little pieces, but some of them have proved too tuneful for their own good: numbers such as the "Bee's Wedding", "Andante and Rondo Capriccioso", "Funeral March" and "Spring Song" have been repeatedly quarried by jingle-writers and other hacks.

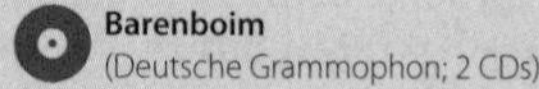
Barenboim
(Deutsche Grammophon; 2 CDs)

Daniel Barenboim's account of the complete set is suitably light and unfussed, with none of the didactic ponderousness that sometimes creeps into his playing. He gives relaxed and engaging performances, which are ideally captured on a well-engineered recording.

Olivier Messiaen (1908–1992)

The greatest twentieth-century French composer after Debussy and Ravel, Olivier Messiaen was an intriguing mixture of the ascetic and hedonistic. On the one hand he was a devout Catholic who found inspiration in medieval chant, wrote a vast opera on the life of St Francis of Assisi, and had the Trinité church in Paris as his postal address. Yet his music is also an ecstatic celebration of earthly life, deriving much of its material from the natural world – when Messiaen went on a pilgrimage to the Holy Land in the last decade of his life, he spent the time between prayer transposing the songs of the local birds. The inventor of a thrillingly sensuous music of bright acoustic colours and resonant fades, he single-handedly created a vocabulary that was eagerly seized on by Xenakis, Boulez and, most importantly, Stockhausen, who applied Messiaen's detailed work on note durations, attack and intensities to electronic music. Furthermore, minimalists such as Steve Reich and Philip Glass owe their interest in non-Western music to Messiaen's wide-ranging precedent.

Born in Avignon, Messiaen was a self-taught musician, and he was composing by the age of seven. After World War I he attended the Paris Conservatoire, where his brilliant piano playing won all available prizes, while he began privately studying Eastern musical scales and rhythms. His first major composition, *Préludes* (1929), owed much to Debussy but shimmered with the exotic

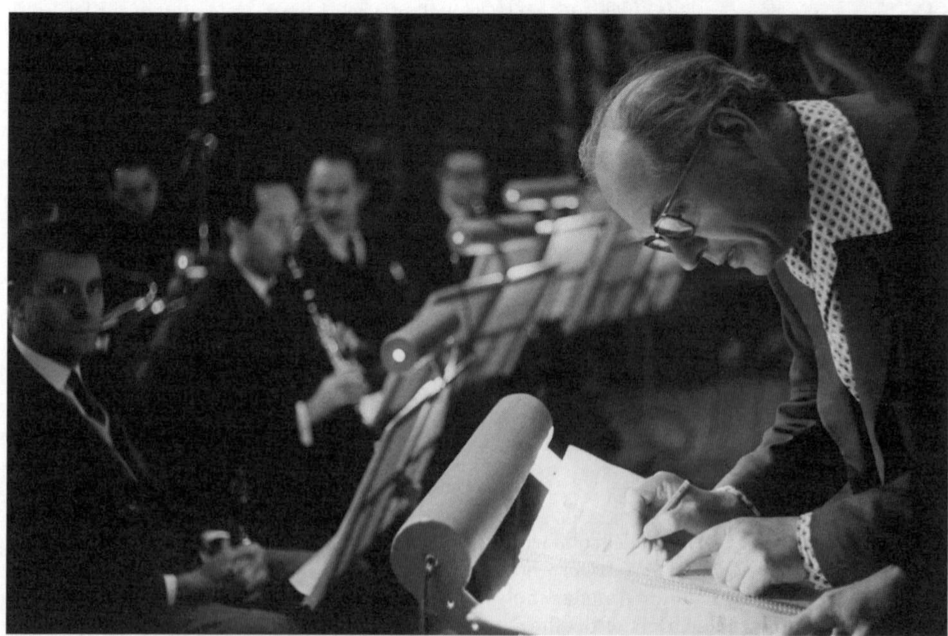

Olivier Messiaen in rehearsal at Sainte-Chapelle, 1965.

sound of what he termed his "modes of limited transposition", special scales which lent his music a strange harmonic richness. It was during this period that he was appointed organist at the church of La Trinité, where he was to play for over five decades.

From 1936 to 1940 he was professor of music at the École Normale in Paris, where he demonstrated his fierce nationalism by founding La Jeune France, a group advocating a French music aesthetic that countered the influence of the Germanic tradition. The outbreak of war saw Messiaen conscripted as a medical auxiliary, but he was then interned by the Germans in Stalag VIIIA at Görlitz. In an astonishing case of art overcoming adversity, Messiaen composed the *Quatuor pour la fin du temps* (Quartet for the End of Time) for himself and three other prisoners. It was to prove one of the seminal works of the twentieth century.

After his repatriation, he was made professor at the Paris Conservatoire, a post he held until 1978 and which was to provide a platform for the dissemination of his immensely influential ideas. In 1944, during the liberation of Paris, he wrote *Vingt regards sur l'enfant Jésus*, a twenty-part meditation on the nativity for solo piano. Then in 1945, entranced by the pianist Yvonne Loriod (who he finally married seventeen years later, after the death of his first wife, the violinist Claire Delbos), Messiaen wrote *Harawi*, a song cycle full of birdsong, Peruvian lore and echoes of the Tristan myth. He subsequently visited the USA, where he conceived the monumental *Turangalîla-symphonie* (1948), an epic celebration of America's vistas and of his passion for Loriod. Featuring the unique tones of the Ondes Martenot (see p.348), and shot through with the bell-like sounds of the Javanese gamelan, it was an instant classic.

From 1953, Messiaen committed himself wholly to notating the sounds of birds, roaming rural France with pen and paper in hand to transpose every song. The project bore fruit with the massive piano piece *Catalogue d'oiseaux* (1956–58), in which Messiaen utilized Greek and Indian rhythms to convey the cries of the alpine chough, tawny owl and numerous other species. His love of nature reached overflow with *Chronochromie* (1960); meaning "the colour of time", it was a ten-part homage to the Alps, full of luminous percussion and shifting dense string parts.

A visit to Japan left an Eastern imprint on *Et Exspecto Resurrectionem Mortuorum* (1964), written for woodwind and percussion, and intended for "vast spaces, churches, cathedrals and the open air of the mountainside". Returning to America in the early 1970s, he was amazed by the landscapes of Utah, which resulted in the intoxicating *Des canyons aux étoiles* (1971–74) for piano and orchestra, a ninety-minute merging of natural sounds, Christian contemplation and the grander themes of American symphonic music. In a search for a "music that touches everything and at the same time touches God", Messiaen then spent nearly a decade on the most ambitious of all his works, *Saint François d'Assise* (1975–83), a four-hour opera which assailed audiences with blocks of almost static sound.

Throughout his life, Messiaen's religious dedication expressed itself above all in his music for organ, much of which was developed during improvisations for services at La Trinité. His very first work to be published was written for organ – the exquisite *Le banquet céleste* (1928) – and nearly sixty years later, he was still intrigued by the colourful possibilities of the instrument closest to his heart. The epic *Livre du Saint Sacrement*, from 1984, is not just a compendium of his favourite compositional techniques, but a perfect embodiment of the experimentalism that illuminates all his music.

Turangalîla-symphonie

Messiaen's richest and most colourful creation, the vast *Turangalîla Symphony* was completed in 1948. Turangalîla is a Sanskrit word combining "turanga", the speed of a galloping horse, and "lîla", meaning play – in particular the play of the gods in creating the world. In Messiaen's own words, the work is a "a love song … a hymn of joy … a joy that is superhuman, overflowing, blinding, unlimited." This sense of cosmic abundance and energy is communicated by an orchestra of more than a hundred players, with piano as part of a shimmering percussion array, and the unearthly quaver of the Ondes Martenot. From this unique palette, Messiaen creates ten dazzling, pulsating movements with a cumulative power that is overwhelming. Among the most memorable movements are the fifth, "Joie du sang des étoiles" (Joy of the Blood of the Stars): "a frenetic dance of joy" according to Messaien, but sounding like a number from a demented Broadway musical. This is followed by "Jardin du sommeil d'amour" (Garden of the Sleep of Love), in which the Ondes Martenot combines with the strings to form a gentle bed of sound over which the piano wanders in imitation of birdsong.

The Ondes Martenot

Along with the Theremin and the Hammond organ, the Ondes Martenot ("ondes" meaning waves) has proved the most popular of the many electronic musical instruments invented in the first half of the twentieth century. Maurice Martenot, a cellist and radio telegraphist, was inspired to invent it after meeting Léon Theremin in 1923. Theremin's instrument consisted of a box with two vacuum-tube oscillators that produced a note, a radio antenna for controlling the dynamics and a rod for controlling pitch. As the hands of the performer move in proximity to the antenna and rod, so the notes and volume are modified.

The Ondes Martenot works on the same principle but has a different playing technique. Two oscillators – one with a fixed frequency and the other a variable one – produce a single note. In the later versions of the instrument, the pitch can be varied via a keyboard or by a finger ring attached to a ribbon (which is slid to create a sliding effect). The performer can add vibrato via the keyboard or ribbon, and alter dynamics and timbre by using the left hand to operate a lever under the keyboard. The resulting eerie wail is projected through three speakers, one of which is fitted with resonators.

The greater expressive range of the Ondes Martenot meant that more composers wrote for it than the Theremin (although the latter has the edge in sci-fi movie soundtracks). Perhaps unsurprisingly, most of these were French, or based in France. As well as the *Turangalîla Symphony*, Messiaen wrote other works with a part for it, including his opera *Saint François d'Assise* and the *Trois petites liturgies de la présence divine*. Other composers to have employed the instrument are Pierre Boulez, Henri Dutilleux and Tristan Murail (see p.371). Murail – a former Messiaen pupil – not only writes for the Ondes Martenot but plays it as well, and can be heard in performance on the Sony recording of the *Turangalîla Symphony* conducted by Esa-Pekka Salonen.

Aimard, Kim; Berlin Philharmonic Orchestra; Nagano (Teldec)

Aimard, the Berlin Philharmonic and Nagano are as cultivated as their distinguished pedigree would imply. Messiaen's love themes are caressed with rare tenderness, but this is a performance unafraid to hit ruder extremes: the fifth movement and finale are dispatched with unheralded physicality and lashings of orchestral detail.

Loriod, Loriod; Orchestre de l'Opéra Bastille; Chung (Deutsche Grammophon)

A recording that comes with the imprimatur of Messiaen himself, and you can hear why. Chung takes a luxuriant view of the score, underlining Messiaen's own view of it as a "love song" and lingering over its more ingratiatingly sensual side.

Et Exspecto Resurrectionem Mortuorum

Written to commemorate the dead of two world wars, Messiaen's *Et Exspecto Resurrectionem Mortuorum* (And I Await the Resurrection of the Dead) was commissioned in 1964 by the writer André Malraux in his capacity as minister of culture. Written for wind, brass and percussion, it was "conceived", as he put it, "to be played in a church, taking resonance for granted, also the ambience and even the echoing of sounds … I even wanted it to be played in the open air and on a mountain height." This, then, is one of Messiaen's most monumental works: its five sections, each headed by a biblical quotation, move gradually from a state of despair to one of joyous exultation by way of a range of extraordinarily rich and varied sonorities. There's an overriding feeling of mystery to this work with its dramatic bursts of sound and silence being applied in abstract blocks or delicate touches of colour. The fourth-section climax alternates the sombre plainsong of the brass with the animated chirruping of the woodwind, the latter representing the song of the Calandra lark – a symbol of heavenly joy for the composer.

Cleveland Orchestra; Boulez (Deutsche Grammophon; with *Chronochromie* & *La ville d'en haut*)

Boulez's second recording of this work is more meditative and spiritual than his earlier Sony version. There's a fantastic spatial dimension in evidence and some beautifully controlled brass playing from the Cleveland Orchestra.

Quatuor pour la fin du temps

Quatuor pour la fin du temps is one of the twentieth century's supreme examples of transcendent art, its symmetry and quiet beauty belying the terrible circumstances of its composition. Detained in a

German camp during World War II, Messiaen found himself in the company of three other French musicians – a clarinettist, a violinist and a cellist – and he strove to overcome the hunger, squalor and bitter cold by writing an eight-part quartet to "bring the listener closer to eternity in space, to infinity". Based on the Book of Revelation, it was premiered with a banged-up piano and a broken cello in front of five thousand prisoners on 15 January, 1941.

The free-flowing, 45-minute score contains hauntingly beautiful music, its labyrinthine sounds replete with shimmering harmonies. The piano, "enveloped in pedal", insistently keeps time through most of the piece, while the clarinet often follows a birdsong-like path. And there are some delightful contrasts, such as when a surprisingly light, dancy interlude gives way to the seductive slow cello phrases of "Louange à l'éternité de Jésus". This fervently devotional work reaches its climax with the last movement's "Louange à l'immortalité de Jésus", an extensive violin meditation in which the instrument is slowly extended to its highest register, expressing Messiaen's spirituality at its most direct.

Chamber Music Northwest
(Delos; with Bartók *Contrasts*)

This is a superlative recording of a joyful performance, with especially fine interplay between piano and violin. Interesting sleeve notes by pianist Williams Doppmann provide an added bonus.

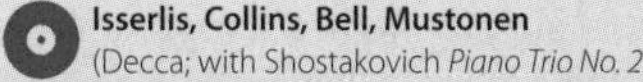

Isserlis, Collins, Bell, Mustonen
(Decca; with Shostakovich *Piano Trio No. 2*)

An extremely lucid interpretation: Michael Collins' clarinet really draws out the notes and he is well supported by some sweet-toned string playing and Oli Mustonen's superb piano. But it misses the cohesiveness of the Delos disc.

Organ Music

Messiaen was the twentieth century's most daring and original composer of organ music. His earliest published work, *Le banquet céleste* (The Heavenly Banquet, 1928), written for the Cavaillé-Coll instrument at Saint-Trinité, attempts to depict the mystery of the Eucharist by a building up of near-static legato chords which are punctuated by a pedal melody representing Christ's blood dripping from the cross. *La Nativité du Seigneur* (1936), nine meditations on Christ's Nativity, is even more adventurous, decking the composer's melodic and harmonic experimentalism – inspired for the first time by Indian music – with a glittering array of aural effects. It closes with an ecstatic toccata, "Dieu parmi nous" (God Among Us), in which the modal themes underpinning the whole cycle explode into frenetic celebration.

Messiaen's final masterpiece, the sprawling *Livre du Saint Sacrement* (1984), was honed during his weekly improvisations at La Trinité. Its eighteen sections, which return to the subject of the Eucharist, incorporate birdsong, Indian melody and a host of other esoteric devices, the work's vast silences and sustained chords assembling a sound-world never previously envisaged for the organ.

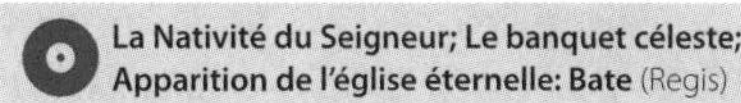

La Nativité du Seigneur; Le banquet céleste; Apparition de l'église éternelle: Bate (Regis)

Jennifer Bate is a passionate advocate of Messiaen's organ music, and her version of these early masterpieces – wonderfully recorded on the organ of Beauvais Cathedral – is highly persuasive. Part of a complete Messiaen organ set, it is also available as a single budget disc – a great place to start if you're exploring this repertoire for the first time.

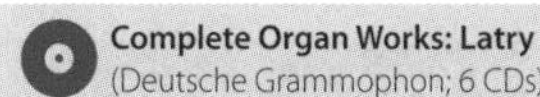

Complete Organ Works: Latry
(Deutsche Grammophon; 6 CDs)

For a definitive account of the complete organ works, Olivier Latry's inspirational set is hard to beat. Latry's playing is technically flawless and beautifully paced, but it's his sense of daring that makes these performances so utterly gripping. The recently restored Cavaillé-Coll organ at Notre-Dame Cathedral sounds tremendous.

Vingt regards sur l'enfant Jésus

Vingt regards sur l'enfant Jésus is a two-hour work for solo piano which seeks to convey, in Messiaen's words, "the various contemplations of the child Jesus in the crib and the Adorations which are bestowed upon him". Written in 1944, the background behind the creation of this masterwork was highly charged. Messiaen's wartime experiences had given him a completely new understanding of musical colour and he was currently fascinated by the music of the East and by the striking sound of the Ondes Martenot. On top of this, he had recently become infatuated with a young pupil at the Conservatoire, the pianist Yvonne Loriod. In *Vingt regards* you can hear all of this, for spread over its intense trance-like passages is every aspect of Messiaen's musical knowledge up to 1944 – extended to its limits by Loriod's extraordinary pianistic capabilities. The faster, more compressed passages are utterly dazzling (and notoriously difficult for the performer) while the slower sections, like "Regard du Fils sur Fils", hover in the air like gossamer, enticing one around their delicate filigree of sound. Messiaen's love of the piano music of Debussy and Ravel is frequently revealed, but his repeated chords and recurring themes reveal

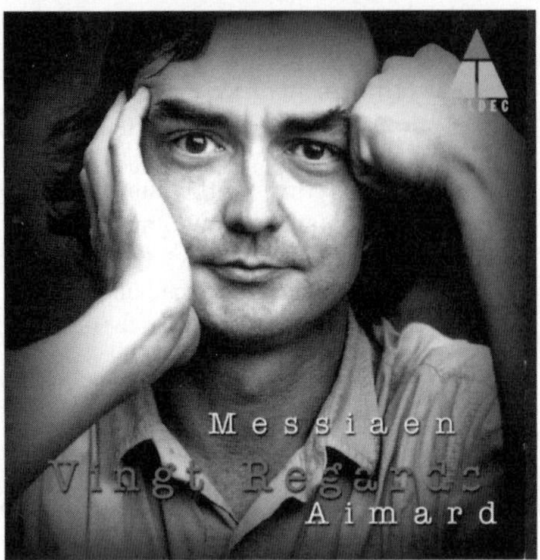

a mind that had just glimpsed a vast new world of sonic possibilities at his disposal.

Aimard
(Teldec; 2 CDs)

Pierre-Laurent Aimard's reading is extraordinary, and contains some of the most technically accomplished pianism on record. He takes many of the movements at hair-raising tempi, yet is always able to create an inexhaustible range of colours and effects, from marimba-like timbres to ghost-like echoes and shimmering arpeggios.

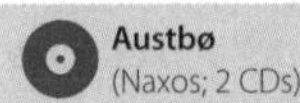
Austbø
(Naxos; 2 CDs)

Hakon Austbø's approach makes a startling contrast to Aimard: drier and more understated, he lets the music, rather than his own brilliant technique, do all the persuading. The result is completely convincing.

Darius Milhaud (1892–1974)

The key to Milhaud's musical personality lies in the very first words of his autobiography: "I am a Frenchman from Provence". He was born into a wealthy Jewish family in Aix-en-Provence, and his musical style is underpinned by his enduring affection for his native region. His unselfconscious ability to soak up folk materials can be traced to the earthy culture of Provence, while his characteristic polytonality (the simultaneous use of more than one key), was not a mere trendy musical excursion, but – at least in part – a further legacy of the Provençal landscape, as refracted by the painter Cézanne.

Showing prodigious musical talent, Milhaud started to learn the violin at the age of 7 and made brilliant progress. Although he entered the Paris Conservatoire as a violin student he soon became convinced that composing was his true vocation, and he began to take lessons from such illustrious teachers as Paul Dukas and Charles-Marie Widor. In the late 1910s Milhaud became a central figure in Les Six (see p.409), an iconoclastic group of young composers (that included Poulenc and Honegger) who rejected not only the inflated Romanticism of Wagner but also what they regarded as the imprecision of Debussy and Ravel. The voice-piece for the group was the writer Cocteau, a charmingly unscrupulous man who used people very much to his own ends. At the instigation of Cocteau, Milhaud found himself composing a self-conscious ballet called *Le boeuf sur le toit* (1920), and overnight he became the talk of Paris – not as a serious musician but rather as a joker who had jumped on the bandwagon of high fashion. It took him a good few years to shake off the tag.

Milhaud was already highly receptive to the folk music of the Americas, having accompanied the poet and diplomat Paul Claudel to Brazil, an episode that was the inspiration for the nostalgic piano pieces titled *Saudades do Brasil*. Then in 1920 he visited London and got his first taste of jazz, which prompted him to set off to New York in order to explore this new musical language at first hand. After that he developed strong sympathies with Viennese expressionism, doing much to help the success in Paris of Schoenberg's *Pierrot Lunaire*. Throughout this decade and the 1930s Milhaud broadened his composing activities to include writing for the cinema (including the score for Renoir's *Madame Bovary*, 1933), for children's and amateur groups, and for the stage (most notably *L'annonce faite à Marie*, 1932, and *Le trompeur de Seville*, 1937).

Fleeing France in 1940, he took refuge in the USA, where he started teaching at Mills College in Oakland, California, a post he was to hold in tandem with the professorship of composition at the Paris Conservatoire after 1947. Much of the vitality went out of Milhaud's work now that he was distanced from his rural roots, but he found some compensation for his dislocation through his growing awareness of his Jewish heritage – the stimulus for fine pieces such as the ballet *Moïsé* (1940) and the *Service sacré* (1947). Crippling rheumatoid arthritis finally forced him to quit Mills College, and he retired with his wife to Geneva in 1971. Tenacious and optimistic as ever he went on composing into his 81st year – his last work was a cantata written for the 1973 Festival of Israel.

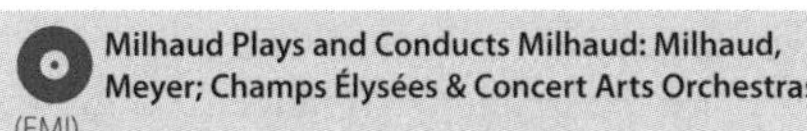

Milhaud Plays and Conducts Milhaud: Milhaud, Meyer; Champs Élysées & Concert Arts Orchestras (EMI)

The sound quality is fairly poor in places (most of the sessions are from the 1950s, and the oldest was cut in 1932), but this is a fascinating document, with the composer in charge of what is in effect a "greatest hits" programme, comprising *Le boeuf*, *La création*, *Suite provençale*, *Saudades do Brasil* and the two-piano version of *Scaramouche*.

Le boeuf sur le toit

Despite his large output as an orchestral composer (including twelve symphonies), Milhaud's most durable pieces have proved to be the two stage works, written in the early 1920s, which established him as French music's *enfant terrible*. *Le boeuf sur le toit* (The Ox on the Roof) is one of several homages by Milhaud to Brazilian music: "I assembled a few popular melodies, tangos, maxixes, sambas, even a Portuguese fado, and transcribed them with a rondo-like theme recurring between each two." The work was named after a Brazilian popular song and Milhaud originally envisioned it being used as music for a Charlie Chaplin film. When Cocteau got his hands on it, he devised a scenario set in an American bar involving a number of bizarre characters (played by the famous Fratellini troupe of clowns) including a policeman who gets beheaded by the overhead fan. Musically it's a highly exhilarating romp to which Mihaud's distinctive polytonality adds a certain acidity.

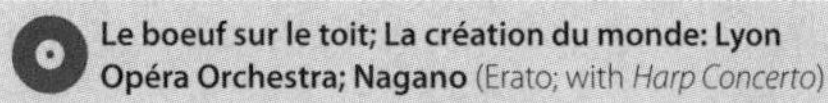

Le boeuf sur le toit; La création du monde: Lyon Opéra Orchestra; Nagano (Erato; with *Harp Concerto*)

Bright and effervescent playing from the Lyon Opéra Orchestra under Nagano, who bring out all the fresh-faced humour and *joie de vivre* of *Le boeuf* without making the piece seem raucous as some do. In addition there is a good performance of the 1953 *Harp Concerto*, a fluent enough work but not especially memorable.

La création du monde

While in London for a production of *Le boeuf* Milhaud heard jazz for the first time: such was his enthusiasm that two years later he went to New York in search of the real thing. Entranced by the melodic lines, rhythms and percussion playing he heard in the jazz clubs of Harlem, on his return to Paris he composed *La création du monde* (1923), the first major jazz-inspired piece by a classical composer (predating Gershwin's *Rhapsody in Blue* by a few months). This seminal ballet (scenario by Blaise Cendrars and designs by Léger) portrays the creation of the world as told in African legend, and is scored for a small ensemble modelled on those Milhaud had seen in New York. It's a near-perfect synthesis of syncopated jazz elements with classic Western procedures, including an overtly Bachian opening (recalling the opening of the *St John Passion*) given a sultry twist by the presence of an alto saxophone.

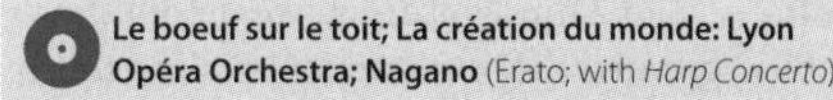

Le boeuf sur le toit; La création du monde: Lyon Opéra Orchestra; Nagano (Erato; with *Harp Concerto*)

With Milhaud's masterpiece, *La création du monde*, Nagano and his Lyon forces are no less convincing, treating the work with complete seriousness while at the same time bringing out its sensuous, smouldering colours.

Claudio Monteverdi (1567–1643)

Monteverdi's career coincides with a period of profound change in European music. From the time of Josquin (see p.275), composers had become increasingly concerned with how best to communicate the meaning of the words that they set to music. By the end of the sixteenth century progressive composers were beginning to reject polyphony for a new form of music, called monody, in which the melody was confined to just one part – any additional parts provided a supportive role, filling in the harmony underneath the melody, usually in

The earliest known portrait of Monteverdi (c.1597).

the form of chords. The increased verbal clarity of this new method gave composers greater scope for expressing ideas and emotions, and no composer was more concerned with affecting the emotions than Monteverdi. However, he did so not by concentrating on one style alone but by choosing a particular style whenever it seemed most appropriate.

His greatest works, the operas and the *Vespers*, combine a range of musical methods – from monody to madrigalian choruses – which succeed in creating an exuberantly varied and, above all, dramatic whole.

Monteverdi was born in Cremona in northern Italy, the son of a pharmacist-cum-barber-surgeon. After studying with Marc'Antonio Ingegneri, the *maestro di cappella* at Cremona Cathedral, he joined the ducal court of the Gonzaga family at Mantua, where he was employed for over twenty years. This was a highly cultivated if somewhat claustrophobic working environment: Duke Vincenzo I was tyrannical and demanding, and Monteverdi frequently felt underappreciated. The Gonzagas were not one of Italy's most politically powerful families but they lived in great style, employing several important artists including the painter Rubens and, as their *maestro di cappella*, Giaches de Wert (see p.553) – an important influence on his younger colleague.

In 1599 Monteverdi married one of the court singers, Claudia de Cattaneis, and by 1601 had become *maestro di cappella* at the ducal chapel of Santa Barbara. His first opera, *Orfeo*, was performed in 1607, at the instigation of the duke's eldest son Francesco. In the same year, the death of his wife sent Monteverdi into a deep depression. He returned to his father in Cremona but was summoned back to court in 1608 to write a new opera, *Arianna*, for the wedding of Francesco Gonzaga. The work was an enormous success but, unlike *Orfeo*, it was never published and only a fragment of it, the beautiful lament of Arianna, has survived.

Monteverdi's final years in Mantua seemed to have been frustrating, and his famous *Vespers* of 1610 was published with a dedication to the pope in an attempt to find employment in Rome. Nothing came of it, and when Francesco Gonzaga succeeded to the dukedom in 1612, Monteverdi found himself out of a job. Once again he returned to Cremona before unexpectedly being offered the post of *maestro di cappella* at St Mark's in Venice. He greatly improved musical standards at St Mark's, and in turn he was properly appreciated, enjoying a substantial and regular salary.

Following the terrible plague that hit Venice in 1630 he became a priest and his final years might have passed quietly but for the opening of the first public opera house in Venice, the San Cassiano, in 1637. For the remaining years of his life he wrote regularly for the opera but unfortunately only two works have survived: *Il ritorno d'Ulisse* (1640) and, one of his greatest works, *L'incoronazione di Poppea* (1642).

Orfeo

Monteverdi's first opera tells of the death of Euridice, and how the poet and singer Orpheus journeys to the underworld in an attempt to bring her back from the dead. The power of his music persuades Pluto into letting her return, but Orpheus must not look back as he leads her to the upper world; but at the last moment he does so and loses her again.

Recitative is the dominant form of vocalizing, while the aria, as a clearly distinct vocal style, is hardly apparent. Even the pivotal moment of the opera, "Possente spirito" (Powerful Spirit), in which Orpheus shows off his vocal skill in order to enter Hades, is essentially ornamented declamation. The strongest melodies in *Orfeo* are found in the ritornelli, short instrumental passages that punctuate the drama. The opening ritornello – which recurs at the end of Act 2 and at the beginning of Act 5 – takes on an almost emblematic function, signifying both the world of mortals and the healing power of music. This symbolic aspect is also evident in the scoring, with a clear distinction between the underworld, represented by darkly sonorous trombones, and the world of the living, which is scored mainly for strings.

Ainsley, Gooding, Bott; New London Consort; Pickett (L'Oiseau-Lyre; 2 CDs)

From the sparkling attack of the opening toccata, this is a truly spirited account. The instrumental work brilliantly communicates the freshness and intimacy of the drama. Orfeo's complex, self-centred character is well conveyed by John Mark Ainsley; Julia Gooding's poignant Euridice and Catherine Bott (in three separate roles) are also excellent.

Il ritorno d'Ulisse in patria

A gap of over thirty years separates *Orfeo* from Monteverdi's second surviving opera, *Il ritorno d'Ulisse*, which was first staged at the San Cassiano theatre in 1640. Its libretto, by Giacomo Badoaro, is based on Homer's *Odyssey*. While Ulysses has been away for twenty years (fighting at Troy and then attempting to return home to Ithaca), his wife Penelope has remained faithful to him, despite the attentions of several suitors. At the opera's conclusion Penelope holds a contest: whoever can draw the bow of Ulysses will win her hand. They all fail with the exception of Ulysses who, disguised as a beggar, not only draws the bow but kills all of the suitors. Penelope, fearing a trick, refuses to acknowledge that it is indeed her husband until he describes the embroidered cover of their wedding bed. *Il ritorno d'Ulisse* is the most neglected of Monteverdi's surviving operas, perhaps because it is the most courtly, yet its fabric is more varied than that of *Orfeo*. *Recitativo* is still the major vehicle for expression here, but arias occur regularly to intensify the drama – the most notable being Penelope's moving "Illustratevi, o cieli" in Act 3.

Pregardien, Fink, Hogman, Hunt; Concerto Vocale; Jacobs (Harmonia Mundi; 3 CDs)

This is a rather more epic work than *Orfeo* and here receives a correspondingly more operatic performance. The instrumental combinations are darker than in *Orfeo*, and René Jacobs' choice of singers tends towards the overtly expressive, particularly in the near-neurotic Penelope of Bernarda Fink. The recording's one drawback is that it occasionally lacks the energy and spontaneity of Pickett's *Orfeo*.

L'incoronazione di Poppea

Monteverdi selected another classical theme for his last and greatest opera, but this time from history rather than mythology – the first known example of an opera based on fact. The choice of subject for *L'incoronazione di Poppea* might seem strange, since it concludes with the complete triumph of immorality. The Roman emperor Nero decides to cast aside his wife Ottavia and to marry his new mistress, Poppea. When his tutor, the philosopher Seneca, is critical of his decision, Nero – goaded on by Poppea – orders his execution. Ottone, Poppea's former lover, is blackmailed by Ottavia into making an attempt on Poppea's life. He does so disguised as Ottavia's maid Drusilla, who is in love with him. His failure duly brings him capture and exile. Nero then divorces and exiles his wife, and the opera ends with Nero and Poppea luxuriating in their success and their love for each other in a highly sensual and disturbingly moving duet.

There are several features that distinguish *L'incoronazione* from its predecessors, apart from the likelihood that it contains music by more than one composer. Its orchestration is pared down from that used in *Il ritorno*, and the music is characterized by more marked contrasts between juxtaposed sections, as when Seneca's preparations for suicide are followed by the badinage of Nero's decadent flunkies. The arias here are longer and more prominent as well, and the characterization is more complex than anything Monteverdi had attempted before – Nero is the most rounded of his creations.

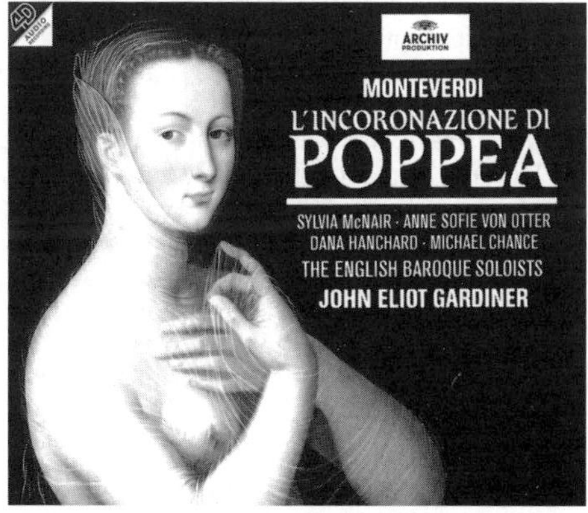

McNair, von Otter, Hanchard, Chance; English Baroque Soloists; Gardiner (Archiv; 3 CDs)

If theatricality is what you want, look no further than this 1993 live recording. Gardiner conducts an orchestra that's smaller than on the rival sets, pushing the voices into sharp relief. Sylvia McNair is a very sexy Poppea and Diana

The Birth of Opera

The major impetus behind the emergence of opera came from a series of theoretical discussions about the nature of Greek tragedy, conducted by the Camerata, a society of Florentine poets and musicians who met from about 1580. The Camerata sought to re-create what they supposed to be the musico-dramatic tradition of ancient Greece, but were rather hampered by knowing almost nothing about the character and performance of Greek dramatic music. With no extant material available, opera's pioneers derived their inspiration from literary sources, primarily Aristotle, whose *Poetics* – written over a century after the works of Sophocles and Euripides – confirmed that music had played a significant role in the performance of tragedy: "Tragedy, then, is an imitation of some action that is important, entire and of a proper magnitude – by language rendered pleasurable ... language that has the embellishments of rhythm, melody and metre ... in some parts metre alone is employed, in others, melody."

So Greek tragedy was performed in a declamatory manner that resembled a semi-musical form of speech. That, at least, was the conclusion of the Florentine scholar Girolamo Mei, a regular correspondent with the two leading members of the Camerata: Count Giovanni Bardi, at whose house the Camerata met, and the musical theorist Vincenzo Galilei, father of the great astronomer. Hitherto, the predominant style of sixteenth-century vocal music had been polyphony, in which several independent lines of music were combined to create a rich and complex layer of overlapping sounds. Such music, Galilei argued, was inadequate to convey the meaning of the words being sung: and word-setting had become the major aesthetic issue for composers during the Renaissance. Madrigal composers, in particular, had become ever more inventive in the musical colouring of words, employing devices like a falling note to convey a sigh, or a clash of notes to suggest anguish. Indeed some composers saw a dramatic potential in the madrigal, and in madrigal cycles such as *L'Amfiparnaso* (The Slopes of Parnassus), written by Orazio Vecchi and performed in 1594, songs were presented in a sequence that made up a simple narrative. Galilei, however, felt that the ornate musical word-painting employed by the madrigalists was ridiculous. What he advocated was a type of monody – that is, a single line of music – in which the natural rhythms of speech were suggested and the words clearly enunciated.

The first significant composer to fully develop these ideas was Jacopo Peri (1561–1633), whose *Dafne*, written to a text by Ottavio Rinuccini and first performed in 1594, is generally regarded as the very first opera. Only fragments of *Dafne* have survived, but Peri's next collaboration with Rinuccini, *L'Euridice*, has fared better. In this work Peri was employing a new musical style of declamation, halfway between speech and song, in which the voice was accompanied by a bass instrument that often employed one sustained note until reaching a moment in the text that needed emphasis, at which point the note would change. The new style of singing was called "stile rappresentivo" or recitative; the accompaniment was called the continuo.

L'Euridice was written for the celebrations surrounding the marriage of Maria de' Medici and Henri IV of France in 1600, and festivities such as these played a crucial role in the evolution of the new genre. Eleven years earlier, Peri had contributed to the enormously lavish entertainments, devised by Bardi, in honour of another Medici wedding, that of the Grand Duke Ferdinando to Christine of Lorraine. On that occasion Peri provided music for one of the intermedi accompanying the comedy *La pellegrina* (The Pilgrim). Intermedi were musical interludes performed between the acts of a play, involving dance, song and often spectacular scenic effects, and early opera owed more to these diverting episodes than it did to madrigal cycles, even if – even at their most atmospheric – intermedi were essentially stylized allegorical tableaux rather than real dramatic narratives.

Hanchard is an imperiously hard Nero, but Anne Sofie von Otter's Octavia almost steals the show, especially in her moving farewell to the city and her friends.

Vespers

The Gonzagas employed Monteverdi primarily as a composer of secular music and, despite becoming *maestro di cappella* in 1601, his religious output was fairly small before his appointment to St Mark's in Venice. Undoubtedly his greatest achievement in the field of religious music was the *Vespro della Beata Vergine*, a collection of music mostly for the service of Vespers, published in 1610. Which occasion – if any – this music was written for has proved difficult to establish, but it is fairly certain that Monteverdi intended its publication as a showcase for his skills, above all for his ability to write effectively in a variety of styles both old and new. The Vespers provides an extraordinarily theatrical approach to church music, with a range of startling effects throughout the service, from the opening fanfare to the use of an echo in the motet *Audi coelum*, or the dramatic ornamentation of the part for three tenors at the end of *Duo Seraphim* – not to mention the consistently sumptuous instrumental writing.

Sampson, Outram, Daniels, Gilchrist, Harvey; King's Consort & Choir; King (Hyperion; 2 CDs; with *Missa in illo tempore & Magnificat a 6*)

Robert King's recent recording is the only one to include all the music (not just the Vespers) from the 1610 publication. It's a scintillating performance with a handful of fine, distinctly English-sounding, soloists supported by a medium-sized choir in exuberant voice. There's no "liturgical context", just the music presented in radiant but natural sound.

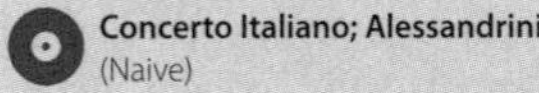

Concerto Italiano; Alessandrini (Naive)

Rinaldo Alessandrini adopts a radical approach to this music and very different from the above. The chorus is made up of the sum of the soloists, all of whom are Italian and with a distinctly darker timbre than their English counterparts. The result is madrigalian rather than ceremonial, even with the brilliant instrumental support. But what is lost in grandeur is gained by the passionate intensity of the performance.

Madrigals

Secular songs for a number of different voices, called madrigals, developed in Italy in the sixteenth century reaching their peak at the beginning of the seventeenth (see p.205). Monteverdi had already published two collections of madrigals by the time he reached Mantua in 1592. These standard five-part settings had great charm but, under the influence of de Wert, Monteverdi became bolder, especially in his use of dissonance and a tendency towards a more declamatory mode. This prompted a conservative theorist named Artusi to launch a biting attack on him. Monteverdi's defence, later amplified by his brother Giulio Cesare, appeared in the preface to the fifth book of madrigals (1605), where he makes a distinction between the old style of composing (the *prima prattica*), where the music governed the words, and his new style (the *seconda prattica*), where the words governed the music. From his fifth book of madrigals onwards Monteverdi becomes increasingly radical: instruments are introduced, the harmony becomes increasingly expressive, and the vocalists are divided into contrasting groups.

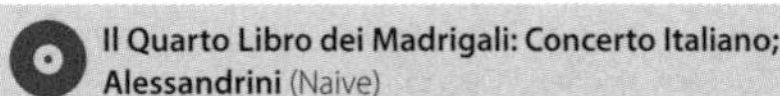

Il Quarto Libro dei Madrigali: Concerto Italiano; Alessandrini (Naive)

The fourth book of madrigals was published in 1603 but contains several works written considerably earlier. The music is unaccompanied five-part polyphony, but the harmonies are more adventurous and there is an increased emphasis on declamation. Concerto Italiano are exemplary performers of this repertoire: sensitive, passionate, theatrical when necessary, but always making the often extreme harmonies seem natural and unforced.

Il Quinto Libro de' Madrigali: Concerto Italiano; Alessandrini (Naive)

Lovers' quarrels dominate the texts of the fifth book, many of which come from the recently published pastoral poem "Il pastor fido" by Guarini. Monteverdi responds with some truly unnerving dissonances, over which the Concerto Italiano linger with real relish.

Il combattimento di Tancredi e Clorinda

In the eighth book of madrigals, subtitled "Madrigals of War and Love", Monteverdi outlines his aesthetic agenda in a foreword. Harking back to classical ideas, he argued that music should be able to evoke in the listener the contrasting states of calmness, love and war. This is exemplified by one of his finest Petrarch settings, "Hor ch'el ciel a la terra", a startlingly dramatic example of word-setting in which changes of mood are reflected in changes of speed and sonority. This move towards a more graphic form of musical realism (called *stile concitato* or "excited style") can be seen even more clearly in a dramatic piece included in the eighth book, *Il combattimento di Tancredi e Clorinda* (The Battle of Tancredi and Clorinda), an oddly unclassifiable work that's not quite an opera but more than a madrigal. First performed in 1624 at the home of a Venetian nobleman, it tells the story (mainly through a narrator) of a duel between a disguised Saracen woman, Clorinda, and a Crusader knight, Tancredi. Monteverdi employs several startling imitative effects, including the trotting of the horse and the clashing of swords, but the essence of *Il combattimento* is its expressive vocabulary. The original performance is said to have reduced its audience to tears.

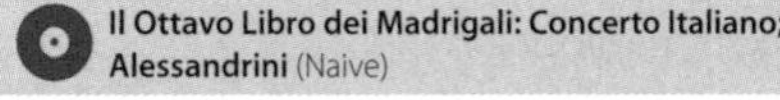

Il Ottavo Libro dei Madrigali: Concerto Italiano; Alessandrini (Naive)

Yet another outstanding release from Concerto Italiano. This selection from the eighth book of madrigals really shows off the individual vocal quality within the group, since Monteverdi continuously varies the combination of voices with songs for solo and duet as well as three-, four-, five-, and even eight-part settings.

Il combattimento di Tancredi e Clorinda: Concerto Italiano; Alessandrini (Naive; 2 CDs; with *Il ballo delle Ingrate*)

Rinaldo Alessandrini's direction really pushes the dramatic intensity of this work, relishing the dynamic extremes and dissonances in Monteverdi's instrumental writing. He's helped by a technically daring and adept narrator in Roberto Abbondanza, who makes the story compellingly poignant. *Il Combattimento* comes with another dramatic work included in Book Eight, *Il ballo delle ingrate*.

Wolfgang Amadeus Mozart (1756–1791)

"It is a mistake to think that the practice of my art has become easy to me – no one has given so much care to the study of composition as I have. There is scarcely a famous master in music whose works I have not frequently and diligently studied." Thus wrote Wolfgang Amadeus Mozart to his father, Leopold. The idea that Mozart had to work at anything doesn't quite match the received image. We know Mozart as the artless child of nature, producing music in unconscious, effortless profusion, untrammelled by knowledge of the heights and depths of human experience. It's an immensely alluring image, as attested by the success of the film *Amadeus*, which marketed a caricature of the composer as a prodigious and foul-mouthed superbrat. Like any caricature, it necessarily bears a recognizable relationship to reality – there are numerous stories of Mozart completing an entire symphony in the course of a coach journey, and many of his manuscripts are entirely free of second thoughts, as if he had been taking dictation from the Almighty. But to categorize Mozart as a brilliant freak who exhaled music as others exhale air is to diminish him. Mozart possessed a profound and profoundly self-aware mind, and his unequalled facility was founded upon a comprehensive knowledge of the traditions within which he was working. He crammed more work into a couple of decades than many composers managed in a lifetime. An attempt to catalogue his vast output, published in 1862 by Ludwig von Köchel, ran to more than six hundred works and began a chronological numbering system (Köchel numbers) which is still favoured by musicologists.

Mozart started working earlier than most, of course. He learned how to play the keyboard at the age of three and was composing from five. From 1762, his father toured Wolfgang and his gifted older sister, Maria Anna, throughout Europe, during which the six-year-old learned to play the violin with a minimum of formal teaching. During these tours, he met and played for some of the world's most powerful figures, including Louis XV at Versailles and George III in London. Not until 1766, when he was ten, did he return home to Salzburg. Two years later he completed two operas and journeyed to Italy, where he was acclaimed as the "greatest genius in all music". While he was in Rome, he heard a performance of Allegri's *Miserere* (see p.9) and wrote it down from memory to spite the authorities, who had refused him access to a copy of the score. After returning to Austria then making further trips to Italy, he came home to work for the new Archbishop of Salzburg, Hieronymus Colleredo. Neither of them liked the other, however, and after five frustrating years Mozart once again left on tour, this time with his mother.

In 1778, while they were in Paris, Mozart's mother died, leaving the 22-year-old in a state of deep distress. Unable to find a court position such as Haydn had procured, Mozart again returned to Salzburg, where he spent the next two years as court and cathedral organist to the archbishop. Unfortunately their relationship deteriorated to such a degree that in 1781, having been granted his request to leave, Mozart was ignominiously booted out of the room by the archbishop's chamberlain. The following year he moved to Vienna, where he married the singer Constanze Weber (he had previously fancied her older sister). There he gave many concerts as conductor and pianist, and spent a great deal of energy on composing opera, an area in which he excelled even his own standards by writing *Don Giovanni* in only a few months in 1787 – shortly after his father's death. But despite his success as an opera composer, Mozart's finances were constantly in bad shape and he was forced to use his contacts as a Freemason to borrow money, in particular from the ever-loyal Michael Puchberg.

The six-year-old Mozart performing with his father Leopold and sister Maria Anna.

His last three years were ones of hectic activity and increasing financial difficulty. *Così fan tutte* was successfully premiered in 1790, while the old-fashioned *La clemenza di Tito* and the populist *Die Zauberflöte* were written more or less simultaneously in the summer of 1791. Fatigued by overwork and with a sick wife, it is hardly surprising that Mozart began to imagine that the *Requiem*, commissioned by an anonymous patron, was being written for himself. He died – without completing it – on 5 December of that year. Constanze was too distressed to attend the funeral and Mozart was buried in a communal grave which has never been identified. The popular theory (central to the film *Amadeus*) that he was poisoned by his colleague, Antonio Salieri, has some evidence to support it, but is not widely accepted.

These brief facts give no idea of the complexity of his short life, but his music is easier to break down. As with most composers, his early music is very much of its time and there is little that's remarkable about his first works except that they were composed by a boy. His "middle period" begins in his sixteenth year, a curious passage of nine years during which much of Mozart's composition reflected his general unhappiness with life, ruled as it was by his strict patron, the Archbishop of Salzburg. As he wrote to his father in 1778: "Frequently I fall into a mood of complete listlessness and indifference; nothing gives me any pleasure."

In his twenty-fifth year he broke free from the archbishop, and what followed was one of the most remarkable decades in musical history. The list of pieces composed between 1781 and 1791 takes in almost everything for which Mozart is best known – music which has no parallel in its achievement of depth without pomposity, clarity without banality and simplicity without shallowness. This music is a synthesis of many different elements, each adopted, modified and then outgrown. As a travelling virtuoso he absorbed an enormous variety of

European music – England, Germany, France and, most importantly, Italy (especially Italian opera) all left indelible marks on his musical character.

Except in the world of opera, Mozart broke no new ground, but – unlike Haydn and Beethoven, who did – he excelled in every genre current in his time. To his contemporaries Mozart's skill was almost too dazzling: the composer Dittersdorf felt that he left "his hearer out of breath: for scarcely has one thought through one idea, than stands there already in its place another which drives out the first, and this goes on..." Today, having become accustomed to this profusion of ideas, we admire Mozart for the way he breaks through the Rococo artifice of eighteenth-century forms to produce music which both seduces by its brilliant melodic facility but which also frequently reaches the very depths of human emotion.

OPERAS

The most obvious distinction between Mozart and the majority of opera composers is that he was the master of all other branches of composition. Almost every great composer of opera after Handel specialized in writing operas and left it at that. Mozart's operas are the product of a mind that thought symphonically – so even if you haven't got a clue what's going on, you can tell that you're listening to an extended piece of music in which the dramatic incidents form part of a perfectly coherent whole. Mozart set some excellent libretti, yet the music is always the dominant element, giving the action inflections of meaning that the words alone wouldn't bear. Furthermore, until Mozart's emergence operatic characters were generalized and typical, often superhuman or supernatural. He was the first to succeed in putting real people on the stage, individuals whose emotions were inconsistent and whose personalities were evolutionary.

In all, Mozart wrote 22 operas, half a dozen of which are performed regularly in all the world's major opera houses, with another half-dozen receiving attention from smaller companies. To discuss all of them in any detail would obviously take up an entire book – we've singled out what we think are the four finest.

Le nozze di figaro

Le nozze di Figaro (The Marriage of Figaro) was first performed in Vienna on 1 May, 1786. In keeping with that decade's vogue for Italian rather than German opera, Mozart chose to set a text by Vienna's most gifted librettist, Lorenzo Da Ponte. Da Ponte's text was based upon Beaumarchais's recently banned comedy *La folle journée, ou le mariage de Figaro*, in which a libidinous count attempts to seduce the fiancée of his servant, but is outwitted by an alliance between the serving classes and his own long-suffering wife. The plot is bursting with intrigue and misunderstanding, and Mozart responded to it by creating an extraordinarily witty piece of music, in which even the most minor characters are precisely characterized. But the magic of *Figaro* lies not in the panache with which Mozart handles the logistics of farce, but rather in the profundity of emotion that he reveals, through some of his most moving arias and perhaps the greatest ensembles ever written. There is no more potent demonstration of Mozart's economy of means than the opening of the second act: virtually everything up to that point has been knockabout humour; within the space of a single two-minute aria from the heartbroken countess, Mozart changes the mood of the opera completely.

Ramey, Popp, Allen, Te Kanawa, von Stade, Moll, Tear, Langridge; London Opera Chorus; London Philharmonic Orchestra; Solti (Decca; 3 CDs)

Recorded in 1981, this was the first digital *Figaro*. It was also Solti's finest operatic recording – graceful, refined and tender. Frederica von Stade indulges her lyrical gifts to the full as Cherubino, but the highlight is Kiri Te Kanawa's countess. Her voice was especially rich in 1981, but there is also a freshness and spontaneity to this portrayal that has scarcely ever been matched.

Siepi, Gueden, Poell, Della Casa, Danco, Rossl-Majdan, Corena; Vienna State Opera Chorus; Vienna Philharmonic Orchestra; Kleiber (Decca; 3 CDs)

Eric Kleiber's 1955 recording has one of the greatest Mozart casts ever assembled. The characterization and dramatic direction are impeccable from first to last, and the singing is a testament to one of opera's golden ages – this set would be worth the money just for the vitality and freshness of Hilda Gueden's Susanna and Lisa Della Casa's countess.

Don Giovanni

Mozart's next opera was commissioned from the Prague opera house as a result of *Figaro*'s success there, and again he turned to Da Ponte for his libretto. The plot of *Don Giovanni* is the familiar morality play concerning the philandering Don Juan and his eventual damnation, but Mozart transforms this cautionary tale into an enthralling assembly of character studies. The Don himself is a monster, but he is an irresistible monster: the seductive beauty of his famous serenade (sung to the servant of one of his thousands of deceived lovers), the superhuman energy of the "champagne aria", and the ambiguous passions he inspires in the women he encounters, all prompt the suspicion that Mozart was, as Blake said of Milton, "of the Devil's party without knowing it." The action of *Don Giovanni* oscillates between high farce and deep tragedy, culminating in an extraordinary banquet scene, during which Giovanni refuses to repent and is dragged to hell by the ghost of the man whom he had murdered in the first scene. Two hundred years later, it is still one of the most terrifying scenes in opera.

Wächter, Sutherland, Schwarzkopf, Sciutti, Alva, Taddei, Cappuccilli; Philharmonia Chorus and Orchestra; Giulini (EMI; 3 CDs)

This is the most melodramatic recording of a melodramatic opera, full of exaggerated colour and generally fast-paced. Eberhard Wächter's Don is the nastiest on record – he employs his large voice with ringing clarity. Taddei's Leporello can appear both repulsive and lovable within the space of ten bars, while the women are magnificent.

Gilfry, Silvestrelli, Orgonasova, Prégardien, d'Arcangelo; Monteverdi Choir; English Baroque Soloists; Gardiner (Archiv; 3 CDs)

This 1994 live period-instrument performance is highly dramatic: fast but flexible tempi create an unnerving feeling of tension. The cast work brilliantly together: d'Arcangelo is a scene-stealing Leporello, Silvestrelli is a Commendatore you wouldn't pick an argument with, while Prégardien's Ottavio is the most beautiful on record.

Così fan tutte

After *Don Giovanni*, Mozart and Da Ponte produced their last opera together, *Così fan tutte* – or, in full, *Così fan tutte, ossia la scuola degli amanti* (Thus Do They All, or The School for Lovers). Though repeated ten times in 1790, the year of its premiere, *Così* did not achieve the popularity of the other Mozart–Da Ponte operas, and by the 1830s it had disappeared from the repertoire, resurfacing only when the likes of Mahler and Strauss began to promote its cause. Beethoven attacked the "immorality" of *Così*, and squeamishness about its apparent cynicism probably goes a long way to explaining its neglect. The plot has the dovetailed perfection of farce: two young men, riled by a friend's insinuations about the trustworthiness of their girlfriends, disguise themselves in order to attempt to seduce them. They expect to fail but in fact succeed; a reconciliation is finally achieved. Mozart takes this formulaic plot and makes it the vehicle for some uncomfortable irony, writing superlatively melodious music whose cheerfulness often has an undertow of melancholy and disillusionment. It's an opera with no hero, not even in the sense of a main character – the six lead roles are all equally important, and more than any other opera this one is carried by its ensembles.

Gens, Fink, Güra, Boone, Spagnoli, Oddone; Kölner Kammerchor; Concerto Köln; Jacobs (Harmonia Mundi; 3 CDs)

René Jacobs' 1999 period-instrument recording is the freshest interpretation for many years. The singing is faultless throughout and Jacobs provides light, intelligent and imaginative support. The three CDs come with a multimedia CD-Rom (formatted for both PC and Mac), that includes the complete opera, a full libretto and more.

Schwarzkopf, Ludwig, Steffek, Kraus, Taddei, Berry; Philharmonia Chorus and Orchestra; Böhm (EMI; 3 CDs)

This 1962 performance of *Così* has few equals. Schwarzkopf, as Fiordiligi, gives a fine display of character singing, and her silvery voice makes an ideal contrast with Christa Ludwig's darker, more mature sound. None of the men had sung their roles before, but all are utterly convincing, with Alfredo Kraus especially delightful as Ferrando.

Die Zauberflöte

After the comparative failure of *Così*, Mozart made an unexpected return to the fantasy and magic of Gluckian opera. Mozart was a Freemason for most of his adult life and the masonic subplot of *Die Zauberflöte* (The Magic Flute) has provoked reams of academic commentary since the opera's first performance in 1791. The ritualistic element of *Die Zauberflöte* is undeniable, but you do not need to know anything of masonic esoteric teaching to enjoy this opera, for it can be heard simply as an incident-packed tale of love tested and found true. *Die Zauberflöte* ranges from buffoonery to hieratic solemnity, and features some of the most unusual and vivid characters in all opera – such as Papageno the guileless bird-catcher, the flamboyantly evil Queen of the Night (who gets two of the most startling arias you'll ever hear), and the comically thuggish Monostatos. In short, *The Magic Flute* is a sort of cerebral pantomime for grown-ups.

Lear, Peters, Wunderlich, Fischer-Dieskau, Crass, Hotter, Otto, King, Talvela; Berlin RIAS Chamber Choir; Berlin Philharmonic Orchestra; Böhm (Deutsche Grammophon; 2 CDs)

Böhm's later *Zauberflöte* is superior to his earlier Decca set – it includes much of the dialogue and the sound is fresher. Above all, it boasts a one-in-a-million cast: Fritz Wunderlich's Tamino is honey-toned and uniquely beguiling; Fischer-Dieskau re-creates one of his greatest successes as Papageno and Roberta Peters is an electrifying Queen of the Night.

Mannion, Kitchen, Blochwitz, Scharinger; Les Arts Florissants; Christie (Erato; 2 CDs)

In this 1996 recording William Christie's identification with the opera's mercurial character is total, and his period-instrument orchestra brings unusual warmth and colour to their playing. None of the principals is outstanding, but the way they enter into the spirit of this performance more than compensates and, with even the smaller parts well cast, this is a high point among recent Mozart recordings.

ARIAS & SONGS

As well as the many operas he wrote, Mozart was frequently called upon to compose occasional pieces for voice and orchestra. Most of these were arias written for other composers' operas, either to replace an inferior number or in order to showcase a particular singer's talents. Then there were those that were produced for concert performance by leading singers and which were geared towards their specific vocal requirements. In both cases, these works are now performed relatively rarely. Equally neglected are Mozart's songs for voice and piano. Like their grander counterparts, they were composed throughout his career, and range in style from the simple efforts of his early years to the more sophisticated, through-composed works of his maturity.

Arias

The classic *da capo* aria consisted of two contrasted stanzas, with the first repeated after the second – hence *da capo* (from the top). By the 1780s, it was more usually in two parts: slow followed by fast. In either case the aria was a chance to combine emotional intensity with vocal artistry, and Mozart was unusually adept at tailoring his music to the qualities of particular singers. One of the most gifted of these was Aloysia Lange (neé Weber), a vocalist with a huge range and a brilliant technique, with whom Mozart was in love and whose sister, Constanze, he married when Aloysia turned him down. Among the most dazzling works written for her are "Vorrei spiegarvi, oh Dio", which contains a tender exchange between the singer and an oboe soloist, and "Ah se in ciel, benigne stelle" with its abundance of rapid, and extremely high, runs. Other favoured singers include the sopranos Nancy Storace and Louise Villeneuve, and the tenor Anton Raaf. But it was for another soprano, Josepha Duschek, that he wrote the most dramatically sustained and moving of his shorter vocal works, the recitative and aria, "Bella mia fiamma, addio … Resta, o cara".

Dessay; Orchestre de l'Opéra de Lyon; Guschlbauer (EMI)

A light-voiced soprano of exceptional dexterity and extraordinary range, Nathalie Dessay has made a speciality of Mozart singing, excelling in the stratospheric role of the Queen of the Night in *Die Zauberflöte*. Five of the eight works chosen for this recital disc were written for Aloysia Lange; all are performed by Dessay with a breathtaking fluency and an innate musicality.

Janowitz; Wiener Symphoniker; Boettcher (Deutsche Grammophon)

Gundula Janowitz, an outstanding Mozartian soprano of an earlier generation, made this recording in her prime in the mid-1960s. It's a fuller and creamier voice than Dessay's, and, significantly, she avoids the showier arias concentrating instead on works such as "Bella mia fiamma…" and "Vado, ma dove? Oh Dei!" which show off the fullness of her tone and her eloquent phrasing.

Songs

In Mozart's day the German lied had not assumed the richness that it was to do so a few generations later. Nevertheless, many of Mozart's songs have a directness of utterance that is highly appealing, while several attain a profundity that anticipates the best of Schubert. All, save two early French songs and an Italian aria with keyboard accompaniment, are in German and cover a wide variety of moods – from the simple tenderness of his very first setting, "An die Freude" (To Joy), written when he was twelve, to the jovial humour of the "Lied der Freiheit" (Song of Freedom). Several of his most touching songs were written in the mid-1780s, including his one setting of Goethe, the delicate "Das Veilchen" (The Violet), and the dramatic "Als Luise die Briefe" (When Luise Burnt the Letters). Best of all are his two longest songs: the melancholic "Abendempfindung" (Evening Thoughts) and the tragic "Das Lied der Trennung" (The Song of Separation). In both of these the depth of feeling is enhanced by an increased degree of subtlety and complexity in the piano writing.

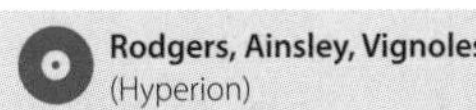

Rodgers, Ainsley, Vignoles (Hyperion)

Of the twenty-five songs included on this disc, twelve are sung by tenor John Mark Ainsley and the rest by soprano Joan Rodgers. Both singers are highly sensitive to the expressive possibilities of even the simplest songs without ever being forced, while in the more dramatic pieces they are outstanding.

SACRED MUSIC

Ever since Mozart's day it has been suggested that the bulk of his sacred music was written as a means of remaining in favour with his patrons. This is unlikely, but even if it is true it makes no difference to the meaning of the music, for even the earliest of his masses (he wrote nearly twenty) express a deep, childlike and unquestioning faith. Following the appointment of Hieronymus Colleredo as Archbishop of Salzburg, Mozart's liturgical music takes on a greater concision in line with the archbishop's reformist views that music should not obscure the audibility of the words. It is possible that this was a contributing factor to Mozart's frustration with his life as Colleredo's employee. But, of his three finest masses, only one, the so-called *Coronation Mass*, was written for Salzburg. The unfinished *Mass in C Minor* was probably written for personal reasons, while the unfinished *Requiem* was commissioned by an aristocrat in the last months of Mozart's life.

Mass in C – The Coronation Mass

The *Mass in C*, the penultimate mass for Salzburg, derives its nickname either from the annual coronation of a local miracle-working statue of the Virgin Mary or, as is more likely, from the fact that it was performed (under the direction of Salieri) at the coronation of Leopold II in Prague in 1791 – twelve years after it was written. It's a short work but it manages to sound extraordinarily grand – especially the opening Kyrie – partly because of the ample brass section of two horns, two trumpets and three trombones. Much of the choral writing is homophonic; that is, the words are sung in each part to the same rhythmic values, and the effect, in movements like the joyous Gloria, has a thrilling directness and simplicity. The solo writing is marginally more complex and operatic, culminating in the soprano's Agnus Dei, which has all the intense fervour of a love song.

Kirkby, Robbin, Ainsley, George; Winchester Cathedral Choir & Quiristers; Academy of Ancient Music; Hogwood (Decca; with *Vesperae solennes de confessore & Epistle Sonata in C Major*)

There are some very good recordings of this imposing work in the catalogue. Christopher Hogwood's impresses in particular because he manages to convey a sense of ceremony and occasion without recourse to sluggish tempi. Emma Kirkby makes the most of her glorious solos.

Mass in C Minor

The *Mass in C Minor*, Mozart's first non-commissioned mass, was probably written in celebration of his marriage to Constanze, which may well explain the music's breathtaking sense of personal utterance. What remains unexplained is why he chose to leave the score incomplete (the Credo ends after the beautiful "et incarnatus est" and there is no Agnus Dei). A number of suggestions have been made – the most watery-eyed being that he did not know how to finish a score already beyond perfection – but nothing convincing has yet emerged and, in fact, Mozart reused much of the music for his cantata *Davidde Penitente*. Whatever the truth, movements such as the Qui tollis, with its soul-shuddering *subito piani* (sudden quiet), eclipse anything in the *Requiem*, and only the latter half of Beethoven's *Missa Solemnis* stands comparison with this extraordinarily solemn and God-fearing work. Much of its solemnity derives from the work's deliberately "antique" style – the start of the Credo, for instance, reveals Mozart's interest in the music of Handel.

McNair, Montague, Rolfe Johnson, Hauptman; Monteverdi Choir; English Baroque Soloists; Gardiner (Philips)

For his recordings of the *Mass in C Minor* John Eliot Gardiner struck gold. The depth and range of expression are overwhelming, and in Sylvia McNair (then largely unknown) he found the perfect soprano – in particular, her performance of "et incarnatus est" has a wondrous, unaffected purity.

Requiem Mass in D Minor

The anonymous commission for the *Requiem* is now known to have come from Count von Walsegg, who wished to pass the composition off as his own. Walsegg did not kill Mozart but he might as well have placed a pistol in the sick man's hand, so disastrous was the commission's effect on Mozart's health. Other than a small funeral motet *Ave verum corpus*, it was his first sacred composition since the abandoned *Mass in C Minor* and it too was to remain incomplete – Mozart died while working on it, and it was left to one of his pupils, Sussmayr, to finish it. If Sussmayr was telling the truth (and many people think he aggrandized his contribution), then he composed a substantial amount of the *Requiem*, using Mozart's sketched bass parts as a guide to harmonic and melodic direction. Whatever Sussmayr's role, much of the *Requiem* bears Mozart's unmistakable stamp, and its strong contrapuntal element reflects Mozart's immersion in the music of Bach and Handel towards the end of his life. It's impossible to hear the *Requiem* as anything other than Mozart's acceptance of fragile mortality, the last testimony of the man who wrote: "I never lie down in my bed without reflecting that perhaps I, young as I am, may not live to see another day."

Bonney, von Otter, Blochwitz, White; Monteverdi Choir; English Baroque Soloists; Gardiner
(Philips; with *Kyrie*)

There's some superb vocal talent on display here and Gardiner achieves a palpable sense of occasion from start to finish. The rock-steady voices of Barbara Bonney and Anne Sofie von Otter are perfectly suited to the plainer and more linear style of the *Requiem*, and the small orchestra and choir contribute greatly towards the intimacy of expression.

SYMPHONIES

Mozart's 41 symphonies represent but a fraction of his enormous output of orchestral music. It's an amazing volume of work, especially when you consider that, unlike Haydn, Mozart was not working in circumstances that guaranteed performance of whatever he wrote. But, also unlike Haydn, Mozart's symphonies do not constitute a great body of work – the first dozen or so are the weightless creations of a prodigiously adept boy, and even in the "middle period" symphonies there are traces of hackwork. There is thus no point, unless you have a mania for completeness, in buying a colossal set of the Mozart symphonies. With the later works, however, it's a different story – the last three in particular represent one of the most remarkable feats of composition ever accomplished. All three – nearly an hour and a half's music – were uncommissioned and were completed in less than six weeks, a period in which Mozart was busy writing other (money-earning) music. These three masterpieces are the expression of an inner compulsion that demanded satisfaction.

Symphonies Nos. 29 & 35

Written in Salzburg when he was a mere nineteen years old, the *Symphony No. 29* is justifiably one of Mozart's most popular orchestral works. Its brilliant opening is instantly engaging: restless upper strings over a smooth steady line in the lower strings establish a tension that increases throughout the movement. The elegant Andante and Minuet seem to look back to earlier statelier times while the energetic finale veers between wit and urgency. Eight years later Mozart wrote a serenade in celebration of the ennoblement of Sigmund Haffner – a friend of the family – hence its nickname, the "Haffner", when he worked it up into a symphony. This is another light but powerful work with a dramatic opening, this time an upwardly leaping octave which fixes the celebratory mood of the whole movement. The other movements seem to disclose its serenade origins – lyrical slow movement, lively Minuet, and opera buffa finale to be played "as fast as possible".

Academy of St Martin-in-the-Fields; Marriner
(Philips; with *Symphony No. 41*)

Neville Marriner is an extremely distinguished Mozartian who, in combination with the light but sinewy sound of the Academy, delivers near-perfect accounts of these two symphonies. These are modern instrument accounts, notable for the suavity and finesse of the playing which at the same time conveys a real sense of passion.

Symphonies Nos. 36 & 38

In October 1783 Mozart and his wife were returning to Vienna from Salzburg (where he had introduced Constanze to his disapproving father) when they stopped at the small town of Linz – home of the music-loving Count Thun. Needing a symphony for an unscheduled concert, Mozart simply wrote one on the spot "… at breakneck speed". The "Linz" symphony, as it is known, is a richly scored ceremonial work that even retains its trumpets and drums during the slow movement. Its sophisticated mixture of the intimate and the grandiose made a great impression at its Vienna premiere and it remained one of Mozart's own favourite works. Three years passed before Mozart wrote *Symphony No. 38*, this time with the idea of capitalizing on his great popularity at Prague where *The Marriage of Figaro* was about to be staged. The "Prague" symphony is a temporary return to the three-movement Italian-style symphony, but it is also suffused with the mood of *Figaro* in its sparkling finale, and seems to prefigure *Don Giovanni* in its brooding introduction and sombre slow movement. It makes a fitting prelude to his three greatest symphonies.

 **Symphonies Nos. 36 & 38: Prague Chamber Orchestra; Mackerras** (Telarc)

Charles Mackerras's approach is a little more gutsy than Marriner's, with a more emphatic string sound and some characterful wind playing. It works well in the "Linz" and even more so in the "Prague" symphony, a grander work which benefits from a more dynamic sound.

 **Symphonies Nos. 36, 38, 40 & 41: English Chamber Orchestra; Tate** (EMI; 2 CDs)

Jeffrey Tate conducts a smaller orchestra than Mackerras or Marriner, and some might find the sound a little too thin. However, these are immensely characterful and spontaneous readings, which do full justice to Mozart's quicksilver imagination.

Symphonies Nos. 39–41

The *Symphony No. 39* seems a smiling work, full of sunlight and mellow, flowing lines. But it begins with a harsh and angry introduction and the autumnal glow of its slow movement is broken up by dark minor-key interruptions. Much of the ambivalence of mood comes from the way Mozart exploits the rich colours of the woodwind – two clarinets, two bassoons and a flute. The *Symphony No. 40* is a more obviously tragic utterance quite unlike anything previously written by Mozart. The tone is set by its remarkable first movement, a brilliant conception which, like the opening of Beethoven's fifth symphony, is built upon a single urgent idea whose interest is primarily rhythmical. The slow movement is as profoundly spiritual a moment as anything in the symphonic repertoire although commentators are divided as to whether the prevailing mood is one of gloom or optimism. It was the haughty and imperial nature of the first movement of the *Symphony No. 41* that earned it the title "Jupiter" early in the nineteenth century – when you hear the opening's march-like progress and forceful trumpets and drums, you'll know why the association caught on. Haydn echoed the wonderful middle movement in the slow movement of his *Symphony No. 98*, as a tribute to his friend and one-time pupil. For complexity and sheer excitement, there is nothing comparable to the finale: there are no fewer than six distinct themes here, and Mozart juggles each throughout the movement until, in the coda, he unites them all in a dazzlingly inventive display.

 **Symphonies Nos. 40 & 41: English Baroque Soloists; Gardiner** (Philips)

As in his choral conducting, John Eliot Gardiner takes full advantage of the dramatic moments in the last two symphonies, with fast movements that are splendidly vigorous yet never undermine the dignity and architectural splendour of these works.

 **Symphonies Nos. 39–41: New York Symphony Orchestra; Walter** (Sony)

Bruno Walter, one of the great Mozartians, comes into his own with the last three symphonies. This is broad and expansive conducting which could be called old-fashioned were it not for the sheer grandeur and sense of energy which Walter gets from his players – the "Jupiter" symphony can rarely have had such a powerful and coherent reading.

CONCERTOS

Mozart's 27 piano concertos dominate his concerto output, and they are remarkably consistent in form. Eighteenth-century pianos were incapable of offering any dynamic challenge to the orchestra – small though it was – and so much of the writing follows the simple system of exchange, whereby the orchestra plays a theme which is then repeated or developed by the pianist and vice versa. All but one of the concertos opens with a straightforward orchestral statement, presenting the main-movement subject as well as any other relevant themes, and then the piano takes over. But if the structure remains essentially the same, the inventiveness within that structure is astonishing. The music can seem brittle at first but beneath the elegant facade is a spirit of immense strength and imagination. Mozart didn't write a proper piano concerto until he was seventeen, and so – unlike the symphonies – they comprise a body of work that's of consistently high quality. If you don't want to commit yourself to the lot straightaway, sample the eight we've selected below – the first will give you a taste of middle-period Mozart, the others reveal him at his peak.

At the age of nineteen Mozart wrote five violin concertos at the instigation of his father (a noted violin teacher), who believed that they would make his name abroad. Composed within a matter of months, for performance by the

Italian violinist Brunetti and his court orchestra in Salzburg, they are all extremely pretty, but the fifth is superior to the rest. Of his other concertos, the *Clarinet Concerto* is the finest of his numerous works for wind instruments (he also wrote two for flute, one for flute and harp, and four for horn).

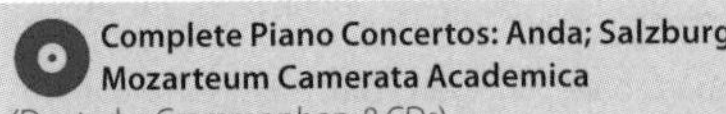

Complete Piano Concertos: Anda; Salzburg Mozarteum Camerata Academica (Deutsche Grammophon; 8 CDs)

Geza Anda's concerto cycle established a benchmark back in the 1960s and, though it now has several excellent rivals, none has surpassed it. Anda's style is intimate, romantic and unfussy, the sound is good for the time, and the set is excellent value for money.

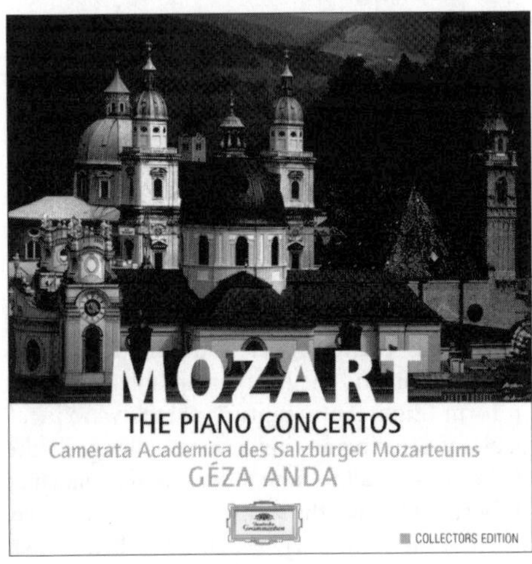

Complete Piano Concertos: Perahia; English Chamber Orchestra (Sony; 10 CDs)

Murray Perahia's more recent set is the obvious alternative. Perahia is a consummate Mozartian with an unerring sense of line and a wonderfully precise and pellucid tone. There's a joyous celebratory quality to this set which makes it hard to resist. All of the twelve discs are available individually.

Piano Concerto No. 12

The delightful *Piano Concerto No. 12* was written in 1782, soon after Mozart had resigned from the service of the Archbishop of Salzburg. Perhaps the plethora of melodic inventions in the first movement is a sign of Mozart's relief. Only the solemn slow movement, which opens with a theme by the recently deceased J.C. Bach, subdues the concerto's predominant cheerfulness. It was one of a set of three concertos, of which Mozart wrote to his father: "These concertos are a happy medium between what is too easy and too difficult; they are very brilliant, pleasing to the ear, and natural without being vapid. There are passages here and there from which connoisseurs alone can derive satisfaction; but these passages are written in such a way that the less learned cannot fail to be pleased, though without knowing why."

Perahia; English Chamber Orchestra (Sony; with *Concertos Nos. 11 & 14*)

Perahia's sprightly intelligence is perfectly suited to the delightful early concertos. There's a marvellous rapport between him and the orchestra, which he directs from the keyboard, as Mozart would have done.

Piano Concerto No. 15

This concerto marks a turning point in Mozart's development of the form into something more expressive and sophisticated. Taking his lead from the Mannheim school of composers, who enriched orchestral sonority by employing a wide range of instruments, Mozart introduced a clearly defined wind section in this concerto, which he uses to telling effect, mainly through conversational exchanges between wind and strings in the outer movements. The meditative slow movement is the first time that the variation form is employed by Mozart in a concerto; it's a movement of great subtlety, which reaches a peak of textural elegance midway when the wind section plays the theme against a background of pizzicato strings and undulating arpeggios in the piano part. The concerto closes with a typically invigorating Mozartian Rondo.

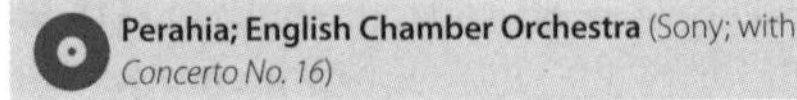

Perahia; English Chamber Orchestra (Sony; with *Concerto No. 16*)

This is another superb demonstration of Murray Perahia's graceful and tender style. The sense of these works as a dialogue between soloist and orchestra has never come across so freshly.

Piano Concerto No. 20

The concertos initiated in 1785 by *No. 20* mark a broadening of the emotional content of the genre, in particular – in this work – a marked darkening of mood. The menacing opening of the first movement, in which insistent syncopation contributes to a brooding tension, seems to anticipate the harsh and shadowy world of *Don Giovanni*, written about two years later. This mood is alleviated by the calm and sunny Romanze, a movement which has been criticized for being rather too placid. Almost certainly Mozart would have expected that the repeated main theme would have been ornamented by the soloist each time it returned. The finale is a breathtaking helter-skelter of a movement which opens with a dramatic upward-moving arpeggio known as a "Mannheim rocket"! This movement also has shades of the last act of *Don Giovanni* in the way it contrasts furious energy with moments of opera buffa comicality.

Curzon; English Chamber Orchestra; Britten
(Decca; 2 CDs; with *Concertos Nos. 23, 24, 26 & 27*)

This is an absolutely classic performance from Clifford Curzon, an immaculate stylist whose Mozart-playing often takes on a Beethoven-like grandeur, as is the case here. The ECO, under the direction of Benjamin Britten, provide nimble and fluent support.

Pires; Lausanne Chamber Orchestra; Jordan
(Warner; with *Concerto No. 27*)

Recorded for Erato about twenty years ago, Maria João Pires's performances of the Mozart piano concertos are characterized by great poise and the most elegant of touches. She's more reserved than Curzon, but these are beautifully assured accounts which are steely when they need to be.

Piano Concerto No. 21

Like the preceding concerto, *No. 21* seems to inhabit the same harmonic world as Mozart's late operas, though here it's more *Così* than *Don Giovanni*. The march-like and jaunty opening soon gives way to piano writing that is especially song-like. Many people know the dreamy slow movement of this concerto in which a glorious rising piano line is set over throbbing orchestral triplets. It was used for the soundtrack of the rather soppy film *Elvira Madigan* and, indeed, it now appears as "The Elvira Madigan" on concert programmes, as if Mozart had thought up the title. The association does the concerto a disservice, for this is a serene rather than a sentimental work full of exquisite melodies and limpid textures, only giving rein to the virtuosity expected by Viennese audiences in the brilliant passage work of the last movement.

Anda; Salzburg Mozarteum Camerata Academica
(Deutsche Grammophon; with *Concertos Nos. 6 & 17*)

Geza Anda's lyrical performance is beautifully constructed, and the recording is bright and well focused. This was the recording used in the film *Elvira Madigan*, and Anda's reading of the slow movement might be thought, by some, to be a little too Romantic.

Perahia; English Chamber Orchestra
(Sony; with *Concerto No. 23 & Rondos*)

In the most popular of the piano concertos Perahia is a model of sensitivity and good taste. Speeds are perfectly judged and, as usual, there is a perfect rapport between soloist and orchestra.

Piano Concerto No. 22

Mozart completed this concerto in 1785 while working on *Figaro*, hence its comparably bright and engaging mood – an effect enhanced by the use of clarinets rather than oboes in the wind section. A fanfare-like opening immediately gives way to something more refined, and this interchange between bold declamation and delicate passage work is extended throughout the first movement. The Andante, in the sombre key of C minor, seems subdued by comparison but then, rather startlingly, the mood changes with the appearance of two wind interludes – as if a wind band had inadvertently stumbled into someone's private meditation. Another surprise appears in the rollicking last movement, whose middle section takes the form of a solemn minuet before returning seamlessly to the original Rondo theme.

Brendel; Scottish Chamber Orchestra; Mackerras
(Philips; with *Concerto No. 27*)

Alfred Brendel is another outstanding Mozartian who has recorded the main concertos more than once. This was made when he was seventy, but you would never guess it given the sprightly energy of his attack. It's a breathtakingly radiant performance, unsentimental and completely focused.

Piano Concerto No. 23

No. 23 is one of the most popular of all Mozart's piano concertos, largely because of the sunny and easy-going disposition of its first theme. Near the end of the movement this is replaced by a rather more wistful second subject played by the orchestra, around which the piano weaves a delicate filigree variation. The slow-movement Adagio, in the rarely used key of F sharp minor, is one of the most beautiful of all. It makes its impact largely through the simplicity of its tender theme which is strongly reminiscent of the slow movement of the earlier *Piano Sonata in F*, K280. Another exhilarating finale, with woodwind very much to the fore, brings the concerto to a close.

Curzon; London Symphony Orchestra; Kertész
(Decca; 2 CDs; with *Concertos Nos. 20, 23, 26 & 27*)

Clifford Curzon's brilliance as a Mozart pianist is very much on show here: there's a sense of complete immersion in the material as well as a delicacy and a grace to his reading of *No. 23* that is utterly infectious.

Gulda; Royal Concertgebouw Orchestra; Harnoncourt
(Warner; with *Concerto No. 26*)

This is a more highly characterized account from Friedrich Gulda, who, aided by lively support from Harnoncourt and the Concertgebouw Orchestra, manages to extract every inch of joyful wit from this concerto.

Piano Concerto No. 24

Though Mozart wrote *No. 24* in 1786 shortly after *No. 23*, it couldn't be more dissimilar. It marks a return to the dark style of *No. 20* and is the grandest in scale of all the concertos, augmenting the already sizable wind section with trumpets and drums. These are used to create the kind of threatening atmosphere which, again, recalls the more ominous moments of *Don Giovanni*. The long first movement is dominated by the stirring opening theme, which establishes a feeling of defiance. A subdued slow movement is followed by an Allegretto in variation form – one of Mozart's most brilliant – which re-establishes the concerto's original tragic mood. The finale's fiery coda was particularly admired by Beethoven and was an influence on his *Appassionata Sonata*.

Curzon; London Symphony Orchestra; Kertész (Decca; 2 CDs; with *Concertos Nos. 20, 23, 26 & 27*)

In *No. 24* Clifford Curzon stresses the proto-Romantic aspects of the work in a performance of controlled power. Orchestral support isn't quite as good as on *Concertos Nos. 20 & 27*, but it is more than adequate.

Piano Concerto No. 27

The *Piano Concerto No. 27* was Mozart's last: he completed it on 5 January, 1791, eleven months before his death. It followed two years of extreme hardship, in which his financial situation had become critical and his relationship with Constanze placed under great strain. The least virtuosic of all his concertos, it is characterized by an autumnal mood of introspection and resignation that is typical of his late work. Some critics have rather fancifully perceived a consciously valedictory tone in this concerto.

Gulda; Vienna Philharmonic Orchestra; Abbado (Deutsche Grammophon; with *Concertos Nos. 20, 21 & 25*; 2 CDs)

Friedrich Gulda has alternated classical concerts with performing and writing jazz, and an improvisatory approach infuses this immensely flexible performance. An illuminating sense of the unexpected is also to be found in the other performances on this double-disc set.

Violin Concertos

The five violin concertos, all written at Salzburg in 1775, may also have been intended for a specific performer (though Mozart is known to have played some of them himself). The way that they rapidly progress in sophistication is truly astonishing. What distinguishes the fifth violin concerto from the rest of the set is the greater responsibility given to the orchestra – in the other four, the orchestra does little more than merely accompany the soloist. The melodies are engaging and instantly memorable: virtuosic in the first movement, tender in the second, and wild in the third. The finale is especially memorable for its "Turkish" episode, a piece of music which reflects the then craze for all things Ottoman.

Concertos Nos. 1–5: Grumiaux; London Symphony Orchestra; Davis (Philips; 2 CDs; with *Violin Sonatas*)

If you want to explore all the concertos, then, once again, Philips offer outstanding value for money. Arthur Grumiaux's 1960s performances are models of their kind: poised, elegant and with a tone that is both sweet and incisive.

Sinfonia Concertante for Violin and Viola

Four years after the five concertos for violin, Mozart wrote the finest of all his concertos for strings. Calling it a sinfonia concertante – rather than a concerto – aligns it with the Baroque concerto grosso in which the solo players were more closely integrated with the full orchestra than in the Classical concerto. The magical first entry of the violin is a case in point: it simply emerges on a long sustained note as the orchestra falls away. From there ensues a marvellous series of conversational interchanges between the two instruments, the viola sounding less gravelly than usual since Mozart specified that it be tuned a semi-tone higher. The high point is the slow movement, an operatic lament of great feeling in which the two instruments have long solo passages before weaving a delicate canonical phrase around each other. Both this and the boisterous final movement contain quotations from works by Michael Haydn (brother of Joseph), who may well have played the viola part in the original performance.

Dumay, Hagen; Camerata Academica Salzburg (Deutsche Grammophon; with *Violin Concerto No. 2*)

A wonderful pairing of Augustin Dumay on violin and Veronika Hagen on viola in which there seems to be a real rapport between them. This is magical music-making, with the soloists weaving a web of the most exquisite sounds around each other in what is one of Mozart's most beautiful works.

Clarinet Concerto

Mozart's *Clarinet Concerto* has for many years been the subject of controversy. While it is quite clearly the finest ever written for the instrument (and almost certainly by Mozart), no one really knows how much of it is actually Mozart's – but for 199 bars of the first movement, there is no complete manuscript in the composer's hand. Written in Mozart's last year (so, like much of his last works, seen as valedictory) the music has a consistently melancholy beauty, reserving its deepest emotion for the elegiac slow movement. It was written for Mozart's friend and fellow Mason Anton Stadler, a performer in the Vienna court orchestra, who devised a downward extension to the instrument and was admired for his playing in the lower register. Mozart exploited this ability and there are several passages which seem to wallow in the instrument's chocolatey lower notes.

King; English Chamber Orchestra; Tate
(Hyperion; with *Clarinet Quintet*)

Thea King plays this concerto on the instrument for which it was written, the basset clarinet, and the result is a darkly refined sound which is extremely beguiling. There is a natural directness to her playing which is well matched by Tate and the ECO.

Goodman; Boston Symphony Orchestra; Munch
(RCA; with *Clarinet Quintet*)

Benny Goodman's recording of Mozart's concerto is probably the most famous ever made: the recording is old but its age is more than compensated for by Goodman's shimmering beauty of tone.

Horn Concertos Nos. 1–4

One of Mozart's longest friendships was with another member of the Salzburg court orchestra, the horn player Joseph Leutgeb – a regular butt of Mozart's heavy-handed humour. In 1777 Leutgeb moved to Vienna to continue his musical career but also to set himself up as a cheesemonger. He requested a concerto from Mozart, but in the end he got four, plus a horn quintet. Rather confusingly, *No. 1* is now known to have been the last and was incomplete at the time of Mozart's death. Though not Mozart's most profound works, each of these concertos is great fun and *Nos. 3* and *4* are especially enjoyable: both have serene slow movements which show off the purity of the instrument's tone, and both finish with rollicking "hunting"-style finales. In Mozart's day the soloist would have used a horn without valves – an extraordinarily difficult instrument to play well.

Pyatt; Academy of St-Martin-in-the-Fields; Marriner
(Warner; with Haydn *Quintet for Horn and Strings in E Flat*)

David Pyatt is a true horn virtuoso but one who wears his authority lightly: his playing is fresh, debonair and technically flawless. His exceptionally rich tone comes into its own in the slow movements, and he throws off the final movement of each concerto with extraordinary panache.

SERENADES

In addition to writing a lot of the large-scale music – operas, symphonies and the like – Mozart was a jobbing composer who also produced a large quantity of lighter music for special occasions of varying degrees of formality, often held out of doors. Such music was usually called a serenade or a divertimento, the two names being virtually interchangeable, although a serenade carried the connotation of an evening entertainment and was often referred to by its German name, *Nachtmusik*. This was essentially background music, against which you could eat, talk or party as the occasion demanded, but such restrictions did not prevent Mozart from writing works of great style and sophistication. A serenade did not conform to any particular form, although they often had several movements: thus *Serenade No. 7*, the "Haffner", is a kind of scaled-down sinfonia-concertante, *No. 10* is mainly for wind instruments, and *No. 13* – the most famous of all – was originally written for string quartet and double bass.

Serenades Nos. 6 & 7

Both of these serenades were written in Salzburg in 1776, and both have concerto-like characteristics. *No. 6* (known as the *Serenata notturna*) is a very short three-movement work in which four string players (two violins, viola and double bass) are set against a full string orchestra and timpani. Probably written for an indoor event, this is light, charming music that is never meant to plumb the depths but achieves an element of wit in the way the grandiosity of the full orchestra is undermined by the more playful solo group.

The *Serenade No. 7* (the "Haffner") is a much more grandiose work. Commissioned by Siegmund Haffner to celebrate the wedding of his sister Marie Elisabeth, it lasts over fifty minutes and is in eight varied movements, three of which feature some brilliant solo violin writing. If the overall effect seems heterogeneous, it should be remembered that this was occasional music: some movements may well have had long gaps between them or indeed been repeated over the course of the celebrations.

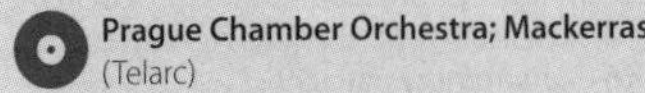
Prague Chamber Orchestra; Mackerras
(Telarc)

Charles Mackerras has a very strong relationship with the Prague Chamber Orchestra and it really bears fruit in the excellent series of Mozart recordings they have made together. Both serenades here receive engaging and ebullient performances with the resonant acoustic adding to the sense of immediacy.

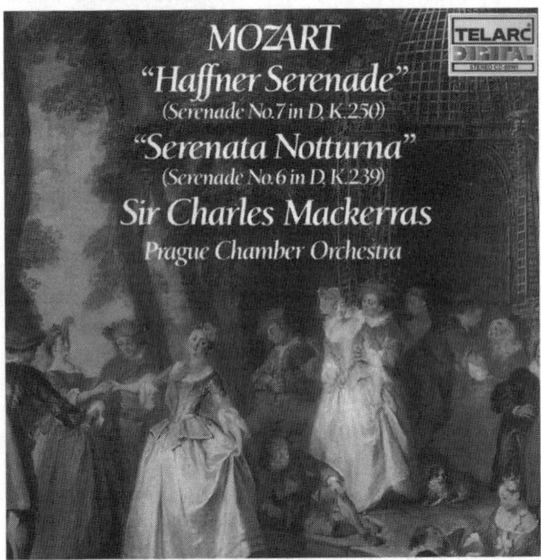

Serenade No. 10 – Gran Partita

Wind bands were highly fashionable in Vienna in the early 1780s – even the emperor had one – and several arrangements of Mozart's operas were made for such ensembles. Mozart's wind-band masterpiece is known as the *Serenade for 13 Wind Instruments*, although it is actually for twelve plus one double bass. There is some doubt as to whether it was written for Mozart's own wedding celebrations or, as seems more likely, for a benefit concert for his old friend the clarinettist Anton Stadler. Clarinets and basset horns (a lower-pitched version of the instrument) make up four of the instruments, but the great glory of this work is the way the various instruments move in and out of the limelight dictating the mood of its seven movements. The core of the work is the third-movement Adagio which begins with a rather unassuming, lilting introduction from which a long sustained note on the oboe suddenly appears. It's a moment of heart-melting magic.

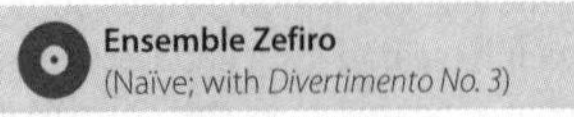
Ensemble Zefiro
(Naïve; with *Divertimento No. 3*)

The *Gran Partita* benefits from so-called period instruments, with the occasional blips and wheezes only underlining the fact that this type of music derives from the ad hoc village wind bands of central Europe. In fact, the Ensemble Zefiro play this work with consummate finesse without neglecting the wit that lurks in its more lively passages.

Serenade No. 13 – Eine Kleine Nachtmusik

This is the piece which practically everybody who has had any contact with classical music can recognize and even hum the beginning of – though they might not be able to put a name to it. Notwithstanding its popularity, it remains a bit of a mystery. It was composed in 1787, at the same time as the second act of *Don Giovanni*, but for what occasion is not known. The scoring, for string quartet and a double bass, is quite specific, although nowadays it is more commonly played by a small string orchestra. It is undoubtedly one of Mozart's most effortlessly sunny works, from its attention-grabbing opening to its sparkling finale. Only in the languid second movement is there any hint of disquiet – a momentary flutter of agitation – otherwise, all is serene and easy-going.

Orpheus Chamber Orchestra (Deutsche Grammophon; with *Musical Joke, German Dances & Contredanses*)

One of the most over-recorded pieces of music here gets the kind of fresh-faced performance you might expect from a group discovering this music for the first time. The Orpheus Chamber Orchestra can sometimes produce a somewhat homogenized sound, but here the sheer energy and sweetness of their playing seems totally appropriate.

CHAMBER MUSIC

By the middle of the eighteenth century various instrumental combinations had become established as permanent ensembles, with a corresponding demand for music. Such music was usually commissioned by aristocratic patrons or written with a view to publication – middle-class, amateur music-making being then very much on the increase. Mozart produced a vast body of chamber music beginning at the age of twelve and continuing right up to his death. He was no innovator; rather he assimilated, with remarkable insight, the developments and innovations made by others. Above all he built on the great achievements of Haydn in making chamber music, especially the string quartet, a vehicle for complex musical argument and personal vision. In Mozart's greatest chamber music – the last ten quartets, the middle two string quintets and the clarinet quintet – thematic development and the most intensely personal expression achieve a perfect equilibrium.

Clarinet Quintet

Mozart first met the clarinettist Anton Stadler in 1782, and the two men – both Freemasons – quickly became close friends, with Stadler frequently taking financial advantage of the far from wealthy composer. This never dented Mozart's admiration for the way Stadler played the clarinet, an admiration that resulted in a concerto, a quintet and a trio. The first two are masterpieces, showing a complete mastery of the instrument's particular tone and blending capabilities. The quintet was composed in 1789 and received its first performance late that year, with both Stadler and Mozart taking part. Mozart included plenty of opportunities for Stadler to show off his and the instrument's dexterity, but this is not merely an exercise in great technique – the second movement is intensely Romantic, for example, and the final movement has moments of almost unbearable yearning. With its wide palette of colour, extreme emotional contrasts, wonderful melodies and innovative exploration of the clarinet's range, "Stadler's Quintet" (as Mozart titled it) is one of the composer's most brilliant and characterful creations.

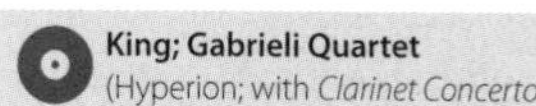

King; Gabrieli Quartet
(Hyperion; with *Clarinet Concerto*)

On the same disc as the *Clarinet Concerto* (see p.366) is Thea King's equally refined and sensitive performance of the quintet. Her restrained and intimate playing is well served by the excellent Hyperion sound.

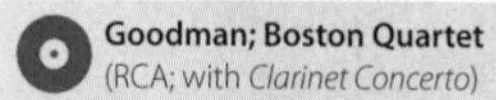

Goodman; Boston Quartet
(RCA; with *Clarinet Concerto*)

Benny Goodman's second recording of the *Clarinet Quintet* was made at the same time as his account of the concerto (see p.366). The Boston Quartet are not quite as good as the Budapest Quartet on Goodman's 1938 recording, but the soloist is on sparkling form and the sound is much better.

String Quintets Nos. 3 & 4

In Mozart's day a string quintet constituted a string quartet augmented by an extra viola – the enriched inner voices allowing for greater contrapuntal elaboration. In the spring of 1787, shortly after the success of the *Le nozze di Figaro* in Prague, Mozart composed two such quintets – one in C and one in G minor. Written at a time when he had become resigned to the indifference of the audiences in his home city of Vienna, both works seem to have been composed solely to satisfy his own requirements and both are highly personal. C major is not a key that is normally associated with complex feelings, but *No. 3* is a work of almost disturbing mood swings, in particular in its long first movement. The G minor quintet seems even more deeply felt: it speaks of resolution and self-reliance in the face of mounting despair. Its dreadfully bleak third movement (some have seen it as a premonition of death) is almost certainly the most powerful thing Mozart ever wrote for a chamber ensemble.

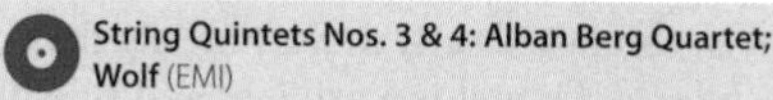

String Quintets Nos. 3 & 4: Alban Berg Quartet; Wolf (EMI)

There are only a few recordings that couple these two quintets on a single disc and it's this one, on which the Alban Berg Quartet are joined by violist Markus Wolf, that best conveys the extraordinarily variegated nature of these profound works. It's also available on a seven-CD set which includes *Quartets Nos. 17–23*.

String Quintet No. 4: Heifetz, Baker, Primrose, Majewski, Piatigorsky (RCA; with *Violin Concerto No. 5, Violin Sonata No. 26*)

This historical recording of *Quintet No. 4* is something special. Recorded in 1961, with Heifetz joined by Gregor Piatigorsky, William Primrose and two of the finest session musicians of the day, this is a highly charged and profound interpretation. Heifetz is the dominant voice, but this performance radiates a sense of complete accord.

STRING QUARTETS

Mozart wrote a total of 23 string quartets, though it was not a genre that came particularly easily to him. Haydn was the absolute master of the form and it was the publication of his Op. 33 set of quartets in 1782 that pushed Mozart to new levels of achievement. How the two met is unknown, but their friendship was probably cemented at "quartet" parties, at which Haydn played second violin to Mozart's viola, with two other respected composers, Dittersdorf and Vanhal, playing violin and cello respectively.

Quartets Nos. 14–19 – The "Haydn" Quartets

Between 1782 and 1785 Mozart wrote six quartets ("the fruits of a long and laborious effort"), which he dedicated to Haydn. The second of the set is a particularly strong and determined work: according to Constanze, the trio of its second movement was her husband's response to her difficult labour prior to the birth of their first son. The third (*No. 16*) is remarkable for the rich sonorities and unpredictable harmonies of its mysterious slow movement.

The two best-known of the so-called *"Haydn" Quartets – Nos. 17* and *19*, known as the *"Hunt"* and the *"Dissonance"* – have proved the most popular of all Mozart's compositions in this genre. The *Hunt*, named after its galloping opening with its hunting-horn motif, is a clear attempt by Mozart at mastering not just four-part harmony but four-part "discourse". The Adagio boasts some richly organized textures that could easily have been composed early in the nineteenth century, while the Minuet is a brilliant and suitably brief study of sophisticated invention.

The startling discords that open the last of the *Haydn Quartets* earned it the subtitle the *Dissonance* after Mozart's death. It is an astonishingly complex piece of music and plunges to depths that remained beyond Haydn's grasp. The dissonant opening turns out to be a ruse, misleading the listener into believing that the remainder of the work will be of a similarly haunting sobriety. Nothing of the sort happens, although the second movement does hark back to the gravity of the first. Mozart may have been no innovator, but the chromaticism of this quartet is an instance of him employing musical language that would not really become acceptable until the following century.

The "Haydn" Quartets: Quator Mosaïques (Naïve; 5 CDs; with *Quartets Nos. 20–23*)

Acclaimed for their performances of the quartets of Haydn, the Quator Mosaïques are equally strong in Mozart. And their firm, burnished tone (they play on period instruments) is especially well suited to the rich sonorities of the *"Haydn"* set. The five discs are also available individually.

Quartets Nos. 17 & 19: Alban Berg Quartet (Warner)

The Alban Berg Quartet deliver a briskly driven performance of the *Hunt Quartet*, but they can be equally ruminative when the music demands it – as in the opening of the *Dissonance*. Recorded in the late 1970s, the sound is fresh and bright.

Quartets Nos. 20–23

Mozart immediately followed the six *Haydn Quartets* with *Quartet No. 20* (known as the "Hoffmeister"), a Classically elegant and rather demure work which forms a bridge between the *Haydn Quartets* and the last three. These, the *"Prussian" Quartets*, were begun in 1789 following a trip to Berlin where Mozart had been introduced to (and offered a job by) the king of Prussia, Friedrich Wilhelm II. Intending to dedicate them to the cello-playing king, Mozart found them particularly difficult to write, perhaps through trying to make the cello part more interesting than was customary. Certainly they are markedly different from the earlier set – more concentrated, with the weight of each work shifted from the first movement to the last, and with several passages in which the cello does, indeed, dominate. Though written at a time of great crisis for Mozart, their overall mood – in particular in the slow movements – is less melancholy and more wistful than the *Haydn Quartets*. The original idea was to write a set of six but Mozart died after the first three and the king of Prussia, almost certainly, never got to play them.

The "Hoffmeister" and "Prussian" Quartets: Quator Mosaïques (Naive; 5 CDs; with *Quartets Nos. 14–19*)

With the last of Mozart's quartets, the Quator Mosaïques triumph yet again: it's partly the mellow beauty of their tone which is so impressive and partly the way they respond so flexibly to the subtle shifts of moods in the music.

PIANO MUSIC

Mozart was, for the first half of his career, primarily a performer rather than a composer. In

Mitsuko Uchida – a consummate Mozart pianist.

fact he was the first great exponent of the then relatively new pianoforte. As a performer and teacher he encouraged clarity above keyboard wizardry – he loathed the playing of Clementi (see p.142) – and this attitude is largely reflected in the relative simplicity of his solo piano works. His first piano compositions were variations and sonatas for four hands written for himself and his sister. He did not begin writing sonatas until 1774, but within six months he had composed six, all of which reveal the influence of Haydn. The later sonatas display a far greater harmonic ingenuity and melodic richness than the earlier ones, though they are no more technically demanding. Virtually all eighteen of Mozart's piano sonatas are neglected by pianists and record buyers alike, almost certainly because they have little of the colour, emotional range or virtuosity of a nineteenth-century piano work. What they do have is spareness, charm and elegance and an almost endless supply of sparkling melodies.

Complete Sonatas; Fantasia in C Minor: Uchida (Philips; 5 CDs)

In the wrong hands, Mozart's outwardly simple sonatas can sound uninteresting, even formulaic. But Mitsuko Uchida brings out all their delights. Her delicate phrasing creates a feeling of innocent melodiousness, yet each movement is intelligently worked out, and Uchida's subtle manipulation of timing conveys a strong sense of Mozart's playful and quick-witted compositional approach.

Piano Sonatas Nos. 11 & 14, and Fantasia in C Minor

Alone among Mozart's solo piano music, these three works are regularly performed and recorded. *Sonata No. 11* is very much a showpiece work written to show off Mozart's wide-ranging skills at the piano. It begins not with the customary fast movement but with a gentle, almost folk-song-like lullaby which goes through a series of sprightly, if conventional, variations. The ensuing Minuet and Trio leads without a break into the infectiously animated Rondo "Alla Turca" – a whirling dance which, like the fifth violin concerto, reflects the fashion for all things Turkish. The *Sonata No. 14 in C Minor*, written in 1784, could hardly be more different. It is Mozart's grandest solo work: terse, pithy and inward-looking in a way that seems to anticipate Beethoven. Seven months after completing it, Mozart wrote an introduction to the sonata in the form of a Fantasia. A studious and intense work, with a startling range of moods, it provides the most vivid portrait of Mozart the brilliant keyboard improviser.

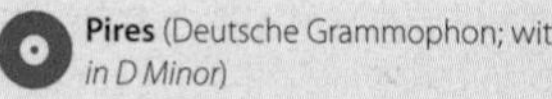

Pires (Deutsche Grammophon; with *Fantasia in D Minor*)

Maria-João Pires has recorded nearly all of Mozart's keyboard works (available as a six-CD set), for which her steely but lyrical style is perfectly suited. Some pianists treat the solo piano music as essentially decorative, but in Pires's readings there is always a degree of grit beneath the filigree surface.

Tristan Murail (1947–)

The leading exponent of so-called "spectral" music, Tristan Murail has done more than any other living composer not only to challenge accepted ways of writing music, but to redefine our understanding of the very nature of musical material itself. Returning to the fundamental acoustic properties of sound for his inspiration, Murail has invented (or simply discovered) a musical world of huge originality and often disconcerting strangeness. But for all his work's theoretical novelty and sophistication, his overwhelming interest in harmony, sonority and musical colour places him firmly in the line of great French composers stretching back through Boulez to Messiaen, Ravel and Debussy.

It was with Messiaen that Murail studied composition at the Paris Conservatoire (1967–72), having already received degrees in Arabic and economics. Messiaen's idiosyncratic attitude to harmony proved an important influence, as did early Ligeti pieces like *Atmosphères* and *Lontano*, with their emphasis on "sound masses" rather than individual notes. Murail subsequently spent two years in Italy as the recipient of the Prix de Rome, where he met the maverick Italian composer Giacinto Scelsi, whose work was another important example of the use of sound for sound's sake.

Returning to Paris in 1973, Murail (along with Gérard Grisey) founded Ensemble l'Itinéraire and began to establish the theoretical and technical bases of what would later come to be known as spectral music. Reacting against the abstract restrictions of serialism championed by the likes of Boulez and Stockhausen, spectral music took as its guiding principle the natural acoustic qualities of sound itself, often using the analysis of particular sounds (or sound "spectra") as its creative starting point. As Murail has put it: "I make music by working the sound matter like a sculptor, revealing the form that is hidden within the block of stone, rather than constructing it with bricks, as is the case in a traditional approach and counterpoint." Early works such as *Mémoire/Erosion* (1976) and *Ethers* (1978) used formal processes – often inspired by studio techniques such as frequency modulation and tape loops – and unorthodox instrumental sounds to blur the distinction between harmony and timbre, and between music and noise. This early phase reached its culmination in the majestic orchestral work *Gondwana* (1980), a kind of spectral symphony that encapsulates the tropical luxuriance of Murail's music in all its rich, outlandish beauty.

Starting in 1980, Murail began a long-term association with IRCAM (see p.91), where computer-music studios allowed him to further explore the inner life of sound, and to make live electronics an increasingly significant element of his music. *Désintégrations* (1983) is typical of this period, the entire piece being based on the analysis and deconstruction of certain instrumental timbres, with an important part for computer-generated tape. In subsequent works like *Time and Again* (1985) and *Serendib* (1992), the smooth, evolutionary style of *Gondwana* and earlier pieces gives way to a more discontinuous and unpredictable approach to form in which the characteristic colours and harmonies of spectral music are invigorated with a new sense of fluidity, drama and unpredictability.

During the 1990s, Murail began to work with ever more complex sound objects. In place of instrumental timbres and electronically generated harmonies, later works such as *L'esprit des dunes* (1994) and *Partage des eaux* (1995) use sources as disparate as Mongolian overtone singing, Tibetan traditional instruments and even natural sounds such as the noise of water flowing against rocks. Murail now lives in New York where he is a professor of composition at Columbia University.

Early Works

Several of Murail's early works use a combination of solo instrument and ensemble to explore the way in which a clearly defined musical object can be metamorphosed by the accompanying group – a kind of instrumental version of the type of acoustic analysis Murail was performing in the electronic studio. In *Mémoire/Erosion* every note played by the solo horn is imitated by the nine-strong ensemble, so that the soloist's music becomes increasingly dense and acoustically "dirty", until it approaches the condition of pure noise. Similarly in *Ethers* the solo flautist's music (including quasi-electronic sounds produced by singing into the instrument whilst playing, and "multiphonics", a technique which allows the instrument to produce multiple notes simultaneously) is freely imitated and transformed by the accompanying six instruments, who also employ a range of unorthodox playing techniques to conjure up a fantastically strange sound-world.

The grandest of these early works, *Les courants de l'espace*, for Ondes Martenot and small orchestra, mirrors many of the processes in *Ethers*, but achieves even greater harmonic richness (bordering on sci-fi weirdness) using electronics to transform the notes of the Ondes Martenot, with the complex resultant harmonies then being further echoed and transformed by the orchestra.

Mémoire/Erosion; Ethers; Les courants de l'espace; C'est un jardin secret: Orchestre National de France; Ensemble l'Itinéraire; Loriod; Altenburger; Bruck; Mercier; Prin (Accord)

This disc offers a snapshot of Murail's early works, with a sequence of magnificently committed performances featuring Ensemble l'Itinéraire, a group with a strong association with spectral music. The three works discussed above are joined with the haunting *C'est un jardin secret, ma soeur, une source scellée, une fontaine close…* for solo viola – a very long title for a very short piece.

Gondwana & Désintégrations

The *locus classicus* of early spectral music, *Gondwana* is the most expansive and dramatic of Murail's earlier works, and the one in which the theoretical and the musical are most successfully balanced. The originality of Murail's approach is everywhere apparent, couched in a sequence of saturated harmonies that sometimes achieve a positively Messiaenic luxuriance. The work's opening few minutes, in which a single chord is gradually transformed and ultimately dissolved into a flurry of trills, is a good example of Murail's spectral technique, both in the strange initial harmony (a complex, bell-like sonority generated using the studio technique of frequency modulation) and in the way Murail shapes his music in long, seamlessly evolving paragraphs – an apt musical parallel to the geological processes which led to the formation of the ancient supercontinent from which the work takes its name.

Composed after an extended stint in the basement at IRCAM, the futuristic-sounding *Désintégrations* is one of Murail's most important works of the 1980s, and a good example of his attempts to achieve a convincing union between electronic tape and live instruments. Before composing the work, Murail made detailed analyses of the timbres of various instruments, and these acoustic deconstructions – the "disintegrations" of the title – provide the harmonic foundations for both the tape and instrumental music, with its characteristically rich palette of surreal sonorities.

Orchestre National de France; Ensemble l'Itinéraire; Orchestre du Beethovenhalle de Bonn; Prin; Rickenbacher (Montaigne Naive; with *Time and Again*)

Fine performances of *Gondwana* by the Orchestre National de France and *Désintégrations* by Ensemble l'Itinéraire. The latter benefits from a brighter sound than the Ensemble Intercontemporain version listed below. The CD also includes *Time and Again*, another work combining live instruments with computer-generated tape.

Serendib & L'esprit des dunes

Like *Gondwana*, *Serendib* has a geographically inspired title, this time an old Arab name for the island of Sri Lanka that later became the root of the word "serendipity" – the making of happy discoveries by chance. One of Murail's most exuberant, colourful and appealing works, *Serendib* neatly illustrates the evolution in his style since *Gondwana*, with a far more discontinuous musical narrative whose mercurial and unpredictable progress – so different from the rather deterministic unfolding of earlier works – seems to evoke something of the fortuitous, accidental pleasures of composition which Murail had previously eschewed.

Begun the year after *Serendib* was completed, *L'esprit des dunes* (Spirit of the Dunes) is a kind of miniature desert symphony, suffused with a plangent melodic writing which sounds almost Arabian, though in fact the underlying harmonies of the work are derived from Mongolian overtone singing and Tibetan religious music. Even more than *Serendib* the work displays an expressive directness and descriptiveness – complete with computer-generated suggestions of whispering sands and other desert phantasmagoria, plus the brief, disembodied chanting of monks – which shows just how far Murail has travelled from his rather abstract early works, and the success with which his music has bridged the gap between studio and concert hall, and between theory and practice.

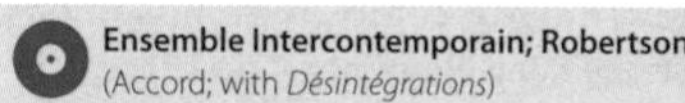

Ensemble Intercontemporain; Robertson (Accord; with *Désintégrations*)

France's premier new-music ensemble gives a virtuoso account of the sparkling score of *Serendib*, coupled with a second recording of *Désintégrations* and the haunting *L'esprit des dunes*. This is radiantly beautiful music, here getting the kind of performance it deserves.

Modest Mussorgsky (1839–1881)

Of all the composers in the Russian nationalist school known as "The Five" or "The Mighty Handful", Mussorgsky is arguably the greatest. True, Rimsky-Korsakov's highly colourful style left its mark on the likes of Glazunov and Stravinsky, but Mussorgsky's works were invariably ground-breaking, though few in number. Indeed, Mussorgsky's music was too innovative. Rimsky-Korsakov, while recognizing that Mussorgsky was "talented, original, full of so much that was new and vital", asserted that his manuscripts also revealed "absurd, disconnected harmony, ugly part-writing, sometimes strikingly illogical modulation ... unsuccessful orchestration" and began a dedicated project to make his music more performable, either by completing

Ilya Repin's portrait of the hard-drinking Mussorgsky.

works Mussorgsky had failed to finish or by the wholesale rewriting of complete compositions. Yet these are the very elements – power, earthiness and sheer invention – that gave Mussorgsky his unique musical personality.

Mussorgsky was born into a land-owning family and led a rather dilettantish early life. He found his way into Balakirev's circle in the late 1850s and began composing in earnest, under Balakirev's guidance. After the emancipation of the serfs in 1861, his family lost much of its wealth and he had to find work with the engineering department of the Ministry of Communications, and later with the forestry department of the Ministry for State Property. (As with many of his contemporaries, composition was always a spare-time activity, though his dipsomania probably had a more deleterious effect on his writing than did his lack of time.)

In the meantime, he had been gaining a growing reputation for his songwriting abilities, bringing a new sense of realism and integration to the form. He also worked on a couple of operas that he never got round to completing, *Salammbô* (1863–66) and *The Marriage* (1868) – from the former emerged one of his best-known works, *St John's Night on the Bare Mountain* (1867). He then embarked on an operatic adaptation of Pushkin's play *Boris Godunov*, which went through two versions in his own lifetime (1869 and 1872), and found lasting success in the second. In 1874 he wrote his best-known work, *Pictures at an Exhibition*, a piano suite more often heard today in orchestral guise. His last great projects, which vied for his attention and thus were never finished, were another historical opera, *Khovanshchina* (1872–80, completed by Rimsky-Korsakov and revised by Shostakovich), and the Gogol-based comedy *Sorochintsy Fair* (1874–80, completed by Liadov).

Boris Godunov

Boris Godunov is roughly based on the life of the man who became tsar in 1598, having murdered his rival, and the plot depicts the attempt of a pretender to the throne, who knows of the murder, to usurp him. Mussorgsky exploits the dramatic potential of this scenario to the full, creating a powerful contrast between the spectacle of the coronation scene and Boris's inner torment as he tries and fails to come to terms with his guilt. His greatest achievement, however, is his musical characterization, in which the words, thoughts and moods of the protagonists are mirrored in the orchestral accompaniment. Composers as diverse as Debussy and Janáček were undoubtedly influenced by Mussorgsky's skill in word-setting, in particular his way of setting dramatic prose so that the music reflects the inflections of the spoken text.

The work exists in three versions: Mussorgsky wrote two (in 1872 he added two scenes set in Poland, but cut a scene in the last act), and Rimsky-Korsakov produced one soon after the composer's death with the intention that it should help the reception of the opera, while admitting that a time might come when it was superseded by a reappraisal of Mussorgsky's original. This has now happened and, while Rimsky's version is undoubtedly colourful, it misses the profundity and dark hues of the original orchestration.

Putilin/Vaneev, Lutsuk/Galusin, Ohotnikov, Pluzhnikov; Kirov Opera Chorus and Orchestra; Gergiev (Philips; 5 CDs)

Valery Gergiev's 1998 recording of *Boris* is terrific value: it contains both of Mussorgsky's versions in a five-disc box that sells for the price of three CDs. Both performances are astonishingly powerful, but the later version has the edge for Vladimir Vaneev's resonantly physical portrayal of the title role, and the dramatic tenor Vladimir Galusin's sensational performance as Grigory.

Pictures at an Exhibition

When Mussorgsky's close friend, the architect-painter Victor Hartmann, died in 1873, a mutual friend named Vladimir Stasov arranged a memorial exhibition of the artist's work in St Petersburg. Visiting the exhibition, Mussorgsky conceived his own tribute in the form of a suite of piano pieces depicting a selection of the works on show, with a recurring theme (the "Promenade") representing the viewer walking between the Romantic and often fantastical pictures. There are ten pictures in total, each one a superbly atmospheric miniature which utilizes the piano's expressive potential in a way that suggests the influence of Liszt but reveals greater psychological insight. A wide range of moods is depicted, from the sinister melancholy of "Gnomus", through the playfulness of "Les Tuileries" (which seems to presage Debussy) to the grand triumphalism of "The Great Gate of Kiev". Although completed in 1874, the suite wasn't published until after Mussorgsky's death, and the pictorial quality of these pieces inevitably drew the attention of other composers and arrangers – it's only surprising that Rimsky didn't attempt an orchestral arrangement himself. Of the many subsequent orchestrations, the most successful, if hardly the most Russian, is that made by Ravel in 1922.

Piano Version: Pletnev (Virgin; 2 CDs; with Tchaikovsky/Pletnev, *Sleeping Beauty* & Tchaikovsky, *The Seasons*)

Mikhail Pletnev gives a strong reading of the original piano suite, with bold and dramatic playing that makes one think that orchestration didn't really add anything really substantial to this work.

Ravel Orchestration: Berlin Philharmonic; Abbado (Deutsche Grammophon; with *St John's Night on the Bare Mountain* and choral works)

Abbado is a highly enthusiastic promoter of Mussorgsky but his latest recording of Ravel's version of *Pictures* can't prevent the piece sounding less like Mussorgsky than like Ravel, but there is still plenty of character and excitement here.

St John's Night on the Bare Mountain

Mussorgsky's only major orchestral work – *St John's Night on the Bare Mountain* – is another piece that Rimsky wouldn't leave to fend for itself. It exists in two versions, Mussorgsky's original (intended as an episode in his opera *Sorochintsy Fair*) and Rimsky's beefed-up recomposition, incorporating other Mussorgsky fragments. The work is a portrait of midsummer night when, according to Russian folklore, a witches' Sabbath is held on the Bare Mountain near Kiev; the musical whirlwind at the heart of the piece is one of those bits of music that hi-fi shops use to impress customers.

Berlin Philharmonic; Abbado (Deutsche Grammophon; with *Pictures at an Exhibition* & choral works)

Although not nearly as well-known as Rimsky's reworking, the original is arguably a more effective portrait of the midsummer mayhem, and Abbado's fine recording of it comes coupled with Ravel's version of *Pictures* plus an invaluable collection of rarely heard choral works.

Songs

Mussorgsky is arguably the greatest nineteenth-century songwriter after Schubert and Schumann, though this aspect of his music is not well enough known outside of Russia. In his songwriting, as in his operas, he was especially concerned with realism and attempted, wherever possible, to follow the rhythms of natural speech. He also, more than any other composer of the period, had no qualms about introducing the modality of folk song into his vocal music, though actual quotation from folk music is relatively rare in his output. As well as many fine individual songs, he wrote two outstanding cycles: *The Nursery* (1872) deals with childhood fears and imaginings on going to bed, while *Sunless* (1874) is striking for its simple and highly original harmony. The *Songs and Dances of Death* (1877) were originally intended as a set of twelve songs, but finished up as four amazingly intense and startling depictions of death.

The Nursery, Sunless, Songs and Dances of Death: Christoff, Labinsky (EMI; with *Lullaby, Hopak, King Saul, The Wild Winds Blow & Song of the Flea*)

Boris Chistoff's is a big resonant bass voice but he uses it with extraordinary sensitivity and psychological insight. This is an outstanding disc by one of the greatest Mussorgsky interpreters, recorded in the 1950s when he was in his vocal prime. Sixteen of the twenty-four songs are accompanied by pianist Alexandre Labinsky, the rest are with orchestral accompaniment.

The Nursery, Sunless, Songs and Dances of Death: Lipovšek, Johnson (Sony; with *Gopak, Hebrew Song & Song of the Flea*)

Though the songs are usually a male preserve, like those of Schubert they work just as well when sung by a female singer – especially one as subtly beguiling as mezzo-soprano Marjana Lipovšek.

n

Conlon Nancarrow (1912–1997)

For all the modern world's obsession with technology, Conlon Nancarrow remains the only classical composer to have established a lasting reputation on the basis of pieces written almost entirely for a machine. His remarkable sequence of player-piano studies demonstrates that dispensing with human performers does not necessarily result in arid music, and offers a compelling exploration of the myriad new structures and sonorities made available through mechanical means.

Born in 1912 to a family of Arkansas worthies, Nancarrow spent a wayward youth learning trumpet, developing a passion for jazz and resolving to become a musician. In 1934, braving parental displeasure, he trooped off to Boston to study composition with arch-academics Roger Sessions and Walter Piston, an experience that seems to have borne little immediate fruit, although he would later emphasize the value of Sessions' obsessive contrapuntal training. Having joined the Communist Party, in 1937 he went to Spain, fighting for two years in the Civil War as a foot soldier with the Republican forces.

In 1940, after being denied a passport by a government that was suspicious of his Communist past, Nancarrow decided to leave the increasingly repressive political climate of the States for Mexico City, where he lived for the remaining 57 years of his life, acquiring Mexican citizenship in 1956. By the time of this self-imposed exile, he was the equal of virtually any American composer then living, as the small corpus of works for live performers that he allowed to survive proves.

The immediate effect of Nancarrow's move to Mexico was less than propitious. Already politically ostracized, he now found himself almost entirely cut off from US musical life and the chance to have his increasingly challenging music performed. Making a virtue of necessity, in 1947 Nancarrow acquired a player piano, or pianola – a mechanical piano operated by a roll of punched paper – on which he could "perform" his own music. The player piano's ability to execute any sequence of notes, no matter how fast or rhythmically complex, also allowed Nancarrow to explore the arcane rhythmic structures which became the basis of his mature music, and whose difficulties would have defeated even the best performers of the time.

The following quarter-century was one of extreme artistic isolation, as Nancarrow laboured on the immense series of *Studies for Player Piano* that forms the bulk of his output. The first step towards recognition was a 1969 Columbia

Conlon Nancarrow checking the punched holes on his score sheets, 1985.

recording of twelve of the studies, but it wasn't until 1977, and the first part-publication of the sequence, followed by further recordings, that Nancarrow's work began to be widely known. In 1981, in the wake of his burgeoning reputation, he returned to the US for the first time since 1947 – though subsequent enquiries about the possibility of his going back to live in his home country were stymied by the unrelenting American officialdom.

More positively, Nancarrow also found a new generation of virtuoso performers rising to the challenge of his music: Yvar Mikhashoff's pioneering orchestrations of selected player-piano studies were brilliantly realized and recorded by the Ensemble Modern, whilst the wizardry of performers such as pianist Ursula Oppens and the Arditti String Quartet persuaded Nancarrow to return to writing for live performers after a gap of some forty years.

Studies for Player Piano

A kind of *Well-Tempered Clavier* for the machine age, Nancarrow's fifty-odd *Studies for Player Piano* constitute one of the twentieth century's most original bodies of music. Where Bach's encyclopedic opus had offered a comprehensive exploration of every major and minor key, Nancarrow's studies comprise a no less thorough exploration of the possibilities of rhythm, using the player piano's ability to transcend the limits of what is humanly performable to create pieces in simultaneous multiple tempi, frequently exploring the outermost intelligible limits of speed and complexity. The earliest – and most approachable – studies extrapolate from Nancarrow's previous instrumental works, heavily influenced by popular music and jazz, such as the crazily accelerated boogie-woogies of *Study No. 3* or the flamenco-on-speed effects of *Study No. 12*. The later studies, from around *No. 20* onwards, are more abstract, and the flights of rhythmic fantasy ever more abstruse, as in the infamous *Study No. 40*, a canon based on the proportions between the irrational numbers π and e.

Complete Studies for Player Piano
(Wergo; 5 CDs)

This five-CD set of the complete player-piano studies was recorded under the composer's supervision on his own player pianos in his studio in Mexico City. It's a gargantuan undertaking, and nobody's idea of easy listening, but taken in small doses it offers one of the twentieth century's most absorbing musical odysseys. For the faint-hearted, a two-CD extracts set is also available.

Music for Live Performers

The fact that an isolated and dispirited Nancarrow gave up writing for live performers for four decades is regrettable, since the few non-mechanial works that do survive contain some of his finest music. These include a number of impressive early compositions – such as the jazzy *Sonatina* for piano and the bucolic *String Quartet No. 1* but arguably the best are the handful of pieces from his final years, most notably the *String Quartet No. 3*, the *Piece No. 2 for Small Orchestra* and *Three Canons for Ursula* (for piano). The small number of live works has also been partly rectified by Yvar Mikhashoff's marvellous arrangements for chamber orchestra of some of the player-piano studies, which not only bring Nancarrow's seminal music into the concert hall, but also replace the monochromatic and antiquated sound of the player piano with a full range of instrumental colouring and incident – not to mention the voyeuristic thrill of hearing live performers attempting to master this supremely difficult material.

Selected Studies for Player-Piano (orch. Mikhashoff); Piece No. 2 for Small Orchestra; Tango; Toccata; Trio; Sarabande & Scherzo: Ensemble Modern; Metzmacher
(RCA)

This disc is the perfect introduction to Nancarrow's music, containing Mikhashoff's orchestrations of eleven of the earlier and more accessible studies, along with a few works written for live performers, including the marvellous *Piece No. 2*. The Ensemble Modern play these consummately taxing pieces with extraordinary verve and assurance.

Carl Nielsen (1865–1931)

Carl Nielsen, Denmark's most celebrated composer, was born into the peasant island community of Funen in eastern Denmark (also the birthplace of Hans Christian Andersen). The son of a painter and a village musician, as a child Carl played in the village dance band and in the local amateur orchestra. At the age of fourteen he joined the military band in Odense as a trombonist, and after two years at the Royal Academy was employed as second violinist at the Royal Theatre Orchestra in Copenhagen. A scholarship took him to Germany where he met the sculptress Anne Marie Brodersen and married her. During this trip he was highly impressed by performances of Wagner's *Ring* and *Die Meistersinger*, but Brahms was an even greater influence, particularly on his early symphonies. Further guidance came from the music director at the Royal Theatre, the composer Johan Svendsen. Nielsen's first symphony was premiered by the orchestra in 1894 and from then on his rise was rapid. His two operas, *Saul and David* (1902) and *Maskarade* (1905), were both performed under his direction; he then left the orchestra to concentrate on composing but returned three years later as principal conductor, a post he held for six years.

The rest of his life was taken up with composition – he once wrote that his life was lived through music rather than out in the everyday world – and sustaining the rather tempestuous relationship with his wife. Towards the end of his life he worked, with his friend Thomas Laub, on producing simple songs, based on traditional

Carl Nielsen aged nineteen.

Danish styles, appropriate for singing in school. He also published a remarkably frank and unsentimental autobiography, *My Childhood in Funen*. Arguably his unique combination of the lyrical and the dynamic is derived largely from his memories of childhood – the songs his mother sang to him and the music of the village dance band. He wrote concertos for flute, clarinet and violin, a popular wind quintet and some fine tone poems, including *Helios* (1903), a short evocation of sunrise, and *Pan and Syrinx* (1918), an impressionistic depiction of characters from Ovid.

Nielsen's fame rests solidly on his symphonies, works which are characterized by an emotional directness devoid of sentimentality, and by a constant search for clarity in line and orchestral texture, spinning out long lines of melody that build into complex yet clearly defined contrapuntal melees. His orchestration can often be stark in its sustained concentration on just a few instruments, yet come the climax of a movement or work Nielsen can unleash the orchestra's full force in a blaze of energy.

SYMPHONIES

Nielsen's six symphonies are almost contemporary with the seven of Sibelius, yet they could hardly be more different in style, form and intent: where Sibelius seemed to be aiming for ever greater concision, Nielsen's symphonies get more adventurous and wide-ranging as the cycle progresses, culminating in the experimental and sardonic sixth. The ones to explore first are numbers 3, 4 and 5, the first of these being the most immediately appealing.

Complete Symphonies: San Francisco Symphony Orchestra; Blomstedt (Decca; 4 CDs; with *Little Suite, Hymnus Amoris, Maskarade Overture & Aladdin Suite*)

Herbert Blomstedt's Nielsen symphonies cycle is as close to definitive as it's possible to be. He brings a sense of spontaneity to the early symphonies and an extraordinary depth to the later ones. Radiant and heartfelt playing from the San Franciscans and superlative sound make for an unbeatable combination. Currently available as two separate two-CD sets.

Symphony No. 3 – Sinfonia Espansiva

Expansiveness is the theme of Nielsen's third symphony (1910–11), and the musical material seems always to be pushing inexorably forward beyond its rightful bounds – through repetitive rhythms, onward-forcing harmonic progressions, endless melodies and typically Nielsenesque dramatic contrasts. A note of foreboding is established by an insistently repeated unison note from the whole orchestra, but this soon gives way to some highly energized counterpoint before the unexpected appearance of a delicate waltz that gets increasingly brash as it is repeated. An almost cosmic spaciousness is achieved in the marvellous slow movement: a horn solo heralds a unison string line which moves tentatively over the first of a series of pedal points. The music becomes increasingly luxuriant, culminating in the entry of two solo voices rhapsodizing worldlessly over the orchestra. An intense but often playful Scherzo follows, and then a finale with an almost Elgarian grandiloquence.

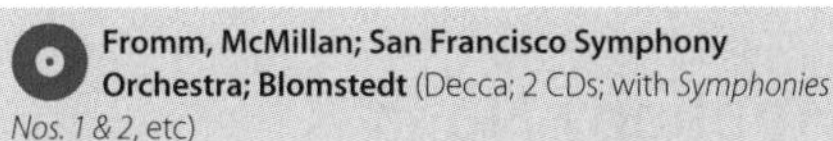

Fromm, McMillan; San Francisco Symphony Orchestra; Blomstedt (Decca; 2 CDs; with *Symphonies Nos. 1 & 2*, etc)

The third gets a truly scintillating reading from Blomstedt. He seems to have an almost instinctive feel for the organic flow of this work and it rides along with all the powerful energy of a wave.

Guldbaek, Møller; Royal Danish Orchestra; Bernstein (Sony; with *Symphony No. 5*)

This is a classic reading from Bernstein and the Royal Danish Orchestra, with a really majestic flow to the opening movement. Coupled with a brilliant version of the fifth (see below), this would be a good starting point for those new to the symphonies.

Symphony No. 4 – The Inextinguishable

The idea of the life force is at the heart of the third symphony and the same is true for *Symphony No. 4 – The Inextinguishable* (1914–16). Its title was explained by the composer as an attempt "... to indicate in one word what only music has the power to express in full: the elemental Will of Life. Music is Life and, like it, inextinguishable." Written when Nielsen's marriage was floundering and shortly after his resignation from the Copenhagen Opera, this symphony abounds in conflict and contradiction. Its opening is frenetic, with percussion, strings and wind seeming to vie with each other in clamorous discourse before giving way to an ardent, affirmative melody in the clarinets. The brief second movement suggests the carefree sounds of a village wind band, but the slow movement – with its angular string lines – is unremittingly bleak. The finale culminates in a musical battle between two sets of spatially separated timpani, a battle that is only resolved by the recall of the lyrical melody from the first movement.

City of Birmingham Symphony Orchestra; Rattle
(EMI; with *Pan and Syrinx* & Sibelius *Symphony No 5*)

Simon Rattle's great achievement here is in managing to balance the rich contrasts in mood and character while sustaining the elemental musical current. At the end he avoids the traditional slowing down when the "big tune"' returns and the whole character of the music changes: not a clear-cut triumph but a kind of defiant joy.

San Francisco Symphony Orchestra; Blomstedt
(Decca; 2 CDs; with *Symphonies Nos. 5 & 6, Little Suite & Hymnus Amoris*)

Though not as structurally satisfying as Rattle's account (see above), Blomstedt's is nonetheless one of the most exciting performances currently available, and recorded with splendid presence and bite.

Symphony No. 5

A sense of conflict is also evident in Nielsen's *Symphony No. 5* (1921–22), but this time there's a decidedly militaristic edge to it – perhaps reflecting Nielsen's response to the nightmare of World War I. Here a tense sparely scored opening gradually breaks out into a protracted battle for supremacy between a solo side drum and the rest of the orchestra, representing – according to the composer – the struggle between good and evil. The orchestra triumphantly subsumes the side drum's martial improvisations and, after a warmly scored Adagio, the first movement ends quietly with the side drum heard again in the distance over a plangent clarinet solo. As this movement had contained both the traditional opening and slow movements, so the second combines the Scherzo and finale. The latter is characterized by a near-demented fugue followed by a slower, more reflective one, before the fury of the first movement returns, building in intensity until some kind of resolution is achieved.

San Francisco Symphony Orchestra; Blomstedt
(EMI; with *Symphonies Nos. 4 & 6*, etc)

Performances and recordings of this symphony often disappoint in the most vital place – the side-drum battle, which can often sound too easily won. Not so in Blomstedt's excellent account, which makes a worthy partner to his recordings of the fourth and sixth.

New York Philharmonic Orchestra; Bernstein
(Sony; with *Symphony No. 3*)

Leonard Bernstein and the New York Philharmonic really get under the skin of this great symphony. Throughout the performance, they generate a tension that is nothing short of electrifying. The coupling is an equally brilliant recording of the third symphony.

Symphony No. 6 – Sinfonia Semplice

The most misunderstood of his symphonies, Nielsen's sixth (1924–25) seems to communicate his uncertainties about the way music was going in the 1920s. As with much of his later music, it is full of paradoxes, not least of which is the fact that he frequently breaks his large orchestra down into small chamber-like groupings. In the first movement a kind of jovial, innocent march is undermined by increasingly anxious, and even aggressive, interventions – including some *Psycho*-style slashing strings – which then unexpectedly move into an affirmative hymn-like "big tune". The second movement (entitled "Humoresque") seems to be a sardonic dig at Schoenberg (and modern music in general) combined with Nielsen's own brand of grotesquerie in what sounds like a village band interrupted by rowdy bystanders. There's an icily austere, but haunting, slow movement, before the demented finale kicks in. The whole enigmatic work ends with an unmistakable bassoon "fart". Whether Nielsen intended his audience to laugh or scream at this music (the premiere met with a mostly negative reaction), this is one of his most fascinating and phantasmagorical works; one that looks forward to the more extreme irony of Shostakovich and nostalgically backwards at his own achievements.

San Francisco Symphony Orchestra; Blomstedt
(Decca; 2 CDs; with *Symphonies Nos. 4 & 5*, etc)

Blomstedt is more restrained than some in this, the most chilling of Nielsen's symphonies, but the requisite nightmare quality is certainly in evidence and, as in the whole of this series, the sound quality is outstanding.

Swedish Radio Symphony Orchestra; Salonen
(Sony; with *Symphony No. 3*)

Arguably Esa-Pekka Salonen gets closer to the chilly, sardonic heart of this great work. It's an immensely powerful performance which really brings out the originality of Nielsen's vision.

CONCERTOS

Nielsen wrote three concertos – for violin (1911), flute (1926) and clarinet (1928). The former is the best, benefiting from a warmth and geniality that seems to reflect Nielsen's affection for both the violin (his own instrument) and the work's dedicatee, his son-in-law Emil Telmányi. The two later concertos are less immediately appealing – the *Clarinet Concerto* in particular is rather austere – but they are well worth investigating.

Violin Concerto

Nielsen's *Violin Concerto* is a buoyant and expansive work which deserves to be better known. Constructed in two sections, it pitches soloist (and listener) straight into the action with an extended cadenza that leads into a first movement proper of gentle poetry and quixotic charm (marked "Allegro cavalleresco"). It's a movement of great variety, mainly optimistic but with moments of an almost Elgarian wistfulness. This mood is developed in the second section, where a ruminative and subdued theme is exchanged, at first between soloist and woodwind and then with the whole orchestra. The work ends with a rather quirky Rondo which just occasionally hints at the village band music that Nielsen had once played himself.

Lin; Swedish Radio Symphony Orchestra; Salonen
(Sony; with Sibelius *Violin Concerto*)

Cho-Liang Lin, one of the most underrated of top violinists, gives a brilliant account of this concerto. His articulation and phrasing are immaculate, but what is especially impressive is the way he avoids a vibrato-thick tone in favour of an emphasis on a clear line. He's helped by a forward position in the natural-sounding recording.

Wind Concertos

After Nielsen had composed his *Wind Quintet* in 1922, he decided to write a concerto for each of the players who had first performed it. In the end, he completed only two before he died, but both are impressive compositions. The *Flute Concerto* is a predominantly high-spirited and lyrical work, and there is some highly beautiful writing within its single-movement structure. The *Clarinet Concerto* is in a different vein, with Nielsen embracing – or parodying – the unsentimental angularity of modernists like Stravinsky. It can be a little hard work in the hands of the wrong performers, but it is undoubtedly an exciting and unusual work.

Christiansen, Thomsen; Danish RSO; Schønwandt
(Chandos; with *Violin Concerto*)

Flautist Toke Lund Christiansen and clarinettist Neils Thomsen make excellent soloists in these pieces, the latter's intelligent performance being especially impressive. With first-rate orchestral work from the DRSO under Schønwandt, and Kim Sjøgren's impressive reading of the *Violin Concerto*, this is an excellent single-disc survey of Nielsen's concertos.

CHAMBER & INSTRUMENTAL

Symphonic music forms the core of Nielsen's output, but there are other areas well worth exploring. The four string quartets (all composed by the time he was thirty), show true feeling for the medium, and it's a pity there are no quartets from his full maturity. Later we have the powerful *Second Violin Sonata*, the delightful and highly original *Wind Quintet*, and piano music ranging from imposing masterpieces like the *Chaconne* to the amateur-friendly *Piano Music for Young and Old*.

Wind Quintet

Nielsen's Puckish sense of humour and a very Danish conviviality emerge above all in the delightful *Wind Quintet*, apparently inspired by overhearing (on the telephone) the five members of the Copenhagen Wind Quintet arguing about how to play Mozart. No work of Nielsen's better exemplifies his claim that he thought "through the instruments themselves, almost as though I crept inside them." The kind of intimate, tender, witty instrumental dialogue one encounters in Mozart's chamber music is translated brilliantly into twentieth-century terms. But this is very different from Stravinsky's neo-classicism – no self-distancing irony here, rather an attempt to re-create something of the spirit of Classicism in Nordic pastoral terms. Gentler – on the whole – than the symphonies, it is however just as original and substantial. Indeed it's said that the

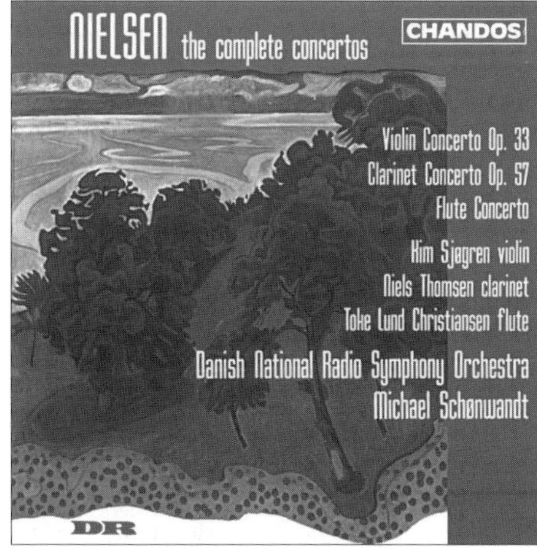

arch-modernist Schoenberg was so impressed with the work that he wrote his own *Wind Quintet* in response.

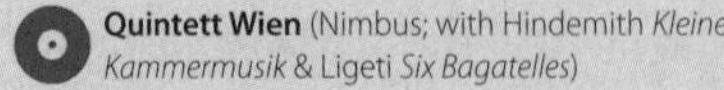

Quintett Wien (Nimbus; with Hindemith *Kleine Kammermusik* & Ligeti *Six Bagatelles*)

A beautifully controlled and balanced performance of the *Wind Quintet*, which misses none of the humour and tenderness in the first two movements, and also manages to touch on darker, more disruptive things in the finale before the homely hymn tune restores order.

Piano Music

The neglect of Nielsen's piano music is hard to understand. Though no keyboard virtuoso, his feeling for the piano is as strong as it is idiosyncratic. The fact that he had no conventional Romantic schooling at the instrument may ultimately have had a positive effect on his writing. Chopinesque Romanticism is in short supply, but the writing in the *Chaconne*, *Theme and Variations* and the *"Luciferian" Suite* is imaginative, dramatic and searching. There are textures and colours in the *Chaconne* and *Suite* as haunting as anything in Prokofiev, Bartók or Ravel, yet the character is unique – Nielsen couldn't be derivative if he tried. Even the pieces for amateurs are full of life, while the modestly entitled *Piano Pieces* give some of the most tantalizing hints of how he might have developed if he'd taken his doctor's warnings a little more seriously.

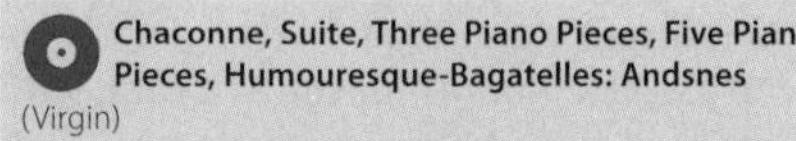

Chaconne, Suite, Three Piano Pieces, Five Piano Pieces, Humouresque-Bagatelles: Andsnes (Virgin)

Listening to Lief Ove Andsnes's penetrating performances one wonders how anybody could have missed the vitality and many-layered originality of this music. It may not be obviously voluptuous, but as Andsnes shows, it has brilliance and sensuous beauty of its own – along with a fantastical streak not always so apparent in the symphonies.

Luigi Nono (1924–1990)

Of the three major composers – Boulez, Stockhausen and Nono – who dominated the European avant-garde in the 1950s, Luigi Nono alone believed that the new revolutionary language of total serialism was compatible with revolutionary politics. Even in Nono's earliest works, such as the *Variazioni canoniche* (1950), his Marxist ideology is allied to the formality of serialist technique, albeit a technique tempered slightly by a characteristically Italian lyricism. There's also a strong dramatic element in much of his music, so it's not surprising that he was the first truly experimental post-war composer to tackle opera, a genre that many of his modernist colleagues affected to despise.

Nono was born in Venice and went on to study law at Padua University as well as taking composition lessons with Malipiero in Venice. An early champion of his work was the conductor Hermann Scherchen, who introduced Nono's work to Darmstadt (see p.384). Nono adopted Schoenberg's serialism (and married his daughter Nuria), but he always regarded technique as the servant of political radicalism, to which ends he also deployed chance methods, *musique concrète* and electronics. His first major composition with an overt political message was the cantata *Il canto Sospeso* (1956), in which he set the letters of various condemned anti-Fascists. His first opera, *Intolleranza 1960*, is an attack on racism, capitalism and colonialism presented as a montage of fragmentary images and ideas loosely centred on the story of an immigrant worker. Its premiere in Venice caused a riot.

The 1960s saw him turn to electronics, in particular the use of taped sounds, to produce a music that was more brashly political and more rooted in the raw material of working life. At the same time, Nono reacted against what he saw as the middle-class elitism of conventional performing venues, and had his work performed in factories and workers' canteens. Finally, in the mid-1970s, Nono's music underwent an astonishing stylistic change of direction: the bold, strident gestures of his most radical statements were replaced by a seemingly introspective language of poetic meditation in which complex literary allusions were frequently woven into the fabric of the music. But as Nuria Schoenberg-Nono recently said: "The audience participate through the intensity of their listening. When there is a silence what you've just heard is contained within your body. There's ten-

Luigi Nono conducting his own work in 1963.

sion throughout." This late style is exemplified by *Fragmente-Stille* (1980), a string quartet of tremulous delicacy which calls on its players silently to read and project into their playing quotations from the poetry of Hölderlin. *Prometeo* (1984) projects those same obsessions onto an ambitious multi-media stage: vocal soloists and a chorus, instrumentalists and electronics are spatially dispersed around a performance space with the audience sitting in the middle. Nono viewed the Prometheus myth as an allegory for the journey of the human condition, now symbolized by sound moving and transforming across physical space.

Il canto sospeso

Il canto sospeso is one of the masterpieces of post-war serialism. Scored for chorus, soloists and orchestra, it's a work in which the harsh, pointillist style (the music presented in dots rather than as melodic phrases) is perfectly matched to the unbearable poignancy of the words – the final messages of Resistance fighters before their execution. The mysterious title – "The Song Suspended" – makes sense when you hear it: Nono creates an extraordinary feeling of time having stood still, a frozen moment of both terrible pain and enormous dignity. In the chorus sections this is achieved in a remarkably effective way by spreading the text out (dividing words and sometimes syllables) across the different voices so that the words seem to flit, like a troubled spirit, between one vocal register and another. There are also several less dislocated moments, in particular the penultimate vocal section in which the soprano solo carries a sustained line of lyrical intensity over a ghostly chorus of women's voices. This is a disturbing and difficult work, but ultimately an extremely rewarding one.

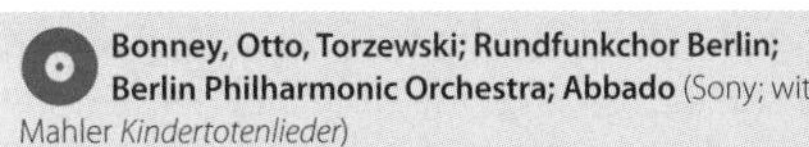

Bonney, Otto, Torzewski; Rundfunkchor Berlin; Berlin Philharmonic Orchestra; Abbado (Sony; with Mahler *Kindertotenlieder*)

Recorded in the Philharmonic Hall in 1992, this is a wonderfully rapt and concentrated live performance, particularly from the Rundfunkchor and an ethereal-sounding Barbara Bonney. A minor drawback is the recitation by two actors of the original letters at the beginning and middle of the performance. Currently deleted but worth searching for.

Fragmente-Stille, An Diotima

Nono's only work for string quartet, *Fragmente-Stille, An Diotima* (Fragments-Silence, To Diotima), was completed in 1980. It's a strangely conceived and oddly affecting work. Nono places a series of enigmatic quotations from the poetry of Hölderlin over the notes as a way of helping the musicians inhabit the music more deeply. The music acts as a meditation on the text, and if a string quartet traditionally represents a varying conversation between four equal voices, then this is more like a collective effort at articulation in the face of an overwhelming silence. There's a real vulnerability in the way the instruments speak: sometimes tentatively, sometimes with a startling rush of energy, but always as if every statement was one that had to be made. *Fragmente-Stille* is a spiritual work, but demands a high level of concentration from the listener – only then will its seemingly arbitrary gestures and nervous fervour begin to make sense.

Total Serialism and the Darmstadt School

The revolution which swept through Western classical music in the aftermath of World War II is inextricably associated with the small German town of Darmstadt, whose summer music school acted for a few years during the 1950s as the ideological headquarters of the new avant-garde movement, the so-called Darmstadt School. Darmstadt's leading protagonists were Pierre Boulez, Karlheinz Stockhausen and Luigi Nono, three composers who – despite the different musical paths they would subsequently follow – found themselves briefly united in their common search for a musical language which would break decisively with the past, establishing a fresh method and aesthetic.

The group's point of departure was Arnold Schoenberg's system of 12-note composition, though their guiding inspiration was not Schoenberg (whose music they regarded as being too bound up with the essentially retrospective German tradition) but the austere work of his pupil Anton Webern, in whose pared-down musical language and obsessive quest for forms of quasi-mathematical purity they saw the germ of a new aesthetic. The 12-note system took as its starting point the idea that a piece of music could be based on a fixed sequence of musical pitches, obviating the need to work with traditional harmonies. Taking up a suggestion first mooted by Messiaen in his piano piece *Mode de valeurs et d'intensités*, Boulez argued that just as pitch could be numerically ordered, so too could every other compositional element, including rhythm, dynamics and register – thus producing a kind of automatic music which would permanently break free from the European musical inheritance. Boulez went on to expound this method, known as total serialism, in his seminal *Structures* for two pianos (1951), whose first movement represents the style at its purest, while Stockhausen, in works such as *Kontrapunkt* and *Zeitmasse*, and Nono, in *Il canto sospeso*, followed his lead.

In fact, total serialism proved to be more a gateway into a new way of writing and thinking about music than an end in itself. Boulez himself immediately tired of the robotic automatism of *Structures*, while both Stockhausen and Nono soon began to explore highly idiosyncratic paths in which electronics, politics and a utopian world music became the major themes. Even so, serialism of one kind or another remained the dominant aesthetic of the 1950s and 1960s – even the elderly Igor Stravinsky, so long the figurehead of the anti-Schoenberg forces, converted to the serial cause (and produced, in works such as *Movements* and the *Requiem Canticles*, some of its most successful compositions). And though few of the erudite and abstruse works of the period have found much favour with the concert-going public, the serial ideal – with its belief that music is not only an art but a kind of science – has continued to influence the work of many younger composers, not least the alumni of Boulez's own musical research centre IRCAM, among them Kaija Saariaho and Magnus Lindberg.

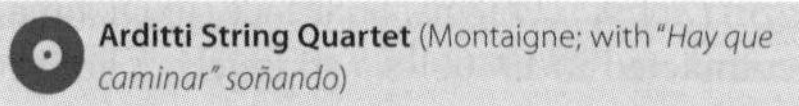

Arditti String Quartet (Montaigne; with *"Hay que caminar" soñando*)

The Ardittis' playing combines virtuosity and intensity in equal proportions, qualities which bring to their performance of *Fragmente-Stille* a touchingly raw fragility. The disc also contains Nono's last work, *"Hay que caminar" soñando*, another introspective piece, written for two violins who take up different positions within the performing space.

Michael Nyman (1944–)

One of the most successful British composers of recent times, Michael Nyman has often courted controversy through the sheer eclecticism of his music. Initially he was part of a group of British experimental musicians who, influenced by Cage, wanted to escape the straitjacket of serialism and embrace a more pluralistic – even anarchic – approach. It has taken him nearly a quarter of a century to move from avant-garde film composer to somewhere near the mainstream, but although he is championed by major companies like Decca and EMI the more entrenched section of the British classical music establishment still finds him beyond the pale.

Nyman attended London's Royal Academy of Music in the early 1960s, and his earliest compositions reflect an enthusiasm for Shostakovich and the post-serialist works of Harrison Birtwistle. But in 1964, disenchanted with the rigid attitudes of the modernist establishment, he abandoned composition and concentrated on musicology, editing Purcell and Handel, and travelling to Romania to study its folk music. By the late 1960s he had become a critic, notably for *The Spectator*, in the pages of which he supported Stockhausen and The Beatles in equal measure and was the first person to use the term "minimalism" (borrowed from the visual arts) in a musical context.

In 1968, a BBC broadcast of Reich's *Come Out* helped to revive Nyman's interest in composing, and led him to develop an enthusiasm for the more melodic strain of pattern music emerging from the USA. Around the same time he penned the libretto for Harrison Birtwistle's *Down by the Greenwood Side*. Nearly a decade later, it was Birtwistle, now music director of the National Theatre, who gave Nyman his big break, inviting him to provide music for a production of Goldoni's play *Il campiello*. Nyman assembled the loudest band he could think of, with banjo and soprano saxophone alongside rebecs, sackbuts and shawms. He liked the sound so much that he kept the band together – initially as the Campiello Band, and then as the Michael Nyman Band, complete with his own pumping piano.

At about this time he also wrote *1–100* for a film by Peter Greenaway, with whom he became a regular collaborator, his music perfectly suited to the esoteric and self-referential imagery of films such as *The Draughtsman's Contract* and *The Cook, The Thief, His Wife and Her Lover*. In the end, the collaboration was terminated by mutual disagreement, but Nyman has continued to write film scores, most famously for Jane Campion's *The Piano* (from which he has extrapolated a *Suite* and a *Piano Concerto*).

More recently, Nyman has been involved in a number of experimental projects, including *The Commissar Vanishes* – an audio-visual work created with David King and Chris Kondek and first performed in London in 1999 – and *Sangam*, in which the Nyman Band collaborated with Indian classical musicians. In 2005 Michael Nyman launched his own label, MN Records, with a recording of his opera *Man and Boy: Dada*. As well as recording new works, the label has issued previously unreleased material and reissued discs which have dropped out of the catalogue.

The Draughtsman's Contract

When Peter Greenaway called on Nyman in 1981, all he had was an idea for the outline of a plot: a seventeenth-century draughtsman is employed to create twelve drawings of an English country house. Nyman would write the music and Greenaway would shoot the film around it. The resulting drama was as hard, glittering, formally intricate, amoral and heartless as the society it depicted. Nyman's contribution stands among his spikiest and cleverest scores, threaded through with ground basses and chaconnes borrowed from Purcell and with the cyclical harmonies of minimalism. "Chasing Sheep is Best Left to Shepherds" is a dynamic combination of piercing fanfares, pulsing bass and climbing reed and woodwind lines, while in "The Disposition of the Linen" simple repetitive motifs are layered and interwoven against staccato wind figures to produce dense, shifting designs.

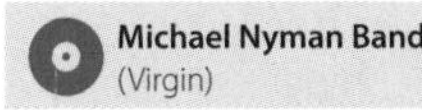

Michael Nyman Band
(Virgin)

With a band including longtime associates Alexander Balanescu (violin), John Harle (soprano sax) and Malcolm Bennett (bass guitar), Nyman is aided by David Cunningham's accomplished production. Although the music fits the action so perfectly, it triumphantly survives its separation from the onscreen complexities.

String Quartets

In 1989 Nyman provided music for Agnieszka Piotrowska's documentary on the aftermath of the Armenian earthquake – a very different kind of filmmaking from Greenaway's cool cerebralism, and one that resulted in a beautiful choral work, *Out of the Ruins*. Later that year, following the Romanian revolution, Nyman decided to turn this piece into his third string quartet, weaving folk tunes around a framework derived from the choral piece. This new work deploys Nyman's trademark repetitions and strong rhythms, but is unusually elegiac, displaying an emotional dimension that is rarely evident in his music. The *String Quartet No. 2*, written in 1988 for Shobana Jeyasingh's dance piece *Miniatures*, succeeded in being unmistakably Nymanesque while evoking and appropriately complementing the essence of South Indian dance. His first quartet, commissioned by the Arditti Quartet in 1985, creates a compelling fusion out of borrowings from Schoenberg's *String Quartet No. 2* and from the seventeenth-century composer John Bull's variations on the popular song "Walsingham".

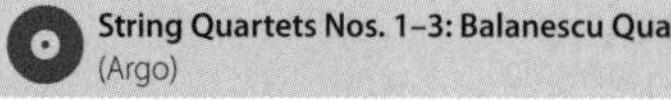

String Quartets Nos. 1–3: Balanescu Quartet (Argo)

The textural and rhythmic tightness of Nyman's writing and the intensity of the playing give this record a compressed timbre which, despite digital technology, makes it sound like something by the veteran Busch Quartet. As the Busch Quartet set a standard that has seldom been emulated, that's as good a recommendation as you could get.

The Upside-Down Violin

The Upside-Down Violin refreshed Nyman's work with an injection of practices from a non-European musical tradition. It was commissioned for Expo '92 in Seville, and teamed Nyman's band with the distinguished Moroccan ensemble, the Orquestra Andaluzi de Telouan. Nyman described the work as a departure from the "knitting pattern" techniques of the early minimalist pieces, and he developed its final form after listening to what the Moroccan musicians did with his melodies during rehearsals. He neither required them to adopt his style nor tried to imitate their music. Instead, he wrote melodies which he hoped they would find congenial, then added material for his own band before bringing the two groups together. The first movement ("Slow") unfolds an undulating melody in the strings and reeds against the flowing rhythms of the tambourine and derboliga (drums), with the laud (lute) moving from rhythm to melody at the end. At the end of this middle movement ("Faster") the music was devised by the Orquestra Andaluzi in response to Nyman's Stockhausen-like admonition, "make music suggested by what you have just played". The final movement ("Faster Still") is a glorious, headlong celebration of instrumental virtuosity.

Michael Nyman Live: The Nyman Band; Orquestra Andaluzi de Telouan (Virgin)

Recorded in concert in Albecete and Madrid in 1994, this disc includes a fine performance of *The Upside-Down Violin* alongside *Water Dances*, *Queen of the Night*, *Bird List*, *In Re Don Giovanni* and *The Piano* concert suite. Despite too much applause, this is an excellent CD, both for the immediacy of the performances and for the exhilarating interplay between the two sets of musicians.

O

Johannes Ockeghem (c.1420–1497)

When Ockeghem died, Josquin Desprez – who may have studied with him – wrote a lament describing him as "Music's very treasure and true master", a fair reflection of the esteem in which he was held during his lifetime. This esteem virtually vanished with his death and, when musical scholarship finally caught up with him in the nineteenth century, he suffered the indignity of being dismissed as too clever by half, a purveyor of over-elaborate formal tricks. This is certainly not a conclusion you would reach about much of Ockeghem's music, for works such as the motet *Intemerata Dei Mater* displays a pellucid and ethereal beauty.

Unlike his two great Franco-Flemish contemporaries, Dufay (see p.165) and Josquin (see p.275), very little documentary information about Ockeghem's life has survived. He may have been born at the village of Ockeghem in eastern Flanders and may have studied with Binchois (on whose death he wrote a lament), but there is no real evidence to support either theory. It is known that in the mid-1440s he served at the court of the Duke of Bourbon at Moulins, and that by 1453 he was in the service of the king of France, Charles VII. He remained a favoured member of the royal chapel until his death, serving Charles VII, Louis XI and Charles VIII as their premier chaplain, and was awarded the honorific and highly lucrative position of treasurer at the abbey of St Martin-de-Tours.

Ockeghem's contemporaries admired him not just for his music but also for the remarkable sweetness of his singing voice. Several accounts also suggest an exceptionally attractive character; one, by Francesco Florio, states that "you could not dislike this man, so pleasing is the beauty of his person, so noteworthy the sobriety of his speech and of his morals and his grace".

Chansons

Considering that he lived so long and was so revered, Ockeghem was a curiously unprolific composer. About twenty secular songs have survived, just four motets that can be confidently ascribed to him, and some fifteen masses, including the earliest surviving polyphonic setting of the Requiem. As a songwriter Ockeghem continued the manner of Machaut (see p.316) and Dufay, using the traditional forms of ballade, rondeau and virelai (all of which employed textual refrains). Each form was thought appropriate for different moods. Thus we have "Fors Seulement", a rondeau of unrequited love, the virelai "Tant fuz gentement", which again deals with love but in a more ambivalent fashion, and the solemn ballade (favoured for serious themes) which Ockeghem employs for his moving lament on the death of Binchois, "Mort tu as navré".

Orlando Consort
(Archiv; with *Missa de plus en plus*)

The Orlando Consort (a group of four male voices) combine seven of Ockeghem's *chansons* with a mass based on a song by Binchois. They present the songs unaccompanied and with a more intensely expressive quality than most, employing an almost tremulous quality for "Mort tu as navré".

Sacred Music

Ockeghem's reputation for complexity derives from his four-part *Missa Prolationum*, in which two separate canons are sung simultaneously. In contrast, the middle-period three-part *Missa Ecce Ancilla Domine*, the only mass by Ockeghem based on a plainsong cantus firmus, is a model of simplicity, though its later sections contain some fairly florid and thick writing. On the whole, Ockeghem's later works achieve an amazingly economic expressivity. Masterpieces like the *Missa fors seulement* (based on a rondeau of that name) and the motet *Intemerata Dei Mater* have a fluidity and directness which is inspiring.

The *Requiem* is a more problematic work. It may have been composed for the funeral of Charles VII in 1461, but each of its movements is so varied in style that it may have been cobbled together from a number of different works. It incorporates the plainsong chants traditionally used for the Requiem into the texture of the polyphony, usually placing it with some ornamentation in the highest voice.

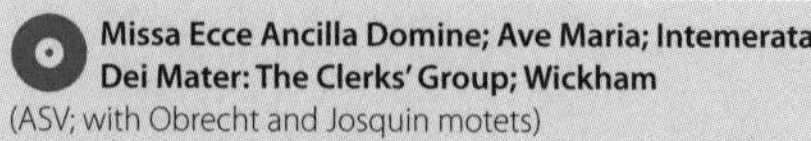

Missa Ecce Ancilla Domine; Ave Maria; Intemerata Dei Mater: The Clerks' Group; Wickham
(ASV; with Obrecht and Josquin motets)

The Clerks' Group have a fresh and clear sound that effectively brings out the elasticity of Ockeghem's vocal lines – notably in their bright performance of the motet *Intemerata Dei Mater* (Inviolate Mother of God), in which they employ women's voices on the top line. All the other Ockeghem works on the disc are sung by the men alone.

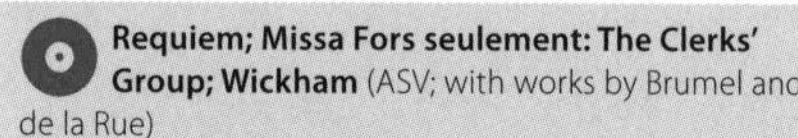

Requiem; Missa Fors seulement: The Clerks' Group; Wickham (ASV; with works by Brumel and de la Rue)

The Clerks' Group are equally impressive on this disc, which includes the song *Fors seulement*, the mass based on it, and the *Requiem*. All the performances are excellent, but the account of the mass is particularly beautiful. The coupled works by two slightly later composers make for a pleasing contrast.

Jacques Offenbach (1819–1880)

Jacques Offenbach, "the Mozart of the Champs-Élysées", was the composer who made operetta an international art form, and so paved the way for Lehár (see p.298), Sullivan (see p.556) and the musicals of the twentieth century. Fusing dialogue and show-stopping set pieces in productions of unrivalled musical verve and satirical bite, he deflated the morals and manners of the Second Empire in its prime – and they paid him for it.

Jacob, as he was named, was born in Cologne in 1819, seventh of ten children. He was taught music in his native city, then in 1833 the family resettled in Paris, allowing him to study at the Conservatoire. Joining the orchestra of the Opéra-Comique, he published waltzes and concert pieces for his own instrument, the cello. Throughout the 1840s he survived as a virtuoso performer, failing to get his stage works performed except when he paid for the privilege, but his luck changed in the following decade. In 1850 he was made conductor of the Théâtre Français, which in 1855 accepted his *Oyayaie, ou La reine des îles*. Its success gave him the cash and the credibility to set up as composer and stager of his own music, despite the disdain of Paris's "respectable" cognoscenti.

His two-act *Orphée aux enfers* (Orpheus in the Underworld) unleashed the Can-Can on the world in 1858, and typified Offenbach's irreverence – the opera's starting point is that Orpheus is bored with Eurydice, while she is being driven to distraction by his violin playing. His big hit of 1864, *La belle Hélène*, was concerned with the infidelities of Helen of Troy, lampooning Donizetti and Wagner in the process. Two years later came *Barbe-Bleu*, in which Bluebeard searches for his sixth wife, and *La vie parisienne*, a glittering portrait of contemporary Paris society. His mordantly satirical *La Grande-Duchesse*

The heavily bewhiskered Jacques Offenbach.

de Gérolstein (1867) was described by George Bernard Shaw as "an original and complete work of art which places its composer heavens-high", and was a colossal box-office success. The risqué *La Périchole* (1868), which concerns the adventures in Lima of a pair of down-at-heel street singers, marked the end of Offenbach's heyday, a period during which he had composed some ninety operettas.

He had made his name amid the frivolous decadence of the Second Empire. Public taste changed after the Franco-Prussian War of 1870–71, and Offenbach, once made a Chevalier of the Legion of Honour, was now branded "the great corrupter" of decorous taste. He fled to the admiring audiences of England and the USA, and from 1877 was occupied with the work that would become his masterpiece, *Les contes d'Hoffmann*. When he died, in 1880, much of it was still in piano-score but was completed and orchestrated by Ernest Guiraud and received a triumphant premiere early in 1881.

Orphée aux enfers

For their assault on the Second Empire's pomposity and hypocrisy, Offenbach and his librettist Ludovic Halévy retained just the bare outline of the story as told in Gluck's hallowed *Orfeo ed Euridice* (see p.215): Orpheus travels to Hades to retrieve Eurydice from Pluto, but looks back on the way out of the underworld and as a result loses her. But in this version Orpheus is a talentless fool who is desperate to get rid of Eurydice, who is a nagging trollop. Public Opinion is pitted against the bored and feckless gods (caricatures of members of the government), the boss of whom, Jupiter (i.e. Napoleon III), is derided for everything from his ugliness and stupidity to his profligacy and roving eye.

When it came to setting the libretto Offenbach created a score almost unique in operetta in that there are no tedious episodes, no flat jokes and no limp melodies. The best-known episode is of course the "galop infernal", universally known as the "Can-Can" – "at last something you can dance to" sing the revellers at the farewell party for the gods. There are many other fantastic orchestral effects, such as Jupiter's "buzzing" transformation into a fly and Pluto's explosive entrance in Act 2, and a number of the more extended solos have entered the repertoire of recital songs – notably John Styx's "Quand j'étais roi de Béotie" (When I was King of the Beotians).

Sénéchal, Mesplé, Burles; Toulouse Capitole Chorus and Orchestra; Plasson (EMI; 2 CDs)

In this 1978 recording Michel Plasson brilliantly captures the wild decadence of *Orphée*. Mady Mesplé is splendidly outré as Eurydice, making the most of her sighing over the irresistible Aristeus, Michel Sénéchal's Orpheus is the soul of artistic pretension, and the show is all but stolen by Charles Burles's degenerate Jupiter.

Beuron, Dessay, Fouchécourt, Naouri; Grenoble Chamber Orchestra; Opéra National de Lyon Chorus and Orchestra; Minkowski (EMI; 2 CDs)

Minkowski's 1997 recording is lighter and brighter than that of Plasson. He uses his own edition of the score, which is essentially the original version with selections from the 1874 revision. The star of the show is, without doubt, the effervescent Eurydice of Nathalie Dessay whose comedic touch is wonderfully deft and assured.

Les contes d'Hoffmann

Produced in 1881, *Les contes d'Hoffmann* (Tales of Hoffmann) was Offenbach's first and last opera, in that it was his only through-composed work without spoken dialogue, but it is a close relative of his other stage works, as he simply adapted his operetta style to fit the more sombre tone of the libretto. The three central acts (framed by a Prologue and Epilogue) recount three tales by the German Romantic writer E.T.A. Hoffmann. The first concerns an inventor and his mechanical doll, Olympia, by whom Hoffmann is seduced; the second involves another of Hoffmann's passions, Antonia, a consumptive singer who falls prey to the evil Dr Miracle; and the third tells of Giulietta, who tries to trick Hoffmann into selling his soul.

Offenbach's trademark wit is in evidence throughout, but it plays a relieving rather than a defining role, so that music-hall episodes such as Olympia's coloratura "mechanical" aria, in which her voice drops in a huge glissando from high above the stave every time her mechanism runs low, serve to leaven the menace of the inventor's rival, Coppélius. Similarly, the comic minor character Frantz, who in Act 4 fails to reach the notes at the end of his scales (a parody of a real tenor who was then past his prime), is an entertaining diversion in an act dominated by minor-key music, stentorian outbursts and a darkly coloured atmosphere, such as the apparently gentle but superbly ominous "Barcarole" that opens the act.

Domingo, Sutherland, Tourangeau, Bacquier, Cuénod; L'Orchestre de la Suisse Romande; Radio Suisse Romande Chorus; Bonynge (Decca; 2 CDs)

The sweep and wit of Offenbach's score is supremely caught by Bonynge in a reading that tingles with frenetic urgency while bringing out the lushness of Guiraud's orchestration. Domingo is in his richest voice, summoning the impetuous ardour of Hoffmann, and Sutherland excels in the bravura arias. A highlights disc of this performance is also available.

Alagna, Dessay, Jo, Vaduva, van Dam, Dubosc; Lyon Opera Chorus and Orchestra; Nagano (Erato; 3 CDs)

This 1995 set was Kent Nagano's first major recording of a full-scale French opera. On the whole it's a great success and – for those who think Offenbach warrants extra élan – arguably a first choice for this work. The casting is outstanding, the chorus and orchestra play with real panache and Nagano provides inventive, sensitive direction.

Carl Orff (1895–1982)

Carl Orff is generally known as the creator of the elemental and hedonistic *Carmina Burana*, one of the most popular of all twentieth-century choral works, but he was both more prolific and more versatile than his reputation suggests. As well as composing nearly twenty music-theatre works, he was a highly influential educationalist, whose teaching methods, the Orff Schulwerk, are still in use all over the world.

Scion of an old Bavarian military family, Orff showed precocious musical gifts and quickly learned to play the piano, cello and organ. He held the position of *Kapellmeister* at the Munich Kammerspiele from 1915 to 1917, going on to work at Mannheim's Nationaltheater and the Landstheater in Darmstadt. His earliest compositions show the influence of Debussy, but this soon gave way to that of Austro-German masters such as Schoenberg and Richard Strauss.

However, Orff later disowned all his compositions written before 1924, the year he and Dorothy Günther founded the Güntherschule in Munich. Working from the belief that everyone has inherent musical understanding and that movement and music cannot be separated, this innovative institution took its young adult students through a coordinated course of music, gymnastics and dance. In the early 1930s the Ministry of Culture recommended that a simplified version of the Güntherschule curriculum be adopted in elementary schools, but the project was thwarted by the Nazis, who objected to the radicalism of the school, with its emphasis on improvisation and percussion-based music.

In 1930 Orff found time to take up the post of conductor of the Munich Bach Society, and during his three-year tenure he became steeped in the compositions of the seventeenth and eighteenth centuries. Augmented by his fascination with classical tragedy, Bavarian peasant life, primitive musical forms and Christian mysticism, this immersion in early music led to the creation of *Carmina Burana*, which was premiered at Frankfurt am Main in 1937. Orff's involvement with the Nazis has been the subject of much debate since his death: along with his fellow-Bavarian Richard Strauss, he composed music for the 1936 Olympics – very much a showcase for the Nazis – and, more controversially, agreed to write new incidental music for Shakespeare's *A*

Midsummer Night's Dream to replace that of the Jewish Mendelssohn (see p.343). In his defence it has been argued that he was an essentially apolitical person who was completely focused on his art to the exclusion of almost all else.

After World War II Orff continued to refine his ideas about a "total theatre" in which music, speech and movement would combine to produce a spectacle both mentally stimulating and visually exciting. Turning to the classic stage for his raw material, he composed a number of ambitious works: *Antigonae* (1949) and *Oedipus der Tyrann* (1959) were derived from Sophocles, *Ein Sommernachtstraum* (1966) from Shakespeare.

Although Orff continued composing into old age (for example, writing a piece for the opening of the Munich Olympics in 1972), it was as a teacher that he was most influential. His educational activities were given fresh impetus when, in 1948, the German radio authorities commissioned him to adapt the Güntherschule's exercises as a series of broadcasts for children. Then in 1961 Orff was invited to set up the Orff Institute in Salzburg so that his methods could be taught at first hand. In the final analysis, those methods, and *Carmina Burana*, are his chief legacy.

Carmina Burana

Though nowadays performed as a choral concert item, *Carmina Burana* was conceived as a "scenic cantata" for the stage. Orff took the libretto from a sequence of medieval Latin lyrics that mix Christian piety with a celebration of the world's delights, but the latter element sets the dominant tone here, as you can tell from the titles of the work's three parts: "Spring", "In the Tavern" and "Love". The musical style of *Carmina Burana* owes a considerable debt to Stravinsky's *Les noces* and *Oedipus Rex*, a connection most evident in Orff's use of the chorus and his rich percussive orchestration. Unlike Stravinsky, however, Orff makes little use of extended melodic writing, thematic development or polyphony – with him the rhythm is paramount (Stravinsky dubbed his style "Neo-Neanderthal"). Allied to explicit harmonies, this rhythmic drive is what gives *Carmina Burana* its sense of wild abandonment.

Janowitz, Stolze, Fischer-Dieskau; Berlin German Opera Orchestra & Chorus; Schöneberger Sängerknaben; Jochum (Deutsche Grammophon)

Bearing the imprimatur of Orff himself, this recording has been a benchmark since its release in 1968. Dietrich Fischer-Dieskau hams it up convincingly, Gundula Janowitz's creamy voice is as seductive as ever, and the CD remastering has augmented the dynamism of Jochum's orchestra.

Matthews, Brownlee, Gerhaler; Berlin State and Cathedral Boys' Choir; Berlin Radio Chorus; Berlin Philharmonic Orchestra; Rattle (EMI)

For a more modern, and sonically dynamic, recording, Simon Rattle and his Berlin forces deliver the goods in this exciting 2004 live performance. Speeds are on the lively side and the characterization of baritone Christian Gerhaler somewhat broad, but the performance thrills in all the right places.

p

Johann Pachelbel (1653–1706)

Along with the spurious Albinoni *Adagio* (see p.8), Pachelbel's *Canon and Gigue* has, in recent times, become a Baroque popular hit to rival Vivaldi's *Four Seasons*. First published in 1920, it didn't achieve its modern status until the early 1970s when a number of recordings – in particular one by the Stuttgart Chamber Orchestra – plus films and television commercials began to fix it in the popular consciousness. Ironically, however, its very popularity has tended to obscure rather than enhance Pachelbel's reputation as one of the leading European composers of his time. As an organist (which also meant a composer for the organ), his contemporaries valued him more highly than anyone else, with the possible exception of Dietrich Buxtehude (see p.121). He was intimate with the Bach family and among his many pupils was Johann Christoph Bach, the elder brother and teacher of Johann Sebastian. His music even reached America via his second son Charles Theodore, an organist who settled there around 1730. Though primarily a composer for the organ, Pachelbel wrote a substantial body of choral music (mostly at Nuremberg) and some chamber music, little of which seems to have survived.

Johann Pachelbel's outstanding ability – both intellectual and musical – was apparent from an early age. A native of Nuremberg, at seventeen he was awarded a scholarship to the Gymnasium Poeticum at Regensburg where, outside of school hours, he studied music with Kaspar Prenz. In 1673 Pachelbel, who was a Lutheran, was appointed deputy organist of the Catholic cathedral of St Stephen in Vienna, where he remained for four years, possibly taking lessons with J.K. Kerll, one of the leading composers of the day. A series of prestigious appointments followed, the first at Eisenach where he was briefly court organist to the Duke of Saxe-Eisenach, and then, in 1678, at nearby Erfurt as organist of the Predigerkirche. Erfurt is where he established his reputation, started a family and consolidated his friendship with the Bach family. But after twelve years he moved on, initially to Stuttgart, then on to Gotha before returning to his home town in 1695, having been specifically invited by the authorities to fill the position of organist at St Sebald's church, the most important in the town.

Canon and Gigue

The simple, short but extremely effective *Canon and Gigue in D Major*, for three violins and continuo, is of course the best known of all Pachelbel's creations. The *Canon*, which is often performed on its own, takes the form of 28 variations over an eight-note ostinato pattern in the bass and continuo. The piece has proved so appealing partly because the strictness of the form (ground bass plus canon) gives it a predictable and solid underpinning which the freedom of the variation form works against in a rather playful fashion. Perhaps its sunny and unemotional disposition serves also as a foil to the rather lugubrious solemnity of the Albinoni *Adagio* with which it is inevitably coupled on recordings.

The chamber music form which Pachelbel most consistently turned to was the Partie – or Suite – written for various sizes of string ensemble and consisting of six contrasted dances. Among the few sets of Partie to be published was a collection entitled *Musicalische Ergötzung* (Musical Delight). Although this kind of music was used as courtly background music (Tafelmusik) or played by amateur musicians for their own enjoyment, it is frequently extremely inventive and often quite technically demanding. Like his contemporary Biber (see p.79), Pachelbel sometimes employed unconventional violin tuning (known as *scordatura*) although not quite with such spectacularly dramatic results.

Chamber Music: London Baroque
(Harmonia Mundi)

It's rare to find a Pachelbel chamber disc with more than just the *Canon and Gigue* on it. This one contains all six suites from the *Musicalische Ergötzung* in wonderfully forthright performances from London Baroque. The *Canon and Gigue* sounds as splendid as ever but no less impressive is the inventive *Ciacona* that closes the Partie in E minor.

Canon and Gigue: Orpheus Chamber Orchestra
(Deutsche Grammophon; with Albinoni *Adagio* etc)

Here's a mellow and refined performance of *Canon and Gigue* on a menu of Baroque "greatest hits", which includes Handel's *Arrival of the Queen of Sheba* and J.S. Bach's *Jesu, Joy of Man's Desiring*. The Orpheus is not a period instrument band and there is a satisfying richness to the group's string sound.

Organ Music

The chorale or metrical hymn formed the heart of the Lutheran liturgy (see p.413), and an organist had to be able to compose pieces of music – chorale preludes – that took the chorale's melody as a starting point and transformed it into a single variation. How this was achieved varied from organist to organist and gradually became increasingly sophisticated. Several of Pachelbel's chorale preludes involve a fugal treatment of the chorale's first phrase while the ensuing phrases are voiced in extended note values. This rather intellectual approach, in contrast to Buxtehude's more poetic one, is also evident in Pachelbel's keyboard variations, of which the most distinguished examples are the six arias with variations collected under the title *Hexachordum Apollinis* (1699) and dedicated to Buxtehude. Here Pachelbel follows a strict numerical system for determining keys, which possibly had some kind of arcane symbolism. All the airs have a stately elegance and easy grace and the variations are brilliantly inventive. The grandiose *No. 6* seems to have had some special significance: named after the church of St Sebald, it breaks the rule of the collection's key system and is the only one in triple time.

Hexachordum Apollinis: Butt
(Harmonia Mundi)

The modern organ recorded on this disc may lack that final ounce of character that you associate with an older instrument, but in the choice of registration and generally flexible approach John Butt brings out the composer's playfulness and his formality. The airs and variations are framed by two chaconnes, the first of which, in D major, is very clearly from the same hand as the *Canon and Gigue*.

Nicolò Paganini (1782–1840)

Nobody had ever played the violin like Nicolò Paganini. The first musician to employ an agent, he was part Jascha Heifetz, part P.J. Barnum. People flocked to hear him play, not just for the promise of astonishing technical virtuosity but also because of the whiff of scandal that surrounded him. One persistent rumour suggested that his extraordinary talent was a result of a pact with the devil. Certainly there was something demonic about him: as a boy he mutilated his left hand in order to increase the spread of his fingers, and most contemporary portraits of the adult Paganini present an almost demented figure: gaunt, long-haired and with an intense, piercing gaze. Like all virtuosos of the time he mostly performed his own compositions,

Caricature of Paganini by Edwin Landseer.

works which were designed to show off the whole range of his skills, from the lyrical to the acrobatic – his party piece was to break three strings on his violin and still keep playing. His music is rarely if ever profound, but its combination of easy-going charm and flagrant exhibitionism exerts a fascination above that of mere curiosity.

Paganini's worldwide reputation as the greatest violinist of the age followed a series of recitals that he gave in Vienna in 1828, and his triumphant progress throughout Europe continued for the next six years. Some musicians, like Spohr, denigrated him for the superficiality and trickery of his playing, but his many admirers included Chopin and Schumann – both of whom wrote musical tributes to him – and above all Liszt, who successfully transformed himself into the Paganini of the piano. By 1834 Paganini was pretty well burnt out, worn down by exhaustion, illness and persistent press rumours of his miserliness and immorality. He retired to Parma and performances became increasingly infrequent. A venture in 1837 to start a casino in Paris bearing his name lost him large sums of money, and three years later he died in Nice from a disease of the larynx, resolutely refusing to see a priest.

Violin Concerto No. 1

Of Paganini's six violin concertos only the first two are now performed with any regularity. The first, the most uninhibited and most enjoyable, was written in 1817–18, when Paganini's fame was still confined to Italy. Like many virtuoso concertos of the period, including the piano concertos of Hummel (see p.265), the influence of Italian opera, particularly of Rossini, looms large. The work begins with a long and extremely bouncy orchestral introduction (with a lot of cymbal crashing) before the soloist enters with a theme full of leaps and runs which eventually leads into a sweet if rather simpering melody. The short slow movement is darker and more thoughtful, and it's not until the last movement that the technical stops are pulled out, with high chords, brilliant runs and "ricochet" bowing, a Paganini speciality in which several bouncing notes are played on one stroke of the bow.

Perlman; Royal Philharmonic Orchestra; Foster
(EMI; with Sarasate *Carmen Fantasy, Zigeunerweisen & Introduction and Tarantella*)

Several violinists are technically capable of playing this music, but few bring to it the finesse and the panache that Itzhak Perlman achieves. The warmth and sweetness of his tone are beguiling, but on top of this is the fact that he enters so fully into the spirit of the music, treating the insinuating first-movement melody completely seriously, but injecting a witty playfulness where necessary.

24 Caprices

Paganini's *24 Caprices*, published in 1820, are the most famous of all his compositions. Like Chopin's *Études* (which they directly inspired), the *Caprices* are technical exercises that transcend the pedagogic limitations of the genre to become virtuosic miniatures – not as wide-ranging in mood as Chopin's pieces but no less brilliant. Paganini dedicated them "Agli Artisti" (To the Artists), but there could have been few artists capable of performing them, apart from himself. Each one explores a different aspect of violin technique: fast passages of double stopping, trills, harmonics and the combination of pizzicato and bowing are just some of the more spectacular examples. *Caprice No. 24*

The Rise of the Virtuoso

Having once been enthusiastically praised for his virtuosity at the organ, J.S. Bach is said to have replied: "There is nothing remarkable about it. All you have to do is hit the right notes at the right time, and the instrument plays itself." Bach is widely thought to have been the greatest organist in history, but by most people's standards he was not a virtuoso. For a start, he was an organist, which meant that he spent most of his working life in churches, where all musical performance was conceived for the service of God. Nevertheless, an element of showmanship – not to say competition – certainly existed in the Baroque period: Scarlatti and Handel competed at the keyboard when their paths crossed in Italy, and Bach himself was not above showing off his skills at the expense of other performers. The most famous such incident involved the leading French organist, Louis Marchand, who on a visit to Dresden in 1717 agreed to take part in a contest of improvisation with Bach. The story, which appears in Bach's "Obituary" of 1754, suggests that Marchand on hearing his rival practising the night before was so rattled that he made his excuses and left for Paris.

Fifty years after Bach's death the balance of priorities had shifted, with the piano the dominant keyboard instrument, and audiences filing out of the churches and into secular, ticket-selling halls, where the performer was promoted from the service of God into a god himself.

In the early part of his career, Beethoven was universally revered as a pianist and as a showman of exceptional skill and dexterity. On one occasion, having sat through a long-winded piano quintet by one of his rivals, Daniel Steibelt, he marched to the piano, seized the cellist's sheet music off his stand, turned it upside down and, using the first eight notes as his theme, proceeded to stupefy the audience with a set of twenty improvised, ever more complicated variations. Such prodigious feats of exhibitionism would have appalled Bach, but Europe's enlightened concert-going public wanted to be entertained as well as moved, and substance began to lose out to surface as performers vied with one another for their share of the public's purse, and a slice of its adulation.

But with the arrival of Paganini, and later of Liszt, the performance, composition and presentation of classical music were virtually reinvented. In their blurring hands, the serious business of art was refashioned as entertainment, and they made a spectacular virtue of brilliance. Performing their own works, written to best illustrate their skills, they reversed the polarity of appreciation, and made the method of performance more important than the work being performed. Their elevation to the status of gods was exacted through careful stage management (women were hired, for example, to faint at their concerts), calculated publicity and frantic touring. Despite (or, perhaps, because of) Paganini's ghoulish appearance he and Liszt became the first sex symbols of classical music, with reputations to match.

Paganini, in particular, transformed the entire vernacular of appreciation, with Schumann declaring him to be "the turning point of virtuosity". Over a century and a half on, Paganini's influence continues to be felt. The performer and his prowess now dominate the entire culture of serious music, with proficiency compensating for the absence of original creativity. Very few instrumentalists now write their own music, but with such a surfeit of talent it is still at least possible to imagine what Heinrich Heine meant when, having witnessed Paganini in concert in 1829, he bemoaned "this vampyr with a violin, who would suck … the money from our pockets … but such thoughts had perforce to vanish instantly, at the moment in which the marvellous master placed his violin under his chin and began to play."

is the best known, having been used by a wide number of composers (Brahms, Rachmaninov, Lutosławski, Andrew Lloyd-Webber) as the theme for sets of variations.

Perlman
(EMI)

As with the concertos, many violinists can now play the *Caprices* (selections are often employed as encore pieces), but few can make their pyrotechnical bravura and quirkiness seem really musical. Itzhak Perlman manages it with ease: whether in the Bach-like opening of *No. 2*, the mysterious trilling of *No. 6*, or the sheer chutzpah of *No. 24*.

Ehnes
(Onyx)

Here's another violinist who takes these pieces completely seriously, not simply as excuses for display. Like Perlman, James Ehnes is blessed with both a formidable technique and a wonderfully rich and insinuating tone: he uses both to maximum effect and generates a sense of excitement in the music that is utterly infectious.

Violin and Guitar Duos

Though he is remembered primarily as a violinist, Paganini was also a virtuoso guitarist. He claimed at least once that he disliked the instrument, but he frequently used it when composing and wrote nearly 200 pieces for solo guitar, guitar and violin, or guitar with string trio. Though there are exceptions, most of these works demonstrate a relatively relaxed and intimate side to the Devil's Fiddler, and they make a good contrast to the pieces discussed above. Generally the guitar serves an accompanying role, though there are examples in which the guitar dominates, such as the *Grand Sonata*. This piece was written after Paganini's regular guitarist-accompanist requested a more interesting part to play; the composer agreed to swap instruments to perform a new piece, but then composed the new sonata giving nearly all the impressive and melodic material to the guitar.

Paganini for Two: Shaham, Söllscher
(Deutsche Grammophon)

Violinist Gil Shaham and guitarist Göran Söllscher make ideal exponents of this lesser-known section of Paganini's output. On a selection including the slow movement from the *Grand Sonata* and the lovely *Sonata Concertata*, the two play accurately but informally, and in effortless ensemble. Shaham's violin work is beautifully clear and well articulated, and Söllscher proves a sensitive player throughout.

Giovanni da Palestrina (c.1525–1594)

Giovanni Pierluigi da Palestrina wrote music for the Catholic Church during one of the most traumatic periods of its history, a period during which its leaders were looking for ways to reverse the damage caused by the Reformation and the rising popularity of Protestantism. The function of church music was one of the many subjects discussed at the Council of Trent, which sat from 1545 to 1663. To its critics polyphony had become an overelaborate web of sound that obscured rather than enhanced the meaning of the sacred words. Some, like the Bishop of Modena, even advocated an exclusive diet of plainsong for church services.

Palestrina is often credited as the composer who single-handedly saved polyphony: with the Church on the brink of abolishing it, he was requested to compose a mass that would show decisively that the polyphonic style was not irreconcilable with clarity of meaning or a truly devotional spirit. The result, the *Missa Papae Marcelli* (Mass of Pope Marcellus), swayed the critics and saved the day, at least till the end of the century. Although the story is now regarded as more legend than fact, there is an important element of truth in it. Palestrina had indeed begun his career by learning and assimilating the techniques of the great Franco-Flemish composers, such as Josquin Desprez (see p.275), but had gone on to forge his own more simple and direct style, one which combined polyphony with sections of more simple homophony – music in which the individual parts are melodically different, but are rhythmically in step with each other.

Palestrina's name derives from the hill town near Rome where he was born. After serving as a chorister at the church of Santa Maria Maggiore in Rome he returned to Palestrina in 1544 to be the organist at the cathedral of Sant'Agapito. He might well have remained in provincial obscurity had not the Bishop of Palestrina been elected Pope Julius III and in 1551 appointed him *maestro da cappella* at the Cappella Giulia, one of the choirs at St Peter's. Palestrina also sang in the Sistine Chapel choir, and may have composed his *Missa Papae Marcelli* on the accession of Pope Marcellus II in 1555, possibly in response to the new pope's directive to his singers that the music for his enthronement "must be sung in a proper manner".

Dismissed in the same year from the Sistine Chapel for being married (it was meant to be a choir of celibates), Palestrina spent five fruitless years at the underfunded church of St John Lateran before being appointed to the rather more affluent Santa Maria Maggiore. By the 1560s his fame was such that several aristocratic patrons sought him out. In 1571 he was reappointed *maestro* to the Cappella Giulia, a post he kept until his death. The deaths of both his sons in the 1570s and of his wife in 1580 led him to consider joining the priesthood but instead he got married again, to a wealthy widow with a thriving business in the fur trade, thus enabling him to spend his final years in relative financial security.

Although Palestrina wrote many madrigals (a source of pious embarrassment to him in later years), the main body of his work is made up of sacred music. Obviously such a long and prolific career is bound to contain a great deal of variety; nevertheless Palestrina's name, especially after his death, came to be synonymous with the classic style of Catholic church music, a style characterized by clarity, sweetness of sound and a serenely optimistic mood. Comparisons are sometimes made with the Renaissance painter Raphael, another artist striving to create an ideal world of balance and harmony. Some have found this ordered and reverential approach unrewarding and even boring, but at its best Palestrina's music creates a powerful impression of spiritual joy, unencumbered by doubt.

Masses

Palestrina wrote over a hundred masses, although only a handful of them are performed with any regularity. The most famous, the six-part *Missa Papae Marcelli*, may have been one of the masses performed for a committee of cardinals who wished to "...test whether the words could be understood." It certainly conforms to the recommendations of the Council of Trent: there's an emphasis on clarity and the musical ideas unfold in slow, steady steps – there are rarely any great interval leaps. The music is subtly varied, however, by different groupings of the voices and by mixing contrapuntal and homophonic writing – that is music made up of independent, overlapping voices (as in the Kyrie) contrasted with music where the voices sing the words together in the same rhythm (as in much of the Gloria and Credo). Of his other masses, the four-part *Missa Brevis* has a similar lucidity and directness, but is rather more lively and less rarified, while the beautiful Christmas mass, *Missa Hodie Christus Natus Est*, bases its musical material on a motet of the same name.

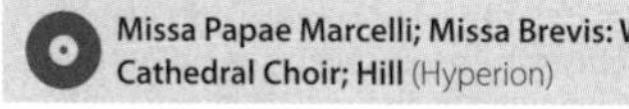

Missa Papae Marcelli; Missa Brevis: Westminster Cathedral Choir; Hill (Hyperion)

The *Missa Papae Marcelli* would have originally been sung by a choir of adult men at a lower pitch than on this disc. But the work's ethereal purity is well served by the Westminster Cathedral choir. The trebles' bright, strong sound is especially appropriate for the sense of line and momentum in Palestrina's melodies.

Missa Hodie Christus Natus Est: King's College Choir Cambridge; Ledger (Decca; with *Stabat Mater* and Lassus *Missa Bell' Amfitrit' altera*)

Written for Christmas Day, the *Missa Hodie Christus Natus Est* (Today Christ is Born) is one of Palestrina's most buoyant and energetic masses. A mass for double choir, it is based on the motet of the same name, which is also included on the disc (along with four others by Palestrina). All get appropriately radiant and serene performances from the fine King's choir of the late 1970s.

Stabat Mater & Canticum Canticorum

After the *Missa Papae Marcelli*, Palestrina's most celebrated work is his short setting of the *Stabat Mater*, the fourteenth-century Latin poem outlining the suffering of the Virgin Mary at the foot of the Cross. Written for double choir, the writing is mostly homophonic but the essential tranquillity of the music helps underline the poignancy of the words, as does the unruffled interchange of the two choirs. A rather more lively response to a text can be found in the *Canticum Canticorum* (Song of Songs), his setting of part of the Old Testament love poem which the Church interpreted in various ways, including as an allegory of Christ's love for the Church or God's love for the Virgin Mary. Palestrina's setting was published in 1584 as a book of motets, but stylistically the twenty-nine verse settings are closer to madrigals with – for Palestrina – some especially vivid word-painting.

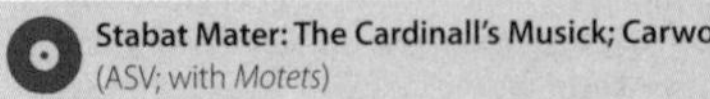

Stabat Mater: The Cardinall's Musick; Carwood (ASV; with *Motets*)

An outstanding account of the *Stabat Mater* from The Cardinall's Musick, with resplendent vocal tone and great warmth to the recording. The disc also contains several motets, many of them associated with Easter, in no less glorious accounts.

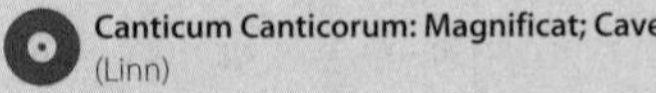

Canticum Canticorum: Magnificat; Cave (Linn)

Philip Cave directs powerful and expressive performances of the various motets that make up the *Canticum Canticorum*. Shifts in mood are nicely conveyed, as in the rapturous excitement of "Surge propera amica mea" ("Rise up, my love, my fair one").

Hubert Parry (1848–1918)

Hubert Parry seems doomed to be known solely as the composer of "Jerusalem", a piece of music written in the depths of World War I which, like Elgar's "Land of Hope and Glory", has become a sort of alternative national anthem. However, Vaughan Williams was acutely aware of the magnitude of Parry's contribution: "We pupils of Parry have … inherited from him the great English choral tradition which Tallis passed on to Byrd, Byrd to Gibbons, Gibbons to Purcell, Purcell to Battishall and Greene and they in turn through the Wesleys to Parry. He has passed the torch to us, and it is our duty to keep it alight." As composer, scholar and teacher (he became director of the Royal College of Music), Parry exercised a revitalizing influence upon British musical life at a time when it desperately needed it.

Parry was a sufficiently gifted child to gain an Oxford B.Mus while still a pupil at Eton. He went on to read law and modern history at Pembroke College, Oxford, and then – following family pressure – became an underwriter at Lloyd's of London. He continued with music, however, studying with Schumann's friend William Sterndale Bennett, and later with Edward Dannreuther (a friend to both Tchaikovsky and Wagner). Parry's first piano concerto was performed in 1880 but it was the premiere, seven years later, of his cantata *Blest Pair of Sirens* that established him as one of England's leading composers. His deep affection for Wagner's music and his immersion in the British sacred traditions nurtured a distinctively Romantic voice that found clearest expression in his work for the voice – and, in particular, choral music, much of it written for English choral music festivals. Hymns and anthems comprise but part of an output that was perhaps too vast for the good of Parry's reputation. At its best, however, Parry's music is a tuneful and enjoyable alliance of late-Victorian grandiosity and highly original polyphony.

Choral Music

Parry was an avowed agnostic yet he produced some of Britain's finest sacred choral music. Apart from the hymn "Jerusalem" and the coronation anthem *I was Glad*, his best-known choral work is the cantata *Blest Pair of Sirens* (1887), a setting for eight-part chorus and orchestra of Milton's "At a Solemn Music" which despite some bombastic moments contains some genuinely poignant melodies. Its success led to the commissioning of the oratorio *Judith*, forgotten today except for the marvellous melody that was later used for the hymn "Dear Lord and Father of Mankind". Arguably his finest work is the dramatic cantata *The Soul's Ransom (A Psalm for the Poor)*, first performed at the Three Choirs Festival of 1906 and then not heard again until its revival in 1981. The text was created by Parry from carefully chosen biblical passages, ending with one of Parry's own poems and offering divine harmony to suffering humans. Parry also composed many secular choral works, including *The Lotos Eaters* (1892), his ravishingly lyrical setting for soprano, chorus and orchestra of the Choric Song from Tennyson's poem of the same name.

The Soul's Ransom; The Lotos Eaters: Jones, Wilson Johnson; London Philharmonic Choir and Orchestra; Bamert (Chandos)

A fascinating recording of a pair of choral works which challenge the stereotyped image of Parry as stuffy late Victorian. Matthias Bamert has also recorded all Parry's symphonies (as well as other works) for Chandos and is deeply committed to upgrading the status of this neglected composer.

Blest Pair of Sirens; I was Glad; Jerusalem; My Soul, There is a Country: Choir of Winchester Cathedral; Wayneflete Singers; Bournemouth Symphony Orchestra; Hill (Decca; with *20 English Lyrics*)

David Hill, one of the most accomplished of British choral conductors, directs an impassioned performance of *Blest Pair of Sirens* and equally convincing accounts of "Jerusalem" and *I was Glad*. The high point, though, is the radiant singing of the Winchester Cathedral choristers in "Long Since in Egypt's Plenteous Land" from the oratorio *Judith*.

Orchestral Music

Parry's *Symphony No. 1* of 1882 is an extraordinary achievement. It's a work bursting with youthful enthusiasm, and is full of beguilingly simple tunes that at times recall Mendelssohn. Parry wrote four more symphonies, the best of which is the cyclic *Symphony No. 5*, first performed in 1912, and an especially fine example of an ardent Romanticism very much influenced by Brahms. The subtitles of the four linked movements ("Stress", "Love", "Play" and "Now") suggest a musical exploration of the human condition. As a group, Parry's symphonies may not reach the exultant heights of Elgar's two, and they lack the humanist gravity of Vaughan Williams's symphonies, but there is much to enjoy here. His other orchestral works include the dramatic *Symphonic Variations*, first performed in 1897, and the moving *Elegy for Brahms*, written in the same year and given a posthumous premiere, conducted by Stanford, in 1918.

Symphony No. 5; Symphonic Variations; Elegy for Brahms: London Philharmonic Orchestra; Boult (EMI; with *Blest Pair of Sirens*, etc)

Recorded in 1978 when Sir Adrian Boult was 89, this was the last recording he ever made – a clear indication of the high regard he had for Parry ("I do hope this will help put him where I feel he ought to be in our history", he wrote). His conviction about the quality of Parry's music shines through in performances that are heartfelt and uplifting.

Arvo Pärt (1935–)

If any one composer can be said to be responsible for creating a public receptive to the "holy minimalism" of John Tavener and Górecki's third symphony, it's the monkish Estonian composer Arvo Pärt. After completing his national service as an army drummer, Pärt trained at Tallinn's conservatory while working as a technician in the music department of Estonian Radio. He gave up this job in 1967 when he began to earn his living from composing, and subsequently scored over 50 films. He rejects his film scores now, but still has a fondness for the music he wrote for children's theatre, an affection that includes piano pieces like "Dance of the Ducklings" and "Puss in Boots".

At around the same time he began to explore serialism, using the dissonances of atonal music to kick against the Soviet system. *Necrology* (1959) outraged Soviet sensibilities, although in the same year Pärt won a prestigious prize in Moscow with the much more conventional *Our Garden* for children's choir and orchestra. He soon abandoned serialist techniques in favour of a collage approach, which also displeased the authorities. After composing the *Symphony No. 2* (1966) in a polystylistic vein, he temporarily abandoned composition and embarked on a study of medieval Franco-Flemish choral music. This resulted in his first religious work, *Credo* (1968), which was banned by the secularist state. The hostility generated, coinciding with a personal crisis, had a damaging effect on his health, but from then on the influence of medieval music and religious ideas was unmistakable, and was certainly not lost on the authorities. The serene *Symphony No. 3* (1971), mixing seventeenth-century elements with Orthodox chant, illustrates the way Pärt's music was to move forward by looking back. In the 1970s he married for the second time, and, realizing how central religion was to both his music and life, joined the Russian Orthodox Church.

Years of meditation, religious consultation – and another break from composing – yielded the small but seminal piano piece *For Alina* (1976) which initiated the "tintinnabulist" period (see below). Three stunning instrumental compositions followed in 1976–77 – *Tabula Rasa*, *Fratres* and *Cantus in Memory of Benjamin Britten*, all potent and beautiful examples of Pärt's unique species of highly charged minimalism. His music continued to annoy the authorities, however, and in 1980 he, his wife, who is Jewish, and two children were granted permission to go to Israel: instead he fled to Vienna, where he lived for eighteen months before settling in Berlin. Since the late 1970s he has unwaveringly followed a spiritual path, producing a succession of small-scale vocal works such as *Summa* (1978) and *De Profundis* (1980) as well as lengthy choral pieces such as the eighty-minute *Passio* (1982), the *Te Deum* of 1986, and the *Kanon Pokajanen* (1998).

In describing his work Pärt frequently invokes the term "tintinnabulation" (the sound or music of bells): "I have discovered that it is enough when a single note is beautifully played. This one note, or a silent beat, or a moment of silence, comforts me. I work with very few elements – with one voice, with two voices. I build with the most primitive materials – with the triad, with one specific tonality. The three notes of a triad are like bells. And that is why I call it tintinnabulation." A form of this pealing device can sometimes be heard in traditional song and Orthodox liturgy, and Pärt's spirituality, as well as his musical heart, is rooted in the Eastern Orthodox church, whose musical tradition has remained largely consistent throughout its history. However, Pärt has also written music for the Catholic liturgy, though here his inspiration comes from music of the early Renaissance and before. Much of the timeless quality of his work derives not just from its apparent simplicity, but from the fact that the harmony does not modulate (change key), so there is none of that sense of movement towards a climax that exists in nearly all post-Renaissance music. That is not to say that the music is entirely static – rather that its energy seems permanently rooted in the present.

Instrumental Music

Scored for string orchestra and tubular bells, Pärt's short but powerful homage to the recently deceased Benjamin Britten, the *Cantus in Memory of Benjamin Britten* (1976), has an amazingly pared-down simplicity: a slow descending minor scale (recalling Britten's ballad "Old Abram Brown is Dead and Gone") is interspersed with the tolling of bells. As the music gradually slows down, it intensifies in volume before the strings cease, leaving the thin but resonant echo of a lone bell.

Fratres, written the following year, is an equally sombre work in which a chorale-like melody is repeated over a drone of a fifth. The occasional beat of a drum underlines the processional quality of the work and its title surely hints at a monastic inspiration. *Tabula Rasa*, also written in the late 1970s, is another work based on a hypnotic series of repetitions. An animated flurry of strings – like a group of people moving towards you – is punctuated by static and subdued moments for violin and prepared piano. The second half is more contemplative: slow-moving and ethereal strings answered by the bell-like middle register of the prepared piano.

Tabula Rasa; Fratres; Cantus: Kremer, Jarrett, Schnittke, Sondeckis; Lithuanian Chamber Orchestra; Berlin Philharmonic cello section; Stuttgart State Orchestra; Russell Davies; (ECM)

Tabula Rasa is given a fittingly intense performance by Alfred Schnittke (on prepared piano) and the violinist Gidon Kremer – a frequent collaborator with the composer. *Fratres* is performed here in two versions, a dramatic one for violin and piano and a more solemn one for twelve cellists.

Fratres; Cantus: Hungarian State Orchestra; Benedek (Naxos; with *Summa* & *Festina lente*)

For those who find the intense ambience of the ECM recording a little too precious, this recording provides a more meaty alternative. Recorded in Budapest, it contains several different versions of *Fratres* and a more elemental but less spiritual version of *Cantus* which is a full two and a half minutes longer than the ECM performance.

Stabat Mater

As with the orchestral works, variety in Pärt's choral music is achieved largely though a build-up of dynamics and by contrasting sonorities, but if this makes for any sense of progression in the music it is strictly of a circular nature. In longer works, like the *Stabat Mater* (1985), there is still that sense of a unifying image pervading the whole work. The verses, concerning the emotions of the Virgin Mary as she stands at the foot of the Cross, are among the most poignant of all Christian writings. But Pärt does not wallow in the pain (though there are several loud declamatory passages from both voices and strings); rather he imbues the sadness with a ritualistic element by way of the gentle rocking motion that forms the basis of the work.

Kremer, Dawson, Bowers-Broadbent; Stuttgart State Orchestra; Hilliard Ensemble; Russell Davies (ECM; with *Arbos, Pari Intervallo, An den Wassern zu Babel, De Profundis, Es sang vor langen Jahren* & *Summa*)

Most of this 1987 disc consists of still and contemplative choral works. These are all exquisitely performed by the Hilliard Ensemble whose then director, Paul Hillier, was and still is very much a Pärt expert. Phrases are beautifully moulded, not least in the *Stabat Mater* and the exquisite *An den Wassern zu Babel* (By the Waters of Babylon).

Kanon Pokajanen

Pärt's longest work is the *Kanon Pokajanen* (Canon of Repentance, 1998), a setting of an eighth-century text by St Andrew of Crete which is particularly dear to him. It deals with the symbolism of transformation: night into day, prophecy and fulfilment, sin and redemption. Pärt sets it as a series of odes in which subdued supplicatory music is contrasted with more refulgent songs of praise. There is both an element of communal worship and something intensely personal in the mesmerizing repetitions and subtly varied voice combinations. Much of the spare harmony is redolent of Orthodox music but, for all its archaisms, this is clearly a modern work, with spicier harmonies for the higher voices which calls to mind Britten's *Ceremony of Carols*.

Estonian Philharmonic Chamber Choir; Kaljuste
(ECM; 2 CDs)

Written to commemorate the 750th anniversary of Cologne Cathedral, the *Kanon Pokajanen* was first performed there in March 1998 and recorded shortly afterwards. It's hard to imagine a more radiant and enraptured performance than the one it gets from the Estonian Philharmonic Chamber Choir. They are a much bigger group than the Hilliard Ensemble but there is a similar attention to detail.

Krzysztof Penderecki (1933–)

Until his contemporary Henryk Górecki (see p.216) became an unlikely New Age icon in the 1990s, Penderecki was the most-performed living Polish composer, more so than his older compatriot Witold Lutosławski (see p.311). He studied then taught at the Krakow Conservatory, and burst on the scene in 1960 with *Threnody for the Victims of Hiroshima*, an anguished piece of expressionism tolerated by the Communist authorities because of its subject matter. Penderecki's use of note-clusters, extreme registers and other effects constituted one form of 1960s "texture music", of which less violent manifestations are found in Lutosławski and Ligeti.

Penderecki on a balcony in Warsaw, 1959.

The Polish regime of the 1960s and 1970s was liberal in comparison to others in Eastern Europe, and its relative tolerance of contemporary music was manifested in the Warsaw Autumn Festival (founded in 1956), which enabled some of Europe's leading avant-gardists to pursue a thriving career on the "wrong" side of the Iron Curtain. The politically quiescent Penderecki was given a certain latitude and so prospered, while Górecki, less diplomatic in attending to the regime's sensitivities, languished in obscurity.

The *St Luke's Passion*, completed in 1966, marked Penderecki's arrival as a composer of international status. His first opera, *The Devils of Loudon*, followed in 1969. Then suddenly, during the 1970s, he turned conservative. His lurch to neo-Romantic symphonism, apparently without a hint of irony, was much criticized, but Penderecki commented later: "Now is the time of synthesis. What we should do now is to find a sort of universal language, which we don't have in our century." During the 1980s Penderecki developed a blend of Romanticism and modernism. His penchant for the big theme and the grand gesture is epitomized by the *Polish Requiem* (1980–84), which was linked with the political programme of the Solidarity trade union – the *Lachrymosa*, composed for Solidarity leader Lech Walesa, is dedicated to the victims of the 1970 Gdansk rising.

Like his English contemporary Peter Maxwell Davies, Penderecki now comes across as an advocate of modernity rather than thoroughgoing modernism. Critical characterization of him as a merchant of hollow rhetoric and incoherent expressionism has some force, as has the charge that he is a stylistic chameleon. But, though he is certainly an uneven composer, Penderecki is capable of powerful utterances, and the "neo-Romantic" symphonies and concertos are impressive achievements despite their bombast and occasional clichés.

St Luke's Passion

Scored for huge forces – three solo voices, narrator, three mixed choirs, boys' choir and orchestra – the *St Luke's Passion* was Penderecki's most ambitious concert work up to the time of its composition (1962–66). Following on from the extreme expressionism of the early 1960s, the *Passion* marks a synthesis of avant-garde techniques with the great traditions of Western choral music – in particular the works of Bach, Palestrina and Gregorian chant. Commissioned to commemorate the 700th anniversary of Münster Cathedral, the work employs angular dissonances and some unconventional but dramatic effects (such as crowd noises), but communicates a genuinely devotional mood and tells its story with undeniable authority and intensity. The earliest and most concentrated section is the a cappella *Stabat Mater*, which is often performed as a separate work.

Cracow Boys' Choir & Warsaw National Philharmonic Chorus; Polish National Radio Symphony Orchestra; Penderecki (Argo)

This is Penderecki at his most impressive, as both composer and conductor. The majestic solo voices are well projected and the recording has great presence; but also, perhaps due to a combination of close and distant miking, there's an exceptional amount of reverberation, producing a very immediate effect.

Warsaw Boys' Choir & Warsaw National Philharmonic Choir and Orchestra; Wit (Naxos)

If Penderecki's own recording proves hard to track down then this more recent one will prove a good alternative, not least because it uses very similar forces and Antoni Wit's interpretation is close in spirit to that of the composer, even though the acoustic is far less resonant. The one drawback is the absence of the text.

Symphonies

Penderecki maintains that he is a symphonist first and foremost. The appearance of his first in 1973 (commissioned somewhat incongruously by Perkins Motors of Peterborough) caused surprise, although the appropriately mechanistic and often expressionist sound-world was recognizably continuous with Penderecki's famous earlier pieces. But it was the *Symphony No. 2* of 1980 that occasioned real astonishment – "the most Romantic piece I ever wrote", Penderecki says. "Pages from the Symphony Writer's Handbook, chapters on Bruckner and Mahler" was how one ill-tempered critic responded. Despite a tendency to meander, the work does achieve a kind of Brucknerian dignity and pace by using simple motivic material, including the carol *Silent Night* – hence its subtitle, the "Christmas Symphony".

The *Symphony No. 4* (1989) began life as an Adagio movement but, at over thirty minutes in length, the composer decided it should stand as a symphony in its own right. It's an unreservedly Romantic work with distinctly Tristanesque touches to the harmony.

Symphonies Nos. 2 & 4: NDR-Sinfonieorchester; Penderecki (Wergo)

The two symphonies are given expansive, measured interpretations by the composer. The orchestral sound is sumptuous in a state-of-the-art live recording in which audience noise is minimal.

Symphonies Nos. 2 & 4: National Polish Radio Orchestra; Wit (Naxos)

Antoni Wit, who studied with Penderecki, once again proves himself a powerful advocate of the composer's work. He concentrates on realizing the best aspects of these two symphonies – their varied tone colour – and succeeds in making the musical arguments unfold in a compelling way.

Threnody & Anaklasis

At a time when the avant-garde was a ghetto within the wider ghetto of modern music, Penderecki popularized the gestures of Stockhausen and Xenakis by making them even more brutally expressive. Works such as the *Threnody for the Victims of Hiroshima* (1959–61), in which tone-clusters eradicate the boundary between noise and pitch, are the last word in textural music. With its sickening glissandos, piercing high-note passages and sepulchral pizzicato and knocking effects, it's a shattering musical evocation of the effects of nuclear destruction. *Anaklasis* (1959) is no less visceral in its impact: this time a dialogue is set up between 42 strings and an armoury of assorted percussion. These works of the 1960s seem to hang together by emotional effect alone, and it's not clear how far Penderecki could have gone in this direction. It has become fashionable to deride the result as dated 1960s avant-gardism, but this is music that still creates a powerful impression, and the shorter works from the 1980s and 1990s seem paler efforts in comparison.

Polish Radio National Symphony Orchestra; Penderecki (EMI; 2 CDs; with other orchestral works)

There are some searing performances in this admirable two-disc collection of Penderecki's orchestral pieces of the 1960s and early 1970s. *Anaklasis*, *Eminationem* and the *Threnody* are definite high points; the rest is mostly dense and anguished, including the *Symphony No. 1* – the high-water mark of Penderecki's own brand of modernism.

Chamber Music

Penderecki's two string quartets, written in 1960 and 1968 respectively, find him at his most expressionistic and direct. Both works are concentrated – lasting less than ten minutes each – and replete with the composer's trademark avant-gardisms. The performers are required to play with quarter-tone vibrato, draw their bows across the tailpiece, knock on the body of their instruments, and strum like guitarists – all techniques that make a dramatic and immediate impact.

The chamber pieces Penderecki wrote in the 1980s and 1990s are slightly less effective, though impressive nonetheless. The short *String Trio* (1991) mixes ferocious slashing chords with rhapsodic cantilenas for each soloist, in a manner clearly derived from Bartók; the *Clarinet Quartet* (1993) is a more assured and original synthesis, combining modernism with an obvious relish for specific instrumental timbres.

String Quartets Nos. 1 & 2; Prelude for Clarinet Solo; String Trio; Clarinet Quartet: Tale Quartet; Fröst (BIS)

These are fine performances by the Tale Quartet, a young ensemble from Scandinavia. There is both fervour and sensitivity in their accounts of the two string quartets, and the later works – the *Clarinet Quartet* in particular – are given persuasive interpretations.

Giovanni Pergolesi (1710–1736)

Though only a moderately successful composer during his extremely short life, Pergolesi managed to write two works that not only brought him posthumous fame but significantly influenced the direction of vocal music in the eighteenth century. The first, *La serva padrona* (The Maidservant as Mistress), was an early example of comic opera, or opera buffa, in which the characters were drawn from everyday life. Pergolesi worked mainly in Naples, a major operatic centre, where a style had developed which emphasized the beauty and virtuosity of the solo voice, often at the expense of dramatic unity. *La serva padrona*, a short intermezzo performed between the acts of Pergolesi's opera seria *Le prigionier superbo*, introduced a more naturalistic tone, but its notoriety came about after the composer's death, when a performance in Paris in 1752 instigated a furious theoretical debate about the respective merits of Pergolesi's opera buffa as opposed to the more formal and serious French opera.

The second, a setting of the *Stabat Mater* for two solo voices and strings, pioneered a style of church music which combined emotional directness with an elegant and graceful expressiveness. Here, as in his operatic work, Pergolesi epitomized a progressive tendency which was championed by the philosopher Jean-Jacques Rousseau, who described the opening of the *Stabat Mater* as "the most perfect and most touching to have come from the pen of any musician".

La serva padrona

La serva padrona should be approached with a little bit of caution. Several of the arias are charming and inventive (and sound surprisingly Mozartian) but over a third of the opera takes the form of long recitatives which, though tolerable with accompanying stage business, can be wearisome on record. The plot tells of how a tyrannical maid-servant (Serpina) tricks her elderly master (Umberto) into marrying her by disguising a fellow servant (Vespone) as a prospective suitor.

Much of the comedy derives from the fact that the role of Vespone is mute, thus providing scope for several comic misunderstandings. The characterization is simple but vivid and the players' primary emotions are neatly established through direct and tuneful writing. Serpina's "Stizzoso, mio Stizzoso" establishes her as a demanding shrew, and neatly sets the scene for her Part 2 aria "A Serpina penserete" in which she proves, through music of almost introverted beauty, that she is not

Stabat Mater Dolorosa

"At the cross her station keeping/stood the mournful mother weeping/close to Jesus to the last."
Opening lines of the *Stabat Mater* (transl. Father Edward Caswall)

The Christian story, as told in the four gospels, features very few women. Even Mary, the mother of Jesus, figures only intermittently. But the apparent need for a mother figure within the Church meant that, over the centuries, Mary's importance grew, and those elements of her life absent from the gospels were fleshed out in stories and verses. By the early Middle Ages her religious status had risen to such an extent that many churches were dedicated to her, and she was widely celebrated in both images and music.

One of the most moving manifestations of the medieval Marian cult was the *Stabat Mater*, a long poem written in Latin in the thirteenth century as a meditation on the suffering of Mary as she witnesses her son's crucifixion. It's not known who wrote it but it was probably someone connected to the Franciscans, an order of friars whose mission to the poor emphasized the humanity of the Christian story, above all in the narrative of events leading to Jesus' death. By the late fifteenth century, the poem was being used in Catholic worship as a hymn – its plainchant melody dates from this period – and it was fully incorporated into the Catholic liturgy in 1727, as part of the Mass of the Seven Sorrows of the Virgin.

Among the earliest harmonized settings of the *Stabat Mater* are three versions from the Eton Choirbook, a manuscript of music compiled c.1500 for use by the choir of Eton College (a foundation dedicated to the Virgin Mary). The composers of these early settings were Richard Davy, William Cornysh the elder and John Browne, all of whom wrote in the highly ornate, polyphonic style favoured immediately prior to the Reformation (see p.000). All three versions are strikingly beautiful, but the one by Browne, with its invigorating rhythmic suppleness, is one of the great – though largely unknown – glories of English music.

Not much of the emotional intensity of the words is communicated in the Eton Choirbook settings, or in those by other Renaissance composers such as Josquin or Palestrina. It was during the Baroque period, when composers sought to communicate the meaning of the words through the music, that the most expressive versions appeared. Many were written in Italy: Pergolesi's *Stabat Mater*, for just two voices, was the most famous example, but there were others including settings by Vivaldi, Antonio Caldara, Agostino Steffani, and both Scarlattis.

Later in the eighteenth century versions appeared by Boccherini and Joseph Haydn, while in the nineteenth the *Stabat Mater* became as much of a concert work as one performed in church. Schubert, Liszt, Gounod, Dvořák, Rossini and Verdi were among those to set all or part of the text – the last two regarded as the most successful. Of the twentieth-century composers included in this book, Poulenc, Penderecki and Syzmanowski all made settings of the *Stabat Mater*, of which Syzmanowski's is the most celebrated.

The Crown of Thorns: The Sixteen; Christophers (CORO)

The second of a five-volume selection from the Eton Choirbook contains all three of its settings of the *Stabat Mater*, versions which use a variant text for the second half of the poem. Richard Davy's has the most sedate and ordered music, the one by John Browne (about whom nothing is known) the most ornate and expressive. The Sixteen clearly relish the joyous syncopation as much as the serenity.

Steffani's Stabat Mater: Chorus and Baroque Orchestra of the Dutch Bach Association; Leonhardt (Deutsche Harmonia Mundi; with Biber *Requiem à 15*)

An exact contemporary of Corelli, Agostino Steffani was a high-powered cleric and diplomat as well as a composer. Though scored for relatively small forces, his *Stabat Mater* has a sombre ceremonial quality, especially in the choral passages. But Steffani is also highly sensitive to the pathos of the text and the solo passages have a dramatic expressiveness. Gustav Leonhardt and his forces do full justice to this little-known masterpiece.

so bad after all. The opera ends with a wonderful ensemble in which Umberto finally confesses his love and Serpina celebrates her victory.

Zanello, Govi; Ensemble Reggia Accademia; Dallara
(Tactus)

There are several recordings of *La serva padrona* but few remain in the catalogue for long. This is the best recent version with a genuine whiff of the theatre to it. Soprano Federica Zanello makes a spirited Serpina and works well with the blustery bass of Michele Govi. The slightly reverberant acoustic adds to the atmosphere.

Stabat Mater

The *Stabat Mater* is Pergolesi's masterpiece: the great medieval text, detailing the Virgin's suffering at the foot of the Cross, drew an enormously intense response from him, in which the expressive use of pauses and of dissonances is much in evidence. It was commissioned by a religious brotherhood, the Cavalieri della Vergine dei Dolori, to replace a slightly earlier setting by Alessandro Scarlatti. If it sounds rather operatic for a religious work, it is largely because Pergolesi (like Scarlatti) dispenses with a chorus in order to present the text through the immediacy of the solo voice – each of the twelve sections is allocated either to the soprano or to the alto, or to both in duet. The music is astonishingly varied given that the prevailing mood is one of pain and supplication, though there are a couple of sections of relative liveliness. According to legend it was the last work Pergolesi wrote before his death, probably from consumption, at the Franciscan monastery in Pozzuoli near Naples. What is certainly true is that it became one of the most popular and enduring works of the entire eighteenth century.

Gens, Lesne; Il Seminario Musicale
(Virgin; with *Salve Regina in F Minor* & *Sinfonia a tre*)

Recordings of the *Stabat Mater* used to sentimentalize the work with lush orchestral playing and big operatic voices. More recently there has been a tendency to pare down the accompaniment and use a male alto with a female soprano. With Véronique Gens and Gérard Lesne (who also directs) you get a near-perfect balance of well-rounded voices that emphasize the sensuous quality of the music.

Mingardo, Harnisch; Orchestra Mozart; Abbado
(Archiv; with *Salve Regina in C Minor* & *Violin Concerto in B Flat*)

This is grander and more operatic than the above but still relatively pared down compared with Claudio Abbado's recording of thirty years ago. Soprano Rachel Harnisch and the rich-toned mezzo Sarah Mingardo don't blend as effectively as Gens and Lesne but it's a powerful performance nevertheless. A sparkling violin concerto and a movingly intense account of the *Salve Regina* in C by Julia Kleiter are welcome bonuses.

Perotin (c.1170–c.1236)

The earliest composers of polyphonic music whose names have come down to us are Leonin (c.1159–1201) and Perotin, both of whom were part of an extraordinary flowering of culture that took place in Paris in the late twelfth century. Almost nothing is known of their lives, the scant information we have coming from the writings of an English monk, now referred to as Anonymous 4, who studied for a while at the University of Paris. They probably had some connection with the new cathedral of Notre Dame, but the theory that Perotin was taught by Leonin and succeeded him as choirmaster of Notre Dame is now generally discredited. Assuming Anonymous 4's attributions are correct, Leonin composed relatively simple two-part music whereas Perotin wrote in three and sometimes four parts, creating strange but utterly compulsive

Notation

It's impossible to overstate the importance to Western music of the notation system that started to develop around a millennium ago. For one thing, this system of notes, staves and bars has allowed musical works to be accurately preserved through time. But that's not all. Notation was also the catalyst that ushered in the basic foundations of the Western musical tradition: harmony and counterpoint, and the concept of the composer.

The ancient Greeks developed the first European notation system, writing note names above the words of a song text. But this didn't take off with the Romans, and for the first millennium of its existence, the Catholic Church was still struggling to find a reliable way to save monks and priests having to memorize its vast chant repertoire. A few systems were tried, including placing each word higher or lower than the previous one to show if the tune should rise or fall. But the most popular technique was to put little symbols, called "neumes", above the words to indicate the shape of the melody. But this was rough at best: more an *aide-mémoire* than a precise system. And the fact that each church had its own version didn't help.

The breakthrough came in the eleventh century, when an Italian monk named Guido d'Arezzo (c.995–1050) had the simple but ingenious idea of drawing a straight line – in red – above the words. Instead of floating around in space, the neumes now had a reference point: on the line meant "F", and anything above or below could be read in relation to that. Guido soon added a second line for "C" – in yellow – and then two more, creating the first stave (or staff). The colour-coding system didn't live long, but Guido's other technique for specifying which line was which, namely writing F on one line and C on another, did: our modern clefs are simply elaborations of letters, each identifying the pitch of a specific line. (Incidentally, the tireless Guido also came up with the Do-Re-Mi teaching system, which helped popularize his staves).

It took a bit longer for the neumes to develop into a standard system of "notes" for specifying rhythm (hence the exact rhythm implied by many medieval music manuscripts is still unclear) but within a few hundred years the system still used today was basically complete. Five-line staves became the norm, bar lines were added to break up the music into regular units of time to make it easier to read, and key signatures were put on each stave to show which notes should be sharpened or flattened throughout the piece. The system's only competitor – graphical tablature, in which each line represents an instrument's string – died out with the lute in the eighteenth century (at least until rock guitarists championed it again two hundred and fifty years later).

Though basic Western notation has changed very little since Bach's time, some post-war modernist composers started to feel restrained by the system. Varèse (see p.593) felt the world was "waiting for a new notation … a new Guido d'Arezzo" so that music could "move forward at a bound". And though that never really happened, the 1950s and 1960s saw various composers having a good go at developing new ways to represent radical new compositional approaches such as indeterminism, where the exact pitch and duration of notes was unspecified. The Americans were pioneers of these so-called "graphic scores", with Morton Feldman (see p.194) using blocks and lines to get his ideas across and John Cage (see p.125) trying out a whole manner of diagrammatic methods. Others, such as the British composer Cornelius Cardew, started paying increasing attention to how the scores looked, effectively turning musical notation into an art form in its own right.

The practice of writing music down has undoubtedly been central to the development of classical music, and to the survival of compositions through time. But some consider that it has also led to a stolid classical music scene in which most musicians are entirely reliant on having a page in front of them, and are unable to improvise. It's certainly true that today's classical musicians are rarely great improvisers, but it would be wrong to blame this on notation, as opposed to contemporary music teaching and performance practices. After all, Baroque keyboardists were expected to be perfect sightreaders, but also to be able to elaborate spontaneously from a "figured" bass part, with just a few numbers to suggest the harmony (rather like an upside-down version of a jazz pianist's lead sheet). And fluency with written music did nothing to temper the improvisational genius of Bach, Mozart, Beethoven and countless other masters. Which is no surprise considering Busoni's view of notation: "primarily an ingenious expedient for catching an inspiration … to improvisation as the portrait is to the living model".

music, in which harmonic plainness is carried joyously along by rhythmic suppleness.

Up to the time of Perotin, the dominant musical form of the Christian Church had been monophonic chant (see p.256), but some time in the ninth century another voice with its own independent line of music was added, marking the beginning of polyphony. At first it was very simple: the added line moved in parallel to the plainsong melody, usually beneath it, at a fixed interval. The plainsong melody was known as the cantus firmus (fixed song), the voice that sang it was the vox principalis and the added voice the vox organalis. This simple form of polyphony was called organum and it was employed as an occasional, ornate addition to liturgical plainsong rather than as a replacement for it.

The parallel duplication of a fixed melody had obvious limitations, and freer styles soon began to appear. The most important was florid, or melismatic, organum, in which the vox organalis was placed above the cantus firmus and made rhythmically independent and melodically dominant, employing as many as twenty notes to each one in the lower part. Since the cantus firmus was drawn out to accommodate the ornate phrases above it, the voice singing this line became known as the tenor (from the Latin "to hold"). Florid organum existed alongside the older note-on-note style, which became known as discant.

Magnus liber organi

The most important record of early polyphony is the *Magnus liber organi* (The Great Book of Organum). Probably written specifically for Notre Dame, this large corpus of work consists of plainchant and polyphony and is the earliest example of precise rhythmic notation. According to Anonymous 4, a first version was composed by Leonin, before "the great Perotinius made a redaction of it" – probably meaning that Perotin reworked many of the pieces in a more lively and exciting modern style, and added many compositions of his own. In reality, many composers probably contributed to the *Magnus liber*, though some pieces can be confidently attributed to Leonin and Perotin. Leonin's contributions represent the older rhapsodic, melismatic organum style, in contrast to Perotin's newer, highly disciplined and rhythmically clear approach. Two of Perotin's most moving contributions are the extraordinary *Viderunt omnes* and *Sederunt principes*, the earliest examples of Western music written in four parts. Both contain startlingly dance-like rhythms in the higher voices, which lilt and weave their way around the drawn-out line of the cantus firmus, echoing each other's material in a way that dissolves the dominant melodic line to create, in Paul Hillier's words, "a kaleidoscope of constantly shifting textures".

Perotin: The Hilliard Ensemble; Hillier
(ECM)

These performances are direct and deeply moving, their wonderfully flexible approach creating an image of the Gothic as something delicate and light-filled. Of the nine pieces on this disc, four (all by Perotin) are organum while the other five (two by Perotin) are conductus, a simple form of music not based on chant, which was employed for ceremonial or processional occasions within the church.

The Mystery of Notre Dame: Orlando Consort
(Archiv)

This disc draws on music from the *Magnus liber* for three major feasts of the liturgical year. A variety of polyphonic styles are covered, from two-part organum to Perotin's colossal four-part *Sederunt principes*. The Orlando Consort bring wonderful shape and motion to the simpler pieces and musical clarity to the most dense. The polyphony is broken up by plainchant, sensitively sung by Westminster Cathedral Choir.

Francis Poulenc (1899–1963)

For years Francis Poulenc was pigeonholed as the playboy of French music, and superficially there's some justice to the charge. He was born into money and had a privileged social position. Through his piano teacher Ricardo Viñes he gained access to the fashionable Parisian artistic scene, and became a key member of a group of iconoclastic young composers called Les Six (see box on p.409). Of all the group, Poulenc seemed the most facile and clownish, the man with the permanent grin on his face. But he was also a serious craftsman, who had made a careful study of counterpoint and was the only one of Les Six to develop in new directions.

Cocteau and Les Six (minus Durey) at the Eiffel Tower in 1921: from left to right, Tailleferre, Poulenc, Honegger, Milhaud, Cocteau and Avric.

By no stretch of the imagination could Poulenc be described as a modernist, yet he always had a keen interest in the international scene, and in 1921 travelled to Vienna with Darius Milhaud in order to meet Schoenberg and his pupils.

Like many young French composers of the interwar years, he was immensely taken by the wit of Erik Satie (see p.468) and by the taut discipline of Stravinsky's early neo-classical works. His masterstroke was to take the irony, implicit in both men's work, and turn it into something beguilingly French. In this project, the influence of his friend Jean Cocteau was never far away, and the rather brittle, jewel-like works of these years show Poulenc taking to heart Cocteau's principle that artists must aim for a coolly elegant modernity, braced with a classical sense of proportion. There is artifice aplenty in the *Aubade* for small orchestra, the ballet *Les Biches* (written for Diaghilev's Ballets Russes), but there was also much ingenuity in the way he achieved fresh sounds with conventional materials.

But there was also a dark side to Poulenc's personality, and in the 1930s a series of disastrous love affairs (mostly with younger men) and the death of a friend, the composer-critic Pierre Octave-Ferroud, precipitated a return to the Catholic Church and a spate of powerful religious works which begin with the *Litanies à la vierge noire* (1936). Poulenc also began a long association with the baritone Pierre Bernac, who became the greatest interpreter of his songs and introduced him to the Surrealist poet Paul Éluard, many of whose poems he later set. Éluard, whose Surrealism was of a decidedly emotional and sensual strain, encouraged Poulenc to modify his rather detached Stravinskian style and embrace the spicier soundworld of Chabrier and Ravel.

Arguably Poulenc's greatest strength was as a lyrical melodist and a writer for the voice: few could match the exquisite delicacy of his word-setting, which was capable of revealing every nuance of his native tongue. But, despite a childhood wish to be an opera singer, he turned to opera relatively late in his career. *Les mamelles de Tirésias* (1944), a setting of Apollinaire's Surrealist comedy, epitomized Poulenc at his most ebullient and light-hearted. It was followed, nine years later, by a work utterly different in tone and mood. *Les dialogues des Carmélites*, based on the true story

Jean Cocteau and Les Six

An antipathy towards Romanticism was very much a badge of honour among progressive European artists at the end of World War I (see p.259). In Paris it found one of its most articulate champions in the artistic polymath and brilliant self-publicist, Jean Cocteau, who in 1917 achieved a certain notoriety when he devised the scenario for *Parade*, a bizarre ballet performed by the Ballets Russes with music by Erik Satie and Cubist costumes by Picasso. The next year Cocteau followed this up with a pamphlet on new music, *Le coq et l'arlequin*, which rejected both the influence of German music and the impressionism of Debussy and Ravel, and advocated instead a French music that took its inspiration from the circus, the music hall and the jazz band. Satie – the exemplary figure for Cocteau – was already a mentor for a group of young musicians who sometimes gave concerts with him as "Les nouveaux jeunes". *Le coq et l'arlequin* became a kind of unofficial manifesto for the group, and in 1920 they were dubbed "Les Six" in an article by critic and composer Henri Collet.

Made up of Louis Durey (1888–1979), Arthur Honegger (1892–1955), Darius Milhaud (1892–1974), Germaine Tailleferre (1892–1983), Francis Poulenc (1899–1963) and Georges Auric (1899–1983), Les Six functioned only briefly as anything like a coherent group, and worked on only two collective projects. The first, *L'album des Six* (1920), was a collection of piano miniatures lasting just over ten minutes; the second was a light-hearted dance work, *Les mariés de la Tour Eiffel* (The Eiffel Tower Newlyweds) commissioned by the avant-garde Ballets Suédois with Cocteau again providing a provocative scenario. He conjured up a bourgeois wedding celebration that rapidly disintegrates into a surreal pantomime complete with an escaped ostrich, a pompous general, a bathing beauty and a small boy representing the future. Two actors declaim the "libretto" over a wittily inventive suite of short pieces that is part homage to popular music and part parody of traditional forms. Durey, who had had enough of what he saw as Cocteau's frivolity, refused to be involved.

Premiered in June 1921 at the Théâtre des Champs-Élysées, *Les mariés* caused the predictable critical uproar. But thereafter Les Six went their separate ways. In truth they were united mostly by friendship and their musical differences had always been as marked as their similarities: Honegger (see p.264) never rejected the German tradition and was not an admirer of Satie, both Durey and Tailleferre were close to Ravel, and only Poulenc and Milhaud (see p.350) retained an element of brittle humour in their ensuing work.

Of the three lesser-known members, Auric went on to become a successful film composer, writing scores for Cocteau's *La Belle et la Bête* (1946) as well as the British comedies *Passport to Pimlico* (1949) and *The Lavender Hill Mob* (1951). Tailleferre settled into a largely neo-classical idiom (her 1924 piano concerto was compared to Bach by pianist Alfred Cortot) but also wrote many scores for film and TV. Durey remains the most forgotten figure, partly because he rejected the social and artistic hothouse of Paris for communism and the south of France, and partly because he returned to writing more traditional and Romantic music (including settings of the writings of Ho Chi Minh).

As for Cocteau, he continued to work with several of the group, writing libretti for Milhaud's chamber opera *Le pauvre matelot* and Honegger's one-act opera *Antigone*, both of which were premiered in December 1927. Over thirty years later, he adapted his own play *La voix humaine* for Poulenc, who skilfully transformed it into a one-person opera for the soprano Denise Duval. But, arguably, Cocteau's most fruitful collaboration was with Stravinsky – not a big fan of Les Six – for whom he provided a text (in French but then translated into Latin) for the opera-oratorio *Oedipus Rex* (1927), one of the great masterpieces of early twentieth-century music (see p.534).

L'album des Six: West, Beynon (Hyperion; with works for flute and piano)

L'album des Six is enjoyable, if lightweight stuff, with Poulenc's *Valse* the most idiomatic and witty piece. Andrew West gives a sound but underwhelming performance on this disc, which also includes all the Six's flute works. There are some gems among them: the Poulenc *Sonata* and the *Sonatine* of Durey get especially sparkling accounts from flautist Emily Beynon.

Les mariés de la Tour Eiffel: Philharmonia Orchestra; Simon (Chandos; with *L'Éventail de Jeanne*)

Les mariés's impact depended as much on its other collaborators as its composers, and musically it remains a curiosity. The Philharmonia and Geoffrey Simon treat it more seriously than perhaps it deserves. The coupling is *L'Éventail de Jeanne*, a children's ballet with contributions from Auric, Milhaud, Poulenc, Ravel and others.

of a group of persecuted nuns during the French Revolution, confirmed Poulenc's transformation from young turk to arch conservative. His final opera, *La voix humaine*, chronicles the psychological disintegration of a desperate woman as she converses on the telephone with her apparently indifferent lover. It is Poulenc's rawest and most extreme work, in which he revealed the vulnerability and pain of his own emotional life.

The best summary of Poulenc's place in the history of modern music is contained in a letter he wrote in 1942: "I know perfectly well that I'm not one of those composers who have made harmonic innovations like Igor [Stravinsky], Ravel or Debussy, but I think there's room for new music which doesn't mind using other people's chords. Wasn't that the case with Mozart-Schubert?" For all his chic use of spicy dissonances and his flirtation with advanced techniques such as polytonality, Poulenc was quite happy to be seen as part of a French tradition stretching back through Chabrier deep into the nineteenth century and beyond.

Concertos

Poulenc was a very gifted pianist and all of the four concertos that he composed were for keyboard instruments, beginning with the *Harpsichord Concerto*, known as the *Concert champêtre*, which he wrote for Wanda Landowska in 1928. Though inspired by the example of Stravinsky's *Concerto for Piano and Wind Instruments*, Poulenc's own brand of neo-classicism is, by contrast, a rather superficial affair more concerned with eighteenth-century flavouring than with structural cohesion. Rather more successful is the delightful *Concerto for Two Pianos* (1932), in which Poulenc's unashamed eclecticism is given full rein. Plenty of affectionate homage is paid to his classical forebears (including a substantial chunk of Mozart in the slow movement) but this is constantly undermined by a wonderful mixture of madcap buffoonery, mock heroics and Ravelian exoticism – all three occurring in the work's scintillating first movement. Six years later, after his return to the Church, Poulenc wrote an organ concerto which he described as existing "on the fringe of my religious music". It's a grandiose and serious work that ranges far and wide in its exploitation of the organ's endlessly rich sonorities. The spirit of Bach presides (specifically his *G Minor Fantasia*) but, once again, there is a profusion of near-incongruous mood swings – meditative, melodramatic and even playful – in its single-movement span. Poulenc's last concerto, for solo piano, was written in 1949 for the Boston Symphony Orchestra. It's not as focused as the *Concerto for Two Pianos*, and the familiar element of pastiche (a Mahlerian slow movement) had rather lost its bite.

Piano Concerto; Concerto for Two Pianos; Organ Concerto; Concert champêtre: Rogé, Deferne, Hurford, Malcolm; Philharmonia Orchestra; Dutoit
(Decca; 2 CDs; with *Gloria* & *Sonata for Two Pianos*)

This is a great survey of the concertos, with Pascal Rogé making a strong case for the uneven *Piano Concerto* and – with Sylviane Deferne – giving a hugely enjoyable account of the double concerto. All the stops get pulled out for the *Organ Concerto*, with Peter Hurford doing full justice to the kaleidoscopic nature of this work. George Malcolm is the eloquent soloist in the *Concert champêtre*.

Choral Works

Poulenc had no doubts as to which of his works gave him most satisfaction: "I think I put the best and most authentic side of myself into my choral music." Certainly it reveals a more emotional side to his personality, although he was not one to differentiate between what was musically appropriate for sacred texts and what was fitting for more earthly subjects. Indeed, when the words required it, Poulenc's religious choral music could be as warm and humane as his secular songs. That said, he often chose to set quite sombre texts: in the *Litanies à la vierge noire* (Litanies of the Black Madonna), for female chorus and organ, monophony, simple harmony and startling dissonance all reinforce the text's supplicatory intensity. Similarly, in the *Stabat Mater* (1950), for soprano, divided chorus and orchestra, the prevailing darkness of mood is achieved through a kind of Baroque solemnity in which there is a lot of unison singing and repetition. There are even echoes of Mozart's *Requiem* in the animated *Cujus animam gementem*, but the eclecticism of the *Stabat Mater* doesn't leap out at you as in so much of Poulenc's work, because the overall emotion seems so heartfelt. It's certainly the masterpiece among his sacred works, though the more extrovert *Gloria* (1959), written for similar forces, is often rated more highly. From its magnificently ceremonial opening, this is a work that exudes confidence and energy and some momentary glimpses back to the Poulenc of the 1920s. Between its two most tender moments – both for soprano solo – are sandwiched some mischievously insouciant orchestral writing which scandalized some members of the original audience.

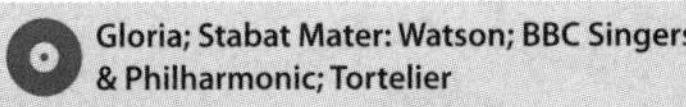

Gloria; Stabat Mater: Watson; BBC Singers & Philharmonic; Tortelier
(Chandos)

Radiant and refined singing plus sensitive orchestral playing make this an obvious first choice. Jan Pascal Tortelier, a specialist in French music, treats singers and players as one force and maximizes the dramatic impact. Janice Watson makes the most of her passionate and intense solos.

Les soirées de Nazelles; Trois novelettes; Pastorale; Trois mouvements perpétuels; Improvisations: Rogé
(Decca)

Such hedonistic music needs delicacy and sensitivity in equal measure, and it certainly gets them from Pascal Rogé. His crystalline touch and subtle pedalling reveal aspects of these pieces that other pianists only hint at, revealing them as multifaceted jewels that may be undemanding but are never bland.

Solo Piano Music

At the age of 17 Poulenc began studying with the brilliant Spanish pianist Ricardo Viñes. As a performer Viñes specialized in contemporary music (he premiered works by Debussy and Ravel) so that, according to Poulenc, "... if the classics were at the basis of Viñes' teaching, it didn't mean Schumann excluded Satie from my lessons". Satie was the major influence on Poulenc's piano music – both his irreverent humour (evident in the quirky titles of his pieces) and his textural clarity made a lasting impact. Odd, then, that Poulenc's first published piece, the mysterious *Pastorale*, shows the equal influence of Satie and Ravel, the latter a composer whose music Poulenc claimed to dislike. A greater impact was made with the *Trois mouvements perpétuels* (1918), three short pieces whose Stravinskian rhythmic drive is modified by an insinuating charm. Charm is a quality that dominates much of Poulenc's piano music, especially that written during the 1930s. Both *Les soirées de Nazelles* and *Improvisations* are sets of poetic mood pieces that evoke a milieu of easy-going friendships and relaxed evenings in the country. These unassuming, light-hearted vignettes are occasionally, as in the last two *Improvisations*, coloured by feelings of melancholy and regret.

Songs

It's arguable that Poulenc's talent was best expressed in his many songs, or *mélodies*, where he could reveal every aspect of his quixotic temperament. He tended to favour French poets of the avant-garde, in particular the work of his friend Paul Éluard and Guillaume Apollinaire. The latter had a genius for conveying complex ideas in simple language, and whose poetry, with its mixture of melancholy and buffoonery, found a reflection in Poulenc's own, troubled spirit. *Le Bestiare*, written just after World War I, was Poulenc's first Apollinaire setting, touchingly spare animal poems which elicit an unfussy and direct response from him. With *Banalités*, written some twenty years later, there's a more fluid approach, with each of the five songs brilliantly balanced between cabaret-style populism and a Schubertian subtlety. In his development as a songwriter Poulenc was aided by his closeness to several outstanding singers, most notably soprano Denise Duval and baritone Pierre Bernac, with whom he regularly performed recitals.

Nuit d'étoiles: Gens, Vignoles (Virgin; with songs by Fauré and Debussy)

This disc (already recommended in the Fauré and Debussy entries) makes an exquisite introduction to twentieth-century French *mélodies*. Véronique Gens has a pure voice but one with a real warmth and bloom to it. Only eight Poulenc songs are featured but they include all five *Banalités*, delivered with great wit and style, and "Les chemins de l'amour" which is sung with just the right degree of *tendresse*.

Michael Praetorius (1571–1621)

Though largely self-taught and something of a late starter, Michael Praetorius was the first great composer for the Lutheran Church. He wrote a wide range of sacred music, much of it based on the chorales – hymns – that Martin Luther had established at the heart of the liturgy (see p.413). However, Praetorius was also interested in secular music, and, with the exception of his delightfully simple settings of the carols "Es ist ein Ros entsprungen" (A Rose has Come to Blossom) and "Joseph, lieber Joseph mein" (Joseph, My Dearest), he is best known today for *Terpsichore*, a collection of over three hundred dances that he arranged and published in 1612. He was an influential musical pedagogue, too, and in 1614–15 published *Syntagma Musicum*, a three-volume encyclopedia that provided practical musical instruction as well as descriptions and illustrations of instruments.

The son of a pastor who had been a pupil of Martin Luther, Praetorius was born at Creuzburg an der Werra near Eisenach but spent his childhood at nearby Torgau. The family name was actually Schulteiss, but Praetorius later Latinized it (Schulteiss means a village mayor while a praetor was a Roman legal official), perhaps as a reflection of his own sense of achievement. Although he had some musical training at Torgau he was mostly educated at Frankfurt an der Oder and Zerbst. In 1587, at the age of sixteen, he became organist of the church of St Marien, Frankfurt, remaining in the post for three years. Five years after this, he was in Wolfenbüttel as the organist of Duke Heinrich Julius of Brunswick. Praetorius flourished at the ducal court, and in 1604 was appointed *Kapellmeister*, with control over about fifteen musicians. He was further rewarded, a year later, for displaying conspicuous bravery during an ambush on the duke and his retinue at Brunswick.

Praetorius travelled fairly widely, not just in the service of the duke but in his own capacity as an organist and a designer of organs. Following the death of Duke Heinrich Julius in 1613 he was granted permission to work at the more lavish and prestigious court of the Elector of Saxony at Dresden, where he stayed for three years. It was at Dresden that he met his younger colleague Heinrich Schütz (see p.508) and became familiar with the very latest styles of Italian music. During the same period he was *Kapellmeister* to the administrator of the Magdeburg bishopric, and also worked at Halle, Sondershausen and Kassel. This heavy workload seems to have contributed to his failing health, and in 1620 his position at Wolfenbüttel was terminated. He died the following year having accumulated a sizeable fortune, most of which he left for the purpose of establishing a foundation for the poor.

Sacred Music

Although he was only active as a composer for about twenty years, Praetorius published over

Praetorius as he appears in *Syntagma Musicum*.

twenty collections of church music, much of which comprised settings of Lutheran chorales or hymns (the nine-volume *Musae Sioniae* contains over a thousand such settings). In Praetorius's time, chorales were usually sung *alternatim*, meaning that sections of them (verses or even lines) were sung alternately between the congregation and the choir (or several choirs) who might be placed in a gallery – depending on the scale and facilities of the church. This practice of spatially divided singing, with or without instrumental accompaniment, was known as polychoralism. It was developed in Venice by Giovanni Gabrieli (see p.196) and was soon adapted to the Lutheran liturgy, as was the Italian practice of dividing the work into solo and tutti sections (the concertante style) and including rich instrumental parts. As well as chorales, Praetorius wrote motets, psalms and settings of the Lutheran mass, many incorporating a chorale melody in some way or other. Unlike Schütz, who was writing exclusively for professional court musicians, Praetorius aimed at universality and his work ranges from simple two-part hymns to complex multi-part settings with connecting instrumental sections. One of his last collections, the *Polyhymnia caduceatrix* (1619), illustrates the range and sophistication of his later church music.

Luther and Music

"...next to the Word of God, the noble art of music is the greatest treasure in the world."
Martin Luther

In 1517 Martin Luther, a German priest and theologian, nailed his *Ninety-Five Theses* to the door of a church in Wittenberg. In this document he set out the case against the Catholic Church's selling of indulgences, whereby members of the clergy would accept money in exchange for the promise that a sinner would spend fewer days in purgatory. Luther's intention was to reform the Church rather than conflict with it, but when in 1521 he refused to retract any of his objections he split the Church and effectively launched the Protestant Reformation.

Luther was highly musical (he sang and played the flute) and a great admirer of the polyphonic masters of the period – especially Josquin Desprez – and when he began reforming the liturgy, music maintained its central role. Indeed, when he composed his *Deutsche Messe* (German Mass) in 1526 he did so with the help of two leading musicians, Conrad Rupsch and Johann Walther. The German Mass was an attempt to establish a simple model for liturgical practice. As such, Luther retained much of the Roman rite but included German paraphrases of some of the Latin, as well as a greater number of hymns at fixed points in the service. The melodies written for the German Mass were relatively simple, avoided melismas (elaborate decorative variants to a chant) and were largely syllabic. Though these melodies had an obvious kinship with Gregorian chant, their accents and cadences made them closer to the patterns of speech and therefore easier to understand.

At the heart of these changes was the idea of greater congregational engagement and involvement in the liturgy. To that end Luther advocated the singing of hymns, called chorales, at all church services. His first hymnal, the *Achtliederbuch* (1524), contained eight of these, four of which were written by Luther himself. There was soon a great demand for chorales, which meant not only writing new words and melodies but just as frequently adapting already existing ones: folk songs and popular songs were used and existing Latin hymns were given German texts. Early examples still in use today include *In dulci jubilo* (Good Christian Men, Rejoice) and *Ein' feste Burg* (A Mighty Fortress), the former adapted from a lullaby, the latter written (and probably composed) by Luther.

In its purest form, a chorale consisted of a melody and a text that could be sung by the congregation in unison. Obviously, however, these melodies could be harmonized, either in a simple homophonic form (as with modern hymn singing) or in more complex contrapuntal ways. So, like plainsong, chorales existed in their own right but also functioned as the raw material from which other music could be fashioned. Thus Philipp Nicolai's famous chorale *Wachet auf* forms the basis of both a motet by Praetorius, in which phrases of the chorale are treated in imitative counterpoint, and of a cantata by J.S. Bach, where sections of the chorale are interspersed with recitatives and arias. Chorales also punctuate the unfolding drama of Bach's two great Passion settings, the *St John* and the *St Matthew*. Incidentally, the melody of the principal chorale in the *St Matthew*, sung to the words "O Haupt voll Blut und Wunden" (O Sacred Head, Sore Wounded), was originally from a love song by Hans Leo Hassler, "Mein Gmüth is mir verwirret" (My Mind is all Confused), written about 100 years earlier.

Chorale melodies were also used as the starting point for organ works, most obviously in chorale preludes. Initially, these were short, usually improvised, pieces intended to provide an introduction to the singing of a chorale, though later examples, particularly those by Bach, are major performance pieces probably never intended for liturgical use.

Just how elaborate the music was in a Lutheran service depended on how musically well-endowed a particular church might be. In Bach's Leipzig churches, the main Sunday service could last as long as five hours, with a motet, the mass, several chorales and a cantata. But, whatever the case, a large degree of congregational participation in the form of chorale singing was always at the heart of the action.

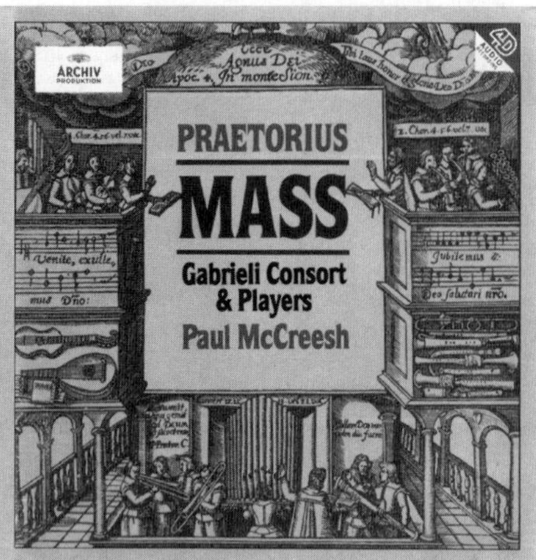

Mass: Gabrieli Consort & Players; Roskilde Cathedral Choirs; McCreesh (Archiv)

This re-creation of a performance of a Lutheran Christmas mass of around 1620 consists, in the main, of music by Praetorius (including three of the motets and the Kyrie and Gloria contained on the disc above). Recorded in the vast resonant space of Roskilde Cathedral, there is undoubtedly a powerful sense of occasion but bear in mind that everything is sung – including the epistle and gospel.

Christmas Motets; Chorale Concertos: Hassler Consort; Raml (Dabringhaus und Grimm)

Given the vast amount of Praetorius's extant liturgical music it's a little odd that the same works are repeatedly recorded, namely motets and hymns for the Christmas celebrations. This is one of the best of such recordings, combining wonderfully fresh and buoyant singing with some outstanding instrumental playing. This is a fine disc that really communicates the outstanding quality of Praetorius's music.

Terpsichore

According to his *Syntagma Musicum*, Praetorius planned to publish eight volumes of secular music, but in the end only one was completed. *Terpsichore*, named after the muse of dancing and song, is a collection of 312 mostly French (plus some English) dances written for the purpose of courtly entertainment. Praetorius dedicated the work to Duke Heinrich Julius, and was at pains to point out that the pieces were brought from France "by your Highness's dancing master Antoine Emeraud". Some of these were arranged by another Frenchman, Pierre Francisque Caroubel, who spent time at the Wolfenbüttel court in 1610, others by Praetorius himself. Designed to be played by a wide range of different instruments, *Terpsichore* is a compendium of the various French dance forms that were popular at the time. These include the courante, a rapid dance usually in 3/2 or 6/4; the volte, a physically intimate dance in triple time; the bransle, a circle dance of peasant origin; and the galliard, a showpiece dance also in triple time.

New London Consort; Pickett (L'Oiseau Lyre)

Philip Pickett's approach to *Terpsichore* is to distribute the dances between a wide variety of instrumental combinations – shawms, crumhorns, rackets, etc – to produce some truly extraordinary (and often bizarre) sounds. The result, appropriately enough, is utterly exhilarating and makes you realize that the Renaissance dance floor must have been a pretty lively place.

The Parley of Instruments Renaissance Violin Band; Holman (Hyperion)

Musician and scholar Peter Holman argues that these dances were intended for a French-style string orchestra accompanied by theorbos and lutes. So in place of Pickett's richly colourful sound-world, we get something rather more sedate and well-behaved. It's a perfectly valid alternative that makes you listen to the pieces (several of which overlap between discs) in a completely different way.

Sergey Prokofiev (1891–1953)

Though he was regarded as impossibly avant-garde in his youth, Sergey Prokofiev belongs squarely to the same great tradition of Russian music as Tchaikovsky and Mussorgsky, a tradition resonant with a sense of the country's history. His best-known scores are written in an immediately recognizable style which reconciles progressive technique with melodic directness, and rank among the most enjoyable of all twentieth-century compositions. His prolific output covers almost every musical genre – an achievement all the more remarkable in view of the fact that his creative impetus continued unabated despite the dogmatic repression of Stalinism, and in the midst of Russia's suffering in World War II.

Born in Sontsovka in the Ukraine at a country estate managed by his agronomist father, he soon displayed prodigious talent as a composer and as a pianist. His relative youth compared to other composition students at the St Petersburg Conservatory went hand in glove with a self-confidence which did not endear him to many of his elders, notably the conservative Alexander Glazunov (see p.212), who was a professor at the Conservatory. Feeling stifled by his homeland, Prokofiev went abroad after graduating in 1914, and soon made contact with Diaghilev and Stravinsky. The latter's music made a deep impact on the young man, and the relationship with the impresario of the Ballets Russes was equally productive. Following Stravinsky's successes with *The Firebird, Petrushka* and *The Rite of Spring*, Diaghilev commissioned Prokofiev to write a ballet, *Ala and Lolly*, much of which was reworked into the *Scythian Suite,* a piece that created a scandal at its Russian premiere in 1916. Work on another ballet for Diaghilev, *Chout*, and a full-length opera based on Dostoyevsky's *The Gambler* for the Mariinsky Theatre, were delayed by World War I and the 1917 Revolution; *Chout* was staged in 1921 and *The Gambler* had to wait for a thorough revision and a 1929 premiere in Brussels.

In 1918 Prokofiev set out for America by way of Japan on the last Trans-Siberian Express to leave Russia that year. He had only intended to stay for a few months, but world events dictated otherwise. Struggling to make his name as a pianist and composer in America and then Europe, he gradually established a reputation with such relatively simple works as *The Love for Three Oranges* and the *Piano Concerto No. 3*. A successful tour of the new Soviet Union in 1927, fascinatingly chronicled in a detailed diary, properly re-established links with the motherland, and he returned more frequently, finally settling in Moscow for good with his wife Lina, a singer, and his two sons in 1936.

His musical language had become increasingly complex during the 1920s in Paris, but now he felt a need to write more directly and simply, an urge that happened to coincide with Soviet cultural policy. Unfortunately Prokofiev landed in Moscow at the very time when Stalin was showing the strength of his arm in the arts. The ensuing years were hard. Despite attempts to write broad, accessible music for the people in his own distinctive style, his relationship with the authorities rapidly disintegrated. So, too, did his marriage; in 1939 he met an intelligent young

The young Prokofiev at the keyboard, 1910.

woman, Mira Mendelson, and subsequently left his family to live with her. The consequences were terrible for Lina: arrested on trumped-up charges of spying as a resident alien, she spent many years in a Siberian labour camp.

For all that he suffered, Prokofiev wrote some superb music during the war years, including the opera *War and Peace*, the three so-called "war" sonatas for piano (numbers 6 to 8), the film score to *Ivan the Terrible* and the ballet *Cinderella*. Through works such as these he attained a dominant position within the Russian musical world, and for the first few years after the war it seemed that he was above persecution. In 1948, however, it became clear that Prokofiev's position was not as secure as he had imagined. The Central Committee of the Communist Party held a meeting at which Prokofiev, Shostakovich and many others were accused of "formalism", a catch-all term applied to any music that had no immediately utilitarian function. The errant composers were charged with "anti-democratic tendencies that are alien to the Soviet people and its artistic tastes" and condemned for writing music "strongly reminiscent of the spirit of contemporary modernistic bourgeois music of Europe and America". Unequivocal apologies were wrung out of all the "defendants".

After this idiotic and brutal farce, all sense of purpose was knocked from Russia's composers and Prokofiev, whose health was already fragile, lost much of his creative confidence. Even so, such astonishing gestures as the *Symphony-Concerto* for cello and orchestra (reworked for the young Mstislav Rostropovich from his *Cello Concerto No. 1* of the mid-1930s) and the delicate, misunderstood *Symphony No. 7* – a very different work from its epic predecessors – confirm his fragile genius. Unlike his younger colleague Shostakovich, Prokofiev was not to see beyond the darkest years of the Soviet Union's history; he died on 5 March, 1953 – a few hours before Stalin.

OPERAS

Prokofiev's lifelong relationship with the theatre was rarely straightforward. Following several childhood works, he started a one-act opera called *Maddalena*, which was left only one-quarter orchestrated, and his first full-length work, based upon Dostoyevsky's *The Gambler*, was beset by so many problems that it wasn't performed until 1929. *The Love for Three Oranges*, his first successful opera, was completed in 1921 while he was living in America. Awaiting its staging, he began another – *The Fiery Angel*, based on one of the few Russian novels he could find in America. The most frustrating project of his earlier years, the opera took eight years to complete, only for its first production to be cancelled. The Soviet-era operas range from the compromised *Semyon Kotko* and the Sheridan comedy *Betrothal in a Monastery* to his most ambitious work, *War and Peace*, which reached the stage only in incomplete form before his death.

The Love for Three Oranges

Reworking the *commedia dell'arte* traditions of Gozzi's eighteenth-century play *Fiaba dell'amore delle tre melarancie*, *Three Oranges* is whimsical, melancholy and very strange, as you can tell from a glance at the cast list, which features ten "ridiculous people", a chorus of "little devils", a "Gigantic Cook" and a smattering of princesses. Prokofiev was deeply impressed by director Meyerhold's theories on drama, which included "the diminution of the role of the actor and a challenge to conventional audience relationships", and in Gozzi's lunatic plot he found the perfect vehicle for such a challenge. Displaying Prokofiev's talent for musical grotesquerie, *Three Oranges* places mock neo-classicism against barbarically rhythmic modernism, and interweaves bizarre choruses with tortuous solo parts. The orchestration is sparse yet colourful, but the only real tunes materialize in the well-known March and Scherzo.

Kit, Akimov, Pluzhnikov, Diadkova, Shevchenko, Morozov, Netrebko; Kirov Opera Chorus and Orchestra; Gergiev (Philips; 2 CDs)

The first recording of *Oranges* on CD to use the original Russian text so sensitively set by Prokofiev, Gergiev's interpretation has more variety than the previous contender, Nagano's sparkling performance on Virgin (which was sung in French). The Kirov ensemble is excellent, running the gamut from Larissa Shevchenko's dramatic-soprano witch to Konstantin Pluzhnikov's character-tenor Truffaldino.

SYMPHONIES

Prokofiev's seven symphonies span the years 1916 to 1952, beginning with the spiced-up Classicism of the first before moving on to the extreme dissonance of the second and the theatre music which provided the basis for its two successors. Fourteen years separate the first version of the *Symphony No. 4*, reworked from the ballet *The Prodigal Son*, from the fifth – a very different proposal, as Prokofiev worked to reflect the demands of the true Soviet symphony. Not as simplistically optimistic as some have suggested, the *Symphony No. 5* has more to please a wider audience than the bleak and despairing sixth. The last of the cycle is the most misunderstood of all. Far from a simple "children's symphony", it reveals the composer relating the sadness of his later years in a language that harks back to Tchaikovsky and Rimsky-Korsakov.

Symphonies Nos. 1–7: London Symphony Orchestra; Gergiev (Philips; 4 CDs)

Recorded live at London's Barbican Hall in 2004, these performances have that compelling combination of refinement and raw energy for which Valery Gergiev has become famous. This is now the most exciting set of all the symphonies, although for those who prefer a studio recording, the Neeme Järvi set with the Scottish National Orchestra on Chandos is excellent if less gutsy than the Gergiev cycle.

Symphony No. 1 – Classical

Prokofiev's most accessible orchestral work is the twenty-minute *Symphony No. 1*, a tuneful homage to Haydn and Mozart that is sometimes linked to the neo-classicism of Stravinsky – although Prokofiev got there first. Prokofiev imagined that "if Haydn were writing today ... he would keep to his way of writing, whilst at the same time incorporating newer ideas. I wanted to compose just such a symphony. I gave it the name *Symphonie classique* – firstly because it was so simple; also in the hope of annoying the philistines." The symphony was begun in 1916, completed in the idyllic Russian countryside far from the centres of struggle in 1917 and successfully premiered the following year shortly before Prokofiev left Russia. Seldom has twentieth-century music sounded so transparent or so free from care: and it was welcomed keenly into the mainstream Western repertoire, thanks above all to the advocacy of Prokofiev's friend, the conductor Serge Koussevitsky.

Chamber Orchestra of Europe; Abbado (Deutsche Grammophon; with *Peter and the Wolf* & *Overture on Hebrew Themes*)

Claudio Abbado is one of the finest modern interpreters of Prokofiev's music, and his account of the first symphony is an exemplary combination of easy elegance and rhythmic elasticity. He really lets the music breathe and the result is both refined and refreshing.

Boston Symphony Orchestra; Koussevitsky (RCA; with *Symphony No. 5* & *Romeo and Juliet Suite No. 2*)

Koussevitsky commands this music as if it had been written for him. The second movement is made a true Larghetto – most modern performances sound lugubrious in comparison. In the fifth, he clarifies Prokofiev's orchestral writing and makes the development really flow. The mono recording, taken from 78s, sounds surprisingly good.

Symphony No. 3

Prokofiev began work on his *Symphony No. 3* in 1928, when production of his thorny and audacious opera *The Fiery Angel* ran into difficulties (it was never staged in his lifetime). The opera was based on a novel of demonic possession in medieval Germany, so it's scarcely surprising that this symphony is one of his most intense: the heaviest thrash in the opera became the climax of the first movement; the eerie anticipation of demonic intrusions became the basis of the second movement; the raising of spirits was transformed into the truly avant-garde Scherzo; and the shattering conclusion of *The Fiery Angel*'s second act became the finale. "Grandiose masses gape and topple", wrote the pianist Sviatoslav Richter of his first impressions, describing it as "the end of the universe". In a truly committed performance, the symphony is every inch as hair-raising as its parent opera.

Scottish National Orchestra; Järvi (Chandos; with *Symphony No. 4*)

The dramatic charge of the symphony is unflagging in the hands of Järvi. The reverberant sound occasionally muddies the waters of this thickly scored work, but the performance is full of atmosphere and terror. The disc also includes the first version of the fourth symphony, derived from the ballet *The Prodigal Son*.

Symphony No. 5

After the *Symphony No. 1*, the loftily heroic *Symphony No. 5* is the most popular of the seven. Starting work on it as the imminent ending of the war was becoming self-evident, Prokofiev claimed that he conceived it as "a symphony of the greatness of the human spirit, a song of praise of free and happy mankind". This, of course, is Soviet-speak, and the music is much more ambiguous. A broad, Soviet-style epic of a first movement, arming itself for grim combat, is followed by a darkly satirical Scherzo; after a lamenting slow movement, based on a theme from Prokofiev's incidental music to a discarded film of *The Queen of Spades*, the finale destroys all illusions of celebration. Nevertheless, its premiere in Moscow on 13 January, 1945, as artillery salvos marked the German retreat, added to the legend of unquenchable heroism. And it was immediately acclaimed at home and abroad.

Berlin Symphony Orchestra; Karajan
(Deutsche Grammophon; with Stravinsky *Rite of Spring*)

This outstanding account has recently been remastered and emerges even more majestically than before. Karajan's approach is commendably straightforward; he allows the music to speak for itself, bringing out its essential steely power with an assured control and authority.

Vienna Symphony Orchestra; Szell
(Orfeo; with Haydn *Symphony No. 93*)

George Szell's conducting was at its most athletic in Slavic music where rhythmic considerations predominate. His thrilling, uninhibited account of Prokofiev's greatest symphony is one of the finest available – a live recording in every sense of the word.

Symphony No. 6

Written in 1947, the *Symphony No. 6* is a response to the war years as well as a chronicle of Prokofiev's own failing health. It's a remarkably daring work, in which Prokofiev writes deeply heartfelt music which seems to function, like the contemporary symphonic writing of Shostakovich, on several levels of meaning. The central Largo has a particularly grief-stricken opening which then opens out into something more lyrical. After this the finale, with its boisterous toe-tapping energy, comes as a startling surprise. But the mood is not sustained and the warning signs accumulate until the liveliness implodes. The ending is one of the most shattering in the repertoire. The symphony was one of several targeted in the 1948 denunciations of "formalism in music".

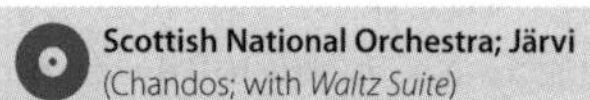

Scottish National Orchestra; Järvi
(Chandos; with *Waltz Suite*)

This was the first release in Järvi's Prokofiev symphonies series and played a large part in the rehabilitation of a neglected masterpiece. Järvi brings to the symphony an intensity and a commitment which is electrifying. The work's somewhat baggy structure is given a greater sense of shape than usual and the sound quality is exceptional.

OTHER ORCHESTRAL MUSIC

The greater part of Prokofiev's orchestral music is made up of suites from his operas, ballets and film scores, a series of works that crystallize his genius for the right theatrical gesture. The selections range from a dozen movements taken from his first Diaghilev ballet to be staged, *Chout* (The Buffoon), to the concise quarter-of-an-hour's worth of music from *The Love for Three Oranges* (although the composer was less proud of this assortment than many of his others). Prokofiev's readjustment for the concert hall was not always a simple matter of cut-and-paste: the suites for *Romeo and Juliet* and *Cinderella* involve a certain amount of re-orchestration and some new links.

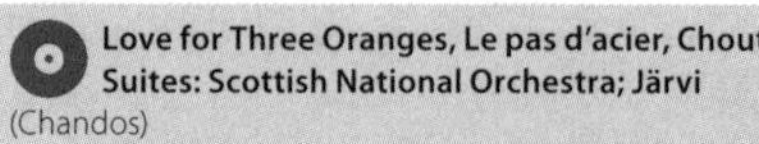

Love for Three Oranges, Le pas d'acier, Chout Suites: Scottish National Orchestra; Järvi
(Chandos)

Much of the knockabout action of *The Love for Three Oranges* is condensed into the Suite; *Chout* is a Russian folk tale, about wife-beating and mock-wizardry, with some wonderfully tuneful dance themes, while *Le pas d'acier*, Prokofiev's 1927 ballet about Soviet progress, is drier, but undoubtedly skilful. Järvi is the best possible advocate for these scores and the sound is brilliant.

Lieutenant Kijé

Prokofiev's first commission to write film music came from the director Alexander Feinzimmer in the spring of 1933. A satirical tale of a soldier who never was, *Lieutenant Kijé* was the perfect vehicle for Prokofiev's quirky sense of humour, and he spent a blissful Parisian summer working on what was to become his frothiest and most popular score. The symphonic suite begins with Kijé's "birth", announced by a cornet solo followed by the lightest of military marches. The "Romance", a beautifully orchestrated pastiche of a nineteenth-century sentimental song, precedes the two best-known movements: the "Wedding" and famous "Troika" with its jingling sleigh-bells. The tale ends mock-mournfully, with the burial of the nonexistent soldier and a distant reprise of the original cornet solo.

Chicago Symphony Orchestra; Abbado
(Deutsche Grammophon; with *Alexander Nevsky* & *The Scythian Suite*)

Abbado resists any temptation to make *Kijé* an exercise in gallumping jollity. The melodic lines are accented to the point of jauntiness, but their snap is used to emphasize the pathos as well as the exuberance of Prokofiev's dazzling invention. Not a bar here is cloying or inert, and the effect is magical.

Romeo and Juliet

The ballet music for *Romeo and Juliet* (1936) is one of Prokofiev's greatest achievements. The emotional scope and scale of this piece has no rival in ballet music and no other composer has so perfectly interpreted this play – indeed, only Verdi's late Shakespearean operas, *Falstaff* and *Otello*, can compare with it as a translation of Shakespeare into music. Prokofiev was long troubled by the ending of the ballet for, as he said, "living people can dance, the dying cannot". As did Rossini with his *Otello*, Prokofiev rewrote the ending so that Romeo arrives just in time to prevent disaster, thus ending the ballet happily. However, he had his mind changed for him by the choreographers, who assisted the composer in following the play almost to the letter – Juliet gets rather longer to expire than Shakespeare allowed her.

Romeo and Juliet – Three Suites: Scottish National Orchestra; Järvi (Chandos)

Romeo and Juliet is a long ballet which works marvellously well in the theatre. As a recording it is best heard as one or all of the three suites into which Prokofiev divided the work's main numbers. Järvi's is a wonderful account, principally because he adopts some undanceably slow tempi – these would incite onstage revolt, but on CD his approach is inventive, original and entirely successful.

Peter and the Wolf

January 1936 brought the beginning of an official crackdown on avant-garde composers in the Soviet Union, prompted by Stalin's horrified reaction to Shostakovich's *Lady Macbeth of Mtsensk* (see p.515). Prokofiev was smarting with disappointment over the belittlement he had received for *Romeo and Juliet*, and already had felt the effects of censorship with *The Gambler* and *Le pas d'acier*. Perhaps in despair, seeming to lose his way, he turned to writing little pieces for children. But *Peter and the Wolf* is one of the few masterpieces of music written specifically with children in mind. A simple story, written by Prokofiev himself, it tells of the capture by a boy of a dangerous wolf. All the principal characters – which also include a duck, a cat and Peter's various querulous relatives – are represented by a theme and a different instrument of the orchestra. The result is immensely charming; for this is a suite which has proved magical for a young audience, and wittily mock-innocent for everyone else.

Sting; Chamber Orchestra of Europe; Abbado (Deutsche Grammophon; with *"Classical" Symphony, Overture on Hebrew Themes & March in B Flat*)

Sting has rewritten the narration a little, but his changes are just right. His laconically stylish and no-nonsense manner is ideal for children, while Abbado's sly and bouncy accompaniment is perfect for anyone. Recording quality is exceptional, and there's an outstanding performance of the *"Classical" Symphony* as well.

Alexander Nevsky

In the course of a 1938 trip to the USA, Prokofiev was able to visit Hollywood and study the techniques of composing for film. The first fruit of these labours was a commission from the Soviet director Sergei Eisenstein, for a score which depicted the struggle on the River Neva between Alexander Nevsky's Russian army and Swedish invaders. It was a collaboration made in heaven: two virtuosos came together from separate spheres and from the start were able to comprehend each other's art. The climax of Eisenstein's film is the famous battle on the ice for which Prokofiev wrote music from Eisenstein's storyboard, and the sequence was then filmed to fit in with the idea of the music. The result is the most thrilling synthesis of sound and vision, in which a gradual momentum builds to a brilliant climax as the ice breaks and the Teutonic knights are drowned. For the concert hall Prokofiev rearranged his soundtrack as a dramatic cantata ("Arise you people free and brave, defend our fair native land!"), culminating with Nevsky's triumphant entry into the city of Psov.

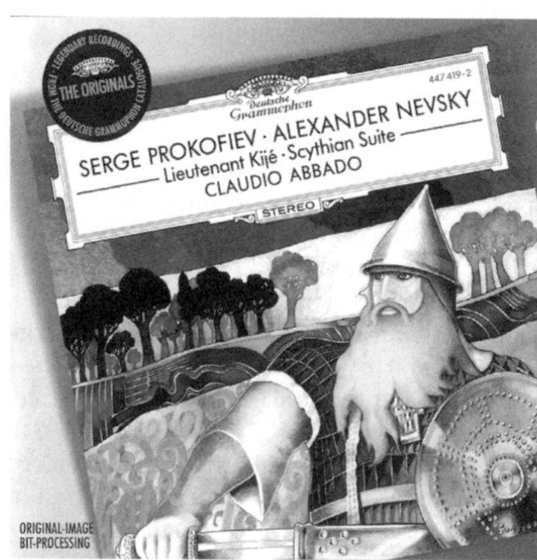

Chicago Symphony Orchestra; Abbado (Deutsche Grammophon; with *Lieutenant Kijé & The Scythian Suite*)

Claudio Abbado's account is thrilling, with a compelling atmosphere of desperate, stabbing intensity. A mood of despair pervades his interpretation – due, in part, to Abbado frequently hanging back almost to the point of stasis, so that explosive climaxes can be unleashed with real ferocity.

CONCERTOS

Not surprisingly, the piano was Prokofiev's first candidate for concerto treatment, and he produced the perfect vehicle for his own very distinctive vein of audacious virtuosity. More poetry surfaces in the violin concertos, and the move from the straightforward lyricism and grotesquerie of the first to the darker tones of the second marks a change of direction. As he moved away from performing himself, a new generation of artists began to inspire him, and while Sviatoslav Richter benefited from the more intimate form of the piano sonata, young cellist Mstislav Rostropovich forced Prokofiev to look again at the rather dry and angular *Cello Concerto* he had composed in 1938. It became the *Symphony Concerto*, a final flourishing of genius in the last, troubled Stalin years.

Piano Concertos

It's baffling that Prokofiev's piano concertos are so infrequently performed, as they are among the most inventive ever written. The first was written in 1912; two years later Prokofiev used it to get back at his piano teachers when he graduated not with the standard performance of an established classic, but with a piece of his own. He won first prize and widespread resentment. The second is notable for the terrifying difficulty of the piano part and, especially, for the maniacal demands of the opening movement's cadenza. The third, the most popular, was composed as a virtuoso vehicle for himself and, though its stylistic diversity lends a sense of detachment to the music, much of it is demonically exciting.

The fourth, composed ten years later, was commissioned by Ludwig Wittgenstein's brother Paul, a brilliant pianist who lost his right arm in World War I (he also commissioned a one-handed concerto from Ravel). It dominated Prokofiev's attention over the summer of 1931, and emerged modest in scale but awesomely demanding; Wittgenstein didn't understand it and never played it, but held onto the score until 1956, when it finally had its premiere. Prokofiev's last concerto began as a slight, almost backward-looking composition, but the performer in him took over and the concerto evolved as yet another barnstorming test of digital prowess. Its five movements are more like a suite than a concerto, and its consequent lack of cohesion has contributed to its lack of popularity.

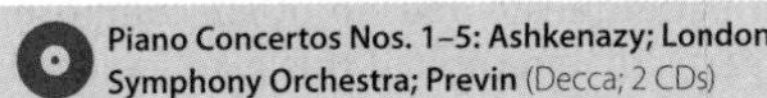

Piano Concertos Nos. 1–5: Ashkenazy; London Symphony Orchestra; Previn (Decca; 2 CDs)

These performances from the 1970s were a landmark in Ashkenazy's recording career: lyrical, audacious, and as cheeky as Prokofiev's idiom demands. Ashkenazy was clearly unafraid of these works' technical difficulties, while relishing their more astringent and angular moments.

Piano Concerto No. 3: Argerich; Berlin Philharmonic Orchestra; Abbado (Deutsche Grammophon; with Ravel *Piano Concerto & Gaspard de la Nuit*)

Argerich is rightly famous for her playing of the third concerto. Its explosive energy and sharply contrasted character suit her mercurial temperament perfectly and, though the studio removes some of the fire from her playing, this recording is required listening.

Violin Concertos

Together with those by Bartók and Shostakovich, Prokofiev's two violin concertos are the finest written last century. The first was composed in 1917, shortly before he left Russia for his long sojourn in Europe, and was premiered by the leader of a Paris orchestra, Marcel Darrieux, after a string of much grander names had declined to learn the very difficult score. Though it ends in a dreamy, lyrical mood, this concerto is far more prickly than the later one, being pivoted on a fierce and angular central Scherzo. It was Prokofiev's intention that the second concerto be "altogether different", and so it is. Composed after his return to Russia in 1935, it has a quality of emotional transparency similar to *Romeo and Juliet*, on which he was working at the same time. The soloist dominates far more than in its predecessor, and the only real harmonic irregularities occur in the first movement. The second movement is one of Prokofiev's most inspired creations, a huge and plaintive melody coloured by rapturous modulations and a jaunty accompaniment. A sprightly dance-like finale rounds off the concerto.

Oistrakh; London Symphony Orchestra; von Matacic; Philharmonia Orchestra; Galliera (EMI; with *Violin Sonata No. 2*)

David Oistrakh was the supreme Russian interpreter of these two concertos during the Soviet era and his recordings form a good starting point for getting to know these works. Unlike some violinists, he stresses the lyrical rather than angular aspects of both works, giving his rich and warm tone free rein throughout.

Shaham; London Symphony Orchestra; Previn (Deutsche Grammophon)

For an outstanding modern recording of both concertos on a single disc Gil Shaham takes the prize. With his rich tone and a marvellous sense of line, Shaham is never afraid to bring out the expressivity of these works. The recorded sound is bright and natural, and Previn and the LSO provide exemplary support.

Symphony-Concerto

The title of the *Symphony-Concerto* hints at the scale of this late, great work: it is symphonic especially in the scheme of its huge central movement, but also makes fiendish demands of the soloist. This is very much to do with Mstislav Rostropovich, the young cellist who worked with Prokofiev on the work's evolution from the austere *Cello Concerto* of 1938. Meeting regularly in the summer of 1951, Prokofiev and Rostropovich thrashed out between them a masterpiece which gives the cello far more opportunity than its predecessor to sing – above all in the generous, extended melody at the heart of the middle movement. The finale's variations are also more concise and better shaped than in the original version, and a whirlwind coda brings back earlier terrors to let the cello end in high-pitched ambiguity.

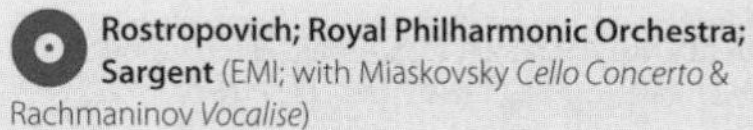

Rostropovich; Royal Philharmonic Orchestra; Sargent (EMI; with Miaskovsky *Cello Concerto* & Rachmaninov *Vocalise*)

As with Du Pré and the Elgar concerto, so Rostropovich's various recordings of this work act as a yardstick by which all others are measured. In this studio recording of the mid-1960s he completely inhabits the work: his technical adroitness is always assured, but it's the way he sustains the long flights of solo writing with such gloriously varied tone colouring that takes the breath away.

CHAMBER MUSIC

The piano was Prokofiev's first love and duty, and music for other combinations of solo instruments only came later – the *Quartet No. 1* at the generous behest of Elizabeth Sprague Coolidge, the *Quartet No. 2* as a thanksgiving offering for his hosts as he joined a group of artistic refugees on their flight southeastwards in World War II. Of all these works, the *Violin Sonata No. 1* ranks with its contemporary numbers in the piano-sonata cycle as an exposure of the bleakness at the heart of those terrible years in the Soviet Union.

String Quartets

Prokofiev's two string quartets epitomize his stylistic schizophrenia. *String Quartet No. 1* was commissioned during a visit to America in 1929–30 and received its first performance in 1931 at the Library of Congress in Washington. At that time, Prokofiev had recently immersed himself in the quartets of Beethoven, so it is no surprise that the opening movement is Classical in feel, though this Classicism is tempered by pungent dance-like rhythms that colour a string of memorable tunes. This energetic movement leads to an Andante of deceptive tranquillity but almost immediately the quartet breaks into a forceful Scherzo, which leads into a disturbing section where the players are directed to use the heel of their bows, a technique that puts violent pressure on the strings. The finale is the work's slow movement, which by Classical rules should have preceded the Scherzo; profoundly expressive, and detailed with moments of sweet lyricism, it closes with a mournful recapitulation of the movement's opening theme.

String Quartet No. 2 was completed a decade later, "for the people", and is too much a product of its environment; evidently the work of a composer working under constraint, it contains none of the idiosyncratic wit of the first.

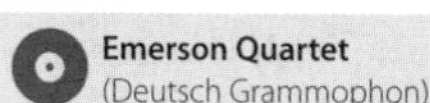

Emerson Quartet (Deutsch Grammophon)

The Emersons are one of the best quartets in the world and have matured in recent years to produce performances of unfailing clarity and freshness. With these two quartets they are heard at their finest, giving performances full of wit and genuine emotion. Currently unavailable but likely to be reissued.

Violin Sonatas

The first violin sonata, begun in 1938 and completed eight years later, is a bleak and sombre work, arguably the most austere and intellectual of Prokofiev's career. Its four movements alternate slow, fast, slow, fast but the sonata ends quietly with a ghostly echo of one of the first movement themes. Prokofiev intended it to shock its first audience, and likened the flickering violin line of the first movement to "wind in a graveyard". Appropriately, the first and third movements were played by David Oistrakh at Prokofiev's own funeral. In contrast to the first, the second (completed in 1944) is a positively sunny composition that conveys no sense of the strain the composer was under. It was written as a flute sonata (and has been recorded as such many times) and was only later transcribed for the violin, at the insistence of David Oistrakh. Although flautists might not agree, it works better in the hands of a good violinist, benefiting from the far wider range of tone colour.

Shaham, Shaham
(Canary Classics; with *Five Melodies* & Heifetz Prokofiev transcriptions)

Gil Shaham, who proved his Prokofiev credentials with an outstanding Concertos disc, here teams up with his sister Orli for equally impressive accounts of both sonatas. The players respond well to each other and invest the *Sonata No. 1* with all the requisite edginess and poignancy.

PIANO MUSIC

Prokofiev's piano style grew naturally out of the characterful pieces – full of rhythmic energy and quirky humour – that he composed as a child. His first piano miniatures, including the hair-raising *Suggestion Diabolique*, remained on his recital programmes for many decades; but the sarcasm and "wrong notes" gave way to a surprising lyricism in the *Visions fugitives* and the *Tales of an Old Grandmother*, composed in 1919, shortly after arriving in America. He wrote surprisingly little for the solo piano during the mid-1920s, but he then renewed his interest in piano music with a vengeance, writing the three so-called "War" sonatas, which stand among the great monuments of twentieth-century piano literature.

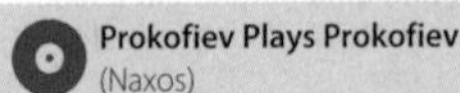

Prokofiev Plays Prokofiev
(Naxos)

Prokofiev was a prodigiously talented pianist and a fine exponent of his own work. In the mid-1930s he recorded several of his compositions – including the third piano concerto, nine of the *Visions fugitives* and the fourth sonata – for HMV in London. They make fascinating listening, not least because his performances are less percussive but more rhythmically flexible than most modern interpreters.

Piano Sonatas

As can be heard on his own recordings (on the Pearl label) Prokofiev possessed an awesome piano technique, and as a young man his muscular approach confused and shocked his contemporaries, who were then revelling in the meanderings of the Scriabin and post-Debussy schools of performance. The tempestuous music of his nine piano sonatas demands a flawless technical command, but many pianists allow them to sink into empty ostentation – this is sharply characterized music that demands a sense of structure and momentum, as well as fingers of flexible steel. Prokofiev's two greatest (and most extreme) works for solo piano are the sixth and the seventh sonatas. Both have an almost violent energy: the sixth contains what Richter called "the shattering pulse of the twentieth century", while the seventh is a titanic construction with a piston-driven last movement that distils the fury and violence of World War II – it's a fierce, draining experience, making terrible demands on the pianist.

Piano Sonatas Nos. 1–9: Nissman
(Pierian; 3 CDs)

The brilliant American pianist Barbara Nissman plays all nine sonatas (plus the incomplete fragment of the tenth) with a wide tonal range and sharply drawn contrasts that single her out as someone fully in command of the music's intricate detail. The energy and sense of occasion make this the best complete sonata cycle.

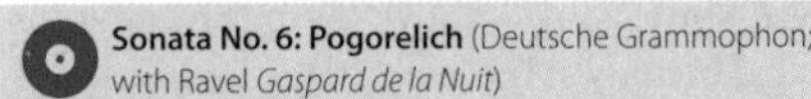

Sonata No. 6: Pogorelich (Deutsche Grammophon; with Ravel *Gaspard de la Nuit*)

This is a fantastically virtuosic performance of one of Prokofiev's greatest sonatas. Pogorelich plays like a man possessed, but the breathtaking variety of his touch means that the less hard-driven passages have an unparalleled degree of subtlety and nuance.

Sonata No. 7: Pollini (Deutsche Grammophon; with pieces by Stravinsky, Boulez and Webern)

Maurizio Pollini's recording of the seventh sonata is a performance that has acquired legendary status since its release in 1977. Pollini commands unrivalled power, concentration and dynamic range, assaulting the listener in a scorching performance that becomes almost diabolical in the last movement.

Visions fugitives

The twenty miniatures of the *Visions fugitives*, snapshots of Prokofiev's idiosyncratic moods, were assembled between 1915 and 1917. Like most miniatures, they are meant to be accessible – a touring virtuoso's calling cards, his intimate confessions, splinters from grander experiments. The title quotes the poem "I Do Not Know Wisdom" by Konstantin Balmont: "In every fugitive vision I see whole worlds. They change endlessly, flashing in playful rainbow colours."

The *Visions fugitives* are Prokofiev's most popular piano work. They are, as David Fanning has put it, "sometimes grotesque, sometimes incantatory and mystical, sometimes simply poetic, sometimes aggressively assertive, sometimes so poised as to allow the performer and the listener leeway to make up their own minds." The composer himself claimed that *No. 19* reflects the excitement of crowds at the time of the February Revolution.

Berman (Chandos; with *Sarcasms*, *Sonata No. 7* & *Tales of an Old Grandmother*)

Boris Berman may lack a little of Richter's audacity and insight (see below), yet he offers an affectionate and complete account which never descends into the routine. A feeling for the composer's playful streak is always apparent, as is an awareness that much of this music draws its inspiration from an older vein of impressionism.

Richter (RCA; 2 CDs; with *Piano Sonata No. 6* and pieces by Haydn, Debussy, Rachmaninov & Ravel)

There are several recordings of Sviatoslav Richter playing selections from the *Visions*, few as electrifying as this live performance at Carnegie Hall in 1960. There's a palpable air of excitement, and Richter rises to the occasion with breathtaking virtuosic flair. A set to be snapped up.

Giacomo Puccini (1858–1924)

It has been said that Wagner's music is better than it sounds. Conversely, Puccini's often sounds better than it is. Puccini had a taste for melodrama, and possessed in abundance the talents necessary to achieve his ends, principally a highly developed sense of theatre and an uncanny facility for memorable melodies. His genius for emotional blackmail soon settled upon the most effective techniques and then stuck to them – from his third opera, *Manon Lescaut*, to his twelfth and last, *Turandot*, his style evolved only slightly. He was frequently accused of decadence, as he still is, but judged by box-office receipts Puccini is the most successful of twentieth-century composers.

Giacomo Puccini in rakish pose.

He was born into a long line of Italian church musicians and, as was expected, first became a church organist. Then in 1880 he entered the Milan Conservatory, where he took lessons with Amilcare Ponchielli, who steered Puccini towards opera. With Ponchielli's encouragement he entered the Sonzogno opera competition in 1883, submitting the one-act *Le Villi*; it was not a success, but it did indirectly lead to a commission, five years later, for a second opera, *Edgar*. Premiered the following year, it too was a failure, but in 1893 Puccini produced his first major work, *Manon Lescaut*; though based on an eighteenth-century novel, this was a verismo opera to rank with those of Mascagni and Leoncavallo.

Remarkably, his next opera didn't get the same acclaim as *Manon* when it was first produced in 1896, but within a year *La Bohème* had become what it remains today – the most popular opera ever written. It established Puccini as Italy's supreme master of the human voice, a reputation further enhanced by the similarly effulgent *Tosca*, premiered in 1900. His career suffered a slight hiccup with the disastrous opening of *Madama Butterfly* at La Scala in 1904; he withdrew the work, rescored it in three acts, and gave it a second premiere three months later, when it was duly acclaimed as a triumph. Puccini turned to the author of *Butterfly*, Belasco, for his next opera, *La fanciulla del West*, but even though Caruso sang at its first performance it never attained the popularity of its predecessors, chiefly because it contains no show-stopping arias.

La Rondine didn't set the world alight, but the composer's ailing fortunes were restored by his penultimate work, *Il Trittico*, which comprised three brief operas – a thriller, *Il Tabarro*, a sentimental religiose drama, *Suor Angelica*, and a comedy, *Gianni Schicchi*. Puccini's last opera, *Turandot*, remained incomplete at his death in 1924; however, Toscanini engaged Franco Alfano to complete the work and the opera received its first performance in front of an ecstatic Milanese audience on 25 April, 1926.

Puccini was prone to glutinous sentimentality, and a sadistically misogynistic streak is evident in the casting of most of his heroines, who are generally helpless and weak creatures at the mercy of callous, domineering men. While he was unquestionably a verismo composer, his plots are often absurd or trivial, and many of his realistic details – such as the bells in *Tosca*, the Americanisms in *Fanciulla* – amount to little more than cheap motivic imitation. For most audiences, however, these objections ultimately don't matter. The important thing is that Puccini's twelve operas contain some of the most beautiful vocal music ever written, carrying into the twentieth century the bel canto tradition of Bellini, Donizetti and Verdi.

La Bohème

La Bohème is the finest lyric opera ever written. Based on Henri Murger's *La vie de Bohème*, and set in Paris around 1830, the drama unfolds amongst a group of impoverished students, one of whom – Rodolfo – is a struggling poet. He meets and falls in love with the seamstress, Mimi, but by the third act they have agreed to separate, largely because Rodolfo can't cope with the fact that Mimi is dying from consumption. At the opera's close, Mimi duly expires in Rodolfo's arms surrounded by their distraught companions.

From the opening ensemble the opera is dominated by an astonishing melodic richness, as the big-hitting arias rise with great dramatic impact from the fast-moving "conversational" dialogue. From the bustling camaraderie of the bohemians in Act 1 emerge two of the most popular operatic songs ever written: Rodolfo's "Che gelida manina" (Your Tiny Hand is Frozen), and Mimi's "Mi, chiamano Mimi" (They Call Me Mimi). These arias, recalled through the repetition of motifs or more subtle echoes, dominate the entire opera, tying it together in a way that distinguishes a Puccini creation from the more rough-and-ready assembly techniques of many of his contemporaries. This subtlety contributes greatly to the work's emotional impact, including the final scene, which has a poignancy unmatched by any other Italian opera of the period.

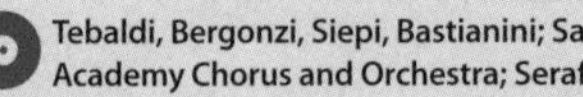

Tebaldi, Bergonzi, Siepi, Bastianini; Santa Cecilia Academy Chorus and Orchestra; Serafin (Decca; 2 CDs)

This 1958 recording, conducted by Tullio Serafin, is arguably the finest of them all. The meltingly lyrical voice of Carlo Bergonzi is perfectly suited to the part of Rodolfo and he is ably matched by the equally fresh-sounding Renata Tebaldi. Both singers are well supported by Serafin's assured sense of pace and style.

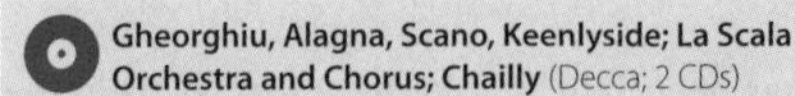

Gheorghiu, Alagna, Scano, Keenlyside; La Scala Orchestra and Chorus; Chailly (Decca; 2 CDs)

Though this recent *Bohème* presents a more detached and objective approach to Puccini than most, the husband and wife partnership of Angela Gheorghiu and Roberto Alagna work well in the roles of Mimi and Rodolfo. The recording quality is excellent and gives a bright reproduction of the orchestra, who play consistently well.

de los Angeles, Björling, Amara, Merrill; RCA Victor Chorus and Symphony Orchestra; Beecham (EMI; 2 CDs)

Another classic recording from the 1950s and perhaps the most celebrated *Bohème* on record, thanks to its two stars. Jussi Björling's Rodolfo stirs a rush of emotion with each succeeding phrase, and there is an innocent abandon to his performance. Victoria de los Angeles is similarly effusive as Mimi, revelling in her stupendous voice.

Tosca

Based on a play that had been a great success for Sarah Bernhardt, *Tosca* was soon labelled "A shabby little shocker". It is indeed a heady mixture of sex and violence. The beautiful singer Tosca loves the painter Mario Cavaradossi, but she suspects him of having an affair with a local noblewoman. Meanwhile, Tosca is being lecherously pursued by the chief of police, Baron Scarpia (one of the most loathsome characters in opera), who is consumed by hatred for the revolutionaries – one of whom, Angelotti, is being protected by Cavaradossi. For this Cavaradossi is arrested by Scarpia and horribly tortured (offstage). After murdering Scarpia with a table knife and seeing her lover executed by firing squad, Tosca hurls herself off the walls of Castel Sant'Angelo, one of Rome's most famous landmarks.

Puccini spent a long time working on *Tosca* and the effort paid off. The harmonies are even richer than *La Bohème*, and Puccini's recurrent themes (or leitmotifs) – a feature of *Bohème* – are refined to the point that anyone can recognize, for example, the Baron's signature tune. The opera has a dozen classic moments, including the two arias for Cavaradossi, the Act 1 duet between him and Tosca, the Scarpia's "Credo", the final duet "O dolci mani" – and, most famous of all, Tosca's Act 2 aria "Vissi d'arte", in which she laments the misery of her fate. This "prolonged orgy of lust and crime", as it was called, is the perfect foil to the slightly saccharine sadness of *La Bohème*.

Nilsson, Corelli, Fischer-Dieskau, Maionica; Santa Cecilia Academy Chorus and Orchestra; Maazel (Decca; 2 CDs)

This 1966 version is the most impressively sung *Tosca*. Birgitt Nilsson is clearly not Italian, but her power, range and colour are such that you overlook her lack of insight. Franco Corelli's lyrical fluency and hammy masculinity make his Cavaradossi outstanding. Supported by Lorin Maazel's urgent, temperamental conducting, the two stars set the performance alight.

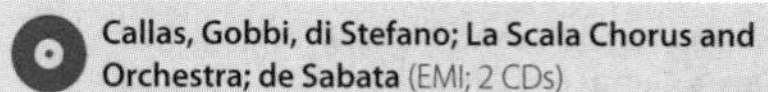

Callas, Gobbi, di Stefano; La Scala Chorus and Orchestra; de Sabata (EMI; 2 CDs)

In the early 1950s Maria Callas was at her thrilling, unself-conscious peak as Tosca. Tito Gobbi's portrayal of the vile Scarpia is similarly convincing, and though di Stefano is miscast he manages a committed portrayal of Cavaradossi, relishing Victor de Sabata's inspired conducting. Though the mono sound has its limitations, this blistering *Tosca* remains a landmark recording.

Madama Butterfly

Butterfly is the archetypal Puccini woman, crushed by the selfishness and cruelty of a man. Based upon a David Belasco play which in turn was based on real events, *Madama Butterfly* is set in Nagasaki during the early part of the twentieth century. A geisha called Cio-Cio-San (Madama Butterfly) marries Pinkerton, an American naval officer, who duly deserts her shortly after the service. Butterfly, bearing their child, faithfully awaits his return. When Pinkerton does come back, it's in the company of Kate, his American wife; Butterfly kills herself with her father's ceremonial sword, leaving the child to the care of Pinkerton and Kate.

In one respect at least, *Madama Butterfly* is even more gruesome than *Tosca*, for the cruelty is accompanied by some of the most seductive music Puccini ever composed – even when Pinkerton is finally revealed as a heartless monster, the music is light, reflecting nothing of his crimes. The growing sophistication of Puccini's technique is demonstrated by the first act's closing twenty-minute duet between Butterfly and Pinkerton, a gorgeous piece of writing in which the Japanese harmonic traits associated with Butterfly are blended with Pinkerton's more robust New World style. Although he dominates the opening act, Pinkerton hardly makes another appearance, leaving the opera almost entirely to Butterfly. When performed by a singing actress capable of impersonating the fifteen-year-old bride of Act 1 as well as the mature woman of Act 3, *Madama Butterfly* becomes one of Puccini's most moving operas.

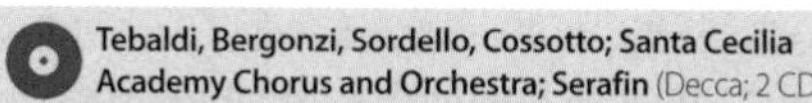

Tebaldi, Bergonzi, Sordello, Cossotto; Santa Cecilia Academy Chorus and Orchestra; Serafin (Decca; 2 CDs)

Both Tebaldi and Bergonzi recorded this opera twice but neither managed to recapture the glorious performances they produced in their first studio recording, in 1958. This is one of the great lyric partnerships of the post-war years, rising to rapturous heights of emotion – the duet is sung magnificently, even if Serafin's tempi do not quite generate the requisite sense of sexual ecstasy.

Price, Tucker, Maero, Elias; RCA Italiana Opera Chorus and Orchestra; Leinsdorf (RCA; 2 CDs)

This energetically conducted *Butterfly*, with Leontyne Price as a vocally luscious Butterfly, reflects Leinsdorf's obsession with detail. Richard Tucker as Pinkerton is a powerful, virile tenor – less seductive than Bergonzi but more exciting. The love duet – a feverish outburst of passion – trumps all others, not in elegance or sweetness, but in sheer theatricality: it's a feverish outburst of passion, leaving you wondering who is seducing whom.

Gheorghiu, Kaufmann, Shkosa, Capitanucci; Santa Cecilia Academy Chorus and Orchestra; Pappano (EMI; 2 CDs)

Fifty years on from Serafin, Antonio Pappano – teamed with the same orchestra and chorus – ratchets up the musical tension in this thrilling recent recording. Angela Gheorghiu delivers an exquisitely sung Butterfly and Jonas Kaufmann's Pinkerton has great vocal presence even though he lacks the true Italianate style. The supporting roles are more than adequate, if not as dramatically convincing as in the versions above.

Turandot

Pavarotti's rendition of "Nessun dorma" was a great choice of signature tune for the 1990 World Cup, but it gave people the wrong idea about the opera from which it's taken, for *Turandot* is a grand but profoundly unpleasant work. Set in Peking during "legendary" times, the story tells of the evil Princess Turandot, who announces that she will marry the first man to answer her three riddles; unsuccessful candidates will be decapitated. Calaf, son of deposed King Timur, loves Turandot and resolves to solve her riddles, but she ridicules him and is unhappy when he answers her questions correctly. Unexpectedly, Calaf tells Turandot that if she can guess his name she may have him killed instead of marrying him. Turandot orders that his name be discovered, and Timur and Liù (a slave girl who loves Calaf) are captured. Liù kills herself rather than give up the name of the man she loves. Finally, Calaf professes his love for Turandot and melts her icy heart.

The score shows Puccini's absorption of contemporary trends (Debussy and Schoenberg are recognizable in the orchestral textures), but *Turandot* is still essentially a work of committed Romanticism. It contains some marvellous vocal writing for Calaf – "Nessun dorma", "Non piangere, Liù" and "Principessa di morte" – plus Turandot's "In questa reggia", one of the most powerful and chilling arias ever composed for a dramatic soprano. The use of exotic harmonies and melodies is more subtle here than in *Butterfly*, and the roster of leitmotifs is considerably larger. On the other hand, it lacks something with regard to dramatic cohesion, and the sadism of the opera can leave a bitter aftertaste.

Sutherland, Pavarotti, Caballé, Ghiaurov; John Alldis Choir; London Philharmonic Orchestra; Mehta
(Decca; 2 CDs)

This 1972 recording was one of Pavarotti's earliest ventures into the heavy repertoire and is among his most successful. Sutherland never sang Turandot on stage and, like Pavarotti, her voice is best in lighter music, but she manages superbly, producing some meatily theatrical tone. Montserrat Caballé's Liù suffers from some lazy pronunciation, but she gives a distinctive, potent reading.

Nilsson, Corelli, Scotto, Mazzini, Ricciardi; Rome Opera Chorus and Orchestra; Molinari-Pradelli
(EMI; 2 CDs)

This recording was made four years after Franco Corelli and Birgit Nilsson headed the Met's first revival of *Turandot* for thirty years, bringing the opera much wider popularity in the US. Corelli's stupendous, wildly emotional Calaf is the finest ever recorded and, with the equally powerful Nilsson, he produces a truly electrifying atmosphere.

Henry Purcell (1659–1695)

Henry Purcell is the greatest composer England has ever produced, and his premature death, at the age of 36, was a terrible blow which curtailed the development of a specifically English musical identity until the emergence of Elgar (see p.181). In the intervening two hundred years, the high points of English musical life were achieved either by foreigners who lived there (like Handel) or by those who were merely passing through (Haydn and Mendelssohn). Not that Purcell was in any way an insular figure: though his youthful training was in the English choral tradition, he assimilated the latest trends of continental music that were so popular with the newly restored King Charles II. Purcell is therefore a pivotal figure, one through whom the art of the Renaissance polyphonists flows into the Baroque era of J.S. Bach, and his importance was fully recognized during his lifetime.

Like J.S. Bach (who was six years old when Purcell died) Purcell came from a family of professional musicians. His father, also named Henry, and his uncle Thomas were both musicians at the court of Charles II, and his brother Daniel was a composer and organist. Unsurprisingly the young Henry had very close connections with the leading English musicians of the day: first as one of the twelve Children of the Chapel Royal, and later as a student with Matthew Locke, whom he succeeded as court composer for the violins in 1677, and with John Blow, whom he succeeded as organist of Westminster Abbey in 1679. Purcell spent all of his life in the environs of Westminster, and his principal places of work – Whitehall Palace, the Chapel Royal at St James's, and Westminster Abbey – were all within walking distance of his home.

From 1680 he travelled further afield, supplementing his official income by writing music for the Dorset Garden Theatre in the City of London. From 1682 he was one of three organists at the Chapel Royal and in 1685 he produced his first major work – the anthem *My Heart is Inditing*, composed for the coronation of James II. Four years later, the Catholic James II was overthrown and Purcell had to provide music for the coronation of the new monarchs, James's daughter Mary and her husband William III – an occasion at which he fell out with the Dean and Chapter over his right to sell tickets to the organ loft. His theatrical activities intensified after the frugal William and Mary cut down on musical activities at court, and it was around this time that Purcell's opera, *Dido and Aeneas*, was staged at a girls' school in Chelsea run by the dancing master Josias Priest.

In 1690 both Purcell and Priest were engaged by Thomas Betterton, the leading actor-manager, to work on his adaptation of Fletcher and Massinger's play *The History of Dioclesian*. Though Purcell had written a substantial amount of incidental music for Betterton, this was his first semi-opera (a play with musical interludes). Staged at the Dorset Garden Theatre, it was an enormous success and led to three more: *King Arthur* in 1691, *The Fairy Queen* in 1692, and *The Indian Queen* in 1694–95, completed on Purcell's death by his brother Daniel. Of these three *The Fairy Queen* was the most ambitious, costing an extraordinary £3000, much of it presumably spent on the machinery needed to effect the spectacular transformation scenes that were required. Despite the fact that "the Court and the Town were wonderfully satisfied with it", the show lost money – the only semi-opera to do so.

Purcell's last years were extremely busy: as well as his work for the theatre, he produced a large amount of extraordinary church music, including the funeral music of Queen Mary – a work performed at his own Westminster Abbey funeral a few months later.

Like his French contemporary Charpentier (see p.135), part of Purcell's achievement was his success in synthesizing certain aspects of the French style – the two-part overture, rhythmically defined dances, and declamatory vocalizing – with the more lyrical and expressive style of the Italians. However, what makes his musical language unique is the way these elements are suffused by a sense of national identity, typified by heavy chromaticism, elaborate counterpoint, extended melody and, above all, an emotional immediacy.

OPERAS

In the history of opera, Henry Purcell is often presented as one of the great might-have-beens: despite having, in the words of a contemporary, "a peculiar Genius to express the Energy of English Words", his career coincided with a period in which opera repeatedly failed to establish itself in England despite the enthusiastic support of Charles II. He wrote just one short operatic masterpiece, *Dido and Aeneas*, and four full-length "semi-operas" – populist extravaganzas that mixed singing, dancing and speech with spectacular scenic effects but which did not integrate its musical moments with its spoken ones, placing them, instead, at the end of each act in the form of a masque.

Dido and Aeneas

Dido and Aeneas, perhaps more than any other of his works, displays Purcell's remarkable skill as a setter of words. This is particularly evident in his recitatives, in which emotional nuance is communicated by an arioso vocalizing of extraordinary subtlety. It can be heard in Dido's recitative "Thy Hand, Belinda", which immediately precedes her famous lament, "When I am Laid in Earth". The recitative is highly chromatic – that is, it uses notes foreign to the key that it is in – with the voice moving in a series of small intervals on the syllable "dar" of the word "darkness". The effect is like someone feeling their way in the dark step by step, or, in Dido's case, coming to a true realization of the enormity of her imminent death. The opera is full of such telling details, with Dido's lament having pride of place. This episode has almost talismanic status in English music, and its fame is justified: indeed the single-note repetition of the words "Remember me" must be one of the most agonized and vulnerable moments in the whole of opera.

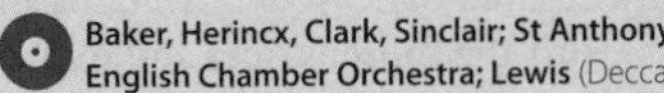

Baker, Herincx, Clark, Sinclair; St Anthony Singers; English Chamber Orchestra; Lewis (Decca)

Vocally, this remains the most gratifying recording of Purcell's opera. Janet Baker's attention to the music's emotional substance has rarely been equalled and never bettered. Anthony Lewis's direction of the ECO is reliable and frequently lively, and Baker is ably supported by Raimund Herincx's baritone Aeneas and Patricia Clark's Belinda.

Bott, Kirkby, Ainsley, Thomas; Academy of Ancient Music Choir and Orchestra; Hogwood (Decca)

Christopher Hogwood's 1994 account is among the best of the period instrument performances. Catherine Bott and Emma Kirkby are well paired as Dido and Belinda respectively, and while Bott doesn't quite wring the withers in the lament it's a powerfully affecting performance overall. The only minor quibbles are the slightly obtrusive thunderclaps and the fact that the sailor is sung by a treble!

von Otter, Varcoe, Dawson, Rogers; English Concert Choir and Orchestra; Pinnock (Archiv)

Trevor Pinnock's 1989 account still holds up well. Anne Sofie von Otter is a well-judged Dido and is well supported by Lynn Dawson's bright-toned Belinda. Stephen Varcoe's Aeneas is solid rather than inspiring, and Nigel Rogers' doubling of the sailor and the sorceress merely irritating. Where this performance loses out is in its failure to convey a real sense of theatrical excitement.

The Fairy Queen

Purcell manages to convey the essential qualities of Shakespeare's *A Midsummer Night's Dream* (on which *The Fairy Queen* is based) without actually setting a word of it. There is an astonishing variety of music, from the spine-tingling air "Hush No More", with its eloquent silences, to the knockabout comedy of the "Dialogue Between Coridon and Mopsa" adapted in the 1693 revision of the work for a countertenor who specialized in comic drag roles. There is also a range of highly theatrical musical devices, such as the echo effect in "May the God of Wit Inspire", or the sopranino recorders imitating birdsong in the prelude to Act 2. This last piece uses a ground bass, a form that occurs frequently in *The Fairy Queen*, most famously in Act 5's "O Let Me Weep", added in the 1693 revision to cover a scene change, and markedly similar to the lament in *Dido and Aeneas*.

Argenta, Dawson, Corréas, Deletré, Desrochers, Gens, Piau, Daniels, Randle; Les Arts Florissants; Christie (Harmonia Mundi; 2 CDs)

This is music-making of great vividness and immediacy, and it stands out from rival recordings precisely for that reason. Despite the lack of any real narrative in the masques, Christie never treats them as a mere collection of songs, but instead turns them into a real theatrical event. This is also true of the dance music, which always sounds spring-heeled and lively.

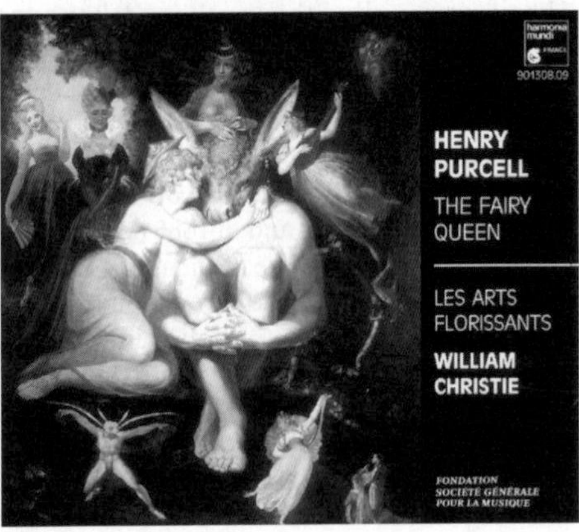

SACRED MUSIC

As well as introducing continental practices into court music, Charles II was determined to liven up the music that he heard in the Chapel Royal. Not everyone approved. John Evelyn, on hearing a large body of violins playing "after the French phantastical light way", pronounced it to be music "better suited to a Tavern or Playhouse than a church". Purcell had first-hand experience of the "new" music from an early age (he joined the Chapel Royal aged eight), so that when he came to write sacred music himself he had none of the difficulty of the older generation in embracing the new style. The result was the most opulent and expressive music ever written for the church in England, though in many ways it was untypical, since no other establishment could match the musical resources available at Westminster.

Anthems

English church music in the seventeenth century made a distinction between the full-anthem, which was choral throughout, and the more dramatic verse-anthem, in which solo sections were contrasted with sections for chorus. Under the influence of French composers like Lully (see p.310) and Charpentier, the verse anthem became an ever more splendid display piece and included lavish orchestral preludes and ritornelli. These are sometimes known as festival anthems since they were usually produced for special occasions like a coronation. Purcell excelled in all three forms. One of the festival anthems, *My Heart is Inditing* (written for the coronation of James II), exemplifies the splendid heights to which the form could rise. It begins with a long instrumental introduction or "symphony" from which the tune of the verse emerges and which is repeated before the final chorus. In between – in the more delicate ensemble writing – Purcell shows that his brilliance as a word-setter was even in evidence for the most ceremonial of music.

Choral Works: Christ Church Cathedral Choir; English Concert; Preston (Archiv; 2 CDs)

Recorded in the early 1980s, when Christ Church Cathedral Choir under director Simon Preston were on top form, these performances of a good cross-section of the major sacred choral works (including the Morning and Evening Service, the *Te Deum* and the *Jubilate*) still sound fresh and lively.

Funeral Music for Queen Mary II

Queen Mary died of smallpox at the end of 1694 at the age of 32. Her funeral, held the following year, was one of the most lavish and grandiose ever accorded an English monarch and there was a great public outpouring of grief. As the Westminster Abbey organist, Purcell was responsible for the music and he responded magnificently, composing a special processional march and canzona – both for the recently introduced "flat" trumpets. This is music of amazing poignancy, profoundly melancholic but full of great dignity. It is followed by the choir singing a slow and reverential setting of *Thou Knowest Lord the Secrets of Our Hearts*, accompanied by the trumpets. The other Purcell music associated with the funeral – *Man That is Born of a Woman*, *In the Midst of Life*, and another setting of *Thou Knowest Lord* – may or may not have been sung at the royal funeral (scholars are currently at odds about this). All three of these funeral sentences are characterized by a stark simplicity and a chromatic foundation that is astonishingly advanced for its time. Additional musical obsequies included three elegies for the queen – two by Purcell and one by John Blow. Of these, Purcell's duet for two altos *O dive custos Auriacae domus* is one of the most exquisitely beautiful works he ever wrote – highly Italianate in its interweaving of florid lines and clashing dissonances.

Lott, Brett, Williams, Allen; Monteverdi Choir & Orchestra; Equale Brass; Gardiner (Warner; with *Come Ye Sons of Art*)

This is one of the finest of all John Eliot Gardiner's period performances. Absolute restraint and discipline are maintained throughout, accentuating the air of doom established by the opening march, and purging all sentimentality in the choral sections.

Countertenor Duets and Solos by Purcell and Blow: Bowman, Chance; The King's Consort; King (Hyperion)

Purcell's two *Elegies for the Queen* are included on this marvellous disc, which brings together two of the finest English countertenors of recent years, James Bowman and Michael Chance. Their rendition of *O dive custos* is an utterly spine-tingling blending of voices which should make this great work better known. The disc also includes Blow's powerful *Ode on the Death of Mr Henry Purcell*.

ODES

The ceremonial splendour of the Stuart court led the poet and playwright Ben Jonson to revive the Pindaric ode – a celebratory lyric poem derived from the Greek examples of Pindar. Purcell's immediate forebears – Locke and Blow – both set odes to music, but it was Purcell who perfected the form, exploiting the expressive riches of the Baroque orchestra. He wrote them for a wide range of different occasions (including the *Yorkshire Ode* for an annual feast of Yorkshiremen in London), but the most important were written either for royal events or for the annual celebration of St Cecilia's Day (the patron saint of music) first organized by London musicians in 1683.

Birthday Odes for Queen Mary

For each of the six birthdays of Queen Mary's reign, Purcell composed a celebratory ode on a poem written especially for the occasion. All are contrasted in style, two of them are masterpieces. Sir Charles Sedley's rather stilted verses for *Love's Goddess Sure Was Blind* (1692) inspired an intimate, if rather mournful, setting from Purcell, dominated by the soloists. There's just one incongruous section when the soprano sings a solo verse over a bass line derived from a Scottish ballad (favoured by the queen), but the ode closes with a really magical moment – a quartet of soloists sing a lament, in canon, for Mary's inevitable death. *Come Ye Sons of*

Saint Cecilia – Patron Saint of Music

Saint Cecilia, allegedly martyred in the second century under Marcus Aurelius, did not acquire her widespread status as the patron saint of music until the Renaissance. Her cult received a boost when what was thought to be her incorrupted remains were found in St Cecilia in Trastevere, a church which had been built in Rome over the house in which she supposedly lived and was killed. During the sixteenth and seventeenth centuries St Cecilia was painted by many artists, including Raphael, Domenichino, Saraceni and Pietro Ricchi. She is depicted with a wide range of instruments but is most commonly associated with the organ which legend credits her as having invented.

The earliest musical event in Cecilia's honour seems to have been at Evreux in Normandy in 1570, which included a competition in which Roland de Lassus (see p.294) won a prize for a motet. In England, just over a hundred years later, her saint's day, 22 November, became the occasion for an annual celebration beginning in 1683. Among the group of London musicians who instigated the first St Cecilia's Day commemoration was Henry Purcell. The celebrations consisted of a church service, followed by a banquet at which an ode, specially written and set to music, was performed. There was a certain competitive, as well as celebratory, aspect to these festivities, and since Purcell's initial contribution of 1683 (*Welcome to All the Pleasures*), the music had become increasingly opulent. In 1687 Giovanni Battista Draghi composed a grandiose setting of a new poem by Dryden (the poet laureate) in which trumpets were included in the orchestra. Purcell's 1692 ode *Hail, Bright Cecilia!* aimed at – and succeeded in – outstripping all previous offerings in scale and splendour, despite an indifferent text by Nicholas Brady. No other composition made such an impact until Handel's two Cecilian odes, *Alexander's Feast* in 1736 and his *Ode for St Cecilia's Day* of 1739, both with words by Dryden.

In more recent times, Benjamin Britten collaborated with his then friend the poet W.H. Auden on a *Hymn to St Cecilia*. It was a work with a special significance for Britten because St Cecilia's Day was also his birthday, and, coincidentally, it was on St Cecilia's Eve, during the night of the 21 to 22 November 1695, that the death of Henry Purcell occurred.

Art (1694) is a much grander and more festive affair with a large Baroque orchestra complete with trumpets and drums. The verses, possibly by Nahum Tate, are crude and unmetrical but, as is so often the case, the poorer the text, the more brilliant Purcell's response. There are no weak moments, just a wonderful series of contrasted solos and duets which include the sparkling "Sound the Trumpet" for two altos, an amazingly deft setting for bass and chorus of the clumsy fourth verse, and – best of all – a glorious melismatic soprano solo ("Bid the Virtues") with an ornate oboe obbligato.

Gooding, Bowman, Robson, Crook, Wilson-Johnson, George; Choir and Orchestra of the Age of Enlightenment; Leonhardt
(Virgin)

Though more associated with German Baroque music, Leonhardt is a distinguished Purcellian who brings a new perspective to three of the birthday odes. In particular he emphasizes the ceremonial aspects with some slow tempi and some luxuriant orchestral playing.

Ode for St Cecilia's Day – Hail, Bright Cecilia!

Although Nicholas Brady's verses for *Hail, Bright Cecilia!* are mediocre, with Purcell it was often the case that the more lacklustre the words the more imaginative was his response. In this particular case, his setting was deemed such a success that the first audience demanded to hear the whole work all over again.

The ode is scored for the grandest of forces – an orchestra of strings, recorders, oboes, trumpets and kettle drums, six soloists and a six-part choir – and begins with a long orchestral sinfonia, after which a varied succession of solos, ensemble and choruses begins to unfold. The profoundest music is reserved for the text's more speculative moments, in particular the extraordinary solo "'Tis Nature's Voice" which describes the emotional impact music has on the listener. It was written for a high male voice as an incredibly free-flowing and heavily ornamented declamation and may have been performed by Purcell himself at the first performance. It's followed by a rousing chorus, "Soul of the World", in which the divided choir – their division suggesting the "scatter'd atoms" of the text – overlap a broad, noble melody which turns into a fugue before all the voices come together on the words "perfect harmony". The ensuing musical vignettes of individual instruments ("the airy violin", "the Am'rous flute", etc) are largely conjured up in order to show their inferiority to that "Wondrous machine" the organ (the instrument at which St Cecilia is usually depicted), which is described in an extremely jaunty bass solo. A final chorus brings all the forces together in a triumphant homage to the "Great Patroness of Us and Harmony!"

Gabrieli Consort and Players; McCreesh (Archiv; with *My Beloved Spake & Sing Unto the Lord*)

The most outstanding quality of this 1994 recording is the sheer energy and élan of the orchestra and chorus, who never let you forget that this is a festive work. The soloists, who are enlisted from the chorus, are good and occasionally outstanding. Best of all is the bass Peter Harvey, who projects just the right degree of expressiveness in what is a highly theatrical work.

INSTRUMENTAL MUSIC

Purcell's instrumental music, mostly written in his early twenties, constitutes a minute fraction of his total output, but its quality is outstanding. As a pivotal figure, standing between two epochs, his instrumental music has proved difficult to classify and has, until recently, been unfairly neglected. His fifteen fantasias (or fancyes) for viol consort (see p.296) brought to an end a genre that had thrived in England since the middle of the sixteenth century, whereas his *Trio Sonatas* were the first attempt by a leading English composer in this "new-fangl'd" Italian form.

Fantasias and Sonatas

Written for upper-class amateurs, the fantasia was essentially a free form in several movements performed by a consort of between three and seven players. It eschewed individual virtuosity in favour of a largely equal exchange of voices. Purcell's fantasias, composed at great speed during the summer of 1680, are an astonishing summation of the genre and possess a contrapuntal inventiveness that has been compared to Bach's *Art of Fugue*. They are shot through with a very Purcellian introspection yet at the same time have a restless energy and internal tension which often sounds extremely modern. In fact when Purcell wrote them, the fantasia was already regarded as old-fashioned, and had largely been replaced by the more formally tight trio sonata.

Purcell wrote two sets of trio sonatas shortly after completing his fantasias. Scored for two violins, viola da gamba and keyboard, their textures are lighter, and the sound is much brighter due to the greater incisiveness of the violin. Even so, there is still a melancholy quality to this music, which one contemporary described as "very artificiall and good", but "clog'd with somewhat of an English vein".

Complete Fantazias: Fretwork (Harmonia Mundi)

The excellent recording by Phantasm (on Simax) is currently unavailable so it's good to be able to recommend an equally compelling performance by Fretwork, who return to these pieces fourteen years after first recording them. It's an even more powerful performance than the earlier one, with the contrapuntal conversation between the instruments having a dark intensity that is unnervingly beautiful.

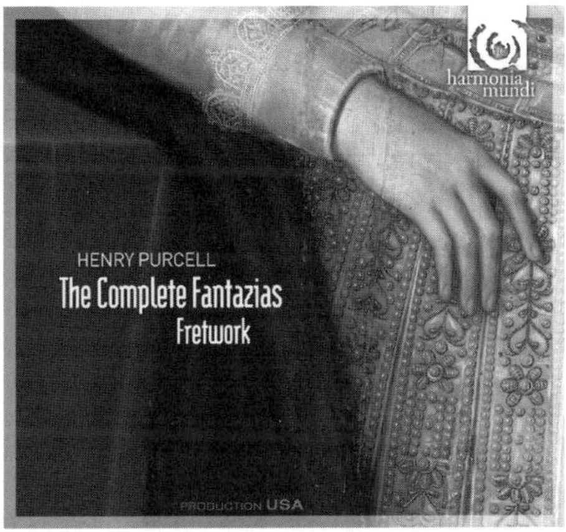

Sonatas Nos. 8–14: Purcell Quartet (Chandos; with *Three Parts Upon a Ground, Chacony & Two Pavans*)

The excellent Purcell Quartet have spread the fourteen trio sonatas across three discs and augmented them with a selection of other chamber works. This volume (the second) contains the last seven, and makes a good introductory disc. The sound is beautifully fresh and clear, a quality enhanced by the decision to employ a chamber organ for the continuo part.

Sergey Rachmaninov (1873–1943)

Sergey Rachmaninov was a displaced person in more than one sense – a Russian who spent much of his life outside the mother country, and a Romantic who embodied a brooding stereotype that belonged to a previous era. A virtuoso of Liszt-like abilities, and a composer of music as expansive as any nineteenth-century symphony, he upheld the Romantic tradition – in particular the tradition of his idol, Tchaikovsky – with a granitic integrity, unmoved by the onslaughts of modernism or the disdain of progressive critics. Stravinsky summarized him thus: "Rachmaninov's immortalizing totality was his scowl. He was a six-and-a-half-foot-tall scowl … he was an awesome man."

Rachmaninov's doom-laden appearance and taciturn manner were acquired quite young: he was born into wealth but his father was profligate, so by the time Rachmaninov was 9 the family was left with nothing. In 1885 he moved to Moscow where he began piano lessons, which in turn led to his first attempts at composing. In 1891, after further studies with various teachers, he completed his *Piano Concerto No. 1*, following it a year later with his most celebrated work for solo piano, the *Prelude in C Sharp Minor*. His opera *Aleko* met with similar acclaim in 1893, but his first symphony was a complete disaster (see p.434). Rachmaninov's reputation as a pianist continued to blossom, yet from 1897 he put almost all his energies into his conducting position with the Moscow Private Russian Opera Company. It was in this capacity that he made his first professional trip abroad, when he journeyed to London in 1899.

Around this time Rachmaninov began to suffer bouts of self-doubt so severe that he lost all faith in his abilities as a composer. A doctor named Nikolai Dahl came to the rescue with a course of hypnosis, through which Rachmaninov overcame his insecurities and began work on his second piano concerto. The first performance in 1901 was an enormous success, and the work has remained his most popular. From then on, he composed fluently but for the next three years he was possessed by an enthusiasm for opera, an area of his output that's now all but forgotten. By 1906 he was becoming worried by Russia's social instability, and he spent extended periods of time outside the country – in 1909, for example, he toured all over America, playing nothing but his own music, including the recently completed *Piano Concerto No. 3*. Shortly after the 1917 Revolution, an invitation to conduct in Stockholm was the catalyst for the inevitable decision, and Rachmaninov and his family left Russia for the last time.

Rachmaninov at home studying a score.

Shrewdly, if reluctantly, he recognized America as the answer to his financial worries and it was in New York that he finally settled in November 1918. His remaining years were dominated by performing engagements, with little time to spare for composing: the fourth piano concerto, the *Paganini Rhapsody*, the third symphony, the *Corelli Variations* and the *Symphonic Dances* were the only major works he produced in the last third of his life. His last American home was a metaphor for his career and his music – it was a complete replica, down to the food and drink, of his home in Moscow.

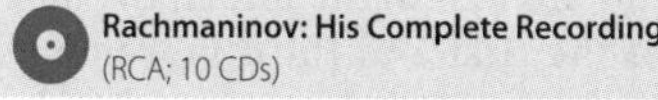

Rachmaninov: His Complete Recordings (RCA; 10 CDs)

Rachmaninov had enormous hands, enabling him to play what other pianists would find almost impossible, and very few recordings of his works approach his own. This dazzling set includes all four piano concertos, the *Paganini Rhapsody*, the third symphony (conducted by Rachmaninov) and a large selection of his solo piano music. You also get recordings of music by Beethoven, Grieg, Schumann, Mendelssohn, Schubert, Tchaikovsky, Scriabin, Liszt, Debussy and others. The one drawback of this set is how poorly documented it is.

The Bells

Rachmaninov composed *The Bells*, his self-styled "choral symphony", at the height of his creative powers in 1913, and two decades later he told a reporter that he valued it as the best of all his works – adding that it was "unfortunately rarely performed". Recordings of this extraordinary work are now, thankfully, plentiful, though the demanding single-movement appearances of tenor, soprano and bass-baritone, as well as a choral part of considerable difficulty, militate against frequent concert performances. The composer took as his inspiration four poems by Edgar Allen Poe in a Russian translation by the poet Konstantin Balmont. The first movement, evoking the enchantment of silver bells on a winter sleigh-ride, is unusually joyous for both composer and author, while "Wedding Bells" blends the yearning of Wagner's *Tristan* with a more ominous undercurrent. The second half of the work darkens the hue: the chorus has the limelight in the panic of "Alarm Bells", but most characteristic of all is the funereal fourth movement, led by the doleful bass-baritone and relieved only at the last minute as the music glides out of its overwhelming despondency into a radiant benediction.

Troitskaya, Karczykowski, Krause; Concertgebouw Orchestra & Chorus; Ashkenazy (Decca; 3 CDs; with *Symphonies Nos.1–3, The Isle of the Dead & Symphonic Dances*)

Although some Russian versions have a more exciting edge, this is perhaps the only recording in which the choruses are given enough space to make their full impact; the solo roles are also well handled. With excellent versions of all three symphonies, *The Isle of the Dead* and *Symphonic Dances*, this box set provides the perfect survey of Rachmaninov's non-concerto orchestral works at a competitive price.

Shumakaya, Dovernan, Bolshakov; Moscow Philharmonic Symphony Orchestra & RSFSR Chorus; Kondrashin (Melodiya; with *Symphonic Dances*)

If you want a single disc with all the requisite Russian intensity and an authentically Slavic choir, then Kiril Kondrashin's recording from the mid-1960s is the real deal. One of the most exciting (and underrated) of Soviet-era conductors, he brings out the full dramatic scope of this great work aided by three excellent soloists. The sound is a little raw but perfectly acceptable.

Vespers

Rachmaninov might have been ambivalent about the Church, but he was far from irreligious; and taking his cue from Tchaikovsky he had already composed a succession of choral works when he began to write the *Vespers* during a concert tour in 1913. It is the culmination of a great tradition, outstripping all predecessors in terms of colour and choral virtuosity. Rachmaninov clearly relished the sepulchral resonance of Slavic basses, the tolling of great bells, and traditional thematic material itself, which he quotes in both his *Symphony No. 1* and *Symphonic Dances*. By turns haunting, serene and magnificent, the *Vespers* proved an instant success, and were repeated four times in the 1915 concert season.

St Petersburg Capella; Chernushenko
(Harmonia Mundi)

Russian choirs bring a special quality to the *Vespers*, and the St Petersburg Capella are as good as any. They have recorded it several times under Vladislav Chernushenko, most recently in this highly charged version (but also in an earlier version with the same choir under its Soviet name). Both are powerful and moving but both flit in and out of the catalogue with an irritating regularity.

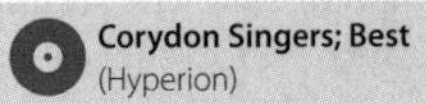

Corydon Singers; Best
(Hyperion)

This British alternative is completely different, representative of another choral tradition; the performance is lighter, sweeter and more elegant, especially in the spot-on intonation of the chorus. A more than interesting complement to the above.

Symphony No. 2

The premiere of Rachmaninov's first symphony was a spectacular failure, thanks to its conductor, Glazunov (see p.212), who arrived at the podium tanked up on vodka and turned the performance into a humiliation for the young composer. In the wake of this debâcle, Rachmaninov pronounced the symphony "weak, childish, strained and bombastic", withdrew it from public use, and never heard it again. The *Symphony No. 2*, however, is a work of immense power and maturity – coming, as it did, twelve years later. It may be overlong, but it's more disciplined than its predecessor, and the richness of its themes makes it the most absorbing of Rachmaninov's three symphonies. In particular, the Adagio is one of the greatest symphonic movements in all Russian music. A song for orchestra, the Adagio becomes perilously sentimental in places, but its lush harmony and exquisite orchestration are so genuinely felt that you'll forgive any excesses.

St Petersburg Philharmonic Orchestra; Jansons
(EMI; with *Vocalise & Scherzo*)

Perhaps the finest recording of recent years is Mariss Jansons' second account of the score, with the St Petersburg Philharmonic. It might be at times too slick and precise, but overall the passion of the interpretation is thrilling, and Jansons maintains a tight balance and responsive tempi throughout.

Philadelphia Orchestra; Ormandy
(RCA; with *Isle of the Dead*)

Eugene Ormandy and the Philadelphia Orchestra worked regularly with Rachmaninov, recording the *Symphony No. 2* on several occasions. This, the last, dates from 1973. It' makes a strong alternative to Jansons, emphasizing the sheer lushness of the score, and gaining in lyricism what it, perhaps, loses in dynamism.

Symphony No. 3

The *Symphony No. 3* was composed in Switzerland between 1935 and 1936 – nearly thirty years after its predecessor. It's very nearly as powerful: a great surge of orchestral energy follows the hushed Orthodox chant of the opening, the singing interludes between the music's recurring motifs are of Rachmaninov's most alluringly heartfelt kind, and before the symphony's hovering ghosts are laid to rest a last fugato is wittily spun in which the composer's *idée fixe,* the Dies irae, insinuates itself as a counterpoint. This is a work to stand by the best of Rachmaninov's Indian summer.

St Petersburg Philharmonic Orchestra; Jansons
(EMI; with *Symphonic Dances*)

Jansons repeats the success of the second symphony with a mesmerizing performance of the third, in which his close attention to detail does the work a lot of favours. It's coupled with a scintillating account of the *Symphonic Dances*, the last of Rachmaninov's orchestral works.

Symphonic Dances

Most fascinating of the few major works Rachmaninov composed during his last years in America, the *Symphonic Dances* of 1940 turned out to be the composer's Requiem. Quoting from several of his major works – crucially the "Resurrection" sequence from his *Vespers*, a vigorous answer to the Dies irae in the third movement's "Dance of Death" – this piece is, as the title suggests, an intriguing hybrid: dance rhythms are well to the fore in the outer sequences of the first and third movements, and the second is a swooning *valse triste*, but there is also symphonic weight in the treatment of short, often simple motifs. Rachmaninov's original plan to give titles to the movements – "Noon", "Twilight", "Midnight" – also gives some support to the listener's impression that ghosts are gathering to hold their revels in the later stages of the work.

St Petersburg Philharmonic Orchestra; Jansons (EMI; with *Symphony No. 3*)

Mariss Jansons' account of the *Symphonic Dances* is one of the most thrilling on record. He never relaxes or takes his foot off the throttle and the results are electrifying, securing a particularly tight reading of the difficult third movement.

Moscow Philharmonic Symphony Orchestra; Kondrashin (Melodiya; with *The Bells*)

The engineered sound may not be up to the Jansons recording but the performance is every bit as exciting. Kondrashin relishes every detail of the score, bringing out both the dance qualities of the music and its emotional depth with great flair.

The Isle of the Dead

The *Isle of the Dead* (1909), Rachmaninov's first orchestral masterpiece, owes its inspiration to Arnold Böcklin's famous painting of an upright shrouded figure being rowed by boat to a cypress-covered island – the painting also inspired Reger (see p.438). Through a steadily repeated rhythmic motif, Rachmaninov brilliantly conveys the movement of oars across the water and the journey's inexorable progress. But this glowering early masterpiece also owes much to the Wagner of *Tristan* with its "immortal longings" for the oblivion and bliss of death (the Dies irae makes another appearance). It's an amazingly powerful piece, whose simple repetitions and sepulchral air work their way insidiously into the memory.

Rachmaninov specialist Vladimir Ashkenazy.

Concertgebouw Orchestra; Ashkenazy (Decca; 3 CDs; with *Symphonies Nos. 1–3, Symphonic Dances & The Bells*)

The sombre weight of Rachmaninov's tone poem is magisterially caught by Ashkenazy. The way in which he makes inflections surge and die, as if themselves caught on the waves, creates just the right atmosphere of brooding heaviness and tense expectation.

Chicago Symphony Orchestra; Reiner (RCA; with *Symphony No. 2*)

If you want a single disc account of this atmospheric work, Fritz Reiner's 1958 recording is one of the best. Reiner was a disciplinarian and his control of the dynamics and shaping of this piece creates a magical reading, with some awe-inspiring brass playing. It's coupled with a strong version of the second symphony from the Philadelphians under Ormandy.

Piano Concerto No. 2

In view of Rachmaninov's complete technical command of the piano, it's amazing that he should so rarely have succumbed to the temptation to write bravura music. His piano concertos are all very difficult to play, but, with the exception of the blatantly taxing third concerto, there are few moments where it sounds like it. Of the four, the *Piano Concerto No. 2* is understandably the most popular. Dedicated to Doctor Dahl, the hypnotherapist who restored Rachmaninov to composition, it is a wonderfully optimistic work, opening with a famous eight-chord progression and crammed with soaringly beautiful music. Remarkably, at no point in the first movement does the soloist take up the main opening theme, and there is a notable sense of self-denial throughout the solo part – which is not to say that the orchestral music doesn't have its moments of wallowing.

Richter; Warsaw National Philharmonic Orchestra; Wislocki (Deutsche Grammophon; with Tchaikovsky *Piano Concerto No. 1*)

Sentimentality has no place here. The powerful authority of Sviatoslav Richter dominates the proceedings, above all in the sheer daring of an interpretation that hangs fire as if possessed of a deep despair and then explodes as if suddenly bursting into flame.

Ashkenazy; London Symphony Orchestra; Previn (Decca; with *Rhapsody on a Theme of Paganini*)

Vladimir Ashkenazy is one of the finest of modern interpeters of Rachmaninov, blessed with a superb technique but always responsive to the music's emotional ebb and flow. This same performance also comes as part of a four-CD set by the same team of all the piano concertos and as a six-CD set with the Rachmaninov *Rhapsody* and solo pieces.

Piano Concerto No. 3

Rachmaninov's *Piano Concerto No. 3* is a production of the fruitful years following his aberrant "operatic" period. Commenced at the same time as the second symphony and completed in 1909, it is his grandest concerto, reflecting a confident mastery of melodic writing and the resources of the orchestra. Here he finally overcomes his habit of signposting the introduction of new material by bringing the music to a screeching halt, and his subtle metamorphosis of the first movement's thematic core into a leitmotif for the whole work gives the concerto a continuity unprecedented in Rachmaninov's work. However, the most important aspect of the *Piano Concerto No. 3* is its scale and violently Romantic vision: it was dedicated to the great pianist Josef Hofmann, and although Hofmann never played the piece it was clearly written with his thunderous abilities in mind. The fourth concerto offers none of the expansive melodies of its predecessors, but its fragmentary nature is part of its fascination: a special case indeed.

Horowitz; RCA Victor Symphony Orchestra; Reiner (RCA; 2 CDs; with Tchaikovsky *Piano Concerto* & solo pieces by Chopin, Schumann, Scriabin etc)

The third concerto was very much Horowitz's calling card and he made several recordings of it. This 1951 RCA recording is among the best. Horowitz is in staggering form, producing one of the most thrilling percussive performances of his life. Now part of a two-CD survey of the pianist at his peak.

Argerich; Berlin Radio Symphony Orchestra; Chailly (Philips; with *Suite No. 2 for Two Pianos*)

An edge-of-the-seat live performance makes a great modern alternative to Horowitz. There's a vibrant and unpredictable edge to Martha Argerich's playing that imparts a sense of discovery and breathes life into the concerto's more prolix moments. She teams up with the brilliant Brazilian Nelson Freire for the rarely recorded *Suite No. 2*.

Rhapsody on a Theme of Paganini

The last of Paganini's *24 Caprices* (see p.394) has spawned more sets of variations than almost any other piece of music. Rachmaninov's response to it, the immensely popular *Rhapsody on a Theme of Paganini* (1934), is a set of variations for piano and orchestra, a sequence that's strictly constructed (the main theme is never far away) but has as strong a Romantic sweep as any of the symphonies or concertos – indeed, it's perhaps best described as a quasi-concerto. Particularly effective episodes are variation number seven, which invokes the Dies irae chant so popular with Romantic composers (for example Berlioz), and the swoony variation eighteen, perhaps Rachmaninov's greatest hit. The last six variations form a highly charged coda, but the work ends with a barely audible flutter of notes that is almost as capricious as Paganini's original.

Ashkenazy; London Symphony Orchestra; Previn (Decca with *Piano Concerto No. 2*)

Ashkenazy is responsive to the music's exuberance as well as its nostalgia, and Previn's accompaniment is superbly attentive. The famous inversion of Paganini's theme, when it comes, is particularly simply done, and quietly moving in its intimacy.

Piano Sonata No. 2

Neither of Rachmaninov's piano sonatas has entered the standard repertoire, a neglect attributable to their extreme technical demands and to a *fin-de-siècle* opulence that many find offputting. In the case of the first sonata this is fair enough, but the *Sonata No. 2* is a different proposition. It was written between January and September 1913, and it soon became a mainstay of Rachmaninov's own concert programmes. In the 1930s, having doubts about the volume of "surplus material" in his early music, he cut the sonata down, but the revision did nothing to improve a work that succeeds by its very expansiveness. The opening is a declamatory and rugged movement that moves into a central Adagio in which the harmonies recall Scriabin. None of this prepares you for the breathtaking finale, a polyphonic Romantic drama of immense grandeur and virtuosity. The wild and jubilant final section is almost crazed with energy.

Horowitz (Sony; with a selection of the *Études tableaux* & *Preludes*, and works by Scriabin and Medtner)

Vladimir Horowitz's playing of the sonata was monumental and Rachmaninov took the pianist's advice on how the work could be improved, approving Horowitz's version, which restored most of the passages trimmed by the revision. This 1968 performance is tremendously exciting, sounding in places like the most glorious of improvisations. Currently out of the catalogue but likely to return.

Preludes

Like Chopin's, Rachmaninov's *Preludes* comprise a sequence of miniatures in every major and minor key and, as with Chopin, the self-imposed constraints inspired some of the composer's most original ideas. Comprising the famous C sharp minor *Prelude* (Op. 3 No. 2) plus two later sets (Op. 23 and Op. 32), the *Preludes* are on the whole more economical than the ripe piano music of Rachmaninov's early career. Melody is a less dominant element than you might expect, for many of these pieces are built upon rhythmic patterns that lead towards the establishment of a melodic pattern that reflects the rhythmic pulse. This is not especially warm music – and you certainly shouldn't tackle the whole series in one sitting – but the *Preludes* are essential listening if you want to get a rounded picture of Rachmaninov.

Weissenberg
(RCA)

Alexis Weissenberg's punchy sound is well-suited to this frequently percussive music, and his searching approach highlights Rachmaninov's inner, contrapuntal voicing to great effect.

Études tableaux

As with the Chopin of the *Ballades*, *Études* and *Preludes*, the *Études tableaux* take a motif or a technical challenge as their starting point, and weave poetically from that. Mordant, terse and visionary in their endless chromaticism, luminously simple or spectrally poignant, they are distinguished by a brevity and a new, virtuosic level of pianism. The title of the set suggests pictures in sound, but Rachmaninov was reticent about revealing exactly what pictures he had in mind. "I do not believe in the artist disclosing too much about his images. Let them paint for themselves what they most suggest." The first set was composed straight after the Opus 32 *Preludes*: chips from the creative block of the composer who had just written *Symphony No. 2* and the *Isle of the Dead*. The Opus 39 collection was one of the last works Rachmaninov wrote in Russia, and one of his least Russian: his imagination was fast outstripping the straitjacket of any parochial idiom that others wanted to impose upon him.

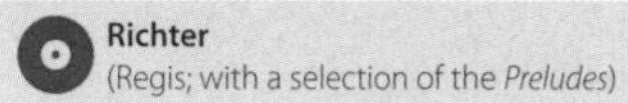

Richter
(Regis; with a selection of the *Preludes*)

Sviatoslav Richter was an extraordinary performer of these works, always revealing the visionary glow behind their melancholy or virtuosic exteriors. As well as the complete *Études*, this disc also includes Richter's personal selection of the *Preludes*, all of which receive equally magnificent readings.

Cello Sonata

As with the majority of nineteenth-century Russian composers, Rachmaninov wrote a small amount of chamber music, and the only work in this field that shows him at his best is the *Cello Sonata* of 1901. It displays an exceptionally detailed knowledge of the expressive qualities of the instrument, a knowledge doubtless acquired with the help of his cellist friend Brandukov, to whom the work is dedicated and by whom it was first performed. After a brief introduction, the cello plays the opening movement's yearning first subject but the piano is given the responsibility of carrying the second. Thereafter, the piano is the dominant partner, and only in the elegiac Andante – one of Rachmaninov's greatest achievements – does the cello come back into its own.

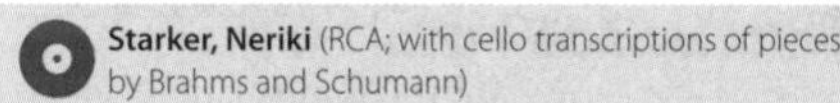

Starker, Neriki (RCA; with cello transcriptions of pieces by Brahms and Schumann)

Janos Starker is highly suited to music that thrives off the projection of a sweet tone. This is a surging, urgent performance: the outer movements are dashed off with considerable passion, while the Andante's emotional assault course is traversed with dignity as well as great feeling.

Jean-Philippe Rameau (1683–1764)

Rameau achieved fame as a composer relatively late in his career. In 1733, when he was fifty years old, his first opera, *Hippolyte et Aricie*, created a storm of controversy because it dared to challenge the model for French opera established by Lully some fifty years earlier. In fact Rameau claimed to be a follower of Lully, but his music is much more dynamic and harmonically adventurous – qualities that his critics decried as being forced and unnatural. Success had been long in coming, partly because he had spent the first forty years of his life in provincial obscurity, and partly because what reputation he had made was as a music theorist, an occupation thought to be incompatible with the actual business of composing, though Rameau himself rated it more highly. Despite his academic background, his music does not sound especially intellectual – rather it has the charm and elegance of Couperin (see p.148), but with rather more bite and vigour.

Drawing of Rameau by Antoine Watteau.

Rameau was born in Dijon, the seventh of eleven children. His father – who taught him music – was the organist of the cathedral of Notre Dame in Dijon, a post to which Jean-Philippe succeeded in 1709. His early career was spent largely as an organist at a series of other French cathedrals, including Clermont-Ferrand, where in 1722 he published his *Traité de l'harmonie* (Treatise on Harmony), in which he examined the origins of harmony and the relationships of chords.

The following year he left for Paris but achieved only modest success writing light theatrical works and teaching the harpsichord, before being taken up by one of the city's greatest artistic patrons, the financier La Riche de la Pouplinière. One of the wealthiest men in France, La Pouplinière was prodigal in his expenditure on art. Among his several homes was a chateau at Passy near Paris, where he had a private chapel, kept an orchestra of fourteen players, and gave regular concerts and musical festivities. Rameau was his music director from 1731 to 1753, and it was La Pouplinière who provided the contacts and the money that launched his late-flourishing operatic career. Within just a couple of decades Rameau's status as a radical innovator had been reversed, and he was held up as exemplifying all that was best about the French operatic tradition in the quarrel that followed the performance of Pergolesi's *La Serva Padrona* in 1752 (see p.403).

Castor et Pollux

Castor et Pollux is arguably Rameau's operatic masterpiece, but its initial reception in 1737 was unenthusiastic and Rameau made extensive revisions (mainly cuts) in 1754. The libretto is based on the classical tale of two half-brothers: one mortal, Castor (tenor), the other the son of Jupiter, Pollux (baritone). When Castor dies, Pollux intercedes with his father, who allows Castor to return to life only if Pollux takes his place in Hades. The story is a simple one of fraternal love and loyalty, made complicated by the fact that Pollux is in love with his brother's lover, Telaira, but not in love with the woman who loves him, Phoebe. Rameau clothes the story in extraordinarily rich and varied music, often juxtaposing profoundly contrasting moments, as when Telaira's meltingly tender lament for Castor's death in Act 1 ("Tristes apprêts, pâles flambeaux") is immediately followed by the warlike music that heralds Pollux's arrival. His orchestration is always highly imaginative, with novel combinations of instruments creating specific descriptive effects (like the storm scene and its sunny aftermath in Act 5). It was precisely for this pictorial skill that Rameau was so admired during his lifetime.

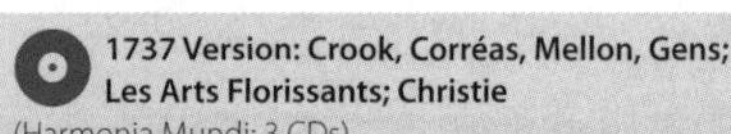

1737 Version: Crook, Corréas, Mellon, Gens; Les Arts Florissants; Christie
(Harmonia Mundi; 3 CDs)

The one failing of this opera (especially in the earlier version used here) is that the two brothers are just too good to be true, a drawback compounded by Howard Crook's rather watery Castor. The recording's strengths are its women (Agnes Mellon is particularly convincing as Telaira) and some superbly atmospheric orchestral playing. A highlights disc is also available.

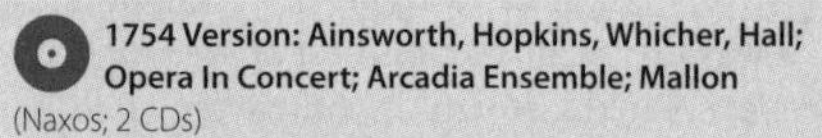

1754 Version: Ainsworth, Hopkins, Whicher, Hall; Opera In Concert; Arcadia Ensemble; Mallon
(Naxos; 2 CDs)

This recent budget recording by a mainly Canadian team under an Irish conductor has a lot to recommend it. While it may lack the sheer dramatic oomph that William Christie brings to French Baroque music, the orchestral playing is assured and the soloists are consistently good: Colin Ainsworth's high tenor Castor working particularly well with the baritone of Joshua Hopkins as Pollux.

Les Indes galantes Suites

As well as writing opera, Rameau also wrote for a peculiarly French theatrical hybrid, the opera-ballet, in which each section has a separate plot and equal importance is given to both song and dance. Rameau's first venture into this genre was *Les Indes galantes* in 1735, a light-hearted work concerned with romance in exotic climes, and reflecting the vogue for the "noble savage". Made up, in its final form, of a prologue and four acts, the action takes place in Turkey, Peru, Persia and America. The fashionable exoticism of *Les Indes galantes* allowed Rameau to display his mastery of a wide range of dance forms. Between the conventional formality of the opening overture and the ceremonial splendour of the chaconne with which it ends, there's a medley of highly contrasted pieces including "L'air pour les sauvages", whose hard-driven jauntiness is said to have been inspired by the singing and dancing of two Louisiana Indians. The work was so successful that Rameau arranged it for harpsichord and as four orchestral suites, in which form it has become one of his most popular works.

Orchestra of the Eighteenth Century; Bruggen (Philips)

In this selection of suites from *Les Indes galantes*, Frans Brüggen's measured direction lets the music unfold graciously and naturally, never underlining its agitated or odder aspects. What emerges is the way in which Rameau's orchestral colouring creates alluring combinations of elegance and passion.

Sacred Music

Rameau is little known, even in France, as a composer of sacred music. But before achieving fame as a composer of operas, he wrote some outstanding *Grands Motets*, in the tradition of Lully and Charpentier, which seem to presage his achievements in the theatre. The French *Grand Motet*, with its mixture of solos, ensembles and instrumental writing, always has had a dramatic element, but in a work like *Deus noster refugium* (1715) there is a level of intensity and excitement (including a musical description of a storm) that is positively startling.

Deus noster refugium; In convertendo; Quam dilecta: Daneman, Rime, Agnew, Rivenq, Cavallier; Les Arts Florissants; Christie (Erato)

An outstanding release which displays all the characteristics which make Christie the doyen of conductors of French Baroque music. All of the more tender moments are exquisitely shaped, but what sticks in the memory is the richness of sound and the sheer excitement that is generated.

Keyboard Music

Rameau wrote four books of harpsichord pieces, amounting to 65 pieces, of which only books two and three – the best of them – were published during his lifetime. As with Couperin, many of these pieces are fancifully named miniatures, and they are among his most charming creations, less elusive and mysterious than Couperin's but no less beautiful. Among them is a late work, *La Dauphine*, which was extemporized for the wedding of the dauphin to Maria-Josepha of Saxony, and is full of cascading runs and daring harmonies. Perhaps his finest achievement as a keyboard composer, though, is the glorious *Suite in A Major* from the third book – its powerful opening Allemande can stand comparison with the finest of Bach's Allemandes from the *English* and *French* suites.

Pièces de clavecin: Rousset (L'Oiseau-Lyre; 2 CDs)

This set by the outstanding French player Christophe Rousset gives you almost all of Rameau's harpsichord works in sparklingly vivid performances. Just occasionally his speeds seem a little fraught, but mostly tone and style seem admirably judged. For variety's sake, he divides the music between two instruments.

Nouvelles suites: Tharaud (Harmonia Mundi with Debussy *Hommage à Rameau*)

This CD features the two *Nouvelles suites* performed on a modern piano – relatively rare for Rameau's keyboard music. Alexandre Tharaud's playing is occasionally a little over-elaborate and jazzy, but he demonstrates greater flair than Angela Hewitt on a comparable recording. Overall it's a beguiling performance, with the suites taking on a whole new dimension courtesy of the piano's varied and softer timbres.

Pièces de clavecin en concerts

Rameau's *Pièces de clavecin en concerts* – his only work for chamber ensemble – marked an advance on forerunners such as the trio sonatas of Corelli, in that the harpsichord, having previously done little more than provide the continuo bass, was now assigned a place at the heart of an ensemble in which the leading role is continuously swapped from instrument to instrument, creating a new intricacy and textural variety. Published in 1741 and written for harpsichord (*clavecin*) with violin or flute, plus viol or second violin (it was common practice to be flexible in the instrumentation of chamber pieces), they are divided into five *concerts* of three or four brief movements, many of which – in characteristically French style – bear a title. Several are named after acquaintances of Rameau (such as Marais), while others take their names from character traits ("La Timide", "L'Indiscrète") or places ("Le Vézinet"); the music is not necessarily an illustration of the title: in several instances Rameau and his friends devised the label after the piece had been written.

Podger, Pinnock, Manson
(Channel Classics)

The playing of Trevor Pinnock (harpsichord), Rachel Podger (violin) and Jonathan Manson (viola da gamba) is dazzlingly vivacious, and it's remarkable what a range of timbres so small an ensemble can produce. The one drawback is the sound engineering which has given the performances a slightly abrasive edge.

Einojuhani Rautavaara (1928–)

Though the resurgence of religious spirituality in late twentieth-century music is usually attributed to the trinity of "holy minimalists" – Pärt, Górecki and Tavener – some of the most profoundly spiritual music of recent years has come from the elder statesman of Finnish contemporary music, Einojuhani Rautavaara. Unlike Pärt and the others, Rautavaara does not write "religious" works as such, yet his music is imbued with a powerful mystical quality that is largely inspired by the elemental qualities of his native landscape. In recent years Rautavaara has developed a near-obsession with the idea of the angel as Jungian archetype: "They repeat in my mind like a mantra that radiates musical energy", he has said. Angels have inspired several works, including the serene and expansive *Symphony No. 7* (1994), subtitled by the composer "Angel of Light".

Rautavaara regards himself as a Romantic composer because of the stylistic freedom he insists upon: "A Romantic has no co-ordinates. In time he is in yesterday or tomorrow, but never in today." In an interview in April 2000 he further emphasized this need for fluidity: "If an artist is not a modernist when he is young, he has no heart, and if he is a modernist when he is old, he has no brain." During his long career his music has undergone several transformations. As a student of Aare Merikanto at the Sibelius Academy in Helsinki, his work conformed to the neo-classicism then prevalent in Finland. At the recommendation of the 90-year-old Sibelius, he was given a scholarship for further study in the US, where he enhanced his already considerable orchestral technique under Vincent Periscetti at the Juilliard School, and Roger Sessions and Aaron Copland at Tanglewood. In 1954 he won the Thor Johnson competition in the USA with *A Requiem in Our Time*. Travel and yet more study in Europe in the late 1950s led him to embrace dodecaphony, but even when he followed the principles of serialism, as in the *String Quartet No. 2* (1958), the music has an emotional charge that is much closer to the expressionism of Berg than the austerity of Webern. By the 1970s, however, Rautavaara had embraced an openly Romantic idiom exemplified by his best-known work, the extraordinary *Cantus Arcticus* (1972). Rautavaara has also composed a number of operas, including *Vincent* (1990) and *Aleksis Kivi* (1997).

Cantus Arcticus

Written in 1972 for the new university of Oulu in northern Finland, *Cantus Arcticus* is described by the composer as a concerto for birds and orchestra. Divided into three sections ("The Bog", "Melancholy" and "Swans Migrating"), it juxtaposes Rautavaara's own recordings of arctic birds with orchestral music of great subtlety and lyricism. The result is a mysterious and exotic sound-world, with the birdcalls emerging and disappearing in the sombre half-light of Rautavaara's orchestral landscapes. This is music with a strong sense of place, which – while not being in any sense programmatic – conjures up vivid images of the great forests and lakes of arctic Finland.

Leipzig Radio Symphony Orchestra; Pommer
(Ondine; with *Symphony No. 4* & *Symphony No. 5*)

This CD makes the perfect introduction to Rautavaara's music: it contains the best of several recordings of *Cantus Arcticus* plus excellent performances of the *String Quartet*

No. 4 (its austerity in marked contrast to the sonorous textures of the *Cantus*) and the *Symphony No. 5*.

Symphony No. 5

Scored for a huge orchestra in one continuous movement, Rautavaara's monolithic *Symphony No. 5* (1986) battles to reconcile the contradiction which lies at the heart of its opening statement – a major triad that slowly pulses and crescendos to fortissimo only to shatter into dissonance. This dramatic opening dissolves into a darkly chromatic theme for cellos and violas (reminiscent of the fugue in the first movement of Bartók's *Music for Strings, Percussion and Celesta*), which is gradually drowned out by a cacophony of babbling woodwind. Originally entitled "Monologue with Angels", this is a broodingly Romantic work despite momentary outbursts of modernist angst. Its stark juxtaposition of conflicting elements encapsulates an important element of Rautavaara's style, one that he continues to explore in later works such as the *Symphony No. 7*.

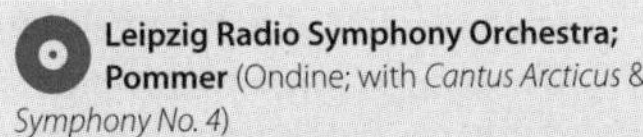

Leipzig Radio Symphony Orchestra; Pommer (Ondine; with *Cantus Arcticus* & *Symphony No. 4*)

The meat of the disc is the *Symphony No. 5*, which under Pommer's sensitive direction has a Sibelian power and recalls Rautavaara's own definition of the symphony as "an epic flow of thinking" – not a description borne out by the challenging *Symphony No. 4*, a serialist work of the most dessicated variety.

Symphony No. 7 – Angel of Light

Rautavaara's angel fixation has little to do with the benign anthropomorphic figures of Christianity, but is more closely related to the stark and terrible presences of Rilke's *Duino Elegies* or the visions of William Blake. It emerged after a visit to a former benefactor, Olga Koussevitsky, who had suggested he write a double-bass concerto. On the flight home Rautavaara looked out of the plane window and saw a cloud formation shaped like an angel. Two works emerged: an overture, *Angels and Visitations* (1978), and a double-bass concerto, *Angel of Dusk* (1980). *Angel of Light* (1994) is the most incandescent and serene of all these "angelic" works. The opening music breathes in a slow pulse, like a huge astronomical clock with a gentle, undulating ostinato in the upper strings punctuated by icy vibraphone chords and granite-like pedal notes in the double basses. Equally impressive is the unfettered violence of the second movement, the fury of which stands in marked contrast to the luminous quality of the work as a whole.

Helsinki Philharmonic Orchestra; Segerstam (Ondine; with *Annunciations*)

Segerstam is a renowned interpreter of Romantic music – Sibelius and Mahler in particular – and he brings to Rautavaara's symphony a sense of vast empty spaces and controlled power. Any tendency to wallow in the sumptuous melodic writing is resisted and the result saves the work from displaying its transcendental aspirations too blatantly.

Maurice Ravel (1875–1937)

Nineteenth-century France made a speciality of failing to recognize its home-grown talent (Berlioz being the most spectacular instance of neglected genius), thereby encouraging composers such as Gounod, Massenet and Saint-Saëns to look to Germany – and Wagner in particular – for inspiration. The inevitable consequence of this trend was a reaction against Wagnerism, a reaction which came to a head around the beginning of the twentieth century with the re-emergence of a completely French school of composition. At the head of this resurgence was Debussy; and the greatest of his lieutenants was Maurice Ravel.

Ravel's music might at times be redolent of Debussy's later work, but these two composers followed quite different paths. Whereas Debussy pushed his music into a world of extreme formal and tonal ambiguity, Ravel never renounced traditional tonality and form, and cultivated a style that combined the Classical with the contemporary. He was fascinated by the grand pianistic tradition of Liszt (as shown by his *Gaspard de la nuit*), and even more obviously drawn towards the purity of Rameau and the eighteenth century (as in *Pavane pour une infante défunte* and *Le tombeau de Couperin*), an interesting enough hybrid without the addition of other enthusiasms, such as Gypsy

Maurice Ravel (right) playing a duet with the ballet dancer Nijinsky.

music, jazz, Spanish culture and the music of the Far East. This last major influence can be traced to Debussy's encounter with Javanese music in Paris in 1889, a seminal moment from which one can follow the thread of Orientalism through much of France's twentieth-century music, right down to Messiaen and, less obviously, Boulez.

Ravel bound all these strands together with brilliant wit and an unrivalled understanding of orchestration, though his mastery of instrumental colour has sometimes been used as a charge against him – Stravinsky, for example, suggested that something was missing in the substance of a work if the thing you noticed above all was the dazzle of its sound. This is to overlook Ravel's marvellous sense of melody and structure, but it's true that he often expended too much energy refining the surface of his compositions or orchestrating piano works that were already perfect in themselves. Ravel relied excessively on spontaneous inspiration, a precarious thing at the best of times, and perhaps made even more precarious by this perfectionism. As he himself admitted – "I can be occupied for several years without writing a single note … one must spend time in eliminating all that could be regarded as superfluous in order to realise as completely as possible the definitive clarity so much desired."

He spent his childhood in Paris, and enrolled at the Conservatoire in 1889. In the course of the next six years he studied with Fauré, among others, and developed a personal style that was characterized above all by unconventional harmonies. His progressiveness offended his conservative elders: in 1901, 1902 and 1903 he entered the Prix de Rome and was failed on each occasion, and his final attempt, in 1905, caused an outcry when Ravel was eliminated in the preliminaries. This setback did not inhibit Ravel's creativity and the next ten years saw the composition of his greatest works, including the *Rapsodie espagnole*, *Gaspard de la nuit* and *Daphnis et Chloé*. With the outbreak of World War I he tried to enter the services, but neither the army nor the air force wanted him (he was two kilos underweight, and too short), so he became an ambulance driver. He wrote: "They tell me that Saint-Saëns announced that during the war he has composed theatre music, songs … If instead he had been servicing Howitzers, his music might have been the better for it."

Ravel, however, did not gain from his engagement in the war, even though his beautiful *Le tombeau de Couperin* was written as a tribute to the dead. He was released from his duties in 1916 after suffering a complete physical collapse, and the death of his mother shortly afterwards seemed to push him into a slow but inexorable decline. From 1918, with the death of Debussy, Ravel was regarded as France's greatest composer, and was fêted all over Europe, but his creative powers were diminishing. The last two decades certainly produced some outstanding works – *L'enfant et les sortilèges*, the *Piano Concerto*, *Tzigane*, the *Violin Sonata* and *Boléro* – but most of his time was spent tampering with earlier compositions. In the last year of his life he was struck by a virulently degenerative brain disease; eventually he could not even sign his name. In December he risked a brain operation, and never regained consciousness.

L'enfant et les sortilèges

Written in 1925, to a libretto by Colette, *L'enfant et les sortilèges* (The Child and the Spells) is one of the most entertaining operas of the twentieth century. The central character is a spoiled brat who gets his comeuppance when the household objects he has abused – the sofa, the armchair, the clock and others – suddenly come to life. The trees and animals in his garden are equally hostile, and only when the child attends to a wounded squirrel do they forgive him. He is then returned home and, by implication, restored to innocence. The pictorial clarity of the whole opera is astonishing but perhaps the most magical moments are the scenes in the garden in which, through highly original instrumental colour, Ravel creates an utterly convincing world that is both seductive and sinister.

Ogéas, Collard, Berbie, Gilma, Herzog, Rehfuss, Maurane, Sénéchal; French Radio Chorus; French Radio National Orchestra; Maazel (Deutsche Grammophon)

Lorin Maazel is not known primarily for his work in the opera house, but this is a fine performance of Ravel's shimmering score – come the moment of reconciliation he is in his element, revelling in the opulent orchestral sonorities. The cast sings well, with the soprano Françoise Ogéas excelling as the child.

Daphnis et Chloé

Daphnis et Chloé, the finest of all French ballets, was commissioned by Serge Diaghilev for his Ballets Russes in 1909 (see p.547). Work on the score occupied the composer from then on until 1912, the same time that Stravinsky was working on another Diaghilev commission, *The Rite of Spring*. The two composers became friends at this point, and Stravinsky was later to recall that Ravel "was the only one to understand the *Rite*". Like Stravinsky's ballets, *Daphnis et Chloé* now survives not so much in the theatre as in the concert hall, through performances of the two orchestral suites into which Ravel split the ballet. However, the ballet really needs to be heard in its complete form, for *Daphnis et Chloé* is a tone poem in all but name, achieving, through adroit orchestration, vivid characterization of the two lovers, Daphnis's rival (the brutish Dorcon), and the gang of pirates who abduct Chloé (the story is taken from a third-century pastoral poem). In Ravel's words: "The work is constructed symphonically, according to a strict tonal plan by the method of a few motifs, the development of which achieves a symphonic homogeneity of style."

Boston Symphony Orchestra; New England Conservatory Chorus and Alumni Chorus; Munch (RCA)

In 1955, the date of this recording, no French orchestra approached the standard of the Boston Symphony, yet no US conductor was the equal of Charles Munch, who here achieves remarkable extremes of colour without affecting the intricate musical structure, and without recourse to sentimentality. Now available as a Hybrid SACD.

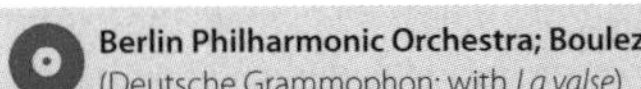

Berlin Philharmonic Orchestra; Boulez (Deutsche Grammophon; with *La valse*)

With *Daphnis et Chloé*, the combination of Pierre Boulez and a Berlin Phil in top form is a marriage made in heaven. More than any other recent recording Boulez makes this sound like a dramatic narrative, with beautifully judged tempi and a wide dynamic range. Not as sensuous as Munch's classic recording but even more exciting and with a fantastically high-octane reading of *La valse*.

Rapsodie espagnole & Pavane

Daphnis et Chloé might be Ravel's masterpiece, but he's better known for a number of smaller orchestral works, beginning with the *Rapsodie espagnole* of 1908. This four-movement evocation of Spain – all glittering colours and exotic atmosphere – manages to transcend a certain indebtedness to Rimsky-Korsakov and Chabrier, by way of its brilliantly dramatic orchestration: the first movement "Prelude à la nuit", in particular, creates a wonderful air of mystery and expectation. It was followed a few years later by another ostensibly "Spanish" piece, the *Pavane pour une infante défunte*. Originally written as a piano piece, its distinctly eighteenth-century soundworld conjures up a kind of fairy-tale solemnity (an infanta is a Spanish princess). Popular from its first performance, it's an extremely tender piece, with an apparent simplicity that belies the demands it makes on the performers – especially the horn player.

Detroit Symphony Orchestra; Paray (Mercury; with *La valse, Tombeau de Couperin, Alborado del gracioso* & Ibert *Escales*)

Like Munch, Paul Paray was a great interpreter of French music, and his performances of Ravel for Mercury are remarkable. As with Munch, the combination of French inspiration and American technique produces outstanding results – particularly in an intoxicating rendition of the *Rapsodie espagnole*.

Boléro: Montréal Symphony Orchestra; Dutoit (Decca; 2 CDs; with *La valse, Tombeau de Couperin, Boléro & Daphnis and Chloé Suite No. 2 etc*)

If you're looking for a more modern version of Ravel's major orchestral works, this Double Decca set provides top notch performances at outstanding value. The "Spanish" works, in particular, receive wonderfully idiomatic readings.

La valse & Boléro

It was largely thanks to Diaghilev's insistence that Ravel wrote the "choreographic poem" *La valse*, a work he finally completed in 1920. This is a waltz of sorts, but it's waltz music scarred by the experiences of wartime, turning the dance form that had recently been the toast of decadent Vienna into a vehicle for biting satire. Diaghilev rejected it and in 1928 the dancer Ida Rubinstein (whose company first performed *La valse*) asked Ravel to orchestrate some of Albéniz's piano music as a dance score. Instead he gave her *Boléro*, a piece that made his name internationally known. Commenting on its success, Ravel ruefully summarized the piece as "orchestration without music". It's built from an unwavering repeated phrase in C major, announced and maintained throughout by a snare drum, which the various orchestral instruments join at regular intervals until reaching the famous climax, a quarter of an hour later.

Boston Symphony Orchestra; Munch (RCA; with *Rapsodie espagnole* & Debussy *Images*)

For *Boléro* and *La valse* Munch is again a skilful advocate. *Boléro* is much more difficult to conduct than might be thought: the hardest task is for the snare-drummer to hold a steady tempo throughout. The drummer never loses concentration here, and Munch adopts a well-judged pulse, moulding a wonderfully rich orchestral texture.

Montréal Symphony Orchestra; Dutoit (Decca; 2 CDs; with *Rapsodie espagnole, Pavane, Tombeau de Couperin & Daphnis and Chloé Suite No. 2 etc*)

Dutoit never quite reaches the manic heights of Boulez in his performance of *La valse*, but it's a highly convincing version nevertheless. Similarly, his *Boléro* is one of the best accounts around, perfectly paced so that the tension builds to its inexorable conclusion.

Shéhérazade

Having failed to complete an opera based on *The Arabian Nights* (he only managed the overture), Ravel turned in 1903 to the *Shéhérazade* poems of Tristan Klingsor, a young symbolist whose mildly perfumed verses conjured up a fantasy landscape of the exotic Orient. The first of the three poems Ravel set, *Asie* (Asia), is also the longest; its fluid vocal line is borne by an orchestral score that evokes a voyage of discovery, full of rich and colourful sights and sounds (a rocking boat, Chinese princesses, a fierce executioner). "La flûte enchantée" is a simpler mood piece in which the sinewy arabesques of a flute remind Shéhérazade of her lover's kisses. The last song, "L'indifférent", is the most beautiful of all – its gentle languor feels close to the *Pavane pour une infante défunte*, as does its undertow of subdued melancholy.

Crespin; Orchestre de la Suisse Romande; Ansermet (Decca; with Berlioz *Les nuits d'été*)

Fantastically seductive singing from the great French soprano Régine Crespin: all the music's heavy-lidded, *fin de siècle* beauty comes across magnificently, while at the same time the words are conveyed with precision and poise. Ernest Ansermet's conducting is a model of sensitivity.

Hendricks; Orchestre de l'Opéra de Lyon; Gardiner (EMI; 2 CDs; with *Deux mélodies hébraïques & Cinq mélodies populaires grecques*, Duparc *Six mélodies avec orchestre*, Britten *Les Illuminations* & Berlioz *Les nuits d'été*)

Ravel's *Shéhérazade* simultaneously contains both a langu-orous heaviness and a fresh innocence of vision. Both these qualities are beautifully and dramatically conveyed by Barbara Hendricks, whose slightly hard but focused tones are softened by some exquisite orchestral playing.

Piano Concertos

"The music of a concerto ... should be light-hearted and brilliant, and not aim at profundity or at dramatic effects." Ravel's G major piano concerto certainly lives up to his dictum, and is one of his most lyrical and captivating scores. It was begun in 1929, when jazz was all the rage among the intelligentsia of Paris. The concerto is deeply infused with the idioms of jazz, but unlike Gershwin's *Rhapsody in Blue* (1924) this is a classically organized, three-movement structure, and it's this combination of opposites that gives the music such zest. It begins with a whipcrack, then hustles and gambols on towards the pivotal slow movement, whose opening unaccompanied tune suggests a Chopin nocturne in its purity and Rachmaninov in its breadth. A glittery yet brooding finale, less than half the length of its predecessor, is a perfect conclusion to this work of brilliant contrasts.

At the same time as he was working on the G major concerto, Ravel was writing a very different concerto for the pianist Paul Wittgenstein, brother of the philosopher. Wittgenstein had lost his right arm in World War I, and had begun to commission leading composers to write works for left hand alone. The astonishing achievement of Ravel's *Piano Concerto for Left Hand* is that it is never apparent to the listener that just one hand is being used, such is the complete integrity of the solo part. If it doesn't quite contradict Ravel's concerto dictum, it is one of the most serious of his works, permeated by a hard-driven energy and a sense of anxiety that borders on the tragic.

Piano Concerto in G Major: Michelangeli; Philharmonia; Gracis (EMI; with Rachmaninov *Piano Concerto No. 4*)

A classic account from Michelangeli: in the punchily rhythmic outer movements you're borne along by his panache and unforced wit, and in the middle movement he achieves a sonority and expressive range that is overwhelming. The finale is brisk, but his technical mastery is such that he almost whispers the piano part, barely touching the keys.

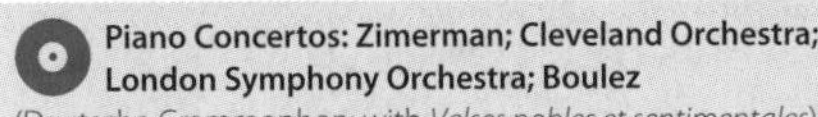

Piano Concertos: Zimerman; Cleveland Orchestra; London Symphony Orchestra; Boulez
(Deutsche Grammophon; with *Valses nobles et sentimentales*)

These are works in which clarity and precision are paramount and this recording really benefits from Deutsche Grammophon's great sound engineering. The performances are no less remarkable, with Krystian Zimerman displaying a breathtaking dynamism and his customary wide range of tonal colour, even in the faster movements.

String Quartet

Ravel was fast making a name for himself when he began composing the *String Quartet* in 1902, and this work – his first foray into chamber music – established him as a mature composer when it was premiered two years later. In his autobiography he stated that the *String Quartet* "more than any of my earlier works, was in line with my ideas of musical structure". Indeed, though the enthusiasm of youth is still very much present, the formal poise of the writing is what strikes you above all. Legend has it that Debussy thought Ravel's quartet bore too close a resemblance to his own, and there are undeniable similarities – both open with a movement in sonata form, for example, and both use the opening theme as the basis for the material of the other movements. However, from the second movement onwards the Ravel quartet displays a rhapsodic, indulgent quality that's miles away from Debussy, and in fact the older composer was a great admirer of the piece; on hearing it for the first time, he wrote to Ravel, saying "in the name of God, you must not tamper with this string quartet".

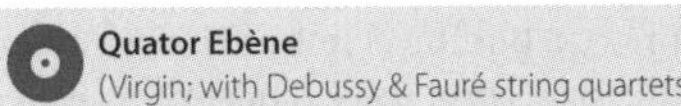

Quator Ebène
(Virgin; with Debussy & Fauré string quartets)

The best of recent versions of the oft-coupled Ravel and Debussy quartets (plus the rare Fauré quartet) comes from four young French men who really get under the skin of these works, bringing a wonderfully organic feel to all three of them. In the Ravel, in particular, the spontaneity of their playing really underlines the work's overriding melancholy.

Quartetto Italiano
(Philips; with Debussy *String Quartet*)

This is a classic recording, full of sinewy vigour and immense charm, recorded when the Quartetto Italiano were at their peak. There's a lot of spontaneity about their performance – particularly appropriate for Ravel's mercurial changes of mood and direction.

Tzigane

Ravel always took a special interest in performers who embodied strong folk traditions, and one of these was the Hungarian violinist Jelly d'Aranyi, whom Ravel heard improvising Gypsy music at the home of a friend in 1923, an event that proved to be the inspiration for *Tzigane*. Styled a "rhapsody for violin and piano", it was composed in the following year and dedicated to d'Aranyi, who gave the first performance. The violin part is vividly Hungarian in feeling but its virtuosity also makes a gesture in the direction of Paganini – *Tzigane* begins with a fearsome cadenza played solely on the G string, an improvisational-sounding passage that's reminiscent of Paganini's *Variations on a Theme from Rossini's Moses*, which is written entirely for the G string. The cadenza culminates with the piano's first entry and the work's main theme (which was heard, in a distended form, in the midst of the opening fireworks), setting up a white-hot exchange that continues right to the final bar.

Vengerov, Vinogradova (Biddulph; with works by Schubert, Tchaikovsky, Debussy and others)

Maxim Vengerov was fifteen years old when he recorded this album of violin showpieces, and his playing is some of the most remarkable ever captured on record. When you've got your breath back after his playing of *Tzigane*, listen to his performance of Ysaye's *Third Sonata* – it's the sort of performance that starts you thinking in terms of Faustian pacts.

Piano Music

The subtle colours and evanescent textures of Ravel's piano music are often compared to those of his older contemporary Debussy, but, in fact, Ravel got there first, defining a new distinctly French style of pianism with *Jeux d'eau* in 1902. The rippling arpeggiated figuration suggestive of water, which recurs throughout his piano works, is derived from Liszt, but Ravel imbues it with a new delicacy. In the six wistful pieces collectively called *Miroirs* (1905), the desire to convey an increasingly wide range of sensations, aural and visual, is even more refined and creates what are, in effect, miniature tone poems. An epic scale is realized in only one work, his piano masterpiece *Gaspard de la nuit* (1908) – a set of three ferocious and morbid pieces derived from the macabre prose-ballads of Aloysius Bertrand. With its broad washes of tonal colour and its gunfire-rapid repeated notes (a hallmark of Ravel's style), *Gaspard* is a barnstorming addition to the Lisztian repertoire, particularly remarkable for the way in which the overall texture is often made up of clearly delineated and individual strands of sound.

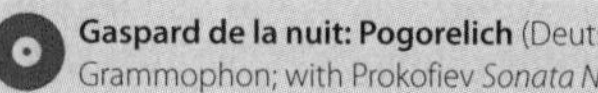

Gaspard de la nuit: Pogorelich (Deutsche Grammophon; with Prokofiev *Sonata No. 6*)

In one of his very best recordings, Ivo Pogorelich brings all his idiosyncratic brilliance to bear on *Gaspard de la nuit*. The variety of his touch and the extraordinary control of dynamics that he is capable of yields breathtaking results. The second movement "le gibet" (The Gibbet) can rarely have sounded spookier.

Complete Music for Solo Piano: Lortie (Chandos; 2 CDs)

This is a very satisfying survey of all Ravel's solo piano music from the consistently fine Canadian pianist, Louis Lortie, who seems to have an especially strong affinity with the music of Ravel. The *Gaspard* is outstanding, not as dangerous-sounding as Pogorelich but no less beguiling. His approach to the other works combines just the right balance between limpid tonal clarity and questing energy.

Max Reger (1873–1916)

Max Reger was the central figure of the "Back to Bach" movement. "For me", he once wrote, "Seb. Bach is the beginning and end of all music. All true progress is based on and rests in him!" However, Reger's respect for tradition was not simply a matter of the resurrection of the old ways of doing things, no more than the music of the similarly inclined Ferruccio Busoni (see p.119). Both men regarded themselves as progressives who, nonetheless, did not reject the past. And while Reger may have sometimes inveighed against the influence of Wagner, he grew up in his shadow and remained essentially a Romantic, albeit one who drew his strength from the tradition of Bach, Beethoven and Brahms.

Brought up in Weiden in Bavaria, Reger's initial musical training was with his father and, from the age of ten, with the town's organist Adalbert Lindner who eventually recommended his young pupil to his own teacher, Hugo Riemann. As a student of Riemann, whose assistant he became, Reger began his serious study of Bach, came into contact with Busoni and Strauss and made friends with the outstanding German organist, Karl Straube. Reger's studies were interrupted by a year of military service in 1897, which precipitated some kind of physical and mental breakdown prompting him to return home to Weiden, where, over the next three years, he composed mostly instrumental music, much of it for organ. In 1901 he moved to Munich, married the next year and, in 1905, got a position at the Akademie der Tonkunst but resigned after only one year. Following his recovery from a stroke – brought on by a combination of overwork and overeating – Reger took up prestigious teaching posts at both the university and the Conservatoire at Leipzig in 1907. By now his reputation as a performer and a composer was firmly established and in 1911 he was appointed conductor of the outstanding Meiningen court orchestra, a position he held until the orchestra was disbanded at the beginning of World War I. Living in Jena from 1915, it was on one of his weekly teaching trips to Leipzig that the composer – who was frequently dogged by ill-health – suffered a fatal heart attack at the age of just 43.

Reger's devotion to German polyphony has led to his being labelled "the second Bach", a nickname that had some justice in the case of his organ music which is the one area of his composition which has maintained its worldwide reputation – at least among organists. During his lifetime his status was close to that of Strauss, Mahler and Schoenberg, with the latter regularly programming Reger's works in the series of progressive music concerts that he organized in Vienna from 1918 to 1925. But like his admirer Hindemith, Reger was arguably too prolific (and too prolix) for his own good and his reputation has declined spectacularly. He produced music with an amazing facility, but it is sometimes hard to sort out the inspired from the merely proficient. Nevertheless, there is more to Reger's music than his enthusiasm for conventional forms (such as variations and fugues) might suggest, and he's a composer capable of assuming several different, and sometimes unexpected, guises.

Four Tone Poems

Reger's most appealing music is his least typical. The *Four Tone Poems after Arnold Böcklin* (1913) are works in which the composer goes some way to betraying his own principles. Suffused with richly chromatic harmonies, this is illustrative music from a composer forever extolling the supremacy of "absolute" music – that is, music that referred specifically to nothing outside itself. His inspiration came from four paintings by the Swiss artist Arnold Böcklin, a rather heavy-handed Symbolist specializing in mythical landscapes. Reger's interpretation of the paintings is powerfully evocative: the first piece, depicting a devout hermit playing his violin is full of longing and sweet despair (with modal harmony similar to Vaughan Williams's contemporary *Tallis Fantasia*). It's followed by the skittish "In the Play of the Waves" which sounds like a Mendelssohn scherzo refracted through the orchestral colouring of Strauss. In Reger's haunting vision of the "Isle of the Dead" – a painting which also prompted a piece by Rachmaninov (see p.435) – the weighted stillness of the scene brings an outpouring of rich, romantic sound, and the tranquillity of the closing music is some of the composer's finest. The uproarious "Bacchanal" ends what is one of Reger's most engaging works.

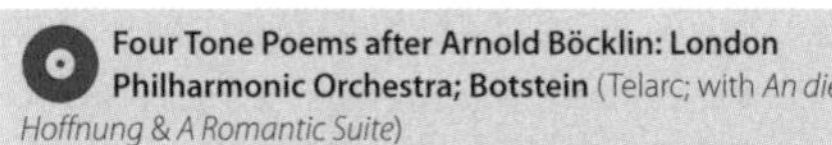

Four Tone Poems after Arnold Böcklin: London Philharmonic Orchestra; Botstein (Telarc; with *An die Hoffnung* & *A Romantic Suite*)

This disc is subtitled "Reger and Romanticism" and as well as the *Four Tone Poems after Arnold Böcklin* it contains the near contemporary orchestral song *An die Hoffnung* and the exquisite *A Romantic Suite* after J.F. Eichendorff. These dazzling and refulgent works, given loving performances by the LPO under Leon Botstein, show that Reger could on occasions be as susceptible to Wagner as he was to Brahms.

Orchestral Variations

Also enjoyable, in a less emotional way, are the sets of orchestral variations that Reger wrote on themes by Hiller and Mozart. Both sets reveal an obvious debt to Brahms's *Variations on a Theme by Haydn*, but they are more ambitious in scope, and each work culminates in a grandiose fugue. The *Variations and Fugue on a Theme by Hiller* (1907) takes a simple melody by the eighteenth-century composer and subjects it to eleven inventive, if sometimes overelaborate, variations in which brilliant orchestration and clever shifts of mood manage to sustain the listener's interest – but only just. The *Mozart Variations* (1914) are more rewarding, although there's something a little perverse in choosing as a theme the opening of the first movement of Mozart's A major piano sonata, which in the original sonata also goes through a series of variations. As with the *Hiller Variations*, Reger's response is always imaginative but this time there is less bombast, considerably more wit and a degree of tension in the eight variations, with a full-blooded climax to the closing the fugue.

Variations and Fugue on a Theme of Mozart; Hiller Variations: New Zealand Symphony Orchestra; Decker (Naxos)

This budget-price coupling of the *Mozart Variations* with the *Hiller Variations* is absolutely first class. Franz-Paul Decker and his New Zealand Orchestra may not be as polished as some, but this is nonetheless a warm and spirited version of two of Reger's most celebrated orchestral works.

Keyboard Music

Reger played the organ since early childhood and was completely steeped in the instrument's repertoire, especially the German Baroque masterworks. He wrote for the organ throughout his career, music of increasing difficulty which challenged his own technical ability and that of his friend Karl Straube, the player who most often championed it. Unsurprisingly, Reger was attracted to the Bachian forms of toccata, passacaglia, fantasia and fugue, bringing to them a monumentalism and a vivid chromatic harmonic language. The results can be amazingly exciting in the right hands but equally easily can feel overwrought and bombastic.

When it came to writing for the piano, Reger continued to think big: his best known work for the instrument, the *Variations and Fugue on a Theme of J.S. Bach* (1904), lasts around thirty minutes. However, the clear inspiration of Brahms's *Handel Variations* means that tensions between Classical constraint and the composer's latent Romanticism frequently favours the latter, and there is no hint of dryness even in the concluding seven-minute fugue. That Reger had a lighter side is evident from such early piano pieces as the *Five Humoresques* (1896), evocative miniatures with an imaginative playfulness and delicacy to rival those of Grieg.

Introduction, Passacaglia and Fugue in E Minor: Barber (Hyperion; with a selection of chorale preludes and the *Chorale Fantasia on Straf'mich nicht in deinem Zorn*)

A great introduction to the range of Reger's organ music, from the grandiose to the contemplative and improvisatory.

Playing on the organ of Limburg Cathedral, Graham Barber's greatest strength is his astute choice of registration (selection of stops) which creates tonal variety, prevents textures from getting muddy and even suggests a degree of wit in this otherwise serious music.

Bach Variations; Five Humoresques: Hamelin (Hyperion; with *Telemann Variations*)

Reger's piano music is finally getting the attention it deserves, and these accounts by Marc-André Hamelin set the bar extremely high. Not only does he meet the technical challenges with his customary flair, revealing unlooked for subtleties by his sheer range of tone colour, he also achieves exactly the right balance between structural cohesion and Romantic abandon.

Steve Reich (1936–)

Although other minimalist composers may have been more commercially successful, and several may be equally rigorous in their methods, none surpass Reich's music for emotional depth or sheer beauty. Born in New York, Reich was reared on Schubert and Beethoven before encountering Stravinsky's *Rite of Spring* at the age of fourteen, an event that helped to widen his musical horizons. After graduating in philosophy at Cornell University, Reich progressed to the Juilliard, where he met Philip Glass and Meredith Monk, then went on to study with both Berio and Milhaud.

In 1965, after a short spell in San Francisco, Reich moved back to New York, bought a batch of tape recorders and – while experimenting with identical tape loops of a street preacher – hit upon the technique of phase-shifting, in which the tapes gradually move out of synch then eventually move back into unison. He produced *It's Gonna Rain* (1965) and *Come Out* (1966) for tape, then began to re-create the effect with instruments, starting with *Piano Phase* (1967).

Continuing to investigate tape-looping and phasing, Reich collaborated with Philip Glass until they fell out, then in 1970 he went to Ghana

Steve Reich rehearsing with the Ensemble Intercontemporain in1986.

on a grant to study the music of the Ewe people. The subsequent *Drumming* (1971), written for bongos, marimbas, voices, glockenspiels, whistle and piccolo, marks the honing of Reich's technique – it's a bright and inventive piece with no melody or changes of rhythm or key, instead using slight changes in timing, pitch and timbre to maintain its momentum. Following on from that, *Music for Mallet Instruments, Voices and Organ* (1973) brought gushing reviews from American writers, while *Music for 18 Musicians* (1974–76) sold like rock music.

Crucial to an understanding of Reich's music, especially the early "process" or "systems" works, is an awareness of his advocacy of the importance of an audible connection between the compositional process and the way the music sounds, a connection he feels is absent from most modernist music. For the listener to fully appreciate and follow the process, he asserted, it must happen gradually.

Restlessly refining his ideas, Reich began studying Indonesian music, and in 1979 went to Israel to study Hebrew chant. The hugely symphonic *Desert Music* appeared in 1983 and was followed by the interlocking orchestral work *Four Sections* (1987) before he switched direction again with the award-winning *Different Trains* (1988) for the Kronos Quartet (plus "found" sounds and voices). His most ambitious project to date is *The Cave* (1993), a four-year work in collaboration with his wife, video artist Beryl Korot, for which he was given a million-dollar grant. Recorded in Israel and America, it presents a series of talking heads whose views on Arab or Israeli history were projected onto five large screens, their speeches punctuated by melodies performed by strings, percussion and four singers. It's an enthralling multimedia experience

More recently, Reich has completed the trilogy *Three Tales* (1998–2001), examining twentieth-century technology. Comprising *Hindenburg*, *Bikini* (as in Atoll), and *Dolly* (as in cloned sheep), the work represented a significant departure from the methods used in *Different Trains* and *The Cave*. In those earlier works Reich let the speech patterns determine the melodic shapes, whereas in *Three Tales* he adjusts the recordings in order to change the pitch and rhythm of the voices.

Early Works

The astonishing early tape works, *My Name Is*, *Come Out* and *It's Gonna Rain*, prefigured *Different Trains*, *The Cave* and *City Life* and anticipated techniques now common in hip-hop and related styles, while using them in ways those

Less is More? The Origins of Minimalism

As a generic description, "minimalism" might have been deployed to define any music of few notes (Webern, Satie, Ravel's Boléro), but in practice, the term evokes a specific sense of time and place, and a definite set of stylistic concerns.

While the public face of minimalism has become largely identified with Philip Glass and Steve Reich, who emerged in downtown New York during the late 1960s, the music's origins can be traced to California rather earlier in the decade. Paradoxically, for a genre that would eventually go mainstream and become a dollar-spinner, its roots were in scuzzy underground performance spaces in San Francisco where local musicians – Terry Riley being the most high profile – wrested an authentic musical language from a combination of rock, modern jazz, Indian and Indonesian music, and drug-fuelled psychedelia.

Such a heady brew was never going to sound like Western classical music, and especially *not* like the twelve-tone compositions that were *de rigueur* in university music departments across the US. This music dealt with another *actualité*. Cheap electric keyboards were available, expensive orchestras were not, and musicians whose world-view had been formed by rock and jazz were more susceptible to this experimental world than players from the local symphony orchestra. Riley's all-night concerts, where he improvised drones and generated repetitive loops with microphone feedback, are now the stuff of legend; and that same open-ended spirit informed his *In C*, written in 1964, and became a blueprint for everything that came later.

Contradicting the Western symphonic archetype of an argument-driven narrative, *In C* stresses the importance of an unfolding process beyond a finished, finite "masterwork". Riley's performance instructions fit onto one sheet of A4 paper that outlines 53 musical fragments – remarkable for a piece that can last over an hour. Players repeat each fragment at will, before jumping to the next module. The resulting free-form counterpoint demands that the musicians zone into each other's patterns as they elect when to move forward. Riley instilled into the performance of composed music the liberating air of democracy.

Associations were forming with Riley's East Coast colleagues. Another California-born composer, La Monte Young, had relocated to New York, bringing with him West Coast drones; and, in fact, it was Reich – on a visit to San Francisco – who suggested *In C*'s most striking feature, a briskly repeated "C" from the top of the piano that could act as a focal point of rhythmical orientation for the musicians.

Reich's own experiments with evolving repetitions were blossoming in sympathy. He created an intricate blurring of sound in two early tape pieces, *It's Gonna Rain* (1965) and *Come Out* (1966), by allowing two identical tapes to run simultaneously, then nudging one machine out of phase. Reich would soon apply this method of "phase shifting" to acoustic means in *Piano Phase* and *Violin Phase* (both 1967), works that used the experience of technology to open up new ways of listening. Meanwhile, Glass had stumbled across yet another method of treating rhythm from his transcriptions of Indian music. His earliest pieces grew from rhythmic cells that added new sub-clauses arranged thus: 1; 1+2; 2+3+4; 3+4+5+6 etc…

For an art music, minimalism quickly developed unheralded levels of popularity. Reich was signed to blue-chip classical label Deutsche Grammophon, and Glass scored a cult success at New York's Metropolitan Opera with *Einstein on the Beach* (1976). John Adams has become America's most performed composer by fusing minimalist principles with Romantic harmony, thereby skipping mid-twentieth century modernism. Although there are those who argue that minimalism is as dominant and dogmatic as the twelve-tone music it once offered an alternative to, every composer has needed to reconcile themselves with its impact – a genre once described as the twentieth century's last great "ism".

In C: Riley and Friends
(Sony)

This classic 1968 recording of *In C* – cleaned up and reissued in 2009 – is where minimalism starts. Terry Riley himself performs on a shrill and lusty soprano saxophone, while a collective of proto-minimalists (including trumpeter Jon Hassell and trombonist Stuart Dempster) create a beautiful, raggedy mess.

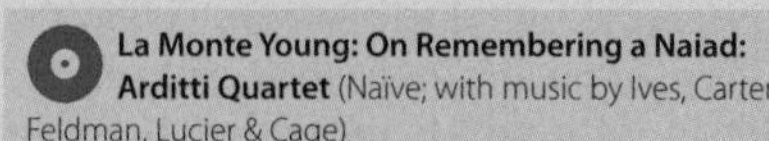

La Monte Young: On Remembering a Naiad: Arditti Quartet (Naïve; with music by Ives, Carter, Feldman, Lucier & Cage)

This early work by La Monte Young belongs to the same experimental tradition as the works by Ives, Feldman and Cage on the same disc, but Young is already pushing boundaries. Twelve-tone music is usually deployed to create a fractured narrative, but here it is employed to create long drone-like continuums.

genres never fully caught on to. *Come Out* (1966) is a quintessential Reich work for a number of reasons: there is the repetition of a small "cell" of material; it is based on a fragment of recorded speech; its rhythms are derived from vernacular speech patterns; it develops by use of phase-shifting; and it has a polemical purpose. *Come Out* was produced for a benefit concert in support of six black youths who had been beaten while in police custody. One of them told how he squeezed his bruises "to let some of the bruise blood come out to show them" so that he could leave the cells and go to hospital. Reich focused on the five words "come out to show them" and subjected them to a simple phasing process. The result is a coruscating counterpoint of syllables and phonemes which gradually lose their meaning and develop into a dense, hypnotic, sibilant screen of abstract sound.

Come Out; Piano Phase; Clapping Music; It's Gonna Rain: Tilles, Niemann, Hertenberger; Reich
(Nonesuch)

A crash course in early Reich, showing the discovery and development of the phase-shifting process, its application to live performers, and the beginnings of Reich's move away from simple phasing. By turns mesmerizing and visceral, this is genuinely ground-breaking stuff.

Music for 18 Musicians

Music for 18 Musicians is "classic" Reich, one of the works which moved the composer and American minimalism into the mainstream. Composed between 1974 and 1976, it marked an expansion of Reich's vocabulary because of its more varied instrumentation (strings, woodwinds, voices, pianos, and wood and metal percussion), its structure and its "harmonic speed" ("there's more harmonic movement in the first five minutes than in any other complete work of mine to date"). Previously, transitions in Reich's works had tended to be gradual but inexorable: pieces would conclude when the system on which they were based had worked itself through. But in *Music for 18 Musicians* Reich made "arbitrary" decisions about the shift from one section to the next, signalled by a phrase on the metallophone. The constant rhythms of piano and percussion are humanized by the voices and wind instruments, which sustain pulsing phrases for as long as their breath holds out. Based on a cycle of eleven chords, the piece is permeated by the spirit of the gamelan and of African pitched percussion, but Reich was also inspired by the music of the Notre Dame school (see p.405). Despite its insistent rhythm, *Music for 18 Musicians* is intricate and graceful, shimmering like sunlight on rippling water.

Reich
(ECM New Series)

The predominantly bright textures and instrumental colours of this piece are well captured by ECM, though the CD has less "top" than the original LP. In compensation, the ebb and flow of the bass clarinets has a more elemental swell. As well as performing and directing, the composer had a hand in mixing this recording.

Tehillim

Though an orchestral version was premiered by the New York Philharmonic in September 1982, *Tehillim* is best known in the chamber version for strings, woodwind, six percussion, three sopranos and an alto. The title is the Hebrew for "praises", and its four movements incorporate verses from Psalms 19, 34, 18 and 150. In contrast to the nimble, restless outer movements, the third ("with the merciful, you are merciful") is slow, translucent and airy, and point toward Reich's interest in Perotin and the Notre Dame school. It's relatively busy harmonically (and more chromatic than most of his works), and in place of the usual short, repeated motivic "cells", Reich uses long melodic phrases. This development arose from "the need to set the text in accordance with its rhythm *and* meaning." *Tehillim* evokes African music through its insistent and intricate percussion patterns; the European classical tradition through the contrapuntal interweaving of the voices; and, most significantly, Hebrew cantillation. Reich's achievement is to weave these complementary strands together in a manner which is mesmerizing, shimmering and utterly engaging.

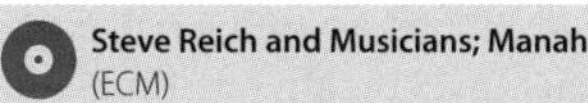

Steve Reich and Musicians; Manahan
(ECM)

This 1981 recording of the chamber version of *Tehillim* was made by the ensemble who premiered it. Both production and the performance impressively realize the bright, intricate yet direct quality of the music, with a sound picture that allows the individual parts to be clearly followed without losing the effect of the overall texture.

Different Trains

During childhood, Reich shuttled from coast to coast, visiting his divorced parents. He later realized that, as a Jew, he would have ridden very different trains if he had lived in occupied Europe. Responding to a commission from the Kronos Quartet, he took fragments from the taped reminiscences of his governess, a Pullman porter and survivors of the Holocaust, and hand-notated the speech rhythms and pitches for the quartet to play. The Kronos made four recordings (in concert, the quartet plays alongside tapes of the other parts), which were combined with train sounds and the speech fragments, sometimes in unison, sometimes echoing and commenting on the memories in an evocative, multilayered antiphony. As in *Come Out*, Reich weaves magical art from grim real-life events, but the complexities of *Different Trains* mark the emergence of a new form of music, which was developed in subsequent works like *The Cave* (1993) and *City Life* (1995).

Different Trains; Electric Counterpoint: Kronos Quartet; Metheny (Elektra Nonesuch)

The Kronos Quartet excel with their characteristic blending of technical precision and emotional commitment. It's coupled with *Electric Counterpoint* (1987), a work written for jazz guitarist Pat Metheny, which generates a complex, pulsing tapestry of sound from the interaction between the soloist and up to twelve taped parts.

Ottorino Respighi (1879–1936)

Such was the success of Verdi and Puccini, and of lesser figures such as Leoncavallo and Mascagni, that by 1900 Italy had almost no composers of instrumental music. A career in music meant a career in opera. The burden of restoring the nation's instrumental tradition fell largely on two men – Ferruccio Busoni (see p.119) and Ottorino Respighi.

Respighi was born in Bologna, where he trained as a violinist. In 1891 he became a student of the composer Giuseppe Martucci (a favourite of Toscanini), then in 1899 left for St Petersburg, where he began composition lessons with Stravinsky's teacher Rimsky-Korsakov, who heavily influenced his approach towards orchestration. He came back to Italy in 1903 and embarked upon a fairly successful career as a solo violinist, but his rapidly developing interest in Baroque and Classical instrumental music eventually led him to concentrate on writing rather than performing music. In 1913, after a stimulating spell in Berlin, he returned to Rome where he was appointed professor at the conservatory of Santa Cecilia. Nine years later, he became the conservatory's director, but resigned within two years in order to devote all his time to composing.

The trouble with Respighi's music is that it wears its influences on its sleeve, and of these influences none is more pronounced than Richard Strauss. The habitual classification of Respighi as the "Italian Strauss" was dismissed by the composer's widow in her biography of her husband, where she stoutly defended his preference for Classical structure. There are indeed many works by Respighi in which he upholds the values of his illustrious predecessors, re-creating the logical lines of the eighteenth century, but much of Respighi's neo-classicism amounts to little more than skilful pastiche. For the foreseeable future, the popularity of his overblown orchestral poems is likely to obscure Respighi's affection for formal clarity.

Orchestral Music

Respighi's most famous compositions are his three technicolour portrayals of Italy's capital city: *Fountains of Rome* (1916), *Pines of Rome* (1924) and *Roman Festivals* (1929). The grandiose and tuneful first part of this "Roman Triptych" is the best, in the sense that it is the most idiosyncratic, even if it does reflect the styles of Debussy, Ravel and, inevitably, Richard Strauss. Melodically, the *Pines of Rome* is heavy going, but the orchestration is vivacious enough to overcome the cumbrousness of the material. The gaudy *Roman Festivals* has been attacked for its fascistic undertones, and it doesn't stand up to comparison with Strauss's earlier treatment of a similar subject in *Aus Italien*.

Respighi had a genuine interest in earlier music, adopting a modal approach for some of his concertos and making an edition of Monteverdi's *Orfeo*. Several of his most popular orchestral works are transcriptions of Renaissance or Baroque pieces – albeit given an extremely lush and somewhat Pre-Raphaelite tint. *Gli uccelli* (The Birds) takes five such pieces (two by Pasquini, one by de Gallot, one by Rameau, and one anonymous) and dresses them up in a manner that all but disguises their origins.

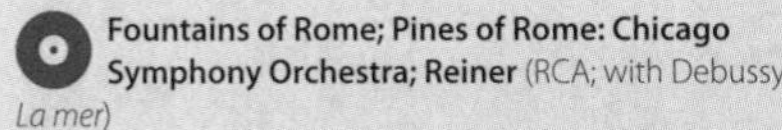

Fountains of Rome; Pines of Rome: Chicago Symphony Orchestra; Reiner (RCA; with Debussy *La mer*)

Recorded in 1959, Reiner's sumptuous, sultry accounts of the Roman diptych have never been bettered. They are available in two different couplings from RCA – the one listed above, and another with Mussorgsky's *Pictures at an Exhibition*. Both are dazzling throughout.

Fountains of Rome; Pines of Rome; Roman Festivals: Royal Philharmonic Orchestra; Bátiz (Naxos)

This budget recording is not very far behind its full-price rivals in terms of quality. A top-class orchestra and conductor give inspired readings, spontaneous, lively and full of character.

Gli ucelli; Trittico Botticelliano; Antiche danze ed arie: I Solisti Veneti; Scimone (Warner)

I Solisti Veneti, a group best known for their performances of Italian Baroque music, turn their attention to more modern music – albeit of an antique hue – with remarkably effective results. Their string sound is warm and intimate, and the emphasis is on the comforting sensuousness of these works.

Violin Sonata

Respighi's predilection for Classical form is perhaps best realized in the *Violin Sonata* of 1916–17, a work championed by many soloists (including Jascha Heifetz), but still little known. Written on a grand scale and demanding a lot of both performers, it is characterized throughout by beautiful melodies, especially in the lyrical opening movement. The finale, a showcase for Respighi's technical dexterity, is a brilliantly written passacaglia, in which a set of twenty variations is built upon a ground first established in a ten-bar bass passage.

Mordkovitch, Benson (Chandos; with Ravel *Violin Sonata & Sonate posthume*)

Lydia Mordkovitch and Clifford Benson give an affectionate and subtle performance of Respighi's sonata, which is characterful without ever degenerating into mere showiness. Their account of the Ravel sonata isn't quite as persuasive, and it's doubtful if anyone could make a strong case for Ravel's youthful *Sonate posthume*.

Wolfgang Rihm (1951–)

In his own words, Wolfgang Rihm is a composer "who writes not only with his pencil, but also with his nerve ends". He is also dauntingly prolific, with a work-list that contains more than 200 pieces in almost every conceivable genre: opera and ballet, quartet and symphony, concerto and lied, oratorio and organ solo. Yet his fecundity is not achieved by resorting to simple formulas: on the contrary, such is his breadth of expression that it is often difficult to fathom what stylistic traits link one work to another.

Rihm studied with Stockhausen in 1972–73, when the latter's own music was expanding in many different directions. By then Rihm had already begun attending the new music courses in Darmstadt, that hotbed of creativity and factionalism (see p.384); since 1978 he has been on the teaching staff there. His already burgeoning reputation was firmly established by his first two operas, *Faust und Yorick* (1977) and *Jakob Lenz* (1979). The former is based on a sketch by the absurdist playwright Jean Tardieu; the latter derives from the novella *Lenz* by Georg Büchner, whose play *Woyzeck* is the source of Alban Berg's opera *Wozzeck*.

The stage has provided a constant stimulus. The ballet *Tutuguri* (1982) uses a text by Antonin Artaud, proponent of the Theatre of Cruelty, whose work and ideas form the basis of the opera *Die Eroberung von Mexico* (The Conquest of Mexico; 1992), a multi-layered spectacle that stands as Rihm's most ambitious stage work. The East German playwright Heiner Müller has also been an important influence, furnishing text for two further stage works, *Die Hamletmaschine* (1987) and *Oedipus* (1987), as well as for *Frau/Stimme* (Woman/Voice), a piece for "soprano and orchestra with soprano".

Away from the stage, it is Rihm's orchestral music that has made the greatest impact. His violin concerto *Gesungene Zeit* (Time Chant; 1992) has gained wide circulation thanks to the advocacy of Anne-Sophie Mutter, for whom it was composed. And he has written several pieces "*in memoriam* Luigi Nono", including *La lugubre gondola/Das Eismeer* (Lugubrious Gondola/Sea of Ice; 1994), while a series of orchestral works

Wolfgang Rihm gets some musical assistance from his daughter Katia.

called *Vers une symphonie fleuve* (Towards a Symphony River) has occupied him through the last decade – there have been four so far, plus *fleuve V*, a kind of pendant premiered in 2000.

Yet Rihm has not neglected chamber music: besides seven solo piano works entitled *Klavierstück* (1970–80), he has written almost as many string quartets as Shostakovich, and many works for piano trio, string trio and other three-instrument line-ups. If the sheer volume of Rihm's work is bewildering, and if his own writings (at least in translation) offer little illumination for the interested listener, he remains a questing and mercurial talent.

Deus Passus

"In my opinion, the suffering God … is the central figure of Christian thought. This is where Christianity differs from other religions." Thus Wolfgang Rihm elucidated the principle underlying his *Deus Passus*, the Passion setting he was commissioned to write by the Stuttgart Bach Academy to mark the new millennium and the 250th anniversary of the death of J.S. Bach. Using fragments from the Luke gospel, interspersed with the *Stabat Mater* and liturgical texts relating to Holy Week, *Deus Passus* – unlike the Bach Passions – is not a dramatic work. Rather, it is a meditation on spiritual pain, not solely of the crucified Christ, but also of humanity in general.

The music is intense and generally sparse, evoking the world of the Bach Passions without resorting to pastiche. Each episode of the ninety-minute piece is eloquently brief, building to a climax that is one of Rihm's most remarkable creations. Following the hushed discovery of the empty tomb, *Deus Passus* concludes with an austere and profoundly moving setting of "Tenebrae" by the great German Jewish poet Paul Celan – a conception that universalizes the whole work by addressing a world in which the values of Christianity have failed.

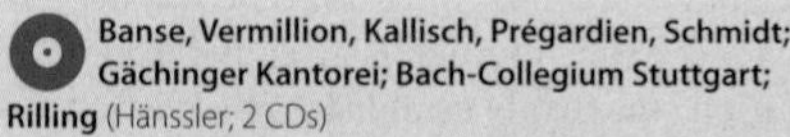

Banse, Vermillion, Kallisch, Prégardien, Schmidt; Gächinger Kantorei; Bach-Collegium Stuttgart; Rilling (Hänssler; 2 CDs)

Conducted by Bach specialist Helmut Rilling, the director of the Stuttgart Academy, this live recording of the world premiere has immense integrity and authority. The soloists are excellent without being over-assertive, as befits a piece that is concerned above all with collective experience.

Gesungene Zeit

A violin concerto in all but name, *Gesungene Zeit* (Time Chant) presents the solo instrument, as the title implies, at its most vocal: "instrumental virtuosity", Rihm says of the piece, and of its dedicatee, Anne-Sophie Mutter, "is an enhancement of vocal abilities." From the first, almost inaudible phrase, the violin is hardly ever silent, singing mostly at the very top of its range.

At first the ear barely notices the small orchestra's presence, so lustrous is the writing for solo violin. A crescendo from low strings and brass, and a disputatious clatter of percussion, briefly rouse the ensemble to greater assertiveness. The soloist, meanwhile, continues in meditative serenity, bow occasionally bearing down hard on the strings to produce a harsh, folk fiddler's rasp. The second movement continues in similar vein, but after a short struggle for dominance, the soloist briefly disappears beneath orchestral turbulence. Loud brass expletives and repetitive string figures disrupt the smooth progress, but Rihm's plaintive "time chant" cannot be subdued so easily. The violin rises again to the surface, leading us back to the silence from which the music shimmered into life half an hour earlier.

Mutter; Chicago Symphony Orchestra; Levine (Deutsche Grammophon; with Berg *Violin Concerto*)

Without a virtuoso soloist, the unvarying tempo of *Gesungene Zeit* might quickly lose our interest, but with a player such as Mutter it is an enchanting rhapsody. Her control of the many high pianissimos is unwavering, and James Levine leads the Chicago orchestra with the utmost discretion. Berg's *Violin Concerto*, eloquently played, makes the ideal companion piece.

String Quartets

Rihm's most characteristic chamber pieces are his ten numbered string quartets. The shadow of Beethoven's late quartets hovers over all these pieces, but as models of dense argument rather than as sources of quotation. *Quartet No. 3* (1977), entitled *Im Innersten* (Into the Innermost), opens with a flourish that briefly coalesces into expansive melody before a mood of restless anxiety establishes itself. The pattern of contrasts continues, leading, in the long final movement, to passages where time seems suspended and the players float free of each other.

The single movement of *Quartet No. 5* (1983) avoids dramatic contrasts. It is agitated, relentless and impatient in its forward momentum. The players' bows pummel rather than caress the strings, pizzicatos have a savage intensity, and the whole has the feel of a rancorous argument in which the participants eventually reach a plateau of exhausted disagreement.

In *Quartet No. 8* (1989), silence plays such a significant part that it might be seen as a fifth instrument. In addition, the performers are called on to rustle paper and, in the final moments, to "write" on their parts with their bows. This addition of a quasi-theatrical element is matched by the dramatic gestures of the music itself, with its ostinatos, harmonics and pizzicatos swirling around the silences with dizzying intensity.

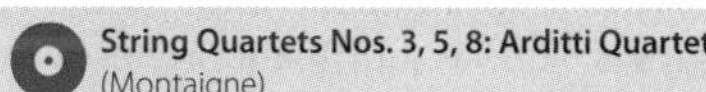
String Quartets Nos. 3, 5, 8: Arditti Quartet (Montaigne)

The Ardittis are famous for the apparent ease with which they take the most testing new music into their repertoire. Rihm stretches them to the limit, but they are equal to the challenge. As dedicatees of all three pieces, their authority is unimpeachable, as are their performances.

Nikolai Rimsky-Korsakov (1844–1908)

Rimsky-Korsakov is honoured as an inspirational teacher and as a fine orchestrator of other composers' music, but of his own compendious output only one orchestral score – *Scheherazade* – has made a really lasting impact outside of his native Russia.

Born into the aristocracy, he received a standard musical education, but his primary ambition was to enter the navy, which he did in 1856, aged only 12. Based in St Petersburg, he was deeply affected by the nationalistic music of Glinka and was encouraged by Balakirev to begin a symphony despite his tenuous grasp of the basics of harmony and tonality. In 1865, after two and a half years at sea, he applied himself to the study of theory and resumed work on his symphony; four years later he completed Dargomyzhsky's opera *The Stone Guest* – the first of several such secondhand projects. In 1871, though still ignorant of the fine details of compositional technique, he was appointed a professor of composition and orchestration at the St Petersburg Conservatory, and worked in private to obtain a better knowledge of the subject he was teaching. It was not until 1876, when he began editing a collection of Russian folk songs, that he perfected his technique and developed a genuine musical identity of his own.

From 1882 he began revising Mussorgsky's music (see p.373) and after Borodin's death in 1887 he assisted Glazunov in the completion of *Prince Igor* (see p.87), a project that coincided with the composition of his own *Scheherazade*. After attending the first Russian performance of Wagner's *Ring* cycle, he devoted most of his remaining years to opera. These years were interrupted by illness, but in 1896 he managed to produce an orchestration and revision of Mussorgsky's *Boris Godunov*.

In 1905 he ran head first into the authorities for openly supporting the revolutionaries, and the subsequent ban on his music spurred him to compose his last opera, *The Golden Cockerel*. Based upon Pushkin's satirical attack on autocracy, this too was banned and was not performed until the year after his death.

Rimsky-Korsakov's music is famous not so much for what it says but for the manner in which it says it. He was a brilliant orchestrator and contributed as much to the development of the craft within Russia as did Berlioz in France. Like Berlioz he was liberated by his lack of proficiency at the piano, and thought primarily in terms of orchestral textures, developing a style that made adventurous use of primary instrumental colours, progressive harmonies and innovative part-writing. *Scheherazade* is one of the greatest works of nineteenth-century Russia, but some have argued that Rimsky-Korsakov's influence is his most important legacy. Had it not been for him, the music of Mussorgsky may have remained unknown, and his efforts to promote Glinka's nationalist ideals proved extremely effective. Of those he taught, Glazunov, Prokofiev and Stravinsky were the most significant; the last of the three said of him, "he made me the most precious gift of his unforgettable lessons", and in *The Firebird* (see p.548) produced a powerful testimony to the depth of Rimsky-Korsakov's impact.

Sadko

Rimsky-Korsakov regarded opera as "essentially the most enchanting and intoxicating of lies", and most of his operas are an exotic blend of supernatural elements within a Russian folk setting. Few productions take place outside of Russia, even though they contain some of his most original and thrilling music. *Sadko* (1896), based on an episode in the eleventh-century epic the *Novgorod Cycle*, he regarded as his best work in the genre, but even here the emphasis is on spectacle rather than coherent narrative, and the work is more of a sprawling musical pageant than an opera. Made up of seven tableaux, it tells of the minstrel Sadko, whose adventures take him from Novgorod to the bottom of the ocean, where he almost marries the sea princess Volkhova. The interplay between fantasy and reality is handled with dazzling skill: chromaticism delineates the fantasy domain; diatonicism, the earthly world. Above all else, *Sadko* is a virtuoso display of picture-painting in music, with Rimsky-Korsakov equally adept at evoking the sombre beauty of Lake Ilmen (Tableau 2) as he is at capturing an undersea party and a riot of storms and hurricanes (Tableau 6).

Galusin, Tarassova, Alexashkin, Tsidipova; Kirov Chorus and Orchestra; Gergiev (Philips; 3 CDs)

This live performance is remarkable for its closely knit ensemble singing: even so, the muscular tenor of Vladimir Galusin as Sadko really stands out. Valentina Tsidipova's Princess and Sergei Alexashkin's Sea King play their supernatural roles with athletic flair, doing much to make Tableau 6 seem like the best thing the composer ever wrote.

Scheherazade

Rimsky-Korsakov's decision to use *The Arabian Nights* as the basis for an orchestral work was symptomatic of the attraction that neighbouring Islamic cultures held for many Russian composers. Each of the "Mighty Handful" (Cui, Balakirev, Borodin, Mussorgsky and Rimsky-Korsakov) wrote Orientalist music, and Rimsky-Korsakov's output is particularly dominated by the trend.

Lasting some forty minutes, *Scheherazade* (1888) contains an abundance of beautiful melodies which are carried on a sensual wash of sound. Different moods and pictures are conjured by the music, but the composer denied that *Scheherazade* was a programmatic piece – it was, he insisted, merely a suite of fairy-tale images of the Orient, rather than a sequence of episodes relating to the stories told by the young Scheherazade to delay her execution. The beguiling, sinuous violin solo in the third of the four movements, "The Young Prince and the Young Princess", is perhaps the most effortlessly beautiful moment in a work which in places sounds like an anticipation of Debussy's hedonistic sound-world.

Kirov Orchestra; Gergiev (Philips; with Balakirev *Islamey* & Borodin *In the Steppes of Central Asia*)

The most viscerally exciting account available of *Scheherazade* is this 2002 live recording from Valery Gergiev and his Kirov forces. There's an amazingly organic feel to this performance, each section seems to grow naturally from the next, and the big moments have never sounded so exhilarating.

Royal Philharmonic Orchestra; Beecham (EMI; with Borodin *Polovtsian Dances*)

This classic account from the late 1950s still holds up very well indeed, thanks to Beecham's remarkable sensitivity to the work's light and shade. In his hands it becomes a brilliant piece of theatre music (though Rimsky-Korsakov is known to have hated dancers interpreting his work).

Antar

Antar, another exotic fairy tale with a Middle Eastern setting, was actually begun before *Scheherazade* in 1868, but Rimsky-Korsakov made several revisions to it, transforming it from his second symphony into "a poem, suite, fairy tale, story, anything you like, but not a symphony". The first of its four movements tells how the warrior poet Antar saves a gazelle that has been attacked by a great bird. The gazelle turns out to be Gul Nazar, Queen of Palmyra, who promises him the three great joys of life – revenge, power and love – which are then depicted in the following three movements. The languid "big tune" that recurs in all three movements is employed somewhat in the manner of Tchaikovsky, though Rimsky-Korsakov lacked his colleague's febrile intensity and, if anything, rather underworks its potential. Nevertheless this is a beautiful piece, full of the subtle instrumental colouring that made Rimsky-Korsakov so revered as an orchestrator, even though it ultimately lacks the thrilling impact of *Scheherazade*.

Philharmonia; Svetlanov (Hyperion; with *Russian Easter Festival Overture*)

Exquisite playing from the Philharmonia, enhanced by Hyperion's wonderfully natural sound. The veteran Russian conductor Yevgeny Svetlanov concentrates on colouristic detail and creating a genuinely fairy-tale atmosphere. It is coupled with a lively performance of the sparkling *Russian Easter Festival Overture*, a work meant to convey the joyous excitement and solemnity of the Easter morning service.

Joaquín Rodrigo (1901–1999)

Outside of his native Spain, Joaquín Rodrigo is one of twentieth-century music's one-hit wonders, although the beautiful *Concierto de Aranjuez* (1939) for guitar and orchestra is quite some hit. Inspired by the rococo palace at Aranjuez in southern Spain, it succeeds in re-creating something of the elegance and formality of Spain in the eighteenth century. Its slow movement, in particular, has assumed an almost talismanic popularity and has even inspired a brilliant jazz tribute by Gil Evans and Miles Davis, *Sketches of Spain*, as well as a surprisingly effective version by the Grimethorpe Colliery Band.

Blind from the age of 3, Rodrigo revealed an innate talent for music in childhood and was sent to study composition with Francisco Antich in Valencia (1920–23). He later became a pupil of Dukas (see p.166) at the École Normale de Musique in Paris, where he met and received encouragement from his compatriot Manuel de Falla. Following his marriage to the Turkish pianist Victoria Kamhi in 1933, he returned briefly to Spain but then, on receiving a grant, went back to Paris to study musicology. With the outbreak of the Spanish Civil War in 1936 he decided to stay in Paris, returning at the end of hostilities. Rodrigo's politics are something of a grey area. It has been argued by his friends that he was a canny individual who merely paid lip service to Franco's repressive regime; outward signs seem to indicate that his views were in accordance with those of Franco's government, and there is no doubt that he was the musician most favoured by the administration after the premiere of the *Concierto de Aranjuez* in 1940.

Thereafter he was firmly ensconced as Spain's leading composer. In 1944 he was appointed music adviser to Spanish Radio, and two years later was appointed to the Manuel de Falla chair, which was created for him at the University of Madrid. A full life as both an academic and a composer followed, though his tendency was to repeat the musical formula of the *Concierto de Aranjuez* in his later concertos for piano, violin, cello and flute. But, while he was undoubtedly musically conservative, Rodrigo nonetheless did Spanish music an important service by helping to preserve the country's musical identity following the traumas of the Civil War.

Guitar Concertos

The guitar is the instrument that Rodrigo is most associated with and although he never learned to play it he had the advantage of close associations with guitarists of the calibre of Regino Sainz de la Maza and Segovia. His musical nationalism is in a different mould from that of Falla, Albéniz and Granados – the big three of modern Spanish music. Whereas they embarked on a deep exploration of the forms of Spanish popular and art music, and transmuted those forms into their compositions, Rodrigo's approach is more generalized, and he is largely content to create attractive melodies and rhythms that generally evoke Spain's sunny atmosphere and traditional culture without recourse to specific folk rhythms. The *Concierto de Aranjuez* is suffused with a Mediterranean spirit, and an underlying nostalgia for an older and more chivalrous Spain. This conservatism is even more marked in the beautifully poised *Fantasia para un gentilhombre* (1954), in which Rodrigo pays homage to the eighteenth century by transforming a selection of dances, collected by the Baroque guitarist Gaspar Sanz, into what is in effect a guitar concerto. The "gentilhombre" is the work's dedicatee, Segovia.

Concierto de Aranjuez; Fantasia para un gentilhombre: Romero; Academy of St Martin-in-the-Fields; Marriner (Philips; with *Invocación y danza* & *Tres pequeñas piezas*)

Spanish guitarist Pepe Romero delivers fine performances of two of Rodrigo's most celebrated works – the flamenco quality of his playing seems completely appropriate for the *Concierto de Aranjuez*. The balance between soloist and orchestra is highly satisfying, with every detail finely etched.

Concierto de Aranjuez; Fantasia para un gentilhombre: Bream; Chamber Orchestra of Europe; Gardiner; RCA Victor Chamber Orchestra; Brouwer (RCA; with *Invocación y danza* & *Tres piezas españolas*)

Julian Bream was a highly sensitive performer and this recently remastered all-Rodrigo disc makes an excellent alternative to the above. Bream is not so hard-edged a player as Romero – his are dreamier, more Romantic interpretations, with a distinctively ripe tone.

Gioacchino Rossini (1792–1868)

Italian operatic life during the first half of the nineteenth century was dominated by one man – Gioacchino Rossini. Between *Demetrio e Polibio*, written before 1809, and *Guillaume Tell*, less than twenty years later, he completed nearly forty operas, taking the first decisive steps towards the establishment of Italian music drama. Donizetti and Bellini worked in his shadow, and it was only when Verdi reached maturity in the late 1850s that Rossini was replaced at the centre of Italian operatic life. His impact upon the development of opera was immense: he was, for example, the first to do away with unaccompanied recitative, thus making the opera a continuous musical fabric, and he was the first to write out all the embellishments for his singers, not leaving anything to chance. But the key to his success was the sheer tunefulness of his music, a quality which seemed to cause him no effort – "Give me a shopping list and I'll set it to music", he once said.

Praise for Rossini was not universal, however. Berlioz was speaking for many non-Italians when he raged against Rossini's conveyor-belt creations: "Rossini's melodic cynicism, his contempt for dramatic expression and good sense, his endless repetition of a single form of cadence, his eternal puerile crescendo and brutal bass drum, exasperated me to such a point that I was blind to the brilliant qualities of his genius, even in his masterpiece, the *Barber*, exquisitely scored though it is." Making an exception for the enduring popularity of the *Barber of Seville*, Berlioz's opinion has become increasingly common, for Rossini's operas do indeed seem simple after Wagner or Strauss.

Rossini was a renowned gourmand.

However, this simplicity is part of Rossini's strength. There is a directness and immediacy to his work that is missing from that of his Italian predecessors and contemporaries, whose plots seem ludicrously entangled alongside Rossini's, and whose characters appear bloodless in comparison.

Rossini was born the son of a trumpeter and a singer. Some time soon after his eighth birthday he composed his first opera and his first commission came before his eighteenth birthday. In 1812 he had a work performed at La Scala, Italy's most prestigious opera house, and in the following year *Tancredi* and *L'italiana in Algeri* established his name outside Italy. Before long he had been appointed music director of the opera houses of Naples and was producing an enormous amount of music for them, including *Otello* and *Il barbiere*, *La Cenerentola*, *La gazza ladra* and *Mosè in Egitto*.

In 1822 he married, and soon after visited Vienna where, reputedly, he met Beethoven. Two years later, aged only 32, he moved to Paris, where he composed the epic *Guillaume Tell* (1829). Whether from doubts about his own powers or sheer exhaustion, he composed no more operas. He did write the extraordinary *Stabat Mater*, but for all its acclaim it did not inspire Rossini to return to full-time composition. Perhaps with the success of Verdi and the advances of Wagner, he thought himself incapable of producing any new opera worthy of his name and reputation.

Viva Rossini
(Testament)

This album of classic Rossini recordings from between 1903 and 1940 makes a fine introduction to Rossini's operas. Among the highlights are Tito Ruffo's grand and idiosyncratic singing of "Largo al factotum" and an even more astounding performance by Luisa Tetrazzini of "Una voce poco fa" from the same opera.

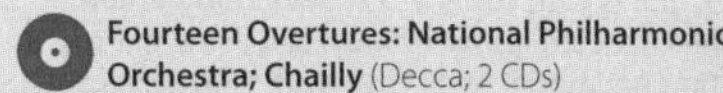

Fourteen Overtures: National Philharmonic Orchestra; Chailly (Decca; 2 CDs)

Rossini's opera overtures are among the most sparkling ever written and create a real frisson of excitement when heard before an opera but function perfectly satisfactorily out of a theatrical context. Chailly directs scintillating performances which include some obscurer ones as well as old favourites like *William Tell* and *The Barber of Seville*.

L'italiana in Algeri

For *L'italiana in Algeri* (The Italian Girl in Algiers), Rossini turned to an established comic libretto by Angelo Anelli, commissioned a quick revision and, so it is claimed, composed the two-and-a-quarter-hour score in twenty-seven days. It was his first successful comic opera, judged by Stendhal to be "perfection … as gay as our world is not." Anelli's tale is a romantic farce with an exotic setting: the Bey Mustafà is bored with his wife Elvira and tells Ali, the captain of his corsairs, to find him a European wife. The Italian girl Isabella, in search of her lover Lindoro (who is being held captive by the Bey), is shipwrecked, along with her elderly admirer Taddeo, and brought to Mustafà, who is captivated by her. When Isabella learns of Lindoro's imprisonment she plans their escape by telling the Bey that she wants to make him her "Pappatacci", the title given to men who allow their women absolute freedom. As Isabella and Lindoro's ship leaves, Elvira and Mustafà are reunited and all ends happily. The pacing is manic and the comedy thoroughly daft – as exemplified by the "sneezing" quintet (part of the Act 2 escape plan) and the Pappatacci coronation (almost certainly a parody of Masonic induction ceremonies). While *L'italiana* has an undertow of seriousness, the traditions of *commedia dell'arte* lie behind the opera's drastic changes of pace and mood, and in the characterization of the buffoonish Mustafà and idiotic Taddeo you can clearly detect the clowning of Italian street theatre.

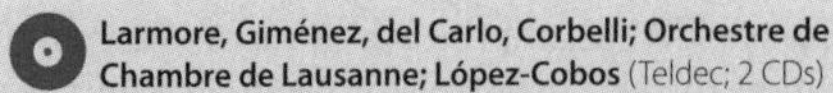

Larmore, Giménez, del Carlo, Corbelli; Orchestre de Chambre de Lausanne; López-Cobos (Teldec; 2 CDs)

Jennifer Larmore's mezzo has an unusually warm lower register and a thrilling top that comes just as easily. The rest of the cast are uniformly splendid. As Lindoro, the underrated Raúl Giménez conjures a portrayal of wit, ease and charm that eclipses every other interpretation on record. Jesús López-Cobos directs a lively, rhythmically precise account of the score.

Simionato, Sciutti, Valletti, Petri; La Scala Chorus and Orchestra; Giulini (Urania; 2 CDs)

Taped in the studio after a 1953 La Scala production, this performance glows with confidence and good humour. Giulini and his orchestra provide some sparkling energy and the casting is a model of its kind, with Graziella Sciutti a spirited Elvira and Giulietta Simionato a graceful and deliciously sly Isabella. The score is cut and the mono sound will be a drawback for some, but this is a very special recording.

Il Barbiere di Siviglia

Operatic folklore has it that *Il Barbiere di Siviglia*, Rossini's comic masterpiece, was composed in just a fortnight, a feat of which he was certainly capable, though the music is so original and the characterizations so rounded that the tale is unlikely. Nowadays it's one of the most popular Italian operas, but it wasn't an immediate hit – indeed the first performance, in Rome in February 1816, was one of operatic history's greatest disasters. Everything that could have gone wrong did go wrong, and by the second act the music was inaudible above the din of the audience. As the critic Castil-Blaze wrote afterwards, "All the whistlers of Italy seemed to have given themselves a rendezvous for this performance".

The source of the libretto is a play by Beaumarchais, covering events in the life of the libidinous Duke of Almaviva – the philandering aristocrat of the later Beaumarchais work that became the text for Mozart's *Le nozze di Figaro* (see p.358). The world of *Il barbiere* doesn't have the ambiguities and depths of *Le nozze*, but as a straightforward, life-affirming comic opera it has no equal. Each of its arias is a highlight, and some of them are truly astonishing – Figaro's "Largo al factotum" is of course one of opera's great bravura set pieces, while Almaviva's "Ecco ridente" is one of the most beautiful things Rossini ever wrote. A characteristic device used to startling effect throughout the opera is the "Rossinian Crescendo", whereby the composer takes a theme and repeats it, each time at a higher pitch and with a larger orchestral accompaniment.

Gobbi, Callas, Alva, Ollendorff, Zaccaria, Carturan, Carlin; Philharmonia Chorus & Orchestra; Galliera (EMI; 2 CDs)

This 1957 studio performance boasts the sublime partnership of Maria Callas and Tito Gobbi. The latter's Figaro has a waggish charm that all but overcomes the restrictions of the studio. Callas is only slightly less convincing (but then, so is the role of Rosina), and Luigi Alva sings Count Almaviva with great elegance and charm.

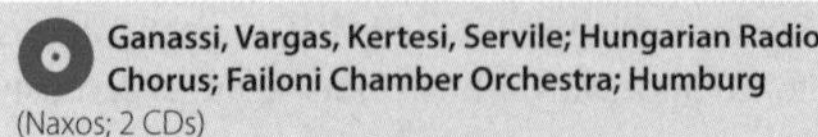

Berganza, Ausensi, Benelli, Corena, Ghiaurov; Naples Scarlatti Chorus and Orchestra; Varviso (Decca; 2 CDs)

Of Teresa Berganza's two fine recordings of Rosina (1964, 1971), the earlier version is the better. Her generous mezzo is ideal for the role and she tackles the coloratura with skill. Her supporting cast is also strong: Ugo Benelli is a cultured Almaviva, while Manuel Ausensi's wild Figaro introduces a devil-may-care frisson that's unrivalled even by Gobbi.

Ganassi, Vargas, Kertesi, Servile; Hungarian Radio Chorus; Failoni Chamber Orchestra; Humburg (Naxos; 2 CDs)

A vivid and vital recording, which at budget price makes a serious rival to the two sets above. Above all it's a truly theatrical experience with some clever, though never obtrusive, sound effects. Apart from Ramón Vargas as Almaviva, none of the soloists are big names, but all acquit themselves admirably, not least the sparky Rosina of Sonia Ganassi.

La Cenerentola

Stendhal referred to Rossini's music as "seldom sublime, but never tiresome", a description that perfectly fits *La Cenerentola*, a semi-comic homily on the value of true love and the speciousness of rank, inspired by Charles Perrault's *Cinderella*. Perhaps the chief reason for its comparative lack of popularity is the florid writing for the title role, a part that demands the combination of a contralto's range with a coloratura's agility. Once in a while a suitable voice comes along – as has happened recently with the arrival of Cecilia Bartoli – and *La Cenerentola* sneaks back into the repertoire, but it's always going to be an opera to hear on disc rather than see onstage. In terms of the proportion of time allotted to them, ensembles predominate over arias in *La Cenerentola*, but, for all Rossini's concentration on multi-voice writing, the main attraction is the title role, one of the finest female roles in Italian opera.

Bartoli, Matteuzi, Corbelli, Dara; Chorus & Orchestra of the Teatro Comunale di Bologna; Chailly (Decca; 2 CDs)

Ricardo Chailly is an inspired conductor of Rossini and in Cecilia Bartoli he has one of the great voices of recent years in a role that completely suits her light and flexible voice. Much more than her recording of *The Barber of Seville*, this is a performance that really works dramatically. A highlights disc is also available.

Berganza, Alva, Capecchi, Montarsolo; Scottish Opera Chorus; London Symphony Orchestra; Abbado (Deutsche Grammophon; 2 CDs)

Claudio Abbado's recording for Deutsche Grammophon boasts the incandescent singing of Teresa Berganza, who transcends mere technical security to give her character an astonishing vivacity and pathos. Claudio Abbado and the LSO tend to smash their way through Rossini's score, but for Berganza's singing alone this recording is worth the money.

Stabat Mater

Just as Verdi's *Requiem* was his only major composition during a long period of inactivity, so Rossini's *Stabat Mater* was his first major composition for twelve years and the last he ever wrote. During a journey to Spain in 1831, Rossini was commissioned by Fernandez Varela to set the text of the *Stabat Mater*, the medieval hymn describing the Virgin Mary's agony at the foot of the cross (see p.404). He completed half the score before asking a friend to take over. This friend, Giovanni Tadolini, did as he was asked but ten years later, under pressure from his Parisian publisher, Rossini replaced Tadolini's work with his own. This revised draft was first performed in Paris on 7 January, 1842, and was received with wild enthusiasm – an appropriate response to a composition that is not so much devotional music as lyric opera in liturgical attire. Leaving aside considerations of piety, the *Stabat Mater* is brilliantly written and contains some superb vocal music, notably the tenor's melodically sumptuous (but inappropriately jaunty) "Cujus Animam" and the unaccompanied quartet, "Quando corpus morietur".

Stoyanova, Lang, Fowler, Borowski; RIAS-Kammerchor; Akademie für Alte Musik Berlin; Creed (Harmonia Mundi)

Marcus Creed achieves an excellent balance between the work's liturgical and theatrical elements. The first-rate young soloists are placed very high in the mix, which emphasizes the operatic style of the piece, and although some may consider that Krassimira Stoyanova and Petra Lang use slightly too much vibrato in places, the arias are consistently expressive and musical.

Poul Ruders (1949–)

The music of Poul Ruders, Denmark's leading contemporary composer, has an elemental quality that is powerfully communicative. Largely self-taught, he uses the raw material of instrumental sound like building bricks, fashioning it – even in small-scale works – into strong, bold statements in which structure is always clearly visible. Absence of complex thematic development can sometimes make his method seem reductive, but when it works – as it does most effectively in his 1989 *Symphony No. 1* – the result has the compelling eloquence and rugged primitivism of a prophetic utterance.

Born at Ringsted in central Zealand, Ruders' first sustained contact with music was as a chorister in the Copenhagen Boys Choir. He later trained as an organist and his first-hand familiarity with church music influenced his own writing, which often contains echoes of, or direct quotations from, liturgical music of the Renaissance and Baroque periods. Equally important was the impact on his musical imagination made by the composers of the Polish avant-garde in the 1960s and 1970s, especially Penderecki, whose *Threnody for the Victims of Hiroshima* (which Ruders heard when he was 17) uses large blocks of sound in a strikingly graphic fashion.

In the 1980s Ruders became a regular visitor to the US with a series of guest lectureships at various American universities. His first major work,

Manhattan Abstraction (1982), dates from this period. Like much of his music, it has a strong visual dimension, being inspired by "the New York profile seen from Liberty Island, one icy cold January day". A definite sense of the city as both beautiful and repellent is expressed by way of starkly juxtaposed types of sound – harsh versus lyrical, heavy and block-like versus light and delicate, etc. It's a technique which can be heard in other orchestral works, such as the apocalyptic *Thus Saw St John* (1984), in which the fearsomely gyrating percussion of the opening moments suddenly subsides into an eerie stasis of extended chords.

Between 1992 and 1995 Ruders produced *Solar Trilogy*, a work which confirmed his ever-growing skill as an orchestral manipulator, as did the single movement of tightly focused activity that is his *Symphony No. 2*, which bears the subtitle *Symphony and Transformation* (1996). Since then he has written two more symphonies and two operas. *The Handmaid's Tale*, based on Margaret Atwood's dystopian novel of the same name, was premiered in 2000 by the Royal Danish Opera. It was followed by *Kafka's Trial* (2005), which interwove parts of Kafka's novel, *The Trial*, with aspects of the author's complicated personal life into a grotesque and disturbing whole.

Symphony No. 1

A BBC Proms commission of 1989 resulted in one of Ruders' most striking and powerful statements. Subtitled with a quotation from Goethe's *Egmont*, "Himmelhoch jauchzend – zum Tode betrübt" ("To heaven rejoicing – cast down unto death"), it is an extreme work (it needs a large orchestra and extended percussion section) which is epic and indeed visionary in its aspirations. It demands a high level of virtuosity from the orchestral players, above all in its opening, where the incessant scurrying of every instrument conjures up a mood of anarchic, cosmic joy – a mood underlined by a quotation from the opening chorus of Bach's *Christmas Oratorio*. This gives way to a more contemplative section, evoking vast empty spaces, in which a sense of vulnerability prevails despite an attempt to return to the movement's joyous opening. Tranquillity pervades the extraordinary second movement, which uses just two alternating chords (like slow regular breathing) to create a feel of time suspended, eventually interrupted by a high solo violin redolent of a frail human presence. A frenetic and short Scherzo moves straight into the last movement marked "Maschera funerale" (Funeral Masque), a nightmarish vision of long suspended chords and a steady inexorable pulse which gradually thins down into near-nothingness save for the final whisperings of a lone violin.

Danish National Radio Symphony Orchestra; Segerstam (Chandos; with *Gong, Tundra & Thus Saw St John*)

This disc gives a pretty clear picture of Ruders' strengths and weaknesses as a composer. *Gong* is a highly effective piece, full of unexpectedly brilliant sounds, but it lacks the coherence of the *Symphony*, which under the vigorous direction of Segerstam has a unity and a dynamic energy that is truly breathtaking.

Solar Trilogy

Although conceived as three free-standing pieces, the *Trilogy* gains from being heard as a single span. The descriptive instructions Ruders provides immediately suggest the sound-world: the first movement (*Gong*) carries the rubric "Throbbing-Dancing-Pulsating-Pounding-Blinding", while *Zenith* is described more pithily as "Dawning", and the restless *Corona* is "Sizzling-Piercing-Sizzling-Majestic". These annotations prepare the listener for an aural onslaught, but Ruders' vast orchestra doesn't simply batter you into submission: much of the music pushes at the outer limits of audibility, and there is never any sense that the composer is merely filling time with volume. His solar landscape seethes with restless energy, as events shoot out in unpredictable directions. *Gong* has passages that resemble symphonic minimalism, with percussion exerting pressure from below to force repeated eruptions throughout the rest of the orchestra. In *Zenith* the tumult subsides and things move more slowly – low brass and high strings generate an ethereal delicacy which eventually expands into a mighty, almost mechanical climax. That, too, fades ominously, preparing the way for *Corona*, an insistent and faintly sinister fast movement that tumbles into silence only after surging to a resolution of old-fashioned Mahlerian magnificence.

Odense Symphony Orchestra; Schønwandt (Marco Polo/DaCapo)

As Michael Schønwandt demonstrates, *Solar Trilogy* has to be heard as a kind of three-movement symphony for the power of each of its components to be fully comprehended. Schønwandt and his orchestra manage the difficult task of maintaining discipline in the tiniest details while suggesting immense forces on the brink of running out of control.

S

Kaija Saariaho (1952–)

The work of Kaija Saariaho offers a tantalizing hint as to what the classical music of the coming century might sound like. More than any other major composer of her generation, Saariaho has made electronic and computer-generated sounds a constant ingredient in her music, while developing a compositional method in which the scientific analysis of instrumental sounds and timbres plays a major role. But what's equally distinctive about her work is its constant ability to transcend its laboratory origins, and to create music not only of startling strangeness and originality, but also of haunting, other worldly beauty.

Although a native of Finland, Saariaho has since 1982 lived mainly in Paris, where she has been closely associated with IRCAM, the music research centre established by Pierre Boulez in 1977 in the bowels of the Pompidou Centre. Funded at vast expense by an obliging French government, IRCAM's charter was nothing less than to lay the ground for the music of the future, bringing together musicians and scientists to investigate new ways of making sound through electronics and novel instrumental techniques. The results of Saariaho's researches at the centre can be heard, most obviously, in her music's extraordinary sound-world, with its myriad new ways of bowing, blowing and plucking – coaxing perplexingly odd sounds from familiar instruments, which are then further enriched through electronic transformation. *Amers* (1992), for cello and ensemble, is a striking example of Saariaho's style at its most uncompromising, using a barrage of unorthodox performing techniques along with a special IRCAM-designed microphone which allows each of the solo cello's four strings to be independently amplified and electronically treated during performance.

Formally, too, Saariaho's works are persuasively novel, often based on natural phenomena and shapes – crystals, spirals, waterlilies, the Northern Lights, to name just a few of her avowed inspirations – which are at once aesthetically pleasing and structurally complex. She's also a composer for whom the spoken or sung word is central, not only in her many vocal works, but also in many of her "instrumental" pieces, in which the performers are often asked to recite fragments of text or verse whilst playing, most memorably in the string quartet *Nymphea* (1987), in which the quartet players' whispered utterances create a secondary tangle of poetic fragments which seem to offer a dream-like commentary on the music itself.

Kaija Saariaho.

Saariaho's interest in exploring the minutiae of instrumental effects meant that until the early 1990s the majority of her pieces were for small-scale instrumental or vocal forces, either without or – most characteristically – with electronics. In more recent works, however, Saariaho has turned increasingly towards larger instrumental forces without electronics, with a consequent paring down of musical detail and a new directness of expression, couched in a luxuriant melodic and harmonic language which often seems to hover tantalizingly at the edge of traditional tonality.

The violin concerto, *Graal théâtre* (1994), was the first major work to signal this new direction, a trend notably accelerated in subsequent pieces such as the sumptuous *Château de l'âme* (1996) for soprano, chorus and orchestra and, perhaps most notably, in her acclaimed opera, *L'amour de loin* (2000) as well as in spin-off works from the opera such as *Oltra Mar* and *Cinq reflets de l'amour de loin* – all of which offer eloquent proof of Saariaho's new-found ability to appeal to the widest audiences whilst remaining recognizably of her time. She continues to work on a big scale, with the anti-war opera *Adriana Mater* (2005) and a further opera, *Emilie*, commissioned by Netherlands Opera for 2010.

Nymphea

Saariaho's use of electronics and unusual instrumental effects to continually blur the borderlines between acoustic and electronic, abstract and programmatic, vocal and instrumental, reaches its apogee in *Nymphea*. Written for string quartet, it magically transforms this most traditional of musical genres into a kind of instrumental theatre, with the quartet's played notes and their electronic echoes intermittently punctuated by the whispered fragments of an Arseny Tarkovsky poem which the performers are asked to recite whilst playing. It's also a wonderful example of Saaariaho's music at its most extravagant and fantastic, with every conceivable type of string sound and texture – from the rasping sound of bow scraping against string to the sweetest of harmonics – flung together in dream-like sequence.

Kronos Quartet; Los Angeles Philharmonic; Salonen; Karttunen; Alanko (Ondine; with *Du cristal ... à la fumée & Papillons*)

The Kronos Quartet give a marvellous account of *Nymphea*, tackling the disconcertingly strange and fiendishly difficult instrumental acrobatics with wonderful conviction. The disc also includes two of Saariaho's finest early orchestral pieces: the twinned orchestral works *Du cristal* and *... à la fumée* (From Crystal ... into Smoke).

Graal théâtre

Graal théâtre ("Grail Theatre", after a poem by Jacques Roubaud), a half-hour violin concerto, written for Gidon Kremer in 1994, is a beautiful example of Saariaho's recent music, with its new-found simplicity and clarity (at least by her complex standards). There are no electronics here, and relatively few of the strange instrumental techniques that typify Saariaho's earlier work, although her characteristic musical fingerprints – the luminous, slowly evolving harmonies, bell-like sonorities and long-spun melodic lines – remain, as the solo violin wends its way slowly through a mysterious and often broodingly subdued orchestral landscape.

Kremer, Upshaw, Karttunen; BBC Symphony Orchestra; Finnish Radio Symphony Orchestra; Avanti! Chamber Orchestra; Salonen (Sony; with *Château de l'âme & Amers*)

Graal Théâtre gets an eloquent reading by Gidon Kremer here on a disc that would make an excellent introduction to Saariaho's work. The coupled works are the "difficult" *Amers* (spectacularly performed by cellist Anssi Karttunen) and the shamelessly hedonistic *Château de l'âme* for soprano, chorus and orchestra – probably the most direct and accessible music Saariaho has ever written.

Cinq reflets de l'amour de loin

Saariaho's most extensive undertaking, the opera *L'amour de loin* (Love from Afar), based on the life of twelfth-century troubadour Jaufré Rudel, has yet to be recorded, but in the meantime *Cinq reflets de l'amour de loin*, an arrangement of scenes from the opera for soprano, baritone and orchestra, offers a beguiling introduction to its poetic and musical world. One of her most accessible works, this ravishing operatic extract is a fine example of her mature music, with its rich harmonies and rapt melodic lines. Best of all is the wonderfully haunting middle section in which the solo baritone performs the quasi-medieval song "L'amour de loin" (from which the opera takes its name). Like a Dufay *chanson* magically recomposed for the twenty-first century, it achieves an effect which is at once oddly familiar and disconcertingly strange.

Suovanen, Freund; Finnish Radio Symphony Orchestra; Tapiola Chamber Choir; Saraste (Ondine with *Nymphea Reflection & Oltra Mar*)

The all-Finnish cast on this disc provide an inspired account of the *Cinq reflets*, as well as impressive performances of two other outstanding recent works: *Oltra Mar*, for chorus and orchestra, another piece derived from the opera and sharing its enchanted musical world; and *Nymphea Reflection* for string orchestra, a kind of musical mirror of Saariaho's string quartet, *Nymphea*.

Camille Saint-Saëns (1835–1921)

A lot of composers began as freakish children, but by any standards Saint-Saëns was an extreme case. As a two-year-old he could read and write, and was picking out melodies on the piano. Shortly after his third birthday he began composing, and by the age of five had given his first piano recital. At seven he was reading Latin, studying botany and developing what was to become an eighty-year interest in lepidoptery. As an encore after his formal debut as a concert pianist, the ten-year-old Camille offered to play any of Beethoven's 32 sonatas from memory. In short, his childhood suggested Mozartian potential, and yet it was a potential that was never realized. Saint-Saëns once remarked that he lived "in music like a fish in water" and that composing was as natural as "an apple tree producing apples". And there lay the problem. As with Mendelssohn, the technique came so easily to him that it virtually extinguished the spark of originality.

That said, for many years he was considered by many to be France's greatest musical revolutionary, though his reputation grew more from his outspoken support of other composers' music – notably Liszt's and Wagner's – than from any work of his own. From 1860 to 1865 Saint-Saëns was professor of piano at the École Niedermeyer where, as well as promoting contemporary music, he threw his energies into researching the work of his forerunners. Along with Mendelssohn, he was one of the first to re-establish the music of Bach (converting the sceptical Berlioz in the process) and he did much to restore Mozart to his rightful place, being the first to play a complete cycle of the piano concertos. Handel was another unfashionable composer to engage Saint-Saëns' attention, and (as with Berlioz) Gluck held a fascination that lasted most of his life.

In his lifetime he was celebrated as much for his organ playing as any of his other musical talents, with Liszt regarding him as the greatest organist in the world. From 1857 to 1875 he was principal organist at the fashionable Parisian church of La Madeleine where – taking full advantage of the new Cavaillé-Coll instrument with its wide range of orchestral sonorities – he amazed listeners with his skill as an improviser. He was succeeded at La Madeleine by his friend and former pupil Gabriel Fauré.

Although he was a co-founder in 1871 of the Société Nationale de Musique (which aimed to promote French music both old and new), by the time Saint-Saëns reached his mid-fifties, the past had won the upper hand over the present. Embittered and ill-tempered, he became an arch-traditionalist, opposing the progressive music of Debussy and Ravel, and bellowing outrage at the premiere of *The Rite of Spring*. Yet for all his reactionary pomposity, he was one of the first neo-classicists, embodying many of the finest traditional qualities of French music – clarity, elegance and dignity. His best epitaph is the rueful one he wrote for himself: "I ran after the chimera of purity of style and perfection of form."

Samson et Dalila

Samson et Dalila is the only one of Saint-Saëns' thirteen operas that has achieved any lasting success. The biblical plot tells how the Hebrew warrior Samson is seduced by the Philistine beauty Dalila; having discovered the secret of his great strength she betrays him to the Philistines; blinded and tied up in the temple, Samson is mocked and taunted, but when he prays to God his strength returns and he brings down the temple.

Although *Samson* has the trappings of Grand Opéra – ballets, big choruses, lengthy ensembles and a fair amount of spectacle – at times it seems more suited to a church. However, much of Act 3 is sensationally dramatic, opening with Samson's melancholic treadmill aria "Vois ma misère, hélas" (See My Misery, Alas) before plunging into the barnstorming barbarism of the bacchanal – Saint-Saëns' most impressive orchestral showpiece. The opera also contains some of the most beautiful vocal melodies in French opera – music that was later to become central to the repertoire of Parisian organ-grinders. Dalila's great Act 2 seduction aria, "Mon cœur s'ouvre à toi" (My Heart Opens to You), is rightly the best-known music, but her Act 1 "Printemps qui commence" (Spring that Comes) and her vibrant, sensual call to love at the beginning of Act 2, "Amour! Viens aider ma faiblesse" (Love, Help Me in My Weakness), are no less fine.

 **Cura, Borodina, Lafont, Silins; London Symphony Orchestra and Chorus; Davis** (Erato; 2 CDs)

Colin Davis's 1997 *Samson* is one of his finest opera recordings. Although made with a British orchestra and chorus, an Argentinian Samson and a Russian Dalila, this is a thoroughly integrated performance that throbs with tension. It stars two of today's outstanding operatic talents: José Cura's tenor is the real thing, with grace as well as power, and the mezzo Olga Borodina makes a strikingly seductive Dalila.

 **Vickers, Gorr, Blanc, Diakov; René Duclos Chorus; Paris Opéra Orchestra; Prêtre** (EMI; 2 CDs)

A marvellous performance from Canadian tenor Jon Vickers in a role for which he was famous. The power of his singing is staggering and he brings a genuinely tragic grandeur to his death scene. Rita Gorr displays great sensitivity as Dalila – it is her dignity as much as her sexuality that conquers the hero. Prêtre's reading is highly impassioned and there are few more epic performances of French opera on CD.

Symphony No. 3

Saint-Saëns' barnstorming *Symphony No. 3* – first performed in London in 1886 – reveals the composer at his crowd-pleasing best. The work's opening is powerfully atmospheric: two darkly lugubrious string chords are followed by brief woodwind solos before pizzicati in the low strings lead into a theme of nervous restlessness. The warmly sentimental Adagio that follows has an almost Mahlerian gravitas, partly through the solemn underpinning provided by the organ part. The third movement is a spine-tingling Scherzo, urgent and compelling, that seems to have strayed in from a lost work by Berlioz. Its lighter central section rather startlingly introduces a pair of pianos who bring an air of carnival jollity to the proceedings. The main theme returns, then transforms itself into a grandiose fugue that gradually thins out almost to nothing before a massive C major chord on the organ heralds the start of the final movement. This is an utterly thrilling hodge-podge of ideas – a fugal introduction, glittering passage work, triumphant fanfares, the return of the Dies irae theme – which concludes with a very long and very loud organ chord.

Preston; Berlin Philharmonic Orchestra; Levine (Deutsche Grammophon; with Dukas *The Sorcerer's Apprentice*)

Levine's account, with Simon Preston, may be a little over-aggressive for some tastes but it is undoubtedly tremendously exciting. It is also very well engineered, with the last movement in particular a tribute to the wonders of digital recording.

Hurford; Montréal Symphony Orchestra; Dutoit (Decca; with *Le carnaval des animaux*)

A more subtle performance, and a cheaper one, comes from Dutoit and another English organist, Peter Hurford. Here the emphasis is less on sonic spectacle – though the last-movement organ entry still packs a real punch – than on clarity and momentum.

Le carnaval des animaux

Saint-Saëns wrote his *Carnaval des animaux* in 1886 as an amusement for his friends and performances were forbidden during his lifetime in case it detracted from his reputation. Scored for two pianos and small orchestra, its fourteen sections depict a wide range of creatures including "Persons with Long Ears" and "Pianists", the latter represented by irritatingly repeated scales. Saint-Saëns' humour is often deft and satirical – "Tortoises" get to amble along to a version of Offenbach's Can-Can played extremely slowly, "Elephants" receive similar treatment, to a dance by Berlioz. There are also moments of great magic: the singing cello melody of "The Swan" (made famous by the ballerina Pavlova) and, most beautiful of all, the rippling arpeggios of the mysterious "Aquarium".

Rogé, Ortiz; London Sinfonietta; Dutoit (Decca; with *Symphony No. 3*)

There are over thirty recordings of *Le carnaval des animaux*, most of them sounding very much like the others. Dutoit's performance has the merit of sharpening the satire, while pianists Rogé and Ortiz add to the flair. It's coupled with a muscular version of the third symphony (see above).

Violin Concerto No. 3

Composed in 1880, the *Violin Concerto No. 3* was written for the Spanish virtuoso Pablo de Sarasate, a brilliant showman in the tradition of Paganini, who liked to stun audiences with his technical expertise. Like the *Symphony No. 3*, it's a crowd-pleaser, full of dramatic contrasts, which opens with one of Saint-Saëns' most striking melodies – a Gypsy-like theme on the lowest of the instrument's strings. The slow movement Adagio, with its jaunty but wistful solo part, is rather less characterful with something of the salon about it, but all the stops are pulled out for the finale: a stupendous creation which lurches between virtuosic flourishes – often accompanied by a thumping Verdian bass line – and a sentimental religiosity.

Wei; Philharmonia; Bakels (ASV; with Bruch *Concerto No. 1*)

The fine Chinese violinist Xue-Wei completely fulfils the music's dramatic potential. He uses gut strings, producing a fuller sound than that made by the routine steel strings, and his playing is among the most natural and instinctive performances available.

Piano Concertos Nos. 2 & 4

Saint-Saëns' *Piano Concerto No. 2* epitomizes much of the composer's output, being pleasant on the ear and murder on the fingers. It was also, typically, a quick job – commissioned in 1868 by the great Russian pianist Anton Rubinstein, it was finished in just seventeen days. Unusually for Saint-Saëns, it opens with an unorthodox gesture, a cadenza that runs into a particularly sumptuous first theme. Thereafter, things run pretty well to pattern: as with the third violin concerto, the central movement is the work's weak spot, but the Presto is a steamroller of a finale, demanding heroic virtuosity from the soloist.

The *Piano Concerto No. 4*, one of Saint-Saëns' most enjoyable works, illustrates – yet again – his tendency to veer disarmingly between high seriousness, maudlin sentimentality and salon frivolity. Indebted to both Liszt and Brahms, its two big movements are divided into two parts in which themes are treated cyclically in the manner of César Franck. Midway through the sombre first movement there is a suggestion of the chorale that is the main feature of the last movement, a lively rondo, which is finally blasted out in triumphant glory at the work's close.

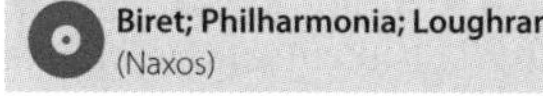

Biret; Philharmonia; Loughran (Naxos)

Idel Biret's enthusiastic account of *Concerto No. 2* displays great technical assurance and sense of forward momentum, with James Loughran giving more than adequate support. The delightful fourth concerto gets an equally spirited reading.

Piano Concerto No. 2: Rubinstein; Symphony of the Air; Wallenstein (RCA; with Falla *Nights in the Gardens of Spain* & Franck *Symphonic Variations*)

A legendary performance from Artur Rubinstein, who championed this concerto and recorded it several times. This is the best of them, and it still sounds startlingly fresh and alive some half-century on.

Violin Sonata No. 1

The majority of Saint-Saëns' chamber music is doggedly formulaic, but the *Violin Sonata No. 1*, composed in 1885, shows him throwing off the shackles to fashion a work of real passion and personality. The insinuating first movement – with its lilting triplets and haunting second subject – may have been the inspiration for the fictitious *Vinteuil Sonata* in Proust's novel *Swann's Way*, although the sonata by César Franck (see p.197) is a more likely candidate. The warmly enveloping Adagio – with the violin and piano engaged in what is very much an exchange between equals – is followed by a Scherzo consisting of a rather melancholy waltz. In the last movement Saint-Saëns sets out to thrill with a brilliant, but technically cruel, moto-perpetuo in which pianist and violinist really have to battle to stay together – an entertaining antidote to Saint-Saëns' habitual propriety.

Wei, Lenehan (ASV; with *Violin Sonata No. 2, Berceuse & Introduction and Rondo Capriccioso*)

Xue-Wei proves himself as persuasive an advocate of the violin sonatas as of the *Violin Concerto No. 3* (see above). In partnership with pianist John Lenehan he finds just the right balance between the work's emotional overdrive and its technical virtuosity.

Erik Satie (1866–1925)

Though dismissed in some quarters as an eccentric lightweight, Erik Satie was one of the most influential figures in twentieth-century music. Ravel never tired of paying tribute to a man he called simply "the precursor", and the young Debussy – for a time his closest friend – was encouraged by Satie to make the final break with Wagnerism and dispense with the heavy Romantic "sauerkraut". Essentially a solitary figure, eking out a living as a pianist in the cafés of Montmartre (dressed always in a grey velvet suit and bowler hat), Satie became famed among the cognoscenti of Paris chiefly for his quirky piano pieces, with their mystifying titles and whimsical performance directions. Compositions such as *Pieces to Make You Run Away*, *True Flabby Preludes* and *Bureaucratic Sonata*, published with such unhelpful tips as "Wonder about Yourself" and "Be Clairvoyant", make Satie a forerunner of Dada and Surrealism, while their combination of wistfulness and satirical wit give them a unique – but distinctly French – flavour.

From the mid-1910s Satie was championed as the supreme anti-Romantic by that arch-trendsetter Jean Cocteau (see p.409), with whom he collaborated on a ballet. *Parade* (1917) was the Russian Ballet's next big scandal after the furore caused by *The Rite of Spring*. This time round, it was not so much Satie's music or Cocteau's scenario that people objected to so much as Picasso's three-dimensional Cubist costumes. The action takes place in front of a fairground booth and involves

Erik Satie – a respectable exterior but an anarchic spirit.

three showmen and their artists – a Chinese juggler, a pair of acrobats and a "Little American Girl". Satie presents them as a series of rather wittily impassive vignettes, "an everyday music" Cocteau claimed, which drew on popular music-hall style and found room for the sound of a typewriter, a revolver, sirens and a xylophone made up of bottles.

Satie himself was largely unstinting in his support of young musicians, most notably the group known as Les Six, two of whom – Poulenc and Milhaud – saw in his independence of traditional musical models a position to emulate. Satie collaborated with Cocteau (and Picasso) again on another entertainment, *Les aventures de Mercure* in 1924, but then, for his final ballet *Relâche*, threw in his lot with the Surrealists. *Relâche* is the term used when a theatre is closed between performances, and when the audience turned up for the "first night" they found the theatre closed (the performance actually occurred three days later). The nonsensical scenario and designs (the set consisted of hundreds of suspended gramophone records) were by Francis Picabia, and a short film by René Clair (in which Satie appeared) was shown in the interval (and entitled *Entr'acte*). As with *Parade*, the music is profoundly inoffensive and indeed somewhat innocuous.

Sadly, just as his star was really on the rise his health began to fail him, due in no small part to the strong drink he consumed in vast quantities over the years. He died of cirrhosis of the liver at the age of 59. Among the tributes heaped on him was this one from Darius Milhaud: "The purity of his art, his horror of all concessions, his contempt for money and his ruthless attitude toward the critics were a marvellous example for us all."

In fact Satie's legacy was more profound than Milhaud's words suggest. The timeless, directionless quality of his music was an important influence on John Cage (see p.125); his idea of *musique d'ameublement* (furniture music) anticipated Muzak by some fifty years; while the simplicity and repetition of much of his work (*Vexations* requests that the same short piano theme be played 840 times in succession) provided minimalism with an inspiring historical precedent.

Piano Music

Satie's mysteriously poignant piano pieces, which make up about three-quarters of his output, are his most representative music. Their frequently absurd titles often have a parodic intention (sometimes poking gentle fun at some of the more absurdly poetic titles of Debussy's piano pieces). But despite their apparent frivolity these miniatures are often deeply lyrical, with a sound-world derived partly from the café-cabarets in which Satie played but also from his interest in the modal music of medieval Christianity. This emphasis on modal techniques and austere "white-key" harmonies is heard to particularly good effect in his two most famous sets of pieces, the languid *Trois Gymnopédies* (1888) and the haunting *Gnossiennes* (1890), which predate Debussy's exploration of such harmonic resources by some fifteen years. Debussy so much admired the *Gymnopédies* that he made orchestrations of two of them, emphasizing their dreamy quality but undermining their quirky incisiveness which is best rendered in their original piano form.

3 Gymnopédies & Other Piano Works: Rogé
(Decca)

Pascal Rogé perfectly captures the composer's mixture of knowingness and naivety, drawing you into this unique sound-world in performances that are full of elegant poise. He's just as successful at bringing out the underlying melancholy of the six *Gnossiennes* as he is at catching the sharp wit of the *Préludes flasques*.

Socrate

If you think that all there is to Satie is laconic Gallic wit and engaging café *chansons*, then you should listen to *Socrate* for voice and piano. With a text extracted from three Platonic dialogues, *Socrate* is a cantata in three parts depicting the last days of the ancient Greek philosopher and sage Socrates who was condemned to death by the citizens of Athens for corrupting the young men of the city. The subtitle, "symphonic drama", belies the understatement and economy of one of Satie's finest works, which is in every way the antithesis of the overblown rhetoric of his *bête noire* Wagner. Over patterns of brisk pulsing ostinati, Satie weaves simple modal melodies, while the vocal line's sequences of repeated notes and avoidance of vivid word painting focus our attention on Plato's text. The result is hauntingly beautiful in its simplicity and total lack of pretension.

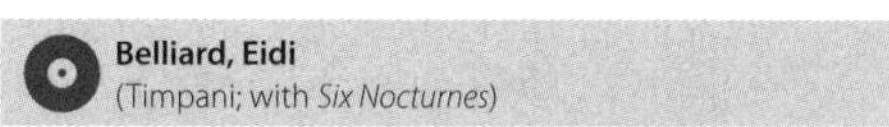

Belliard, Eidi
(Timpani; with *Six Nocturnes*)

Jean Belliard's light reedy tenor, with his sparing use of vibrato and impeccably clear French diction, is ideal. His unrhetorical style fits the music perfectly and, for all its restraint, is intensely moving. Billy Eidi accompanies with appropriate clarity and objectivity. The recording allows just the right amount of space for the singer and piano.

Alessandro Scarlatti (1660–1725)

Alessandro Scarlatti has become the obscure Scarlatti, eclipsed by his son Domenico whose early career he seems to have controlled with a rod of iron. But the older Scarlatti was a figure of great historical importance as one of the major composers of opera before the generation of Handel and Gluck. Immensely successful during his lifetime, his works were published in numerous editions and his operas were frequently produced throughout Italy.

He began his musical studies in Rome with Carissimi (see p.128), under whose guidance he composed his first opera, *Gli equivoci nel sembiante*, in 1679. During the next 46 years he composed more than one hundred stage works (the precise number isn't known) and became a seminal figure in the world of opera seria – the principal operatic genre of the early eighteenth century. At Rome he was employed as *maestro di cappella* by the exiled Queen Christina of Sweden, and counted both Cardinal Pamphili and Cardinal Ottoboni among his influential patrons. In 1684 he settled in Naples where he was employed by the Spanish viceroy. He remained there until 1702 and for the remainder of his life floated in and out of various court appointments.

Scarlatti helped establish Naples as a major centre of Italian operatic life and made several technical advances to the genre, such as his development of the da capo aria, his skilful use of instrumental textures, and his adoption of subjects less high-flown than the mythological themes so loved by Monteverdi. Yet musically his work looks back to the declamatory Venetian tradition of Monteverdi rather than towards the dramatic school that followed. It was perhaps indicative of a recognition of his fundamentally conservative nature that Scarlatti composed fewer and fewer operas from the 1700s, and the overall pallidness of his style isn't likely to win many admirers nowadays. At the moment there is just one complete Scarlatti opera, *La Griselda*, in the catalogue.

But Scarlatti was also a major composer of other types of vocal music closely related to opera. He composed over six hundred cantatas – a genre which was to opera what the short story is to the novel. He also wrote about 34 oratorios, which were essentially sacred operas (though usually scored for fewer voices) – several of which were written during the first decade of the eighteenth century when Pope Clement XI placed a ban on the public performance of opera in Rome.

Motets

Scarlatti's sacred works, which form a relatively small but important part of his output, were mostly composed during his time in Rome. As well as oratorios, he also composed a number of masses and about one hundred motets. Of the latter, some are polyphonic and in a self-consciously archaic style while others (often for solo voice) employ the expressive range and variety that you find in the cantatas and operas, with the text divided into short musically contrasted sections. The *Salve Regina* and the *Stabat Mater*, both hymns to the Virgin Mary written for two voices, fall into the latter category. Both the vocal and the instrumental writing are ornate and sometimes virtuosic and there's an effective but sparing use of dissonance. But above all it's the sense of a personally felt reaction to the words that makes such an impact – a musical emotionalism that was to be a major influence on Pergolesi's *Stabat Mater* (see p.405).

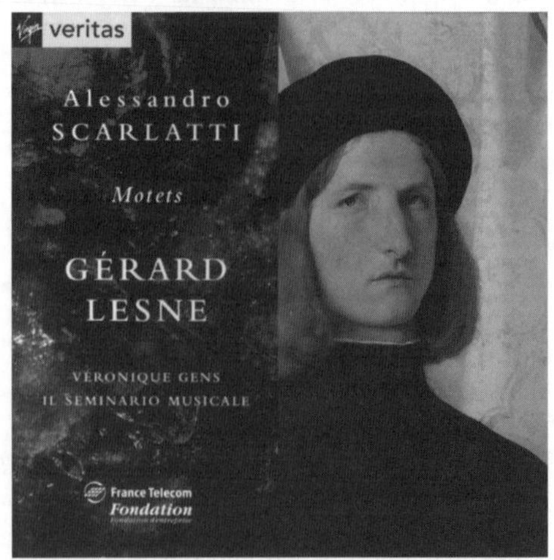

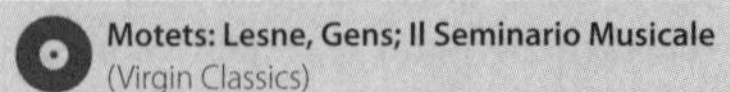
Motets: Lesne, Gens; Il Seminario Musicale
(Virgin Classics)

This is one of the most wholly satisfying recordings of Scarlatti's music to have appeared in recent years.

Countertenor Gérard Lesne is something of a specialist in Italian Baroque vocal repertoire, and he emphasizes the music's warmth and sensuousness without overdoing it. He sings three solo motets and is joined by Véronique Gens for a moving account of the *Salve Regina*.

Stabat Mater: Mingardo, Bertagnoli; Concerto Italiano; Alessandrini (Naïve; with Pergolesi *Stabat Mater*)

Scarlatti's *Stabat Mater* was written for a Neapolitan religious order who commisioned a replacement version by Pergolesi some twenty years later, so it makes sense to put both versions on the same disc. Scarlatti's is the more restrained of the two settings but this intense account by soprano Gemma Bertagnoli and contralto Sara Mingardo makes a more than convincing case for it.

Cantatas

During Scarlatti's lifetime the Italian cantata developed into an extended dramatic scene, usually for a soloist but sometimes employing up to three voices, that employed recitative, aria and arioso (a more lyrical recitative). Their brevity allowed for a concentration and emotional intensity which was heightened by expressive instrumental accompaniment (including an introductory sinfonia) close in feeling to the trio sonatas of Scarlatti's colleague Arcangelo Corelli (see p.147). Cantatas were performed at private gatherings of aristocrats and literati, such as the Accademia dell'Arcadia of which Scarlatti himself was a member, and dealt with a limited range of topics usually involving some aspect of the vicissitudes of love which often related to some classical myth or legend. Creating music appropriate to the text was the challenge for which Scarlatti became particularly renowned, though he rarely achieved the poignancy or power of his contemporaries Alessandro Stradella (see p.535) and Barbara Strozzi (see p.552).

Cantatas Vol. 4: Brandes, Labelle; Arcadian Academy; McGegan (Deutsche Harmonia Mundi)

The last of Nicholas McGegan's four volumes of Scarlatti cantatas is dedicated to duet-cantatas of which the most ambitious is *Puote si poco*, a series of arguments between Cupid and Virtue over their respective skills. The pairing of the clear incisive tones of soprano Christine Brandes with the fuller sound of Dominique Labelle works well, though a nagging doubt over the quality of the music remains.

Domenico Scarlatti (1685–1757)

Domenico Scarlatti is now known almost exclusively for his keyboard sonatas. This is hardly surprising, since between 1719 and his death he wrote around 555 of these single-movement works in one of musical history's most remarkable marathons.

Born in Naples, a city under Spanish rule since 1503, Domenico studied there with his father Alessandro and was appointed organist at the vice-regal court (where his father was *maestro di cappella*) at the tender age of fifteen. A few months later, in 1702, father and son obtained leave of absence to travel to Rome and Florence in the hope of more rewarding employment at the court of Alessandro's princely patron, Ferdinando de Medici. In Florence it is likely that both Scarlattis would have met the famed instrument maker to the prince, Bartolomeo Cristofori (see p.472). Back in Naples the same year, Domenico made his debut as an opera composer with two works for the 1703–04 season. A year later the domineering Alessandro – ambitious for his son – arranged for Domenico to join him in Venice where he hoped that both would make their mark. In the end neither proved successful there, although Domenico did meet and become friends with the young Handel. Alessandro's next move was to secure himself the post of *maestro di cappella* at the church of Santa Maria Maggiore in Rome, where he also managed to find a position for his son.

Domenico remained in Rome from 1708 to 1719. It was there, shortly after he arrived, that he took part in a keyboard contest with Handel at the palace of Cardinal Ottoboni, in which the Italian won the plaudits as a harpsichordist while his rival was thought the superior organist. An important post soon followed, that of *maestro di cappella* to Maria Casimira, the dowager queen of Poland, for whom Domenico wrote several operas and oratorios. In 1713 he was appointed assistant *maestro* of the Cappella Giulia at St Peter's in Rome, becoming *maestro* the following year. At the same time he was also working for Portugal's ambassador to the Vatican as well as writing operas for Rome's main theatre, where he made the acquaintance of the great castrato Farinelli.

The Development of the Keyboard

The first keyboard instrument to arrive in western Europe was an organ, which King Pepin of the Franks received as a gift from Emperor Constantine in 757. At this time the organ was as much a symbol of technology and wealth as a functional musical instrument, but by the turn of the first millennium it had assumed an important role in liturgical music, and organs were found in many churches. They bore little resemblance to the church organs of today, however, only spanning a range of around two octaves, but with keys as much as a foot wide, which were intended to be played not with individual fingers but with fists, or even feet or knees. There were no chromatic keys (the black keys on the modern keyboard), and it wasn't until the fourteenth century that keyboards started appearing with all the notes of the chromatic scale available.

The organ continued to develop in the church, but from around 1400 a new branch of the keyboard family started to emerge, in which the noise was produced not with air but with strings. The earliest of these, the clavichord (literally "key-string"), was a small instrument with a very simple mechanism. When a key was pressed, its back end would seesaw up and hit the string, resulting in a pleasant but very quiet note. The need for more volume caused the rise of a new generation of keyboard instruments – the harpsichord, shaped like an angular grand piano, and its smaller cousins, the virginal and spinet – which created more sound by plucking the strings. Though they dominated from the sixteenth to the eighteenth century, these plucked-string instruments gave players almost no control over volume, and so produced a rather mechanical sound – like "two skeletons copulating on a corrugated tin roof" in the words of the conductor Thomas Beecham.

This lack of expressive potential caused the Italian instrument-maker Bartolomeo Cristofori to revert to the old idea of striking the string. In around 1700 he added a complex hammer mechanism to the harpsichord, producing an instrument which was reasonably loud, produced a warm sound, and most importantly gave the player control over volume. The instrument was called "gravicembalo con piano e forte" (harpsichord with loud and soft), a name that was soon shortened to pianoforte, and then to piano. Cristofori's instrument would completely change the face of keyboard music, but not until the last few decades of the 1700s, when the combination of innovative instrument-makers and brilliant performers, like Mozart, Hummel, Clementi and Beethoven, continually extended the piano's expressive potential. As well as the two main styles of grand pianos – the light-toned Viennese model and more powerful English instrument – the smaller table-shaped "square piano" was invented, soon becoming a must-have in fashionable English households.

By the turn of the century, piano-fever, which had initially been confined to Germany and England, spread to France and then America, where the one-piece cast-iron frame was developed. Capable of holding more and higher-tension strings, this was a major breakthrough, facilitating a bigger register and a stronger tone. Back in Europe, the French manufacturer Sébastien Erard combined the advantages of the Viennese and English actions, and in 1822 added the incredibly clever and complicated "double escapement" mechanism, allowing rapidly repeated notes to be played. By the second half of the century, the piano closely resembled the precision-engineered 10,000-part music machine that is today's concert instrument.

The familiar keyboard layout has remained the same for around 600 years except for the colours of the keys – black and white were often used the other way round – but several new designs have been proposed during this time. As early as 1606, before the introduction of equal temperament (the splitting of the octave into 12 equal semitones) the Italian designer Trasuntino had produced an instrument with 31 notes per octave, allowing the player to achieve good natural tuning in every key. Since then there have been attempts to popularize everything from pianos with only one row of keys (allowing the same fingering to be used in every key) to left-handed keyboards with the bass notes on the right.

Sometime in the early 1720s Scarlatti became court composer to King João V of Portugal, a position whose duties included teaching music to the king's daughter, the Infanta Maria Barbara with whom he established a close relationship. When, in 1729, the Infanta married Prince Fernando, the heir to the Spanish throne, Scarlatti (himself recently married) followed her to Madrid where he remained in her service until three years before his death. In Madrid, Scarlatti resumed his friendship with Farinelli (now also part of the royal household) but never seems to have been involved in writing for the opera. Instead, he was largely a backgound figure at court and the majority of his massive keyboard output was composed solely for the private consumption of Maria Barbara. Only thirty of the sonatas were published during Scarlatti's lifetime, as *Essercizi per gravicembalo* (1738).

The keyboard of Scarlatti's day had a far smaller range than the modern piano, but within these confines he created music of great variety, ranging in character from helter-skelter urgency to the most delicate lyricism. While his music may not possess the depths of his contemporary J.S. Bach, it reveals a seemingly inexhaustible inventiveness. Scarlatti was arguably the first composer really to explore the limits of what ten fingers could achieve: his music is littered with jumps over two octaves, crossed-hand passages and rapid note repetitions.

Keyboard Sonatas

Scarlatti's sonatas bear no resemblance to the multi-movement form mastered by Haydn, Mozart and Beethoven – to Scarlatti the term "sonata" signified nothing more precise than that a piece was purely instrumental (see p.58). Nor does he develop the material of his one-movement compositions in the manner of a Classical sonata, but instead proceeds by the interweaving and juxtaposition of motifs which are repeated throughout a piece. It seems clear that Scarlatti became familiar with popular Spanish music during his long spell in Spain, and his sonatas reflect this indigenous tradition more than the courtly dance forms favoured by his contemporaries. Thus it is possible to discern echoes of guitar strumming, castanets, even the suggestion of foot stamping in the dynamic faster sonatas, and the hint of Andalusian *cante jondo* singing in some of the slower ones. But above all it is the force of Scarlatti's melodies, the quick-wittedness with which he conducts his musical arguments, and the quasi-Romantic expressive effects he achieves that make these works as absorbing as any instrumental music of the Baroque period.

Harpsichord Sonatas, Vol. 1–3: Hantaï
(Mirare; 3 CDs)

The outstanding French harpsichordist Pierre Hantaï has selected around forty-five sonatas which he plays on three different instruments spread across three separate discs. Hantaï regards these innovative works as passionate and exciting, and he plays his selection with tremendous daring and attack, employing dramatic pauses and even, on occasions, exploiting the clatter of the keyboard action for expressive effect.

The Complete Sonatas: Ross
(Warner; 34 CDs)

For those who catch the Scarlatti bug in a serious way, it is now possible to choose between three sets of the complete sonatas played on eighteenth-century keyboards. Of these the earliest, performed by Scott Ross (and first issued in 1986), is the most recommendable and an outstanding achievement by any standards. Employing four different instruments, Ross's consistent freshness of vision for every piece is breathtaking.

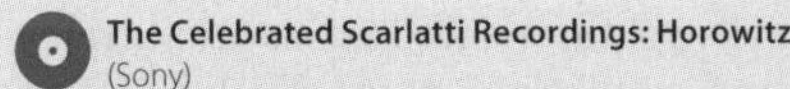

The Celebrated Scarlatti Recordings: Horowitz
(Sony)

Vladimir Horowitz was one of the first pianists to regularly programme Scarlatti's sonatas, usually at the beginning of a recital. These performances, part of Sony's Horowitz Edition, highlight the quirkiness of the music and use the piano's full resources to produce textures beyond the scope of the harpsichord.

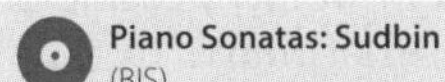

Piano Sonatas: Sudbin
(BIS)

Scarlatti is now in the repertoire of plenty of pianists but few make such a brilliant case for his music on that instrument as does Yevgeny Sudbin in his 2005 debut recording. Hugely receptive to the inner voicing, shifting moods and sheer wit of the sonatas, Sudbin more than holds his own in the company of a master like Horowitz.

Stabat Mater

Scarlatti's harpsichord sonatas so dominate his output that it's almost forgotten that he was a distinguished composer of vocal music, both the secular – in the form of operas and cantatas – and the sacred. In recent years the latter has started to emerge from the shadows, in particular his mysterious and archaic-sounding *Stabat Mater*.

Nobody knows exactly when it was written or for whom, although it may well date from his time at the Cappella Giulia. Compared with his father's dramatically emotional setting of the same text (see p.470), Scarlatti's harks back to an earlier polyphonic tradition as exemplified by Palestrina – a style still felt in some quarters to be appropriate for church music. Written for ten voices, though rarely employing them simultaneously, the magical opening is a gently subdued but intense interweaving of the voices, full of anguished dissonances. What distinguishes it from Renaissance polyphony is the harmony, but also the way Scarlatti varies the writing from verse to verse, employing different vocal groupings and often abrupt changes of speed, culminating in a closing Amen in particularly exuberant triple time.

Concerto Italiano; Alessandrini
(Naïve; with *Missa quator vocum*)

There are now several recordings of the *Stabat Mater* available, of which this is the most wholly satisfying. Employing just one voice per part (plus some beautifully discreet continuo playing), Alessandrini allows his singers to retain their individuality which lends the work the immediacy and intimacy of a madrigal. The similarly archaic Mass is also extremely beautiful.

Giacinto Scelsi (1905–1988)

Count Giacinto Scelsi D'Ayala Valva, aristocrat, poet and composer, was one of the twentieth century's more unusual musicians. Born in 1905, he grew up in the Scelsi family's ancestral castle at Valva, near Naples, where his studies concentrated – according to the composer's own testimony – on the noble pursuits of fencing, Latin and chess. His youthful enthusiasms also included the piano, an instrument for which he formed a lifelong affection and at which he developed the habit of improvising for hours at a time – a foreshadowing of his later composing method. Although Scelsi never received any formal musical training, as a young man he frequented the house of Respighi in Rome, became an enthusiast for the Futurist music of Luigi Russolo, and later studied briefly in Vienna with a pupil of Schoenberg, writing the first twelve-note music to be composed by an Italian. He subsequently lived in London, where he married a cousin of the queen, and Paris, where he published three volumes of Surrealist poetry in French and established a minor reputation as a maverick composer whose influences ranged from Futurism to Berg and Scriabin. During these years he also travelled in Asia, in particular to India and Tibet, journeys which would later prove of great significance in his artistic development.

The full facts of Scelsi's life are imperfectly known. Following World War II it appears he suffered an extended nervous breakdown during which, as he would later proudly announce, "I forgot everything I ever knew about music". During his recuperation Scelsi fell into the habit of calming his mind by playing single notes over and over on the piano, a form of musical auto-therapy which was, improbably, to form the basis of his mature compositional style. He also became an adept of Buddhism, meditating three times daily and adding a Zen symbol (a circle above a horizontal line) to his signature.

In 1959 his one-note improvisations led to the creation of the seminal *Quattro pezzi chiascuno su una nota sola* ("Four Pieces Each One on a Single Note"), the first unequivocal demonstration of Scelsi's concern with what he called the "three-dimensional" quality of sound. Each piece takes as its starting (and ending) point a single note – a radical paring down of musical subject matter which focuses attention inward, making the listener concentrate on what musical sound *is*, rather than what it does. The obvious comparison is with the Eastern musics Scelsi admired – whether the Indian raga or the Tibetan tantra, with their hypnotic concentration on a single elemental sonority – yet Scelsi's strange genius lifts this and all his later work far above the level of mere musical tourism, creating a unique sound-world which is unplaceable in any tradition except its own.

Though none of Scelsi's subsequent works has quite the stark simplicity of the *Quattro pezzi*, all are based on what is essentially material of extreme spareness. It's music which is totally lacking in theme, melody, rhythm and (often) harmony, but which instead confronts the listener with the phenomenon of pure sound in seemingly natural and spontaneous evolution – the paradox is that (in his finest works at least) Scelsi manages to conjure such luminous musical effects from even the simplest of note-combinations. Always an extremely prolific composer, Scelsi in later life wrote many pieces for strings especially, including a number of string quartets and the wonderful "violin concerto" *Anahit*, and also for wind instruments, such as the haunting *Kya* for clarinet and ensemble – though he gave up writing for his once-favoured instrument, the piano, finding its fixed tuning and uniform sound colour too inflexible for his needs. Scelsi also became famous not only for his unique style, but also for his unusual working methods, whereby pieces were first improvised – either by the composer himself at the keyboard or in collaboration with sympathetic performers – and then written down by amanuenses. (In a subsequent twist, one of Scelsi's assistants, the composer Vieru Tosatti, later claimed that he rather than Scelsi was the true author of the works.) Scelsi stopped composing around 1975, but enjoyed belated fame as musicians from all over the world discovered his work.

Anahit

Scelsi's later works include many for strings, these instruments being particularly well suited to his musical style, given the range of different tone colours they're able to produce (different bowing effects, glissandos, pizzicatos, harmonics), and the ease with which they can play microtones, the tiny pitch divisions which are such an important ingredient in Scelsi's later music. Arguably Scelsi's finest work, *Anahit* (1965), for solo violin and eighteen instrumentalists, subtitled "Lyric Poem on the Name of Venus", encapsulates his style at its richest and most cogent. As in all his mature works, the musical material is of the utmost simplicity – essentially nothing more than a sequence of slowly ascending pitches – yet the work produces an effect of extraordinary, strange voluptuousness, as simple tonal chords drift gradually in and out of focus, while the solo violinist describes a slow and wayward ascent, climbing higher by infinitesimal degrees over the course of the piece.

Bik; Klangforum Wien; Zender
(Kairos; with *Yamaon, I presagi, Tre pezzi* & *Okanagon*)

This is a marvellous performance of *Anahit* by Annette Bik and Klangforum Wien – though the other pieces on the CD go to prove that the prolific Scelsi tended to miss the mark rather more often than he hit it.

Kya

Kya, for solo clarinet and a small ensemble of mainly wind instruments, shows Scelsi's incantatory style at its simplest and most persuasive. It dates from 1959, the same year as the seminal *Quattro pezzi*, and though it's rather more freewheeling in material and effect than that reductionist work, the influence of the one-note style can be strongly felt in the long-held drones which underpin the solo clarinet's haunting melody, and in the way in which that melody returns obsessively to the same few pitches. Meditative and static for the most part, *Kya*'s hypnotic repetitions gradually flower into melodic lines of ever-greater complexity before, in a characteristic gesture, the piece suddenly stops – as if the work itself is only a fragment of an infinite music which continues out of hearing before and after the written limits of the composition.

Lerner; Ensemble 2E2M; Méfano
(Musicdisc; with *Pranam* and other chamber works)

This disc offers a good general introduction to Scelsi's music, including the best of the three versions of *Kya* currently available (with Rémi Lerner the idiomatic soloist) along with the haunting *Pranam* (1973), one of the most beautifully mysterious of Scelsi's later works, and an interesting selection of pieces for one or two performers.

String Quartets

Scelsi's five string quartets span virtually his entire career – the first dates from 1944; the fifth, his last work, from 1984 – and offer a concise introduction to his evolving style. The first quartet shows how, by the age of forty, Scelsi had absorbed all the lessons of modernism and turned them into something which is already some way removed from the musical norms of its time. Quartets 2–4 were written in close succession in the early 1960s: the volatile second and serene third quartets form something of a contrasting pair. Most extraordinary, however, is the fourth quartet. Here, each individual string of each of the four instruments is separately notated – as if Scelsi imagined the piece not as a work for two violins, viola and cello, but for one enormous sixteen-string instrument, capable of producing effects of quasi-orchestral richness unparalleled in the quartet repertoire. In 1984 Scelsi came out of compositional retirement to write one last quartet – the brief and sphinx-like fifth – as a tribute to his friend, the recently deceased French poet Henri Michaux.

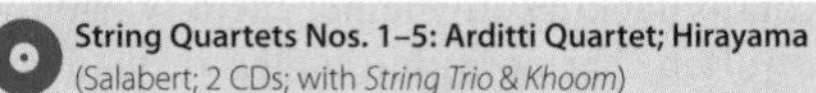

String Quartets Nos. 1–5: Arditti Quartet; Hirayama (Salabert; 2 CDs; with *String Trio* & *Khoom*)

Contemporary music specialists the Arditti Quartet make an eloquent case for these strange creations. The *String Trio* of 1958 and the vocal work *Khoom* of 1962 (entertainingly subtitled "Seven Episodes from an Unwritten Story of Love and Death in a Distant Country") complete the disc.

Alfred Schnittke (1934–1998)

Alfred Schnittke, Russia's most celebrated composer of the late Soviet era, is often seen as the successor to Shostakovich, but the generation gap meant that they were significantly different musicians. Whereas Shostakovich's music was forged in the heat of the early revolutionary period and tempered in the ice of Stalinism, Schnittke was young during the Kruschev thaw and matured under Brezhnev's stagnation. The other crucial factor in Schnittke's background was that his mother was German and his father German-Jewish – though born in the Volga Republic, he spoke German as his first language and always felt an alien in his native land. Thus it's scarcely surprising that if there are any common elements running through his wide-ranging output, they are irony, parody, disguise and wild pastiche. His music can be uncomfortably dissonant and loud, and at times it is ramblingly episodic, but at his best Schnittke was one of the wittiest composers of his time, and the manifest sincerity of his vision helped to secure him a wide following.

Alfred Schnittke with his son Andrei.

Schnittke began his musical studies in Vienna, where his father was posted as a journalist right after the war. The musical traditions of that city – both the Classicism of Haydn, Mozart and Beethoven and the *fin-de-siècle* works of Mahler and Schoenberg – had an enormous effect on him. In 1948 he settled in Moscow (where he was to stay until moving to Hamburg in 1990), and soon began writing music using serial techniques that were almost obligatory for composers in the West, but led to his marginalization by the Soviet establishment. Few official commissions came his way, and rare performances of Schnittke pieces were packed out, becoming more like socio-political events than concerts. Most of his income came from the cinema (he produced sixty film scores in just twenty years), and his work for directors such as Elem Klimov, who was to become an international figure when *perestroika* arrived, helped spread Schnittke's reputation.

Schnittke was one of the first Russian composers to be influenced by post-Webern serialism in the 1960s. But his distinctive and postmodern "polystylism", the mixing of widely disparate styles, emerged in the 1970s, notably with the *Symphony No. 1* (1974). "The goal of my life", he wrote, "is to unify 'E' [*Ernste Musik*, serious music] and 'U' [*Unterhaltungsmusik*, light music], even if I break my neck in so doing!" A number of commissions from Western Europe followed; including the notorious opera *Life With an Idiot* (1992), a scathing "requiem for the Soviet Union" and one of the most provocative, idiosyncratic and lewd scores of the last years. Arguably, critical reaction in the West tended to over-hype Schnittke's music as the Cold War came to an end, but this should not obscure the fact that – though uneven – his output includes some of the most incisive music of the late twentieth century.

Choral Music

Schnittke's 1983 choral masterpiece *Seid nüchtern and wachtet (Faust Cantata)* is his adaptation of the concluding part of Goethe's *Faust* for soloists, choir and orchestra. Constituting the third act of his opera *Faust* (but written many years before the completion of that project, and conceived as a freestanding work), this gothic postmodernist fantasy opens with a liturgical combination of chorus and choir, but with a distant tango beat. The tango comes to the foreground in the climactic scene, where Mephisto describes Faust's blood-spattered room and corpse in a nightmarish monologue. Rather more approachable than this is the *Choir Concerto* (1985), a profoundly devotional score which uses texts by the tenth-century Armenian poet Gregory of Narek and owes much to the Orthodox choral tradition.

Faust Cantata: Malmö Symphony Choir and Orchestra; DePreist (BIS; with *(K)ein Sommernachtstraum, Ritual & Passacaglia*)

This vivid BIS recording of *Faust* powerfully communicates the work's visceral energy and features an outstanding Mephisto from the countertenor Mikael Bellini. It comes coupled with some of Schnittke's best orchestral music.

Choir Concerto; Russian State Symphonic Cappella; Polyansky (Chandos)

Chandos have made two separate recordings of this work with different choirs. This is the better of the two, with the Russian State Symphonic Cappella successfully communicating something of the authentic Orthodox atmosphere.

Symphonies Nos. 1 & 2

Schnittke's landmark *Symphony No. 1* was premiered by Gennadi Rozhdestvensky in 1974 in Gorky, an emblematically out-of-the-way venue for this crazed mish-mash of a work. "The first symphony is the central work for me", says the composer, "because it contains everything that I have ever had or done in my life, even the bad and the kitschy as well as the most sincere ... all of my later works are its continuations and are determined by it." Featuring theatrical entrances and exits for the orchestral players, free-jazz improvisation and undigested fragments from the classics, it's a raucously eclectic piece. By contrast, the consistently powerful *Symphony No. 2* – actually more a mass than a symphony – was inspired by Austria and by Bruckner in particular; permeated by bell sounds and sonorous choral writing, it's a far more homogeneous work than its predecessor. Schnittke completed nine symphonies in all, the later becoming increasingly more spare and chamber-like in texture.

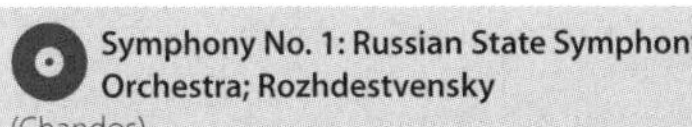

Symphony No. 1: Russian State Symphony Orchestra; Rozhdestvensky (Chandos)

This is a live recording with a fairly noisy audience, clearly enthusiastic about the occasion. Rozhdestvensky (a consistent promoter of his music) does a brilliant job in giving a semblance of order to this unruly pageant of styles and genres. This may not be a great symphony, but as a musical spectacle it's compelling.

Symphony No. 2: Mikaeli Chamber Choir; Stockholm Philharmonic Orchestra; Segerstram (BIS)

The second symphony works far better on CD and has been given several recordings. This is the best of those currently available with Segerstram completely in control of his forces, and managing to make Schnittke's rather heavy-handed symbolism sound less obvious than it actually is.

Concerto Grosso No. 1 & Viola Concerto

The *Concerto Grosso No. 1* (1977), scored for two violins, harpsichord, prepared piano and string orchestra, is quintessential Schnittke polystylism. Its six movements lurch with disarming abandon from style to style and across widely varying moods. Most entertainingly the second-movement Toccata pushes the motor rhythms of a typical Vivaldian concerto to hysterical extremes, while the fifth is a demented tango for harpsichord and strings. Amidst all this mayhem is a long slow lament for strings alone which has all the dark intensity of Shostakovich at his bleakest. The *Viola Concerto*, by contrast, is a more overtly lyrical and expressive work: its two slow outer movements enclose a frenetic middle section at the centre of which comes a moment of uneasy repose, with the viola playing a simple Classical melody, initially over a piano accompaniment, which gradually starts to distintegrate.

Concerto Grosso No. 1: Kremer, Grindenko; Chamber Orchestra of Europe; Schiff (Deutsche Grammophon; with *Quasi una sonata* & *Concerto Grosso No. 5*)

If you wish to explore Schnittke at his most eclectic, this CD makes the best introduction. The *Concerto Grosso No. 1* gets an ideal performance, led by the two violinists Gidon Kremer and Tatiana Grindenko; it's combined with *Quasi una sonata*, a strenuous rearrangement of his second violin sonata, and Schnittke's final *Concerto Grosso* in a live performance by the Vienna Philharmonic.

Viola Concerto: Bashmet; USSR Ministry of Culture Symphony Orchestra; Rozhdestvensky (Regis; with *Cello Concerto*)

The *Viola Concerto*, one of Schnittke's most Mahlerian scores, is given a definitive performance by Yuri Bashmet, for whom it was written. It is coupled with an equally compelling performance of the *Cello Concerto* by Natalia Gutman.

Chamber Music

Although it shares the multi-stylistic character of his large-scale pieces, Schnittke's chamber music contains his purest and most intense expression. Out of his entire output, nothing makes such a powerful impact as the *Piano Quintet* (1976) and the *String Trio* (1985). Both works were written in memoriam. The *Piano Quintet* commemorates his mother and juxtaposes episodes of tortured longing with a bittersweet waltz, using conflicting elements to construct a statement that is imaginative and haunting. The *String Trio*, composed for Berg's centenary, contains a macabre and insinuating motif based on "Happy Birthday to You". It's a powerful, tortured work which seems simultaneously to acknowledge the past, and point to a new way forward. The *String Quartet No. 3* is one of Schnittke's most performed works. Perhaps the use of quotation – from Lassus, Beethoven and Shostakovich – is more obviously stated than other polystylistic works, but this is immediately attractive and extremely powerful music.

Piano Quintet; Piano Quartet; String Quartet No. 3: Berlinsky; Borodin Quartet (Virgin)

The Borodin Quartet's close relationship with Schnittke really comes through on this disc; with Ludmilla Berlinsky on piano they produce a towering performance of the *Piano Quintet*, one which grippingly captures the desolation of the work – the second movement, a haunting waltz, projects a deep foreboding from the very start.

Piano Quintet; String Trio: Mason; Capricorn (Hyperion; with *Three Madrigals* & *Serenade*)

A rather different approach to the composer prevails in this recording: the players of Capricorn play down the agony of these works, concentrating instead on the musical arguments. The result is relatively subdued but still compelling, especially in the rarely recorded *Serenade*.

Arnold Schoenberg (1874–1951)

In 1909 Arnold Schoenberg wrote his *Three Pieces* for piano, Op. 11, the first wholly atonal piece of music and arguably the most significant composition of the twentieth century. In these three epigrammatic works, Schoenberg abandoned the time-honoured methods of musical expression – tonal centres, key signatures and the traditional application of harmony – in favour of one in which all the notes of the chromatic scale were assigned equal importance. As might be imagined, this brought the heavens down upon Schoenberg's head, and even today there are many people who find his subsequent work violent and incomprehensible.

Born in Vienna to Jewish parents, Schoenberg first learned the violin and cello, and taught himself theory until 1894, when Alexander Zemlinsky – whose sister he later married – began instructing him in counterpoint. By the time he was 25, Schoenberg had seen each of Wagner's major operas more than twenty times, and although his earliest music reflects an admiration for the Classical discipline of Brahms, the influence of Wagner soon became all-consuming, as was clear from the opulent string sextet *Verklärte Nacht* and the grandiose choral work *Gurrelieder*. With the latter project under his arm he applied for a teaching post in Berlin. On Richard Strauss's recommendation he was accepted at the Stern Conservatory, where he stayed for three years, a period during which he composed his Straussian tone poem *Pelleas und Melisande*.

But, whereas Strauss seemed content to live off the harmonic legacy of Wagner, to Schoenberg it seemed evident that Wagnerian chromaticism had exhausted the conventional vocabularies without offering any way forward. Schoenberg shared the preoccupation of many *fin-de-siècle* artists: how to find a way of expressing an inner vision – the subjective and the abstract. Between 1900 and 1910 Schoenberg set off in a new direction: developing a style that gradually moved away from the opulence of Symbolism towards the more economical and increasingly personal language of expressionism (see p.259). All his music of these years possesses a raw, passionate emotionalism that sometimes reflects his own troubled personal life and completely belies his later image as a dry intellectual. With the *String Quartet No. 2*, written in 1907, he came to the brink of composing music that was in no identifiable key, and with the *Three Pieces* of 1909 he finally made the complete break with tonality, following it up in the same year with the bleak atonal opera *Erwartung*.

By the following year, Schoenberg and Strauss (by now estranged) were the *enfants terribles* of European music, but whereas Strauss was hugely successful Schoenberg was the subject of venomous derision – though he had two devoted supporters in his pupils Anton Webern (see p.625) and Alban Berg (see p.67), the other key members of what became known as the Second Viennese School. The Viennese premiere of *Pierrot Lunaire* in 1912 produced outright hostility, in marked contrast to the premiere of the *Gurrelieder* early the following year, which was an unqualified success.

Schoenberg served in the ranks during World War I, and immediately after the war returned to Vienna, where, together with Berg and Webern, he organized and played in concerts of new music, events from which the critics of the Viennese press were barred. He composed little until 1924, when he announced his "re-emergence" with the creation of twelve-tone serialism, the method by which he brought order to the potential chaos of atonalism. Whereas pure atonalism gave the composer freedom to select notes at will from the entire chromatic scale, the twelve-tone technique arranged the twelve notes in a specific sequence (or tone-row) for each piece. The tone-row could be played note by note, simultaneously, even upside down, but no note could be repeated until the whole series had been played. By giving all twelve notes of the chromatic scale equal value, the conventional sense of movement to and from the tonic was eliminated, as it had been with atonalism, but this new method gave modern music a sense of focus that had been lacking in atonal works.

Egon Schiele's portrait of Schoenberg, 1917.

In 1925 Schoenberg moved back to Berlin, where he taught composition at the Academy of Arts, but with the advent of Nazism he was dismissed from his post. He left Germany in 1933 and eventually emigrated to the United States, where he settled in Los Angeles, and taught at the University of California. In the remaining years of his life he produced a large body of music in a range of styles. In 1944 he applied for a Guggenheim grant to enable him to complete his opera *Moses und Aron*, which he had begun in 1930; his application was refused, and he died leaving the third act incomplete. The opera is Schoenberg's largest staged work and the most complete dramatic expression of serialist techniques. The deeply philosophical libretto – written by the composer – is set to music of such complexity that Schoenberg doubted that a performance would be possible.

Schoenberg is one of the most remarkable figures in the history of music, as inspirational in his dedication to his art as in his published work. Driven by an inner compulsion to create new foundations for Western music, he was spurred

The Crisis of Tonality

There are twelve different notes in Western music – C, C#, D, Eb, E, F, F#, G, Ab, A, Bb, B – though each note can appear at various different *octaves*: you can have a very high C, a very low C, and a whole number of Cs in between. This is why the piano keyboard displays a repeating twelve-note pattern of black and white keys. Most passages of music, however, don't use all twelve of the available notes, instead focusing on a particular selection: a scale. There are many types of scale, but most music written between the times of Monteverdi and Mahler is based on two types – major and minor. And if a piece is based on the major scale that starts on the note D, for example, it is said to be in the "key" of D major.

Major and minor scales are the basis of tonality, not only defining how traditional melody and harmony work but also providing composers with an organizing principle. They aren't musical straitjackets, though: a piece may be based on the notes of a particular scale, but other notes, called *chromatic* notes, can be introduced, and though most pieces start and end in the same key, composers "modulate" to other keys in between.

In the nineteenth century, composers started using increasingly prominent chromatic notes and modulating to ever more "distant" keys. Their musical language became increasingly rich and complex – you only need to try humming along to Beethoven's *Grosse Fuge* (see p.57) to realize that chromaticism had come a long way since Mozart. The result was that music began to feel less secure and stable, and it became harder for the listener to predict what world happen next. Many composers such as Schubert, Liszt and Chopin built on Beethoven's chromaticism, but it was Wagner – specifically with the opera *Tristan und Isolde* – who took tonality to the edge of breaking point, with music in which there are so many and such extreme modulations that it is very difficult to keep up. The famous "Tristan chord", the first chord heard in the prelude and the musical seed of much of the rest of the opera, is the ultimate paradigm of tonal ambiguity: each time it is used it can lead the music into one of many different keys, creating a sense of moving towards ever-shifting harmonic goalposts.

Wagner's precedent was taken up by many composers such as Strauss, whose musical language is characterized by unpredictable changes of key – one can feel almost musically seasick listening to *Metamorphosen* – and Mahler, who exploited large-scale tonal ambiguity and sometimes ended symphonies in different keys to which they had begun. But for Schoenberg and Debussy, Wagner's language represented only a starting point.

In the first decade of the twentieth century Schoenberg abandoned the chromatic Wagnerian tonality of *Verklärte Nacht*, described by one critic as sounding as though "someone had smeared the score of *Tristan* whilst the ink was still wet", and attempted to let his compositions flow directly from the subconscious. But before long he began to crave for a structural principle to replace tonality, which he eventually found in his twelve-tone techniques.

While Schoenberg deliberately exhausted and then abandoned tonality, Debussy took a more evolutionary approach, gradually dissolving traditional scales and harmony in a beguilingly evocative sound-world. Instead of seeking a replacement for the goal-orientated structures of traditional tonal music, Debussy placed priority on the moment, making sensation as important as ongoing development. In pieces like *Prélude à l'après-midi d'un faune* and his opera *Pelléas et Mélisande* tonal scales and chords are present, but not consistently, and are not used in a traditional way.

to ever greater determination by the hostility he encountered. In 1947 he accepted an award from the American Academy of Arts with the words, "That you should regard all I have tried to do in the last fifty years as an achievement strikes me as in some respects an overestimate. My own feeling was that I had fallen into an ocean of boiling water; and, as I couldn't swim and knew no other way out, I struggled with my arms and legs as best I could ... The credit must go to my opponents. It was they who really helped me."

CHORAL, VOCAL & STAGE WORKS

Of all Schoenberg's choral works, the most important is the mighty *Gurrelieder*, perhaps the greatest Austro-German choral composition of the twentieth century. After Mahler's *Symphony No. 8* it requires the largest forces of any concert work, and each of Schoenberg's subsequent stage works also demands a large-scale orchestra.

However, these later pieces – *Erwartung, Die glückliche Hande, Von Heute auf Morgen* and *Moses und Aron* – are of completely different character from *Gurrelieder*, for they all come after his shift into atonality. Lyricism and melody are not wholly absent from the stage works (indeed, *Erwartung* is littered with moments of lush expressionism), but on the whole they are challengingly dissonant and extreme works. The orchestra is heavily subdivided, so that often only a few instruments are playing at any one time, while the vocal parts are typified by extreme leaps and the use of *Sprechgesang*, a style of declamation that is midway between speech and song, and is used to even more disconcerting effect in *Pierrot Lunaire*, a work described by Stravinsky as "the solar plexus" of twentieth-century music.

Gurrelieder

Of all Schoenberg's scores, none has won such wide popularity as *Gurrelieder* (Songs of Gurre). Its success has a lot to do with its scale, for *Gurrelieder* deploys a veritable army of players, including at least seventy strings, four choirs, five soloists, a narrator, eight flutes, ten horns, seven trumpets, seven trombones, five tubas, four harps, six percussionists and iron chains.

Schoenberg started it in 1900 but didn't complete the orchestration until 1911. Based upon a poem by Jens Peter Jacobsen, the ninety-minute work dramatizes the love between King Waldemar and Tove, resident of Castle Gurre. Set in the fourteenth century, it's a tale that would have appealed to Wagner, and indeed the music of *Gurrelieder*, though in part a homage to Strauss, is especially indebted to Wagner, whose *Tristan und Isolde* is the prototype for the febrile emotionalism of Part 1. This section is dominated by a long and luxuriant duet for Waldemar and Tove, which is interrupted after each verse by sumptuous orchestral commentaries, and is followed by the murder of Tove and a lament for her, sung by a wood dove. Part 2 sees Waldemar cursing his fate, but Part 3 builds to a final, pantheistic chorus of outrageous, wondrous dimensions.

Dunn, Fassbaender, Jerusalem, Becht, Haage, Hotter; Berlin St Hedwige's Cathedral Choir; Dusseldorf Musikverein; Berlin Radio Symphony Orchestra; Chailly
(Decca; 2 CDs; with *Chamber Symphony No. 1 & Verklärte Nacht*)

A superb achievement from both Chailly's combined forces and Decca's engineers. In this superbly dramatic performance, everything is present and correct: the soloists are all excellent (Susan Dunn in particular) but it's the way Chailly creates such a thrilling sense of occasion that is ultimately so impressive.

Erwartung

Erwartung (Expectation), for soprano and large orchestra, is a thirty-minute monologue of gruelling concentration. Though moments of tonality and tantalizing Classical motifs do punctuate the score, it's essentially a stream of dream-like images and jagged musical gestures – one of the most extreme examples of musical expressionism. It was written a year after the painter Richard Gerstl – who taught both Schoenberg and his wife Mathilde – committed suicide after Mathilde had ended their affair and returned to her husband.

The plot, by Marie Pappenheim, is a typical product of Freud's Vienna. A lone, unnamed woman is seen wandering at night through a forest which may be real or may be the landscape of her subconscious. The woman is searching for her lover, whose corpse she stumbles across fairly early in the work; leaving unanswered the question of the motive and identity of the murderer, the rest of *Erwartung* is given over to the woman's disjointed, distracted recollections of their life together. The rapidity of the mood swings – moments of lucidity next to near-incoherence – are brilliantly communicated by the music's extraordinary rhythmic freedom, while the absence of a clear pulse, like the absence of tonality, contributes to a sensation of rootlessness and timelessness.

Norman; Metropolitan Opera Orchestra; Levine
(Philips; with cabaret songs)

James Levine's performance of this dense score is a revelation, unleashing tremendous power at the climaxes as well as perfectly controlling the orchestra in the delicate, introspective passages. The disc is dominated, however, by an awesome performance from Jessye Norman – this is perhaps her greatest half-hour on record.

Pierrot Lunaire

At the time of *Erwartung*, Schoenberg was almost equally active as a painter – indeed, he exhibited at the famous *Blaue Reiter* exhibition organized by Kandinsky in 1911. Many of his paintings from this period are preoccupied with nightmare images of staring mask-like faces, and he had little hesitation when the actress Albertine Zehme commissioned him to write her a vocal melodrama around the Pierrot poems of Albert Giraud. The result was *Pierrot Lunaire* (1912), another startling work of raw expressionism. Scored for a small ensemble (flute, clarinet, strings and piano) and a soprano employing *Sprechgesang* (a form of vocalizing halfway between speaking and singing), *Pierrot Lunaire* focuses on a dislocated, splintered personality in the same way *Erwartung* did. This time, however, there's a strong element of grotesquerie – madness even – as Pierrot (traditionally a figure of pathos) rasps out his tortured and often violent fantasies. The lightness of the accompaniment (the instrumentalists were hidden at the original performance) means that it functions as a kind of ghostly commentary.

Schäffer; Ensemble Intercontemporain; Boulez
(Deutsche Grammophon; with *Herzgewächse* & *Ode to Napoleon*)

Although she never compromises on the harsher aspects of the score, this is a highly musical performance from Christine Schäffer with a wide range of vocal colouring on offer. Combined with the meticulous ensemble of the Ensemble Intercontemporain, this makes the most fully satisfying recording of *Pierrot*.

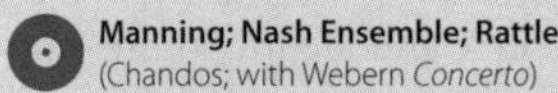

Manning; Nash Ensemble; Rattle
(Chandos; with Webern *Concerto*)

A tart, acerbic and uncompromising performance from Jane Manning, who growls and swoops her way through the increasingly disturbing verses. Recorded in 1977, the Nash Ensemble, under Simon Rattle, provide virtuosic but discreet accompaniment.

ORCHESTRAL WORKS

It was his orchestral music that first earned Schoenberg his reputation as a dangerous radical. The premiere of the "tuneless" *Five Orchestral Pieces* caused an outrage, as did the later *Variations for Orchestra*, an uncompromising example of fully developed serialism. To appreciate the origins of these works you should approach them via his early *Pelleas und Melisande*, which shows Schoenberg at his most Romantic. These three works represent only a small selection of Schoenberg's orchestral output, but they will give you an excellent introduction to the composer's range.

Pelleas und Melisande

Debussy wrote his *Pelléas et Mélisande* in the mid-1890s; though unaware of Debussy's opera, Schoenberg also considered writing a stage work based on Maeterlinck's play at this time, but in 1902 he decided instead to turn the story into a symphonic poem. Whereas Debussy's opera is all about understatement and implication, Schoenberg's music is a tightly strung, blatantly hedonistic piece, explicitly portraying Melisande's illicit love for her brother-in-law – the love duet in particular is breathtakingly effective, containing some brilliantly dramatic counterpoint. In places *Pelleas und Melisande* does suggest that Schoenberg's grasp of the technicalities of orchestration was not yet complete, yet his only symphonic poem is obsessively involving, and contains some of the most erotic music ever written.

Berlin Philharmonic Orchestra; Karajan
(Deutsche Grammophon; with *Verklärte Nacht*)

With Karajan at the helm, this is perfect repertoire for the Berlin Phil to show off their mastery of luscious, late Romantic writing. *Pelleas* is pretty dense in its orchestration, but in this recording you are made aware of more of the textural strands than usual. A must for anti-Schoenbergians wanting to be converted.

Chamber Symphony No. 1

With the *Chamber Symphony No. 1* the grandiosity of *Pelleas und Melisande* has been condensed into something much more spare and sinewy. This is a concentrated single-movement work for fifteen solo players: a semblance of Classical four-movement structure still remains as does the passionately rapturous quality of the earlier orchestral works. Where the old fixities start to break down is in the way that melody is gradually undermined, rather than reinforced, by its underlying harmony. There is plenty of energetic momentum to this work (it's one of Schoenberg's most positive pieces), but it is sustained through lively contrapuntal writing against a background of unstable tonality which is both disconcerting and liberating.

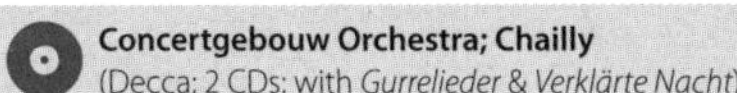

Concertgebouw Orchestra; Chailly (Decca; 2 CDs; with *Gurrelieder* & *Verklärte Nacht*)

Ricardo Chailly's dynamic 1990 performance of *Gurrelieder* has been coupled with his superb reading of the *Chamber Symphony No. 1*, made with players from the Concertgebouw a couple of years later. It's a bold and assertive reading that brings out all the work's coiled energy.

Five Orchestral Pieces

Composed in the *annus mirabilis* of 1909, the *Five Orchestral Pieces* shows Schoenberg moving further into the free-floating world of atonalism, yet this is not a schism so much as a transition. The rather unwieldy orchestrations betray an affinity with the *fin-de-siècle* aesthetic of *Pelleas*, as do some of the titles originally appended to each of the five pieces: "Premonitions", "Yesteryears", "Summer Morning by a Lake", "Peripetia" and "The Obbligato Recitative". The first and the last of the set are laden with the kind of angst associated with expressionism, but the second piece is a restrained and essentially Romantic episode which in turn leads into the extraordinary "Summer Morning by a Lake", the work's high point. Here Schoenberg explores the possibilities of what was termed *Klangfarbenmelodie* ("sound-colour melody"), in which a melodic effect is transformed simply by changing the timbre of a single note or a simple harmony. Just as colour can alter the eye's perception of an object's shape, so a chord or run of notes is here modified by playing with its tone-colour. The tranquillity of this third movement is extremely affecting, and its stylistic impact upon Webern and subsequent generations is incalculable.

London Symphony Orchestra; Dorati (Mercury; with orchestral works by Webern and Berg)

Aware of every inflection of the music's colour and internal shape, Antal Dorati makes the most of Schoenberg's orchestration; combined with other fine examples of the Second Viennese School, this brightly engineered recording serves as an excellent starting point for atonal orchestral music.

Variations for Orchestra

The *Variations for Orchestra*, Schoenberg's most successful orchestral application of the twelve-tone method, was premiered by Wilhelm Furtwängler on 3 December, 1928, and prompted such tumultuous scenes that the concert came close to being abandoned. Nonetheless the critic Max Marschalk was moved to comment: "Schoenberg convinces us with the *Variations* that he has succeeded in discovering new vistas in music in which we can feel comfortably at home … The music he presents in the *Variations* is without precedent." This is not strictly true, for Schoenberg had created his own precedents, but this music certainly did mark a new direction in its rigorous formal cohesion. You cannot hear the variations taking place – Schoenberg himself said that this was impossible – but you can detect an underlying momentum generated by the music's complex rhythmic patterns, and the rich orchestral detail builds to a climax as fulfilling as that of any conventional variation sequence. The more often you listen to this piece, the more easily you'll be able to follow the many layers from which it is constructed and so appreciate its fundamentally Classical architecture.

BBC Symphony Orchestra; Boulez (Sony; with *Verklärte Nacht* & *Die Glückliche Hand*)

Boulez has a reputation for being a somewhat cool interpreter of the great modernist classics; that's not the case on this disc, where there seems to be the perfect marriage between rigorous attention to structure and a relish of the score's colouristic detail.

CHAMBER & PIANO MUSIC

Schoenberg's string quartets and his piano music comprise two categories of his output within which you can clearly trace the dominant pattern of his career, from chromatic Romanticism through atonality to serialism. Besides these works, there is one other piece of essential listening in his chamber-music output: the string sextet *Verklärte Nacht*, the composer's most seductive creation.

Verklärte Nacht

Verklärte Nacht (Transfigured Night) was one of Schoenberg's earliest pieces and it gave him his first taste of success when it was performed in 1903, four years after its composition. It was liked both by the public and by its creator, who produced orchestrated versions of it in 1917 and 1943, each of which proved as popular as the orginal sextet.

Verklärte Nacht was written shortly after Schoenberg's immersion in the Symbolist poetry of Richard Dehmel, whose words he used for a set of early songs. The Dehmel poem that specifically inspired the sextet concerned a woman racked by guilt and fear, like the figure portrayed in *Erwartung*. However, whereas *Erwartung* ends in unease, *Verklärte Nacht* ends with a resolution: she confesses to her lover that she is pregnant by another man; he replies that through their love the child will be born his, and thus the night is transfigured. However, no knowledge of this programme is really necessary to enjoy a piece of music that is one of the peaks of late Romanticism and which possesses a highly charged, near-neurotic expressiveness which is completely unique. In this work Schoenberg manages to achieve a sort of reconciliation between Brahms and Wagner: the lyricism, instrumentation and sheer tunefulness of *Verklärte Nacht* reflect the influence of the former, while its chromaticism and overall construction bear the marks of the latter.

Chamber version: Raphael Ensemble (Hyperion; with Korngold *Sextet*)

The Raphael Ensemble deliver a pulsating but sensitively drawn performance, in which the intricately balanced counterpoint is made to sigh with erotic yearning – in the final part, introduced by the second cellist's beautiful solo theme, the music seems about to burst its banks.

Orchestral version: Berlin Philharmonic; Karajan (Deutsche Grammophon; with *Pelleas und Melisande*)

Coupled with a refulgent account of *Pelleas und Melisande* (see p.482), this is an immaculately detailed performance, carefully paced so that by the time the coda is reached, the feeling of transcendence is all the more uplifting.

String Quartets

Schoenberg's *String Quartet No. 1* of 1905 is a Brahms-like piece, forward-looking in the sense that it is written as a single extended movement, but basically conservative in its language. In extreme contrast, the third and fourth quartets (1927 and 1936) are thorough-going serial works. Bereft of anything that could be termed conventional melody, they are immensely intellectual pieces that are best approached after you've become familiar with the earlier works. The *String Quartet No. 2* (1907) is the one most likely to excite you if you're coming fresh to Schoenberg. In the last two movements this amazing quartet steps over the line into the shifting, eerie soundscape of atonality, a move announced by a soprano soloist who sings Stefan George's prophetic words, "I breathe the air of other planets." More than any other of Schoenberg's works, the *String Quartet No. 2* dramatizes the transition from the old to the new.

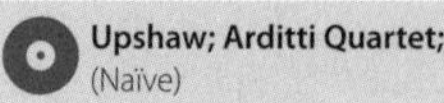
Upshaw; Arditti Quartet; (Naïve)

These are exceptionally fine readings of all the music for string quartet. The playing is rigorous and lucid without being merely efficient. Schoenberg's densely argued last two quartets have rarely sounded so impressive, and if the first two are given less Romantic accounts than usual they are still utterly compelling performances.

Piano Works

Schoenberg was not a pianist and published only six works for solo piano, but no part of his oeuvre provides so complete and concise a survey of his compositional development. Aside from the rather clumsy unpublished *Piano Pieces* of 1894, Schoenberg's first work for the instrument was the epoch-making atonal music of the *Three Piano Pieces* Op. 11, works in which the hegemony of the major and minor scales – and the sense that some episodes in a piece are more important than others – is rejected. This radical approach is furthered by the aphoristic *Six Little Piano Pieces* Op. 19 (1911), which rejects all motivic development in favour of a reliance upon tone colour and vertical relations between notes, which obey no other logic than Schoenberg's intuitive sense of what works. These pieces still split opinion: some people find them insubstantial and uncomfortably dissonant; others regard them as masterpieces of expressive concision in which everything happens in the present tense.

The *Five Piano Pieces* Op. 23 was the first published example of rigorous serial music, a technique that is further refined in the wonderful *Piano Suite* Op. 25 (a distant relative of the keyboard suites of Bach), and shown at its most polished in the two *Piano Pieces* of Op. 33. To really understand the formal intricacies of these works requires careful study of the scores, but the non-specialist simply needs concentration and open ears: the radical dynamic shifts, eventful rhythmic changes and startling juxtapositions of tones make these small-scale pieces as engrossing, if not as comforting, as any Chopin study or Schumann miniature.

Pollini (Deutsche Grammophon)

Mauricio Pollini's recording of the complete published piano music is a magnificent achievement. Few pianists have matched the intellectual and emotional cohesion he brings to this music. If anyone tells you that Schoenberg is all about composing by numbers or by random selection, just listen to this CD – Pollini reveals the passion behind the method.

Franz Schreker (1878–1934)

In the decade prior to World War I, Franz Schreker was regarded as the third member of German music's avant-garde triumvirate, alongside Richard Strauss and Arnold Schoenberg. Nowadays he is little more than a footnote to the history of modern music, even though his operas are among the most intriguing works of the early twentieth century. At times reminiscent of both Richard Strauss and Debussy, Schreker creates an impressionistic sound-world of ever-changing moods and colours, a style perfectly suited to the post-Freudian psychology of his subjects. But if his music deserves to regain its former reputation, then his lurid and morbid libretti – which he wrote himself – suggest just why the operas have always had their critics.

Born in Monaco to Austrian parents, Schreker lived most of his life in Vienna where, in 1892, he was enrolled at the conservatory. His first success as a composer came in 1908 with *Der Geburtstag der Infantin* (The Birthday of the Infanta), a ballet based on a story by Oscar Wilde (later set as an opera by his colleague Zemlinsky, see p.641). Four years later the premiere of the first of Schreker's major operas, *Der ferne Klang* (The Distant Sound), established him as a leading modernist, and both Schoenberg and Berg expressed great admiration for the score. For a short time Schreker's influence on the development of new music was crucial. He conducted the premiere of Schoenberg's *Gurrelieder* in 1913, and in 1920 was appointed to the prestigious position of director of the Hochschule für Musik in Berlin, where he presided over an impressive teaching staff that included Hindemith.

Two more operas, both written during World War I, consolidated his reputation: *Die Gezeichneten* (The Stigmatized Ones) and *Der Schatzgräber* (The Treasure Seeker) were two of the most frequently performed operas of the immediate post-war period, but by the mid-1920s Schreker's opulent style was rapidly going out of fashion as the more acerbic manner of composers such as Weill and Hindemith began to find favour. He produced four more operas but his later works were not well received. The first performance of *Christophorus* in 1931 was cancelled as a result of Nazi pressure, but the premiere of *Der Schmied von Gent* (The Blacksmith of Ghent) the following year was allowed to continue – only to be shouted down by an anti-Semitic mob.

In 1932 the composer Max von Schillings became the new president of the Prussian Academy of Arts, accepting the task of purging the Academy of all "racially undesirable" members. Schreker was duly dismissed from his teaching post and he found himself at the mercy of some of modernism's most virulent opponents. Quite apart from any musical criticism, he was attacked for "sexual deviancy", with disastrous consequences. Condemned for his Jewishness, his homosexuality and his music, Schreker suffered a fatal heart attack, dying just two days short of his 56th birthday. Only in very recent years has there been any serious attempt to reassess his achievements as an opera composer.

Der ferne Klang

Der ferne Klang tells how Fritz, a young composer haunted by a magical sound, abandons his lover, Grete, to go in search of it. She falls into prostitution, but they are finally reunited as Fritz is dying, whereupon he realizes that the "distant sound" – the natural world, the power of love, Grete – was within his grasp all the time. The opera's incredible success established Schreker as one of Germany's leading modern composers but for all the daring of its subject matter and Schreker's advanced harmonic language this is essentially a Romantic work, characterized by muscular instrumentation and extremely atmospheric sonorities that augment the moods and emotions of the protagonists. In terms of dissonance it is not as extreme as Strauss's *Elektra*, which was composed around the same time, and it was the opera's luxuriant and diaphanous textures that so appealed to contemporary audiences.

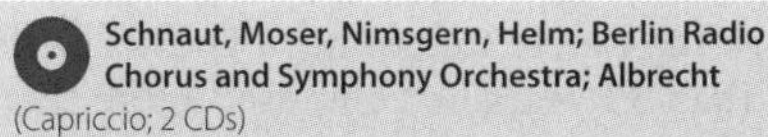

Schnaut, Moser, Nimsgern, Helm; Berlin Radio Chorus and Symphony Orchestra; Albrecht
(Capriccio; 2 CDs)

Of the two recordings of *Der ferne Klang* Gerd Albrecht's is preferable in most respects, with a rich, indulgent sound and a fine orchestra, to whom the music is clearly second nature. Gabriele Schnaut is a powerful, chesty mezzo and she copes well with Grete's difficult music. Thomas Moser is reliable in the baritone role of Fritz but no more; the remaining cast all give solid – if not top-flight – performances.

Orchestral Works

Prior to *Der ferne Klang*, Schreker had experienced some success as an orchestral composer, notably with the short *Intermezzo* (1901), a ravishingly beautiful work for string orchestra whose hushed, rapturous opening is distinctly Wagnerian. In the best of his later orchestral works he adapted the highly charged music of the operas into something akin to tone poems. The most exhilarating of these is the twenty-minute *Vorspiel zu einem Drama* (Prelude to a Drama), which takes the themes from his decadent opera *Die Gezeichneten* and transforms them into an ebullient display of orchestral fireworks – full of long, arching melodies and shimmering instrumental colouring. In the even grander *Vorspiel zu einem großen Oper* (Prelude to a Grand Opera; 1933) the orchestration is more varied – startlingly lean in the opening Mahlerian march – and suggests the direction Schreker might have followed had he lived.

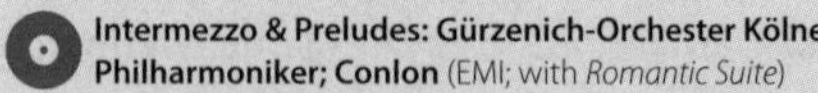
Intermezzo & Preludes: Gürzenich-Orchester Kölner Philharmoniker; Conlon (EMI; with *Romantic Suite*)

James Conlon and his Cologne orchestra have made something of a speciality of the neglected music of *fin-de-siècle* Vienna, and their familiarity with the details of these four works really pays off. When performances are this engrossing it begs the question why a work such as *Vorspiel zu einem Drama* isn't a standard part of the orchestral repertoire.

Franz Schubert (1797–1828)

The neglect that Schubert suffered for most of the nineteenth century now seems incredible. None of his symphonies was performed during his lifetime and not one was published until some fifty years after his death. In 1827 a music dictionary was published in which Schubert's name did not so much as feature once. A century later, another book attacked him as a "conventional music-machine, contentedly turning out work after work, day after day". A partial explanation for this situation is that – unlike Beethoven or Mozart – Schubert was not a virtuoso musician, and he found no other means of promoting himself. Ironically, however, his unfettered talent for melody and his attachment to Classical forms also contributed significantly towards his neglect. In the high Romantic period, when complexity and ambiguity were the order of the day, Schubert's lucid and tuneful music was often dismissed as the product of a naive mind. But even in the area of his output where melody predominated – his lieder (songs) – there is so much more to his work than mere tunefulness. During a life of less than 32 years he composed more than six hundred songs, and few other composers have displayed such an ability to match music to poetry so closely that the words seem to have been written expressly for this purpose. He remains the greatest of all songwriters, but that is not the limit of his achievement, for in his late chamber music, piano sonatas and symphonies Schubert created works that mark him down as the first great Romantic. The progressive element to this late music suggests that, had he lived longer, he would have gone on to produce music of daunting originality. The epitaph on his monument, written by his friend Grillparzer, says as much: "The art of music here entombed a rich possession, but even fairer hopes."

Schubert was born in Lichtenthal, a suburb of Vienna, and at the age of nine or ten was sent to study with the local church organist, Michael Holzer. As Holzer later wrote: "If I wished to instruct him in anything fresh, the boy already knew it. So I gave him no actual tuition but merely talked to him and watched him with silent astonishment." Every moment Schubert had to himself was spent composing, and in 1812 he was accepted as a student by Salieri, under whose guidance he composed his first symphony. Two years later, to Salieri's astonishment, the seventeen-year-old presented him with the 341 pages of his fully orchestrated first opera. (Despite repeated attempts, mastery of operatic form was always to elude him.) On 19 October, 1814, Schubert wrote his setting of Goethe's poem "Gretchen am Spinnrade" (Gretchen at the Spinning Wheel) – his first real masterpiece. Unlike the young Beethoven, composing came completely naturally to Schubert. On the first anniversary of "Gretchen

Schubert by his friend Leopold Kupelweiser.

am Spinnrade" he composed no fewer than eight songs in one day, and in the course of 1815 he produced some 144 songs.

From 1814 to 1817 Schubert worked in his father's school, spending all his spare time writing – students who interrupted him received short shrift. Towards the end of this period he began to gather around him a close and influential circle of friends, including the rich and rather disreputable Franz von Schober, the melancholy poet Johann Mayrhofer, and the operatic baritone Michael Vogl, for whom Schubert composed many of his greatest songs. Although his music was now sporadically performed in concert as well as at private gatherings called "Schubertiads", Schubert was regarded as an esoteric taste and he was in desperate need of money, a plight that was to dog him throughout his life.

In the summer of 1818 he moved to Zseliz in Hungary to take up the position of music tutor to the daughters of Count Johann Esterházy. Initially happy there (he particularly liked the girls) he soon started to miss Vienna and his friends. On his return the following year he took rooms with Mayrhofer and a new friend, Josef Huttenbrenner, who devoted himself to the composer, collecting and cataloguing his music. This was an especially productive period, with two operas commissioned by the Court Theatre and an extended summer holiday with Vogl in the countryside at Steyr providing the inspiration for the *Trout Quintet*. In 1821 the song "Erlkönig" was published by Diabelli – his first published composition – and in the same year he sketched, but never orchestrated, a seventh symphony.

What seemed like the beginnings of a great career began to fall apart in 1822. The Court Theatre, which had continued to favour Schubert despite his failure to produce a popular success, brought in new, Italian management (Vienna had gone Rossini-mad) who cancelled two commissions. Worse was to follow: around this time Schubert contracted syphilis, then rife in Vienna, and in 1823 his health began to fail, resulting in his admission to the Vienna general hospital. Though the mental and physical shock was overwhelming, his illness and subsequent depression did nothing to inhibit his creativity and while in hospital he began work on his first song cycle, *Die schöne Müllerin*.

In 1825 he and Vogl spent five restorative months touring Austria, in the course of which Schubert is known to have sketched a symphony – possibly an early draft of *Symphony No. 9*. At some point during the next two years Schubert met Beethoven (by now totally deaf) and, although there are no details of any strong ties between the two men, Beethoven clearly recognized the younger man's talent and Schubert is known to have been one of the torchbearers at Beethoven's funeral in 1827. As with Beethoven, Schubert's last years saw him reaching a new level of achievement, as if the prospect of death had forced out of him the creation of his finest works. The *Quintet in C Major*, the *Winterreise* song cycle, the last three piano sonatas and his final symphony all plumb the most astonishing emotional depths. In March 1828 he gave a concert of his own music and, although the Viennese turned out in force, the concert's success was completely eclipsed by the Vienna debut of Paganini three days later. Eight months later Schubert was dead at the age of 31. His brother Ferdinand interpreted his dying words as a wish to be buried near Beethoven, and so he was; in 1888 both bodies were exhumed to be placed in the Zentralfriedhof in Vienna, where they now lie side by side.

SYMPHONIES

Schubert lived in Beethoven's shadow all his life and yet his symphonies owe less to Beethoven's style than you might expect. Devoid of the Promethean defiance so common to Beethoven's works, they generally have a lightness, openness and thematic profusion that owes more to Haydn and Mozart than to Beethoven. However, while it's true that Schubert's symphonies as a whole are not as individualistic as his smaller-scale works, the last two symphonies display an approach to orchestral colouring that looks forward to the expansive symphonies of the mid-nineteenth century – the opening of the *Unfinished Symphony*, for example, is more Romantic than Classical in feel. As with all his works, the symphonies are dominated by a succession of seraphic melodies, but unlike the highly melodic symphonies of Schumann and Mendelssohn, Schubert's are never facile, and their range of emotion, from capricious gaiety to deep melancholy, marks them out as one of the great cycles of the century.

The numbering of Schubert's symphonies can be confusing, as *Symphony No. 7* was never orchestrated by Schubert (though others had a go). Thus, although Schubert composed nine symphonies, only eight are played and some authorities label *Symphony No. 8* (the *Unfinished*) as *Symphony No. 7* and *Symphony No. 9* (the *Great*) as *Symphony No. 8*.

Complete Symphonies: Concertgebouw; Harnoncourt (Teldec; 4 CDs)

Harnoncourt's Beethoven cycle reaped every award on offer, but his Schubert set is even better – refreshingly instinctive conducting that is at once lyrical and brisk. If you've heard more traditional recordings, the sound of the much-reduced Concertgebouw orchestra might surprise you, but nothing is done merely to surprise.

Complete Symphonies: Chamber Orchestra of Europe; Abbado (Deutsche Grammophon; 5 CDs; with *Rosamunde Overture* & *Grand Duo*)

A good alternative to Harnoncourt is this excellent cycle from Claudio Abbado and the Chamber Orchestra of Europe, who generally deliver somewhat sunnier interpretations. Abbado put a lot of textual research into his recordings, so there are small but significant differences between the scores used for the two sets. The five CDs are all available separately.

Symphony No. 4 – The Tragic

Composed at the age of nineteen, the *Symphony No. 4* shows that a dark strain was present in Schubert's music from the very beginning. Its epithet "tragic" was added by Schubert himself and it is indeed a sombre work, revealing more than any other the influence of Beethoven, not least in the choice of key – C minor. It opens with a slow introduction, which gives way to a development of great urgency and vigour that recalls the *Symphony No. 40* of Mozart. The subsequent broad-themed Andante is twice interrupted by agitated episodes, and this mood of restlessness is continued in the ensuing minuet and Allegro.

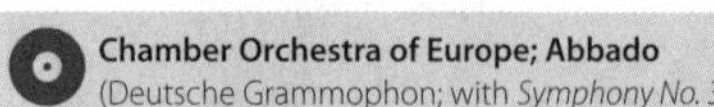

Chamber Orchestra of Europe; Abbado (Deutsche Grammophon; with *Symphony No. 3*)

Instead of overplaying the tragic element in this performance Abbado manages to generate an atmosphere of real tension and excitement from an orchestra who have, on previous occasions, sounded rather too suave.

Symphony No. 5

Begun a mere five months after *Symphony No. 4*, the *Symphony No. 5* is of an altogether more cheery disposition and has proved one of the most popular of all Schubert's orchestral works. It is certainly a work of far greater confidence than the previous four symphonies, with a Mozartian orchestral and architectural scale but a personality very much Schubert's own. The exquisite slow movement, characterized by poignant, uniquely Schubertian key modulations, features a magical duet between the strings and wind section near the end, while its coda is perhaps the most affecting conclusion in all his symphonic music. He was still only nineteen when he completed this masterpiece, and its captivating finale embodies all the optimism and clear-sightedness of youth.

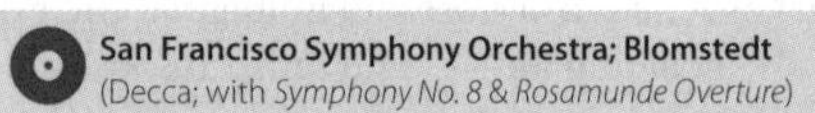

San Francisco Symphony Orchestra; Blomstedt (Decca; with *Symphony No. 8* & *Rosamunde Overture*)

Blomstedt's account is marked by finely judged balance and exquisite melodic colour, best shown in the slow movement, where a beguiling attention to detail creates a chamber-like intimacy. It's coupled with an excellent version of the eighth symphony (see below).

Symphony No. 6

Sometimes known as the "Little" C major symphony to distinguish it from *Symphony No. 9*, the *Symphony No. 6* is one of the least known of Schubert's major works. Its neglect probably stems from the fact that, though its orchestration is heavier than in earlier symphonies, it has a somewhat throwaway air despite several moments of grandiloquence. This insouciance can be traced to the influence of Rossini apparent throughout, but, in particular, in the opening introduction which recalls a Rossini opera overture and in the bustle of the dotted rhythms that dominate the last-movement Allegro.

Royal Philharmonic Orchestra; Beecham
(EMI; with *Symphonies Nos. 3 & 5*)

Thomas Beecham's scintillating performance, made in 1955, should really have rescued this symphony from its unjustifiable neglect. It's poised, elegant and fleet-footed and comes with equally seductive performances of *Symphonies Nos. 3* and *5*. An irresistible bargain.

Symphony No. 8 – The Unfinished

Schubert's *Symphony No. 8* was composed in 1822, and then abandoned for reasons about which one can only speculate. It may be that he was simply unable to find the inspiration to continue with the last two movements or, more likely, that he was repulsed by the work's association with the painful events that had accompanied its composition: arguments with Vogl, a regrettable publishing agreement, and the emergence of the symptoms of syphilis. Its truncated form has been no handicap to success, however, and this is now the best known of all Schubert's orchestral music.

The first movement is ushered in by the basses, playing a darkly hued theme of ominous power. This leads to a gentle rustle of strings over which an intensely yearning theme is played by oboe and clarinet in unison. Then the dominant idea is introduced: a sweeping melody which, for extra weight, is given over to the cellos. It is one of the most profound openings in all symphonic music. In the second movement the first movement's intimations of doom are transformed into radiant optimism, and Schubert shows himself to be a master of orchestration as well as form. From here on, no one could categorize him as a songwriter with unseemly aspirations.

Vienna Philharmonic Orchestra; Kleiber
(Deutsche Grammophon; with *Symphony No. 3*)

Carlos Kleiber's recording of the *Unfinished* is the most dramatic on record, highlighting the dynamic contrasts without impeding the flow. It's coupled with a quicksilver interpretation of the third symphony.

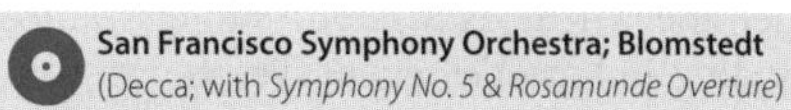

San Francisco Symphony Orchestra; Blomstedt
(Decca; with *Symphony No. 5 & Rosamunde Overture*)

Blomstedt concentrates on the essentially lyrical nature of the *Unfinished* – nothing is forced and everything has its place. Something of the composer's contradictory psychology might be missed, but this is immensely accomplished playing.

Symphony No. 9 – The Great

Schubert's orchestral masterpiece is the mighty *Symphony No. 9*, better known as the "Great". It was written in the year of his death for the Gesellschaft der Musikfreunde (Society of Friends of Music), who found the music too difficult for their tastes. The spurned manuscript went missing for a number of years until Schumann found it in 1838, whereupon he sent it to Mendelssohn, who gave the symphony its premiere in Leipzig on 21 March, 1839.

Schubert's slow movements are frequently the high points, and the blissful, ardent slow movement of the ninth symphony is very special indeed. Schumann, for one, admired it immensely, extolling its "heavenly length". He was especially taken by the section leading towards the recapitulation of the main theme, when the horn plays a series of delicate repeated notes – the instrument, Schumann said, was "calling as though from … another sphere. Everything else is hushed, as though listening to some heavenly visitant hovering around the orchestra." The symphony as a whole is characterized by an exceptional rhythmic energy, while Schubert's radically advanced orchestration places much greater weight on the brass sections, anticipating the bias of much Romantic orchestral music.

In brief, the "Great" is Schubert's longest, most demanding and most eloquent symphony.

Vienna Philharmonic; Solti
(Decca; with Wagner *Siegfried Idyll*)

Georg Solti had a reputation as a somewhat frenetic conductor, but this beautiful reading of Schubert's last symphony shows a mellower, more reflective side of his character. Recorded in 1981, this is arguably the finest of the post-Furtwängler accounts.

Berlin Philharmonic Orchestra; Furtwängler
(Deutsche Grammophon; with Haydn *Symphony No. 88*)

The sound quality is superior but this is not as exciting and emotionally charged as Furtwängler's live recording of 1942 (currently available on the Tahra label) but it still makes an incredible impact. Furtwängler's vision and discipline bring a dimension to this music that few other conductors have realized on disc.

CHAMBER MUSIC

Schubert composed an astonishing amount of chamber music, much of it before the age of twenty, but it's the work that he carried out in his last years which really justifies the use of superlatives. Overall his chamber music is marked by a vein of intensely lyrical melody to which, in the later works, is added a strengthening of resources on several fronts. Increasing chromatic boldness and a greater flexibility of form become notable, as do a scrupulous attention to the details of instrumentation, a more aggressive use of rhythm, and a sometimes overwhelming sense of urgency. Schubert's final chamber masterpieces – the last three string quartets, the piano trios and the string quintet – were written at about the same time that Beethoven was working on his final series of quartets. Both bodies of work are profoundly personal and, while Schubert's may not possess the same degree of discursiveness or complexity, not even Beethoven conveys the sheer implacable momentum that runs through these last works.

Quintet for Piano & Strings – The Trout

In 1819, during a walking tour with Michael Vogl in Upper Austria, Schubert stayed in Vogl's home town of Steyr, a place he thought "inconceivably lovely". Here the two men met a wealthy patron of the arts named Sylvester Paumgartner, who asked Schubert to compose a work for one of his musical gatherings. Paumgartner made some stipulations: the piece should employ the same instrumentation as Hummel's *Quintet* (piano, violin, viola, cello, double bass) and at least one of the movements should be a theme and variations based upon Schubert's song "Die Forelle" (The Trout). The resulting *Trout Quintet*, completed the following year, is an irresistibly good-natured piece of music, and there is no better introduction to Schubert. The dramatic Allegro, soulful Andante, lively Scherzo, rippling variations and Gypsyish finale all display a staggering wealth of invention and thematic contrast. The piano part is marvellously integrated with the textures of the strings, with a high, lightly written role that beautifully balances the weight of the double bass.

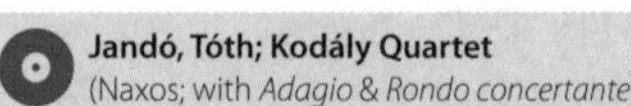

Jandó, Tóth; Kodály Quartet
(Naxos; with *Adagio & Rondo concertante*)

Star-name recordings are often dominated by an overbearing pianist, but Jenö Jandó and the Kodály Quartet are brilliantly coordinated in their light-footed approach. This 1992 recording is completely convincing and great value.

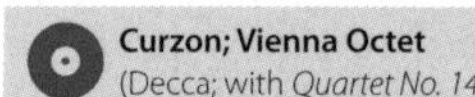

Curzon; Vienna Octet
(Decca; with *Quartet No. 14*)

Recorded in 1957, this is an utterly winning account, full of wit and sparkle though the rather thin sound may deter some. Curzon was a natural Schubert performer and here his playing sounds particularly joyous and spontaneous – especially in the variations. Also available in a Decca two-CD set with the *Arpeggione Sonata*, *Violin Romance* and *Octet*.

Piano Trios Nos. 1 & 2

Schubert's two complete piano trios were probably composed in fairly quick succession in 1827. The first, in B flat, is one of his ripest creations: stuffed with long melodies of effortless lyricism, it is a perfectly balanced composition. Whereas Beethoven's trios give preference to the piano part, each of Schubert's three players is accorded an equal bite of the very sweet cherry. All four movements are immensely attractive but the second is its finest: a journey of musical discovery, it begins with one of the most marvellous of all his tunes, played first by the cello over rippling triplets and then by the violin. The *Trio No. 2 in E Flat* was performed at Schubert's public concert in March 1828. It opens with a similar flourish to the earlier work but, on the whole, it's a rather more delicate and sombre work, full of passages of quiet yearning. This is especially true of the marvellous slow movement (used in the film *Barry Lyndon*) in which a plaintive song-like melody on the cello is heard against a repeated strumming accompaniment. The weakness of the work is its overlong last movement which, though full of glorious moments, seems to go around in circles.

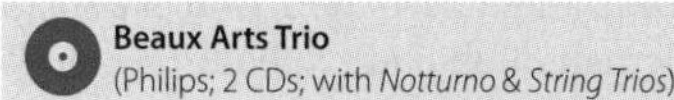
Beaux Arts Trio
(Philips; 2 CDs; with *Notturno* & *String Trios*)

The Beaux Arts Trio may seem a predictable choice, but once again the amazing rapport between the players and their impeccable style yields winning results. They even succeed in making you forget the prolixity of *No. 2*'s last movement. This two-disc set also includes fine performances by the Grumiaux Trio of the charming but slight *String Trios*.

Arpeggione Sonata

This is the oddity in Schubert's chamber music. In 1824 the instrument maker J.G. Staufer of Vienna invented a new instrument, a kind of bowed guitar, which he called the arpeggione. The guitarist Vincenz Schuster seems to have been its only professional exponent, and in the same year he commissioned a work for it from Schubert. The result was a fine sonata, which is now performed mainly by cellists and occasionally by viola players. It remains an underrated work, although in the right hands it exudes enormous panache, beginning with an opening melody which seems to possess the seemingly contradictory qualities of swagger and melancholy. A beautiful Adagio – another quasi-song – leads into a thematically rich but slightly underdeveloped Allegretto.

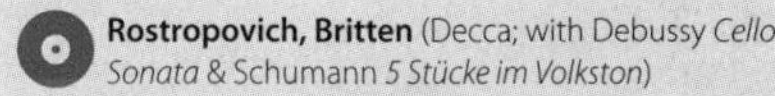
Rostropovich, Britten (Decca; with Debussy *Cello Sonata* & Schumann *5 Stücke im Volkston*)

Stravinsky famously dismissed Benjamin Britten as "a talented accompanist", an enviable skill displayed at its best in the wonderful partnership he established with Rostropovich. There's a warmth and tangible sympathy on display here which brings out all the sonata's wit and sly charm. A classic recording.

Octet in F

Schubert's serenely confident *Octet* is doubly unique: it is his only work for eight players, and no other major composer has written for the same combination: two violins, viola, cello, bass, clarinet, horn and bassoon. It was commissioned by a Viennese nobleman named Ferdinand Troyer, a fine clarinettist, who wanted a companion piece to Beethoven's *Septet*, a work of immense popularity at the time. Schubert completed his commission on 1 March, 1824, but it was not performed until 1827 and did not appear in print until 26 years later. The *Octet*'s six movements last over an hour, but the piece is so light-hearted that the time flies past. Similarities between Beethoven's and Schubert's works are few, and the only real acts of homage are Schubert's imitation of Beethoven's use of folk-based variation form for the fourth movement, and the use of a slow introduction to the finale – exactly eighteen bars in length, just like Beethoven's. Highly appealing is Schubert's delicate, unfussy counterpoint and, as ever, his concentration upon song-like melody, but the most remarkable feature of the *Octet* is his effortless unification of the potentially disparate instrumental colours, with the clarinet and violin taking the dominant roles.

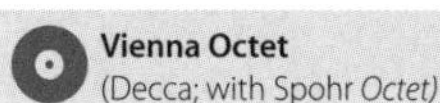
Vienna Octet
(Decca; with Spohr *Octet*)

There are a number of fine recordings of this work, but the Vienna Octet's 1958 classic is perhaps most ideally suited to the music's optimistic nature, and their attention to ensemble playing produces an endearing through-flowing momentum. Excellently recorded and fantastic value.

String Quartets Nos. 13–15

In March 1824, despite describing himself as "the most unhappy and wretched creature in the world", Schubert completed the *String Quartets* in A minor and D minor – his first for over three years. He'd been inspired to write them through contact with the famous quartet led by Ignaz Schuppaznigh who duly performed *No. 13* a few weeks later. It's the most intimate and highly concentrated of the quartets, with an opening theme of brooding sadness played by the first violin over a restless accompaniment. It's a work full of Schubertian ambivalence – sad songs interrupted by flurries of almost manic energy. This ambivalence is pushed to extremes in *Quartet No. 14*, which he wrote shortly after. This is arguably the greatest of the three late quartets, chiefly on account of its harrowing emotional honesty, which reaches an almost unendurable pitch in the second movement, a set of variations based upon Schubert's song "Der Tod und das Mädchen" (Death and the Maiden) – hence the quartet's customary title. The quartet is characterized by its unrelenting rhythmic force, which is introduced by the opening movement's furious principal theme, then carried by the desperate song of the variations, and in turn followed by a whirling Presto like a grim dance of death. Schubert's final quartet, in G major, is less driven than *No. 14* but it has a similar rawness with an unnerving tension set up between major and minor in its long first movement. An elegiac cello melody in the slow movement establishes a mood of calm, broken by angry interruptions, while another whirligig dance rounds the whole thing off – this one with a somewhat theatrical display of menace.

Lindsay Quartet (ASV; 4 CDs; with *Quartets Nos. 8 & 12 & String Quintet*)

The Lindsay Quartet are best known for their passionate performances of Beethoven, but if anything their Schubert recordings are even better, bringing out every gradation of light and shade with thrilling directness. There's an apparent spontaneity to their playing which, of course, comes from knowing the work so thoroughly that it sounds absolutely fresh and exciting.

Quartetto Italiano
(Philips; 2 CDs)

If it's just the late quartets you want, this is an excellent choice at mid-price. The Italian Quartet was always a tightly knit ensemble, and this set shows them at their best. As you'd expect from a mid-1960s set, the sound isn't quite as crisp as the ASV recordings, but it's more than acceptable.

String Quintet

Schubert's *String Quintet in C Major*, his greatest chamber work, was also his last – on 2 October, 1828, just seven weeks before his death, the composer wrote to a friend that he had "finally turned out" a quintet. Rather than compose for a string quartet plus extra viola, which is the conventional setup for a string quintet, Schubert scored his work for an extra cello, thus creating a darker, more sonorous tone for this tragically beautiful music. Every moment is magnificent – no other composer could surpass the lyricism of the cello duet in the opening movement, the simple grace of the third movement and the rhythmic bite of the finale. But the emotional centre of gravity is the Adagio, a desperately poignant, valedictory statement which seems to hover between two worlds.

Lindsay Quartet; Cummings
(ASV)

This wonderful performance is courageously restrained, with none of the self-indulgent emotionalism that mars many other recordings. Delicate yet full of strong contrasts, this intense, but never overstated, account does full justice to Schubert's masterpiece. The performance can also be obtained in the four-disc set discussed above.

Stern, Schneider, Katims, Casals, Tortelier
(Sony; with *Symphony No. 5*)

This 1952 performance is one of the greatest of all chamber music recordings. At the heart of it is the cello of Pablo Casals – a musician whose deep sensitivity and awareness of the music's emotional ebb and flow makes for an experience that is even more moving than usual.

LIEDER

Schubert's "Gretchen am Spinnrade", written at the age of seventeen, announced the arrival of a song-writer of preternatural abilities. Nobody previously had brought such complexity and sophistication to this salon genre. In "Gretchen am Spinnrade" the piano is no mere accompaniment to the singer but a protagonist in its own right, playing its part in the creation of the emotional drama. Through the music you hear the motion of the spinning wheel and sense every fluctuation of Gretchen's ever-changing emotions, which build to a crisis at the extraordinary moment when the wheel stops, only to begin again as she recovers herself.

More than anything else by the composer, Schubert's songs live or die with the talents of their performers. Like the plays of Shakespeare (several of whose verses he set), the songs respond to a variety of interpretations while always needing a singer who can strike the right balance between characterization and vocal beauty, and a pianist who knows when to step into the limelight and when to withdraw. Broadly speaking, interpretative styles range between those who tend to let the music alone bring out

The great lieder exponent Dietrich Fischer-Dieskau.

the meaning and those who dramatize the songs – sometimes to an extreme extent.

There are many ways to enter the vast terrain of Schubert's song catalogue. Our selection below represents the tip of the iceberg. The two anthology discs by young singers make a good starting point (and there are equivalent individual recital discs by Dietrich Fischer-Dieskau). On the other hand, if you want to start at the top, listen first to *Die schöne Müllerin* and *Winterreise*, where an unforgettable impact is created by the cumulative effect of one connected song after another.

An die Musik – Favourite Schubert Songs: Terfel, Martineau (Deutsche Grammophon)

The Welsh baritone Bryn Terfel has a big dramatic voice, some might think too big for song, but one with a wide range of colours which are employed with wonderful control – he's equally at home in the wild melodrama of "Erlkönig" as he is in the serene beauty of "Du bist die Ruh".

Schubert Lieder: Bonney, Parsons (Warner)

American soprano Barbara Bonney not only has a beautiful voice, but her interpretations communicate very strongly the meaning of the words. There is some overlap with the Terfel disc, but she includes a highly introspective account of "Gretchen am Spinnrade" as well as the famous "Shepherd on the Rock" with its clarinet obbligato.

Lieder: Fischer-Dieskau, Moore (Deutsche Grammophon; 21 CDs)

Nobody has lived with Schubert's songs for as long as Dietrich Fischer-Dieskau, and he has produced scores of recordings of them, often returning to the same pieces several times. Deutsche Grammophon's colossal budget-price boxed set, a splendid testament to a great artist, includes nearly all of Schubert's songs. The 21 CDs are also available in three mid-price volumes.

The Hyperion Schubert Edition: Various Singers, Graham Johnson (Hyperion; 37 single CDs)

Masterminded and accompanied by Graham Johnson, this wonderful series includes every single Schubert song (including fragments and piano-accompanied part songs). The songs are grouped thematically, with singers selected for their suitability for each group of songs. Not every voice appeals, so it is worth taking advantage of the budget-price sampler by way of an introduction.

Die schöne Müllerin

In 1823, during a time of great physical and mental distress, Schubert discovered a collection of verses – *Poems from the Posthumous Papers of a Travelling Hornplayer* – by a contemporary, Wilhelm Müller. The poems had a simple directness which clearly made a strong impact on him and he set twenty of them as a cycle entitled *Die schöne Müllerin* (The Fair Maid of the Mill). The verses outline a rather sketchy story about a young miller setting out on his travels. Constant throughout the cycle is the presence of the millstream, which Schubert evokes, notably in the first six songs, through a torrent of rippling semi-quavers in the piano part. The cycle begins with an opening song, "Das Wandern", of jaunty optimism, but gradually the general air of lightness begins to darken as it becomes clear that the young man's love for the miller's daughter is unrequited. Jealous anger is provoked by a rival, the hunter, and a new tinge of tragedy emerges with "Die Liebe Farbe" in which the miller meditates on the colour green – the favourite colour of his beloved. This, essentially conventional, tale of doomed innocence is transformed by Schubert into an acute study of the pain of disillusionment. Its unhappy denouement foreshadows the even darker world of *Winterreise*.

Fischer-Dieskau, Moore (EMI)

Fischer-Dieskau has recorded this cycle several times. Of his three versions with Gerald Moore, this 1961 account is the best as a first-time buy. His partnership with Moore produces some dramatically spontaneous singing and his wonderfully crafted voice comes into its own in the more sombre songs.

Bostridge, Johnson (Hyperion)

Light-voiced English tenor Ian Bostridge brings home how much *Die schöne Müllerin* is a young man's tragedy. It is a very detailed performance where every nuance and subtlety has been carefully pondered, but without a hint of contrivance. In an interesting addition, all of the unset Müller poems are recited by Dietrich Fischer-Dieskau.

Winterreise

In *Winterreise* (Winter Journey), Schubert takes the despondency which closed *Die schöne Müllerin* and pushes it to extremes, creating a desolate landscape (both inner and outer) of unrelenting pessimism – indeed his friends, when they first heard the complete cycle in the autumn of 1827, were dismayed by its bleakness, while understanding the personal pain from which it was created. The 24 verses are again by Müller, but Schubert altered their order so that the occasional flashes of consolation offered by the poet in the original sequence are no longer visible. The protagonist, a rejected lover, seems on the verge of madness as we follow his lonely peregrinations through a snowbound landscape. Unlike the earlier cycle, nature is here represented as something cruel and unsympathetic to his fate. As his journey progresses, so his vision becomes all the more inward and the subjectivity of the songs all the more pronounced. The final song, "Der Leiermann", is a masterstroke: the traveller meets a destitute hurdy-gurdy player, whose rustic music Schubert mimics with a drone and a quirky figure in the piano. The wanderer wonders whether he should go with him but his question is left hanging in the air and the song simply drifts away.

The Lieder Poets

The golden age of German poetry began as the spirit of the eighteenth-century Enlightenment began to shade into early Romanticism. One supreme genius, Johann Wolfgang von Goethe (1749–1832) found an unprecedented range of musical possibilities in the German language, to which composers from Beethoven and Schubert to Wolf and Strauss responded in a tidal wave of great settings. Goethe's two-part drama *Faust* and his novel *Wilhelm Meisters Lehrbuch* (Wilhelm Meister's Apprenticeship) contain verses specifically designed as lyrics, and these have been set again and again – notably the songs for the frail, enigmatic girl Mignon in the novel, which inspired masterpieces by Schubert, Schumann and Wolf.

Themes touched on by Goethe – the poetry of night, God or the gods revealed in nature, desperate unrequited love, the ideal balance and harmony revealed in ancient Greek art – were echoed or further developed by such outstanding figures as Friedrich Schiller, Heinrich Heine, Novalis and Friedrich Hölderlin, and by lesser poets whose verse can still be strongly musically suggestive: Friedrich Gottlieb Klopstock, Wilhelm Müller, Joseph von Eichendorff, Friedrich Rückert, Eduard Mörike and Schubert's friend Johann Baptist Mayrhofer. Heine and Müller's poems of rejected love turning to madness form the basis of the two greatest song cycles with piano in German: Schubert's *Winterreise* (Winter Journey) and Schumann's *Dichterliebe* (The Poet's Love), while Mahler raised Rückert's verse to new heights in his orchestral *Kindertotenlieder* (Songs on the Deaths of Children) and the five *Rückert Lieder*.

To some modern listeners, such morbidly obsessive literary themes can be off-putting, even when the musical settings are so beautiful and touching. Why this obsession with pathological despair and rejection, with alienated, often frankly egoistical wanderers, and above all with death? It makes more sense when put in historical context. Whilst Romanticism in German poetry was emerging well before the end of the eighteenth century, the lieder tradition really took flight after the final defeat of Napoleon, and the demise of French revolutionary politics. The German-speaking world became much more repressively conservative, and the younger Romantic poets and composers felt compelled to seek their ideal world not in some future utopia, but in nature, dreams and death mysticism. A line from Schiller's "Die Götter Griechenlands" (The Gods of Greece) as set by Schubert – "Schöne Welt, wo bist du?" (Beautiful world, where are you?) – distils this attitude hauntingly.

Intriguingly, although this strain almost disappeared in German poetry after the failed revolutions of 1848, German composers continued to revisit it in such late Romantic masterpieces as Brahms's Goethe-based *Alto Rhapsody* and Mahler's most exquisite Rückert setting, "Ich bin der Welt abhanden gekommen" (I am Lost to the World). Was this nostalgia, a longing to escape the effects of growing industrialization, or simply a response to the musicality of these verses? Yet there was a forward-looking element too. In exploring these new worlds of imagination and extreme emotion the German Romantic poets discovered a new world of psychological insight. And it is probably through the settings of Schubert, Schumann, Wolf and others that these poetic insights have been conveyed most widely to non-German-speaking peoples.

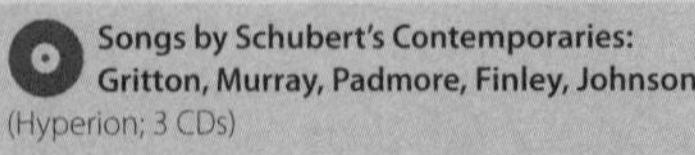
Songs by Schubert's Contemporaries: Gritton, Murray, Padmore, Finley, Johnson
(Hyperion; 3 CDs)

This set manages to be both richly instructive and a treat to listen to. It underlines the fact that Schubert didn't invent the lied single-handed. There are plenty of fine settings, not only by the big names: Carl Friedrich Zelter and especially Johann Friedrich Reichardt stand out, and it's fascinating to have some of Conradin Kreutzer's Müller settings to compare directly with Schubert. All are performed with compelling sympathy by Graham Johnson and his A-list team. While Schubert did take the German art song to new heights and depths, the foundation was already there.

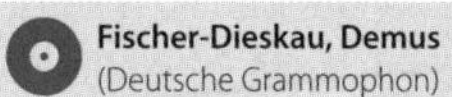
Fischer-Dieskau, Demus
(Deutsche Grammophon)

Fischer-Dieskau recorded *Winterreise* no fewer than eight times. This one dates from 1966 when the singer was in his early forties, and the combination of a rich and authoritatve vocal sound with mature interpretative insights is completely convincing. Jorge Demus, his sensitive accompanist, is more reticent than most, but this simply highlights the emotional veracity of Fischer-Dieskau's performance.

Schreier, Schiff (Decca; 3 CDs; with *Die schöne Müllerin & Schwanengesang*)

Some people find a baritone voice rather overdoes the gloom of *Winterreise*, and that a tenor actually enhances the drama through the contrast between vocal tone and meaning. Peter Schreier's performance with Andras Schiff was made when the singer was in his mid-fifties, but it is the best of his recordings of the work and a most persuasive argument in favour of the tenor approach.

Schwanengesang

The fourteen songs of the aptly named *Schwanengesang* (Swan-Song) were not conceived as a cycle by Schubert, but were cobbled together after his death by the publisher Haslinger, who had bought them from Schubert's brother. The songs set verses by three young poets – seven are by Rellstab, six by Heine and one by Seidl – and, while there is no unifying narrative, the selection and settings do create a coherent psychological landscape. *Schwanengesang* isn't coloured by the unremitting grief of *Winterreise*, but the mood is fairly sombre. In particular the Heine settings have a pared-down style which is especially effective in the two vignettes of the uncanny – "Die Stadt" and "Der Doppelgänger". The one anomaly is the somewhat twee final song "Die Taubenpost", in which the poet tells of his carrier pigeon – a rather cumbersome metaphor for constancy – but even here there's a suggestion in the music that the whole thing could just be wishful thinking.

Terfel, Martineau
(Sain)

Bass-baritone Bryn Terfel recorded *Schwanengesang* in 1991 for the Welsh company, Sain. It's an outstanding performance and well worth tracking down. Sain favour a less forward sound than many companies, which has the effect of increasing the sense of tension and concentration – *Der Doppelgänger* in particular gets a rapt and marvellously controlled reading.

Quasthoff, Zeyen (Deutsche Grammophon; with Brahms *Vier Ernste Gesänge*)

Thomas Quasthoff is one of the outstanding lieder singers of recent years. Blessed with an absolutely solid, warm-toned baritone, he's an artist who avoids any hint of melodrama and his interpretations are understated but still powerfully convincing.

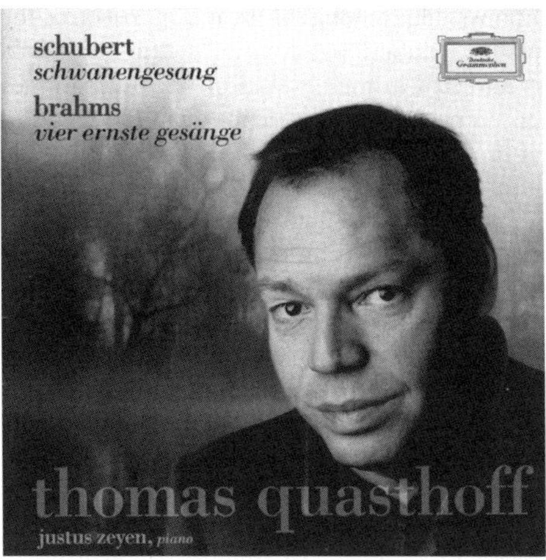

Goethe Lieder

Schubert was a huge admirer of Goethe and wrote over seventy settings of his poems from 1814 onwards. They vary hugely in style and subject: from the passionate "Gretchen am Spinnrade", the spine-tingling ballad "Erlkönig" to the playful "Der Musensohn" and the beautiful and pensive contemplations of nature "Auf dem See" and "Wandrers Nachtlied II". Schubert seems to have been especially fascinated by the songs sung by the innocent, childlike Mignon and her father the harper in Goethe's novel *Wilhelm Meisters Lehrbuch*. He set them several times, the most poignant of which are the three Mignon songs of 1826 – his last Goethe settings. Sadly, Goethe (a lover of music but conservative in his taste) did not return the compliment, and never replied when Schubert sent him some of his compositions.

Fischer-Dieskau, Moore, Demus
(Deutsche Grammophon)

Fischer-Dieskau gives a particularly atmospheric and powerful performance of 24 Goethe songs on this disc. Highlights include a dramatic "Erlkönig", a wonderfully fleet-footed and joyful "Der Musensohn" (superbly accompanied by Jörg Demus) and an exquisite pianissimo "Wandrers Nachtlied II".

Baker, Moore, Parsons
(EMI; 2 CDs)

It is surprisingly hard to find a good selection of Schubert's Goethe lieder for female voice. Luckily this two-CD set covers many of them, including the erotic Suleika songs, the 1826 Mignon settings and "Gretchen am Spinnrade". Janet Baker sings with enormous sensitivity, superbly characterizing each of Goethe's women – from the sensual Suleika to the desperate Gretchen and the waif-like Mignon.

PIANO MUSIC

Almost alone among the great composers for the piano, Schubert was himself no virtuoso. This is reflected in the absence of bravura passages in his piano works which, with the exception of the *Wanderer Fantasy*, make no great technical demands on a performer. Instead Schubert translated his matchless lyric gift into practically everything he wrote for the piano – from the numerous lighthearted dance pieces to the profoundly personal late sonatas. It is with the sonatas that his reputation as a piano composer stands, even though they were completely neglected for a hundred years after his death until the pianists Artur Schnabel and Edward Erdmann rediscovered them. Schubert was the last great composer for whom the sonata was the primary genre of piano music. His loyalty to the form goes some way to explain his neglect in the era of Chopin, Liszt and Schumann, for whom the traditional imperatives of the sonata made it less attractive than the étude, prelude and other vehicles for spontaneous-sounding expression. However, Schubert's relationship to the sonata tradition was not one of straightforward allegiance. Most of his piano sonatas – especially the last three – display a flexibility of structure and an adventurous handling of harmony and tone that is the key to their profoundly dramatic character. Schubert the proto-Romantic is more clearly revealed in the *Wanderer Fantasy* and in his short lyric pieces, in which the minimum of formal constraints is placed on his melodic expansiveness.

Complete Piano Sonatas: Schiff
(Decca; 7 CDs)

Schiff is an outstanding Schubertian, particularly alive to the undercurrents of feeling that are a constant presence in the sonatas. He plays on a Bosendorfer piano precisely because its gentler, warmer tone and touch correspond to his view of Schubert as, above all, a creator of multilayered and translucent texture.

Complete Piano Sonatas: Kempff
(Deutsche Grammophon; 7 CDs)

Not as sweet-toned nor as ingratiating as Schiff, nevertheless these are immensely assured performances – elegantly phrased and with a full, strong tone. Just occasionally, in the late sonatas especially, the internal drama seems underplayed but, with outstanding sound (from the late 1960s) and at budget price, this set has no serious faults.

Sonata No. 14

The *Piano Sonata No. 14* in A minor, written in 1823, a few months after the *Wanderer Fantasy*, signals a change of direction in Schubert's sonata writing. Though only in three movements, it possesses a breadth of feeling and a grandness of design which is positively symphonic in scope. The opening – a short phrase in stark octaves that manages to be both simultaneously expansive and reticent – sets the tone for a piece which abounds in startling contrasts. The most dramatic occur in the first movement, which travels from a mood of sombre yearning through agitated tremolandos into a rich melody shot through with resignation. It's an encapsulation of Schubert at his most quixotic.

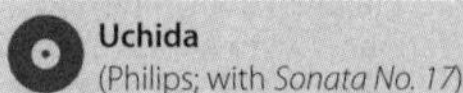

Uchida
(Philips; with *Sonata No. 17*)

An intensely probing, analytical artist, Mitsuko Uchida here plays two of the most highly polarized of the composer's piano works, the fourteenth and seventeenth, with an effortless flow and a communicative power that's rarely encountered. Uchida has recorded many of the Schubert sonatas for Philips; all are fascinating, but this CD is perhaps the peak of the series.

Cooper
(Ottavo; with *Sonata No. 18 & 12 German Dances*)

Imogen Cooper, who has recorded all the major Schubert piano works for Ottavo, is one of the most eloquent of Schubert interpreters. More than most she lets the music do the work for her, her acute musical intelligence bringing out the constant interplay of darkness and light through perfectly judged dynamics and deftly applied variations in colour.

Sonatas Nos. 17 & 18

In August 1825 Schubert was at the mountain spa of Gastein, halfway through his extended holiday with Vogl. This was one of the happiest times of his troubled life and it produced one of the most exuberant of all his piano sonatas, *No. 17* in D major. The opening Allegro is especially energetic, with a bold fanfare-like figure followed by rapid triplets which scurry around for most of the movement. The subsequent three movements redress the balance by way of a series of sweet melodies that, at times, border on the simpering. *Sonata No. 18* in G major, written a year later, is a work of more subtly shifting moods, quintessentially Schubertian in the way the lilting dream-like opening is developed to incorporate angry outbursts and troubled asides without in any way upsetting the overall cohesion of the movement. This is piano music as discursive soliloquy – each idea clearly develops out of another – with an overriding sense of a rather fragile consciousness gradually revealing itself.

Piano Sonata No. 17: Uchida
(Philips; with *Sonata No. 14*)

This scintillating account of the D major sonata, like the movingly eloquent reading of the A minor sonata with which it's coupled, is as fine as any version ever recorded. The sound quality, too, is excellent.

Piano Sonata No. 17: Cooper
(Ottavo; with *Moments Musicaux*)

Piano Sonata No. 18: Cooper
(Ottavo; with *Sonata No. 14* and *12 German Dances*)

What is so impressive in Cooper's reading of *Sonata No. 17* is the variety of touch that she brings to bear on the sonata: bold but unmelodramatic in the first movement, and delicate and playful in the other three. In *Sonata No. 18* she judges the overall shape of the long first movement to perfection, controlling the sudden changes of musical and emotional direction with consummate ease.

Late Sonatas

The last three sonatas – *No. 19* in C minor, *No. 20* in A major and *No. 21* in B flat major – were all composed around the same time as the *String Quintet*, and Schubert died two months after finishing his work on the last of the group. Comparison with Beethoven's final sonatas is inevitable, and to an extent the comparison is just: like Beethoven's last five, these works are overcast by the imminence of death, and they represent the furthest extremity of the composer's keyboard music in more than a merely chronological sense.

But, whereas the late Beethoven sonatas are marked by a desperate need to communicate, to arrive at a means of conveying something that ultimately eludes expression, the Schubert sonatas look inward, constantly repeating and reformulating themes as if they were persistent memories. Deep pessimism pervades this music – the Andantino of *Sonata No. 20*, for example, is built on a melody that returns again and again to the same single note, as if to an unassuageable pain, and is then interrupted by a terrifying outburst of splintered motifs within which no melody can be found. The late sonatas are long musical soliloquies in which the forceful direction of Beethoven's music is replaced by structures that seem to circle round their subjects without ever coming to rest. This is not to say that these works are in any way self-indulgent or prolix. It is rather that the conventional perception of linear time is here suspended. The philosopher Theodor Adorno summarized what is astounding about these three sonatas when he talked about their "landscape-like quality"; they do indeed define an emotional terrain that is unique to Schubert.

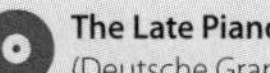

The Late Piano Sonatas: Pollini
(Deutsche Grammophon; 2 CDs; with *Drei Klavierstücke & C Minor Allegretto*)

So perfectly judged are the tempi, tone and weight of Mauricio Pollini's performances that there's always a point to each repetition; what can seem like meandering diversions in other hands here come across as essential qualifications and revisions. These superb accounts are coupled with four late Schubert miniatures, each as melancholy as the sonatas.

Sonata No. 21: Kovacevich
(EMI; with *Six Moments Musicaux & Allegretto in C Minor*)

Some pianists tend to play up the Romantic agony of the late sonatas, underlining the desperation with slow speeds and dramatic pauses, while others emphasize the lyricism. Stephen Kovacevich falls more into the former than the latter category, but he maintains a constant tension between the tender and the clamorous elements, and always makes the music sound entirely cogent rather than capricious.

Piano Sonatas Nos. 20 & 21: Schnabel
(EMI; 2 CDs; with *Sonata No. 17, Moments Musicaux & March*)

These 1939 recordings, finely transferred, are by the man who, more than anyone else, revealed Schubert's piano music as essential repertoire material. Despite some odd tempi, these are still remarkable performances – convincing, above all, for their intellectual probity and resistance to any false sentimentality.

Moments Musicaux

The concentrated poetic miniature for the piano was the mainstay of the Romantic piano repertoire. Schubert's major contribution to the genre consisted of six pieces published together, in 1828, under the title *Moments Musicaux*, and two sets of *Impromptus*. Most of the *Moments Musicaux* almost certainly date from Schubert's last years, though two of them were published separately at an earlier date: *No. 3*, with its jaunty rhythm, as *Air Russe*, and the melancholy *No. 6* as *Les plaintes d'un troubadour*. All six pieces display Schubert's ability at distilling a feeling without recourse to the kind of virtuosity that you frequently find in the miniatures of Chopin and Liszt. And although their range is limited – the dominant mood is one of introspection – the emotional fine shading which the *Moments Musicaux* possess is unprecedented in its detail and intensity.

Brendel (Philips; 2 CDs; with *Impromptus, Allegretto* and other pieces)

Alfred Brendel is another marvellous Schubert player, clear-sighted and unfussy, he's especially good in the smaller pieces, where his attention to detail and concentration create performances of poised perfection.

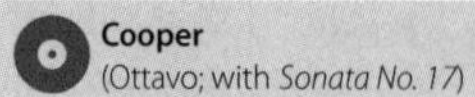
Cooper
(Ottavo; with *Sonata No. 17*)

This is deeply sensitive and elegant playing which more than holds its own in comparison with that by better-known names. Every phrase is given just the right weight and emphasis to draw out its internal meaning. The elegiac *No. 3* gets an especially fine reading.

Impromptus

Schubert once wrote to his father, "people assured me that the keys became singing voices under my hands", and nowhere is the vocal nature of his piano writing more evident than in the two sets of four *Impromptus* he composed in the last year of his life. Perhaps best described as large-scale miniatures, these brief but expansive pieces have the appearance of spontaneous personal utterance, veering from one mood to another with all the unpredictability that the title "Impromptu" suggests. The second set has sometimes been read as a loose-limbed sonata: it certainly is not one in any conventional sense, but certainly there's an element of interconnection to the sequence, which culminates in a fierce, scherzo-like episode. In their roaming exploration of fleeting emotion and piano texture, the *Impromptus* are Schubert's most direct connection to the music of Chopin, Schumann and Liszt.

Brendel (Philips; 2 CDs; with *Moments Musicaux*, *Allegretto* and other pieces)

These eloquent accounts of the *Impromptus* are among the highlights of Alfred Brendel's hugely distinguished recording career, and are coupled with rapt renditions of the *Moments Musicaux*. These recordings are also available on a single full-price disc.

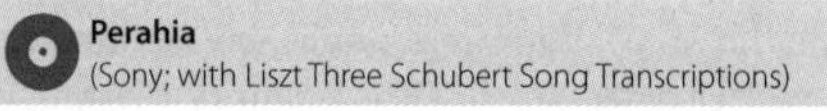
Perahia
(Sony; with Liszt Three Schubert Song Transcriptions)

Perahia's recording of the *Impromptus* was deservedly hailed as a classic on the day of its issue, in the mid-1980s. Elegant and perfectly paced, Perahia's playing is so subtle and profound that you are left with something different after every hearing.

Wanderer Fantasy

Comprising four movements to be played without a break, the *Wanderer Fantasy* of 1822 is at once a homage to the Classical sonata and a subversion of it. The overall shape resembles that of the great Beethoven sonatas, but it is used to contain quasi-improvisatory elements which, as it were, break down the ordained structure from inside. Thus the second movement is a set of variations that sounds more like a sequence of impressionistic mood pieces, while the finale opens as a fugue that evolves quickly into a blazing outbreak of unfettered passion. A degree of formal unity comes from the motif with which the fantasy opens, for it provides the basic material from which all the subsequent major themes are constructed. In the second movement this motif becomes recognizable as a theme from Schubert's song "Der Wanderer", a link that introduces a Schumann-like element of autobiographical confession. The array of free-ranging ideas within a plan of overarching unity marks the *Wanderer Fantasy* as an ancestor of Liszt's B minor sonata and, indeed, this is one of the few Schubert piano works in which the succeeding generation showed any interest.

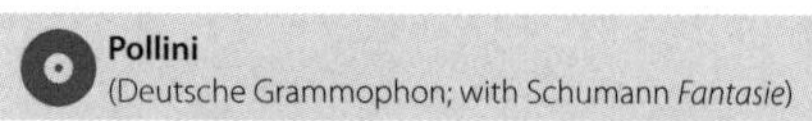
Pollini
(Deutsche Grammophon; with Schumann *Fantasie*)

Pollini's version of the *Wanderer* is an ideal performance: highly charged but not reckless, tautly structured but not inflexible. It's coupled with an equally compelling performance of the Schumann *Fantasie in C*, played with a magisterial authority.

Fantasie in F Minor

That Schubert wrote so much music for piano duet is often taken as a measure of just how convivial a man he was. Much of it was written during his time teaching the Esterházy girls at Zseliz, and several pieces involve a fair amount of stretching over a partner's arms (implying, for some, a desire for intimacy that conflicted with his alleged homosexuality). Of the half-dozen or so masterpieces that he wrote for piano duet, the outstanding work is the *Fantasie in F Minor*, written in the last year of his life and dedicated to his favourite Esterházy pupil, the Countess Caroline. Like so many of his piano pieces, it is technically unchallenging but demands an acute sensitivity from both players, particularly in the control of dynamics. The opening is one of the most strikingly mysterious that he ever wrote, with a desperately yearning upper part set against a darkly murmuring passage below. Given the prevailing sadness, Schubert succeeds in communicating such a variety of feelings in its four continuous sections as to suggest a work of intensely personal significance.

Perahia, Lupu
(Sony; with Mozart *Sonata in D for 2 Pianos*)

This utterly beguiling performance possesses the essential prerequisite for the *Fantasie* – a real rapport between the players that allows for some immensely hushed and delicate playing from the very beginning.

Robert Schumann (1810–1856)

Robert Schumann died a failure in his own eyes, yet he occupies a key position in the music of the nineteenth century. The first Romantic with a deep knowledge of literature and philosophy, Robert Schumann saw it as his mission to fuse all the arts in music that spoke profoundly of its creator. He once wrote: "I am affected by everything extraordinary that goes on in the world and think it over in my own way … then I long to express my feelings and find an outlet for them in my music: a poem, something infinitely more spiritual, the result of poetical consciousness." His music came to be the confessional for his inner life. Schumann composed four symphonies and some fine chamber music, but it is his transparently candid piano works that truly reveal this enigmatic, complex composer. Despite his respect for Classical forms (he was in awe of Beethoven), Schumann was quick to break away from them, creating instead music which reads like the pages of a diary – fragmented, condensed and profuse in invention. Schumann's compositions have a uniquely changeable emotional climate, shifting from passion to nostalgia, or from pain to ingenuous optimism, in the passage of a moment.

He was a middle-class boy from the provinces, born in Zwickau, Saxony, in 1810. His father, a bookseller and novelist, died in 1826, whereupon Robert's sister committed suicide, an event from which he never recovered. He enrolled at Leipzig University to study law, enjoyed the good life and the customary grand tour of the continent, and was told by his professor that he had no talent whatsoever. Yet he continued with his musical studies under Friedrich Wieck, a notable teacher in whose house he took lodgings. There he met Wieck's daughter Clara, a nine-year-old who was already showing signs of extraordinary ability as a pianist. Robert's own hopes of becoming a virtuoso were soon wrecked by the crippling of his left hand – ostensibly the result of a machine designed to strengthen his fourth finger, but more likely due to poisoning by the mercury he took when he realized he had syphilis ("My whole house is like a chemist's shop", he told his mother). Fortunately he had already begun to show talent as a composer.

Robert Schumann by Eduard Bendemann.

His Opus 1 *Variations* derived their central motif from the letters of the surname of Meta Abegg, an early love. Schumann would often use such codes to devise thematic fragments, which he then developed into musical dialogues between imagined characters who reflected the ambivalences of his nature. In Jean Paul's novel *Die Flegejahre* (Years of Indiscretion) he came across Walt and Vult, introvert and extrovert, from whom he derived his two creative demons, christened Florestan and Eusebius. The personae of Florestan and Eusebius recur in his work "in order to express contrasting points of view about art", as the composer explained, since he perceived music as having the cut and thrust of Hegelian dialectic. Then there was the Davidsbund (The Band of David), a fictitious band of musicians at war against the artistic philistines; their names swarm through his scores and their signatures peopled the

Clara Schumann (1819–96)

In her day, Clara Wieck – later Clara Schumann – was one of the world's leading piano virtuosos. Admired early on not just by her future husband but also by Goethe, Mendelssohn, Paganini and others, this young woman "with an inclination to melancholy" was proclaimed a *wundermädchen* by the Emperor of Austria and praised by Liszt for her "complete technical mastery, depth and sincerity of feeling." When she died in 1896 she had performed over a thousand public recitals in Russia and Europe, having also found the time to compose a handful of impressive works and raise eight children.

Robert Schumann first heard Clara play when she was just nine years old and he was nineteen, and he immediately signed himself up as a pupil and boarder with her father, Friedrich, the strict and domineering man who taught her to play and planned what he envisaged as her future. Years later, when Robert and Clara fell in love, Friedrich put every obstacle in the way of their relationship, and they were only married in 1840 after appealing to the courts. Robert was full of admiration for his wife – "in the house such a housewife, in my heart a beloved and loving wife, for the world an artist" – and encouraged her to compose, but she was busy as a mother and breadwinner, and also very low in confidence: "I once believed that I had creative talent but I have given up this idea: a woman must not wish to compose". If, as is often said, Clara was such a matchless pianist that she killed Robert's hopes of becoming a performer, the reverse was true in the field of composition, where she was overshadowed both by her husband and by Brahms, a close friend and passionate admirer of Clara for many decades.

Her compositions are mostly songs and works for solo piano, though later on, encouraged by Brahms, she also wrote violin romances and a piano trio (a vigorous and skilful piece which she nonetheless wrote off in typically self-critical fashion as being "effeminate and sentimental"). Her early piano works include the *Romance Variée* Op. 3, dedicated to Robert, and a concerto that her future husband orchestrated; from that point on Clara and Robert shared many ideas and themes, including a motif of a descending fifth that they both used in their works to signify each other. Her later piano works, which combine a Romantic sensibility with a proud dignity, include two sets of beautiful *Romances* and the gently melancholic *Variations on a Theme of Robert Schumann* – based on a theme that Brahms also used for a set of variations.

In the field of songwriting, Clara also doubted her abilities – she once wrote that "to compose a song, to grasp a text thoroughly, one needs genius for that" – and it's true that she wasn't quite a melodist on a par with her husband. But her skilful use of rhythm, harmony and pianistic colours raises her fifteen published songs well above the ordinary. The year after their wedding, the Schumanns jointly published twelve songs (without indicating the composer of each), including Clara's ecstatic "Er ist Gekommmen" (He Comes in Storm and Rain). Her *Sechs Lieder* Op. 13, to words by Heine, was reviewed as the "tender gracious outpourings of a bounteous heart, quiet and unadorned", and one of the set, "Die Stille Lotusblume", with its unresolved ending and a rush of Romantic archetypes, including the moon, a lotus flower and a white swan, was thought by some commentators to be the quintessential Romantic lied. In 1853, a move to Düsseldorf prompted six songs set to texts by Hermann Rollett, who wrongly assumed Robert had written these spirited and exalted pieces.

All told, Clara was one of the most important musical figures of her day. Not only was she a phenomenal pianist, a talented composer and an extremely important inspiration both to her husband and to Brahms (who once wrote that he could "no longer love an unmarried girl. They but promise heaven while Clara shows it revealed to us"). She was also, despite her extraordinary pianistic gifts, an important figure in the school of musical thought that shunned the outward virtuosity of the "new school" composers such as Liszt in favour of a more restrained approach, something typified by her regular scheduling of earlier masters such as Beethoven at her recitals.

Piano Music: Iwai (Naxos)

In the absence of Cristina Ortiz's exquisitely played selection, this recording by Yohsiko Iwai makes a good introduction to Clara Schumann's piano music. As with the Ortiz recording, the high points are the *Romances* and the *Variations*, which Iwai plays with real elegance and refinement.

Schumann Lieder – Robert & Clara: Bonney, Ashkenazy (Decca)

This wonderful CD includes eleven songs each by Clara and Robert in performances of such sensitivity and intimacy by Barbara Bonney that you feel almost like an eavesdropper throughout. Listen blind and it's hard to tell who wrote which songs.

pages of *Neue Zeitschrift für Musik*, an iconoclastic musical journal of which Schumann was editor.

The 1830s began with the "Abegg" variations and produced most of his finest music: *Papillons*, *Carnaval*, *Davidsbündlertänze*, *Fantasiestücke*, the piano sonatas, *Kinderszenen*, the *Fantasie in C Major*, the beginnings of the *Études Symphoniques*. Yet it was also a decade of despair, for his attempts to marry Clara were blocked by her father. There were good reasons for the obstructiveness: Clara's blossoming career (unquestionably sacrificed in later years by the demands of life with Schumann); and the frivolities of a young man who showed little sign of being able to establish a serious career. In 1840 Schumann won legal action to overturn Wieck's veto and the couple were married one day before Clara's 21st birthday.

In that same year Schumann composed two great song cycles, *Dichterliebe* and *Frauenliebe und Leben*, both relating to his feelings for Clara. The following year his first symphony appeared, then in 1843 Mendelssohn offered him a piano professorship at the new Leipzig Conservatory. But Schumann's manic depression was now taking the form of increasing bleakness of vision and creative sterility, and led to serious breakdowns. He resigned and moved to Dresden, but Clara's triumphant concert tours, triumphs for herself as a concert artist, only emphasized how widespread indifference to her husband's music had become. He lacked the training to dash off musical money-spinners: operas, festival cantatas, frothy salon pieces. His spell as conductor in Leipzig, beginning in 1850, ended in recriminations and disaster. The next year, following his appointment as music director at Düsseldorf, his behaviour became increasingly erratic. In 1854 he attempted suicide by throwing himself in the Rhine and was committed to the Endenich asylum near Bonn. There he died in July 1856, almost certainly from the final ravages of tertiary syphilis.

Symphonies

Schumann for years tinkered with sketches for a major orchestral work, but like Brahms he lacked the courage to pursue them further. His discovery of Schubert's ninth symphony gave him the encouragement to try again, and in January and February of 1841 he wrote his *Spring Symphony*. It's an exuberant work, as indicated by the titles Schumann originally gave to its four movements – "Spring's Awakening", "Evening", "Merry Playmates" and "Full Spring".

The second symphony, written in the wake of a nervous breakdown in 1845, is the darkest, most conventional and least popular of the cycle, but the third, the *Rhenish*, is his most joyous and spontaneous. Conceived as a celebration of the landscape, legends and history of the Rhineland, it progresses from a thrilling, syncopated opening to a stately polyphonic finale that was inspired by a mass celebrated in Cologne Cathedral – he marked it to be played "In the manner of an accompaniment to a solemn ceremony". The *Symphony No. 4*, written in 1841 but massively revised in 1851, is an extremely intense work, and is of revolutionary originality, being through-composed as one seamless development – almost every significant theme is generated by the motifs that appear in the slow introduction to the opening movement.

It has to be admitted that Schumann's symphonies are not masterpieces of orchestration. Schumann's first thoughts came to him as piano music, and his efforts to reorchestrate them invariably made them more opaque. It may be that he was deliberately making the music easier for inept orchestras and conductors (Schumann had experience of both) but, whatever the reason, they sometimes sound clumsy. For all that, they are essential to a full understanding of the composer, and there's a great deal in the symphonies to dispel the myth that Schumann's final years were a period of unmitigated decline.

Staatskapelle Dresden; Sawallisch
(EMI; 2 CDs)

Sawallisch exerts more control than most over Schumann's more slovenly moments – the *Symphony No. 2*, for example, really moves under his direction. But what really convinces is the sheer euphoric vitality of his readings, notably in the fourth, which travels along with all the inevitability of a wave.

Orchestre Révolutionnaire et Romantique; Gardiner
(Archiv; 3 CDs; with *Symphony in G & Konzertstück*)

Comprising three full-price CDs, this is an expensive alternative to Sawallisch, but John Eliot Gardiner and his period-instrument orchestra offer a thrilling overview of Schumann's symphonic work, in a survey that includes both versions of the fourth symphony as well as the *Symphony in G*, which was left incomplete in 1832.

Piano Concerto

In 1841 Schumann composed a single-movement piece for piano and orchestra, "something between a symphony, a concerto and a large sonata". When it was turned down by the publishers, he decided to transform it into a full-length concerto, but it was not until 1845 that he completed its Intermezzo and finale, extracting the motifs for both added movements from the woodwinds' opening theme. Liszt called the end result "a concerto without piano" and, anticipating its rejection, Schumann had declared he was unable to write a display piece. It certainly is not a vehicle for hair-raising virtuosity, but the concerto is a supremely eloquent piece, placing its emphasis on intimate dialogue between the soloist and orchestra. Its most obvious antecedent is Beethoven's fourth concerto; its descendants are the concertos of Brahms and, especially, the concerto by Grieg.

Kovacevich; BBC Symphony Orchestra; Davis (Philips; with Grieg *Piano Concerto*)

This performance, now remastered for Philips' "Great Recordings" series, stands out for its clarity of thinking, and gets right to the heart of the music. Kovacevich has a fine rapport with the orchestra, and between them they develop a sense of line that sounds as natural as breathing.

Perahia; Bavarian Radio Symphony Orchestra; Davis (Sony; with Grieg *Piano Concerto*)

Perahia brings a magical impulsiveness which, coupled with his bright tone, creates a sharp, crystalline surface. There's an effervescent spontaneity to this performance, but also a sense of constant qualification, of building effects and redefining them.

Cello Concerto

In 1849 Schumann had been offered the directorship of the Düsseldorf Orchestra, but despite his new duties his composing continued unabated. The *Cello Concerto* was finished in two hurried weeks, "a concert piece for cello with orchestral accompaniment", the composer called it – revealing his affinity for the instrument to which he had turned since the crippling of one hand and an end to his hopes as a concert pianist. It is, indeed, a quietly revolutionary piece made up of three linked movements and an accompanied cadenza. Its most memorable virtue is a solo line embedded in the orchestral fabric as a leading voice amongst civilized equals; its highlights are the exquisitely poetic opening and the twilight song which makes up the slow movement. It's the only nineteenth-century cello concerto of substance until that of Saint-Saëns and yet it was not performed in public before 1860.

Isserlis; Deutsche Kammerphilharmonie; Eschenbach (RCA; with *Funf Stücke im Volkston*)

Steven Isserlis has long proclaimed his huge enthusiasm for Schumann, and it shows in this outstanding recording. It's a much more full-blooded account than that of Starker (below) but such is Isserlis's identification with the music that the passion seems absolutely appropriate. Comes with equally fine accounts of the music for cello and piano.

Starker; London Symphony Orchestra; Skrowaczeski (Mercury; with Lalo *Cello Concerto* & Saint-Saëns *Cello Concerto*)

Janos Starker's bold sinewy tone and sophisticated phrasing draw real intensity from what can sometimes seem a sombre and four-square work. It's a more vigorous performance than most, one which refuses to wallow.

Papillons

Schumann once referred to himself as a chrysalis, and he spoke of his initial inspirations as butterflies – motifs which appeared and then as suddenly disappeared in a flitter of colour and uncertain shape. The image is perfectly suited to the Opus 2 *Papillons*, which were written as a suite of twelve waltzes inspired by Jean Paul's novel *Die Flegejahre*. Beginning with a motif that fades past vanishing point at its end, *Papillons* contains the most capricious and diaphanous music Schumann wrote, a supreme instance of art concealing art: completed in 1831, they represent three years of intermittent but intense work, distilling countless sketches and rearrangements.

Richter (EMI; with *Fantasie & Faschingsschwank aus Wien*)

Richter's live 1963 performance is both majestic and mercurial. The prevailing spirit is one of mischievous reminiscence, in which a grand rhetorical gesture can suddenly dissolve into an almost imperceptible whisper. It's a dramatic approach to this music which is highly effective.

Perahia (Sony; with *Davidsbündlertänze & Fantasiestücke*)

Perahia is a more decorous pianist than Richter but one with wonderful tonal control and rhythmic flexibility. His marvellous account of *Papillons* would be worth the money on its own – coupled with his beautiful readings of the *Davidsbündlertänze* and *Fantasiestücke*, it's irresistible.

Piano Sonatas

Schumann's three sonatas were all started in the same year, 1833, but were completed at intervals over the next five years – the first in 1835, the second in 1836, the third in 1838. Shortly after finishing the last one, Schumann thus expressed his thoughts on the sonata as a genre: "it seems that the form has outlived its life cycle. This is of course in the natural order of things: we ought not to repeat the same statements for centuries, but rather to think about the new as well. So let's write sonatas or fantasies" – adding the comment, "what's in a name?" In essence, Schumann's

Romanticism and the Austro-German Tradition

As a term applied to music, Romanticism (in its simplest sense) denotes the period from the beginning of the nineteenth century to the start of the twentieth – from the late works of Beethoven, say, to the death of Mahler. But Romanticism was also a movement, in the sense that the composers of the nineteenth century, despite their stylistic diversity, shared some underlying beliefs about creativity which emphasized the primacy of the individual imagination.

To a large extent, Romanticism (in literature and painting as well as in music) was a reaction against the philosophy of the Enlightenment and its belief in the supremacy of reason. The Romantics, on the contrary, stressed the validity of subjectivity and emotion, often embracing the fantastical, the weird and the exotic. Writing on Beethoven's *Symphony No. 5*, in 1810, the writer and composer E.T.A. Hoffmann describes how "Beethoven's ... music opens to us the realm of the colossal and the immeasurable. Glowing beams of light shoot through the deep night of this realm and we perceive shadows surging back and forth, closer and closer around us..."

Hoffmann also perceived Romantic characteristics in the works of earlier composers, and it's true that examples can be found throughout the eighteenth century of music that was dark, fervent and extremely dramatic. Notable examples would include the *empfindsamer stil* (expressive style) works of C.P.E. Bach, the *Sturm und Drang* symphonies of Haydn, and the opera *Don Giovanni* and some of the late piano concertos of Mozart. But such works, however turbulent, were still closely tied to established formal models.

The great Romantic composers, following the example of Beethoven, pushed against the limits of the symphony, sonata and other genres, often transforming them into something completely new. This experimental impulse was fuelled both by a sense of the individual genius needing to break free of restrictions – with the concomitant emphasis on the personality of the performer (see The Rise of the Virtuoso, p.395) – and by a desire to convey extra-musical elements. The piano miniature became a vehicle for encapsulating a particular mood or feeling, while the orchestral tone poem attempted to capture the essential qualities of a landscape or a great work of literature.

But not all composers who we think of as Romantics completely rejected the principles of Classicism. Schumann, who for a time was an admirer of Liszt, came to be dismayed not just by the Hungarian pianist's carefully cultivated personality cult but more especially by his music. Schumann's own piano works eschewed virtuosity for its own sake, nowhere more so than in his only piano concerto which went against the grain of the times, integrating the solo part with the orchestra rather than pitching it against it. Schumann's concerto was performed by his wife Clara, one of the greatest pianists of the nineteenth century, whose programmes deliberately avoided the kind of flashy showpieces beloved of Liszt and Thalberg (see p.141), in favour of a repertoire which balanced Classical masterpieces with the works of her husband and later of his disciple Brahms.

As the century progressed, German music was seen as being polarized between the traditionalists, led by Brahms, who maintained Classical structures within their works, and the progressives, dubbed the "New German School", who rejected the past and had Liszt and above all Wagner at their head. Battlelines were somewhat artificially drawn up by critics, in particular Eduard Hanslick (see p.112) who while acknowledging the genius of Wagner was vehemently opposed to the way his later music dramas abandoned the traditional divisions of the "number" opera in favour of through-composed works of epic proportions.

Even more upsettingly, Wagner and to a lesser extent Liszt were whittling away at the traditional major–minor basis of Western harmony – Liszt in his late piano work, Wagner most radically in *Tristan und Isolde* where any sense of stability and progression is constantly undermined by an extreme chromaticism which points to no definite tonal centre (see The Crisis of Tonality, p.468). While this erosion of tonality was pursued by Schoenberg to its logical conclusion of atonality, a melodically rich and harmonically lush late Romanticism survived well into the twentieth century in the work of such composers as Richard Strauss and Korngold – the latter giving it a new lease of life via the medium of cinema (see Composers at the Movies, p.287).

sonatas are fantasies braced by a desire to live up to the example of Beethoven's sonatas. They are not as episodic as his other major works for solo piano (there are, for example, numerous motivic links between the movements), but neither do they adhere to the principles enshrined in the great Germanic tradition – in the *Sonata No. 1*, for example, the four movements are so disparate that really there's no reason why the work couldn't just as easily have been six movements long, or three or five. With their sudden changes of key, dramatic thematic transformations and juxtaposition of rapt self-absorption with outbreaks of expansive emotion, the sonatas are quintessential Romantic piano music. The first two are more rewarding than the third – a revision of an earlier work, it is far less frequently recorded.

Sonata No. 1: Pollini (Deutsche Grammophon: with Schubert *Sonata No. 16*)

Lesser players can make the first sonata sound like nothing more than a stream of fugitive ideas, but Pollini's precise articulation and his sense of overall form ensure that the music's impetuousness never degenerates into incoherence – every gesture has a context.

Sonata No. 2: Argerich (Deutsche Grammophon ; with Liszt *Sonata in B Minor* and Brahms *Rhapsodies*)

In the second sonata, Martha Argerich gives a performance of fearless virtuosity: whole passages of notes are at once perfectly transparent yet gorgeously coloured, and there's a sense of tightly disciplined improvisation about the entire piece.

Carnaval

Carnaval is the Schumann piece in which spontaneity, invention and superlative technique coexist most vividly. Written in September 1834, *Carnaval* is a series of tableaux, a masked ball in which one character after another takes centre stage. It was described by the composer as "Little scenes on four notes", a reference to the exercise in creative cryptography by which Schumann proclaimed his love for Ernestine von Fricken through the music. The letters ASCH, which spell Ernestine's birthplace as well as a fragment of his own name, translate in German musical notation into the notes A, E flat, C and B. Permutations of these notes litter the entire score, generating the themes for the carnival characters, some of them historical (Chopin and Paganini), others folkloric (Pierrot and Harlequin), and others incarnations of Schumann's various personae (Florestan and Eusebius). It concludes with a "March of the Davidsbündler", in which the Philistines are put triumphantly to flight.

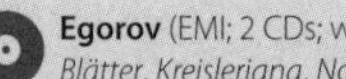

Egorov (EMI; 2 CDs; with *Toccata, Arabesque, Bunte Blätter, Kreisleriana, Novelettes & Papillons*)

Yuri Egorov can't match Michelangeli's tonal palate and aura of infallibility (see below), but his reading of *Carnaval* is highly dynamic and full of feeling. Some might find his approach too unyielding at times, but this is a generous and generally persuasive all-Schumann programme.

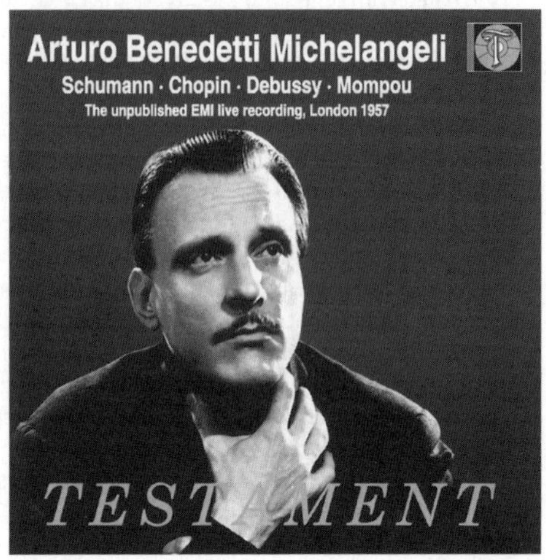

Michelangeli (Testament; 2 CDs; with *Faschingsschwank aus Wien* and pieces by Chopin, Debussy and Mompou)

This is a recording of a 1957 Festival Hall recital, and it captures the volatile perfectionist at the very peak of his form. Listen to this and you'll understand why the mere mention of Michelangeli makes some people go glassy-eyed with awe.

Davidsbündlertänze

Written three years after *Carnaval*, the *Davidsbündlertänze* (Dances of the Band of David) is an assembly of eighteen mood-pieces that epitomize the multifariousness of Schumann's art. The sequence begins with a musical motto composed by Clara, and most of the dances use this motto's interval of a falling second as their starting point. Schumann attached a traditional poem as the epigraph – "In all and every time, pleasure and pain are linked" – and each of the pieces bears a phrase sketching the atmosphere: "Rather cockeyed ... wild and merry ... as if from afar". If you don't find the *Davidsbündlertänze* irresistible, you're not going to get on with Schumann.

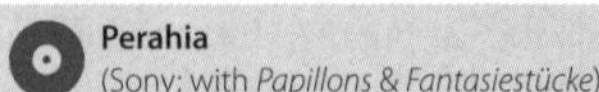

Perahia (Sony; with *Papillons & Fantasiestücke*)

Murray Perahia's first disc after winning the Leeds Piano Competition in 1972 was an LP that combined his authoritative version of *Davidsbündlertänze* with an equally fine

Fantasiestücke. Add to this a sublime *Papillons* and you have one of the finest Schumann piano CDs in the catalogue.

Kreisleriana

"One hardly dare breathe whilst reading the works of E.T.A. Hoffmann", Schumann confided to his diary in 1831. The *Kapellmeister* Johannes Kreisler was Hoffmann's own fictional alter ego, and the "fragments" of Hoffmann's novel depict an ardent and overwhelmingly restless Romantic personality, spun helplessly by secret visions and fancies as if "on through an eternally stormy sea ... He seemed to seek in vain the haven that would finally give him the peace and tranquillity without which an artist can seek nothing". Such demons and glimpses of "heavenly luminescence" were also Schumann's creative byword, and nobody has given us a more compelling or rounded musical self-portrait than in these eight dazzling vignettes.

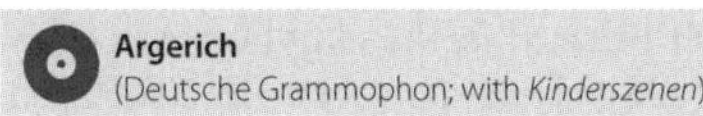

Argerich
(Deutsche Grammophon; with *Kinderszenen*)

There are many fine recordings of *Kreisleriana* but Martha Argerich's version is perhaps the best single-disc account of this mercurial work. There's a sense of brilliant fantasy in this high-voltage performance, tempered by intellectual rigour.

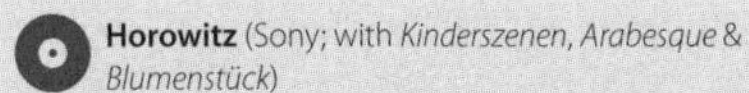

Horowitz (Sony; with *Kinderszenen, Arabesque & Blumenstück*)

Horowitz's vintage account from the early 1960s is one of his finest recordings but it's only available as a special import. Never has *Kreisleriana* been played with greater imagination: its refinement and passionate enchantment make an overwhelming impression.

Fantasiestücke

The Opus 12 *Fantasiestücke* (there's another, less interesting *Fantasiestücke* set, Op. 111) was composed between May and July 1837, shortly after Clara had returned all Schumann's letters. The ever-volatile composer dedicated the work to a Scottish pianist by the name of Roberta Laidlow. The *Fantasiestücke* catches the fragility of inspiration, which Schumann felt sprang from hidden depths to vanish as consciousness was reached, and the titles of its chimerical scenes evoke the higher realities of Romanticism – the worlds of night, twilight and dreams. Some of Schumann's most touching and delicate writing is here: "Warum" (Why?), for example, in which the music is the subject of momentary dialogue rather than formal development, or "Des Abends" (Of the Evening), which moves into unexpected keys to create a sense of revelation within stasis.

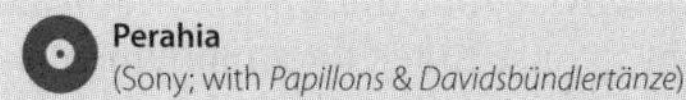

Perahia
(Sony; with *Papillons & Davidsbündlertänze*)

Perahia brings a lightness of touch and a transparency to the *Fantasiestücke* which is completely captivating. Even more so than with *Papillons*, these are elusive and delicate pieces which demand great sensitivity – and here receive it.

Argerich
(EMI; with *Fantasie*)

Argerich's quicksilver playing really penetrates to the soul of these pieces, capturing all their evanescent magic. At the moment this disc is only available as an EMI import, but it's worth the hassle of ordering it.

Kinderszenen

Written in February 1838, *Kinderszenen* (Scenes from Childhood) was suggested by Clara's comment that Schumann sometimes seemed to her like a child. These tiny, exquisite pieces are very much the recollection of an adult, yet one whose affinity with the innocence and vulnerability of childhood was painfully acute. *Kinderszenen* opens with "Of Strange Lands and People" (the storyteller's "once upon a time") and progresses through evocations of emotions in their purest state, until at last the adult steps forward in "The Poet Speaks" (the titles of the episodes suggested themselves after the music was written). Trance-like and apparently artless, *Kinderszenen* contains moments of disarming enchantment: the floating syncopations of "Almost Too Serious", for instance, or the phrase with which "Entreating Child" opens and closes, so that the piece ends as it began, and hangs quizzically in space.

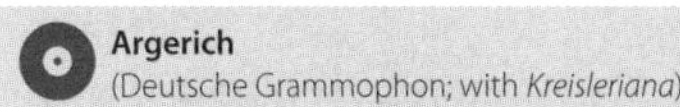

Argerich
(Deutsche Grammophon; with *Kreisleriana*)

Highly responsive but surprisingly controlled playing from Martha Argerich – especially after the inspired volatility of her *Kreisleriana* – as if her vision of childhood was tinged with a certain degree of sadness.

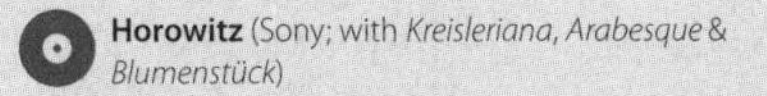

Horowitz (Sony; with *Kreisleriana, Arabesque & Blumenstück*)

Kinderszenen is the perfect conjunction of naivety and experience, and to conjure it up you need to be a master of fleeting effects. Vladimir Horowitz has this quality in abundance, but also brings a cohesive shape to the music.

Fantasie in C Major

In 1838 Schumann wrote to Clara: "I have just finished a fantasy in three movements that I sketched in all but the detail in June 1836. The first movement is, I think, the most passionate thing I have ever composed – a deep lament for you." Possibly so, but the work's origins lie in an attempt to raise funds for a monument to Beethoven. Schumann thought he could contribute best with a commemorative sonata, and the original titles of its movements are suitably redolent of tribute: "Ruins", "Triumphal Arch" and "Wreath of Stars". The *Fantasie* has Beethoven-like drive and verve, and indeed draws part of its thematic material from a Beethoven song. But if its march – "it makes me hot and cold all over", Clara wrote – is worthy of Beethoven's *Hammerklavier* (see p.61), its ardent and tender finale reveals a different, more diffused world. In the words of the philosopher Theodor Adorno, it seems to "open upon an undefined vastness". Subtle chromaticism, cross-rhythms, syncopation, countermelodic chords and a host of other stylistic subtleties give substance to the Schiller quotation that Schumann appended to the score: "Through all sounds in the coloured earthly dream resounds a quiet sound drawn for him, who secretly listens."

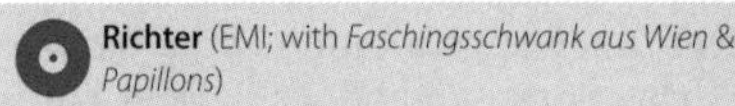
Richter (EMI; with *Faschingsschwank aus Wien & Papillons*)

Superhuman playing, in which every phrase seems to have been rethought and made Richter's own. The song-like tenderness of this music has never been better brought out, and the finesse makes its great climaxes all the more telling.

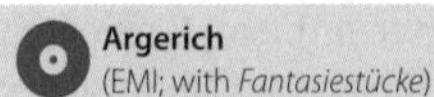
Argerich
(EMI; with *Fantasiestücke*)

The perfect marriage of artist and repertoire: Martha Argerich was born to play this music, and she brings a spontaneous-sounding energy to what is Schumann's most driven and passionate work.

Études Symphoniques

The *Études Symphoniques* began life in 1834 simply as variations on a theme written by Ernestine von Fricken's father. After years of dogged gestation, they emerged in 1852 as one of the cornerstones of Romantic piano literature, a dazzling exposition of the "symphonic" possibilities of the instrument for blending, contrasting and superimposing timbres. The variation technique still forms the structural armature of the *Études Symphoniques*, but at the heart of this work is the exhilaration of experiment – of clarifying dense planes of polyphony, presenting themes against a background of tonal reverberation (in a way that anticipates Debussy), exploring the borders of sound and silence.

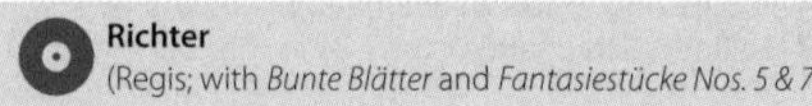
Richter
(Regis; with *Bunte Blätter* and *Fantasiestücke Nos. 5 & 7*)

In this 1970 recording Richter thinks through the organic structure of this music in playing of extraordinary richness and power; there's an unflagging urgency to this account, yet he never loses the crucial sense of private meditation. This is a performance which thinks on the move.

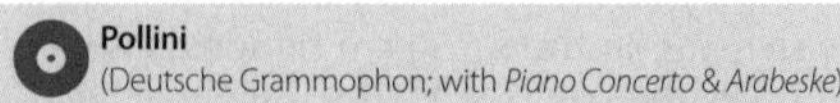
Pollini
(Deutsche Grammophon; with *Piano Concerto & Arabeske*)

Pollini's version doesn't project quite the same degree of personal commitment as Richter's, but it has an even greater analytic rigour and range of tone. It's coupled with a fine version of the *Piano Concerto* and a touching account of *Arabeske*, a marvel of considered innocence.

String Quartets Nos. 1 & 3

1842 was Schumann's year of chamber music, beginning with the three string quartets written in June and July of that year. While the piano music and the songs abound in private allusions, the chamber works (like the symphonies) are less obviously personal and more formally structured. In the opening of *No. 1*, for instance, Schumann clearly relishes the contrapuntal interplay of the four voices, but it's a counterpoint suffused with Romantic yearning. A skittish Mendelssohnian Scherzo follows, then a tender Adagio in which he pays obvious homage to the slow movement of Beethoven's ninth symphony.

Robert and Clara frequently used the interval of a descending fifth in their compositions as a coded reference to each other and it dominates the first movement of *Quartet No. 3*. Both here and in the second movement variations, Schumann's quixotic way with rhythm often makes it hard to locate a precise pulse and gives the work its restless excitement. As in the first quartet, the slow movement's overriding gravity suggests late Beethoven while the rondo finale has all the spirited energy of the ballroom.

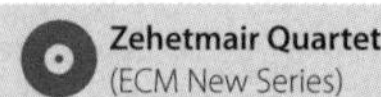
Zehetmair Quartet
(ECM New Series)

Though fairly regularly recorded, Schumann's string quartets have always been overshadowed by his chamber masterpiece, the *Piano Quintet*. This unprecedently dynamic performance can be credited with forcing a reassessment of their quality. Adopting rather faster speeds than most, the Zehetmair Quartet highlight Schumann's contrapuntal inventiveness and his sheer bravura.

Piano Quintet

Before Schumann, no composer of importance had attempted to combine piano with string quartet. But the piano was Schumann's instrument, and it gave him the foothold that he needed to tackle and conquer the field of chamber music – something he had resolved to do after his thirty-second birthday. Schumann started work on the *Piano Quintet* in September of 1842 and tried it out privately less than a month later, with Mendelssohn at the piano, stepping in for a heavily pregnant Clara.

That the sonata-form first movement surges with such high spirits is a tribute to Schumann's sheer bravura. Between this, and an ebullient Scherzo in which prodigies are accomplished through simple ascending and descending scales, lies a funereal sonata-rondo. The quintet concludes with an exhilarating finale, which reveals Schumann's increasing preoccupation with unity through thematic metamorphosis. All in all the *Piano Quintet* is a masterly piece of craftsmanship, but also one of the boldest and most brilliant declarations of its composer's creative spirit – and by far the best of his chamber music.

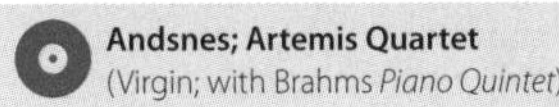

Andsnes; Artemis Quartet
(Virgin; with Brahms *Piano Quintet*)

Leif Ove Andsnes and the Artemis Quartet give a performance that's lyrical and vigorous, without ever sacrificing clarity of articulation. Indeed, it's perhaps a degree cooler than some rivals, but there are few other accounts in which the accord between pianist and strings is so complete.

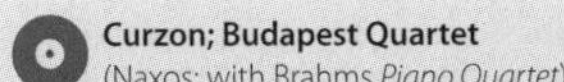

Curzon; Budapest Quartet
(Naxos; with Brahms *Piano Quartet*)

The Budapest Quartet recorded the Schumann quintet at least three times, including this radiant account in the early 1950s with the English pianist Clifford Curzon. What comes across most strongly is the sheer *joie de vivre* of the music-making plus the refined but energetic quality of Curzon's pianism.

Dichterliebe

Dichterliebe (Poet's Love), a cycle made up of sixteen songs, takes its text from Heinrich Heine and introduces to German song a new mingling of sentiment and irony, much as Heine's poems had done for German verse – this is a world of disillusionment in which nature acts as an adjunct and reflection to a bittersweet love story. *Dichterliebe* takes the song to a higher level of evolution: the piano here becomes an equal partner with the singer, appearing sometimes as combatant, sometimes as commentator, and is given long solo preludes and postludes which add an extra dimension to the possibilities of the genre. In a sense *Dichterliebe* is a continuation of Schumann's character pieces for piano, adding a second layer of tone-colour, liberating the lyrical element and defining the emotional content more precisely. They offer, as the composer put it, "a deeper insight into my inner musical workings".

Wunderlich, Giesen (Deutsche Grammophon; with Schubert and Beethoven songs)

Fritz Wunderlich, one of the last century's finest tenors, made this recording in 1966, shortly before his premature death. His rich, honeyed tones bring out the sadness and tenderness of Schumann's settings to an almost painful extent.

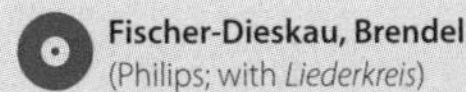

Fischer-Dieskau, Brendel
(Philips; with *Liederkreis*)

The baritone Dietrich Fischer-Dieskau has a profound sense of dramatic narrative, and in Alfred Brendel he has a creative partner rather than a mere accompanist. Where Wunderlich was all youth and freshness, Fischer-Dieskau impresses through valedictory power and anger.

Frauenliebe und Leben

Frauenliebe und Leben (A Woman's Love and Life) was written at a fraught time for Schumann: the courts had just given permission for him to marry Clara, but her father Friedrich Wieck had ten days to appeal against the decision. Between 11 and 12 July, 1840, in his anguish, Robert snatched a cycle of poems by Adelbert von Chamisso,

Anne-Sofie von Otter.

depicting a woman who loves her husband and lives only for him. It is very much a nineteenth-century male's conception of womanhood: and Schumann edits the text so as to reinforce further the impression that the girl's happiness can exist only alongside that of her man (ironically Clara had an extremely successful career and finished up as the family breadwinner). But, matters of sexism aside, *Frauenliebe und Leben* has maintained its key place in the repertoire as a supreme embodiment of *Innigkeit:* inwardness, intimacy and sincerity of feeling.

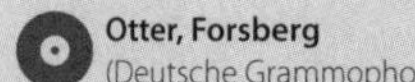

Otter, Forsberg
(Deutsche Grammophon; with *Five Songs* etc)

Anne-Sofie von Otter has the measure of this cycle, perfectly judging its moods – from initial yearning through exuberant delight to final disappointment. Her control of dynamics is particularly effective; the emotion she can wring from a whisper is something to marvel at.

Banse, Johnson
(Hyperion; with *Seven Songs of Elisabeth Kulmann* etc)

This is a subtle and original reading of this popular song cycle with Juliane Banse's creamy lyric soprano creating both a sense of the character's youthful excitement and her tenderness towards her husband. Graham Johnson is the excellent pianist.

Late Songs

For years, the popular belief was that Schumann composed his best lieder during his 1840 "year of song". However, he continued to produce many beautiful songs until the early 1850s, and these often sound strikingly modern. While the piano generally plays a less prominent role in the later lieder, Schumann shows a greater understanding of the voice, gained from his work with singers in the 1840s. Among the finest examples of these late songs are the boldly experimental settings of Mignon and the Harper's songs from Goethe's novel *Wilhelm Meisters Lehrbuch* and the *Sechs Gedichte und Requiem*, Opus 90, which range from a folk-song-like expression of pleasure in a peasant girl's singing to an exultant meditation on the release of a soul in death. Other fine settings include the "biographical" song cycle to texts by the child prodigy Elisabeth Kulmann, and five dignified yet impassioned poems believed to be by Mary, Queen of Scots.

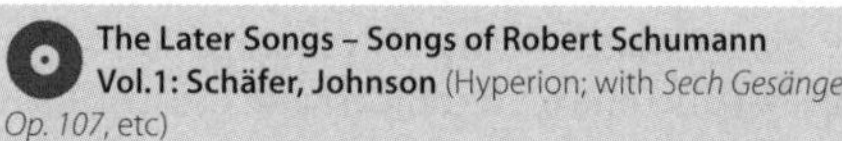

The Later Songs – Songs of Robert Schumann Vol.1: Schäfer, Johnson (Hyperion; with *Sech Gesänge, Op. 107*, etc)

This disc focuses exclusively on Robert Schumann's late lieder. Christine Schäfer's clear, bell-like soprano is perfect for the five "Mignon" songs, conveying Mignon's dreamy, childlike character, and also rich enough in tone to create a moving interpretation of the *Sechs Gedichte und Requiem*.

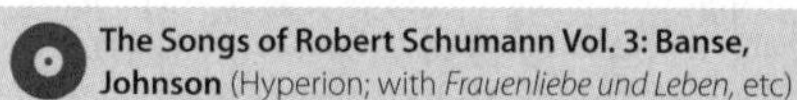

The Songs of Robert Schumann Vol. 3: Banse, Johnson (Hyperion; with *Frauenliebe und Leben*, etc)

Soprano Juliane Banse is wonderfully versatile on this disc, conveying the alternating playfulness and wistfulness of the Elisabeth Kulmann settings, each of which she introduces with a short passage of text, and giving a poised, yet passionate performance of the five songs to texts by Mary, Queen of Scots.

Heinrich Schütz (1585–1672)

Heinrich Schütz was the greatest German composer before J.S. Bach, a status that has a lot to do with the four years he spent in Venice, assimilating the polychoral style of Giovanni Gabrieli (see p.199). Schütz took this declamatory and dramatic style back to Germany, where he applied it to the texts of the Lutheran Church to produce some of the most powerful and pious music of the seventeenth century.

Schütz was born in Kostritz in Saxony into a family of legal officials. He began studying law at Marburg University in 1608, but was encouraged to turn his attention to music by the Landgrave of Hesse, who sponsored his studies in Venice. Schütz returned in 1612 and was made organist at the landgrave's chapel at Kassel before being poached by the more powerful, but less sympathetic, Elector of Saxony at Dresden. He was officially appointed the elector's *Kapellmeister* in 1618, the same year that the Thirty Years War broke out – a religious conflict that was to devastate northern Europe.

In 1628 Schütz returned to Venice to recruit new musicians for Dresden and to familiarize himself at first hand with the new style of

Monteverdi. To escape further the ravages of the war, which had severely depleted the musical forces at Dresden, Schütz requested extended leave of absence, and between 1633 and 1635 he was at Copenhagen reorganizing the court chapel there. Back in Dresden his duties at the court became increasingly onerous, but the elector was not prepared to pension him off, and much of Schütz's time was spent petitioning for funds to pay the few court musicians who remained. He finally retired when he was 72, to his sister's house at Weissenfels, where he spent the final years of his life occasionally composing but mostly studying and reading the Bible.

During Schütz's long composing career his style underwent some quite radical changes, including a shift from monumental choral works such as the *Psalmen Davids* (1619) to the more intimate madrigalian style of the *Cantiones Sacrae* (1625). There is however a consistent tone of grave solemnity that runs through his extraordinary sacred output, punctuated by many dramatic and highly expressive moments.

Musikalische Exequien

One of Schütz's greatest works is the *Musikalische Exequien* of 1636, a Lutheran Requiem composed for the funeral of one of his early benefactors, Prince Heinrich von Reuss. The prince had specified that certain texts should be inscribed on his coffin and set to music for performance at his funeral. Schütz assigns these contemplative words to his soloists, and inserts them within a setting of the Kyrie, sung by a chorus. This is followed by a choral motet and culminates in an extraordinarily powerful setting of the Nunc Dimittis in which a spectral-sounding reduced choir periodically interrupts the main chorus with the words "Selig sind die Toten, die in dem Herren sterben" (Blessed are the dead who die in the Lord).

Musikalische Exequien, Motetten und Konzerte: The Monteverdi Choir; English Baroque Soloists; His Majesties Sagbutts and Cornetts; Gardiner (Archiv)

This is a wonderful selection of some of Schütz's most startling and intense music, featuring the *Musikalische Exequien* and four short motets, one of which, *Auf dem Gebirge* (In the Mountains), has a mysterious opening in which the overlapping vocal lines of two countertenors seem to float across the dark, stolid tones of the sackbuts (early trombones).

Historia der Geburt Jesu Christi

A setting in German of the gospel story of the Nativity, Schütz's *Historia der Geburt Jesu Christi*, or *Christmas Story*, does for Christmas what the Passion settings of Bach do for Easter. Written around 1660, Schütz employs the then new vocal style of recitative for the role of the Evangelist, which is sung by a tenor. The other parts are taken by combinations of different singers, and a chorus which appears on just three occasions. Schütz's achievement is to create a sense of drama not just by varying the style of music for the different sections but also by associating specific instruments with each character. Thus the angel's three interjections are accompanied by two viols, the appearance of the shepherds by two recorders and a dulcian (a forerunner of the bassoon}, while for the Chief Priests a suitable element of formality and menace is achieved by means of the dark sonority of a pair of sackbuts.

Christmas Vespers: Gabrieli Consort and Players; McCreesh (Archiv)

On this excellent disc, Paul McCreesh re-creates the music within a specific liturgical and historical context, in this case a Christmas Vespers at the court of Dresden. So the marvellous performance of the *Christmas Story* is complemented by two hymns by Martin Luther, organ music by Samuel Scheidt, Schütz's *Magnificat* and more. With performers of such high quality, the result is startlingly dramatic and conveys a real sense of a joyous, ceremonial occasion.

The Christmas Story: Oxford Camerata; Summerly (Naxos; with *Psalm 100, Cantate Domino, Spes mea & O bone, O dulcis*)

Musically this budget recording by the ever-reliable Oxford Camerata is as good as the Gabrieli Consort version, with Paul Agnew particularly strong as the Evangelist. Where the Archiv recording has the edge, however, is in generating a greater sense of narrative momentum.

Il libro primo de Madrigali

Schütz is remembered almost entirely as a composer of sacred music, but his output was more diverse than this reputation suggests. He composed several operas – including *Dafne*, the first ever written in German – and though none of these have survived, we do have his Opus 1, a remarkable book of secular madrigals, *Il libro primo de Madrigali*. Completed by 1611, after Schütz's period with Gabrieli, the nineteen pieces in the collection display an effortless compositional virtuosity and demonstrate the young Schütz's masterful command of this most Italian of genres. His sensitive word setting is in evidence even at this early stage, such as in the eighth madrigal, where the darting sprightly setting of "Fucci o mio core" (Flee, O my heart) finally gives way to a sighing mournful expression of "Ma lasso, ecco un sospir nunzio infelice" (But alas, behold a sigh, unhappy messenger".

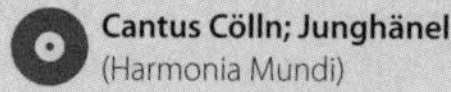

Cantus Cölln; Junghänel
(Harmonia Mundi)

Schutz's madrigals are brilliantly realized here. Everything is beautifully phrased and balanced, and the group's superbly clear tone is matched by an exceptional recording quality. The singers, who are in perfect ensemble (listen, for example, to the cohesion of the tempo changes in "Selve beate"), treat every line with meticulous attention to dynamics, and emphasize the dramatic treatment of the texts.

Alexander Scriabin (1872–1915)

Alexander Scriabin was the embodiment of E.T.A. Hoffmann's dictum: "Only in the truly Romantic does comedy mix so fittingly with tragedy that both are fused in a total effect". Scriabin's egomaniacal delusions – sustained by the attentions of countless adoring aunts, wives, lovers and nurses – grew to a grandiosity unrivalled even in the history of music. He came to believe that he was one with God and that he would ultimately be absorbed into the rhythm of the universe, becoming a revivifying deity who would one day unite the world. Grand ambitions for someone who died from a septic boil on his lip. However comical his writings and beliefs, there is no question about the merits of Scriabin's music. He lived out the transition from Romanticism to modernism, initiating a musical language that moved decisively towards a break with tonality. Only slightly less radical than Schoenberg or Debussy, he could have become one of the major figures of twentieth-century music had he not died so young.

He was Rachmaninov's immediate contemporary, attending the same class and graduating from the Moscow Conservatory in the same year. Like Rachmaninov he was a virtuoso pianist. But whereas Rachmaninov remained an ardent traditionalist, Scriabin quickly arrived at conclusions that placed him at the forefront of contemporary musical thought. His earliest piano music reflected his obsession with Chopin, although there are certain hints at what was to come. The *Sonata No. 1* bore reflections of Rachmaninov, Prokofiev and early Stravinsky, but by the *Sonata No. 3* his style was clearly shifting towards the shimmering exoticism with which he is now associated. The breakthrough came in 1907 with the completion of his *Sonata No. 5*, a single-movement work of extreme difficulty and tonal dissolution.

From then on, Scriabin's musical experimentation led him as far away from his peers as could be imagined, while his extreme hypochondria and his fascination with his own personality assumed Wagnerian dimensions. Influenced by the spiritual ideas of theosophy, Scriabin was fascinated by synaesthesia – the notion that all the senses stimulated each other – and the idea that musical keys corresponded to specific colours. In 1909, building on the success of his symphonic poem *Prometheus*, he unveiled a project more ambitious than anything Wagner ever dreamed up. The *Mysterium* was an extraordinary, cataclysmic idea, synthesizing all the arts and senses into an extravaganza involving a "colour organ", pianos, a huge orchestra, choirs, dancers, "visions" and clouds of perfume. His friend and publisher, the conductor Serge Koussevitzky, bought the rights. Scriabin designed a temple to be built in India expressly for the performance of the *Mysterium*, and in preparation for the great day bought himself a sunhat and a book on Sanskrit grammar. The project died with him.

Symphonies

Completed in 1900, Scriabin's *Symphony No. 1* shows him thinking in typically immodest terms: lasting fifty minutes, it's in six movements, the last of which boasts a chorus and soloists singing "visionary" texts of his own writing. The circulation and repetition of thematic ideas is used to bind together the work's ambitious length, and Scriabin's extensive use of triple time (finally broken in the finale), progressive tonality and highly dramatic melody all contribute towards a sweeping fluency that makes this one of the most powerful of all Russian Romantic symphonies.

The *Symphony No. 2*, composed the following year, is the same length as the first and is similarly marked by religio-mystical inebriation, but it is neither as bombastic nor as engaging. It's chiefly of interest for its orchestration, for in its use of bold instrumental colour and its quotation of birdsong it looks towards the style of Messiaen, another composer for whom music was an aspect of the spiritual world. The extra-musical dimension of the *Symphony No. 3* or *Divine Poem* (1904) was helpfully summarized by its composer: "The *Divine Poem* represents the evolution of the human spirit which, freed from the legends and mysteries of the past that it has summoned and overthrown, passes through pantheism and achieves a joyful and exhilarating affirmation of its liberty and its unity with the universe." As you may imagine, this is his most opulent creation. There is a conservative, formal architecture beneath the gorgeous, kaleidoscopic orchestral colour, but really it's best to treat the *Symphony No. 3* as an aural wallow.

Symphonies Nos. 1–3; Poem of Ecstasy; Prometheus: Myers, Toczyska; Philadelphia Orchestra; Westminster Chorus; Muti (Brilliant; 3 CDs)

Ricardo Muti's is the finest available set – he gives wonderful cogency to these massive works. The Philadelphia Orchestra plays with bright and responsive enthusiasm, while the solo soprano and tenor in the last movement of *Symphony No. 1* are suitably ecstatic.

Poem of Ecstasy & Prometheus

Scriabin took his symphonic journey to the limits of tonality in his two single-movement tone poems, the *Poem of Ecstasy* (1908) and *Prometheus* (1910) – the orchestral counterparts of his late piano sonatas. Melodies and conventional thematic material are conspicuously elusive here; instead harmonic progressions generate the material and Scriabin employs what he called a "mystic" chord of his own devising. The *Poem of Ecstasy* is a masterpiece of orchestration and harmonic modulation, with shifting sound colours that reflect the composer's intense interest in Debussy's music. Its early performances generated extraordinary excitement in the musical world; Prokofiev noted how as students he and his fellow-composer Miaskovsky were taken aback by the novelty of the piece after the relatively familiar territory of the *Divine Poem* and had to hear it several times. *Prometheus,* taking its name from the bringer of fire to mankind in Greek mythology, was the forerunner for the *Mysterium*. It includes a complex filigree role for piano, a chorus introduced at the last minute and an optional part in the score for a "colour organ" to project coloured light, instead of sound, to correspond with certain chords.

The visionary Russian Alexander Scriabin.

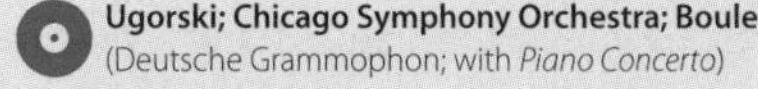

Ugorski; Chicago Symphony Orchestra; Boulez (Deutsche Grammophon; with *Piano Concerto*)

The analytical mind of Pierre Boulez is not associated with the perfumed hedonism of Scriabin, but he does lend a compelling shape and urgency to *Prometheus,* a piece that can easily drift in the wrong hands. There are Russian performances of the *Poem of Ecstasy* which blaze more sensually than this one; yet here, too, Boulez makes a compelling argument for structural tautness.

Piano Concerto

Scriabin's *Piano Concerto* is something of a surprise – a rose among the hothouse plants of his very idiosyncratic output. He completed it in 1896 while still a young man; the qualities then noted in him of candour and lightness of touch are very much to the fore. Although much of the piano writing scintillates, there is little bravura for its own sake, and the theme of the central variations – written even earlier than the concerto – is a real charmer. The Rachmaninov and Tchaikovsky piano concertos occasionally come to mind, but this is a surprisingly modest work with a sincerity all its own – definitely Scriabin's most accessible work for orchestra.

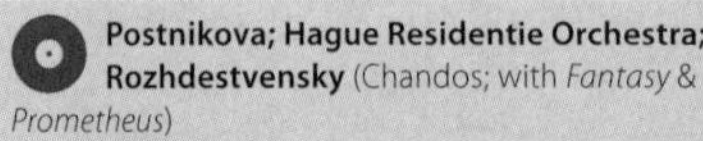

Postnikova; Hague Residentie Orchestra; Rozhdestvensky (Chandos; with *Fantasy* & *Prometheus*)

The Ugorski performance on the previously recommended Boulez disc is good but this is even better. Subtlety and tender atmosphere are not qualities one normally expects from Rozhdestvensky and his wife, the pianist Victoria Postnikova; but they find it in spades for this performance. The *Prometheus* hangs together less well.

Piano Sonatas

Scriabin's extensive output for piano is dominated by his sonatas, which cover his entire creative life: he wrote his first (unnumbered) sonata in 1892, and his last in 1913. The first four of the ten numbered sonatas are for the most part routinely Romantic, relying heavily on the legacy of Chopin and featuring a lot of aimless, overripe material. As examples of turn-of-the-century expressionism they are fascinating, but the *Sonata No. 5* (1907) is extremely interesting in itself. A brooding creation, it poses severe musical challenges, not least the dissonant, violent introductory bars, in which the music rises from the growling bass to the uppermost reaches of the keyboard in a startling flash of inspiration. From this work onwards, the sonatas become increasingly fiendish in their technical difficulty, exploring every recess of piano sonority. Scriabin's extremely complicated chromaticism – effectively borderline atonalism – reaches its expressive extreme in the so-called *Black Mass Sonata* and in its successor, the tenth. Concentrating myriad themes into the span of a single, multilayered movement, these last two sonatas are as scintillating as the virtuosic piano works of Liszt.

Complete Sonatas: Ashkenazy
(Decca; 2 CDs; with other Scriabin piano works)

There may be more subtle accounts of individual sonatas, but Vladimir Ashkenazy's cycle of the ten sonatas, recorded in the 1970s, set the standard against which modern performances are judged. His percussive, frequently belligerent tone is ideal for Scriabin's Mephistophelean music, and the recorded sound is excellent.

Sonatas Nos. 2, 5 & 9: Sudbin (BIS; with 4 Mazurkas and other Scriabin piano works)

As with Rachmaninov, Scriabin is core repertoire for Russian pianists (both Soviet and post-Soviet), and there are many great – if elusive – recordings by such legends as Sofronitsky, Horowitz and Richter. This 2007 recital by the young virtuoso Yevgeny Sudbin is in that great tradition. His performances of a cross-section of key works convey a profound identification with the music, and make an ideal introduction for those new to this composer.

Preludes, Opus 11

Scriabin wrote a total of ninety preludes, but the 24 selected for Opus 11 formed his first and most popular cycle. Sketched between 1888 and 1896, these pieces cover the years between his studies at the Moscow Conservatoire and his career as a travelling composer and virtuoso. Alternately daring and coy, but always with an awareness of the possibilities of the instrument, this is the work of a young man still finding his feet, and it would be another decade before his writing would take on its own peculiarly transcendental quality. But if the inspiration for the 24 *Preludes* is clearly Chopin's own *Préludes*, Op. 28, then they are given a Russian twist of mordant and far-sighted chromaticism. Already Scriabin's occasional moments of naivety are surmounted by a command of shifting harmonies and of complex, impassioned rhythmic pulses which seem, just as much as Liszt ever did, to shine a light into the future.

24 Preludes, Opus 11: Pletnev
(Virgin; with *Sonatas Nos. 4 & 10* and other pieces)

Mikhail Pletnev ratchets up the excitement in scintillating accounts of the Opus 11, in which Scriabin's colourful miniatures are met by a formidable technique and an unindulgent approach. The result is a revelation, Pletnev's wonderful tonal clarity somehow enhancing the Romantic focus of these pieces.

Complete Preludes: Lane
(Hyperion; 2 CDs)

If you want to hear the entire 75 or so preludes, then Piers Lane certainly has the measure of this elusive music without quite reaching the heights of a Sofronitsky or a Pletnev. What is impressive is the way he manages to convey the impulsiveness behind Scriabin's vision without lapsing into histrionics.

Études

With Chopin the étude ceased to be an exercise for the rehearsal room and became instead a celebration of what the pianist-composer could achieve: an exploration and extension of language for the nineteenth century's greatest instrument. This is the agenda Scriabin inherited, an agenda given an added charge by the otherworldly brilliance of Liszt's *Transcendental Études*. Scriabin wrote études throughout his career and they lie at the heart of his imaginative world. Functioning as a means for experiment as well as for private pleasure, they evolve from an early happy innocence through to music which seems to exist only as some spectral coalescence of rhythm and timbre. Though his Opus 8 remains the set favoured most by virtuosos, the principal later collections, Opus 42 (1903) and Opus 65 (1912), are just as rewarding.

Richter Edition Vol. 10 (Melodiya; with *Piano Sonata No. 6*, Prokofiev *Sonata No. 7* & Miaskovsky *Sonata No. 3*)

In this superlative 1952 recital, Sviatoslav Richter plays the whole of Op. 65 and substantial extracts from Opp. 8 and 42. Where other performers hammer the notes, Richter finds a dizzy and teeming world in which ideas float and dart like fish in some exotic lagoon. Hard to find but worth searching for.

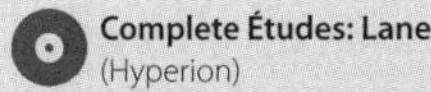

Complete Études: Lane
(Hyperion)

If you can't get hold of the Richter set (or are put off by the slightly dry sound), then this highly impressive performance of the complete études from Piers Lane, in a wonderfully natural acoustic, makes a worthwhile alternative.

Vers la flamme

Lasting less than seven minutes, the strange piano essay of *Vers la flamme* dates from 1914, when Scriabin was striving for a hedonistic fusion of the arts into a total sensory experience. This is powerful and progressive music, a breakthrough work inspired by theosophy and mysticism, in which Scriabin pushes tonality to its very limits and where deliberate harmonic irresolution opens up audacious and visionary possibilities. Throughout this late music there is an overwhelming sense of darkness made visible and of an attempt to suggest a dissolution of time itself.

Richter the Master Vol. 3: Richter
(Philips; 2 CDs; with *Poème Nocturne, Danses Op. 63, Fantasie Op. 28*, Prokofiev *Sonatas Nos. 4 & 6*, etc)

Scriabin's brooding mysticism has never been animated as brilliantly as it is here. The opening hesitancy of *Vers la flamme* is handled through dissolving sonorities which Richter treats in an almost improvisatory manner. Yet the inner lines and tensions are beautifully controlled, driving the music on to its ecstatic culmination.

Late Russian Romantics: Horowitz
(Sony; with 8 études, Rachmaninov *Sonata No. 2* and music by Medtner)

Vladimir Horowitz was an enthusiastic advocate of Scriabin's music and his performances are powerfully convincing. His approach to *Vers la flamme* is less inward-looking and more percussive than Richter's. The range of dynamics on display is extraordinary, especially in the clamorous tintinnabulation of the piece's last third.

Dmitri Shostakovich (1906–1975)

Dmitri Shostakovich died in 1975, four years after Stravinsky, and was the last composer whose qualities were acknowledged throughout the Western world, in both the modernist and the traditionalist camps. Within weeks of his death, memorial concerts were held throughout the world and he was being celebrated as the finest composer of the century. For many that claim still holds true, and even among those who rate him not quite so highly none would argue that he is one of modern music's most fascinating characters. Unlike Prokofiev, who grew up and was educated in Tsarist Russia, Shostakovich spent his entire life under the Soviet system, and he was the first successful composer to emerge because of and not despite the Communist regime.

Shostakovich was taught initially by his mother, but his first major musical influence came from Glazunov, who encouraged the boy when he entered Petrograd (St Petersburg) Conservatory in 1919. Four years later Shostakovich graduated from Glazunov's piano course and began giving concerts. In 1926, his diploma work – the *Symphony No. 1* – was performed in Moscow and Leningrad (the renamed Petrograd), earning the composer international fame before his 21st birthday. The idealistic Shostakovich believed that it was his responsibility to serve the state as an artist, and he settled down to composing "realist" music, albeit with a progressive edge. He was impressed by much of the music of the Second Viennese School, and by Berg's *Wozzeck* in particular, and developed an eclectic style that was rooted in tonality yet incorporated some more abrasively Germanic and avant-garde tendencies. His mission was to produce work that was accessible without being regressive, and it was to bring him into conflict with the musical arbiters within the government.

Two years after the successful 1934 premiere of his opera *Lady Macbeth of Mtsensk*, the work was savaged in *Pravda*, where an article titled "Chaos instead of Music" deplored *Lady Macbeth* for its "confused stream of sounds" and "petty bourgeois sensationalism". The state made it clear that "Soviet art can have no other aim than the interest of the people and the state" and, while Shostakovich sympathized in part with these vague dictates, he was appalled by the extremes to which the state was willing to go. When you have a country of over 180 million people, speaking 108 different languages, it is hard to find a common musical ground, but Shostakovich was relentlessly bullied for his deviations from the ill-defined path of Socialist Realism.

From 1938 until 1955 Shostakovich devoted himself chiefly to symphonic music, and also began his vast cycle of string quartets. During the two months before he was airlifted out of the besieged Leningrad in October 1941, he fought fires and helped the wounded. In 1943, following his time with other evacuated artists further east in Kuibyshev, he settled in Moscow, where he was appointed a professor of composition at the conservatory. Even though he toed the party line with humiliating obedience, Shostakovich still fell foul of the government in 1948, when he and many other prominent Russian composers were singled out and denounced for "formalism" and the creation of "anti-people art". He was dismissed from his teaching post, and subsequently composed almost nothing but film scores and patriotic music until after Stalin's death in 1953. The last twenty years of his life were much calmer: free from state intrusion, he produced some particularly fine music, and saw the first performance of several major pieces written during the Stalinist repression. One of his most consistent pleasures in later years was his friendship with Benjamin Britten and the group of Russian musicians for whom he composed, including Nikolayeva, Oistrakh and Rostropovich.

Shostakovich's style is heterogeneous yet immediately recognizable, combining the three strands of "high-spirited humour, introspective meditation and declamatory grandeur", in the words of musicologist Boris Schwarz. As Schwarz goes on to say, in much of his music Shostakovich allows one of these elements to prevail, and the result can be monotonous and wearisome. But in his greatest works, notably the symphonies and string quartets, he encompasses exceptionally wide emotional extremes, juxtaposing tragic intensity and grotesque wit, sublimity and banality, folksy jauntiness and elemental darkness, in a manner that recalls Gustav Mahler, a composer he especially admired.

Shostakovich contemplates one of his scores.

OPERAS

Intoxicated by the anything-goes artistic freedom of the early years in the new Soviet Russia, Shostakovich completed his first opera, *The Nose*, in 1928, just as the liberal tide was beginning to turn. As a result, performances of this sharp and biting musical satire were all too few. *The Nose* includes a spluttering monologue and an orchestral interlude scored for percussion only, and there are comparably audacious moments in Shostakovich's only full-length opera, *Lady Macbeth of Mtsensk*, including a graphic sex scene that was removed from its reincarnation as *Katerina Izmailova*. Shostakovich's only other operatic projects were a 1942 attempt to set every word of Gogol's drama *The Gamblers* (abandoned as the piece would have lasted more than four hours) and a 1958 operetta,

Moskva Cheryomushki. The latter was written with little involvement, and sounds like it, but has nonetheless been revived in recent years.

Lady Macbeth of Mtsensk

Lady Macbeth of Mtsensk was heralded as a work of great power and originality after its 1934 premiere in Leningrad. Productions outside the Soviet Union soon followed, but in December 1935 Stalin went to see the show. The result was a *Pravda* editorial decrying this "fidgety, screaming, neurotic music" and deriding the composer for sympathizing with a thoroughly wicked heroine – a bored adulteress who murders her husband, is exiled to Siberia with her lover, and ends up committing suicide. The authorities entirely missed the opera's mordant social satire, and demanded a revision; Shostakovich duly toned down what he termed the "animal eroticism" of *Lady Macbeth*, and the work re-emerged in 1956 under the new title *Katerina Izmailova*.

The original version now seems one of the most powerful and dramatically effective operas of the twentieth century. Its compelling protagonist is a desperate young woman whose extreme and murderous behaviour is explained by the domestic and social constraints that entrap her. By employing a wide range of disparate musical styles and colours, the composer makes it absolutely clear what he thinks of the characters. This highly graphic approach is heard at its rawest in Katerina's first bout of love-making with her lover Sergey, the orchestra – complete with braying brass – providing a frantic accompaniment which culminates in downward, post-coital trombone glissandi. Powerful and uncompromisingly modern, *Lady Macbeth* warrants comparison with Berg's *Wozzeck*.

Vishnevskaya, Gedda, Petkov, Krenn, Tear, Valjakka; Ambrosian Opera Choir; London Philharmonic Orchestra; Rostropovich (EMI; 2 CDs)

This is one of Mstislav Rostropovich's most successful recordings as a conductor, his sensitivity to the orchestral colours and his vigorous tempi perfectly serving the opera's sudden contrasts and black humour. Rostropovich's wife, Galina Vishnevskaya, sings with a thrilling, elemental power, and Nicolai Gedda is also impressive, even though he was past his prime in 1978.

SYMPHONIES

From the daring precocity of the *Symphony No. 1* (1923–24) to the anguished bitterness of the *Symphony No. 15* (1971), Shostakovich's symphonies display a range unequalled by any other modern cycle. His style, however, was largely consistent from the *Symphony No. 4* onwards: a harmonic language that borrowed a little from Prokofiev and a little from Russian folk song, a tendency (shared with Mahler) to juxtapose music that is startlingly different in mood and feeling, and a mordant sense of humour that often finds expression in the grotesque. Since the publication of the composer's supposedly dictated "memoirs" (*Testimony*) in 1979, and even more so since his death, critics have speculated at length about encoded messages in his symphonies which reveal his "true" feelings about the ideological and aesthetic constraints placed upon him. Such speculation is sometimes enlightening but more often tendentious: Shostakovich's work stands on purely musical grounds, irrespective of the always interesting circumstances in which it was written. The symphonies are best bought individually, starting with the six selected below. For those wanting the complete cycle, the Haitink set (recorded in the 1970s and 80s) is still the best option.

Complete Symphonies: Concertgebouw Orchestra; London Philharmonic Orchestra; Haitink
(Decca London; 11 CDs)

Bernard Haitink's symphony cycle is a remarkable achievement. The LPO and the Concertgebouw are both on top form throughout, and their playing is matched by consistently excellent recorded sound. Haitink's interpretations occasionally lack the visceral power of certain other versions, but the architecture is always conveyed and, unlike some recordings, these don't cloy on repeated listening.

Symphony No. 1

Hackwork, and the onset of tuberculosis, frustrated Shostakovich's progress on the work planned for his graduation from the St Petersburg Conservatoire. His first symphony, the "symphony-grotesque", as he christened it, was begun early in 1923 and completed, after much hard grind, in June 1925. In Moscow, a crush of students came to blows in order to hear it, and its success was repeated in the West where it was conducted by Bruno Walter. It is indeed a tremendous debut: clean and deft, tightly integrated and structured with many of the resources that would serve Shostakovich well in later life, not least a natural symphonist's manipulation of interludes and anticlimax. It is the work of a composer turning his back on specifically Russian music to forge a new modern language (for new Revolutionary times) that was witty, ironic and bursting with energy.

Philadelphia Orchestra; Ormandy (Sony; with the *Festive Overture* and selections from *The Gadfly*, *The Age of Gold*, *Moskow-Cheryomushki* & *Ballet Suites Nos. 1 & 2*)

This razor-sharp performance from Ormandy catches exactly the right element of burlesque and always allows the wit to shine through. There are hints at the undercurrent of sedition and the profound disquiet which run through this work. A well-played selection of Shostakovich's most flamboyant film and stage music completes an irresistible disc.

Scottish National Orchestra; Järvi (Chandos; with *Symphony No. 6*)

Järvi's is probably the best of the modern interpretations: it lacks the keenness and individuality of Ormandy but combines style and sensitivity in equal measure. It's coupled with a splendid performance of the underrated *Symphony No. 6* and the recording is excellent.

Symphony No. 5

Shostakovich began the *Symphony No. 5* a year after *Pravda* had attacked his *Lady Macbeth*, and the work was premiered on 21 November, 1937. A journalist referred to it as "A Soviet Artist's Practical Creative Reply to Just Criticism" and Shostakovich let the description stand. It was a sensational success, for, in accordance with the Politburo's dictum that "all aspects of music should be subordinated to melody and such melody should be clear and singable", Shostakovich produced a work bursting with tunes. The treatment is less ambitious than in its immediate predecessor, but the symphony is still constructed along grand lines – though Shostakovich's confidants attest to the irony of its optimistic finale.

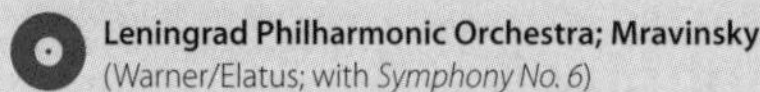

Leningrad Philharmonic Orchestra; Mravinsky (Warner/Elatus; with *Symphony No. 6*)

Yevgeny Mravinsky was for years Shostakovich's own favoured interpreter, and he generally has no equal in the composer's music. Here he conducts with incision and an utter lack of sentimentality or strain. Nobody else brings off the last movement so compellingly.

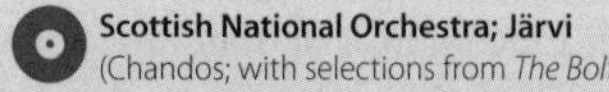

Scottish National Orchestra; Järvi (Chandos; with selections from *The Bolt*)

Järvi's disc has more technical polish than Mravinsky's live recording, and there is no doubting the sincerity of this performance or the dignity with which its desolate vision is communicated. For those who might be concerned about Mravinsky's lack of gloss, Järvi is ideal, though Mravinsky flows better – conspicuously so in the Scherzo.

Symphony No. 7 – The Leningrad

The *Symphony No. 7* was written during the siege of Leningrad when maybe as many as a million people died of cold and starvation. Shostakovich was evacuated near the beginning of the siege, by which time he had already written the symphony's first three movements. Once completed, it was performed (with the siege still going on) not just in Moscow and Leningrad but also in London and across America. It is therefore inextricably tied up with the war and comes with even more extra-musical baggage than usual (including a detailed programme by Shostakovich). To confuse matters the composer later declared: "I have nothing against calling the 7th the *Leningrad* ... but it's not about the Leningrad under siege, it's about the Leningrad that Stalin destroyed and Hitler finished off." Famously, the opening movement is dominated by a long, rather banal, march that builds ever more menacingly to a shuddering climax. This "War" or "Invasion" motif has divided critics, but the way the composer creates an atmosphere that is both cheap and exhilarating before having it subside into something spare and elegiac is highly effective. In the rest of the symphony there is an equally profound tension between bitterness and hope, not least in the beautifully judged slow movement, which resolutely refuses to succumb to sadness.

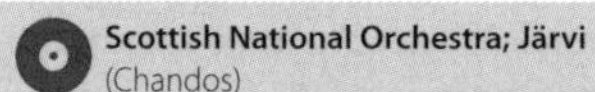

Scottish National Orchestra; Järvi (Chandos)

In Järvi's hands the *Leningrad* becomes truly great music: this is a mesmerizing reading, in which the opening builds like a wave. Yet Järvi's crisp phrasing keeps the slower episodes nimble, allowing him to pull back the tempo without any sense of disruption. Rarely has the humanity of Shostakovich's desolate grotesquerie been more finely judged or so passionately communicated.

Chicago Symphony Orchestra; Bernstein (Deutsche Grammophon; 2 CDs; with *Symphony No. 1*)

This live performance is a determined rethink, adding a level of gravitas beyond the usual rhetoric. Leonard

Bernstein manages to create an extra breadth for Shostakovich's white-hot inspiration, even if more than once the work's overriding tension is somewhat reduced.

Symphony No. 8

Critics tend to consider the *Symphony No. 8* a more considered and effective response to the experience of war. It is certainly a work that exudes a profound feeling of tragedy, and when Shostakovich was criticized by Zhdanov in 1948 the symphony was singled out for its "extreme subjectivism" and "unrelieved gloom". Its opening is immensely powerful: a long, inward-looking Adagio punctuated by a faster development that seems to mock the original material. There is little let up in this work but the third-movement Allegro is positively demented in its hard edge and its machine-like rhythms. It culminates in a fulsomely expansive passacaglia before leading straight into a final movement in C major, usually a key associated with joyous ceremonial, but here shot through with an unnerving ambiguity which suggests that hope is just too expensive a commodity to enjoy unreservedly.

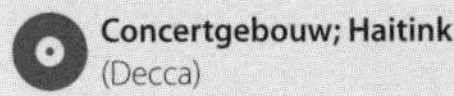

Concertgebouw; Haitink
(Decca)

Haitink finds a highly satisfactory middle ground between the impassioned extremity of some Russian recordings and the sleek angst-free tones of many Western interpreters. This is one of the most successful of his complete cycle of Shostakovich symphonies – there's energy as well as pain in this hard-driven performance.

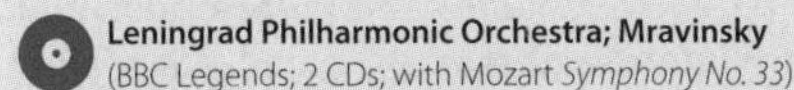

Leningrad Philharmonic Orchestra; Mravinsky
(BBC Legends; 2 CDs; with Mozart *Symphony No. 33*)

Mravinsky's intense, anguished and powerfully dramatic vision of this work was recorded many times. Though only available as part of a double CD, this 1960 performance, recorded in London with the composer in attendance, offers the best balance of sound quality and interpretative power (despite the plethora of coughing).

Symphony No. 10

Shostakovich's *Symphony No. 10* is one of the least programmatic of his works but it was performed soon after the death of Stalin, and the bleak power of the first three movements could be taken as a commentary on the dark age that had just passed. Galina Vishnevskaya has called this symphony "a composer's testament of misery, forever damning a tyrant". But what impresses most is the way in which this music commands and subverts symphonic decorum on purely abstract terms to produce a profound disquiet. It is a reinvention of the symphony at the hands of a master, whose thoughts here have undergone years of secretive gestation. There's an epic scope to it: indeed the first movement – an immense autumnal essay of gradually built momentum – could almost stand alone. As it is, its solemnity is shattered, in typical fashion, by a shrill and aggressive Scherzo. The finale is also built on a striking contrast, this time between the poignant Mahlerian Andante which begins it, and the frantic *danse macabre* which dominates the rest of the movement.

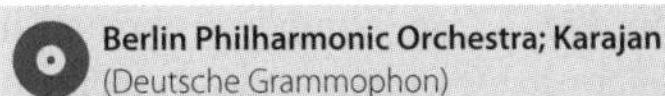

Berlin Philharmonic Orchestra; Karajan
(Deutsche Grammophon)

The second of Karajan's two recordings, with its marvellously rich sound, is the outstanding version of this symphony. He gives it a darkly lustrous and noble stature, spinning out the long lines, merging its interlocking structures in a sweeping but cohesive vision.

Symphony No. 15

Shostakovich's orchestral swansong of 1971 marks a return to the standard four-movement symphony after the song-cycle form of its predecessor. Yet its overall proportions are, as always, unconventional. Instead of an epic first movement, we have what is in effect a speeded-up version of the usual Shostakovich drama, where droll references to Rossini's *William Tell* overture sit with deliberate unease alongside spikier themes that come very close to Schoenberg's use of the twelve-tone scale. A lean, funereal slow movement is followed by a skeletal Scherzo, before references to Wagner's *Gotterdämmerung* and *Tristan und Isolde* launch a dramatic finale which fades away into the utterly original infinity of percussion whirrings and clickings. Here, as ever, Shostakovich was reaching out into new areas of sound and feeling.

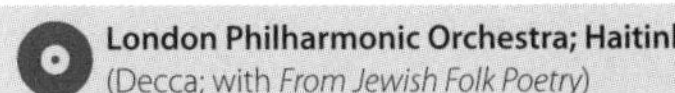

London Philharmonic Orchestra; Haitink
(Decca; with *From Jewish Folk Poetry*)

Haitink's polished sonorities and focused interpretative approach pay off richly here, especially when pages of the score pass without more than a handful of instrumental lines. The accompanying item is Haitink's Concertgebouw reading of the song cycle *From Jewish Folk Poetry*, a daring statement of solidarity composed during Stalin's virulently anti-Semitic last years.

CONCERTOS

Compared with his fifteen symphonies and fifteen string quartets, Shostakovich's concerto output was relatively meagre. There are six in total (two each for piano, violin and cello) and all of them were written with a specific performer in mind – himself for the first piano concerto, his son Maxim for the second, David Oistrakh for the violin concertos, and Mstislav Rostropovich for the cello concertos. All have been recorded on several occasions, but only the two piano concertos and the first violin concerto have gained a permanent foothold in the concert hall.

Piano Concertos

Shostakovich's *Piano Concerto No. 1*, written in 1933, is scored for strings, piano and solo trumpet, a combination as unusual as the concerto's form, which consists of four through-flowing movements which sound like just one. Because of its wit, its clarity and its sharply etched contours it has been compared to the concertos of Poulenc but Shostakovich's humour is far more sardonic and barbed. It's always been a popular work, chiefly because of its plenitude of uplifting tunes, its frequent, provocative changes of mood and a wonderfully high-spirited last movement which is pure Keystone Kops. The second concerto, written for his son Maxim in 1957, is for the conventional combination of piano and orchestra, and is a lighter work than its predecessor. Like the *Violin Concerto No. 1*, it has a slow movement of exquisite pathos – its unabashed Romanticism would not be out of place in a concerto by Rachmaninov – while the last movement presents a corrective dose of Shostakovich's very own brand of flippancy.

Alexeev, Jones; English Chamber Orchestra; Maksymiuk (Classics for Pleasure; with *The Assault on Beautiful Gorky*)

This is the best modern coupling of both concertos, with Dmitri Alexeev a brilliant and assertive soloist throughout. As a bonus there's a fine mini-concerto taken from one of Shostakovich's many film scores.

Shostakovich; French National Radio Orchestra; Cluytens (EMI; with selected *Preludes and Fugues*)

Quirky, frenetic playing from Shostakovich himself in 1958 – at times he makes the music rear up like a ferocious beast. A selection of the *Preludes and Fugues*, superbly laconic, completes a delightful disc that is a wonderful discovery and an indispensable historic document.

Violin Concertos

Shostakovich composed two violin concertos, both of them written for and first performed by David Oistrakh, one of the twentieth century's finest violinists. The first was composed in 1947–48 but remained unperformed until 1955, and was perhaps altered during the intervening years. This work features some of the finest music ever written for the violin, and in its third movement Shostakovich created his most beautiful concerto episode – a deeply spiritual passacaglia, in which a regular rhythmic pattern announced by the timpani forms the backdrop to the soloist's desperately mournful lament. As a whole, it's a multifaceted work of great difficulty for the soloist but of complete immediacy for the listener.

The *Violin Concerto No. 2* was composed two decades after the first and is not quite such an immediately beguiling creation. Written, curiously, in C sharp minor (an awkward key for the solo instrument), it lacks the melodic ease of its predecessor, but it is powerful nonetheless, especially the central Adagio, which builds from brooding melancholy to an impassioned cadenza-like climax.

Vengerov; London Symphony Orchestra; Rostropovich (Teldec)

The spirit of Oistrakh seems to inform Maxim Vengerov's playing, which has a burnished intensity. The guidance of Rostropovich is also an influence that Vengerov has been happy to acknowledge, and it shows here in the breadth of his bowing and tone, which ranges from an anguished whisper to a raucous outcry.

Cello Concertos

The situation with the two cello concertos is superficially the same as with their violin counterparts: the first is often heard in the concert hall, the second very rarely. But while the daunting ambitions of the *Violin Concerto No. 1* perhaps deservedly overshadow the more understated qualities of its successor, the pared-down ambiguities of the *Cello Concerto No. 2*, composed in 1967, make it a richer work than the exciting and effective piece that precedes it by eight years. *No. 1* is certainly an extraordinary creation, notable not least for its massive, tempestuous cadenza, but *No. 2*, in the words of the cellist who inspired both concertos, Mstislav Rostropovich, "is less striking ... but its profundity is second to none".

Mørk; London Philharmonic Orchestra; Jansons (Virgin)

Truls Mørk's noble performances of both concertos make this disc the first choice among the modern recordings. Mørk's searching, introspective account of the second concerto is particularly outstanding – one of the most compelling Shostakovich performances available on disc.

Cello Concerto No. 1: Rostropovich; Philadelphia Orchestra; Ormandy (Sony; with *Violin Concerto No. 1*)

Rostropovich has recorded both concertos more than once, but there's no CD available that contains his readings of both works. If you want to try just one disc, this classic 1959 recording of *No. 1* is a good choice, not just for Rostropovich's breathtaking playing, but also for Oistrakh's equally authoritative account of the first violin concerto.

CHAMBER & PIANO MUSIC

Many of Shostakovich's finest works were written for small instrumental ensembles that allowed for an intimacy and a directness of expression. The most celebrated of all his chamber music are the fifteen string quartets, which for several critics is the most significant twentieth-century quartet cycle after Bartók's. Shostakovich was a fine pianist – not as good as Rachmaninov or Prokofiev but good enough to enter the 1922 Chopin competition in Warsaw. His intensely idiomatic piano writing is very much concerned with Classical forms, such as sonatas and preludes. Best of all are his *24 Preludes and Fugues*, which were inspired by hearing the pianist Tatiana Nikoleyeva play Bach preludes and fugues, and are worthy successors to them.

String Quartets

Shostakovich wrote fifteen symphonies and fifteen string quartets, but the numerical equality might be misleading – he didn't compose his first quartet until 1938, when he had already completed his fifth symphony, and waited another six years before embarking on the second. Each of the quartets displays an understanding of the interrelationship of string instruments that is as fine as that shown by Schubert or Beethoven, and as with the Beethoven quartets these pieces are a vehicle for the composer's most intimate utterances. In comparison with Bartók's quartets, the century's other great cycle (see p.39), Shostakovich's are extremely melodic and direct, sometimes to the point of obviousness, but his gift for the unexpected turn of phrase is evident in every one.

Two of the finest of this astonishingly sustained sequence are the first and the eighth quartets. The former contains some gorgeous melodic writing, particularly in the second movement, which possesses the sort of tune that sets you thinking of divine inspiration. The latter was written in 1960 but was inspired by the firebombing of Dresden, a disaster that was also a source for Strauss's *Metamorphosen*. Unlike *Metamorphosen*, however, this is a bleak creation that offers no sense of hope or reconciliation. Written "In Memory of the Victims of Fascism and War", it's also a coded autobiography, for the music quotes from Shostakovich's own *Piano Quintet* and from *Lady Macbeth*, while the dominating theme is his musical "signature" D-S-C-H (D-E flat-C-B), which he also used in the *Symphony No. 10* and in other places.

Complete String Quartets; Emerson Quartet
(Deutsche Grammophon; 5 CDs)

The Emersons are slightly cooler and more objective than the Fitzwilliams (see below), but their approach works brilliantly. With their interpretative intelligence and astonishing technical skill, they bring verve, theatricality and a gorgeous tone to the pieces, highlighting not only their expressive power but also the frequently profound tension between internal anguish and external calm.

Complete String Quartets: Fitzwilliam String Quartet
(Decca; 6 CDs)

More than the symphonies, this is a cycle worth exploring from beginning to end, and this superb recording allows you to do so for a very reasonable price. The Fitzwilliam players may lack that final, emotionally driven edge of the Borodins or the technical precision of the Emersons, but these are wonderful performances, deeply felt and densely argued.

Quartets Nos. 2, 3, 7, 8 & 12: Borodin String Quartet
(Virgin; 2 CDs)

The Borodins, notable for their extraordinarily powerful and hard-hitting Shostakovich readings, have made three recordings of the complete cycle. This two-for-the-price-of-one set is drawn from the most recent, which benefits from better sound quality. Excellent value and superlative performances, including a breathtaking account of *No. 8*, make this an excellent introduction to the quartets.

Piano Quintet

After the failure of his *Symphony No. 6*, Shostakovich's income was sustained by film commissions (for which he received the Order of the Red Banner of Labour). But in 1940 there was the chance to rekindle his fame with chamber music on a grand scale – the *Piano Quintet* in G minor. It's a work that is impressive, above all, for its propulsive force – the opening prelude is like Bach with a searing modernist edge. The second movement is music cut back to bare sinews, from which the piano is all but absent. The finale exploits the open diatonic intervals through which Mahler used to envelop music in buoyant euphoria, but for Shostakovich the emotions soon become more complex than that, as if optimistic resignation were the best one could hope for. When Shostakovich appeared in the Hall of the Conservatoire to give its first performance with the Beethoven Quartet, his audience rose and their final ovation had all the fervour of a political demonstration.

Leonskaya; Borodin Quartet (Teldec; with *Piano Trio No. 2*)

Shostakovich was rarely more economical in his writing than he is in this score; and filled with such warmth as the Borodins give it, the sense of suffering is almost unbearable. It's a reading in whose machinery the heroic and the hopeless are equally realized, and it comes across with the biting intensity of an assault.

Sonata for Violin & Piano

The *Sonata for Violin and Piano* was composed in 1968 to celebrate the sixtieth birthday of David Oistrakh. Abounding in private allusions and coded messages, this haunting sonata is written in Shostakovich's most sparse and desultory style. It's a work whose expressive compass ranges from a meditation on twelve-note chromaticism, through ironic vehemence, to a series of stratospheric variations, as noble as Bach – indeed, the finale repeats the passacaglia structure which had already been put to such powerful effect in Shostakovich's *Violin Concerto No. 1*.

Mordkovitch, Benson (Chandos; with pieces by Prokofiev and Schnittke)

Lydia Mordkovitch prevents this sardonic piece of writing from descending into crabbiness, deploying timbres that range from a crepuscular sotto voce to sinuous resilience. However much she holds in reserve, she keeps enough metrical buoyancy and power to drive on Shostakovich's bitter narrative.

Preludes and Fugues

Shostakovich's penchant for musical "signatures" derived from his study of the music of Bach, who wrote pieces in which the notes signified by the letters of his name were used as thematic material. A more interesting product of his immersion in Bach was the *24 Preludes and Fugues* Op. 87, which was written in 1950–51 for Tatiana Nikolayeva. Comprising a prelude and fugue in each key, this huge composition mirrors the structure of the *Well-Tempered Clavier*, but this music is a world away from the decorum of the Baroque era. These are intensely personal pieces, covering an emotional spectrum almost as wide as that of the quartets. From the simplicity of the first in C major to the quasi-symphonic grandeur of the last in D minor, the *Preludes and Fugues* bare the composer's soul with uncompromised honesty.

Nikolayeva (Hyperion; 3 CDs)

A Bach recital by Tatiana Nikolayeva gave Shostakovich the idea of writing these pieces, and she advised him throughout their composition. Powerhouse playing is required by these works and Nikolayeva plays them as if her life depended on it. A superb document and a lasting testament to a great musical personality.

Scherbakov (Naxos; 2 CDs)

Scherbakov plays with a greater range of colours and dynamic variety than does Nikolayeva, and his grasp of the different voices in the fugues certainly comes close to hers. This is a first-rate performance at any price, but with all 24 *Preludes and Fugues* accommodated on two bargain-price CDs it is exceptionally good value.

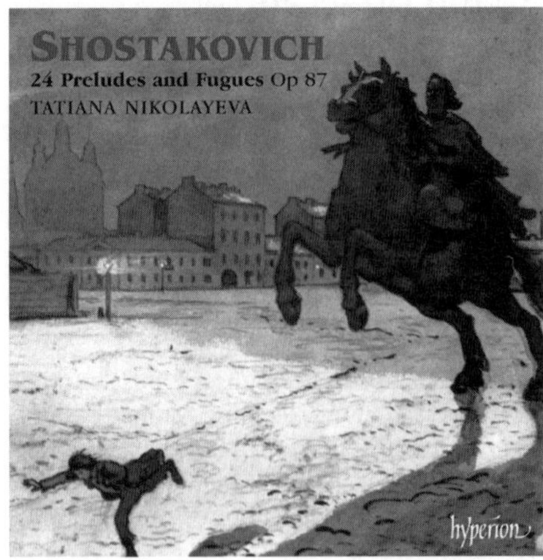

Jean Sibelius (1865–1957)

Nineteenth-century Finland was a grand duchy of Tsarist Russia, ruled by a Swedish-speaking minority. It was one of Sibelius's greatest achievements to reassert Finnish culture as something distinct from that of both Russia and Sweden. He became the cultural figurehead of Finnish nationalism, a status achieved largely through writing some of the greatest symphonic music of the nineteenth and twentieth centuries.

Johan (later Jean) Julius Christian Sibelius was born into a Swedish-speaking doctor's family in a small town in southern Finland, Hämeenlinna, but spent much of his school life in a Finnish-speaking environment. He was composing by the age of ten and at first saw his future as a violinist, though he entered Helsinki University to study law, before turning to music when he came under the influence of Ferruccio Busoni (see p.119), then on the university's staff. Sibelius continued his musical studies in Berlin and then in Vienna.

Returning to Finland in 1891, he completed his first major work, the choral symphony *Kullervo* (1892), the first of many compositions based on the mythology of the Finnish national epic, the *Kalevala* – the closest Finnish equivalent to the Arthurian legends or the Nordic sagas. Championed by the conductor Robert Kajanus, the success of this work led to the commissioning of *En Saga* and enabled Sibelius to marry his fiancée Aino Järnefelt. His *Symphony No. 1* (1899) consolidated a reputation in his home country, which had already honoured him with a small pension for life, partly as recompense for his not getting the post of director of music at Helsinki University. His fame now spread abroad and several ensuing works were first performed in Berlin, including the *Violin Concerto* (1903–05), which was given its premiere under Richard Strauss.

The first decade of the century also saw Sibelius develop a more personal style, away from the Tchaikovsky-inspired early symphonies towards something sparer, more refined and more organic in structure. In 1907 Gustav Mahler visited Helsinki, where he had several conversations with Sibelius about music. Famously, they discussed the symphony, with Sibelius (as he later recalled) stating his admiration for "its severity of style and the profound logic that creates an inner connection between the themes." Mahler disagreed; for him "the symphony must be like the world. It must embrace everything." The exchange is highly revealing of Sibelius's insistence that a composition be determined by the development of thematic material, a process that became ever more visible as his style got more austere.

In 1908, Sibelius was diagnosed with cancer of the throat, thus depriving him of his beloved tobacco and alcohol. He responded by darkening and paring down his style even further, a process clear in works such as the *Symphony No. 4* (1911). Further deprivation was to come: the outbreak of World War I obliterated his income from royalties, then an attempted communist coup in Finland – which had achieved independence in the wake of the Russian Revolution – forced Sibelius to leave his home in the forests to the north of Helsinki.

The elderly Sibelius enjoying a cigar.

After the war Sibelius composed the last two of his seven symphonies and the great tone poem *Tapiola* (1926). The following year, with restored royalties and his state pension giving him a secure future, he simply retired from composing and conducting, and for the next twenty years kept the musical world waiting for an eighth symphony that never materialized.

SYMPHONIES

Sibelius was the most original symphonist since Beethoven, in that he found unique solutions to the problems of symphonic form. His earliest symphonies follow a fairly traditional nineteenth-century model, but he soon went on to develop a highly complex structural approach, in which the music was conceived in terms of a great arch. As a broad generalization, the mature symphonies of

Sibelius progress from scattered and fragmentary ideas into fully formed themes and sections, as if the compositional process were happening in the presence of the audience. The high point of this process is the *Symphony No. 7*, where Sibelius manages to combine the usual four movements into a single continuity, in which it is impossible to tell where one section ends and another begins.

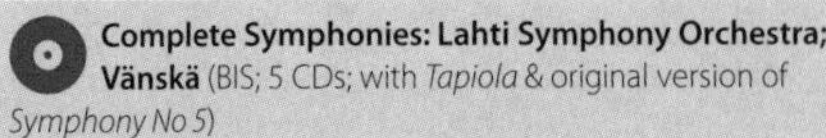
Complete Symphonies: Lahti Symphony Orchestra; Vänskä (BIS; 5 CDs; with *Tapiola* & original version of *Symphony No 5*)

Osmo Vänskä is one of the most penetrating Sibelians of modern times. He may be less Romantic than some, but his understanding goes way beyond abstraction. His performances of *No. 4* and *No. 7* are amongst the most stirring ever recorded, while in the ever-popular *No. 5* he brings the kind of visceral engagement that forces you to listen afresh.

Symphony No. 1

Sibelius was still under the influence of Tchaikovsky when he wrote his first symphony, but these Russian overtones coexist with assuredly individualistic orchestral textures and themes. At the very opening, for example, in a highly original stroke, a clarinet over a gentle timpani roll introduces the main theme, which achieves its apotheosis at the climax of the finale. In the second movement the debt to Tchaikovsky is clearly revealed in the way the languidly mournful opening theme is developed prior to a stormy climax. An emphatically rhythmic Scherzo reveals another influence: Bruckner, a composer whose music Sibelius had first encountered in Vienna in 1890. The finale, marked "Quasi una Fantasia", veers between frenzied agitation and a grandly refulgent "big tune" in which the strings predominate.

Oslo Philharmonic Orchestra; Jansons (EMI; with *Karelia Suite* & *Finlandia*)

In the right hands, the first symphony can be an extremely exciting work. Mariss Jansons finds just the right level of energy as the symphony unfolds, and the Oslo Philharmonic respond with a brilliance that is never forced.

Symphony No. 2

The *Symphony No. 2* (1901), one of the most popular of the cycle, marks a transition between the youthful and the mature Sibelius. Much of it was composed in Italy, and the Russian influence has here been replaced by something more southern in feeling: textures are more open, the thematic writing more ingratiating and there is a general atmosphere of warmth. That said, a mood of foreboding emerges at the start of the second movement, with a theme inspired by the tale of Don Juan being confronted by the figure of Death – an idea originally intended for a tone poem. Oppressiveness eventually gives way to a warmer, affirmative second theme. The finale is a real epic – pulsating and elemental – which, like the first symphony, has that most Russian of concepts, a stirring "big tune" as the work's crowning glory.

Gothenburg Symphony Orchestra; Järvi (BIS; with *Romance in C*)

Neeme Järvi's recording with the Gothenburg Symphony Orchestra is among the most thrilling available – full of exhilarating power and energy yet always alert to the demands of the symphony's formal structure.

Symphony No. 3

Perhaps because it lacks the broad sweep and the overt emotionalism of the earlier symphonies, *Symphony No. 3* (1907) is one of Sibelius's least-known works. Significantly, it shows him moving towards a new pared-down style, with restraint, subtlety and clarity of texture the most obvious characteristics. The orchestra is now relatively small and the strings dominate the presentation of the main thematic material, which has a direct, straightforward quality to it. The first-movement Allegro is virtually a *moto perpetuo* of scurrying energy, with a hint of peasant dance music occasionally obtruding before the movement reaches its broad hymn-like ending. By contrast, the slow movement is a model of restraint, with a gentle melody in triple time being exchanged by different instrumental groupings within the orchestra. This idea of a conversation between orchestral sections is even more marked in the finale – a *tour de force* of layered sounds culminating in a grand, brass-laden peroration for the whole orchestra.

London Symphony Orchestra; Davis (LSO Live; with *Symphony No. 7*)

Colin Davis, one of the great Sibelians of the last forty years, has recorded three complete cycles: the earliest with the Boston Symphony Orchestra, the other two with the LSO. All have their supporters, but the recent live recordings from London's Barbican Hall really up the emotional temperature, with an especially compelling account of *Symphony No. 3*.

Symphony No. 4

The increasing austerity and reduction of scale is even more marked in the *Symphony No. 4* (1911), a work that has been compared to chamber music and can be seen as Sibelius's riposte to the grandiose tendencies of Bruckner and Mahler. Sibelius's fear of death (he had been seriously ill with throat cancer) seems to be another strong factor in this symphony, which is characterized by a generally grey orchestral palette and an emphasis on themes and harmonic relationships based on the tritone, a musical interval traditionally employed to represent the devilish or the sinister (as in Liszt's *Mephisto Waltzes*). A mournful cello soliloquy establishes the main theme of the slow first movement, a movement that is part funeral march, part threnody. Not all is bleakness: both the Scherzo and the finale have flashes of playfulness, though even here the music is shot through with ambivalence – especially in the unnerving epilogue of the Scherzo. The mood of the slow movement is unremittingly chilly: initially dominated by woodwind and brass, there's a Wagnerian feel to the later string writing, which suggests an emotional landscape akin to the last act of *Tristan*.

Lahti Symphony Orchestra; Vänskä
(BIS; with *Symphony No. 1*)

Osmo Vänskä's account of the fourth symphony has a truly magisterial authority; his control of the mood of the work – its gradations of bleakness – is utterly convincing, and the orchestral sound is beautifully realized by the BIS recording. An outstanding achievement.

Berlin Philharmonic Orchestra; Karajan
(Deutsche Grammophon; 2 CDs; with *Symphonies Nos. 5–7, The Swan of Tuonela & Tapiola*)

This is a classic performance from Karajan, who frequently performed the fourth and recorded the work three times. This version dates from 1966, and it has an intensity and feeling of mounting despair that has rarely been equalled on disc.

Symphony No. 5

The *Symphony No. 5* is one of Sibelius's most original reworkings of symphonic form, and he had great difficulty in getting it completed to his satisfaction. He withdrew it after the premiere in 1915 (given to celebrate his fiftieth birthday) and the final version didn't appear until 1919. Originally it was in four movements, but during the revision he merged the first and second into one, with a transition passage that miraculously glides from one into the other. The formal concision of the fifth is astonishing – a horn call at the start of each movement defines a chord that then becomes the basis for that movement's material. After the pessimism of *Symphony No. 4,* this symphony is one of his most heroic and confident statements, with a triumphant finale whose main theme was memorably described by music writer Donald Tovey as "Thor swinging his hammer". The conclusion is the composer's most radiant and dramatic: a thunderous chord seems to signify the end, but as it dies away another crashing chord is struck, and so it goes on, leaving you on tenterhooks for the final resolving cadence.

City of Birmingham Symphony Orchestra; Rattle
(EMI; with *Symphony No. 7, Nightride and Sunrise & Scene with Cranes*)

Simon Rattle has recorded the work twice, once with the Philharmonia and later with the CBSO. Both versions display a refinement and structural integrity that is enormously impressive. This CBSO version comes coupled with an equally fine performance of *Symphony No. 7*.

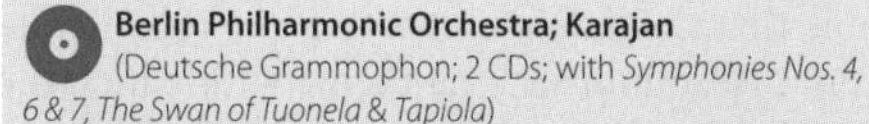

Berlin Philharmonic Orchestra; Karajan
(Deutsche Grammophon; 2 CDs; with *Symphonies Nos. 4, 6 & 7, The Swan of Tuonela & Tapiola*)

Another triumphant reading from Karajan and the Berlin Philharmonic recorded in the mid-1960s. There's a cumulative force to this performance that makes the great brass climax a thoroughly overwhelming experience.

Symphony No. 6

The *Symphony No. 6* (1923) is another restrained work, more subtle and less physical than the others, described by the composer as "very tranquil in character and outline". It seems to combine the sound-worlds of the third and fourth symphonies, though it was actually conceived alongside the fifth (Sibelius even sketched passages for one that ended up in the other). The music is based on modal rather than traditional major or minor harmonies and melodies, and the effect of this on the work's mood is well summed up in Sibelius's suggested motto:

"When shadows lengthen". That said, it contains one of the most beautiful openings of all his symphonies, with shimmering high strings suggesting a restful forest landscape. This is perhaps the most linear of all his works, not least in the finale, which can be heard as a set of variations on the movement's initial theme, all growing out of each other.

Lahti Symphony Orchestra; Vänskä
(BIS; with *Symphony No. 7* & *Tapiola*)

The fleet, linear quality of the sixth symphony demands the subtlest of treatments and gets it here from Vänskä and his team. Never one to overplay the drama of this work, he prefers to place the emphasis on textural clarity and phrasing and the result is by far the most convincing of recent accounts.

Berlin Philharmonic Orchestra; Karajan
(Deutsche Grammophon; 2 CDs; with *Symphonies Nos. 4, 5 & 7, The Swan of Tuonela* & *Tapiola*)

Karajan's recording of the sixth symphony is as insightful as the rest of this fine set – he manages to penetrate better than most the symphony's mysterious heart. It should come as no surprise to learn that the composer regarded Karajan as one of his most talented advocates.

Symphony No. 7

The *Symphony No. 7*, completed in 1924, represents the summit of Sibelius's search for symphonic fluency. The work's four movements are played as one piece: vestiges of the traditional symphonic structure – such as a Scherzo and an Adagio – are discernible, but the development of the material is so tight and its progress so inevitable that the music seems to grow organically from the ominous string theme with which the work begins. If the fifth symphony is an essentially confident and optimistic work, then the seventh is more ambivalent, with an overriding sense of restless struggle between opposing forces that is exemplified, about halfway through, by a swirling "whirlwind" motif in the strings, over which the steady presence of the brass intones. Extraordinarily fluid, expressive and even epic in character, the symphony nonetheless has a concision and brevity (it lasts just twenty minutes) that anticipates the structural rigour of Webern. For many it's the greatest of all Sibelius's works.

City of Birmingham Symphony Orchestra; Rattle
(EMI; with *Symphony No. 5, Night Ride and Sunrise* & *Scene with Cranes*)

Simon Rattle excels in this most complex of works, building it slowly but with an inexorable and steely logic. This is a performance of real integrity and the playing of the City of Birmingham Symphony Orchestra is absolutely first-rate.

Berlin Philharmonic Orchestra; Karajan
(Deutsche Grammophon; with *Symphonies Nos. 4–6, The Swan of Tuonela* & *Tapiola*; 2 CDs)

Karajan's seventh may not have the white-hot intensity of his recordings of the fourth and fifth, but it is still a highly impressive account, with a muscular energy and a probing intelligence that penetrates to the very heart of the work.

OTHER ORCHESTRAL WORKS

Though Sibelius's output is dominated by his seven symphonies, by the time he had written the first of these he had already honed his craft with a series of orchestral pieces on national themes written during the 1890s. Formally, these are just as original as the best of the symphonies, and make especially vivid use of the orchestra to conjure up the atmosphere of the northern forests and Finland's mythical tales. In addition to this, Sibelius wrote an outstanding violin concerto, a work that, despite a problematic early history, has become one of the mainstays of that instrument's repertoire. There is also a wealth of music for the theatre, and orchestral pieces composed for specific occasions – of which the best-known is *Finlandia*.

Kullervo

Kullervo, written in 1892 and scored for chorus, orchestra and two soloists, was classified by Sibelius as a choral symphony, but it could be more accurately described as a choral symphonic poem, since its form is determined by a literary source – the five movements depict the exploits of the eponymous mythological hero of the *Kalevala.* Preceding his first "abstract" symphony by some eight years, it was *Kullervo* that first brought Sibelius to prominence in Finland, and its importance to his development is crucial. Although the influence of Tchaikovsky and Bruckner can be discerned, Sibelius had also spent time with a traditional Karelian singer, noting down the rhythms and inflections of her singing. The resulting work is unmistakably his own, yet he withdrew it after the premiere, and it was not performed again until after his death.

Mattila, Hynninen; Gothenburg Symphony Orchestra; Järvi (BIS)

Neeme Järvi's recording with the Gothenburg Symphony is the most successful of the handful of versions in the CD catalogue. Both the chorus and the two exemplary soloists (Karita Mattila and Jorma Hynninen) provide a dramatic urgency, and the immediacy of the work is intensified by fine recorded sound.

En Saga & Karelia Suite

As a result of the great success of *Kullervo*, the conductor Robert Kajanus asked Sibelius for another orchestral work. This result was *En Saga* (A Saga), which was premiered by the composer in 1893 but significantly revised nine years later. The longest of his symphonic poems – at around twenty minutes – it's a brilliantly colourful and tuneful piece, rather in the manner of (though shorter than) Rimsky-Korsakov's *Scheherazade*, written four years earlier. Sibelius brilliantly establishes a "once-upon-a-time" feel with the subtlest of orchestral touches, before building up the atmosphere that climaxes in the third and boldest of its melodies.

Karelia, a region spread over eastern Finland and neighbouring Russia, is the heartland of Finnish traditional culture and the place where many stories in the *Kalevala* are set. In 1892, shortly after his marriage, Sibelius wrote music to accompany a student production of scenes based upon the area's history, and the rousing three-movement *Karelia Suite* evolved from this music as a separate concert work. The opening and closing movements are march-like in character, while the middle movement, entitled "Ballade", is more lyrical, having originally accompanied the tale of a musician entertaining his king.

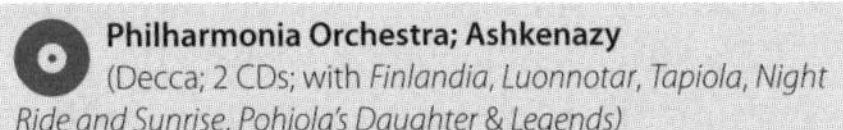

Philharmonia Orchestra; Ashkenazy (Decca; 2 CDs; with *Finlandia, Luonnotar, Tapiola, Night Ride and Sunrise, Pohjola's Daughter & Legends)*

Ashkenazy is outstanding in the *Karelia Suite,* the outer movements of which he invests with great sweep. His *En Saga* is also impressive, with the Philharmonia showing great form. All in all, this two-for-the-price-of-one set (with the lesser tone poems excellently played by the Suisse Romande orchestra under Horst Stein) makes an excellent introduction to Sibelius's non-symphonic orchestral works.

Lemminkäinen Suite & Finlandia

The *Lemminkäinen Suite* (1895), also known as *Four Legends*, is another early work based on the *Kalevala*. It's best known for its second movement, "The Swan of Tuonela", in which a cor anglais, singing mournfully over sombre string and low wind harmonies, evokes the swan gliding on a dark river. The excerpt is heard far more often on its own than in its original context, but the other three movements are equally worth getting to know for Sibelius's distinctive way of creating drama and atmosphere.

Four years later saw the creation of a rather less subtle approach to the question of national identity: *Finlandia*, a work which evolved in a similar way to the *Karelia Suite*. Originally written to accompany a series of tableaux staged in Helsinki in 1899 representing events in Finnish history, the show was put on in the guise of a charity event, but was designed to encourage anti-Russian sentiment in the wake of Tsar Nicholas II's recent repressive policies. First known under the title *Finland Awakes*, it struck an immediate chord – so much so that the authorities banned people from whistling its melodies in the streets.

Lemminkäinen Suite: Gothenburg Symphony Orchestra; Järvi (BIS)

Neeme Järvi conducts a particularly satisfying performance of the whole suite on this disc from BIS. The interpretation is aided by the warm spacious acoustic in which the Gothenburg Symphony was recorded.

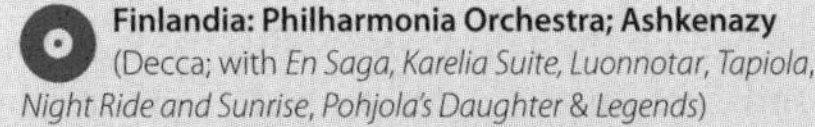

Finlandia: Philharmonia Orchestra; Ashkenazy (Decca; with *En Saga, Karelia Suite, Luonnotar, Tapiola, Night Ride and Sunrise, Pohjola's Daughter & Legends*)

Ashkenazy's performance of *Finlandia* is the most stirring available, with a ripe recording and a particularly pungent sound from the Philharmonia's tuba. It's coupled with excellent performances of *En Saga* and the *Karelia Suite* (see above).

The Tempest & Tapiola

Sibelius composed a fair amount of music for theatrical productions (in those days many theatres had orchestras), and the finest example was his last: music for a 1926 production of Shakespeare's *Tempest* in Copenhagen. Beginning with a wonderful evocation of the storm, cleverly composed almost entirely of held chords and swishing cascades of chromatic scales, it consists of over thirty separate numbers, including character studies and settings of the play's songs. Written immediately after *The Tempest*, *Tapiola* was Sibelius's very last work, and it's one of his greatest. Inspired by Tapio, the ancient Finnish god of the forest, this symphonic poem – like the early *En Saga* – is a broadly pictorial and atmospheric composition rather than a musical depiction of a specific train of dramatic events. It's as tautly conceived as any of his symphonies and as evocative in its tone-painting as anything in his entire oeuvre.

The Tempest: Tiihonen, Paasikivi, Hirvonen, Kerola, Keinonen; Lahti Opera Chorus & Symphony Orchestra; Vänskä (BIS)

There have been several recordings of the suites compiled from Sibelius's *Tempest* music, but none matches the magnificence of this version of the complete score. Vänskä has recently made a name for himself as an outstanding Sibelian and this performance is full of exquisite detail.

Tapiola: Gothenburg Symphony Orchestra; Järvi (BIS; with *Pohjola's Daughter, Rakastava & Impromptu*)

The epic northern landscape is marvellously conjured up in Järvi's Gothenburg account of *Tapiola*, which is coupled with a fine version of *Pohjola's Daughter* (1906), another *Kalevala*-inspired tone poem. Järvi's stunning performance does full justice to both pieces' wide-ranging and sumptuous orchestral colouring.

Violin Concerto

Sibelius's *Violin Concerto* got off to a terrible start, receiving such a mauling after its premiere in 1903 that the composer made extensive revisions; this second draft is the version usually played today. A boldly Romantic work, its magical opening features the soloist's drawn-out, Slavic melody emerging plaintively over tremolo strings, which then alternates with passages of rhapsodic yearning. After a mysterious introduction, the slow movement's ardent melody begins low on the instrument and rises higher and higher – always on the instrument's lower two strings – against a melancholy background of horn and bassoon. Like the first movement, however, there is an urgent, ominous undertow that emerges in its second half. Sibelius finally allows sunlight to penetrate the shadows in the work's dynamic finale. The critic Donald Tovey referred to this movement as "a polonaise for polar bears", a joke that gives an idea of the orchestral music's enjoyably lumbering gait but scarcely does justice to the soloist's scintillatingly brilliant contribution in which the very highest level of virtuosity is demanded.

Lin; Philharmonia Orchestra; Salonen (Sony; with Nielsen *Violin Concerto*)

This is an immensely subtle reading from Cho-Liang Lin and the Philharmonia. If anything the sense of teamwork is more pronounced in this performance: there's an exemplary balance between soloist and orchestra – the first movement, in particular, conveys a powerful sense of the violin as an optimistic, but still troubled, voice emerging from the dark orchestral texture.

Neveu; Philharmonia Orchestra; Susskind (EMI; with Brahms *Violin Concerto*)

Recorded four years before her death in 1949, Ginette Neveu's performance offers a compelling emotional journey. In the slow movement the sense of love and loss seems to come right from the heart of the music, while the finale provides edge-of-the-seat excitement right to the last note. Yet it's all done with such musical tact that it never feels exaggerated. Also available in a non-digital transfer from Opus Kura.

SONGS

The prominence given to Sibelius's symphonies and tone poems might suggest that he was only truly at home writing for the orchestra. But his vocal music is a rich, underexplored country – his writing for the female voice in particular can be searingly beautiful. The great themes of love and death are central but – as one would expect with this composer – nature also plays a vital recurring role. The biggest surprise for the newcomer is how this great symphonist was also able to say so much, and so exquisitely, in small forms.

Orchestral Songs

Sibelius conceived most of his nearly one hundred solo songs for voice and piano, and on the whole he preferred to keep them that way. However there were some he realized could benefit from a larger, more colourful orchestral palette: generously melodic "hits" such as "Demanten på marssnön" (The Diamond in the March Snow) or the openly romantic "Våren flyktar hastigt" (Spring Flies Fast) are fine examples. Others – like the haunting "Säv, säv susa" (Sigh, Sigh Rushes) – he entrusted to his conductor son-in-law Jussi Jalas, who generally did an excellent job at translating the piano writing into Sibelian orchestral terms. But then there are masterpieces like "Höstkväll" (Autumn Evening) – a miniature tone poem in its own right – that Sibelius felt cried out for the expressive weight of the orchestra. On the other hand the powerfully atmospheric *Luonnotar* – described as a tone poem by Sibelius – could only have been conceived in orchestral terms.

Orchestral Songs: Isokosi; Helsinki Philharmonic Orchestra; Segerstam (Ondine)

If Sibelius's vocal music is new territory, there's no better place to start. Finnish soprano Soile Isokoski has rarely sounded so beautiful and profoundly absorbed as in these songs, while conductor Leif Segerstam is just about ideal as her musical partner. *Luonnatar* is a highlight, of course, but there are so many other, smaller treasures here. A disc to go back to again and again.

Songs with Piano

Sibelius's solo piano music has come in for a lot of criticism – some of it justified. But when writing piano accompaniments for songs he seems to have lost a lot of his awkward self-consciousness and let his imagination run much freer. And while Sibelius was happy to orchestrate a select few of his songs, there were many more he felt were best left alone: "One can't express small ideas with a large orchestra." In addition many of the songs with piano have all the soaring eloquence of *Luonnatar*, but with added intimacy and subtlety. Sibelius's word setting was usually at its best when he was working with his first language, Swedish, and particularly with favourite poets such as Johan Ludwig Runeberg and Viktor Rydberg, to whom he returned again and again, as in the great collections of Opuses 13, 38 and 90. But there are also several glorious settings of Finnish and German verse.

Sibelius Songs, Opp. 13, 50 & 90: Von Otter, Forsberg (BIS)

A splendid collection. The Opus 13 and Opus 90 sets are outstanding, but as a programme the whole disc is beautifully balanced. Anne Sofie von Otter approaches every song like a new discovery, each with its own world of sound and feeling. Bengt Forsberg is her superb accompanist – discreet, but still a strong presence.

Bedřich Smetana (1824–1884)

Czech classical music did not spring into existence with the arrival of Bedřich Smetana – Prague, after all, was one of the great musical centres of the eighteenth century. However, Smetana almost single-handedly established Czech musical nationalism, being the first to integrate folk-based material into his compositions. His music may reflect a prominent Germanic influence – hardly surprising considering that he spent his formative years under Austrian rule – but his impact upon the more overtly nationalistic Dvořák, Janáček and Martinů is incalculable.

Born in Bohemia, the son of a brewer, Smetana showed incredible ability as a child: he was playing in a string quartet from the age of five and three years later produced his first symphony. He was educated at the Proksch Institute in Prague, where he wrote some Lisztian tone poems that received little recognition. Obliged to teach in order to make ends meet, he was almost penniless when Liszt prompted him to try his fortune in Sweden, away from the oppressive atmosphere of Austrian-ruled Prague. From 1856 to 1861 he lived in Gothenburg and it was there that he composed his first successful symphonic poem, *Richard III*; written as a tribute to Liszt, it was heavily Romantic and Germanic, giving no hint of a Czech national style.

In 1861, with the easing of the Austrian regime, Smetana returned home. His financial instability forced him to tour as a pianist for a while, but exciting possibilities appeared with the opening in 1862 of the Provisional Theatre, Prague's first theatre built exclusively for Czech use. Four years later Smetana's first opera, *The Brandenburgers in Bohemia*, was performed there, and its success led to Smetana's appointment as the theatre's chief conductor. Later the same year, a draft of Smetana's most remarkable opera, *The Bartered Bride*, received its premiere at the Provisional, but it was the performance of the definitive three-act version in 1870 that effectively created a Czech national opera.

It was to prove the apex of his public career. His subsequent operas were attacked for their Wagnerian tendencies, and Smetana's enemies plotted for his removal. In the event, he was forced to resign in 1874 when he went deaf as a result of syphilitic infection. He continued to compose (*Má Vlast*, his best-known work, comes from this period), and he became recognized as something of a national institution, but Smetana's life ended tragically. Suicidally depressed and ravaged by syphilis, he eventually went mad, and was committed to Prague's lunatic asylum early in 1884. He died in May, and was buried with full Czech honours.

The Bartered Bride

The Provisional Theatre was not the best-appointed opera house in Europe. Bewailing its meagre facilities, Smetana wrote: "How can we possibly play opera in a house as small as ours? In *Les Huguenots*, the armies barely number eight on each side ... and thus provoke laughter." Yet it was in this theatre, in 1866, that *The Bartered Bride* heralded the birth of Czech opera. Smetana later wrote that he had composed the opera "out of spite, because I was accused after *The Brandenburgers* of being a Wagnerian who was incapable of writing anything in a lighter vein." Even though he was working on it some time before *The Brandenburgers* was staged, there is something to Smetana's claim, for the style of this opera is indeed unlike the declamatory Wagnerian manner of *The Brandenburgers*.

Set in a Bohemian village, *The Bartered Bride* is an engagingly direct love story in which boy gets girl after just the right amount of comic misunderstanding, and the music is full of broad strokes and bold contrasts – with plenty of Czech "numbers", such as drinking-choruses and polkas, to keep things moving. An equally important aspect of the work is Smetana's vivid characterization. Each of the leads is assigned clearly recognizable musical features that are maintained throughout the opera, and Smetana brilliantly uses key signatures to reflect their changing moods.

Beňačková, Dvorský, Kopp, Novák; Czech Philharmonic Orchestra and Chorus; Košler
(Supraphon; 3 CDs)

Many recordings of *The Bartered Bride* use a translated libretto, but Smetana's operas lose much of their musical style if not performed in Czech. The earthy qualities of the original are best heard in this excellent recording from Kocler Košler. Lyrical performances from Gabriela Beňačková and Peter Dvorský, and exemplary chorus and orchestral work, make this a highly entertaining production.

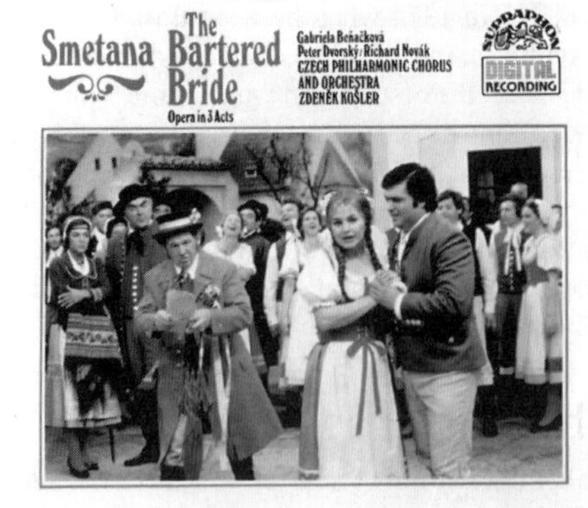

Má Vlast

The six symphonic poems of *Má Vlast* (My Homeland) were begun in 1872 and completed a full seven years later. At the end of this process, Smetana had created his fullest expression of the Czech national spirit – although, ironically, the principal theme of "Vltava", the second and most famous of the six, is a derivation of a Swedish (rather than a Czech) folk song. Characterized by expansive melodies and dramatic rhythms, *Má Vlast* presents a vision of Czech legend, history and landscape, packing an incredible array of battles, celebrations and other scenes into fifty minutes' music. Specifically, the first section is a graphic description of the river flowing through Prague; the second is a portrait of the Czech countryside; and the remaining four refer to episodes from Czech history, making repeated use of a nationalist hymn in the last two sections. It's heroic, astonishingly well-crafted music, meriting comparison with the orchestral poems of Liszt – Smetana's inspiration – and Richard Strauss.

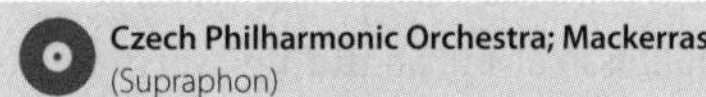

Czech Philharmonic Orchestra; Mackerras
(Supraphon)

Sir Charles Mackerras has a profound rapport with Czech music, and he brings many illuminating insights to bear on this recent recording of Smetana's masterpiece. The superior sound quality means that many details of orchestral colouring are revealed with an unusual clarity but in the end it's the sheer passion of Mackerras's direction that sweeps you along.

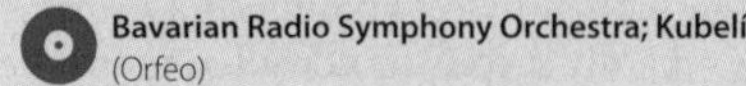

Bavarian Radio Symphony Orchestra; Kubelík
(Orfeo)

This 1984 recording is arguably the most musically satisfying of Rafael Kubelík's several accounts of this work. Both orchestra and conductor are so in control of the material that the smallest details are revealed in all their subtlety. A beautiful performance well recorded.

String Quartets

The first of Smetana's two stupendous string quartets was composed in 1876, two years after he had gone deaf from the disease which eventually was to kill him. Subtitled "From My Life", the *String Quartet No. 1* is Smetana's autobiography in music; as he put it himself, the four movements comprise a "recollection of my life and the catastrophe of total deafness". The folk rhythms and rustic harmonies are allied to a heightened comprehension of the instruments' expressive potential, a development which, as with Beethoven, was surely connected with the composer's isolation. In a moment of desperate poignancy, the end of the jaunty last movement is interrupted by a shattering, dissonant high E on the first violin. This is the note which tormented the composer in his deafness; Smetana grimly referred to it as his "little joke".

The *Quartet No. 2* is not blatantly autobiographical, but the music does relate to the suffering of his later years, and its bittersweet themes can be deeply distressing. It was composed in 1882, when Smetana's mind was in such a state that he found concentration all but impossible, and he would frequently forget a theme within seconds of writing it down. The movements are therefore episodic and brief, but they constitute an amazingly advanced essay in the form. Schoenberg judged that in its treatment of rhythm, harmonic obscurity, melodic richness and tendency to terseness, Smetana's *Quartet No. 2* was decades ahead of its time.

Lindsay Quartet
(ASV; with Dvořák *Romance* & *Waltzes Nos. 1 & 2*)

This is a typically assertive recording from the Lindsay Quartet, who are perfectly attuned to the anxiety of Smetana's music. Now that the excellent recording from the Talich Quartet has become almost impossible to find, this is a clear first choice if you want both quartets on one disc.

Ethel Smyth (1858–1944)

Ethel Smyth is finally beginning to achieve the attention she deserves, with much of her music now available on CD. The daughter of an army general, Smyth was a quite extraordinary person, determined to study music at a time when professional careers for women were frowned on, fighting with a most unladylike tenacity for recognition as a composer and for performances of her powerfully vital music. After a fierce tussle with her family, Smyth went to Leipzig to study composition. Her first works, chamber music and songs, were published and performed there, and show a decidedly Germanic flavour. On her return to England she had a few successful performances of various orchestral works and her compelling *Mass in D* (1891), but she found it difficult to interest most conductors and promoters in such large-scale music. Women were thought to be incapable of producing complex compositions, being expected to write nothing but pretty songs and delicate piano pieces. Undaunted, Smyth turned to opera, the most complex of all musical genres, even though at that time new operas had little chance of success in Britain, and her first three operas, *Fantasio* (1892–94), *Der Wald* (1899–1901) and *The Wreckers*, were first performed in Germany.

Smyth devoted two years to the militant suffragette campaign, spending a few weeks in Holloway prison for throwing a stone through the colonial secretary's window. It was Holloway where she wrote her best-known work, the rousing suffragette anthem *March of the Women*, which was sung by a choir of imprisoned suffragettes in the exercise yard, conducted by the composer from her cell window, with a toothbrush for a baton. After her release Smyth produced *The Boatswain's Mate* (1913–14), a comic opera with a decidedly feminist theme – Mrs Waters, the strong-willed heroine, constantly outwits a bumbling suitor who is determined to prove that she needs a man to protect her. Smyth also wrote two other operas, *Fête galante* (1922), a neo-classical "dance-dream" set in the eighteenth century, and another comic opera, *Entente Cordiale* (1925). Works in other forms included the lively unaccompanied chorus, *Hey Nonny No* (1911), the beautiful orchestral songs, *Three Moods of the Sea* (1913), and *The Prison* (1930), an intense work for soloists, chorus and orchestra. Smyth had realized that she was beginning to lose her hearing during the 1910s and, although she continued to compose, in later life she concentrated more on her ten volumes of memoirs and essays, in which she expressed her views on subjects ranging from women's creativity to golf and sheepdogs.

Mass in D

Now that the one recording of *The Wreckers* has dropped out of the catalogue, the only readily available large-scale work by Ethel Smyth is the *Mass in D* (1891), which was written while the composer was infatuated with the devoutly Catholic Pauline Trevelyan, and first performed in January 1893 after intense lobbying by Smyth's aristocratic friends, such as the Empress Eugénie, widow of Napoleon III. The audience and most critics were impressed: "This work definitely places the composer among the most eminent composers of her time", wrote the (male) reviewer in *The Times*, who went on to observe that its most striking feature was "the entire absence of the qualities that are usually associated with feminine productions; throughout it is virile, masterly in construction and workmanship, and particularly remarkable for the excellence and rich colour of the orchestration." Yet it was not until 1924 that the work received a second performance, which is no reflection of the quality of the *Mass*, for it's a compelling piece, from its sombre opening to the expansive exultation of the final Gloria.

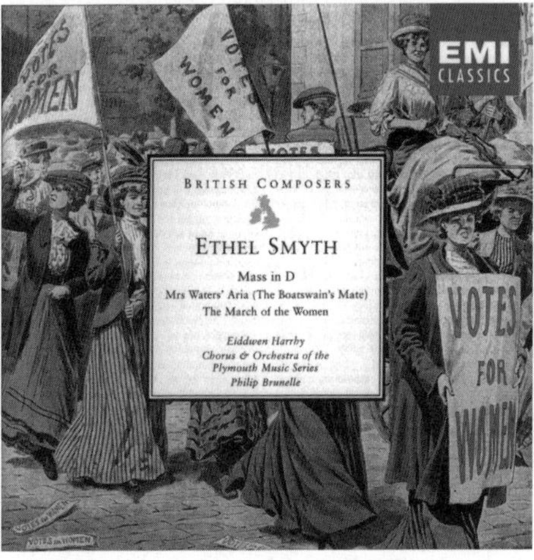

Harrhy; Plymouth Festival Chorus & Orchestra; Brunelle (EMI; with *The March of the Women & What if I Were Young Again*)

Philip Brunelle conducts a powerful performance of the *Mass* on a CD that offers the bonuses of *The March of the Women* and Mrs Waters' beautiful aria, "What if I Were Young Again" from The Boatswain's Mate. The latter uses the tune of the Scottish traditional folk song, "Lord Randal", which Smyth orchestrates with subtle delicacy.

Orchestral Works

When Smyth's orchestral works, the *Serenade in D* and *Overture to Anthony and Cleopatra* (both written in 1889), were first performed in London, several critics expressed surprise that a woman had written such powerful and dramatic music. The *Serenade* is a large, four-movement work which is symphonic in scope and remarkably assured for a first orchestral work. Smyth did not write another purely orchestral work until the *Concerto for Violin, Horn and Orchestra* of 1927, although several interludes from her operas (such as *On the Cliffs of Cornwall* from *The Wreckers*) achieved widespread popularity in the concert hall. Skilfully orchestrated, the *Concerto* is a delightful work with another of Smyth's deeply felt slow movements but also a sense of fun as the unusual solo pairing of violin and horn weave with the orchestra an intricate and often joyful pattern of diverse themes.

Serenade in D; Concerto for Violin, Horn and Orchestra: Langdon, Watkins; BBC Philharmonic; de la Martinez (Chandos)

A recording that provides two very different examples of Smyth's writing, separated by nearly forty years. Odaline de la Martinez has long been a champion of Smyth's music and brings energy and passion to these gripping performances, which clearly demonstrate the composer's importance.

Chamber Music

Most of Smyth's chamber music was written while she was at Leipzig in the 1880s, and the best of her work from this period is represented by the Brahmsian *String Quintet* (1883), an eloquent, large-scale composition with a beautifully poignant slow movement, and the impressive four-movement *Violin Sonata* (1887), which a contemporary reviewer found "deficient in the feminine charm that might have been expected of a woman composer". The dramatic and more strikingly individual *String Quartet* is one of her few post-Leipzig chamber works: the first two movements were written in 1902 but not performed until 1912, when they were heard at the first public concert of the Society of Women Musicians. On hearing them, Smyth decided to complete the work by adding two more movements, an expressive Andante and the exuberantly contrapuntal finale.

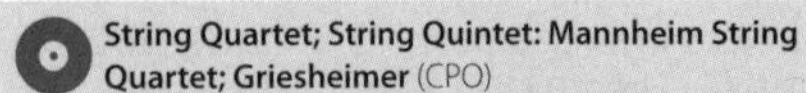

String Quartet; String Quintet: Mannheim String Quartet; Griesheimer (CPO)

These two works clearly show the development of Smyth's musical language. They are given thoughtful and fluent performances by the Mannheim Quartet, who are more convincing in the slower movements than the faster ones, where they lack the sparkling vitality that is so much part of Smyth's music.

Karlheinz Stockhausen (1928–2007)

Karlheinz Stockhausen was one of the most seminal figures of twentieth-century music and its most controversial. His audacious output includes a 29-hour opera complete with a quartet featuring four flying helicopters. Yet this high priest of post-war modernity has nonetheless influenced musicians ranging from Frank Zappa to The Beatles (the debt is most glaringly obvious on the *White Album*'s "Revolution No. 9"). And his pioneering work in the field of electronic music set the stage not just for computerized art music but also for the sampling techniques central to much of today's pop, rock, hip-hop and electronica.

Brought up near Cologne, Stockhausen absorbed music from his mother (who played piano and sang) and from the radio and gramophone. The war shattered his childhood: his mother, who had been recuperating in a mental home, fell victim to the Nazi's inhuman euthanasia programme; his father, a schoolteacher, was reported missing and never seen again. Conscripted as a stretcher-bearer, the orphaned Stockhausen witnessed brutal carnage and many times came within an inch of losing his life. By the war's end he had become a devout Christian, and was playing jazz piano for American GIs to finance his courses at Cologne's music school and university, where he studied German literature, philosophy, piano and musicology.

Under the influence of Arnold Schoenberg and Anton Webern, Stockhausen composed some brilliant serial pieces, including *Choral* (1950), a haunting evocation of the bleak North Rhine landscape. By the following year he was attending new-music courses in Darmstadt (see p.384), where he became entranced by the work of Olivier Messiaen. He soon moved to Paris to study with Messiaen, who promptly proclaimed him a genius and took him (along with fellow-student Pierre Boulez) to meet Pierre Schaeffer, the *musique concrète* pioneer working on innovative forms of tape composition at the ORTF radio studio.

Still fascinated by Messiaen and Webern, Stockhausen – like Boulez – went on to advocate "total serialism", music in which every element is determined by impersonal parameters, though he did not long adhere to this strict doctrine. Performances of his work at Darmstadt were greeted mostly with shock and dismay, as audiences struggled with music that lacked any discernible melodic or rhythmic sense. Nonetheless, Stockhausen's early pieces, born in a climate which regarded recent history as so tainted that even its art had to be rejected, were significant steps in the development of post-war music.

Stockhausen in the studio.

At the age of 24, Stockhausen landed a job at the WDR radio station in Cologne to continue his search for a "pure electronic music", and in 1953 created *Studie I*, the first piece of music constructed entirely of sine waves. During the next few years he studied phonetics, acoustics and communications science at Bonn University, while also tirelessly experimenting with white noise, feedback and chance operations. From this period came the mighty *Gruppen* for three orchestras – a piece that moved music through space as well as time – and the thirteen-minute *Gesang der Jünglinge* (Song of the Youths), a *tour de force* for boy soprano and electronic sound. The debut of the latter work – at which the audience were made to sit down and experience this "electronic space music" through loudspeakers alone – caused as much uproar as Stravinsky's *Rite of Spring* nearly half a century before, and Stockhausen's fame quickly spread. Musicians such as Ligeti (see p.300) made pilgrimages to Cologne to see the inspirational German innovator, and in 1957 he was invited back to Darmstadt, where he gave a series of provocative lectures.

The 1960s were a stage of consolidations and expansion. *Kontakte* (1960) pushed the tape machine to its limits, and *Momente* (1962) applied to acoustic instruments his electronic discoveries about the importance of sound-colour and silence-duration. In 1966, after a visit to Japan, he wrote *Telemusik*, a meta-collage of ethnic musics; after a visit to America in 1967 he completed the epic *Hymnen*, based on the world's national anthems; and his openness to non-European music was further explored in *Stimmung*, a vocal work inspired by Aztec and Maya mythology.

In May 1968 the disintegration of his relationship with Mary Bauermeister precipitated a personal crisis from which Stockhausen extracted himself through the writing of *Aus den sieben Tagen* (Out of the Seven Days), a sequence of fifteen works that he commenced during a seven-day fast. Termed "Intuitive Music" by the composer, *Aus den sieben Tagen* in its written form consisted of prose texts to be interpreted by its performers, who were required to bring the music into being through the filter of their own beliefs, moods and experiences. In its loosely structured procedures and its incorporation of raw material from its creator's life, this cathartic sequence foreshadowed much of Stockhausen's future work. From this point on, everything he saw, heard or in any way experienced was now assimilated into a continuous production system – meticulously annotated, logged and transcribed into music. The thousand hours of "musical space travel" presented at the Osaka Expo of 1970 was a typically audacious project.

The apotheosis of Stockhausen's inexhaustible ambition came in 1977, when he announced the genesis of the twentieth century's closest equivalent to the gigantic musical projects of Wagner. He had set himself the task of creating *Licht* (Light), a seven-part opera (one for each day of the week) for solo voices and instruments, dancers, choirs, orchestras, mimes and electronics. The first part – *Donnerstag* (Thursday) – was completed in 1980, with the final touches added to the final day more than twenty years later, on the last day of 2002.

In 1991 Stockhausen returned to WDR to remaster his entire oeuvre on CD. The dazzling results are now available through Stockhausen-Verlag, a company based at the composer's self-designed house in Kürten. Together with Stockhausen's own insights into his music and life, detailed in his six-volume *Texte zur Musik*, the Stockhausen-Verlag series is the composer's definitive career statement. For a catalogue and order form, visit *www.stockhausen.org*.

Gruppen

The gestation of *Gruppen* (Groups) began before the creation of *Gesang der Jünglinge*, and at the outset it was conceived as a work for tape and orchestra. Yet when Stockhausen recommenced work on *Gruppen* in 1957, it transmuted into a piece for three orchestras, each comprising six woodwind instruments, seven or eight brass, six percussion (including keyboards and electric guitar) and sixteen or eighteen strings. As with *Kontakte*, the music is underpinned by the perception of rhythm, tempo and pitch as aspects of the same phenomenon (slow any note far enough, for example, and you start to hear it as a beat). *Gruppen* is innovatory in the way it treats tempo to the sort of serial techniques that composers had been applying to tones since the breakthrough compositions of Schoenberg (i.e. subjecting tempo to systematic organization); but in performance, however, it's the spatial dimension of this piece that makes the immediate impact. Arrayed on three sides of the audience, and each with its own conductor (at the premiere the roles were taken by the formidable trio of Stockhausen, Boulez and Bruno Maderna), the three orchestras merge in accelerations and crescendos, then separate into a tripartite dialogue in which independent tempi are combined or fragments of sound fly between the groups – as in the work's climax, when a great brass chord swirls around the hall.

Berlin Philharmonic Orchestra; Abbado (Deutsche Grammophon; with Kurtág *Grabstein für Stephan* & *Stele*)

Claudio Abbado, one of the few top-flight conductors to consistently champion the music of the post-war avant-garde, gives a thrilling reading of *Gruppen*. No CD could adequately convey the experience of being hemmed in by Stockhausen's triple orchestras, but the DG engineers have achieved a superb illusion of space on this live recording.

Stimmung

Written in Madison, Connecticut, during the early months of 1968, *Stimmung* (Tuning) is a hypnotically static work for six unaccompanied voices, in 51 brief sections. Using only a series of

Electronic Music – The First Seventy Years

The roots of electronic music go all the way back to 1897, when Thaddeus Cahill patented the Telharmonium, a kind of gargantuan proto-synthesizer – early models were 60 feet long, weighed 200 tons and interfered with local telephone networks. Not surprisingly, this musical behemoth was a roaring failure, despite being championed by Busoni in his famous *Sketch of a New Aesthetic of Music* (1907). During the 1920s and 1930s a steady stream of electronic instruments were produced, such as the Ondes Martenot (1928; see p.348), Trautonium (1930) and Hammond Organ (1935), though these proved more successful in film music than concert performance, despite capturing the attention of composers as diverse as Messiaen and Hindemith (who in 1931 penned a now sadly forgotten *Concerto for Trautonium and Orchestra*).

The real history of electronic music began in the years immediately after World War II, and was initially dominated by two studios. The RTF studio in Paris, under the guidance of Pierre Schaeffer and Pierre Henry, was the centre for *musique concrète*, a style of composition using electronically manipulated recordings of real sounds – anything from pianos to railway engines. By contrast, the WDR studio in Cologne, established by composer Herbert Eimert and scientist Werner Meyer-Eppler, focused on building a new musical language from scratch out of purely electronic sounds: so-called *elektronische Musik*. Despite their considerable artistic differences, at both studios composers focused initially on creating pieces entirely on tape, completely eradicating live musicians in performance and (usually) in the preparation of the taped sounds themselves.

Artistically, the Cologne studio was the more successful of the two, thanks to the young Karlheinz Stockhausen, who produced seminal works there such as *Gesang der Jünglinge* (1956) and *Kontakte* (1960) – the first significant works to use electronics in combination with live performers. RTF and WDR were soon joined by the RAI studio in Milan, where young Italian composers Luciano Berio and Luigi Nono pursued a path midway between those of Paris and Cologne, and produced music that was perhaps more interesting than either. During the 1950s, virtually every significant young European composer worked in some capacity at one of these studios, including those, such as Xenakis and Boulez, who would later play key roles in the development of electronic and computer music, and others, such as Ligeti and Dutilleux, whose interest in the medium lasted only briefly.

During the 1960s and 1970s, further studios were established on both sides of the Atlantic, including an important one at Princeton in the USA, which served as a focus for North American research and attracted composers as varied as Milton Babbitt and John Cage. The latter had for many years been following a characteristically eccentric investigation of electronics – concentrating on their use in performance rather than in producing tape pieces – beginning in 1939 with *Imaginary Landscape No. 1*, employing variable speed turntables playing recordings of RCA Victor test frequencies, and continuing with oddities such as *Music for Amplified Toy Pianos*.

These studios remained primarily concerned with the production of tape works, but commercial developments were rapidly changing the technological landscape in which composers operated. The massive popularity of the electric guitar had already brought electronic sound production (albeit of a very simple kind) firmly into the popular music mainstream; and the Moog Synthesizer, launched in 1966, combined many of the functions of the traditional studio into a single instrument at a fraction of the size and cost, spawning classics such as Walter Carlos's massively popular *Switched on Bach* (1968) and *The Well Tempered Synthesizer* (1969).

Back in the studio these developments led to a growing interest in live electronics: transforming and manipulating sounds during performance rather than using an inflexible pre-recorded tape. Again Stockhausen was in the vanguard with works such as *Mikrophonie I* (1964) and *Mixtur* (1964), while later in the decade he produced, in *Telemusik* (1966) and *Hymnen* (1967), two classics of electronic music that summed up developments thus far. These were to be two of the last such works, however, and with the emergence of digital sound-processing and so-called "computer music" in the early 1970s, the old analogue studio techniques rapidly became obsolete.

In reality, the two post-war decades of studio research produced little of lasting musical value – even the finest works of the period now sound dated and clumsy. But in ushering music into the technological age they opened up a momentous new phase in its history, one whose effects are now with us everywhere – from pop music and film scores to computer games and mobile ringtones.

harmonics of a low B flat, the six singers recite and transform speech sounds based on various "magic names" (mostly gods and goddesses) and erotic texts written for Stockhausen's partner, Mary Bauermeister. The lyrics, when audible, are often pretty gauche, but the music is mesmerizing. The notes are sung softly, without vibrato, beginning with overtone singing that produces sounds like a kind of delicate, higher-pitched didgeridoo, and the bewitching journey continues with swirls of vowels, phonemes and chords, the luminous clouds of abstract syllables shot through with startling, clearly enunciated words.

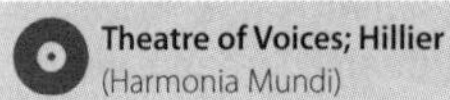
Theatre of Voices; Hillier
(Harmonia Mundi)

Paul Hillier has been involved with *Stimmung* performances since the early 1980s, allowing him to penetrate this riddle-filled score at a deeper level than most. His Theatre of Voices operate at such a refined level of technique – overtones impeccably articulated – that radically fresh expressive territory is plucked from the ether.

Electronic Music

Stockhausen is a crucial figure in the history of electronic music (see p.533), and was one of its most accomplished exponents. He first began his explorations in 1952 with *Etude*, a brief piece constructed from processed recordings of piano strings struck with an iron beater, and continued in 1953–54 with two electronic "studies" based on entirely synthesized material and exploring the application of serial principles to timbre and frequency. However, the work that brought electronic music to maturity, and set the agenda for future developments, was *Gesang der Jünglinge* (1955–56). Conceived as part of a projected mass, the work interweaves synthesized elements with a boy's voice half-singing and half-reciting syllables and words from the third Book of Daniel. Though condemned as blasphemous after its performance at Cologne Cathedral, it's a devout, exultant and at times quite magical piece, with the voice moving in and out of the mix of strange, unidentifiable electronic sounds.

Some 35 minutes long, *Kontakte* (1960) is the lengthiest of Stockhausen's seminal electronic pieces. Its fundamental concern is one that he explored in several works of the period: the way that frequencies are perceived differently – as pulsation, rhythm, focused note, etc – depending on their speed. Replete with previously unheard sonorities, *Kontakte* embodies the aesthetic of "Moment Form", in which each sound event is intended to be viable in itself, rather than deriving validity from its place in the overall process or structure.

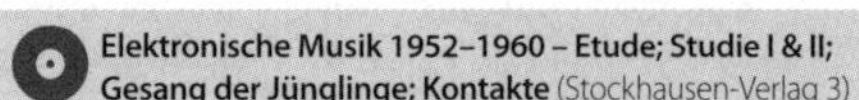
Elektronische Musik 1952–1960 – Etude; Studie I & II; Gesang der Jünglinge; Kontakte (Stockhausen-Verlag 3)

This disc collects Stockhausen's crucial early contributions to the genre, and comes with exhaustive notes by the composer. *Gesang der Jünglinge* was conceived for five channels with the boy's voice assigned to its own overhead speaker, but it nonetheless sounds amazing on CD. The version of *Kontakte* here is purely electronic (a version with piano and percussion soloists is available on Stockhausen-Verlag 6).

Hymnen

Whereas pieces such as *Gesang der Jünglinge* and the later *Telemusik* were compacted into a dense agglomerate, *Hymnen* lays out its processes for inspection. Begun in 1965 and informed by trips to Japan and America, *Hymnen* is an ambitious two-hour work divided into four regions or movements. Stockhausen builds the work by juxtaposing forty songs and national anthems, upending them and turning out their jingoistic baggage. He mixes them with natural sounds, electronic interventions and the reactions of live performers. Listeners have to be content with meditating on the journey rather than fretting about the destination, as *Hymnen* unfolds slowly through the extended transformations (Stockhausen often puns with sound, as when crowd noises mutate into the calls of swamp-ducks) and passages of near-silence. Using short-wave radios, he literally plucks sounds from the air, drawing on every culture to produce a genuine "music of the world".

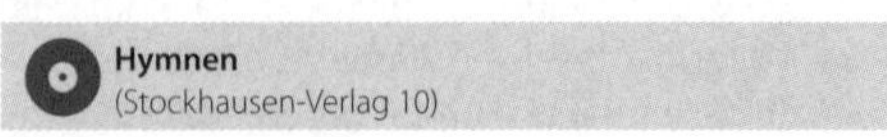
Hymnen
(Stockhausen-Verlag 10)

Like a number of Stockhausen's other works, including *Kontakte*, *Hymnen* exists in more than one version. It can be "performed" purely on tape, or with soloists who are encouraged to introduce improvisatory elements. Both of these versions are included here.

Alessandro Stradella (1644–1682)

Alessandro Stradella was a notorious womanizer whose sexual adventures led to his murder in Genoa at the age of 37. This has tended to obscure the fact that he was also a notable composer of opera and oratorios – one of the latter, *San Giovanni Battista*, being among the most dramatically compelling works of the seventeenth century. In both his oratorios and his purely instrumental works Stradella was one of the first composers to employ the concerto grosso form, in which the music was divided between the full ensemble and a smaller group within it, for the purpose of dramatic contrast.

Stradella was born in Rome into the minor nobility, a distinction that allowed him entry into exalted aristocratic circles. His patrons included the powerful Colonna and Pamphili families as well as Queen Christina of Sweden, who was living in Rome in voluntary exile and in whose household Stradella served from the age of fourteen. In 1669 the discovery of his involvement in a plot to embezzle money from the Church forced him to leave the city, though he returned in time for the opening of a new theatre, the Teatro Tordinona, which was to perform several of his works.

In 1673 in Florence he attempted to abduct a young nun, Lisabetta Marmonari, who had been the object of his attentions for several years. Four years later in Venice, having been hired by Alvise Contarini to give music lessons to his young mistress, Stradella instead eloped with her to Turin. An incensed Contarini pursued the couple and eventually two of his hired thugs left Stradella seriously wounded after a murder attempt. He fled to Genoa early in 1678, but four years later yet another amorous involvement with a high-ranking lady led to his assassination at the hands of a hired killer in the city's main square.

San Giovanni Battista

San Giovanni Battista was written for the Confraternity of Florentines in Rome, who in 1675 (declared a Holy Year by the Pope) commissioned fourteen oratorios on the subject of their patron saint, St John the Baptist. Stradella's effort is a masterpiece of dramatic sophistication, with fully rounded characters, a huge range of emotions and a remarkable immediacy that's heightened by the fact that the text is in Italian rather than Latin. Though San Giovanni is the protagonist, it is the corrupt and incestuous court of Erode (Herod) that generates the piece's psychological complexity. The libretto maintains the tension by dispensing with a narrator, but it is the music that builds up the atmosphere of degeneration and moral panic. In several arias Stradella seems to anticipate Handel's florid lines, but he doesn't have Handel's tendency to spin out the luxuriant moments at the expense of dramatic momentum – here, the mood often changes within the space of a single aria. Thus when Erodiade (Salome) requests the death of San Giovanni, she begins her exchanges with Erode nervously, becoming insinuating then petulant, and finally pleads with him in a stunningly beautiful aria, "Queste lagrime". Only Monteverdi's *L'incoronazione di Poppea* (see p.353) creates such a splendid frisson from the apparent triumph of evil.

Bott, Lesne, Huttenlocher, Batty, Edgar-Wilson; Les Musiciens du Louvre; Minkowski (Erato)

Minkowski's performance is exceptionally well cast, with an emphasis on characterful rather than merely beautiful singing. Phillippe Huttenlocher (though a little woolly sounding) perfectly projects the tyrant's bluster and fearfulness; Gerard Lesne is equally strong; and Catherine Bott's rendition of the demented aria "Su coronatemi" (Come Now Crown Me) is a fantastic moment.

Cantatas

Scarcely less impressive than *San Giovanni Battista* are the many cantatas which Stradella wrote. These short dramatic works, usually written for a single voice, exist as discrete units, as if an aria had been plucked from within an opera. They were highly popular in seventeenth-century Italy, but it demanded great skill to make such a compressed form seem musically and dramatically coherent. Stradella's best cantatas are particularly brilliant, rivalling those of his Venetian contemporary Barbara Strozzi (see p.552) in their emotional intensity. *Fuor della Stigia sponda* tells the story of Orpheus returning from the Underworld having lost Eurydice for ever: it starts with a scene-setting introduction in recitative before Orpheus begins his restrained but impassioned lament. *Ferma il corso*, another lament, sung by Arianna (Ariadne) as she bewails her abandonment by her lover Theseus, is even more highly charged with abrupt changes of mood conveyed through a range of frequently extreme effects, including rich chromaticism and some demandingly virtuosic passages.

Brandes, O'Dette, Springfels, Matthews, Weiss (Harmonia Mundi; with *Sinfonias Nos. 12 & 22*)

Soprano Christine Brandes seems slightly less at ease with her material than Catherine Bott in *San Giovanni Battista*, but she acquits herself well in the sombre *Fuor della Stigia*. In the other, more technically demanding, cantatas, she's a little shrill in the higher passages, but two utterly beguiling Stradella instrumental works more than compensate.

The Strauss Family

When Johann Strauss died in 1849 at the age of 45, a Viennese obituarist suggested that the city should mourn not just because a great man had gone but because once again Vienna's resident genius had been struck down prematurely. Fifty years later the same writer made the same claim for Johann Strauss the Younger (1825–99), and again courted controversy by suggesting that waltz-manufacturers should command as much respect as Schubert, or indeed any composer of symphonies and sonatas. Admirers of the Strauss family still face an uphill struggle to convince people that their music is anything more than the froth of Viennese high society, but it's a mistake to patronize the talent required to write hundreds of memorable pieces within the extreme technical limitations of the waltz. Strauss senior's compositions may often have been convention-bound and short-winded, yet in his flamboyant *Radetzky March* he produced a work that became the very symbol of Habsburg military might, just as his son's *Blue Danube* was to epitomize the glittering hedonism of imperial Vienna.

In addition to the two Johanns there was also a Josef (1827–1920) – Johann the Younger's brother – who composed some 280 pieces, but couldn't match the fertility of his sibling, the so-called "Waltz King". Johann Strauss the Younger set the standards for every writer of "light" music in the next half-century, not just by enriching the Viennese waltz and other dance forms, but also through the creation of *Die Fledermaus* (The Bat), a magnificent operetta that has a claim to be his finest composition. Nobody would make out that there is any great depth here, but Johann the Younger has few rivals as uncomplicated melodist and orchestrator, and his music has retained the nostalgic attraction to which the obituary referred when it called him "the last symbol of cheerful, pleasant times".

Die Fledermaus

Premiered in 1874, *Die Fledermaus* is a brilliantly clever commentary on Viennese moral laxity cloaked in sparklingly tuneful music. The management of the Theater an der Wien found it too close to the knuckle and, even after editing, it caused something of a scandal. Within two years, however, it was playing in some 170 theatres. On paper the plot is complicated to the point of unintelligibility, but on stage this tale of infidelity, mistaken identity and excessive champagne consumption works as well as any piece of music-theatre. Offenbach's witty, hedonistic operettas obviously influenced the musical style of *Die Fledermaus*, but Strauss's quintessentially Viennese decorum softens the edge of the satire.

The most important stage work of its sort ever written, *Die Fledermaus* established a tradition that saw its apogee in the works of Lehár, and Richard Strauss paid homage to its waltz rhythms in *Der Rosenkavalier*.

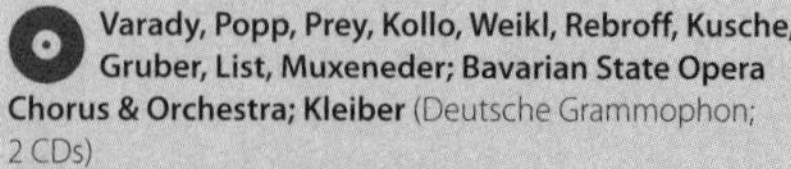

Varady, Popp, Prey, Kollo, Weikl, Rebroff, Kusche, Gruber, List, Muxeneder; Bavarian State Opera Chorus & Orchestra; Kleiber (Deutsche Grammophon; 2 CDs)

For its flair and wit, Carlos Kleiber's superbly conducted recording is the obvious choice. Few other conductors have been able to get such downright erotic sounds out of an orchestra. His cast isn't ideal, but Hermann Prey gives one of the best performances of his career, and Julia Varady and

Lucia Popp are very good indeed – their singing of Act 1's "So muss allein ich bleiben" is truly wonderful.

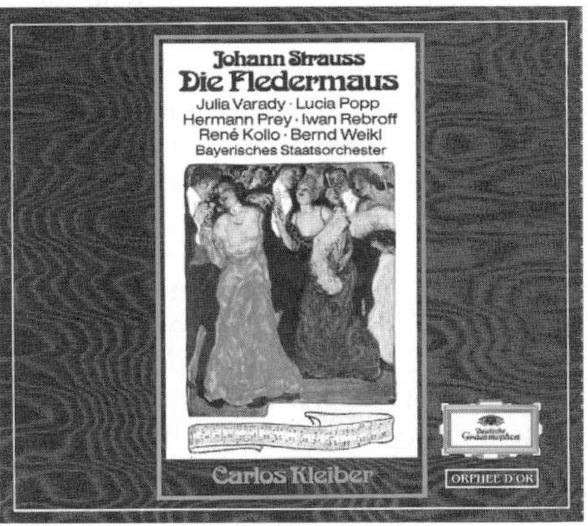

Dance Music

Johann I's *Radetzky March* is played every year at the New Year's Day Concert at the Vienna Musikverein, an outbreak of white-tie jollity to celebrate the city's kings of dance music. That piece aside, however, it's Johann II's waltzes that dominate the dynasty's output, and pieces such as *Thunder and Lightning*, *Vienna Blood*, *Acceleration*, *Tales from the Vienna Woods* and *The Blue Danube* are among the best-known tunes of the nineteenth century. (*The Blue Danube* has been recorded more than seventy times, putting it in the same league as many of Beethoven's symphonies.)

Johann II once claimed that he merely took over the waltz form from his father, and indeed the structure of his waltzes is similar to the later works of his elders: slow introduction, five repetitions of the waltz and a quick coda. However, Johann II greatly increased the length of the central sections, introduced a greater sense of homogeneity to the whole piece, and enhanced the textural complexities, which makes his waltzes much more satisfying as concert music. But ultimately, of course, this is music to move to. If you don't have a ballroom at your disposal, sample the following CDs sparingly, because you can only listen to so many waltzes before going berserk. Taken in measured doses, however, they'll cheer you up in almost any circumstances. Schoenberg was so fond of them that he made transcriptions of two of them and set others as transcription exercises for his pupils Berg and Webern.

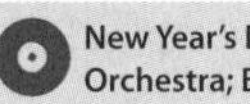

New Year's Day Concert 1979: Vienna Philharmonic Orchestra; Boskovsky
(Decca)

It has long been a Viennese tradition to have a New Year's Day Concert in the Musikvereinsaal. Many fine conductors have done the honours with the Vienna Phil over the years, but the orchestra's concertmaster, Wili Boskovsky, has this music in his blood. 1979 was his farewell year and the concert has a tremendous sense of occasion.

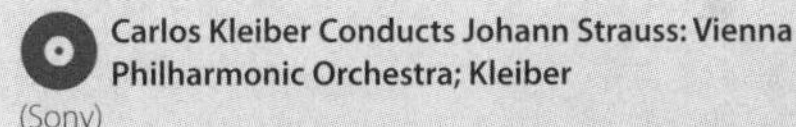

Carlos Kleiber Conducts Johann Strauss: Vienna Philharmonic Orchestra; Kleiber
(Sony)

Carlos Kleiber is most commonly associated with heavyweight repertoire such as Beethoven and Brahms, but this disc shows that he can let his hair down with the best of them. Including famous pieces by Josef, as well as Johann II, it features great performances in which the Vienna Phil respond to Kleiber with obvious enjoyment.

Richard Strauss (1864–1949)

Richard Strauss was the last great German Romantic, but the trajectory of his career was more convoluted than such a definition suggests. Having burst onto the scene as the composer of feverishly ardent orchestral pieces, he went on to produce operas as progressive and discomforting as any of their time, before switching to decorous, slightly decadent and often ironic conservatism. However, through each phase of Strauss's long life – from the electrifying brilliance of *Don Juan* to the ersatz eighteenth-century charm of the late opera *Capriccio*, there runs a fundamentally consistent harmonic and melodic style, marked above all by a Mozartian tunefulness. Like Mozart, Strauss possessed an amazing technical facility, and if his abilities did sometimes lead to passages of superficial note-spinning, he was constitutionally incapable of writing anything slipshod. Often depicted as the traditionalist opponent of modernism, even the

The elderly Richard Strauss.

epitome of bourgeois complacency (few composers ever enjoyed Strauss's financial success), he has now come to seem like a prophet of the postmodern age, in which irony and pastiche are perceived as radical procedures. His work is dismissed as shallow kitsch in some quarters, but such critical disapproval has not affected his standing as one of the two most popular opera composers of the twentieth century (Puccini being the other).

Born in Munich, Strauss was the only son of Franz Strauss, the brilliant principal horn player in the Bavarian Court Opera, who instructed him in music's fundamentals. Strauss senior was an arch-conservative who hated Wagner and brought up his son with a profound reverence for Bach, Mozart and Beethoven. Strauss junior took piano lessons from the age of four, began composing two years later and, requiring no formal musical tuition, received a traditional, rounded education. After the composition of his Brahmsian *Symphony No. 1* in 1880, he scored something of a success with his *Serenade* for wind instruments, which in turn induced the conductor Hans von Bülow to commission a suite from him in 1882. By 1885 he had succeeded von Bülow as principal conductor at Meiningen, a post he left the following year to journey to Italy, where he composed his first symphonic poem, *Aus Italien*. Upon his return, he was appointed conductor at the Munich Opera.

Having achieved provincial success as a conductor, Strauss struck international success as a composer in 1888 with *Don Juan*, a flamboyant tone poem that established him as the most exciting composer in Germany, a position secured by a string of virtuosic orchestral pieces written between 1895 and 1899. During the next six years he concentrated chiefly on conducting, though in 1901 he produced his first successful opera, *Feuersnot*. In 1905 he shocked audiences with his interpretation of Oscar Wilde's *Salome*, then four years later repeated the outrage with *Elektra*: both works were decried for their moral corruption, while the music was deemed dissonant and unintelligible. After *Elektra* it seemed inevitable that Strauss would cross over into outright atonality, but *Der Rosenkavalier*, composed only two years later, turned out to be a sumptuously tonal and charmingly elegant comedy. The volte-face caused much consternation, but *Der Rosenkavalier* established itself immediately as his operatic masterpiece, and its reputation has remained intact ever since.

In 1915 Strauss completed *Ein Alpensinfonie*, which, with the exception of *Metamorphosen* and the *Four Last Songs*, turned out to be his last large-scale non-operatic work. From then on, having completely mastered his craft, Strauss settled into the composition of opera, never looking back to the extremes of *Elektra*, and never tempted by the formal innovations of Schoenberg and the Second Viennese School. Living in a plush villa in Garmisch, not far from Munich, Strauss wrote prolifically and was amply rewarded for his work, but a problematic chapter in his life began in 1933, when the Nazis appointed him president of the Reichsmusikkammer, a job that effectively made him the national representative of German music. For two years he seems to have been content to fulfil the function required of him, disingenuously maintaining the belief that he

Music in the Third Reich

Although Plato warned against music's latent capacity to influence mass feeling and opinion, the first systematic abuse of music as an instrument of political propaganda was during the Third Reich, when Adolf Hitler directed Joseph Goebbels to reinvent the course of German music history, and plot its future, to accommodate his broader restructuring of the country. The inter-war years of the Weimar Republic had, it was claimed, allowed for the rise in modernism and internationalism (bywords for Jewishness) which had set in motion a corresponding decline in supposedly German music and musicians. It is true that the country's cultural landscape in January 1933 was characterized strongly by Jewish talent, but the vast majority of these Jews thought of themselves, first and foremost, as Germans. They were, regardless, targeted as the cause and effect of the alleged German musical decline, and during the first eighteen months of National Socialist rule a panoply of laws and regulations – known as *Entjudung* ("Jewish purges") – were introduced which led to the exile, banishment, imprisonment and, in many cases, murder of Jewish musicians while, at the same time, restoring to influence a host of pure-blood Germans who had, so it was claimed, been squeezed from power during the Weimar years.

This process was overseen by the *Reichsmusikkammer* (RMK), the Nazi music council whose president and vice-president were Richard Strauss and Wilhelm Furtwängler. Neither man considered himself a political animal, but as Goebbels announced in April 1934, everything in Nazi Germany was unavoidably politicized, since even the most begrudging collaboration served an inevitably approbatory means to what was an unavoidably political end. While Furtwängler struggled against the system, striving for the rights of Jews across Austro-Germany, Strauss devoted himself to the feathering of his own nest – oblivious to, or in denial of, the moral and ethical issues raised by his collaboration.

Strauss's response to events was no more nor less than typical of the newly Aryanized world of German music. A host of second- and third-rate composers found themselves in a position of relative authority on account of nothing more than their race and political disposition. Talent – once the only measure of success in Germany – was now a secondary consideration when it came to writing music that served the wider interests of New Germany. Alongside such major figures as Werner Egk, Carl Orff and Hans Pfitzner – each of whom was involved in making music for the Nazis – were a stable of inferior, albeit highly regarded Nazi stooges, including Max von Schillings, Hermann Reuter, Paul Höffer, Kurt Thomas, Paul Graener, Max Trapp and Edmund Nick, who at the behest of the RMK provided an "Aryanized" replacement for Mendelssohn's incidental music to *A Midsummer Night's Dream* in 1934.

Performers were no less important to the Nazis, and a depressing number of the century's greatest talents – including the pianist Walter Gieseking and the conductor Karl Böhm – handed their influence to the Nazi political machine. And for an emerging artist, membership of the Party could be an extremely useful short cut to success. Both conductor Herbert von Karajan and soprano Elisabeth Schwarzkopf were Nazi Party members, in Karajan's case joining extremely early, on 8 April, 1933, only two months and eight days after Hitler came to power. Schwarzkopf became a student member after joining the Berlin Hochschule für Musik in 1934, later holding the office of "Führerin", one of whose responsibilities was to watch over other students and to make sure that they said nothing disparaging about the Führer or the Party. Any performer actively resisting the Nazis was dealt with in no uncertain terms. In 1943 the exceptionally gifted young pianist Karlrobert Kreiten was overheard criticizing Hitler. This was reported to the local Gauleiter, who oversaw Kreiten's execution on 7 September, 1943. Ultimately, music may well have been the most potent medium for propaganda employed by the Nazi machine, but had it not been for the weakness, vanity and fear of its servants a great deal less might have been accomplished.

could serve German music in the Reich without serving the Reich itself. However, two years later he had to choose between loyalty to the abstraction of German culture and loyalty to a Jewish individual, the writer Stefan Zweig, with whom he was working. He refused to condemn Zweig, was removed from his post, and from that point on was merely tolerated by the Nazis. He remained in Germany until the war's end, when he was investigated as a Nazi collaborator, and acquitted. In 1947 he took his first flight in an aeroplane to travel to London, where he was honoured as the greatest living German composer. Strauss died in his villa shortly after celebrating his 85th birthday.

OPERAS

The major part of Strauss's life was dedicated to opera, and of all twentieth-century operatic composers only Puccini could match his fluency. His first opera, *Guntram*, was a Wagnerian experiment, interesting solely for one glorious tune in the final act. Similarly, his Bavarian folk tale, *Feuersnot*, though showing Strauss's ever-increasing understanding of the orchestra and human voice, is little more than a Wagnerian homage. With *Salome* and *Elektra* he arrived at a unique expressionistic style, to which he returned – after the recidivistic *Der Rosenkavalier* and his delightful chamber opera *Ariadne auf Naxos* – in the extremely complicated and not altogether successful symbolist drama, *Die Frau ohne Schatten*, composed in 1919. After *Die Frau* Strauss produced nothing of comparable quality until 1933, when he wrote *Arabella*, a work along the same mock-classical lines as *Rosenkavalier*. Five years later came *Daphne*, followed in 1942 by his fifteenth and final work for the stage, *Capriccio*.

The vividness of characterization in Strauss's work is partly attributable to the quality of the writers with whom he collaborated. Of all these librettists the greatest was Hugo von Hofmannsthal, with whom Strauss established a relationship as productive as that of Mozart and da Ponte: four of the five operas they produced together – *Elektra, Der Rosenkavalier, Ariadne auf Naxos* and *Arabella* – represent the pinnacle of Strauss's operatic art. Precise delineation of character is only part of the appeal of Strauss's operas, however, for they provide some of the most hedonistic pleasures to be found in twentieth-century music. Above all, they are typified by lushly expressive harmony, elastic and extended melody, ingenious orchestrations and an unrivalled understanding of the female voice.

Salome

It was the premiere of *Salome* in December 1905 that catapulted Strauss into superstardom. Oscar Wilde's drama, originally in French, translated into German by Hedwig Lachmann and cut into shape by Strauss himself, formed the basis for the shocking libretto. Herod arrests and jails John the Baptist (Jokanaan), who then rejects the advances of Salome, Herod's stepdaughter. Salome performs the "Dance of the Seven Veils" for Herod on condition that he give her anything she asks for. Herodias, her mother, tells her to ask for the head of Jokanaan. The severed head is brought out on a platter and in a final scene of immense length and power, she kisses its lips. In disgust, Herod has her crushed to death.

Salome is an intoxicating evocation of depravity and madness. The headily erotic decadence of the narrative is conveyed by music of unprecedented colour, and Strauss's portrayal of Herodias's necrophilic daughter is of awesome emotional strength. Strauss described the title part as a role "for a sixteen-year-old-girl with the voice of Isolde" and this is indeed one of the most demanding soprano roles, as Salome is rarely off stage during the continuous ninety minutes of the opera. Though *Salome* is not imitative of Wagner in the way Strauss's earliest efforts were, this through-composed opera still owes much to Wagner in its use of the orchestra (which is dominant throughout), in its system of leitmotifs and in its vocal writing, which alternates between declamation and sustained melodic lines of thrilling richness.

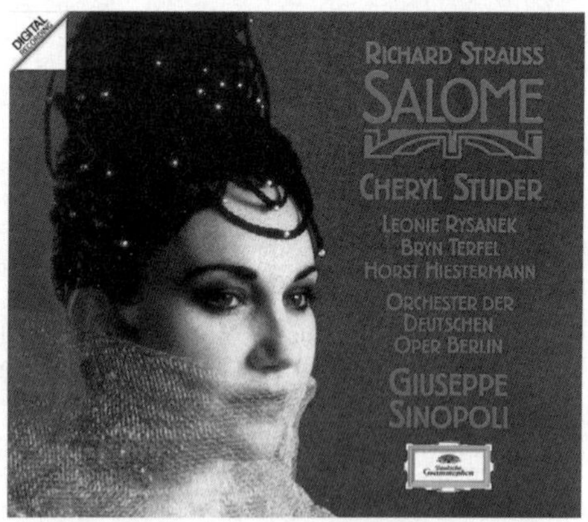

Studer, Terfel, Hiestermann, Rysanek, Bieber; Berlin Deutsche Opera Orchestra; Sinopoli
(Deutsche Grammophon; 2 CDs)

Giuseppe Sinopoli's 1990 recording is the finest *Salome* of recent years, chiefly thanks to Cheryl Studer. Her light soprano, with its quivering, uncertain quality, is ideal for the portrayal of Strauss's unstable heroine, whose burgeoning sexuality she captures brilliantly. Bryn Terfel's Jokanaan is hugely sumptuous, and the Herods (Horst Hiestermann and Leonie Rysanek) are memorably vile.

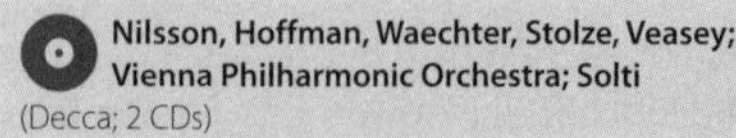

Nilsson, Hoffman, Waechter, Stolze, Veasey; Vienna Philharmonic Orchestra; Solti
(Decca; 2 CDs)

Birgit Nilsson's Salome generates the sort of tension more commonly found in the theatre than on record, while Eberhard Waechter is a grand but lyrical Jokanaan. Solti's conducting is the best testimony to his gift for Strauss's music, and the Vienna Phil make an indecently sumptuous sound, revelling in the sweatiness of Strauss's colossal score.

Elektra

Elektra (1909) was the first Strauss opera with a text by Hofmannsthal, who here provided Strauss with a libretto (based on his own play) that remains one of the greatest of all operatic texts. The immediacy of Elektra's hatred for her mother Klytemnestra, her love for her brother Orestes and her disgust with her sister Chrysothemis inspired Strauss to heights even he could never equal. Elektra's savage desire for her mother's death (in revenge for Klytemnestra's killing of Agamemnon, Elektra's father) is realized in a characterization of chilling dramatic depth and, though all the characters are essentially grotesque, Klytemnestra, for whom Strauss composed his only atonal music, is the most disgusting creation in his entire output. Orestes is the opera's weakest portrayal but his contribution is of little relevance until the climax.

This astonishing one-act opera is sumptuously Romantic yet dissonant, so that its dozens of melodies are not immediately apparent, but rather blossom to surface as your ear becomes accustomed to the textures. The first audiences had problems with Strauss's complicated and heavy counterpoint, his virtuosic orchestrations and his insistent use of polytonality, but the superb vocal writing quickly made it a soprano's favourite. Especially memorable are Elektra's and Chrysothemis's monologues, the recognition scene between Elektra and Orestes, and the final duet for the two sisters, when Elektra performs a hysterical, fatal victory dance.

Borkh, Madeira, Schech, Uhl, Fischer-Dieskau; Dresden Staatskapelle Chorus & Orchestra; Böhm
(Deutsche Grammophon; 2 CDs)

Jean Madeira is suitably fragile as Chrysothemis and Fischer-Dieskau copes well with Orestes's extended range, but it is the instinctive partnership between Inge Borkh and Karl Böhm that marks this performance out as the finest on record. The former is just about perfect in the title role, while Böhm's tempi are very quick, creating a momentum that is only briefly stilled in the magical recognition scene.

Der Rosenkavalier

After the excesses of the one-act shockers, Strauss and Hofmannstahl turned in 1911 to Mozartian comedy with *Der Rosenkavalier*, which has always been the most popular Strauss opera. Subtitled "A Comedy for Music", it is set in Vienna in the middle of the eighteenth century, and adopts a neo-classical framework for its bittersweet tale of romantic love, in which Baron Ochs (a "rural Don Giovanni", in Strauss's words) intends to marry the young Sophie, but is thwarted when she ends up falling for Octavian, the lover of the Marschallin and the "Rose Cavalier" of the title. In the end the young lovers are united, and the ageing Ochs and the Marschallin withdraw from the scene. Boasting a subtle and clever libretto, and Strauss's most delicate and seductively tuneful score, *Der Rosenkavalier* is a perfect combination of good humour, high farce, deep sentiment and pleasant sentimentality. The smoothness of the dramatic action, the fullness of characterization and the graceful profusion of melody make *Der Rosenkavalier* a worthy homage to the art of Mozart.

Central to *Der Rosenkavalier* are its waltzes, which are derived from the music of Schubert, Lanner and Johann Strauss the Younger but treated in so refined a way as to cheat the ear into believing they could have been a feature of eighteenth-century musical life. The enchanted atmosphere of these waltzes is sustained in moments of intense lyrical beauty: the tenor's "Italian" aria and final scene of Act 1, the presentation of the rose in Act 2 and the famous final soprano Trio of Act 3 are among the most overwhelmingly beautiful music composed in the last century.

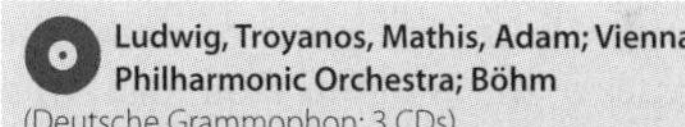

Ludwig, Troyanos, Mathis, Adam; Vienna Philharmonic Orchestra; Böhm
(Deutsche Grammophon; 3 CDs)

Böhm recorded *Rosenkavalier* in the studio in 1958, but that set pales beside this 1969 live recording from the Vienna Staatsoper. The beauty and warmth of Christa Ludwig's Marschallin, the urgency of Tatiana Troyanos's Octavian and the fragile innocence of Edith Mathis's Sophie have never been bettered, while Böhm's feel for the opera's overall shape, orchestral texture and phrasing is unsurpassed.

Schwarzkopf, Ludwig, Stich-Randall, Edelmann; Philharmonia Orchestra; Karajan
(EMI; 3 CDs)

Schwarzkopf was famous in two of the principal female leads in *Rosenkavalier* but it was with the Marschallin that her name was most frequently associated. In this 1957 account Schwarzkopf, Christa Ludwig (Octavian) and Theresa Stich-Randall (Sophie) produced an ensemble performance of deep humanity. Karajan presides over the glowing pit of sound with extreme sensitivity.

ORCHESTRAL MUSIC

Strauss first achieved fame for his mastery of the orchestra, as demonstrated in the set of tone poems he produced in the last years of the nineteenth century: principally the sparkling miniatures *Don Juan* and *Till Eulenspiegel*, and the more epic *Tod und Verklärung*, *Also sprach Zarathustra*, *Don Quixote* and *Ein Heldenleben*. Notable for their flamboyant gestures, complicated counterpoint and remarkable melodies, these pieces are the lineal descendants of the tone poems of Berlioz and Liszt, but their musical stories are even more expansive and dramatic. The expressive, pictorial and narrative elements of these orchestral works paved the way for his operas, and once he had embarked on his operatic career Strauss rarely returned to purely instrumental composition. However, towards the end of his life he created possibly his finest orchestral work, *Metamorphosen*, then brought the full panoply of his orchestral skills to bear in his valedictory *Vier letzte Lieder* (Four Last Songs).

Don Juan

Don Juan set the musical world on fire in 1888. In less than twenty minutes of music Strauss showed himself to be both a Classical master of his craft and a radical innovator, for the demands upon the orchestra (especially the horns) were more strenuous than anything even in Berlioz, and the sheer scale and drama of the scoring was shocking. The piece recounts the loves and losses of the amorous Don Juan, who is characterized throughout the score by a horn call of Wagnerian intensity. Some gushingly exciting string writing leads to a love scene in which the oboe solo prefigures many of the sentimental tunes that were to come in Strauss's operas. The finale, leading to the antihero's damnation, is a blazing crescendo that, when well played, can knock your socks off.

Berlin Philharmonic Orchestra; Karajan
(Deutsche Grammophon; with *Also sprach Zarathustra* & *Till Eulenspiegel*)

Strauss's tone poems are a work well suited to Karajan's flamboyant style and to the Berlin Philharmonic's rich and refulgent tone. In this 1973 recording both conductor and orchestra hit the mark in thrilling fashion.

Also sprach Zarathustra

Nietzsche's book *Also sprach Zarathustra* (Thus Spake Zarathustra) had only been published a few years when Strauss chose, in 1896, to write a tone poem inspired by it. Nietzsche's philosophy of the Superman and his celebration of human power and energy clearly appealed to Strauss's overwhelming self-belief and sense of destiny. His response was a work of enormous proportions, a free-flowing fantasia which, apart from its philosophical aspirations, creates some truly awe-inspiring orchestral sounds. Not least of these is the work's inspired "sunrise" opening used by Stanley Kubrick in his film *2001*. Nothing else quite lives up to this and, taken as a whole, the work's eight episodes (each with a heading from Nietzsche) can seem a little meandering in all but the most brilliant performances. It's not without humour, however: Zarathustra's dance, towards the end of the work, is cast in the form of a Viennese waltz – albeit one with a decidedly rustic flavour.

Berlin Philharmonic Orchestra; Karajan
(Deutsche Grammophon; with *Don Juan* & *Till Eulenspiegel*)

Karajan takes *Zarathustra* completely seriously, and achieves a quality of sound so rich, but also so incisive, as to overcome the work's bombast and prolixity. What he cannot disguise – indeed he revels in it – is the often brash exhibitionism of Strauss's orchestral writing, an aspect of the music which many people have found unbearably vulgar and even sinister.

Chicago Symphony Orchestra; Reiner
(RCA; with *Ein Heldenleben*)

A stupendous recording; the Chicago SO play with adventure and excitement under Fritz Reiner's dynamic leadership. Few other versions manage to give such a convincing sense of shape to this work. The early stereo sound of 1954 is amazingly good.

Don Quixote

The following year Strauss turned to another literary character, Cervantes' *Don Quixote*, for inspiration. Subtitling his work "Fantastic Variations on a Theme of a Knightly Character", the unworldy Don Quixote is assigned to a solo cello, while his robust sidekick Sancho Panza is a viola. The work is thus a kind of concerto in variation form, each variation depicting an incident from the novel by developing new material out of the main themes. There's a chamber-music dimension to *Don Quixote*, which makes it the least draining of his long tone poems, but the orchestration is as brilliantly inventive as ever – the Don's battle with the sheep is full of disturbingly dissonant bleating – and Strauss's luxuriant side, most stirringly presented in Variation 3, is never far away. A long and melancholy cello solo, representing the Don's death, brings this affectionate portrait to a close.

Meneses, Christ; Berlin Philharmonic Orchestra; Karajan (Deutsche Grammophon; with *Till Eulenspiegel*)

Don Quixote needs a cellist with a brilliant technique who can also characterize with wit and restraint. Paul Tortelier, who recorded the work at least four times, was such a one, but his best performances are only available in box sets. This recording makes a more than adequate alternative: Antonio Meneses has a beautiful tone, the death scene is touchingly conveyed, and Karajan and the BPO provide excellent support.

Ein Heldenleben

When *Ein Heldenleben* was premiered in 1899 it caused a sensation, not because of its musical audacity but because of the arrogance of a composer who, at the age of 35, could present the world with an autobiographical piece titled "A Hero's Tale". There's no point trying to argue away Strauss's egotism – he did, after all, once remark that he found himself "every bit as interesting as Caesar or Napoleon". The music itself, however, is a vigorous affirmation of life, realized in orchestration of sensational colour and imagination. The hero battles against the critics, who are portrayed by a bleating and dissonant wind section, and is both soothed and frustrated by his wife, depicted by the lead violin. His victory is hailed in "The Hero's Works of Peace", an eight-minute section in which Strauss packs in some thirty excerpts from his own catalogue, including all his other tone poems. "The Hero's Retirement from the World" ends the work: its tender duet for horn (himself) and violin (his wife) is perhaps the most beautiful bit of music outside his operas.

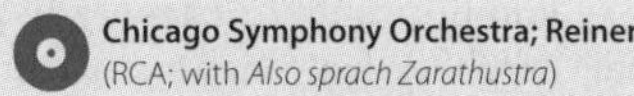

Chicago Symphony Orchestra; Reiner (RCA; with *Also sprach Zarathustra*)

Fritz Reiner, a friend and colleague of Strauss, gives a reading that is muscular and hard-driven (the battle scene is suitably cacophonous) without being brutal. He brings out the part-writing with exemplary lucidity, and in the final section he employs the sweetest of tones to create a great Romantic wash of sound.

Metamorphosen

Strauss spent much of his life expressing the emotions of others; in *Metamorphosen* he expressed himself, pouring out his grief over the destruction of Dresden, Weimar and Munich in 1945. As he wrote shortly after: "history is almost entirely an unbroken chain of acts of stupidity and wickedness, every sort of baseness, greed, betrayal, murder and destruction. And how little those who are called upon to make history have learned from it." A single movement for 23 strings, *Metamorphosen* is based upon a motif taken from the funeral march of Beethoven's *Eroica*, and as the piece progresses its emotional state is transformed from grief-stricken sombreness to grudging reconciliation, via music of the most trenchant anger.

Berlin Philharmonic Orchestra; Karajan (Deutsche Grammophon; with *Tod und Verklarüng* and *Vier letzte Lieder*)

In the absence of Furtwängler's desperately moving live performance made shortly after the war, this is the version to go for. Karajan, who made the first recording of this work in 1947, controls and shapes the almost supernatural string sound of the BPO as if he were moulding it. The result is both mysterious and moving in its valedictory pathos.

Four Last Songs

Like Grieg, Strauss learned most about the quality and capacity of the female voice from his wife, for whom he wrote a great deal of music, including his finest group of chamber songs, the four Op. 27, which were composed as a wedding present for her. The great majority of his two hundred songs are for soprano, and Strauss ended his life as a composer with a grandiloquent piece for soprano and orchestra, the *Vier letzte Lieder* (*Four Last Songs*). They were not composed as a cycle – after Strauss's death, his publisher brought them together, gave them an opus number and saw to their first performance – but they indubitably work as one, for they share a mood of autumnal peace and absolute honesty in the face of death, and the music is of a consistent simplicity and

clarity. After settings of three poems by Hermann Hesse, the *Four Last Songs* conclude with a text by Eichendorff, "Im Abendrot" (At Sunset), where Strauss alters the last line from "Is that perhaps Death?" to "Is this perhaps Death?" This final song portrays an ageing couple watching the setting sun: as they close their eyes, their lives end to the sound of trilling flutes, signifying skylarks and the liberation of their souls. Some might find it maudlin, but for many people it's an acutely moving conclusion to one of the most intriguing careers in the history of music.

 **Schwarzkopf; Berlin Radio Symphony Orchestra; Szell** (EMI; with *12 Orchesterlieder*)

Almost alone among the great interpreters of these songs, Elisabeth Schwarzkopf performs them as if the words really mattered. In this 1965 recording George Szell conducts what on paper seems to be a second-division orchestra but which produces some truly ravishing sounds, including an exquisitely vibrant violin solo in "Beim Schlafengehen".

 **Janowitz; Berlin Philharmonic Orchestra; Karajan** (Deutsche Grammophon; with *Metamorphosen & Tod und Verklärung*)

Gundula Janowitz is one of the most celebrated of post-war Straussian sopranos and this 1974 recording is justly famous. The rounded richness of her voice is never used in an indulgent fashion and her vocal strength allows the orchestra to play out. The one problem is that the CD transfer seems to have constricted the voice in the upper register.

 **della Casa; Vienna Philharmonic Orchestra; Böhm** (Decca; with excerpts from *Arabella, Ariadne auf Naxos & Capriccio*)

Lisa della Casa's 1953 recording of the *Four Last Songs* is one of the finest ever made. Her limpid, tranquil tone is beautifully supported by Karl Böhm, who prevents the music from descending into sentimentality. A dry-eyed and dignified account, this recording is a wonderful testament to all those involved.

Igor Stravinsky (1882–1971)

Like his friend Pablo Picasso, Igor Stravinsky became a modernist icon, an artist as well known to the general public as he was to the cognoscenti. And, as with Picasso, people were never quite certain what Stravinsky was going to do next. He made his name with *The Firebird, Petrushka* and *The Rite of Spring*, Dionysian masterpieces that shocked and enthralled their first audiences. He then rejected the legacy of Romanticism and went into a neo-classical phase, an audacious change of direction, but not quite as extraordinary as the last volte-face of his career, when, in ripe old age, he threw in his hat with the serialist enemy. However, through all his metamorphoses Stravinsky remained a Classicist at heart. Above all other things he loved precision, order and structure, and all his works have a consummate sense of poise. The Swiss writer C.F. Ramuz, who collaborated with Stravinsky on *L'histoire du soldat*, once wrote: "His writing desk resembled a surgeon's instrument case. Bottles of different coloured inks in their ordered hierarchy each had a separate part to play in the ordering of his art … One was reminded of the definition of St Thomas: beauty is the splendour of order."

Stravinsky's early years gave little hint of the *enfant terrible* to come. Born near St Petersburg, he was a musical child and diligent student, but on the advice of his parents he studied law, thinking that profession a safer bet than a life devoted to music. In 1903 his encounter with the composer and pedagogue Rimsky-Korsakov (see p.455) changed the direction of his life. Rimsky took on Stravinsky as a private pupil, and Stravinsky soon resolved to try to make it as a composer, albeit against his teacher's advice.

By a stroke of good fortune, Russia's leading impresario, Serge Diaghilev, happened to catch his first mature compositions – *Scherzo fantastique* and *Feu d'artifice* – at a St Petersburg concert in 1909, and promptly asked Stravinsky to write two numbers for a ballet he was producing. Stravinsky acquitted himself so well that Diaghilev commissioned from him a score for his new Paris-based dance troupe, the Ballets Russes – and, as Diaghilev had predicted, the *Firebird* made Stravinsky famous overnight. Knowing that he was on to a good thing, Diaghilev persuaded Stravinsky to write an even more exotic Russian-style ballet for the next season. The result was *Petrushka*, a work which caused a stir with its daring polytonality and tart rhythms. This was nothing compared to the impact of Stravinsky's next ballet, *The Rite of Spring*. A score of unprecedented rhythmic and

Igor Stravinsky in rehearsal..

harmonic ferocity, it caused a riot at its premiere on 29 May, 1913, and established Stravinsky as the prince of the avant-garde.

During World War I Stravinsky and his family found refuge in Switzerland, where wartime deprivation obliged him to think in terms of writing for small ensembles. *Les noces* (1914–17) and *L'histoire du soldat* (1918) showed Stravinsky developing leaner textures, and he spoke of the latter as his "final break with the Russian orchestral school". With the coming of peace in 1918, Stravinsky and his family settled in Paris, where the composer took up French citizenship. (Their planned return to Russia became impossible after the Communists confiscated their property and blocked Stravinsky's royalties.) At the behest of Diaghilev, Stravinsky began fashioning music for a ballet called *Pulcinella* (1920) out of some pieces by the eighteenth-century composer Pergolesi, a commission that marked the beginning of his neo-classical phase. Whereas Schoenberg devised the twelve-tone method as a modernist discipline to supplant the prescriptions of the past, Stravinsky reinvented older forms and styles, using traditional conventions as vessels for modern ideas. His neo-classicism was immensely fluid, adapting Handel and Gluck for *Oedipus Rex* (1927) and Mozart for *The Rake's Progress* (1951), but running through most of his work for the next thirty years was an emphasis on Classical elegance and clarity.

By the end of the 1930s Stravinsky was tiring of Europe: his wife and one daughter had both died of tuberculosis, war was once again about to break out, and the French critics who had once vilified *The Rite* were now carping about his supposed sell-out to neo-classicism. The USA seemed the obvious place to go: he had wealthy admirers there, and the conductor Serge Koussevitsky was proving a hugely influential champion of his work, having already commissioned the *Symphony of Psalms* for the fiftieth anniversary of the Boston Symphony Orchestra. In 1939 he made the move, taking with him his mistress, the painter Vera de Bossett, whom he married the following year. In 1940 Stravinsky and his family settled in Hollywood, where the cell of exiled European artists included Arnold Schoenberg, whom Stravinsky seems to have avoided.

During the 1940s he composed some magnificent neo-classical works, including the *Symphony in C* and *The Rake's Progress*, but then came his dramatic conversion to the serialist cause. The young American conductor Robert Craft discreetly introduced him to various key serial works, and

Stravinsky became particularly taken with the crystalline scores of Anton Webern, declaring that "the serial composers are the only ones with a discipline that I respect". He now turned to twelve-note techniques with characteristic inventiveness and a vigour that was typified by the creation of the astringent *Agon* (1957) at the age of 75. By now, such was Stravinsky's reputation that each new work was guaranteed several performances and a recording, however prickly its musical language. In his last decade he achieved a degree of celebrity unmatched by any composer since Mozart, being feted by Pope John XXIII, by the Kennedys and, in a triumphant visit to Russia in 1962, by Nikita Khrushchev. He died in New York on 6 April, 1971, and was buried where he had asked to be – near to his old comrade Diaghilev, on Venice's cemetery island of San Michele.

The Igor Stravinsky Edition
(Sony; 22 CDs)

Towards the end of his life Stravinsky gave a lot of his time to conducting and supervising performances of his works. Sony have gathered all of Stravinsky's performances of his own music, supplemented by recordings of those pieces he didn't conduct himself, into this immense set, available as a 22-CD box or in twelve separate volumes. It has to be said that Stravinsky was not an outstanding conductor, and there are better recordings of much of his music. But this is nonetheless a great historical document – and Stravinsky's output was so vast that in several instances the *Stravinsky Edition* offers the only available recording of a piece.

OPERAS & BALLETS

Stravinsky composed in a wide range of genres, but his output is dominated above all by ballet music, a field that he did more than any other composer to reinvent for the twentieth century. His ballets trace his entire development as a composer – from the bejewelled Romanticism of *The Firebird*, through the hard-hitting orchestral coruscation of *The Rite of Spring* and the smaller-scale neo-classicism of *Pulcinella*, to the serialism of *Agon*. As well as the key examples discussed further below, Stravinsky's ballets include a number of less well-known works: *Renard* (Fox; 1916), *Le baiser de la fée* (The Fairy's Kiss; 1928), *Perséphone* (1933), *Jeu de cartes* (Card Game; 1936) and *Orpheus* (1947). Stravinsky was not quite such an outstanding composer for voice as he was for orchestra, and his music-theatre works involving singers and narrators haven't achieved quite the same degree of popularity as his straightforward ballets. Nonetheless, from his one full-length opera, the neo-classical *The Rake's Progress*, to the mixture of spoken and sung passages in *Oedipus Rex*, they are always questing and add up to a unique body of work.

Oedipus Rex

Based on Sophocles's most famous tragedy, Stravinsky's *Oedipus Rex* (1927) is a semi-abstract, ritualistic music drama that narrates its events in the simplest, starkest terms. The sense of Oedipus's story as the exemplar of inexorable fate is enhanced by the absolute detachment of the presentation, in which the arias and choruses are punctuated by short and simple texts delivered in French by a narrator who stands apart in modern clothes from the rest of the costumed cast, who are themselves not empowered to act or express any individuality.

For the text of the vocal parts, Stravinsky and his collaborator Jean Cocteau (the provocative cultural fixer behind "Les Six"; see p.409) settled on Latin as "a medium not dead, but turned to stone, and so monumentalized as to have become immune from all risk of vulgarization". Narrative momentum and cohesion are created above all by the music: the drama of *Oedipus Rex* is static, but the score is awesomely powerful. This is also one of the most impressive displays of Stravinsky's allusive neo-classical technique, with its evocations of such composers as Monteverdi, Handel, Mussorgsky and Verdi.

Cole, von Otter, Estes, Sotin, Gedda, Chereau; Eric Ericson Chamber Choir; Swedish Radio Symphony Orchestra & Chorus; Salonen (Sony)

This version from Finnish conductor Esa-Pekka Salonen is the finest account of Stravinsky's opera-oratorio yet committed to disc. It is gripping from the first bar to the last, with the chorus and top-class singers as incisive as the orchestra.

The Rake's Progress

Stravinsky's only full-length opera was inspired by Hogarth's *Rake's Progress*, and its libretto (by W.H. Auden and Chester Kallman) fleshes out the story told in Hogarth's series of eight paintings, charting Tom Rakewell's descent through dissipation into madness. Appropriately enough, the musical language of this eighteenth-century morality tale is heavily indebted to Mozart – *The Rake's Progress* is constructed from solo and ensemble numbers, which are accompanied by a small orchestra and strung together by recitatives accompanied by harpsichord. With its subtle anachronisms the music mirrors a world in which the natural order – epitomized by marriage – is subverted by Tom's feckless career, and in its extremely knowing (some might say cold-hearted) exploitation of opera's heritage, *The Rake's Progress* marks the culminating point of Stravinsky's neo-classical style. Almost everything in this opera appears in quotation marks, so to speak, and its libretto is perhaps the richest operatic text of the last century. It demands a little effort but it does include some episodes of

Diaghilev and the Russian Ballet

As a young man, the great Russian impresario Serge Diaghilev briefly aspired to be a musician – until Rimsky-Korsakov persuaded him that he lacked sufficient talent. So he moved into the visual arts, staging exhibitions and, from 1898, editing a progressive arts magazine, *The World of Art*. The stir the magazine created led to Diaghilev's appointment as an assistant at the Imperial Theatres, but his career there was cut short when a contretemps with senior officials effectively barred him from any further Imperial employment.

Russia's loss was Europe's gain: Diaghilev became an unofficial ambassador for Russian culture. In Paris an exhibition of Russian art was followed, in 1907, by a season of Russian music featuring Rimsky-Korsakov, Scriabin, Glazunov, Rachmaninov, the pianist Josef Hoffmann and the young bass, Chaliapin. But 1909 was the real turning point: at the Châtelet Theatre, with a company recruited from the Imperial Theatres, Diaghilev presented a mixed season of opera and ballet, with the ballet – by then almost moribund outside of Russia – causing an absolute sensation. None of the works presented were entirely new and several of the dancers had already performed in Europe, but the sheer finesse of the performers and the way each work fused music, dancing and decor into a single kaleidoscopic spectacle was completely revolutionary.

Emboldened by his success, Diaghilev's next Paris season was even more ambitious: new works included a ballet to Rimsky-Korsakov's score *Scheherazade* (in which the animal physicality of Nijinsky's dancing made a huge impact), and a new commission, *The Firebird*, by the young and unknown Igor Stravinsky. With their brightly coloured Leon Bakst designs, both ballets exemplified the bejewelled exoticism of the Russian Ballet's early productions, an aesthetic which made the company as fashionable as it was critically acclaimed.

Adopting an ever more experimental approach, the Russian Ballet's notoriety reached a ferocious climax on 29 May, 1913 with the first night of Stravinsky's *The Rite of Spring*. Shocked as much by the awkwardness of the dancing as the rhythmic savagery of the music, many in the audience screamed their disapproval, thus forcing Nijinsky, who had choreographed the work, to stand in the wings shouting out instructions to his dancers.

Though the company's initial work drew upon a core group of compatriots presided over by the tyrannical genius of Diaghilev, the net was gradually thrown wider to exploit some of the extraordinary wealth of talent then resident in Paris. In 1912 Debussy's languorous orchestral piece *L'après-midi d'un faune* became a *succès de scandale* when it was turned into an erotic Hellenic fantasy by designer Bakst and choreographer Nijinsky (who danced the central role), while the same year also saw the staging of Ravel's especially commissioned *Daphnis et Chlöe*. Other commissions included Debussy's *Jeux* (1913), Strauss's *Josephslegende* (1914), Satie's *Parade* (1917), Falla's *The Three-Cornered Hat* (1919), Poulenc's *Les biches* (1924), Milhaud's *Le train bleu* (1924) and three scores by Prokofiev – *Chout* (1921), *Le pas d'Acier* (1927) and *The Prodigal Son* (1929). Diaghilev also employed several leading artists as designers such as Matisse, Braque, Utrillo, Derain, de Chirico and, most notably, Picasso whose fantastical "Cubist" costumes for *Parade* and witty *commedia dell'arte* designs for *Pulcinella* (1920) perfectly complemented each score.

Pulcinella represents one of the high points of the company's twenty-year history, with Diaghilev's idea of orchestrating some pieces by the composer Pergolesi transformed by Stravinsky into an unmistakably modern homage to the forms of the eighteenth century. Arguably, several of the other ballets of the 1920s were less successful, and Diaghilev's skill at bringing together and managing so many disparate talents began to seem less assured. But while his death in 1929 brought one of the great enterprises of modern art to an end, much of what he achieved in transforming the ballet into a total theatrical event lived on in the work of company members, notably choreographer George Balanchine who continued a highly fruitful working relationship with Stravinsky in the USA.

extraordinary directness: the final scene in Bedlam is saturated with desperate tragedy, and Anne Trulove's farewell to Tom is probably Stravinsky's most tender creation.

Hadley, Upshaw, Ramey, Bumbry; Chorus and Orchestra of Lyon Opera; Nagano (Erato; 2 CDs)

Kent Nagano has made *The Rake's Progress* something of a speciality, and his studio recording pretty much redefines the standard, presenting an ideally cast and exactingly prepared performance that gets as close to the opera's mercurial character as anything yet recorded.

The Firebird

The Firebird (*L'oiseau de feu*) is a straightforward fairy tale, in which the Firebird helps a young prince to rescue a beautiful princess from an evil ogre and win her heart. Aspects of its musical language would have been familiar to its first Parisian audience in 1910, for Stravinsky borrows much from his teacher Rimsky-Korsakov: for example, in his use of chromaticism for the ballet's magic creatures and of a modal-diatonic style for the mortals. Knowledgeable onlookers, however, realized that there was something much deeper here than another piece of Rimsky-style exoticism. Debussy for one was thrilled by its latent barbarism, and revelled in its "unusual combinations of rhythms".

Chicago Symphony Orchestra; Boulez (Deutsche Grammophon; with *Four Études; Fireworks*)

Boulez's second recording of *The Firebird* is as colourful and vivid as his first, but even more tightly focused. The playing of the Chicago Symphony is characterized by great finesse and power.

Petrushka

To quote Stravinsky, the central figure of *Petrushka* is "the immortal and unhappy hero of every fair in all countries"; more specifically, he is a "puppet, suddenly endowed with life, exasperating the patience of the orchestra". On 13 June, 1911, the title role was danced by the legendary Nijinsky, ensuring that what was happening onstage was as remarkable as what was coming out of the orchestra pit. The ballet's burlesque and parodic elements are heightened by ever-shifting rhythms and a startling polytonal harmonic language – the juxtaposition of the two unrelated keys of C major and F sharp major in one section is typical of Stravinsky's brazen innovation. These advanced musical devices, which are primarily used for the appearances of Petrushka himself, are contrasted with the predominantly diatonic harmonies of the vivid crowd scenes.

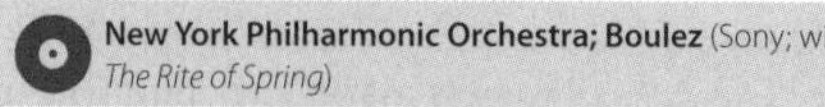

New York Philharmonic Orchestra; Boulez (Sony; with *The Rite of Spring*)

This is a brilliant, scintillating account from Boulez and the New York Phil, which brings out all the angularity and awkwardness in the score. Rarely has Petrushka's plight, and the sheer bustle of the fair, sounded so vital.

Cincinnati Symphony Orchestra: Järvi (Telarc; with *The Firebird Suite & Scherzo à la Russe*)

For a more forward-moving and impassioned account, try Paavo Järvi and the Cincinnati Symphony. They make everything sound charged and luminous, both in this work and the coupled account of the *Firebird Suite*.

The Rite of Spring

The idea for *The Rite of Spring* (*Le sacre du printemps*) came to Stravinsky several years before he actually wrote it, as he was later to recount. "One day, when I was finishing the last pages of the *Firebird* in St Petersburg, I had a fleeting vision … a solemn pagan rite: sage elders, seated in a circle, watched a young girl dance herself to death. They were sacrificing her to propitiate the god of spring." In 1913 he unleashed the visceral music that this vision prompted, and the result was the most notorious premiere in the history of modern music. The catcalls started only seconds after the music, and soon Debussy was pleading vainly for people to calm down, while Ravel yelled "Genius, genius!" in the midst of fist-fights and screams of abuse so loud that the dancers were unable to hear the orchestra. It is not difficult to understand why *The Rite of Spring* had such a profound effect. Written for a huge orchestra, it's unrelentingly barbaric in its dissonances and asymmetrical rhythms, jolting the listener into attention from first to last. The *Rite*'s defining quality is its thumping, irregular pulse, a rhythmic propulsion achieved through frequent changes in time signature – sometimes, as in the "Sacrificial Dance", in every successive bar.

Kirov Orchestra; Gergiev
(Philips; with Scriabin *Poem of Ecstasy*)

Valery Gergiev's *Rite* has an unmatched sense of earthiness, breadth and unbridled power. The Kirov Orchestra play brilliantly, and with a wide range of sonorities: often the sound-world is positively luminous, yet the strings are unusually weighty and rosiny, making maximum impact in big entrances such as the opening of the "Rondes printanières".

New York Philharmonic Orchestra; Boulez
(Sony; with *Petrushka*)

Pierre Boulez's reading brings out less of the work's primeval quality than does Gergiev's. Instead we get a more analytical, though still exciting, account in which the radical, experimental nature of Stravinsky's complex score is made especially clear.

Les noces

Stravinsky had the idea for *Les noces*, a dance cantata depicting a Russian peasant wedding, while working on *The Rite of Spring*. The text, arranged into four scenes, is derived from Russian folk poems and is meant to suggest "scraps of conversation without the connecting thread of discourse". It's one of the most Russian of his works, with a strong ritualistic element of repeated words and insistent rhythms, a quality reinforced in the first production of 1923 by Bronislava Nijinska's austere and abstract choreography. After much experiment, Stravinsky decided to accompany the predominant vocal part with a largely percussive accompaniment which included four pianos, xylophone, timpani and bells. It is this extraordinary instrumentation which gives *Les noces* much of its unforgettably raw energy.

Pokrovsky Ensemble; Pokrovsky (Elektra Nonesuch; with *Traditional Russian Wedding Songs*)

There's no ideal version of this piece available, but Dimitri Pokrovsky and his ensemble get close with a hard-hitting account in which the authentic Russian vocal sound is an extra bonus. The odd, but effective, aspect of this disc is that the instrumental parts have been produced through a computer.

L'histoire du soldat

L'histoire du soldat was devised by Stravinsky, in collaboration with the Swiss writer Ramuz, as a small-scale, low-budget theatre piece that could be toured around Switzerland on the back of a lorry. Although the story, a morality tale about a soldier who makes a pact with the Devil, is based on a Russian folk tale, the music turns its back on a distinctly Russian style in favour of a more contemporary and eclectic idiom – ragtime and tango both feature in typically acerbic guise as well as a concluding chorale. Because the soldier gives his violin to the Devil, that instrument leads the small ensemble of trumpet, trombone, double-bass, clarinet, bassoon and percussion – an unusual combination from which Stravinsky produces some wonderfully rich and acid timbres. Despite its vivid picture-book colours, *L'histoire du soldat* is rarely staged partly because of its length but also because of its unusual mixture of music, spoken roles and dance.

Members of the Cleveland Orchestra; Boulez
(Deutsche Grammophon; with *Le chant du Rossignol* etc)

Stravinsky arranged *L'histoire du soldat* as a suite, which seems the best way to hear the music outside of the theatre. Using seven virtuoso players plucked from the ranks of the Cleveland Orchestra, Boulez produces a crisp and vigorous account in which Stravinsky's rhythmic playfulness is always to the fore.

Pulcinella

The ballet *Pulcinella*, written in 1920 for Diaghilev and the choreographer Massine, inaugurated Stravinsky's neo-classical period. Stravinsky's source material was a melange of operas, cantatas, trio-sonatas and other pieces ascribed to Pergolesi (see p.403), which he turned into the music for a *commedia dell'arte* story. Although the orchestration of *Pulcinella* recalls a lean, eighteenth-century ensemble, Stravinsky gives the eighteenth-century melodies a modernist spin through a range of devices. The orchestration is wonderfully quirky (there's a rare double-bass solo in one movement); harmonies are decidedly non-authentic; its rhythmic accents shift about ceaselessly, while its melodies sometimes seem to start in midstream, or stop short of a satisfactory resolution. The whole effect of *Pulcinella* is of an oscillation between passages of giddy energy and elegant if tentative repose.

Murray, Rolfe Johnson, Estes; Ensemble Intercontemporain; French National Orchestra; Boulez (Warner; with *Le chant du Rossignol*)

As a young man Pierre Boulez was fond of heckling at premieres of new works from Stravinsky, in his capacity as standard-bearer of the avant-garde. He went on to become one of the finest conductors of twentieth-century music, and this meticulously lucid and sprightly reading of

Pulcinella is a marvellous example of Boulez's ability to think himself into an aesthetic that is miles away from his own.

Apollon musagète

Apollon musagète (Apollo, Leader of the Muses), the most serene of all Stravinsky's ballets, was commissioned in 1927 for a festival of contemporary music at the Library of Congress in Washington DC. It's a paradoxical work in that, though Stravinsky conceived it as embodying a classical ideal, devoid of "many-coloured effects and of all superfluities", by restricting himself to an orchestra of strings alone he produced one of his warmest and most luscious-sounding works. Much of *Apollon musagète* really doesn't sound like Stravinsky at all, and it has none of the astringent edge of many of his other neo-classical works. Diaghilev thought it "extraordinarily calm, and with greater clarity than anything he has done so far ... somehow music not of this world, but from somewhere above". It was the perfect vehicle for the clean, linear vision of choreographer George Balanchine, and the first of several marvellous collaborations between him and Stravinsky.

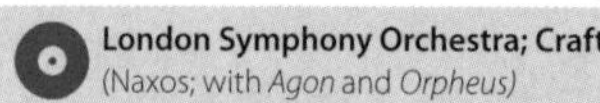

London Symphony Orchestra; Craft (Naxos; with *Agon* and *Orpheus)*

Stravinsky expert Robert Craft has had the bright idea of recording all three ballets inspired by classical Greece on one disc. Despite their markedly different styles, they are united by Craft's meticulously clean readings in which rhetorical gestures are avoided. *Apollon*, in particular, has a marvellous transparency and supple grace.

Agon

Completed in 1957 for George Balanchine's New York City Ballet, *Agon* is as abstract a dance piece as it's possible to write. The title means "contest" in Greek, and the work can be read as a kind of dialectic between tradition and modernity. Starting with neo-classical fanfares, it becomes increasingly chromatic until it reaches a form of fully fledged serialism, then at its conclusion returns to the tonal fanfares. Along the way you'll hear some of the finest dance music written in the twentieth century, and if any single piece is going to convince you that serialism does not have to be hard work, *Agon* is it.

London Symphony Orchestra; Tilson Thomas (RCA; with *Circus Polka, Huxley Variations, Scènes de ballet*, etc)

Agon is strangely under-represented in the CD catalogue. Stravinsky gives an assured and atmospheric account in a Sony three-CD set of the later ballets, but this recent performance by the LSO has exceptional poise while maintaining a strong sense of theatre.

SYMPHONIES & CONCERTOS

Stravinsky wrote five works with the word "symphony" in the title, though only three of these are recognizably symphonic in any standard sense: his Op. 1 *Symphony in E Flat*, an enjoyable if unremarkable Romantic piece written under the guidance of Rimsky-Korsakov, and the much more characterful and distinguished *Symphony in C* and *Symphony in Three Movements*. The other two are the *Symphony of Psalms*, a stern but never stolid Biblical setting for chorus and orchestra, and the *Symphonies of Wind Instruments*, a short but delightful piece assembled from blocks of distinct themes and textures.

Stravinsky's other non-theatre orchestral works range from the early showpiece *Feu d'artifice* (Fireworks), via the jazzy but not wholly successful *Ebony Concerto*, to the lively *Dumbarton Oaks*, which betrays the influence of Bach's *Brandenburg Concertos*. But the outstanding piece here is the *Violin Concerto*, a scintillating composition that shows the composer at his pared-back neo-classical best.

Symphony of Psalms

Despite its title, the treatment of chorus and orchestra in the *Symphony of Psalms*, dating from 1930, looks back to the choral works of the Baroque period rather than to archetypal Classical symphonic models. Dedicated "to the glory of God", it was written not long after Stravinsky's conversion to Christianity and is imbued with the intensity of the first flood of faith. The Latin texts of the three movements are taken from the Psalms, which the composer saw as "poems of exultation, but also of anger and judgement", and he responded with music in which self-expression is expunged in favour of humble devotion. The sound-world of *Symphony of Psalms* is austere, due in large part to the absence of the "warm" sonorities of the violin, viola and clarinet.

Berlin Philharmonic Orchestra; Berlin Radio Chorus; Boulez (Deutsche Grammophon; with *Symphony in Three Movements & Symphonies of Wind Instruments)*

Boulez brings a great sense of clarity to the *Symphony of Psalms* without sacrificing any of the weight and solemnity that really make the work special. Every sonority and polyphonic strand is meticulously brought out, and the

Deutsche Grammophon engineers achieve an excellent balance between orchestra and choir.

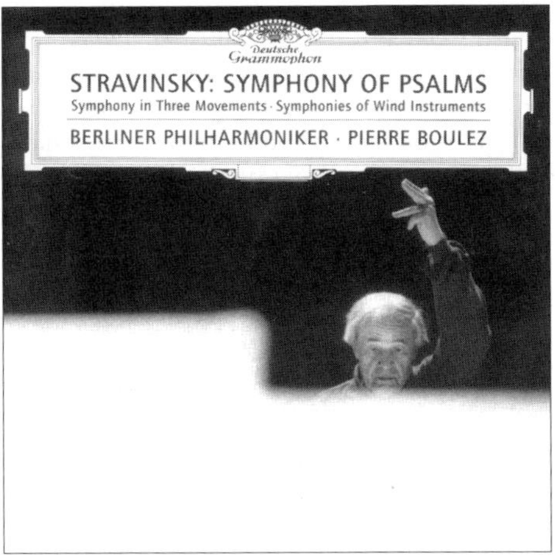

Symphony in C

Eight years after the composition of the *Symphony of Psalms* Stravinsky received a commission from the Chicago Symphony Orchestra, which resulted in the *Symphony in C*, a more obvious orchestral showpiece. It's a work that shows Stravinsky's great capacity for synthesis. There are clear formal and thematic references to other works – in the first two movements an unlikely mélange of Beethoven, Haydn and Tchaikovsky – but the whole work has a typically Stravinskian acerbity, with crisp woodwind writing, bustling counterpoint, and heavily accented motor rhythms.

 **Philharmonia Orchestra; Craft** (Naxos; with *Dumbarton Oaks Concerto, Octet & Symphony in Three Movements*)

Robert Craft has a unique authority as a Stravinsky interpreter having acted as his unofficial assistant during the composer's final creative period. It shows in the supreme confidence of this performance, in which the work's energy is conveyed with great panache and, on occasions, a leavening degree of wit. At budget price this is superb value.

Symphony in Three Movements

The *Symphony in Three Movements* (1943–45) was described by Stravinsky as his "War Symphony", and it is indeed one of the most significant compositions to come out of World War II – although, unlike the war music of Prokofiev, Shostakovich and Richard Strauss, the *Symphony in Three Movements* reflects images seen on newsreels, rather than the direct experience of a country ravaged by armies. Stravinsky's hallmark techniques – prominence of wind instruments, rapid changes of time signature, astringent harmonies – are all employed to telling effect, and Stravinsky's loathing of fascism is nowhere better depicted than in the third movement, with its relentless march rhythms and sharp brass-band orchestration.

Berlin Philharmonic Orchestra; Berlin Radio Chorus; Boulez (Deutsche Grammophon; with *Symphony of Psalms & Symphonies of Wind Instruments*)

Though other conductors bring more drama to the *Symphony in Three Movements*, no one combines power, weight and structural transparency as well as Boulez. He masterfully controls the BPO's supremely intense and technically excellent playing, and the sound quality is superb.

Violin Concerto

L'histoire du soldat was the only work that Stravinsky had written with a substantial violin part when, in 1931, he was approached to write a concerto for the young virtuoso Samuel Dushkin. Stravinsky was reluctant to accept until he met Dushkin, who became an active collaborator in the technical detailing of the violin part. The composer studied other violin concertos, but the only apparent model seems to have been Bach. Stravinsky's concerto is in four movements with the pointedly Baroque titles of Toccata, Aria I, Aria II and Capriccio. Its parodic neo-Baroque characteristics include the bouncy motor rhythms of its opening movement, and the leaping violin line of the Capriccio. The second of the slow movements, an effusive Bach-inspired cantilena, belies many critics' insistence that this concerto is a purely abstract work with little emotional content.

 **Mutter; Philharmonia Orchestra; Sacher** (Deutsche Grammophon; with Bartók *Violin Concerto No. 2* & Dutilleux *Sur le même accord*)

Conductors frequently get the balance wrong between soloist and orchestra in this work, which is why it often fails in the concert hall. In Mutter's fresh and invigorating performance, the balance sounds just right (easier to achieve in the studio) and both soloist and orchestra exude enjoyment.

CHAMBER & PIANO MUSIC

Stravinsky was a very accomplished pianist and composed a fair amount of music for the instrument – the best-known being his stupendous arrangement of three movements from *Petrushka*. However, other than piano music, he wrote comparatively little for solo instruments or chamber ensembles. There are various wonderful miniatures, such as the *Three Pieces for String Quartet* and the

Three Pieces for Clarinet, and, on a slightly bigger scale, a *Septet* from 1953 scored for three winds, three strings and piano. But the best of Stravinsky's chamber music is the *Octet*, one of the highlights of his middle-period neo-classicism.

Octet

With the *Octet* for wind instruments of 1922, Stravinsky completely embraced neo-classicism. The inspiration seems more Bach than Mozart, with counterpoint and strong rhythmic propulsion very much to the fore. Stravinsky claims the idea for the instrumentation came to him in a dream – whatever its origins, the combination of two trumpets, two trombones, two bassoons, a flute and a clarinet makes for a wonderfully transparent texture which, in Stravinsky's own words, "renders more evident the musical architecture". Objectivity was the point of the exercise and Stravinsky was adamant that the *Octet* was "not an 'emotive' work but a musical composition based on objective elements which are sufficient in themselves". All of which makes it sound dry, which it isn't. As in so many of his neo-classical works an element of witty subversion is constantly present – from the over-insistent bassoon ostinato that seems a foretaste of minimalism to the syncopated coda in the finale with its heavy-footed but light-hearted rumba.

Twentieth Century Classics Ensemble; Craft (Naxos; with *Symphony in C, Symphony in Three Movements* and *Dumbarton Oaks Concerto*)

Stravinsky thought that the issue of interpretation was irrelevant to this work because of the almost mechanical interaction of the voices. Still, it needs players with as much flair as ability and the scratch players assembled for this recording certainly earn their fee in a taut and extremely enjoyable performance.

Piano Music

Other than the extraordinary *Petrushka* arrangements, prepared for Artur Rubinstein, Stravinsky's piano music is largely overlooked. But there are some great pieces, the best of which are the two piano sonatas, the *Four Études* and the offbeat *Circus Polka*. The heavily Romantic early sonata was composed under Rimsky-Korsakov's guidance in 1903–04, and is extremely similar to the first sonatas of Rachmaninov, Prokofiev and Scriabin. The other sonata, written twenty years later, is also highly entertaining but in a rather different manner – it's a fiendishly difficult piece, in places giving every finger its own clearly delineated role in the musical texture.

The *Four Études* (1908) are just as difficult to play, with their complex rhythmic and polytonal experiments, but they are by no means esoteric compositions. They are light, tuneful and witty – the performer is the one who suffers, not the listener. Even wittier is the *Circus Polka* of 1942, a piece commissioned by the Barnum and Bailey Circus, who wanted a work that could be danced by the troupe's elephants. Originally written for orchestra, it was later made into a wonderfully effective showpiece for piano.

Three Movements from Petrushka: Pollini (Deutsche Grammophon; with music by Prokofiev, Boulez and Webern)

Maurizio Pollini's recording of the *Three Movements from Petrushka* is a bewilderingly brilliant performance, taking the music at a speed that defies belief. Coupled with equally stunning accounts of other key modernist piano works, this is a classic recording that nobody interested in twentieth-century music should be without.

Sonatas; Four Études; Circus Polka; Serenade; Tango; Piano Rag Music; Scherzo; Three Movements from Petrushka, etc: Jones (Nimbus; 2 CDs)

This well-recorded double-CD from Martin Jones includes most of Stravinsky's work for piano. Though Jones lacks some of Pollini's technical finesse, his performances are lively, percussive and idiomatic, making this an attractive and good-value overview.

Barbara Strozzi (1619–c.1677)

In seventeenth-century Italy the cantata – which originally simply meant music that was sung rather than music that was played (sonata) – developed into a short dramatic piece, usually for just one voice, that employed recitative, aria and arioso (a more lyrical recitative) in contrasted sections. Cantatas were privately performed by leading professional

Concerto di Donne

The exalted status of the soprano voice in Western music can be partly traced to the personal obsession of one man. In the small ducal state of Ferrara in northern Italy, Duke Alfonso II d'Este (1533–97) gathered together a select group of virtuoso female musicians to perform at his court. His fascination with the female voice led him to search out exceptional singers, not only in his own duchy but from neighbouring states, and to bring them to Ferrara. The resulting consort of women – the *concerto di donne* – was Alfonso's "musica secreta", hidden away from the public eye and the pomp of the court and its official *musica di cappella*. They would perform in the duke's private apartments for distinguished guests or for Alfonso's pleasure alone.

From a sixteenth-century perspective this was radical and, initially at least, shocking. Although women had sung and played at court before, they had done so as "donne di palazzo" – courtiers displaying the artistic accomplishments that Baldesare Castiglione had laid down in his bible of courtly manners, *The Book of the Courtier* (1528). The only professional female performers at the time were actors in the vibrant, popular theatre, the *commedia dell'arte*, who had – by courtly standards – no claims to respectability. So when the duke set about recruiting singers in 1580, he had to avoid any suggestions that these daughters of the upper middle classes, who had trained their voices in the hope of a courtly life, were being employed as professionals, since this would imply the role of servants or courtesans, rather than courtiers.

The solution was to make them ladies-in-waiting, but on the clear understanding that they sing every night on demand and be trained by his *maestro di cappella*, Luzzascho Luzzaschi, to the highest professional standard. No expense was spared in indulging the duke's passion; as one visitor observed in 1581, "the duke is so inclined to and absorbed in this thing, that he appears to have placed there not only all his delight but also the sum total of his affection. One can give him no greater pleasure than by appreciating and praising his ladies who are constantly studying new inventions."

Arranged marriages and generous salaries compensated the women for their precarious position and ambiguous status. The soprano Laura Peverara, who arrived at Ferrara in 1580, was given an apartment in the palace, 10,000 scudi as a marriage dowry, plus 300 scudi per annum each for herself, her husband (Count Annibale Turco) and her mother. In comparison, Luzzaschi was only paid 135 scudi. Peverara was joined by Anna Guarini (sister of the poet), Livia d'Arco and later the widow Tarquina Molza, whose ravishing voice had first entranced Alfonso at Modena in 1568.

At Ferrara the women would accompany themselves on the lute or viol, sometimes with Luzzaschi at the harpsichord and occasionally with an additional male singer. Their repertoire was the "beautiful and delicious" madrigals (see p.205) of Cipriano di Rore and his followers Giaches de Wert, Luzzaschi and Marc'Antonio Ingegneri, all specially rearranged as solos, duets and trios. Written in the new expressive style (the *seconda prattica*), that was closely responsive to the meaning of the words, the range of emotions in these dramatic pieces could pass swiftly through rage, anger, hope, scorn, sorrow, love and despair. It was as if, in Ferrara, the birth of opera had been anticipated by thirty years. As the fame of the women grew, so imitations flourished and before long few courts were without their own *concerto di donne*. The groundwork had been laid for the professional female musicians who, like Monteverdi's wife Claudia de Cattaneis, began to flourish in the next century.

Despite their fame and fortune, the women remained highly dependent on male protection, and in more than one case their lives ended in scandal and tragedy. Despite her best efforts to appear as respectable as possible (she refused to wear make-up or dress fashionably), Tarquina Molza was dismissed in 1589 on the unproven accusation that she was conducting an affair with a musician (said to have been Giaches de Wert). Anna Guarini fared even worse: accused of adultery by her husband, Count Alfonso Trotti, the duke insisted that she should not be harmed, but within a few months of the accusation she had been assassinated.

Dangerous Graces: Musica Secreta
(Linn)

Musica Secreta are a group of highly experienced singers dedicated to researching and performing Renaissance and Baroque music for female vocal ensemble. *Dangerous Graces* offers a selection of songs by four composers with strong links to Ferrara – de Rore, Ignegneri, Luzzaschi and de Wert – in beautifully judged and often exquisite performances.

singers before an aristocratic, and classically educated, audience.

Barbara Strozzi was one of the period's most prolific composers of cantatas. She also wrote madrigals and arias, eventually publishing seven volumes of secular pieces and one of sacred music. A virtuoso singer and lutenist, she was born illegitimately to Isabella Garzone, a servant in the household of the Venetian poet and librettist Giulio Strozzi, who may well have been her father. Giulio adopted her and seems to have planned a musical career for her, sending her to Francesco Cavalli (see p.132) to learn composition – an unusual move for a woman in the early seventeenth century.

The cultural and political elite of Venice, of which Giulio was a member, regularly met in various private salons or academies for intellectual debate. When Barbara was about eighteen Giulio founded the Accademia degli Unisoni, an offshoot of the free-thinking Accademia degli Incogniti, as a showcase for her talents. Barbara was the muse and mistress of ceremonies at these all-male gatherings which met in the Strozzi home. She would choose topics for debate, award prizes and sing to an audience of adoring men.

Despite the high status and rewards which could be achieved by women singers in this period, there was a tradition of linking female music-making with courtesans – especially in Venice. Scurrilous rumours about Barbara's virtue were rife. Though under Giulio's protection, Barbara must have been conscious that the coquettish and sensual love songs that she wrote were doubly alluring when performed by a seductive young girl, but whatever went on behind the closed doors of the Accademia degli Unisoni, only the debates were documented.

In 1652 Giulio Strozzi died and although Barbara was named as his sole heir there was little to inherit and she had to contribute to his funeral expenses out of her own pocket. Unmarried and with four illegitimate children to look after, it remains unclear whether she managed to support herself entirely through her music. Despite humble dedications of her work to wealthy aristocrats, no one took her under their protection; nor did she become involved in the burgeoning Venetian opera world, even though she had close connections with virtually all its leading figures. As far as is known, Barbara Strozzi only ever performed in private, but the mere fact that she published so much testifies to a reputation of some considerable standing.

Cantatas

Barbara Strozzi practised the "new style" of Baroque monody that reacted against the heavily textured polyphony of the Renaissance, and which took the solo voice as its musical ideal (though she also wrote some two-, three- and four-part songs). Many Venetian poets wrote texts for her – usually on the theme of the agonies of unrequited love – which she set in a free lyrical style which revealed an acute sensitivity to textual nuance and emotional content. Although she never wrote opera, her style often recalls her teacher Cavalli, especially in longer works. The difference lies in an even greater expressiveness and a formal freedom – the longer cantatas are often composed of several, highly varied sections. The cantata *Lagrimie mie* opens with a cry of grief and then seems to fuse tears and song in an eloquent chromatic outpouring, in which occasional melismas (florid note-spinning on a single vowel) underline the significance of key words. Not all the songs are melancholy: the witty *La sol fi mi re do* is positively skittish, while very clearly pointing up a connection between singing and prostitution.

To the Unknown Goddess: Bott, Chateauneuf, Kelly, Roberts (Carlton Classics)

Though it's currently unavailable, this disc is well worth seeking out for anyone interested in Strozzi's music. Few singers balance the music's mixture of formality and near-improvisatory flair as convincingly as Catherine Bott, whose fresh soprano helps re-create a sense of the domestic intimacy of the original performances.

Rydén; Musica Fiorita (Harmonia Mundi)

If you can't get hold of the above disc, this recent recording – mostly of cantatas from the Op. 2 set of 1651 – makes a good substitute. With her light, flexible voice, Susanne Rydén adopts an understated approach to this music, but with subtle word-painting and effectively florid ornamentation.

Motets

Strozzi's collection of religious pieces, mostly motets to the Virgin Mary, was published as *Sacri Musicali Affetti* in 1655 and dedicated to Anne of Austria, Archduchess of Innsbruck. The approach is more formal and restrained than in her secular works but essentially the same, with the texts

being treated in a highly personal and sometimes ecstatic fashion. High points include *Erat Petrus*, in which Strozzi creates two distinct voices to illustrate the story of St Peter's release from jail, and the lyrical motet *Mater Ana* (in praise of the Virgin Mary's mother) which has a dreamy, meditative quality.

Sacri Musicali Affetti: Kiehr; Concerto Soave
(L'Empreinte Digitale)

On this disc a selection of motets from Strozzi's only sacred collection is interspersed with instrumental works by her Venetian contemporaries Gianocelli, Merula and Biagio Marini. Soprano Maria Cristina Kiehr has a fuller and darker tone than Bott, which, along with the more powerful accompaniment of organ and strings, gives the music a definite public feel.

Josef Suk (1874–1935)

Before he had reached the age of twenty, Josef Suk was being hailed as the musical heir of Antonín Dvořák, his father-in-law and teacher. He did indeed produce work that was remarkably similar to Dvořák's – the light-hearted and tuneful *Serenade for Strings* of 1892, for example. Yet the resemblances are less important than the differences between Dvořák and a composer he once accused of writing too much in the melancholic minor keys. Suk's music has almost nothing of the joyful pastoralism that's so common to Dvořák, and in his orchestral pieces – in particular *Asrael* – Suk's use of huge orchestral forces to create vast expressions of anguish suggests closer affinities with Mahler.

Suk received his first lessons from his father, a schoolmaster and choir director in Bohemia. In 1885 he entered the Prague Conservatory where, three years later, he began studying chamber music with the cellist Dennis Wihan – a friend of both Dvořák and Richard Strauss. After six years he graduated, but remained at the conservatory for a further year in order to pursue his lessons with Wihan and begin studies with Dvořák. It was at this time that Suk joined the Czech Quartet, an ensemble with whom he was to play some four thousand concerts until his retirement in 1933. In 1898, he married Dvořák's daughter Otylka, and was by then acknowledged as one of the most important Czech composers.

When Dvořák died in 1904, followed, the next year, by Suk's wife, the ensuing emotional devastation resulted in a more ambitious type of music – epic, richly coloured and profoundly melancholic. However, his music never really established itself outside his native country, and for the rest of his life Suk remained something of a peripheral figure, bathing in the light shed by his father-in-law more than in the glory of his own reputation. Nowadays, although sporadic attempts are made to bring his music to wider audiences, he is still widely known for just one work.

Asrael Symphony

Suk was at his best working on a large scale, and his most popular work, the massive symphony of mourning called *Asrael*, is the finest example of his expressive, late-Romantic style. Taking its title from the name of the Islamic angel of death, the symphony was written in direct response to the death of Dvořák and Otylka. The five-movement symphony, with its concentration of slow movements, is saturated with a sense of loss, conveyed in music of cathartic intensity – in the depths of his grief, Suk wrote how "such a bitter blow either destroys one or bears one up on all the strength which has been lying dormant … I was saved by music". Though to an extent indebted to Mahler in its funereal idiom and to

Strauss in its orchestration, *Asrael* is one of the finest orchestral works of its time.

Bavarian Radio Symphony Orchestra; Kubelík
(Panton)

Of the various recordings available, Kubelík's powerful 1981 performance is particularly convincing, always alive to the work's many mood swings. The Bavarian RSO is in fantastic form producing a touchingly sweet sound for the Adagio, Suk's portrait of his wife.

Summer Tale

Summer Tale (1909) is another epic and highly personal work, a symphonic poem in five contrasting movements, each of which is given an evocative title. The first, "Voices of Life and Consolation", opens with a slow brooding introduction which gradually builds to a big surging melody, as if to suggest a slow return to life. The second, "Noon", is a piece of brilliantly orchestrated impressionism which suggests the perfumed heaviness of a hot summer's day. The strangest movement is the lightly scored third, "Blind Musicians", in which a pair of cor anglais play a yearning Slavic melody over strumming harps. All in all, it's another astonishingly rich and imaginative work, a brilliantly orchestrated exercise in late Romanticism, which deserves to be better known.

Czech Philharmonic Orchestra; Mackerras
(Decca; with *Fantastic Scherzo*)

This marvellously radiant account stresses Suk's artistic kinship with his contemporary Mahler, with the Czech Philharmonic really relishing the rich sonorities. The earlier *Fantastic Scherzo*, a lighter but no less rewarding work, gets a scintillatingly fresh and invigorating performance.

Arthur Sullivan (1842–1900)

"They trained him to make Europe yawn" ran George Bernard Shaw's obituary of Arthur Sullivan, referring to the "serious" music – long since forgotten – that the composer claimed he always wished to devote more time to. But Sullivan hangs on as the composing half of Gilbert and Sullivan, creators of a uniquely English blend of social satire, burlesque and sophisticated musical parody.

He was born in Lambeth in 1842, and was accepted into the Royal Academy of Music in 1856. Studies at the Leipzig Conservatory between 1858 and 1861 culminated in a performance of his Mendelssohnian overture to *The Tempest*. He wrote a ballet and in 1867 visited Vienna, where he discovered a lost Schubert score, which did his credentials as a serious musician no harm at all. In the same year he met W.S. Gilbert.

The first fruit of their partnership, *Thespis*, closed to mixed reviews, and Sullivan returned to teaching and religious composition – including the hymn "Onward Christian Soldiers". His permanent reunion with Gilbert was brought about by the impresario Richard d'Oyly Carte, who suggested the plot of what became *Trial by Jury* (1875), a work so successful that a string of collaborations followed, including *The Sorcerer* (1877), *HMS Pinafore* (1878), *The Pirates of Penzance* (1880), *Patience* (1881) and *Iolanthe* (1882).

In 1882 Sullivan was knighted. Honours notwithstanding, his frustration at his diet of

Bust of Arthur Sullivan near the Savoy Theatre.

musical frivolity came to a head with *Princess Ida* (1884), and off he stormed to tour Europe. Carte negotiated a truce between him and Gilbert, and after a lot more bickering *The Mikado* took shape. It was, in the view of Ethyl Smyth (see p.529), their masterpiece; within four years *The Gondoliers* and *The Yeomen of the Guard* were to follow.

A quarrel and lawsuit between Gilbert and Sullivan in 1890 was later patched up, but it ended their creative streak. Sullivan died ten years later, in his own estimation a shadow of what he should have been. A jaunty *Symphony in E* (1866) hints at what might have happened had Gilbert never turned up. As it is, he's forever shackled to Gilbert, with whom he created a sequence of crisp, witty and untranslatable works of art. Sullivan represents the acceptable face of Little Englandism.

The Pirates of Penzance

The inspiration for *The Pirates of Penzance* came from Stevenson's *Treasure Island*; the occasion in Gilbert's childhood when he was kidnapped by Neapolitan bandits; and from the playwright's less-than-respectful feelings for the army, the police and the House of Lords. Gilbert put his pirates at the opera's moral centre, where they display a courage and a dignity notably lacking in the authorities. The Pirate King is the very model of decency, with a nice line in vicious social commentary: his attitude is justified when it turns out that the pirates are really misdirected noblemen.

Sullivan, as was his wont, plagiarizes effectively, using Italian sources for romances such as Frederic's bel canto tenor lament "Oh is there not one maiden here", and employing Victorian oratorio pastiche for the first act's lovably pompous "Hail, Poetry!" The array of marches and dance tunes (famously Mabel's coloratura waltz "Poor Wandering One") adds much to the work's appeal, and the rich orchestral support is both more expressive and more pictorial than in anything Sullivan had written before.

Reed, Adams, Masterson, Brannigan; D'Oyly Carte Opera Chorus; Royal Philharmonic Orchestra; Godfrey (Decca; 2 CDs)

Isidore Godfrey achieves a wonderful sense of theatre, and were the singing and orchestral playing not so perfect, you might think it was a live set. Donald Adams is magnificent as the Pirate King, Owen Brannigan is gloriously over the top as the Police Sergeant, and John Reed is secure as the Major-General. But the vocal highlight is Valerie Masterson's affectionate, even seductive, Mabel.

The Mikado

Librettist and composer were at their most epigrammatic and imaginative in *The Mikado*, which was their longest-running show. A hugely popular exhibition of Japanese products in Knightsbridge suggested the setting, but the work's orientalism is only skin-deep: the absurdly convoluted tale, tying together such characters as Ko-Ko the Lord High Executioner, Pooh-Bah "the Lord High Everything Else", the wandering minstrel Nanki-Poo and the lovely Pitti-Sing ("Pretty Thing" in baby talk), is a satire aimed at the absurdities of British society. The wit of Sullivan's music can be gauged by the fact that *The Mikado* manages to incorporate a genuine Japanese tune (used for the entrance of the Mikado himself), an English madrigal and a Bach fugue, while still sounding completely coherent. Victorian ballads are nicely set against the more acerbic pastiches, and the essential cruelty of much of Gilbert's text is perfectly balanced by the overall sunniness of Sullivan's sparkling music. Many of the work's best numbers have lodged in the English collective unconscious: Ko-Ko's "Tit-willow" refrain, for example, will be recognized by many who think they don't know any Gilbert and Sullivan.

Adams, Rolfe Johnson, Suart, van Allan, McLaughlin; Welsh National Opera Orchestra and Chorus; Mackerras (Telarc)

This is the finest of Mackerras's G&S recordings for Telarc, and is certainly the best-sung *Mikado* on disc, with a world-class operatic cast really letting their hair down. However, not only is the dialogue omitted, but the overture is cut, and though there's an economic benefit to editing the score to fit onto a single CD, you are left with a savagely trimmed object. That said, the performance is unmatched, and no rival recording is complete anyway.

Karol Szymanowski (1882–1937)

Karol Szymanowski, the most prominent Polish composer of the twentieth century, is sometimes compared to Bartók in the way he forged a distinctive style out of the folk music of his native land. But there's another important component to his achievement: many of his greatest scores constitute a personal celebration of Dionysus and ecstatic love, exemplified by works such as the opera *King Roger*, *Symphony No. 3*, and the two violin concertos, all of which create an opulent sound-world full of yearning melodies and filigree decoration. If any music could be said to be heavily perfumed, it's Szymanowski's.

Szymanowski was born in Tymoszówka in the Ukraine, then part of the Russian empire. One of five children of well-to-do and highly cultured parents, his early life seems to have been a continuous round of dances, plays and music. Of the five children in the family, three went on to become professional musicians – his sister Stasia became an opera singer and starred as Roxana in the first performance of *King Roger*.

Yet in his early years Szymanowski found little to inspire him in Poland, a country then partitioned between Germany, Russia and the Habsburg empire. His musical interests lay with foreign composers such as Richard Strauss, Debussy, Scriabin and Stravinsky, and he felt a deep affinity with Italy, Sicily and North Africa, regions he explored in 1911 and 1914 with Stefan Spiess, who was probably his lover. The cultures of ancient Greece, Norman Sicily and the Arab world had a huge and lasting impact on his music.

Exempt from military service, Szymanowski spent most of World War I in Tymoszówka where, despite anxiety about the conflict, he wrote much of his finest music. However, the Russian Revolution of 1917 completely overturned Szymanowski's world and he was forced to leave his beloved family home which was later destroyed by the Bolsheviks. Unable to compose amidst the upheaval, instead he wrote a novel called *Efebos*, an exploration of homosexual love, most of which was destroyed by fire in Warsaw in 1939.

An independent Poland emerged out of the chaos of World War I and, like many Polish intellectuals, Szymanowski was determined to create a truly national art. In the exotic pieces for which he first gained international recognition – the *Symphony No. 3*, the *Violin Concerto No. 1* and *King Roger* – he resisted using folk material out of a fear of its limitations ("Poland's national music should not be the stiffened ghost of the polonaise or mazurka"). It was his ongoing analysis of the music of Stravinsky that finally revealed to him how folk elements could be used in a modern and unsentimental fashion.

Woodcut of Szymanowski by E. Ricardo (c. 1921).

Though continuing to travel widely as a pianist (to France, England, the USA and Cuba), much of his time was spent at the resort of Zakopane, a small town at the heart of the distinctive folk culture of the Tatra mountains. A key member of a group who called themselves "the emergency ambulance service of Tatra culture", Szymanowski befriended the Obrochta family – a leading group of village musicians – and began to notate the strange and idiosyncratic sounds of *góral* (highland) music. The main work to emerge from this research was the ballet *Harnasie* (1923–31), a tale of highland brigands culminating in a village wedding, a score which includes many genuine *góral* dances. Alongside *Harnasie*, Szymanowski worked on his austerely beautiful *Stabat Mater* (1926), a piece that uses the ancient traditions of Polish church music, but in a less self-conscious and bombastic way than *Harnasie* uses folk melodies.

During the last decade of his life Szymanowski took over the directorship of the Warsaw conservatory but suffered increasingly from health problems as the first signs of tuberculosis appeared. This was not a fruitful period as a composer, but he completed two major works, the *Symphonie concertante* for piano and orchestra and the *Violin Concerto No. 2*, both of which have characteristics of Polish folk music, combined with the lush exoticism of his earlier style. His last years were a sad story of failing health, financial hardship and neglect in Poland, but at least he had growing success abroad – *King Roger* was triumphantly received in Prague, and *Harnasie* likewise in Paris. Szymanowski died in a sanatorium in Lausanne and received a huge state funeral in Kraków, with the Obrochta family playing beside his tomb.

King Roger

The opening of *Król Roger* (1924) is extraordinary: the curtain rises on a service in Palermo cathedral during the twelfth-century reign of King Roger, as choral music evokes clouds of incense and glistening mosaics. A mysterious shepherd arrives to preach a new faith of ecstasy and love ("My god is as young and beautiful as I am") – he is the embodiment of the union between Christ, Dionysus and Eros, an idea sketched by Szymanowski in his novel *Efebos*. Roger's wife Roxana and many of his subjects find the shepherd's message intoxicating, and the opera culminates in a ritual in an ancient Greek theatre: the shepherd is transformed into Dionysus, while Roger – also transformed by the experience – salutes Apollo and the rising sun.

The opera is rarely performed, perhaps because it is essentially contemplative rather than dramatic. The music, though, has some breathtaking set pieces – the opening religious service, the arias of the shepherd and Roxana, a wild Dionysiac dance and the final hymn. Szymanowski was working on the score just after hearing Ravel's *Daphnis et Chloé* in America, and it shows the composer indulging in orientalist fantasy at its most full-blown.

Hampson, Szmytka, Langridge, Minkiewicz; City of Birmingham Symphony Chorus and Orchestra; Rattle (EMI; 2 CDs; with *Symphony No. 4*)

Simon Rattle has made Szymanowski a speciality and his sumptuous 1998 *King Roger* is the most satisfying recording available. The singers are excellent, with Thomas Hampson conveying the king's authority and psychological confusion. But what raises this recording above its rivals is the way Rattle relishes every colouristic detail of the scoring while also managing to generate real dramatic tension.

Symphony No. 3

Szymanowski's *Symphony No. 3*, subtitled "Song of the Night" (1916), is the most exotic of his large-scale compositions. Fascinated by Eastern mysticism, he turned to a Polish translation of the thirteenth-century Persian poet Rumi, the founder of the Mevlevi (or whirling dervishes). Like other Sufi sects, the Mevlevi strove to attain an ecstatic union with God, and the poem which inspired the symphony celebrates the wonder and mystery of the divine as manifest in a glorious night sky. Szymanowski's response is to conjure up an extraordinarily opulent soundscape, in which the vivid orchestral writing is enriched by the addition of a tenor soloist and chorus, and extra percussion including celesta and piano. Written in one continuous, tripartite movement, the work often seems more tone poem than symphony, not least in the way exquisite instrumental combinations are contrasted with the full force of the orchestra. Amidst all the languor and opulence, there's a continuous sense of anguished striving, which reaches fulfillment in two overwhelming climaxes at the end of each of the outer movements.

City of Birmingham Symphony Orchestra; Rattle (EMI; with *Stabat Mater & Litany to the Virgin Mary*)

All Szymanowski's colouristic effects shine through on this wonderful recording, particularly the languorous melodies on the solo violin and the glittering flashes on piano, harp and percussion. After this performance you can understand Lutosławski's comment that listening to this music was like opening a gate onto a fantastic garden.

Violin Concertos

The violin concertos are a good place for those new to Szymanowski to start. The first, written in 1916, seems to have been inspired by Tadeusz Micinski's poem, "May Night", a fervent evocation of love amid the rich fecundity of nature. In this rhapsodic one-movement fantasy (like the *Symphony No. 3*, a virtual tone poem), the violin soloist resembles an elusive and volatile free spirit, travelling – sometimes anxiously, sometimes ecstatically – through the multi-hued landscape of the orchestral writing. The second concerto (1933), which like the first was dedicated to Szymanowski's friend the violinist Pavel Kochanski, is also in one movement but with four clear divisions. This time the solo part is leaner, earthier, more pensive and frequently in the violin's lower register – a possible reflection of Szymanowski's immersion in Polish folk music. The folkish elements are most apparent following a mid-point cadenza (written by Kochanski), after which a melancholy lullaby alternates with wild dance tunes.

Zehetmair; City of Birmingham Symphony Orchestra; Rattle (EMI; with *Three Paganini Caprices & Romance*)

There are now several excellent versions of the violin concertos in the catalogue, but this one is in a league of its own. It sounds as though Zehetmair and Rattle have pondered long and hard over these superb works, to produce multidimensional readings which have an almost organic feel.

Harnasie

Though sometimes called the Polish Bartók, Szymanowski is far less rigorous and economical with his material, favouring a more rhapsodic and colourful approach. Typical of the composer's late style is *Harnasie*, his most ambitious attempt at reworking highland folk music in symphonic form. Written as a "Ballet-pantomime" between 1927 and 1931, the scenario tells of the abduction of a peasant bride-to-be by the outlaw Harnas and his followers, the Harnasie. Divided into nine scenes, the music is scored for a massive orchestra plus tenor soloist and chorus. The work begins with a beautiful evocation of spring's arrival and the leading of sheep to the mountain pastures. While the vivid clarity of the orchestration suggests Stravinsky's early ballets, Szymanowski's treatment of the typical *góral* melodies and dances of a small village band is much more overblown. Nevertheless, there is no denying *Harnasie*'s vigour and sheer dramatic impact.

Robinson; City of Birmingham Symphony Orchestra and Chorus; Rattle (EMI; with *Songs of a Fairy-Tale Princess* and *Eight Love Songs of Hafiz*)

Once again Simon Rattle's flair for revealing every strand of the rich orchestral colouring, the sheer vivid immediacy of the work, is what makes this particular recording so alluring. It would have been good to have had a more idiomatic tenor than Timothy Robinson, but it in no way detracts from the impact of the performance.

Stabat Mater

Szymanowski made a study of sixteenth-century Polish church music in preparation for writing the *Stabat Mater*, and the results are plain in the simplicity and purity of the piece, which makes an interesting counterweight to the lush scores of *King Roger* and *Symphony No. 3*. Gone is the over-chromatic harmony that dominates so much of his earlier work, replaced by simpler chords and finely placed tensions and dissonances. Szymanowski was not a religious man, and perhaps his indifference to the established Church helped him to maintain the detachment that makes this his masterpiece. Either way, the work certainly contains some of the composer's most beautiful music. Szymanowski described it as a peasant Requiem (the text is in Polish, not Latin), and it has the same qualities of naive directness as the paintings that adorn some of the ancient wooden churches of southern Poland.

Szmytka, Garrison; City of Birmingham Symphony Orchestra; Rattle (EMI; with *Symphony No. 3 & Litany to the Virgin Mary*)

If this triumphant recording can't win new fans for Szymanowski, then nothing can. Rattle controls the ebb and flow perfectly, moving from rapt intensity to outbursts of passion, and the opening of the last movement, with the soprano solo rising from soft dissonances with the clarinets to a glowing major chord with the chorus, is truly sublime.

Hossa, Marciniek, Brek; Warsaw Philharmonic Orchestra and Choir; Wit (Naxos; with *Veni Creator, Litany to the Virgin Mary, Demeter* and *Penthesilea*)

The Naxos Szymanowski series provides a sound (and cheap) alternative to Rattle on EMI. Many are conducted by a superb Polish Szymanowski advocate, Antoni Wit. His recent *Stabat Mater* recording is especially fine – not least for the radiantly beautiful singing of soprano Iwona Hossa.

String Quartets

String quartets do not come much more febrile than Szymanowski's *Quartet No. 1* in C. Written in the autumn of 1917, it has the same rapturous quality as the *Violin Concerto No. 1*, with the first violin seemingly possessed of a restless desire to pull itself away from its more earthbound colleagues. Sudden changes of mood abound, but the first two movements seem to occupy the same mental landscape as Schoenberg's *Verklärte Nacht* – the slow movement contains some of the most mysterious and exotic sounds you are likely to hear in a quartet. Ten years later Szymanowski entered his *String Quartet No. 2* for a competition in Philadelphia. The tone is fractionally bleaker and more astringent (the first movement alternates lushness with extreme spookiness) and may reflect both an awareness of the more aggressive quartet writing of Bartók (whose *Quartet No. 3* won the Philadelphia competition) and Szymanowski's study of Polish folk music.

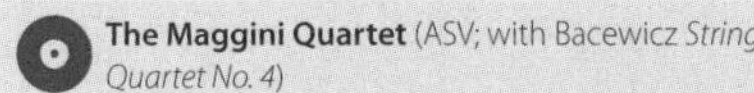
The Maggini Quartet (ASV; with Bacewicz *String Quartet No. 4*)

Both quartets, with their kaleidoscopic changes of sonority and texture, are very difficult to play well. The constant flow of ideas, and the different vocal groupings which seem to emerge from within the quartet, can tax the most experienced players. The Maggini Quartet captures all the shades of these colourful pieces with the greatest subtlety and an almost uncanny sense of ensemble.

Mythes

Szymanowski's passion for the sensuous beauty of the Hellenistic world finds its perfect expression in the best of his works for violin and piano, the *Mythes* of 1915. Written while staying on a friend's estate in the Ukraine, the three poetic movements are remarkable for the way the virtuosity of the violin part is always at the service of atmosphere rather than display. Inspired by three sexually charged Greek myths ("La fontaine d'Aréthuse", "Narcisse" and "Dryades et Pan"), the prevailing mood is one of rapturous otherworldliness: dreamlike yet vividly intense. The Debussy of *L'après-midi…* is a clear influence but there's a startling originality in the way Szymanowski exploits the full sonic range of both instruments to conjure up the natural world – rippling water, buzzing bees, an impending storm and, most magically of all, the pipes of the god Pan himself.

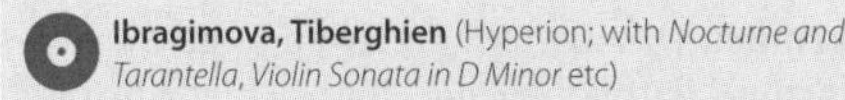
Ibragimova, Tiberghien (Hyperion; with *Nocturne and Tarantella*, *Violin Sonata in D Minor* etc)

It's hard to imagine a better recording of Szymanowski's complete music for violin and piano. Alina Ibragimova has a wonderfully full and rich tone but also great control and she brings a fiery intensity to this music which is wholly appropriate. Her pianist partner, Cédric Tiberghien, is no less sensitive and together they achieve the perfect balance between feverish excitement and hushed rapture.

Piano Music

Szymanowski was a gifted pianist who composed a wealth of fine music for the instrument. His early works, championed by his friend and compatriot Artur Rubinstein, reveal a profound debt to Chopin (his respect for whom never diminished) but he was also receptive to more harmonically daring composers (Scriabin in particular) and from the very beginning his piano music had a highly coloured exoticism. His musical horizons widened during World War I and he developed his own individual impressionist style, composing atmospheric short pieces – often with a literary inspiration – that resembled concentrated, condensed tone poems.

Overt references to the indigenous music of Poland only appear in Szymanowski's later compositions, following his discovery of the *góral* music of the Tatra mountains. Outstanding among these folk-inspired piano pieces are the *Twenty Mazurkas*, Opus 50, written in the mid-1920s. Like Chopin, Szymanowski pushes the form way beyond its origins as a dance in triple time to create a set of varied and idiosyncratic pieces coloured by the melodic shape and harmonies of *góral* music.

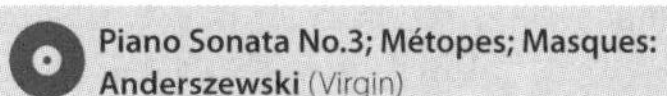
Piano Sonata No.3; Métopes; Masques: Anderszewski (Virgin)

Piotr Anderszewski brings out the inner voicings and the magical colouring of the miniatures with the most assured and delicate touch. "Shéhérazade", the first and longest of the *Masques*, dazzles through the variety of his tone but he is no less convincing in the sonata, relishing the sheer energy of its assertive last moment fugue.

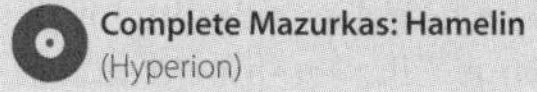
Complete Mazurkas: Hamelin (Hyperion)

Absolutely thrilling playing from Marc-André Hamelin, who really gets the measure of this complex, quixotic music, both in the delicacy of the Satiesque *Mazurka No. 1* and in the more assertive and outgoing works. He makes the rhythmic quirkiness of these pieces seem entirely natural, with a brilliantly applied and completely idiomatic rubato.

Toru Takemitsu (1930–1996)

Largely self-taught, Toru Takemitsu turned his back on Japanese music in favour of Western models in the wake of his wartime experiences. The textural delicacy of his work is clearly indebted to Debussy and Messiaen, and the eloquent silences recall Cage, and yet his love of timbre for its own sake has always indicated the strength of his native musical heritage, which he eventually came to embrace openly. On occasions, his music can seem a rather glib fusion of East and West, but at his best, Takemitsu is a refined sensualist whose shimmering soundscapes evoke a magical world that is both aurally precise and yet intensely dreamlike. Many of the poetic titles that he gave to his pieces evoke the presence of water, and there is a recurring quality of purity and evanescence in much of his work.

Although Western music was banned in Japan during the war, Takemitsu's first contact with it came during his military service (he had been conscripted) when he heard a recording of the-French popular song, "Parlez-moi d'amour". After the war Takemitsu worked at an American military base where he was able to listen to the US Armed Forces Network which played both classical and popular music. Throughout his life he was to remain extremely receptive to a wide range of music (he even made arrangements of Beatles songs), but during the 1950s he was especially interested in the European avant-garde. Together with a group of fellow musicians and artists, he set up an "experimental workshop", Jikken Kobo, in 1951. Influenced by *musique concrète*, his electronic works included *Mizu no kyoku* (1960), a piece (the title of which translates as *Water Music*) made exclusively from the recorded sounds of water.

The first work to make a real impact in the West was the *Requiem for Strings* (1957), which was highly praised by Stravinsky, and in 1964 Takemitsu was invited to Hawaii to give a series of lectures with John Cage. It was chiefly through Cage's fascination with Japanese culture that Takemitsu came to realize the value of his native traditions. In the early 1960s Takemitsu began a serious reassessment of traditional Japanese instruments, which he employed for the first time in the film score *Seppuku* (1962). The combination of the lute-like *biwa* and *shakuhachi* (bamboo flute) can be heard in his most famous orchestral score, *November Steps* (1967), and in *Ran* (1985) – one of the best of his 93 film scores.

Takemitsu's work is sometimes criticized for a lack of structure and thematic development. But these are Western musical preoccupations and it is better, when listening to his work, to let the

Toru Takemitsu.

music unfold in its particular unruffled way. The aesthetics of Japanese gardens (which Takemitsu loved) make a useful analogy when describing his music: there's a similar interplay between nature and artifice as well as a sense of an exquisite placing of aural elements to create a balanced and harmonious whole.

Orchestral Music

Takemitsu's orchestral works vary considerably, but his overriding preoccupations – sonority and slow-paced musical unfolding – are ever-present. In *November Steps* (1967) an almost competitive dialogue between the Japanese instruments takes place well in front of the orchestra, which ebbs and flows in and out of the soloists like a multi-voiced and eloquent chorus. The language is gestural and splintered (not unlike Boulez), greatly increasing the overall impression of highly coloured abstraction. Ten years later another large orchestral work entitled *A Flock Descends into the Pentagonal Garden* proved a popular success. It was inspired by a particularly vivid dream of the composer's and is more cohesive in its orchestration, with an almost Mahlerian sumptuousness. Even richer is the *Viola Concerto* (1984), subtitled "A String Around Autumn", in which the soloist functions as an observer in "an imaginary landscape". An appropriately warm-hued and mellow work, at times it reaches a rhapsodic fervour reminiscent of Szymanowski.

Quotation of Dream (1991), for two pianists and orchestra, is subtitled with a line from Emily Dickinson ("Say sea, take me!"). Typical of Takemitsu's later music, the work is episodic in structure but lent an overall unity by a principal idea, in this case a harmonic one. However, *Quotation of Dream* is unusual in the composer's output in that quotations from another work – Debussy's *La Mer* – are woven subtly into the score.

November Steps; Eclipse; Viola Concerto: Imai, Yokoyama, Tsuruta; Saito Kinen Orchestra; Ozawa (Philips)

Seijri Ozawa is a specialist in the more impassioned masters of modern music, and he brings a somewhat full-blooded approach to Takemitsu's work. In *November Steps* he manages to make the often dense orchestral writing markedly clean and clear, while in the *Viola Concerto*, with its closer relationship between soloist and orchestra, he provides a vigorous counterpart to Nobuko Imai's splendidly ripe tone.

Day Signal; Quotation of Dream; How Slow the Wind; Twill by Twilight; Archipelago S; Dream/Window; Night Signal: Crossley, Serkin; London Sinfonietta; Knussen (Deutsche Grammophon)

This disc features a fine selection of orchestral and ensemble works written in the latter years of Takemitsu's life. Pianists Paul Crossley and Peter Serkin give a subtle and transparent performance of *Quotation of Dream*, and the London Sinfonietta realize Takemitsu's post-Debussian textures brilliantly under the supervision of Oliver Knussen, who was a good friend of Takemitsu.

Chamber Music

The individuality of Takemitsu's voice can arguably be heard best in his small-scale works, where his diaphanous textures and subtle colours make an intense and startling impact. The string quartet *A Way a Lone* (1980) and the piano trio *Between Tides* (1993), for example, both inhabit opulent sound-worlds and feature string writing that recalls that of Berg in its timbral variety. And the seeming consistency of pacing in both of these pieces hides finely controlled gradations of tempo. A more rarefied atmosphere pervades the string quartet *Landscape I* (1961), thanks to subtle use of repetition and silence, and the direction that the musicians should play entirely without vibrato.

Takemitsu also wrote chamber works for more idiosyncratic combinations of instruments. *Waves* (1977), for example, is a much more dramatic work for the startling combination of clarinet, bass drum, French horn and trombones. This is a highly atmospheric piece, with the looming background presence of the drum – sometimes soft, sometimes loud – suggesting an impending but never realized violence. Throughout much of the piece the other instruments, the clarinet in particular, seem to simulate the breathy vitality of the *shakuhachi*. A more bluesy final section subsides into the ghostly sounds of the wind players breathing into their instruments.

Between Tides; Landscape I; Distance de fée; Rocking Mirror Daybreak; Hika; A Way a Lone: Ensemble Kaï (BIS)

The works gathered together on this disc span Takemitsu's compositional career, providing an excellent overview of his chamber output. The Ensemble Kaï play in impressive ensemble and admirably achieve the all-important timbral subtlety, something that is helped by the clear and well-balanced sound quality.

Thomas Tallis (c.1505–1585)

Tallis's powerful but ethereal sacred music was written during one of the most turbulent periods of English history (see p.565). Each of the four Tudor monarchs whom he served possessed widely different attitudes to religious affairs. This not only meant that he was forced to write sometimes in Latin and sometimes in English, but also resulted in regular changes of musical style. His earliest music adopts a peculiarly English, florid style of polyphony, quite similar to that of Taverner (see p.571); then during the reforms of Edward VI he was obliged to write much more simple and direct music, in line with the rationalization of the liturgy; finally, in Elizabeth I's reign, he developed a tighter and more lucid polyphonic manner, one which became increasingly sensitive to the meaning of the words being set.

Next to nothing is known of Tallis's early life, but in 1540 his livelihood was directly influenced by the volatile religious climate when he lost his job as organist at Waltham Abbey in Essex, following the dissolution of the monasteries. He received twenty shillings' payment and a further twenty shillings as compensation. After brief employment at Canterbury Cathedral, Tallis joined the royal household in 1543 as a Gentleman of the Chapel Royal, a position he maintained until his death. His duties as composer and organist earned him significant rewards from his royal patrons: in 1557 the Catholic Queen Mary granted him a 21-year lease on a lucrative property in Kent, and in 1575 the Protestant Queen Elizabeth gave him, and his younger colleague William Byrd (see p.122), the exclusive right to print and publish music. Their first publication, which came out in the same year, was the *Cantiones Sacrae*, a collection containing seventeen Latin motets by each composer. It was not a financial success, and the two men petitioned the queen as a result of which they were granted a joint lease on another property. Tallis died in 1585 and was buried in the church of St Alphege at Greenwich.

There has been some debate over Tallis's religious convictions: it is thought by some that he was merely a pragmatist who adapted to the demands of successive monarchs, but there is strong evidence to suggest that (like Byrd) he remained a committed Catholic throughout his life, probably managing to escape persecution because of his connections with highly placed recusants, such as the Roper family. Evidence of recusancy can also be seen in later works, such as the *Lamentations of Jeremiah*, which contain a heartfelt plea to Jerusalem to turn to the one true God, widely interpreted as a call for a return to the Catholic faith.

Though best known for his sacred choral music, Tallis also wrote a number of instrumental works. As an active organist for well over fifty years, it is likely that he wrote many more than the small number of keyboard compositions that survive – the best of which are highly original. His handful of works for viol consort include arrangements of partsongs and two accomplished *In Nomine* settings. These last two are interesting for their signs of a development of a style more suited to string instruments, rather than voices, particularly evident in the repetition of short phrases separated by rests at the end of the piece as a way of heightening tension.

Music and Reformation in England

No one escaped the political and religious upheavals that convulsed England in the sixteenth century. Though the period is usually known as the English Reformation, that straightforward phrase belies the seismic changes that occurred between the dissolution of the monasteries by Henry VIII in the 1530s and the accession of James I seventy years later. In little more than two generations, England witnessed Henry's bad-tempered break with Rome, the aggressively Protestant policies of his son Edward VI, a militant return to Catholicism under Mary I, and finally the so-called "Elizabethan Settlement", by which Elizabeth I and her ministers attempted to hold together the fractured wings of English religion.

Church musicians found themselves balancing on a series of religious faultlines, yet what resulted was arguably the most exciting period ever to occur in English music. Up to the 1540s, the country's choral traditions had been tied to the ancient practices of worship at the monasteries and chantries, in which florid polyphony was the dominant style. The first major turning point came in 1549 under Edward VI, with the publication of the *Book of Common Prayer*, an English-language volume influenced by Luther and Calvin (see p.413). The reformist Thomas Cranmer signalled the new regime when he wrote – somewhat ominously – that music should "not be full of notes", but instead communicate the meaning of the words, ideally in a strictly syllabic arrangement for full congregation. It was a call heeded by John Marbeck, organist at St George's Chapel, Windsor, who the next year produced his homely setting *The Common Praier Noted*.

Yet the authorities did permit some choral singing, and under composers such as Christopher Tye (c.1505–c.1571), John Sheppard (1515–c.1559) and William Mundy (c.1529–c.1591), polyphony cautiously began to reappear – often in the form of imitative counterpoint balanced by solid homophony. The new prayer book also offered opportunities to perform non-liturgical texts, the main result being the development of English-language anthems. Early anthems simply reworked Latin motets with English translations, but they evolved into a fully mature genre: the so-called "verse" anthem, which alternates expressive solo lines with passages for full choir. A colleague of Marbeck's, Richard Farrant (d.1581), wrote several innovative examples, though his most memorable works hark back to the earlier syllabic style.

The period's most talented musicians were undeniably Thomas Tallis (c.1505–1585) and William Byrd (c.1537–1623), for whom crisis seems to have acted, if anything, as impetus rather than impediment. Tallis found himself unemployed after the monasteries went, but soon gained work in Windsor, and went on to write music for no fewer than four English monarchs, moving from sparse Edwardian anthems to elaborate Marian polyphony with impressive ease. Several of Tallis's works exist in rival English and Latin versions; appropriately enough, scholars disagree about which represent his final intentions.

Byrd, by contrast, clung obstinately to the old faith, and composed some of his finest religious music in the teeth of official opposition – although he was lucky enough to enjoy the protection of powerful Catholic patrons. The motets in his second volume of *Cantiones Sacrae* (1589) linger pointedly on desolation and exile, themes of bitter significance for English Catholics. Even more striking are the three masses Byrd wrote in the early 1590s, in defiance of rulings outlawing the rite (see p.123). Agonized as often as they are ecstatic, full of anguish as well as joy, these works attest to the force of Byrd's belief, but never seem able to escape the fraught circumstances of their composition.

Mary and Elizabeth at Westminster Abbey: Westminster Abbey Choir; O'Donnell (Hyperion)

An excellent place to begin: major works by Sheppard, Tallis and Byrd alongside a selection of exquisite rarities by Mundy, Tye and Robert White. The performances are alert and beautifully judged, O'Donnell coaxing impressively sensitive singing out of his all-male choir – the trebles are particularly airy during Byrd's *O Lord, Make thy Servant Elizabeth*.

Treasures of Tudor England: The Sixteen; Christophers (CORO)

This superlative recording by a mixed-voice choir offers music by two of Byrd's contemporaries, Robert Parsons and Robert White, and an exact contemporary of Tallis, Christopher Tye. Though all three wrote for various Protestant authorities, it's their Latin music that feels most vivid, its arching lines harking back to a much older compositional tradition.

Chirk Castle Part-Books: The Brabant Ensemble; Rice (Hyperion)

All the music on this beautifully sung disc is in English and comes from the choir books of Chirk Castle chapel. Nine composers are represented, and it's a measure of the wealth of the talent then available that the lesser known figures, such as Edmund Hooper, Thomas Caustun and William Deane, are not eclipsed by the likes of Byrd, Tallis, Mundy and Sheppard.

Thomas Tallis – The Complete Works: Chapelle du Roi; Dixon (Signum; 9 CDs)

To coincide with the five hundredth anniversary of Tallis's birth, Signum released this nine-CD boxed-set containing the composer's complete works, admirably performed by Chapelle du Roi under Alistair Dixon. Recorded over the best part of a decade, it's a splendid achievement, and gathers together every last fragment of Tallis's music, including all his instrumental works, some never recorded before.

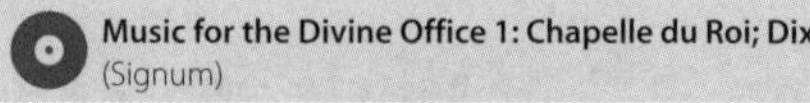

Music for the Divine Office 1: Chapelle du Roi; Dixon (Signum)

The plainchant, which forms such an integral part of this music, sometimes feels slightly rushed, but it's beautifully intoned nonetheless, while the polyphony is characterized by warm and expressive singing. This group doesn't strive for the ethereal blend of, say, the Tallis Scholars, but takes a more soloistic approach, with individual voices rising out of and falling back into the texture.

Music for the Latin Liturgy

A significant proportion of Tallis's output was written for the cycle of eight services that would have been sung daily in Latin Christendom – Matins, Lauds, Prime, Terce, Sext, None, Vespers and Compline – but now survive only in monastic rites. Spanning the middle decades of the sixteenth century, these works take the form of plainchant alternated with polyphonic refrains and show Tallis's musical technique evolving and absorbing continental influences. He begins to explore the device of imitation, perfected earlier by Flemish composers such as Josquin Desprez, and also starts harmonizing around a cantus firmus (a plainchant "tune") – already a standard procedure on the continent. With this latter technique he produced very expressive and solemn music, such as the seven-part *Loquebantur variis linguis*, in which the multiple voices chatter and weave their way around the plainchant melody to create a complex and dense texture. A similar effect is achieved in the six-part *Videte Miraculum*, technically and imaginatively one of Tallis's truly great works; the slowly unfolding lines convey a sense of hushed awe and the listener is caught up by the music's spellbinding power.

English Church Music

Tallis was one of the first composers to write for the new Anglican liturgy, introduced in 1549. The Protestant clergy wanted clarity and ease of understanding: this meant services in English and simple music that didn't distract from the words – "one syllable one note" was Archbishop Cranmer's famous injunction. Despite the severe constraints this placed on the composer, Tallis rose to the challenge admirably, producing uncomplicated, yet artistically satisfying works. His wonderfully concise anthem *If Ye Love Me*, for example, shows that he was able to conform to the requirement for plainly heard words, unobscured by elaborate musical detail, while still managing to convey a range of emotion through simple melodies enhanced by bold harmonies. Equally perfect in their simplicity are the metrical psalm settings Tallis wrote for Archbishop Parker's psalter, among the finest of early harmonized tunes for congregational use. Many are still in current use as hymn tunes, while one, "Why fum'th in fight", inspired Vaughan Williams's celebrated *Fantasia on a Theme by Thomas Tallis* (see p.597).

The Complete English Anthems: The Tallis Scholars; Phillips (Gimmel)

The Tallis Scholars at their incomparable best. Each anthem is subtly and sensitively shaped, and the singers' remarkable clarity of tone perfectly serves the simplicity of the music; Archbishop Cranmer himself could not have asked for more.

Elizabethan Motets

Elizabeth, although Protestant, retained an affection for Latin liturgy and ceremony, and composers in her employ, such as Tallis, were free to compose Latin-texted music. Tallis, by now in his sixties, was at the height of his powers; he had fully mastered the continental technique of imitation, and the natural rhythm and meaning of the words now took greater place in shaping the music. This can be seen in the motet *Salvator Mundi*, for example; the striking rising intervals on the word "salvator" point heavenwards, while the homophony used for the words "auxiliare nobis" gives added directness to the appeal for help. Similar techniques, combined with choice use of dissonance, are used in the two celebrated settings of the *Lamentations of Jeremiah*. These are sombre and heartfelt pieces that convincingly express the spirit of their melancholy words, but are still characterized by restraint – it would be left to younger, bolder composers, such as Byrd, to invest polyphonic writing with even greater intensity and imaginative power. That said, nothing in English choral music can quite compare with Tallis's masterpiece, the extraordinary and unforgettable motet *Spem in Alium* for five eight-part choirs. Possibly written for the fortieth birthday of Queen Elizabeth, *Spem in Alium* uniquely combines complex and delicate polyphonic writing with clamorous tutti passages, and is one of the greatest achievements of all English music.

Spem in Alium; Lamentations of Jeremiah; Salvator Mundi: Winchester Cathedral Choir; Hill
(Hyperion; with other Tallis vocal works)

This recording is remarkable both for the outstanding Winchester Cathedral Choir and for the resonant acoustic of that vast cathedral, which adds an extremely dramatic quality to the sound. The opening of *Spem in Alium*, with its gradual accumulation of voices, is particularly thrilling, while the lighter-textured five-part motets have a suitable quality of rapt concentration.

Lamentations of Jeremiah: The Hilliard Ensemble
(ECM)

The all-male Hilliard Ensemble is renowned for the ethereal beauty of its sound, and the group doesn't disappoint in this recording of the *Lamentations*. The five voices all enjoy equal status, allowing the listener to appreciate the interplay of the parts. The disc also contains the little-known *Mass for Four Voices*; it's a plainer work but is beautifully crafted and sung here with consummate mastery.

Giuseppe Tartini (1692–1770)

Of the many Italian composer-violinists who followed in the wake of Arcangelo Corelli, none was more highly regarded than Giuseppe Tartini. Like Corelli he was unusual in that he wrote only instrumental music, extending the technical range of the violin in ever more expressive directions. Tartini composed in the new *galant* style, favouring strong singable melodies and simple, often dissonant, harmonies. As with his younger contemporary, C.P.E. Bach, the emphasis was on translating powerful feelings into sound, and several works are prefaced by poetical quotations indicating the inspiration behind a piece. But of the many concertos and sonatas that he wrote, only one – the so-called *Devil's Trill Sonata* – has become a staple of the violin repertoire.

Tartini was born in Pirano, on the Adriatic coast (then on the edge of the Venetian republic, now part of Slovenia), the son of a merchant in the salt trade. His parents intended him for the Church, but in 1708 he left his native region to study law at Padua University and, according to legend, perfect his fencing skills. Two years later, shortly after his father's death, his marriage to Elisabetta Premazore incurred the combined wrath of her guardian, the Bishop of Padua, and Tartini's own supporters. Forced to leave for Assisi, he remained there for three years, improving his violin playing and studying composition – probably with the organist of the Franciscan basilica, Bohuslav Cernohorsky.

From around 1714 he started earning his living as a violinist, in churches, academies and opera houses, but a performance by a leading virtuoso, Francesco Veracini, made him realize that he still needed to work on his technique – in particular his bowing. By now able to return to Padua, in 1721 he was appointed to the important position of leader of the orchestra of St Anthony's basilica. He remained in the job for the rest of his life, apart from a three-year spell in Prague (1723–26) where he worked for the aristocratic Kinsky family and performed at the coronation of Emperor Charles VI as king of Bohemia.

In 1728 Tartini founded an important violin school in Padua which attracted students from across Europe and became known as "the school of the nations". His favourite pupil, Pietro Nardini, became the leading player of the next generation and helped refine Tartini's style into something even more elegant and sensitive. Another pupil, Maddalena Sirmen, was the recipient of a "Letter" outlining the fundamentals of violin playing, in which special emphasis was placed on mastery of the bow. This, along

Contemporary portrait of Giuseppe Tartini.

with his treatise on ornamentation, were Tartini's major contributions to violin pedagogy.

Throughout his life Tartini was fascinated with musical theory, and he claimed to have discovered the combination tone (*terzo suono*), a psycho-acoustical phenomenon whereby the playing of two tones produces a lower third tone. Sometimes referred to as a "Tartini tone" or "ghost tone", this became the starting point for a "natural" theory of harmony, which was set out in his *Tratatto di musica* of 1754. Such speculations, and the hostility with which they were often met, became the preoccupation of his later years, when, because of a stroke, he performed less frequently.

Concertos

Tartini wrote more than 130 violin concertos, 50 of which exist in manuscript form. Though some were published during his lifetime, the many that weren't were constantly modified and revised by the composer – whose style changed throughout his career. In general, Tartini's concertos are based on the concerto grosso model of Corelli (see p.147), but with something of the more florid and virtuosic approach of Vivaldi. Above all, both in his concertos and sonatas, Tartini regarded the singing voice as the ideal to which the violinist should aspire, and his most exquisite writing appears in the slow movements. This means that the interest of these works is firmly located in the solo part, and the writing for full ensemble can sometimes sound routine and predictable. Ultimately this is quite simple music, designed to showcase the soloist, and it needs inspired playing for it to rise above the ordinary.

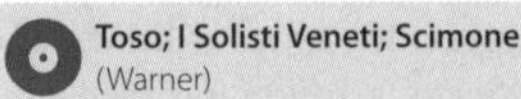

Toso; I Solisti Veneti; Scimone
(Warner)

Recorded over thirty years ago (on modern instruments), these performances of six violin concertos from across Tartini's career still sound fresh and exciting. Piero Toso is the excellent soloist – virtuosic without being showy and always alive to the mood of each movement.

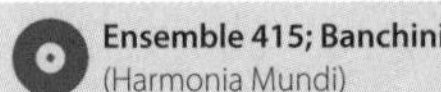

Ensemble 415; Banchini
(Harmonia Mundi)

There are just two violin concertos on this disc, along with a cello concerto and two concerti grossi transcribed from violin sonatas by a Tartini pupil. Played on period instruments, the high point is undoubtedly the A minor concerto, which gets an alert and sensitive performance from Enrico Gatti.

Sonatas

Tartini was even more prolific as a composer of sonatas than he was of concertos, writing at least 170 examples. As with the concertos, these are firmly modelled on the Corellian prototype. Most begin with a slow movement (which provides a showcase for the soloist's singing tone), which is followed by a usually contrapuntal fast movement, and finally a lighter fast movement – often based on a dance form.

The composition of his most celebrated sonata, *The Devil's Trill*, had a peculiar origin which Tartini explained in a letter to J.G. de Lalande: "One night I dreamt I had made a pact with the devil … I found myself handing him my violin to see what he could do with it. Imagine my astonishment when I heard him play a sonata so original and beautiful, and so skillfully performed, that it transcended anything I could have conceived. So overwhelmed was I that my breath stopped and I awoke. Seizing my violin, I tried to recall something of what I had just heard, but to no avail. The piece I then composed is the best I ever wrote … but it falls well below the one that so impressed me." The dream is described in the last extended movement, which alternates fast and slow sections and contains the fiendishly difficult trill of the title.

There is Nothing Like a Strad

As the popularity of the violin rose during the sixteenth and seventeenth centuries, so the demand for instruments grew apace. Northern Italy was the laboratory where the violin was developed, the city of Cremona, in particular, becoming virtually synonymous with the instrument. Andrea Amati (d. 1577) was the first great Cremonese *luthier* (a maker of all stringed instruments) and it was he who more or less standardized the form of the violin, which was then simply refined by succeeding generations – including Andrea's grandson Nicolò (1596–1684).

Although it is not certain whether he was an apprentice of Nicolò Amati or not, Antonio Stradivari (1644–1737) was his most famous follower and the undoubted star of the next generation of makers. Stradivari worked over a seventy-year period, introducing many improvements both to the look and the sound of the violin, and creating instruments to a level of craftsmanship which, in the opinion of many, has never been bettered. Because of his longevity, a relatively large number of Stradivari's instruments have survived – between six and seven hundred is the usual estimate – but even with so many about, a Stradivarius (the label inside each instrument bears the Latinized version of his name) remains a highly desirable object, especially one made during the "golden period" of 1700–20. The most expensive Stradivarius to be sold at auction (and private deals can make even more) was a 1727 violin that went for £947,500 ($1.6 million) at Christie's in London in 1998. This was the so-called "Kreutzer" Strad, bought (with the help of a benefactor) for the Russian virtuoso Maxim Vengerov.

Nearly all the top virtuosos either own a Strad, have one on loan – or wish they did. But what exactly is it about these instruments that makes them so sought after? Performers speak of their depth and sweetness of sound and wide range of tonal colour; the cellist Steven Isserlis describes them as having "souls". And yet sorting out the myth from the reality is surprisingly difficult. There have been many attempts to crack the "secret" of their quality: some have put it down to the density of the wood employed, caused by slow-growing trees during a "mini ice age" at the end of the 1600s; others have concentrated on trying to discover the recipe of Stradivari's mysterious deep-red varnish. Joseph Nagyvary, a biochemist in Texas, is convinced that the high quality of nearly all Cremonese violins of the period is due to the rich stew of micro-organisms soaked up by the wood as it was transported downriver, combined with the various chemicals used to prevent mould and insect damage.

But the heretical question has to be asked: are Strads really so much better than other instruments? Most top players insist that they are, although a select group (including Paganini, Fritz Kreisler and Yehudi Menuhin) have preferred the even rarer instruments of Stadivari's Cremonese competitor Giuseppe Guarneri del Gesù (1698–1744). Interestingly, however, few non-specialists have been able to tell the difference between one instrument and another in the various "blind" tests that have been carried out over the years. Perhaps one explanation for the near unanimity of virtuosos in maintaining the Stradivarius mystique is that it links the player with tradition: to play a violin of a legendary maker that has been played by a succession of equally legendary performers is to be part of history and part of a lineage.

Recently, one leading violinist who has questioned received opinion is Christian Tetzlaff, who used to play a 1713 Strad but gave it up, not for a Guarnerius but for a modern instrument made by Stefan-Peter Greiner. Tetzlaff makes the point that no two Strads are the same, either qualitatively or in their size of sound, and that it's possible to pay a lot of money for a mediocre instrument just because it's old and Italian. Of his current Greiner, which was made in 2001 and cost £10,000, he says: "I can play everything on it … and I can play very loud and very soft. With the Strad, I just couldn't give as much." Which, given that a regularly played old instrument has a limited lifespan, is probably good news.

Current player	Strad name	Former player
Izthak Perlman	Soil (1714)	Yehudi Menuhin
Anne-Sophie Mutter	Lord Dunraven (1710)	Jelly D'Aranyi
Joshua Bell	Gibson (1713)	Bronislaw Huberman
Maxim Vengerov	Kreutzer (1727)	Rodolphe Kreutzer
Yo-Yo Ma (cellist)	Davidoff (1712)	Jacqueline Du Pré
Steven Isserlis (cellist)	Feuermann (1730)	Emanuel Feuermann

Manze
(Harmonia Mundi)

Andrew Manze breaks with custom by dispensing with a continuo part for *The Devil's Trill*, a decision that is fully vindicated by his electrifying performance, which utilizes an astonishing range of tone colour and rubato. The approach is no less convincing in the lively variations on a theme by Corelli and the *Pastorale* for scordatura (retuned) violin.

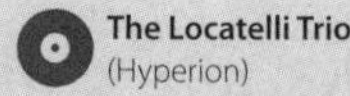

The Locatelli Trio
(Hyperion)

A more conventional approach prevails on this recording of six sonatas plus the *Pastorale*, with violinist Elizabeth Wallfisch supported by harpsichord and cello. Compared to Manze's performance of *The Devil's Trill*, this one sounds a little safe, but Wallfisch's wonderfully suave tone comes into its own on the sonata known as *Didone abbandonata*.

John Tavener (1944–)

If John Tavener seemed unexcited by the 1993 chart success of his sumptuous work for solo cello and strings, *The Protecting Veil*, it's hardly surprising – he has seen it all before, and it turned sour the first time round. Back in 1968 the critics pronounced Tavener the new composer to watch: *The Guardian* described the premiere of his *In Alium* as "nothing less than a musical love-in"; he found himself courted by The Beatles to record for their Apple label; London's Trinity College of Music invited him to join their staff as a professor of composition; and, to cap it all, Covent Garden commissioned him to write a full-length opera, *Thérèse*, on the recommendation of Benjamin Britten. The pressure soon began to tell, and by the early 1970s Tavener was finding that it took a progressively longer time to compose each work, and there were worrying "dry" periods. He was in danger of burning out. Salvation came in the shape of the Russian Orthodox Church.

Ever since Tavener converted to the Orthodox faith in 1977, he has held the view that art is inseparable from religion – "Music is a form of prayer, a mystery." His fervent spirituality was not the result of some blinding revelation – on the contrary, he has been concerned with such things from the start. As a boy of 12 he was profoundly influenced by a broadcast of Stravinsky's *Canticum Sacrum*, a remarkable synthesis of ancient and modern, Eastern and Western, sacred and secular, with which he felt an instant affinity. His parents brought him up a Presbyterian and some of his earliest compositions were written for that church. Apart from the works produced in the late 1960s, when he became something of an apostle of flower power, Tavener has devoted himself to exploring the connection between art and the sacred.

Despite a conventional British musical training, Tavener is, by his own admission, "not very interested in Western art music", reserving special disdain for "angst-ridden serial music". Tavener instead looks for inspiration to Greek, Persian, Indian and Sufi music, exotic languages from which he has distilled a style that conveys spiritual depth through simple textures and forms. His music is non-developmental – "iconic" is his preferred term. For Tavener "the icon is the supreme example of Christian art", and the severe shapes and limited colours of a Byzantine icon are, in his view, analogous to the spartan means by which his music seeks to inspire a sense of spiritual wonder.

Tavener has his detractors, for whom his static simplicity is merely musical nostalgia of the most sentimental and retrogressive kind. But his backward-looking music, like the similarly devotional works of Górecki (see p.216) and Pärt (see p.399), seem to strike a chord among people seeking refuge from the neuroses and struggles of contemporary life: he has become one of the most frequently performed living composers, and recordings of his works sell in large numbers. He has also been taken to the heart of the British establishment, receiving a knighthood in 2000 and being commissioned to write a large-scale millenial work, *Fall and Resurrection*, which was premiered in St Paul's Cathedral and dedicated to the Prince of Wales (another unabashed traditionalist).

Tavener's most ambitious work to date was completed in 2003. Based on texts from medieval and Renaissance Serbian poetry, the *Veil of the Temple* is a seven-hour all-night Vigil for performance by no fewer than 120 singers.

The Protecting Veil

Commissioned for a BBC Promenade Concert and written with the cellist Steven Isserlis in mind, *The Protecting Veil* (1987) for cello and orchestra takes its inspiration from the Orthodox feast of The Protecting Veil of the Mother of God, which commemorates the alleged appearance of the Virgin Mary in tenth-century Constantinople. The music is divided into eight sections, but there is little feeling of development in a Western sense; instead the intensely rhapsodic solo part rises, like a vocal lamentation, slowly but steadily against a subdued orchestral background. Tavener strives for an Eastern ideal of perfection in this music, a timeless spirituality untrammelled by the Western artist's struggle for individuality and self-advertisement. *The Protecting Veil* never grabs your attention (despite an insistent pealing figure in the high strings) but this is no mere background music: it demands an undivided attention, a willingness to surrender to its meditative atmosphere and devotional purpose.

Isserlis; London Symphony Orchestra; Rozhdestvensky (Virgin; with *Thrinos* & Britten *Cello Suite No. 3*)

Over the last few years the creative partnership between Tavener and cellist Steven Isserlis has grown closer, but the impact of *The Protecting Veil* has not been surpassed by his subsequent works for cello. In this superbly produced disc, both soloist and orchestra manage to convey a rapt and inward-looking quality that many have found truly uplifting.

Choral Music

Tavener's choral music constitutes the most substantial part of his output, with many of the best pieces prompted by the composer's need to come to terms with death. When his own mother died in 1985, Tavener was unable to write for several months but then responded with a number of deeply felt works which include the ritualistic *Eis Thanaton* and the *Two Hymns to the Mother of God*. This preoccupation with death continues with two very different works completed in 1995. *Syvati* (O Holy One) was shaped by the news of the death of a friend and includes some luminous writing for chamber choir as well as an important role for cello, an instrument that Tavener has come to regard as the perfect avatar for the spiritual essence of his music. *Innocence*, meanwhile, is a sombre eulogy to innocent victims of oppression throughout history, its startling theatricality partly due to the way Tavener divides the vocal forces around the space it was written for – Westminster Abbey. Most famously, the *Song for Athene* (1993) shows Tavener's ability to touch people by the most simple means. Written in memory of a young Greek actress, its slow processional quality and continuous underlying bass drone create a mood of both solemnity and serenity (it provided the musical climax at the funeral of Diana, Princess of Wales).

Innocence; The Lamb; The Tiger; The Annunciation; 2 Hymns to the Mother of God; Hymn for the Dormation of the Mother of God; Song for Athene: Rozario; Westminster Abbey Choir; Neary (Sony)

This recording presents a representative selection of Tavener's choral works in outstanding performances. Westminster Abbey's vast and resonant acoustic moderates the bleakness of *Innocence*, but the smaller pieces get slightly lost in the spaciousness. Nevertheless, the disc makes a near-ideal place to start with this composer.

John Taverner (c.1490–1545)

John Taverner was the outstanding talent of pre-Reformation English music and one of the greatest of all polyphonists. To a large extent his music was the culmination of an extremely rich English polyphonic tradition which employed highly florid vocal writing and a variety of contrasted voice combinations within the same piece. To this tradition Taverner added the continental device of imitation, whereby a phrase sung by one voice would be repeated by another, thus giving his works a greater sense of shape and direction than those of his English predecessors.

Taverner was probably born in Lincolnshire: the earliest record of his musical activities is in 1525 as a lay clerk at the collegiate choir of Tattershall, northwest of Boston. The following year, on the recommendation of the Bishop of Lincoln, he was appointed choirmaster to the newly founded Cardinal (later Christ Church) College, Oxford. This was a prestigious position but a short-lived one, due to the fall from power in 1529 of the college's founder, Cardinal Wolsey. The year before that, Taverner was briefly arrested for his involvement with a group sympathetic to Lutheranism, an incident treated with leniency at the time, but which gave rise to the legend that Taverner eschewed both Catholicism and music to dedicate his remaining years to the destruction of the monasteries. This is the subject of Peter Maxwell Davies's 1970 opera, *Taverner*, on the life of the composer, but the truth seems to be rather less dramatic. Taverner returned to Lincolnshire to become a lay clerk and possibly choirmaster at the church of St Botolph's at Boston. Once again it was not an appointment that he held for long – this time he left because of the collapse of the guild that paid his wages. From 1537 his musical activities seem to have ceased and the rest of his life was spent in the role of a well-to-do local dignitary, one well enough regarded to be honoured at his death with burial beneath the great tower of St Botolph's church.

Sacred Music

Eight of Taverner's masses have survived, of which the most beautiful is the early six-part *Missa Gloria Tibi Trinitas*. This employs a plainsong cantus firmus which is located in the alto part, thus making it more audible than usual since only the treble part is higher. The work is remarkable for its variety and for the liveliness of its counterpoint – there are several moments of richly florid writing, notably near the beginning of the Credo, when the treble line weaves ever more complex patterns above the bass part. Its most famous section, the In Nomine from the Benedictus, was used by subsequent English composers, from Tallis to Purcell, as the thematic material from which to write short pieces for viol consorts, which were duly known as "in nomines".

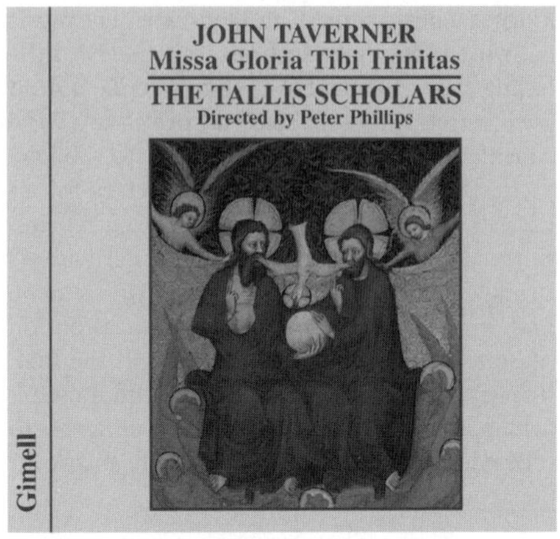

Missa Gloria Tibi Trinitas; Leroy Kyrie; Dum Transisset Sabbatum; Western Wynde Mass: The Tallis Scholars; Phillips (Gimell)

The Tallis Scholars bring their customary precision and textural clarity to the *Missa Gloria Tibi Trinitas*, but also a greater degree of flexibility and warmth than is usual. Occasionally the incisiveness of the female voices in the upper parts brings a slightly top-heavy quality to the sound, but this is a small distraction. The other works included are less animated, and make a more solemn and serene impression.

Pyotr Il'yich Tchaikovsky (1840–1893)

If any one composer can be said to encapsulate the essence of Russianness, it is Pyotr Il'yich Tchaikovsky, and yet he was the one major composer of nineteenth-century Russia who cannot be bracketed with the Russian nationalist school. Although he associated with prominent nationalist figures, particularly Balakirev, Tchaikovsky followed a fiercely independent path, and he paid heavily for his determination to be true to himself above all else – few major artists have ever suffered the sort of critical savaging that was meted out to Tchaikovsky. Nowadays it's difficult to understand why his music aroused such antipathy, for Tchaikovsky is the most powerful and direct of composers: characterized above all by its tunefulness and sweeping orchestral sound, Tchaikovsky's music appeals directly to the heart. Certainly he was prone to bombastic gestures and sentimentality, but these weaknesses are the obverse of his chief strength, which is his sincerity. The emotional fluctuations and contradictions of his work reflect the turbulence of an extraordinary life.

Tchaikovsky was born in the provincial town of Votkinsk, where his father was a mining engineer. His formal tuition began at home, where his parents played him pieces by Mozart and Rossini, and gave him lessons in piano and music theory. In 1848 the family moved to St Petersburg, and in 1850 he was sent to a boarding school in the city; nine years later, after intensive and extended law studies (and the death of his mother, a trauma that was to scar him for the rest of his life), he found employment at the Ministry of Justice. Aged 22 he left the ministry and entered the city music conservatory to study with Anton Rubinstein, a composer and stupendous pianist. In 1866 he went to Moscow, where Anton's brother Nikolai appointed Tchaikovsky professor of harmony at the conservatory.

In Moscow he came into contact with Rimsky-Korsakov and his cabal of young nationalists, and for a short while Tchaikovsky was swept up by their enthusiasm for Russia's folk heritage. He even composed a nationalist symphony – the *Symphony No. 2*, known as the *Little Russian* – but it was not long before his cosmopolitan instincts prevailed. By the time of the first performance of his *Piano Concerto No. 1* in 1875 he had created a style that was strongly individual while being accessible to any audience raised on the wider European tradition – indeed, the concerto found greater acclaim abroad than at home.

Pyotr Il'yich Tchaikovsky.

1877 was the most crucial year in Tchaikovsky's life, and the point from which his music radically expands its emotional depth and profundity. Bizarrely, this transformation was prompted by his contact with two women hitherto unknown to him. The first was Nadezhda von Meck, a wealthy widow who, impressed by some of his early music, now commissioned Tchaikovsky to produce some violin and piano arrangements of his more recent works. Thus began a relationship between the two that lasted fourteen years, during which time they never once met. Convinced of Tchaikovsky's genius, she supplied him with an annuity that would enable him to devote all his time to composition.

The second woman was Antonina Milyukova, who in May 1877 started sending Tchaikovsky infatuated love letters in which she threatened to take her life unless he responded. Initially cautious, Tchaikovsky seems suddenly to have seen in his unstable admirer a solution to the problem of his homosexuality (homosexual acts were punishable by death in Russia). Within seven weeks of meeting her, and unbeknown to most of his family, the two were married. Predictably it was an unmitigated disaster: Tchaikovsky immediately sank into an overwhelming depression and the couple separated after just a few weeks.

The love of his family and friends, in particular his increasingly intimate correspondence with Nadezhda von Meck, helped Tchaikovsky over the breakdown caused by his marriage and, remarkably, this period corresponds with the composition of two of his greatest works, the *Symphony No. 4*, dedicated to "my best friend" (i.e. Nadezhda), and the best-loved of his eight surviving operas, *Eugene Onegin*, which he completed in 1878.

By the 1880s his music was being played as far afield as the USA, and in 1885 he ended his nomadic existence by moving to a house at Klin, the first of several houses he was to rent in the Russian countryside. He lived there in almost complete isolation until 1887, when he ventured back to Moscow to begin a second successful career as a conductor. In this capacity he toured Europe in the following year, and in the winter of 1889–90 he spent a long period in Florence, where he composed the opera *The Queen of Spades*. The work's triumph was marred by the collapse of his relationship with von Meck, but although he was deeply distressed by their falling out he made an incredibly successful visit to the USA in 1891, conducting at the opening night of what was to become Carnegie Hall.

Two years later he completed his *Symphony No. 6*, the *Pathétique*, a creation that typifies the work of a composer who poured the whole of his life into his music. It was premiered in St Petersburg on 28 October, just nine days before his death. The circumstances of Tchaikovsky's last days remain controversial. The official version was that he had died from cholera after drinking unboiled water. Many people surmised that Tchaikovsky had hoped this reckless act would bring about his death, but in the 1970s a Russian scholar produced a new theory, which claimed suicide was the cause of death. In this version of events, Tchaikovsky was caught in flagrante with a nephew of a high-ranking official; the composer's law-school colleagues, determined to avert a scandal, summoned Tchaikovsky before a "court of honour" on 31 October and ordered him to commit suicide. Two days later, he took arsenic.

OPERAS

Tchaikovsky's operas are the distillation of what he termed his "lyrical idea", the notion that everything can be characterized or made real through melody. His technique was always at the service of melody, and his music was first and foremost conceived for the voice – whether or not it was actually written for voice, all his music can be sung. Tchaikovsky was not, however, an effortless tune-writer in the manner of Mendelssohn or Strauss. He worked hard at honing his skills, making an intensive study of his European precursors, not just as a student in Russia, but also in later life as a touring celebrity. For his operatic music Tchaikovsky immersed himself in Italian bel canto as well as in the operas of Mozart, and the breadth of Tchaikovsky's schooling is a major distinction between him and his Russian contemporaries. He wrote no fewer than ten operas, though he destroyed two of them and only *Eugene Onegin* and *The Queen of Spades* have found a regular place in the repertoire.

Eugene Onegin

Tchaikovsky was initially sceptical about a friend's suggestion to turn Pushkin's great verse-novel *Eugene Onegin* into an opera, but when he reread the passage where the heroine Tatyana writes a declaration of love to Onegin, he was struck by the similarity to his own situation and the letter he had received from Antonina Milyukova. His identification with Tatyana prompted him to begin work on the "letter scene", which became the emotional core of the opera; it also prompted his disastrously sympathetic response to Antonina.

Eugene Onegin contains some of the composer's most graceful, untroubled music. Where Pushkin's poem explores the social and moral discrepancies between the worlds of Tatyana, the country girl, and Onegin, the cynical aristocrat, Tchaikovsky focuses on their aborted relationship. Onegin spurns Tatyana, then flirts with her sister Olga; when Olga's fiancé and Onegin's friend, the poet Lensky, protests, Onegin reluctantly fights a duel, killing Lensky. Six years later Onegin returns from abroad to find Tatyana married; he tempts her to leave with him, but eventually she rejects him.

Lensky is a fine tenor role (his aria is one of the work's highlights) but it's the characterization of Tatyana that really makes this opera. There are few more realistic or sympathetic heroines, and her "Letter Scene" is just about the most moving twenty minutes that Tchaikovsky ever devised.

Allen, Freni, von Otter, Schicoff; Staatskapelle Dresden; Levine (Deutsche Grammophon; 2 CDs)

Levine's thrilling version is the most impressive modern recording. Thomas Allen's Onegin is perfectly shaped and the surprise casting of Mirella Freni works amazingly well – she conveys, with equal ease, youthfulness in her first meeting with Onegin and maturity in their final confrontation. A highlights disc is also available.

The Queen of Spades

The Queen of Spades – aka *Pique Dame*, *La dame de pique* and *Pikovaya Dama* – is also based upon a story by Pushkin. The protagonist, a young army officer called Hermann, becomes obsessed with discovering a secret to success in gambling known only to the countess – the grandmother of Lisa, who he loves. He breaks into the countess's room to attain the secret of the "three cards", but she dies of shock, later returning as a ghost and telling Hermann the secret. He abandons Lisa (who drowns herself) and prepares to make his fortune. But when he turns the third card, expecting a winning ace, it turns out to be the Queen of Spades. In despair, he kills himself.

Premiered in St Petersburg in 1890, the opera is far more sophisticated than *Onegin*, combining nineteenth-century realism with the elegance of Mozart and the rococo style of Catherine

the Great's St Petersburg. The focus upon Fate – a recurrent idea in Tchaikovsky – is handled brilliantly, with the "three cards" motif strongly colouring the work's fabric. Hermann (a high, dramatic tenor) and the Countess (a contralto) interact in some immensely impressive scenes, especially the blood-curdling appearance of her ghost. But then *The Queen of Spades* is littered with memorable moments; as Tchaikovsky wrote to his brother, the co-librettist, "Unless I'm terribly mistaken, the opera is a masterpiece."

Grigorian, Guleghina, Putilin, Arkhipova, Chernov, Borodina; Kirov Opera Chorus and Orchestra; Gergiev (Philips; 3 CDs)

Gergiev has consistently proved the most involved and impassioned interpreter of this rich and subtle score, and for this superb recording he joins forces with the quicksilver tenor of Gegam Grigorian and the experienced diva Irina Arkhipova. A highlights disc is available.

BALLETS

Russian ballet music before Tchaikovsky was vapid stuff, amounting to little more than background music for displays of the dancers' qualities. Tchaikovsky introduced a greater range of rhythms, an increased richness of melody and orchestration, and above all gave the ballet a sense of symphonic construction – in short, he gave respect to ballet music as an art form. Classical ballet owes more to Tchaikovsky than to any other composer, and if *Swan Lake*, *The Sleeping Beauty* and *The Nutcracker* met with little more than polite approval during Tchaikovsky's lifetime, they are now the world's most frequently performed dance scores.

Ballet Suites: Berlin Philharmonic Orchestra; Rostropovich (Deutsche Grammophon)

This recording of the suites from *Swan Lake*, *The Sleeping Beauty* and *The Nutcracker* is a bargain at mid-price. Rostropovich is not the greatest conductor but his Tchaikovsky performances are always full-blooded and he is given ravishing support from the Berlin Philharmonic. Both he and the orchestra clearly enjoy every minute of this music.

Swan Lake

Tchaikovsky was commissioned to write *Swan Lake* at the end of May 1875 by the Imperial Theatre. He gladly accepted the work, partly because of his poor financial situation, and partly because, as he wrote to Rimsky-Korsakov, "I have long had the wish to try my hand at this kind of music." Tchaikovsky duly produced the first ballet that had overall musical coherence, for rather than being the customary series of dances strung together by the vaguest of plots *Swan Lake* is constructed of extended quasi-symphonic movements, unified by a system of themes and key structures. Tchaikovsky's brilliantly orchestrated musical narrative flows perfectly, and features more memorable tunes than any of the composer's other scores. The first production was nonetheless a resounding failure. Petipa, the pre-eminent choreographer of his day, and Drigo, a ballet composer of the old school, then set about revising the work, but it was still considered undanceable. Time has told a different story.

Philharmonia Orchestra; Lanchbery (Classics for Pleasure; 2 CDs)

John Lanchbery, a ballet conductor who worked frequently with Fonteyn and Nureyev, made this budget-price recording in 1982, and it remains the best version on record. This is a delicate, flowing performance with fine orchestral playing and a spacious dynamic range that highlights even the subtlest of touches.

The Sleeping Beauty

Tchaikovsky's second ballet is a work of his maturity, coming between the fifth and sixth symphonies. It was premiered in 1890, with choreography by Petipa, and this time Tchaikovsky had learned his lesson – he allowed Petipa to guide him, section by section, through the ballet's composition. (On certain occasions Petipa would go so far as to specify the number of bars required.) Unlike its predecessor, *The Sleeping Beauty* is a happy-ending tale. But for all the sweetness of the story line, this is Tchaikovsky's finest ballet, for if *Swan Lake* marked the establishment of a symphonic style of ballet music, *Sleeping Beauty* went a stage further – it was even attacked at the time for being "too symphonic". Elaborately constructed, it contains movements within movements that are, effectively, miniature concertos for the orchestral section leaders.

Concertgebouw; Dorati
(Philips; 2 CDs)

Antal Dorati's recording of the complete *Sleeping Beauty* is magnificently coherent. Dorati's aggressive manner and almost impatient tempi, exemplified by his performances of music by Stravinsky, are a gift to music that can easily become sickly sweet.

The Nutcracker

The Nutcracker, based on E.T.A. Hoffmann's story of a little girl and her Christmas presents, was written at the end of Tchaikovsky's life but it reflects nothing of his misery or self-hatred – rather it evokes a world of innocence where everything is as it should be. Again, Petipa worked closely with the composer on the production of a detailed scenario, and much of Hoffmann's ironic juxtaposition of reality and fantasy was lost in the process. Yet this is still an enchanting work, containing many of Tchaikovsky's best-loved tunes – notably the variation for the Sugar-Plum Fairy, which spotlights the celesta, a new instrument that Tchaikovsky was desperate to keep secret from his rivals, in particular Rimsky-Korsakov. The celesta's finest hour was to come courtesy of Bartók (see p.39).

London Symphony Orchestra; Dorati
(Mercury; 2 CDs; with *Serenade*)

The Nutcracker is shorter and considerably less ambitious than *Sleeping Beauty*, but it is in no way lacking in drama or colour. Dorati's calm direction is perfectly delicate and yet he produces a wash of sound of the type that few have achieved on record. A wonderful, superbly engineered recording.

SYMPHONIES

Tchaikovsky viewed the symphony as the mould into which to pour his most profound thoughts and feelings, and his seven completed symphonies are the emotional graph of a lifetime, from the relative calm of the *Symphony No. 1* (*Winter Daydreams*) to the desolation of the *Symphony No. 6* (the *Pathétique*). They are uniformly revealing but not uniformly excellent. The first three have plenty of Tchaikovsky's outgoing melodies and thrilling rhythms, but they also have slack episodes that you won't find in the last three numbered symphonies. These represent the high-water mark of the Romantic symphony and are discussed below. The seventh, written between the fourth and the fifth, is known as the *Manfred Symphony* since it was inspired by Lord Byron's poem of the same name. It has some truly thrilling moments but is rather shapeless and tends to overwork its big tune.

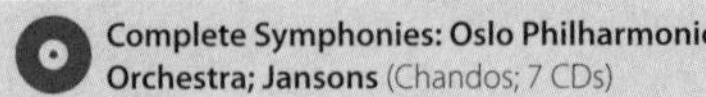

Complete Symphonies: Oslo Philharmonic Orchestra; Jansons (Chandos; 7 CDs)

Mariss Jansons' survey of Tchaikovsky's symphonies is a remarkable achievement, bringing something fresh to each one. He and the Oslo players give a sense of conviction to the early symphonies that is lacking from the majority of alternative versions, and with the late masterpieces they are at least the equal of any rivals. These fine recordings are available on separate, full-price discs, or as a specially reduced set – in the latter format they represent a very good investment.

Symphony No. 4

The composition of the *Symphony No. 4* was interrupted by the breakdown of Tchaikovsky's marriage and by a consequent, pathetic attempt at suicide – he waded into the Moskva river, hoping to catch pneumonia. Yet when he completed the piece in December 1877, he was convinced that it was his greatest work: "in technique and form it represents a step forward in my development, which has been proceeding extremely slowly". The fourth symphony shows a greater control of the orchestral palette, and a stronger grasp of the means of integrating melodic material into an overall structure. The first movement is an expansive conception, dominated by a bleak "Fate" motif that colours the entire movement, while the second is a mournful song of poignant beauty. The third movement features some amazingly original scoring for plucked strings, but it is the charging, ebullient finale that justifies the use of superlatives – incorporating variations on a Russian folk song, this is the composer's most exciting symphonic invention, ending in a torrent of enthusiasm after the violent incursions of the "Fate" motif.

Leningrad Philharmonic Orchestra; Mravinsky
(Deutsche Grammophon 2 CDs; with *Symphonies Nos. 5 & 6*)

Mravinsky was one of the finest of all Soviet conductors, whose Tchaikovsky performances were admired for their rigour and their athleticism. Under his baton, the Leningrad Phil became one of the world's great orchestras and this performance shows them at their very best. In this symphony the prevailing sense of tension created by finely shaded dynamics is breathtaking.

Symphony No. 5

Tchaikovsky wrote of the *Symphony No. 5* (1885): "I have become convinced that the symphony is unsuccessful. There is something repellent about it, a certain patchiness, insecurity and artifice … All this causes me a keen torment of discontent … it is all most distressing." This certainly is a distressing work, but chiefly because of its unguarded candour rather than because of any compositional failings. Fate is more capricious and cruel in this symphony than it was in its predecessor: the piece begins in despairing mood, and the frequent, massive emotional climaxes generate a sense of hysteria that rarely featured in the fourth. The symphony's "Fate" motif destroys even the song-like melody of the slow movement, and only at the close of the finale does the tragic atmosphere lift – even then, you feel it's a case of putting a brave face on things.

London Symphony Orchestra; Dorati (Mercury; with *Marche Slave* and excerpts from *Eugene Onegin*)

Dorati's discipline prevents the emotional climate of the symphony from becoming too oppressive, and the potentially cloying textures are balanced with precision and imagination. The first four movements are evenly paced, but the finale is driven with an insatiable energy that is well served by a clear and resonant recording.

Leningrad Philharmonic Orchestra; Mravinsky (Deutsche Grammophon; 2 CDs; with *Symphonies Nos. 4 and 6*)

Mravinsky's fifth is as controlled as Dorati's, but he stresses the work's melancholy side more: the beginning of the slow movement is particularly poignant, with the dark brass sound – so characteristic of Russian orchestras – bringing a touching frailty to the first statement of the movement's big tune.

Symphony No. 6 – The Pathétique

"I give you my word of honour that never in my life have I been so contented, so proud, so happy in the knowledge that I have written a good piece." Within months of writing this to his publisher, Tchaikovsky was dead, possibly pushed towards suicide by the hostile reception accorded to his *Symphony No. 6*. The title *Pathétique* was added by the composer's brother, and is undeniably appropriate to a work which, despite a number of positive interludes and beautiful thematic writing, is overwhelmingly melancholic.

Although the opening movement contains one of Tchaikovsky's loveliest themes, a sense of intense internal struggle is conveyed by extremes of dynamics – no previous symphony had displayed such violent ranges between soft and loud. The second movement is a ghostly piece written in a rhythm that seems to be imitating a waltz but never quite becomes one. In the third movement a hectic march takes over, but any hints of momentary triumph are soon dispelled. Unusually the symphony ends with a slow movement, and it's the most anguished music Tchaikovsky ever composed – the emotional weight of this Adagio becomes ever more burdensome until, breaking down with grief, the music disappears into the darkness from which it emerged.

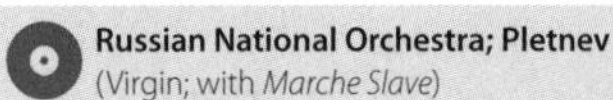

Russian National Orchestra; Pletnev (Virgin; with *Marche Slave*)

The pianist Mikhael Pletnev's transition to conducting began with this staggering performance of the *Pathétique*, in which he achieves a perfect balance of strength and pathos. The orchestra's playing is breathtakingly urgent and the expressive range truly harrowing. It is disappointing to add that his subsequent Tchaikovsky symphony set for Deutsche Grammophon only hits such heights sporadically.

Leningrad Philharmonic Orchestra; Mravinsky (Deutsche Grammophon; 2 CDs; with *Symphonies Nos. 4 & 5*)

Yergeny Mravinsky recorded the *Pathétique* several times, and there is an authority to this performance which is awe-inspiring. The conductor's restraint pays great dividends: there is a convincing sense of emotional connection between the four movements which makes the final movement's despair all the more shattering.

OTHER ORCHESTRAL WORKS

When the level of Tchaikovsky's invention is below the standard of his finest works, his music can seem tremendously banal and short-winded. This perhaps explains why, out of the substantial body of orchestral music that he wrote, apart from the symphonies, only a handful of pieces have permanently entered the repertoire outside of Russia. Of the works that have, the *1812 Overture* is the best known, but *Romeo and Juliet* represents his highest achievement, both because it is rich melodically and because it succeeds in developing its thematic material in a dramatically convincing way.

Romeo and Juliet

The idea of a fantasy overture on Shakespeare's *Romeo and Juliet* was suggested to Tchaikovsky in 1869 by his friend and fellow composer

Balakirev, who had no qualms about giving advice as to the exact form it should take. In fact Balakirev's suggestions were sound ones, and Tchaikovsky revised *Romeo and Juliet* twice, giving it its final form in 1880. It's rightly one of his most celebrated works, and possesses a vitality as well as a structural tightness that is very satisfying. Clearly its big love tune, with its rapturous swooping horn accompaniment, has become as big a cliché as the *Mona Lisa*. But it still retains its impact, largely because, before you get there, you travel through some startlingly vivid music in which tension and anticipation are brilliantly handled, first with the solemn, stately opening (a chorale represents Friar Laurence) through more sunny expansive music into the feverish violence of the brawl scene. The work's relationship to the play is not a slavish one; nevertheless it's a highly sympathetic attempt to encapsulate in music the helter-skelter of emotions that Shakespeare drags us through and, on the whole, it's a highly successful one.

London Symphony Orchestra; Dorati
(Mercury; with *Symphony No. 6*)

Recorded in 1959, this fine performance still has enormous impact. Dorati's Tchaikovsky interpretations never push too hard on the throttle and this one is no exception. The pacing of the drama is always perfectly controlled and the final ringing chords bring to an end a perfectly integrated reading in which every element seems to grow out of another.

Royal Liverpool Philharmonic Orchestra; Edwards
(Classics for Pleasure; with *Francesca da Rimini*, *1812 Overture* & *Marche Slave*)

Sian Edwards studied conducting with the doyen of Russian conductor-professors, Ilya Musin, and her performances of the Russian repertoire have a genuinely idiomatic feel to them. This *Romeo and Juliet* has very strong contours and a firm sense of direction. It doesn't quite have the tautness of Dorati but it's still very impressive.

Francesca da Rimini

It's hard not to see a special significance in Tchaikovsky's choice of Francesca da Rimini as the subject for his epic and sprawling tone poem of that name. In Dante's *Inferno* Francesca and her lover Paolo are punished for their illicit passion by spinning for ever, locked in a permanent embrace. Written in 1876 at a time when Tchaikovsky was contemplating marriage as a means of providing a smokescreen for his homosexuality, it's an enormously passionate work which at times borders on the excessive. It begins with a kind of brooding horror which then rapidly builds to the brilliant depiction of the relentless whirlwind conveyed by a rich chromatic sweep of orchestral sound. Francesca's story appears as the still lyrical centre of the piece, a long cantabile melody which begins tentatively and goes through several guises before building to a richly passionate and intricately orchestrated climax. The storm music returns and culminates, with a terrible finality, in a coda of almost frantic desperation.

New York Stadium Symphony Orchestra; Stokowski
(Everest; with *Hamlet*)

This work was a Leopold Stokowski speciality; one that matched his own oversized personality. He recorded it more than once, but this is the one to go for: a completely over-the-top performance with some superbly deployed percussion vividly conjuring up the Second Circle of Hell.

1812 Overture

The *1812 Overture* was composed by Tchaikovsky in 1881 with a great deal of reluctance. A state commission, the composer rattled it off in a week and was particularly scathing about it: "The overture will be very loud and noisy … but I wrote it with no warm feelings of love, and therefore there will probably be no artistic merits in it." Critics have tended to agree with him, but popular opinion deems it among his most thrilling works. Commemorating the Russian rout of Napoleon's forces, it weaves together a number of original and historically significant themes, including the *Marseillaise*, the Russian national anthem and an Orthodox hymn, into a veritable hodgepodge of breathless excitement culminating in the ringing of bells and the explosion of cannons. Bombastic vulgarity or history brought thrillingly to life? Who cares? In the right circumstances it's a supremely enjoyable and extravagant romp.

Minneapolis Symphony Orchestra; University of Minnesota Brass Band; Dorati (Mercury; with *Capriccio Italien* & Beethoven *Wellington's Victory*)

A sonic spectacular, recorded in the 1950s with a genuine French cannon and a real carillon of bells, this is also a great performance led by one of the finest Tchaikovsky conductors of the twentieth century. And as an added bonus, the legendary classical music commentator, Deems Taylor, explains just how it was all put together.

Royal Liverpool Philharmonic Orchestra; Edwards
(Classics for Pleasure; with *Francesca da Rimini*, *Romeo and Juliet* & *Marche Slave*)

If you insist on a more modern recording, then this budget disc gets the balance right between going for audiophile overload and taking the music too seriously. Under Sian Edwards's expert direction the dances swing, the cavalry caper, and the cannons crash with the requisite degree of swagger and panache.

CONCERTOS

Tchaikovsky composed one concerto for violin, one for cello (the *Variations on a Rococo Theme*) and three and a half for piano – if you count the glittering *Concert Fantasia* and the one-movement torso of a third concerto (which various other composers, including Tchaikovsky's pupil Taneyev, have attempted to complete). The *Violin Concerto* and *Piano Concerto No. 1* are particularly grand conceptions, boasting an exceptional orchestral expertise in addition to the customary large-scale emotionalism. The other piano concertos have never really entered the repertoire, but the *Rococo Variations*, Tchaikovsky's charming homage to the music of the eighteenth century, is something of a showcase for those cellists with the technique and style to play it.

Piano Concerto No. 1

Nikolai Rubinstein, the intended dedicatee of the *Piano Concerto No. 1*, pronounced it "worthless, unplayable and clumsy". He later agreed to play it subject to substantial revisions, but by this stage Tchaikovsky had rededicated the piece – first to his lifelong friend Sergei Taneyev and then to the German conductor Hans von Bülow, who premiered the piece in Boston. It went down a storm in the USA (though not at first in Russia), and in time even Rubinstein came to love it. No one would argue that it's the most coherent of concertos – there's little discernible link between the opening movement and what follows, and the last movement is anticlimactic in all but the most sparkling performances. But Germanic rigour is not what Tchaikovsky is about, and the heroic bravado and typically Russian "big tunes" have made this one of the most popular of all piano concertos. Incidentally, its most famous flourish, the grandiose piano chords which accompany the opening melody – one of classical music's great attention-grabbing effects – was in large part the creation of Alexander Siloti, who helped arrange the score for its third edition.

Argerich; Berlin Philharmonic Orchestra; Abbado (Deutsche Grammophon; with *The Nutcracker Suite* arranged for two pianos)

Of the hundreds of recordings of this work that have been made, two artists stand out: Vladimir Horowitz and Martha Argerich. Both have recorded it several times and each performance has its own insights. This live version by Argerich is marked by a tumultuous drive; there's a feeling of the notes just tumbling out, but they're guided by a restless intelligence that makes everything seem freshly written.

Horowitz; NBC Symphony Orchestra; Toscanini (RCA; with Beethoven *Piano Concerto No. 5*)

Vladimir Horowitz and his father-in-law Arturo Toscanini gave this legendary 1943 Carnegie Hall performance to raise money for the war effort. Though the sound is constricted, it's the performance of a lifetime, bursting with energy and old-fashioned virtuosity. At the time of writing, it's out of the catalogue; if you can't find it, the same performers' studio version is almost as good.

Violin Concerto

The history of Tchaikovsky's *Violin Concerto* is similar to that of the *Piano Concerto No. 1*. Written in just one month in 1877, it was intended for the violinist Leopold Auer (Heifetz's teacher), who promptly refused to perform it when he saw the difficulty of the solo part. Instead, Adolf Brodsky gave the premiere in Vienna, in 1881. Europe's pre-eminent music critic, Eduard Hanslick, was in the audience – "stinking music" was his verdict. The reaction was hardly unexpected, for the conservative Wagner-hating Hanslick was Brahms's biggest fan, whereas Tchaikovsky loathed everything that Brahms stood for – and had been singularly unimpressed by the Brahms violin concerto, which appeared in 1879. The two works are in the same key (the D major of Beethoven's concerto), but that's where the resemblance ends. Whereas tension and constraint are essential to Brahms, Tchaikovsky creates a largely effortless, song-like part for the violin, while the orchestral score is packed with rumbustious energy and bold melodies. If the Brahms concerto is like a well-scripted dialogue, Tchaikovsky's is more like an uninhibited duet for soloist and orchestra.

Mullova; Boston Symphony Orchestra; Ozawa (Philips; with Sibelius *Violin Concerto*)

Viktoria Mullova's thrilling interpretation is distinguished by ringing tone, impeccable technique and Russian flair; one of her first projects for Philips after winning the Tchaikovsky competition, it comes generously coupled with an equally fine account of Sibelius's concerto.

Heifetz; London Philharmonic Orchestra; Barbirolli (Naxos; with concertos by Sibelius and Wieniawski)

Heifetz recorded the work a number of times but the finest version is his first, made in 1937. With Barbirolli's sympathetic, flexible accompaniment, Heifetz hurls himself into the score, producing an extraordinarily exciting sound.

Rococo Variations

Tchaikovsky followed the unbridled passion and fury of *Francesca da Rimini* with the relatively cool and elegant *Rococo Variations*. As the title suggests, the inspiration is the eighteenth century, and the theme (Tchaikovsky's own) is a short and dainty dance tune similar to a gavotte. The seven variations which follow are refined and sophisticated, with only two of them – the one in C major and the one in D minor – really giving a glimpse of the composer's emotional side. Tchaikovsky originally wrote eight variations, but William Fitzenhagen, for whom they were written, discarded the last one and changed the order of the remaining seven – much to Tchaikovsky's annoyance. This is the most frequently performed version, although since its recent publication Tchaikovsky's original version is often preferred.

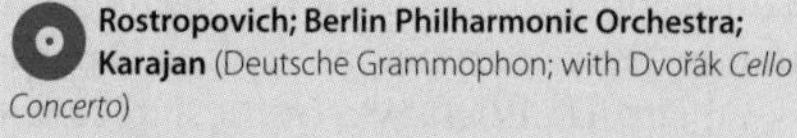

Rostropovich; Berlin Philharmonic Orchestra; Karajan (Deutsche Grammophon; with Dvořák *Cello Concerto*)

This is a wholeheartedly Romantic account, with Rostropovich wallowing in the slower variations but always keeping on the right side of mawkishness. His tone is warm but incisive and, though he doesn't quite make a convincing moment of the difficult octave passage work in the coda, few other cellists have managed it either.

CHAMBER MUSIC

In the eyes of many of the Russian intelligentsia, chamber music was almost as trivial a genre as ballet, but Tchaikovsky created some fine work in this field, even without a strong indigenous tradition to support him. It's in his chamber music that Tchaikovsky's style is most clearly indebted to the great Germans, and to Brahms in particular but, as with everything he wrote, the overriding tone is quintessentially Russian. The three string quartets plus the *Piano Trio* represent the best of his chamber music, though newcomers to the latter may find it relatively turgid.

String Quartets

The *String Quartet No. 1* (1871) is Tchaikovsky's most attractive chamber work. The majority of the music is jauntily lyrical and folk-inspired, free of the melancholy and fatalism so common to Tchaikovsky's music. That said, its reputation rests on its incredibly mournful second movement, the Andante cantabile, which has become one of his most popular pieces – both in its original form and in orchestral transcription. The *Quartet No. 2*, written three years later, lacks the unity of the first and is notably less tuneful; the *Quartet No. 3* (1876), although well constructed, seems to strain for originality, and it is uncomfortably dominated by the first violin, no doubt in response to the death of the violinist Laub, the work's dedicatee.

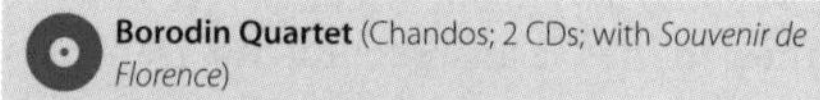

Borodin Quartet (Chandos; 2 CDs; with *Souvenir de Florence*)

The Borodin Quartet made these recordings in the 1960s. Now remastered, they approach perfection, especially their accounts of the *Quartet No. 1* and the *Souvenir de Florence* sextet, with Rostropovich as the second cellist, which combines a supple instrumental balance and extraordinary fluidity of melodic line.

Piano Trio

With the colossal two-movement *Piano Trio* Tchaikovsky set an example that was followed by several later Russian composers, above all Shostakovich, when they composed piano trios as a gesture of commemoration. In this case the recently deceased dedicatee was Nikolai Rubinstein, who – for all his occasional hostility to Tchaikovsky's music – had played a major role in the younger composer's development. Tchaikovsky celebrates his colossal technique in the piano part, which supports the vast structure of the effusive first movement on its broad back before going on to play a virtuoso part in many of the second movement's theme and variations. So protracted are these variations that Tchaikovsky suggested several optional cuts before the music steers back to the elegiac mood of the trio's opening.

Richter, Kagan, Gutman
(Live Classics)

There are so few truly outstanding performances of this demanding work that it's worth putting up with the slightly wonky live recording of these three great artists. Richter alone would be worth the investment, but the phenomenal violinist Oleg Kagan and his wife, cellist Natalia Gutman, match Richter's inspiration at every point.

The Moscow Rachmaninov Trio
(Hyperion; with Glinka *Trio Pathétique in D Minor*)

Those worried by sound quality should investigate this stirring performance by the Moscow Rachmaninov Trio. It's not as characterized as the above recording but it's still a highly passionate account which manages to make the sometimes rambling second movement sound coherent.

PIANO MUSIC

Tchaikovsky, who had studied with the great virtuoso and pedagogue Nikolai Rubinstein, was a fine pianist but he never seriously considered it as a career. Instead he expressed his affection for the instrument in over one hundred piano works, mostly poetic miniatures, such as the *Six Pieces*, Opus 21. He also began at least three sonatas but only one of them, the *"Grand" Sonata* in G major (1878) – described by its composer as "somewhat dry and complicated" – was published during his lifetime. Popular with Russian pianists, few of Tchaikovsky's piano works have won wider acceptance; the sole exception is his collection of twelve miniatures, *The Seasons*.

The Seasons

The idea of writing a collection of twelve short pieces representing the months of the year came from Nikolai Bernard, editor of the music magazine, *Nouvellist*. The pieces duly appeared in the appropriate issue of the magazine throughout 1876, with a subtitle (by Bernard) and a short poem (by various Russian poets) appended to each one. Tchaikovsky was an admirer of Schumann and his influence is clearly apparent in such pieces as "January: By the Fireside" or the quirky "March: Song of the Lark", which reveals a kinship with the earlier composer's "Vogel als Prophet". But while they display his skill as a melodist, these aphoristic pieces also reveal Tchaikovsky's ability to create delicate harmonies and subtle internal lines – nowhere more so than in the hauntingly beautiful "June: Barcarolle". There's plenty of ebullience to balance the poetry, however, with a spirited Allegro for "August: Harvesting" and an appropriately festive Christmas waltz to round the set off.

Pletnev (Virgin; 2 CDs; with Tchaikovsky/Pletnev Sleeping Beauty & Mussorgsky *Pictures at an Exhibition*)

Mikhail Pletnev is a great champion of Tchaikovsky's piano music and has recorded *The Seasons* more than once. He is also a highly individual interpreter, and these pieces really benefit from his strong but sensitive approach: each piece is clearly characterized, through deft voicings of inner lines and the pianist's unforced rubato, and the cumulative effect raises the collection to the highest level.

Georg Philipp Telemann (1681–1767)

Telemann was the greatest German composer of the first half of the eighteenth century – at least that's what they thought at the time. Nowadays his friend and colleague J.S. Bach (who became cantor at Leipzig only because Telemann turned it down) is regarded as infinitely superior, while Telemann is treated as an overproductive and superficial also-ran. He was certainly incredibly prolific, writing among other things about forty operas, forty-six Passions and five complete cycles of cantatas for the Lutheran liturgical year. And there's some justice to the charge of superficiality: able to write in pretty well any style that was demanded of him, he wrote no single work that stands out distinctly as his own. Yet, at its best, the music of Telemann has a bright melodiousness that looks forward to that of Haydn and Mozart.

Telemann was born at Magdeburg into an affluent middle-class family. His father and brother, like several of his ancestors, were clergymen, and despite showing musical aptitude from an early age (he wrote his first opera aged twelve), Georg Philipp was intended for a similarly respectable career. In 1701 he went to the University of Leipzig to study law, but once his musical talents were discovered by others it was impossible for him to do anything else. He founded the Collegium Musicum (a society that gave public concerts, and which Bach later directed), became organist of the Neue Kirche, then director of the Leipzig Opera, and so dominated the city's musical life that its ostensible music director, Johann Kuhnau, became extremely irritated.

Telemann left Leipzig in 1705, and after positions at Sorau and Eisenach became music director of the city of Frankfurt, and *Kapellmeister* of the Barfusserkirche (church of the Barefoot Friars). He was there for nine years, from 1712 to 1721, before being invited by the city of Hamburg to be cantor of the Johanneum, the grammar school, and to be responsible for music at the city's five principal churches. A dispute with the civic authorities led to his applying for the Leipzig cantor's job in 1722, but things were patched up (his salary was increased) and he remained at Hamburg until his death, when he was succeeded in the post by his godson, C.P.E. Bach (see p.16).

Orchestral Music

In Telemann's time the dominant orchestral forms were the concerto and the orchestral suite, which was made up of a French-style overture and a series of formalized dance movements. One of Telemann's employers, Count Erdmann II of Promnitz, distinctly favoured the French style of music and Telemann consequently composed several suites for him. It was while at the count's court at Sorau that he came into contact with the indigenous music of Upper Silesia, and folk elements – both rhythmic and instrumental – became a feature of his music throughout the rest of his career. In his concertos the influence is more Italian than French, with the model of Vivaldi particularly apparent in the way he frequently employs quite strange combinations of instruments as the solo group – for example, the delightful *Grillen-Symphonie*, in which a double bass, a piccolo and a *chalumeau* (an early clarinet) combine with a string quartet to startling effect.

Concerto in D Major; La Bouffonne Suite; Grillen-Symphonie; Alster-Ouverture: Collegium Musicum 90; Standage (Chandos)

This disc shows off Telemann's versatility, from the rather formal and slightly bland elegance of the *Bouffonne Suite* to the light-hearted scene-painting of the *Alster-Ouverture*, a piece with one movement of weird harmonies and unexpected key changes representing the music of the local peasantry. Utterly compelling, and played with great spirit and enthusiasm by Collegium Musicum 90.

Chamber Music

Telemann published an enormous amount of chamber music for a wide range of musical combinations and in several different styles, including sonatas, quartets and Corellian trio sonatas. Much of it was aimed at amateur players and was not especially difficult. For this reason it was highly successful and his fame became so widespread that when his largest collection of chamber music, *Musique de table*, was published in 1733, 52 of the 206 subscriptions came from abroad. The predominant style is what the eighteenth-century dubbed "galant", meaning music in which simple melodies and clear textures convey a mood of easy-going elegance and charm.

The Ensemble Florilegium disc is a fine selection of consistently first-rate and beautiful music, even though much of it recalls other composers. Four of the five works use a recorder or flute to carry the melody, the exception being the *Sonata in F Major*, an uncannily accurate evocation of Corelli's chamber music.

Solo Instrumental Music

Of the relatively small amount of solo instrumental music that Telemann wrote, the *Twelve Fantasies* for flute and the *Twelve Fantasies* for solo violin are outstanding. The latter pieces invite comparison with J.S. Bach's slightly earlier works for solo violin, but Telemann's approach is rather different. Though the first six fantasies have contrapuntal elements, including fugues, they don't have Bach's sense of organic development (the exception is the

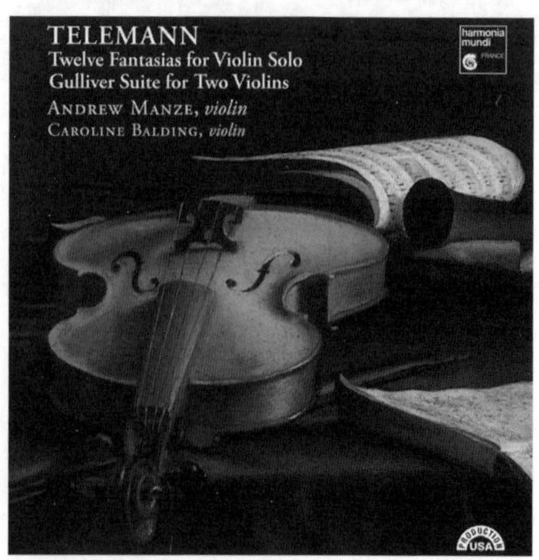

last one), placing more emphasis on the contrast between the movements. Fantasies six to twelve are in more of a "galant" style, full of delightfully bright and sprightly melodies. They have neither the emotional range nor the musical complexity of Bach's solo violin pieces, but these fantasias are among Telemann's most personal and rewarding works.

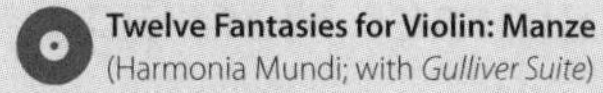
Twelve Fantasies for Violin: Manze
(Harmonia Mundi; with *Gulliver Suite*)

Andrew Manze's informative sleeve notes suggest that Baroque unaccompanied instrumental works derived from a lost tradition of extemporizing. His performance certainly possesses a refreshing air of spontaneity and elan, as well as a gracious wit and a seemingly effortless virtuosity. As a fill-up he performs, with Caroline Balding, a suite for two violins inspired by *Gulliver's Travels*.

Michael Tippett (1905–1998)

Michael Tippett was nearly thirty years old when Elgar died, yet he was more obviously a modern composer than his immediate contemporaries Walton and Britten. A late starter, he did not produce his first recognized score until he was thirty, and attracted virtually no public attention until he was nearly forty. When he did, however, his neo-Romantic notions of self-expression attracted considerable, if far from universal, enthusiasm. Tippett always remained a maverick belonging to no category except his own. On the one hand he had little sympathy with the ideas of modernity represented by serialism, but on the other he wrote music that is markedly more complex and demanding than that of a more traditional composer such as Malcolm Arnold (see p.12).

He did not begin to study music properly until he was eighteen years old, but then applied himself vigorously to the mechanics and fundamentals of composition while at the Royal College of Music. In characteristic style he passed up the chance to study with Vaughan Williams, fearing to become a mere imitator of such a powerful figure. A spell as a schoolteacher and the first performances of his own works were followed by further study with R.O. Morris, a leading expert on counterpoint. It was only in the mid-1930s that his work began to develop a personality of its own, culminating in the remarkable *Concerto for Double String Orchestra* (1939).

Tippett was one of the most widely read and intellectually curious of modern composers, and his beliefs play a conspicuous part in much of his work. In coming to terms with his homosexuality he underwent Jungian analysis and this had the most profound and far-reaching effect on his music. Much of his work, beginning with the oratorio *A Child of Our Time* (1941), represents a quest for wholeness, a reconciliation of the dark and the light contained – he believed – within everyone. A committed pacifist, he had a spell in Wormwood Scrubs in World War II for refusing to carry out his noncombatant military duties.

Apart from composing, Tippett exerted a profound influence as a teacher, most notably in his eleven years as director of music at Morley College, London. As great an encourager of amateurs as of professionals, he was a passionate if erratic conductor, with a special passion for the music of his great English forebear, Henry Purcell.

In 1946, inspired by the success of his friend Benjamin Britten's *Peter Grimes*, Tippett began work on his first full-scale opera, *A Midsummer Marriage*. Though it contained some of the most refulgently lyrical music by an English composer, its libretto (which he wrote himself) was attacked by most critics for its alleged obscurity and pretentiousness – a criticism that was repeated for all his subsequent operas with the possible exception of *King Priam* (1961). Even so, by the 1960s he was at last beginning to be acknowledged as a major figure in his native England and, following a trip to America in 1965, something of a cult figure in the US.

In the end it is the humanity that shines out of Tippett's complicated music, an essentially optimistic and affirmative vision that has attracted as many people as it has irritated: "I have to sing songs for those who can't sing for themselves. Those songs come from the torments and horrors that have happened. I can't lose faith in humanity."

The Midsummer Marriage

The Midsummer Marriage is a quest opera inspired by two great fantasies: Mozart's *The Magic Flute*, in the way two sets of lovers undergo a trial before they can be united; and Shakespeare's *A Midsummer Night's Dream*, in the way that the lovers' world overlaps with a supernatural world which may be a dream. The principal set of lovers, Jennifer and Mark, reach a spiritual maturity by recognizing those elements of each other that exist in themselves, and in this they are obliquely assisted by the He-Ancient and the She-Ancient – guardians of the temple in the woods – and opposed by Jennifer's father, the dark and materialistic King Fisher. Central to the work are the "Four Ritual Dances" that enact the constant seasonal cycle of death and rebirth.

Critics were initially baffled by all this symbolism, but what makes *The Midsummer Marriage* convincing is the sheer vigour and richness of the music, which conveys – more clearly than the words – a genuine sense of transcendence, and which reaches extraordinary heights of ecstatic lyricism. Tippett's score is determinedly tonal and lyrical, with its roots planted firmly in the English pastoral tradition.

Carlyle, Harwood, Remedios, Burrows, Herincx; Royal Opera House Chorus and Orchestra; Davis (Lyrita; 2 CDs)

Recorded in 1971, this fine performance stands as one of Colin Davis's greatest achievements. Resisting the temptation to wallow in the splendour of the writing, Davis's disciplined approach illuminates the often thickly Romantic orchestration. Alberto Remedios brings a true sense of impetuous vitality to Mark, and is nicely matched by the delicate beauty of Joan Carlyle's Jennifer.

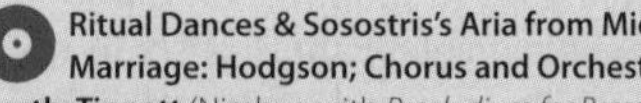

Ritual Dances & Sosostris's Aria from Midsummer Marriage: Hodgson; Chorus and Orchestra of Opera North; Tippett (Nimbus; with *Praeludium for Brass, Bells and Percussion & Suite for the Birthday of Prince Charles*)

If you want a brief sample of the opera, then this disc is the place to start. The *Ritual Dances*, which are frequently performed as concert pieces, sound particularly mysterious and evocative under Tippett's direction, and Alfreda Hodgson gives a powerful account of Sosostris's aria (though unfortunately the sleeve notes do not include the words).

King Priam

King Priam marked a radical shift from the lyrical and celebratory nature of *Midsummer Marriage* to something more bitter and clamorous. The opera was first performed at the Coventry Festival of 1962, which celebrated the building of a new cathedral from the ashes of the old one destroyed in World War II. It is a story and a landscape filled with the suffering and pain of seemingly arbitrary and pointless killing, presented from the perspective of the losers.

The most obvious musical difference between *King Priam* and *The Midsummer Marriage* is the way the lush and largely contrapuntal orchestral writing of the earlier work is replaced by something leaner and more focused. The raucous opening fanfare sets the dark background mood for the whole work, against which individual scenes are set in relief. Achilles gets the most lyrical moment in the opera, the guitar-accompanied "O rich-soiled land", and also the most chilling, when – hearing of Patroclus's death – he puts on his armour and gives forth his terrible war cry.

Bailey, Harper, Allen, Palmer, Langridge, Minton, Tear, Roberts, Murray, Wilson-Johnson; London Sinfonietta Chorus; London Sinfonietta; Atherton (Chandos; 2 CDs)

This outstanding recording was originally issued on Argo in 1981, and it's hard to imagine it being bettered. Norman Bailey brings both authority and vulnerability to Priam, and Robert Tear makes a commanding Achilles. The extraordinary tension and violence of Tippett's score is brought out by conductor David Atherton with considerable energy and panache.

A Child of Our Time

Tippett began his oratorio *A Child of Our Time* at the beginning of World War II but it was not performed until 1944. During the Depression years Tippett had been profoundly affected by the social deprivation caused by unemployment, but it was the 1938 Nazi pogrom known as Kristallnacht that was the work's real catalyst. T.S.

Eliot agreed to write the libretto but when he saw Tippett's scenario he felt that the composer's own text would be less distractingly poetic. Tippett modelled his composition on Handel's *Messiah* and the Bach *Passions*, employing recitatives, arias and dramatic choruses. In place of Bach's Lutheran chorales he had the inspired idea of punctuating the work with five negro spirituals, to which each episode returns. There's a wintry feel to the work and many of Tippett's operatic ideas are foreshadowed in the powerfully emotional and dramatic music. The most telling line – "I would know my shadow and my light, so shall I at last be whole" – stands as a kind of encapsulation of Tippett's beliefs.

Robinson, Walker, Garrison, Cheek; City of Birmingham Symphony Orchestra and Chorus; Tippett (Naxos)

There are now several recordings of Tippett's choral masterpiece in the catalogue. This one – conducted by the composer when he was 85 – has the advantage of a straightforward directness and sincerity. It's a studio recording, but the spacious sound creates the ambience of a live performance.

Orchestral Works

Beethoven was the young Tippett's musical idol and his first three symphonies (spread over nearly thirty years) are knotty contrapuntal reinterpretations of the Classical, while the single-movement fourth (1977) is looser in form, closer to a symphonic poem. On the whole Tippett's smaller orchestral works have proved more popular, in particular the *Concerto for Double String Orchestra* (1939) and the *Fantasia Concertante on a Theme of Corelli* (1953). The former is Tippett's finest work from the 1930s, a rhythmically dynamic homage to the Baroque concerto grosso whose two outer movements have a gloriously spring-heeled linearity which frame the serenely melodious (and unmistakably English) Adagio cantabile.

Commissioned by the Edinburgh Festival in 1953 to celebrate the tercentenary of Corelli's birth, the *Fantasia Concertante on a Theme of Corelli* is a densely elaborate set of variations for two violins and cello and double string orchestra on a theme from Corelli's *Concerto Grosso Op. 6 No. 2*. It's a less obviously neo-classical work than the *Concerto for Double String Orchestra*, having the same textural density of *The Midsummer Marriage* as well as a similar sense of symbolic transformation. The work progresses through five sections of increasingly fanciful flights of imagination, culminating in a Bach-quoting fugue that subsides into a radiant lyricism before returning to an almost exact replica of the initial variation.

Concerto for Double String Orchestra; Fantasia Concertante on a Theme of Corelli: The Scottish Chamber Orchestra; Tippett (EMI; with *Songs for Dov*)

Unlike many composers, Tippett was an excellent conductor of his own works. Though recorded at the end of his career, these performances are remarkable for their vitality and freshness. The EMI engineers succeed in capturing the all-important separation of the orchestra groupings.

Piano Concerto

Tippett's other major orchestral work from this period is the *Piano Concerto*. In the composer's own words, this piece "had its precise moment of conception years before, when I was listening to a rehearsal of Beethoven's *No. 4 Piano Concerto* with Gieseking, who had just returned to England after the war. I felt moved to create a concerto in which once again the piano might sing." The first of the three movements (the longest at around fifteen minutes) sets smooth-flowing lines of melody against agitated orchestral effects, creating an engaging sense of momentum. Overall the concerto is a heavily contrapuntal composition, but in the slow movement it approaches a more rhapsodic sense of form; the last movement is basically an orchestral rondo, culminating in a marvellous duet for piano and celesta.

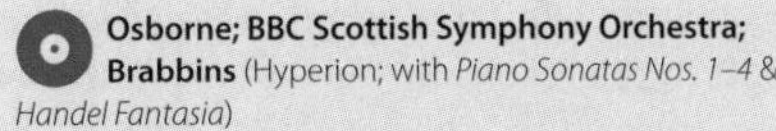

Osborne; BBC Scottish Symphony Orchestra; Brabbins (Hyperion; with *Piano Sonatas Nos. 1–4 & Handel Fantasia*)

John Ogdon's exceptional account of the *Piano Concerto* has gone from the catalogue but this is, arguably, an even more exciting performance. Steven Osborne brings an incisiveness and a focus to this work, and in so doing makes it an even more powerful presence. He's equally persuasive in all four of Tippett's highly original piano sonatas.

String Quartets

Spanning his entire creative life, Tippett's five string quartets allow you to chart the evolution of his distinctive, essentially contrapuntal, style in which the example of Beethoven's chamber music is never too far away. The first three are the most appealing, especially the tuneful *Quartet No. 1* of 1935 (the first piece Tippett was prepared to acknowledge), which successfully reconciles the influences of Sibelius, Beethoven and English folk song. The second and third quartets, dating from 1942 and 1946, are grandly expressive creations, distinguished by close attention to the textures and intricacies of part-writing – three of the movements of *Quartet No. 3*, for example, are fugal in structure. The last two quartets are more difficult. The *Quartet No. 4* is an abrasive piece that illustrates a sometimes too obvious cradle-to-grave programme (also the theme of the *Symphony No. 4*), while *Quartet No. 5*, using material from the opera *New Year*, clearly aspires to a visionary radiance which is only fitfully achieved.

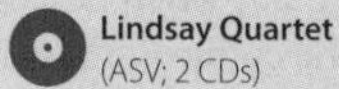

Lindsay Quartet
(ASV; 2 CDs)

In general Tippett's energetic counterpoint is well suited to the vigorous and exuberant style of playing of the Lindsay Quartet, for whom the fourth and fifth quartets were written specifically. Although other fine performances of the quartets exist on CD, these have an authority and a confidence that are extremely persuasive.

Michael Torke (1961–)

Michael Torke, one of the brightest stars to emerge on the American music scene in the last 25 years, has been described as both a post-minimalist and a postmodernist. The former label has been applied to him because his highly energetic music appears to have its roots in the tightly organized rhythmic systems of Glass and Reich, while the latter is due to his cool, polystylistic eclecticism. One of his first works to make a strong impact, *The Yellow Pages* (1986), typically combines a bass line taken from a Chaka Khan song with the bright, clean sonorities of Stravinsky's neo-classical phase carried along by a pulsating, toe-tapping beat. His music is an exhilarating mix that seems to work best in the texturally uncluttered world of chamber music, although several of Torke's full orchestral scores have proved popular as ballet music – especially with the American choreographer Peter Martins – and some of his vocal works, such as *Four Proverbs* (1993), have met with critical acclaim.

Born and brought up in Milwaukee, Wisconsin, Torke was something of a prodigy, studying the piano and composing from the age of five. As a teenager he won prizes for both piano and composition and began learning the bassoon. Surprisingly, considering his later development, popular music made very little impact on him at this time and it was only when attending the Eastman School of Music that he discovered jazz and rock and began attempting to instil some of their vitality and spontaneity into his own music. Further study took place at Yale University with Jacob Druckman and Martin Bresnick, and it was there that he wrote *The Yellow Pages* and his first "colour" work for orchestra, *Ecstatic Orange* (1985).

The many colour references in Torke's work reflect his interest in synaesthesia – the ability to perceive one sensory stimulus in terms of another. Works like *Ecstatic Orange* and *Bright Blue Music* (1985) are his attempt to make a

Michael Torke.

Postmodernism and After

One of the most striking – and confusing – aspects of contemporary classical music is the bewildering range of styles employed by today's composers, from the quasi-medieval simplicity of Arvo Pärt's *Fratres* to the computer-assisted complexities of Kaija Saariaho's *Nymphea* (to name just two examples). The roots of this diversity extend back to the 1960s, the decade in which the modernist tradition which had begun with Schoenberg's early atonal works and culminated in the serial experiments of the Darmstadt School (see p.384) lost its pre-eminent position: composers finally tired of its prescriptive laws, and many grew bored with the monochrome and angst-ridden music which it tended to produce, even in the hands of its finest exponents.

One of the most notable breaks with modernism came with the advent of minimalism, whose various practitioners – Riley and Reich in the US, Andriessen in Holland, Pärt and Górecki in Eastern Europe – all rejected serialism's anarchic complexity in favour of simpler and more consonant styles. Other composers soon followed suit by returning to previously outlawed types of material. In England and Germany, musicians such as Maw, Holloway and Rihm began to look back to late-Romantic music for their inspiration, while Alfred Schnittke in Russia developed his notion of "polystylism", with its free mingling of musics past and present. Subsequently, younger composers like the post-minimalist Michael Torke and the eclectic Mark-Anthony Turnage have continued to open up the previously tightly guarded frontiers of classical music to a host of new influences, not only from the classical past but also the worlds of pop, jazz and world music.

This collective turn towards a more inclusive and less dogmatic aesthetic – often described as postmodernism – is much more than a simple act of artistic nostalgia or escapism. For many composers, the failure of serialism to provide a coherent universal language was proof that the Western musical tradition had reached an impasse, and that the only way was back, or at least sideways – a fact acknowledged even by modernist giants such as Berio and Ligeti, whose later music was enriched by influences ranging from Mahler symphonies to the music of Central Africa. Not that the modernist tradition is absolutely dead: younger composers such as Magnus Lindberg and George Benjamin continue to pave distinctly innovative paths. But for the time being, the promised land of a totally new music – perhaps using the potentially limitless resources of computer-generated sound – remains some way over the horizon. Meanwhile, one of postmodernism's most positive by-products has been the way in which contemporary classical music has increasingly re-entered the musical mainstream, with the works of audience-pleasers like Górecki and Tavener achieving a mass popularity never enjoyed by their more challenging predecessors – though whether this signals true artistic health, or simply the increasing commodification of Western art music, remains to be seen.

coherent aural equivalent of specific colour sensations. With their rich orchestration (*The New York Times* called him "the Ravel of his generation"), the "colour" pieces constitute Torke's most self-conscious mixing of disparate stylistic elements. In *Ash* (1989), for instance, it's as if the first movement of a rather nondescript nineteenth-century symphony has got permanently locked into its opening moments. This is postmodernism at its most pompous and banal, and fortunately an avenue of exploration that Torke seems to have abandoned.

When Torke's oddball stylistic matches and unpredictable rhythmic variations are applied with a lighter touch, however, the results can be both thrilling and illuminating. His great gift is that he can unify apparently contradictory material into coherent statements while maintaining the clarity and integrity of individual elements. And he has a unique way of exploiting a tension between free-form spontaneity and tight structural control. The result, comparable to the collages of Robert Rauschenberg, has an unblinking confidence that seems to encapsulate a very particular American optimism.

Many of Torke's works were recorded on the Argo label, but the composer has subsequently acquired the rights to these performances and re-released them (along with other recordings) on his own Ecstatic Records. They are available via his own website, *www.michaeltorke.com*. His first opera, about the great Brazilian Formula 1 driver Ayrton Senna, is due to be premiered by English National Opera in 2011.

Chamber Works

In nearly all of Torke's music there's an implicit tension between a kind of free-form spontaneity and the tight structural control that he likes to impose on his material. An early work, the jazz-inspired *Vanada* (1984) bustles with a restless urban energy but, like fast-moving people in a modern city, each element knows precisely where it is heading. It's one of Torke's harshest scores, close in spirit to the aggressive European minimalism of Louis Andriessen (see p.10). An American tint can also be heard in *Adjustable Wrench* (1987), which introduces a new melodic element but also shows Torke the stylistic magpie, changing the mood by introducing the unexpected, such as a bass guitar riff followed by sustained brass chords in big-band-style. In *Rust* (1989) there's a return to the metallic sound-world of *Vanada*, but broken into by a section of surprising lyricism. Torke's great gift is that he can unify apparently contradictory material into coherent statements while maintaining the clarity and integrity of individual elements.

Rust; Vanada; Slate; Flint; Music on the Floor: London Sinfonietta; Nagano; Miller (Ecstatic Records)

These recordings have a beautifully balanced and crystalline sound that is perfectly suited to Torke's high-energy music, permitting every strand of his often complex textures to emerge clean and true. The performances are hard to fault – the energy and chutzpah of the playing are completely winning.

Adjustable Wrench; Overnight Mail; Monday & Tuesday: Zagrosek, Hempel; Orkest De Volharding; London Sinfonietta; Nagano (Ecstatic Records)

This disc combines a tight yet characterful performance of *Adjustable Wrench* with two other works for large chamber ensemble. *Monday & Tuesday*, inspired by the periodicity of the Earth's rotation, is full of dazzling rhythmic energy, while *Overnight Mail* focuses on resolving dissonances in melodic leaps rather than in the traditional stepwise motion.

Four Proverbs & Book of Proverbs

Completed in 1993, *Four Proverbs* is one of Torke's most original and interesting works. Scored for female voice, five strings and pairs of clarinets, saxophones and keyboards, it's a predominantly light and airy work full of typically Torkean syncopation. Its most characteristic feature is the treatment of the texts, drawn from the biblical Book of Proverbs, in which Torke finds a beautiful "intersection of poetry and ethics". He starts conventionally, setting a line of text to a melody, but each word remains "pinned" to the note that it was initially sung on. Then, as the thematic material is developed and reworked, the words reappear, but re-arranged, acting, in the composer's words, as "a signifier, a flag mounted on the back of each note giving the listener an idea of where those notes are going in the course of musical development". Torke employs the same technique on a bigger scale in *Book of Proverbs* (1996), a longer piece scored for soprano and baritone soloists, orchestra and choir.

Bott, Anderson, Ollmann; Argo Band; London Sinfonietta; Netherlands Radio Choir and Philharmonic Orchestra; Torke; De Waart (Ecstatic Records)

Catherine Bott and the Argo Band give an excellent performance of the *Four Proverbs*, bringing off the lilting melodies and softly driving rhythms with a suitably cool sense of forward movement. The account of the *Book of Proverbs*, conducted by Edo De Waart, is no less impressive.

Mark-Anthony Turnage (1960–)

Mark-Anthony Turnage exploded into prominence in 1988 when his opera *Greek*, a brash and brutish vision of Thatcher's Britain, was premiered first in Munich and then in London. A retelling of the Oedipus myth set in the East End of London, *Greek* was attacked by some critics (including Steven Berkoff, on whose play it was based) for being crude, strident and simplistic. But even those who disliked it were impressed by the brilliance of the orchestral writing – music that pinpointed a mood or an emotion with more directness than the work's rather relentless vocal style. After *Greek*, Turnage expressed considerable ambivalence about opera as a genre and concentrated on orchestral writing, steadily forging a distinctive and powerful style of smouldering colours and dark intensity.

Brought up in Grays, Essex (one of the gloomier London satellites), Turnage began composition lessons with Oliver Knussen (see p.280) at the age of 15, later continuing his studies at the Royal College of Music, where Knussen taught. In 1983 a scholarship to Tanglewood led to further study with Gunther Schuller and Hans Werner Henze (see p.253), who commissioned *Greek* for the Munich Biennale. An even more profound influence on the evolution of Turnage's style was jazz. Increasingly, his orchestral scores seemed to occupy the same emotional terrain as the work of artists like Gil Evans and Miles Davis, and it is clear that Turnage regards the directness of expression and formal freedom of jazz as better able to communicate the anxieties and ambiguities of modern urban life than what he sees as the formulaic language of classic modernism.

Another catalyst in the development of Turnage's style was a four-year stint as composer in association with the City of Birmingham Symphony Orchestra. This afforded him the luxury of working out ideas in close collaboration with performers, and resulted in increasingly bold and complex orchestral textures. A similar arrangement with English National Opera resulted in a full-length opera, *The Silver Tassie*, based on a play by Sean O'Casey and premiered in 2000. Though it generated less hype and was less immediately hard-hitting than *Greek*, it showcased a more refined and mature Turnage at work. Since then, Turnage's output has included a number of overtly jazz-based compositions, including *Scorched* (2002), a collaboration with guitarist John Scofield for jazz trio and orchestra, and the orchestral pieces *Scherzoid* (2005) and *Chicago Remains* (2007). He is currently working on a commission from the Royal Opera House of an opera based on the life of the late Anna Nicole Smith, a former glamour model and *Playboy* centrefold.

Orchestral Music

Night Dances (1981), the first orchestral piece to get Turnage noticed, already displays many typical stylistic touches. Written "to evoke feelings and emotions aroused by my first encounter with Black music", this is an overwhelmingly atmospheric work that employs a highly original mesh of instrumental voices – shimmering percussion, an amplified solo group and offstage string quintet – that manages to be both sensual and slightly unnerving.

Time and again, the raw and anguished eloquence of the saxophone figures strongly in Turnage's work and in 1994 he wrote *Your Rockaby* – a saxophone concerto in all but name. Partly inspired by a Samuel Beckett monologue of the same name, the piece pitches the solitary voice of the saxophone against a kaleidoscopic orchestral backdrop that is part Ravel, part urban sleaze. Another remarkable concertante work is *Dispelling the Fears*, in which two solo trumpets gradually move from harsh insistency to touching lyrical rapture. Originally scored for full orchestra, it was later scaled down to become the final movement of *Blood on the Floor* (see below).

Your Rockaby; Night Dances; Dispelling the Fears; Some Days: BBC Symphony Orchestra; London Sinfonietta; Philharmonia Orchestra; Davis; Knussen; Harding (Decca; 2 CDs; with *Blood on the Floor*)

Contemporary works often suffer from under-rehearsal, but in these superb recordings, Turnage's sound-world seems well and truly lived-in. The soloists in particular bring a degree of finesse and nuance which raise this music to a very high level. The sound, too, is stunning throughout, combining lucidity with warmth and naturalness.

Blood on the Floor

Turnage's tendency to place the violent in close proximity to the tender can be heard at its most extreme in a, highly personal work: *Blood on the Floor* (1996). This suite in nine movements takes its title from a Francis Bacon painting, but much of it is a response by Turnage to his brother's death from a heroin overdose (as evidenced by movements with titles such as "Junior Addict" and "Needles"). Turnage worked closely with long-time collaborator Martin Robertson and two American jazz musicians, guitarist John Scofield and drummer Pete Erskine, in shaping the work, and it's they who take centre stage improvising and interacting, concertante style, within the bustling, abrasive sounds of the ensemble. It is Turnage's richest score to date, and shows his remarkable ability to fuse elements from the world of rock and classical jazz – there's a definite element of Miles Davis in "Elegy for Andy" – without any feeling of jarring contradiction or contrivance.

Scofield; Erskine, Robertson, Ensemble Modern; Rundel (Decca; 2 CDs; with *Your Rockaby, Night Dances, Dispelling the Fears & Some Days*)

This is the only available recording of *Blood on the Floor*, but there's no need for alternatives. Turnage wrote it expressly for these performers, and they do the composer proud from first bar to last, weaving perfectly into the highly varied textures of the Ensemble Modern, who play with their customary verve and conviction.

U

Viktor Ullmann (1898–1944)

In 1938, mirroring the infamous *Entartete Kunst* (Degenerate Art) exhibition in Munich, the Nazis organized an exhibition of *Entartete Musik* in Düsseldorf, where the public was invited to sneer at recordings of the offending creations. "Degenerate" in this instance meant anything vaguely avant-garde, anything with jazz or black American associations, and anything written by a Jew. Blacklisted composers such as Korngold, Schoenberg, Weill, Zemlinsky and Hindemith soon emigrated; some of the lesser known were to endure marginalization and neglect, but at least they escaped with their lives. Others, such as Hans Krása, Erwin Schullhof and Viktor Ullmann, were not so lucky. A generation of composers was annihilated by the Nazis, and it's only in recent years that their music has been rediscovered, so that at last we can assess the true history of twentieth-century music in central Europe.

Viktor Ullmann sketched at Terezín by Petr Kien.

Ullmann was born into a German-speaking family in Teschen (now Tecín) on the Moravian–Polish border, but received his musical education in Vienna, where he joined Schoenberg's composition class in 1918. Schoenberg, Zemlinsky and Berg all became personal friends and strong influences, though Ullmann's highly chromatic music resisted the atonality of the Second Viennese School and always retained a strong tonal centre. In the 1920s he worked as assistant to Zemlinsky in Prague, then took up posts in Aussig and Zürich before giving up his musical career to run the Anthroposophic Society's bookshop in Stuttgart, devoting himself to the dissemination of Rudolf Steiner's philosophy of self-knowledge. Hitler's rise to power forced him back to Prague in 1933, but it was to prove a temporary haven.

After the Nazi occupation of Czechoslovakia it is thought he tried, but failed, to emigrate. Soon after he was sent to the Jewish ghetto established by the Nazis in the town of Terezín, otherwise known as Theresienstadt. On his arrival in September 1942, Ullmann was excused the customary work assignment and asked to organize concerts and musical activities. He wrote reviews and set up a group to give performances of works by Terezín composers – Gideon Klein, Hans Krása, Pavel Haas and Ullmann himself – as well as by Mahler, Schoenberg and Zemlinsky. During his two years in Terezín, Ullmann was more prolific than at any other time in his life, writing three piano sonatas, the beautiful *String Quartet No. 3*, several songs and orchestral scores, and perhaps his most remarkable work, the satirical opera *Der Kaiser von Atlantis*. In October 1944, not long after the first performance of *Der Kaiser* had been banned by the SS, Ullmann and the majority of the composers and musicians in Terezín were transported to the gas chambers of Auschwitz.

Der Kaiser von Atlantis

Ullmann wrote two operas in Prague immediately before the war – *Der Sturz des Antichrist* (The Fall of the Antichrist) and *Der zerbrochene Krug* (The Broken Jug) – but his most remarkable work, *Der Kaiser von Atlantis* (The Emperor of Atlantis), was written in the appalling conditions of the Terezín ghetto and designed for performance there. The opera portrays a paranoid emperor fighting wars on all fronts until Death, "an old-fashioned craftsman of dying", refuses to work any longer, in protest at the infernal mechanization of killing. With the sick and wounded now condemned to live on in agony, the emperor pleads with Death to return to work, but he will do so only on one condition – that the emperor agrees to be his first victim.

Der Kaiser was prepared up to the dress rehearsal, but then banned after the slow-witted SS officers at last saw it as a satire of Hitler, and the opera only got its premiere in 1975. Ullmann's score is an eclectic mixture of cabaret music, pastiche (there is a daring minor-key version of the German national anthem), operetta and lush Romanticism, for a band that includes saxophone, banjo and harmonium. Death is depicted in music of ecstatic beauty, dripping with sumptuous harmonies – not a fearsome character, but a reliable and faithful friend, merciful and welcoming. The ultimate message is one of hope mingled with resignation, as Death himself declares: "It's not the other side we need fear, but rather this world that is veiled in darkest shadow."

Mazura, Kraus, Berry, Vermillion; Leipzig Gewandhaus Orchestra; Zagrosek
(Decca; with *Hölderlin-Lieder*)

This premiere recording is extremely fine, if not completely ideal. The serious moments are extremely well done, but the lighter ones just lack that final sense of dangerous fun. Walter Berry as Death is too old and crusty to bring over the role's lyrical seductiveness, but the other voices are well suited, with Michael Kraus deeply powerful in the emperor's farewell aria. The closing chorale is unutterably moving.

Orchestral Works

Ullmann wrote some impressive orchestral pieces before the war, including the uncompromising *Variations and Double Fugue on a Piano Piece of Schoenberg* (1934) and the powerfully lyrical *Piano Concerto* (1939). As with his operas, though, the extremity of Terezín produced his finest work. The manuscript of Ullmann's *Piano Sonata No. 7*, which he completed only a few weeks before he was transported to Auschwitz, was covered with notes for its orchestration into a symphony. Now completed by the German composer Bernhard Wulff, this *Symphony in D* is a final summation of Ullmann's savagely curtailed career – including a quotation from *Der Sturz des Antichrist* and a waltz from Heuberger's operetta *Der Opernball*, which Ullmann worked on in Prague, it ends with an impressive *Variations and Fugue on a Hebrew Folksong*. The source tune for this resilient final movement, a Zionist song which would have been familiar to many inmates of Terezín, is transformed into a Czech Hussite hymn whose message of national liberation would also not have been lost on the symphony's intended audience.

Symphony in D; Piano Concerto; Variations and Double Fugue on a Piano Piece of Schoenberg: Richter; Brno Philharmonic; Yinon (Bayer)

This first recording of the *Symphony in D* reveals it as a very fine work indeed, with Israel Yinon keeping a grip on the fluid scoring. In the *Piano Concerto* Konrad Richter finds just the right balance of power and gentle lyricism, and a compelling reading of the *Variations and Double Fugue* completes the best all-round CD of Ullmann's works.

Chamber & Piano Music

Ullmann's most accomplished piece in Terezín, and the one most likely to enter the standard concert repertoire, is the *String Quartet No. 3*, which was written in January 1943 although it isn't known whether it was ever performed in Terezín. It has a beautiful lyrical opening tinged with a melancholy typical of his Viennese background, while in the slow movement he ventures into the world of Schoenberg and Berg with a twelve-note motif, though he always retains an underlying sense of tonality. Ullmann's seven piano sonatas – the final three written in Terezín – are of more specialized interest, but they show him as a distinctive voice in the central European musical tradition. The writing can seem a little indigestible at first, but it's worth persevering with.

String Quartet No. 3; Piano Sonatas Nos. 5–7: Kolben Kraus Group for New Music, (Koch International)

Volume 1 in Koch's Terezín Music Anthology features a fine performance of the *Quartet No. 3*, with an appropriately luscious opening and beautifully blended lines. Edith Kraus, who plays the sixth sonata, premiered this piece in the ghetto, and it's the most attractive of the three sonatas on this disc (the seventh sounds better orchestrated as the *Symphony in D*). This disc is now hard to find, but the identical programme is also available on the Praga label well played by the Kocian Quartet and pianist Radoslav Kvapil.

V

Edgard Varèse (1883–1965)

As early as 1917 Edgard Varèse spoke of instruments which could offer "a whole new world of unsuspecting sounds", foreshadowing the use of synthesizers and computers in contemporary music. He devoted his life to new ideas, new instruments and new music, and though his output is fairly meagre by comparison with many of the twentieth century's great innovators he was to be a prime influence on the post-war avant-garde, rejecting melody in favour of a rhythmically propelled aural abstraction. "I am not a musician", he once said. "I work with rhythms, frequencies and intensities. Tunes are the gossips in music."

Of Franco-Italian parentage (the pianist Alfred Cortot was a cousin), Varèse's serious musical studies began at the Schola Cantorum in Paris, where his independent spirit led to clashes with the director, Vincent d'Indy. By 1909 he was in Berlin, where he became friends with Busoni (see p.119) and was impressed by his ideas for "a new music". Varèse found employment there as a conductor but by 1913 he was back in Paris. He attended the riotous premiere of *The Rite of Spring*, a work with which he felt an immediate sympathy – the audience around him screamed abuse at the stage, but Varèse remarked: "The music seemed very natural to me."

Conscripted in 1914, he was discharged through illness and escaped to America the following year. Varèse's arrival in New York – where he was to spend the rest of his life – was the start of his career as an evangelist for new music. He organized an International Composers Guild for the presentation of works by Schoenberg, Stravinsky and Webern, and his first major composition, *Amériques* (1922), displayed his espousal of Stravinsky's anti-Romantic intensity, using plentiful brass and woodwind to invoke the pounding presence of the new world. "I refuse to limit myself to sounds that have already been heard", he declared. After labouring for years on *Arcana,* a huge work for 120 musicians but no string sections, his search for new sonorities led to *Ionisation* (1931), in which sirens, anvils, gourds and sleigh bells compete for attention.

In the 1930s and 1940s he explored the sonic potential of various electromechanical devices and new instruments such as the theremin and the Ondes Martenot – the latter famously employed by Messiaen in a number of works (see p.339). In the 1950s Varèse went on to compose *Déserts* (1954), a pioneering work for magnetic tape and, in 1958, the vast *Poème électronique* for tape and 400 loudspeakers. This was co-created with Xenakis (see p.638) as the main feature of the Philips Pavilion at the Brussels World's Fair of that year. He died seven years later, hailed as a visionary by Stockhausen, the composer whose work did most to realize Varèse's vision of an electronic future.

Complete Works: Royal Concertgebouw Orchestra; Asko Ensemble; Chailly (Decca; 2 CDs)

This recording of Varèse's complete works is quite an achievement. It's headed by Riccardo Chailly, who conducts with great sensitivity and insight, evincing superbly subtle timbres and biting rhythms from the RCO. As well as the famous pieces and Varèse's original tape of *Poème électronique*, there are unpublished and previously unrecorded pieces such as *Tuning Up* and the original of *Amériques*, prepared by Varèse's friend and pupil Chou-Wen Chung.

Amériques & Ionisation

Varèse's search for new sonic possibilities was influenced by Luigi Russolo, the Italian Futurist who created noise machines and whose manifesto *The Art of Noises* proposed a new world of organized sound which simulated the disparate soundscape of modern urban life. In *Amériques*, premiered by members of the Philadelphia Orchestra under Stokowski, Varèse calls for nine percussionists including two sets of timpani, a siren and the roar of a lion (later changed to Ondes Martenot). It's a work of raw rhythmic energy – with the occasional moment of lyrical repose – which evokes the brash, angular and violent sounds of the city. Varèse described it as being about "new worlds on earth, in the sky or in the minds of men" and it marks the beginning of his fascination with the expressive possibilities of percussion.

In *Ionisation* (1931) Varèse dispenses with all conventional instruments in favour of percussion. The title rather unhelpfully comes from physics, and refers to the process by which an atom liberates an electron and assumes a positive electric charge. The 37 percussion instruments include bells, piano, glockenspiel, Chinese blocks, anvils, bongos, tam-tams, all manner of drums and two sirens. Its highly concentrated six minutes contrast an astonishing range of sonorities with great virtuosity: a particular tension is set up between sounds that have a hard, abrasive quality and those of a more mellow and softer character. The result suggests an often terrifying dreamscape where images of primeval jungle, of modern urban bustle, and even of warfare, jostle for dominance in the listener's imagination. *Ionisation* was greeted with horror and alarm at its first performance at Carnegie Hall in 1933.

Amériques; Arcana; Density 21.5; Intégrales; Ionisation; Octandre; Offrandes: Beauregard, Yakar; New York Philharmonic & Ensemble Intercontemporain; Boulez (Sony)

This is the best available single CD of Varèse's music. Pierre Boulez has been one of Varèse's greatest champions, and he regularly programmed his music with the New York Phil in the 1970s. This disc contains most of Varèse's major works in powerful and authoritative performances plus some smaller-scale pieces, including the meditative *Density 21.5* for solo flute and the haunting *Octandre* for wind instruments.

Ralph Vaughan Williams (1872–1958)

With his friend and colleague Gustav Holst (see p.262), Vaughan Williams spent many years researching and cataloguing English traditional songs that had never previously been written down, thereby spurring a resurgence in English music comparable to the similar folk-inspired movements within eastern and central Europe. He stands, alongside Elgar and Britten, as one of the most popular twentieth-century English composers, thanks to music that is affirmatively humanistic and individual. Though an almost exact contemporary of Schoenberg, Vaughan Williams was never an experimental composer ("Why need music be original to be enjoyed?" he once asked). But it is wrong to categorize him – as do his detractors – as a nostalgic sentimentalist, forever evoking a fantasy idyll of a rural England that never was. His range is far wider than such a caricature, above all in his nine symphonies, the scope and invention of which can be compared to the seven symphonies of Sibelius – a composer he greatly admired.

As a composer Vaughan Williams showed an early talent but was something of a slow developer. Two bouts of study at the Royal College of Music (first with Parry, then with Stanford) were interrupted by a spell at Cambridge where he read history and obtained his Bachelor of Music degree. He then travelled to Germany for further study with Max Bruch, and as late as 1908 he was in France for lessons in orchestration from Ravel (three years his junior). Ravel, in particular, helped to make Vaughan Williams's sometimes cloggy textures much more transparent, and on his return to England he wrote one of his best-known and most beautiful works – the *Fantasia on a Theme by Thomas Tallis*. By 1914 he had produced a considerable body of music, including two symphonies, and was beginning to find an audience. After World War I – during which he served in the medical corps and the artillery – he threw himself into musical activity, not just composing but also conducting the Bach Choir and Handel Society, and teaching at the Royal College.

During the 1920s his music began to be heard overseas, with notable performances given in Salzburg, Venice, Prague, Geneva and the US. By the middle of the following decade he was established as the figurehead of English music, and was very much in demand as a conductor of his own work. His recordings – notably his 1937 version of the *Symphony No. 4* – testify to a greater talent than he would have admitted. He once began a concert saying, "You start and I'll follow", a self-deprecating joke typical of his modesty.

Success eluded him as an opera composer in spite of several attempts at the genre. Nevertheless much of his finest music can be found in his operas: in particular the short, bleak *Riders to the Sea* (1932) and the epic *The Pilgrim's Progress* (1951). The latter was based on John Bunyan's seventeenth-century religious "novel", a work Vaughan Williams was obsessed with for much of his life, and despite the fact that he referred to himself as an agnostic his several settings of Christian texts display a fervour and an intensity of feeling that seems almost mystical. Like his younger colleague, Tippett (see p.583) – who he stood up for during World War II – he was a lifelong socialist and possessed an essentially optimistic and affirmative view of humanity. He once defined his role with the words, "the composer must not shut himself up and think of art; he must live with his fellows and make his art an expression of the whole life of the community."

Vaughan Williams during World War I.

SYMPHONIES

Without doubt Vaughan Williams's nine symphonies (which span a period of some fifty years) form the finest cycle ever produced in England; ironically so because, as a young composer, he had no intention of writing any. All nine have a distinctive and individual voice, although the first two – the choral *Sea Symphony* and the exuberant *London Symphony* – reveal a small but discernible debt to Elgar. By *Symphony No. 3* (1921) Vaughan Williams had found his own voice, and the ensuing three symphonies reflect his complete confidence in handling large-scale forms. If these four constitute his symphonic masterpieces, then the final three (written in his last decade) are still highly impressive. *Symphony No. 7* was drawn from the music that he wrote for the film *Scott of the Antarctic*, *No. 8* is a relatively light work that is, nonetheless, brilliantly orchestrated, while the epic *No. 9* is, arguably, the most visionary of all his symphonies – a richly scored work partly inspired by Hardy's novel *Tess of the D'Urbevilles*.

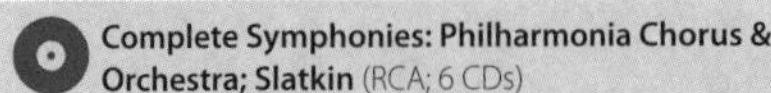
Complete Symphonies: Philharmonia Chorus & Orchestra; Slatkin (RCA; 6 CDs)

Vaughan Williams has been fortunate in interpreters of his symphonies. John Barbirolli and Adrian Boult were skilful advocates; more recently André Previn and Bernard Haitink have brought fresh insights. But of the five complete cycles available, Leonard Slatkin's is the most consistently satisfying. Slatkin never flinches from the more aggressive moments – the fourth and sixth symphonies have a violence that belies Vaughan Williams's cosy pastoral image.

Symphony No. 3 – The Pastoral

Vaughan Williams's belief "that to attach meanings to music is a mistake" could well have been prompted by reactions to his *Symphony No. 3*. Completed in 1921, its four slow movements and modal melodies suggesting folk song (though none are present) were long taken to be a kind of homage to the English countryside. In fact the work was his highly personal and deeply felt response to the recent war: "a great deal of it incubated when I used to go up night after night with the ambulance waggon at Écoivres ... and there was a wonderful Corot-like landscape in the sunset – it's not really lambkins frisking at all, as most people take for granted." Neither is it the sound of guns and actual battle (though the second movement contains a distant bugle call), but rather an internal monologue encapsulating feelings of loneliness, pain and sorrow. But despite its slowness and introspection, its finale seems to offer an image of hope and reconciliation as a lone soprano intones a wordless text.

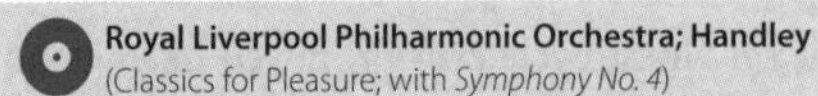
Royal Liverpool Philharmonic Orchestra; Handley (Classics for Pleasure; with *Symphony No. 4*)

Beautiful and measured as it is, Vernon Handley's *Pastoral* leaves one in no doubt that this is one of Vaughan Williams's subtlest works, uniquely mingling rapture and unease. The surface may seem relatively calm, but the underlying slow current is strong, leading eventually to a powerful but ambiguous climax.

Price; New Philharmonia Orchestra; Boult (EMI; with *Symphony No. 5*)

Boult was one of the finest conductors of Vaughan Williams, and his eloquent and emotional vision of the *Pastoral* symphony is wonderfully realized by the New Philharmonia. The recordings, which date from 1968, benefit from good digital remastering.

Symphony No. 4

Premiered by the BBC Symphony Orchestra under Adrian Boult in 1935, it is extremely difficult not to interpret this cataclysmic work as, in some way, representing the mounting crisis in Europe. In particular the first movement, with its brass-heavy, strident opening, evinces a constant sense of anxiety and unspecific threat. Needless to say, Vaughan Williams denied any such reading, claiming that he wrote it "not as a definite picture of anything external ... but simply because it occurred to me like that." While it's perhaps the most tightly structured of his symphonies, with some brilliantly realized contrapuntal writing, the bleakness never lets up, least of all in the long second-movement Andante in which an angular melody played by high strings floats precariously above pizzicato cellos and basses. Even when a hint of humour appears in the finale, in the form of a lumbering fugue, a mood of foreboding soon returns, culminating in the reprise of the symphony's clamorous opening.

London Symphony Orchestra; Hickox (Chandos; with *Mass in G Minor*)

This overwhelming account from Hickox and the LSO captures all the work's violent energy with startling vividness. At the same time Hickox is always conscious of the ebb and flow of Vaughan Williams's long phrases, shaping them with real sensitivity.

BBC Symphony Orchestra; Vaughan Williams (Dutton; with *Symphony No. 5*)

Vaughan Williams knew his own technical limitations as a conductor, but that sense of an orchestra flying by the seat of its pants only adds to the excitement of this 1937 recording. The passion, rage and driven desperation are almost frightening. Coupled with a fine *No. 5* with the same orchestra under Barbirolli.

Symphony No. 5

Dedicated to Sibelius, the *Symphony No. 5* was begun in 1938, while Vaughan Williams was at work on *The Pilgrim's Progress*. Doubting that he would ever complete his operatic magnum opus, he used some of the opera's material for the symphony, which he completed in 1943 but then revised in 1951. The final version is perhaps the very best of all Vaughan Williams's symphonies. The first movement begins with a particularly haunting idea, stated softly by the horns, which is followed by ominously shifting music that foreshadows what's to come beyond the ghostly, muted Scherzo. Everything is leading towards the huge span of the wonderful slow movement, where Vaughan Williams introduces overwhelmingly emotive solos for oboe and violin. Its mood of reverence extends to the finale, a harmonic and rhythmic kaleidoscope that builds to an exalted climax before subsiding into a quietly contemplative state.

Royal Liverpool Philharmonic Orchestra; Handley (Classics for Pleasure; with *Flos Campi* & *Oboe Concerto*)

The opening soft horn-call is pure magic, but what's even better is the way the whole performance seems to grow from this pregnant opening. The flickering elf-lights of the Scherzo, the elegiac nobility of the Romanza and the quasi-choral hymn of serenity at the close all feel woven together into one great musical tapestry.

London Philharmonic Orchestra; Boult (EMI; with *Symphony No. 3*)

Boult's ability to really penetrate Vaughan Williams's scores is clearly in evidence in this 1969 recording of the fifth symphony. The conductor achieves a wonderfully lucid sense of line, and balances the orchestral forces perfectly. The LPO respond well, and the result is a beautifully warm and tender performance.

Symphony No. 6

With the *Symphony No. 6* (1947) Vaughan Williams returns to the brooding world of the fourth, but without that work's unrelenting violence and acerbity. There's an extraordinary energy and power to it, however, built around a tension between major and minor, and between the light, evanescent string writing and the thick, dense sound-world of the brass. This creates a feeling of agitation in the first movement which is briefly dissipated towards the end by a radiant and uplifting folk-style melody. Thereafter the edginess returns: from the anxious, funereal march of the slow movement, with its insistent, percussive rat-a-tat-tat, through the Scherzo's wild dance of death in which a snaky saxophone solo adds a touch of the exotic. Even more disturbing is the eerie quietness of the finale where a delicate counterpoint of strings creates a sense of aimless drifting in an inhospitable landscape. A vision of post-war nihilism is how some critics have interpreted it, although once again the composer rejected any such programmatic readings.

BBC Symphony Orchestra; Davis (Warner; with *Tallis Fantasia* & *The Lark Ascending*)

When it comes to the tortured and turbulent sixth symphony, Andrew Davis and the BBC SO lead the field. This is a performance that really gets to the heart of this often uncomfortable music, helped by the wonderfully natural recorded sound.

OTHER ORCHESTRAL MUSIC

The reputation that Vaughan Williams gained for having a limited range exclusively based around folk-inspired modal melodies (what Elizabeth Lutyens called "cow-pat music") partly derives from the "rustic" opera *Hugh the Drover* (good tunes, patronizing libretto) as well as from a series of orchestral miniatures that seem to conjure up an Edenic picture of England. Vaughan Williams certainly had a visionary picture of the countryside as a haven against the creeping industrialization that seemed to be destroying it. This vision is exemplified by the rhapsodic *The Lark Ascending*, and less poetically in the *Five Variants of "Dives and Lazarus"* based on a folk song that had greatly impressed him. His sense of a native tradition also surfaces in his interest in early English composers, finding expression in both his work on the English Hymnal and in his much-loved orchestral masterpiece *Fantasia on a Theme by Thomas Tallis*. The only later orchestral work to match the depth of the *Fantasia* is the Blake-inspired *Job* (1930), originally commissioned as a ballet but finishing up in its final form as a concert piece.

Fantasia on a Theme by Thomas Tallis

Termed a "Jacobean Fantasy" by the composer, the *Fantasia on a Theme by Thomas Tallis* (1910) is Vaughan Williams's homage to the music of Renaissance England. Specifically it grew out of his work editing the English Hymnal, during which he came across a melody of Thomas Tallis written as a psalm setting in 1567. Vaughan Williams took this basic theme and developed it into music that is both intensely devotional and sumptuously Romantic. Commissioned for the Three Choirs Festival in Gloucester, the *Fantasia* is scored for two string orchestras, the smaller of which was arranged to produce an antiphonal effect, even in acoustics less resonant than the cathedral in which it received its first performance. The *Fantasia* also assigns separate parts to a string quartet, and the numerous independent voices confused many of those present at the premiere – one critic called it "a queer, mad work by an odd fellow from Chelsea". He was probably in the majority, but the work soon secured Vaughan Williams's place as the spiritual leader of English music, and nowadays it's by far the best known of all his works.

Allegri String Quartet; Sinfonia of London; Barbirolli (EMI; with *Fantasia on "Greensleeves"*, Elgar *Introduction and Allegro & Serenade for Strings*)

Barbirolli elicits an absolutely spell-binding account from his forces, which combines delicacy and warmth in equal amounts. This is justifiably regarded as a classic recording with a no less moving performance of the *"Greensleeves" Fantasia* and two works for string orchestra by Elgar.

New Queen's Hall Orchestra; Wordsworth (Decca; 2 CDs; with other orchestral works by Vaughan Williams)

This account, played on period instruments and supposedly in period style, has a uniquely sweet sound, and conductor Barry Wordsworth encourages just about the right amount of gushing. This two-CD set, which gathers together eleven of the composer's orchestral works (conducted by Neville Marriner and Adrian Boult as well as Wordsworth), makes a great introduction to the composer.

The Lark Ascending

Four years after the *Tallis Fantasia*, Vaughan Williams composed *The Lark Ascending* – one of his most simple and direct utterances but also one of the most effective. Described as a Romance for violin and small orchestra, the score was prefaced with some lines by George Meredith that conclude: "Our valley is his golden cup,/ And he the wine which overflows/ To lift us with him when he goes./ Till lost on his aerial rings/In light, and then the fancy rings." A brilliant evocation of the song of the lark, the piece opens with a short orchestral introduction before holding a sustained chord over which the solo violin, tentatively at first, begins its short trilling birdsong phrases which gradually build into an upwardly climbing cadenza of great eloquence. The feel of a hot and hazy summer's day is created by the lilting phrase which marks the orchestra's return. The middle section culminates in a sturdy folk-like melody before the "lark-song" cadenza returns once more.

Brown; Academy of St Martin-in-the-Fields; Marriner (Decca; 2 CDs; with other orchestral works by Vaughan Williams)

Neville Marriner directs the leader of the orchestra, Iona Brown, in a radiant performance of *The Lark Ascending*. The soloist rises from the warm, refulgent glow of the St Martin's string sound which comes even more into its own on the three other works. Part of the same two-CD set as the above.

Job

Inspired by William Blake's engravings of scenes for the biblical Book of Job, and based on a scenario devised by Blake expert Geoffrey Keynes, *Job (A Masque for Dancing)* is one of Vaughan Williams's finest works, with a rich variety of music in twelve sections that, nonetheless, makes a unified whole. Commissioned as a ballet, the composer completed it as a concert work when staging seemed unlikely, beefing up the orchestra and including parts for organ and alto saxophone. Much of the music has a modal simplicity, but is frequently shot through with piquant harmonies and vigorous counterpoint. In particular "Satan's Dance of Triumph" achieves a wonderfully sinister-comic quality through a combination of angular strings and edgy percussion. No less startling is the "Dance of Job's Comforters" which has an ingratiating alto sax "miaowing" over pizzicato strings, a perfect encapsulation of insincerity. For the celestial music, Vaughan Williams is at his visionary best, with a radiantly affirmative melody for the "Saraband of the Sons of God" and a near-reprise of *The Lark Ascending* for "Elihu's Dance of Youth and Beauty".

BBC Symphony Orchestra; Davis (Warner; with Walton *Belshazzar's Feast*)

This is a highly charged and deeply convincing account of *Job* from the BBC Symphony Orchestra under Andrew Davis. The more contemplative music is played with a rapt and spine-tingling intensity, a quality that serves to highlight the comedic sleaze and jazzy energy of the darker passages.

VOCAL & CHORAL MUSIC

Like Elgar and Parry, Vaughan Williams projected a rather hearty public persona that served to disguise an acute artistic sensitivity. He was a widely read man, and his choice of texts for musical setting reflects this. As an agnostic from a nonconformist background, he tended to favour writers with an intensely individual vision, most notably William Blake and John Bunyan. As a young man he was passionate about Walt Whitman and used his verses on several occasions, notably for the choral *Sea Symphony*, the cantata *Dona Nobis Pacem* and *Toward the Unknown Region*. He also set several verses from A.E. Housman's *A Shropshire Lad*, but interestingly balanced the more morbid side of Housman's output with examples of his rarer rapturous moments.

Sancta Civitas

Vaughan Williams wrote many choral works, but none have established the same kind of position in the repertoire as Elgar's *The Dream of Gerontius*, Walton's *Belshazzar's Feast* or Britten's *War Requiem*. His own favourite among his choral works, and the one that most exemplifies the emotional intensity of his beliefs, is the oratorio *Sancta Civitas* (The Holy City; 1925).

Unfortunately, its difficulty, its shortness – it lasts about thirty minutes – and the large forces it requires mean that performances are infrequent. Using words from the Book of Revelation and Walt Whitman, it presents an incredibly vivid vision of the afterlife which, though it begins and ends in a concentrated stillness, is far from the warm enveloping sound-world of *Gerontius*. *Sancta Civitas* contains some of Vaughan Williams's most startling and most sensuous music and its very concentration makes it an unforgettably powerful experience in performance.

Langridge, Terfel; St Paul's Cathedral Choir; London Symphony Chorus and Orchestra; Hickox (EMI; with *Dona Nobis Pacem*)

This marvellous performance (one of only three in the catalogue) should do much to re-establish this work at the very centre of Vaughan Williams's achievements. Hickox marshals his forces brilliantly, keeping the textures ringingly clear, and it is hard to imagine two more incisive soloists than Philip Langridge and Bryn Terfel.

Songs

Solo songs make up a substantial part of Vaughan Williams's output, of which the Housman settings *On Wenlock Edge* (1908) are the best known. Four years earlier he wrote another fine cycle, *Songs of Travel*, to words by R.L. Stevenson, which Vaughan Williams scholar Michael Kennedy has called "a kind of English *Winterreise*". They combine a typically Edwardian manly vigour with an element of melancholy. At their best (as in "The Vagabond" and "Bright is the Ring of Words") they reveal an acute feeling for word-setting and a rare melodic gift.

On Wenlock Edge was written soon after returning from his studies with Ravel and it contains what Vaughan Williams referred to as "several atmospheric effects". These can be discerned in the scoring for piano quintet, and in certain delicate pictorial passages – the wind blowing in the title song, the chiming of bells in "Bredon Hill". The latter is the longest and most telling song, in which the composer brilliantly captures the changes of mood from the joy of an English summer's day to the wintry presence of death, with the tolling of bells finally taking on a doom-laden oppressive quality.

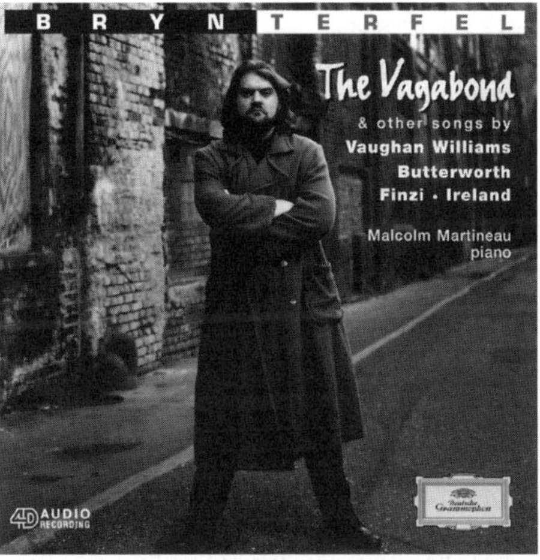

Songs of Travel: Terfel, Martineau (Deutsche Grammophon; with songs by Butterworth, Ireland and Finzi)

This performance by baritone Bryn Terfel has an extra dimension that makes other recordings seem pallid. He's almost unique among modern singers in making every word sound like a real expression of his thoughts and the result, here, is to make what is good (but not great) material sound absolutely first-rate.

On Wenlock Edge: Partridge; Music Group of London (EMI; with *Ten Blake Songs, Four Hymns & Merciless Beauty*, Warlock *The Curlew* etc.)

The lyric tenor of Ian Partridge was at its prime in the early 1970s when this recording was made. It's a very English voice – not unlike Peter Pears – with a pure tone, near-perfect control and an understated fervour that is heard at its best in "Bredon Hill" and the short, intensely beautiful "From Far, from Eve, from Morning".

Giuseppe Verdi (1813–1901)

Verdi's operas are paragons of high Romanticism, with their lavish emotionalism, demanding vocal and instrumental writing, complex plots, high-voltage characterizations and so forth. Yet political engagement was not a notable feature of the lives of most Romantic composers, and Verdi was a supremely political artist. In the aftermath of the Napoleonic wars, Italy was divided into a mosaic of kingdoms and duchies, a situation that prevailed for most of the century, in the face of a burgeoning movement for national unification. Many of the plots of Verdi's earlier operas can be read as allegories related to the aspirations of the Italian people – the well-known "Chorus of the Hebrew Slaves" from *Nabucco* struck a particular chord in an audience living under the rule of countless princelings and foreign oppressors.

Censorship was a bugbear: although Verdi managed to smuggle a topical message into such works as *Nabucco* and *La battaglia di Legnano*, where centuries of history provided a disguise of sorts, in other instances his plots had to be tampered with in order to ensure performance. Such interference achieved nothing, however. As the nationalist movement gathered force in the 1850s and 1860s, and Victor Emmanuel, liberal ruler of Piedmont, became the popular choice for king of a united Italy, the chant "Viva Verdi!" was heard at performances of his work and on the streets – the composer's name being also an acronym for "Vittorio Emmanuele, re d'Italia" (Victor Emmanuel, King of Italy). Verdi himself came to be seen as a figurehead for the unification movement, and once the goal had been achieved he became an active politician, and was elected to the Italian senate in 1874.

There is little in Verdi's early upbringing that foreshadows the cosmopolitan operatic master. His parents ran a village inn in the northern plains of Parma, and everything about his education and early life suggests provincialism. After private studies in Milan (he failed to gain entrance to the city's conservatory) he returned to his home area as music director for the town of Busseto, where he yearned to get back to the Lombard capital. In the end he found it impossible to stifle his ambition to see an opera of his performed at La Scala: in 1839 he resigned his post in Busseto and headed with his family back to Milan. He was fortunate in that his first opera, *Oberto*, was almost immediately accepted for performance, even though his previous compositions of any consequence amounted to just a few academic exercises and liturgical works. *Oberto* was first heard in November of the same year, and it made the Milanese public sit up and take notice of the ambitious 26-year-old.

His second opera, *Il Giorno di Regno* (1840), was a flop, but two years later he produced *Nabucco*, which really saw his career take off. In the wake of its success came a steady stream of commissions from other Italian cities and from

Giuseppe Verdi.

abroad, resulting in thirteen operas in just eight years: *I Lombardi alla prima crociata* (1843), *Ernani* (1844), *I due Foscari* (1844), *Giovanna d'Arco* (1845), *Alzira* (1845), *Attila* (1846), *Macbeth* (1847), *I masnadieri* (1847), *Jérusalem* (1847), *Il corsaro* (1848), *La battaglia di Legnano* (1849), *Luisa Miller* (1849) and *Stiffelio* (1850). By the end of this sequence his mastery of the operatic stage was well established and he had earned so much money he could have retired had he wished. The pace of composition relaxed in the 1850s, but it was in this period that Verdi wrote his most popular operas, beginning with the trio of *Rigoletto* (1851), *Il trovatore* (1853) and *La traviata* (1853), followed by, among others, *Simon Boccanegra* (1857), *Un ballo in maschera* (1859), *La forza del destino* (1862), *Don Carlos* (1867) and *Aida* (1871).

There then followed a gap of some fifteen years before the premiere of another Verdi opera, a phase during which he composed his only non-operatic work of any standing, the *Requiem* (1874), and otherwise concentrated on revising some of his earlier works, whenever new productions or new translations of the libretto brought an opportunity to tighten up structure or expand scenes. *Macbeth*, *La forza del destino*, *Simon Boccanegra* and *Don Carlos* were all overhauled at this time. The revised *Boccanegra* benefited from the involvement of the poet and composer Arrigo Boito, who provided the librettos for Verdi's last two operas, *Otello* (1886) and *Falstaff* (1893). His final years were spent on more religious music, the *Four Sacred Pieces*, and masterminding the foundation of the Casa di Riposa, a retirement home for musicians in Milan, funded by his royalties. He died of a stroke in January 1901 and was buried in the grounds of the Casa di Riposa; a quarter of a million people attended his funeral cortège.

OPERAS

During his time studying in Milan, Verdi had a subscription seat at La Scala and thus became thoroughly conversant with all the latest developments of Italian opera. Accordingly, even his earliest operas revealed a mature knowledge of what was possible on stage. Admittedly, in his earlier work the style is not always up to the demands of the drama: *Macbeth*, for example, for all its wonderful tunes and its dramatic speed, often resorts to rum-tum-tum accompaniments that suggest comedy more than tragedy. It's a stylistic mannerism that even affects mature works such as *La traviata* and *Rigoletto*, but the late works – *Otello* and *Falstaff* in particular –are masterpieces of consistency and continuity. By this stage, too, Verdi's music had gained a much broader harmonic vocabulary, with more subtlety and ease than the rather four-square harmonic language of the early works. And of course one skill he always displayed in profusion was his talent for melody, and it is the striking originality of Verdi's arias and choruses that have made him, with Puccini, the most popular operatic composer in history.

Rigoletto

Rigoletto was the work that revealed Verdi's operatic maturity, and it's always been one of his most popular. The tragic tale of the cursed hunchback jester Rigoletto, the heinous Duke of Mantua, and Rigoletto's daughter Gilda, was based on Victor Hugo's *Le Roi s'amuse*, but thanks to the Venetian censors the action had to be moved from the French royal court to the sixteenth-century ducal court of Mantua. This was admittedly closer to home for its audience, but at least the setting didn't depict a womanizing monarch – Venice was at that time ruled by the monarchist Austrians. *Rigoletto* is an immensely accessible opera, moving swiftly and coherently through a series of memorable arias, choruses and confrontations. Yet it's also a very dark work: Gilda sacrifices her life to the philandering duke, whose role is assigned to a tenor, normally the voice of the good guy. The villain gets the opera's best tune as well – "La donna è mobile" (Women are Fickle).

Milnes, Sutherland, Pavarotti, Talvela; Ambrosian Opera Chorus; London Symphony Orchestra; Bonynge (Decca; 2 CDs)

This 1971 recording was Pavarotti's first go at the duke, and his firmness of tone, confident extension (listen to the unending high C in "La donna") and beautiful portamento make for a dangerously beguiling villain. Sherrill Milnes is outstanding too – a wounded, roaring, spitting Rigoletto – and Sutherland produces some beautiful sounds, even if her characterization of Gilda is rather thin.

Gobbi, Callas, di Stefano, Zaccaria; La Scala Chorus and Orchestra; Serafin (EMI; 2 CDs)

Of the Italian tenors of the 1950s who played the duke, only Giuseppe di Stefano achieved the right mix of licentiousness, cruelty and charm. The other lead roles on this recording are similarly superb: Callas is by far the most convincing Gilda on disc and Gobbi is the most subtle Rigoletto. Serafin gives smooth and attentive support and the mono sound is perfectly acceptable.

Il trovatore

Best known for its almost incomprehensible plot, *Il trovatore* (The Troubadour) is another fast-moving drama of revenge with a parent–child relationship at its centre, this time one of mother (Azucena) and supposed son (Manrico, the "troubadour" of the title). In some ways the opera backslides into pre-*Rigoletto* freestanding musical forms, in that the arias tend to hold up the action rather than move it on. Nonetheless, there's some wonderfully tuneful music, the most famous episode being sung by the chorus of Gypsies who, in Act 2, get to pound their anvils in time with the music. But the most moving passages are created through dialogue, notably the Act 4 "Miserere" duet between Manrico and Leonora, in which she sings to the imprisoned troubadour above a chorus of praying monks, and the final exchanges between the lovers, beginning with the tenor's fearsome outburst "Parlar non vuoi". Moments such as these raise *Il trovatore* way above the level of period-costume melodrama.

Bonisolli, Price, Cappuccilli, Obraztsova; Berlin Chorus; Berlin Philharmonic Orchestra; Karajan (EMI; 2 CDs)

Recorded in1977, this is an unrelievedly intense performance with orchestral playing that is electrifying. Such a background places a strain on the soloists, but Leontyne Price as Leonora is more than up to the challenge, while Obraztsova is a forthright Azucena. Bonisolli's voice is too thick to give the music its natural ring, but he manages the notes and copes well with Karajan's full-throttle direction.

Corelli, Tucci, Merrill, Simionato; Rome Opera Chorus and Orchestra; Schippers (EMI; 2 CDs)

This recording, made at the 1962 Salzburg Festival, captured one of those rare occasions on which everything worked. Franco Corelli – the most famous Manrico of his day – was at his magnificent best and Leontyne Price, also in her prime, gives an extraordinary performance. Both Bastianini and Simionato impress as di Luna and Azucena. If the sound isn't perfect, then the performance is.

La traviata

After a pair of operas with historic settings, Verdi wrote one placed in his own time. *La traviata* (The Fallen Woman) is based on Alexandre Dumas the Younger's play *La dame aux camélias*, about a consumptive "society hostess" (Violetta) whose love for upper-class Alfredo provokes the disapproval of his class-conscious father, Germont. After the costume melodrama of *Rigoletto* and *Il trovatore*, *La traviata* is a much more intimate piece, played out among the three principals against a high-society background. Nowadays this is perhaps Verdi's most popular opera, yet initially it was one of his few flops, though the reasons for its failure are to be found in the inadequacy of the original casting (including an implausibly unfrail Violetta) and in the fact that the director had for no obvious reason set it in the eighteenth rather than the nineteenth century. The role of Violetta is one of the most demanding in the repertoire, and there's scarcely a high-profile soprano who hasn't at some time in her career had a go at one of her poignant arias.

Gheorghiu, Lopardo, Nucci; Covent Garden Chorus and Orchestra; Solti (Decca; 2 CDs)

Violetta was the role that established the international reputation of Angela Gheorghiu, and this 1992 recording shows what the fuss is all about – she has a gorgeous voice but, like Callas, she does much more with that voice than merely convey the notes. She acts with every inflection. Her Alfredo is a warm-voiced Frank Lopardo, and Georg Solti gives a splendidly vital and well-paced account of the score.

Callas, di Stefano, Bastianini; La Scala Chorus and Orchestra; Giulini (EMI; 2 CDs)

Callas recorded the role of Violetta several times, but this 1955 live recording stands out for its completeness and intimacy. At once naive and worldly, she creates an image as varied and contradictory as Verdi intended, and her voice contains a rainbow of tones, with none of the hardness to which it was later prone. The sound certainly shows its age but Giulini shapes and phrases with intelligence, and the entire production hums with energy.

Don Carlos

Verdi's next opera, a work on an even larger scale, was originally composed in French for Paris, but then was pruned drastically following its poor reception – hence the existence of two versions, the French-language *Don Carlos* and the four-act Italian-language *Don Carlo*. (To complicate things further, several recent productions and recordings have used an Italian translation of the Paris text.) Its starting point is a fictional account of events in the lives of historical figures. Here Verdi adapts Schiller's play about the sixteenth-century Spanish king Philip II and his son Don Carlos, whose fateful love for his young stepmother, Elisabeth, leads to his downfall. The welter of political intrigue and emotional drama is most effective in the five-act version, from which Verdi later excised some scenes crucial to the dangerous relationship between Don Carlos and Elisabeth.

Alagna, Mattila, Meier, van Dam, Hampson; Orchestre de Paris; Pappano (EMI; 3 CDs)

This recording of the French *Don Carlos*, following a production at the Châtelet, is superb. Roberto Alagna as Carlo and José van Dam as Philip are finely matched, but the outstanding performance is the gorgeous and very moving Elisabeth of Karita Mattila. The orchestral sound isn't top-class, but that's the only problem with an interpretation that looks set to be the first-choice *Don Carlos* for many years.

Carreras, Freni, Baltsa, Cappuccilli, Ghiaurov, Raimondi, van Dam, Gruberova; Berlin Opera Chorus; Berlin Philharmonic Orchestra; Karajan (EMI; 3 CDs)

Karajan's passion makes this 1978 recording of the four-act *Don Carlo* unbelievably intense. The young José Carreras is in magnificent voice easily the most impressive Don Carlo on record. The rest of the cast are equally strong, and the whole performance reaches almost hysterical levels of dramatic tension.

Aida

In November 1869 Khedive Ismail, the ruler of Egypt, announced plans to open a new opera house in Cairo as part of the celebrations surrounding the opening of the Suez Canal. He asked Verdi to compose a new work for its opening night, which was planned for November 1870; Verdi missed his deadline (the opera house opened instead with *Rigoletto*), but a year later, just weeks before the premiere in Egypt, he completed *Aida*, the spectacular successor to *Don Carlos*. Associated above all with its "Triumphal March", it is regularly subjected to the most lavish treatment that stage technicians can muster – every year in Verona, for example, the Roman amphitheatre is turned into a replica of Pharaonic Egypt for a cast-of-thousands production of *Aida*. But, as with *Don Carlos*, the spectacle is essentially a backdrop to an intense emotional drama. In essence, *Aida* is another of Verdi's tragedies of divided loyalty, focusing on the Ethiopian slave girl Aida, daughter of the captured Ethiopian king, and her love for the Egyptian Captain of the Guard, Radames.

Tebaldi, Bergonzi, Simionato, MacNeil; Vienna Philharmonic Orchestra; Karajan (Decca; 3 CDs)

Karajan's first *Aida*, recorded in 1959, was also the first in stereo, and it has never been surpassed. Tempi are swift, but not unduly so, and Karajan elicits some gorgeous sounds from the Vienna Philharmonic. Renata Tebaldi and Carlo Bergonzi, a well-matched pairing, produce consistently beautiful tone and both give unerringly stylish and intelligent readings.

Freni, Carreras, Baltsa; Vienna Philharmonic Orchestra; Karajan (EMI; 3 CDs)

The second of Karajan's two recordings of *Aida* encompasses both the grandeur and excitement of the big public moments and the intimacy of the real drama beneath. His cast is equal to the conception, with José Carreras an ardently youthful Radames, Mirella Freni spinning out beautiful lines as Aida, and Agnes Baltsa sonorous as her rival in love, Amneris.

Otello

In 1879 Verdi began to sketch an opera based on Shakespeare's *Othello*, a project that was to take more of his time than any of his other works. *Otello* was completed in 1886, some sixteen years after *Aida*, and shows Verdi achieving an extraordinary level of dramatic sophistication. This opera marks the culmination of the evolutionary development of the perfectly through-composed Italian opera (German opera already had Wagner), in which each act is a continual dramatic sweep within which the set pieces are intrinsic parts of the whole, intensifying the action rather than arresting it.

Some of this credit for *Otello*'s economy must go to Verdi's librettist Boito, who ditched the entire first act of Shakespeare's play to create a piece that focuses entirely on the characterization of the central trio, giving greater prominence to Iago than accorded by Shakespeare – indeed, for years Boito and Verdi used the working title *Jago*.

Domingo, Studer, Leiferkus, Vargas; Paris Opéra-Bastille Chorus and Orchestra; Chung (Deutsche Grammophon; 2 CDs)

This hard-driven and dramatic reading is the third time Placido Domingo has recorded *Otello*. It's also the best, even if his vocal resources are not what they were. Cheryl Studer makes a light, somewhat brittle Desdemona, but gives a touchingly vulnerable reading of the "Willow Song".

The obviously Russian Sergei Leiferkus is easily the most interesting Iago to feature on a Domingo recording.

Vickers, Rysanek, Gobbi, Andreolli; Rome Opera Chorus & Orchestra; Serafin (RCA; 2 CDs)

Although he possessed one of the most powerful tenor voices of his day, Jon Vickers is a vulnerable rather than a heroic Otello in this 1960 recording. The love duet is achingly moving, and his death scene has a haunting dignity. Leonie Rysanek is a little too grand for Desdemona, but Tito Gobbi – using his open-throated voice to great effect – is a thrilling Iago, especially during his villainous "Credo".

Falstaff

Rossini once remarked that Verdi was "too melancholic and serious" to write a comedy. Verdi's riposte came right at the end of his life – premiered in 1893, the composer's eightieth year, *Falstaff* displays the wit and *joie de vivre* of a work created by a man half Verdi's age. He and Boito concentrate almost exclusively on the Falstaff of *The Merry Wives of Windsor*, and the fat knight's forlorn attempt to seduce Alice Ford and Meg Page simultaneously, with inevitable consequences. *Falstaff* has the formal perfection of *Otello*, yet was not immediately as successful – whereas the audience had packed the streets outside Verdi's hotel after the premiere of the latter, at the opening night of *Falstaff* the atmosphere was one of deep respect rather than spontaneous joy. It was mainly due to the efforts of Toscanini, who conducted the work in opera houses all over the world, that *Falstaff* achieved its due acclaim as one of Verdi's masterpieces.

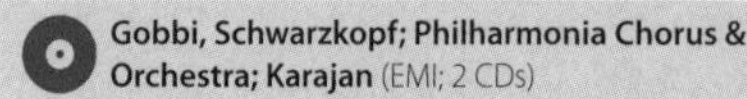
Gobbi, Schwarzkopf; Philharmonia Chorus & Orchestra; Karajan (EMI; 2 CDs)

Falstaff requires an almost Haydnesque lightness of touch which it gets in Karajan's classic recording – one of the first stereo recordings of the mid-1950s. Tito Gobbi – the greatest Falstaff of the age – is joined by equally distinguished colleagues, including Elisabeth Schwarzkopf as Alice, Anna Moffo as Nannetta and Rolando Panerai as Ford. The fleet-footed playing of the Philharmonia is no less impressive.

Lafont, Michaels-Moore, Palombi, Martinpelto; Monteverdi Choir; Orchestre Révolutionnaire et Romantique; Gardiner (Philips; 2 CDs)

In setting out to re-create the sort of orchestral sound and balance that Verdi might have recognized, Gardiner and his orchestra have transformed our perception of a score. The pungent brass, fruity wind and delicately weighted strings reveal layers of detail and character that have often been lost. Jean-Philippe Lafont as Falstaff excels throughout, and the rest of the cast impart a genuine sense of ensemble.

SACRED MUSIC

Apart from a string quartet, the only non-operatic music that Verdi wrote was a handful of sacred choral works – of which the famous *Requiem* is by far and away the most distinguished. Despite his decidedly lukewarm view of Christianity, the sixty-year-old composer was moved to write the *Requiem* as a memorial to the poet and novelist Alessandro Manzoni, whose novel *I promessi sposi* (The Betrothed) had immense patriotic appeal for Italians during the campaign for Italian unity. As well as this, Verdi composed four unrelated religious works: an *Ave Maria*, written in response to a challenge by a publisher to harmonize a bizarre scale ("scala enigmatica"); a *Stabat Mater*; a setting of Dante, *Laudi alla Vergine Maria*; and a *Te Deum*. He reluctantly permitted all four to be published together in 1898 as *Quattro Pezzi Sacri* (Four Sacred Pieces), and they have been performed as a group ever since.

Requiem

The conductor Hans von Bülow sneeringly described Verdi's *Requiem* as his "latest opera in theatrical vestments", and there is little doubt that this is a mass that has rather more fire and brimstone than compassion and consolation. Ignoring the prevailing idioms of Catholic usage, Verdi fell back on what he knew best, creating a score of wild extremes, emotional ensembles and a vocal score of quasi-operatic arias. Much of the orchestration recalls *Aida*, and the origin of one of the numbers (the Lacrymosa) is a discarded duet from the opera *Don Carlo*. The work's most dramatic sequence is the extended Dies irae, in which Verdi conjured hair-raising visions of the Last Judgement, using the huge chorus and mighty percussion section to thrilling effect, above all in the opening bars. Verdi added to the impact by scoring a series of fanfares for widely spaced ensembles, grouped in fours (an idea borrowed from Berlioz) and while this is inevitably more effective live, the effect can still be heart-stopping on disc.

Schwarzkopf, Ludwig, Gedda, Ghiaurov; Philharmonia Chorus and Orchestra; Giulini
(EMI; 2 CDs; with *Four Sacred Pieces*)

This famous 1963 performance, freshly remastered, has long been a benchmark. The four superb soloists (Schwarzkopf is not really a Verdian soprano but still impresses) were all at the peak of their careers, and they are well integrated under the intense but never melodramatic or sentimental direction of Giulini. Chorus and orchestra are superb.

Filipova, Scalchi, Hernández, Colombara; Hungarian State Opera Chorus and Orchestra; Morandi
(Naxos; 2 CDs; with *Four Sacred Pieces*)

The best of the budget recordings (by a long way) and a fine performance by any standards. The chorus, though not as good as the Philharmonia, are spirited and sound genuinely involved. The soloists are even better (with the soprano Elena Filipova outstanding), while the conducting has both energy and warmth.

Tomás Luis de Victoria (1548–1611)

Of all the great polyphonists of the sixteenth century, Victoria is the one whose music makes the most powerful impact. Whereas the music of his contemporary, Palestrina (see p.396), creates a mood of serene repose and contemplation, Victoria transforms the polyphonic technique into a vehicle for more fervent and passionate feelings, which suggest a direct and personal relationship with God. It is a quality that has its roots in a particularly Spanish form of Catholicism, an intense piety that can be found in the writings of the mystic St Teresa of Ávila (whom Victoria probably knew), and in the visionary intensity of El Greco's paintings.

Victoria was born at Ávila, where he later served as a chorister at the cathedral and attended the Jesuit school of San Gil. Around 1565, with King Philip II as his benefactor, he was sent to Rome to complete his education at another Jesuit institution, the Collegium Germanicum. While there he would almost certainly have come into contact with Palestrina, who may even have given lessons to the younger man. Victoria held several important positions during his time in Rome, culminating in that of *maestro di cappella* at the Collegium Germanicum (1573–78). Ordained a priest in 1575, he joined the community of Filippo Neri, the creator of the oratorio form (see p.128). The community was based at the church of San Girolamo della Carità and Victoria held a chaplaincy there between 1578 and 1585.

In the mid-1580s he expressed a wish to return to Spain and was made the personal chaplain to Philip II's sister, the Dowager Empress Maria, who was then living in retirement at the Convent of the Descalzas Reales in Madrid. He returned just once to Rome, between 1592 and 1594, to supervise the printing of his works and to attend the funeral of Palestrina; otherwise he remained in Madrid, serving the empress until her death in 1603, after which he continued at the convent until his own death eight years later.

Compared with Palestrina, Victoria's output is extremely small, but it has a far wider emotional range which conforms perfectly to the recommendations for liturgical music laid down after the Council of Trent (see p.397): from the rapturous opening of the motet *O Quam Gloriosum* to the dark intensity of the *Tenebrae Responsories*, there's an acute awareness of marrying music with the meaning of the words. The support of wealthy patrons meant that nearly everything Victoria wrote was published during his lifetime and was disseminated across the Spanish empire, travelling as far as Mexico City and Bogotá in Colombia.

Masses

Victoria wrote a mere twenty masses, fifteen of which are "parody" masses, based on already existing material. Surprisingly, the *Missa O Quam Gloriosum* does not quote from the glorious rising phrase which opens the motet on which it is based, but it does have the same rapturous energy and variety – joyful in the Gloria, reverent in the Benedictus. The *Missa Ave Maris Stella* is one of four "paraphrase" masses, works which are based on a plainchant melody. Written in a minor key, it's a more obviously soulful and introspective work than the *Missa O Quam Gloriosum.* It contains much striking music including, at the close of the second Agnus setting, one of the most exquisitely beautiful moments in all of Victoria's music.

O Quam Gloriosum (mass & motet); Missa Ave Maris Stella: Westminster Cathedral Choir; Hill (Hyperion)

This prize-winning recording from 1983 is one of the glories of David Hill's tenure as music director at Westminster Cathedral. The singing is highly expressive – the well-drilled trebles particularly strong – but at the same time it always sounds beautifully clean and accurate, allowing the individual vocal lines to be heard clearly as they weave around each other.

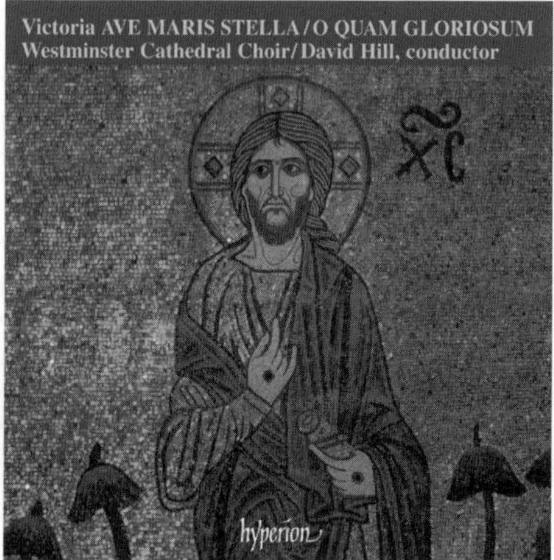

Officium Defunctorum

Victoria's greatest work is the *Officium Defunctorum*, which was written for the funeral of the Dowager Empress Maria in 1603, and includes music for both the Mass of the Dead and the services that preceded it. It begins with the second lesson of Matins, Taedet animam meam, which establishes a mood of austere solemnity, but the *Requiem Mass* itself is far richer, the opening Requiem aeternam hinting at spiritual aspiration through the slowly swelling chords of its opening. Unity is provided between the different sections by a plainsong *cantus firmus*, or fixed melody, which is mostly sung by the second soprano part. The music culminates in the long Libera me in which the word-setting is especially acute. At this point the assembled dignitaries, dressed in black, gathered around the catafalque which was sprinkled with holy water and had incense wafted over it.

Officium Defunctorum: Magnificat; Cave (Linn Records)

This performance, which uses light but incisive women's voices for the two upper parts, is expressive without ever being forced, changes of mood in the different sections of the Libera me are conveyed through subtle changes of dynamics. A sense of the original liturgical context is provided by plainsong, which is here sung in a manner that makes it sound of a piece with the polyphony.

Heitor Villa-Lobos (1887–1959)

Heitor Villa-Lobos was living proof that a conventional musical education is not a prerequisite to becoming a composer. Born in Rio de Janeiro, he received most of his music lessons from his amateur cellist father, and then taught himself to play many other instruments besides – including the guitar, on which he achieved a remarkable facility. His close friend and compatriot, the conductor Burle Marx, once asked Villa-Lobos if there was anything he did not play. "Only the oboe", was the reply; but when the two men met again soon afterwards, Villa-Lobos was already well on the way to mastering that instrument. Villa-Lobos became Brazil's leading composer partly because this lack of academic training gave him the space to develop his uniquely free-ranging approach to form, style and source material.

On his father's death, instead of pursuing a medical career as his mother wished, he preferred to spend his time playing guitar with the street bands of Rio, and for several years led a dissipated, bohemian life. In his late teens and early twenties he undertook a long tour of Brazil to research its folk music. Villa-Lobos was fond of telling Rio's chattering classes that during his travels he had been captured by cannibals, who spared him only because of his musical capabilities; more plausibly, he claimed that the map of Brazil was his first harmony book. On returning to Rio he enrolled at the National Music Institute to further his technical studies, but soon found the atmosphere stifling, and decided to abandon his training in midstream. However, he gained the respect of the teaching staff, who continued to provide help, support and advice after he had left.

Although money was hard to come by, he spent the next few years building up a strong local reputation, and caused a sensation when his compositions were performed at a series of concerts in Rio in 1915. With scant concern for academic niceties, he had amalgamated a vast range of material into music that was eclectic and original. Indigenous Brazilian music went into the mix alongside Wagner, Puccini, Debussy, Milhaud, Stravinsky, Gregorian chant, Palestrina and Johann Sebastian Bach, the composer who meant most to him and who provided the inspiration for his most famous works, the *Bachianas Brasileiras* – a series of nine little suites that attempt to fuse the style of Bach with the idioms of Brazilian folk music. His fourteen *Chôros* were more populist but no less ground-breaking, representing, to quote the composer, "A new form of musical composition, synthesizing different types of Brazilian, Indian and popular music".

The pianist Artur Rubinstein, on hearing some of the composer's work in Brazil in 1919, helped persuade wealthy patrons to sponsor Villa-Lobos's first journey to Paris in 1923. Parisian audiences immediately warmed to his music, and he was fêted by the press and artists of all descriptions, including people of very different temperament from his own, such as Edgard Varèse (see p.593). On returning to Brazil he became a figurehead for young musicians. In 1930 he was appointed director of the National Music Academy and two years later he was given charge of the country's music education. In 1942 Villa-Lobos founded the Conservatorio National de Canto Orfeonico, with the aim of providing music teachers for Brazilian schools. Leaving aside the merits of his compositions, as a pedagogue and administrator, as well as folklorist and musicologist, Villa-Lobos made an incalculable contribution to Brazilian music.

Bachianas Brasileiras

Villa-Lobos wrote music at all hours of the day and night, wherever he happened to be, jotting down ideas as they occurred to him, and rarely bothering to revise them. Thus his output is immense (around 1500 officially listed works) and highly uneven. At his best he achieved a Romantic, strongly coloured amalgam of indigenous Brazilian music and the Classical tradition of Western Europe, and nowhere is this better demonstrated than in his remarkable *Bachianas Brasileiras*. They're a fairly disparate collection of pieces in which chugging Baroque motor rhythms suddenly subside into lyrical effusion. *No. 1*, written for eight cellos, is a case in point; its opening movement begins and ends with some hard-driven ostinati but also contains melodies of a more folksy complexion. *No. 2*, an arrangement of mostly cello pieces for a chamber orchestra, is much more overtly Romantic music, being essentially a set of four exotic and occasionally gushing tone poems that attempt to evoke the colours and flavours of his native land. Rather more Hollywood than Bach is in evidence here – though the last movement, "The Little Train of the Caipira", is justly famous as an exuberant picture of an energetic train journey across Brazil. Most celebrated of all, and Villa-Lobos's best-known work, is the *Bachianas Brasileiras No. 5*, for soprano solo and eight cellos. It's in two movements: the first a rhapsodic and sensual night poem over pizzicato strings, the second an animated celebration of birdsong. It's a colourful and mysterious work, and a good showcase for any soprano able to communicate its uniquely rhapsodic fervour.

Bachianas Brasileiras Nos. 1 & 5: Gomez, Manning; Pleeth Cello Octet (Hyperion; with *Suite for Voice and Violin & Arrangements of Bach preludes and fugues*)

This CD from Hyperion makes an excellent introduction to Villa-Lobos. Jill Gomez is in ravishing voice and the Pleeth Cello Octet provide a winning combination of expressive power and voluptuousness in the *Bachianas Brasileiras No. 5*, with Peter Manning giving warm and characterful support in the *Suite*. Completing a fascinating disc are Villa-Lobos's transcriptions of various Bach preludes and fugues.

Bachianas Brasileiras Nos. 2, 4 & 8: Cincinnati Symphony Orchestra; López-Cobos (Telarc)

The Cincinnati Symphony Orchestra provide spirited accounts of three of the Bachianas Brasileiras – the luscious *No. 2* and two of the less well-known ones. They produce a warm and expansive sound which is at times a little too refined (the little train should surely clatter along in a rather more noisy fashion), but nonetheless these are very persuasive performances.

Music for Guitar

Villa-Lobos, himself a proficient guitarist from an early age, made the acquaintance of the great Spanish guitarist Segovia during his stay in Paris in the 1920s. Segovia's brilliant technique had completely revolutionized guitar playing and the instrument was starting to be taken seriously by contemporary composers and in the concert hall. The *Twelve Études* (1929), the first result of this fruitful contact, function as a kind of compendium of what the instrument was capable of in the right hands: a range of techniques are explored – glissandi, arpeggiation, harmonics – but Villa-Lobos's idiosyncratic harmonies means that they rarely sound like mere exercises. The *Five Preludes* (1940) – less virtuosic and more emotional than the *Études* – have proved his most popular guitar pieces. They are wonderfully fresh and imaginative poetic miniatures, whose prevailing melancholy is established at the very beginning with the yearning melody of *Prelude No. 1. Guitar Concerto* (1951), commissioned by Segovia, is a rather more elusive work which rather suffers in comparison with the bright colours and seductive melodies of Rodrigo's concerto. There's a languid, almost throwaway quality to Villa-Lobos's work, which is permeated by an almost suffocating ennui that is only partly shaken off halfway through the final movement.

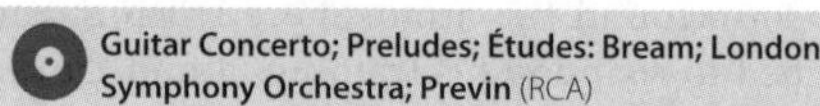

Guitar Concerto; Preludes; Études: Bream; London Symphony Orchestra; Previn (RCA)

The warmth of Bream's playing and the variety of his tone and touch are well suited to Villa-Lobos's guitar music, which can be deadened by too technical an approach. These performances, which date from the 1970s, are justly celebrated. In particular the *Preludes* have a lyrical intensity which has rarely been matched. It is no surprise to learn that Villa-Lobos was himself an admirer of Bream's playing.

Antonio Vivaldi (1678–1741)

"The same concerto four hundred times" is how Stravinsky dismissed his work, but no musical reputation has mushroomed more in recent times than that of Antonio Vivaldi. At the turn of the twentieth century, he was an unknown name whose works were turned into salon pieces by the violinist Fritz Kreisler; now his *Four Seasons* is bought by people who have never listened to any other piece of classical music.

The life behind the music is elusive. His father was a musician at St Mark's in Venice, and Antonio – the youngest of six children – is said to have studied at the church under the *maestro di cappella*, Giovanni Legrenzi. Vivaldi was ordained as a priest of a minor order in 1703 (he was later known as the "Red Priest" on account of his hair colour) but he rarely celebrated mass, due – so he claimed – to a debilitating illness which was probably asthma. In the same year he entered the service of the Conservatorio della Pietà, the most famous of four Venetian orphanages for foundling girls, all of which placed special emphasis on musical education. In addition to teaching the violin, Vivaldi composed music for the Pietà's outstanding choir and orchestra, and seems to have made himself well liked by the governors, who in 1713 granted him leave of absence to supervise the performance of the first of over 45 operas, *Ottone in Villa*, in Vicenza.

By now his fame was beginning to spread as a result of the publication of *L'estro armonico* in Amsterdam in 1711. These twelve concertos were greatly admired, especially in Germany, where Bach copied and arranged six of them. Much of Vivaldi's time was soon devoted to opera, both as composer and as manager of the Sant'Angelo and San Moisè theatres. Though he continued to work in Venice, from 1718 he was also in the service of Mantua and then spent several years travelling throughout Italy.

The governors of the Pietà, trying to rein in their increasingly errant maestro, contracted him to provide two concertos per month, and for a while the scheme paid off. Shortly before Christmas 1725 he produced his last works for them – *Il cimento dell'armonica e dell'inventione* (Contest Between Harmony and Invention), another series of twelve concertos, of which the first four were *Le quattro stagioni* (The Four Seasons).

From this period stems his close association with Anna Girò, a young soprano (and former Pietà protégée) who often took the principal roles in operas staged at the Sant'Angelo Theatre. Throughout the 1730s Vivaldi resumed his extensive travelling, accompanied by Anna and her sister Paolina, an arrangement that caused a fair amount of scandal and led to the Archbishop of Ferrara trying to ban him from that city.

He was invited to Amsterdam, where *Il cimento* had been published, and proved a major attraction there, but when he returned to Venice in 1739, to supervise a festival in honour of a visit from the son of the King of Poland, he found that his reputation – particularly as an opera composer – had considerably waned in his native city. The following year Vivaldi departed for Vienna in the hopes of gaining patronage from the emperor, but this plan came to nothing. At his death in 1741 he was almost forgotten, and was buried a pauper outside the Vienna city walls. One of six choristers at his funeral was the young Joseph Haydn.

Characterized by dramatic contrasts of dynamics and harmony, Vivaldi's music was often criticized by his contemporaries as eccentric, and after his death it lay forgotten until the 1930s. Yet as a violin virtuoso he was fascinated by the range of possibilities in string sound, and he greatly extended the boundaries of instrumental technique. The slow movement of his B minor concerto for four violins, for example, is an exploration of different methods of spreading a chord and bowing it. Moreover, Vivaldi's contribution to the development of the solo concerto was immense (see p.610). His first movements are notable for their taut economy and the rhythmic drive of opening themes; his slow movements have the eloquence of operatic arias; and his finales anticipate those of the Classical symphony in their buoyancy and pace.

Caricature of Vivaldi by Pier Leone Ghezzi.

Farnace

Vivaldi wrote at least 49 works for the stage, and yet it's only in recent years that this huge part of his output has begun to emerge from almost three centuries of oblivion. The composer's own favourite among his operas was *Farnace*, which was first performed during the Carnival of 1727, and was such a hit that he went on to produce six different versions of it in the ensuing decade.

Antonio Maria Lucchini's libretto is typical of the tortuous texts that Vivaldi and his contemporaries tended to favour. Farnace, King of Pontus, having been defeated by the Roman general Pompeo, orders his wife, Tamiri, to kill herself and their son – but Tamiri's mother, Berenice, is plotting with Pompeo to kill Farnace. Romantic entanglements further complicate the issue, as is often the case with Vivaldi, but all is well in the end. *Farnace* may not score highly for concision and plausibility, but Vivaldi delivers in abundance what his audience wanted: vivacious orchestral writing, dazzling and varied vocal solos, and dashes of acute characterization.

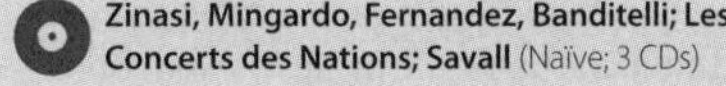
Zinasi, Mingardo, Fernandez, Banditelli; Les Concerts des Nations; Savall (Naïve; 3 CDs)

Jordi Savall's 2001 recording, re-edited and repackaged as part of Naïve's Vivaldi Edition, makes a terrific introduction to Vivaldi's stage works. The orchestra playing is vivid and pacy, and the singing is generally excellent: Sara Mingardo, as Tamiri, is especially remarkable. Taped from live performances in Madrid's Teatro de la Zarzuela, the sound is at times reverberant, but not offputtingly so.

The Concerto

The word concerto comes from the Latin concertare, which has two contradictory meanings: to come together and to compete. During the initial stage of concerto writing, the first meaning was the important one. In the sixteenth and early seventeenth centuries, composers such as Giovanni Gabrieli, Lodovico Viadana and Claudio Monteverdi wrote concertos which required singers and instrumentalists to "come together". Mostly sacred works, vocal concertos became very popular in Germany as well as Italy, and remained an important church genre right up until the time of Bach (many of whose cantatas were actually titled concerts).

However, the second meaning of concerto – to compete – is the one that has endured, referring to instrumental works in which one or more solo instrumentalists are pitted against an orchestra. The earliest style was the concerto grosso (literally "large ensemble"), which developed in late seventeenth-century Italy, initially in works by Stradella but most importantly in the output of Corelli. Usually made up of a number of movements, a concerto grosso consists of an ensemble split into a concertino (two or more soloists, often violins) and a ripieno (an orchestra of violins, viola and cellos), all supported by a continuo (a keyboard and bass instrument). Musically, the early concerto grosso is very similar to the trio sonata and other instrumental forms, but a whole new dimension is added by the dramatic alternation of soloists and orchestra.

Though the concerto grosso achieved great popularity, by the early eighteenth century it was becoming increasingly overshadowed by the solo concerto, in which just one soloist competed with the rest of the orchestra. Influenced by opera arias as well as instrumental forms, this new genre allowed for a greater degree of melodic clarity and lyricism. Giuseppe Torelli led the way with his violin concertos, establishing three movements (fast–slow–fast) as the norm, and casting his fast movements in ritornello form, in which orchestral statements of the opening material alternate with developmental passages performed by the soloist. His lead was taken up by Vivaldi, who wrote over 350 solo concertos as well as more than 100 for two or more instruments. Writing for a vast range of instruments – everything from mandolin to recorder – and placing an increased emphasis on the virtuosity of the soloist, Vivaldi developed the solo concerto into a dazzling, cogent genre.

The Italian concerto models were quickly taken up by composers across Europe. J.S. Bach's contribution was especially significant: he brought a new complexity and subtlety to ritornello form – nowhere more impressively than in the famous concerti grossi he dedicated to the Margrave of Brandenburg – and wrote the first concertos for harpsichord, laying the foundation for the piano concerto. By the time of Bach's death in the middle of the eighteenth century, the concerto grosso had almost completely fallen from favour, but the solo concerto continued to thrive. Bach's sons and their contemporaries composed many examples (including the first concertos for piano), but it wasn't until the piano concertos of Mozart that the Classical concerto reached maturity. Though in many ways his concertos are among his more conservative works, Mozart brought a new level of lyricism to the concerto and developed a style in which elements of Classical sonata form (see p.58) were fused with Baroque ritornello.

The concertos of Beethoven continue the Mozartian tradition, but are more dramatic in style, adventurous in harmony and complex in form, with the solo and orchestral parts intricately woven together. Beethoven also increased the virtuosity of the solo writing, setting a trend that would continue throughout the nineteenth and twentieth centuries. Though composers right back to Vivaldi had relished the opportunity provided by concertos for displays of virtuosity, Romantic composers such as Paganini, Chopin and Liszt took the dazzle factor to a new level.

One manifestation of this is the increased length and complexity of the cadenza. What was once simply the embellishment of the penultimate note by the lead violinist, and then an improvised solo section at the end of a fast movement, became a super-virtuosic display in which the performer would sum up the whole piece in miniature.

Though the solo concerto has remained the most popular type, modernist composers (such as Hindemith and Stravinsky) rejected the idea of Romantic display and looked to the examples of the Baroque when writing their concertos. Around the same time, the concerto for orchestra – which showcased the flexibility and virtuosity of the orchestra rather than an individual performer – was developed by composers such as Bartók, Bacewicz, Tippett and Carter.

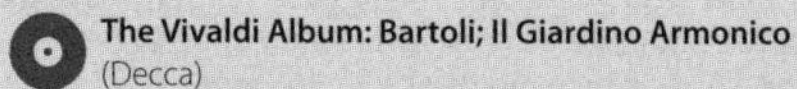

The Vivaldi Album: Bartoli; Il Giardino Armonico
(Decca)

If you'd prefer to dip your toes in the water before plunging into the ocean of Vivaldi's operas, consider mezzo-soprano Cecilia Bartoli's powerful – if ocasionally histrionic – recital CD, which includes one mighty set piece from *Farnace* ("Gelido in ogni vena"), plus a dozen other arias, all delivered with amazing virtuosity.

L'estro armonico

Of one of Vivaldi's concerts a contemporary wrote, "At the end he improvised a fantasy which quite confounded me, for such playing has not been heard before and can never be equalled. He played with his fingers but a hair's breadth from the bridge, so that there was hardly room for the bow. He played thus on all four strings, and at unbelievable speed." The stupendous technique is confirmed by the twelve concertos of *L'estro armonico*, yet there is much more than mere virtuosity to what has been called the most influential collection of instrumental music from the eighteenth century. The title is the key, for *l'estro* means "inspiration", and indeed the impersonal stateliness of Corelli's Opus 6, the precedent for these concertos, pales beside Vivaldi's music. The scholar H.C. Robbins Landon tallied the qualities of *L'estro armonico* when he wrote of the music's "freshness, the vigour, the variety and – in the slow movements – the mysterious tenderness". It was, he concluded, "unlike anything published before".

Standage; English Concert; Pinnock
(Deutsche Grammophon; 2 CDs; with *Flute Concertos*)

It was the metrical abruptness and crispness of *L'estro armonico* that lifted the composer above his predecessors, as Trevor Pinnock makes clear in this agile and exhilaratingly alert performance. Originally on the Archiv label, this is now available as part of a mid-price double-CD with Vivaldi's flute concertos.

La stravaganza

The *Capriccio stravagante* of Carlo Farina, published in 1626, was crammed with every trick of current violin technique. To the virtuosic Vivaldi the challenge must have been irresistible, and he rose to it in his Opus 4 set, *La stravaganza*, which he dedicated to Vettor Delfino, a former pupil and member of a celebrated Venetian noble family. "I cannot wish for a better protection of my feeble works", the composer wrote, "than that of Your Excellency." They have been neglected by comparison with *L'estro armonico*, but the concertos of *La stravaganza* are anything but "feeble". They display a winning flair throughout, with slow movements every bit as lyrical as their predecessors', and their astringent modulations, so bewildering to Vivaldi's contemporaries, make them vibrantly fresh for modern audiences.

Podger; Arte Dei Suonatori Baroque Orchestra
(Channel Classics; 2 CDs)

This is a wonderfully fiery performance from Baroque violinist Rachel Podger and the Arte Dei Suonatori ensemble, whose playing is dazzlingly vivid and charged with energy. Podger's light-touched virtuosity is as subtle as ever – especially in the aria-like slow movements – but the overall impression is sparkling and supercharged.

Le quattro stagioni – "The Four Seasons"

Once a potent enough force to influence Haydn, *Le quattro stagioni* was not republished until 1950 but is now the most recorded piece of classical music, with over 150 versions issued to date. The first four of a collection of twelve violin concertos, collectively entitled *Il cimento dell'armonica e dell'inventione* (The Trial of Harmony and Invention), each one depicts a season, beginning with *Spring*, and takes its structure from four sonnets (possibly written by Vivaldi himself). It is thus both an early example of programme music and a bravura showpiece for its violin soloist. One of the most dazzling examples of musical scene-painting, the listener is treated to musical evocations of buzzing flies, drunkards and goatherds dozing in the sun, dripping rain and so on. The imagination with which Vivaldi manipulates rhythm and timbre to achieve each effect is crucial to its success, and the opening motif (a bouncy alternation of quavers and semi-quavers) gives the work a sense of forward movement which is never lost.

Carmignola; Venice Baroque Orchestra; Marcon
(Sony; with three violin concertos)

In this superb recording Andrea Marcon achieves a good balance between clarity, forward-moving festivity and the programmatic elements of the work. Giuliano Carmignola creates a wonderful sound on his Baroque violin and displays frightening virtuosity, while the VBO's tightly knitted playing is impressively varied in tone colour and well captured by the very clear, forward sound quality.

Huggett; Raglan Baroque Players; Kraemer
(Virgin; with *Violin Concertos Op. 8 Nos. 5, 6, 10 & 11*)

This is a bargain at mid-price: not only do you get an exhilarating performance without excessive ornamentation and with Monica Huggett in sparkling form, but the generous length of the disc means that you also get another four violin concertos from Opus 8.

Flute Concertos

In 1726 Venice played host to the virtuoso flautist Johann Joachim Quartz, and immediately afterwards the flute enjoyed an unprecedented vogue in the city. Vivaldi promptly wrote an ornate flute part into his opera *Orlando*, which was premiered in 1727, the year before an Amsterdam publisher commissioned the Opus 10 flute concertos from him. In a few cases Vivaldi was able to recycle music from existing movements, but the instrument also drew from him some of his freshest feats of imagination, and as a compendium of flute technique it had no rival at the time. The concertos' haunting evocations of night and birdsong compare with any of the onomatopoeic effects in *The Four Seasons*.

Beznosiuk; English Concert; Pinnock (Deutsche Grammophon; 2 CDs; with *L'estro armonico*)

Liza Beznosiuk's fluidity of phrasing and articulation draws the best from these concertos and minimizes any sense of routine in Vivaldi's less inspired patches. The English Concert, under the direction of Trevor Pinnock, provide fresh and vigorous support throughout.

Gloria in D

It has taken a fair amount of time for Vivaldi's choral works to get the same amount of attention as his instrumental pieces. The exception to this rule is the *Gloria in D Major*, catalogued as RV589 (rather confusingly, he wrote another in the same key). This is the most popular of all Vivaldi's sacred music, and has been in the repertory since it was revived in 1939 by Alfredo Casella, a pupil of Fauré. Notable for its fusion of festive brilliance with moments of profound sadness, it was composed in Venice some time between 1713 and 1717 for two female soloists, choir and an orchestra that includes a prominent solo part. It's a highly theatrical work, full of unashamedly operatic excess, with the text divided between soloists and chorus into no less than twelve sections. The lack of male soloists confirms that it was almost certainly composed for the Pietà, but the *Gloria*'s bold contrasts and striking sonorities are also an acknowledgement of the Venetian polychoral tradition of Monteverdi and Gabrieli.

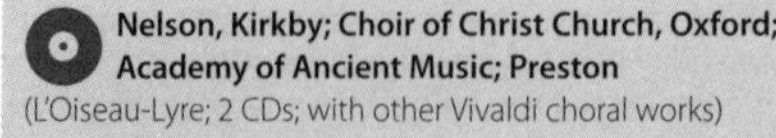
Nelson, Kirkby; Choir of Christ Church, Oxford; Academy of Ancient Music; Preston (L'Oiseau-Lyre; 2 CDs; with other Vivaldi choral works)

This refreshingly joyful account of the *Gloria* comes from Simon Preston at the helm of the Choir of Christ Church, Oxford, in its heyday. There's a feeling of airy lightness to the performance that is enhanced by the light open tones of the two soloists: Emma Kirkby and Judith Nelson.

York, Biccire, Mingardo; Akademia; Concerto Italiano; Alessandrini (Opus 111; with *Magnificat*)

With Rinaldo Alessandrini attacking the music like a man possessed, this recording may well irritate as many as it thrills. The opening is faster than you'd believe possible, with an incredible rasping attack from the strings. Startling contrasts abound; for instance when the highly spirited "Domine Fili" is followed by a slow and sombre account of the "Domine Deus", which has all the air of a classical tragedy.

Stabat Mater

Vivaldi also wrote a substantial amount of sacred music for solo voice, of which the most celebrated is the *Stabat Mater*, composed in 1712 for the church of the Oratorian Order in Brescia. The text, probably written by a Franciscan poet in the thirteenth century (see p.404), is a meditation on the Virgin Mary's suffering as she stands at the foot of the cross. Vivaldi uses just over half of the text, but he pours into its setting some of his most intense and heartfelt music. It was written for a high male voice (either a falsettist or a castrato) and a string orchestra, and much of the pathos is derived from their exquisite interaction – in the penultimate stanza, for instance, where the harsh angularity of the dotted string introduction is followed by a legato phrase from the soloist, "Eia Mater" (O Mother), before the strings re-enter, nagging away underneath him. This is followed by a more ardent rocking arpeggiated figure in the strings, which is matched by the soloist's legato, which in turn leads into the relatively joyful (and fugal) Amen which closes the work.

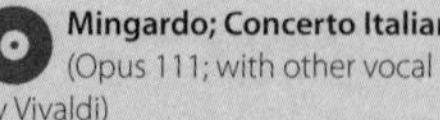
Mingardo; Concerto Italiano; Alessandrini (Opus 111; with other vocal and instrumental works by Vivaldi)

This reading of the *Stabat Mater* is overwhelming in its dramatic impact. The playing of the Concerto Italiano is as incisive and exciting as ever, but it's the anguished intensity of the contralto Sara Mingardo that makes this a great interpretation. She's equally powerful in the jubilant *Clarae Stellae, Scintillate*.

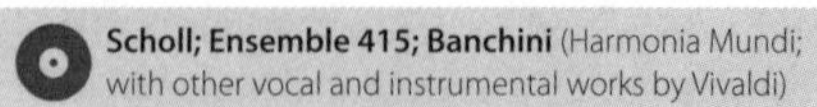
Scholl; Ensemble 415; Banchini (Harmonia Mundi; with other vocal and instrumental works by Vivaldi)

Andreas Scholl's beautifully clear and penetrating countertenor voice has no hint of hoot, and he uses it intelligently, judging the work's sequential runs with a natural grace. Greater dynamic contrast from the string ensemble would have been welcome, but this is nonetheless a wonderfully well-projected and unsentimental account.

Richard Wagner (1813–1883)

No composer ever polarized opinion as violently as Richard Wagner. Nowadays, as in his lifetime, he attracts a cult following, and every year thousands of people make a pilgrimage to the small Bavarian town of Bayreuth, where in 1876 he inaugurated a festival entirely devoted to his own music. For many others, Bayreuth is the embodiment of the composer's megalomania, and the adoption of Wagner's music as a cultural and political icon by the Nazis is seen not as a propagandist perversion of his art but as the apotheosis of a man who prefigured the Teutonic, anti-Semitic triumphalism of the Third Reich. To his admirers, Wagner's vision of the *Gesamtkunstwerk*, the "total art work" in which music, poetry, drama and the visual arts were synthesized, is one of the mightiest achievements of European culture, on a par with the drama of ancient Greece. To the sceptics, the four-part *Ring des Nibelungen* is a boring tale of dwarfs and giants, while *Tristan und Isolde* is an impossibly long-winded love story with pseudo-medieval trappings. Yet none of Wagner's contemporaries was untouched by his music, even if they felt his influence to be malign, and to ignore his music is to turn away from a figure as seminal as Beethoven. You might never find Wagner appealing; it is equally likely that you'll hear the prelude to *Tristan* and be hooked for life.

Wagner was the archetypal Romantic artist, with a life story as fantastic as his plots. His true parentage has never been fully established: his father was either his mother's husband, Carl Friedrich Wagner, or her lover, the actor and painter Ludwig Geyer. (This uncertainty surely has some connection with the number of characters in his operas whose fathers were equally unknown to them – Siegmund, Siegfried, Parsifal.) Whatever the truth, Carl Friedrich died a year after Richard's birth, and his widow married Geyer. Wagner thus grew up in a theatrical milieu, and he was already writing plays in his early teens. His need for incidental music for these dramas sent him in search of composition teachers, and his first musical works (now lost) date from 1829, when he was sixteen. His first completed opera, *Die Feen*, dates from only four years later, a period when he was gaining his first experiences of working in the theatre as chorus-master.

By 1843 his reputation had been firmly established with the premieres of *Rienzi* and *Der fliegende Holländer* (The Flying Dutchman) in Dresden, where, as a result of these successes, he was appointed *Kapellmeister* to the Saxon court.

Richard Wagner.

There he worked on *Tannhäuser* and *Lohengrin*, and made preliminary drafts for *The Ring* and *Die Meistersinger*, at the same time becoming involved in the republican movement that swept across Europe in the late 1840s. In 1849 a warrant was issued for his arrest. With the help of Liszt, who was to be a devoted ally throughout his life, he fled to Zürich, where he wrote many of his most influential essays, among them "The Artwork of the Future" and "Opera and Drama", in which he set out his theories of the *Gesamtkunstwerk*.

During this period of exile he finalized the libretto for the four dramas of *The Ring* and began composing their music, but he found himself distracted by his infatuation with Mathilde Wesendonck, the wife of one of his wealthy Swiss patrons. Showing his customary propensity for self-mythologizing, Wagner's thoughts now turned towards the Tristan legend, and soon he had interrupted work on his colossal operatic cycle to concentrate on *Tristan und Isolde*, a work he hoped would finance the building of the theatre he had realized would be necessary to stage *The Ring* as he had conceived it. The Wesendonck affair was the most damaging in a succession of infidelities that his wife, the actress Minna Planer, had been forced to endure since their marriage in 1836. Suffering from a heart condition, Minna spent much of her time in the 1850s either seeking cures or following Wagner around his various lodgings, with a dog and parrot in tow, trying to lure him back. But before long he was obsessed with yet another woman: Cosima von Bülow, Liszt's daughter and wife of the renowned conductor Hans von Bülow. Minna died in 1866, by which time Cosima and Wagner had been living together for a couple of years; in 1869 the Bülows' marriage was annulled, and the following year Cosima married Wagner, having already produced three children by him.

In the meantime, Wagner had found a new patron in King Ludwig II of Bavaria, the "mad King Ludwig", whose enthusiasm for Wagner's music was such that his fairy-tale castles in the Bavarian alps had interiors based on images from *Lohengrin*. It was through Ludwig's limitless largesse that Wagner could at last realize his planned theatre, though political intrigue made it impossible to build it in the first-choice location, Munich. In 1872 the foundation stone was laid in the backwater town of Bayreuth, and four years later the inaugural Bayreuth Festival opened with the first complete performances of *The Ring*. The ensuing financial loss, like most of Wagner's debts in his later years, was borne by Ludwig. The premiere of his last music-drama, *Parsifal*, took place at Bayreuth in 1882, a little over six months before Wagner died of a heart attack in Venice.

OPERAS

Der fliegende Holländer (The Flying Dutchman; 1840–44) is the work which marks the emergence of Wagner's distinctive stagecraft and musical style, a style that evolved through *Tannhäuser* (1843–45) and *Lohengrin* (1845–48) to achieve maturity in *Der Ring des Nibelungen* (text 1848–53, music 1853–74). Even though the same thematic material extends through the whole of this four-part epic, a growing sophistication of technique is manifest within the *Ring* cycle. In the third epi-

The Leitmotif

By the time he came to write *The Ring*, Wagner had mastered a means of weaving long spans of music into a continuous fabric, chiefly by the use of thematic leitmotifs ("leading motifs"), short phrases associated with either a character, an object or a dramatic idea. Debussy dismissed these motifs as "musical calling cards", and at their most basic they are indeed little more than this – thus character X mentions character Y, and the leitmotif of character Y duly appears in the music. However, Wagner's technique became far more subtle than this. For example, in *The Ring*, the River Rhine has a swelling theme of arpeggios from which, ultimately, all the opera's other leitmotifs are derived – a horn call for Siegfried, a fanfare-like theme for his sword, an ominous motif for Alberich's curse of death on future holders of the ring, and so on. Furthermore, these leitmotifs are not static: each is modified by its contact with other motifs, thus mirroring and qualifying the action of the opera. The climactic destruction of Valhalla at the end of *Götterdämmerung* takes place against a sort of symphonic recapitulation into which some ninety leitmotifs are blended.

The term leitmotif was invented by F.W. Jähns and used in his study of the music of Weber (1871). However, the idea of linking themes to programmatic elements or characters goes back further, most notably to the *idée fixe* that Berlioz employed in his *Symphonie fantastique* to represent the recurring idea of the beloved (see p.77).

sode, *Siegfried*, there is a stylistic shift between the second and third acts, for it was here that Wagner broke off composition of *The Ring* to compose *Tristan und Isolde* (1856–59) and *Die Meistersinger von Nürnberg* (1862–67), both of which are vast, single-evening works. His final drama, the "sacred stage festival play" *Parsifal*, occupied him from 1877 to 1882.

Superficially, the chief characteristic of Wagner's major operas is their length: ranging from three to five hours in duration. However, Puccini's witticism that Wagner contains "wonderful moments but terrible quarters of an hour" is wide of the mark, for these massive creations are emphatically not composed as a succession of highlights padded out with narrative material. Containing very few arias, Wagner's works are not so much operas as vocal dramas structured symphonically (and with the aid of musical signifiers known as *leitmotifs*; see box). So you shouldn't be daunted by Wagner's epic scale. That said, it is perhaps better to start with his most concise mature work, *The Flying Dutchman*, before moving on to *The Ring* and the late works.

Preludes & Other Orchestral Excerpts: New Philharmonia; London Philharmonic Orchestra; London Symphony Orchestra; Boult (EMI; 2 CDs)

More than any other composer, Wagner is misrepresented by so-called "bleeding chunks" torn out of the operas, but you might nonetheless want to sample extracts before committing yourself. Adrian Boult's two-disc collection of the best-known preludes and orchestral passages contains performances of great drama and passion.

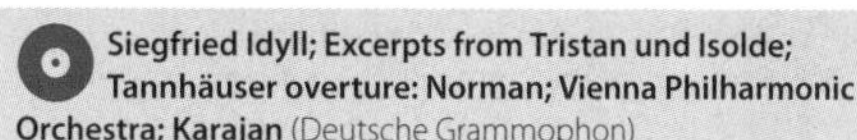

Siegfried Idyll; Excerpts from Tristan und Isolde; Tannhäuser overture: Norman; Vienna Philharmonic Orchestra; Karajan (Deutsche Grammophon)

Herbert von Karajan, one of the great Wagner conductors of the post-war period, conducts a deeply moving performance of the *Siegfried Idyll*, Wagner's lyrical reworking for chamber orchestra of themes from *Siegfried*. In addition there's a stirring account of the *Tannhäuser Overture*, plus the prelude and "Liebestod" from *Tristan*, the latter with Jessye Norman in full, glorious voice.

Der fliegende Holländer

The idea of salvation through love is a common theme in Wagner's work, and it first emerges in *Der fliegende Holländer*, a work inspired by the legend of a Dutch sea captain whose blasphemy led to his being condemned to sail the seas for eternity, unless he could be redeemed by a faithful woman. The action begins in a Norwegian fjord, where a sailor named Daland is sheltering his vessel from a storm. A ghostly ship pulls in alongside and its captain, the Dutchman, offers Daland vast wealth in exchange for a single night's hospitality. Daland's daughter, Senta, who is obsessed by the tales she has heard of the Dutchman's fate, vows to be his salvation. When the Dutchman overhears Senta's forsaken lover Erik complain to her that she is pledged to him, he believes he has lost her. But she proves her fidelity by throwing herself into the sea after him. In a climax that foreshadows that of *Tristan*, the lovers are finally seen transfigured, rising above the waves.

Der fliegende Holländer is in three acts, but is often performed as a continuous two-and-a-half-hour whole. It is Wagner's most compact drama, though there is an imbalance between the rather leisurely first half and the swift pattern of events in the second. There is a certain imbalance too in the musical treatment, which ranges from strophic ballads and arias with definite Italianate overtones to more Germanically dramatic choruses and arias – something that was not helped by Wagner's piecemeal revisions in 1860, when parts of the opera were reworked in his more advanced *Tristan* style.

Estes, Balslev, Salminen, Schunk, Clark; Bayreuth Festival Chorus and Orchestra; Nelsson (Philips; 2 CDs)

This 1985 recording brilliantly captures the cohesion and fluency of *Der fliegende Holländer*. Made at the end of a long-running Bayreuth production, the performance has a conspicuous unity of vision. Simon Estes' full-voiced, bass-baritone Dutchman has an anguish and desperation rarely matched on record. Most of the remaining cast sing superbly, especially Matti Salminen's resonant Daland.

Weikl, Studer, Domingo, Seiffert; Choir and Orchestra of the Deutsche Opera, Berlin; Sinopoli (Deutsche Grammophon; 2 CDs)

Giuseppe Sinopoli's recording of the *Dutchman* is tremendous, with orchestra and chorus in glowing form. The approach is typically fluid, as is the cast, with the sweet and effortless voices of Cheryl Studer as Senta, Plácido Domingo as Erik and Peter Seiffert as the Helmsman. A more declamatory style is evident in Bernd Weikl's resonant, noble portrayal of the Dutchman.

Der Ring des Nibelungen

Nothing in Wagner's output prefigures the sheer scale of *Der Ring des Nibelungen*, and indeed it was not initially envisaged on anything like the scale it ultimately attained. In 1848 Wagner began searching for a subject that could express the political fervour engendered by the Europe-wide uprisings of that year. He wanted a theme that would possess the power of ancient Greek theatre, with its emphasis on myth and communal experience, and he found it in the Norse-Germanic myth of the hero Siegfried, through whom an old, corrupt world was destroyed and replaced by one of hope.

Soon he had sketched the libretto for an opera called *Siegfrieds Tod* (Siegfried's Death), but then realized he needed to elaborate upon the events that led up to the hero's demise, and thus wrote a "prequel" called *Der junge Siegfried* (The Young Siegfried). Even that was not enough, so he drafted a scenario that added two more dramas, *Das Rheingold* (The Rhinegold) and *Die Walküre* (The Valkyrie). Having written the libretti for the four dramas in reverse order he began composing the music in sequence, beginning with *Rheingold*, the shortest part of the cycle, described merely as a prelude to the main drama (though it's longer than many full-length operas). Having completed *Walküre* and much of *Siegfried* (formerly *Der junge Siegfried*), in 1857 he broke off composition of *The Ring* to write *Tristan* and *Die Meistersinger*. Resuming *Siegfried* in 1865, he then composed the gargantuan finale, *Götterdämmerung* (Twilight of the Gods), as *Siegfrieds Tod* had now become. From a single opera, his project had grown to a length of some fifteen hours, spread over four evenings.

Obviously enough, the plot is impossible to convey in a few sentences, though one wit summarized it as a moral tale about what happens when a god defaults on the repayments on his house. This might well sum up *Das Rheingold*, in which the ruler of the gods, Wotan, tricks a power-wielding ring from the Nibelung dwarf Alberich (who in turn has stolen gold from the Rhinemaidens), then is obliged to use it to pay the giants Fafner and Fasolt for building his fortress, Valhalla. In a nutshell, the rest of the cycle depicts the attempts of both Wotan and Alberich to retrieve the ring from Fafner (who guards it in the form of a dragon) by fathering offspring to do the deed for them. Wotan's grandson Siegfried kills the dragon and then, with Brünnhilde (his betrothed, and Wotan's daughter), foils Alberich's son Hagen's plan to gain the ring, which is returned to the Rhinemaidens as the old world is cleansed by fire and water.

In outline *The Ring* sounds a bit like a "Sword and Sorcery" fantasy yarn, but it's in fact a drama so complex that it can bear – and has borne – scores of different interpretations. At Bayreuth, where they don't take kindly to frivolous cleverness, it has been presented both as a ritualistic exploration of such eternal verities as Love and Death, and as a quasi-Marxist study in power relations. The musical structure of *The Ring* is even more rich than its text, and includes some of the most powerful scenes in all opera: the very opening, for example, which conjures up the Rhine in a single, extended and elaborated chord; or the entry of the gods into Valhalla at the end of *Rheingold*; or the "Ride of the Valkyries" and "Magic Fire Music" in the third act of *Die Walküre*; or Siegfried's "Funeral March" from *Götterdämmerung*. But these are just moments of extreme intensity in an epic that is highly charged from start to finish. Take the plunge – this is one of the great musical journeys.

The Strange Case of August Bungert

For all that Wagner achieved as an individual, his impact on the course of German opera was uniquely suffocating and, in the final analysis, utterly destructive. Even before his greatest triumphs, dozens of his contemporaries were leaping onto his coat-tails, so that less than a year after the completion of *Tannhäuser* in 1845 a rival composer called Karl Mangold produced a romantic opera titled *Tannhäuser*, while only a few months after Wagner began working on the poetry for a cycle of operas on the myth of the Nibelungen, one Heinrich Dorn produced an epic opera entitled *Nibelungen*. With every step that Wagner took, a thousand others followed in imitation, and a host of rival composers were reduced passively to the status of disciples, as if an entire generation of once aspiring musicians had been hypnotized by the sheer force of will that characterized Wagner's personality, invention and ambition. Even those composers who claimed independence, such as August Klughardt, ended up throwing the towel in – spectacularly so in Klughardt's case, when in 1882 he produced a Wagnerian photostat titled *Gudrun*. Felix Draeske did precisely the same thing two years later, with his own take on *Gudrun*, and during the decade following Wagner's death in 1883 hardly a month passed without one or another myth and leitmotif-saturated work of pseudo-Wagnerian deference appearing (albeit briefly) in a German opera house.

Almost everyone had a go, and the margins of German music history around the turn of the twentieth century are littered with lost or forgotten manifestations of the Wagner cult – a process that reached its natural end with *Guntram*, the operatic debut of the young Richard Strauss. However, the most spectacular case of Wagnerian devotion was that of August Bungert, a gloriously mad and justifiably forgotten composer, born in 1845, whose life work for the theatre was devoted to outdoing Wagner in everything but talent. Like his idol he secured for himself a royal patron, the German-born Queen Elisabeth of Romania, who supported his work in return for Bungert agreeing to set her doggerel verse to music under the pseudonym Carmen Sylva.

His "greatest" achievement, in that it emphasized the virtues of a Protestant work ethic, was *Die Homerische Welt* (The Homeric World). Where Wagner had restricted himself to one cycle of four operas for his *Der Ring des Nibelungen*, Bungert set out during the 1880s to create in *Homerische Welt* two cycles totalling seven operas for which, like Wagner, he would write both the words and the music. The scale of his ambition was worthy of Odysseus, and it stands as a monument to his industry that he managed to progress as far as he did. The first cycle of three operas remained unfinished, but he did complete the second cycle of four, entitled *Die Odyssee*. Like the *Ring* on which it was modelled, Bungert's tetralogy was scored for monstrous, economically suicidal forces, and each opera suffered from the appearance of more named characters than *Die Meistersinger*. He nonetheless managed to oversee the first performances of each of the operas, in Dresden between 1896 and 1903, and even persuaded his patron to consider the construction of a Bungert Festival Theatre, at Bad Godesberg on the Rhine, to rival Wagner's monument in Bayreuth. Despite the support of a band of enthusiasts (the "Bungert Bund") led by one Max Chop, Bungert's plans never left the drawing board, and the unrelieved tedium of his music consigned *Homerische Welt* to an eternity of indifference and neglect. He died in 1915 convinced that his work would be discovered and resurrected after his death.

Various Artists; Bayreuth Festival Chorus and Orchestra; Keilberth
(Testament; 14 CDs)

A strong contender for the finest *Ring* on record, these live performances were taped in 1955 but released only recently. In terms of casting it would be hard to imagine better: Wolfgang Windgassen is in peak form as Siegfried, while Hans Hotter is uniquely authoritative as Wotan – both in better voice than on the later Solti set. Keilberth is a less showy conductor than his rivals but he offers a refreshingly unforced quality, one to which his performers are deeply responsive.

Various Artists; Bayreuth Festival Chorus and Orchestra; Böhm
(Philips; 14 CDs)

Karl Böhm's *Ring*, recorded live at Bayreuth between 1966 and 1967, is the most viscerally exciting, with an outstanding cast and vital sound. Some find Böhm's conducting too calculating, but few performances carry such a weight of personality. Some of the casting overlaps with both the Keilberth and Solti sets, but this recording captures these remarkable voices in wonderfully theatrical form.

Various Artists; Bayreuth Festival Chorus and Orchestra; Barenboim (Warner; 14 CDs)

This *Ring*, recorded live at Bayreuth in 1993, is the most rewarding since Böhm's. The carefully prepared voices, sublime orchestral sonorities and clear, naturally balanced sound would satisfy the most pedantic score-follower, but the spirit of Wagner's gothic imagination is also present throughout, with some remarkably percipient and imaginative conducting. All four operas are available separately.

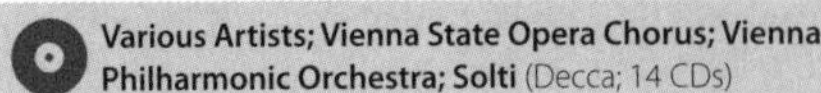

Various Artists; Vienna State Opera Chorus; Vienna Philharmonic Orchestra; Solti (Decca; 14 CDs)

The first studio *Ring* is for many the finest: the sumptuous orchestral presence, the superb singing, the sound quality and the special effects (eighteen real anvils for *Rheingold*) have never been bettered. As a reading it falls slightly short of the Keilberth and Böhm sets, because incident rather than structure seems to be the main preoccupation, but there is no more impressive-sounding *Ring* on record.

Tristan und Isolde

Arthurian legend provided the raw material for Wagner's greatest opera, but his treatment of the story was inspired by the philosophy of Schopenhauer, specifically its contention that bliss can only be found through the negation of the will and of desire. Schopenhauer is certainly a presence in the completed opera, which ends in blissful annihilation, but desire is its governing force. *Tristan und Isolde* is in essence a five-hour love song.

The plot is refreshingly simple. Tristan has been sent to Ireland to bring back the Irish princess Isolde as bride for his uncle, King Mark of Cornwall. But Tristan has fallen passionately in love with Isolde himself and she reciprocates. They conclude that death is the only way out and on the voyage to Cornwall they take a potion they believe to be poison, but Isolde's maid Brangäne has substituted a love draught and their passion is only reconfirmed. They continue their affair until caught in the act, when Tristan is wounded by one of Mark's knights. He is taken back to his castle in Brittany, where he dies just as Isolde arrives. Mark forgives them for their love and Isolde sinks onto Tristan's body, united with him in death.

Right from the prelude, with its sinuous melodic lines and suspended harmonies, a sense of heady sensuality and physical longing saturates *Tristan und Isolde*. The long love duet of the second act is as explicitly sexual as any piece of music ever written, complete with a musical coitus interruptus when the two lovers are discovered. The ever-present unfulfilled yearning is only satisfied in the closing bars of the whole opera, as Isolde's famous "Liebestod" (Love-Death), in which she sings herself into ecstatic oblivion, finally achieves harmonic fulfilment. *Tristan* is revolutionary in its chromatic language, which stretches tonal harmony to its very limits, casting the listener adrift in a world that has no reliable markers.

Windgassen, Nilsson, Ludwig, Talvela, Waechter; Bayreuth Festival Orchestra; Böhm (Philips; 3 CDs)

Tristan's hothouse atmosphere is ideally caught in Böhm's live 1966 Bayreuth performance, featuring Wolfgang Windgassen and Birgit Nilsson at the height of their powers. Böhm directs the performance of his life: tempi are swift and the orchestra plays at white heat, never allowing the tension to flag. Not a recording for the faint-hearted.

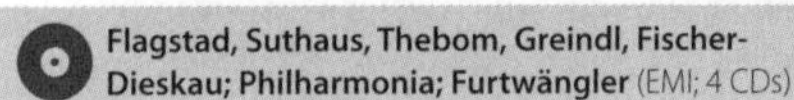

Flagstad, Suthaus, Thebom, Greindl, Fischer-Dieskau; Philharmonia; Furtwängler (EMI; 4 CDs)

For many people the greatest of all Wagner conductors was Wilhelm Furtwängler, and his 1952 account of *Tristan* has classic status. The sound quality doesn't match the Böhm set and the cast isn't ideal (even the legendary Kirsten Flagstad is past her best), but such is the cohesion and passion of this performance that these considerations really don't matter. An outstanding achievement.

Die Meistersinger von Nürnberg

As if to cleanse his system of the excesses of *Tristan*, Wagner next turned to comedy and the purer world of C major. *Die Meistersinger von Nürnberg* is not, however, a simple comedy: it is a hymn to German art and a celebration of progressiveness in culture.

The setting is medieval Nuremberg and its society of trade guilds. The most revered of these is the guild of Mastersingers, one of whom, Pogner, has decided to offer his daughter Eva to the winner of the Midsummer Day song contest. Eva is already in love with an itinerant knight, Walther von Stolzing, who attempts to gain admittance into the guild. Only the cobbler-poet Hans Sachs, a widower who himself is not immune to Eva's charms, sees the potential in his modern style of song and promises to help him. Walther has a rival in the shape of the fussy, carping town clerk Beckmesser – a caricature of Wagner's arch-critic in Vienna, Eduard Hanslick. At the contest, Beckmesser is laughed off after his catastrophic performance of a song he believes to be by Sachs; but it is actually by Walther, who sings it properly and, of course, wins Eva's hand.

Although less musically extreme than *Tristan*, it is nonetheless a great work, particularly in its characterization – Sachs is Wagner's most sympathetic creation, and the pomposity of the Mastersingers is wonderfully delineated. There are several magnificent set pieces in this most social of Wagner's works: the nocturnal comedy of Act 2, where Beckmesser tries to lure Eva with a serenade, is a bewitching piece of scene-setting; the first scene of Act 3, in which Sachs relinquishes his claim on Eva, is an extremely moving episode; and the final song contest is genuinely funny.

Holl, Schmidt, Seiffert, Magee, Wottrich, Hölle; Chorus and Orchestra of the Bayreuth Festival; Barenboim (Teldec; 4 CDs)

This is the obvious first choice for anyone new to *Der Meistersinger*. Robert Holl may lack the vocal weight of some, but he creates an enduring portrayal of the venerable Sachs. Andreas Schmidt is a more rounded Beckmesser than most, Peter Seiffert reasserts his credentials as an outstanding heldentenor, and Emily Magee and Birgitta Svenden are near-perfect as Eva and Magdelene. Barenboim directs a kaleidoscopic interpretation – in short, an instant classic.

Adam, Evans, Kollo, Donath, Hesse, Ridderbusch; Dresden State Opera Chorus and Orchestra; Karajan (EMI; 4 CDs)

In Karajan's 1970 *Meistersinger* the atmosphere is noticeably theatrical. Theo Adam brings weight and intensity to Sachs, Karl Ridderbusch positively glows as Pogner, and Geraint Evans sings beautifully as Beckmesser, but with little characterization. The women are uniformly superb, with Helen Donath swooningly lovely as Eva, and Ruth Hesse delightful as Magdalene.

Parsifal

Wagner's last opera has always divided even the composer's admirers. Some think it's his masterpiece, others find it depraved in its celebration of ascetic virtue through music of sometimes overwhelming sensuality. The climactic scene of this Arthurian morality drama takes place on Good Friday, and the opera is replete with Christian imagery such as the Grail, baptism, Holy Communion and the Crucifixion. Into this scheme Wagner mixes Buddhist notions of self-denial and elements of Schopenhauer's philosophy, to produce a distinctively Wagnerian exploration of the theme of enlightenment through purification.

As with Wagner's previous Arthurian opera, the action is more straightforward than the music. Amfortas, one of the senior knights guarding the Holy Grail, has succumbed to the temptation of lust and has thereby lost the sacred spear that pierced Christ's body on the cross. The spear has fallen into the possession of the magician Klingsor, who has inflicted on Amfortas a wound that can only be healed by a man "made wise through compassion". Parsifal at the start of the opera witnesses Amfortas's plight but doesn't understand it; eventually, having been similarly tempted by the sinful Kundry, he renounces sexuality in order to recover the spear and bring salvation to Amfortas and his knights.

Parsifal takes the harmonic experiments of *Tristan* one step further, dissipating the energies of tonal music to such an extent that the opera sometimes approaches the very verge of stasis. Though *Parsifal*'s slow-building crescendos and languid cadences express the seductiveness of spiritual goals and the duration of suffering, rather than the sexual ecstasy of *Tristan*, the overall dynamics of the two operas are very similar. In each opera a long prelude creates a state of suspension which lasts all the way through to the last moments – in the case of *Parsifal*, until the heavenward-reaching choral writing as the hero conducts Communion for the Knights of the Grail.

Thomas, London, Hotter, Dalis, Neidlinger, Talvela; Bayreuth Festival Chorus and Orchestra; Knappertsbusch (Philips; 4 CDs)

This 1962 Bayreuth recording is a triumph: not only are the performances faultless, but the remastered early stereo captures the Bayreuth sound to perfection. Jess Thomas is magnificent as Parsifal, George London makes a remarkably moving Amfortas, while Irene Dalis's Kundry, hurling caution to the wind, is the most compellingly dislocated interpretation on disc.

Hofmann, van Dam, von Halem, Moll, Nimsgern, Vejzovic; Berlin Philharmonic Orchestra; German Opera Chorus; Karajan (Deutsche Grammophon; 4 CDs)

This was one of Karajan's last recordings, and one of his greatest. Peter Hofmann is not altogether comfortable in the title role, but the rest of the cast is strong, and the playing of the Berlin Philharmonic is astonishingly beautiful. But above all this is Karajan's performance: the experience of a lifetime lies behind his shaping of the immense and slow trajectory of this climactic work.

William Walton (1902–1983)

Although he dabbled briefly with atonality in his early *String Quartet*, William Walton was an unrepentant neo-Romantic for most of his life. By his late twenties he had settled on a style that reconciled the essentially lyrical Englishness of Elgar with the pungency of Prokofiev and Stravinsky, a style characterized by earthy rhythms, wide intervallic writing, colourful and unstable harmonies, and a predilection for melancholy. Walton may not be the most challenging of modern composers, but his music is always extremely well crafted and two of his works – *Belshazzar's Feast* and the *Symphony No. 1* – have proved to be among the most durable of the twentieth century.

Born in Oldham, Lancashire, the son of a choirmaster and singing teacher, Walton spent his formative years in Oxford, where he was a chorister at Christ Church Cathedral. It was there that he began to compose, and in 1918 he was taken up by the aristocratic and artistic Sitwell family who introduced him to the leading cultural figures of the day, including the composer Constant Lambert, who had a powerful influence on him. Four years later he achieved notoriety with *Façade*, a self-consciously modernist "Entertainment" for six players and a speaker who recited poetry by Edith Sitwell through a megaphone. *Façade* gave Walton's name widespread currency, while his reputation was enhanced by his elegiac *Viola Concerto*, which Paul Hindemith (see p.258) premiered in 1929.

Walton's style reached maturity in 1931 with *Belshazzar's Feast*, a dramatic cantata which was acclaimed as the finest English choral work since Elgar's *Dream of Gerontius*, while attracting accusations of modernistic and eclectic tendencies from some quarters. Less equivocal success was achieved with the *Symphony No. 1* (1935), and the *Violin Concerto* commissioned by Jascha Heifetz in 1939. During World War II Walton was encouraged to pursue his obvious gift for the dramatic, and he began an opera on the life of the composer Gesualdo, but the project foundered after a couple of years. A rather more fruitful collaboration was with Laurence Olivier, for whom Walton wrote a number of brilliant film scores, beginning in 1944 with *Henry V*. Walton's music for Olivier reveals his acute sensitivity to narrative pace, as well as a sure touch in creating exactly the right mood for a particular scene.

His only full-length opera, *Troilus and Cressida*, was commissioned by the BBC in 1947. The troubled relationship between Walton and his librettist Christopher Hassall delayed work and it was not until 1954, after Walton had married and moved to the Italian island of Ischia, that the score was finally completed. *Troilus* was premiered at Covent Garden in the same year, but its dreadful reception proved a terrible disappointment. Walton spent the rest of his life in Italy, producing less and less music as his brand of Romantic traditionalism became ever more unfashionable.

Belshazzar's Feast

Walton's reputation was established primarily by *Belshazzar's Feast*, a fine piece of biblical gothic, scored for baritone solo, full choir and large orchestra to a text selected by Osbert Sitwell. In his handling of these vast forces Walton displays remarkable abilities for orchestration and ensemble-writing, and his music is typified by ardent, sometimes violent, thematic material. There's an obvious nod to the English oratorio tradition, above all in the sheer scale of the piece, but there's a much more wild imagination at work here that produces an unbridled theatrical energy comparable to Orff's *Carmina Burana*. Indeed its pulsating quasi-paganism upset many of those present at the first performance in 1931, and the Three Choirs Festival wouldn't touch the piece until 1957.

Terfel; BBC Singers, Chorus & Symphony Chorus & Orchestra; Davis (Warner Apex; with Vaughan Williams *Job*)

With the outstanding Decca recording (conducted by Andrew Litton and with Bryn Terfel as soloist) currently only available as a four-CD set, this live recording makes an obvious and satisfying alternative. Taped at the Last Night of the 1994 Promst it has a real sense of occasion, with Bryn Terfel once again making the most of his dramatic solo interventions.

Symphony No. 1

Walton's next major score after *Belshazzar*, the *Symphony No. 1*, gave him such difficulties that it took three years to complete, and the work conveys a strong sense of personal victory and fulfilment. Opening with a gorgeous extended flute solo, the movement builds with an ever-mounting tension to a tumultuous climax. Ideas tend to be developed in a way similar to the symphonies of Sibelius: a sparky, colourful Scherzo (Walton marks it "con malizia") is followed by an Andante of an almost Elgarian melancholy. There is also a debt to Hindemith – in particular the fugal passage in the finale is almost a homage to Walton's German friend. With its broad emotional horizons, Walton's first symphony stands in the forefront of English symphonic achievement and stands comparison with Vaughan Williams's contemporaneous fourth symphony.

London Symphony Orchestra; Previn (RCA; 2 CDs; with *Violin, Viola & Cello Concertos* and *Sinfonia Concertante*)

This is one of André Previn's finest achievements on disc: consistently exciting throughout, the air of tension is built with consummate skill but he also gives full rein to the symphony's more expansive moments.

English Northern Philharmonia; Daniel (Naxos; with *Partita*)

Like Previn, Paul Daniel knows how to distil the drama of this symphony, and although his approach is not quite so unrelenting he achieves a truly exciting performance. Only the slightly blurry sound mars this outstanding disc.

Viola & Violin Concertos

It may not be a crowded field, but Walton's is the outstanding concerto for the viola, its introspective mood perfectly matching the mellow subdued tone of the instrument. Completed in 1929, it begins with a slow movement in which a long lilting melody for the soloist gradually takes on a rather edgy character before returning to its initial calmness. Another of Walton's spiky, mischievous Scherzos is followed by a broad Elgarian finale. The concerto was composed for the English viola player Lionel Tertis at the suggestion of Sir Thomas Beecham, but Tertis rejected it – which is why Paul Hindemith gave its first performance.

Arguably the most seductive of all Walton's music is the *Violin Concerto* (1938–9), a work designed to display the virtuosity and beautiful tone of Jascha Heifetz. The soloist's opening theme, a lyrical idea which sets the emotional tone of the work, leads to a staccato section in which the violinist battles with the orchestra for dominance; having won, the violinist is rewarded with yet another captivating solo episode. This movement's sensuousness is carried through into the Scherzo, while the finale makes much of the composer's brilliant facility for orchestral writing.

Kennedy; Royal Philharmonic Orchestra; Previn (EMI; with Vaughan Williams *The Lark Ascending*)

There are surprisingly few recordings that couple these two concertos, but in any case it would be difficult to imagine more sympathetic accounts than Nigel Kennedy's. He taps straight into the *Viola Concerto's* elegiac spirit and pulls out all the stops for the more extrovert and virtuosic *Violin Concerto*.

Heifetz; Philharmonia Orchestra; Walton. Bashmet; London Symphony Orchestra; Previn (RCA; 2 CDs; with *Symphony No. 1, Cello Concerto & Sinfonia Concertante*)

Jascha Heifetz, who commissioned the work, gives an electrifyingly intense account of the violin concerto under the direction of the composer in what is very good sound for 1950. Yuri Bashmet's 1994 performance of the viola concerto is excellent, marginally more introspective than Kennedy's which still leads the field.

Cello Concerto

Walton's last concerto, commissioned by the great Russian-born cellist Gregor Piatigorsky, was completed in 1956, but as with the other two, the composer made a number of revisions to it later on. Regarded by Walton as the best of his concertante works, it's a wonderfully compelling piece in the hands of the right soloist. The work is essentially two slow outer movements with a central Scherzo which the composer described as "technically more spectacular". After a few spooky opening chords the cello enters with an elegant and wistful theme, creating a melodious and melancholy atmosphere, which, despite some animated passages in the middle movement, is sustained throughout the work.

Hugh; English Northern Philharmonia; Daniel (Naxos; with *Violin Concerto*)

In the *Cello Concerto* Tim Hugh finds the perfect middle ground between the cerebral and the instinctive. The disc is completed by a fantastically clear and graceful account of the *Violin Concerto* from Dong-Suk Kang.

Piatigorsky; Boston Symphony Orchestra; Munch (RCA; 2 CDs; with *Symphony No. 1, Viola & Violin Concertos* and *Sinfonia Concertante*)

The second of the 1950s premiere recordings featured on this bumper Walton set is the outstanding rendition of the *Cello Concerto* by dedicatee Gregor Piatigorsky. Originally released in 1957 as part of RCA's "Living Stereo" series, the sound is still extremely vivid, with the authoritative soloist placed quite far forward in the mix.

Façade

First "staged" at the Aeolian Hall, London, in 1923, *Façade* was performed from behind a decorated curtain by six instrumentalists, plus Edith Sitwell reciting 21 of her verses. Her exotically surreal poetry now seems camp and orchidaceous in a delightfully English way. Walton's music precisely matches its mood of quirky nostalgia, with a light parodistic mixture that includes suggestions of jazz, music hall and even folk music. There's an obvious formal debt to Schoenberg's *Pierrot Lunaire* (see p.481), especially in the way the reciter must follow precise rhythmic notation, but stylistically it is closer in feel to the similarly irreverent "Entertainments" organized by Jean Cocteau and his musical protégés, Les Six. Subsequent performances established the work's notoriety, assisted by Noel Coward's revue sketch "The Swiss Family Whittlebot", which parodied both it and the Sitwell siblings. A definitive version of the score was established in 1951 and a supplement of eight additional poems (*Façade 2*) premiered in 1979.

Sitwell, Pears; English Opera Group Ensemble; Collins (Alto; with *Henry V & Coronation March "Orb and Sceptre"*)

Too many recent recordings have celebrity reciters who tend to overact and can't quite manage the rhythms. There are no such problems in this mono recording from the 1950s: Dame Edith has a finesse and an eccentric delicacy that is completely appropriate, while Peter Pears brings a musician's precision to his rather more deadpan delivery.

Carl Maria von Weber (1786–1826)

If any single person can be credited with the creation of German Romantic opera, it is Carl Maria von Weber. His *Der Freischütz*, with its magical orchestral atmospherics and its use of Germanic folklore, established a lineage that would lead ultimately to Wagner. Weber was also in his time a highly regarded music critic, a pianist of international renown and one of the first conductors to establish the importance of that role.

Weber was born near Lübeck in northern Germany into a musical and theatrical family (he was a cousin of Mozart's wife Constanze). The fact that he was a sickly child did not prevent his father, Franz Anton, from planning a career for his young son as a prodigy in the style of Mozart. Carl Maria soon learned to play the piano and his subsequent training included a period with Joseph Haydn's brother Michael in Salzburg, where, aged twelve, he wrote his earliest compositions. The following year he completed his first opera, although the manuscript was destroyed by fire shortly after its completion. After further training with the Abbé Vogler in Vienna, he secured the post of *Kapellmeister* at the theatre in Breslau at the tender age of seventeen, staying for two years until he fell seriously ill by accidentally swallowing some engraver's acid. A position as financial secretary to the profligate Duke Ludwig, brother of the King of Württemberg, led to friendship with the composer Franz Danzi and the completion of the opera *Silvana*, but ended

Portrait of Weber by Ferdinand Schimon.

disastrously when Weber's father purloined some official funds to pay his debts – an action that eventually resulted in the banishment of both father and son.

For the next two years Weber pursued a career as a itinerant virtuoso pianist basing himself first in Mannheim and then in Darmstadt. A prolonged trip to Munich resulted in a fruitful musical partnership with the clarinettist Heinrich Bärmann, the two men performing together across Germany. Then, in 1813, he was unexpectedly made director of the Prague opera house where he resumed his efforts at operatic reform, placing the emphasis on Mozart and contemporary French opera, in opposition to the prevalent taste for all things Italian. He also got married, after a stormy courtship, to Caroline Brandt, a singer he had recruited to the company.

Weber's reforming ideals were taken even further in his next major appointment, as Royal Saxon *Kapellmeister* in Dresden, a post he took up in 1817. His endeavours to develop a German national opera company led to years of antagonism within the court, where the music of Rossini was greatly preferred. Until, that is, *Der Freischütz* was performed in Berlin in 1821. Its success was instant: it received dozens of productions throughout Germany within a year of its premiere, then was played throughout Europe. *Der Freischütz* was to remain the most popular German opera throughout the first half of the century.

Weber made two attempts to follow up his success with *Euryanthe* (1823) and *Oberon* (1826), but – despite much powerful and dramatic music – neither lived up to the promise of their predecessor, chiefly because of their terrible libretti. While in London to conduct the premiere of *Oberon*, years of ill health caught up with him and he died, aged only 39, the day before he was due to return home to his family. He was buried in Moorfields Chapel, but in 1844, Richard Wagner, his successor in Dresden, arranged for his body to be returned to that city.

Der Freischütz

The structure of *Der Freischütz* (The Marksman), in which the musical numbers are linked by spoken dialogue, derives from the Germanic genre of music-theatre known as *Singspiel*, of which Mozart's *Magic Flute* is the best-known example. However, Weber's opera is an advance on its predecessors in its use of recurrent motifs to achieve musical continuity, notably in the use of horns to underline the huntsman theme. Furthermore, in its fusion of the supernatural, the folkloric and the rustic, *Der Freischütz* brought together some of the dominant strands of German Romanticism for the first time in the history of opera.

The hero of the piece is the huntsman Max, who makes a pact with the forces of darkness to gain some magic bullets that will allow him to win a shooting contest, and thus gain the hand of his sweetheart, Agathe. At the heart of the opera is the scene in which the magic bullets are forged in a gloomy, inhospitable mountain valley called the Wolf's Glen. This wonderful musical evocation of evil is Weber's most impressive creation, but his command of orchestral colouring is deft throughout the opera, especially in his use of folk-like melodies for his choruses.

Grümmer, Schock, Otto, Kohn, Prey, Frick; Berlin Deutsche Opera Chorus; Berlin Philharmonic Orchestra; Keilberth (EMI; 2 CDs)

Joseph Keilberth's 1958 recording of *Freischütz* is an outstanding achievement. Elizabeth Grümmer's flowing soprano gives an urgent, sensitive characterization of Agathe, while Lisa Otto makes a delicious Ännchen and Rudolph Schock is a powerful, earnest Max. The dialogue is included and the sound is orchestrally thin but vocally sumptuous.

Schreier, Janowitz, Weikl, Adam, Vogel, Mathis; Leipzig Radio Chorus; Dresden Staatskapelle; Kleiber (Deutsche Grammophon; 2 CDs)

Carlos Kleiber adopts some extreme speeds in his 1973 recording of *Der Freischütz*, but he conveys the dramatic energy of the score like no other conductor. He gets wonderful playing out of the Dresden Staatskapelle and his cast is generally good, though Peter Schreier's Max sounds a little strained at times, and Gundula Janowitz's Agathe, though exquisitely sung, might just as well be singing a shopping list.

Clarinet Music

While Weber's main claim to fame is as an opera composer, his music for the clarinet is another significant legacy. As with Mozart, Weber was inspired by a particular musician, in his case Heinrich Bärmann, the brilliant principal clarinettist of the Munich court orchestra, for whom he wrote a concertino, two concertos, and a set of variations (all 1811), plus a quintet (1814) and a showpiece for piano and clarinet, the *Grand Duo Concertant* (1816). Though Weber's instrumental music is ostentatiously virtuosic, especially so in the *Clarinet Concerto No. 2*, there are also some startlingly dramatic changes of

The Clarinet Comes of Age

The clarinet first appeared toward the close of the seventeenth century, and it developed around the same time as another single-reed woodwind instrument, the chalumeau. Its invention is usually credited to one Johann Christoph Denner of Nuremberg, who manufactured both chalumeaux and clarinets, and it was some time before the latter emerged as the dominant voice. Telemann, Handel, Vivaldi and Rameau all occasionally wrote works that had clarinet parts; J.S. Bach – more conservative in his instrumentation – did not.

But it was in Mozart, whose favourite instrument it was said to have been, that the clarinet found its first real exponent. Clarinets appeared in Mozart's later piano concertos and symphonies, while his *Clarinet Concerto* (see p.366) and *Clarinet Quintet* (see p.369) are the greatest of all works for the instrument. Mozart was largely inspired by the technical brilliance of his friend Anton Stadler who played a five-key instrument and a unique basset clarinet – made for him by Theodor Lotz – which had two extra lower tones. Around the same time, a seemingly inexhaustible craze for wind band music (known as *Harmoniemusik*) proved fertile ground for many composers, the most gifted – after Mozart – being the Bohemian Franz Krommer (1759–1831).

By the end of the century a pattern had been established: makers created clarinets which were much easier to play, which in turn inspired composers to write ever more ambitious works – often with specific performers in mind. By 1800 the clarinet had become an important solo instrument, prized not simply for its expressive "vocal" tone but also for the opportunities it offered for out-and-out virtuosity. The next two decades proved a golden age for clarinet composition, much of it written for the three greatest players of the time, Heinrich Bärmann (1784–1847), Simon Hermstedt (1778–1846) and Bernhard Crusell (1775–1838). All three had graduated from the ranks of military bands (where the clarinet was now firmly established) to become prestigious court musicians, and each of them had studied with one of the greatest players of the previous generation, Franz Tausch.

Weber's association with Bärmann, which began soon after they met in Munich in 1811, produced a handful of dazzling masterpieces, made playable by the addition of extra keys on the newest clarinets. Weber was especially impressed by Bärmann's "welcome homogeneity of tone from top to bottom", and his two concertos exploit the clarinettist's sensitivity as much as his virtuosity. Hermstedt, who was based at the ducal court at Sondherhausen, had a similar relationship with the composer Ludwig Spohr (1784–1859), commissioning a concerto from him in 1808 and another shortly after. Spohr was a violinist and, arguably, his four clarinet concertos are less idiomatic than those of Weber, though just as demanding. The second is the most rewarding with a short slow movement that cleverly contrasts the instrument's high and low registers. Crusell, the principal clarinettist with the Royal Court Orchestra of Stockholm, wrote three clarinet concertos as well as a delightful set of variations. Though no less talented a player than Bärmann and Hermstedt, Crusell's clarinet writing is remarkable for the way it avoids the kind of flashy passage work found in the Weber and Spohr concertos, nor is he as brilliant an orchestrator. Instead, his music is characterized by craftsmanship and restraint, with the soloist working alongside the orchestra rather than ostentatiously against it.

Spohr's Clarinet Concertos Nos. 2 & 4; Krommer's Double Clarinet Concerto: Meyer, Bliss; Academy of St Martin-in-the-Fields; Sillito (EMI)

Julian Bliss plays Spohr's *Concerto No. 2* (the only one in a major key) with sufficient flair and panache to overcome the occasionally bombastic orchestral writing. Sabine Meyer is the equally excellent soloist in the grandly symphonic *Concerto No. 4* written for the warmer-toned clarinet in A; the pair of them clearly relish Krommer's sparkling double concerto of 1815, a frequently witty work that deserves to be better known.

Crusell's Clarinet Concertos Nos. 1–3: Kriiku; Finnish Radio Symphony Orchestra; Oramo (Ondine)

Finns claim Bernhard Crusell as their own so it's appropriate that the phenomenally gifted Finnish clarinettist Kari Kriiku should do the honours here. By choosing to take the fast movements at breakneck speeds he invests all three concertos with a compelling verve and a playful sense of danger that the orchestra is swift to respond to.

Mendelssohn's Concert Pieces for Clarinet, Basset Horn and Orchestra Nos. 1& 2: Meyer, Meyer; Academy of St Martin-in-the-Fields; Sillito (EMI; with Weber *Clarinet Quintet* & Bärmann *Clarinet Quintet No. 3*)

Bärmann was also a good friend of Mendelssohn and extracted two display pieces from him (in exchange for cooking the composer a meal) which he played with his son Carl – a gifted basset horn player. He also composed himself, and his own clarinet quintets (especially *No. 3*) reveal his debt to Weber. On this disc all the works, fluently played by Sabine Meyer and her brother Wolfgang, are supported by a chamber orchestra.

mood. The central movements of both concertos are slow episodes that highlight the instrument's vocal sonority, but in the finales everything is subservient to display.

The charming *Clarinet Quintet* follows a slightly different pattern, its opening movement alternating between moments of introspection and a rather manic jauntiness. The mournful slow Fantasia conforms to the song-like nature of Weber's slow movements. It's followed by a quirky Minuet and the obligatory Rondo finale designed to show off the instrument's range. The *Grand Duo* is notable for its operatic brilliance and the extreme difficulty of the two evenly balanced roles. The last movement, in particular, is a sensational battle for supremacy between the two players.

Clarinet Concertos Nos. 1 & 2; Concertino Op. 26; Clarinet Quintet: Kriiku; New Helsinki Quartet; Finnish Radio Symphony Orchestra; Oramo (Ondine)

Truly breathtaking performances of the concertos from Kari Kriiku, who clearly relishes their technical challenges which he shrugs off with aplomb. He is equally assured in the *Quintet*, finding just the balance between the flashy and the sensitive that Weber's finest chamber work demands.

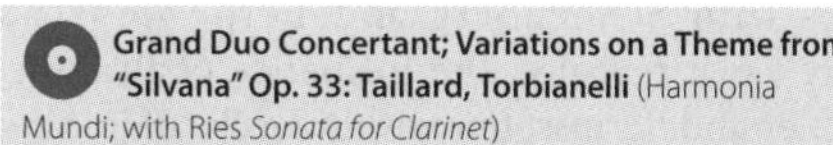

Grand Duo Concertant; Variations on a Theme from "Silvana" Op. 33: Taillard, Torbianelli (Harmonia Mundi; with Ries *Sonata for Clarinet*)

Pierre André Taillard plays on a copy of an instrument of around 1800 and is accompanied by Edoardo Torbianelli on a pianoforte of the same period. Far from being an academic exercise, it adds a dimension of warmth to the two most showy pieces Weber wrote for Bärmann.

Anton Webern (1883–1945)

Like Alban Berg (see p.67), Anton Webern began studying with Arnold Schoenberg (see p.478) in 1904, and soon realized that all his ideas about composition had to change. The path that Webern followed, however, took an entirely different direction from Berg's. Where the latter went on to write large-scale works in which the dictates of modernism were reconciled with the Romantic tradition of Wagner and Mahler, Webern worked relentlessly towards a state of absolute economy, compressing a vast range of emotions into a few wisps of music. He did, however, acknowledge links to Mahler, links which can be clearly heard in such works as *Six Orchestral Pieces* (1909), albeit worked out on a distinctly un-Mahlerian scale.

An assiduous, self-critical perfectionist, Webern assigned opus numbers to only 31 compositions, the vast majority of which last less than ten minutes, and some of which seem like mere splinters or tissues of sound. Yet these are among the most important works of the twentieth century. Webern once finished a lecture with the words "There is no other way", and in the aftermath of World War II the generation of Boulez and Stockhausen took this as truth in a quite fundamentalist way. It remains an open question whether Webern would have seen himself as their mentor.

Webern was born into prosperity in Vienna, and took his first piano lessons with his mother at the age of five. He began composing at an early age, and from the age of fourteen studied with Edwin Komauer in Klagenfurt, where the family had moved. In 1902 he entered the University of Vienna, where he quickly became dissatisfied with educational routine. He decided to take up studies with the arch conservative Hans Pfitzner, but stormed out of his first meeting with him when Pfitzner expressed a lack of enthusiasm for the music of Mahler. Instead he enrolled in Schoenberg's extracurricular classes in composition, and remained a Schoenberg student until 1908.

As with Schoenberg and Berg, Webern's early work revealed the influence of Brahms, Mahler and Strauss, but within weeks of joining Schoenberg's course he had begun to revise his ideas on tonality. The *String Quartet* of 1905 (one of the works to which Webern did not assign an opus number) already foreshadows his later style, and by the time he moved out from under Schoenberg's wing he was wholly committed to atonality (not a word either he or Schoenberg liked), as well as to a lifelong friendship with Berg. Webern's first major atonal work, the *Five Movements for String Quartet*, appeared in 1909 – the same year as Schoenberg's trailblazing *Three Piano Pieces*.

For the next nine years Webern devoted himself to composition and conducting. Much of the music he composed during this period was for voice, and all of it was of a revolutionary brevity: Schoenberg wrote that the *Six Bagatelles* for string quartet of 1913 (total duration less than four minutes) expressed "a novel in a single gesture, a joy in a breath". He served as a non-combatant during World War I before poor eyesight led to his being discharged. He renewed close contacts with Schoenberg, with whom he and Berg formed the "Society for Private Musical Performances" to promote new music (by no means exclusively their own). The Society's inauguration, in November 1918, followed closely after the end of the war.

When the Society ceased operating in 1922, Webern at last found himself in demand as a conductor. For twelve years he was the conductor of the Vienna Workers' Symphony Orchestra and Chorus, and he gave numerous concerts for the BBC between 1929 and 1936. Meanwhile he found time to produce an intermittent flow of predominantly vocal music, although when, following Schoenberg's lead, he adopted the serial method, he found himself able to return to writing for instruments alone, first with the *String Trio* (1927), then with the *Symphony* (1928). Always obsessed with structural precision (his works include the formal application of fugues, canons and passacaglias), Webern established a more complete form of serialism, applying rigorous principles not just to the intervals between the notes, but to aspects of timbre, rhythms and dynamics, thereby laying the foundations for the "total serialism" espoused by the modernist vanguard after World War II.

Although the Nazis banned his music as an example of "cultural Bolshevism", Webern had pronounced Nazi sympathies. He stayed in Austria throughout the war, earning his money by proofreading other composers' works, and completing three major works, *Cantatas Nos. 1* and *2* (1939 & 1943), and the *Variations for Orchestra* (1940). A terrible accident made him one of the war's last casualties, months after hostilities had ceased. On 15 September, 1945, visiting his daughter, Webern stepped outside for a cigar and was shot by an American soldier in the mistaken belief that he was involved in the black marketeering activities of his son-in-law. He died before medical help arrived.

Complete Works with Opus Numbers: Harper, Rosen, Stern, Piatigorsky; Julliard Quartet; London Symphony Orchestra; Boulez (Sony; 3 CDs)

Recorded in the 1960s and 1970s, Boulez's first "complete" set comprises all the works with opus numbers. Despite some wrong notes in the vocal recordings and a generally hard-edged approach, the performances are good, making this the best-value way to get acquainted with Webern's core output.

Complete Works: Oelze, Pollet, Finley, Cascioli, Hagen, Kremer, Zimerman; Emerson String Quartet; Ensemble Intercontemporain; Berlin Philharmonic Orchestra; Boulez (Deutsche Grammophon; 6 CDs)

This set, recorded throughout the 1990s, includes practically every Webern work known. The best pieces are undoubtedly those with opus numbers, but the others give a fascinating overview of Webern's development from late Romanticist to meticulous modern miniaturist. The recorded sound is good, and the performances excellent and Boulez is more outwardly expressive than in the Sony set.

Passacaglia

The *Passacaglia* was the first work of which Webern felt sufficiently confident to assign it an opus number, and Opus 1 it remains, although earlier pieces are now part of the Webern canon (notably the "idyll for large orchestra" *Im Sommerwind*, written in 1904). The *Passacaglia* marked an enormous advance on the quasi-Romanticism of *Im Sommerwind*, being a highly individual interpretation of variation form. A theme of radical sparseness is stated in the strings, then followed by no fewer than 23 variations and a coda: all in the space of ten minutes. Already there is an impressive concentration on the quality of each note, and on the musical architecture. Webern later wrote to Berg that all his works from the *Passacaglia* on "relate to the death of my mother", and indeed there is a haunting and haunted sense of tragedy lurking just beneath their often suave surfaces.

Berlin Philharmonic Orchestra; Boulez (Deutsche Grammophon; with *Five Movements, Six Pieces for Orchestra, Im Sommerwind* & Bach/Schubert arrangements)

In this excellent recording from Boulez (part of his second complete Webern set), the conductor elicits spacious and luxuriant performances from the Berlin Phil. The CD includes Webern's Bach and Schubert arrangements, which are fascinating tributes from one master to his forebears.

Symphony

Webern adopted Schoenberg's twelve-tone method of composition in 1924 in *Three Traditional Rhymes*, but it was with the *Symphony*, written three years later, that the change truly registered. Here, in two compact movements, Webern returned for the first time in fifteen years to writing for orchestra, albeit one tailored to his own highly individual needs: strings (no double basses), a harp, pairs of clarinets and horns. There is a distilled clarity to Webern's scoring that was to sustain the rest of his career and, if it is built on a technical mastery that is dauntingly complex, the results are bracing, as if the ear is at last cleansed of the previous century's detritus.

Oelze, Finley; Berlin Philharmonic; BBC Singers; Boulez (Deutsche Grammophon; with *Cantatas Nos. 1 & 2, Variations for Orchestra, Three Orchestral Songs & Das Augenlicht*)

Boulez never allows the music to sag and the performances throughout are superb, not least from soprano Christiane Oelze. In the *Three Orchestral Songs* she finds beauty and tension where many others achieve only an antiseptic purity, and in the second cantata her feeling for the expressiveness of Webern's idiom is well matched by Gerald Finley.

Variations for Orchestra

Webern heard very little of his music performed, and often overestimated how long it would last: the *Variations for Orchestra*, he calculated, would take "about twenty minutes". In the event, they last not much more than seven, but those seven minutes are packed with incident. Webern derives the whole piece from the briefest four-note phrase heard at the work's beginning. That fundamental material is then shaped and reshaped in six variations, as if one were to examine a tiny gem from every angle to see the light it cast. The composer described the work as an "overture", which suggests its dramatic potential, but for the composer it was all but a finale, and its 1943 premiere in Switzerland was the last time Webern heard his own work performed.

Vienna Philharmonic; Abbado (Deutsche Grammophon; with *Passacaglia, Six Pieces for Orchestra, Five Pieces for Orchestra*, Bach/Webern *Ricecare* & Schoenberg *A Survivor from Warsaw*)

His reputation may be based on different repertoire, but Abbado excels in twentieth-century music. The same might be said of the Vienna Phil, which produces performances of airy transparency in music that can easily sound clogged. Abbado finds a restless tension in the score that makes Boulez's otherwise excellent version with the BPO (see above) seem almost demure.

String Quartet Op. 28

Webern wrote comparatively often for the string quartet, although he only allowed four such works into his official oeuvre. None is more quintessentially Webern than the last, Op. 28, completed in 1938 to a commission from Elisabeth Sprague Coolidge. Its austerity is at first abrasive, yet the work grew from Webern's reflections on his daughter's pregnancy, and in the right hands there is warm eloquence as well as astringency in its three movements. As usual, the music grows from the smallest seeds (the metaphor appropriate here) as Webern manipulates rhythm, tempo and duration into mercurial patterns that shift even as we think we've managed to fix them in our mind.

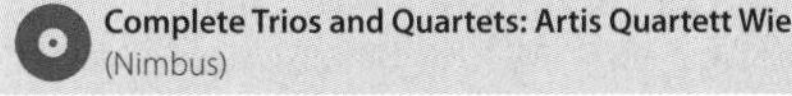
Complete Trios and Quartets: Artis Quartett Wien (Nimbus)

Marvellously well-judged performances of all the pieces for quartet and string trio from the Artis Quartett of Vienna, played in the order that they were written. The playing is always clear and precise but there is also considerably more expressive warmth than is the norm in such music. A masterful achievement.

Kurt Weill (1900–1950)

If Weill had lived and worked into a reasonable old age, the end of his career would have coincided with the beginning of Andrew Lloyd Webber's. What would Weill, whose work helped shape the modern musical, have made of what the form had become? A supremely practical composer, might he have adapted his style to suit the needs of the time? Perhaps we should be grateful that we shall never know. As it stands, Weill's oeuvre (and not only the stage works) remains one of the linchpins of twentieth-century repertoire, attracting audiences and interpreters far removed from the conventions of opera house and concert hall.

Weill was born in Dessau, where his father was cantor of the synagogue, and his earliest musical studies were as a pianist. Later he studied composition with Humperdinck and Busoni. While still a teenager, he coached singers at the Dessau Opera, and in 1920 became *Kapellmeister* at the municipal theatre in Ludenscheid. His first compositions flirted with current styles, whether the neo-classicism of Hindemith or, as in the *Symphony No. 1* (1921), the atonality of Schoenberg. Nevertheless, something personal was already beginning to emerge.

In 1924 Weill met the actress Lotte Lenya and the two married in 1926. By the time Weill met Bertolt Brecht in 1927, he had already established himself as a successful theatre composer with acerbic pieces such as *Der Protagonist* (1926) and *Royal Palace* (1927). Now with Brecht, he embarked on one of the most significant collaborations in twentieth-century music. The first work they produced was *Mahagonny, A Songspiel* (1927), a setting for Lenya and five opera singers of pre-existing Brecht texts attacking American capitalism. This was the basis of the full-scale opera *Aufstieg und Fall der Stadt Mahagonny* (Rise and Fall of the City of Mahagonny; 1930), but before that Weill, Brecht and Brecht's largely unacknowledged collaborator Elisabeth Hauptmann wrote *Die Dreigroschenoper* (The Threepenny Opera; 1928), a "play with music" marvellously derived from John Gay's *The Beggar's Opera* (1728). Acridly modern, bitingly satirical, it was a huge success. Brecht and Weill were now in demand, and another collaboration,

Kurt Weill and Lotte Lenya in California, 1944.

Happy End, soon followed. The text for this "play with music" was again by Brecht and Hauptmann.

After *Mahagonny* came *Der Jasager* (1930), then *Der Burgschaft* (1932), for which Weill collaborated on the text with Caspar Neher. Shortly after the premiere he and Lenya broke up, and by now his relationship with Brecht had soured because, as Lenya later declared, Weill was not prepared "to set the Communist Manifesto to music". But the darkest shadow of all was cast by the growing power of the Nazis. Hitler became chancellor in 1933, and three weeks later, Weill's *Der Silbersee* (text and lyrics by Georg Kaiser) was premiered. Nazis demonstrated against the second performance, and hurled anti-Semitic abuse at Weill.

Weill knew what was coming, and fled to Paris. He never returned to his homeland. In Paris he wrote *Die sieben Todsünden* (The Seven Deadly Sins), his final and greatest collaboration with Brecht, and his *Symphony No. 2*. He and Lenya were reunited in London before sailing for New

York, where the Manhattan Opera House was to premiere a version of the unperformed *Der Weg der Verheissung*, now called *The Eternal Road*.

Weill later confessed, "I never felt the oneness with my native country that I do with the United States; the moment I landed here I felt as though I'd come home." He thought America offered a way out of what he saw as the dead end of the European avant-garde. Here at last he could write music that would speak, not to the faceless masses of political philosophy, but to real audiences. He and Lenya remarried in 1937 shortly after the lavish premiere of *The Eternal Road*. New projects came thick and fast: besides the "musical play" *Johnny Johnson* (premiered in 1936) he wrote a score (not used) for the movie *Blockade*, as well as incidental music for several plays, a radio cantata and Broadway musicals like *Knickerbocker Holiday* (1938) and *Lady in the Dark* (1941).

Perhaps the greatest work of his American period was *Street Scene* (1947), Weill's "Broadway opera"; "75 years from now", he predicted, "*Street Scene* will be remembered as my major work." If it's customary to divide Weill's work into European and American periods, Weill himself saw no such discontinuity; his music was always a commentary on society in the most direct way possible. As he told an interviewer in 1940, "Schoenberg has said that he is writing for a time fifty years after his death ... For myself, I write for today. I don't give a damn about writing for posterity."

The Threepenny Opera

Within months of the Berlin premiere, European theatres were clamouring to stage the work: there had been a reputed ten thousand performances by January 1933, and songs like "Mack the Knife" were international show stoppers. *The Beggar's Opera* of 1728 was a scathing musical satire that played the realities of London's seedier side against the pompous conventions of opera seria. In the same way, Brecht and Hauptmann's libretto for *The Threepenny Opera* set out to undermine the self-deluding niceties of Germany's bourgeoisie, while Weill's music aimed at "the complete destruction of the concept of music-drama", being cast in verse-song with pauses for spoken dialogue and any necessary action. The writers and first cast anticipated a flop, but in the event *The Threepenny Opera* proved to be Brecht and Weill's greatest success. It remains a savage work, too often betrayed by playing it purely as lowlife farce when its target is the bourgeoisie, every bit as roguish and thieving as the criminal underclass the piece ostensibly portrays. Brecht may have relocated the action to Soho, but Weimar Germany was clearly intended. Weill's insidious tunes were written for singers from cabaret, musical comedy and operetta, and in the right hands their suavity conceals their savage subversiveness: songs such as "Mack the Knife" and "The Song of Sexual Dependency" still pack a powerful punch.

Lenya, Neuss, Trenk-Trebitsch, Hesterburg; Chorus and Orchestra of Radio Free Berlin; Brückner-Rüggeberg (Sony)

By the time Lenya took the role of Jenny in this 1958 recording, her voice was an octave lower than it had been in the 1930s. As a result, much of the music had to be transposed downwards. If her contribution remains controversial, it's certainly characterful, and the rest of the cast responds well. Wilhelm Brückner-Rüggeberg directs a performance full of salty vigour.

Berliner Requiem

Weill wrote his *Requiem* (for tenor, baritone, male chorus and wind orchestra) only weeks after the premiere of *The Threepenny Opera*, and it occupies the same musical world. Commissioned for radio, it takes its texts from poems by Brecht, but was never satisfactorily completed. The radio authorities refused to broadcast the section lamenting the murder of the revolutionary Rosa Luxemburg, and Weill himself added and subtracted sections, using the finale in *Mahagonny*. Nevertheless, in David Drew's performing version it's a powerful piece, as bitter in its wind harmonies as in its irony. The use of a very churchy organ only adds to the sarcasm.

Laiter, Kooy; La Chapelle Royale; Ensemble Musique Oblique; Herreweghe (Harmonia Mundi; with *Vom Tod im Wald & Concerto for Violin & Wind Orchestra*)

Philippe Herreweghe is best known for his clean-cut period-instrument performances of Bach. Here he brings the same clarity of texture to Weill in a performance of ringing immediacy. He also includes the song "Vom Tod im Wald", which Lenya called "gruesome but powerful", and which was originally intended for the *Requiem*.

Violin Concerto

After being inspired by hearing a performance by violinist Joseph Szigeti, Weill wrote his *Concerto* in 1924 with a young man's open-minded approach to musical possibilities – the work partakes of the neo-classicism of Busoni and Hindemith, the atonality of Schoenberg, and the objective clarity of Stravinsky. However, there are also foreshadowings of the mature Weill in the work, not least in the decision to give the accompaniment to an unusual ensemble of wind and brass instruments with percussion and double bass. A youthful but by no means immature work, the *Violin Concerto* is well worth exploring.

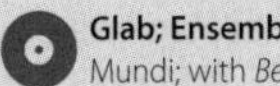
Glab; Ensemble Oblique; Herreweghe (Harmonia Mundi; with *Berliner Requiem* & *Vom Tod im Wald*)

Elisabeth Glab perhaps makes the *Concerto*'s solo part a touch more emotive than it needs to be, but this is still a winning performance. The Ensemble Oblique under Herreweghe provide fine support, full of grace and playful energy.

Die sieben Todsünden

Properly staged, *Rise and Fall of the City of Mahagonny*, with its slavetraders, its brothel and its climactic electric-chair execution, fully retains its power to shock. *Die sieben Todsünden* (The Seven Deadly Sins) is, if anything, even more powerful. Here Weill deploys his full armoury of spicy harmonic ambiguities, spiky instrumentation and witty dance rhythms, all in the service of a mordant attack on the hypocrisies of capitalist morality. There is arguably no more tragic figure in twentieth-century music than Anna, one woman split into two "sisters", a singer and a dancer, the former providing a commentary on the ruin of the latter while the family quartet (bass taking the role of the mother) look on, singing admonitory homilies. Although the piece works wonderfully well on record, it is a stage work, a *ballet chanté* (sung ballet), that reeks of the theatre.

Fassbaender, Brandt, Sojer, Komatsu, Urbas; Radio-Philharmonie Hannover des NDR; Garben (Harmonia Mundi; with songs)

Brigitte Fassbaender deploys her considerable skill as a singer of both opera and lieder here, but her performance lacks none of the theatrical intensity of the rasp-and-rant school of Weill interpretation. Although her colleagues are not quite so convincing, this remains the most searing of many distinguished recordings of the piece.

Judith Weir (1954–)

Judith Weir has the rare distinction of being as popular with audiences as with critics and she has produced vivid music for film, ballet and the theatre as well as numerous concert-hall works in a variety of genres. Her music, which uses modal or tonal techniques, is clear and direct yet always with hidden depths. She draws frequently on sounds and images from folk music, and, like John Tavener (see p.570), with whom she studied while still at school, she also makes frequent gestures – often of a playful nature – towards the music of the distant past. Her interest in medieval culture has led to two works based on the music of thirteenth-century composer Perotin (see p.405). Homage of an even more direct kind is found in her reworkings of Mozart (*Scipio's Dream*, 1991) and Monteverdi (*Combattimento II*, 1992). But Weir's music is distinguished above all by her talent for lucid narrative structure, a talent most apparent in her operatic and music-theatre works.

Her first full-length adult opera, *A Night at the Chinese Opera*, was premiered in 1987 and was the first of her works to reach a wide audience. Weir wrote her own libretto from a thirteenth-century Chinese play about a collaborator with the Mongolian regime, and the music – which is mostly based around the fundamental intervals of the octave and the fifth – has a clear and open texture, showing Weir's abiding concern that her texts should be heard and understood. In 1990 came another opera, *The Vanishing Bridegroom*, retelling three traditional Scottish tales in which the supernatural obtrudes into everyday life. It's a work in which Weir's attachment to her Scottish heritage is especially noticeable, both in her use of Celtic folklore and literature, and in her quotations of fragments of Scottish music. Weir's third full-length adult opera, *Blonde Eckbert*, was first performed in April 1994; once again she wrote her own libretto, deriving it from an enigmatic German tale of incest, deception and betrayal.

More recently, Weir has turned increasingly to orchestral writing, with pieces for the City of Birmingham Symphony Orchestra (for whom she was composer in residence) culminating in *We are Shadows* (1999), a meditation on death for chorus and orchestra. Further commissions include *The Welcome Arrival of Rain* (2001) for the Minnesota Orchestra, a song-cycle for Jessye Norman on the subject of a woman's life, entitled *woman.life.song* (2000) and an opera, *Armida* (2005), written for television.

Short Music Dramas

King Harald's Saga (1979), billed as a "Grand Opera in Three Acts" for solo soprano, packs the story of King Harald's unsuccessful 1066 invasion of Britain into less than ten minutes. The soprano sings eight clearly differentiated solo roles as well as that of Harald's entire Norwegian army, a technique which – combined with the matter-of-fact quality of Weir's text – emphasizes the absurdity of the violence depicted. The *Consolations of Scholarship* (1985) is a music drama for mezzo-soprano and nine instruments, which, like *A Night at the Chinese Opera,* draws on Chinese sources. Like that later work, it carries much of the narrative through rhythmically notated speech, a style that re-creates the transparent formality of classical Chinese theatre. In *Missa del Cid* (1988), a work for ten singers, Weir's text combines the medieval Spanish epic of El Cid with the liturgy of the mass, each section being introduced by a speaker who tells the story of El Cid's bloodthirsty campaign against the Moors. Offsetting rich music for unaccompanied voices against the stark facts of slaughter, *Missa del Cid* shows Weir's predilection for simple, eloquent dramatic devices.

King Harald's Saga; The Consolations of Scholarship; Missa del Cid: Manning; Lontano; Combattimento; de la Martinez; Mason (CALA)

This CD provides a fascinating cross-section of Weir's earlier vocal dramatic music. The performances are excellent and are given by the musicians for whom the works were originally written. Soprano Jane Manning is outstanding, presenting vivid portrayals of all the characters in *King Harald's Saga*.

Chamber Music

Weir's chamber music, often written for friends, makes an excellent introduction to her absorbing and essentially melodic musical language, as well as demonstrating the range of her influences and her dry and unassuming wit. Most of it has a role for the piano, which is often set in engaging contrast or competition with different string ensembles. In the playful *Piano Concerto* (1997) – essentially a chamber work – small-scale Mozartian moments are subverted by the accompaniment of what seems, at times, like a demented Palm Court Orchestra. *I Broke Off a Golden Branch* (1991), a string quintet written for the same instrumentation as Schubert's "Trout" Quintet, makes use of a haunting Croatian melody in the second movement of a work that "moves from brightness at the beginning to darkness at the end". Even more stylistically diverse are the *Piano Trio* (1997) and *Piano Quartet* (2000), in which Poulenc-esque wit rubs shoulders with Ivesian sonorities, with flashes of gamelan and Scottish folk song thrown in for good measure. Somehow Weir manages to make these scraps and allusions seem both disjointed and coherent.

Tomes, Howard, Casén; Schubert Ensemble of London; Domus (NMC; 2 CDs)

These two discs present a variety of Weir's chamber music (all the works mentioned above, plus more) performed by the musicians for whom the works were originally written and are the obvious place to start if you're new to this composer. There is a palpable air of enjoyment about the playing, particularly in the delightful *I Broke Off a Golden Branch* and *Piano Concerto*.

Sylvius Leopold Weiss (1686–1750)

Sylvius Leopold Weiss was the last great star in the story of the lute. He was not only the greatest player of the eighteenth century – possibly the greatest ever – but also the most gifted and prolific composer for the instrument, leaving behind him a remarkable corpus of around 650 exquisite pieces. Though he is relatively little-known today, in his lifetime Weiss was greatly revered by musicians and the aristocracy alike, and was ranked with outstanding contemporaries like Bach, Handel and Scarlatti.

Born in Breslau (now Wrocław, Poland), Weiss was introduced to music by his lutenist father and gained his first position as a performer in 1706. From 1708 to 1714 he worked in Rome in the service of Prince Alexandre Sobieski, learning a great deal about Italian music and almost certainly meeting Alessandro and Domenico

Scarlatti. When his employer died in 1714, Weiss headed north again, visiting Prague, London and various other cities before landing the prestigious post of chamber musician in the court of Dresden in 1718. He remained based there for the rest of his life, though made numerous trips to other cities, building a widespread reputation as a matchless performer, improviser and composer on both the lute and theorbo (a large cousin of the lute, often used for orchestral playing).

In 1728 he visited Berlin, impressing the future king Frederick the Great and giving lute lessons to Frederick's sister Wilhelmine. She later wrote in her memoirs that Weiss "has never had an equal, and those who come after him will only have the glory of imitating him". In 1739 he met J.S. Bach in Leipzig, though it is probable that these two masters were acquainted already. Some of Bach's lute works are said to have been written for Weiss, and Bach transcribed one of Weiss's lute pieces for harpsichord and violin. According to one commentator the two masters even engaged in a competition, performing and improvising fugues and fantasias – Bach on the keyboard, Weiss on the lute.

Weiss's time at Dresden must have been relatively comfortable. By 1744 he was the highest-paid instrumentalist in the court, and he was also a much sought-after teacher, with lutenists flocking from far and wide to try and master the famous "Weissian method". His life wasn't without its upsets, however: in 1722 an enraged French violinist bit Weiss's thumb so hard that it was almost severed, making playing impossible for much of that year, and in 1738 he was arrested and imprisoned for "offensive" behaviour towards a senior court functionary. He was released only when the music-loving Count Keyserling, commissioner of Bach's *Goldberg Variations*, stepped in with a character reference.

In the second half of the eighteenth century the lute disappeared from the European musical scene and Weiss's work, written down in a format that was incomprehensible until relatively recently, remained ignored from the time of his death until the late twentieth century. The 1980s and 1990s saw an increased interest in his music, but as it's written entirely for an archaic instrument it seems unlikely that Weiss will ever receive his due as one of the most significant composers of Baroque Germany.

Works for Lute

Apart from the accompaniments of a handful of lost ensemble works, Weiss's surviving output consists entirely of pieces for solo lute. Like Bach in his instrumental music, Weiss combined elements of the French and Italian styles, but the approaches of the two composers are markedly different. Weiss's pieces tend to be more rhapsodic and lyrical than Bach's, and less contrapuntally dense. His style is highly recognizable, making frequent use of unusual harmonic progressions and daring modulations, and integrating melodic passages, arpeggiated figures and subtle counterpoint to great effect.

The majority of Weiss's pieces are sonatas, written in the form of the suite. Most have six movements, and feature a sombre allemande, a sprightly courante and a lyrical sarabande. The early sonatas are generally bright in spirit and possess a virtuosic flair, while later examples are characterized by emotional gravity and lengthy developmental movements. Weiss also wrote many single-movement works, the most famous of which is the *Tombeau sur la mort de M. Comte de Logy*. Written as a tribute to a count who was one of the best lutenists of his time (and an influence on the young Weiss), the *Tombeau* is a stately and profoundly melancholic work, full of funeral-march motifs and sombre melodies.

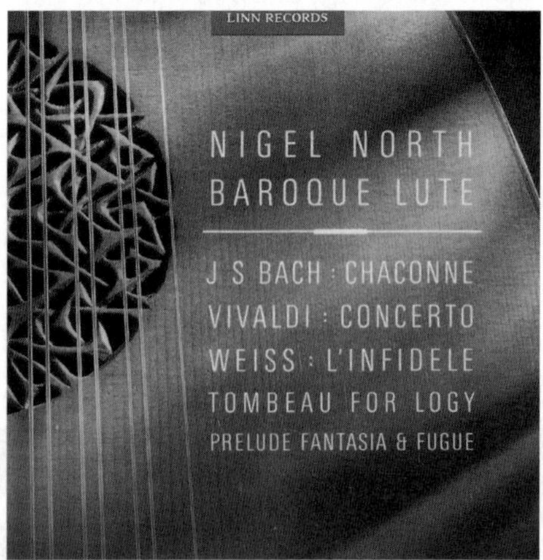

Tombeau sur la mort de M. Comte de Logy; Prelude Fantasia and Fugue; Sonata in A Minor: North (Linn; with lute music by Bach and Vivaldi)

Released in 1992, this lute recital disc from Nigel North features subtly expressive accounts of the *Tombeau* and one of Weiss's very best sonatas. With such outstanding playing, and impressive accounts of Bach's D minor *Chaconne* and transcriptions of Vivaldi concertos, this is an ideal recording for newcomers and seasoned lute music fans alike.

Sonatas Volume 3: Barto
(Naxos)

Featuring three sonatas, each from a different period, the third volume in Naxos's Weiss survey makes a great introduction to the composer. The 35-minute *Sonata in D Minor* is especially impressive, encompassing an enormous range of musical ideas. Barto's performances are natural, fresh and idiomatic throughout, his subtle rubato and sensitive dynamics ideally suited to Weiss's music.

Charles-Marie Widor (1844–1937)

With the possible exception of Bach's *Toccata and Fugue in D Minor*, Widor's *Toccata* must be the most popular organ work ever written. Numerous newly-weds have processed down the aisle to its jubilant flurry of semi-quavers, but at barely six minutes long it provides its otherwise unknown composer with a rather fleeting claim to fame. In fact the piece is merely the last movement of a much longer work, the *Cinquième symphonie* (1887), a grandiose, five-movement blockbuster written by Widor for the Parisian church of St Sulpice where he was organist for an incredible 64 years.

Widor's father, who was both an organ-builder and an organist, gave Charles-Marie his first lessons, but the boy's main training took place in Brussels where he studied composition with Fétis and the organ with J.N. Lemmens, the latter a brilliant performer and teacher whose pedagogical lineage could be traced back to J.S. Bach. Four years later, at the age of eighteen, Widor returned to his home town of Lyons where he took over from his father as organist of the church of St François.

In 1870 Widor's appointment to the magnificent Baroque church of St Sulpice in Paris proved contentious: he was still only 25 and there were plenty of organists who felt they had a stronger claim to the post. He had been recommended by the composer Gounod and the builder of St Sulpice's new organ, Aristide Cavaillé-Coll (see p.634). The "grand orgue" of St Sulpice (situated in the west gallery of the church) is Cavaillé-Coll's masterpiece, its 5 manuals, 118 stops and 7000 pipes capable of producing a dazzling array of instrumental sounds.

As Widor's reputation as a brilliant performer rapidly grew, so the fashionable world beat a path to St Sulpice, attracted both by his virtuosity and the essentially secular nature of much of his music, which evoked the salon as much as it did spirituality. His legacy as a composer is firmly based on the ten organ symphonies written between 1872 and 1900. Inspired, in part, by a César Franck organ work, the *Grande pièce symphonique*, Widor's organ symphonies combined the epic scale of contemporary orchestral writing with the bravura of great keyboard virtuosos like Liszt and Alkan, while taking full advantage of the amazing sonic range of the St Sulpice organ.

In 1890, following the death of César Franck, Widor became professor of organ at the Paris Conservatoire, where, despite the initial resistance of Franck's more devoted pupils, he successfully introduced a more disciplined pedagogical approach. Six years later he switched professorships from organ to composition and proved to be a sympathetic and flexible teacher, even to more forward-looking students such as Honegger, Milhaud and Varèse.

As well as his duties at St Sulpice and the Conservatoire, Widor was a welcome figure in several Parisian salons, those cultural and political hothouses presided over by brilliant, usually aristocratic, women. Most of Widor's chamber music and songs were written for such gatherings. His *Piano Quartet* in A minor (1891) – the most passionate of all his works – was dedicated to the beautiful Comtesse Potocka with whom he almost certainly had an affair. He also had some success as a composer of orchestral and theatre music, notably with the ballet score *La Korrigane* (1880), but today he's known exclusively as a writer for the instrument on which he so brilliantly excelled – the organ.

Organ Symphonies Nos. 5 & 6

Of Widor's ten organ symphonies, *No. 5* and *No.6* are the most popular and the most

Cavaillé-Coll and the French Organ Tradition

Widor's early career received valuable guidance from Aristide Cavaillé-Coll, the most significant French organ maker of the nineteenth century. Since the French Revolution, organ playing and organ building had been in the doldrums in France. By using the latest science and technology to help him develop instruments of an unprecedented scale, power and range, Cavaillé-Coll helped to reverse the decline. His innovations provided, among other things, a far greater variety of tone colour, and greater control of volume from soft to loud. In short, his organs aspired to the sonic opulence and grandeur of the orchestra, which in France meant the Romantic orchestra of Berlioz. The nearly 500 organs that he built (mostly in France) included instruments for Notre Dame Cathedral and the Paris churches of Ste Marie-Madeleine (1846), Ste Clotilde (1858), St Sulpice (1862) and Ste Trinité.

These fantastic instruments needed gifted players to fulfil their huge potential. Unfortunately the prevailing taste within the more fashionable Parisian churches was for music of astonishing vulgarity and banality, as exemplified by Widor's popular predecessor at St Sulpice, Lefébure-Wély. Gradually things started to improve: Saint-Saëns was appointed organist at the Madeleine in 1857, César Franck arrived at Ste Clotilde the next year, Widor took over at St Sulpice in 1870, and Alexandre Guilmant (another pupil of Lemmens) at the Ste Trinité in 1871. Between them these men established a thriving tradition of French organ playing, in which the ability to improvise was paramount. The tradition was continued by a wealth of equally talented players, who included the Widor pupils Vierne, Tournemire and Dupré (his successor at St Sulpice) as well as later figures such as Duruflé and Messiaen.

frequently recorded. Both are in five, highly varied, movements, making them more like suites than symphonies. *No. 5* begins with a brilliant set of variations, shamelessly veering from the skittish to the solemn. The ingratiating lyricism of the Allegro that follows comes straight from the salon, while the ensuing Andante is built around a slightly comical opening pedal theme. If the hymn-like Adagio is the only movement to suggest a religious character, it also serves to set up the fiery toccata finale, in which Widor generates an extraordinary momentum through the insistent repetition of a relatively simple phrase.

Though not so well known, *No. 6* is a more profound work than its predecessor and reveals a clear debt to Bach in the rapid figuration of its magnificent first movement. Bach's influence is also evident in the fourth-movement Cantabile, which has the character of a chorale prelude, despite its rather flighty main tune. In the brilliant finale Widor develops the principal rondo theme in a way that builds to a mounting sense of tension and excitement.

Organ Symphonies Nos. 5 & 6: Latry
(BNL)

Played on the Cavaillé-Coll organ of Notre Dame Cathedral by the current organist, this is a superb introduction to Widor's finest works. It is, of course, a hugely resonant space but the sound engineers have done a great job: all the brilliance of Latry's articulation and subtle registration are revealed while retaining the atmospheric reverberance of the acoustic.

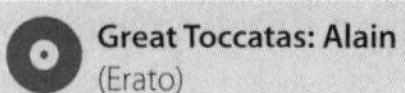
Great Toccatas: Alain
(Erato)

There are plenty of discs of wedding music selections, if you just want the Widor *Toccata* on its own. This is a rather more interesting collection which – apart from the Bach *Toccata and Fugue* in *D Minor* – focuses on the French tradition and is played on the Cavaillé-Coll organ of Orléans Cathedral by Marie-Claire Alain, one of the finest French organists of the last fifty years.

Hugo Wolf (1860–1903)

Hugo Wolf was the archetypal Romantic artist: manically driven, misunderstood, impoverished, mad and short-lived. He was also, after Schubert, the finest of all composers of German art songs. As a musician he was not in the same league as his great precursor, but where he arguably surpassed him was in his sensitivity to words. Wolf conceived the music of his songs as exact translations of the poems that provided their texts: thus, unlike Schubert's songs, in which the music follows the mood of the text rather than the semantics, Wolf's make no sense without a complete grasp of what is being sung. He reconciled the dramatic and theatrical intensity of opera with the discipline of song, employing a Wagner-influenced style that took the form as far as tonality would allow. In short, Wolf's songs are highly wrought and complex creations, perhaps something of an acquired taste but deserving a far wider audience than they currently enjoy.

Born in Slovenia, Wolf was taught by his father until 1875, when he entered the Vienna Conservatory, where one of his contemporaries was Gustav Mahler. He was a fractious student, and in 1877 – the year he contracted the syphilis that was to kill him – he was expelled from the conservatory, although Wolf maintained he had resigned over the college's inflexible conservatism. For the next decade he made his money chiefly from teaching, but in 1884 his songs aroused the interest of the greatly influential critic Eduard Hanslick, who recommended Wolf to two publishers, neither of whom was prepared to back the young composer. In emulation of Hanslick he began writing criticism, but in siding with the recently deceased Wagner against the very much alive Brahms he made many enemies in Vienna.

Until the great explosion of songwriting that began at the age of 28, Wolf had composed extensively for chamber groups, solo piano and orchestra. Most of these pieces were left unfinished, and the few that Wolf did complete met with little or no success. He submitted his string quartet to the Rosé Quartet, who sent it back covered with derisory comments, and the Vienna Philharmonic were reduced to tears of laughter at the rehearsal for his tone poem *Penthesilea*. Wolf began to realize that, contrary to the advice given to him by Wagner, Brahms and Liszt, he was better suited to songs than to orchestral or instrumental music.

Hugo Wolf

In 1888 he composed dozens of songs, including much of the *Spanisches Liederbuch* (Spanish Song Book), a work that established him in certain quarters as the finest songwriter of his time. By the mid-1890s a Hugo Wolf Society had been established in Berlin and even the Viennese were beginning to acknowledge his talent. In 1896 he completed his greatest body of songs, the *Italienisches Liederbuch* (Italian Song Book), but in the same year his mind began to collapse. The following year he fell into syphilitic dementia – he announced, for example, that he, and not Mahler, was director of the Vienna State Opera, and that the opera house would perform nothing but his music in future. He was committed to an asylum and remained incarcerated until his death, except for a brief period in 1898, when he was deemed to be cured, only to attempt suicide as soon as he was released. In belated recognition of his achievement, he was buried next to Schubert and Beethoven in the city's central cemetery.

SONGS

Wolf's most important songs date from the years between 1888 and 1898, and fall into several large groups. His preferred working method was to immerse himself in the works of a particular poet and produce nothing but settings of that writer's work until he had exhausted the material. Thus the clusters of Eichendorff, Mörike, Goethe, Michelangelo and Keller settings dominate his output, alongside two books of songs inspired by poetry from Spain (*Spanisches Liederbuch*) and from Italy (*Italienisches Liederbuch*). His settings cover an extraordinary range of moods and feelings, which he probes with the most acute psychological insight: the characters in his poems have a real living presence. For Wolf the words always come first, and his task as a composer was to clothe the words in music that most communicated their inner meaning, rather than simply letting the words inspire a generalized musical interpretation of what they were about. In this he was closer to Schumann than to Schubert, and listeners with no German may find the songs initially rather dry. They are certainly worth persevering with, none more so than the songs of the *Italienisches Liederbuch*.

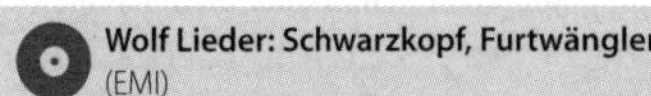

Wolf Lieder: Schwarzkopf, Furtwängler
(EMI)

Elisabeth Schwarzkopf championed Wolf's music throughout her career. Her outstanding 1958 Salzburg recital with Gerald Moore is currently unavailable, but her recording of five years earlier, with the conductor Furtwängler at the piano, is equally impressive. It features a wide range of songs including excerpts from the Italian and Spanish books plus some of the Möricke, Goethe and Eichendorff lieder.

Mörike Lieder

Eduard Mörike was a Swabian pastor who wrote some of the finest German lyric poetry after Goethe. The tone of his poetry is ardent but never overstated, and he often dealt in the most fleeting of half-emotions inspired by the landscape or the coming of spring. Many of his verses touch on his own unhappy love life but he also wrote comic verses which appealed to Wolf as much as the lyric poems. Wolf's 52 settings did much to give Mörike an international profile as a poet and they are among his most inventive songs. They are not a cycle and vary considerably in mood from the solemn religiosity of "An die Geliebte" (To the Beloved), to the ridiculous comicality of "Storchenbotschaft" (Stork's Message), in which a stork's awkward gait is mimicked in a dissonant piano introduction. All the *Mörike Lieder* have a concentration that is highly communicative; there is nothing redundant in the music and very little repetition. Had Wolf written nothing else, he would still be regarded as one of the most gifted writers of German song.

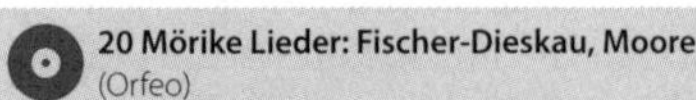

20 Mörike Lieder: Fischer-Dieskau, Moore
(Orfeo)

Fischer-Dieskau has recorded these songs many times over, but this selection of twenty – recorded live at Salzburg in 1961 – displays his voice in its finest condition. His interpretative skills have all the effortless ease of a great actor.

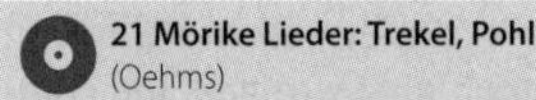

21 Mörike Lieder: Trekel, Pohl
(Oehms)

Those wanting a more recent performance of the Möricke lieder should look no further than this outstanding recital by Roman Trekel. As with Fischer-Dieskau, he combines a beauty of tone with interpretative skills that get to the psychological heart of these powerful songs.

Eichendorff & Goethe Lieder

As well as his mighty set of *Mörike Lieder*, Wolf published a collection of twenty lieder to texts by Eichendorff in 1889, and fifty-one by Goethe in the following year. In setting Eichendorff, Wolf claimed that he wanted to get away from the concept of the poet as a melancholy Romantic, focusing instead on Eichendorff's deft character sketches of soldiers, students, minstrels, and Gypsy girls. With a few exceptions, these are among the most optimistic and energetic of Wolf's songs. His *Goethe Lieder*, on the other hand, are hugely varied in both style and subject. Like Schubert and Schumann, he was fascinated by Mignon's and the Harper's songs from *Wilhelm Meister*, and his Mignon lieder are especially popular. His other Goethe settings range from a large selection of sensual love poems from the Persian-inspired *West-östlicher Divan* to gentle contemplations of nature such as "Anakreons Grab" to humorous texts, such as "Epiphanias" (a song about the Magi, originally written for children) and the hyperactive "Der Rattenfänger".

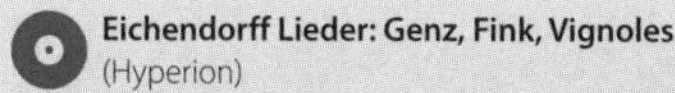

Eichendorff Lieder: Genz, Fink, Vignoles
(Hyperion)

A disc entirely devoted to Wolf's Eichendorff songs is unusual and doubly welcome when it's as good as this. Stephan Genz's character shifts are highly effective and his velvety baritone is always pleasing. In the few songs written for the female voice, mezzo Bernarda Fink is no less effective.

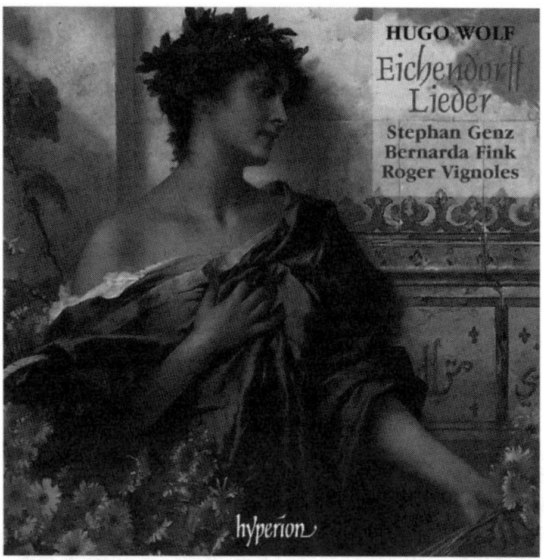

Goethe Lieder: McGreevy, Johnson
(Hyperion)

In a disc focusing mainly on songs specifically for female voice, soprano Geraldine McGreevy is perfect as the troubled Mignon (a character of more violent emotions than Schubert's Mignon). The quasi-Wagnerian "Ganymed" is also outstanding – performed with great sweetness and warmth.

Italienisches Liederbuch

Of the 46 songs that make up the *Italienisches Liederbuch*, the first 22 were composed in 1890–91, while the remaining 24 were completed five years later. The texts were taken from a translation by Paul Heyse of anonymous Italian poems published in the year of Wolf's birth, and the obscurity of the verses evidently liberated him. Because these poems came with no burden of previous interpretation, Wolf was free to read himself into them and thereby produce his most profoundly personal music. The verses Wolf selected were mostly Tuscan love poems, which form a kind of narrative in which two lovers express devotion, quarrel, make up and generally carry on as lovers do. They are usually performed by a soprano and a baritone singing (mainly) alternative songs. Often very terse and to the point, these are not the most obviously engaging of songs, though the beauty of several is immediately apparent. Concentration brings great rewards, however, and their cumulative impact when performed by really good singers is overwhelmingly poignant.

Schwarzkopf, Fischer-Dieskau, Moore
(EMI)

Schwarzkopf, Fischer-Dieskau and Moore are again at their best on this milestone recording of the *Italienisches Liederbuch* from the mid-1960s. The delivery of both singers is incredibly subtle, and the nurturing of the often fractured melodic lines is unimaginably beautiful.

Bonney, Hagegård, Parsons
(Teldec)

Of more recent interpretations of the cycle, none has displayed such a unanimity of mood and intention between the three interpreters as this 1992 recording by Barbara Bonney, Håkan Hagegård and Geoffrey Parsons. There's a real sense of the listener eavesdropping on intensely private and often painful moments.

Iannis Xenakis (1922–2001)

Iannis Xenakis is known for three things: he's the only famous composer whose name begins with the letter X; he's one of only two Greek composers famous outside Greece (the other is Mikis Theodorakis); and, most importantly, he's one of the crucial figures in the development of electronic music. Rejecting the straitjacket of serialism, Xenakis aimed to liberate sound from all *a priori* rules. His inspirations were the mythologies of Greek culture and natural phenomena – such as the sounds of rain or the slow movement of shifting sand on a beach. His tools were chance operations, computer technologies and mathematical procedures, and at its best his music combines organic yet meticulously thought-out design with intense emotion.

Born into a wealthy Greek family in Romania, Xenakis went to school in Greece and then studied architecture and engineering in Athens. The next phase of his life reads like a parable of triumph over adversity. Deeply involved with the anti-Nazi resistance, he had half his face blown away in a street battle. After the war, his involvement in the Greek nationalist movement in British-occupied Athens led to a death sentence. In 1947 he escaped under a false passport to Paris, where he took a job with the architect Le Corbusier, for whom he worked for twelve years, most notably on the monastery of Sainte-Marie de la Tourette. In 1958 Xenakis designed the futuristic Philips Pavilion, the venue for Varèse's ground-breaking *Poème électronique* (see p.593), and for his own *Concret pH* for indeterminate mathematically generated sound. Xenakis was heavily influenced by Varèse's radicalism, especially the way that he worked "on the very flesh of sound … His music is colour and sonorous force. No more scales, no more themes, no more melodies – to the devil with music called 'musical.'"

After creating the orchestral sound-blast of *Metastaseis* in the mid-1950s, Xenakis took up composing full-time. Encouraged by Messiaen to be true to his own vision, he set about applying probability theories and computer programs to the processes of composition, a method he defined as stochastic, meaning governed by the laws of probability. The pieces produced during the 1960s were often characterized by dense clusters and explosions of sound, and revealed a dazzling talent for stretching timbres to their limits. In 1966, Xenakis founded the Centre for Automatic and Mathematical Music in Paris and subsequently set up a similar unit at Indiana University, turning out work that impressed Pierre Boulez and led to his association with IRCAM and the Ensemble Intercontemporain. Subsequent sound-and-light

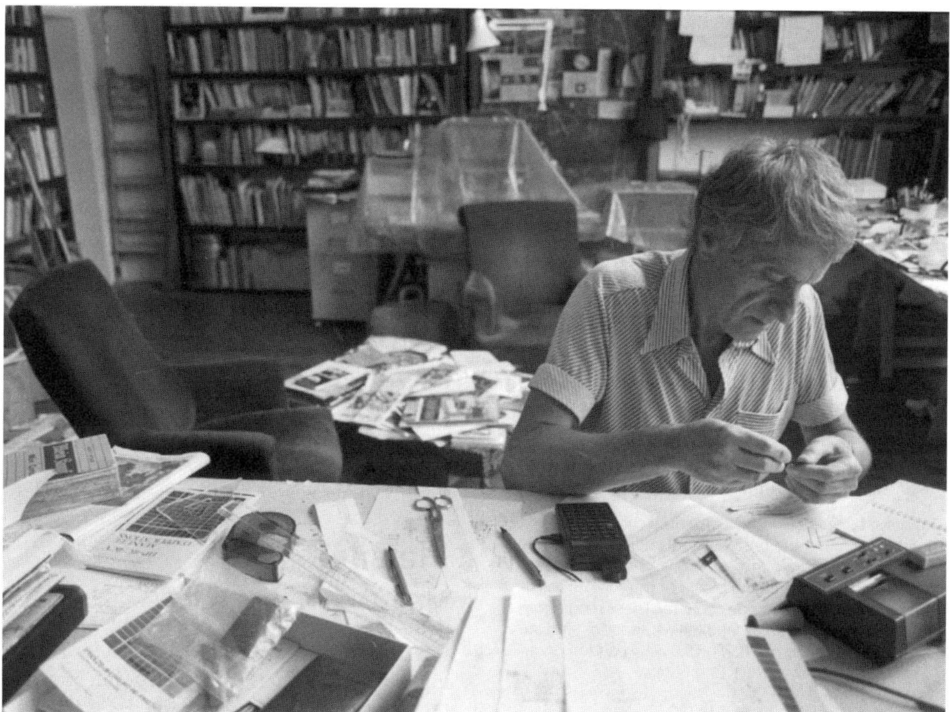
Iannis Xenakis at work in his study.

works such as *Hibiki-Hana-Ma* (1970), for twelve tapes and eight hundred speakers, displayed the composer's unparalleled technical virtuosity, but in later years the mythic and spiritual element of his music came to the fore, conveying his Christian faith and his profound feelings about his homeland, to which he returned after twenty years of exile. Xenakis's health gradually deteriorated in the last years of the millennium, and he died in Paris in 2001.

Electronic Music

Although Xenakis's electronic music accounts for a numerically tiny percentage of his entire output, his pioneer status in the field was incalculable. After assisting Edgard Varèse on the preparation of his *Poème électronique*, Xenakis's earliest electronic pieces *Diamorphoses* (1957) and *Concret PH* (1958) – the latter shaping a continuum from the crackle of burning charcoal – shared Varèse's vision of otherworldly sound masses that disperse, re-configure and climax in feral glissandi that burst the sound barrier. Later Xenakis worked electronics into a sequence of installations he called Polytopes, where architecture and monolithic sonic blocks, packed with inner light and shade, were harvested from the same abstract designs. During the 1970s, Xenakis refined his UPIC software, a computer-based drawing tablet that allowed composers to sketch sounds and structures onto a screen, while listening to a real-time playback. Electronics go to the marrow of how Xenakis created a new syntax for sound without reference to Classical tradition.

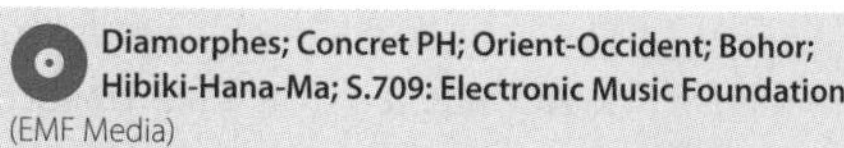
Diamorphes; Concret PH; Orient-Occident; Bohor; Hibiki-Hana-Ma; S.709: Electronic Music Foundation
(EMF Media)

This invaluable anthology of Xenakis electronica, beginning with *Diamorphoses* (1957) and ending in 1992 with the bracing *S.709*, has been transferred with crystal clarity by those boffins at the Electronic Music Foundation in New York. *Hibiki-Hana-Ma* – sounds transformed from acoustic instruments – is like hearing familiar instrumental hooks put through a shredder and re-formed as a purist soundscape.

Choral Music

Xenakis's music is often linked with the harsh landscape of Greece and the bitter, fateful world of Greek tragedy. This aspect of his output is most directly expressed in his vocal and choral music which, like so much of his work, seems to aspire to the pure and the primitive. *Medea* (1967) is a setting of a classical text (albeit a Latin one) in which the ritualistic world of the original is conveyed by chanting male voices and struck stones, while various instruments – notably a cello, clarinet and rasping trombone – provide a kind of astringent commentary. Even in Xenakis's non-theatrical choral music, there is a highly dramatic quality. *Nuits*, written in response to the 1967 military coup in Greece, is a searingly intense work for twelve mixed unaccompanied voices, dedicated to the victims of the military junta. Having experienced loss of freedom himself, Xenakis fully identified with the victims of oppression, and the result is a nine-minute emotional cry for liberty – part lamentation, part political protest.

Nuits; Medea; A Colone; Serment; Knephas: New London Choir; Critical Band; Wood (Hyperion)

This brave recording of Xenakis's radical choral works is superbly animated and breathtakingly skilful. All of these works have an almost plastic quality, as if Xenakis were moulding shapes or creating blocks of sound from the dazzling range of vocal techniques on offer. These range from the declamatory to scarcely audible whisperings, and are carried off with incredible flair by the New London Choir.

Chamber & Instrumental Music

If you're new to Xenakis, perhaps the best place to start is with his chamber and instrumental works, which are less dense and demanding than his larger-scale pieces. *Nomos Alpha* (First Law) for solo cello replaces scales and traditional harmony with a sound continuum that places great demands on the player. It extends the dynamic range of the instrument by the use of rapid glissandi and the overlaying of low notes with high-pitched harmonics. From the mid-1970s onwards, Xenakis abandoned strict mathematical processes in favour of a more expressionistic, though still abstract, musical language. *Ikhoor* (1978) for string trio is full of gratingly harsh sequences of sounds, and obsessively repeated rhythms whose raw but controlled energy recalls the pulsating dynamism and ethereal beauty of Bartók's late string quartets. *Evryali* (1973) for solo piano is more lyrical, despite its toccata-like propulsion, which forms a constant tension with the ringing and often delicate sonorities. More recent works, like the 1990 string quartet *Tetora*, have an austerity and terseness of utterance, occasionally tempered by fragments of melody.

Chamber Music 1955–1990: Helffer; Arditti String Quartet (Naïve; 2 CDs)

This nicely packaged set provides a revealing introductory compendium of Xenakis's work, including all the pieces discussed above. The Arditti Quartet play to their customarily high standards and, in pianist Claude Helffer, Xenakis has an advocate with the technique and insight to make his glittering piano works sparkle with an extra brilliance.

Pleiades

Like Varèse, Xenakis was particularly drawn to the sonic possibilities of percussion. Of several works for percussion ensemble, *Pleiades*, a strikingly beautiful quartet of pieces which evokes the richness of the Balinese gamelan, is the most exciting and aurally seductive. Written in 1978, it is divided into four sections which group the percussion timbres by family – keyboards, metallophones, skins. The Claviers section is particularly rich, utilizing Indonesian scales and the bright timbres of vibraphone, xylophone and marimba to produce a fascinating ethno-minimalist concoction.

Kroumata Percussion Ensemble (BIS; with *Psappha*)

The vindictive vigour of this performance has a physicality that stretches beyond the usual reach of classical performance. Subtler shadings are certainly heard as required, but the ecstatic clatter of the Kroumata Percussion Ensemble's gorgeously tuned instruments is something special. As a bonus, there's the seminal solo percussion piece *Psappha*.

Z

Alexander Zemlinsky (1871–1942)

Arnold Schoenberg once wrote: "I owe almost everything I know about composing and its problems to Alexander Zemlinsky … I always thought he was a great composer." Yet until the 1980s Zemlinsky was likely to feature in an A–Z of music only in order to justify its title, or in his secondary role as Schoenberg's mentor. Zemlinsky's essential problem was that he was too advanced for his conservative contemporaries, but not interesting enough for the radicals. To make matters worse, he was physically unprepossessing (Alma Mahler uncharitably described him as a "horrid little gnome – chinless, toothless and stinking of the coffee-houses"), and was uncomfortable pushing his own work. The result was relegation to the margins of history until the last decade, which has seen a reassessment of Zemlinsky's sumptuous late Romanticism.

Zemlinsky was a typical example of Viennese multiculturalism. His father was Slovakian, his mother from a Bosnian Jewish family in Sarajevo, and Zemlinsky went on to become one of the cabal of Viennese musicians who formed around Gustav Mahler, the reforming force in the city's musical life. When Zemlinsky left the conservatoire in the 1890s, he became a member of the Wiener Tonkünsterverein (Viennese Society of Composers), whose honorary president, Johannes Brahms, encouraged the young composer.

Opera and song were to comprise the greater part of his output: *Sarema*, the first of his eight completed operas, was performed in Munich in 1897, and his second, *Es war einmal* (Once Upon a Time), was premiered by Mahler at the Court Opera in Vienna in 1900. His career as a conductor developed in parallel: from 1899 he was conductor at the Carltheater in Vienna, then he moved on to the Volksoper and was invited by Mahler to the Court Opera. He and Schoenberg founded a society to promote new music in Vienna, and his star seemed to be rising under the patronage of Mahler, who was going to present his next opera, *Der Traumgörge* (Görge the Dreamer). However, after numerous disagreements Mahler was forced out of the Court Opera in 1907, prompting Zemlinsky to walk out in protest. *Der Traumgörge* wasn't performed until 1980.

After another spell at the Volksoper, Zemlinsky went to work in the Deutsches Landestheater in Prague, where he was to remain for sixteen years. Under his direction it became one of the most important opera houses in Europe – Stravinsky, though usually begrudging in his praise, once described Zemlinsky conducting Mozart as one of the most satisfying experiences of his life. This was the most successful period of Zemlinsky's life as a composer too – it was in Prague that he wrote his best operas and the *Lyric Symphony*, his most famous work. In 1927 he went to work with Otto Klemperer at the Kroll Opera in Berlin, where his last completed opera, *Der Kreidekreis* (The Chalk Circle), was given a performance in 1934, before being suppressed by the Nazis. Zemlinsky fled first to Vienna and then, in 1938, to America, where he died a forgotten man.

Der Zwerg

The most remarkable of Zemlinsky's eight operas is the one-act *Der Zwerg* (The Dwarf), first given under Otto Klemperer in 1922 and the work most frequently performed in Zemlinsky's lifetime. Based on "The Birthday of the Infanta", a short story by Oscar Wilde, the opera tells of a dwarf given as a birthday present to a spoilt young girl. She adores him and he falls in love with her, but she eventually forsakes him, and he dies of a broken heart. *Der Zwerg* brings out all Zemlinsky's strengths in orchestral colour, lyricism and highly charged emotion – the dwarf's achingly beautiful music (with soft violins, chromatic harmony and the searing melody of a cor anglais) no doubt gains some of its power from Zemlinsky's own feelings at his rejection by Alma Mahler.

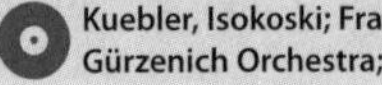

Kuebler, Isokoski; Frankfurter Kantorei; Cologne Gürzenich Orchestra; Conlon (EMI)

This 1996 recording is of the original version of the opera, incorporating revisions made in 1926. The luxurious recording enhances the orchestral sound and Soile Isokoski is in fine voice as the Infanta. David Kuebler is good as the dwarf, though he lacks the pathos and the lyrical ease that Kenneth Riegel brings to the role in the only other recording.

Orchestral Music

Like Mahler's *Das Lied von der Erde*, Zemlinsky's remarkable *Lyrische Symphonie* (1923) is a cross between an orchestral song cycle and a symphony. A setting of seven love poems by the Bengali poet Rabindranath Tagore, it's typically Viennese in its fascination with yearning, parting and death, and clearly illustrates Zemlinsky's place between the Classical Austro-German tradition and the innovative Second Viennese School. Alban Berg, one of the key figures of that school, underlined the work's importance by quoting it in his *Lyric Suite*, which he dedicated to Zemlinsky. Of Zemlinsky's other orchestral works, the best is the wonderful tone poem *Die Seejungfrau* (The Mermaid), which had the misfortune to be performed on the same programme as Schoenberg's *Pelleas und Melisande* in 1905. Zemlinsky's piece was overshadowed and the composer lost interest in its future – it was not heard again until 1984.

Lyric Symphony: Goerne, Schaefer; Orchestre de Paris; Eschenbach (Capriccio)

There are several fine recordings of the *Lyric Symphony*, but this one seems to generate the greatest passion, with Christoph Eschenbach securing some beautifully nuanced and detailed playing from the orchestra. Rarely has the vocal exchange between baritone and soprano been so sympathetically realized as here, Mathias Goerne and Christine Schäfer complementing each other perfectly.

Die Seejungfrau: Czech Philharmonic Orchestra; Beaumont (Chandos; with *Symphony in D minor*)

Antony Beaumont is a scholar as well as musician, and he has studied *fin de siècle* Austro-German music in great depth. In this engrossing performance of *Die Seejungfrau* his enthusiasm for Zemlinsky's opulent sound-world shines through in every bar. The early *Symphony in D Minor* gets an equally committed performance.

String Quartets

Zemlinsky's four string quartets are a little-known part of his output, yet they are skilfully wrought works, each with considerable strengths – from the jubilantly romantic *Quartet No. 1* (1896) to the sometimes sardonic *No. 4* (1936). The finest of all is *Quartet No. 2*, which contains much hauntingly dark and incisive writing, as well as a highly poignant lyricism. Composed in 1913–14 (a particularly unhappy period of the composer's life), it's a good example of Zemlinsky's compositional sophistication, with the six parts of its forty-minute structure containing several personal references, such as themes derived from the letters of his own name as well as those of his sister Mathilde (Schoenberg's wife).

Quartets Nos. 1 & 2: Artis Quartett Wien (Nimbus)

In these remarkable performances of the first two quartets, the Artis Quartett Wien (who have also recorded the third and fourth quartets) play with a suitably rich and generous sound which is well captured by the Nimbus engineers. With beautiful phrasing and tight ensemble, this compelling performance suggests that these works should be core quartet repertoire.

GLOSSARY

Absolute music
A purely abstract music that makes no references to events, paintings, literature and so forth; as opposed to programme music.

A cappella
Literally "in the church style". Unaccompanied choral singing.

Accelerando
Gradual increase in speed.

Accent
A stress on a particular note or beat, highlighting its place within a musical phrase.

Adagio
Slow and drawn-out tempo.

Ad libitum
Instruction to play or improvise "at will".

Alberti bass
In keyboard music, a running figure for the left hand that arpeggiates (see "Arpeggio") a simple series of chords, allowing the right hand to concentrate on melody. Highly popular in the eighteenth century.

Aleatory music
Derived from *alea*, the Latin word for "game of dice". Music composed by random procedures, often computerized. Popular from the 1950s with experimental composers, particularly John Cage.

Allegro
Fast and lively tempo. The customary marking for the opening movement of a symphony.

Alto
1. The highest of the male voices.
2. The lowest of the female voices.
3. Prefix to an instrument that is lower in pitch and darker in tone than a treble instrument – e.g. alto saxophone, alto flute.

Andante
Moderate tempo. Slightly faster than Adagio – literally "walking pace".

Anthem
Brief, solemn composition for church choir; Protestant equivalent of the Latin motet. Masters of the form include Gibbons and Purcell. Also used to define a patriotic vocal composition.

Antiphon
In the Catholic and Orthodox churches, a form of liturgical singing in which responses are exchanged between a solo voice and a choir, or between two separate choirs.

Aria
Term used since the time of Alessandro Scarlatti to describe an independent solo vocal piece within an opera, frequently created to display the artist's vocal facility.

Arpeggio
Literally "like a harp". A chord in which the notes are spread, or played separately, either from top to bottom or vice versa.

Atonal
Music that is not tonal (that isn't in a major or minor key). With atonal music the traditional harmonic language no longer applies and the twelve notes of the octave function independently of any key centre. Atonality is associated above all with Schoenberg and his chief followers, Berg and Webern.

Authentic
Term used to describe a performance that attempts to reproduce, as accurately as possible, the way the music would have originally sounded. Many prefer the alternative terms of "period instrument" or "historically informed".

Ballade
Term used by Chopin to describe an extended single-movement piano piece in which narrative is suggested, without reference to any extramusical source. Later adopted by Grieg, Brahms, Liszt and Fauré.

Ballet
Dance form in which a story is told through the unification of music and dance. Originated in the French court of the sixteenth century. Used by Lully as an interlude in his operas, then evolved into hybrid opera-ballet. Later became an independent art form, dominated by the French until the emergence of Tchaikovsky. Since the end of the nineteenth century many composers have written for the ballet, notably Prokofiev and Stravinsky.

Barcarolle
A composition (usually a song) that was originally associated with Venetian gondoliers' songs; usually has a gentle swaying motion, imitating the movement of the gondola.

Baritone

The male voice between tenor and bass.

Baroque

Music composed between 1600 and 1750, spanning the period from Monteverdi and Gabrieli to Bach and Handel. The period before Classical (see p.236).

Bass

1. The lowest of the male voices.
2. The lowest part of a chord or piece of music.
3. The lowest of an instrument family – e.g. bass clarinet.

Bel canto

Literally "beautiful song". An eighteenth- and early nineteenth-century school of singing, characterized by a concentration on beauty of tone, virtuosic agility and breath control. Bellini, Rossini and Donizetti are the main bel canto composers.

Berceuse

A lullaby. The most famous instrumental example is the piano piece of this name by Chopin.

Binary form

A short work in two evenly balanced sections. Infrequently used since the death of Handel. Predated sonata form.

Bitonal

Music that uses two distinct keys at the same time. Employed by composers like Milhaud and Stravinsky in the first half of the twentieth century.

Cabaletta

An heroic but brief aria (or end to an aria) built upon an unchanging rhythm. The most famous example is "Di quella pira" (for tenor) from Verdi's *Il trovatore*.

Cadence

The closing sequence of a musical phrase or composition. The "perfect cadence" gives a sense of completion; the "imperfect cadence" leaves the music hanging in mid-air.

Cadenza

A solo passage designed to show off the soloist's abilities, occurring at the end of a concerto movement (generally the first), using material based upon the movement's main themes. Originally improvised, but composers began writing them out in the eighteenth century.

Canon

The strictest of contrapuntal forms. A work in which the same melody is played or sung by two or more voices, each beginning slightly after the preceding one. Famous examples include "London's Burning" and "Frère Jacques".

Cantabile

A "singing" style. Generally applied to instrumental and orchestral music.

Cantata

Literally "sung piece".

1. In seventeenth-century Italy, a cantata was a dramatic vocal work, often for a single voice, with instrumental accompaniment.
2. In eighteenth-century Germany the cantata was extended to include several soloists and a chorus, and was often a setting of a religious text.

Cantilena

1. A melodic line which is smooth and lyrical.
2. In choral music, the vocal part that carries the main theme.
3. A vocal exercise which employs all the notes of the scale.

Cantus firmus

Literally "fixed song". A melody borrowed from a religious or secular source as the basis to a polyphonic composition in which other melodies are set in counterpoint against it. Popular between the fourteenth and seventeenth centuries.

Castrato

A male singer castrated as a child, developing a soprano or contralto voice. Very popular during the seventeenth and eighteenth centuries – the last castrato died in the twentieth century (see p.233).

Cavatina

A lyrical operatic song or aria in one section, or an instrumental work in imitation of such a song – e.g. the fifth movement from Beethoven's *Quartet No. 13*.

Chaconne

A dance-piece in a slow three-beat time, consisting of variations upon a repeated theme in the bass part. Finest examples are the final movement of Bach's *Violin Partita No. 2* and Purcell's "When I am Laid in Earth", from *Dido and Aeneas*.

Chamber music

Instrumental music composed for a small number of players. Sometimes applied to solo instrumental pieces, but more commonly used for duos, trios, quartets, quintets etc.

Chanson

French song form of the fourteenth to sixteenth centuries; generally polyphonic.

Chorale

Metrical hymn-tune, with its foundations in the Lutheran Church of sixteenth-century Germany. Originally sung in unison, but Bach extended the form into separate parts for soprano, alto, tenor and bass.

Chord
Any simultaneous combination of notes.

Chromaticism
Use of notes not belonging to the diatonic scale – i.e. using sharps, flats or naturals alien to the key. The chromatic scale comprises twelve ascending or descending semitones. Chromaticism is a strong element of Romantic music – Wagner's in particular.

Classical
1. The post-Baroque period, roughly between 1750 and 1830. Pre-eminent Classical composers were Haydn, Mozart and Beethoven, who refined the sonata, symphony and concerto forms.
2. General term used to distinguish Western music intended for a formal context, e.g. a church or concert hall, from more informal, popular music (rock, folk, etc).

Cluster
Dissonant chord made up of several adjacent notes played simultaneously.

Coda
The closing section to a movement. Originally made a basic summary of what had gone before, but Mozart and Beethoven developed the coda into a substantial subsection, sometimes introducing new ideas.

Coloratura
Soprano voice capable of great agility and delicacy. The most famous coloratura role is the Queen of the Night in Mozart's *Magic Flute*.

Colour
Term used to describe the varieties and gradations of timbre that an instrumentalist or vocalist can produce.

Concertante
1. Like a concerto. A sinfonia concertante is a work for soloist(s) and orchestra which is closer in form to a symphony than a concerto.
2. Name for the group of soloists in a concerto grosso.

Concerto
Originally an orchestral work in several movements, with or without soloists, but in the eighteenth century it developed into a large-scale work in which one or more solo instruments are contrasted with an orchestral ensemble. The form was refined by Mozart, whose three-movement concertos became the model for the genre. For a more detailed discussion, see p.610.

Concerto grosso
An orchestral work in which two bodies of instruments (one large and one small) play off against each other. Popular in the seventeenth and eighteenth centuries, and with twentieth-century neo-classicists.

Continuo
A figured bass part (see below), or the instruments performing it (usually keyboard or lute plus cello or viol da gamba).

Contralto
The lowest of the female voices – same as an alto, but alto is associated with sacred and choral music, whereas contralto is applied to opera singers.

Contrapuntal
Adjective derived from "counterpoint".

Counterpoint
The placing of two or more parts or voices against each other in such a way that they have both harmonic coherence and a degree of independence.

Countertenor
The highest male voice.

Crescendo
Gradual increase in loudness.

Cyclic form
The repetition or modification of a single theme in two or more of a work's movements. The most perfect use of cyclic form can be found in Franck's *D Minor Symphony*; Berlioz's *idée fixe* and Wagner's leitmotif are related concepts.

Da capo
Means "repeat from the beginning".

Diatonic
Music using the major and minor scales; music constructed exclusively from the notes defined by the key.

Diminuendo
Gradual decrease in loudness.

Dissonance (or discord)
A combination of notes that sounds harsh on the ear and requires resolution. The contrast between dissonance and its opposite, consonance, is a central element of Western music.

Divertimento
A light and entertaining suite or movement. Mozart's are supreme examples; popular also with neo-classicists.

Dodecaphonic
See "Serialism".

Double-stopping
Simultaneous playing of two strings on a bowed instrument.

Dynamics
The qualities and degrees of softness and loudness in music.

Étude
A "study", or essay in technique. Paganini, Chopin, Liszt and Debussy – among others – developed the étude into an expressive form rather than a merely technical exercise.

Expressionism
As in the visual arts, a term used to describe works in which the artist's emotional or mental state is the primary subject. Applied to German music of the early twentieth century – above all to the pre-serialist works of Schoenberg and Berg. For a more detailed discussion, see p.259.

Fantasia (or Fantasie or Fantaisie)
A loosely structured (usually instrumental) composition, with a suggestion of extemporization, which allowed more freedom of expression than the Classical forms. Also associated with English viol consort music, see p.296.

Figured bass
A bass part with numbers specifying the harmonies to be played above it. Used extensively during the Baroque period for keyboard or lute accompaniments.

Fugue
A complicated contrapuntal style in which two or more voices explore a single theme called the subject. Bach was the greatest master of the form, which he is said to have characterized as resembling "people engaged in rational conversation". For a more detailed discussion, see p.30.

Galant
The light, elegant and melodic style that first developed in the early Classical period in the music of composers such as C.P.E. Bach and Tartini.

Gavotte
An old French dance in 4/4 time, but beginning on the third beat of the bar. Popularized by Lully.

Gesamtkunstwerk
Literally "total art work". Wagner's term for his dramatic ideal in which music, drama and poetry would unite to create a completely unified art form.

Gigue
A sprightly dance in binary form. Much used by Bach and other eighteenth-century composers as a finale to a dance suite.

Glissando
Principally applied to string instruments. The sliding of a finger over a number of consecutive notes, thus creating an extended slither of sound.

Gregorian chant
A type of solo and unison plainsong employed in the liturgy of the Roman Catholic Church. It was thought to have been codified during the papacy of St Gregory the Great (590–604), though his precise involvement is a matter of conjecture (see p.256).

Ground bass
A bass line, usually quite brief, that is constantly repeated in a piece or movement, serving as the foundation for the melody, counterpoint and harmony in the upper parts. The basis of passacaglias and chaconnes.

Harmony
The simultaneous grouping of notes to form a musically significant whole; the basic unit of harmony is the chord. Harmony can colour any single melodic line in innumerable different ways and a composer's harmonic language is one of his or her most immediately identifiable characteristics.

Homophony
Music in which the parts move as one, in grouped chordal patterns, with no independent movement. The opposite of polyphony.

Hymn
A congregational work of praise in which the structure is invariably strophic and the words specially written.

Idée fixe
Berlioz's term for the motto theme that recurs throughout his *Symphonie fantastique*. A forerunner of leitmotif.

Impressionism
Term taken from painting, to describe music in which suggestion and atmosphere were dominant considerations; typified by Debussy and his followers.

Impromptu
A short, improvisatory piece of song-like piano music – Schubert's are the best known examples.

Instrumentation
The scoring of music for particular instruments – not the same as orchestration, which refers to a composer's skill in writing for groups of instruments. Thus Schubert's *Octet*, which shows a remarkable awareness of the qualities of each component, is a superb example of instrumentation.

Intermezzo
1. A brief instrumental or orchestral diversion performed during an opera's scene changes, to denote the passing of time. The Intermezzo in Mascagni's *Cavalleria rusticana* is perhaps the best known.
2. A single-movement concert piece, usually for piano. Brahms wrote many.

Interval
The distance between two notes. Intervals are expressed numerically – thirds, fourths, etc (though "octave" is used rather than "eighth"). Composers' preferred intervals are highly recognizable aspects of style.

Inversion
The turning upside down of a chord or melody. Used in traditional counterpoint and in the twelve-tone system.

IRCAM
Institut de Recherche et de Co-ordination Acoustique/Musique. Electronic studios attached to the Pompidou Centre in Paris, established in 1977 by Pierre Boulez as a research centre into new compositional techniques.

Key
Any piece of tonal music is based on the notes of one of the major or minor scales (there are twelve of each), though other notes, called accidentals, can be introduced. If a piece is based on the notes of the D minor scale, for example, it is said to be in the "key" of D minor, and D will be the most stable and important note, known as the "keynote". Though a piece usually starts and ends in the same key, other keys can be visited in between. Each key has a certain number of flats and sharps, signified by a key signature, written at the beginning of each stave on the music.

Klavier
German word for "keyboard" – can apply to harpsichord, piano or any domestic keyboard instrument.

Largo
Slow and broad tempo.

Legato
Instruction to play smoothly.

Leitmotif (or leitmotiv)
Literally "leading motif". A short, constantly recurring musical phrase that relates to a character, emotion or object. Associated above all with Wagner. For a more detailed discussion, see p.615.

Libretto
The text of an opera.

Lied
German word for "song", commonly applied to the art songs of Schubert, Schumann, Brahms and Wolf.

Madrigal
A secular (frequently unaccompanied) polyphonic vocal style that reached its height in sixteenth- and seventeenth-century Italy in the works of Monteverdi, Gesualdo and others. For a more detailed discussion, see p.205.

Mass
The main service of the Catholic Church. Most mass settings use the so-called "Ordinary" of the mass, the unchanging five-part core of Kyrie, Gloria, Credo, Sanctus and Agnus Dei. Settings of the "Proper" of the mass have additional sections required by special circumstances – the best-known example being the Requiem.

Melisma
A group of several notes sung to the same syllable, common in Gregorian chant.

Melodie
French art song, the equivalent of the German lied.

Mezzo or Mezzo-soprano
The lowest soprano voice (one above contralto).

Minimalism
A predominantly American school of music which rejected the strictures of the European avant-garde in favour of a more accessible sound-world often involving an almost hypnotic texture of repeated short patterns. Associated most famously with Steve Reich, Philip Glass and John Adams (see p.451).

Minuet
A brisk French dance in triple time, developed by Lully, then highly popular during the eighteenth century. Became the standard third movement in Classical sonata form, where it is coupled with a trio. It later grew into the Scherzo.

Mode/Modal
A mode can be any scale of notes–classical or non-classical, Western or non-Western. However, the term is most commonly used to refer to the "church modes", the scales used in European music prior to the seventeenth century. From that point, just two of the modes, now referred to as major and minor, dominated completely. Certain twentieth-century composers returned to the church modes.

Modulation
The movement from one key to another.

Monody
Term used to describe the style of writing in which a single line or melody is given a continuo accompaniment. Developed around 1600, in reaction to the complexities of polyphonic composition.

Motet
1. In the thirteenth to fifteenth centuries, a short polyphonic vocal work.
2. In the Renaissance and after, a sacred unaccompanied choral composition usually in Latin.

Motif (or Motiv or Motive)
A brief, recognizable musical idea, usually melodic but sometimes rhythmic.

Movement
A self-contained section of a larger work; so called because each section had a different, autonomous tempo indication.

Multiphonics
Chords played on instruments that are designed to play only one note at a time, such as the oboe and clarinet. They have been employed by various avant-garde composers such as Berio.

Musique concrète
Music made from recorded sounds such as birdsong or traffic noises. Pioneered by the French sound technician Pierre Schaeffer (1910–96), it influenced electronic composers like Stockhausen.

Nationalism
The expression of distinctive national characteristics in music, usually through the adaptation of folk material. A prevalent tendency all over Europe in the latter half of the nineteenth century; associated with such diverse figures as Glinka, Liszt, Smetana, Dvořák, Bartók, Kodály, Grieg, Vaughan Williams, Janáček and Sibelius.

Neo-classicism
A trend that became particularly strong during the 1920s, in reaction to the indulgences of late Romanticism. Typified by the adoption of Baroque and Classical forms, and the use of heavily contrapuntal writing. Much of Stravinsky's output can be classified as neo-classical. For a more detailed discussion, see p.259.

Nocturne
1. In eighteenth-century music, a short serenade in several movements for a small group of instruments.
2. A brief, lyrical piano piece; associated especially with Chopin.

Note-row
The foundation of serialism; the order in which a composer chooses to arrange the composition's basic twelve notes, none of which can be repeated until the other eleven have been deployed (see "Serialism").

Obbligato
An accompanimental part that is important and therefore "obligatory". The term is commonly used to describe either a counter-melody played by an instrument in an ensemble (often complementing a vocal line) or a Baroque keyboard accompaniment that is written out in full rather than with the standard figured bass notation (a written-out bass line with numbers indicating the harmony).

Octave
The interval that divides two notes of the same written pitch – e.g. from C to C.

Opera buffa
A form of opera in which everyday characters are placed in comic situations. Mastered by Mozart in *Le nozze di Figaro*, by Rossini in *Il barbiere di Siviglia* and Donizetti in *Don Pasquale*.

Opera seria
The dominant operatic genre during the seventeenth and eighteenth centuries. Characterized by heroic or mythological scenarios, often with extensive florid writing for castrati. The last and greatest example was Mozart's *La clemenza di Tito*.

Oratorio
An extended dramatic musical setting of a religious text (often written in the vernacular) usually for solo voices, chorus and orchestra. Originated in Rome around 1600 (see p.128), about the same time as opera. Developed in scale during the eighteenth century. Later examples are Handel's *Messiah*, Mendelssohn's *Elijah* and Elgar's *The Dream of Gerontius*.

Orchestra
The first regular orchestras appeared in the Baroque era, and consisted of strings, oboes and bassoons, plus a widely changing list of solo instruments. The layout became standardized during the Classical period, when Mozart and Haydn made specific demands regarding the number and quality of players for their symphonies. This Classical orchestra established the basic division of the players into four sections: strings; woodwind (flutes, oboes, bassoons and clarinets); brass (horns and trumpets); and percussion (kettledrums). Beethoven's symphonies demanded more (and better) players, and Berlioz, Wagner and Mahler required yet further expansions of the orchestra's resources. Though some instruments have been refined over the years, the orchestra of today is not much different from that of 150 years ago.

Orchestration
1. The art of writing for an orchestra, demanding an understanding of the qualities of each instrumental section, and an ability to manage and combine them.
2. The scoring of a work not originally intended for the orchestra – e.g. Mussorgsky's *Pictures from an Exhibition*, which was orchestrated by Ravel.

Ornaments (or Embellishments)
Notes added to the printed score in performance by a singer or instrumentalist. In the seventeenth and eighteenth centuries, composers generally indicated where such additions were required; by the start of the nineteenth century this improvisatory element had been virtually quashed.

Ostinato
Literally "obstinate". A persistently repeated melodic or rhythmic figure (see "Ground bass").

Overture

1. An orchestral introduction to an opera, oratorio or play.
2. A single-movement orchestral piece composed for the concert hall, otherwise known as a "Concert Overture". Examples include Mendelssohn's *Hebrides Overture* and Brahms's *Academic Festival Overture*.

Parody

1. A work that ridicules the pretensions of another work by distorting its most characteristic features.
2. An already-existing piece of music which is used to set entirely different words.
3. A sixteenth- or seventeenth-century mass in which the musical material has been derived from another source, like a motet or chanson.

Passacaglia

Instrumental work (originally a dance) with a continually repeated theme – not necessarily in the bass, and thus not the same as a chaconne.

Pedal point

A sustained bass note over which changing, and sometimes discordant, harmonies occur.

Pentatonic

A scale of five notes (often without semitones) and the music based on those notes. The tune of "Auld Lang Syne" is pentatonic, but examples are worldwide.

Pitch

The position of a sound in relation to the whole range of tonal sounds, depending on the frequency of sound waves per second (hertz). A high frequency is heard as a high pitch, a low frequency as a low pitch. In the US and the UK, pitches are named using the first seven letters of the alphabet.

Pizzicato

The plucking of bowed string instruments.

Plainchant (or Plainsong)

Medieval unaccompanied liturgical music in which a single vocal line (monophony) is notated in free rhythm, like speech. The principal form of plainsong in the West is Gregorian chant. For a more detailed discussion, see p.251.

Pointillism

Originally applied to the paintings of Seurat, in which colour is applied in small dots. Used by critics to describe those serialist works in which the notes seem placed in isolation rather than in melodic phrases.

Polyphony

Music in which a group of voices are combined contrapuntally. The heyday of polyphonic music was from the thirteenth to the late sixteenth century. The contrapuntal works of Bach and other later composers can also be described as polyphonic, even though it is governed by different harmonic principles.

Polystylism

Term applied to those contemporary composers (e.g. Alfred Schnittke) who employ a number of different styles within the same work.

Polytonality

The use of two or more keys at the same time. Mostly a twentieth-century technique; Stravinsky's music is full of examples.

Portamento

A continuous sliding from one pitch to another in vocal and instrumental music.

Prelude

1. An introductory piece of music, e.g. one that precedes a fugue or an act of an opera.
2. A self-contained piano piece, as in the *Préludes* of Chopin and Debussy.

Programme music

Music that attempts to describe a specific story, painting, text, character or experience. Most often used in connection with the "symphonic poems" or "tone poems" of various Romantic composers. Examples include Tchaikovsky's *Francesca da Rimini* and Richard Strauss's *Also sprach Zarathustra*.

Quarter tone

A note with a pitch that is halfway between two adjacent standard notes such as C and C sharp. Quarter tones, which cannot be played on the piano, have been used considerably since the middle of the twentieth century, by such composers as Scelsi.

Rallentando

Gradual decrease in speed.

Recitative

Semi-sung dialogue and narrative in opera and oratorio. Its rhythmic freedom is close to dramatic speech.

Rhapsody

A Romantic term, applied to compositions suggestive of heroic endeavour or overwhelming emotion. Best-known examples are Brahms's *Alto Rhapsody*, Rachmaninov's *Rhapsody on a Theme of Paganini* and Gershwin's *Rhapsody in Blue*.

Ritornello

Literally "little return". A short, recurring passage in Baroque orchestral music, or a recurring instrumental section in early Baroque opera.

Romanticism

The cultural epoch heralded in music by Beethoven, which dominated the nineteenth century. Characterized by the abandonment of traditional forms, a predilection for extra-musical subjects, an increase in the scale of composition, and an affection for chromaticism. For a more detailed discussion, see p.503.

Rondo

A form in which one section, or theme, recurs a number of times throughout a work or movement – e.g. A B A C A D A – usually in the same key each time.

Rubato

Literally "robbed". A subtle flexibility of pace that alters the shape of a phrase but does not affect its pulse, tempo or structure.

Scale

Any collection of notes that are important in a piece or style of music, arranged in order from lowest to highest or vice versa. In Western music, the term usually refers to the major and minor scales (which form the basis of tonality) or the chromatic scale (which contains all twelve notes used in traditional Western music). But there are also many other scales, such as the whole tone and octatonic scales, often used by Debussy and Stravinsky among others.

Scherzo

Literally a "joke". Began as a lively movement derived from the minuet, but developed into an autonomous genre in which the original humour is replaced by a free-ranging, rather tempestuous expressiveness – Chopin's piano *Scherzi* are the most famous examples.

Sequence

1. A type of hymn in the Catholic mass which follows the Alleluia. The earliest, from the ninth or tenth centuries, were written in prose, later ones (e.g. the Dies irae from the Mass of the Dead) were in rhymed verse.
2. The repetition of a phrase at a higher or lower pitch, much employed in Baroque music. In a "real sequence" the phrase is repeated exactly, whereas a "tonal sequence" is one in which the phrase is slightly altered to avoid a key change. In the chorus of the carol "Ding Dong Merrily on High" the word "Gloria" begins with a tonal sequence.

Serenade

1. A love song.
2. In the eighteenth century, an evening entertainment for orchestra – e.g. Mozart's *Eine kleine Nachtmusik*.

Serialism

Also known as twelve-tone or dodecaphonic music, serialism was developed by Schoenberg as a replacement for traditional harmonic and tonal languages. A serial composition is based on a twelve-note theme (the tone-row or note-row), which can then be used in different ways: forwards, backwards, upside down, upside down and backwards, or superimposed to create chords. Its most extreme form, in which predetermined rules govern every aspect of the piece, including volume and speed, is known as total serialism, and is associated primarily with the music of Boulez and Nono.

Singspiel

A German term for a comic opera with spoken dialogue instead of recitative. A good example is *The Magic Flute*.

Sonata

1. From around 1600 to the mid-eighteenth century, a solo instrumental composition not in any strict form – literally "sounded" rather than sung.
2. From the era of Haydn, an instrumental work, usually in three or four movements, for solo instrument and keyboard, or for solo keyboard. The form of the first movement became known as sonata form.

Sonata form

One of the crucial inventions of the Classical era, sonata form was used in most instrumental and symphonic music until the Romantic era, and even then the likes of Brahms kept it alive, as did the great symphonists of the twentieth century. Sonata form is basically a three-part scheme consisting of an exposition, a development and a recapitulation. For a more detailed discussion, see p.58.

Sonority

A combination of different timbres which produce a specific sound quality.

Soprano

The highest female voice.

Spectral music

A method of composing based on the computer analysis of the acoustic properties of sounds and timbres (or so-called "sound spectra", hence the name). Particularly associated with Tristan Murail, the technique has also influenced Kaija Saariaho, Jonathan Harvey and others.

Spinto

Urgent, heroic Italian tenor voice.

Sprechgesang

Literally "speechsong", a singing style midway between song and speech. Invented by Schoenberg, the technique requires the singer to approximate the pitch of the note and deliver it with the right amount of colour. Used by Schoenberg in his *Pierrot Lunaire*, but the finest example is Berg's *Wozzeck*.

Staccato

The opposite of legato. A direction for a note to be played shorter than is marked, detaching it from the note that follows.

Stretto

1. In a fugue, the overlapping of the entries created by the subject starting up in one voice before the previous statement of it has finished.
2. Increase in tempo.

Strophic
Term used to describe a song which uses the same music for each new verse.

Study
See "Étude".

Suite
1. In the seventeenth and eighteenth centuries, a piece of instrumental music in several contrasting movements based on dance forms; in particular the Allemande, Courante, Sarabande and Gigue.
2. A set of movements assembled from a ballet or other stage composition.

Suspension
A note that is held, often creating a dissonance, before being "resolved" by falling to the next note down.

Symphonic poem
An orchestral composition with a programmatic basis, i.e. that tells a story or evokes a scene; the genre was devised by Liszt and perfected by Richard Strauss.

Symphony
First used to designate an orchestral interlude or overture to a vocal work, but since the mid-eighteenth century the term has been used for a large-scale orchestral work, generally in four movements, sometimes in three or five. The Classical symphony was developed by Haydn, Mozart and Beethoven, and many of the greatest subsequent composers have added to the repertoire – Schubert, Brahms, Mahler, Bruckner, Sibelius, Nielsen, Shostakovich and Vaughan Williams being notable masters of the form.

Syncopation
Accentuation of the offbeat (i.e. not the main beat). Characteristic of jazz, much used in jazz-influenced early twentieth-century music.

Tempo
The pace of a work.

Tenor
The second highest male voice.

Ternary form
An instrumental or orchestral composition in three sections, in which the first section is repeated.

Tessitura
The natural range of a voice, or the range within which lie most of the notes of a role.

Texture
The quality of a composite musical sound or sequence of sounds as determined by the number of voices involved, and the timbre and spacing of those voices.

Timbre
The particular quality (literally "stamp"), or character, of a sound that enables a listener to distinguish one instrument (or voice) from another. Synonymous with tone colour.

Time signature
The numbers at the beginning of a composition, movement or section (or midway through a phrase in some twentieth-century scores) to indicate the number and kind of beats in a bar – 4/4, 3/4, 9/16, etc.

Tonality/Tonal
Tonality is the system of major and minor scales and keys that forms the basis of all Western art music from the seventeenth century until Schoenberg. Tonal music is music that adheres to the principles of tonality. For a more detailed discussion, see p.480.

Tone poem
See "Symphonic poem".

Triad
A three-note chord consisting of a root note plus the intervals of a third and a fifth. The four types of triad are: major (e.g. C–E–G), minor (e.g. C–E flat–G), augmented (e.g. C–E–G sharp), and diminished (e.g. C–E flat–G flat).

Trio
1. A combination of three performers.
2. A work for such a combination.
3. The central section of a minuet, so called because these sections were often written for three instruments in the seventeenth century.

Triplets
A group of three notes of equal duration, played in the time of two as indicated by the time signature.

Tritone
A highly dissonant interval of three whole tones (e.g. C–F#).

Tutti
Literally "all" or "everybody". A direction indicating all the performers should play (or sing) as opposed to a smaller group of soloists.

Twelve-tone
See "Serialism".

Vibrato
Rapid but small vibration in pitch, especially those created by string players, singers and wind players.

Waltz
A dance in triple time. Especially popular throughout the nineteenth century in Austria, most famously through the music of the Strauss family.

It's not what we do.
It's the way that we do it.

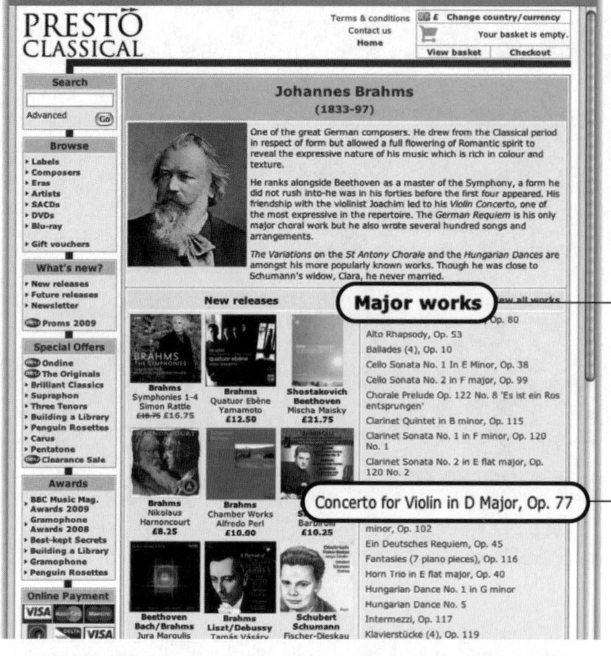

There are many on-line sources of classical music. But no other site does it like Presto Classical.

No other site is arranged in such a logical and accessible format.

There is a huge catalogue from which to choose, with 117 different versions of Brahms' Violin Concerto.

But we'll help you make the right choice with our unique listing of reviews and recommendations from the Gramophone, the Penguin Guide, BBC Music Magazine and Building a Library.

PRESTO CLASSICAL

It's the way that we do it.

www.prestoclassical.co.uk

The most user-friendly classical music site on the internet.

INDEX OF COMPOSERS & WORKS

Titles are listed in *italic*; composers are listed in **bold** face. Standard forms, such as concertos and symphonies, are not listed unless they are known by a popular name, for example Mahler's *Symphony No. 2* is under its alternative name of the *Resurrection Symphony*. Wherever a work is given a separate entry, the definite and indefinite article has been omitted from the title wherever it is the first word of the title – thus *La Traviata* is to be found under T for *Traviata*, *Der Freischütz* under F for *Freischütz*, and *A Midsummer Night's Dream* under M for *Midsummer*.

C

D

E

F

G

H

I

J

K

L

M

N

O

P

Q

R

S

T

U

Picture credits

Lebrecht Music & Arts: 6, 16, 45, 74, 134, 153, 162, 164, 174, 191, 214, 224, 241, 269, 335, 378, 408, 412, 415, 438, 468, 499, 511, 521, 558, 573, 590, 595, 609, 614, 622, 635; Betty Freeman/Lebrecht Music & Arts: 10, 194, 278, 377, 454; Suzie Maeder/Lebrecht Music & Arts:144; Nigel Luckhurst/Lebrecht Music & Arts: 65; Laurie Lewis/Lebrecht Music & Arts: 82; Misha Donat/Lebrecht Music & Arts: 130; Decca/Lebrecht Music & Arts: 169; Moravské Zemské/Lebrecht Music & Arts: 272; E. Comesana/Lebrecht Music & Arts: 284; Marion Kalter/Lebrecht Music & Arts: 292, 639; P.B. Martinů/Lebrecht Music & Arts: 332; Sammlung Rauch/Interfoto/Lebrecht Music & Arts: 374; T. Martinot/Lebrecht Music & Arts: 449; Victor Bazhenov/Lebrecht Music & Arts: 476; Kurt Weill Foundation/Lebrecht Music & Arts: 628; Lebrecht Music & Arts/Corbis: 2; Suzie Maeder/Lebrecht Music & Arts/Corbis: 91; Anne Purkiss/Lebrecht Music & Arts/Corbis: 227; Bettmann/CORBIS: 19, 27, 79, 94, 111, 119, 147, 182, 189, 202, 263, 266, 285, 306, 322, 343, 352, 394, 423, 442, 459, 479, 538, 545; Hulton-Deutsch/CORBIS: 104, 126, 258, 266, 340, 383, 389; Allen Ginsberg/Corbis: 210; Corbis: 220, 432; The Art Archive/Corbis: 36, 137, 231, 244, 283, 568; Christopher Felver/Corbis: 72; Steffano Bianchetti/Corbis: 600; Van Parys/CORBIS Sygma: 217; The Gallery Collection/Corbis: 357; Jacques Haillot/Apis/Sygma/Corbis: 346; Edmund Uchymiak/PAP/Corbis: 401; Michael Nicholson/CORBIS: 487; Underwood & Underwood/CORBIS: 514; Patrick Ryan: 56; Stockhausen-Verlag: 531; Chris Lee/IMG: 338; Roger Bardon: 556; Schott: 563; Naïve Records: 150; Vivianne Purdom/Decca: 435, 586; Walter Schels/Decca: 370: Mat Hennek/Deutsche Grammophon: 492; Gabriela Brandenstein/Deutsche Grammophon: 50; Edition Wilhelm Hansen: 312; Maarit Kytöharju/Chester Music: 464; Gunter Glücklich/Warner Classics: 301